SPECIAL UPDATE FOR DSM-5

The Developing Person
Through Childhood and Adolescence

NINTH EDITION

KATHLEEN STASSEN BERGER

Bronx Community College
City University of New York

Custom Edition for Grossmont College

WORTH PUBLISHERS

Executive Publisher: Catherine Woods

Executive Editor: Jessica Bayne

Developmental Editor: Tom Churchill

Executive Marketing Manager: Katherine Nurre

Supplements and Media Editor: Sharon Prevost

Assistant Editor: Lukia Kliossis

Associate Managing Editor: Lisa Kinne

Director of Print and Digital Development: Tracey Kuehn

Production Editor: Vivien Weiss

Supplements Production Editor: Jennifer Chiu

Art Director: Barbara Reingold

Interior Designer: Lissi Sigillo

Photo Treatments: Lyndall Culbertson

Layout Designer: Paul Lacy

Photo Editor: Cecilia Varas

Photo Researcher: Jacqui Wong

Senior Illustration Coordinator: Bill Page

Illustrations: Todd Buck Illustrations, MPS Limited, TSI Graphics, Inc.

Production Manager: Barbara Seixas

Supplements Production Manager: Stacey Alexander

Composition: TSI Graphics

Printing and Binding: RR Donnelley

Cover Art: Katherine Dunn

Library of Congress Control Number: 2011942454

ISBN-13: 978-1-3190-0360-9

ISBN-10: 1-3190-0360-5

Printed in the United States of America

First printing

Worth Publishers

41 Madison Avenue

New York, NY 10010

www.worthpublishers.com

Credit is given to the following sources for permission to use the photos indicated:

Part Openers

Jose Luis Pelaez Inc./Jupiter Images, p. xxxii

Jose Luis Pelaez Inc./Jupiter Images, pp. vii, ix, 1

Alex Cao/Getty Images, p. 124

John Lund/Annabelle Breakey/Jupiter Images, pp. vii, x, 125

BLOOM Images/Getty Images, p. 222

© Vinicius Ramalho Tupinamba/istockphoto, pp. vii, xi, 223

Ronnie Kaufman/Larry Hershowitz/Getty Images, p. 320

George Doyle/Getty Images, pp. vii, xi, 321

Tyler Edwards/Getty Images, p. 408

Mark Anderson/Getty Images, pp. vii, xii, 409

Chapter Openers

Hugh Sitton/Photolibrary, pp. ix, 2

Fancy/Alamy, pp. ix, 34

David M. Phillips/Photo Researchers, Inc., pp. ix, 62

Rick Gomez/Corbis, pp. x, 92

Angelo Cavalli/Robert Harding, pp. x, 126

Vanessa Davies/Getty Images, pp. x, 160, 221

Bruce Yuan-Yue Bi/Lonely Planet, pp. x, 190

Joanne Lane/Photographers Direct pp. xi, 224

Dynamic Graphics/Creatas, pp. xi, 256

© Little Blue Wolf Productions/Corbis, pp. xi, 288

Cindy Miller Hopkins/DanitaDelmont, pp. xii, 322

Holger Winkler/Corbis, pp. xii, 350

Sean Sprague/The Image Works, pp. xii, 376

Paul Miles/Axiom, pp. xii, 410

Hill Street Studios/Blend Images/Corbis, pp. xii, 438

Digital Vision/Getty Images, pp. xiii, 470

Exotica IM/Age Fotostock, pp. xiii, 504

LaunchPad

LaunchPad is an intuitive, online course tool where your instructor can post assignments for you to do, and you can see all your course content, including ebook, online.

To Register for your course you need to have:

- The specific URL/internet address from your instructor
- An access code purchased with your text

OR

- Means of online payment for access

Dear Students,

My online course is open for student registration—follow the simple steps below to get started.

1. Go to http://www.worthpublishers.com/launchpad/myers10e/299437
2. **Bookmark** the page to make it easy to return to.
3. If you have an **access code**, click the button "Register an activation code" in the upper right corner and follow the instructions.
4. If you don't have an access code, click the **"Purchase Access"** button.
5. If you have any questions or problems logging in, please **contact Technical Support.** Technical support will need a technical support incident ID if you continue to have trouble, so be sure to save that ID when you report your issue. You can reach a representative:

   - by phone at (877) 587-6534
   - through our online form

Tech Support Hours (all times EST)
Monday - Thursday 9:00 AM - 3:00 AM
Friday 9:00 AM - 11:00 PM
Saturday 11:30 AM - 8:00 PM
Sunday 11:30 AM - 11:30 PM

System Requirements: www.macmillanhighered.com/sysreq

Your instructor should have sent an email or posted instructions on how to access YOUR course. This includes the URL you should use.

- If you DO NOT have this, STOP and request this URL from your instructor.
- If you DO have this, click on or paste the link into a browser.

If you have an access code, click "Enter Your Student Access Code" and follow the instructions provided. You will be asked to set up an account and register for the class.

If you do not have an access code, either purchase a text package that includes one OR click "Purchase Access" and follow the instructions.

If you have any questions, go to macmillanhighered.com/getsupport for FAQs and information on how to contact Tech Support.

Good luck this semester!

The Basics of Scientific Writing in APA Style

Pam Marek
Kennesaw State University

This chapter was prepared with the expert assistance of Terrence D. Jorgensen, M.S., Applied Statistics, Kennesaw State University (Ph.D, Quantitative Psychology, University of Kansas, expected 2016)

For quite some time, the three Rs—Reading, 'Riting, and 'Rithmetic—have been the cornerstone of education. When it comes to "'Riting," scientists use specific scientific writing styles to communicate their findings in a way that generalizes across many disciplines. By utilizing these styles, they effectively organize their material; communicate with clarity, precision, and logic; and cite source materials to avoid plagiarism (inappropriate use of someone else's ideas or expressions). Familiarity with the elements of scientific writing in the field of psychology—specifically, APA (American Psychological Association) style—will enhance successful report writing and assignment preparation in psychology courses. An understanding of scientific writing style also provides a tool that sharpens critical thinking about ideas and evaluation of conclusions.

Scientific writing, like all formal writing, requires a firm foundation in English sentence construction, usage, and punctuation. The abbreviated communication used in instant messages or tweets among friends—such as "RUOK with this?" would likely cause confusion and, possibly, consternation from those who read scientific writing. When studying this chapter, consider its contents a challenge to learning how to organize ideas about science and to expressing science-related thoughts with clear but formal language. Use the chapter as a reference to guide formal scientific writing and APA style, specifically.

Writing for any discipline involves a cycle (or multiple cycles) that includes (1) planning, which encompasses locating and reading source materials; (2) writing a rough draft; and (3) editing and proofreading. Writers aim for continuity and a logical flow of ideas. In scientific writing, all ideas must be supported by evidence, with appropriate citations of the source of the evidence. Of course, different instructors have different requirements for writing assignments. Thus, it is important for you to be thoroughly familiar with the criteria for specific assignments and to assume responsibility for clarifying the answers to questions that arise.

In psychology courses, the "ultimate source" for appropriate writing style is the *Publication Manual of the American Psychological Association,* 6th edition.* The guidelines for APA style include instructions for formatting, organization, content, citations, lan-

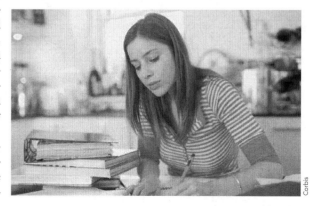

Corbis

* This content is adapted from Publication Manual of the American Psychological Association (6th ed.). Washington, DC, US: American Psychological Association (2010). Copyright (c) 2010 by the American Psychological Association. Adapted with permission.

This content is not a substitute for the *Publication Manual of the American Psychological Association,* 6th edition (2010), which contains broad and comprehensive guidance on all aspects of scientific writing.

APA has a number of resources to help individuals learn APA style, including free tutorials, FAQs, and an APA Style blog. Visit http://www.apastyle.org for more information, and join APA Style on Facebook http://www.facebook.com/APAStyle and Twitter http://twitter.com/#!/APA_Style.

guage, and sentence construction. Unless your instructor says otherwise, use formal language when writing APA-style papers because the typical audience includes researchers and academics. Precise and clear writing is crucial, with adjectives or adverbs used only to advance accurate and objective description. For instance, a scientific writer might describe participants in an experiment as "preschool children"; in this case, the adjective "preschool" helps to clarify the age and experience of the subjects. If this writer had written "cute little children," the word "cute" would express only the writer's opinion, and the word "little" would be a less precise description of the participants' age or experience.

When learning about the elements of APA style, students are sometimes surprised to find that many psychology textbooks do not use it. For example, to engage a student such as yourself, many textbooks (and this very chapter!) frequently use a more conversational tone, addressing the reader as "you." As you will notice in the "Things to Avoid in APA Style" section of this chapter, when writing in APA style, writers avoid the word "you." Instead, rather than addressing the reader directly, they use terms such as "people" or "individuals." To help you make these kinds of distinctions, this chapter outlines several "dos and don'ts" for writing in APA style (see Table 6, page 20).

Further, to illustrate APA style items, Appendix A (pages 1–16) presents an annotated manuscript for an article published in the *Psi Chi Journal of Undergraduate Research* (http://www.psichi.org/pubs/journal/). The annotated comments point out ways in which science writing may or may not meet APA criteria and emphasizes correct APA style. Appendix B (pages B-1–B-2) summarizes and illustrates important rules for proper sentence construction. All examples are drawn from students' final reports of an experimental psychology class project that focused on ageism in the workplace. Armed with this information, you will be prepared to complete written assignments effectively in a variety of psychology courses.

COMMON GENRES OF APA-STYLE ARTICLES

The types of written assignments that instructors may ask you to complete will vary across courses. In an introductory psychology class, for example, your instructor may require an article summary, a book review, or a brief paper on a specific topic. In research methods, experimental psychology, and laboratory courses (e.g., some cognitive psychology or learning and behavior courses), your instructor may require a laboratory report, an empirical report on a project you have completed, or a research proposal. In senior-level courses, instructors may also require an empirical report on an individual project, or they may require that you prepare a comprehensive review paper to compare and contrast different theoretical perspectives on a particular topic. Thus, during the course of your academic career, you will most likely be using APA style to prepare a variety of different types of reports.

To prepare for most of the assignments described above, you will be reading articles from professional journals. Typically, these articles will be classified as empirical reports or review articles. An **empirical report** describes original research that the authors have conducted, typically with human participants or animals. In these reports, authors provide a structured framework for their new research by topically integrating relevant findings of existing studies in a literature review, presenting their hypotheses, describing their methodology and results, and then concluding with a discussion to position the new research in the context of existing knowledge. A **review article** integrates, summarizes, and provides suggestions for extending prior research on a particular topic. Rather than initiating a new investigation with individual participants, authors of review articles study the existing literature on a topic. The information contained in a review article is an expansion of the information contained in the literature review portion of the introduction to an empirical report.

APA style specifies guidelines for the order of report sections. Table 1 lists these sections sequentially. To guide both your reading and writing, it also includes a brief

TABLE 1 **Organization of Empirical Reports and Review Articles**

Section	Information in Section	Page (typed manuscript)
Title page	Identifies topic/variables studied and provides authorship information	1
Abstract	Provides very brief summary of information from major sections of report	2
Introduction (or Body of empirical report)	Indicates purpose and importance of research and reviews prior research literature and theory • In an empirical report, the introduction typically concludes with specific hypotheses that follow from information in the literature review • In a review article, the literature review and theoretical information are more extensive than in an empirical report and constitute the body (main part) of the report	Start on p. 3
Method	In an empirical report, provides sufficient information about participants, design, materials, and procedures so that interested readers might replicate (repeat) the research	No new page
Results	In an empirical report, provides detailed information about the findings and includes results of statistical analysis for quantitative research	No new page
Discussion (or Conclusion)	Offers interpretation of results, their theoretical implications, limitations of the research, potential applications of the findings, and ideas for further research • In an empirical report, the discussion typically includes a focus on whether results supported specific hypotheses presented in the introduction and an explanation of why hypotheses were (or were not) supported	No new page
References	Lists authorship and source information for all items cited in report or article to enable readers to locate original sources	Start on new page

statement of the information contained in each section. Finally, it indicates which sections should start on a new page in a manuscript.

Supplementary information (e.g., Appendix, tables) follows the References section, and page numbers continue from the end of the References section. In a typed manuscript, you would present supplementary information in the following order, with each section starting on a new page: tables, figures, and then appendices. In a published article, these sections are integrated within the text rather than appearing in a separate section.

STEP 1: PLANNING—LOCATING, READING, AND TAKING NOTES ON SOURCE MATERIAL

Scientific papers are not written in a vacuum; rather, they build on and extend prior research. Thus, becoming familiar with existing scientific literature on the topic of interest is a crucial first step in planning a paper. Planning a scientific writing assignment involves locating appropriate source articles, reading the articles, and taking notes in a manner that will ultimately facilitate preparation of a first draft that includes accurate citations.

Locating Appropriate Source Material

When locating appropriate source material, it is important to distinguish between scientific material and articles targeted at the general public that may or may not be firmly based on scientific research. Multiple sources are available on the internet, in books, in newspapers, and in trade publications that may be tempting to use. However, unlike articles in professional, peer-reviewed literature, these sources often do not contain citations to support their claims, may be based on anecdotal evidence such as personal experience, or may include conclusions that are not justified by the data presented. In other words, there may be no "check" on the accuracy of the facts or logic of the arguments.

The peer review process is a safeguard against these weaknesses. If an article is peer reviewed, it means that professionals who are experts in a particular field have carefully evaluated the article on dimensions such as inclusion and citation of relevant background material, methodology, analysis, and interpretation of results. Thus, before you begin a writing project, you will often need to search the professional, peer-reviewed literature on your topic. Computerized databases typically allow users to limit their searches to peer-reviewed sources. PsycINFO is a comprehensive database for psychology-related sources. After entering search terms, you will be able to retrieve a listing of published articles, books, and book chapters. In this database, as in many others, searches can be restricted to terms found in specific fields (e.g., author, title, abstract, source) of database records. As shown below, a search for the term "writing" in the title and "assessment" in the abstract yielded 541 results.

These results suggest that your initial topic may be too broad to cover in a single paper. Generally, a literature review is more effective if writers probe deeply into a more limited topic rather than skim over a wide range of material. A more limited topic allows you to compare and contrast different approaches or theories rather than simply describing them. Careful selection of articles will make it easier to write a cohesive literature review. Reading the abstract will indicate how closely an article relates to your specific topic of interest. Often, you may decide to restrict your search to specific subtopics or populations. For example, narrowing the results above by adding the term "college students" in the "subjects" field led to a list of 31 potential items.

After locating appropriate sources, the next step is to obtain the full text of the material. In some instances, full text articles are available for downloading directly from the database. When given the choice between .html and .pdf, the .pdf version is preferable because it integrates tables and figures in the text for ease of reference. Although some students are tempted to limit their sources to those that are available for immediate download, yielding to such temptation often leads to the omission of highly relevant information from the literature review. To avoid this potential problem, attempt to locate the material by checking the catalogue at your school's library. If the library does not have the material, check with a librarian (or on the library web page) to determine the procedures for ordering material via interlibrary loan. Typically, school libraries share materials with each other; thus, if the material is not available at your school, your library may be able to borrow it from another school for your use. The time needed to obtain materials from other libraries varies across institutions and by the type of resource requested.

Prior to searching for sources or after reading just a few that have been collected, it is helpful to develop a topical outline for the literature review. This outline can guide the search process, and you can refine it as the search progresses. Then, when reading and taking notes about theories, findings, and relevant terms in the source articles, you can position the notes in the appropriate section of the outline.

Reading Source Material

It takes considerable time to select and collect sources and to extract the appropriate material from each source. Professional articles are not necessarily easy to read and "digest." Reading the abstract first will give you an idea of what to expect. However, if you just read the abstract, you definitely will not have a sufficient depth of understanding (or content) to integrate information into a literature review.

Before reading an article thoroughly, familiarize yourself with the article's structure (the information contained in each section). Table 1 on page 3 indicates what to expect in each section. Then, as you read the article more carefully, direct your attention to issues such as the research purpose and importance, how it relates to prior research on the topic, the hypotheses, general methodology, major findings, and interpretation of the findings. As you read, consider how the material relates to what you plan to write.

As you confront potentially unfamiliar terminology and theories, your first experience reading articles from the professional literature is apt to be quite challenging. If you plan to include information from a source in your written report, be sure that you take the time to understand it. Otherwise, you will not be able to express the ideas correctly in your own words or to integrate them with related material in your report. Early in your academic career, the material in the Results section, which often includes multiple statistical tests, is particularly daunting. To gain a better understanding of the results, read the verbal information that indicates, for example, whether one group performed better than another did or whether one variable predicted another variable. In addition, in the Discussion section, authors often reiterate key results in a straightforward verbal form when they examine support for a hypothesis or explain the findings.

Constructing an Outline and Taking Notes

It is important to develop a topical outline. Do this as early as possible in the literature review process. A topical outline helps overcome the tendency to summarize one article after another. Organizing information by topic encourages you to compare and contrast the findings from one study with those of other studies on the same topic in a single paragraph (integrating information from multiple sources). Your topical outline serves as a framework for presentation of past research and provides an underlying structure for writing.

> *Note:* For a review article, you may opt to use your outline to develop headings for subsections. The outline for a review article encompasses the entire article, leading to the conclusions. For an empirical study, the items in an outline will guide the flow of information relevant to explaining the particular research question, illuminating prior research related to the variables being investigated, and providing a rationale for the research hypothesis.

Good note taking during a literature review typically leads to a higher quality paper. Because a source article may address one or more topics, it is helpful to categorize notes topically and to include identifying information from source articles for citation purposes. To avoid plagiarism in the writing stage, do not copy phrases directly from articles and do not simply change one or two words in a sentence when you add the information to your notes. Instead, describe the ideas and findings in your own words. *Be sure that your notes include all the information you need for citations* that are required for each factual item that is not very common knowledge. If in doubt, cite! Although using quotations in psychological writing is discouraged, if it seems absolutely necessary to use a brief quote (and assignment criteria permit doing so), remember to include quotation marks (and a page number) as well as a citation! Highlighting the sections of source articles from which you draw information will assist subsequent self-checks for signs of plagiarism, which encompass both missing or incorrect citations and use of similar words or expressions. (See Table 5 on page 10 for more details about these topics.)

STEP 2: WRITING A FIRST DRAFT

This section focuses on the types of information that you need to organize and include in each section of a research report. It begins with general guidelines for formatting and provides additional information about formatting for each individual part of the paper. To emphasize the importance of citations in APA-style writing, it includes a special section about citations and their formatting both in the text of the report and in the References section.

General Information About APA-Style Formatting

APA-style formatting includes rules for margins, line spacing, alignment, and font as outlined in the table below. Using the options provided by word processing software, select the appropriate formatting choices before starting your first draft. When preparing the paper, adjust the formatting options for the Abstract and References as noted in Table 2.

There are also APA-style formatting rules for the headings and subheadings, which do not include what APA-style considers section labels (e.g., "Abstract," the title, and "References"). On her APA-style blog, Chelsea Lee includes a table that concisely summarizes these rules at http://blog.apastyle.org/apastyle/2009/07/five-essential-tips-for-apa-style-headings.html or http://tinyurl.com/ykqzm6s. For their respective sections, the words Method, Results, and Discussion are typed using Level 1 bold-faced headings. However, the first section of an APA-style report (the Introduction) begins with the title of the paper (not the word "Introduction"). Although it is centered, the title is not shown in boldface font. "Abstract" and "References" titles are also centered, but not boldfaced.

TABLE 2 How to Format APA-Style Manuscripts

Line spacing	• Double-spaced throughout • No extra spaces between paragraphs
Spacing after punctuation	• Use two spaces after punctuation at the end of a sentence; otherwise, use one space after punctuation
Alignment	• Left for all paragraphs and most headings, but Level 1 headings (for major sections, see illustration) are centered
Margins	• All (top, bottom, left, right) set at 1" for the body of the manuscript, with header ½" from top
Typeface	• 12-point font, Times New Roman

First line of paragraph	• Set indent at .5" paragraph
	• Exceptions:
	  ■ The abstract is a single block paragraph (without .5" indent for the first line)
	  ■ Reference items are formatted using a "hanging" indent (with the first line of each citation beginning at the margin and subsequent lines using a .5" ["hanging"] indent)

Page number & running head	• On the first line of the header in a Word document, the running head appears at top left of all pages, and the page number appears at top right on the same line • Explained in Title Page section

There are five levels of headings in APA style. An example illustrating the use of the first three levels from an empirical paper is shown at right. Level 1, used for the main section heading (Method), is centered and in boldface font. If there were multiple words in the Level 1 heading, all words with four letters or more would begin with a capital letter. Level 2, used for the Participants and Materials subsections in the example, is also in boldface font, but it is positioned flush with the left margin. Capitalization rules are the same as those for Level 1 headings. Level 3, used for Scenarios and related questions in the example, is positioned .5" from the left margin (as is the indent for the first line of a new paragraph), is in boldface font, and is followed by a period (with text beginning thereafter). Only the first word of Level 3 headings is capitalized unless the heading includes proper nouns, which would also be capitalized.

Level 4 and Level 5 headings, if needed, would also be positioned .5" from the left margin and would be followed by a period. Level 4 and Level 5 headings are italicized and follow the same capitalization rules used for Level 3 headings. However, the font style used for Level 4 and Level 5 headings differs: boldface for Level 4 and regular for Level 5.

>

Method

>
> **Participants**
>
> Participants included 301 individuals from a community sample (180 women and 115 men, $M_{\text{age}} = 38.64$, $SD_{\text{age}} = 14.15$.
>
> Participants had a variety of ethnic backgrounds, (text continues)
>
> **Materials**
>
> **Scenarios and related questions.** Participants read a brief scenario about a mother (Maggie) who was offered the measles, mumps, and rubella (MMR) vaccine for (text continues)

Title Page

The title should clearly and concisely (maximum 12 words) indicate the topic of the manuscript. For an empirical report, it should include the primary variables that you are studying. For a review article, it should contain the major issue that you are investigating. Use Table 3 as a guide for the Title Page.

TABLE 3 **What to Include on a Title Page**

Title	• Centered horizontally on upper half of page • Capitalize first letters of important words and all words of four of more letters
Author's name and	• Centered, on a line double-spaced below title, including first name, middle initial, last name • If there are two authors from the same institution, both names are typed on the same line with "and" between them
Institutional affiliation	• Centered • On a line double-spaced below author's name
Running head (appears at top of page in published articles) IMPORTANT NOTE	• In header area (use header feature in word processing programs) • Type the words "Running head:" left-justified • After the words Running head: (on the same line in the header area) type an abbreviated title *in all capital letters* (maximum 50 characters including spaces and punctuation) • The actual running head appears on all pages, but the words "Running head:" appear on the title page only. For instructions on creating a unique header for the first page, see http://www.apastyle.org/learn/faqs/running-head.aspx
Page number	• In header on every page, on same line as running head, on right • Title page is page 1 • Do not use dashes or the word "page," just the number • Use automatic page numbering feature in word-processing programs

In manuscripts submitted for publication, title pages also contain an Author's Note. Guidelines specify that an Author's Note should include departmental affiliation, acknowledgments, and contact information for the author. However, your instructor may not require an Author's Note on student papers.

The Abstract

An abstract summarizes a report in 120 to 250 words with maximum length requirements varying across journals (and instructors). When you search databases, the abstract is the only section of a manuscript shown in the database record. By reading the abstract, you typically learn whether a source is directly relevant to your paper.

When you actually write a report, you prepare the Abstract last because it summarizes the entire paper (see Table 4). The Abstract should not contain any information that is not included in the actual paper. Moreover, information in the Abstract should be consistent with information that is included in the body of the report. Abstracts are concise, specific, and self-explanatory.

TABLE 4 **What to Include in an Abstract**

Empirical Reports	Review Articles
Purpose/problem investigated	Topic/purpose or thesis
Number, type, age, sex (or species) of participants	Types of sources used
Method (materials used, basic procedures)	
Major findings	Major findings
Conclusions and implications	Conclusions and implications

In manuscripts submitted for publication, authors itemize keywords used for database searches. To do so, double-space after the last line of the abstract, indent .5", and type *Keywords* (italicized and followed by a colon). Then, add a few words that indicate key topics of your manuscript. For example, keywords for the manuscript in Appendix A (see pages 1–16) might include "communication" and "self-disclosure." Your instructor may not require keywords on student papers.

The Introduction

The Introduction of an empirical report or the body of a review article begins on page 3 (after the Title Page and Abstract) with the title of the paper. The opening paragraphs highlight general information about the issue under investigation and prepare readers for the detailed literature review that follows. For example, in the opening paragraphs of their Introduction in the sample manuscript, Bruss and Hill (2010) incorporated key facts about communication and self-disclosure that indicated why the issue is important. The paragraphs included specific statements, supported by citations, rather than broad generalities without citations. Typically, the opening paragraphs also include a statement of the goal or purpose of the research. However, in the sample manuscript, the explicit statement of purpose was positioned as a lead-in to the hypothesis at the end of the introduction.

The Thesis Statement

When you write a review article (or an analytical, explanatory, or argumentative paper), you typically begin with a thesis statement, a short, precise statement that indicates what issue you are analyzing, what you are explaining to readers, or what argument you are making. The thesis statement presents the main idea of your paper. If you have prepared an outline, check to be sure it includes information relevant to your thesis statement. You may need to add topics (perhaps searching for additional sources), or you may need to eliminate topics that are only peripherally related to your thesis. An outline that conforms to your thesis will serve as an effective framework for your paper, guiding your subsequent writing.

The Literature Review

As described at http://www.writing.utoronto.ca/advice/specific-types-of-writing/literature-review or http://tinyurl.com/mt22ly, the purpose of a literature review is "… to convey to your reader what knowledge and ideas have been established on a topic, and what their strengths and weaknesses are" (para. 1). In a literature review, do not simply summarize a series of articles sequentially. Rather, integrate material from multiple articles into paragraphs focused on specific subtopics linked to the purpose of your research. In the sample manuscript, Bruss and Hill (2010) integrated information about self-disclosure, online communication, and face-to-face communication in their literature review. For articles published in professional, peer-reviewed journals, literature reviews are quite comprehensive. However, instructors' expectations for literature reviews typically reflect the extent of your experience with reading professional literature and preparing scientific reports. Regardless of requirements for length or a minimum number of sources, typical expectations include thorough reading of source articles, precise and accurate reporting, appropriate organization, proper citations, and use of formal grammar and sentence construction.

An outline helps you integrate the information from multiple articles into a series of paragraphs about a specific topic rather than summarizing one article after another. If coverage of a particular topic area seems weak, the weakness should be a cue that you need to search for additional articles on the topic. If you do not understand something that seems important when you read it, make sure to clarify the meaning before using the information in a written assignment. Avoid simply trying to reorganize the original author's words without understanding them! Such "reorganization without understanding" tends to result in plagiarism. If there are conflicting findings or opinions on a topic, compare and contrast them in the same paragraph, perhaps commenting on the possible reason (e.g., different methodologies) for the conflict. You seldom need to report detailed information about the number of participants or methodology in a literature review unless the methodology relates to a point about a particular finding. Instead, emphasize the research findings and their theoretical underpinnings. In an empirical report, the literature review provides information needed to justify the hypotheses. In a review article, the literature review provides evidence to support the conclusion.

Concluding the Introduction of an Empirical Report

The final paragraphs of the Introduction of an empirical report typically lead in to the Method section. To do so, they provide a brief description of the research design, a rationale for the hypotheses, and specific hypotheses. A rationale is a statement that indicates the reasoning that underlies a hypothesis based on prior findings or theories introduced in the literature review. In the sample manuscript, Bruss and Hill (2010) clearly stated their rationale for each of two hypotheses based on prior findings about online anonymity and on the concept of reciprocity. Their actual hypotheses identified specific variables and indicated how they expected these variables to relate to or influence each other.

Citations in Scientific Writing

Scientific writing relies heavily on providing evidence from existing research and theoretical perspectives. One of the most important requirements for scientific writing is the obligation to cite the original source of ideas or findings (see Table 5). Not only is such citation an indication of academic "etiquette," but the lack of citation of ideas is considered *plagiarism*. Principle 8.11, Plagiarism, of the Ethical Principles of Psychologists and Code of Conduct, states, "Psychologists do not present substantial portions or elements of another's work or data as their own, even if the other work or data source is cited occasionally" (see http://www.apa.org/ethics/code/index.aspx?item=40 or http://tinyurl.com/749vrw6). The phrase "elements of another's work" refers to even single sentences!! Moreover, although it may be tempting to adapt someone else's sentence from a source article by changing a few words, such minor changes are NOT permissible, *even if you cite the source article*. Rather, in addition to citing sources, use paraphrasing (expressing ideas using your own words and sentence structure).

TABLE 5 **Focus on Citations and Plagiarism**

Paraphrases

Paraphrasing involves reading something that someone else has written (the original source); "digesting," synthesizing, and otherwise integrating the material with other topically relevant information; and showing accurate understanding of the material by presenting it in your own words. Rather than attempting to paraphrase a single sentence, carefully read an entire paragraph. Then, present the gist of the paragraph in your own words. Below you will find an original source and examples indicating inappropriate paraphrasing (plagiarism) and acceptable paraphrasing.

- **Original source** (Fallahi, Wood, Austad, & Fallahi, 2006): "In conclusion, we recommend that instructors of undergraduate psychology courses incorporate a student-friendly didactic model into their course curricula. Our findings demonstrate that the instructors' time and effort is well spent because it improved students' basic writing skills. Writing proficiency is an essential element of effective communication for future psychology clinicians or academicians that requires ongoing training and feedback, and students are unlikely to master it in a single college-level English course."
- **Plagiarized version #1** (missing quotation marks and ellipsis dots [three dots with spaces between them] to indicate omitted material): Writing proficiency is an essential element of effective communication that requires ongoing training and feedback (Fallahi, Wood, Austad, & Fallahi, 2006).
- **Plagiarized version #2** (a few words changed, sentence structure not changed): Writing well is a key component of meaningful communication that entails continuous training and feedback (Fallahi, Wood, Austad, & Fallahi, 2006).
- **Acceptable paraphrase:** Because writing is an important communication skill, instructors should incorporate writing assignments and provide feedback in multiple courses (Fallahi, Wood, Austad, & Fallahi, 2006).

Quotations

A quotation is an exact copy of the language from a source. If you do use a quote, be sure to include quotation marks, cite the source, and include a page number.

Quotations are very rare in scientific writing. Overuse of quotations may detract from a paper in both style and content. On occasion, instructors may perceive that use of quotations reflects a lack of effort or understanding. Thus, it is extremely important that you thoroughly understand the material that you incorporate into your manuscripts; otherwise, it will be extremely difficult to accurately paraphrase and integrate the material into a written report without using quotes. If your instructor permits you to use quotes, remember the quotation marks, citation, and page number! If you do not include quotation marks, the material may be considered plagiarized even if the source is cited! Below is the correct format for quotations, based on the Fallahi et al. (2006) example:

- **Correct quotation** (Illustrates use of ellipsis dots for omitted material): "Writing proficiency is an essential element of effective communication . . . that requires ongoing training and feedback" (Fallahi, Wood, Austad, & Fallahi, 2006, p. 174).

Citation Format

APA style incorporates author–date referencing for all citations in all sections of any report. The application of this author–date referencing varies slightly (e.g., in the use of "and" versus "&") for citations that are included in the body of a narrative (see Example 1) or in parentheses (see Example 2). The first time a source is cited, if the source includes fewer than six authors, an APA-style citation includes the surnames of all authors, followed by the year of publication.

- Example 1 (in body of narrative): Marek, Griggs, and Christopher (1999) noted that students prefer pedagogical aids that relate directly to test content.
- Example 2 (parenthetical): Students prefer pedagogical aids that most directly assist in preparing for tests (Marek, Griggs, & Christopher, 1999).

If there are more than two authors, all subsequent citations include the name of the first author followed by et al. (and others). There is no period after "et," but there is a period after "al" (an abbreviation for alia).

- Within body of narrative: Marek et al. (1999) indicated that introductory psychology textbooks differed in the number and type of pedagogical aids used.
- Parenthetical: Introductory psychology textbooks differed in the number and type of pedagogical aids used (Marek et al., 1999).

If a source contains six or more authors, only the surname of the first author followed by et al. appears both in the first and subsequent citations. For example, Lynn Fuchs collaborated with five other authors on an article about assessment of learning. Even the first time this source is cited, the citation would read either Fuchs et al. (2011) or (Fuchs et al., 2011), depending on its positioning in the body of narrative or in parenthesis.

If an article has a single author, the author's name is included in all citations. If an article has two authors, both authors' names are always included in all citations. For citations in the body of the narrative, include the year the first time the article is cited in each paragraph but omit the year for subsequent citations to the same article in the *same* paragraph. For parenthetical citations, the year is included in *all* citations. If you include more than one citation in the same parenthesis, put the citations in alphabetical order (by last name of first author) and separated by semicolons. Do not change the order of authors for any citation!

Instructors may require that you obtain copies of all sources cited in your writing. However, in some instances, instructors will permit you to cite a source mentioned in your textbook (or in another published work) when you are unable to obtain the source itself. In such instances, you must distinguish what you actually read from the item cited (the original source of the information). For example, suppose you were reporting information from a textbook by Richard Griggs that included coverage of an article by Schwartz (1999). Although textbooks are seldom cited in formal APA writing, suppose your instructor permits you to do so without obtaining the primary source article. In that case, the citation would read as follows:

> When constructing a survey, researchers should remember that question wording may influence participants' answers (Schwartz, 1999, as cited in Griggs, 2012).

The unread, original source is *not* included in the Reference list. Remember, before citing a source that you did not personally read, *check the criteria for your assignment!* Remember that such citations, whether they are from a textbook, another article, an edited book, or a book chapter, are extremely rare in published manuscripts.

Method Section of an Empirical Report

The Method section provides enough information for readers to replicate the research and to determine if findings are valid and reliable. This section is typically divided into three subsections: Participants, Materials (or Apparatus), and Design and Procedures. Although content of specific subsections may vary somewhat, the paragraphs below highlight typical content, as does the sample manuscript in Appendix A (see pages 1–16).

Participants

This subsection includes information about the number of participants, the overall "group" to which they belong (e.g., college students, workers at Company ABC, children from a specific day care center), and basic demographic characteristics (e.g., age, gender, ethnicity). In addition, this section often includes information about recruiting participants (e.g., random sample from Registrar's list, convenience sample of adults, sign-up sheet posted in a particular area) and incentive offered (entered in drawing for prize, small amount of money or credit, no incentive). In some manuscripts, information about recruiting and incentive is included in a Design and Procedures subsection instead of in the Participants subsection.

Materials (or Apparatus)

The description of materials provides sufficient detail for readers to replicate the research. For an experiment, the Materials section includes a description of the stimuli, and explicitly identifies differences in materials used for different groups. For a survey, the Materials section includes a description of the overall questionnaire (number of questions asked, type of answer options), and identifies key topics covered. For each existing scale (a series of items measuring the same construct) included in a questionnaire, descriptions often encompass the following information: what it measures, original source/citation, number of items, type of answer options, anchor points and descriptions, sample item, and reliability and validity data.

Design and Procedures

This subsection describes how the investigation was conducted. For an experiment, it indicates whether the design was between subjects (each participant was in only one condition) or within subjects (each participant was in all conditions). For a between-subjects design, it clarifies how you assigned participants to conditions. For a within-subjects design, it clarifies how you counterbalanced the order of conditions (systematically changed the order for different participants). It includes information about participants' tasks, the order in which tasks were completed, instructions, and time limits if applicable. For a survey, this section includes information about how questionnaires were distributed and collected, instructions given to participants, and the approximate time it took participants to complete the questionnaire.

Results Section of an Empirical Report

This section contains verbal and statistical information describing the findings. Section organization varies according to the types of analyses involved and the research hypotheses. An opening paragraph often includes information about the type of analyses used and clarification of variables analyzed. Next, following specific rules for formatting of statistics, it presents the results that relate to the hypotheses. For example, in the sample manuscript, Bruss and Hill (2010) reported results for an independent-samples t test, an analysis designed to compare ratings or scores for two unrelated groups of participants. If assignment criteria indicate that you should provide tables or figures to clarify complex arrays of data, refer to and comment on the highlights of each table or figure in the text of the Results section even though the actual tables and figures appear at the end of the report.

Discussion Section of Empirical Report

This section serves as an arena for interpretation of the results. It often begins with an explicit statement or statements regarding whether results supported the hypotheses. Subsequent discussion positions the results in the context of theoretical perspectives and explains similarities to and differences from prior research on the topic. The Discussion section also contains information about the limitations of the study (e.g., the generalizability of findings). It includes coverage of the implications of the findings and potential applications of the results. The section often concludes by indicating how the research extends the existing literature and by offering suggestions for future investigations that emanate from questions raised by the results of the current study. In Appendix A, annotations identify the elements of a discussion section.

References

This section contains a listing in a standardized format (with "hanging indent") of all sources that you have read and cited in your paper. Unlike a bibliography, the References section does *not* include any material that you read but do not cite in the manuscript. Each item in the References contains detailed information that enables readers to obtain the source material. Alphabetize reference entries by the surname (last name) of the first author. Do not change the order of authors for any source!

Individual Reference Entries

Authors' names appear in the same order as they appear on the original source, because the ordering of names typically reflects the extent to which authors contributed to the article or book. The components of each reference entry typically include the authors' names, year of publication, title, and publisher-related information. Authors' names include both surnames and initials. For the most common types of references used in scientific writing, the year is shown within parentheses and then followed by a period. References without a doi (digital object identifier) end with a period. The *doi* (digital object identifier) is a recently added reference component designed to facilitate location of items on the internet (http://www.doi.org/). It is most often applicable to articles in professional journals rather than other types of sources. The order of reference components varies somewhat. Instructions for and examples of reference entries to three common sources (journal article, book, and chapter in edited book) and to an online resource follow. Additional examples of references to journal articles, books, and an online newsletter are included in the sample manuscript in Appendix A (see pages 1–16).

A Citation to a Journal

Include the following components in the following order: author(s) name(s), year, article title, journal name, volume number, page numbers, and doi (digital object identifier). As illustrated, when there are multiple authors, an ampersand (&) is used before the name of the last author. The date and title are also followed by a period. In the title, only proper nouns, the first word, and the first word after a colon (if applicable) are capitalized. The journal name, followed by a comma and a volume number (also followed by a comma) are both italicized, but the page numbers are not. Here is an example of a reference to a journal article.

> Luttrell, V. R., Bufkin, J. L., Eastman, V. J., & Miller, R. (2010). Teaching scientific writing: Measuring student learning in an intensive APA skills course. *Teaching of Psychology, 37,* 193–195. doi:10.1080/00986283.2010.488531

If a doi is not available, include the words "Retrieved from" followed by the URL (web site address) of the journal's publisher. In the References of the sample manuscript, the citation for Chiou (2006) illustrates use of a journal URL when a doi has not been assigned.

A Citation to a Book

Include the following components in the following order: author(s) name(s), year, book title, publisher's location, and publisher's name. Information about the publisher is found in database records and on one of the first pages in a book. The title of the book is italicized and follows the same capitalization rules used for article titles. Regarding publisher location, standard (postal code) abbreviations are used for states (e.g., GA for Georgia). If the publisher is an association or a press, as in the example below, the publisher's name should be complete; however, if the publisher's name ends with Publishers, Company, or Incorporated, these words are not included in the citation.

> Graham, S., MacArthur, C. A., & Fitzgerald, J. (2007). *Best practices in writing instruction: Solving problems in the teaching of literacy.* New York, NY: Guilford Press.

A Citation to a Chapter in an Edited Book

Include the following components in the following order: author(s) name(s), year, chapter title, editors' names, book title, pages for chapter, publisher's location, and publisher's name. For editors' names, initials precede surnames. The editors' names are followed by the abbreviation "Eds." within parentheses and then followed by a comma. The title of the book is italicized and follows the same capitalization rules used for article titles. Unlike a reference to an article, the abbreviation "pp." precedes the chapter page numbers that are in parentheses. Here is an example of a reference for a chapter in an edited book.

> Schmidt, M. E., & Dunn, D. S. (2007). Teaching writing in statistics and research methods: Addressing objectives, intensive issues, and style. In D. S. Dunn, R. A. Smith, & B. Beins (Eds.), *Best practices for teaching statistics and research methods in the behavioral sciences* (pp. 257–273). Mahwah, NJ: Erlbaum.

If there are eight or more authors for a chapter (or for a journal article or book), APA style follows a somewhat unusual guideline for the citation in the References section. The citation should include the surnames and initials for the first six authors, followed by an ellipsis (three periods with a space between them . . .) and the surname and initials of the last author. An example for a chapter with eight authors in an edited book follows.

> Rijlaarsdam, G., Van den Bergh, H., Couzijn, M., Janssen, T., Braaksma, M., Tillema, M., . . . Raedts, M. (2012). Writing. In K. R. Harris, S. Graham, T. Urdan, A. G. Bus, S. Major, & H. Swanson (Eds.), *APA educational psychology handbook, Vol 3: Application to teaching and learning* (pp. 189–227). Washington, DC: American Psychological Association. doi:10.1037/13275-009

A Citation to an Online Resource

To cite a web page or nonperiodical web document, include the following components in the following order: author(s) name(s), year, title of resource, and URL (website address).

> Seas, K., & Brizee, A. (2010). *APA style workshop.* Retrieved from http://owl.english.purdue.edu/owl/resource/664/01/

STEP 3: EDITING AND PROOFREADING

After the first draft is written, the next step is the initial proofreading, a task that encompasses grammar, sentence construction, punctuation, spelling, and use of APA style, as well as a review of the content. The following sections illuminate rules that are specific to APA-style writing and general rules that apply to all formal writing. These general rules are available in most grammar books. The Purdue Online Writing Lab (OWL, http://owl.english.purdue.edu/) is an excellent source of information for both grammar and APA-style guidelines.

Other online educational sites also offer a variety of exercises for practicing grammar and the mechanics of writing. For clarification and additional practice, you are encouraged to consult any (or all) of the following sites:

> Butte College
> http://www.butte.edu/departments/cas/tipsheets/grammar/parts_of_speech.html
> or http://tinyurl.com/6vvclno

> Indiana State University
> http://libguides.indstate.edu/content.php?pid=18359&search_terms=
> writing+center

> University of North Carolina at Chapel Hill
> http://www.unc.edu/depts/wcweb/handouts/index.html or
> http://tinyurl.com/72ykcmk

> Diana Hacker's *A Writer's Reference* http://bcs.bedfordstmartins.com/
> writersref7e or http://tinyurl.com/6mnqmop

Grammar and Punctuation Rules for All Writing

The principles outlined below (and summarized in Appendix B, pages B-1–B-2) are applicable to scientific writing across disciplines. The principles include fundamental rules of formal English grammar and punctuation. Some of the topics covered include construction of complete sentences, subject-verb agreement, noun-pronoun agreement, parallel construction, and punctuation. *When editing your manuscript, it is particularly important to leave sufficient time to check these items and to correct any errors.*

Construct Complete Sentences and Avoid Sentence Fragments.

A sentence must contain an independent clause (a clause containing a subject and a verb that expresses a complete thought). In contrast, a group of words (including a subject and a verb) that does not express a complete thought is called a dependent (or subordinate) clause. An independent clause can stand alone as a sentence, but a dependent clause is not a sentence; if you use a dependent clause alone, you have created a sentence fragment (e.g., "Because consumers perceive that generic brands are not as healthy as name brands"). To help you identify dependent clauses that cannot stand alone, remember that they often begin with words such as "although," "because," "if," or "when."

Use Parallel Construction.

Parallel construction applies to using the same grammatical form to express a series of elements in the same sentence. Using parallel construction tends to improve the clarity of a sentence. For example, the sentence "People at the sporting event were either cheering, talking, or had a program to look at" does not use parallel construction. The words "had a program to look at" involve a different grammatical form than do "cheering" and "talking." An improved version of the sentence would read as follows: "People at the sporting event were cheering, talking, or looking at a program."

Make Sure the Subject "Agrees With" the Verb.

The subject of a clause is who or what the clause is about, and the verb describes the action or state of being. If the subject is plural, then the verb must be in the plural form as well. For example, it is *incorrect* to say, "One reason for smoking habits are that young adults may tend to conform." The subject "reason" is singular; thus, the verb should be "is." The correct sentence would read, "One reason for smoking habits is that young adults may tend to conform."

Make Sure a Pronoun "Agrees With" the Noun to Which It Refers.

A pronoun is a word that takes the place of a noun (a name of a person, place, or thing). A pronoun must "agree in number" with the noun that it replaces. If a noun is singular (e.g., participant), then the pronoun must also be singular (e.g., he or she). If a noun is plural (e.g., participants), then the pronoun must also be plural (e.g., they). For example, it is *incorrect* to say, "Each participant was assigned to a group based on a number they had chosen." The subject "participant" is singular; thus, the pronoun should be "he or she." Because the use of "he or she" (to avoid gender bias) may seem somewhat awkward, most sources suggest that you change the sentence so that the subject is plural (e.g., Participants were assigned to a group based on a number they had chosen).

Make Sure a Pronoun Clearly Refers to a Specific Noun or Noun Phrase.

Although the referents for words such as "this," "that," or "it" may be clear to you as a writer, the referents may be unclear to readers. For example, the referent for the word "this" in the second sentence that follows is ambiguous. "To identify each participant, I will assign a number to each individual who submits an informed consent form. This will serve as identification for later analysis." The word "this" could refer to the informed consent form or to the number (the intended meaning). To correct the ambiguity, you may simply add the word "number" after "this."

Use Similar Words Appropriately.

Words such as "then" and "than" are sometimes confused. "Then" typically refers to a point in time (e.g., "Then, we ended the session with a debriefing."), whereas "than" is used in comparisons (e.g., "Women responded more quickly than did men."). Other word sets or pairs that tend to be confused include "there," "their," and "they're"; "to," "too," and "two'; "affect" and "effect"; "who's" and "whose"; "accept" and "except"; "adolescents" and "adolescence"; and "compliment" and "complement." If you have any doubt about which word is appropriate in a particular context, checking a dictionary should resolve the uncertainty.

Use Apostrophes Appropriately.

Apostrophes indicate possession (e.g., the participant's scores). When a sentence involves a plural noun (e.g., participants), the apostrophe is placed after the "s" (e.g., the participants' scores). *One particularly confusing situation involves the use of "its," a* possessive form that does *not* require an apostrophe (e.g., "The committee was doing its work."). There is no such word as "its'." In forms of writing other than APA style, "it's" is used as a contraction for "it is." However, in APA style, you should avoid using contractions.

Punctuation

It is sometimes difficult to notice errors in punctuation if you are not actively looking for them. With this in mind, prior to editing, you might develop a list of the types of errors you are personally most apt to make. You can then use this list to systematically check for and correct these types of errors.

- *Use a comma before a coordinating conjunction that connects two independent clauses.* Seven coordinating conjunctions are available for connecting two independent clauses in the same sentence. To help remember these connecting words, you may use the acronym FANBOYS, which represents For, And, Nor, But, Or, Yet, and So. When you use one of these words as a coordinating conjunction, you should use a comma before the word (e.g., "The independent variable will be the condition, and the dependent variable will be attitudes toward the anti-smoking policy."). In contrast, the following sentence is incorrect because it lacks a comma before the coordinating conjunction: "Some parents claimed that health care professionals provided vaccination-related information that was too general and other parents noted that information about side effects was vague or lacking (Austvoll-Dahlgren & Helseth, 2010)." Please remember that the rule about using a comma before FANBOYS applies *specifically* to the use of these words to connect two independent clauses. Do *not* place a comma before every "and" in your manuscript (see section about avoiding unnecessary commas)!

- *Use a comma after introductory phrases, clauses, or words* before *the main independent clause but not if the dependent clause* follows *the main clause.* In the sentence "Because people are distracted, they may not notice changes in their environment," the dependent clause precedes the main clause; therefore, it is correct to use a comma between the two. The sentence "People may not notice changes in their environment because they are distracted" is also correct. In this second example, the dependent clause follows the main clause; therefore, there is no comma separating the two.

- *Use a comma after each item in a series of three or more items.* The following sentence illustrates correct use of commas in a series because it includes a comma after both "eggs" and "bacon": "Ten patrons ordered a combination of eggs, bacon, and waffles." The next sentence is *incorrect* because it is missing a comma after "equity theory": "Theories of work motivation emphasizing the cognitive effects of information include expectancy theory, equity theory and goal-setting theory."

- *Avoid comma splices.* A comma splice occurs when you use only a comma to separate two sentences (independent clauses)—for instance, "Many public emergency rooms are understaffed, some may attract homeless people who are seeking shelter." There are two equally acceptable ways of creating a correct compound sentence. One way is to add a conjunction such as "and" after the comma (e.g., "Many public emergency rooms are understaffed, and some may attract homeless people who are seeking shelter."). A second way is to change the comma to a semicolon (e.g., "Many public emergency rooms are understaffed; some may attract homeless people who are seeking shelter."). You may also solve the problem by creating two simple sentences.

- *Avoid using commas when they are not necessary.* There are three relatively common types of "comma abuse." First, commas are not used between a subject and a predicate. The subject indicates who or what the sentence is about. The predicate includes a verb or verbs that tell something about the subject. The sentence "One important attribute of learning, involves elaboration of material" is *incorrect* because it has an unnecessary comma between "learning" and "involves." Second, commas are not used between two parts of a compound subject (a subject with more than one noun). The sentence "Magazines, and televisions often portray models who are very slim." is *incorrect* because it includes a comma between "magazines" and "and." Third, commas are not used between two parts of a compound predicate. The sentence "Fifteen women talked on their cell phones, and crossed the street." is *incorrect* because it includes an unnecessary comma between "phones" and "and."

- *Use semicolons correctly.* The most common use of a semicolon is to separate two closely related sentences (independent clauses) that are not connected with a conjunction (e.g., "and"). The following example illustrates the correct use of a semicolon: "People show remorse in different ways; some cry, and others are apologetic." A semicolon should *not* be used to separate an independent from a dependent clause. The following example illustrates an *incorrect* use of a semicolon: "Students in a cooperative learning environment typically enjoy it; particularly when a single grade is given for a group assignment." To correct this sentence, remove the semicolon and replace it with a comma.

- *Use colons correctly.* The most common use of a colon is to separate a grammatically complete (independent) clause from a final phrase that extends it. The following example illustrates the correct use of a colon: "The routine included three types of exercises: knee bends, sit ups, and running in place." A colon should *not* be used after a clause that is not an independent clause. The following example illustrates an *incorrect* use of a colon: "According to Freud, the mind is made up of: the ego, the id, and the superego." To correct this sentence, remove the colon.

Rules Pertaining Specifically to APA Style

In addition to rules about grammar and mechanics that apply to formal writing in general, APA style also includes specific guidelines that relate to unnecessary words, use of numerals, use of abbreviations, use of active voice, and distinctions between words such as "while" and "since." These guidelines are summarized in this section.

Economy of Expression

Avoid redundancy by using as few words as possible to express your ideas. For example, the phrase "due to the fact that" can be consolidated to a single word, "because." Another way to reduce redundancy is to consider the precise meaning of words. For example, because "unanimous" means endorsed by everyone, it is redundant to use the phrase "completely unanimous."

Use of Numerals Versus Numbers Expressed as Words

When referring to numbers 10 and above, use numerals except when the number begins a sentence (in which case use words to express the number). To express numbers less than 10, APA style requires that you use words rather than numerals most of the time. For example, the description of a sample of students might read, "The sample included 14 first-year students, nine sophomores, 10 juniors, and five seniors." The most common exceptions to the rule about using words to express numbers less than 10 include using numerals in the Abstract and in tables; for values that precede a unit of measurement (e.g. 9 cm) including time (e.g., 5 min); and for values designating age, scores, points on a scale, or placement in a sequence (e.g., Test 3). Numbers that begin a sentence are always expressed in words (e.g., Thirty-five participants did not complete the survey.").

Use of Abbreviations

The examples for numerals illustrate two of the more common abbreviations in APA style: "cm" for centimeters and "min" for minutes. Other common abbreviations include "hr" for hour, "s" for second, "m" for meter, and "v" for volt. However, APA guidelines state that you should not abbreviate the words "day," "week," "month," and "year." Before using other abbreviations (e.g., "CG" for control group), consider whether the abbreviation is helpful or potentially confusing. With a few exceptions for words familiar to psychologists (e.g., IQ), abbreviations are explained when initially used. You might say, for example, that participants in the control group (CG) did not listen to any type of music. After an abbreviation is introduced, use it consistently throughout the paper.

Use of Active Voice

In general, APA-style guidelines suggest that you use active voice whenever possible. In sentences that use active voice, the subject of the sentence performs an action. For example, the sentence "men completed the task in small groups" is in active voice. In contrast, the sentence "the task was performed by the men" is in passive voice.

Use "While" and "Since" to Refer Only to Time.

To be precise, APA guidelines suggest that you should use the word "while" only when referring to events that occur simultaneously. For example, it is correct to say, "While participants were learning the words, they heard either music or static." It is incorrect to say, "While many reasons parents offered for not vaccinating their children related to potential side effects, others emphasized emotional factors rather than risks (Wroe, Turner, & Salkovskis, 2004)." In this latter instance, you should substitute "although" or "whereas" for "while." Similarly, you should use the word "since" only to indicate that an event occurred after another event. For example, it is correct to say, "Since the time when the data were initially published, there have been divergent interpretations of the findings." It is incorrect to say, "Since studies (e.g., Hedge, 2000) indicate that people spend a majority of the time indoors, it is important to investigate the effect of different types of artificial lighting on performance." In this latter instance, you should substitute "because" for "since."

Things to Avoid in APA-Style Writing

Although the APA guidelines explicitly mention only some of the items in Table 6 (on the next page), the listing encompasses widespread conventions for scientific writing in psychology. Reviewing your writing to adhere to these suggestions will improve the quality of your manuscript!

CONCLUDING THOUGHTS

Manuscript editing and revision completes your first writing cycle. Ideally, if you have time, put the manuscript away for a few days. After some time has elapsed, read it again. Some sources even suggest that you take the time to read your work aloud in order to locate possible discontinuities or awkward phrases. Prior to submitting your written assignment, it is particularly important to check that you have cited all sources accurately and that all articles cited in the body of the report are included in the manuscript. Overall, although you may find these guidelines cumbersome at first, continued practice with formal, scientific APA-style writing, complemented by instructors' feedback and the material included in this chapter, should enable you to develop and enhance your scientific writing skills. In turn, you may approach your written assignments with greater confidence and with heightened potential for academic success.

TABLE 6 **Clarification of and Commentary on Items to Avoid**

Items to avoid	Clarification	Comment
Using sexist language	Do not use "he" to refer to a person in general.	Unless you are specifically referring to a man or woman, it is often easier to work with plurals (with the nouns "participants" or "people") and the gender-neutral pronoun "they."
Using informal language and colloquial expressions	Phrases such as "kind of," "sort of," "lots of," "pretty much," and "write up," although used in conversation, are not appropriate in formal writing.	Be as precise as possible. Find data that allow you to specify numbers or percentages if possible, or use words such as "many" or "few."
Using the word "prove"	Seek alternatives such as "support the hypothesis" or "gathered evidence for."	In psychology, conclusions are generally probabilistic, not certain, which is why we avoid the use of "prove."
Using the word "you" to refer to the reader	Rather than stating "it is important for you to exercise regularly," report "it is important for people to exercise regularly."	
Using the words "we," "us," or "our" to refer to people in general	Seek alternatives such as "individuals," "students," "respondents," or "people."	"We" or "our" is appropriate only to refer to the opinions or behaviors of the authors if there is more than one author (e.g., "We recruited a convenience sample.").
Using phrases such as "The first article indicated," "The next article demonstrated."	Use citations such as "Myers (2008) reported" or "_____ and _____ indicated."	In a literature review, integrate material topically, using meaningful transitions such as "Similarly," "In contrast," or "Moreover."
Using titles of articles (except in References) or authors' first names.	Use citations as illustrated above.	
Using males and females as nouns	Use "men" and "women" as nouns (e.g., 30 men and 30 women).	Use "male" and "female" as adjectives (e.g., Male participants read a scenario.)
Using contractions	Write "have not" rather than "haven't."	

References

Austvoll-Dahlgren, A., & Helseth, S. (2010). What informs parents' decision-making about childhood vaccinations? *Journal of Advanced Nursing, 66,* 2421–2430. doi:10.1111/j.1365-2648.2010.05403.x

Bruss, O. E., & Hill, J. M. (2010) Tell me more: Online versus face-to-face communication and self-disclosure. *Psi Chi Journal of Undergraduate Research, 15,* 3–7. Retrieved from http://www.psichi.org/pubs/journal/

Chiou, W. (2006). Adolescents' sexual self-disclosure on the Internet: Deindividuation and impression management. *Adolescence, 41,* 547–561. Retrieved from http://www.vjf.cnrs.fr/clt/php/va/Page_revue.php?ValCodeRev=ADO

Fallahi, C. R., Wood, R. M., Austad, C., & Fallahi, H. (2006). A program for improving undergraduate psychology students' basic writing skills. *Teaching of Psychology, 33,* 171–175. doi:10.1207/s15328023top3303_3

Fuchs, L. S., Compton, D. L., Fuchs, D., Hollenbeck, K. N., Hamlett, C. L., & Seethaler, P. M. (2011). Two-stage screening for math problem-solving difficulty using dynamic assessment of algebraic learning. *Journal of Learning Disabilities, 44,* 372–380. doi:10.1177/0022219411407867

Griggs, R. A. (2012). *Psychology: A concise introduction* (3rd ed.). New York, NY: Worth.

Hedge, A. (2000). Where are we in understanding the effects of where we are?. *Ergonomics, 43,* 1019–1029. doi:10.1080/001401300409198

Marek, P., Griggs, R. A., & Christopher, A. N. (1999). Pedagogical aids in textbooks: Do college students' perceptions justify their prevalence?. *Teaching of Psychology, 26*(1), 11–19. doi:10.1207/s15328023top2601_2

Schwarz, N. (1999). Self-reports: How the questions shape the answers. *American Psychologist, 54,* 93–105. doi:10.1037/0003-066X.54.2.93

Wroe, A. L., Turner, N., & Salkovskis, P. M. (2004). Understanding and predicting parental decisions about early childhood immunizations. *Health Psychology, 23,* 33–41. doi:1037/0278-6133.23.1.33

Appendix A

Sample Annotated Manuscript

Note: The copy above the line below constitutes the name of this section. The material below this line and in the running head above is part of the sample copy itself.

Tell Me More: Online Versus Face-to-Face Communication and

Self-Disclosure

Olivia E. Bruss and Jennifer M. Hill

Wisconsin Lutheran College

> Page numbering starts on the title page, right-justified in the header area.

> Running head—The running head is left-justified. The words "Running head" (followed by a colon, with only the R capitalized) appear in the header area for the title page only. The actual running head that appears on all pages is typed in all capital letters

> Key words (and all words with four or more letters) in the title begin with capital letters. The title, authors' names, and byline (affiliation) are all centered.

> Authors' names are on a line double-spaced below the title and affiliation is on the next double-spaced line.

The abstract is a single block paragraph. Length limits vary for different journals.

Information from Introduction (purpose).

Information from Method (participants and design).

Citations in the Abstract do not "count" as the first citation within the text of the manuscript.

Information from Results that includes specific measure used.

Information about Discussion.

Abstract

The purpose of this study was to examine the effect of type of communication (online or face-to- face) on self-disclosure. A group of 58 college students engaged in a conversation either face-to-face or using an instant-messaging system. Those who conversed online reported a significantly higher amount of personal and perceived partner self-disclosure as measured by an adapted version of the Revised Self-Disclosure Scale (Wheeless, 1978) than those who conversed face-to-face. Implications regarding online communication and its impact on counseling, educational, and personal relationships are discussed.

In the Abstract, *all* numbers are expressed as numerals. Do not begin a sentence with a number in the Abstract. Elsewhere in the manuscript, any number greater than or equal to 10 is also expressed as a numeral (unless it begins a sentence). However, numbers less than 10, with some exceptions, are expressed in words.

Tell Me More: Online Versus Face-to-Face Communication and

Self-Disclosure

In today's technology-centered world, people are no longer required to communicate and form relationships in face-to-face situations alone. In fact, the use of electronic forms of communication, such as text-messaging or online interaction, is rapidly becoming a primary tool for many people to form and maintain many of their relationships. For instance, a recent online survey of 439 college students showed that nearly 20% of college students spent over 20 hr per week online (Burst Media, 2007). This shift in communication impacts several different categories of relationships people have: familial relationships, friendships, romantic relationships, professional relationships, and educational relationships. Consequently, the impact of online communication on building and maintaining relationships is important to understand.

Self-disclosure has been viewed as a key component in developing close relationships (Altman & Taylor, 1973). Jourard and Lasakow (1958, p. 91) defined self-disclosure as "the process of making the self known to other persons." According to this perspective, self-disclosure builds trust which leads to closer relationships. When one individual takes a risk by disclosing to another individual, the receiver feels as though he or she is trusted. In return, the receiver is more likely to disclose information as well. Trust and security are developed when two people respond to one another positively over repeated interactions, which continually strengthen the relationship. A key element of the relationship is that the individuals involved must perceive that their disclosures are being accepted. Therefore, the process is mutually reinforcing (Bennis, Schien, Berlew, & Steele, 1964).

With the rapid growth of technology, people can now self-disclose

---

Margin notes:

The introduction begins with the title, not the word Introduction.

There are two spaces between sentences.

Note the comma after the introductory phrase.

Abbreviate units of time.

Note the use of a colon after an independent clause that is extended with additional information.

Initial paragraph emphasizes the relevance of the topic.

Example of parenthetical citation with use of an ampersand (&).

Example of citation in narrative with use of "and." Because this citation involves a quote, it also includes a page number.

If a citation contains three to five authors, all are included in the first citation in the text, with a comma between them and between the last author and the year.

Note the use of a comma before the coordinating conjunction that separates two independent clauses.

If multiple citations are included in the same parentheses, the citations are listed in alphabetical order by the name of the first author.

Note the appropriate use of a semicolon between two closely related independent clauses.

The year is always included in parenthetical citations.

Notice the logical organization of information in this paragraph about disparate results. The systematic use of the terms first, second, and third provide a structure to the coverage.

If a citation includes more than two authors, only the first author's name (followed by et al.) is used after the initial citation. Et al. means "and others." There is a period after "al" (because it is an abbreviation for alia) but not after "et" (because it is an unabbreviated word).

using more indirect means like the Internet, and several recent studies have begun to more closely examine self-disclosure during online communication (Chiou, 2006; Punyanunt-Carter, 2006; Valkenburg & Peter, 2007). One of the most common explanations proposed for people's tendency to self-disclose online is the fact that online communication increases anonymity. This anonymity can then produce a state of deindividuation in which others are not seen as individuals; consequently, people lose their inner restraints (Chiou, 2006). In other words, people may feel more comfortable with self-disclosure online because others do not necessarily know who they are as individuals and their disclosures online are less likely to produce immediate social repercussions.

Online Versus Face-to-Face Communication and Self-Disclosure

Although numerous researchers have compared the self-disclosure of participants in online situations versus those in face-to-face situations, results have been mixed. Tidwell and Walther (2002) found that participants in online situations demonstrated higher self-disclosure than those in face-to-face situations. Conversely, others found that participants in a face-to-face situation reported greater self-disclosure than those interacting online (Mallen, Day, & Green, 2003; Skinner & Latchford, 2006).

Factors that may have contributed to the different results should be noted. First, researchers have studied the relationship between type of communication and self-disclosure in different ways. Some have assigned participants to one of two communication conditions (online versus face-to-face) and looked for differences in self-disclosure (Mallen et al., 2003; Tidwell & Walther, 2002). Others examined differences in perceived self-disclosure between those who self-reported using online communication regularly, compared to those who said they used it less frequently (Cho, 2007; Skinner & Latchford, 2006). Second, different forms of computer-mediated communication (CMC) were used in these studies, including synchronous (instant messaging) and asynchronous (e-mail and support group webpage) methods. Third, these studies differed in their measurements of self-disclosure as well; some employed self-reports and some used judges to rate the degree and quality of self-disclosure, often by rules of linguistics.

Another facet of self-disclosure is the phenomenon of reciprocity. This states that if people perceive that their discussion partners are self-disclosing to them, they will in-turn self-disclose more to their partners (Barak & Gluck-Ofri, 2007). The extant literature indicates that reciprocity does occur online (Barak & Gluck-Ofri, 2007) and describes the factors that impact reciprocity online (Rollman, Krug, & Parente, 2000; Rollman & Parente, 2001). However, to our knowledge, no studies exist that have investigated whether people perceive their partners as self-disclosing more in an online situation or a face-to-face situation. This would be necessary to determine if reciprocity occurs to a greater degree online than face-to-face.

Purpose and Hypotheses

The goal of the present research is to gain more clarity regarding the relationship between type of communication and self-disclosure. Specifically, the current study extends previous research in the area by (a) employing an experimental rather than retrospective design and (b) comparing whether the perception of partner self-disclosure is greater online or face-to-face situation. First, we hypothesized that because online communication increases anonymity (Chiou, 2006), participants in the online group will report higher levels of personal self-disclosure than those in the face-to-face group. Second, based on the concept of reci-

---

An abbreviation is initially introduced by putting it in parentheses after the term to which it refers. In subsequent mentions of the concept, only the abbreviation is used. Although APA guidelines suggest that it is preferable not to introduce an abbreviation for a term that is subsequently used less than three times, this manuscript does not follow that guideline.

In this paragraph, after introducing the topic of reciprocity, the authors discuss a gap in the literature that provides justification for their own study.

The authors state explicitly the goal of their research.

Within this sentence, notice how the authors identify elements in a series by lowercase letters in parentheses.

In the hypotheses, the authors identify specify variables and how they expect them to influence each other.

procity (Barak & Gluck-Ofri, 2007), we hypothesized that those participating in online discussions would perceive that their conversation partners disclose more to them than those participating in face-to-face discussions.

Method

Participants

Participants were recruited through an undergraduate psychology department-sponsored research activity. Initially, 60 participants completed the study, but two participants were not included in the final analyses due to incomplete data. The remaining participants included 58 (25 men, 33 women) undergraduate students attending a small liberal arts college in the Midwest, and the majority of the sample was Caucasian (97%). The participants' ages ranged from 18 to 28 ($M = 20.10$, $SD = 1.78$). Two conditions existed: the online communication group and the face-to-face communication group. The participants in the online group consisted of 14 men and 15 women, whose ages ranged from 18 to 28 ($M = 20.38$, $SD = 2.19$). The participants in the face-to-face group consisted of 11 men and 18 women, and their ages ranged from 18 to 22 ($M = 19.83$, $SD = 1.23$).

Instruments and Apparatus

The researchers employed an adapted version of the Revised Self-Disclosure Scale (RSDS; Wheeless, 1978) to determine participants' level of self-disclosure. Nineteen items from the original scale were reworded to be more applicable to the interaction in this particular experiment. Nine items were used to measure the amount and quality of each participant's disclosure in this situation (personal self-disclosure). Sample items include "In this experience, I often disclosed intimate personal things about myself without hesitation" and "In this experience, I did not often talk about myself."

The heading of the Method is centered and is in boldface type.

This Level 2 heading is flush left and boldface.

Numbers less than ten are typically expressed using words (with some exceptions). More common exceptions include consistent use of numbers for time, age, scores, points on a scale, and for numbers that indicate a position in a series (such as Table 2).

Note the appropriate placement of an apostrophe to indicate plural possessive.

Abbreviations for statistics (mean and standard deviation) are italicized.

This Participants section contains basic, required demographic information about number of participants, age, gender, and ethnicity.

This Level 2 heading is flush left and boldface with capital letters at the beginning of key words.

Always use words to express a number that begins a sentence.

In this and the following paragraph, notice the detailed information provided about the scale (source, number of items that measured each construct, sample items, the type of answer options, and the numerical and verbal anchors for the answer options).

The remaining 10 items measured the amount and quality of disclosure from the partner in this situation (perceived partner self-disclosure). Sample items included "In this experience, my partner talked about his/herself for fairly long periods at a time" and "In this experience, my partner did not seem honest in his/her self-disclosures." Participants were asked to indicate their agreement with the items on a 7-point Likert scale ranging from 1 (*strongly disagree*) to 7 (*strongly agree*).

> Numbers representing points on a scale are expressed in numerals, an exception to the rule about using words to express numbers less than 10.

> Verbal anchor points for a scale are italicized.

The participants used five of Aron, Melinat, Aron, Vallone, and Bator's (1997) Closeness-Generating Questions, which were designed to encourage self-disclosure. One example question is, "If you have to move from where you consider home, where would you go, and what would you miss the most about home?". Lastly, participants responded to an eight-question demographic survey on which they reported their age, gender, year in school, and the extent to which they felt they knew their partner before this experiment.

> Typically the period goes inside the quotation marks when the material occurs at the end of a sentence, but in this case the material is a question, even though the sentence itself is not.

In addition, the participants in the online condition used computers in the following manner. The researchers placed 15 laptops in two rooms (A and B) on two different floors. Each computer had a number 1 through 15. Each computer also had a mock instant messaging (IM) account already on the screen. The individual IM accounts on each screen allowed the participant to communicate with only one other account, which was already up on the screen of the corresponding computer in another room on a different floor. Therefore, participants communicated online with the person in the other room sitting at the computer with the same number. For instance, the participant seated at Computer 1 in Room A communicated online only with the person seated at Computer 1 in Room B. Each participant was assigned a gender-neutral pseudonym that appeared at the top of each IM account (e.g.,

> This is example of the use of a numeral to express a number less than 10 that designates a place in a series.

> Capitalize words that indicate placement within a series.

Sam024689753, Taylor035798642, and Jess035798642). In addition, all participants were asked not to reveal their real names to their partners.

Procedure

The independent variable was type of communication (online versus face-to-face) and participants were assigned to one of these two conditions as they arrived at the study. We randomly assigned partners only in the face-to-face condition. The dependent measures were personal self-disclosure and perceived partner self-disclosure.

Online condition. Participants entered the room and picked a computer by seating themselves. Consequently, pairs were created through convenience sampling. Each pair then was given five questions to discuss, and each topic was designed to encourage self-disclosure (Aron et al., 1997). The researchers asked participants not to reveal their names to each other and to stop the conversation and notify the researchers if they suspected that they knew their partner. This, however, did not occur. The researchers then informed the participants to keep conversing until instructed to do otherwise. After 15 min, the researchers stopped the conversations and the participants filled out the survey packet, which included an adapted version of the RSDS (Wheeless, 1978) and a demographic survey. Participants took approximately 3 min to complete these surveys.

Face-to-face condition. All participants entered the same room and received an informed consent. The researchers randomly assigned pairs by having participants pick numbers out of a container and pair up with the person with the same number. Participants were asked if they knew their partners (more than just in passing) before this interaction, and if they did, they would have been reassigned. However, this did not hap-

In this opening paragraph of the Procedure, the authors describe the experimental design and identify the independent and dependent variables.

Min is the standard APA style abbreviation for minutes. The abbreviation is not followed by a period.

Numbers referring to time are also always expressed in numerals, another exception to the less than 10 rule.

This description of the face-to-face condition includes information about informed consent and debriefing.

pen. Pairs then were given the same choices of topics as the online con-

dition and the same time limit. After 15 min, the researchers stopped the

conversations and handed out the survey packets, which contained all the

same instruments as the packets for the online group. The participants in

both the online and face-to-face groups were given debriefing statements

after they handed in their survey packets.

Results

For the entire sample, mean response scores for personal self-dis-

closure on the adapted version of the RSDS (Wheeless, 1978) ranged

from 3.56 to 6.56 ($M = 5.09$, $SD = 0.68$) on a scale from 1 to 7. The

Cronbach's $\alpha\alpha$ for the personal self-disclosure items was .64. An inde-

pendent t test was conducted to explore the impact of communication

group (online or face-to-face) on levels of personal self-disclosure. Mean

personal self-disclosure responses for the online group ($M = 5.30$, $SD =$

0.66) were significantly higher than the face-to-face group ($M = 4.88$, SD

$= 0.65$), $t(56) = 2.45$, $p = .02$. The partial eta squared statistic was .10,

indicating a large effect.

For perceived partner self-disclosure, entire sample mean

response scores on a scale from 1 to 7 ranged from 1.90 to 6.10 ($M =$

4.80, $SD = 0.69$). The Cronbach's $\alpha\alpha$ for perceived partner self-disclo-

sure items was .71. An independent t test was conducted to explore the

impact of communication group (online or face-to-face) on levels of

perceived partner self-disclosure. Mean perceived partner self-disclo-

sure responses for the online group ($M = 5.02$, $SD = 0.57$) were signifi-

cantly higher than the face-to-face group ($M = 4.58$, $SD = 0.74$), $t(56)$

$= 2.49$, $p = .02$. The partial eta squared statistic was .10, indicating a

large effect.

The opening paragraph is the analysis of the first dependent variable. Cronbach's alpha is a measure of internal consistency, which means that it measures how closely all the items on a scale relate to each other.

This sentence describes the results of one type of inferential statistical test, a t test. This type of t test is used to determine whether the difference between two sample groups is likely to occur in the population or whether the difference is attributable to random fluctuation (chance). The authors state that the difference was significant, meaning that the difference is likely to be attributable to the independent variable (communication group) rather than to chance.

Discussion

Type of Communication and Self-Disclosure

The purpose of the study is restated.

The authors explicitly state whether the hypothesis about the predicted results was supported.

Current findings are placed in the context of existing literature.

A possible explanation is offered for why results differ from those of a prior investigation.

Information in this paragraph expands on possible reasons for personal self-disclosure results in the present research.

This research study sought to examine the relationship between online or face-to-face communication and self-disclosure. As predicted, the participants in the online communication group reported higher levels of personal self-disclosure and perceived partner self-disclosure than those in the face-to-face group. These results are in line with Tidwell and Walther's (2002) findings, but contradict Mallen et al.'s (2003) results, which indicated that those in face-to-face pairs self-disclosed more than those in online pairs. These differences may reflect measurement issues. Mallen et al. (2003) measured self-disclosure with one item that focused on the amount of self-disclosure. Specifically, they asked participants to rate their own self-disclosure from 1 (*no self-disclosure*) to 6 (*extreme self-disclosure*), whereas the present study's measure contained nine items that were also meant to assess one's perception of both the quality and amount of self-disclosure.

Results from the current study suggest that online communication may increase people's personal self-disclosure in general, helping them along in the early stages of relationship building. Several previous researchers have provided possible explanations for the present results. A common explanation is the anonymity that an online environment provides, which allows people to feel safer self-disclosing (Chiou, 2006). Tidwell and Walther (2002) proposed another explanation for greater disclosure in an online setting. They noted that many of the ways people get to know others (e.g., reading and interpreting nonverbal cues) are not possible in online communication. Therefore, people communicating online may actually be limited to using self-disclosure as a means to get to know one another. Because this form of communication is fairly commonplace in present times, people may now expect self-disclosure by themselves and others in online communication because no other means of getting to know each other is possible. If this norm of self-disclosure does in fact exist online, it may explain why the online group in this study reported higher personal self-disclosure.

Finally, results indicated that people perceive their communication partners as disclosing more in an online situation than in a face-to-face situation. This suggests that the phenomenon of reciprocity may occur to a greater degree online than face-to-face. Therefore, these findings may serve as another explanation of why people disclose more online in general. The online participants may have felt that their partners were self-disclosing more than the face-to-face participants felt their partners were self-disclosing. In turn, this may have then influenced the online group to self-disclose more to their partners than the face-to-face group felt necessary to disclose to theirs.

> This paragraph focuses on participants' perceptions of their partners' disclosure. Again, potential explanations are offered, expanding readers' understanding of the results rather than just iterating the findings.

Practical Applications and Future Directions

> In this section, the authors highlight the importance of their study by indicating how results can be applied. In the first paragraph, the authors discuss clinical applications; in the second paragraph, they discuss academic applications. Such organization enhances readers' understanding.

Due to the prevalence of online communication in the world today, the results of this study can be applied to practical situations. This study can contribute to the debate concerning the effectiveness of online counseling (Mallen & Vogel, 2005; Murphy & Mitchell, 1998; Rochlen, Zack, & Speyer, 2004; Young, 2005). Because online communication elicited more self-disclosure, online communication may be an effective venue for forming therapeutic relationships. Online therapy may appeal to and benefit clients for several other reasons, which are discussed extensively in other research articles; therefore, we provide only a brief overview of the benefits here. The anonymity of online communication may make clients feel more open when disclosing to counselors (Chiou, 2006). Furthermore, because the Internet can hide the client's and therapist's age, race, other physical features, and clothing style or quality, the harmful assumptions and judgments about others that people often make in person will not exist. This may allow for less biased communication from the client and genuine therapeutic guidance (Rochlen et al., 2004). Despite the possible benefits of online therapy, research on its effectiveness is still needed. Therefore, counselors should practice online counseling cautiously by taking extra ethical precautions, such as ensuring confidentiality, formulating an emergency protocol, and obtaining informed consent for treatment (Casper, 2004).

Furthermore, the present results may also be useful in academic settings. Because online communication elicited more self-disclosure, teachers may consider using it to form closer relationships with their students so they can better meet their students' needs. Using online communication may make students feel more comfortable asking teachers or other students' questions because of the anonymity it can provide. Similarly, online communication may be used in this way for students to assist each other with academic assignments. Naturally, the present study's results suggest that future research examine whether online communication may be used to increase disclosure and strengthen new business relationships between colleagues as well as personal relationships (familial, romantic, and platonic).

This paragraph addresses limitations of the present research and possible ways to overcome them in future investigations.

Given that online communication will likely continue to grow rapidly, research about the impact of online communication on self-disclosure and relationships is necessary. Due to the small and racially homogenous sample size, future studies should employ a larger and more ethnically diverse sample. Because this study took place on a small campus of less than 1000 students, the anonymity of online communication may have played a role in producing more self-disclosure in the online group. This may have occurred because participants in the face-to-face group may have guarded their disclosures more than those in the online group if they thought they were likely to see their partners on campus later. This phenomenon may not occur in a larger sample from a bigger university or from a noncollege sample.

Additionally, future researchers should consider other important moderating variables to better understand the relationship between type of communication (online versus face-to-face) and self-disclosure. In particular, it would be helpful to consider the impact of certain personal characteristics, such as age, personality, race, culture, socioeconomic status, intelligence, and writing ability. Furthermore, the present study did not consider the effects of large amounts of self-disclosure on relationships; for example, future studies could examine how and in which situations excessive self-disclosure can harm a relationship. Finally, it would be beneficial to examine how online versus face-to-face communication impacts self-disclosure for particular types of relationships, such as student–teacher, client–therapist, romantic, and familial.

The concluding paragraph also addresses future research, highlighting specific variables that researchers may investigate.

References

- Every reference included in the article is listed in the References section.
- References are listed in alphabetical order by the last name of the first author.
- Citations use a "hanging" indentation.
- There is only a single space after the period that follows each reference element (e.g., year, title,).
- If there is more than one author, an ampersand (preceded by a comma) is used before the last author's surname.

For books and book chapters, include city and state (or city and country, if not in the United States).

This citation is an example of a reference to an entire book. For a book, the title is italicized.
- If an author's middle initial is provided in the article, the middle initial is included in the citation (with a space after the period between initials).

This citation is an example of a reference to a journal article, the most common type of source in a typical article.
- Note the order of reference elements, the use of capitalization in the article compared to the journal title, and the use of italics for the journal name and volume number (but not for the article title or page numbers).
- There is a period after the page numbers, but not after the doi (digital object identifier).

This citation is for an online newsletter. As is the case for a doi, make sure not to put a period after a URL because it could be confused as part of the URL rather than as punctuation.

If a journal article does not have an assigned doi, provide the URL of the journal's home page.

Altman, I., & Taylor, D. (1973). *Social penetration: The development of interpersonal relationships*. New York, NY: Holt, Rinehart, & Winston.

Aron, A., Melinat, E., Aron, E. N., Vallone, R. D., & Bator, R. J. (1997). The experimental generation of interpersonal closeness: A procedure and some preliminary findings. *Personality and Social Psychology Bulletin, 23,* 363–377. doi:10.1177/0146167297234003

Barak, A., & Gluck-Ofri, O. (2007). Degree and reciprocity of self-disclosure in online forums. *CyberPsychology & Behavior*, *10*, 407–417. doi:10.1089/cpb.2006.9938

Bennis, W. G., Schien, E. H., Berlew, D. E., & Steele, F. I. (1964). *Interpersonal dynamics*. Homewood, IL: Dorsey Press.

Burst Media (2007). *Online insights*. Retrieved from http://www.burst-media.com/assets/newsletter/items/2007_07_01.pdf

Casper, F. (2004). Technological developments and applications in clinical psychology and psychotherapy: Introduction. *Journal of Clinical Psychology, 60,* 221–230. doi:10.1002/jclp.10260

Chiou, W. (2006). Adolescents' sexual self-disclosure on the Internet: Deindividuation and impression management. *Adolescence, 41,* 547–561. Retrieved from http://www.vjf.cnrs.fr/clt/php/va/Page_revue.php?ValCodeRev=ADO

Cho, S. H. (2007). Effects of motivations and gender on adolescents' self-disclosure in online chatting. *CyberPsychology & Behavior, 10,* 339–345. doi:10.1089/cpb.2006.9946

Jourard, S. M., & Lasakow, P. (1958). Some factors in self-disclosure. *Journal of Abnormal and Social Psychology, 56,* 91–98. doi:10.1037/h0043357

Mallen, M. J., Day, S. X., & Green, M. A. (2003). Online versus face-to-face conversations: An examination of relational and disclosure variables. *Psychotherapy: Theory, Research, Practice, Training, 40,* 155–163. doi:10.1037/0033-3204.40.1-2.155

Mallen, M. J., & Vogel, D. L. (2005). Introduction to the major contribution: Counseling psychology and online counseling. *The Counseling Psychologist, 33,* 761–776. doi:10.1177/0011000005278623

Murphy, L., & Mitchell, D. (1998). When writing helps to heal: E-mail as therapy. *British Journal of Guidance & Counseling, 26,* 21–32. doi:10.1080/03069889800760031

Punyanunt-Carter, N. M. (2006). An analysis of college students' self-disclosure behaviors on the Internet. *College Student Journal, 40,* 329–331. Retrieved from http://www.projectinnovation.biz/csj_2006.html

Rochlen, A. B., Zack, J. S., & Speyer, C. (2004). Online therapy: Review of relevant definitions, debates, and current empirical support. *Journal of Clinical Psychology, 60,* 269–283. doi:10.1002/jclp.10263

Rollman, J. B., Krug, K., & Parente, F. (2000). The chat room phenomenon: Reciprocal communication in cyberspace. *CyberPsychology & Behavior, 3,* 161–166. doi:10.1089/109493100316003

Rollman, J. B., & Parente, F. (2001). Relation of statement length and type and type of chat room to reciprocal communication on the Internet. *CyberPsychology & Behavior, 5,* 617–622. doi:10.1089/109493101753235214

Skinner, A. E. G., & Latchford, G. (2006). Attitudes to counseling via the Internet: A comparison between in-person counseling clients and Internet support group users. *Counseling and Psychotherapy Research, 6,* 158–163. doi:10.1080/14733140600853641

This citation illustrates the correct use of capitalization after a colon.

Alphabetize entries with the same first author according to the first difference between the two citations (ignoring "&"), not necessarily by the year of publication.

This article title illustrates correct use of a hyphen; all "self" compounds should be hyphenated.

Tidwell, L. C., & Walther, J. B. (2002). Computer-mediated communication effects on disclosure, impressions, and interpersonal evaluations: Getting to know one another a bit at a time. *Human Communication Research, 28,* 317–348. doi:10.1111/j.1468-2958.2002.tb00811.x

Valkenburg, P. M., & Peter, J. (2007). Preadolescents' and adolescents' online communication and their closeness to friends. *Developmental Psychology, 43,* 267–277. doi:10.1037/0012-1649.43.2.267

Wheeless, L. R. (1978). A follow-up study of the relationships among trust, disclosure, and interpersonal solidarity. *Human Communication Research, 4,* 143–157. doi:10.1111/j.1468-2958.1978.tb00604.x

Young, K. S. (2005). An empirical examination of client attitudes towards online counseling. *CyberPsychology & Behavior, 8,* 172–177. doi:10.1089/cpb.2005.8.172

This article title illustrates correct usage of apostrophes for plural possessives.

Appendix B

Constructing Grammatical Sentences

Proper sentence structure	Explanation	Correct example	Incorrect usage (see bolding)
Construct complete sentences and avoid sentence fragments.	A sentence expresses a complete thought and typically contains a subject and a verb. A fragment does not express a complete thought.	Because employers may consider being young as a plus (Finkelstein & Burke, 1998), older applicants may have difficulty obtaining an interview.	**Because employers may consider being young as a plus (Finkelstein & Burke, 1998).**
Use parallel construction.	Use a similar grammatical form to express each item in a series.	Limitations of this online research included convenience sampling, potential for socially desirable responding, and lack of control over the experimental environment.	Limitations of this online research included convenience sampling, **participants who may have responded in a socially desirable manner,** and the fact that the researcher did not control the experimental environment.
Make sure the subject agrees with the verb. (Remember, the word "data" is pural.)	The verb should be consistent with the subject in number (singular or plural) and person (1st, 2nd, or 3rd).	High scores on the ageism scale indicate more negative attitudes about older individuals.	High **scores** on the ageism scale **indicates** more negative attitudes about older individuals.
Make sure a pronoun agrees with the noun to which it refers.	A pronoun should be consistent in number (singular or plural) and person (1st, 2nd, or 3rd) with the noun that it replaces.	When individuals feel stereotyped, they may fall victim to self-fulfilling prophecies (Hilton & Von Hippel, 1996).	When **an individual** feels stereotyped, **they** may fall victim to self-fulfilling prophecies (Hilton & Von Hippel, 1996).
Make sure pronouns have a clear referent.	There should be no doubt about the noun to which a pronoun refers.	If older job applicants are viewed as resistant to change, employers may be less likely to hire them particularly when the pool of job applicants is large. This stereotyping of older applicants could lead to problems of discrimination.	If older job applicants are viewed as resistant to change, employers may be less likely to hire them particularly when the pool of job applicants is large. **This** could lead to problems of discrimination.
Use similar words appropriately.	Correctly distinguish between words that sound or look alike (e.g., "then" and "than," " "their" and "there").	Participants perceived that younger workers performed more efficiently than did older workers (Finkelstein & Burke, 1998).	Participants perceived that younger workers performed more efficiently **then** did older workers (Finkelstein & Burke, 1998).
Use apostrophes appropriately.	Apostrophes indicate possession or contraction, never whether a word is plural, and their placement differs for singular and plural nouns.	Kwong See and Heller (2004) explained how shifting standards for what is good across age groups may affect participants' responses.	Kwong See and Heller (2004) explained how shifting standards for what is good across age groups may affect participant**'s** responses.
Use a comma before a conjunction that separates two independent clauses.	Use a comma before a "coordinating conjunction" when the conjunction is used to connect two independent clauses. Coordinating conjunctions include For, And, Nor, But, Or, Yet, and So (FANBOYS).	Martens et al. (2004) reported that people do not want to be reminded of their own mortality, and older adults only serve as a reminder of the reality of aging and dying.	Martens et al. (2004) reported that people do not want to be reminded of their own **mortality and** older adults only serve as a reminder of the reality of aging and dying.

Proper sentence structure	Explanation	Correct example	Incorrect usage
Use a comma after introductory phrases, clauses, or words before the main independent clause.	If a sentence begins with a phrase or clause that does not express a complete thought, put a comma at the end of that phrase or clause.	Because of the increasing number of older workers, ageism in employment has become a topical issue (William & Nussbaum, 2001).	Because of the increasing number of older workers ageism in employment has become a topical issue (William & Nussbaum, 2001).
Do not use a comma between clauses when the dependent clause follows the main clause.	If a sentence includes an independent clause followed by a dependent clause, do not put a comma between the two clauses.	Ageism in employment has become a topical issue because of the increasing number of older workers (William & Nussbaum, 2001).	Ageism in employment has become a topical **issue, because** of the increasing number of older workers (William & Nussbaum, 2001).
Use a comma after each item in a series of three or more items.	If a sentence includes a series of items, put a comma between them.	Laczko and Philipson (1991) found that older workers exhibited high energy, flexibility, and a willingness to learn.	Laczko and Philipson (1991) found that older workers exhibited high energy, **flexibility and** a willingness to learn.
Avoid comma splices.	When only a comma connects two independent clauses, it is called a comma splice. Avoid this error by using a semicolon or a period.	We hypothesized that participants would perceive older workers as more resistant to change than younger workers. We derived this hypothesis from Reio and Sanders-Reio's (1999) findings that older adults were set in their ways.	We hypothesized that participants would perceive older workers as more resistant to change than younger **workers, we** derived this hypothesis from Reio and Sanders-Reio's (1999) findings that older adults were set in their ways.
Do not use a comma between a subject and a predicate (the part of a sentence including the verb).	There is no comma used between these two primary sentence components.	Another factor that may influence the reporting of discrimination is the accountability of employees.	Another factor that may influence the reporting of **discrimination, is** the accountability of employees.
Do not use a comma between two parts of a compound subject.	A subject may include more than one noun. If it does, do not put a comma between them.	Media and advertisements may reinforce ageist attitudes.	**Media, and** advertisements may reinforce ageist attitudes.
Do not use a comma between two parts of a compound predicate.	A predicate may contain more than one verb or verb phrase. If it does, do not put a comma between them.	Older employees can contribute considerably to a company and should be valued for their achievements.	Older employees can contribute considerably to a **company, and** should be valued for their achievements.
Use semicolons correctly.	The most common use of a semicolon is to separate two independent clauses not connected with a conjunction.	Lawmakers enacted the Age Discrimination Act to protect older workers from discrimination; legislators designed the Act to provide guidance to employers.	Lawmakers enacted the Age Discrimination Act to protect older workers from discrimination; **providing** guidance to employers.
Use colons correctly.	The most common use of a colon is to separate a grammatically complete (independent) clause from a final phrase that extends it.	Fraboni, Saltstone, and Hughes (1990) indicated that their ageism scale included three primary factors: antilocution, avoidance, and discrimination.	The three primary factors of the ageism scale **were:** antilocution, avoidance, and discrimination (Fraboni, Saltstone, & Hughes, 1990).

References

Finkelstein, L. M., & Burke, M. J. (1998). Age stereotyping at work: The role of rater and contextual factors on evaluations of job applicants. *Journal of General Psychology, 125,* 317–345. doi:10.1080/00221309809595341

Fraboni, M., Saltstone, R., & Hughes, S. (1990). The Fraboni Scale of Ageism (FSA): An attempt at a more precise measure of ageism. *Canadian Journal on Aging, 9,* 56–66. doi:10.1017/S0714980800016093

Hilton, J. L., & von Hippel, W. (1996). Stereotypes. *Annual Review of Psychology, 47,* 237–271. doi:10.1146/annurev.psych.47.1.237

Kwong See, S. T., & Heller, R. B. (2004). Judging older targets' discourse: How do age stereotypes influence evaluations?. *Experimental Aging Research, 30,* 63–73. doi:10.1080/03610730490251487

Laczko, F., & Philipson, C. (1991). *Changing work and retirement.* Buckingham: Open University Press.

Martens, A., Greenberg, J., Schimel, J., & Landau, M. J. (2004). Ageism and death: Effects of mortality salience and perceived similarity to elders on reactions to elderly people. *Personality and Social Psychology Bulletin, 30,* 1524–1536. doi:10.1177/0146167204271185

Reio Jr., T. G., & Sanders-Reio, J. (1999). Combating workplace ageism. *Adult Learning, 11*(1), 10–13. Retrieved from http://www.aaace.org

Williams, A., & Nussbaum, J. F. (2001). *Intergenerational communication across the life span.* Mahwah, NJ: Lawrence Erlbaum Associates.

About the Author

Kathleen Stassen Berger received her undergraduate education at Stanford University and Radcliffe College and earned an M.A.T. from Harvard University as well as an MS and PhD from Yeshiva University. Her broad experience as an educator includes directing a preschool, serving as chair of philosophy at the United Nations International School, teaching child and adolescent development to graduate students at Fordham University and undergraduates at Montclair State University in New Jersey and at Quinnipiac University in Connecticut, as well as teaching social psychology to inmates at Sing Sing Prison.

Throughout most of her professional career, Berger has taught at Bronx Community College of the City University of New York, first as an adjunct and for the past two decades as a full professor. She has taught introduction to psychology, child and adolescent development, adulthood and aging, social psychology, abnormal psychology, and human motivation. Her students—who come from many ethnic, economic, and educational backgrounds and who have a wide range of ages and interests—consistently honor her with the highest teaching evaluations.

Berger is also the author of *The Developing Person Through the Life Span* and *Invitation to the Life Span.* Her developmental texts are currently being used at more than 700 colleges and universities worldwide and are available in Spanish, French, Italian, and Portuguese, as well as English. Her research interests include adolescent identity, multigenerational families, immigration, and bullying, and she has published many articles on developmental topics in the *Wiley Encyclopedia of Psychology* and in publications of the American Association for Higher Education and the National Education Association for Higher Education. She continues teaching and learning every semester and in every edition of her books.

BRIEF CONTENTS

CONTENTS

Preface

"Another edition? Has anything really changed?" people often ask.

I suppress the impulse to tell them that if they understood child development from infancy through adolescence, they would realize that change is pervasive. Scientists know more about the brain, culture, genes, education, and much else today than they did just a few years ago. Humans themselves change, too, as each cohort experiences new events around the world—electronic media, chemicals in the food supply, globalization, HIV, longer lives, fewer babies . . . . The list of sociocultural shifts that affect all our lives is long indeed.

Instead I talk about my own life, a small window on the larger changes around us. For example, in the past two years, my first grandchildren, Asa and Caleb, were born. As I watch them develop, I learn, again, about early childhood and motherhood. Among the dramatic changes since I first became a mother are recommendations to breast-feed longer, heightened worry about toxins, anticipated maternal employment, saving for college some day. And some of the accoutrements are new: bigger and better strollers and paper diapers, no-slip slippers, automatic rockers, books for babies, attractive mobiles.

Where does the science of child development fit into all this? Consider my experience.

When my daughter Bethany was pregnant, she knew of my extensive knowledge of development and asked me to be her birth partner, a great honor. We went to classes together, and I felt ready for the big day. She was told to also find a good midwife and doula—fortunate for me because, although I knew what was happening, understood the monitored vital signs, and had confidence in the professionals taking care of my daughter in labor, tears flowed down my cheeks as I watched.

I stayed in a corner, where Bethany could not see how emotional I was. At the birth, I helped her push, holding one leg as a nurse held the other—just as the midwife had told us. Caleb was born, small and perfect; Bethany cradled and fed him. A miracle.

And then I fainted.

I suddenly found myself on the floor, with six medical people clustered around me instead of attending to my daughter and new grandson.

"I'm fine," I assured them, telling them to focus on Bethany. They did not. They insisted that, per hospital policy, I'd have to be wheeled down to emergency intake. I protested until one nurse said, "You can refuse treatment when you're there."

So, to get them to focus on Bethany, I sat in the wheelchair—and soon told a triage nurse that a night of high emotion without food, water, or sleep made me faint. Then, I said, "I refuse treatment." She checked with her supervisor and then allowed me to return to Bethany. The midwife was patiently waiting for the placenta to be expelled.

How does all this relate to development? In three ways:

1. Emotions can overtake reason. As you will read, we are all dual-process thinkers. My knowledge led me to ignore my emotions—big mistake.

2. Knowledge helps. I have since learned that many family members faint at births. If I had been aware of this, I would have nourished my body rather than deprived it in solidarity with Bethany (she could not eat). I would have noticed that I felt dizzy and lightheaded and thus would have sat down. Lack of knowledge is harmful in many ways—sharing vital information is why I write this book, and why you study development.

3. Development brings change. Personal changes were evident: Giving birth to four wonderful daughters (without ever fainting) is quite different from witnessing one of those daughters give birth herself. Cohort changes are evident as well: Now

that fathers, friends, and grandmothers are often allowed in delivery rooms, new education is needed—like how to avoid fainting. I did not know; now I do. That is why updating developmental textbooks is necessary.

All this makes me remember again why I study human development. We all need to know more; it will help us, our loved ones, and every person develop with more joy and fulfillment and less harm and despair.

Teaching and writing remain my life's work and passion. I strive to make this text both challenging and accessible to every student, remembering that my students were the inspiration for writing a developmental text in the first place. Students deserve a book that respects their intellect and experiences, without making development seem dull or obscure.

Overall, I believe that a better world is possible because today's students will become tomorrow's leaders. My hope is that the knowledge they gain from reading this book will benefit all their family members—children and adults alike—from one generation to the next.

To learn more about the specifics of this text, including the material that is new to this edition, read on. Or simply turn to the beginning of Chapter 1 and start your study.

Human Development and the DSM-5

The *Diagnostic and Statistical Manual of Mental Disorders* (DSM) provides a common language and standard criteria for psychiatrists, psychologists, and other healthcare providers to classify mental disorders. It is also used by schools and insurance companies to set the criteria for who qualifies for services—including everything from government disability benefits to special education.

This edition of the DSM, like many of the editions that came before it, has been hotly debated by everyone from parents of children with disabilities to researchers and politicians. While there are some controversial changes in the new DSM, for the most part it is extremely similar to the editions that have come before. But students of human development will want to be aware of the latest diagnostic categorizations, particularly for disorders like autism spectrum disorder and attention deficit/hyperactivity disorder. Some of the changes to the DSM are too specific and at too high a level to be covered in an introductory human development course; this is an overview and is not meant to be an exhaustive summary of the changes.

This table shows a chapter-by-chapter list of the DSM-5 changes in your textbook. Kathleen Stassen Berger's *Developing Person Through Childhood and Adolescence, 9e Updated for DSM-5*

Chapter, pages	Description of change	Characterization of change
Chapter 7, p. 210	New coverage of Reactive Attachment Disorder	Reactive Attachment Disorder is a highly unusual diagnostic category—evident in young children who have never had the chance to form any attachment, even an insecure one.
Chapter 11, pp. 338–339	Updated coverage of Attention-Deficit/Hyperactivity Disorder	Updated coverage of ADHD as per DSM-5.
Chapter 11, pp. 339–340	Coverage of the new Disruptive Mood Dysregulation Disorder	Thorough overview of this new DSM-5 category.
Chapter 11, p. 342	Updated coverage of Autism Spectrum Disorder	New DSM-5 describes Autism Spectrum Disorder, with Asperger syndrome no longer considered a separate diagnosis.
Chapter 14, p. 422	Updated coverage of eating disorders	New diagnostic criteria for Anorexia Nervosa and Bulimia Nervosa.
Chapter 16, p. 486	Updated coverage of Gender Dysphoria	DSM-5 now focuses on an individual's dissatisfaction with their current gender, "gender incongruence," rather than cross-gender identification.

New Material

Every year, scientists discover and explain new concepts and present new research. The best of these are integrated into the text, including hundreds of new references on many topics—among them the genetics of delinquency, infant nutrition, bipolar and autism spectrum disorders, the importance of early attachment, high-stakes testing, drug use and drug addiction, brain development throughout childhood and into emerging adulthood. Cognizant of the interdisciplinary nature of human development, I reflect research in biology, sociology, education, anthropology, political science, and more—as well as in my home discipline, psychology.

Genetics and social contexts are noted throughout. The variations and hazards of infant day care and preschool education are described; the implications of various family structures (single parents, stepparents, same-sex parents) are explored; the pivotal role of middle school is noted; and so on.

Research on the Brain

Every page of this text reflects new research and theory. Brain development is the most obvious example: Every trio of chapters includes a section on the brain, often enhanced with charts and photos to help students understand its inner workings. The following list highlights some of this material:

Correlation between MAOA production and violent crime, p. 7
A Case to Study feature on brain plasticity, pp. 9–10
A View from Science feature on mirror neurons, pp. 20–21
Piaget's sensorimotor intelligence, pp. 47–49
Fronto-striatal deficits and ADHD, p. 49
Phenylketonuria and harm to the brain, p. 89
Prenatal brain development and age of viability, p. 97
Head-sparing and malnutrition, pp. 129, 154–155
Development of axons, dendrites, and cortex in infancy, pp. 133–135
A View from Science feature on the fusiform face area and face recognition, pp. 137–138
Neurological effects of stress, pp. 138–139
Social deprivation and brain growth, pp. 139–140
Sources of harm to the infant brain, including stress and deprivation, pp. 138–140
Techniques for measuring infant brain activity, pp. 167–168
Infant cognition and information-processing theory, pp. 169–176
Chomsky's language acquisition device, p. 188
Brain maturation and infants' emotional development, pp. 194–195
Synesthesia, pp. 195–196
Brain development, myelination, and speed of thought in early childhood, pp. 229–231
The corpus callosum and lateralization, pp. 232–233
Maturation of the prefrontal cortex, pp. 233–234
The limbic system, pp. 235–237
Stress and the brain, pp. 236–237
A View from Science: Witness to a Crime explores early cognitive competency, p. 265
Brain maturation as basis for theory of mind, pp. 267–269
Gender differences in brain development and emotional regulation, pp. 293–294
Reaction time, attention, automatization in middle childhood, pp. 333–336
Brain scans and IQ, pp. 336–337
Pituitary, hypothalamus, and puberty, pp. 412–414

Worlds Apart This day center in Dhaka, Bangladesh, shows that daycare is needed all over the world.

New Pedagogical Aids

This edition incorporates learning objectives at the beginning of each chapter: The "What Will You Know?" questions indicate important concepts for students to focus on. There is also a new element at the end of each chapter: The "What Have You Learned?" questions help students assess their learning in more detail. Some further explanation follows.

Learning Objectives

Much of what students learn from this course is a matter of attitude, approach, and perspective—all hard to quantify. In addition, there are specific learning objectives, which supplement the key terms that should also be learned. In this edition, for the first time, two sets of objectives are listed for each chapter. Each question in the first set ("What Will You Know?"), asked at the beginning of each chapter, correlates with a major heading in the chapter and focuses on general ideas that students might remember and apply lifelong. At the end of each chapter are more specific learning objectives ("What Have You Learned?") that also connect to each major heading in the chapter but ask more specific questions about the chapter content.

Ideally, students answer the learning objective questions in sentences, with specifics that demonstrate knowledge. Some items on the new lists are straightforward, requiring only close attention to the chapter content. Others require comparisons, implications, or evaluations. Suggestions and grading rubrics for these questions are available in the test bank that goes along with the book.

Balancing the Range of Difficulty

To illustrate, the first "What Have You Learned?" question in Chapter 5 is straightforward: *What specific facts indicate that infants grow rapidly in the first year?* But the nineteenth question is more difficult: *What are the reasons for and against breast-feeding until the child is at least 1 year old?*

The first question might be answered simply as follows: *Birthweight doubles in four months and triples by one year, while infants grow about a foot*—or with several other specific details. However, students may, at first, be stumped by question 19, since the chapter is overwhelmingly in favor of breast-feeding. A good answer might be:

> *There are dozens of strong reasons for breast-feeding, including protection against disease, early immunity, better digestion, easier bonding, and perhaps a positive long-term effect on intellectual ability. Breast-feeding has advantages for the mother and family as well. Disadvantages are more difficult to find. However, if the mother is taking drugs or is unable to breast-feed, formula may be best. And if a woman or culture insists that no other foods, supplements, or vitamins are needed for a year or more, an infant might become malnourished, as occurred with Kiana. [See A Case to Study on p. 153.]*

As you can see from these examples, good answers may vary, but students should always use their own words and critical thinking skills, referring to specifics in the chapter.

Content Changes in the Ninth Edition

Child and adolescent development, like all sciences, builds on past learning. Many facts and concepts are scaffolds that remain strong over time: stages and ages, norms and variations, dangers and diversities, classic theories and fascinating applications. However, the study of development is continually changed by discoveries and experiences, so no paragraph in this ninth edition is exactly what it was in the eighth edition, much less the first. Some major revisions have been made, and hundreds of new examples are cited.

Since many of the students in this class are preparing to be teachers, every chapter now has an "Especially for" question for teachers. Other questions are especially for nurses, parents, police officers, and so on. Some students are planning for careers in early childhood development. To help them, we have provided an alignment of the text in the book with the standards provided by the National Association for the Education of Young Children, in an appendix developed by Wendy Bass Kerr from Pierce College.

Highlights of this updating appear below.

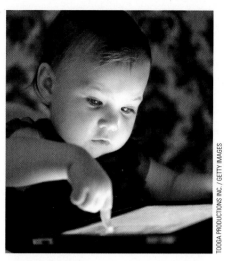

No More Playpens Much has changed since Jacqueline watched a temper tantrum in a playpen. "Little scientists" still "experiment" in order to see, but this 14-month-old uses a digital tablet and may protest if it is taken away.

Part I: The Beginnings

1. Introduction
- Scientific method explained at the outset of the book, with research on SIDS as example of a mystery that became hypotheses and then life-saving practices
- Nature–nurture interaction and critical versus sensitive periods explained in Chapter 1
- Cultural/ethnic differences made clear with example of Chinese and U.S. mothers reading books to toddlers
- Juvenile delinquency as example of multidisciplinary perspective, including genetics, neuroscience, child rearing, and social context
- Critical and sensitive periods brought forward from Chapters 4 and 5; illustrated via language learning
- *A View from Science* feature on mirror neurons

2. Theories of Development
- Distinction between theories, facts, and norms
- Examples of behaviorism include a *Thinking Critically* feature on toilet training
- Information processing now introduced in this chapter
- Humanism highlighted as a major theory
- Evolutionary theory explained, including *A View from Science* feature on sex differences in romantic jealousy

3. Heredity and Environment
- Epigenetics explained in more detail, including methylation and gene expression
- *Thinking Critically* feature on sex selection includes the United States, China, and India
- *Thinking Critically* feature on IVF insemination
- Stem cells explained; possible applications
- ART and multiple births
- Controversy regarding genetic testing for psychological conditions illustrated in *A View from Science* feature that focuses on schizophrenia

4. Prenatal Development and Birth
- Section on birth now directly follows section on prenatal development (in the previous edition, the section on Risk Reduction separated these sections)

- *Thinking Critically* feature on home births, including international comparisons
- Research on the benefits of the doula for high-risk infants and low-risk births
- Greater emphasis on father involvement (or absence) during pregnancy and birth, including couvade
- Various measures of newborn health—weight, age, Apgar score, Brazelton assessment scale, and reflexes
- Teratogens and innate vulnerability
- Complications of risk analysis and advice (e.g., alcohol, fish, prenatal testing)

Part II: The First Two Years
5. The First Two Years: Biosocial Development

- Bed-sharing, co-sleeping, and infant sleep patterns as issues for critical thinking
- New discussion of pain as an aspect of the sense of touch
- The fusiform face area of the brain and the effect of experience on specialized and differentiated recognition of human faces
- Current infant immunization, including California's 2010 whooping cough epidemic
- Infant survival worldwide; specifics include breast-feeding to combat malnutrition, vitamin D to prevent rickets, and bed nets to reduce malaria

6. The First Two Years: Cognitive Development

- Sharper yet more sympathetic coverage of limitations of Piaget's research
- Applications of information processing, especially for infant memory
- Stress on developing language before the first words, including in bilingual families
- *Thinking Critically* feature on the value of educational videos for infants
- Norms and theories of language learning explained with practical examples

7. The First Two Years: Psychosocial Development

- Extensive discussion of the influence of brain maturation on the emotional development of infants and toddlers
- Description of synesthesia and how it might differ in infancy and later on
- Variations in age of toilet training and how toilet-training approaches reflect theories of infant development
- *A View from Science* feature on the persistence or changeability of temperament and the effects of family and culture
- Impact of personal theories and how they can be changed
- Expanded discussion of infant day care, including comparison of day-care policies in 10 nations as well as possible positive and negative effects

Part III: Early Childhood
8. Early Childhood: Biosocial Development

- Expanded discussion of brain development, including maturation of the prefrontal cortex and a reorganized and expanded section on the limbic system and the effects of stress
- *A View from Science* feature on the long-term effects of child maltreatment
- Comparison of social understanding in humans and chimpanzees
- *Research Design* feature, in a section on environmental hazards, presents compelling new research on asthma risk

9. Early Childhood: Cognitive Development

- Role of imitation in children's learning, comparing non-Western and Western children
- New research on early intervention strategies that are effective in enhancing reading ability years later in elementary school.

Words, Don't Fail Me Now Could you describe how to tie shoes? The limitations of verbal tests of cognitive understanding are apparent in many skills.

- Updated research on preschool programs, including Montessori schools and Reggio Emilia schools, and federal evaluation of Head Start programs
- *A View from Science* looks at cognitive competency through children as witnesses to crime

10. Early Childhood: Psychosocial Development

- Expanded discussion of play, including cultural differences and learning from peers
- Major section on moral development, with types and origins of prosocial and antisocial behavior and the moral lessons learned from methods of punishment
- New research on cultural differences in disciplinary practices, including *A View from Science* feature on cultural determinants of effective discipline
- Updated research on the impact of the new media

Part IV: Middle Childhood
11. Middle Childhood: Biosocial Development

- *A Case to Study* looks at SES influences on asthma
- International data on obesity and stress on macrocosm influences
- Variations of intelligence and IQ, including data from brain scans
- Bipolar disorder in childhood explained and contrasted with ADHD
- In psychopathology, examples of equifinality and multifinality
- Discussion of children with special needs expanded, including new section on gifted and talented students

12. Middle Childhood: Cognitive Development

- Cultural differences in methods of learning (individual versus collaborative; discovery versus direct instruction)
- Advent of universal primary education (e.g., India)
- Updates on various measures of learning—TIMSS, PIRLS, NAEP, NCLB
- Who decides what is part of the curriculum (e.g., religion, charter schools, vouchers)

13. Middle Childhood: Psychosocial Development

- Self-esteem presented as complex; problems with high self-esteem and international variations explained
- Updated data on family structures—nuclear, step, extended, single parents, same-sex parents, and others
- SES effects on children from both high- and low-income families
- Moral values, including peer influence, bullying, retribution, and restitution

Part V: Adolescence
14. Adolescence: Biosocial Development

- Specifics about the role that weight and stress play in the onset of puberty
- Problems with early teen sex as contrasted with later teen sex (pregnancy, STIs)
- Complications and benefits of brain development in adolescence
- Eating disorders now in this chapter; drug use now in Chapter 16

15. Adolescence: Cognitive Development

- Logical fallacies now include base rate neglect
- Contrast clarified between college-bound students and high school dropouts
- Methods of student engagement critically examined
- Technology and cognition discussed, with recent data on social networking, cyberbullying, computers in instruction
- International contrasts include results from the PISA

Fourth Grade Challenge How much weight can a bridge hold? Thirty-three students in gifted classes at an elementary school in Idaho designed and built toothpick bridges and then tested them. David Stubbens (shown here) added 61 pounds to the bucket before his bridge collapsed.

AP PHOTO / MOSCOW-PULLMAN DAILY NEWS, GEOFF CRIMMINS

Who and Where? As Erikson explained in 1968, the pride of self-discovery is universal for adolescents: These could be teenagers anywhere. But a closer look reveals gay teenagers in Atlanta, Georgia, where this march could not have occurred 50 years ago.

16. Adolescence: Psychosocial Development

- Identity crisis refers to gender identity and identity politics
- Norms, expectations, and roles of parents and peers presented in cross-cultural contexts—variations by region (e.g., Hong Kong), by SES, and by ethnicity
- Updated data on drug use, including brain changes, depression, anxiety

Epilogue: Emerging Adulthood

- Debate among scholars as to whether contemporary emerging adults are more selfish or more transformative than those of earlier generations
- Risk taking explained as a benefit to society as well as a problem
- Connection between social understanding and maturation of the prefrontal cortex
- New *A Case to Study* feature describes one professor's journey to postformal thought
- Updated data on college, including statistics on 25- to 34-year-olds who are college graduates, in many nations
- Impact of recent cultural and economic changes on ethnic and vocational identity
- Crucial role of parental support during emerging adulthood

Ongoing Features

Many characteristics of this book have been acclaimed since the first edition and have been retained in this revision.

Writing That Communicates the Excitement and Challenge of the Field

An overview of the science of human development should be lively, just as real people are. Each sentence conveys tone as well as content. Chapter-opening vignettes bring student readers into the immediacy of development. Examples and explanations abound, helping students make the connections among theory, research, and their own experiences.

Coverage of Diversity

Cross-cultural, international, multiethnic, sexual orientation, wealth, age, gender—all these words and ideas are vital to appreciating how children develop. Research uncovers surprising similarities and notable differences: We have much in common, yet each human is unique. From the discussion of social contexts in Chapter 1 to the coverage of cultural differences in family dynamics in the Epilogue, each chapter highlights possibilities and variations. New is inclusion of genetic susceptibility, another source of variation.

New research on family structures, immigrants, bilingualism, emerging adults, and ethnic differences in health are among the many topics that illustrate human diversity. Listed here is a smattering of the discussions of culture and diversity in this new edition. Respect for human differences is evident throughout. You will note that examples and research findings from many parts of the world are included, not as add-on highlights, but as integral parts of the description of each age.

Just Like Me Emerging adults of every ethnicity take pride in their culture. In Japan, adulthood begins with a celebration at age 20, to the evident joy of these young women on Coming of Age Day, a national holiday.

Up-to-Date Coverage

My mentors welcomed curiosity, creativity, and skepticism; as a result, I am eager
to read and analyze thousands of articles and books on everything from autism to
zygosity. The recent explosion of research in neuroscience and genetics has challenged me, once again, first to understand and then to explain many complex findings and speculative leaps. My students continue to ask questions and share their
experiences, always providing new perspectives and concerns.

Topical Organization within a Chronological Framework

The book's basic organization remains unchanged. Four chapters begin the book
with coverage of definitions, theories, genetics, and prenatal development. These
chapters function not only as a developmental foundation but also as the structure
for explaining the life-span perspective, plasticity, nature and nurture, multicultural awareness, risk analysis, gains and losses, family bonding, and many other
concepts that yield insights for all of human development.

The other four parts correspond to the major periods of development. Each
part contains three chapters, one for each of the three domains: biosocial, cognitive, and psychosocial. The topical organization within a chronological framework
is a useful scaffold for students' understanding of the interplay between age and
domain. The chapters are color-coded with tabs on the right-hand margins. The
pages of the biosocial chapters have blue tabs, the cognitive chapters have purple
tabs, and the psychosocial chapters have green tabs.

Three Series of Integrated Features

Three series of deeper discussions appear as integral parts of the text, and only
where they are relevant. Readers of earlier editions will remember the *A View from
Science* feature; new to this edition are *Thinking Critically* and *A Case to Study*.

End-of-Chapter Summary

Each chapter ends with a summary, a list of key terms (with page numbers indicating where the word is introduced and defined), "What Have You Learned?"
questions, and three or four application exercises designed to let students apply
concepts to everyday life. Key terms appear in boldface type in the text and
are defined in the margins and again in a glossary at the back of the book. The
outline on the first page of each chapter, the new learning objectives, and the

system of major and minor subheads facilitate the survey-question-read-write-review (SQ3R) approach.

A "Summing Up" feature at the end of each section provides an opportunity for students to pause and reflect on what they've just read. Observation quizzes inspire readers to look more closely at certain photographs, tables, and graphs. The "Especially for . . ." questions in the margins, many of which are new to this edition, apply concepts to real-life careers and social roles.

Photographs, Tables, and Graphs That Are Integral to the Text

Students learn a great deal from this book's illustrations because Worth Publishers encourages authors to choose the photographs, tables, and graphs and to write captions that extend the content. Appendix A furthers this process by presenting numerous charts and tables that contain detailed data for further study.

Supplements

As an instructor myself, I know that supplements can make or break a class. I personally have rejected textbook adoptions because I knew that a particular publisher historically had provided inaccurate test banks, dull ancillaries, and slow service. That is not the case with Worth Publishers, which has a well-deserved reputation for providing supplements that are extensive and of high quality, for both professors and students. With this edition you will find the following.

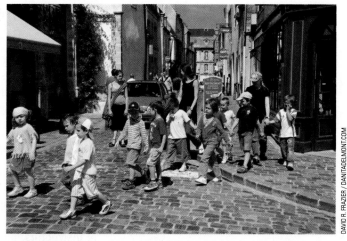

And If He Falls . . . In this example of secondary prevention, the French teacher stands in front of the car, protecting the pre-school children from oncoming traffic, which could do serious injury.

NEW! *Developing Lives:* An Interactive Simulation

The study of child development fully enters the digital age with *Developing Lives.* Using this interactive program, each student raises his or her own unique "child," making decisions about common parenting issues (nutrition choices, parenting style, type of schooling) and responding to realistic events (divorce, temperamental variations, and social and economic diversity) that shape a child's physical, cognitive and social development.

At the heart of this program is interactivity—between students and the simulation as well as among classmates. While the core experience happens on the computer, students can get notices or check in with their child "on the go" on a variety of mobile devices; they can even share photos of their baby with friends, family, and classmates. *Developing Lives* has a student-friendly, "game-like" feel that not only engages students in the program but also encourages them to learn. It features these helpful resources to reinforce and assess student learning: integrated links to the eBook version of your Worth text; readings from *Scientific American;* more than 400 videos and animations, many of them newly filmed for *Developing Lives;* and links to easy-to-implement assessment tools, including assignable quizzes on core topics, discussion threads, and journal questions.

NEW! *LearningCurve:* Formative Quizzing Engine

Developed by a team of psychology instructors with extensive backgrounds in course design and online education, *LearningCurve* combines adaptive question selection, personalized study plans, and state-of-the-art question analysis reports.

LearningCurve is based on the simple yet powerful concept of testing-to-learn, with game-like quizzing activities that keep students engaged in the material while helping them learn key concepts.

A team of dedicated instructors—including Lisa Hager, Spring Hill College; Jessica Herrick, Mesa State College; Sara Lapsley, Simon Fraser University; Rosemary McCullough, Ave Maria University; Wendy Morrison, Montana State University; Emily Newton, University of California, Davis; Curtis Visca, Saddleback College; and Devon Werble, East Los Angeles Community College—have worked together closely to generate more than 5,000 quizzing questions developed specifically for this edition of *The Developing Person Through Childhood and Adolescence*.

NEW! *Launch Pad:* Pre-loaded Assignments for Easy Startup

Launch Pad offers a set of prebuilt assignments, carefully crafted by a group of professors and instructional designers. Each assignable unit contains videos, activities, and formative assessment pieces to build student understanding for each topic, culminating with a quiz to hold students accountable for their work.

Human Development: A Video Tool Kit

This edition of *The Developing Person Through Childhood and Adolescence* is supplemented with the vast library of human development video and student activities on the Human Development Tool Kit. There are **more than 30 new student activities** especially for this edition. The tool kit was prepared by a talented team of instructors, including: Victoria Cross, University of California, Davis; Sheridan Dewolf, Grossmont College; Pamela B. Hill, San Antonio College; Lisa Huffman, Ball State University; Paul Kochmanski, Erie Community College; Thomas Ludwig, Hope College; Cathleen McGreal, Michigan State University; Martina Marquez, Fresno City College; Amy Obegi, Grossmont College; Michelle L. Pilati, Rio Hondo College; Tanya Renner, Kapiolani Community College; Kathleen Ringenbach, Brandman University—Antelope Valley Campus; Catherine Robertson, Grossmont College; Michelle Ryder, Daniel Webster College; Raechel Soicher, California State University, Davis; Stavros Valenti, Hofstra University; and Pauline Zeece, University of Nebraska, Lincoln.

The collection of student activities offers a full range of material, from investigations of classic experiments (like the visual cliff and the Strange Situation) to observations on children's play and adolescent risk taking. For instructors, the tool kit includes more than 400 video clips and animations, along with discussion starters and PowerPoint slides available to download for free. The kit also offers a selection of videos taken from the online library (215, to be exact) on a DVD called "The Human Development Video Collection," as well as a DVD with 40 of the most popular student activities, packageable for students.

PsychPortal

This is the complete online gateway to all the student and instructor resources available with the textbook. PsychPortal brings together all the resources of the video tool kits, integrated with an eBook and powerful assessment tools to complement your course.

The ready-to-use course template is fully customizable and includes all the teaching and learning resources that go along with the book, preloaded into a ready-to-use course; sophisticated quizzing, personalized study plans for students, and powerful assessment analyses that provide timely and useful feedback on class and individual student performance; and seamless integration of student resources, eBook text, assessment tools, and lecture resources. The quiz bank features more than 100 questions per chapter.

eBook

The beautiful and interactive eBook fully integrates the complete text and its electronic study tools in a format that instructors and students can easily customize—at a significant savings on the price of the printed text. It offers easy access from any Internet-connected computer; quick, intuitive navigation to any section or subsection, as well as any printed book page number; a powerful notes feature that allows you to customize any page; a full-text search; text highlighting; and a full, searchable glossary.

Companion Web Site

The companion Web site (at www.worthpublishers.com/bergerca9e) is an online educational setting for students and instructors. It is free, and tools on the site include interactive flashcards in both English and Spanish, a Spanish-language glossary, quizzes, and crossword puzzles. A password-protected Instructor Site offers a full array of teaching resources, including PowerPoint slides, an online quiz gradebook, and links to additional tools.

"Journey Through the Life Span" Observational Videos

Bringing observational learning to the classroom, this video series allows students to watch and listen to real children as a way of amplifying their reading of the text. "Journey Through the Life Span" offers vivid footage of people of all ages from around the world (North America, Europe, Africa, Asia, and South America), as seen in everyday environments (homes, hospitals, schools, and offices) and at major life transitions (birth, marriage, divorce, being grandparents).

Interviews with prominent developmentalists—including Charles Nelson, Barbara Rogoff, Ann Peterson, and Steven Pinker—are integrated throughout to help students link research and theory to the real world. Interviews with a number of social workers, teachers, and nurses who work with children, adults, and the aged give students direct insight into the practical challenges and rewards of their vocations. One hour of unedited footage helps students sharpen their observation skills. Available on VHS and DVD.

Child Development Telecourse

Stepping Stones, developed by Coast Learning Systems and Worth Publishers, teaches fundamentals of human development. The course also explores the variety of individual and developmental contexts that influence development, such as socioeconomic status, culture, genetics, family, school, and society. Each video lesson includes specific real-life examples interwoven with commentary by subject matter experts. The course includes 16 half-hour video lessons, a telecourse study guide, and a faculty manual with test bank. The test bank is also available electronically.

Instructor's Resources

This collection of resources written by Richard O. Straub (University of Michigan, Dearborn) has been hailed as the richest collection of instructor's resources in developmental psychology. The *Lecture Guides* preview learning objectives, springboard topics for discussion and debate, handouts for student projects, and supplementary readings from journal articles. Course planning suggestions, ideas for term projects, and a guide to audiovisual and software materials are also included.

Study Guide

The *Study Guide* by Richard O. Straub helps students evaluate their understanding and retain their learning longer. Each chapter includes a review of key concepts, guided study questions, and section reviews that encourage students' active participation in the learning process. Two practice tests and a challenge test help them assess their mastery of the material.

Interactive Presentation Slides for Human Development

A number of different presentation slides are available. There are two prebuilt slide sets for each text chapter—one featuring chapter outlines, the other featuring all chapter art and illustrations. These slides can be used as is or can be customized to fit individual needs. Video presentation slides provide an easy way to connect chapter content to the selected video clip and follow each clip with discussion questions designed to promote critical thinking.

In addition, a new extraordinary series of "next generation" interactive presentation lectures gives instructors a dynamic yet easy-to-use new way to engage students during classroom presentations of core developmental psychology topics. Each lecture provides opportunities for discussion and interaction and enlivens the psychology classroom with an unprecedented number of embedded video clips and animations from Worth's Video Tool Kit for Human Development Psychology.

Test Bank and Computerized Test Bank

The test bank, prepared by Rosemary McCullough (Ave Maria University) and Wendy Morrison (Montana State University), includes at least 100 multiple-choice and 70 fill-in, true-false, and essay questions for each chapter. Each question is keyed to the textbook by topic, learning objective, and level of difficulty.

The Diploma computerized test bank, available on a dual-platform CD-ROM for Windows and Macintosh, guides instructors step by step through the process of creating a test. It also allows them to quickly add an unlimited number of questions; edit, scramble, or resequence items; format a test; and include pictures, equations, and media links. The accompanying gradebook enables instructors to record students' grades throughout the course and includes the capacity to sort student records, view detailed analyses of test items, curve tests, generate reports, and add weights to grades.

The CD-ROM is also the access point for Diploma Online Testing, which allows instructors to create and administer secure exams over a network or over the Internet. In addition, Diploma has the ability to restrict tests to specific computers or time blocks. Blackboard- and WebCT-formatted versions of each item in the Test Bank are available on the CD-ROM.

Thanks

I'd like to thank the academic reviewers who have read this book in every edition and who have provided suggestions, criticisms, references, and encouragement. They have all made this a better book. I want to mention especially those who have reviewed this edition:

Melanie Arpaio, *Sussex County Community College*

Elaine Barry, *Penn State Fayette, The Eberly Campus*

Kris Bliss, *Mesa Community College*

Paul Boxer, *Rutgers University*

Natasha Fratello Breitenbach, *American River College*

Jamie Brown, *UNC–Charlotte*

Melinda Burgess, *Southwestern Oklahoma State University*

Dominic Carbone, *Sussex County Community College*

Ron Craig, *Edinboro University of Pennsylvania*

Timothy Croy, *Eastern Illinois University*

Laura Dell, *University of Cincinnati*

Patricia Dilko, *Canada College*

Elaine Francisco, *Skyline College*

Kate Fletcher, *University of Florida*

Heather Gelhart, *Cypress College*

Michael Goldblatt, *Bucks County Community College*

DeDee Goldsmith, *Oakton Community College*

Myra Harville, *Holmes Community College*

Tywanda Jiles, *Governors State University*

Jennifer Kampmann, *South Dakota State University*

Deena Kausler, *Jefferson College*

Megan Kelly, *University of Maryland*

Regina Kijewski, *Naugatuck Valley Community College*

Margaret King, *Ohio University*

Larry Kollman, *North Iowa Area Community College*

Kathryn Kotowski, *Cuyamaca College*

Michael Leffingwell, *Tarrant County College*

Kris Leppien-Christensen, *Saddleback College*

Martina Marquez, *Fresno City College*

Krista McClain-Rocha, *Skyline College*

Martha Myklebust, *Mendocino Community College*

Lori Nanney, *Cleveland Community College*

Sherri Palmer, *Truman State University*

Nicole Porter, *Modesto Junior College*

John Prange, *Irvine Valley College*

Melita Baumann Riddle, *Glendale Community College*

Joel Shapiro, *Green Mountain College*

Donna Sims, *Fort Valley State University*

Latoya Smith-Jones, *University of Texas at Arlington*

Cecilia Jane Spruill, *Pensacola State College*

Valerie Taylor, *Washtenaw Community College*

Peggy Thelen, *Alma College*

Sharron Thompson, *Chaminade University of Honolulu*

Tara Vargas, *Lewis and Clark College*

Anne Christine Watson, *Chapman University*

Lois Wedl, *College of Saint Benedict*

Julia Yoo, *Lamar University*

I also need to thank the instructors who reviewed our online materials. We've tried to apply the insights gained from their experiences with using our media materials in the last edition to make materials we've designed for this new edition better.

Patty Dilko, *Canada College*

Tony Fowler, *Florence Darlington Tech College*

Heather Gelhart, *Saddleback College*

Lisa Hagan, *Metropolitan State College of Denver*

Brantlee Haire, *Florence-Darlington Technical College*

Vicky Hammer, *Cloud County Community College*

Kris Leppien-Christensen, *Saddleback College*

Angela Lily, *Houston Community College*

Cheryl McGill, *Florence Darlington Tech College*

Lynn McKinley, *Grossmont College*

Wendy Bianchini Morrison, *Montana State University*

Patricia Puccio, *College of DuPage*

Rodney Raasch, *Normandale Community College*

DeAnna Timmerman, *Eastern Oregon University*

Curtis Visca, *Saddleback College*

Bridget Walsh, *University of Nevada-Reno*

In addition, I wish to thank the instructors who participated in our online survey. We've tried to apply their feedback as well, to further improve this new edition.

Farah Alam, *De Anza College*

Sindy Armstrong, *Ozarks Tech Community College*

Sherri Black, *Western Nevada College*

Deborah Barton, *York College of Pennsylvania*

Don Bower, *University of Georgia*

Diane Brown, *Everett Community College*

Sandra Broz, *Northeast Community College*

Stephen Burgess, *Southwestern Oklahoma State University*

Lanthan Camblin, *University of Cincinnati*

Catherine Camilletti, *University of Texas at El Paso*

Toni Campbell, *San Jose State University*

Donna Carey, *Keystone College*

Maria Casey, *Immaculata University*

Carolyn Cohen, *Northern Essex Community College*

Lauren Cooley, *Napa College*

Catherine Currell, *Central Michigan University*

Jennifer DeCicco, *Hunter College*

Gretchen DeHart, *Community College of Vermont*

Sorah Dubitsky, *Florida International University*
Natalie Ebner, *Yale University*
Robert C. Gates, *Cisco College*
Amy Gerney, *Misericordia University*
Zebbedia Gibb, *University of Northern Iowa*
Margie Goulden, *Pierce College*
Troianne Grayson, *Florida State College at Jacksonville*
Jerry Green, *Tarrant County College*
Christine Grela, *McHenry College*
Robert Hagstrom, *Northern Arizona University*
Danielle Hodge, *California State University–San Bernardino*
Kristin Homan, *Grove City College*
Alishia Huntoon, *Oregon Institute of Technology*
Matthew Isaak, *University of Louisville at Lafayette*
Mehraban Khodavandi, *Lakeland College*
Timothy L. Kitzman, *Blackhawk Technical College*
Kristina Klassen, *North Idaho College*
Jennifer King-Cooper, *Sinclair Community College*
Charles P. Kraemer, *LaGrange College*
Alison Kulak, *Concordia University of Alberta*
Karen Kwan, *Salt Lake Community College*
Krista Morris Lehman, *LeTourneau University*
Kathy Lein, *Community College of Denver*
Pei-Wen Ma, *William Paterson University*
Alisha Marciano, *Lynchburg College*
Dorothy Marsil, *Kennesaw State University*
Kris McAleavey, *Longwood University*
Alex McEntire, *Penn Valley Community College*

Kittie Myatt, *Argosy University–Nashville*
Nancy Neveau, *Northeast Wisconsin Technical College*
Liz O'Dell, *Northwest State Community College*
Alan Oda, *Azusa Pacific University*
Nancy Ogden, *Mount Royal University*
Bonnie Ortega, *Trinidad State Junior College*
Andrea Phronebarger, *York Technical College*
Cynthia Putman, *Charleston Southern University*
Cyd Quarterman, *Toccoa Fall College*
Jennifer Reid Reichert, *Marquette University*
Nancy E. Rizzo, *Valencia Community College*
Michael Rhoads, *University of Northern Colorado*
George Sayre, *Seattle University*
David J. Schieffer, *Minnesota West Community and Technical College*
Sheryl R. Schindler, *University of Utah*
Pamela Schuetze-Pizarro, *Buffalo State College*
Robert Schwartz, *Bergen Community College*
Deborah Sedik, *Bucks County Community College*
Sean Seepersad, *California State University*
Jane Tiedt, *Gonzaga University*
Tonya Toutge, *Bethel University*
Anne Unterkoefler, *Delaware County Community College*
Michel Vallante, *Quinsigamond Community College*
Ruth A. Wallace, *Butler Community College*
Steve Wisecarver, *Lord Fairfax Community College*
Susan Wolle, *Kirkwood Community College*
Rebecca Wood, *Center Connecticut State University*

The editorial, production, and marketing people at Worth Publishers are dedicated to meeting the highest standards of excellence. Their devotion of time, effort, and talent to every aspect of publishing is a model for the industry. I particularly would like to thank Stacey Alexander, Jessica Bayne, Tom Churchill, Lyndall Culbertson, Lukia Kliossis, Tracey Kuehn, Paul Lacy, Katherine Nurre, Sharon Prevost, Babs Reingold, Barbara Seixas, Ted Szczepanski, Cecilia Varas, Vivien Weiss, Jacquelyn Wong, and Catherine Woods.

Dedication

Every edition of this book is dedicated to people who made this textbook better than I could have alone. I dedicate this edition to Cele Gardner, my editor for more than ten years, who died in April 2010. We all miss her.

New York, October 2011

The Developing Person
Through Childhood and Adolescence

I

the beginnings

The first part of this book describes many beginnings: first definitions, research designs, and theories that have become the science of human development and then the beginnings of human life, when two cells become one zygote, eventually becoming a baby (or, rarely, babies).

To be more specific, Chapter 1 introduces what, why, and how we study human development, explaining some basic research strategies and methods. Chapter 2 introduces several theories of development, both grand theories and newer ones. Chapter 3 describes the interacting genes and surrounding chemicals that influence everything from the thickness of toenails to the swiftness of brain waves. And finally, Chapter 4 describes early growth, from one dividing cell to the moment of birth.

The next four chapters, then, begin our study of child development. In all four chapters, it is evident that a swirling multiplicity of disciplines, ideas, and people create the context for a new person.

Introduction

WHAT WILL YOU KNOW?

1. What makes the study of children, with all their variability and unexpected actions, a science?
2. How does culture change the way children develop?
3. Why is development considered dynamic, not static?
4. Why is comparing people of several ages not considered the best way to understand how people change as they grow older?
5. Is it unethical to study children scientifically?

A blizzard overwhelmed the U.S. mid-Atlantic states on December 26, 2010. Was it a force of nature, unrelated to human development? Only at first. Then people reacted, each according to age, history, family, and context.

Workplaces closed, hardware stores sold out of shovels, gloves were lost in frozen drifts, plows became stuck, cars and buses were abandoned mid-block, political leaders' approval ratings soared or plummeted. The mayor of Newark (Cory Booker, age 41, not married) responded to constituents on Twitter. He brought diapers to a snowed-in resident, rebuked another for cursing, shamed a third who was inside tweeting while his mother and wife shoveled. The governor of New Jersey (Chris Christie, age 48, married, father of four), however, flew to Florida because he had promised to take his family to Disney World. He replied to a reporter that his marriage would be in trouble if his wife went without him. Across the river, the mayor of New York (Michael Bloomberg, age 68, divorced) did not declare a Snow Emergency; many streets were impassable for days. Booker was praised, gaining a million Twitter followers; Christie was both defended and attacked; Bloomberg was soundly criticized, and his deputy resigned.

Meanwhile, children of all ages were overjoyed. My toddler grandson eagerly donned mittens and boots to play in Hudson River Park. Remembering my own childhood, I laid him down on virgin snow to make a snow angel and built a small snowman. But he cared little for angel wings or snowmen; he threw lumps of snow into the river.

A father nearby built a big snowman, complete with pine-needle hair and sculpted nose. His 6-year-old son ignored the creature until it was finished and then prepared to topple it. The man wanted to preserve his creation "for other people to admire"; his son argued that "a bully might come and knock it down." Developmental science to the rescue: I had just read about child guidance in China—praise *before* action, not only afterwards.

"You are not a bully; you are a good boy," I told him.

That snowman stayed erect for five days, until it melted.

Development is like weather. Birth, growth, and death come to everyone, and then individuals respond. This chapter describes universals and particulars, beginning with laws of science and sweeping definitions, and then detailing methods and applications. We can all soar, or at least come to the rescue, when needed.

Joy or Trouble? When the forecast is snow, many city children celebrate, as these two do at Columbus Circle in Manhattan. Adults are less enthusiastic.

>> Understanding How and Why

The **science of human development** *seeks to understand how and why people—all kinds of people, everywhere, of every age—change over time.* This definition has three crucial elements: science, people, and change.

Developmental study is a *science*. It depends on theories, data, analysis, critical thinking, and sound methodology just like every other science. Developmentalists ask questions and seek answers, to ascertain "how and why"—that is, to discover the processes of development and the reasons for those processes. In seeking answers, scientists gather evidence on whatever they are studying, be it chemical elements, rays of light, or, here, child behavior. One of the hallmarks of the science of human development is that it is *multidisciplinary*; that is, scientists from many academic disciplines (biology, psychology, sociology, anthropology, economics, and history among them) contribute to our understanding.

Science is especially needed when we study humans because lives depend on the answers. People disagree vehemently about what pregnant women should eat, when babies should cry, how children should be punished, whether teachers should explain sex. Such subjective opinions arise from emotions, culture, and upbringing, not necessarily from evidence. Scientists seek to progress from opinion to truth, from subjective to objective, from wishes to results.

When science concerns development, it leads to practical applications. The first experts on childhood opened schools, advised parents, founded community centers, and legislated to halt child abuse. Some scientists distinguish between basic and applied research, arguing that basic discoveries are valid for their own sake, whether or not applications are forthcoming. However, most developmentalists are eager to apply science to life's problems. As one scientist explains:

> After more than 40 years of concurrent advances in the science of early childhood development, the challenge facing policy makers at the end of the first decade of the 21st century is clear—it is time to leverage new scientific knowledge in the service of generating new intervention strategies.
>
> *[Shonkoff, 2010, p. 361]*

As you surely realize, facts may be twisted and applications may spring from assumptions, not from data. Because the study of development is a science, it is based on *objective* evidence, such as the neuroscience of brain activation, the data on family structure, the specifics of how learning occurs. At the same time, because it concerns human life and growth, it is also laden with *subjective* perceptions, which are open to bias. This interplay of the objective and the subjective, of facts and possibilities, of the universal and the unique makes developmental science challenging, intriguing, and even transformative.

The Scientific Method

To avoid unexamined opinions and to rein in personal biases, researchers follow five steps of the **scientific method:**

1. *Begin with curiosity.* On the basis of **theory** (a comprehensive set of ideas, as explained in Chapter 2), prior research, or a personal observation, pose a question.
2. *Develop a hypothesis.* Shape the question into a **hypothesis,** which is a specific prediction that can be tested.
3. *Test the hypothesis.* Design and conduct research to gather **empirical** (observable, verifiable) evidence (data).
4. *Draw conclusions.* Use the evidence to support or refute the hypothesis.
5. *Report the results.* Share the data, conclusions, and alternative explanations.

science of human development The science that seeks to understand how and why people of all ages and circumstances change or remain the same over time.

scientific method A way to answer questions using empirical research and data-based conclusions.

theory A comprehensive set of ideas.

hypothesis A specific prediction that can be tested.

empirical Based on observation, experience, or experiment; not theoretical.

Verification

Developmentalists begin with curiosity and then seek the facts, drawing conclusions only after careful research. **Replication**—repeating the procedures and methods of a study with different participants—is often a sixth step. Everyone wants to know more about his or her personal issues; that is one reason the study of human life is fascinating. But we need answers that are beyond the personal, valid answers that may or may not confirm our hunches and assumptions. Replication, either exactly or with modifications, can do that.

Scientists study the research procedures and reported results of other scientists who are working on the same issues. They read publications, attend conferences, send e-mails, and sometimes move from one nation to another to collaborate. Conclusions are revised, refined, and replicated. Then, especially when the topic is child development, other people analyze and apply the results.

replication Repeating a study, usually using different participants, perhaps of another age, SES, or culture.

SIDS, an Example

Coverage of every topic in this book is based on research that follows the scientific method. Here we present just one issue, **sudden infant death syndrome (SIDS),** to illustrate the process. Every year until the mid-1990s, tens of thousands of infants died of SIDS, called *crib death* in North America and *cot death* in England. Tiny infants smiled at their caregivers, waved their arms at rattles that their small fingers could not yet grasp, went to sleep seemingly healthy, and never woke up. As parents mourned their dead babies, scientists asked why (*step 1*) and tested hypotheses (the cat? the quilt? natural honey? homicide? spoiled milk?) to no avail: Sudden infant death was a mystery.

A scientist named Susan Beal studied every SIDS death in South Australia for years, noting dozens of circumstances, seeking factors that increased the risk. Some things did not seem to matter (such as birth order) and others seemed to increase the risk (such as maternal smoking and lambskin blankets). A breakthrough came when Beal discovered an ethnic variation: Australian babies of Chinese descent died of SIDS far less often than did Australian babies of European descent. Genetic? Most experts thought so. But Beal's scientific observation led her to note that Chinese babies slept on their backs, contrary to the European or American custom of stomach-sleeping. She developed a new hypothesis (*step 2*): that sleeping position mattered.

To test her hypothesis (*step 3*), Beal convinced a large group of non-Chinese parents to put their newborns to sleep on their backs. Almost none of them died suddenly. After several years of gathering data, she drew a surprising conclusion (*step 4*): Back-sleeping protected against SIDS. Her published reports (*step 5*) (Beal, 1988) caught the attention of doctors in the Netherlands, where pediatricians had told parents to put their babies to sleep on their stomachs. Two Dutch scientists (Engelberts & de Jonge, 1990) recommended back-sleeping; thousands of parents took heed. SIDS was reduced in Holland by 40 percent in one year—a stunning replication (*step 6*).

Replication and application spread. By 1994, a "Back to Sleep" campaign in nation after nation cut the SIDS rate dramatically (Kinney & Thach, 2009; Mitchell, 2009). In the United States, in 1984, SIDS killed 5,245 babies; in 1996, that number was down to 3,050; in the past decade, it has decreased to about 2,000 a year (see Figure 1.1). Such results indicate that, in the United States alone, about 40,000 children and young adults are alive today who would be dead if they had been born before 1990. The campaign has been so successful that physical therapists report

sudden infant death syndrome (SIDS) A situation in which a seemingly healthy infant, usually between 2 and 6 months old, suddenly stops breathing and dies unexpectedly while asleep.

And If I Die Not likely. Death "before I wake" occurred too often in many nations before 1990, but not in Mongolia (shown here) or other Asian countries. The reason, as scientists hypothesized and then confirmed, is that Asian parents put their infants "back to sleep."

Observation Quiz Back-sleeping babies sometimes squirm, making the blankets covering them come loose—another risk factor for SIDS. What detail makes that unlikely here? (see answer, page 6)

SEAN SPRAGUE / THE IMAGE WORKS

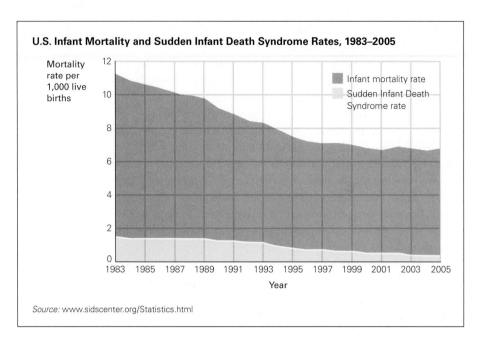

Source: www.sidscenter.org/Statistics.html

FIGURE 1.1

Rates of SIDS Death The dramatic decrease in SIDS deaths is a direct result of a scientific discovery that babies are more likely to survive if they sleep on their backs. The next challenge is to reduce the other causes of infant mortality. These rates are from the United States—some nations have much lower rates and others much higher. As with SIDS, international comparisons may increase survival.

Observation Quiz About what percent of infant mortality in the United States is the result of SIDS? (see answer, page 8)

nature In development, nature refers to the traits, capacities, and limitations that each individual inherits genetically from his or her parents at the moment of conception.

nurture In development, nurture includes all the environmental influences that affect the individual after conception. This includes everything from the mother's nutrition while pregnant to the cultural influences in the nation.

>> Answer to Observation Quiz (from page 5) The swaddling blanket is not only folded under the baby but is also tied in place.

that babies now crawl later than they used to; they therefore advocate *tummy time*—putting awake infants on their stomachs to develop their muscles (Zachry & Kitzmann, 2011).

Stomach-sleeping is a proven, replicated risk, but it is not the only one: SIDS still occurs. Currently, the rate is much lower in Canada and Japan than in the United States but higher in New Zealand, for reasons not yet known. Beyond nationality and sleeping position, other risks include low birthweight, a brain-stem abnormality that produces too little of a particular brain chemical (serotonin, a neurotransmitter), cigarette smoking in the household, soft blankets or pillows, and bed-sharing (when infants sleep in their parents' bed) (Duncan et al., 2010; Ostfeld et al., 2010). Most SIDS victims experienced several risks: Virtually never do babies with none of these risks die from SIDS (Ostfeld et al., 2010).

The Nature–Nurture Debate

This example highlights a historic puzzle, often called the *nature–nurture debate*. **Nature** refers to the influence of the genes that people inherit. **Nurture** refers to environmental influences, beginning with the health and diet of the embryo's mother and continuing lifelong, including family, school, culture, and society. For SIDS, nature includes serotonin in the brain and physiological maturation; nurture includes parental smoking and sleeping position.

The nature–nurture debate has many other names, among them *heredity–environment, maturation–learning, nativist–empiricist*. Under whatever name, the basic question is: How much of any characteristic, behavior, or emotion results from genes and how much from experience? Note that the question is *How much?* not *Which?* Both genes and the environment affect every characteristic. Nature always affects nurture, and nurture always affects nature.

Indeed, some scientists think that the ongoing interaction between genes and experiences is so varied, explosive, and profound that *How much?* is not a valid question (Gottlieb, 2007; Meaney, 2010; Spencer et al., 2009). It implies proportions, as if each part contributes a share. But babies die of SIDS not because of nature added to nurture or vice versa, but because of multiplying risks: No genetic or environmental factor acts in isolation.

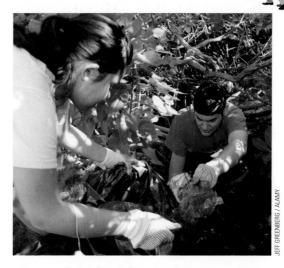

Now consider a more complex example, which further illustrates that not only *How much?* but also *Which?* are the wrong questions regarding nature and nurture.

Genetics

Some young people become violent, hurting others as well as themselves. Indeed, if a person is ever going to kill someone, he (or less often, she) is most likely to do so between ages 15 and 25. Researchers in medicine, psychology, and sociology have found many factors that contribute to youth violence, including past child abuse and current circumstances. The violent delinquent is often a boy who was beaten in childhood, troubled in school, living in a drug-filled, crowded neighborhood (Maas et al., 2008).

Yet some such boys never harm anyone. A fourth discipline—genetics—suggests why. One genetic variant occurs in the code for an enzyme (monoamine oxidase A, abbreviated MAOA) that affects several neurotransmitters. This gene comes in two versions, dubbed short and long, producing people with lower or higher levels of that enzyme. Both versions are normal.

A famous developmental study began with virtually every child born in Dunedin, New Zealand, between April 1, 1972, and March 31, 1973. The children and their families were examined on dozens of measures from early childhood on, yielding literally hundreds of published studies based on a wealth of data, including parental practices and variants of the MAOA gene. About one-third of them had the short gene and thus had lower levels of MAOA. Researchers found that boys who were mistreated by their parents were about twice as likely to be overly aggressive (to develop a conduct disorder, to be violent, to be antisocial, and eventually to be convicted of a violent crime) if, *and only if,* they had the gene for low levels of the enzyme instead of the high-MAOA version (Caspi et al., 2002; see Figure 1.2). Some maltreated boys—usually those with high MAOA—nonetheless became model citizens.

Does this mean that becoming violent is inevitable for those with less of that enzyme? No. As Figure 1.2 shows, *if* they were not maltreated, boys with low MAOA were *more* likely than those with high MAOA to become law-abiding, peaceable adults. Such results were surprising at the time, but recently many other scientists have found genes, or circumstances, that work both ways—they predispose people to be either unusually successful or pathological (Belsky et al., 2011; Keri, 2009).

Differential Sensitivity

Such differential sensitivity is now recognized, especially among developmentalists: Certain versions of particular genes may make it more likely for people to develop specific problems *or* specific strengths. Replications of the Dunedin study have not always confirmed the direct link between MAOA and violence. However, the general finding that genes can act in opposite ways depending on the environment has been confirmed by many other researchers. The social context—including the pregnant mother's diet, the affection bestowed on the infant, the intellectual stimulation of early childhood, bullying or friendship in middle childhood—affects how genetic codes work. Inherited risk influences later behavior, but the impact varies from one place, age, and background of participants to another.

Now consider a study of a very different population: African American 11-year-olds in rural Georgia, the United States (Brody et al., 2009). In this program, parents and children were randomly divided into two groups: (1) a group that had

Doing Good Someone threw that garbage onto this beach in south Miami, but these two teen volunteers are cleaning it up. It is easy to trace such good behavior to culture, family, and community, but genes may also play a role. Some people are naturally more caring about other people.

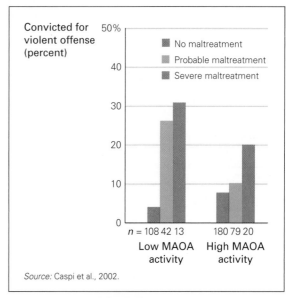

Source: Caspi et al., 2002.

FIGURE 1.2

Genetic Origins for Violent Crime Two variables—parental treatment and a variant of the gene that produces the enzyme MAOA—interact to affect the likelihood that a child will commit a violent crime. Of the boys in the "probable maltreatment" category, 10 percent were convicted of a violent crime if their MAOA level was high, but 26 percent were convicted if their MAOA was low.

>> **Answer to Observation Quiz** (from page 6) It depends on the decade. About 18 percent from 1983 to 1995, but only about 3 percent in 2005.

no intervention and (2) a group that attended seven seminars designed to increase racial pride, family support, honest communication, and compliance with house rules. (These features are in keeping with replicated research that finds that pride and parental involvement protect against early sex and drug use.) A follow-up study found that some participants had the short version of a particular gene (called 5-HTTLPR); others had only the long version.

That small genetic difference turned out to be critical: Those with the long version developed just as well whether they were in the intervention group or not. However, teenagers with the short version who attended the seminars were less likely to have early sex or to use drugs than were those who also had the short gene but not the family training. More of the latter broke the law. (This study is further explained in Chapter 16.) The interaction of nature and nurture was crucial: The special nurture without the sensitivity nature made no difference.

That often seems true regarding the two versions of this particular gene. The short version is fairly common—almost half of those with European ancestors and as many as three-fourths of those with Asian ancestors may have it—but culture and family affect whether it becomes an asset or a liability (Chiao & Blizinsky, 2010). Considering all the research on aggression, both nature and nurture are pivotal, sometimes in complex interactions (Tremblay, 2011).

Critical and Sensitive Periods

The interaction of nature and nurture brings up another issue: timing. Babies are most likely to die of SIDS about a year after conception, usually from 2 to 4 months after birth, when the breathing reflex undergoes a shift. People are most likely to take dangerous risks during adolescence, thus making early adolescence the best time for parents to set guidelines. Late adolescence is the most likely time for violent death. Immigrants who arrive as children are most likely to identify with their new nation; arrival in late adulthood makes identification less likely (Cheung et al., 2011). These are a few examples of the basic theme of development: Age matters. In fact, there are *critical periods* and *sensitive periods* for particular growth.

The Only Time or the Best Time

critical period A time when a particular type of developmental growth (in body or behavior) must happen for normal development to occur.

A **critical period** is a time when something *must* occur to ensure normal development or the only time when an abnormality might occur. For example, the human embryo grows arms and legs, hands and feet, fingers and toes, each over a specific few days between 28 and 54 days after conception. After that it is too late: Unlike some insects, humans never grow new limbs. Tragically, between 1957 and 1961, thousands of newly pregnant women in 30 nations took *thalidomide,* an antinausea drug. This change in nurture (via the mother) disrupted nature (the genetic program). If an expectant mother ingested thalidomide during that critical period, her baby's limbs were malformed or absent (Moore & Persaud, 2007). Specifics depended on the precise day she swallowed the drug. Surprisingly, if a woman took thalidomide only before day 28 or after day 54, no harm occurred.

Life has very few such critical periods. Often, however, a particular development occurs more easily—but not exclusively—at a particular time. Such a time is called a **sensitive period.** An example is language. If children do not start speaking their first language between ages 1 and 3, they might do so later (hence the first three years are not a critical period), but their grammar is often impaired (hence, these years are a sensitive period). Similarly, childhood is a sensitive period for learning to pronounce a second or third language.

sensitive period A time when a certain type of development is most likely, although it may still happen later with more difficulty. For example, early childhood is considered a sensitive period for language learning.

As is often the case with development, sweeping generalizations (like those in the preceding sentences) do not apply in every case. Accent-free speech *usually* must be learned before puberty, but some teenagers or adults with exceptional nature and nurture (naturally adept at speech and then immersed in a new language) master a second language flawlessly (Birdsong, 2006; Muñoz & Singleton, 2011).

Childhood and Adulthood

Language is not the only thing that is best learned in childhood. As you will find out, early development is often the foundation for later life. For example, children who are severely malnourished at age 1 are more likely to become overweight and thus develop diabetes or heart disease in middle age. That makes early life a sensitive period for nutrition. Emotional control is best learned before age 6: Without it, adults typically have quick outbursts that they later regret. Early human relationships—with parents in infancy, with friends in school, with romantic partners in adolescence—affect adults' reactions to their children.

All these connections indicate that childhood is a sensitive period. However, **plasticity** is evident as well. Plasticity denotes two complementary aspects of development: Human traits can be molded (as plastic can be), yet people maintain a certain durability of identity (as plastic does). The concept of plasticity in development provides both hope and realism—hope because change is possible over the life span and realism because development builds on what has come before, for better or for worse. Malnourished children need not become diabetic: Nature and nurture may protect them. An adult whose childhood relationships were troubled may nonetheless become a loving, responsive parent. But in both cases, the adult is at increased risk.

Plasticity works in the other direction as well: Early potential does not necessarily come to fruition. For instance, a review of children who are extraordinarily gifted (fascinated by numbers at age 3, or fluent readers by age 5, or expert violinists at age 9) found that genes, training, talents, and motivation very early in life affected the child's brain and abilities. However, early giftedness did not necessarily endure: Some child prodigies became ordinary adults, and some children who were not notably talented became so later on (Horowitz et al., 2009).

There is a crucial concept here. As is already evident, our understanding of development often benefits from neuroscience and genetics. Once, misbehavior was thought to be caused by bad parenting; we now believe parenting is only one factor. But currently people sometimes blame a child's behavior exclusively on brain immaturity or destructive genes. The crucial concept is that any human behavior has multiple causes and that plasticity is possible, especially in the early years but also lifelong (Nelson, 2011). That is true for everyone, but it is especially apparent when a baby is born with multiple disabilities, as I know from my nephew David.

plasticity The idea that abilities, personality, and other human characteristics can change over time. Plasticity is particularly evident during childhood, but even older adults are not always "set in their ways."

A CASE TO STUDY

Plasticity and David

My sister-in-law had rubella (called German measles) early in her third pregnancy, a fact not recognized until David was born, blind and dying. Heart surgery two days after birth saved his life, but surgery at 6 months to remove a cataract destroyed that eye. Malformations of his thumbs, ankles, teeth, feet, spine, and brain became evident. Predictions were dire: Some people wondered why his parents did not place him in an institution. He did not walk or talk for years.

Fortunately, the traditional view of handicapped children was shifting: Specialists were beginning to recognize plasticity. For example, at 9 months David did not crawl because his parents kept him safe in their arms. Then a consultant from the Kentucky School for the Blind put him on a large rug, teaching him to feel the boundaries and crawl safely. At age 2 he did not talk, but an audiologist found that he could hear, and teachers encouraged my brother and his wife to sing to him. At age

2½ he did not chew, but a nutritionist showed his parents how to force him to eat food that was not pureed. In middle childhood, doctors repaired his heart, removed the remaining cataract, realigned his jaw, replaced the dead eye with a glass one, and straightened his spine. Dozens of other professionals also improved his life. David attended three specialized preschools, then a mainstreamed public school, then a special high school, then the University of Louisville—each with educators guided by research that confirmed plasticity.

Remember, plasticity cannot erase genes, childhood experiences, or permanent damage. David's disabilities are always with him. But the interaction of nature and nurture meant that, by age 10, David had skipped a year of school and was a fifth-grader, reading at the eleventh-grade level. He learned German and Russian, with some Spanish and Korean, and he learned how to circumvent his handicaps—for example, swimming to keep his body fit since he could not play basketball (as most Kentucky boys do).

David now works as a translator of German texts, which he enjoys because, as he says, "I like providing a service to scholars, giving them access to something they would otherwise not have." The child whose birth was a reason for despair has become an adult who contributes to his family and his community. My brother and his wife, their two other sons (see the accompanying photo), hundreds of educators and medical professionals, decades of research, new laws, and David's own determination have enabled him to overcome the odds. He still is dependent on others for reminders to wash his hair, for guidance in social situations, and for scheduling doctor's appointments. However, plasticity is possible; David proves that.

Family Bonds Note the friendly smiles of these three brothers; from left to right, Mike, Bill, and David. No wonder I am proud of my nephews.

SUMMING UP

Human development can be studied in many ways because each person is unique as well as similar to every other human being. The scientific study of development begins with curiosity and then follows a specific sequence, from hypothesis to data collection to conclusions that are based on empirical evidence, not on wishful thinking or prejudice.

Nature and nurture always interact. A critical period is a time when something *must* occur to ensure normal development or the only time when an abnormality might occur. A sensitive period is a time when a specific development can occur most easily. Although many constraints affect development, people alter and transcend their situations, demonstrating plasticity: Change is possible throughout life. ■

>> Including All Kinds of People

The second element of our definition of the science of development—*all kinds of people*—is equally important. Developmentalists study young and old; rich and poor; people of every ethnicity, background, sexual orientation, culture, and nation. To help organize their study, they segment people into discrete age divisions, such as infancy, childhood, adolescence, and adulthood, each with approximate ages (see Table 1.1).

The challenge is to identify both universalities and differences and then to describe them in ways that simultaneously unify humanity and distinguish each individual. The danger is in drawing conclusions based on a limited group or, worse, to consider one's own group normal and every other group abnormal. This is called the **difference-equals-deficit error,** the human tendency to notice differences and then to jump to the conclusion that something important is lacking. In a flash, every

difference-equals-deficit error The mistaken belief that a deviation from some norm is necessarily inferior to behavior or characteristics that meet the standard.

Family Pride Grandpa Charilaos is proud of his tavern in northern Greece (central Macedonia), but he is even more proud of his talented grandchildren, including Maria Soni (shown here). Note her expert fingering. Her father and mother also play instruments—is that nature or nurture?

difference is perceived as a deficit (Gernsbacher, 2010). By studying all kinds of people, of every age and background, developmentalists recognize and try to avoid this danger. Many diversities are differences to be welcomed, not deficits to be remedied.

Sex Differences

Consider the differences between males and females. Of course, both sexes are alike in many ways: In modern nations, boys and girls eat the same foods, learn the same lessons, and wear many of the same clothes—unless the culture insists otherwise. Yet humans tend to focus on differences, evident in the popularity over the past two decades of John Gray's book *Men Are from Mars, Women Are from Venus* (1992/2004) and repeated spinoffs, most recently *Venus on Fire, Mars on Ice* (Gray, 2010). Exaggerating human sex differences is a distortion that developmentalists seek to avoid. As Janet Hyde (2007) puts it, people are from neither Mars nor Venus; they are from Earth, where the similarities among the sexes far outweigh the differences.

The importance of accepting differences in sexual development is apparent when considering sexual orientation. Historically, people who were attracted to others of the same sex were considered deficient, and 50 years ago their suicide rate was much higher than the suicide rate of heterosexual people (Herek, 2010). Gay activism, scientific data, and other factors combined to cause a dramatic reversal: In the 1970s, psychiatrists and psychologists declared, "Homosexuality per se implies no impairment in judgment, stability, reliability" (Conger, 1975, p. 633). The gay suicide rate has plummeted, more in some nations than others.

Culture, Ethnicity, and Race

Confusion about diversity often results when anyone—scientist or nonscientist—refers to *cultures*, *ethnic groups*, or *races*. These terms are **social constructions,** which means they are terms constructed, or made, by a society. Social constructions can be powerful, affecting how people think, but since they arise from society, they can be changed by society.

When the terms *culture, ethnicity,* and *race* are misused, they lead to the difference-equals-deficit error. The following definitions may help us avoid that mistake.

TABLE 1.1	Age Ranges for Different Stages of Development
Infancy	0 to 2 years
Early childhood	2 to 6 years
Middle childhood	6 to 11 years
Adolescence	11 to 18 years
Emerging adulthood	18 to 25 years
Adulthood	25 to 65 years
Late adulthood	65 years and older

social construction An idea that is built on shared perceptions, not on objective reality. Many age-related terms (such as *childhood, adolescence, yuppie,* and *senior citizen*) are social constructions, connected to biological traits but strongly influenced by social assumptions.

culture A system of shared beliefs, norms, behaviors, and expectations that persist over time and prescribe social behavior and assumptions.

What's for Dinner? Markets are universal, but each culture has a unique mix of products, stores, and salespeople. Compare this floating food market in Bangkok, Thailand, with a North American supermarket.

A System of Shared Beliefs

For social scientists, **culture** is "the system of shared beliefs, conventions, norms, behaviors, expectations and symbolic representations that persist over time and prescribe social rules of conduct" (Bornstein et al., 2011, p. 30). Culture is far more than food or ritual; it is a powerful social construction.

Each family, community, and college has a particular culture, and these cultures may clash. For example, decades ago my friend from a small rural town arrived for her first college class wearing her Sunday best: a freshly pressed skirt and blouse with a matching striped jacket. She looked around, embarrassed, and went directly to a used-clothing store to buy jeans and a T-shirt.

Often people use the word *culture* to refer to large groups of other people, as in "Asian culture" or "Hispanic culture." That invites prejudice, since within large groups are many cultures. For instance, people from Korea and Japan are aware of notable differences between them, as are people from Mexico and Guatemala. Furthermore, individuals within those cultures sometimes rebel against their culture's expected "beliefs, conventions, norms, behaviors." It is a short step from generalizations about cultures to the difference-equals-deficit error: Culture needs to be understood in all its fluidity and variations.

Book Reading: An Example

Cross-cultural research uncovers shared behaviors that people are unaware of. One example is reading books to toddlers, a behavior that advances language development. Indeed, a European American criticism of Mexican Americans is that parents rarely read to their children. This criticism may reflect the difference-equals-deficit error, since cross-cultural research finds that many Mexican American families use other ways to foster literacy (Hammer et al., 2011).

Even when parents read to toddlers, they do not necessarily convey the same messages. Scientists designed a picture book (no words) and asked middle-class parents from different nations to look at it with their 20-month-olds. Everything said was recorded and analyzed (see the Research Design).

> ### ▶ Research Design
>
> **Scientists:** Cheri C. Y. Chan, Amanda C. Brandone, and Twila Tardif.
>
> **Publication:** *Journal of Cross-Cultural Psychology* (2009).
>
> **Participants:** A total of 49 mother–toddler pairs, 25 of them from a city in the United States and 24 of them from Beijing, China. The two groups were comparable in age and education.
>
> **Design:** Each pair was brought into a playroom and recorded in three 10-minute play sessions (1) with mechanical toys, (2) with regular toys, and (3) looking at the same picture book. (To equalize both groups, the book was created for this study by laminating an equal number of pages from books used in the United States and China.)
>
> **Major conclusion:** Some universals were evident. For example, all the mothers were influenced by context—using more verbs when the toys were mechanical, for instance. Differences also emerged. The U.S. mothers gave fewer commands, such as "sit down" and "listen," and allowed children to express more irrelevant comments. During the joint book reading, Chinese mothers used more verbs than nouns (about 20 percent more), but U.S. mothers used more nouns than verbs.
>
> **Comment:** This study shows cultural similarities as well as differences. All mothers encourage their children to play and talk. Yet prior research had shown that U.S. children learn object names more rapidly than children elsewhere and that Chinese culture encourages people to see themselves in active relationship to others rather than as isolated individuals. Many Asians tend to perceive objects and experiences in context rather than detached from their uses and surroundings. Might these cultural differences be reflected when mothers explain pictures to toddlers?

A notable cultural difference surfaced. The U.S. mothers used more nouns than verbs; the opposite was true for the Chinese. For example, in a picture of a dandelion, some U.S. mothers pointed out the petals, leaves, and stem, and added colors, as the "yellow flower" and "green leaves." In contrast, the Chinese mothers stressed actions: A dandelion could be picked or smelled, and since this particular dandelion was in a book, the child would need to go outside to pick one (Chan et al., 2009).

It is tempting to see that difference as a deficit. Indeed, the initial data from this study were reanalyzed because some researchers assumed the Chinese mothers were too strict and hypothesized that their frequent verbs were often commands ("sit down," "pay attention"). A detailed reanalysis, excluding all words not relevant to book reading, revealed otherwise. The difference was not a deficit; all the parents were teaching vocabulary and attitudes related to their cultures.

Not the Same At first glance, this seems a standard scene; educated mothers the world over often read books to their toddlers. A closer look reveals differences—in the billboard, in hairstyles, in the mother's ring. However, the pivotal cultural variation cannot be seen: her words and his focus (see text).

Ethnic and Racial Groups

People of an **ethnic group** share certain attributes, almost always including ancestral heritage and usually national origin, religion, and language (Whitfield & McClearn, 2005). Ethnic group is not the same as cultural group: Some people of a particular ethnicity may not share a culture (consider people of Irish descent in Ireland and in North America), and some cultures are widespread, including people of several ethnic groups (consider British culture).

Ethnicity is a social construction, affected by the social context. For everyone, ethnic identity is strengthened if (1) other members of the same group are nearby, and (2) other groups exclude the person. For example, African-born people who are longtime residents of North America typically consider themselves African, but African-born people living on that continent identify with a more specific ethnic group. Similar identities are evident for everyone: Ethnic identity becomes more specific and more salient (Sicilian, not just Italian; South Korean, not just East Asian) when others of the same ethnic group are nearby and when members of other groups focus on differences.

> **ethnic group** People whose ancestors were born in the same region and who often share a language, culture, and religion.

The term **race** has been used to categorize people on the basis of physical differences, particularly outward appearance. However, appearance is not a reliable indicator of biology, genetics, or development (Race, Ethnicity, and Genetics Working Group of the National Human Genome Research Institute, 2005). Skin color (often used as a racial marker) is particularly misleading, since dark-skinned people with ancestors from Africa have "high levels of genetic population diversity" (Tishkoff et al., 2009, p. 1035). And dark-skinned people whose ancestors were not African are typically distinct from Africans in genes as well as culture.

> **race** A group of people who are regarded by themselves or by others as distinct from other groups on the basis of physical appearance, typically skin color. Social scientists think race is a misleading concept, as biological differences are not signified by outward appearance.

Social scientists reject the concept that race is genetic. As one team of psychologists explains: "Race is a social construction wherein individuals [who are] labeled as being of different races on the basis of physical characteristics are often treated as though they belong to biologically defined groups" (Goldston et al., 2008, p. 14). Unlike genetic differences, social constructions can disappear within a few decades: This has occurred with race (Rothenberg, 2010). For instance, Greek and Italian Americans were considered Black in the nineteenth century and White in the twentieth (Jacobson, 1998).

Socioeconomic Status

Another difference between one person and another relates to **socioeconomic status,** abbreviated **SES,** sometimes called *social class* (as in *middle class* or *working class*). SES reflects family income, but not income alone. The education and

> **socioeconomic status (SES)** A person's position in society as determined by income, occupation, education, and place of residence. (Sometimes called *social class.*)

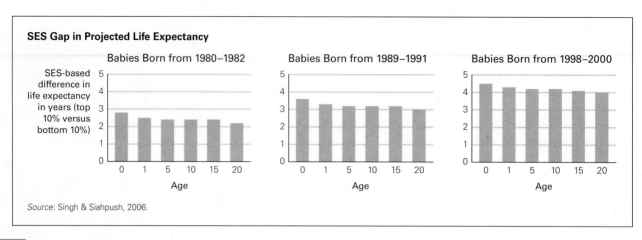

SES Gap in Projected Life Expectancy

Source: Singh & Siahpush, 2006.

FIGURE 1.3

Everyone Lives Longer, But . . . The advances of medical science and public health have added years to life for everyone, no matter what their SES (not shown). However, for those in the top 10 percent and the bottom 10 percent, the gap between years of life expected has increased in the United States. As this graph shows, the most advantaged baby born in 2000 is expected to live 4½ years longer than the least advantaged (about 80 years compared to 75). Economic equality is not keeping pace with health improvements.

occupation of the head of the household, or of both parents, and sometimes the average education or income of the other residents of the neighborhood, are also used to determine SES.

SES affects every aspect of development, even life itself (see Figure 1.3). Social scientists have many theories as to why SES is so influential, some of which are explored later in the text. Not surprisingly, those trained as economists and sociologists tend to emphasize SES differences more than those trained in neuroscience or psychology. However, all developmentalists appreciate that SES impacts each person's life, perhaps even more in the early years than the later ones.

Finding the Balance

As already noted on page 0, the science of human development attempts to find the right balance between the universal and the particular. All humans are the same, yet each individual is unique. Sex, culture, ethnicity, and SES make that abundantly clear. Is that a paradox, a dilemma, or a fascinating challenge?

Be forewarned: Some data from many sources (e.g., the 2010 U.S. Census, United Nations reports, research studies) group people in categories that might be considered races, such as by African, European, Hispanic, and Asian ancestry. Other data distinguish people by gender, sexual orientation, national origin, and SES. Such social constructions are sometimes important to the scientist, the community, and the individual. This is not a criticism: Differences among people need to be noted so that "all kinds of people" are studied, thereby avoiding the assumption that everyone develops in the same way. This point was forcefully made by a leading developmentalist:

> Psychologists and psychiatrists are fond of writing sentences such as "individuals with the short allele of the serotonin transporter [the 5-HTTLPR mentioned earlier] are vulnerable to depression if they experience past stressors." . . . I suggest that they should more often write sentences such as "women with a European pedigree possessing the short allele of the serotonin transporter who live in a large city far from their family, and grew up as a later born child in an economically disadvantaged family are at risk for depression."
>
> *[Kagan, 2011, p. 111]*

Kagan's suggestion is meant to be an exaggeration: The right balance between generalizations and specifics is not obvious, but developmental conclusions should not be "contextually naked," as Kagan explains (2011, p. 112). We must guard against simple conclusions, across groups or within them. A child of one group may develop unlike another child of another group or of that same group. Such differences are not necessarily deficits; all these categories are social constructions, not enduring divides. This leads to the third aspect of our definition, *change over time.*

SUMMING UP

Developing persons of every age, culture, and background teach us what is universal and what is unique. Differences among people are not necessarily deficits, although some people mistakenly assume that their own path is best for everyone. Ethnicity, race, and socioeconomic status all impact development, with much variation and overlap. ∎

❯❯ Observing Changes over Time

Individuals, cultures, and societies *change over time.* Continuity and discontinuity, consistencies and transformations, sudden eruptions and gradual shifts—these are the focus of developmental science. Developmental study would be easier if people grew gradually, at the same pace every year (called *linear growth*), or at least if growth occurred in distinct stages, like steps. Traditionally, developmentalists debated which of those two patterns—continuity or discontinuity—was more accurate. But there are far more patterns of growth than these two (see Figure 1.4).

No matter what the pattern, for developmentalists age is always significant. Is it normal for a boy to throw himself down, kicking and screaming, when he is frustrated? Yes, if he is 2 years old; no, if he is 12. Is it normal for a girl to be interested in boys? Yes, at age 16; no, at age 6. More broadly, children think, play, and learn differently depending partly on their age: Specific patterns and norms at each age are the backbone of developmental science and are significant for anyone who works with children.

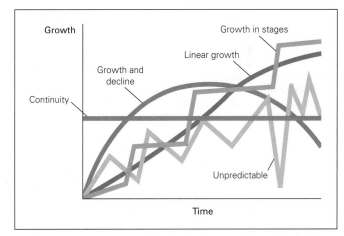

Dynamic Systems

Every aspect of development repeatedly interacts with every other; every person interacts with other people; all conditions and experiences interact continuously over time; each developmental change in a person affects every other aspect of that person as well as everyone else in that person's family, community, and beyond.

Consequently, scientists now envision development as the result of **dynamic systems.** The word *systems* captures the idea that a change in one aspect of a person, family, or society affects all the other aspects because each part is connected to all the other parts (Thelen & Smith, 2006) (see Figure 1.5). The body itself is a system, made up of many other systems (cardiovascular, respiratory, reproductive, and so on); a family is a system; so are neighborhoods, cities, nations, the world. Each small aspect of each person is connected to many systems within that person and affects many other people, and thus many other systems, as time goes on. To pick a simple example, a first birth turns a woman into a mother and a man into a father, a dramatic transformation of the individuals and of the family system that contributes to many other changes—in habits, goals, sleep, sibling rivalry, neighborhood interactions, national birth rates, and so on.

As explained by Esther Thelen (one of the leaders of the dynamic-systems perspective) in the *Handbook of Child Psychology,* "the application of dynamic systems

FIGURE 1.4

Patterns of Developmental Growth Many patterns of developmental growth have been discovered by careful research. Although linear (or nonlinear) progress seems most common, scientists now find that almost no aspect of human change follows the linear pattern exactly.

dynamic systems A view of human development as an ongoing, ever-changing interaction between the physical, cognitive, and psychosocial influences. The crucial understanding is that development is never static but is always affected by, and affects, many systems of development.

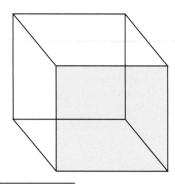

FIGURE 1.5

Dynamic Systems, Simplified Would it still be a box without one of the twelve lines? Which is the front, the top, or the bottom? And if someone flipped it around, would it be the same or not? Hopefully this simple example helps you grasp the complications of dynamic systems—every aspect of development is connected to every other, and the result might change at any moment.

ecological-systems approach A perspective on human development that considers all the influences from the various contexts of development. (Later renamed *bioecological theory.*)

FIGURE 1.6

The Ecological Model According to developmental researcher Urie Bronfenbrenner, each person is significantly affected by interactions among a number of overlapping systems, which provide the context of development. *Microsystems*—family, peer groups, classroom, neighborhood, house of worship—intimately and immediately shape human development. Surrounding and supporting the microsystems are the *exosystems,* which include all the external networks, such as community structures and local educational, medical, employment, and communications systems, that influence the microsystems. Influencing both of these systems is the *macrosystem,* which includes cultural patterns, political philosophies, economic policies, and social conditions. *Mesosystems* refer to interactions among systems, as when parents and teachers coordinate to educate a child. Bronfenbrenner eventually added a fifth system, the *chronosystem,* to emphasize the importance of historical time.

to developmental processes is relatively new" (Thelen & Smith, 2006, p. 258) for social scientists but not for natural scientists. For decades, natural scientists have studied how

> . . . seasons change in ordered measure, clouds assemble and disperse, trees grow to certain shape and size, snowflakes form and melt, minute plants and animals pass through elaborate life cycles that are invisible to us, and social groups come together and disband.
>
> *[Thelen & Smith, 2006, p. 271]*

Given the way the natural world changes over time, it should not be surprising that human growth follows diverse patterns and paces. The assumptions that growth is linear and that progress is inevitable have been replaced by the idea that both continuity and discontinuity are part of every life, that gains and losses are apparent at every age, that changes proceed in many ways (see Figure 1.5).

Although the dynamic-systems approach is "relatively new" to the science of development, similar approaches were evident earlier. One of the most famous and forceful developmentalists of the later twentieth century was Urie Bronfenbrenner, who recommended an **ecological-systems approach** to developmental study (1977). He argued that developmentalists must consider all the systems that surround each person, just as a naturalist examines the ecology of each organism, considering the interrelationships between it and its environment. Toward the end of his life, Bronfenbrenner renamed his theory *bioecological* to ensure that the name reflected the natural settings and biological processes that the theory includes (Bronfenbrenner & Morris, 2006).

Bronfenbrenner described three nested levels that affect each person (diagrammed in Figure 1.6): *microsystems* (elements of the immediate surroundings, such as the family system), *exosystems* (local institutions such as school and workplace), and *macrosystems* (the larger contexts, including cultural values, economic

AP PHOTO / JIM MOORE

Dynamic Interaction A dynamic-systems approach highlights the ever-changing impact that each part of a system has on all the other parts. This classroom scene reflects the eagerness for education felt by many immigrants, the reticence of some boys in an academic context, and a global perspective (as demonstrated by the world map). These facets emerge from various systems—family, gender, and culture—and they have interacted to produce this moment.

Observation Quiz What country is this? (see answer, page 20)

policies, and political processes). To reflect the dynamic interaction among the microsystem, exosystem, and macrosystem, Bronfenbrenner named a fourth system, the *mesosystem*, which encompasses the connections between the other systems.

One example of a mesosystem is the interface between school and family. Some elements of this mesosystem, such as parent–teacher conferences, are obvious. Others, such as promotion standards, curriculum choices, or school schedules that still assume one parent is home at 3 P.M., originate in the macrosystem, as nations recognize the connection between education of the population and economic growth.

Especially for Future Teachers Does the classroom furniture shown in the photograph above affect instruction? (see response, page 21)

The Historical Context

Change over time occurs not only within each person but also in families, communities, nations, and the entire world. Recognizing this, Bronfenbrenner coined the term *chronosystem* (literally, "time system"). Many other developmentalists also emphasize the historical context, for good reason. Children who are 10 years old today have thoughts and experiences—with technology, climate change, globalization, AIDS, school curriculum, and many other phenomena —unlike those their grandparents experienced at age 10. Their bodies differ as well (see Figure 1.7).

All persons born within a few years of one another are said to be of the same **cohort,** a group who travel through life together, experiencing similar circumstances. Members of each cohort are affected by the values, events, technologies, and culture of their era. For instance, young children in developed

cohort People born within the same historical period who therefore move through life together, experiencing the same events, new technologies, and cultural shifts at the same ages. For example, the effect of the Internet varies depending on what cohort a person belongs to.

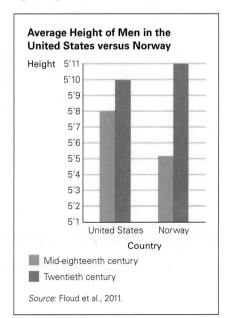

Average Height of Men in the United States versus Norway

Height
- 5'11
- 5'10
- 5'9
- 5'8
- 5'7
- 5'6
- 5'5
- 5'4
- 5'3
- 5'2
- 5'1

United States   Norway
Country

■ Mid-eighteenth century
■ Twentieth century

Source: Floud et al., 2011.

FIGURE 1.7

Systems and Cascades A change in any one part of a system affects all the other systems over time. Machines that made farming more efficient beginning in the eighteenth century improved the nutrition of pregnant women and added height, health, and decades of life to the average adult. This chart shows height specifics for two nations, but similar data are found in every nation that has longitudinal records. Another result is that the average human life span has more than doubled since 1800. Yet another is the population explosion of the twentieth century, which has led to dramatic reductions in average family size in the twenty-first century. So if you wish you had brothers and sisters, don't blame your parents, blame the tractor.

Past Life, Future Life This elderly man is considerably more active than most in his age group. Pausing on the Appalachian Trail, is he thinking about his past 60 years, his future destiny, or simply where he will open his backpack and sleep tonight?

"Hey! Elbows off the table."

Twenty-First-Century Manners If he obeyed his father but kept texting, would Emily Post be pleased?

nations in the twenty-first century almost always attend an early-childhood-education program, where they increase their vocabulary and make friends of their own age, often friends from other ethnic groups. This was not true for the cohort born 50 years ago, and this one historical change affects the intellect, motivation, and values of the current generation in ways older generations never imagined.

If you doubt that national trends and events touch individuals, consider your first name—a word chosen especially for you. Look at Table 1.2, which lists the most popular names for boys and girls born into cohorts 25 years apart, beginning in 1910. Your name and your reaction to it are influenced by the era. Research has found that, in the United States, names are influenced by when a person's birth state entered the union: Controlling for ethnic background, babies born in the "frontier" states of the Pacific Northwest or in "mountain" states (Montana, Oregon, Nebraska, and so on) are less likely to be given popular names than babies born in the original 13 states (Varnum & Kitayama, 2011).

A more general example of historical change is evident in the economy. Changes in SES are common and significant for child development. This is true for each child born into the same family. Typically, over the life of a family, income rises and falls, education and job status change (especially for children born to teenage parents), employment begins or ends, and families move from one neighborhood to another. Having many children reduces the resources for each child; moving into or out of a two-parent family structure changes SES as well. For many reasons, the SES of a first-born child may be quite different from that of a child born to the same parents 20 years later (Conley & Glauber, 2008).

Economic changes in an entire society also affect the development of the people within that society. For example, the global economic crisis that began around 2007 has meant fewer babies born, more children in each school classroom, later marriages, and much more. Each of these affects human development in ways detailed later in this book.

Fresh Fruit Many religious groups provide food for low-income families. Lisa Arsa is fortunate to have found this Seventh Day Adventist food pantry for herself and her son, Isaac. Unfortunately, the food donated to low-income families is usually high in salt, sugar, and fat—among the reasons why the U.S. rates of obesity and diabetes rise as income falls.

TABLE 1.2	Which First Names for U.S. Girls and Boys Were Most Popular in 1910, 1935, 1960, 1985, and 2010?	
Year	Top Five Girls' Names	Top Five Boys' Names
_____	Mary, Susan, Linda, Karen, Donna	David, Michael, James, John, Robert
_____	Mary, Helen, Margaret, Dorothy, Ruth	John, James, William, Robert, George
_____	Isabella, Sophia, Emma, Olivia, Ava	Jacob, Ethan, Michael, Jayden, William
_____	Mary, Shirley, Barbara, Betty, Patricia	Robert, James, John, William, Richard
_____	Jessica, Ashley, Jennifer, Amanda, Sarah	Michael, Christopher, Matthew, Joshua, Daniel

Source: Social Security Administration Web site (http://www.ssa.gov/OACT/babynames), retrieved May 16, 2011.

Guess First If your answers, in order from top to bottom were 1960, 1910, 2010, 1935, and 1985, you are excellent at detecting cohort influences. If you made a mistake, perhaps that's because the data are compiled from applications for Social Security numbers, so the names of those who did not get a Social Security number are omitted.

The Three Domains

Obviously, it is impossible to simultaneously examine all the dynamic changes that occur over the years. Instead, scientists study one aspect of development at a time and then combine many aspects to describe a person. Developmentalists often segment their study into three domains—*biosocial, cognitive,* and *psychosocial*. (Figure 1.8 describes each domain.) Each domain includes several academic disciplines: biosocial includes biology and medicine, cognitive includes psychology and education, and psychosocial includes sociology and anthropology. The two newest disciplines, neuroscience and genetics, contribute to every domain.

Every aspect of growth touches on all three domains. This dynamic reality is expressed with a single word, **biopsychosocial,** a term that expresses the interaction of domains. Biopsychosocial does not imply that biological changes precede the other changes—sometimes the opposite sequence seems more accurate

biopsychosocial A term emphasizing the interaction of the three developmental domains (biosocial, cognitive, and psychosocial). All development is biopsychosocial, although the domains are studied separately.

FIGURE 1.8

The Three Domains The division of human development into three domains makes it easier to study, but remember that very few factors belong exclusively to one domain or another. Development is not piecemeal but holistic: Each aspect of development is related to all three domains.

DOMAINS OF HUMAN DEVELOPMENT

Biosocial Development	Cognitive Development	Psychosocial Development
Includes all the growth and change that occur in a person's body and the genetic, nutritional, and health factors that affect that growth and change. Motor skills—everything from grasping a rattle to driving a car—are also part of the biosocial domain. In this book, this domain is called biosocial, rather than physical or biological.	Includes all the mental processes that a person uses to obtain knowledge or to think about the environment. Cognition encompasses perception, imagination, judgment, memory, and language —the processes people use to think, decide, and learn. Education—not only the formal curriculum in schools but also informal learning—is part of this domain as well.	Includes development of emotions, temperament, and social skills. Family, friends, the community, the culture, and the larger society are particularly central to the psychosocial domain. For example, cultural differences in "appropriate" sex roles or in family structures are part of this domain.

>> **Answer to Observation Quiz** (from page 17) The three Somali girls wearing headscarves may have thrown you off, but these first-graders attend school in Minneapolis, Minnesota, in the United States. Clues include the children's diversity (this school has students from 17 nations), clothing (obviously Western), and—for the sharp-eyed—the flag near the door.

mirror neurons Cells in an observer's brain that are activated by watching an action performed by someone else as they would be if the observer had personally performed that action.

(Cohen, 2010). For example, although babies start speaking because of maturation of the brain and vocal cords (*biosocial*), which allows them to express connections between objects and words (*cognitive*), such developments would not lead to speech unless people talked to the baby (*psychosocial*). In other words, the biology must precede the speech, but if the baby didn't hear speech, brain maturation would not occur. This is literally true: If profoundly deaf infants begin hearing years after the language-learning time, they never talk normally because some brain areas never developed (Buckley & Tobey, 2011).

You can see the quagmire here: Words and pages follow in linear succession and the mind thinks one thought at a time, making it impossible to consider ongoing development in all domains simultaneously. Yet because changes in everything and everybody are connected as time goes on, developmental discoveries from one line of research have the potential to raise questions among scholars in every other discipline. One example comes from **mirror neurons**—the term for parts of the brain that react to actions people see as if the people were actually performing the actions themselves—as explained in the following.

A VIEW FROM SCIENCE

Mirror Neurons

About two decades ago, scientists were surprised to discover that a particular region of a macaque monkey's brain responded to actions the monkey had merely observed as if the monkey had actually performed those actions itself (Gallese et al., 1996). For example, when one macaque saw another reach for a banana, the same brain areas were activated (lit up in brain scans) in both monkeys. Certain neurons, dubbed *mirror neurons,* in the F5 area of the observing macaque's premotor cortex, responded to what was observed. Using increasingly advanced technology, neuroscientists now are finding mirror neurons in several parts of the human brain (Keysers & Gazzola, 2010). Neurons fire in the same action sequences in both actor and observer, as is evident from studies in which ballerinas watch a ballet or soccer players watch another team's game.

Human brains mirror much more than reaching for bananas or scoring a goal. Indeed, the "human mirror neuron system may allow us to go beyond imitating the observed motor acts of others to infer their intentions and perhaps even their states of mind"

Lighting Up In the photograph at left, the arrow points to a web of neurons that are activated not only when a monkey uses motor abilities (as in reaching for a banana) but also when the monkey sees another monkey perform that action. At right, these toddlers in Buenos Aires may be exhibiting mirror neurons at work as they get ready to join other fans in cheering on Argentina's soccer team in a match against Peru.

NATACHIA PISARENKO / AP

(Coward, 2008, p. 1494). Repeated observations over time lead to brain development in much the same way that repeated actions over time might. Scientists in many disciplines continue to explore the implications (Rizzolatti & Fabbri-Destro, 2010):

- Anthropologists hypothesize that mirror neurons might explain cultural transmission and social organization (Losin et al., 2009).
- Psychopathologists describes autism as a "broken mirror" (Marsh & Hamilton, 2011).
- Psychiatrists believe that abnormalities in the mirroring function of the brain may trigger the symptoms of schizophrenia (Buccino & Amore, 2008).
- Linguists believe mirror neurons aid language learning (Corballis, 2010; Rossi et al., 2011).

- Cognitive psychologists suggest that mirror neurons explain newborns' ability to imitate what they see, learning from observation (Diamond & Amso, 2008).
- Social psychologists think mirror neurons help people empathize with one another (Decety, 2011; Iacoboni, 2009).

Although scientists are excited by these multidisciplinary possibilities, they are cautious as well. Research on human brains is notoriously difficult. Neural networks are complex; mirror neurons certainly do not explain all of human learning, or social responsiveness (Plotkin, 2011; Wheatley et al., 2007). Yet because developmental research is multidisciplinary, thousands of scientists studying childhood are pursuing implications and applications suggested by an unexpected discovery in a monkey brain.

SUMMING UP

A dynamic-systems approach finds continuity as well as discontinuity, erratic change as well as linear progress, gains as well as losses throughout life. Developmentalists are interested in learning about the factors that influence a person's biosocial, cognitive, and psychosocial development. Urie Bronfenbrenner's bioecological approach notes that each person is situated within larger systems of family, school, community, and culture. Cohort, culture, and socioeconomic status affect each person's development, and biological factors are always influential. One example is in mirror neurons, which amplify human learning and development. Infants, children, and adults watch what other people do and, neurologically, experience it themselves.

>> Using the Scientific Method

Now we focus on the crux of the scientific method: designing research and analyzing evidence. Statistical measures often help scientists discover relationships between various aspects of the data they collect. (Some statistical perspectives are presented in Table 1.3.) Every research design, method, and statistical measure has strengths as well as weaknesses. You will notice that every chapter in this text includes a Research Design that explains the details of a particular study to help you see the variations and shortcomings that, when properly understood, add to our understanding of development. Now we describe three basic types of research designs—observation, the experiment, and the survey—and in the next section explore three ways developmentalists learn more about change over time.

Observation

We are all observers. Developmentalists have made observation a science, finding many ways to limit subjectivity so that conclusions are based on data, not assumptions. **Scientific observation** requires researchers to record behavior systematically and objectively, using behavioral definitions (noting instances of hitting, for instance, not instances of aggression) and timed data (e.g., what happens every 10 seconds, not just what captures attention). Observations often occur in a naturalistic setting (such as a home, school, or public park), where people behave as

Especially for Parents Who Want Their Children to Enjoy Sports While your baby is still too young and uncoordinated to play any sports, what does the research on mirror neurons suggest you might do? (see response, page 22)

>> Response for Future Teachers (from page 17) Yes. Every aspect of the ecological context affects what happens. In this classroom, tables and movable chairs foster group collaboration and conversation—potent learning methods that are difficult to achieve when desks and seats are bolted to the floor and the teacher sits behind a large desk.

scientific observation A method of testing a hypothesis by unobtrusively watching and recording participants' behavior in a systematic and objective manner—in a natural setting, in a laboratory, or in searches of archival data.

TABLE 1.3	Statistical Measures Often Used to Analyze Research Results
Measure	**Use**
Effect size	Indicates how much one variable affects another. Effect size ranges from 0 to 1: An effect size of 0.2 is called small, 0.5 moderate, and 0.8 large.
Significance	Indicates whether the results might have occurred by chance. A finding that chance would produce the results fewer than 5 times in 100 is significant at the 0.05 level. A finding that chance would produce the results once in 100 times is significant at 0.01; once in 1,000 times is significant at 0.001.
Cost-benefit analysis	Calculates how much a particular independent variable costs versus how much it saves. This is particularly useful to analyze public spending. For instance, one cost-benefit analysis showed that an expensive preschool program cost $15,166 per child but saved $215,000 by age 40, in reduced costs of special education, unemployment, prison, and so on (Belfield et al., 2006).
Odds ratio	Indicates how a particular variable compares to a standard, set at 1. For example, one study found that, although less than 1 percent of all child homicides occurred at school, the odds were similar for public and private schools. The odds of such deaths occurring in high schools, however, were 18.47 times that of elementary or middle schools (set at 1.0) (MMWR, January 18, 2008).
Factor analysis	Hundreds of variables could affect any given behavior. In addition, many variables (such as family income and parental education) may overlap. To take this into account, analysis reveals variables that can be clustered together to form a factor, which is a composite of many variables. For example, SES might become one factor, child personality another.
Meta-analysis	A "study of studies." Researchers use statistical tools to synthesize the results of previous, separate studies. Then they analyze the accumulated results, using criteria that weight each study fairly. This approach improves data analysis by combining the results of studies that used so few participants that the conclusions did not reach significance.

Who Participates? For all these measures, the characteristics of the people who participate in the study (formerly called the subjects, now called the participants) are important, as is the number of people who are studied.

they usually do and ideally where the observer can be ignored or even go unnoticed. Scientific observation can also occur in a laboratory, where scientists record human reactions in various situations, often with wall-mounted video cameras and the scientist in another room.

Observation is the mainstay of anthropologists, who live within a community while they take meticulous notes on its culture. Historians use observation when they pore over old records to gain insight, and many social scientists analyze data collected for some other reason, such as census data. Nonetheless, even with careful training, controlled timing, and the motivation to be objective, observation is limited: It cannot prove what *causes* human behavior.

Remember Beal's observations of Australian infants? She developed an important hypothesis, based on hundreds of detailed observations, but she needed more than observational data. Every observation has several plausible explanations. For SIDS, among the observed differences between Chinese and Australian infants were prenatal care, maternal diet, breast-feeding, facial features, baby blanket fabrics, and more. Proof was needed to support Beal's hypothesis that the crucial difference was sleeping position.

The Experiment

The experiment is the research method that scientists use to establish cause. In the social sciences, experimenters typically give people a particular treatment or expose them to a specific condition and then note whether their behavior changes.

>> **Response for Parents Who Want Their Children to Enjoy Sports** (from page 21) The results of mirror-neuron research imply that people of all ages learn by observing body movements in others. This suggests that such parents should make sure their baby gets many chances to watch them (or someone else) throwing balls, running, and playing sports.

Procedure:

1. Divide participants into two groups that are matched on important characteristics, especially the behavior that is the dependent variable on which this study is focused.

2. Give special treatment, or intervention (the independent variable), to one group (the experimental group).

3. Compare the groups on the dependent variable. If they now differ, the cause of the difference was probably the independent variable.

4. Publish the results.

In technical terms, experimenters manipulate an **independent variable,** which is the imposed treatment or special condition (also called the *experimental variable*). This independent variable may affect whatever they are studying, called the **dependent variable** (which *depends* on the independent variable). Thus, the independent variable is the new, special treatment; any change in the dependent variable is the result. If the experiment is carefully done, the researcher can conclude that the independent variable caused whatever changes occurred in the dependent variable. Beal convinced thousands of non-Chinese parents to put their babies to sleep on their backs (the independent variable) and then tallied infant deaths (the dependent variable).

The purpose of an experiment is to find out whether an independent variable affects the dependent variable. Usually, if an experiment is well designed (see Figure 1.9), at least two groups of participants are studied, with both groups similar in background characteristics (same ages, gender proportions, ethnic backgrounds, and so on). Typically, one group is designated to be the *experimental group*, which gets the particular treatment (the independent variable). The other group is the *comparison group* (also called a *control group*), which does not. The dependent variable in both groups is measured after the experiment, to make sure the independent variable (and not some other variable, such as time or circumstances) caused any change in the dependent variable.

The Survey

A third research method is the **survey.** Information is collected from a large number of people by interview, questionnaire, or some other means. The survey is a quick and direct way to obtain data, which is why it is used in the U.S. Census, political polls, and corporate customer surveys.

However, acquiring valid data is far more problematic than it appears. For example, elections would be easy to predict (never "too close to call") if people always voted as they said they would, if the undecided followed the trends, and if those who refused to tell or who were not asked were similar to those who responded. But none of that is true: People lie or change their minds; the undecided

FIGURE 1.9

How to Conduct an Experiment The basic sequence diagrammed here applies to all experiments. Many additional features, especially the statistical measures listed in Table 1.3 and various ways of reducing experimenter bias, affect whether publication occurs. (Scientific journals reject reports of experiments that were not rigorous in method and analysis.)

Especially for Nurses In the field of medicine, why are experiments conducted to test new drugs and treatments? (see response, page 24)

independent variable In an experiment, the variable that is introduced to see what effect it has on the dependent variable. (Also called *experimental variable*.)

dependent variable In an experiment, the variable that may change as a result of whatever new condition or situation the experimenter adds. In other words, the dependent variable *depends* on the independent variable.

survey A research method in which information is collected from a large number of people by interviews, written questionnaires, or some other means.

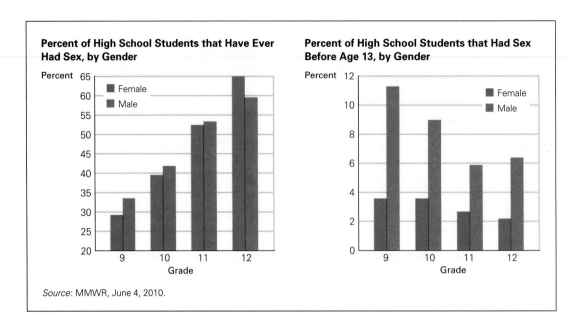

Percent of High School Students that Have Ever Had Sex, by Gender

Percent of High School Students that Had Sex Before Age 13, by Gender

Source: MMWR, June 4, 2010.

FIGURE 1.10

Is Everybody Doing It? No. About one-third of high school seniors and half of all students in grades 9 through 12, both boys and girls, are still virgins. The data for this graph are from the Youth Risk Behavior Survey, a national survey that asks the same questions of thousands of U.S. students in the ninth through twelfth grades each year.

>> Response for Nurses (from page 23) Experiments are the only way to determine cause-and-effect relationships. If we want to be sure that a new drug or treatment is safe and effective, an experiment must be conducted to establish that the drug or treatment improves health.

cross-sectional research A research design that compares groups of people who differ in age but are similar in other important characteristics.

react in unexpected ways; those who never speak to strangers are unlike those who talk freely; college students, prisoners, and cell phone users are less likely to be surveyed but tend to be younger and less predictable than average. Good scientists correct for all this, but some uncertainty is inevitable.

Furthermore, answers are influenced by the wording and the sequence of the questions as well as by selective memory. For example, every year since 1991, thousands of high school students throughout the United States have been asked if they had sexual intercourse before age 13. Every year, about twice as many ninth-graders (8 percent in 2009) as twelfth-graders (4 percent) say yes (see Figure 1.10). How could that be? Do twelfth-graders forget, do ninth-graders lie, does "intercourse" have different meaning, or do sexually active ninth-graders drop out of school? Surveys of more than 200,000 students over the years cannot tell.

Studying Development

Social scientists from every discipline use these same three methods (observations, experiments, and surveys) to explore human behavior. Typically, before conclusions are accepted, not only does replication occur, but so does research on the same topics using other methods.

Developmentalists have an added requirement: to consider dynamic change, not static results. To study change over time, they design cross-sectional, longitudinal, or cohort-sequential research (see Figure 1.11).

Cross-Sectional and Longitudinal Research

The most convenient (quickest and least expensive) way to study developmental change over time is with **cross-sectional research,** in which a group of people of one age are compared with a similar group of people of another age.

For example, in the United States a repeated national survey tallies various medical measures (blood tests, weight, height, and so on) on a cross section of people of many ages. In 2007–2008, the incidence of childhood obesity was about 12 percent for 2- to 5-year-olds, almost 20 percent for 6- to 11-year-olds (Ogden, 2010) (see Figure 1.12), and 32 percent for adults. These data suggest that people get fatter as they grow older, a result found in other nations as well.

CROSS-SECTIONAL
Total time: A few days, plus analysis

2-year-olds	6-year-olds	10-year-olds	14-year-olds	18-year-olds
Time 1	Time 1	Time 1	Time 1	Time 1

Collect data once. Compare groups. Any differences, presumably, are the result of age.

LONGITUDINAL
Total time: 16 years, plus analysis

2-year-olds	→	6-year-olds	→	10-year-olds	→	14-year-olds	→	18-year-olds
	[4 years later]		[4 years later]		[4 years later]		[4 years later]	
Time 1		Time 1 + 4 years		Time 1 + 8 years		Time 1 + 12 years		Time 1 + 16 years

Collect data five times, at 4-year intervals. Any differences for these individuals are definitely the result of passage of time (but might be due to events or historical changes as well as age).

COHORT-SEQUENTIAL
Total time: 16 years, plus double and triple analysis

2-year-olds	6-year-olds	10-year-olds	14-year-olds	18-year-olds

[4 years later]   [4 years later]   [4 years later]   [4 years later]

| 2-year-olds | 6-year-olds | 10-year-olds | 14-year-olds |

For cohort effects, compare groups on the diagonals (same age, different years).

[4 years later]   [4 years later]   [4 years later]

| 2-year-olds | 6-year-olds | 10-year-olds |

[4 years later]   [4 years later]

| Time 1 | Time 1 + 4 years | Time 1 + 8 years | Time 1 + 12 years | Time 1 + 16 years |

Collect data five times, following the original group but also adding a new group each time. Analyze data three ways, first comparing groups of the same ages studied at different times. Any differences over time between groups who are the same age are probably cohort effects. Then compare the same group as they grow older. Any differences are the result of time (not only age). In the third analysis, compare differences between the same people as they grow older, *after* the cohort effects (from the first analysis) are taken into account. Any remaining differences are almost certainly the result of age.

FIGURE 1.11

Which Approach Is Best? Cohort-sequential research is the most time-consuming and complex, but it yields the best information. One reason that hundreds of scientists conduct research on the same topics, replicating one another's work, is to gain some advantages of cohort-sequential research without waiting for decades.

longitudinal research A research design in which the same individuals are followed over time, as their development is repeatedly assessed.

However, cross-sectional data do not always reliably indicate the processes of development: It is not necessarily true that the current cohort of 2- to 5-year-olds will follow what seems to be the age-related trend. Their experiences may be different. When they reach adulthood, in 2030 or so, they may be thinner or fatter than adults now are. (In fact, 50 years ago, adults were lighter as well as shorter, on average, than they are now.)

To discover whether age itself, not historical trends, causes developmental change, scientists undertake **longitudinal research,** collecting data repeatedly on the same individuals. Longitudinal research is particularly useful in studying development over many years (Elder & Shanahan, 2006; Hofer & Piccinin, 2010). For instance, to predict the long-term effects of childhood obesity, one study recorded the childhood weight of almost 5,000 American Indians born between 1945 and 1984 (29 percent were obese) and then noted which ones died before

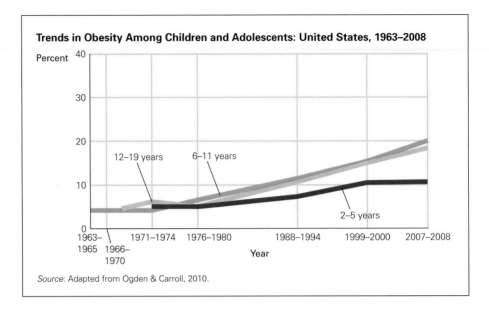

Trends in Obesity Among Children and Adolescents: United States, 1963–2008

Source: Adapted from Ogden & Carroll, 2010.

And It Gets Worse Rates of obesity in the United States rise with age and cohort. Adults are increasingly overfeeding their children as well as themselves—about one-third of all adults are obese while another one-third are overweight but not yet obese.

late adulthood. Those 11-year-olds who were in the top quartile of weight (the heaviest 25 percent) died prematurely at twice the rate of those in the bottom quartile (Franks et al., 2010). However, the reasons for the higher death rate were not the expected ones such as diabetes but rather alcohol-related liver disease.

Are obese adolescents more likely to abuse alcohol? Is the interaction between obesity and alcoholism more deadly than either one alone? Will the higher death rates be apparent in late adulthood and will diabetes then become more lethal? More research is needed, but the questions themselves would not have been asked without longitudinal research.

Developmentalists agree that longitudinal research uncovers links that cross-sectional research does not. However, longitudinal studies require much more effort and time than cross-sectional research, and that limits the number of participants. The famous New Zealand study mentioned on page 7 began with 1,037 participants, but only 13 boys were in the severely maltreated, low-MAOA group. Four of them were convicted of violent crimes as adults, as were 11 of the 42 "probably maltreated" low-MAOA boys. These are high proportions, but they are low numbers.

Compare These with Those These diverse groups seem ideal for cross-sectional research. The younger ones have their hands all over each other and express open-mouth joy—but with age, even smiling classmates, like these graduating high school seniors, are more restrained. However, with cross-sectional research, it is not certain whether such contrasts are the direct result of chronological age or the result of other variables—perhaps income, cohort, or culture.

Six Stages of Life These photos show Sarah-Maria, born in 1980 in Switzerland, at six stages of her life: infancy (age 1), early childhood (age 3), middle childhood (age 8), adolescence (age 15), emerging adulthood (age 19), and adulthood (age 30).

Observation Quiz Longitudinal research best illustrates continuity and discontinuity. For Sarah-Maria, what changed over 30 years and what didn't? (see answer, page 28)

Moreover, when developmentalists want to know the eventual effects of childhood experience, they need to wait decades for conclusions from longitudinal research. Waiting can have disastrous consequences. For example, until the results from longitudinal research were in, millions of teenagers started smoking because their parents, their schools, and their friends thought cigarettes were harmless. Currently, because of fears about adult cancer from industrial compounds (called *phthalates*) in plastic, many parents use glass baby bottles. Might the risk of occasional shattered glass hurt more people than chemicals in plastic? Longitudinal research can tell us—in 50 years.

Combining Methods and Strategies

As you can see, cross-sectional and longitudinal research each have advantages that compensate for the other's disadvantages. Scientists have discovered a third research strategy that involves using these two together, often with complex statistical analysis. In **cohort-sequential research** (or *cross-sequential* or *time-sequential research*), researchers study several groups of people of different ages (a cross-sectional approach) and follow them over the years (a longitudinal approach). A cohort-sequential design lets researchers compare findings for a group of, say, 25-year-olds with findings for the same individuals at ages 20, 15, 10 and 5—as well as with findings for groups who are *currently* age 20, 15, 10, and 5. Cohort-sequential research thus allows scientists to disentangle age and historical context.

One well-known cohort-sequential study (the Seattle Longitudinal Study) discovered something about schoolchildren: Older adults are better at math than younger adults, not because number sense improves with age (it does not) but because decades ago schools emphasized math—a finding that neither cross-sectional nor longitudinal research alone could reveal. For parents and teachers, this is significant: Lessons learned before age 12 can affect intellectual abilities 50 years later.

cohort-sequential research A research design in which researchers first study several groups of people of different ages (a cross-sectional approach) and then follow those groups over the years (a longitudinal approach). (Also called *cross-sequential research* or *time-sequential research*.)

Especially for Future Researchers What is the best method for collecting data? (see response, page 28)

>> **Answer to Observation Quiz** (from page 27) Of course, much changed and much did not change, but evident in the photos is continuity in Sarah-Maria's happy smile and discontinuity in her hairstyle (which shows dramatic age and cohort changes).

>> **Response for Future Researchers** (from page 27) There is no best method for collecting data. The method used depends on many factors, such as the age of participants (infants can't complete questionnaires), the question being researched, and the time frame.

correlation A number between +1.0 and −1.0 that indicates the degree of relationship between two variables, expressed in terms of the likelihood that one variable will (or will not) occur when the other variable does (or does not). A correlation indicates only that two variables are somehow related, not that one variable causes the other to occur.

SUMMING UP

Social scientists use many research methods, each with advantages and disadvantages. Observational research requires careful and systematic recording of whatever actually occurs. Experiments seek to establish cause and effect, as revealed by change in the dependent variable. A true experiment compares at least two groups, similar in many ways except that one receives a particular treatment (the independent variable) that the other does not. A third method, the survey, is useful for large groups. However, the accuracy of a survey depends on factors not always evident, including the wording of the questions and who responds.

Developmentalists need to study change over time, so they use additional strategies. Cross-sectional and longitudinal research designs are both useful, yet each has serious limitations. A combination of these two, often called cohort-sequential, is ideal but complicated statistically and logistically.

■

>> Cautions and Challenges from Science

The scientific method illuminates and illustrates human development. Facts, hypotheses, and possibilities have emerged that would not be known without science—and people of all ages are healthier and more capable because of it. For example, infant death, childhood malnutrition, adolescent suicide, and racism and sexism at every age are much less prevalent today than a few decades ago. Primarily because more children survive to adulthood, the average life span in developed nations is about 80, not 50, as it was a century ago. Science contributed to this; many of us would not be alive without it.

Developmental scientists have also discovered unexpected sources of harm. As detailed in later chapters, sugary drinks, television, lead paint, video games, and parental divorce are less benign in childhood than people first thought. New protections, and newly discovered dangers, are examples of the benefits of science.

However, science can be misused and misinterpreted. We now discuss three possible problems: correlation, quantification, and ethics.

Correlation and Causation

Probably the most common mistake in interpreting research is to think that correlation means causation. It does not. Scientists try to remember the mantra: *Correlation is not causation.* A **correlation** exists between two variables if one variable is more (or less) likely to occur when the other does. A correlation is *positive* if both variables tend to increase together or decrease together, *negative* if one variable tends to increase while the other decreases, and *zero* if no connection is evident.

To illustrate: From birth to age 9, there is a positive correlation between age and height (children grow taller as they grow older), a negative correlation between age and hours of sleep (children sleep less as they grow older), and zero correlation between age and number of toes (barring a rare accident or late-life diabetes, after the eighth prenatal week, humans have 10 toes lifelong). (Now take the quiz on correlation in Table 1.4.)

Expressed in statistics, correlations vary from +1.0 (the most positive) to −1.0 (the most negative). Totally positive or totally negative correlations are virtually never found because there are always exceptions that reduce the strength of the correlation. Indeed, a correlation of +0.3 or −0.3 is noteworthy; a correlation of +0.8 or −0.8 is amazingly high.

Many correlations are unexpected. For instance, first-born children develop asthma more often than later-born children, teenage boys commit suicide more

TABLE 1.4	Quiz on Correlation	
Two Variables	Positive, Negative, or Zero Correlation?	Why? (Third Variable)
1. Ice cream sales and murder rate	_____	_____
2. Reading ability and number of baby teeth	_____	_____
3. Sex of adult and his or her average number of offspring	_____	_____

For each of these three pairs of variables, indicate whether the correlation between them is positive, negative, or nonexistent. Then try to think of a third variable that might determine the direction of the correlation. The correct answers are printed upside down below.

often than teenage girls, and, at least in North America, babies born to immigrants are healthier than other babies. (These findings are discussed in later chapters.) Why? Correlations do not answer that question because, as the mantra says, correlation is not causation.

Quantity and Quality

A second caution concerns how heavily scientists rely on data produced by **quantitative research** (from the word *quantity,* such as more or less, higher or lower, in rank order, in percents, or in numerical scores). Because quantitative data are numerical, they can be translated across cultures and applied to diverse populations. One example of quantitative research is school test scores, used to measure the effectiveness of teachers, or to determine whether a child must repeat a grade, or to decide whether a particular school should win a grant or be shut down.

Since quantities can be easily summarized, compared, charted, and replicated, many scientists prefer quantitative research. Quantitative data are said to provide "rigorous, empirically testable representations" (Nesselroade & Molenaar, 2003, p. 635). Without numbers to measure ability or achievement, students might unfairly be denied college admission because of their ethnicity, religion, or SES.

However, when data are reduced to numbers, nuances and individual distinctions are lost. Many developmental researchers thus turn to **qualitative research** (from *quality*)—asking open-ended questions, reporting answers in narrative (not numerical) form, and generating "a rich description of the phenomena of interest" (Hartmann & Pelzel, 2005, p. 163). Qualitative research reflects diversity and complexity, but it is vulnerable to personal bias and hard to replicate. Particularly if one person, *a single case study,* is used, conclusions may be idiosyncratic. (Earlier in this chapter, I referred to one case, my nephew David. Is he atypical, a misleading example, giving false hope? Would I have been equally likely to tell his story if he had died or remained unable to walk, talk, or think?)

The solution: a combination of quantitative and qualitative methods. Sometimes scientists translate qualitative research into quantifiable data; sometimes they use qualitative studies to suggest hypotheses for quantitative research. In this we return to the scientific method. Although news reports sometimes headline an unexpected result from one study, scientists do not accept a finding as verified until several groups of scientists, ideally after replication and then several qualitative and quantitative methods with diverse groups of participants, reach the same conclusion.

Ethics

All scientists, especially those studying humans, need to uphold ethical standards. Each academic discipline and professional society has a **code of ethics** (a set of moral principles).

quantitative research Research that provides data that can be expressed with numbers, such as ranks or scales.

Answers:
1. Positive; third variable: heat
2. Negative; third variable: age
3. Zero; each child must have a parent of each sex; no third variable

qualitative research Research that considers qualities, not quantities. Narrative accounts and individual variations are often stressed in qualitative research.

Especially for People Who Have Applied to College or Graduate School Is the admissions process based on quality or quantity? (see response, page 31)

code of ethics A set of moral principles or guidelines that members of a profession or group are expected to follow.

Institutional Review Board (IRB) A group within most educational and medical institutions who ensure that research follows established ethical guidelines. Unlike in prior decades, most research in human development cannot begin without IRB approval.

By federal law in the United States, most educational and medical institutions have an **Institutional Review Board (IRB),** a group that permits only research that follows certain guidelines. Although IRBs often slow down scientific study, some research conducted before IRBs were established was clearly unethical, especially when the participants were children, members of minority groups, prisoners, or animals (Blum, 2002; Washington, 2006).

Protection of Research Participants

Central to every IRB is the attempt to ensure that participation in research is voluntary, confidential, and harmless. In Western nations, this entails the *informed consent* of the participants—that is, their understanding of the research procedures and of any risks involved. If children are involved, consent must be obtained from the parents as well as the children. The children and the parent must be allowed to opt out at any time with no penalty. For instance, if children are given toys or parents are paid for participation, those who quit before the study is over must receive the same payment as those who complete the study, and any gifts or payments must be small so that people will not participate merely in order to get the incentive.

Implications of Research Results

Especially for Future Researchers and Science Writers Do any ethical guidelines apply when an author writes about the experiences of family members, friends, or research participants? (see response, page 32)

Once a study has been completed, additional ethical issues arise. Scientists are obligated to "promote accuracy, honesty, and truthfulness" (American Psychological Association, 2010). That precludes distortions to support any political, economic, religious, or cultural position. Results must be carefully presented (Principle 14).

Deliberate distortion is rare, but insidious dangers include unintentionally slanting the conclusions or withholding publication, especially when there is "ferocious . . . pressure from commercial funders to ignore good scientific practice" (Bateson, 2005, p. 645). Similarly, nonprofit research groups and academic institutions may pressure scientists to produce publishable results.

For this reason, scientific training, collaboration, and replication are essential. Numerous safeguards are built into scientific methodology, including the fact that reports in professional journals are typically "peer reviewed," meaning that before an article can be published, it must be evaluated by scientists not connected with the author(s). Reports often include (1) researchers' affiliations and sources of funding, (2) sufficient details to allow for replication, (3) limitations of the research, and (4) alternative interpretations.

What Should We Study?

A crucial question for all scientists is whether their research is ethical and will help solve human problems.

Long before designing and publishing research, the first ethical question for every developmental scientist is: "What research is needed to enable more humans to live satisfying and productive lives?" Consider these questions, for instance:

- Do we know enough about prenatal drug abuse to protect every fetus?
- Do we know enough about poverty to enable everyone to be healthy?
- Do we know enough about sexual drives to eliminate AIDS, unwanted pregnancy, and sexual abuse?
- Do we know enough about learning so that all children develop basic skills and values?

The answer to all these questions is a resounding *NO*. The reasons are many, but a major one is that these topics are controversial. Some researchers avoid them, fearing unwelcome and uninformed publicity (Kempner et al., 2005). Few funders eagerly support scientific studies of drug abuse, poverty, sex, or values, partly because the data may conflict with popular assumptions. Yet developmentalists should study whatever helps the human family. Many people suffer because questions go unanswered—or even unasked. More research and more application are needed (Keating, 2011).

The next cohort of developmental scientists will build on what is already known. The challenge is to find answers to many urgent questions that could improve life for the world's 6.9 billion people. This chapter and this text are only the beginning.

>> **Response for People Who Have Applied to College or Graduate School** (from page 29) Most institutions of higher education emphasize quantitative data—the SAT, the GRE, GPA, class rank, and so on. Decide for yourself whether this is fairer than a more qualitative approach.

SUMMING UP

Science has helped people in many ways over the past century, contributing to longer and happier lives. However, there are several potential pitfalls in scientific research. For instance, although correlations are useful, people may mistakenly assume that they prove cause, not simply connection. Quantitative research is more objective and easier to replicate than qualitative research, but it loses the nuances that qualitative research can reveal.

Scientists follow codes of ethics to make sure they fully inform research participants and safeguard their well-being. Research codes have become more stringent in recent years. Scientists also must be "mindful of implications," which means they must take care that results are not misinterpreted. The most urgent developmental issues are controversial and therefore difficult to study objectively or to report honestly. That is precisely why further scientific research is needed. ■

SUMMARY

Understanding How and Why

1. The study of human development is a science that seeks to understand how people change or remain the same over time. As a science, it begins with questions and hypotheses and then uses various methods to gather empirical data. Researchers draw conclusions based on the evidence.

2. Replication confirms, modifies, or refutes the conclusions of a scientific study. In child development, first replication and then application of research often helps the next generation, as in the application of research that led to far fewer sudden infant deaths.

3. The universality of human development and the uniqueness of each individual's development are both evident in nature (the genes) and nurture (the environment); no person is quite like another. Nature and nurture always interact, and each human characteristic is affected by that interaction. Neuroscience has discovered differential susceptibility—that certain genes increase or decrease the likelihood that a child will be affected by the environment.

4. Time is a crucial variable in studying human development. A critical period is a time when something *must* occur to ensure normal development or the only time when an abnormality might occur. Often a particular development can occur more easily—but not exclusively—at a particular time, called a sensitive period.

5. Throughout life, human development is plastic. *Plasticity* emphasizes that it is possible for individuals to change their characteristics and behavior as they develop, although it is also true that their childhood experiences affect later development.

Including All Kinds of People

6. All kinds of people, of every age, culture, and background, are studied by developmental scientists, who recognize that many variations are the result of social constructions, not biological facts. The goal is to find the universal patterns of human growth while also recognizing that each person is unique.

7. In studying human variations, one pitfall to avoid is the difference-equals-deficit error. For example, the concept that males and females are opposites may lead to the distorted idea that one sex is better than the other.

8. *Culture, ethnicity,* and *race* are social constructions, concepts created by society. Culture includes beliefs and patterns; ethnicity refers to ancestral heritage. The social construction of "race" has been so misused that social scientists prefer not to use it.

9. Socioeconomic status (SES) is an important influence on human development, affecting a person's opportunities, health, and even abilities at every stage. As with other differences among people, developmentalists seek to find the balance between recognizing similarities and respecting differences.

Observing Changes over Time

10. A dynamic-systems approach to development emphasizes that change is ongoing in life, with each part of development affecting every other part. The assumption that growth is linear and progress is inevitable has been replaced by the idea that both continuity (sameness) and discontinuity (sudden shifts) are part of every life, that gains and losses are apparent at every age.

11. Urie Bronfenbrenner's ecological-systems or bioecological approach notes that each child is situated within larger systems of family, school, community, and culture. Changes within a person, or changes in the context, affect all other aspects of the system.

12. Certain experiences or innovations shape people of each cohort because they are members of a particular generation who share the experience of significant historical events. Mirror neurons suggest that observing other people's experiences has a powerful effect on each individual, which may be one reason why cohort effects are strong.

Using the Scientific Method

13. Commonly used research methods are scientific observation, the experiment, and the survey. Each can provide insight and discoveries that were not apparent before the research.

14. An additional challenge for developmentalists is to study change over time. Two traditional research designs are often used: cross-sectional research (comparing people of different ages) and longitudinal research (studying the same people over time). Each has limitations, and for that reason cohort-sequential research (combining the two other methods) is also used. Every method of research has advantages and disadvantages.

Cautions and Challenges from Science

15. A correlation shows that two variables are related. However, it does not prove that one variable *causes* the other: The relationship of variables may be opposite to the one expected, or both may be the result of a third variable.

16. Quantitative research provides data that is numerical, and thus it is best to compare children in different contexts and cultures. By contrast, in qualitative research, information is reported without being quantified. Qualitative research best captures the nuance of individual lives, but quantitative research is easier to replicate, interpret, and verify.

17. Ethical behavior is crucial in all the sciences. Not only must participants be protected and data kept confidential (primary concerns of IRBs), but results must be fairly reported and honestly interpreted. Scientists must be mindful of the implications of their research.

18. Appropriate application of scientific research depends partly on the training and integrity of the scientists. The most important ethical question is whether scientists are designing, conducting, analyzing, publishing, and applying the research that is most critically needed.

>> **Response for Future Researchers and Science Writers** (from page 31) Yes. Anyone you write about must give consent and be fully informed about your intentions. They can be identified by name only if they give permission. For example, family members gave permission before anecdotes about them were included in this text. My nephew David read the first draft of his story (see pages 9–10) and is proud to have his experiences used to teach others.

KEY TERMS

science of human development (p. 4)	critical period (p. 8)	dynamic systems (p. 15)	cross-sectional research (p. 24)
scientific method (p. 4)	sensitive period (p. 8)	ecological-systems approach (p. 16)	longitudinal research (p. 25)
theory (p. 4)	plasticity (p. 9)	cohort (p. 17)	cohort-sequential research (p. 27)
hypothesis (p. 4)	difference-equals-deficit error (p. 10)	biopsychosocial (p. 19)	correlation (p. 28)
empirical (p. 5)	social construction (p. 11)	mirror neurons (p. 20)	quantitative research (p. 29)
replication (p. 5)	culture (p. 12)	scientific observation (p. 21)	qualitative research (p. 29)
sudden infant death syndrome (SIDS) (p. 5)	ethnic group (p. 13)	independent variable (p. 23)	code of ethics (p. 29)
nature (p. 6)	race (p. 13)	dependent variable (p. 23)	Institutional Review Board (IRB) (p. 30)
nurture (p. 6)	socioeconomic status (SES) (p. 13)	survey (p. 23)	

WHAT HAVE YOU LEARNED?

Understanding How and Why

1. What makes the study of human development a science?

2. What are the five steps of the scientific method?

3. How does research on SIDS illustrate the replication and application of the science of child development?

4. What is known and unknown about the causes of sudden infant death?

5. What is the difference between nature and nurture?

6. Why is it a mistake to ask whether a human behavior stems from nature or nurture?

7. What is an example from neuroscience that illustrates differential susceptibility?

8. What is the difference between a critical period and a sensitive period?

9. Why is it important to know when a sensitive period in development occurs?

10. How can both plasticity and the long-term effects of childhood be true?

Including All Kinds of People

11. How is exaggeration of male–female differences an example of the difference-equals-deficit error?

12. How can people of several ethnic groups share a culture?

13. What is the difference between race and ethnicity?

14. What factors comprise a person's SES?

Observing Changes over Time

15. What is implied about human development when it is described as dynamic?

16. Why is it more accurate to consider the systems of development rather than each part in isolation?

17. What did Bronfenbrenner emphasize in his ecological-systems approach?

18. Why does it matter what cohort a particular person belongs to?

19. What are the differences among the three domains of development?

Using the Scientific Method

20. How do scientific observation and experimentation differ?

21. Why do experimenters use a control (or comparison) group as well as an experimental group?

22. How do independent and dependent variables make it easier to learn what causes what?

23. What are the strengths and weaknesses of the survey method?

24. How do cross-sectional and longitudinal research differ?

25. What are the advantages and disadvantages of cross-sequential research?

Cautions and Challenges from Science

26. Why does correlation not prove causation?

27. Why do some researchers prefer quantitative research and others qualitative research?

28. Why do most colleges and hospitals have an IRB?

29. What are the primary ethical principles used when scientists study humans?

30. Why are some important questions about human development not yet answered?

APPLICATIONS

1. It is said that culture is pervasive but that people are unaware of it. List 30 things you did *today* that you might have done differently in another culture. Begin with how and where you woke up.

2. How would your life be different if your parents were much higher or lower in SES than they are? Consider all three domains.

3. Design an experiment to answer a question you have about human development. Specify the question and the hypothesis and then describe the experiment. How would you prevent your conclusions from being biased and subjective? (Look at Appendix B.)

4. A longitudinal case study can be insightful but is also limited in generality. Describe the life of one of your older relatives, explaining what aspects of their development are unique and what aspects might be relevant for everyone.

>>ONLINE CONNECTIONS

To accompany your textbook, you have access to a number of online resources, including quizzes for every chapter of the book, flashcards (in English and Spanish), critical thinking questions, and case studies. For access to any of these links, go to www.worthpublishers.com/bergerca9e. In addition to these free resources, you'll also find links to podcasts, video clips, diagnostic quizzing with personalized study advice, and an ebook. Some of the videos and activities available online include:

- *Ethics in Human Research: Violating One's Privacy?* This video introduces the controversies around a research project in Iceland that collects the genetic and health information about private citizens.

- *What's Wrong with This Study?* This activity allows you to review some of the pitfalls in various research designs.

Theories

WHAT WILL YOU KNOW?

1. How is a theory different from a fact?
2. Does development occur in stages or more gradually, day by day?
3. What limitations do Freud, Erikson, Watson, Skinner, and Piaget all share, according to newer theories of development?
4. Why is it better to use several theories rather than just one?

When I was little, on special occasions we drove to my grandparents' farm, the childhood home of my father, his three brothers, and one sister. My mother sang, "Over the river and through the woods, to grandmother's house we go." When we arrived, my brother and I played with our twelve cousins, including three other girls my age. I remember turkey, mashed potatoes, and lemon meringue pie; horses and hay in the barn; grandma wearing an apron; grandpa resting his big hands over a huge coffee mug; enormous wooden rocking chairs in the sitting room. But my strongest single memory is a bitter one: One Christmas, Grandma gave us girls presents—precursors of Barbie dolls. Mine had a peach-colored gown; my cousin's had a white bride's dress and veil.

Why did I feel rejected? In hindsight, I can think of several laudable reasons that particular cousin got the bride doll. But when I was 6, my simple theory about presents and brides led to resentment.

This chapter outlines five theories of human development, or actually ten, since each theory has at least two versions. There are hundreds more theories about the human life span, some explained later. Before beginning, however, you should know that theorizing is part of human nature. In fact, according to "theory theory," young children spontaneously develop theories to explain whatever they observe, because that is what humans do (Gopnik & Schulz, 2007). My theory led me to believe that Grandma loved my cousin more than me.

>> What Theories Do

A **developmental theory** is a systematic statement of general principles that provides a coherent framework for understanding how and why people change as they grow older. "Developmental theorists try to make sense out of observations . . . [and] construct a story of the human journey from infancy through childhood or adulthood" (Miller, 2011, p. 2). Such a story, or theory, connects facts and observations with patterns and explanations, weaving the details of life into a meaningful whole. A developmental theory is more than a hunch or a hypothesis and is far more comprehensive than my childish theorizing about bride dolls. My assumptions were not "systematic" and did not add up to a "coherent framework." Developmental theories provide insights that are both broad and deep, making them more comprehensive than the many observations and ideas from which they arise.

developmental theory A group of ideas, assumptions, and generalizations that interpret and illuminate the thousands of observations that have been made about human growth. A developmental theory provides a framework for explaining the patterns and problems of development.

As an analogy, imagine building a house. A person could have a heap of lumber, nails, and other materials, but without a plan and labor, the heap cannot become a building. Furthermore, not every house is alike: People have theories (usually not explicit) about houses that lead to preferences for the number of stories, bedrooms, entrances, and so on. Likewise, the observations and empirical studies of human development are essential raw materials, but theories pull them together.

As Kurt Lewin (1943) once quipped, "Nothing is as practical as a good theory." Theories differ; some are less comprehensive or adequate than others (why did we forget a back door?), some are no longer useful (no bathrooms?), some reflect one culture but not another (entrance facing east?), but without theory we have only a heap.

Questions and Answers

As we saw in Chapter 1, the first step of the science of human development is to pose a question, which often springs from a developmental theory. Among the thousands of important questions are the following, each central to one of the five theories described in this chapter:

1. Do early experiences—of breast-feeding or attachment or neglect—linger into adulthood, even if they seem to be forgotten?
2. Does learning depend on specific instruction, punishment, and examples?
3. Do children develop moral principles, even if they are not taught right from wrong?
4. Does culture guide behavior? Is that why Okinawa has more voters than Oklahoma?
5. Is survival a basic instinct, underlying all personal or social decisions?

Each of the five questions above is answered "yes" by one of the five major theories—in order: question 1 by psychoanalytic theory, question 2 by behaviorism, question 3 by cognitive theory, question 4 by sociocultural theory, and question 5 by the two universal theories (humanism and evolutionary theory). Each question is answered "no" or "not necessarily" by several others. For every answer, more questions arise: Why or why not? When and how? So what? This last question is crucial for the science of human development; the implications and applications of the answers affect everyone's daily life.

To be more specific about what theories do:

▪ Theories produce *hypotheses*.
▪ Theories generate *discoveries*.
▪ Theories offer *practical guidance*.

A popular book of child-rearing advice, *Battle Hymn of the Tiger Mother* (Chua, 2011), seems to advocate a parenting style that insists on high achievement. For example, Amy Chua rejected a birthday card, hastily handmade by her 4-year-old daughter, saying:

> I don't want this. . . . I want a better one—one that you've put some thought and effort into. . . . I deserve better.
>
> *[p. 103]*

Reactions to Chua's book are very positive (five-star rating) or very negative (one-star rating). Six months after it was published, of the first 500 reader reviews on Amazon, 42 percent were very positive, 23 percent very negative, with less extreme evaluations (two to four stars) from only 7, 11, and 17 percent of responders. Explaining these reactions, one professional reviewer wrote:

There was bound to be some pushback. All the years of nurturance overload simply got to be too much. The breast-feeding through toddlerhood, nonstop baby wearing, co-sleeping, "Baby Mozart" . . . After "free range" parenting . . . [and] "simplicity parenting" [came] a kind of edgy irritation with it all: a new stance of get-tough-no-nonsense, frequently called—with no small amount of pride—being a bad mother.

[Warner, 2011, p. 11]

Chua herself seems surprised at the extreme reactions. Although many people do not realize it, everyone has strong opinions about child development, sometimes promoted with fierce intensity. These opinions sometimes spring from the five theories soon to be described.

Facts and Norms

A **norm** is an average or usual event or experience. And while it is related to the word *normal*, the term has a slightly different meaning. For instance, it is a norm for brides to wear white in Western culture, symbolizing purity; but in Asian culture, brides wear red to symbolize celebration. And describing something as "abnormal" (not normal) implies that it is wrong, yet norms are not meant to be right or wrong. Norms are averages, though not merely an arithmetical mean or median. Rather, a norm is a mode, a common behavior that results from biological or social pressure. Norms reflect facts and can be calculated (such as the norm for babies beginning to walk or for brides to wear a certain color), but deviations are not necessarily deficits.

Do not confuse theories with facts, either. Theories raise questions, suggesting hypotheses, leading to research that gathers empirical data. Those data are facts that may lead to conclusions. Each developmental theory to be explained soon has led to research, data, and conclusions that have verified as well as refuted aspects of that theory, thereby advancing developmental science.

Thus, a theory is neither true nor false, good nor bad. Ideally, a theory is provocative and useful, leading to hypotheses and exploration. For example, some people dismiss Darwin's theory of evolution as "just a theory," while others believe it is a fact that explains all of nature since the beginning of time. No and no. Good theories should neither be dismissed nor equated with facts. Instead, theories deepen thought; they are useful (like a house plan), leading to new interpretations, studies, and perspectives.

As already explained, developmental theories are comprehensive and detailed, unlike the simple theories of children or the implicit theories that underlie the customs and assumptions of each culture. But to clarify the distinction between theory and fact, we return to the simple theory of the bride doll. My bitterness was one outcome of the dominant theory in my childhood culture—a pro-family theory. The theory led to a series of assumptions, including that everyone should leave their parents by age 20, marry one person and stay married lifelong, have at least two children, and visit their parents periodically. Furthermore, the parents should stay in their own house, not only so the children can visit but also because alternatives were sad and shameful. That led to norms, followed by my paternal grandparents' five offspring and by nine of my maternal grandparents' twelve children. We pitied my mother's unmarried sisters, Aunt Ida and Aunt Marie, as well as Aunt Alma, who had only one child.

True to the dominant theory of my childhood, I fantasized about my wedding, named my seven imagined children, and rejoiced when my Aunt Marie finally married but was sad when my mother said Marie was too old to have children. That theory was reflected in the laws and assumptions of my community: Having

norm An average, or typical, standard of behavior or accomplishment, such as the norm for age of walking or the norm for greeting a stranger.

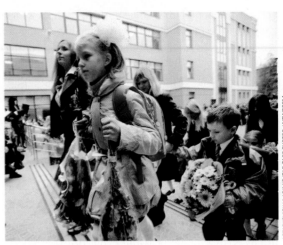

Backpacks or Bouquets? Children worldwide are nervous on the first day of school, but their coping reflects implicit cultural theories. Kindergarten girls in Kentucky bring many supplies, while elementary children in Russia bring flowers for their teachers.

more than one spouse was wrong (bigamists went to jail), divorce meant a "failed" marriage and "broken" family, and "only" children had psychological problems.

However, research has now shown that differences are not deficits, and none of the assumptions above is necessarily true. As flaws in the theory have been revealed, norms have changed accordingly. Longitudinal data found that singleton children (no longer called "only") are often high achievers with successful lives (Falbo et al., 2009) and that China's "one-child" policy led to economic success. Consequently, in some nations (Italy and Japan among them), having one child is the norm.

Some say that the pro-family theory I knew as a child has been replaced, at least in Western middle-class culture, by another untested theory: that personal happiness is the goal of life. This led to an alternate set of ideas: that parents should strive to make their children happy, that unhappy spouses should divorce, that self-esteem is more important than academic success—all of which led to the tiger-mother pushback.

Obviously, more science is needed. Realizing that theories are not facts and that "each theory of developmental psychology always has a view of humans that reflects philosophical, economic, and political beliefs" (Miller, 2011, p. 17), scientists question norms, develop hypotheses, and design studies. Science has thus led to conclusions that undercut some theories and modify others, to the benefit of all.

Theories do more than raise questions. They give insight and guidance, especially when developmental problems (such as a crying infant, an aggressive toddler, a bullied preschooler, a failing schoolchild, a drunk adolescent) occur. Without theories, we would be merely reactive and bewildered, adrift and increasingly befuddled, blindly following our culture and our prejudices. Theories are useful, leading to verification, exploration, and application. Eventually, better theories are developed: Without them we might be stuck with limiting, childish assumptions—as I was with the doll.

SUMMING UP

Theories provide a framework for organizing and understanding the thousands of observations and daily behaviors that occur in every aspect of development. Theories are not facts, but they allow us to question norms, suggest hypotheses, and provide guidance. Thus, theories are practical: They frame and organize our millions of experiences. ■

>> Grand Theories

In the first half of the twentieth century, two opposing theories—psychoanalytic theory and behaviorism (also called *learning theory*)—began as general theories of psychology, each with applications in child development. By mid-century, cognitive theory had emerged, becoming the dominant seedbed of research hypotheses. All three theories are "grand" in that they are comprehensive, enduring, and widely applied (McAdams & Pals, 2006), although they are not universally accepted (as you will soon read).

psychoanalytic theory A grand theory of human development that holds that irrational, unconscious drives and motives, often originating in childhood, underlie human behavior.

Psychoanalytic Theory: Freud and Erikson

Inner drives, deep motives, and unconscious needs rooted in childhood are the foundation of **psychoanalytic theory.** These basic underlying forces are thought to influence every aspect of thinking and behavior, from the smallest details of daily life to the crucial choices of a lifetime.

Freud's Ideas

Psychoanalytic theory originated with Sigmund Freud (1856–1939), an Austrian physician who treated patients suffering from mental illness. He listened to their accounts of dreams and fantasies and to their uncensored streams of thought, and he constructed an elaborate, multifaceted theory. Early childhood, he thought, was crucial.

According to Freud, development in the first six years occurs in three stages. He called each stage *psychosexual* because children derive erotic pleasure from whatever body part is central at each stage. This idea (infantile sexuality) was one reason psychoanalytic theory was rejected at first, because Victorian sensibilities led to the dominant theory that children were innocent, asexual beings. According to Freud, in infancy, the erotic body part is the mouth (the *oral stage*); in early childhood, it is the anus (the *anal stage*); in the preschool years, it is the penis (the *phallic stage*), a source of pride and fear among boys and a reason for sadness and envy among girls. Two more developmental periods then follow early childhood. After the phallic stage, *latency* occurs, and then, at puberty, the *genital stage* arrives, lasting throughout adulthood. (Table 2.1 describes the stages in Freud's theory.)

Freud maintained that at each stage, sensual satisfaction (from stimulation of the mouth, anus, or penis) is linked to major developmental needs and challenges. During the oral stage, for example, sucking provides not only nourishment but also erotic delight for the baby and attachment to the mother. Kissing in adulthood is a vestige of the oral stage. Next, during the anal stage, pleasures that arise from control and self-control—initially with defecation and toilet training—are paramount.

One of Freud's most influential ideas was that each stage includes its own potential conflicts. Conflict occurs, for instance, when mothers try to wean their babies (oral stage) or teachers expect kindergartners to become independent of their parents (phallic stage). According to Freud, how people experience and resolve these conflicts—especially those related to weaning, toilet training, and sexual pleasure—determine personality patterns because "the early stages provide the foundation for adult behavior" (Salkind, 2004, p. 125).

Freud did not believe that new stages occurred after puberty; rather, he believed that adult personalities and habits were influenced by earlier stages. Unconscious conflicts rooted in a childhood stage may be evident in adult behavior—for instance, smoking cigarettes (oral) or keeping careful track of money (anal) or

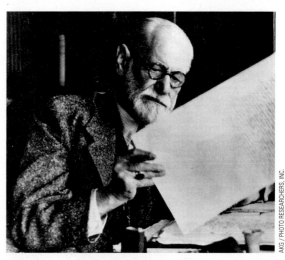

Freud at Work In addition to being the world's first psychoanalyst, Sigmund Freud was a prolific writer. His many papers and case histories, primarily descriptions of his patients' bizarre symptoms and unconscious sexual urges, helped make the psychoanalytic perspective a dominant force for much of the twentieth century.

Art Appreciation or Penis Envy? Freud would say the latter, but most people now believe children are more interested in facial expressions, gestures, and muscles than in genitals.

becoming romantically attracted to a much older partner (phallic). For all of us, psychoanalytic theory contends, childhood fantasies and memories remain powerful lifelong, particularly as they affect the sex drive (which Freud called the *libido*). If you have ever wondered why lovers call each other "baby" or why many people refer to their spouse as their "old lady" or "sugar daddy," then Freud's theory provides an explanation: The parent–child relationship is the model for all forms of intimacy.

Many other aspects of psychoanalytic theory are thought to explain behavior. According to Freud, the personality has three parts: the *id* (unconscious drives, inborn and animal-like, mostly sexual and aggressive), the *superego* (the moral ideal, the conscience, learned from parents and society), and the *ego* (the conscious self).

The id is dominant in infancy, the superego develops in the phallic stage, and throughout life the ego defends itself against attacks from the id and superego. That defense occurs with *defense mechanisms* that keep the id and superego under control. Ideally, during childhood, parents help their children develop a strong ego so that impulses from the id and superego are kept in check.

Erikson's Ideas

Many of Freud's followers became famous theorists themselves. They acknowledged the importance of the unconscious and of early childhood experience, but each of them expanded and modified Freud's ideas. One of them, Erik Erikson (1902–1994), is well respected for his theory of development.

Erikson never knew his Danish father. He spent his childhood in Germany, his adolescence wandering through Italy, and his young adulthood in Austria, working with Freud. He married an American, fleeing to the United States just before World War II. His experiences in many nations—as well as his studies of Harvard students, Boston children at play, and the child-rearing methods of Sioux and Yurok Indians—led Erikson to stress cultural diversity, social change, and psychological crises throughout life (Erikson, 1969).

A Legendary Couple In his first 30 years, Erikson never fit into a particular local community, since he so frequently changed nations, schools, and professions. Then he met Joan. In their first five decades of marriage, they raised a family and wrote several books. If he had published his theory at age 73 (when this photograph was taken) instead of in his 40s, would he still have described his life as a series of crises?

Erikson described eight developmental stages, each characterized by a particular challenge, or *developmental crisis* (summarized in Table 2.1). Although Erikson named two polarities at each crisis, he recognized a wide range of outcomes between those opposites. For most people, development at each stage leads to neither extreme but to something in between. The resolution of each crisis depends on the interaction between the individual and the social environment.

In the stage of *initiative versus guilt*, for example, children between ages 3 and 6 often want to undertake activities that exceed the limits set by their parents and culture. They jump into swimming pools, pull their pants on backwards, make cakes according to their own recipes, and wander off alone. Such efforts to act independently leave them open to feelings of pride or failure, producing guilt if adults are too critical.

Who Are We? The most famous of Erikson's eight crises is the identity crisis, during adolescence, when young people find their own answer to the question "Who am I?" Erikson did this for himself by choosing a last name that, with his first name, implies "son of myself" (Erik, Erik's son). These *hara juko* girls in Japan are among the millions of teenagers worldwide who display an identity unlike that of their parents.

TABLE 2.1	Comparison of Freud's Psychosexual and Erikson's Psychosocial Stages	
Approximate Age	Freud (Psychosexual)	Erikson (Psychosocial)
Birth to 1 year	*Oral Stage* The lips, tongue, and gums are the focus of pleasurable sensations in the baby's body, and sucking and feeding are the most stimulating activities.	*Trust vs. Mistrust* Babies either trust that others will care for their basic needs, including nourishment, warmth, cleanliness, and physical contact, *or* develop mistrust about the care of others.
1–3 years	*Anal Stage* The anus is the focus of pleasurable sensations in the baby's body, and toilet training is the most important activity.	*Autonomy vs. Shame and Doubt* Children either become self-sufficient in many activities, including toileting, feeding, walking, exploring, and talking, *or* doubt their own abilities.
3–6 years	*Phallic Stage* The phallus, or penis, is the most important body part, and pleasure is derived from genital stimulation. Boys are proud of their penises; girls wonder why they don't have one.	*Initiative vs. Guilt* Children either want to undertake many adultlike activities *or* internalize the limits and prohibitions set by parents. They feel either adventurous *or* guilty.
6–11 years	*Latency* Not really a stage, latency is an interlude during which sexual needs are quiet and children put psychic energy into conventional activities like schoolwork and sports.	*Industry vs. Inferiority* Children busily learn to be competent and productive in mastering new skills *or* feel inferior, unable to do anything as well as they wish they could.
Adolescence	*Genital Stage* The genitals are the focus of pleasurable sensations, and the young person seeks sexual stimulation and sexual satisfaction in heterosexual relationships.	*Identity vs. Role Confusion* Adolescents try to figure out "Who am I?" They establish sexual, political, religious, and vocational identities *or* are confused about what roles to play.
Adulthood	Freud believed that the genital stage lasts throughout adulthood. He also said that the goal of a healthy life is "to love and to work."	*Intimacy vs. Isolation* Young adults seek companionship and love *or* become isolated from others because they fear rejection and disappointment. *Generativity vs. Stagnation* Middle-aged adults contribute to the next generation through meaningful work, creative activities, and/or raising a family, *or* they stagnate. *Integrity vs. Despair* Older adults try to make sense out of their lives, either seeing life as a meaningful whole *or* despairing at goals never reached.

As you can see from Table 2.1, Erikson's first five stages are closely related to Freud's stages. Erikson, like Freud, believed that problems of adult life echo unresolved conflicts of childhood. For example, an adult who has difficulty establishing a secure, mutual relationship with a life partner may never have resolved the first crisis of early infancy, *trust versus mistrust*. Even in late adulthood, one older person may be outspoken, while another fears saying the wrong thing, because they resolved their initiative-versus-guilt stage in opposite ways. However, in at least one crucial way, Erikson's stages differ significantly from Freud's: They emphasize not sexual urges but rather each person's relationships to family and culture.

Especially for Teachers Your kindergartners are talkative and always moving. They almost never sit quietly and listen to you. What would Erik Erikson recommend? (see response, page 43)

Behaviorism: Conditioning and Social Learning

The second grand theory arose in direct opposition to the psychoanalytic notion of the unconscious. John B. Watson (1878–1958) argued that if psychology was to be a true science, psychologists should examine only what they could see and measure: behavior, not irrational thoughts and hidden urges. In his words:

> Why don't we make what we can *observe* the real field of psychology? Let us limit ourselves to things that can be observed, and formulate laws concerned only with those things. . . . We can observe behavior—what the organism does or says.
>
> [*Watson, 1924/1998, p. 6*]

An Early Behaviorist John Watson was an early proponent of learning theory. His ideas are still influential and controversial today.

behaviorism A grand theory of human development that studies observable behavior. Behaviorism is also called *learning theory* because it describes the laws and processes by which behavior is learned.

conditioning According to behaviorism, the processes by which responses become linked to particular stimuli and learning takes place. The word *conditioning* is used to emphasize the importance of repeated practice, as when an athlete *conditions* his or her body to perform well by training for a long time.

classical conditioning The learning process in which a meaningful stimulus (such as the smell of food to a hungry animal) is connected with a neutral stimulus (such as the sound of a tone) that had no special meaning before conditioning. (Also called *respondent conditioning*.)

A Contemporary of Freud Ivan Pavlov was a physiologist who received the Nobel Prize in 1904 for his research on digestive processes. It was this line of study that led to his discovery of classical conditioning.

Observation Quiz In appearance, how is Pavlov similar to Freud, and how do both look different from the other theorists pictured? (see answer, page 43)

According to Watson, if psychologists focus on behavior, they will realize that everything can be learned. He wrote:

> Give me a dozen healthy infants, well-formed, and my own specified world to bring them up in and I'll guarantee to take any one at random and train him to become any type of specialist I might select—doctor, lawyer, artist, merchant chief, and yes, even beggar-man and thief, regardless of his talents, penchants, tendencies, abilities, vocations, and race of his ancestors.
>
> *[Watson, 1924/1998, p. 82]*

Other psychologists, especially in the United States, agreed. They developed **behaviorism** to study actual behavior, objectively and scientifically. Behaviorism is also called *learning theory* because it describes how people learn and develop habits, step by step. For every individual at every age, behaviorists describe laws detailing how simple actions and environmental responses shape complex competencies, such as reading a book or making a family dinner.

Learning theorists believe that development occurs in small increments: A person learns to talk, read, or anything else bit by bit over a long time. Because change is cumulative, behaviorists, unlike Freud and Erikson, describe no specific stages of development (Bijou & Baer, 1978). Rather, they focus on the laws of **conditioning,** the processes by which responses become linked to particular stimuli, sometimes called *S–R (stimulus–response) conditioning*. In the first half of the twentieth century, behaviorists described only two types of conditioning: classical and operant.

Classical Conditioning

A century ago, Russian scientist Ivan Pavlov (1849–1936), after winning the Nobel Prize for his work on animal digestion, began to examine the link between stimulus and response. While studying salivation, Pavlov noted that his experimental dogs drooled not only at the smell of food but also, eventually, at the footsteps of the people bringing food. This observation led Pavlov to perform a famous experiment: He conditioned dogs to salivate upon hearing a particular noise.

Pavlov began by sounding a tone just before presenting food. After a number of repetitions of the tone-then-food sequence, dogs began salivating at the sound even when there was no food. This simple experiment demonstrated **classical conditioning** (also called *respondent conditioning*).

In classical conditioning, a person or animal is conditioned to associate a neutral stimulus with a meaningful stimulus, gradually responding to the neutral stimulus in the same way as to the meaningful one. In Pavlov's original experiment, the dog associated the tone (the neutral stimulus) with food (the meaningful stimulus) and learned to respond to the tone as though it were the food itself. The conditioned response to the tone (no longer neutral but now a conditioned stimulus) was evidence that learning had occurred.

Behaviorists see dozens of examples of classical conditioning in human development. Infants learn to smile at their parents because they associate their mother and father with food and play; toddlers become afraid of busy streets if the noise of traffic frightens them; schoolchildren enjoy—or fear—sitting at their desks, depending on past experiences.

Operant Conditioning

The most influential North American proponent of behaviorism was B. F. Skinner (1904–1990). Skinner agreed that psychology should focus on the scientific study of behavior. His famous contribution to the science of psychology was to recognize another type of conditioning—**operant conditioning** (also called *instrumental conditioning*)—in which animals (including people) act and then a consequence occurs. If the consequence is enjoyable, the animal will repeat the behavior. If the consequence is unpleasant, the animal might not repeat that behavior. Usually, learning occurs only after several repetitions with consequences.

Pleasant consequences are sometimes called *rewards,* and unpleasant consequences are sometimes called *punishments.* Behaviorists hesitate to use those words, however, because what some call punishment may actually be a reward, and vice versa. For example, parents punish their children by withholding dessert, by spanking them, by not letting them play, by speaking harshly to them, and so on. But a particular child might dislike dessert, so being deprived of it is no punishment. Or a child might not mind a spanking, especially if that is the only time the parent gives the child attention. Thus, the intended punishment is actually a reward.

SAM FALK / SCIENCE SOURCE / PHOTO RESEARCHERS

Similarly, teachers sometimes punish misbehaving children by sending them out of the classroom or even suspending them from school. However, if a child hates the teacher, leaving class is rewarding. In fact, recent research on school discipline finds that some measures, including school suspension, *increase* later misbehavior (Osher et al., 2010). The true test is the *effect* a consequence has on the individual's future actions, not whether it is intended to be a reward or a punishment. A child, or an adult, who repeats an offense may have been reinforced, not punished, for the first infraction. Consequences that increase the frequency or strength of a particular action are called *reinforcers,* in a process called **reinforcement** (Skinner, 1953).

One of the discoveries arising from behaviorism is that each person responds differently to reinforcements and punishments, as already mentioned with spanking. In another example, a longitudinal study of children's physical activity (playing sports, exercising, and so on) found that, for boys, the father's praise was especially important. For girls, reinforcement helped, but the mother's own physical activity was the more powerful influence (Cleland et al., 2011).

Social Learning

The importance of the mother's example leads to another insight from behaviorism. At first, behaviorists interpreted all behavior as arising from a chain of learned

>> Response for Teachers (from page 41) Erikson would note that the behavior of 5-year-olds is affected by their developmental stage and by their culture. Therefore, you might design your curriculum to accommodate active, noisy children.

operant conditioning The learning process by which a particular action is followed by something desired (which makes the person or animal more likely to repeat the action) or by something unwanted (which makes the action less likely to be repeated). (Also called *instrumental conditioning.*)

Rats, Pigeons, and People B. F. Skinner is best known for his experiments with rats and pigeons, but he also applied his knowledge to human behavior. For his daughter, he designed a glass-enclosed crib in which temperature, humidity, and perceptual stimulation could be controlled to make her time in the crib enjoyable and educational. He wrote about an ideal society based on principles of operant conditioning, where, for example, workers in less desirable jobs would earn greater rewards.

Especially for Teachers Same problem as previously (talkative kindergartners), but what would a behaviorist recommend? (see response, page 45)

reinforcement When a behavior is followed by something desired, such as food for a hungry animal or a welcoming smile for a lonely person.

>> Answer to Observation Quiz (from page 42) Both are balding, with white beards. Note also that none of the other theorists in this chapter have beards—a cohort difference, not an ideological one.

responses, the result of conditioning based either on the associations between one stimulus and another (classical) or on the consequences an individual experienced (operant). Such conditioning does occur, as has been demonstrated by many studies confirming this part of learning theory. However, humans are social and active, not just reactive. Instead of responding merely to their own direct experiences, "people act on the environment. They create it, preserve it, transform it, and even destroy it . . . in a socially embedded interplay" (Bandura, 2006, p. 167).

This insight led to **social learning theory** (see Figure 2.1), which holds that humans sometimes learn without personal reinforcement. This may occur through **modeling,** when people copy what they see others do (also called *observational learning*). Modeling is not simple imitation. Instead, people model only some actions, of some individuals, in some contexts. As an example, you may know adults who, as children, saw their parents hit each other. Some such adults abuse their own partners, while others scrupulously avoid marital conflict. These two responses seem opposite, but both are social learning produced by childhood observation. Still other adults may seem unfazed; differential susceptibility (explained in Chapter 1) may be the reason.

Generally, modeling is most likely to occur when the observer is uncertain or inexperienced (which explains why modeling is especially powerful in childhood) and when the model is admired, powerful, nurturing, or similar to the observer (Bandura, 1986, 1997). If your speech, hairstyle, or choice of shoes is similar to those of a celebrity, ask yourself what made you model that person's behavior. Admiration? Similarity? If children's language includes curses that their parents never utter, who were the models and why are they admired?

Social learning is connected to perceptions and interpretations of experience. One crucial interpretation involves a sense of **self-efficacy,** the belief that personal achievement depends on personal actions. People develop a sense of efficacy when they see other people solve problems successfully, which teaches them to have high aspirations and to strive for notable accomplishments (Bandura et al., 2001). The same applies to ethnic groups, cultures, and nations. Whether or not one nation intervenes in the actions of another depends partly on the national sense of self-efficacy.

Applications of learning theory often combine strategies suggested by all three aspects of behaviorism. In one study, for example, when children (aged 5 to 10) had sleep problems, their therapy involved classical conditioning (a quiet room with blue walls), operant conditioning (encouragement from peers), and the self-efficacy aspect of social learning (convincing children and their parents that improved sleep was possible). According to the researchers, the combination led to markedly fewer arousal problems or nightmares (Schlarb et al., 2011).

Psychoanalytic Versus Behaviorist Theories

Psychoanalytic and behaviorist theories were provocative, innovative, comprehensive, and surprising; they have endured because they offer insights into important aspects of development. Until these theories were developed, few imagined that childhood exerts such power (psychoanalytic) or that adult behavior arises from earlier reinforcement (behaviorist) or observation (social learning).

FIGURE 2.1

Three Types of Learning Behaviorism is also called *learning theory* because it emphasizes the learning process, as shown here.

Learning occurs through:

■ **Classical conditioning** Through association: neutral stimulus becomes conditioned stimulus.

■ **Operant conditioning** Through reinforcement: weak or rare response becomes strong, frequent response.

■ **Social learning** Through modeling: observed behaviors become copied behaviors.

social learning theory An extension of behaviorism that emphasizes the influence that other people have over a person's behavior. Even without specific reinforcement, every individual learns many things through observation and imitation of other people. (Also called *observational learning*.)

modeling The central process of social learning, by which a person observes the actions of others and then copies them.

self-efficacy In social learning theory, the belief of some people that they are able to change themselves and effectively alter the social context.

BIG CHEESE/ GLOW IMAGES

His Pride and Joy This father is proud of his muscles, but he is even more proud of his son—and didn't want to be photographed showing off his biceps alone. The pride is mutual: The boy hopes to become a man like his dad.

Observation Quiz Behind the posturing, what indicates that this boy models himself after his parent? (see answer, page 46)

TABLE 2.2	Psychoanalytic Theory vs. Behaviorism	
Area of Disagreement	Psychoanalytic Theory	Behaviorism
The unconscious	Emphasizes unconscious wishes and urges, unknown to the person but powerful all the same	Holds that the unconscious not only is unknowable but also may be a destructive fiction that keeps people from changing
Observable behavior	Holds that observable behavior is a symptom, not the cause—the tip of an iceberg, with the bulk of the problem submerged	Looks only at observable behavior—what a person does rather than what a person thinks, feels, or imagines
Importance of childhood	Stresses that early childhood, including infancy, is critical; even if a person does not remember what happened, the early legacy lingers throughout life	Holds that current conditioning is crucial; early habits and patterns can be unlearned, even reversed, if appropriate reinforcements and punishments are used
Scientific status	Holds that most aspects of human development are beyond the reach of scientific experiment; uses ancient myths, the words of disturbed adults, dreams, play, and poetry as raw material	Is proud to be a science, dependent on verifiable data and carefully controlled experiments; discards ideas that sound good but are not proven

Both theories have also been soundly criticized. Although Freud considered himself a scientist, many psychologists reject psychoanalytic theory as unscientific (Mills, 2004; Tauber, 2010). Many others reject behaviorism as demeaning of human potential (Chein, 2008). In some ways, the two theories are opposites (see Table 2.2). Another theory, humanism (described later in this chapter), arose in direct opposition to both these theories, contending that neither theory recognized human potential. Nonetheless, like all good theories, both behaviorism and psychoanalytic theory have led to hypotheses that have been examined in thousands of experiments, and both continue to be applied. Here is one example.

>> **Response for Teachers** (from page 43) Behaviorists believe that anyone can learn anything. If your goal is quiet, attentive children, begin by reinforcing a moment's quiet or a quiet child, and soon all the children will be trying to remain attentive for several minutes at a time.

THINKING CRITICALLY

Toilet Training—How and When?

Remember that theories are practical. This is particularly apparent in early childhood. Parents hear opposite advice about the very practical question of when to respond to an infant's cry. They are told that ignoring the cry will stunt the infant's future happiness (psychoanalytic—advocating attachment parenting), whereas others say that responding to every cry will teach the child to be demanding and spoiled (behaviorist—advocating strong character). Neither theory directly predicts such dire results, but each underlies one side or the other of this debate.

Another very specific example is toilet training. In the nineteenth century, many parents believed that bodily functions should be controlled as soon as possible; they began toilet training in the first months of life (Accardo, 2006). Then psychoanalytic theory pegged the first year as the oral stage (Freud) or the time when trust was crucial (Erikson), before the toddler's anal stage (Freud) or autonomy needs (Erikson). Thus, psychoanalytic theory influenced parents to postpone toilet training to avoid serious personality problems later on.

Soon this was part of many manuals on child rearing, including the recommendation of a leading pediatrician, Berry Brazelton, who wrote that toilet training should not begin until the child is cognitively, emotionally, and biologically ready—around age 2 for daytime training and age 3 for nighttime dryness.

> As a society, we are far too concerned about pushing children to be toilet trained early. I don't even like the phrase "toilet training." It really should be toilet learning.
>
> [Brazelton & Sparrow, 2006, p. 193]

By the middle of the twentieth century, many U.S. psychologists had rejected psychoanalytic theory and become behaviorists. Since they believed that learning depends primarily on conditioning, some suggested that toilet training occur whenever the parent wished, not at a particular age (Azrin & Foxx, 1974). In one method of training (an application of behaviorism), children drink quantities of their favorite juice, sit on the potty with a parent nearby to keep them entertained, and then, when the inevitable occurs, the parent praises and rewards them. They soon learn (within a day, according to some behaviorists) to head for the potty whenever the need arises.

Rejecting both of these theories, some Western parents prefer to start potty training very early. One U.S. mother began training her baby just 33 days after birth. She noticed when her son was about to defecate, held him above the toilet, and had trained him by 6 months (Sun & Rugolotto, 2004). Behaviorists would say that the mother was trained, not the son. She taught herself to be sensitive to his body, and she was reinforced when she read his clues correctly.

Which method is best? Dueling theories and diverse parental practices have led the authors of an article for pediatricians to conclude that "despite families and physicians having addressed this issue for generations, there still is no consensus regarding the best method or even a standard definition of toilet training" (Howell et al., 2011, p. 262). One comparison study of toilet-training methods found that the behaviorist approach was best for older children with serious disabilities but that almost every method succeeded with the average child. No method seemed to result in marked negative emotional consequences (Klassen et al., 2006). Many sources explain that because each child is different, there is no "right" way.

Later training may be quickest. One study followed hundreds of toddlers whose parents began training between 18 months and 3 years. Early starters took about a year to be toilet-trained completely (doing everything without help), while later starters took only about three months (Blum et al., 2003). Of course, if the goal is for children to independently go to the bathroom, pull down their pants, relieve themselves, and wash their hands afterward, then substantial maturation is needed, but many parents do not want to wait three years.

These contrasting theories raise the crucial question: What is the goal? What values are imbedded in each theory, each practice? Even the idea that each child is different, making no one method best, is the outgrowth of a theory of child development (sociocultural theory, explained soon). There is no easy answer: Critical thinking is required.

All Together, Now Some cultures teach regular elimination, others do not. These toddlers are in a day-care center in Brandenburg, Germany, where the boys (and soon the girls) all sit on the potty together.

>> Answer to Observation Quiz (from page 44) The swimsuit—in style and color. You might think it makes more sense for a young boy to have a suit that is shorter and tighter—but then it wouldn't be just like his father's.

cognitive theory A grand theory of human development that focuses on changes in how people think over time. According to this theory, our thoughts shape our attitudes, beliefs, and behaviors.

cognitive equilibrium In cognitive theory, a state of mental balance in which people are not confused because they can use their existing thought processes to understand current experiences and ideas.

assimilation The reinterpretation of new experiences to fit into old ideas.

accommodation The restructuring of old ideas to include new experiences.

Cognitive Theory: Piaget and Information Processing

According to **cognitive theory,** thoughts and expectations profoundly affect attitudes, beliefs, values, assumptions, and actions. This theory has dominated psychology since about 1980 and has branched into many versions.

Piaget's Stages of Development

The first major cognitive theorist was the Swiss scientist Jean Piaget (1896–1980), whose academic training was in biology. He became interested in human thought when he was hired to standardize an IQ test by noting at what age children answered each question correctly. However, the wrong answers caught his attention. *How* children think is much more revealing, Piaget concluded, than *what* they know.

In those days, most scientists believed that babies could not yet think, but Piaget used scientific observation with his own three infants, finding them curious and thoughtful. Later he studied hundreds of schoolchildren. From this work Piaget formed the central thesis of cognitive theory: How children think changes with time and experience, and their thought processes affect their conclusions and actions. According to cognitive theory, to understand human behavior one must understand thinking.

Piaget maintained that cognitive development occurs in four age-related periods, or stages: *sensorimotor, preoperational, concrete operational,* and *formal operational* (see Table 2.3). Each period fosters certain cognitive processes; for instance, infants think with their senses, and abstract logic is absent in children but possible at puberty (Inhelder & Piaget, 1958; Piaget, 1952b).

According to Piaget, intellectual advancement occurs because humans at every age seek **cognitive equilibrium**—a state of mental balance. The easiest way to achieve this balance is to interpret new experiences through the lens of preexisting ideas. For example, infants grab new objects in the same way as they grasp familiar objects, children interpret their parents' behavior by assuming that adults think in the same way that children do.

However, achieving equilibrium is not always easy. Sometimes a new experience or question is jarring or incomprehensible. Then the individual experiences *cognitive disequilibrium,* an imbalance that creates confusion. As Figure 2.2 illustrates, disequilibrium can cause cognitive growth if people change their thinking. Piaget describes two types of cognitive adaptation:

- **Assimilation:** New experiences are reinterpreted to fit into, or *assimilate* with, old ideas.
- **Accommodation:** Old ideas are restructured to include, or *accommodate,* new experiences.

Accommodation is more difficult than assimilation, but it produces intellectual advancement. For example, if a friend's questions reveal inconsistencies in your own opinions, or if your favorite chess strategy puts you in checkmate, or if your mother says something completely unexpected, disequilibrium occurs. In the last example, you might *assimilate* by deciding your mother didn't mean what she said. You might tell yourself that she was repeating something she had read or that you misheard her. However, intellectual growth would occur if, instead, you changed your view of your mother to *accommodate* a new, expanded understanding.

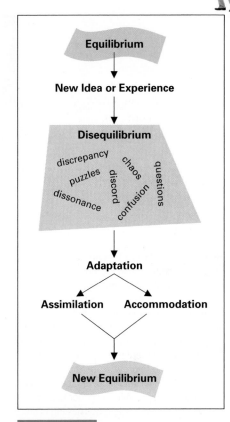

FIGURE 2.2

Challenge Me Most of us, most of the time, prefer the comfort of our conventional conclusions. According to Piaget, however, when new ideas disturb our thinking, we have an opportunity to expand our cognition with a broader and deeper understanding.

TABLE 2.3	Piaget's Periods of Cognitive Development		
Age Range	**Name of Period**	**Characteristics of the Period**	**Major Gains During the Period**
Birth to 2 years	Sensorimotor	Infants use senses and motor abilities to understand the world. Learning is active; there is no conceptual or reflective thought.	Infants learn that an object still exists when it is out of sight (*object permanence*) and begin to think through mental actions.
2–6 years	Preoperational	Children think magically and poetically, using language to understand the world. Thinking is *egocentric*, causing children to perceive the world from their own perspective.	The imagination flourishes, and language becomes a significant means of self-expression and of influence from others.
6–11 years	Concrete operational	Children understand and apply logical operations, or principles, to interpret experiences objectively and rationally. Their thinking is limited to what they can personally see, hear, touch, and experience.	By applying logical abilities, children learn to understand concepts of conservation, number, classification, and many other scientific ideas.
12 years through adulthood	Formal operational	Adolescents and adults think about abstractions and hypothetical concepts. They reason analytically, not just emotionally, and can be logical about things they have never experienced.	Ethics, politics, and social and moral issues become fascinating as adolescents and adults take a broader and more theoretical approach to experience.

How to Think About Flowers A person's stage of cognitive growth influences how he or she thinks about everything, including flowers. *(a)* To infants in the sensorimotor stage, flowers are "known" through pulling, smelling, and tasting. *(b)* At the concrete operational stage, children become more logical. This boy can understand that flowers need sunlight, water, and time to grow. *(c, d)* At the adult's formal operational stage, flowers can be part of a larger, logical scheme—either to earn money or to cultivate beauty. Thinking is an active process from the beginning of life until the end.

Ideally, when two people disagree, or when they surprise each other by what they say, adaptation is mutual. For example, when parents are startled by their children's opinions, the parents may revise their concepts of their children and their ideas, accommodating to new perceptions. If an honest discussion occurs, the children, too, might accommodate. Cognitive growth is an active process, dependent on clashing and challenging concepts.

Information Processing

Piaget is credited with discovering that people's thoughts and perceptions affect their development, an idea now accepted by most social scientists. However, many think Piaget's theories were inadequate. Neuroscience, cross-cultural studies, and step-by-step understanding of cognition have revealed the limitations of Piaget's theories. Here we introduce one newer version of cognitive theory, *information processing*, a theory inspired by the many processes by which computers function so efficiently. According to this theory, the human mind is similar in many ways to a sophisticated computer.

information-processing theory A perspective that compares human thinking processes, by analogy, to computer analysis of data, including sensory input, connections, stored memories, and output.

Information-processing theory "is not a single theory but, rather, a framework characterizing a large number of research programs" (Miller, 2011, p. 266). Instead of merely interpreting responses by infants and children, as Piaget did, information processing explores the processes of thought, that is, how minds work before responding. The underlying theoretical basis of information processing is that the details of process shed light on the specifics of outcome.

For information-processing scientists, cognition begins with input picked up by the five senses; proceeds to brain reactions, connections, and stored memories; and concludes with some form of output. For very young infants, output consists of moving a hand, making a sound, or staring a split second longer at one stimulus than at another. With the aid of sensitive technology, information-processing research has overturned some of Piaget's findings, as explained in later chapters.

Information processing also describes the relationship between one person's thinking and another's. For instance, under some conditions, thinking improves when people are part of a group, but under other conditions, groups slow down thought. Information processing helps us understand the difference (De Dreu et al., 2008). Similarly, some people say that watching television is destructive for young children; others disagree. Information-processing studies help researchers weigh in on this debate: Such studies can pinpoint exactly which cognitive processes are impaired by which images on the screen and at what age (Roseberry et al., 2009).

This approach to understanding cognition has many other applications. For example, it has long been recognized that children with ADHD (attention-deficit/hyperactivity disorder) are not simply excessively active but also tend to have difficulties learning in school, obeying their parents, and making friends. Information processing has led to the discovery that certain brain circuits (called *fronto-striatal systems*) do not function normally in children with ADHD. Consequently, they have difficulty reading facial expressions and voice tone in order to understand emotions (Uekermann et al., 2010). They may not know whether their father's "Come here" is an angry command or a friendly suggestion. Information processing helps in remediation: If a specific brain function can be improved, children may learn more, obey more, and gain friends.

SUMMING UP

The three grand theories originated decades ago, each pioneered by men who are admired for their ability to set forth psychological theories so comprehensive and creative that they deserve to be called "grand." Each grand theory has a different focus: emotions (psychoanalytic theory), actions (behaviorism), and thoughts (cognitive theory) (see Figure 2.3).

Freud and Erikson thought unconscious drives and early experiences form later personality and behavior. Behaviorists stress experiences in the more recent past and focus on learning by association, by reinforcement, and by observation. Cognitive theory holds that to understand a person, one must learn how that person thinks. According to Piaget, cognition develops in four distinct stages; according to information-processing theory, a multiplicity of components eventually result in crucial ideas and perceptions. ∎

>> Newer Theories

You have surely noticed that the seminal grand theorists (Freud, Erikson, Pavlov, Skinner, Piaget) were all men, scientists from western Europe or North America, born more than a hundred years ago. These background variables are limiting. (Of course, female, non-western, and contemporary theorists are limited by their backgrounds, too.) Despite their impressive insights, the three grand theories no longer seem as comprehensive as they once did, in part because their limitations have become more apparent in the twenty-first century.

New theories have emerged that, unlike the grand theories, are multicultural and multidisciplinary and thus are more in accord with the current view of the science of human development. The first theory described here, sociocultural theory, draws on research in education, anthropology, and history; the second one, universal theory, arises from theology, political science, and history (humanism) or from archeology, ethology, and biology (evolutionary theory).

Would You Talk to This Man? Children loved talking to Jean Piaget, and he learned by listening carefully—especially to their incorrect explanations, which no one had paid much attention to before. All his life, Piaget was absorbed with studying the way children think. He called himself a "genetic epistemologist"—one who studies how children gain knowledge about the world as they grow up.

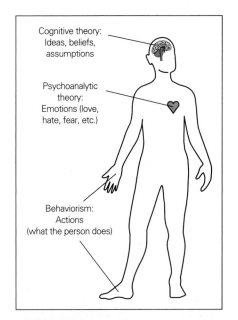

FIGURE 2.3

Major Focuses of the Three Grand Theories This simplified figure emphasizes that although all three of the grand theories recognize that thoughts, emotions, and actions interact within each person, each theory focuses on a different aspect of the person.

The Founder of Sociocultural Theory
Lev Vygotsky, now recognized as a seminal thinker whose ideas are revolutionizing education and the study of development, was a contemporary of Freud, Skinner, Pavlov, and Piaget. Vygotsky did not attain their eminence in his lifetime, partly because his work, conducted in Stalinist Russia, was largely inaccessible to the Western world and partly because he died young, at age 38.

sociocultural theory A newer theory that holds that development results from the dynamic interaction of each person with the surrounding social and cultural forces.

apprenticeship in thinking Vygotsky's term for how cognition is stimulated and developed in people by more skilled members of society.

guided participation The process by which people learn from others who guide their experiences and explorations.

zone of proximal development In sociocultural theory, a metaphorical area, or "zone," surrounding a learner that includes all the skills, knowledge, and concepts that the person is close ("proximal") to acquiring but cannot yet master without help.

Sociocultural Theory: Vygotsky and Beyond

The central thesis of **sociocultural theory** is that human development results from the dynamic interaction between developing persons and their surrounding society. Culture is viewed not as something external that impinges on developing persons but as integral to their development every day via the social context (all the dynamic systems described in Chapter 1).

Social Interaction

The pioneer of the sociocultural perspective was Lev Vygotsky (1896–1934), a psychologist from the former Soviet Union. Vygotsky was a leader in describing the interaction between culture and education. He noted that each community in his native Russia (which included Asians and Europeans, of many faiths and languages) taught its children whatever beliefs and habits its culture valued.

Vygotsky studied cognitive competencies of people of many ethnic groups as well as of children with and without special needs. He studied how farmers used tools, how illiterate people used abstract ideas, and how children of all abilities learned in school. In his view, each person, schooled or not, develops with the guidance of more skilled members of the society, who are tutors or mentors in an **apprenticeship in thinking** (Vygotsky, 1934/1986).

To describe this process, Vygotsky developed the concept of **guided participation,** the method used by parents, teachers, and entire societies to teach novices the skills and habits expected within the particular culture. Tutors engage learners (also called *apprentices*) in joint activities, offering not only instruction but also "mutual involvement in several widespread cultural practices with great importance for learning: narratives, routines, and play" (Rogoff, 2003, p. 285). Active apprenticeship is a central concept of sociocultural theory because each person depends on others to learn. This process is informal, pervasive, and social.

For example, one of my students came to my office with her young son, who eyed my candy dish but did not take any.

"He can have one if it's all right with you," I whispered to his mother.

She nodded and told him, "Dr. Berger will let you have one piece of candy."

He smiled shyly and quickly took one.

"What do you say?" she prompted.

"Thank you," he replied, glancing at me out of the corner of his eye.

"You're welcome," I said.

In that brief moment, all three of us were engaged in cultural transmission. We were surrounded by cultural traditions and practices, including my authority as professor, the fact that I have an office and a candy dish (a custom that I learned from one of my teachers), and the direct authority of the mother, who had taught her son to be polite and obedient. As an apprentice, he needed to be reminded to say "thank you." I guided him as well, in part by saying he could have one piece (encouraging math, authority, and moderation all at once). Specifics differ, but all adults teach children skills expected in their society and culture.

All cultural patterns and beliefs are social constructions, not natural laws, according to sociocultural theorists. They find customs to be powerful, shaping the development of every person, and they also find that some assumptions need to shift to allow healthier development of all people. Vygotsky stressed this point, arguing that mentally and physically disabled children should be educated (Vygotsky, 1925/1994), a cultural belief that has emerged in the United States in the past few decades but is not accepted in many other nations (Rogoff, 2003).

The Zone of Proximal Development

According to sociocultural theory, all learning is social, whether people are learning a manual skill, a social custom, or a language. As part of the apprenticeship in thinking, a mentor (parent, peer, or professional) finds the learner's **zone of proximal development,** the skills, knowledge, and concepts that the learner is close to acquiring but cannot yet master without help.

Through sensitive assessment of the learner, the mentor engages the mentee; together, in a "process of joint construction," new knowledge is attained (Valsiner, 2006). The mentor must avoid two opposite dangers: boredom and failure. Some frustration is permitted, but the learner must be actively engaged, never passive and never overwhelmed (see Figure 2.4).

To make this seemingly abstract process more concrete, consider an example: a father teaching his daughter to ride a bicycle. He begins by rolling her along, supporting her weight while telling her to keep her hands on the handlebars, to push the right and left pedals in rhythm, and to look straight ahead. As she becomes more comfortable and confident, he begins to roll her along more quickly, praising her for steadily pumping. Within a few lessons, he is jogging beside her, holding only the handlebars. When he senses that she could maintain her balance by herself, he urges her to pedal faster and slowly loosens his grip. Perhaps without even realizing it, she is riding on her own.

Note that this is not instruction by preset rules. Sociocultural learning is active: No one learns to ride a bike by reading and memorizing written instructions, and no good teacher merely repeats a prepared lesson. Because each learner has personal traits, experiences, and aspirations, education must be individualized. Learning styles vary: Some people need more assurance than others; some learn best by looking, others by hearing. A mentor needs to sense when support or freedom is needed and how peers can help (they are sometimes the best mentors). Teachers know how the zone of proximal development expands and shifts.

Excursions into and through the zone of proximal development, as illustrated by the boy prompted to say "thank you" and the girl learning to balance on a bike, are commonplace for all of us. Examples are everywhere. At the thousand or so science museums in the United States, children ask numerous questions, and adults guide their scientific knowledge (Haden, 2010). The same process is evident when children are learning to drum in rhythm with another drum: Children need practice, but they learn faster when the other drummer is not a machine but a person, older than they and presumably better at synchronizing a beat (Kleinspehn-Ammerlahn et al., 2011).

In general, mentors, attuned to ever-shifting abilities and motivation, continually urge a new level of competence; learners ask questions, show interest, and demonstrate progress, thereby guiding and inspiring the mentors. When education goes well, both are fully engaged and productive within the zone of proximal development. Particular skills and processes vary enormously from culture to culture, but the overall social interaction is the same.

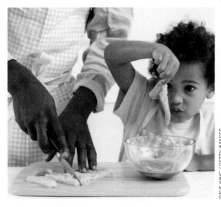

DAVE KING / GETTY IMAGES

Gourmet Cook in the Making Some children have skilled mentors who engage them in learning. It would be much easier for this cook to cut, dip, and fry without help, but the child is an apprentice and will soon learn the skill himself.

What the learner is not yet ready or able to learn (don't teach; too difficult)

Zone of Proximal Development
What the learner could understand with guidance (do teach; exciting, challenging)

What the learner already knows (don't reteach; too boring)

The learner

FIGURE 2.4

The Magic Middle Somewhere between the boring and the impossible is the zone of proximal development, where interaction between teacher and learner results in knowledge never before grasped or skills not already mastered. The intellectual excitement of that zone is the origin of the joy that both instruction and study can bring.

Taking Culture into Account

The sociocultural perspective has led contemporary scientists to consider social context in every study. Earlier theorists and researchers are quickly criticized for having failed to do so.

Research on attachment provides an easy example. As you will see in Chapter 7, a major topic in development is the relationship between infant and caregiver, a social bond that may affect the child lifelong. Secure attachment at 12 months correlates with the mother's responsiveness earlier in the infant's life, a finding that led to "attachment parenting" (the theory that parents should respond to every cry) and then to the "nurturance overload" mentioned early in this chapter.

At first, only attachment between mother and child was studied: It was thought that secure infants (about two-thirds of all babies studied) will play happily when mother is nearby, showing affection but not clinging. This early research was heavily influenced by psychoanalytic theory; it was Freud (1940/1949) who wrote that the mother–infant relationship is "unique, without parallel, established unalterably for a child's lifetime as the first and strongest love-object and as the prototype of all later love-relations" (p. 45).

Later research acknowledged fathers, grandparents, and other caregivers (Hrdy, 2009). Some infants are equally attached to both parents or are more securely attached to their fathers than to their mothers. Indeed, "in the United States and elsewhere, multiple attachment relationships are normative" (Thompson, 2006, p. 43). When researchers began exploring attachment in various cultures, they found a higher proportion of Japanese infants clinging to their mothers rather than exploring (suggesting these infants were insecurely attached) and a higher proportion of German infants exploring but seemingly indifferent to their mothers (also suggesting insecure attachment).

However, the sociocultural perspective has shed new light on cultural differences such as these. The attachment bond is universally important, but the expression of it depends on cultural context. Unless that context is considered, infants who are developing well may be misjudged, as many Japanese and German infants were. Responsiveness of the mother to the infant in the first months of life is thought to influence attachment at 1 year, but it is now apparent that how the mother responds is strongly influenced by her culture (Kärtner et al., 2010). Moreover, the goal of the early actions of the caregiver varies by culture: Most Western families value language and thus respond to infant vocalization; many African families value social responsibility and thus teach sensitive interaction (Super et al., 2011). Attachment is just one of dozens of developmental concepts that have been reevaluated in research with participants from various cultures.

Another intriguing area of research is gender and ethnic prejudice, which may increase at Freud's phallic stage or Piaget's concrete operational stage. Most of the research on this topic has occurred in the United States, where, over the past half-century, research has found that children are increasingly aware of prejudice against Black Americans, yet they are more vulnerable to becoming prejudiced themselves depending not only on cognitive maturation but also on the particular circumstances of their lives (Brown & Bigler, 2005; Nesdale et al., 2005).

In the United States, studies indicate that by adolescence, personal experience counts: Children who attend schools that are almost exclusively European American are less likely to oppose prejudice than are children with more diverse experiences (Killen at al., 2010). The sociocultural perspective, however, reminds us that cultures may differ on such matters.

For example, a recent study among children in Denmark found that they all soundly disapproved of excluding a child from an activity because of that's child's gender or ethnic background (the outgroup were children born in Denmark to

Especially for Adoptive Families Does the importance of attachment mean that adopted children will not bond securely with nonbiological caregivers? (see response, page 55)

Muslim parents who had immigrated in the 1960s) (Møller & Tenenbaum, 2011). Contrary to behaviorism and the conclusions of U.S. research, this study found that attitudes were not affected by whether a child's school had Muslim children or not; and contrary to Piaget, this study found few age differences in attitude. It did find, however, that children distinguished justice from custom—a sociocultural distinction (see the Research Design).

The Universal Perspective: Humanism and Evolutionary Theory

No developmentalist doubts that each person is unique. Yet many social scientists contend that focusing on cultural (or ethnic, or sexual, or economic) differences results in an unbalanced vision of humanity. We are one species, sharing universal impulses and needs. This universal perspective has been articulated in many developmental theories, each time expressed in particular ways but always contending that humans are, at the basic level, alike. Here we describe two of the most prominent of such perspectives: humanism and evolutionary theory.

Humanism

Many scientists are convinced that there is something hopeful, unifying, and noble in the human spirit, something ignored by psychoanalytic theory (which stresses the selfish id and infantile sexuality) and by behaviorism (which seems to ignore free will). The limits of those two major theories were especially apparent to two Americans: Abraham Maslow (1908–1970) and Carl Rogers (1902–1987), both deeply religious. They had witnessed the Great Depression and two world wars and concluded that traditional psychological theories underrated human potential by focusing on evil, not good. They founded a theory called **humanism** that became prominent after World War II, as millions read Maslow's *Toward a Psychology of Being* (1962/1999) and Rogers's *On Becoming a Person* (1961/2004).

As he expressed it first in 1943, Maslow believed that all people—no matter what their culture, gender, or background—have the same basic needs and drives. He arranged these needs in a hierarchy (see Figure 2.5):

1. Physiological: needing food, water, warmth, and air
2. Safety: feeling protected from injury and death
3. Love and belonging: having loving friends, family, and a community (often religious)
4. Esteem: being respected by the wider community as well as by oneself
5. Self-actualization: becoming truly oneself, fulfilling one's unique potential while appreciating all of humanity

At the highest level, when basic needs have been met, people can be fully themselves—creative, spiritual, curious, appreciative of nature, able to respect everyone else. One sign of self-actualization is that the person has "peak experiences" when life is so intensely joyful that time stops and self-seeking disappears. Given the stresses and deprivations of modern life, humanists believe that relatively few people reach the self-actualization of level 5. But everyone *can*—that is the universality of humanism.

Rogers also stressed the need to accept and respect one's own personhood as well as that of everyone else. He thought that people should give each other *unconditional positive regard*, which means that they should see (regard) each other with appreciation (positive) without conditions (unconditional). He did not think that everything people do is good, but he believed that people themselves are good, as in "Hate the sin but love the sinner." Rogers spent the last years of his life trying to

▶ **Research Design**

Scientists: Signe J. Møller and Harriet R. Tenenbaum.

Publication: *Child Development* (2011).

Participants: Questions were asked of 282 Danish majority children, ages 8 to 12, attending seven schools—four of which had no ethnic minority children enrolled and three of which had some ethnic minority children enrolled. The schools were located in the suburbs, not where ethnic differences were most salient.

Design: Children, individually and privately, responded to eight hypothetical vignettes in which a child was excluded by teachers or children because of the child's gender or ethnicity. For example, "Shahar wants to play Ludo, but the teacher says she cannot play because there are already three Danish boys and girls playing. Instead, the teacher says that a Danish classmate can play."

Results: The children not only recognized the prejudice, they were strongly opposed to it. This was true even when the exclusion was based on gender and even when a child was the perpetrator. But opposition was most adamant when a teacher excluded an ethnic minority child (as in the example). Such teachers were strongly criticized by children of all experiences.

Conclusion: Although age and daily life affect children's awareness of discrimination in the United States, because Danish values strongly endorse egalitarian practices, the children with no personal experience of other ethnicities judged ethnic exclusion as morally wrong, especially when perpetrated by a teacher.

Comment: Studies in other nations have also found that children are aware of discrimination and generally oppose it. The strength of these children's attitudes, with little effects of age and experience, suggest that national culture can have a powerful impact. Similar studies need to be performed in cultures in which prejudice is more acceptable, to learn how much children independently seek to be inclusive and how much children respond as a result of sociocultural values.

humanism A theory that stresses the potential of all humans for good and the belief that all people have the same basic needs, regardless of culture, gender, or background.

Hope and Laughter Maslow studied law before psychology, and he enjoyed deep discussions with many psychoanalytic theorists who escaped Nazi Europe. Nonetheless, he believed in the human spirit and that it could overcome oppression and reach self-actualization, where faith, hope, and humor abound.

Especially for Nurses Maslow's hierarchy is often taught in health sciences because it alerts medical staff to the needs of patients. What specific hospital procedures might help? (see response, page 56)

reconcile the factions in Northern Ireland, South Africa, and Russia; he believed all sides needed to learn to listen to each other.

As you can see, humanists emphasize what all people have in common, not their national, ethnic, or cultural differences. Maslow contended that everyone must satisfy each lower level of the hierarchy of needs before moving higher. A starving man, for instance, may not be concerned for his own safety when he seeks food (level 1 precedes level 2), or an unloved woman might not care about self-respect because she needs love (level 3 precedes level 4). Destructive and inhumane actions that prevent people from self-actualization may be the consequence of unmet lower needs. At the end of his life, Maslow explained that the highest level transcended selfishness and became selflessness, when a person is able to appreciate all of humanity (Maslow, 1971).

Although humanism does not postulate stages, a developmental application of this theory is that the satisfaction of childhood needs is crucial for later self-acceptance. Thus, when babies cry in hunger, that basic need should be satisfied. People may become thieves or even killers, unable to reach their potential, to self-actualize, if they were unsafe or unloved as children. Rogers agreed that adults who were deprived of unconditional positive regard in childhood might become selfish and antisocial. He developed a widely used method of psychological therapy to help people become more accepting of themselves and therefore of other people.

This theory is still prominent among medical professionals because they now realize that pain can be physical (the first two levels) or social (the next two) (Majercsik, 2005; Zalenski & Raspa, 2006). Even the very sick need love and belonging (family should be with them) and esteem (the dying need respect).

FIGURE 2.5

Moving Up, Not Looking Back Maslow's hierarchy is like a ladder: Once a person stands firmly on a higher rung, the lower rungs are no longer needed. Thus, someone who has arrived at step 4 might devalue safety (step 2) and be willing to risk personal safety to gain respect.

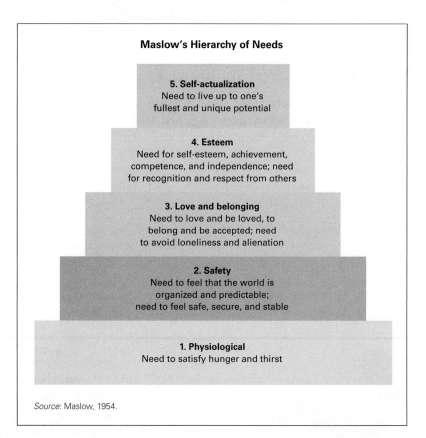

Maslow's Hierarchy of Needs

5. Self-actualization
Need to live up to one's fullest and unique potential

4. Esteem
Need for self-esteem, achievement, competence, and independence; need for recognition and respect from others

3. Love and belonging
Need to love and be loved, to belong and be accepted; need to avoid loneliness and alienation

2. Safety
Need to feel that the world is organized and predictable; need to feel safe, secure, and stable

1. Physiological
Need to satisfy hunger and thirst

Source: Maslow, 1954.

Echoes of humanism are also evident in education and sports: The basic idea here is that people are more effectively motivated when they try to master a body of knowledge or a skill to achieve a "personal best"—that is, to reach the peak of their own potential—than when they strive to be the best in their class or on their team (Ravizza, 2007).

Evolutionary Theory

You are familiar with Darwin and his ideas, first published 150 years ago—essentially that plants, insects, birds, and animals developed over billions of years, as life evolved from primitive cells to humans (Darwin, 1859). But you may not realize that serious research on human development inspired by this theory is quite recent. As two leaders in this field write:

> During the last two decades, the study of the evolutionary foundations of human nature has grown at an exponential rate. In fact, it is now a booming interdisciplinary scientific enterprise, one that sits at the cutting edge of the social and behavioral sciences.
>
> [Gangestad & Simpson, 2007, p. 2]

Evolutionary theory has intriguing explanations for many issues in human development, including women's nausea in pregnancy, 1-year-olds' attachment to their parents, puberty in young adolescents, emerging adults' sexual preferences, and parents' investment in their children. According to this theory, many human impulses, needs, and behaviors evolved to help humans survive and thrive over millions of years, with children particularly protected (Konner, 2010).

To understand human development, this theory contends, humans need to acknowledge the power of emotions that evolved thousands of years ago. For example, why are some people terrified of snakes (which cause 1 death in a billion), but virtually no one fears automobiles (which cause about 1 death in 5,000)? Evolutionary theory suggests that the fear instinct evolved over millennia to protect life when snakes killed people. Now we need to recognize that our fears have not caught up to modern inventions, so we need to use our minds, not be slaves of our emotions. That is happening: The motor-vehicle death rate has been cut in half by better-designed roads, laws, and cars. Other killers—climate change, drug addiction, obesity—are also difficult to manage because instincts are contrary to knowledge: Evolutionary theory contends that recognizing the origins of destructive urges helps to control them.

According to evolutionary theory, every species has two long-standing, biologically based drives: survival and reproduction. Understanding these two drives provides insight into protective parenthood, the death of some newborns, infant dependency, child immaturity, the onset of puberty, and much more (Konner, 2010). Later chapters will explain how in more detail, but here is one example. Human and nonhuman adults find babies appealing—despite the reality that babies (not only human, but also puppies, kittens, and so on) have little hair, no chins, stubby legs, and round stomachs—all of which are considered ugly in adults. The reason, evolutionary theory contends, is that adults of all species are instinctually attuned to protect and love the young.

A basic idea from evolutionary theory—**selective adaptation**—proposes that humans today react in ways that helped survival and reproduction long ago. In one version of selective adaptation, genes for traits that aid survival and reproduction are selected over time to allow the species to thrive (see Figure 2.6). Some of the best human qualities—cooperation, spirituality, and self-sacrifice—may have originated more than a hundred thousand years ago when groups of people endured because they took care of one another. Childhood itself, particularly the

>> Response for Adoptive Families (from page 52) Not at all. Attachment is the result of responsiveness, not biology. In some cultures, many children are adopted from infancy, and the emotional ties to their caregivers are no less strong than for other children.

Especially for Teachers and Counselors of Teenagers Teen pregnancy is destructive of adolescent education, family life, and sometimes even health. According to evolutionary theory, what can be done about this? (see response, page 57)

selective adaptation The process by which living creatures (including people) adjust to their environment. Genes that enhance survival and reproductive ability are selected, over the generations, to become more prevalent.

FIGURE 2.6

Selective Adaptation Illustrated Suppose one of a group of nine mothers happened to have a gene that improved her daughter's survival rate. Suppose most women merely replaced themselves each generation (as was generally historically true), but this gene mutation meant more births and therefore more surviving children, such that each woman who had the gene bore two who survived to womanhood instead of one. As you see, in 100 years, the "odd" gene becomes more common than the normal one—a new normal.

	Women With (Sex-Linked) Advantageous Gene	Women Without (Sex-Linked) Advantageous Gene
Mothers (1st generation)	🧍	🧍🧍🧍🧍🧍🧍🧍🧍
Daughters (2nd generation)	🧍 🧍	🧍🧍🧍🧍🧍🧍🧍🧍
Granddaughters (3rd generation)	🧍 🧍 🧍 🧍	🧍🧍🧍🧍🧍🧍🧍🧍
Great-granddaughters (4th generation)	🧍🧍🧍🧍🧍🧍🧍🧍	🧍🧍🧍🧍🧍🧍🧍🧍
Great-great-granddaughters (5th generation)	🧍🧍🧍🧍🧍🧍🧍🧍 🧍🧍🧍🧍🧍🧍🧍🧍	🧍🧍🧍🧍🧍🧍🧍🧍

long period when children depend on their parents, can be explained via evolution (Konner, 2010).

The process of selective adaptation works like this: If one person happens to have a gene that makes survival more likely, that gene is likely to be passed on to the next generation (because the person has survived long enough to reproduce). Such a beneficial gene might have arisen as a mutation, or it might simply be one end of the natural variation in height, body type, anxiety, or any other characteristic that varies from one person to another. Anyone who inherits such a gene would be more likely to survive to adulthood, to be chosen as a mate, and to have several children—half of whom would inherit that desirable gene.

For example, originally all humans probably got sick after drinking cow's milk, a trait called *lactose intolerance* (Suchy, 2010). Then in a few regions, cattle were domesticated and raised for their meat. In those places, "killing the fatted calf" provided a rare feast for the entire community when a major celebration occurred. In such cattle-raising locations, if a hungry child chanced to have an aberrant gene for the enzyme that allowed digestion of cow's milk, and that child drank some milk intended for a calf, he or she had a better chance of surviving long enough to have children, since malnutrition was a common cause of death among early humans. Indeed, a girl with that gene might become fat enough to experience early puberty, then to sustain many pregnancies, and then to breast-feed her thriving babies longer than her lactose-intolerant, malnourished sisters could. In that way, the next generation would include more people who inherited that gene.

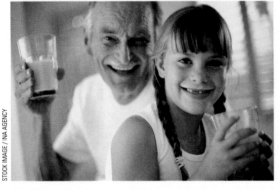

Got Milk! Many people in Sweden (like this pair) and the other Scandinavian countries regularly drink cow's milk and digest it easily. That may be because their ancient occupation of cattle herding coincided with a genetic tendency toward lactose tolerance.

This process of selective adaptation continues over many generations. That odd gene allowing digestion of cow's milk would become widespread in cold climates where plant proteins were scarce and cow's milk meant survival. This might explain why few Scandinavians are lactose-intolerant but many Africans are—a useful fact for Wisconsin dairy farmers who want to ship milk to starving children in Ethiopia. When the farmers realize that their milk might make some children sick, they can find other ways to relieve hunger. Although malnutrition is still a global problem, fewer children are starving than a few decades ago, partly because nutritionists now know which foods are digestible and nourishing for whom.

For groups as well as individuals, the interaction of genes and environment affects survival and reproduction, the two basic drives recognized by evolutionary theory. Genetic variations are particularly beneficial when the environment changes, which is one reason the genetic diversity of humans throughout the world benefits humanity as a whole. If a species' gene pool does not include variants that

>> Response for Nurses (from page 54) Reassurance from nurses (explaining procedures, including specifics and reasons) helps with the first two, and visitors, cards, and calls might help with the next two. Obviously, specifics depend on the patient, but everyone needs respect as well as physical care.

STOCK IMAGE / INA AGENCY

allow survival in difficult circumstances (such as exposure to a new disease or to an environmental toxin), the entire species may become extinct. This explains why biologists are concerned when a particular species becomes inbred—diversity is protective of all creatures. About 90 percent of all species that ever existed have disappeared because as conditions changed, every member died without progeny (Buss et al., 1998).

Genetic variation among humans and inherited flexibility (the plasticity explained in Chapter 1) enable humans to survive and multiply. This is probably true not only for biological traits (such as digestion of milk) but also for traits that originate in the brain (Tomasello, 2009). For example, certain genes foster socialization, communication, and language, which helped humans in the Paleolithic era talk to one another and allowed societies a few thousand years ago to develop writing, then books, and then universities. As a result of this burgeoning of education and communications, humans now learn from history and from the experiences of people on the other side of the globe.

Because of humans' genetic inheritance, therefore, people have come to understand the importance of clean water, good nutrition, and immunization, and the average life expectancy worldwide has increased from about 20 years a thousand years ago, to 35 years a century ago, to about 75 years today (85 years in some nations and only 50 in others, but everywhere much longer than a few decades ago). The very fact that you are reading this book, accepting some ideas and rejecting others, is part of the genetic heritage that will aid future generations, according to evolutionary theory.

In developmental science, evolutionary theory is now considered insightful and intriguing, but some interpretations are hotly disputed. For instance, an evolutionary account of mental illness suggests that disorders are extremes of adaptive traits, such as a vivid imagination or feelings of anxiety. The implications of this interpretation include more acceptance of the unusual people among us. This is controversial. More controversial are evolutionary explanations of the emotional differences between men and women, as the following explains.

>> **Response for Teachers and Counselors of Teenagers** (from page 55) Evolutionary theory stresses the basic human drive for reproduction, which gives teenagers a powerful sex drive. Thus, merely informing teenagers of the difficulty of caring for a newborn (some high school sex-education programs simply give teenagers a chicken egg to nurture) is not likely to work. A better method would be to structure teenagers' lives so that pregnancy is impossible—for instance, with careful supervision or readily available contraception.

A VIEW FROM SCIENCE

If Your Mate Were Unfaithful

Universally, males seek more sexual partners than females do, and brides are younger than grooms. These are norms, not followed in every case, but apparent in every culture. Why? The evolutionary explanation begins with biology. Since females, not males, become pregnant and breast-feed, in most of human history, a woman needed a mature, strong man to keep predators away from her and her children. This would allow her to fulfill her evolutionary destiny, to survive and pass on her genes to children who would live long enough to reproduce. Consequently, a woman kept her man near the campfire with home-cooking and sex.

By contrast, men had a better chance of living on genetically by having as many offspring as possible, which meant having multiple sexual partners of prime childbearing age. That may explain why powerful kings had dozens of young wives and concubines, spreading their genes to many descendents. Because of

those ancient needs, men still are more likely to stray, especially with younger women, whereas women seek one steady marriage partner.

Evolutionary psychologists have some research to support this interpretation. They asked people of many ages, nationalities, and religions to imagine their romantic partner either "forming a deep emotional attachment" or "enjoying passionate sexual intercourse" with someone else. After imagining that, people were asked which of those two possibilities would distress them more (Buss, 2003). One recent replication involved 212 college students, all U.S. citizens, whose parents were born in Mexico (Cramer et al., 2009). As with every other study of this kind, more women (60 percent) were distressed at the emotional infidelity and more men (66 percent) at the sexual infidelity.

Evolutionary theory explains this oft-replicated result by noting that for centuries a woman has needed a soul mate to be emotionally committed, to ensure that he will provide for her and her children, whereas a man has needed a woman to be sexually faithful to ensure that her children are also his. Indeed, worldwide, men are more likely to fly into a jealous rage if they suspect infidelity, sometimes beating their sex partners to death, which women never do (Mize et al., 2009).

This evolutionary explanation is rejected by many women, who contend that patriarchy and sexism, not genes, lead to mating patterns. Similar controversies arise with other applications of this theory.

People sometimes act in ways that are counter to evolutionary predictions: Parents sometimes abandon newborns, adults sometimes handle snakes, and so on. In the survey just cited of Mexican American college students, more than one-third did not follow the typical pattern for their sex (Cramer et al., 2009). Nonetheless, evolutionary theorists contend that, for the future of humankind, developmentalists need to understand people in order to mitigate destructive impulses (e.g., by establishing laws against "crimes of passion") and encourage the best of human nature (Ackerman & Kenrick, 2009; Bulbulia, 2007; Gintis et al., 2007).

Many hypotheses from evolutionary theory have not been scientifically tested, much less accepted, partly because this is the newest theory to be applied to development. Some critics contend that evolutionary theory is an unscientific leap from current behavior to imagined conditions before written history. Nonetheless, this theory offers intriguing explanations for universal human tendencies that are difficult to explain in other ways.

SUMMING UP

Newer theories of development are more multicultural, expansive, and multidisciplinary than the earlier grand theories. Sociocultural theory emphasizes the varied cultural contexts of development, suggesting that even such basic behaviors as caring for infants and educating children are guided by the community. Learning occurs within the zone of proximal development, as the result of sensitive collaboration between a teacher (who could be a parent or a child) and a learner who is ready for the next step.

Universal theories include humanism and evolutionary theory, both of which stress that all humans have the same underlying needs. Humanism holds that everyone merits respect and positive regard in order to become a fully self-actualized human being. Evolutionary theory contends that thousands of years of selective adaptation have led humans to experience emotions and impulses that satisfy two universal needs of every species: to survive and to reproduce. These primitive reactions need to be recognized and understood in order for the species to progress, according to this theory. ■

>> What Theories Contribute

Each major theory discussed in this chapter has contributed a great deal to our understanding of human development (see Table 2.4):

- *Psychoanalytic theories* have made us aware of the impact of early-childhood experiences, remembered or not, on subsequent development.
- *Behaviorism* has shown the effect that immediate responses, associations, and examples have on learning, moment by moment and over time.
- *Cognitive theories* have brought an understanding of intellectual processes and how our thoughts and beliefs affect every aspect of our development.
- *Sociocultural theories* have reminded us that development is embedded in a rich and multifaceted cultural context, evident in every social interaction.
- *Universal theories* stress that human differences are less significant than those characteristics that are shared by all humans, in every place and era.

No comprehensive view of development can ignore any of these theories, yet each has encountered severe criticism. Psychoanalytic theory has been faulted for

TABLE 2.4	Five Perspectives on Human Development		
Theory	Area of Focus	Fundamental Depiction of What People Do	Relative Emphasis on Nature or Nurture?
Psychoanalytic theory	Psychosexual (Freud) or psychosocial (Erikson) stages	Battle unconscious impulses and overcome major crises	More nature (biological, sexual impulses, and parent–child bonds)
Behaviorism	Conditioning through stimulus and response	Respond to stimuli, reinforcement, and models	More nurture (direct environment produces various behaviors)
Cognitive theory	Thinking, remembering, analyzing	Seek to understand experiences while forming concepts and cognitive strategies	More nature (person's own mental activity and motivation are key)
Sociocultural theory	Social context, expressed through people, language, customs	Learn the tools, skills, and values of society through apprenticeships	More nurture (interaction of mentor and learner, within cultural context)
Universal perspective	Needs and impulses that all humans share as a species	Develop impulses, interests, and patterns to satisfy needs and survive as a species	More nature (needs that apply to all humans; genetic evolution)

being too subjective; behaviorism, for being too mechanistic; cognitive theory, for undervaluing emotions; sociocultural theory, for neglecting individuals; and universal theory, for slighting cultural, gender, and economic variations. Most developmentalists prefer an **eclectic perspective,** choosing what they consider the best aspects of each theory. Rather than adopt any one of these theories exclusively, they make selective use of all of them.

Being eclectic, not tied to any one theory, is beneficial because everyone, scientist as well as layperson, tends to be biased. It is easy to dismiss alternative points of view, but using all five theories opens our eyes and minds to aspects of development that we might otherwise ignore. As one overview of seven developmental theories (including those explained here) concludes, "Because no one theory satisfactorily explains development, it is critical that developmentalists be able to draw on the content, methods, and theoretical concepts of many theories" (Miller, 2011, p. 437).

As you will see in many later chapters, theories provide a fresh look at behavior. Imagine a parent and a teacher discussing a child's actions. Each suggests a possible explanation that makes the other say, "I never thought of that"; if they listen with an open mind, together they understand the child better. Having five theories is like having five perceptive observers. All five are not always on target, but it is better to use theory to expand perception than to stay in one narrow groove. A hand functions best with five fingers, although each finger is different, and some are more useful than others.

eclectic perspective The approach taken by most developmentalists, in which they apply aspects of each of the various theories of development rather than adhering exclusively to one theory.

SUMMING UP

Theories are needed to suggest hypotheses, to spur investigation, and, finally, to find answers so that empirical evidence can replace untested personal assumptions. All five of the major theories have met with valid criticism, but they have also all helped to move the scientific process forward. Most developmentalists are eclectic, making selective use of all these theories and more. This helps guard against bias and keeps scientists, parents, students, and everyone else open to alternative explanations for the complexity of human life.

SUMMARY

What Theories Do

1. A theory provides a framework of general principles to guide research and to explain observations. Each of the five major developmental theories—psychoanalytic, behaviorist, cognitive, sociocultural, and universal—interprets human development from a distinct perspective, and each provides guidance for understanding how human experiences and behaviors change over time.

2. Theories are neither true nor false. They are not facts; they suggest hypotheses to be tested. Good theories are practical: They aid inquiry, interpretation, and daily life.

3. A norm is a usual standard of behavior. Norms are not theories, although they may result from theories if a theory suggests that a certain behavior is proper; and norms are not necessarily good or bad, although sometimes differences from the norm are falsely considered deficits.

Grand Theories

4. Psychoanalytic theory emphasizes that human actions and thoughts originate from unconscious impulses and childhood conflicts. Freud theorized that sexual urges arise during three stages of childhood development—oral, anal, and phallic—and continue, after latency, in the genital stage.

5. Erikson described psychosocial, not psychosexual, stages. He described eight successive stages of development, each involving a crisis as people mature within their context. Societies, cultures, and family members respond to each person's development.

6. All psychoanalytic theories stress the legacy of childhood. Conflicts associated with children's erotic impulses have a lasting impact on adult personality, according to Freud. Erikson thought that the resolution of each crisis affects adult development.

7. Behaviorists, or learning theorists, believe that scientists should study observable and measurable behavior. Behaviorism emphasizes conditioning—a lifelong learning process, as association between one stimulus and another (classical conditioning) or the consequences of reinforcement and punishment (operant conditioning) guide behavior.

8. Social learning theory recognizes that people learn by observing others. Children are particularly susceptible to social learning. Self-efficacy is apparent in societies as well as individuals.

9. Cognitive theorists believe that thoughts and beliefs powerfully affect attitudes, actions, and perceptions. Piaget proposed four age-related periods of cognition, propelled by an active search for cognitive equilibrium. Information processing focuses on each aspect of cognitive input, processing, and output.

Newer Theories

10. Sociocultural theory explains human development in terms of the guidance, support, and structure provided by knowledgeable members of the society, via culture and personal mentoring. Vygotsky described how learning occurs through social interactions, when mentors guide learners through their zone of proximal development.

11. The universal perspective focuses on the shared impulses and common needs of all humanity. One universal theory is humanism. Maslow believed that all humans have five basic needs, which he arranged in sequence beginning with survival and ending with self-actualization. Rogers believed that each person merits respect and appreciation, with unconditional positive regard.

12. Evolutionary theory has recently been applied to development. It contends that contemporary humans inherit genetic tendencies that have fostered survival and reproduction of the human species for tens of thousands of years. Some hypotheses from this theory are particularly provocative, such as the explanation for male–female differences in romantic liaisons.

What Theories Contribute

13. Psychoanalytic, behavioral, cognitive, sociocultural, and universal theories have each aided our understanding of human development, yet no one theory is broad enough to describe the full complexity and diversity of human experience. Most developmentalists are eclectic, drawing upon many theories.

KEY TERMS

developmental theory (p. 35)	operant conditioning (p. 43)	cognitive equilibrium (p. 47)	guided participation (p. 50)
norm (p. 37)	reinforcement (p. 43)	assimilation (p. 47)	zone of proximal development (p. 51)
psychoanalytic theory (p. 39)	social learning theory (p. 44)	accommodation (p. 47)	
behaviorism (p. 42)	modeling (p. 44)	information processing (p. 48)	humanism (p. 53)
conditioning (p. 42)	self-efficacy (p. 44)	sociocultural theory (p. 50)	selective adaptation (p. 55)
classical conditioning (p. 42)	cognitive theory (p. 46)	apprenticeship in thinking (p. 50)	eclectic perspective (p. 59)

WHAT HAVE YOU LEARNED?

What Theories Do

1. How can a theory be practical?

2. What is the relationship between norms and facts?

3. How do theories differ from facts?

Grand Theories

4. What is the basic idea of psychoanalytic theory?

5. What is Freud's theory of infantile sexuality?

6. What body parts are connected to the oral, anal, and phallic stages?

7. In what two ways does Erikson's theory differ from Freud's?

8. What is the basic idea of behaviorism?

9. In what way is behaviorism considered "in opposition" to psychoanalytic theory?

10. How do classical and operant conditioning differ?

11. What reinforcers are emphasized by social learning theory?

12. What is the basic idea of cognitive theory?

13. How are Piaget's stages similar to, and different from, Freud's stages?

14. In what ways are assimilation and accommodation similar?

15. Why is information processing not a stage theory?

Newer Theories

16. What are the underlying differences between the newer theories and the grand theories?

17. How is "apprenticeship in thinking" an example of sociocultural theory?

18. What do mentors do when mentees are in their zone of proximal development?

19. How is the religious background of both Rogers and Maslow related to humanism?

20. How does Maslow's hierarchy of needs differ from Erikson's stages?

21. How does evolutionary psychology explain human instincts?

22. Why are aspects of evolutionary theory of human emotions controversial?

23. What does the idea of selective adaptation imply about the nature–nurture controversy?

What Theories Contribute

24. What is the key criticism and key contribution of psychoanalytic theory?

25. What is the key criticism and key contribution of behaviorism?

26. What is the key criticism and key contribution of cognitive theory?

27. What is the key criticism and key contribution of sociocultural theory?

28. What is the key criticism and key contribution of universal theories?

29. What are the advantages and disadvantages of an eclectic perspective?

APPLICATIONS

1. Developmentalists sometimes talk about "folk theories," which are theories developed by ordinary people, who may not know that they are theorizing. Choose three sayings commonly used in your culture, such as (from the dominant U.S. culture) "A penny saved is a penny earned" or "As the twig is bent, so grows the tree." Explain the underlying assumptions, or theory, that each saying reflects.

2. Behaviorism has been used to change personal habits. Think of a habit you'd like to change (e.g., stop smoking, exercise more, watch less TV). Count the frequency of that behavior for a week, noting the reinforcers for each instance. Then, and only then, develop a substitute behavior, reinforcing yourself for it. Keep careful data for several days. What did you learn?

3. Ask three people to tell you their theories about male–female differences in mating and sexual behaviors. Which of the theories described in this chapter is closest to each explanation, and which theory is not mentioned?

Heredity and Environment

1. What is the relationship between genes and chromosomes?

2. Do sex differences result from chromosomes or culture?

3. How can a child have genetic traits that are not obvious in either the mother or the father?

4. If parents are alcoholic, will their children, because of genetics, be alcoholics too?

5. Why are some children born with Down syndrome, and what can be done for them?

"She needs a special school. She cannot come back next year," Elissa's middle school principal told us.

Martin and I were stunned. Apparently the school staff thought that our wonderful daughter, bright and bubbly (Martin called her "frothy"), was learning-disabled—more specifically, spatially disorganized. We had noticed that she misplaced homework, got lost, left books at school, forgot where each class met on which day—but we thought those were insignificant compared to her strengths in reading, analyzing, and friendship.

I knew the first lesson from genetics: Genes affect everything, not just physical appearance, diseases, and cognitive abilities, so I wondered what Elissa had inherited from us. Our desks were covered with papers, and our home had assorted objects everywhere. If we needed masking tape, or working scissors, or silver candlesticks, we had to search in several places. Could that be why we were oblivious to Elissa's failings?

The second lesson from genetics is that nurture always matters. My husband and I had both learned to compensate for innate organizational weaknesses. Since he often got lost, Martin did not hesitate to ask strangers for directions; since I was prone to mislaying important documents, I kept my students' papers in clearly marked folders. Despite our genes, we both were successful; we thought Elissa was fine.

Once we recognized our daughter's nature, we changed her nurture. Martin attached her bus pass to her backpack; I wrote an impassioned letter telling the principal it would be unethical to expel her; we hired a tutor who helped us teach Elissa to make a list of her homework assignments, check them off when done, put them carefully in her bag, and then take the bag to school. Elissa herself began to study diligently. Our efforts succeeded. Elissa aced her final exams, and the principal allowed her to return. She became a master organizer; 15 years later, she was valedictorian of her law school class.

This chapter begins with nature and then emphasizes nurture. Throughout, we note some ethical and practical choices regarding the interaction of genes and environments. I hope you recognize that interaction long before you have a seventh-grade daughter.

>> The Genetic Code

You already know that one sperm and one ovum combine to begin human life and that each newly created cell contains genes that affect every aspect of development. Remember, however, that development is dynamic, ongoing, and interactional; individuals are much more than the product of their genes.

For example, genes dictate the maximum life span for each species: For mice it is 4 years; for humans, 122; for the bowhead whale, about 200 (Austad, 2010). If you were a mouse, you couldn't live past age 4. But the factors that determine whether one person outlives another are dynamic and interactional, depending much more on where each person lives than on his or her genes.

Genes are not the main reason people in some nations live decades longer than those in other nations. From the shortest to the longest average life span, the range is about 40 years—for instance, age 45 in Afghanistan and age 84 in Japan (United Nations, 2011). As you can see, most people die decades before their inherited potential. Similarly, genes for language fluency, diabetes, strong teeth, and even organizational skills are expressed—or not—depending on nurture. To understand development, begin with genes. But never forget: Genetics describes possibilities (you *could* live to 122), not outcomes (you probably won't).

What Genes Are

First, we review some biology. All living things are composed of cells. The work of these cells is done by *proteins.* Each cell manufactures certain proteins according to instructions stored by molecules of **deoxyribonucleic acid (DNA)** at the heart of each cell. These DNA molecules are on a **chromosome.**

Humans have 23 pairs of chromosomes (46 in all), which contain the instructions to make all the proteins that a person needs (see Figure 3.1). The instructions in the 46 chromosomes are organized into genes, with each **gene** usually located at a specific spot on a particular chromosome. Humans have between 18,000 and 23,000 genes, and each gene contains the chemical recipe for making a specific protein (Brooker, 2009).

What exactly is a protein? A protein is composed of a sequence of chemicals, a long string of building blocks called *amino acids.* The recipe for manufacturing a protein consists of instructions for stringing together the right amino acids in the right order.

These instructions are transmitted to the cell via pairs of four chemicals called *bases* (adenine, thiamine, cytosine, and guanine; abbreviated A, T, C, and G). The bases pair up in only four possible ways (A-T, T-A, C-G, and G-C). Humans have more than 3 billion base pairs, which are arranged in triplets (three base pairs) on those 20,000 or so genes.

Variations

Most genes have thousands of base pairs that make the 20 types of amino acids needed to create a human being. The triplets of each particular gene can vary, although usually they do not. Some genes have transpositions, deletions, or repetitions of the triplets not found in other versions of the same gene. Each of these variations is called an **allele** of that gene, and genes that have various alleles are called *polymorphic* (literally, "many forms") or, more formally, *single-nucleotide polymorphisms* (abbreviated SNPs). Most alleles cause only minor differences (such as the shape of an eyebrow); some seem inconsequential; some are notable, even devastating.

---

deoxyribonucleic acid (DNA) The chemical composition of the molecules that contain the genes, which are the chemical instructions for cells to manufacture various proteins.

chromosome One of the 46 molecules of DNA (in 23 pairs) that virtually each cell of the human body contains and that, together, contain all the genes. Other species have more or fewer chromosomes.

gene A small section of a chromosome; the basic unit for the transmission of heredity. A gene consists of a string of chemicals that provide instructions for the cell to manufacture certain proteins.

Especially for Scientists A hundred years ago, it was believed that humans had 48 chromosomes, not 46; 10 years ago, it was thought that humans had 100,000 genes, not 20,000 or so. Why? (see response, page 66)

allele A variation that makes a gene different in some way from other genes for the same characteristics. Many genes never vary; others have several possible alleles.

The interaction of genes from the mother and genes from the father affects the embryo's growth in many ways (more about genetic interaction soon). This complex interaction actually begins the moment a zygote is formed, because everyone inherits alleles from the sperm and the ovum that make him or her unique. Thus, each person has some base pairs that differ from those of other people, and everyone has some extra repeats of a piece of a gene or sometimes of a whole gene. Consequently, each person has several gene pairs that do not quite match. One expert said: "What's cool is that we are a mosaic of pieces of genomes. None of us is truly normal" (Eichler, quoted in Cohen, 2007, p. 1315).

Furthermore, everyone has additional DNA and RNA (another molecule) that are not genes but that are critical to life: In a process called *methylation,* this material enhances, transcribes, connects, empowers, and alters genes (Shapiro, 2009). This nongenetic material used to be called *junk*—no longer. Thousands of scientists seek to discover what these molecules do, but no one thinks they are junk anymore (Wright & Bruford, 2011). It is clear that methylation can stop a gene's expression in a process that begins at the moment of conception or later—even after the person is born.

The entire packet of instructions to make a living organism is called the **genome.** There is a genome for every species and variety of plant and animal—even for every bacteria and virus. Knowing the genome of the human species is only a start (it was fully decoded in 2001). Even before 2001 it was apparent that, with the exception of monozygotic twins, each person has a slightly different code, although the *human genome* is 99.9 percent identical for any two persons. For instance, all humans have two eyes, two legs, linguistic abilities, and much more—major characteristics and capacities ordained by genes. Despite all the shared genes that make humans one species, small differences between individuals make each one of us unique.

genome The full set of genes that are the instructions to make an individual member of a certain species.

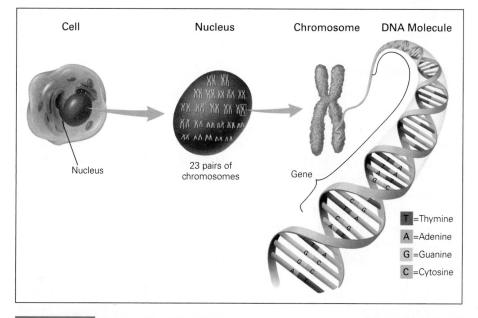

FIGURE 3.1

How Proteins Are Made The genes on the chromosomes in the nucleus of each cell instruct the cell to manufacture the proteins needed to sustain life and development. The code for a protein is the particular combination of T-A-G-C.

>> Response for Scientists (from page 64)
There was some scientific evidence for the wrong numbers (e.g., chimpanzees have 48 chromosomes), but the reality is that humans tend to overestimate many things, from the number of genes to their grades on the next test. Scientists are very human: They are inclined to overestimate until the data prove them wrong.

gamete A reproductive cell; that is, a sperm or ovum that can produce a new individual if it combines with a gamete from the other sex to make a zygote.

zygote The single cell formed from the union of two gametes, a sperm and an ovum.

genotype An organism's entire genetic inheritance, or genetic potential.

homozygous Referring to two genes of one pair that are exactly the same in every letter of their code. Most gene pairs are homozygous.

heterozygous Referring to two genes of one pair that differ in some way. Typically one allele has only a few base pairs that differ from the other member of the pair.

The Moment of Conception This ovum is about to become a zygote. It has been penetrated by a single sperm, whose nucleus now lies next to the nucleus of the ovum. Soon, the two nuclei will fuse, bringing together about 20,000 genes to guide development.

SUMMING UP

The human genome contains hundreds of thousands of molecules, forming about 20,000 genes on 46 chromosomes, using 3 billion base pairs of 4 chemicals to instruct production of 20 amino acids to create proteins that make a human being. Some genes, called alleles, are polymorphic. Because of small differences in their genetic codes (perhaps a change of only one base pair), each future person is unlike any other. Other material, once called junk DNA, affects the expression of the genes—sometimes stopping expression completely, sometimes increasing the power of that gene. The result is that each person is unique yet similar to all other humans. The entire instruction code is the genome, contained in a single cell, smaller than the head of a pin. ■

>> The Beginnings of Life

A reproductive cell is called a **gamete** whether it is a *sperm* or an *ovum*. Each gamete contains 23 chromosomes. When two gametes combine, they create a **zygote,** a single cell of 46 chromosomes that begins a human life.

That one-celled zygote copies itself again and again, creating an embryo, a fetus, a baby, and eventually an adult with trillions of cells, each with the same 46 chromosomes and same thousands of genes of the original zygote. When sperm or ova are created, the parent cell splits neatly in half so that each gamete has only one of the two chromosomes at each location. Thus, for instance, a gamete has only one chromosome number 10 although the man or woman who formed it has two chromosomes at the 10th site. The new zygote will have a pair of number 10 chromosomes as well—one from the sperm and one from the ovum.

The particular member of each chromosome pair from each parent on a given gamete is randomly selected. A man or woman can produce 2^{23} different gametes—more than 8 million versions of his or her own 46 chromosomes. If a given couple conceived a billion zygotes, each would be genetically unique because of the chromosomes of the particular gametes that created them. Alleles, methylation, and other genetic interactions would add even more variations.

Matching Genes

At the moment of conception, the father's chromosomes match up with the mother's chromosomes—his number 10 with her number 10, for instance—so that the zygote's 23 pairs of chromosomes are arranged in father–mother pairs. (This can go awry if a zygote has more or fewer than 46 chromosomes, discussed later in the chapter.) The genes on the chromosomes constitute the organism's genetic inheritance, or **genotype,** which endures throughout life. Growth requires duplication again and again of the code of the original cell.

In 22 of the 23 pairs of chromosomes, both members of the pair are closely matched. Each of these 44 chromosomes is called an *autosome,* which means that it is independent (*auto* means "self") of the sex chromosomes (the 23rd pair). Each autosome, from number 1 to number 22, contains hundreds of genes in the same positions and sequence. At conception, each gene on each autosome matches with its counterpart from the other parent. If the code of all the base pairs of the gene from one parent is exactly like the code on the same gene from the other parent, the gene pair is **homozygous** (literally, "same-zygote").

However, the match is not always letter perfect because the mother might have a different allele for that particular gene than the father has. If a gene's code differs from that of its counterpart, the two genes still pair up, but the zygote (and, later, the person) is **heterozygous.** Usually this is no problem: Indeed, it is better to be

BIOPHOTO ASSOCIATES / PHOTO RESEARCHERS, INC.

Uncertain Sex Every now and then, a baby is born with "ambiguous genitals," meaning that the child's sex is not abundantly clear. When this happens, a quick analysis of the chromosomes is needed, to make sure there are exactly 46 and to see whether the 23rd pair is XY or XX. The karyotypes shown here indicate a normal baby boy *(left)* and girl *(right)*.

heterozygous than homozygous for some traits, as we will soon explain. But first, let us explain the most dramatic example of a disparate pair, the 23rd chromosomes.

Male or Female?

The chromosomes that make up the **23rd pair** are the sex chromosomes. In females, the 23rd pair is composed of two X-shaped chromosomes. Accordingly, it is called **XX.** In males, the 23rd pair has one X-shaped chromosome and one Y-shaped chromosome. It is called **XY.**

Because a female's 23rd pair is XX, every ovum contains either one X or the other—but always an X. And because a male's 23rd pair is XY, half of his sperm carry an X chromosome and half a Y. The X chromosome is bigger and has many more genes, but the Y chromosome has a crucial gene, called *SRY,* that directs the embryo to make male hormones and organs. Thus, the sex of the zygote depends on which sperm penetrates the ovum—a Y sperm with the SRY gene, creating a boy (XY), or an X sperm, creating a girl (XX) (see Figure 3.2). Since Y sperm are smaller, they can swim faster, so slightly more male than female zygotes are conceived.

23rd pair The chromosome pair that, in humans, determines sex. The other 22 pairs are autosomes; inherited equally by males and females.

XX A 23rd chromosome pair that consists of two X-shaped chromosomes, one each from the mother and the father. XX zygotes become females.

XY A 23rd chromosome pair that consists of an X-shaped chromosome from the mother and a Y-shaped chromosome from the father. XY zygotes become males.

FIGURE 3.2

Determining a Zygote's Sex Any given couple can produce four possible combinations of sex chromosomes; two lead to female children and two, to male. In terms of the future person's sex, it does not matter which of the mother's Xs the zygote inherited. All that matters is whether the father's Y sperm or X sperm fertilized the ovum. However, for X-linked conditions it matters a great deal because typically one, but not both, of the mother's Xs carries the trait.

Observation Quiz In the chapter-opening photograph (page 62), can you distinguish the Y sperm from the X sperm? (see answer, page 69)

Thus, for humans, at the moment of conception the future embryo is either XX or XY. In some other species, however, sex is not determined at conception. In certain reptiles, for instance, temperature during incubation affects the sex of the embryo (Hare & Cree, 2010). But humans are male or female from the moment of conception, even though traditionally parents did not know their child's sex until birth. Now, however, parents can find out much earlier, making it easier to choose names, decorate nurseries, and bond with the future child—or not, as the following explains.

THINKING CRITICALLY

Too Many Boys?

Prenatal sex selection is possible; millions of couples do it. Is this a problem?

Historically, some newborns were killed in every culture. One of the moral advances of Islam, in the seventh century, was to forbid female infanticide. Currently, killing a newborn girl is rare because there are three other ways used to prevent female births—(1) inactivating X sperm before conception, (2) in vitro fertilization (IVF), or (3) aborting XX fetuses.

In China, a "one-child" policy initiated in 1990 cut the birth rate in half and increased the number of Chinese newborn girls available for adoption because parents wanted their one child to be a boy. This policy (sometimes enforced with sterilization and abortion) alleviated poverty but also skewed the sex ratio, as many Chinese couples aborted female fetuses. Since 1993, the Chinese government has forbidden prenatal testing to reveal sex, but many aspects of prenatal care (e.g., sonograms) reveal sex, and female fetuses were more often aborted. Recently, the one-child policy has become a two-child policy, and the sex ratio may be more balanced (Greenhalgh, 2008).

Parents elsewhere also prefer boys. The Indian government forbids abortion to prevent female births, but India nonetheless has only 92 girls for every 100 boys. One elderly Indian man said, "We should have at least four children per family, three of them boys" (quoted in Khanna, 2010, p. 66). Worldwide, one estimate is that 100 million fetuses have been aborted since 1990 because they were female (Sharma, 2008), perhaps 20,000 of them in the United States (Abrevaya, 2009).

Many nations forbid abortion solely because of sex. Some nations also forbid sorting sperm to change the proportion of X and Y sperm before insemination, a technique that works for humans about 85 percent of the time (Karabinus, 2009).

In the United States, individuals make their own choices before and after conception. Most fertility doctors and some parents believe that sex selection is a reproductive right and that couples who can afford it should be able to decide to have either a boy or a girl (Puri & Nachtigall, 2010). Some people who themselves would not abort a fetus because it is the less desired sex nonetheless oppose laws that forbid personal freedom—in this case, freedom to "balance" the family.

One consequence of sex selection in China has been a much higher mortality rate for young men than young women, perhaps because many men cannot find wives. Unmarried young men in every culture take risks to show their bravery, become depressed or drug-addicted, or neglect medical advice (Kruger & Polanski, 2011). From what is known about male–female differences, male-heavy societies might have more learning disabilities, drug abusers, violent crimes, wars, heart attacks, and suicides but fewer nurses, day-care centers, or close family bonds.

But wait: Chromosomes and genes do not determine behavior. Every male–female difference mentioned in the preceding paragraph is influenced by culture. Even traits that originate with biology, such as the propensity to heart attacks, are affected more by environment (in this case, diet and stress) than by sex. Answers to this issue are not obvious, which is why this feature is titled Thinking Critically. Is sex selection the parents' right or a social wrong?

My Strength, My Daughter That's the slogan these girls in New Delhi are shouting at a demonstration against abortion of female fetuses in India. The current sex ratio of children in India suggests that this campaign has not convinced every couple.

New Cells, New Functions

Within hours after conception, the zygote begins *duplication* and *division*. First, the 23 pairs of chromosomes carrying all the genes duplicate, forming two complete sets of the genome. These two sets move toward opposite sides of the zygote, and the single cell splits neatly down the middle into two cells, each containing the original genetic code. These two cells duplicate and divide, becoming four, which themselves duplicate and divide, becoming eight, and so on.

Every Cell the Same

By the time a baby is born, the zygote has become about 10 trillion cells, all influenced by the material that was once called junk and by whatever nutrients, drugs, hormones, viruses, and so on came from the pregnant woman. By adulthood, those cells become more than 100 trillion—again, all affected by the environment.

But no matter how old a person, how large the total number of cells, or how much division and duplication occur, almost every cell carries a complete copy of the genetic instructions of the one-celled zygote. This explains why DNA testing of any body cell, even from a drop of blood or a snip of hair, can identify "the real father," "the guilty criminal," "the long-lost brother."

DNA lingers long after death, evident in living African Americans who claimed Thomas Jefferson as an ancestor: DNA testing proved some of them right and some of them wrong (Foster et al., 1998). Indeed, because the Y chromosome is passed down to every male descendent, men have the Y of their male ancestors who died thousands of years ago. Tracing that Y chromosome suggests that thousands of East Asian men are descendants of Genghis Khan—although that twelfth-century leader's bones and thus his DNA have never been found (Stoneking & Delfin, 2010).

Stem Cells

If the two-celled organism is artificially split apart and each of those two separated cells duplicates, divides, and survives (an illegal practice for humans, successful with mice), that creates twins who begin as one zygote. Every cell of both of them would have the same DNA. However, barring dangerous and radical intervention, cells can become a complete creature *only* during the first few hours after conception—not later, even though they still have the same DNA as the original zygote.

The first cells are called **stem cells,** able to produce any other cell and thus to become a complete person. After about the eight-cell stage, duplication and division continue and a third process, *differentiation,* begins. Cells specialize, taking different forms and reproducing at various rates, depending on where they are located. For instance, some cells become part of an eye, others part of a finger, still others part of the brain. As one expert explains, "We are sitting with parts of our body that could have been used for thinking" (Gottlieb, 1992/2002, p. 172).

Scientists have discovered ways to add genes to differentiated cells in a laboratory process that reprograms those cells, making them like stem cells again. However, using those reprogrammed stem cells to cure genetic conditions is not yet feasible because inserting reprogrammed stem cells into a person may wreak havoc, causing cancers and even death. Although thousands of scientists are seeking to overcome that problem, currently reprogrammed cells are used only for testing drugs to treat diseases that are caused by genes, either directly (such as sickle-cell anemia) or indirectly (such as heart disease, diabetes, and dementia) (Vogel, 2010).

Some U.S. restrictions on stem cell research were lifted in 2009, and some states (e.g., California) and nations (e.g., South Korea) allow more extensive research, but

ALL: ANATOMICAL TRAVELOGUE / PHOTO RESEARCHERS, INC.

First Stages of the Germinal Period The original zygote as it divides into *(a)* two cells, *(b)* four cells, and *(c)* eight cells. Occasionally at this early stage, the cells separate completely, forming the beginning of monozygotic twins, quadruplets, or octuplets.

stem cells Cells from which any other specialized type of cell can form.

>> Answer to Observation Quiz (from page 67) Probably not. The Y sperm are slightly smaller, which can be detected via scientific analysis (some cattle breeders raise only steers using such analysis), but visual inspection, even magnified as in the photo, may be inaccurate.

everywhere many ethical and practical issues remain. As the head of the Michael J. Fox Foundation for Parkinson's Research said, "All my exposure was pop media. I thought it was all about stem cells. I have not totally lost hope on cell replacement, I just don't think it's a near-term hope" (Hood, quoted in Holden, 2009).

Twins

One "near-term hope" two decades ago has become reality. Millions of infertile couples have babies, often twins, increasing the demand for twin strollers, rhyming names, and newborn intensive care. To understand this, you need to know the difference between monozygotic and dizygotic twins.

Monozygotic Twins

Although every zygote is genetically unique, about once in 250 human conceptions, a complete split occurs after duplication, creating two, or four, or even eight separate zygotes, each identical to the first single cell. Such a split is illegal in a laboratory, but nature does it occasionally in the womb. (An incomplete split creates *conjoined twins,* formerly called Siamese twins.)

If each of those separated cells duplicates, divides, differentiates, implants, grows, and survives, multiple births occur. One separation results in **monozygotic (MZ) twins,** from one (*mono*) zygote (also called *identical twins*). Two or three separations create monozygotic quadruplets or octuplets. Because monozygotic multiples originate from the same zygote, they have identical genetic instructions for appearance, psychological traits, disease vulnerability, and everything else affected by genes.

Genetic identicals are blessed in at least one way: Monozygotic twins can donate an organ for surgical implantation in their twin with no organ rejection, thus avoiding a major complication with such transplants. They also befuddle their parents and teachers, who may use special signs (such as different earrings) to tell them apart. Usually, the twins themselves find their own identities while enjoying twinship. They might enjoy inherited athletic ability, for instance, with one playing basketball and the other soccer.

As one monozygotic twin writes:

> Twins put into high relief *the* central challenge for all of us: self-definition. How do we each plant our stake in the ground, decide how sensitive, callous, ambitious, cautious, or conciliatory we want to be every day? . . . Twins come with a built-in constant comparison, but defining oneself against one's twin is just an amped-up version of every person's life-long challenge: to individuate, to create a distinctive persona in the world.
>
> *[Pogrebin, 2010, p. 9]*

Dizygotic Twins

Among naturally conceived twins, only about one in three pairs is monozygotic. Most are **dizygotic (DZ) twins,** also called *fraternal twins.* They began life as two separate zygotes created by two ova fertilized by two sperm at the same time. (Usually, women release only one ovum per month, but sometimes double or triple ovulation occurs.) When dizygotic twinning occurs naturally, the incidence varies by ethnicity. For example, about 1 in 11 Yorubas in Nigeria is a twin, as are about 1 in 45 European Americans, 1 in 75 Japanese and Koreans, and 1 in 150 Chinese. Age matters, too: Older women more often double-ovulate and thus have more twins.

monozygotic (MZ) twins Twins who originate from one zygote that splits apart very early in development. (Also called *identical twins*.) Other monozygotic multiple births (such as triplets and quadruplets) can occur as well.

dizygotic (DZ) twins Twins who are formed when two separate ova are fertilized by two separate sperm at roughly the same time. (Also called *fraternal twins*.)

Like all full siblings, DZ twins have about half of their genes in common; they can differ markedly in appearance or they can look so much alike that only genetic tests can determine whether they are monozygotic or dizygotic. Chance determines which sperm fertilizes each ovum, so about half are same-sex pairs and half are boy–girl pairs.

Assisted Reproduction

When a couple are unable to conceive (true for about 12 percent of U.S. couples; international rates vary primarily because of health care), some choose **assisted reproductive technology (ART)**. A woman can take drugs to cause ovulation, often of several ova, which may lead to multiple births (see Figure 3.3). Or ova can be surgically removed from an ovary, fertilized in a glass lab dish, and then inserted into the uterus. This is **in vitro fertilization (IVF)**—*in vitro* literally means "in glass." Younger women and women of normal weight are more likely to have successful IVF pregnancies, but even among healthy young women, less than half of IVF cycles result in a baby.

Same Birthday, Same (or Different?) Genes Twins who are of different sexes or who have obvious differences in personality are dizygotic, sharing only half of their genes. Many same-sex twins with similar looks and temperaments are dizygotic as well. One of these twin pairs is dizygotic; the other is monozygotic.

Observation Quiz Can you tell which pair is monozygotic? (see answer, page 73)

assisted reproductive technology (ART) A general term for the techniques designed to help infertile couples conceive and then sustain a pregnancy.

in vitro fertilization (IVF) Fertilization that takes place outside a woman's body (as in a glass laboratory dish). The procedure involves mixing sperm with ova that have been surgically removed from the woman's ovary. If a zygote is produced, it is inserted into a woman's uterus, where it may implant and develop into a baby.

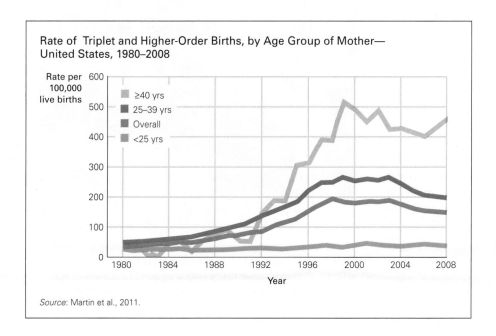

Rate of Triplet and Higher-Order Births, by Age Group of Mother—United States, 1980–2008

Source: Martin et al., 2011.

FIGURE 3.3

Why More Multiple Births? Historically in the United States, the natural rate of multiple births, particularly triplets and higher orders, tended to increase as mothers aged. Women in their mid- to late 30s were more likely to have twins than those who were younger. The advent of assisted reproductive technology (ART) led to a dramatic increase in multiple births overall starting in the early 1990s; it is now women aged 40 and over who are most likely to experience this phenomenon. After peaking in the late 1990s, rates of triplet and higher-order births seem to be on the decline, as the hazards of multiple births are more apparent.

Perfectly Legal Nadya Suleman takes 10 of her 14 children to the park. She was a medical miracle when her eight newborns all survived, thanks to expert care in a Los Angeles hospital. Soon thereafter, however, considerable controversy began: She was dubbed "Octomom" because—even though already a single mother of six children, including twins—she still opted to undergo in vitro fertilization, which resulted in implantation of her octuplets. Many believe implanting more than two zygotes is unethical and should be illegal. The license of Suleman's doctor was revoked, but the debate continues.

In IVF, to improve the odds of fertilization, a sperm can be inserted directly into each ovum, a procedure called *intra-cytoplasmic sperm injection (ICSI),* which is now standard. Then technicians can insert only one zygote, or only XX or XY zygotes, or as many zygotes as seem viable. Since the first "test-tube" baby in 1973, IVF has produced 4 million babies worldwide; in 2010, between 1 and 3 percent of all newborns in developed nations and thousands more in developing nations were the result of IVF.

Couples who once were childless now have children, sometimes children who are not biologically theirs if others provide the sperm and the ova. Donated sperm have been used for decades, resulting in millions of babies born after intrauterine insemination (formerly called *artificial insemination*). Donor ova and donor wombs (when an IVF embryo is implanted in a woman who did not provide the ovum) are increasingly common, although providing donor ova is more difficult for a woman than providing donor sperm is for a man. The word *donor* may be misleading, since people are paid for their sperm (up to $1,100), ova (up to $10,000 per ova), or surrogate pregnancies (up to $22,000) in addition to medical expenses.

Birth defects and later illnesses increase slightly with IVF (Kalra & Barnhart, 2011; Williams et al., 2011). Nonetheless, the risk is small: About 97 percent of all IVF newborns have no apparent defects.

Not small, however, is the risk of prematurity and low birthweight. In the United States, almost half of all IVF babies are low-birthweight twins or triplets (MMWR, June 12, 2009). Many couples who feared they could never have children suddenly have two tiny ones. Is this a problem? Consider the following.

THINKING CRITICALLY

Two Babies for the Price of One?

If you were infertile, would you welcome twins? Most scientists and doctors wish the answer was no, but most couples say yes. Couples want to avoid the cost (psychological and financial) of a second IVF cycle, so twins seem a bonus. If you were in a committed same-sex relationship, would you consider donor sperm, donor ova, or a donor womb? Many such couples say yes, to the consternation of many politicians.

Why do doctors hope for singletons and why do some people find IVF unethical? Ethics are a matter of culture and belief, and thus can be debated without obvious answers. But doctors have good reasons to hope for single births. Multiple births cause medical complications for mothers and infants, and they are costly for fathers, other siblings, and society as a whole. Indeed, twins and triplets have higher rates of death, disease, and disabilities lifelong. Even when compared with equally small singletons, multiples tend to develop more slowly and form weaker social bonds (Feldman & Eidelman, 2004).

Some nations make IVF twins a rare event. Finland allows insertion of only one IVF embryo per cycle, a move that did not reduce the rate of successful pregnancies but did increase the rate of full-term single births (Yli-Kuha et al., 2009). Similar

Mama Is 60 Wu Jingzhou holds his newborn twin daughters, born to his 60-year-old wife after in vitro fertilization. Ordinarily, it is illegal in China, as in most other nations, for women to have children after menopause. But an exception was made for this couple since the death of their only child, a young woman named Tingling, was partly the government's fault.

results were found in the United States when an experiment funded only single-embryo transfer (Stillman et al., 2009). Most European nations limit numbers per IVF cycle when government health care pays for the procedure. China now allows more than one IVF zygote if a couple is infertile or if their only child died—as was the case for one 60-year-old woman who had twins (see photo).

Governments vary in other restrictions, as cultures differ regarding ethics. Switzerland requires that ART be used only "when future child welfare can be guaranteed," which usually means that low-income couples are not eligible. An Italian law in 2004 outlawed donor sperm or ova, required that couples be married and heterosexual, and insisted that three embryos be inserted if three were viable, thereby increasing medical complications and fetal deaths and limiting births (Italy already had the lowest birth rate in the world).

The Italian courts in 2009 lifted some of those restrictions, and more infertile Italian couples gave birth (Levi Setti et al., 2011). U.S. laws vary by state. Many wealthy couples travel to different states or nations if ART is not available where they live.

In the United States, IVF can be costly, but even when it is not, as when military insurance pays for it, Latino couples hesitate whereas rates increase among African and European Americans (McCarthy-Keith et al., 2010). When three or more embryos implant, doctors often recommend selective reduction (abortion) of some embryos to protect the others. Not every woman agrees, as was dramatically illustrated by the eight fragile infants born in California in 2009—a miracle or a disaster? (See photo on page 72.) Is ART an issue for elected officials, for judges, for medical ethicists? Or is every aspect of reproduction a personal choice?

SUMMING UP

People usually have 23 chromosomes from their mother and 23 from their father, with all the genes and chromosomes matched up into mother–father pairs—although the match may not be letter perfect because of alleles. The father's 23rd chromosome pair is XY, which means that half his sperm are X and half are Y, determining the future baby's sex. The genes of the zygote duplicate themselves, as that first single cell becomes two cells, four, eight, and so on. Although those early cells are stem cells, and each could become a whole person, soon the cells begin to differentiate as they multiply. Each cell becomes a particular type, traveling to the location on the body where it will perform whatever is needed, becoming skin, blood, bone, part of the brain, and so on.

Twins are monozygotic (one zygote, from the same stem cells) or dizygotic (two zygotes). Assisted reproduction technology has increased the rate of multiple births. Modern reproductive measures, including IVF, have led to millions of much-wanted, healthy infants but also to new dilemmas, including whether people should be able to choose the sex, the genetic and biological parentage, and the number of newborns they have.

>> **Answer to Observation Quiz** (from page 71) The Japanese American girls are the monozygotic twins. If you were not sure, look at their teeth, their eyebrows, and the shape of their faces, compared with the ears and chins of the boys.

>> From One Cell to Many

As already explained, when sperm and ovum combine into a zygote, they establish the *genotype:* all the genes that the developing person has. Creation of a person from one cell involves several complex processes that form the **phenotype**—the person's appearance, behavior, and brain and body functions. Nothing is totally genetic, not even such obvious traits as height or hair color, but nothing is untouched by genes, not even social traits such as political views or propensity to marry and divorce (Rutter, 2011).

The genotype instigates body and brain formation, but the phenotype depends on many genes and on the environment, influenced from the moment of conception until the moment of death through "the organism's encounters with its prenatal and postnatal environments" (Gottlieb, 2010, p. 26). Most traits are **polygenic** (affected by many genes) and **multifactorial** (influenced by many factors, including biological and psychological ones). A zygote might have the genes for becoming,

phenotype The observable characteristics of a person, including appearance, personality, intelligence, and all other traits.

polygenic Referring to a trait that is influenced by many genes.

multifactorial Referring to a trait that is affected by many factors, both genetic and environmental, that enhance, halt, shape, or alter the expression of genes, resulting in a phenotype that may differ markedly from the genotype.

say, a musical genius, but that potential is not usually realized. Some crucial factors in development of the zygote are in the genome itself, because

> genes occupy only about 1.5 percent of the genome. The other 98.5 percent, dubbed "junk DNA," was regarded as useless scraps . . . most of this supposedly useless DNA now appears to produce transcriptions of its genetic code, boosting the raw information output of the genome to about 62 times what the gene alone would produce.
>
> *[Barry, 2007, p. 154]*

Almost daily, researchers describe additional complexities in polygenic and multifactorial interaction. It is apparent that "phenotypic variation . . . results from multiple interactions among numerous genetic and environmental factors." To unravel this "fundamental problem of interrelating genotype and phenotype in complex traits" (Nadeau & Dudley, 2011, p. 1015), we begin with epigenetics.

Epigenetics

Research over the past two decades has found that every trait—psychological as well as physical—is influenced by genes. At first, some scientists thought that genes *determined* everything, that humans became whatever their genes destined them to be—heroes, killers, or ordinary people. Research quickly revealed the limitations of this hypothesis.

Even monozygotic twins are not totally identical—biologically, psychologically, or socially. Many people mistakenly believe that genes determine biology, but hundreds of factors after conception, beginning with the effects of the nongenetic material surrounding the zygote and the nutrition that results from the particular placement of the embryo in the womb, influence the biology of the person. Genes affect everything but determine nothing.

Instead, all important human characteristics are **epigenetic.** The prefix *epi-* means "with," "around," "before," "after," "beyond," or "near." The word *epigenetic*, therefore, refers to the environmental factors that surround the genes, affecting genetic expression. Some "epi" influences occur in the first hours of life as biochemical elements silence certain genes in methylation that results from the material surrounding the genes. The details of this process are not yet clear: Thousands of biologists are trying to understand exactly how methylation develops and in what ways it alters genetic expression (Margueron & Reinberg, 2010).

For developmentalists, one fascinating finding is that methylation changes over the life span (Mazin, 2009). Another important finding is that all the diseases known to be genetic (including cancer, schizophrenia, and autism) are actually epigenetic (Saey, 2008). Certain environmental influences (such as injury, temperature extremes, drug abuse, and crowding) can impede genetic development, whereas others (nourishing food, loving care, play) can facilitate it. No trait—even one with strong, proven, genetic origins, such as blood pressure or social anxiety—is determined by genes alone because "development is an epigenetic process that entails cascades of interactions across multiple levels of causation, from genes to environments" (Spencer et al., 2009, p. 80).

The inevitable epigenetic interaction between genes and the environment (nature and nurture) is illustrated in Figure 3.4. That simple diagram, with arrows going up and down over time, has been redrawn and reprinted dozens of times since it was first published in 1992, reiterating that genes interact with environmental conditions again and

epigenetic Referring to environmental factors that affect genes and genetic expression—enhancing, halting, shaping, or altering the expression of genes and resulting in a phenotype that may differ markedly from the genotype.

FIGURE 3.4

An Epigenetic Model of Development
Notice that there are as many arrows going down as going up, at all levels. Although development begins with genes at conception, it requires that all four factors interact.

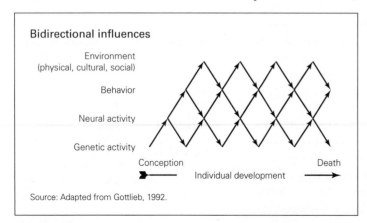

Source: Adapted from Gottlieb, 1992.

again in each person's life (Gottlieb, 2010). All this is a prelude to the explanation of genetic interaction: Epigenetics reminds us that genes are only the beginning.

Gene–Gene Interactions

Many discoveries have followed the completion of the **Human Genome Project** in 2001. One of the first surprises was that humans have far fewer than 100,000 genes, the number everyone believed throughout the twentieth century. The total number of genes in a person is between 18,000 and 23,000. The precise number is elusive because—another surprise—it is not always easy to figure out where one gene starts and another ends, or even if a particular stretch of DNA is actually a gene (Rouchka & Cha, 2009).

Another unexpected finding is that all living creatures share many genes. For example, the eyes of flies, mice, and people all originate from the *Pax6 gene*. Similarly, the legs in many species—including the butterfly, the cat, the centipede, and the person—all begin with the same gene. Perhaps even odder is that chimpanzees have 48 chromosomes and people merely 46, yet humans and chimpanzees have almost all (an estimated 99 percent) of their genes in common. What makes humans unlike other animals? The answer lies partly in that "junk" around the genes (lower creatures have far less of it) and partly in 100 or so "regulator" genes, all of which influence thousands of other genes (Shapiro, 2009), directing formation of a creature who talks in words, walks on two legs, and thinks as people do.

The crucial factor that differentiates humans is in the brain. Adult brain size (about 1,400 cubic centimeters) is highly heritable (monozygotic twins are very alike) and is quite similar among humans worldwide, especially when compared with the small chimpanzee brains (about 370 cubic centimeters). Bigger animals (elephants) have bigger brains, but the proportion of brain to body is much greater for humans than for other creatures.

One caution here: Although brain size among humans correlates with body size (women, on average, have smaller brains than men), human brain size does not correlate with intelligence. Furthermore, some animals have brain capacities that people do not, such as an acute sense of smell. Nonetheless, something genetic in the way our brains function makes us uniquely human (Allen et al., 2008; Damasio, 2010; Ramachandran, 2011).

Additive Heredity

Some alleles are *additive* because their effects *add up* to influence the phenotype. When genes interact additively, the phenotype usually reflects the contributions of every gene that is involved. Height, hair curliness, and skin color, for instance, are usually the result of additive genes. Indeed, height is probably influenced by 180 genes, each contributing a very small amount (Enserink, 2011).

Most people have ancestors of varied height, hair curliness, skin color, and so on, so their children's phenotype does not mirror the parents' phenotypes (although it does always reflect their genotypes). I see this in my family: Our daughter Rachel is of average height, shorter than my husband or I but taller than our mothers. Rachel evidently inherited some of her grandmothers' height genes from us. And none of my children have exactly my skin color—apparent when we borrow clothes from one another and realize that a particular tint is attractive on one of us but not on the other.

How any additive trait turns out depends partly on all the genes a child happens to inherit (half from each parent, which means one-fourth from each grandparent). Some genes amplify or dampen the effects of other genes, aided by all the other DNA and RNA (not junk!) in the zygote.

Human Genome Project An international effort to map the complete human genetic code. This effort was essentially completed in 2001, though analysis is ongoing.

HYBRID MEDICAL ANIMATION / PHOTO RESEARCHERS, INC.

Twelve of Three Billion Pairs This is a computer illustration of a small segment of one gene, with several triplets. Even a small difference in one gene, such as a few extra triplets, can cause major changes in the phenotype of a person.

Especially for Future Parents Suppose you wanted your daughters to be short and your sons to be tall. Could you achieve that? (see response, page 77)

dominant–recessive pattern The inter-action of a heterozygous pair of alleles in such a way that the phenotype reflects one allele (the dominant gene) more than the other (the recessive gene).

carrier A person whose genotype includes a gene that is not expressed in the pheno-type. The carried gene occurs in half of the carrier's gametes and thus is passed on to half of the carrier's children. If such a gene is inherited from both parents, the characteristic appears in the phenotype.

X-linked A gene carried on the X chromo-some. If a male inherits an X-linked reces-sive trait from his mother, he expresses that trait because the Y from his father has no counteracting gene. Females are more likely to be carriers of X-linked traits but are less likely to express them.

Dominant–Recessive Heredity

Not all genes are additive. In one nonadditive form, alleles interact in a **dominant–recessive pattern,** in which one allele, the *dominant gene,* is more influential than the other, the *recessive gene.* The dominant gene controls the characteristic even when a recessive gene is the other half of a pair. When someone inherits a recessive gene that is not apparent in the phenotype, that person is said to be a **carrier** of that gene because the recessive gene is *carried* on the genotype.

Most recessive genes are harmless. For example, blue eyes are determined by a recessive allele and brown eyes by a dominant one, which means that a child con-ceived by a blue-eyed person and a brown-eyed one will usually have brown eyes. "Usually" is accurate, because sometimes a brown-eyed person is a carrier of the blue-eye gene. In that case, in a blue-eye/brown-eye couple, every child will have at least one blue-eye gene (from the blue-eyed parent) and half will have the blue-eye recessive gene from the other parent and thus have blue eyes. The other half will have a brown-eye dominant gene and thus have brown eyes, like the parent who is the carrier of the blue-eye gene. If two brown-eyed parents both have the blue-eye recessive gene, they could have a blue-eyed child (one chance in four)— and no one should raise doubts about the child's paternity (see Figure 3.5).

A special case of the dominant–recessive pattern occurs with genes that are **X-linked** (located on the X chromosome). If an X-linked gene is recessive—as are the genes for most forms of color blind-ness, many allergies, several diseases, and some learning disabilities—the fact that it is on the X chromosome is criti-cal in determining whether it will be ex-pressed in the phenotype (see Table 3.1).

Since the Y chromosome is much smaller than the X, an X-linked recessive gene almost never has a counterpart on the Y chromosome. Therefore, recessive traits carried on the X affect the pheno-types of sons more often than those of daughters because the daughters have another X chromosome, usually with the dominant gene. This explains why males with an X-linked disorder inherited it from their mothers, not their fathers. Because of their mothers, 20 times more boys than girls are color-blind (McIntyre, 2002).

B = Gene for brown eyes   b = Gene for blue eyes

FIGURE 3.5

A Changeling? No. Many brown-eyed people carry a recessive gene for blue eyes. The only way to know for sure is if they have a blue-eyed parent (who gives one gene for blue eyes to every child) or if they have a blue-eyed child. Other recessive genes include red hair, Rh negative blood, and many genetic diseases.

More Complications

As complex as the preceding explanation may seem, it simplifies genetic interaction by making genes appear to be separately functioning entities. But remember that genes merely direct the creation of 20 types of amino acids, which combine to pro-duce thousands of proteins. Those proteins then interact with other proteins, nutri-ents, and toxins, beginning with thousands of RNA molecules and other material at conception, continuing throughout prenatal development and throughout life.

Copy Number Variations

For any living creature, the outcome of all the interactions involved in heredity is difficult to predict. A small deletion, repetition, or transposition in any of the 3 billion base pairs, or several extra repetitions of a triplet, may be inconsequential, lethal, or something in between. When the human genome was first mapped in

TABLE 3.1	The 23rd Pair and X-Linked Color Blindness: Six Possibilities		
23rd Pair	Phenotype	Genotype	Next Generation
1. XX	Unaffected woman	Not a carrier	No color blindness from mother
2. XY	Unaffected man	No color-blind gene	No color blindness from father
3. XX	Unaffected woman	Carrier from mother or father	Half her children will inherit her color-blind X. Half her girls will be carriers; half her boys will be color-blind.
4. XX	Unaffected woman	Carrier from mother	Half her children will inherit her color-blind X. Half her girls will be carriers; half her boys will be color-blind.
5. XY	Color-blind man	Inherited from mother	All his daughters will carry his color-blind X. None of his sons will have his color-blind X. All his children will have normal vision, unless their mother also had an X for color blindness.
6. XX	Color-blind woman (rare)	Inherited from both parents	Every child will have one color-blind X from her. Therefore, every son will be color-blind. Daughters will only be carriers, unless they also inherit a color-blind X from the father.

2001, headlines trumpeted that accomplishment. It was hoped that a specific gene could be located for each genetic disorder and that a cure would soon follow.

That "one gene/one disorder" hope proved to be fantasy, disappointing many doctors who hoped that personalized medicine was imminent (Marshall, 2011). Molecular analysis found, instead, that thousands of seemingly minor variations in base pairs turn out to be influential—each in small ways. Since there are 3 billion base pairs, accumulated variations have notable impact.

Attention has focused on **copy number variations,** which are genes with various repeats or deletions of base pairs. Copy number variations correlate with almost every disease and condition, including heart disease, intellectual abilities, mental illness, and many cancers. Such variations are partly developmental, in that they are often more influential prenatally than in adulthood because that is when the basic brain structures are formed. But remember plasticity—changes can occur lifelong (Chaignat et al., 2011).

Copy number variations are "abundant"—we all have some of them (Mills et al., 2011). Detecting and interpreting such variations may be crucial for the personalized medicine of the future. For instance, many drugs work differently depending on the genetic structure of the recipient; specific factors that lead directly to effective treatment of individual patients need to be better understood (Marshall, 2011).

Parental Imprinting

Sometimes one half of a gene pair switches off during prenatal development, allowing the other free rein but potentially causing a problem if that remaining gene has a deleterious variation. In fact, for girls, one X of the 23rd pair is deactivated early in prenatal life.

Switching-off probably happens during differentiation. This gives rise to a new hope: Perhaps making cells return to the stem cell stage of embryonic development will counter the problem of inactivation and solve some problems of genetic medicine (Lengner, 2010). For girls, it seems random whether the inactive X is

copy number variations Genes with various repeats or deletions of base pairs.

>> Response for Future Parents (from page 75) Yes, but you wouldn't want to. You would have to choose one mate for your sons and another for your daughters, and you would have to use sex-selection methods. Even so, it might not work, given all the genes on your genotype. More important, the effort would be unethical, unnatural, and possibly illegal.

She Laughs Too Much No, not the smiling sister, but the 10-year-old on the right, who has Angelman syndrome. She inherited it from her mother's chromosome 15. Fortunately, her two siblings inherited the mother's other chromosome 15 and are normal. If she had inherited the identical deletion on her father's chromosome 15, she would have developed Prader-Willi syndrome, which would cause her to be overweight as well as always hungry and often angry. With Angelman syndrome, however, laughing, even at someone's pain, is a symptom.

from the ovum or sperm, but geneticists wonder if reactivating genes on that inactive X could treat genetic diseases.

A related complexity is *parental imprinting:* Some genes are affected by whether they came from the mother or the father. The best-known examples of imprinting are two syndromes, Prader-Willi and Angelman. Both result in cognitive impairment, and both are caused by a deletion of the same small part of chromosome 15. However, if that deletion is inherited from the father's chromosome 15, the child will have Prader-Willi syndrome and be obese, slow-moving, and stubborn. If that deletion is from the mother's chromosome 15, the child will have Angelman syndrome and be thin, hyperactive, and happy—sometimes too happy, laughing when no one else does.

Parental imprinting is quite common. Early in prenatal development (day 15), an estimated 553 genes act differently if they come from the mother or from the father—a much higher frequency than previously thought. It is possible that imprinting may differ for XX versus XY embryos. For instance, women are more likely to inherit multiple sclerosis from their mothers than from their fathers, and men are less likely to develop it at all (Gregg, 2010): Could imprinting be involved? Many other traits affect one sex more than the other: Imprinting is one of the dozens of plausible biological and cultural explanations.

SUMMING UP

The distinction between genotype (heredity) and phenotype (manifest appearance and observed behavior) is only one of the many complexities involved in trying to understand the influence of genes on development. All traits are epigenetic, the product of nongenetic influences, beginning with methylation at conception and continuing lifelong. Furthermore, most traits are polygenic, the result of many genes that interact—some additively and some in a dominant–recessive pattern, with thousands of minor variations in base pairs. Some genetic effects vary in ways not yet understood, depending on which genes came from the mother and which from the father. ■

>> Genotype and Phenotype

The goal of this chapter is to help every reader grasp the complex interaction between genotype and phenotype. This is not easy. For the past 100 years in virtually every nation, a million scientists have struggled to understand this complexity. Each new decade brings advances in statistics and molecular analysis, as well as data that uncover various patterns. Each decade also raises new questions.

Current Consensus

Developmentalists today accept four generalities that were surprising when first reported (Gottlieb, 2010; Plomin et al., 2008; Rutter, 2011; Worthman et al., 2010):

1. Genes affect every aspect of behavior, including social interactions, intellectual abilities, even political values and reactions.
2. Most environmental influences on children raised in the same home are *not shared* (more on this in Chapter 13).
3. Genes elicit responses that shape development. Thus, personality may be partly the cause of a person's experiences, not merely the result.

4. Lifelong, people choose friends and environments that encourage their genetic predispositions (called *niche-picking*). Thus, genetic effects *increase* with age.

Every trait, action, and attitude has a genetic component: Without genes, no development could occur. Yet every trait, action, and attitude has an environmental component; without context, genes have no power. An easy example is height, powerfully influenced by genes. However, although Koreans, for instance, share many genes, adults in North Korea are on average 3 inches shorter than those in South Korea. The probable reason is chronic famine in North Korea (Johnson, 2010; Schwekendiek, 2009). A more surprising example is political ideology: Several researchers report that a particular allele of a dopamine receptor gene (DRD4-R7) correlates with being liberal, but one recent study finds this connection only if a person has many friends. Loners with the liberal-leaning gene tend to be more conservative (Settle et al., 2010).

Now we examine two complex traits: addiction and visual acuity. As you read about specific expressions of those traits (alcoholism and nearsightedness), you will see that understanding the progression from genotype to phenotype has many practical implications for child development.

Alcoholism

At various times, people have considered the abuse of alcohol and other drugs to be a moral weakness, a social scourge, or a personality defect. Historically, attention has been on alcohol, since that drug occurs naturally from fermentation and people everywhere have drunk it. In diverse times and places, alcoholics were locked up, doused with cold water, or burned at the stake. Alcohol has also been declared illegal (as in the United States from 1919 to 1933) as well as deemed a sacred part of religious observance (as in many Judeo-Christian rituals). We now know that, because inherited biochemistry affects alcohol metabolism, laws, treatments, and traditions have varied impacts on individuals.

Genes create an addictive pull that can be overpowering, extremely weak, or somewhere in between. To be specific, each person's biochemistry reacts to alcohol, causing sleep, nausea, aggression, joy, relaxation, forgetfulness, sex urges, or tears. How bodies metabolize alcohol allows some people to "hold their liquor" and therefore drink too much, whereas others (including many East Asians) sweat and become red-faced after just a few sips—an embarrassing response that may lead to abstinence. Candidate genes for alcoholism have been identified on every chromosome except the Y chromosome (ironic, since, internationally, more men than women are alcoholics) (Epps & Holt, 2011). Every research scientist agrees: Alcoholism is polygenic and culture is pivotal.

Although the emphasis has been on metabolism, inherited psychological characteristics may be as influential for alcoholism (Macgregor et al., 2009). A quick temper, sensation seeking, or high anxiety encourage drinking. Moreover, some contexts (such as fraternity parties) make it hard to abstain; other contexts (a church social in a "dry" county) make it difficult to swallow anything stronger than lemonade.

Biological sex (XX or XY) and gender (cultural) also affect the risk of alcoholism. For biological reasons (body size, fat composition, metabolism), women become drunk on less alcohol than men, but how much a woman drinks depends on her social context. For example, in Japan, both sexes have the same genes for metabolizing alcohol, yet women drink only about one-tenth as much as men. When Japanese women live in the United States, their alcohol consumption increases about fivefold (Higuchi et al., 1996). It seems as if people of Asian descent who are born in the United States take on the drinking patterns of their fellow Americans, perhaps to the detriment of Japanese American women (Makimoto, 1998).

MARCO C. PEREIRA / SARA WONG / 4SEE / REDUX

Hidden Husband Shyness is inherited, but this mother seems not to have the gene. Probably her husband is the shy one—unless nurture has taught the daughter to be shy and the mother to be outgoing.

AP PHOTO / PELLE RINK / POLFOTO

Is He Drunk? This worker at Carlsberg Breweries in Copenhagen was one of many who benefited from company policy—beer available all day long from coolers placed throughout the work floor. In 2010, the policy changed: No more coolers, and beer could be consumed only at lunch. Many employees walked off their jobs in protest. Social attitudes about alcohol added intensity to this labor–management conflict.

Especially for Future Drug Counselors Is the wish for excitement likely to lead to addiction? (see response, page 81)

Nearsightedness

Age, genes, and culture affect vision as well. First consider age. Newborns focus only on things within 2 feet of their eyes; vision improves steadily until about age 10; the eyeball changes shape at puberty, increasing nearsightedness (myopia), and again in middle age, decreasing myopia, hence distance vision improves.

Now consider genes. A study of British twins found that the Pax6 gene, which governs eye formation, has many alleles that make people somewhat nearsighted (Hammond et al., 2004). This research found *heritability* of almost 90 percent, which means that if one monozygotic twin was nearsighted, the other twin was almost always nearsighted, too.

Heritable?

heritability A statistic that indicates what percentage of the variation in a particular trait within a particular population, in a particular context and era, can be traced to genes.

However, **heritability** is a statistic that indicates only how much of the variation in a particular trait *within a particular population* in a particular context and era can be traced to genes. For example, the heritability of height is very high (about 95 percent) when children receive good medical care and ample nourishment, but it is low (about 20 percent) when children are malnourished. Thus, the 90 percent heritability of nearsightedness among the British children may not apply elsewhere.

Indeed it does not. Visual problems may be caused by the environment. In some African nations, heritability of vision is close to zero because severe vitamin A deficiency is the main reason some children see less well than others. Scientists are working to develop a strain of maize (the local staple) high in vitamin A. If they succeed, heritability will increase and overall vision will improve (Harjes et al., 2008). But what about children who are well nourished? Is their vision entirely inherited? Cross-cultural research suggests that it is not.

One report claims "myopia is increasing at an 'epidemic' rate, particularly in East Asia" (Park & Congdon, 2004, p. 21), and another cites "very strong environmental impacts" on Asian children's vision (Morgan, 2003, p. 276). The first published research on this phenomenon appeared in 1992, when scholars noticed that, in army-mandated medical exams of all 17-year-old males in Singapore, 26 percent were nearsighted in 1980 but 43 percent were nearsighted in 1990 (Tay et al., 1992).

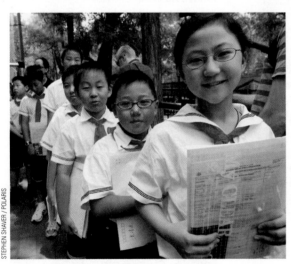

Bright-Eyed and Nearsighted These are star students from Beijing, China, waiting in line for visas to the United States. If they had spent less time studying, would they be here?

Further studies found nearsightedness increasing from 12 to 84 percent between ages 6 and 17 in Taiwan, with increases in myopia during middle childhood also in Singapore and Hong Kong (cited in Grosvenor, 2003). Some of this may be the natural increase in myopia at puberty, but not this much. Nurture must somehow be involved. But how?

Outdoor Play?

One possible culprit is homework. In Chapter 12, you will learn that, unlike earlier generations, contemporary East Asian children are amazingly proficient in math and science. Fifty years ago, most Asian children were working; now all attend school and study more than their peers in other nations. As their developing eyes focus on the print in front of them, those with a genetic vulnerability to myopia may lose acuity for objects far away—which is exactly what nearsightedness means.

A study of Singaporean 10- to 12-year-olds found a correlation between nearsightedness (measured by optometric exams) and high achievement, especially in language (presumably reflecting more reading). Correlation is not causation, but statistics (odds ratio of 2.5, significance of 0.001) suggest a link (Saw et al., 2007).

Ophthalmologists believe that the underlying cause is not time spent studying but inadequate time spent in daylight. Perhaps if Asian children spent more time outside playing, walking, or relaxing, fewer might need glasses. This recommendation is supported by an editorial in a leading U.S. journal for ophthalmologists:

> The probability of becoming myopic by the eighth grade is about 60% if a child has two myopic parents and does less than 5 hours per week of sports/outdoor activity. . . . [It is] about 20% if a two-myopic-parent child does 14 hours or more per week of sports/outdoor activity.
>
> *[Mutti & Zadnik, 2009, p. 77]*

Between the early 1970s and the early 2000s, nearsightedness in the U.S. population increased from 25 to 42 percent (Vitale et al., 2009). Urbanization, television, and fear of strangers have kept many U.S. children indoors most of the time, unlike earlier generations who played outside for hours each day. To prove a causal link, a longitudinal experiment that keeps some children indoors while their siblings (to control for genes) play outside would be helpful, but that is impossible. Nonetheless, the correlational data on nearsightedness, as well as on alcoholism and on other genetic conditions, has many implications.

Practical Applications

Since genes affect every disorder, no one should be blamed or punished for inherited problems. However, knowing that genes do not act in isolation can lead to preventive measures when genetic vulnerability is apparent. For instance, if alcoholism is in the genes, parents can keep alcohol out of their home, hoping their children become cognitively and socially mature before drinking. If nearsightedness runs in the family, parents can make sure that children play outdoors every day.

Of course, outdoor play and abstention from alcohol are recommended for every child, as are dozens of other behaviors, such as flossing the teeth, saying "please," getting enough sleep, eating vegetables, and writing thank-you notes. However, no parent can enforce every recommendation. Awareness of genetic risks helps parents set priorities and act on them.

Ignoring the nature–nurture interaction can be lethal. Consider baseball superstar Mickey Mantle, who hit more home runs in World Series baseball than any other player. Most of his male relatives were alcoholics and died before middle age, including his father, who died of Hodgkin disease (a form of cancer) at age 39. Mantle became "a notorious alcoholic [because he]believed a family history of early mortality meant he would die young" (Jaffe, 2004, p. 37). He ignored his genetic predisposition to alcoholism.

At age 46 Mantle said, "If I knew I was going to live this long, I would have taken better care of myself." He never developed Hodgkin disease, and if he had, chemotherapy developed since his father's death would likely have saved him—an example of environment prevailing over genes. However, drinking destroyed his liver. He understood too late what he had done. When he was dying, he told his fans at Yankee Stadium: "Please don't do drugs and alcohol. God gave us only one body, keep it healthy. If you want to do something great, be an organ donor" (quoted in Begos, 2010). Despite a last-minute liver transplant, he died at age 63—15 years younger than most men of his time.

SUMMING UP

Genes affect every trait—whether it is something wonderful, such as a wacky sense of humor; something fearful, such as a violent temper; or something quite ordinary, such as a tendency to be bored. The environment affects every trait as well, in ways that change as maturational, cultural, and historical processes unfold. Genes themselves can be modified through epigenetic factors, including drugs and nutrition. Furthermore,

>> Response for Future Drug Counselors (from page 79) Maybe. Some people who love risk become addicts; others develop a healthy lifestyle that includes adventure, new people, and exotic places. Any trait can lead in various directions. You need to be aware of the connection so that you can steer your clients toward healthy adventures.

genetic expression can be directed or deflected, depending on the culture and the society as well as on the individual and the family. This is apparent in height, alcoholism, nearsightedness, and almost every other physical and psychological condition. All have genetic roots, developmental patterns, and environmental triggers. ▪

>> Chromosomal and Genetic Problems

We now focus on conditions caused by an extra chromosome or a single destructive gene. These are abnormalities in that they are not the norm (hence called *ab*normal). Three factors make these conditions relevant to our study:

1. They provide insight into the complexities of nature and nurture.
2. Knowing their origins helps limit their effects.
3. Information combats prejudice: Difference is not always deficit.

Not Exactly 46

As you know, each gamete usually has 23 chromosomes, creating a zygote with 46 chromosomes and eventually a person. However, some gametes have more or fewer than 23 chromosomes. One variable that correlates with chromosomal abnormalities is the parents' age, particularly the age of the mother. A suggested explanation is that, since ova begin to form before a girl is born, older mothers have older ova, less likely to be 23–23.

These miscounts are not rare. One estimate is that about 5 to 10 percent of all conceptions have more or fewer than 46 chromosomes (Brooker, 2009); another estimate suggests that the rate is as high as 50 percent (Fragouli & Wells, 2011). Far fewer of such zygotes are born, less than 1 percent, primarily because most such organisms never duplicate, divide, differentiate, and implant. If implantation does occur, many are aborted, spontaneously (miscarried) or by choice. Birth itself is hazardous; about 5 percent of stillborn (dead-at-birth) babies have 47 chromosomes (O. J. Miller & Therman, 2001), and many abnormal but living newborns die within the first few days.

Each abnormality leads to a recognizable *syndrome,* a cluster of distinct characteristics that tend to occur together. Usually the cause is three chromosomes (a condition called a *trisomy*) at a particular location instead of the usual two. Once in about every 200 births, a newborn survives with 45, 47, or, rarely, 48 or 49 chromosomes.

Down Syndrome

The most common extra-chromosome condition that results in a surviving child is **Down syndrome,** also called *trisomy-21* because the person has three copies of chromosome 21. According to one estimate, a 20-year-old woman has about 1 chance in 800 of carrying a fetus with Down syndrome; a 39-year-old woman, 1 in 67; and a 44-year-old woman, 1 in 16. (Estimates vary, although all the data show marked increases with maternal age).

Some 300 distinct characteristics can result from that third chromosome 21. No individual with Down syndrome is identical to another, but most have specific facial characteristics—a thick tongue, round face, slanted eyes—as well as distinctive hands, feet, and fingerprints. Many also have hearing problems, heart abnormalities, muscle weakness, and short stature. They are usually slower to develop intellectually, especially in language, and they reach their maximum intellectual potential at about age 15 (Rondal, 2010). Some are severely retarded; others are of average or above-average intelligence. That extra chromosome affects the person

Down syndrome A condition in which a person has 47 chromosomes instead of the usual 46, with 3 rather than 2 chromosomes at the 21st site. People with Down syndrome typically have distinctive characteristics, including unusual facial features, heart abnormalities, and language difficulties. (Also called *trisomy-21*.)

lifelong, but family context, educational efforts, and possibly medication can improve the person's prognosis (Kuehn, 2011).

Problems of the 23rd Pair

Every human has at least 44 autosomes and one X chromosome; an embryo cannot develop without those 45. However, about 1 in every 500 infants is born with only one sex chromosome (no Y) or with three or more (not just two) (Hamerton & Evans, 2005). Having an odd number of sex chromosomes impairs cognitive and psychosocial development as well as sexual maturation. The specifics depend on the particular configuration as well as on other genetic factors. Sometimes only a part of that 23rd chromosome is missing, or a person with an extra chromosome is relatively unaffected by it. In such cases, the person seems to be a normal adult but typically is infertile (Mazzocco & Ross, 2007).

Gene Disorders

Everyone carries alleles that *could* produce serious diseases or handicaps in the next generation (see Table 3.2). Most such genes have no serious consequences because they are recessive. The phenotype is affected only when the inherited condition is dominant or when a zygote is homozygous for a particular recessive condition, that is, when the zygote has received the recessive gene from both parents.

Dominant Disorders

Most of the 7,000 *known* single-gene disorders are dominant (always expressed). They are usually easy to notice because their effects are evident in the phenotype. Severe dominant disorders are rare because people with such disorders rarely live long enough to reproduce and thus do not pass the gene on to children.

One exception is *Huntington disease,* a fatal central nervous system disorder caused by a genetic miscode—more than 35 repetitions of a particular triplet. Unlike most dominant traits, the effects do not begin until middle adulthood. By then a person could have had several children, and odds are that half would have inherited the same dominant gene. This was true for the original Mr. Huntington (Bates et al., 2002). Another exception is a rare but severe form of Alzheimer disease that causes dementia before age 60.

Recessive Disorders

Several recessive genetic disorders are sex-linked. The most famous of these is hemophilia, a blood disorder carried by Queen Victoria of England. She passed it on to her descendants, including Empress Alexandra, who bore the only male heir to the Russian throne, Crown Prince Alexi (Rogaev et al., 2009). Some historians suggest that X-linked hemophilia was a pivotal cause of antimonarchy revolutions, including the one that led to Communism in Russia in 1917. Alexi's parents were distracted from leading the nation and listened to irrational advice from Rasputin, a psychopathic "healer."

Another X-linked condition, **fragile X syndrome,** is caused by more than 200 repetitions of one triplet on one gene (Plomin et al., 2003). (Some repetitions are normal, but not this many.) The cognitive deficits caused by fragile X syndrome are the most common form of *inherited* mental retardation (many other forms, such as trisomy-21, are not inherited).

Since this is an X-linked, single-gene disorder, fragile X syndrome may be recessive; however, the exact inheritance pattern of fragile X is more complex than that

Universal Happiness All young children delight in painting brightly colored pictures on a big canvas, but this scene is unusual for two reasons: Daniel has trisomy-21, and this photograph was taken at the only school in Chile where normal and special-needs children share classrooms.

Especially for Future Doctors Might a patient who is worried about his or her sexuality have an undiagnosed abnormality of the sex chromosome? (see response, page 84)

Especially for Teachers Suppose you know that one of your students has a sibling who has Down syndrome. What special actions should you take? (see response, page 88)

Especially for Historians Some genetic diseases may have changed the course of history. For instance, the last czar of Russia had four healthy daughters and one son with hemophilia. Once called the royal disease, hemophilia is X-linked. How could this rare condition have affected the monarchies of Russia, England, Austria, Germany, and Spain? (see response, page 88)

fragile X syndrome A genetic disorder in which part of the X chromosome seems to be attached to the rest of it by a very thin string of molecules. The cause is a single gene that has more than 200 repetitions of one triplet.

TABLE 3.2	Common Genetic Diseases and Conditions					
Name	Description	Prognosis	Probable Inheritance	Incidence*	Carrier Detection?†	Prenatal Detection?
Albinism	No melanin; person is very blond, pale	Normal, but must avoid sun damage	Recessive	Carriers more common among Native and African Americans	No	No
Alzheimer disease	Memory loss; increasing mental impairment	Eventual death, often after years of dependency	Early onset—dominant; after age 60—multifactorial	Fewer than 1 in 100 early onset; more common in late adulthood	Yes, for early onset; yes, for risk factors.	No
Cancer	Tumors that can spread	Each type has different rates of cure and fatality	Multifactorial; almost all cancers have a genetic component	Most people eventually develop some type; about one-fourth die	No	No
Cleft palate, cleft lip	The two sides of the upper lip or palate are not joined	Correctable by surgery	Multifactorial	1 in every 700 births; more common in Asians and U.S. Indians	No	Yes
Club foot	The foot and ankle are twisted	Correctable by surgery	Multifactorial	1 in every 200 births; more boys than girls	No	Yes
Cystic fibrosis	Mucous obstructions, especially in lungs, stomach	Most live to middle adulthood	Recessive gene; also spontaneous mutations	1 in 3,200; 1 in 25 European Americans is a carrier	Sometimes	Yes, in most cases
Deafness (congenital)	Inability to hear	Language possible via signs, or cochlear implants	Multifactorial; some forms are recessive	1 in 1,000 births; more common in people from Middle East	No	No
Diabetes	Abnormal sugar metabolism; insufficient insulin	Early onset (type 1) fatal without insulin; later onset (type 2), variable	Multifactorial; for later onset, body weight is significant	Type 1: rare; type 2: 1 in 6, especially non–European Americans	No	No
Hemophilia	Absence of clotting factor in blood	Death from bleeding; blood transfusions prevent damage	X-linked recessive; also spontaneous mutations	1 in 10,000 males; royal families of Europe had it	No	No
Hydrocephalus	Obstruction causes excess fluid in the brain	Brain damage and death; surgery allows normal life	Multifactorial	1 in every 100 births	No	Yes
Muscular dystrophy (30 diseases)	Weakening of muscles	Inability to walk, move; wasting away; death	Recessive or multifactorial	1 in every 3,500 males develops Duchenne's	Yes, for some forms	Yes, for some forms

>> **Response for Future Doctors** (from page 83) That is highly unlikely. Chromosomal abnormalities are evident long before adulthood. It is quite normal for adults to be worried about sexuality for social, not biological, reasons. You could test the karyotype, but that may be needlessly alarmist.

of other X-linked conditions. Repetitions of the damaging triplet increase when the affected X chromosome passes from one generation to the next; more repetitions correlate with lower IQ, especially in boys.

Most recessive disorders are on the autosomes and thus are not X-linked. For example, cystic fibrosis, thalassemia, and sickle-cell anemia are all equally common and devastating in both sexes (see Table 3.2). About 1 in 12 North Americans is a carrier for one of these three. That high incidence occurs because carriers benefit from the gene (Brooker, 2009).

Name	Description	Prognosis	Probable Inheritance	Incidence*	Carrier Detection?[†]	Prenatal Detection?
Neural-tube defects (open spine)	Anencephaly (parts of the brain missing) or spina bifida (lower spine not closed)	Anencephalic—severe retardation; spina bifida—poor lower body control	Multifactorial; folic acid deficit and genes	Anencephaly:1 in 1,000; spina bifida: 3 in 1,000; more common in Welsh, Scots	No	Yes
Phenylketo-nuria (PKU)	Abnormal digestion of protein	Mental retardation, preventable by diet begun soon after birth	Recessive	1 in 100 European Americans is a carrier; higher among Irish, Norwegians	Yes	Yes
Pyloric stenosis	Overgrowth of muscle in intestine	Vomiting, weight loss, death; corrected by surgery	Multifactorial	1 boy in 200, 1 girl in 1,000; less in African Americans	No	No
Rett syndrome	Neurological developmental disorder	Boys die at birth; at 6–18 months, girls lose speech and motor skills	X-linked	1 in 10,000 female births	No	Sometimes
Schizo-phrenia	Severely distorted thought	Drugs, therapy ease symptoms	Multifactorial	1 in 100 people develop it by early adulthood	No	No
Sickle-cell anemia	Abnormal blood cells	Painful "crisis"; heart, kidney failure; treated with drugs	Recessive	1 in 11 African Americans and 1 in 20 Latinos are carriers	Yes	Yes
Tay-Sachs disease	Enzyme disease	Healthy infant becomes weaker, usually dying by age 5	Recessive	1 in 30 U.S. Jews and 1 in 20 French Canadians are carriers	Yes	Yes
Thalassemia	Abnormal blood cells	Low energy, vulnerable to infections, slow growth	Usually recessive, occasionally dominant	1 in 10 from Italy, Greece, India, Egypt are carriers	Yes	Yes
Tourette syndrome	Uncontrollable tics, body jerking, verbal outbursts	Appears at about age 5; worsens, then improves	Dominant, but variable penetrance	1 in 250 children	Sometimes	No

*Incidence statistics vary from country to country. For instance, the rate of PKU is 1 in 119,000 in Japan but is 26 times that in Ireland. Those given here are approximate for the United States, but all these diseases can occur in any ethnic group in any nation. Many affected groups limit transmission through genetic counseling; for example, the incidence of Tay-Sachs disease is declining because many Jewish young adults obtain testing and counseling before marriage.

[†]"Yes" refers to carrier detection. Family history can also reveal genetic risk.

Sources: Benacerraf, 2007; Butler & Meaney, 2005; Cruz-Inigo et al., 2011; Haydon, 2007; Hemminki et al., 2008; Klug et al., 2008; McKusick, 2007; K. L. Moore & Persaud, 2007; Shahin et al., 2002.

The most studied example of the benefits of recessive genes is sickle-cell anemia. Carriers of sickle-cell die less often from malaria, still prevalent in parts of Africa. Indeed, four distinct alleles cause sickle-cell anemia, each originating in a malaria-prone region. Selective adaptation allowed the gene to become widespread because it protected more people (the carriers) than it killed. About 11 percent of Americans with African ancestors are carriers. Similarly, cystic fibrosis is more common among Americans with ancestors from northern Europe; carriers may have been protected from cholera.

Genetic Counseling and Testing

Until recently, after the birth of a child with a disorder, couples blamed witches or fate, not genes or chromosomes. Today, many young adults worry about their genes long before they marry. Virtually everyone has a relative with a serious condition, and everyone wonders what their children will inherit. Researchers now know much more than they did about genes even a few years ago: Not every scientist believes the public is ready for that knowledge, as the following explains.

A VIEW FROM SCIENCE

Genetic Testing for Psychological Disorders

Might your genes increase your chances of developing a psychological disorder—say, schizophrenia, dementia, bipolar disorder, autism, or addiction? Should you seek genetic testing to learn more? The answer from science to these two questions is yes for all five conditions, and then no to testing.

No doubt genes are part of every psychological disorder. Thankfully, parents are no longer blamed for causing their children's autism. Yet the environment is crucial for every disorder —not only what the parents do but also what the community and governments do. You have already seen this with alcoholism. The same is true for almost every psychological condition.

Consider, for example, schizophrenia, a devastating condition that distorts thought and gives rise to hallucinations, delusions, garbled talk, and irrational emotions. When one monozygotic twin becomes schizophrenic, often—but not always—the other identical twin also develops a psychological disorder. For dizygotic twins and other siblings, the risk is much lower—about 12 percent for schizophrenia—but higher than the 1 percent incidence of schizophrenia for people who have no relatives

ASSOCIATED PRESS

Too Cute? This portrait of the Genain sisters was taken 20 years before they all developed schizophrenia. However, from their identical hair ribbons to the identical position of their feet, it is apparent that their unusual status as quadruplets set them apart as curiosities. Could their life in the spotlight have nurtured their potential for schizophrenia? There is no way to know for sure.

with the disease. This leaves no doubt that genes are one factor (Castle & Morgan, 2008), and some genetic-testing companies advertise an ability to detect vulnerabilities.

Yet note that even monozygotic twins differ, which means that schizophrenia cannot be simply genetic. That is apparent for non-twins as well. Children born to schizophrenic parents are at genetic risk but might not develop the disease. One careful study of the entire population of Denmark found that if both parents have the disease, 27 percent of their children develop it; if one parent has it, 7 percent of their children develop it. These same statistics can be presented another way: Even if both parents have schizophrenia, almost three-fourths (73 percent) of their children do not (Gottesman et al., 2010) (see the Research Design).

Among the known environmental causes are undernutrition of the mother during pregnancy, birth in the summer, use of psychoactive drugs in adolescence, emigration to another nation as a young adult, and family emotionality during adulthood. Because environment is crucial and many genes that increase vulnerability to schizophrenia remain to be found, few scientists advocate genetic testing for schizophrenia. Some worry that a positive test would lead to depression, lack of therapy, and more stigma for those who have mental illness than already exists (Mitchell et al., 2010).

In several U.S. states (California and New York among them), selling genetic tests is illegal without a physician's request, and most doctors test only to confirm diagnosis of a problem they already suspect. Nonetheless, many companies profit from genetic testing, and some people break the law to get the information they want. If they learn that they could develop a mental disorder, they might buy term-care insurance—a good investment for them but a bad one for insurance companies (D. H. Taylor et al., 2010). That might lead to more costly insurance for the general population and inferior care for those who cannot afford insurance. Another possibility is that people who learn they have a higher risk of illness or dementia might leave their families or even kill themselves. No wonder some places make genetic testing illegal.

However, any restriction seems unfair to people who want more information. The opposite problem often occurs: Children might be required to get genetic tests they do not want. The most obvious example comes not from tests for psychological conditions but from tests for known physical conditions. Some students who want to play sports in school must be tested for heart abnormalities and for the sickle-cell trait, both of which can cause sudden death if an otherwise healthy student becomes physically exhausted.

However, most young people who test positive never have a problem. If a positive test keeps someone off the team, is that fair? If that is fair, what about a test for behavior disorders? Should kindergartners be tested for antisocial behavior or attention-deficit/hyperactivity disorder so that their teachers or parents can be forewarned? But might that information itself cause a problem?

Finally, marked ethical issues are raised regarding a new blood test for pregnant women that reveals, through cells discarded by the embryo, if the future baby might have any of 100 or more genetic or chromosomal conditions (Greely, 2011). Will that lead to more abortions or more stress? If the test is not rec-

PHOTO BY GARY W. GREEN, USED WITH PERMISSION OF THE ORLANDO SENTINEL, © 2010

Praying Too Late The coaches of this high school football team wish they had known that 15-year-old Oliver Louis was a carrier for sickle-cell anemia. Perhaps then his death could have been prevented before he collapsed in practice, due to exertional sickling. His teammates pray before they play—should they also be tested for genetic vulnerability?

ommended and a baby is born with a genetic condition, will that lead to a lawsuit?

It is easy to understand why scientists hope that people will rely on behavior change (e.g., more exercise) to make us all healthier, not on genetic tests. On the other hand, people want information about themselves. Many researchers debate what data people should have and how they should get it (Couzin-Frankel, 2011). Science has revealed much more about genes than anyone imagined a decade ago. Laws and ethics have not kept up with the possibilities.

▶ **Research Design**

Scientists: Irving I. Gottesman, Thomas Munk Laursen, Aksel Bertelsen, and Preben Bo Mortensen.

Publication: *Archives of General Psychiatry* (2010).

Participants: Everyone born in Denmark between 1968 and 1997 whose parents were listed in the Denmark population archives.

Design: The researchers examined the psychiatric records of all the children in the study (more than 2 million of them), who were aged 10 to 52 at the time the study was done. The researchers also traced the medical records of the children's parents, noting hospital admission for psychiatric disorders. They found 196 couples (with 270 children) in which both the mother and father were hospitalized for schizophrenia and 83 couples (with 146 children) who were both admitted for bipolar disorder.

Results: Children born to parents with psychological disorders had much higher rates than average of developing a disorder. When both parents were schizophrenic, 27 percent of the children were hospitalized for schizophrenia and 12 percent had other severe disorders. Of those with only one schizophrenic parent, 7 percent developed that disorder. When neither parent was hospitalized for schizophrenia, less than 1 percent (0.86 percent) of the children were. Children whose parents had bipolar disorder had higher rates of other disorders (including depression) than the average person, but their illness rate was lower than that for children whose parents had schizophrenia.

Major conclusion: Genes confer vulnerability for serious mental disorders, especially schizophrenia. However, more than half of the children born to a schizophrenic mother and father escaped serious disorders themselves, and about 20,000 Danes who were hospitalized for schizophrenia had neither parent with the disorder.

Comments: This is an impressive study, since it included both parents of more than 2 million children. Such powerful research on a large population group with verified records (not just a selected sample with the researchers' assessment) is possible only in relatively small, developed nations with accurate records. Note, however, that the data are a correlation, not longitudinal. Even in Denmark, where every child gets good medical care, social services, and education, some of the burden of family schizophrenia may result from nurture, not nature.

ROBERT SPENCER / THE NEW YORK TIMES

"The Hardest Decision I Ever Had to Make" That's how this woman described her decision to terminate her third pregnancy when genetic testing revealed that the fetus had Down syndrome. She soon became pregnant again with a male fetus that had the normal 46 chromosomes, as did her two daughters and as will her fourth child, not yet born. Many personal factors influence such decisions. Do you think she and her husband would have made the same choice if they had had no other children?

genetic counseling Consultation and testing by trained experts that enable individuals to learn about their genetic heritage, including harmful conditions that they might pass along to any children they may conceive.

Genetic counseling relieves some worries by providing facts and helping prospective parents discuss sensitive issues. Genetic counselors usually favor testing, reasoning that knowledge is better than ignorance. However, high-risk individuals (who might hear bad news) do not always agree.

Many people, especially when considering personal and emotional information, misinterpret words such as *risks* and *probability* (O'Doherty, 2006). Even doctors do not always understand. Consider the experience of one of my students. A month before she became pregnant, Jeannette was required to have a rubella vaccination for her job. Hearing this, her prenatal care doctor gave her the following prognosis:

> My baby would be born with many defects, his ears would not be normal, he would be mentally retarded. . . . I went home and cried for hours and hours. . . . I finally went to see a genetic counselor. Everything was fine, thank the Lord, thank you, my beautiful baby is okay.
>
> *[Jeannette, personal communication, 2008]*

It is possible that Jeannette misunderstood what she was told, but one of the jobs of the professional is to make sure that the client understands. If sensitive counseling is available, then preconception, prenatal, or even prenuptial (before marriage) testing is recommended for everyone, especially for:

- Individuals who have a parent, sibling, or child with a serious genetic condition
- Couples who have had several spontaneous abortions or stillbirths
- Couples who are infertile
- Couples from the same ethnic group, particularly if they are relatives
- Women over age 35 and men over age 40

Genetic counselors follow two ethical rules: (1) Tests are confidential, beyond the reach of insurance companies and public records, and (2) decisions are made by the clients, not by the counselors.

However, these guidelines are not always easy to follow. One quandary arises when genetic tests reveal that the husband does not carry the gene that caused a recessive disease in a child. Should the counselor tell the couple that they have zero chance of having another baby with this problem because the husband is not the biological father? Counselors vary in how they handle this (Lucast, 2007).

Another quandary arises when DNA is collected for one purpose—say, to assess the risk of heart disease—and analysis reveals another problem, such as an extra sex chromosome or a high risk of breast cancer. This problem is new: Even a few years ago, testing was so expensive that researchers did not discover any conditions except those for which they were testing. Now, DNA collected a few years ago, from people who did not expect to be tested for the condition that was found, often reveals a genetic risk. Must the researcher inform the person?

The current consensus is that information should be shared if and only if (1) the person wants to hear it, (2) the risk is severe and verified, and (3) treatment is available (Couzin-Frankel, 2011). However, scientists and physicians disagree as to how severe, and how treatable, various conditions are. This is particularly true for psychological disorders. Moreover, many researchers are not able to provide the careful and patient counseling necessary. We all are carriers. Do we all want to know the specifics?

Sometimes couples make a decision (such as to begin or to abort a pregnancy) that is not what the counselor would do. People with identical genetic conditions often make opposite choices. For instance, 108 women who already had one child with fragile X syndrome were told they had a 50 percent chance of having another such child. Most (77 percent) decided to avoid pregnancy with sterilization or excellent contraception but some (20 percent) had another child (Raspberry &

>> Response for Teachers (from page 83) As the text says, "information combats prejudice." Your first step would be to make sure you know about Down syndrome, reading material about it. You would learn, among other things, that it is not usually inherited (your student need not worry about his or her progeny) and that some children with Down syndrome need extra medical and educational attention. This might mean you need to pay special attention to your student, whose parents might focus on the sibling.

>> Response for Historians (from page 83) Hemophilia is a painful chronic disease that (before blood transfusions became feasible) killed a boy before he could reach adulthood. Though rare, it ran in European royal families, whose members often intermarried, which meant that many queens (including England's Queen Victoria) were carriers of hemophilia and thus were destined to watch half their sons die of it. All families, even rulers of nations, are distracted from their work when they have a child with a mysterious and lethal illness. Some historians believe that hemophilia among European royalty was an underlying cause of the Russian Revolution of 1917 as well as of the spread of democracy in the nineteenth and twentieth centuries.

Skinner, 2011). Always the professional explains facts and probabilities; always the clients decide.

Sometimes people have no choice because testing is legally required. This is the case for **phenylketonuria (PKU)** in the United States. Newborns with the double recessive gene for PKU become severely retarded if they consume phenylalanine, an amino acid found in many foods. But if their diet has no phenylalanine, they develop almost normally (Hillman, 2005). Newborns need to start the special diet immediately (which is why testing is required), but parents whose child has PKU might treat that child differently (which is why the information needs to be sensitively transmitted).

Tests for dozens of other conditions are routinely administered to newborns (specifics vary by U.S. state and by nation). Although early diagnosis can reduce problems, counseling is needed. In one study of newborn testing, some parents wanted facts and others wanted emotional support. They were distressed if they sought one yet received the other (Tluczek et al., 2006).

Counseling must be individualized because each adult's perceptions are affected by his or her partner, present and future children, work, religion, and community (McConkie-Rosell & O'Daniel, 2007). Without careful explanation and comprehension checking, misunderstanding is common. For example, half of a large group of women misinterpreted an explanation (written for the general public) about tests for genes that make breast cancer more likely (Hanoch et al., 2010).

Some leaders in genetic research stress that changes in the environment, not in the genes, are the most promising direction for "disease prevention and more effective health maintenance" (Schwartz & Collins, 2007, p. 696). Much depends on the family and society. Genes are part of the human story, influencing every page, but they do not determine the plot or the final paragraph.

N03 / ZUMA PRESS / NEWCOM

phenylketonuria (PKU) A genetic disorder in which a child's body is unable to metabolize an amino acid called phenylalanine. Unless the infant immediately begins a special diet, the resulting buildup of phenylalanine in body fluids causes brain damage, progressive mental retardation, and other symptoms.

Reach for the Sky Gavin and Jake Barker both have cystic fibrosis, which would have meant early death had they been born 50 years ago. Now their parents pound on their chests twice a day to loosen phlegm—and they can enjoy jumping on the trampoline while wearing special pneumatic vests under their shirts.

SUMMING UP

Every person is a carrier for some serious genetic conditions. Most of them are rare, which makes it unlikely that the combination of sperm and ovum will produce severe disabilities. A few exceptional recessive-gene diseases are common because carriers were protected by a recessive gene against some lethal conditions in their communities. They survived to reproduce, and the gene spread throughout the population. Most serious dominant diseases disappear because the affected person dies before having children, but a few dominant conditions continue because their effects are not evident until after the childbearing years are over.

Often a zygote does not have 46 chromosomes. Such zygotes rarely develop to birth, with two primary exceptions: those with Down syndrome (trisomy-21) and those with abnormalities of the sex chromosomes. Genetic counseling helps couples clarify their values and understand the genetic risks, but every fact and decision raises ethical questions. Counselors try to explain probabilities. The final decision is made by those directly involved.

SUMMARY

The Genetic Code

1. Genes are the foundation for all development, first instructing the living creature to form the body and brain and then influencing thought and behavior. Human conception occurs when two gametes (an ovum and a sperm, each with 23 chromosomes) combine to form a zygote, 46 chromosomes in a single cell.

2. Genes and chromosomes from each parent match up to make the zygote. The match is not always perfect because of genetic variations called alleles.

The Beginnings of Life

3. The sex of an embryo depends on the sperm: A Y sperm creates an XY (male) embryo; an X sperm creates an XX (female) embryo. Virtually every cell of every living creature has the unique genetic code of the zygote that began that life. The human genome contains about 20,000 genes in all.

4. Twins occur if a zygote splits into two separate beings (monozygotic, or identical, twins) or if two ova are fertilized in the same cycle by two sperm (dizygotic, or fraternal, twins). Monozygotic multiples are genetically the same. Dizygotic multiples have only half of their genes in common, as do all siblings who have the same parents.

5. Assisted reproductive technology (ART), including drugs and in vitro fertilization, has led not only to the birth of millions of much-wanted babies but also to an increase in multiple births and infants who have a higher rate of medical problems. Several aspects of ART raise ethical and medical questions.

From One Cell to Many

6. Genes interact in various ways—sometimes additively, with each gene contributing to development, and sometimes in a dominant–recessive pattern. Environmental factors influence the phenotype as well. Epigenetics is the study of all the environmental factors that affect the expression of genes, including the DNA that surrounds the genes at conception.

7. The environment interacts with the genetic instructions for every trait, even for physical appearance. Every aspect of a person is almost always multifactorial and polygenic.

8. The first few divisions of a zygote are stem cells, capable of becoming any part of a person. Then cells differentiate, specializing in a particular function.

9. Combinations of chromosomes, interactions among genes, and myriad influences from the environment all ensure both similarity and diversity within and between species. This aids health and survival.

Genotype and Phenotype

10. Environmental influences are crucial for almost every complex trait, with each person experiencing different environments. Customs and contexts differ markedly.

11. Genetic makeup can make a person susceptible to a variety of conditions; nongenetic factors also affect susceptibility. Examples include alcoholism and nearsightedness. Cultural and familial differences affecting both of these problems are dramatic evidence for the role of nurture.

12. Knowing the impact of genes and the environment can be helpful. People are less likely to blame someone for a characteristic that is inherited; realizing that someone is at risk of a serious condition helps with prevention.

Chromosomal and Genetic Problems

13. Often a gamete has fewer or more than 23 chromosomes. Usually zygotes with other than 46 chromosomes do not develop.

14. Infants may survive if they have three chromosomes at the 21st location (Down syndrome, or trisomy-21) or one, three, or more sex chromosomes instead of two. In such cases, the affected child has physical and cognitive problems but can live a nearly normal life.

15. Everyone is a carrier for genetic abnormalities. Genetic disorders are usually recessive (not affecting the phenotype); if they are dominant, the trait is usually mild, varied, or inconsequential until late adulthood. When the gene is recessive and carrier status is protective, selective adaptation results in the carried gene becoming widespread, as has been shown with the sickle-cell gene that protects against malaria.

16. Genetic testing and counseling can help many couples. Testing usually provides information about possibilities, not actualities. Couples, counselors, and cultures differ in the decisions they make when risks are known.

KEY TERMS

deoxyribonucleic acid (DNA) (p. 64)
chromosome (p. 64)
gene (p. 64)
allele (p. 64)
genome (p. 65)
gamete (p. 66)
zygote (p. 66)
genotype (p. 66)
homozygous (p. 66)

heterozygous (p. 66)
23rd pair (p. 67)
XX (p. 67)
XY (p. 67)
stem cells (p. 69)
monozygotic (MZ) twins (p. 70)
dizygotic (DZ) twins (p. 70)
assisted reproductive technology (ART) (p. 71)

in vitro fertilization (IVF) (p. 71)
phenotype (p. 73)
polygenic (p. 73)
multifactorial (p. 73)
epigenetic (p. 74)
Human Genome Project (p. 75)
dominant–recessive pattern (p. 76)

carrier (p. 76)
X-linked (p. 76)
copy number variations (p. 77)
heritability (p. 80)
Down syndrome (p. 82)
fragile X syndrome (p. 83)
genetic counseling (p. 88)
phenylketonuria (PKU) (p. 89)

WHAT HAVE YOU LEARNED?

The Genetic Code

1. How many pairs of chromosomes and how many genes does a person usually have?

2. What is the relationship among genes, base pairs, and alleles?

The Beginnings of Life

3. In nature, what determines a person's sex and how can nurture affect that?

4. What are the advantages and disadvantages of being a monozygotic twin?

5. Why does in vitro fertilization increase the incidence of dizygotic twins?

From One Cell to Many

6. Why is a person's genotype not usually apparent in the phenotype?

7. What is the difference between an epigenetic characteristic and a multifactorial one?

8. Why do polygenic traits suggest that additive genes are more common than dominant–recessive ones?

9. What surprises came from the Human Genome Project?

Genotype and Phenotype

10. Regarding heritability, why is it important to know which population at what historical time provided the data?

11. What nature and nurture reasons make one person an alcoholic and another not?

12. What nature and nurture reasons make one person nearsighted and another not?

13. What can be learned from Mickey Mantle's life?

Chromosomal and Genetic Problems

14. Why does this textbook on normal development include abnormal development?

15. What usually happens when a zygote has fewer or more than 46 chromosomes?

16. What are the consequences if a newborn is born with trisomy-21?

17. Why are relatively few genetic conditions dominant?

18. Why are a few recessive traits (such as sickle-cell) quite common?

19. What are the advantages and disadvantages of genetic testing?

20. Why do people need genetic counselors, not merely fact sheets about genetic conditions?

APPLICATIONS

1. Pick one of your traits, and explain the influences that both nature *and* nurture have on it. For example, if you have a short temper, explain its origins in your genetics, your culture, and your childhood experiences.

2. Many adults have a preference for having a son or a daughter. Interview adults of several ages and backgrounds about their preferences. If they give the socially preferable answer ("It does not matter"), ask how they think the two sexes differ. Listen and take notes—don't debate. Analyze the implications of the responses you get.

3. Draw a genetic chart of your biological relatives, going back as many generations as you can, listing all serious illnesses and causes of death. Include ancestors who died in infancy. Do you see any genetic susceptibility? If so, how can you overcome it?

4. List a dozen people you know who need glasses (or other corrective lenses) and a dozen who do not. Are there any patterns? Is this correlation or causation?

>>ONLINE CONNECTIONS

To accompany your textbook, you have access to a number of online resources, including quizzes for every chapter of the book, flashcards (in English and Spanish), critical thinking questions, and case studies. For access to any of these links, go to www.worthpublishers.com/bergerca9e. In addition to these free resources, you'll also find links to podcasts, video clips, diagnostic quizzing with personalized study advice, and an ebook. Some of the videos and activities available online include:

- *Genetic Code.* This activity includes animations of basic genetic processes in our earliest development.

- *Identical Twins.* This video features footage of two identical twins, separated at birth and unknown to each other until adulthood.

Prenatal Development and Birth

WHAT WILL YOU KNOW?

1. When does a fetus become a baby?
2. Does medical assistance safeguard or impede the birth process?
3. What must a pregnant woman do to keep all toxins away from the developing person?
4. Is low birthweight the result of nature or nurture?
5. Why do some new mothers feel depressed after the birth of a baby, and what should fathers do about it?

Birthdays are important. Every February 28, I send a birthday card to my older brother, a 6-foot-tall grandfather of six, born in 1936.

Prenatal care is important, too. Although my brother was full term, he was born underweight because my mother was told to be hungry when she was expecting. Seventy-three years later, when my daughter was pregnant, she was told to eat as much as she wanted. In mid-pregnancy she baked a cake for her husband's birthday and decorated it with a metal figure of Superman. She wrapped Superman's legs in plastic before sticking it on the cake: She worried the figurine might be made of lead and wanted to ensure that slice would be safe to eat.

I think both my mother and my daughter were irrational mothers-to-be, heeding advice that they didn't need to. There are other foolish warnings—no spicy foods, no reaching, no sex, no exercise—that women have followed, and I took some unnecessary precautions myself. There is one universal here: Women everywhere hope for healthy and happy children, and they change their habits to that end.

My brother often asked my mother what time he was born. She said she didn't remember. Finally, when she was in her 90s, he told her "a story."

> When your first precious baby was beginning to be born, it was February 28th. But labor was slow, so your baby was born on the 29th. You felt sorry for your little boy, with a birthday only once in four years, so you persuaded the doctor to lie.
> "Yes," Mom replied. "That is just what happened."

I was shocked; my mother was scrupulously honest. I thought that she would never lie and that no doctor would sign a false birth certificate. But this illustrates another universal truth: Parents imagine their newborn's future lives and do what they can to protect them.

In this chapter, you will learn about the amazing growth of the embryo and fetus, and you will learn how family members and medical professionals try to protect every developing fetus and every newborn. Possible harm is noted, too—causes and consequences of diseases, malnutrition, drugs, pollution, stress, and so on. Birth places and practices vary, from a high-tech operating room to a lowly hut, in a tub of water at home or in a bed in a birthing center. Despite the many variations, remember the universals: We all develop for months before birth, nurtured by our mother's bodies and by thousands of people, who have hopes, plans, and fantasies for the future.

>> Prenatal Growth

The most dramatic and extensive transformation of the entire life span occurs before birth. To make it easier to study, prenatal development is often divided into three main periods. The first two weeks are called the **germinal period;** the third through the eighth week is the **embryonic period;** the ninth week until birth is the **fetal period.** (Alternative terms are explained in Table 4.1, which also explains why sometimes pregnancy is dated from the woman's last menstrual period rather than from conception).

Germinal: The First 14 Days

You learned in Chapter 3 that the one-celled zygote, traveling slowly down the fallopian tube toward the uterus, begins to duplicate and multiply (see Figure 4.1). At about the eight-cell stage, differentiation begins as those early cells take on distinct characteristics and gravitate toward particular locations.

About a week after conception, the multiplying cells (now numbering more than 100) separate into two distinct masses. The outer cells form a shell that will become the *placenta* (the organ that surrounds and protects the developing creature), and the inner cells form a nucleus that will become the embryo.

The first task of the outer cells is to achieve **implantation**—that is, to embed themselves in the nurturing lining of the uterus. This is far from automatic; about 50 percent of natural conceptions and an even larger percentage of in vitro conceptions never implant (see Table 4.2): Most new life ends before an embryo begins (Sadler, 2009).

Embryo: From the Third Through the Eighth Week

The start of the third week after conception initiates the *embryonic period*, during which the formless mass of cells becomes a distinct being—not yet recognizably human but worthy of a new name, **embryo.** (The word *embryo* is often used loosely, but each stage of development has a particular name; here, embryo refers to the developing human from day 14 to day 56.)

First, a thin line (called the *primitive streak*) appears down the middle of the embryo, becoming the neural tube 22 days after conception and eventually developing into the central nervous system, the brain, and spinal column (Sadler, 2009). The head appears in the fourth week, as eyes, ears, nose, and mouth start

---

germinal period The first two weeks of prenatal development after conception, characterized by rapid cell division and the beginning of cell differentiation.

embryonic period The stage of prenatal development from approximately the third through the eighth week after conception, during which the basic forms of all body structures, including internal organs, develop.

fetal period The stage of prenatal development from the ninth week after conception until birth, during which the fetus gains about 7 pounds (more than 3,000 grams) and organs become more mature, gradually able to function on their own.

implantation The process, beginning about 10 days after conception, in which the developing organism burrows into the placenta that lines the uterus, where it can be nourished and protected as it continues to develop.

embryo The name for a developing human organism from about the third through the eighth week after conception.

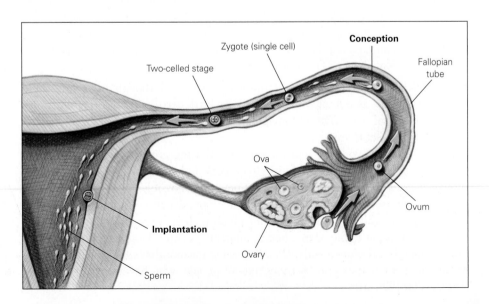

FIGURE 4.1

The Most Dangerous Journey In the first 10 days after conception, the organism does not increase in size because it is not yet nourished by the mother. However, the number of cells increases rapidly as the organism prepares for implantation, which occurs successfully about one-half of the time.

TABLE 4.1	Timing and Terminology

Popular and professional books use various phrases to segment the stages of pregnancy. The following comments may help to clarify the phrases used.

- *Beginning of pregnancy:* Pregnancy begins at conception, which is also the starting point of *gestational age.* However, the organism does not become an *embryo* until about two weeks later, and pregnancy does not affect the woman (and is not confirmed by blood or urine testing) until implantation. Perhaps because the exact date of conception is often unknown, some obstetricians and books for laypeople calculate from the woman's last menstrual period (LMP), usually about 14 days *before* conception.

- *Length of pregnancy:* Full-term pregnancies last 266 days, or 38 weeks, or 9 months. If the LMP is used as the starting time, pregnancy lasts 40 weeks, sometimes expressed as 10 lunar months. (A lunar month is 28 days long.)

- *Trimesters:* Instead of *germinal period, embryonic period,* and *fetal period,* some writers divide pregnancy into three-month periods called *trimesters.* Months 1, 2, and 3 are called the *first trimester;* months 4, 5, and 6, the *second trimester;* and months 7, 8, and 9, the *third trimester.*

- *Due date:* Although doctors assign a specific due date based on the LMP, only 5 percent of babies are born on that exact date. Babies born between three weeks before and two weeks after that date are considered *full term,* although labor is often induced if the baby has not arrived within 7 days of the due date. Babies born more than three weeks early are *preterm,* a more accurate term than *premature.*

TABLE 4.2	Vulnerability During Prenatal Development

The Germinal Period

About half* of all conceptions fail to grow or implant properly and thus do not survive the germinal period. Most of these organisms are grossly abnormal.

The Embryonic Period

About 20 percent of all embryos are aborted spontaneously,** most often because of chromosomal abnormalities.

The Fetal Period

About 5 percent of all fetuses are aborted spontaneously before viability at 22 weeks or are stillborn (defined as born dead after 22 weeks).

Birth

About 31 percent of all zygotes grow and survive to become living newborn babies.

*The rate of very early pregnancy failures could be higher, as often no one realizes that pregnancy occurred when it stops so early.

**Spontaneous abortions are also called miscarriages. The rate of induced abortions varies depending on availability of contraception and on culture; induced abortions are not included in this table.

Sources: Bentley & Mascie-Taylor, 2000; Sadler, 2009; Schorge et al., 2008.

to form. Also in the fourth week, a minuscule blood vessel that will become the heart begins to pulsate. By the fifth week, buds that will become arms and legs emerge. The upper arms and then forearms, palms, and webbed fingers grow. Legs, knees, feet, and webbed toes, in that order, are apparent a few days later, each having the beginning of a skeletal structure. Then, 52 and 54 days after conception, respectively, the fingers and toes separate (Sadler, 2009).

As you can see, prenatally, the head develops first, in a *cephalocaudal* (literally, "head-to-tail") pattern, and the extremities form last, in a *proximodistal* (literally, "near-to-far") pattern. At the end of the eighth week after conception (56 days), the embryo weighs just one-thirtieth of an ounce (1 gram) and is about 1 inch (2½ centimeters) long. It has all the basic organs and body parts (except sex organs) of a human being, including elbows and knees. It moves frequently, about 150 times per hour, but such movement is random and imperceptible (Piontelli, 2002).

The Embryonic Period *(a)* At 4 weeks past conception, the embryo is only about ⅛ inch (3 millimeters) long, but already the head has taken shape. *(b)* At 5 weeks past conception, the embryo has grown to twice the size it was at 4 weeks. Its primitive heart, which has been pulsing for a week now, is visible, as is what appears to be a primitive tail, which will soon be enclosed by skin and protective tissue at the tip of the backbone (the coccyx). *(c)* By 7 weeks, the organism is somewhat less than an inch (2½ centimeters) long. Eyes, nose, the digestive system, and even the first stage of toe formation can be seen.

fetus The name for a developing human organism from the start of the ninth week after conception until birth.

ultrasound An image of a fetus (or an internal organ) produced by using high-frequency sound waves. (Also called *sonogram*.)

There's Your Baby For many parents, their first glimpse of their future child is an ultrasound image. This is Alice Morgan, 63 days before birth.

Especially for Biologists Many people believe that the differences between the sexes are sociocultural, not biological. Is there any prenatal support for that view? (see response, page 98)

Fetus: From the Ninth Week Until Birth

The organism is called a **fetus** from the ninth week after conception until birth. The fetal period encompasses dramatic change, from a tiny, sexless creature smaller than the final joint of your thumb to a boy or girl about 20 inches (51 centimeters) long.

The Third Month

In the ninth week, if a fetus is male (XY), the SRY gene triggers the development of male sexual organs. Otherwise, female organs develop. The male fetus experiences a rush of the hormone testosterone, affecting the brain (Morris et al., 2004; Neave, 2008). Of course, the range of brain and behavioral variations *among* males and *among* females is greater than the variations *between* the average man and woman. Nonetheless, some neurological sex differences begin in the third month. The brain of the male fetus is slightly different from that of the female fetus.

By the end of the third month, the sex organs are visible via **ultrasound** (also called *sonogram*), which is similar to an X-ray but uses sound waves instead of radiation. Fetal similarities far outweigh any gender differences, however. For instance, the head of the developing human of any sex or ethnicity comprises about half of the total body weight, and facial features appear human in placement and shape by the third month.

The 3-month-old fetus weighs about 3 ounces (87 grams) and is about 3 inches (7.5 centimeters) long. Early prenatal growth is very rapid, with considerable variation, especially in body weight, from fetus to fetus (Sadler, 2009). The numbers just given—3 months, 3 ounces, 3 inches—are rounded off for easy recollection. (For those on the metric system, "100 days, 100 grams, 100 millimeters" is similarly imprecise but useful.)

The Middle Three Months

In the fourth, fifth, and sixth months, the heartbeat becomes stronger. Digestive and excretory systems develop. Fingernails, toenails, and buds for teeth form, and hair grows (including eyelashes). The brain increases about six times in size and develops many new neurons (*neurogenesis*) and synapses (*synaptogenesis*). Indeed,

The Fetus At the end of 4 months, the fetus, now 6 inches long, looks fully formed but out of proportion—the distance from the top of the skull to the neck is almost as long as that from the neck to the rump. For many more weeks, the fetus must depend on the translucent membranes of the placenta and umbilical cord (the long white object in the foreground) for survival.

up to half a million brain cells per minute are created at peak growth during mid-pregnancy (Dowling, 2004). Some neurons extend long axons to distant neurons, and, following the proximodistal sequence, first the brain stem above the back of the neck, then the midbrain, and finally the cortex develop and connect. Crucial brain development occurs in every prenatal month, but these three months may be the most important of all (Johnson, 2011).

The reason brain growth is critical at this point is that the entire central nervous system becomes responsive during mid-pregnancy, beginning to regulate basic body functions such as breathing and sucking. That means that advances in neurological functioning allow the fetus to reach the **age of viability,** when a preterm newborn can survive. With intensive medical care, some babies survive at 22 weeks past conception, although many hospitals worldwide do not routinely initiate intensive care unless the fetus is at least 25 weeks old. The age of viability decreased dramatically in the twentieth century, but it now seems stuck at about 22 weeks (Pignotti, 2010) because even the most advanced technology cannot maintain life without some brain response. (Reports of survivors born earlier than 22 weeks are suspect because the date of conception is unknown.) Figure 4.2 indicates survival rates for extremely preterm newborns with advanced medical care.

As the brain matures and axons connect, the organs of the body begin to work in harmony, so the heart beats faster during activity. Both fetal movement and heart rate quiet down during rest (which may not be when the mother wants to sleep). It is during these months that the mother usually feels the first signs of life.

age of viability The age (about 22 weeks after conception) at which a fetus might survive outside the mother's uterus if specialized medical care is available.

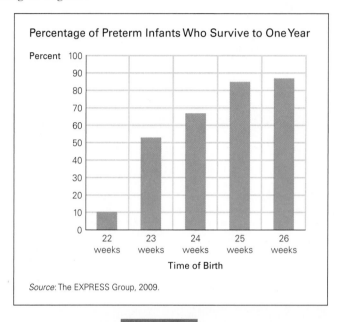

Source: The EXPRESS Group, 2009.

FIGURE 4.2

Each Critical Day Even with advanced medical care, survival of extremely preterm newborns is in doubt. These data come from a thousand births in Sweden, where prenatal care is free and easily obtained. As you can see, the age of viability (22 weeks) means only that an infant *might* survive, not that it will. By full term (not shown), the survival rate is almost 100 percent.

The Final Three Months

Attaining the age of viability simply means that life outside the womb is *possible*. Each day of the final three months improves the odds, not only of survival but also of life without disability (Iacovidou et al., 2010). (More on that later in this chapter.) A preterm infant born in the seventh month is a tiny creature requiring intensive care for each gram of nourishment and every shallow breath. By contrast, after nine months or so, the typical full-term newborn is ready to thrive at home on mother's milk—no expert help, oxygenated air, or special feeding required. For many thousands of years, that is how humans survived: You and I would not be alive if any one of our ancestors required intense newborn care.

The critical difference between life and death, or between a fragile preterm baby and a robust newborn, is maturation of the neurological, respiratory, and cardiovascular systems. In the last three months of prenatal life, the lungs begin to expand and contract, and the fetus exercises breathing muscles by swallowing amniotic fluid as a substitute for air. The valves of the heart go through a final maturation, as do the arteries and veins throughout the body. Among other things, this helps to prevent "brain bleeds," one of the hazards of preterm birth in which paper-thin blood vessels in the skull collapse.

LOYOLA UNIVERSITY HEALTH SYSTEM HO / AP PHOTO

One of the Tiniest Rumaisa Rahman was born after 26 weeks and 6 days weighing only 8.6 ounces (244 grams). Nevertheless, she has a good chance of living a full, normal life. Rumaisa gained 5 pounds (2,270 grams) in the hospital and then, six months after her birth, went home. Her twin sister, Hiba, who weighed 1.3 pounds (590 grams) at birth, had gone home two months earlier. At their one-year birthday, the twins seemed normal, with Rumaisa weighing 15 pounds (6,800 grams) and Hiba, 17 pounds (7,711 grams) (CBS News, 2005).

AT ABOUT THIS TIME
Average Prenatal Weights*

Period of Development	Weeks Past Conception	Average Weight (nonmetric)	Average Weight (metric)	Notes
End of embryonic period	8	1/30 oz.	1 g	Most common time for spontaneous abortion (miscarriage).
End of first trimester	13	3 oz.	85 g	
At viability (50/50 chance of survival)	22	20 oz.	570 g	A birthweight less than 2 lb., 3 oz. (1,000 g) is extremely low birthweight (ELBW).
End of second trimester	26–28	2–3 lb.	900–1,400 g	Less than 3 lb., 5 oz. (1,500 g) is very low birthweight (VLBW).
End of preterm period	35	5½ lb.	2,500 g	Less than 5½ lb. (2,500 g) is low birthweight (LBW).
Full term	38	7½ lb.	3,400 g	Between 5½ lb. and 9 lb. (2,500–4,000 g) is considered normal weight.

*To make them easier to remember, the weights are rounded off (hence the imprecise correspondence between metric and nonmetric). Actual weights vary. For instance, normal full-term infants weigh between 5½ and 9 pounds (2,500 and 4,000 grams); viable preterm newborns, especially twins or triplets, weigh less than shown here.

Can He Hear? A fetus, just about at the age of viability, is shown fingering his ear. Such gestures are probably random; but, yes, he can hear.

N. BROMHALL / PHOTO RESEARCHERS, INC.

>> Response for Biologists (from page 96) Only one of the 46 human chromosomes determines sex, and the genitals develop last in the prenatal sequence, suggesting that dramatic male–female differences are cultural. On the other hand, several sex differences develop before birth.

The fetus usually gains at least 4½ pounds (2.1 kilograms) in the third trimester, increasing to almost 7½ pounds (about 3.4 kilograms) at birth (see At About This Time). By full term, human brain growth is so extensive that the *cortex* (the brain's advanced outer layers) forms several folds in order to fit into the skull (see Figure 4.3). Although some large mammals (whales, for instance) have bigger brains than humans, no other creature needs as many folds as humans do, because the human cortex contains much more material than the brains of nonhumans.

The relationship between mother and child intensifies during the final three months, for fetal size and movement make the pregnant woman very aware of it. In turn, her sounds, the tastes of her food (via amniotic fluid), and her behavior patterns become part of fetal consciousness. Auditory communication from mother to child begins at the 28th week and improves each week as fetal hearing (or newborn hearing if a baby is born early) becomes more acute (Bisiacchi et al., 2009). The fetus startles and kicks at loud noises, listens to the mother's heartbeat and voice, and is comforted by rhythmic music and movement, such as when the mother sings as she walks. If the mother is fearful or anxious, the fetal heart beats faster and body movements increase (DiPietro et al., 2002).

SUMMING UP

In two weeks of rapid cell duplication, differentiation, and finally implantation, the newly conceived organism is transformed from a one-celled zygote to a many-celled embryo. The embryo soon develops the beginning of the central nervous system (3 weeks), a heart and a face (4 weeks), arms and legs (5 weeks), hands and feet (6 weeks), and fingers and toes (7 weeks) while the inner organs take shape. By 8

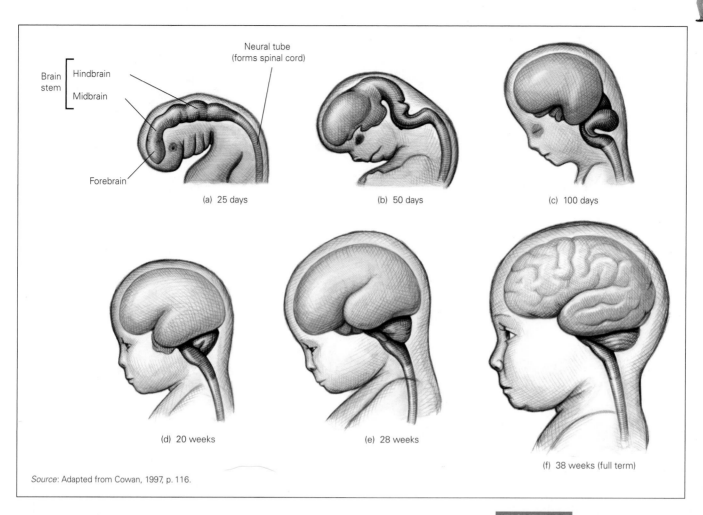

(a) 25 days (b) 50 days (c) 100 days

(d) 20 weeks (e) 28 weeks (f) 38 weeks (full term)

Source: Adapted from Cowan, 1997, p. 116.

weeks, all the body structures, except male and female sex organs, are in place. Fetal growth then proceeds rapidly, including mid-trimester weight gain (about 2 pounds, or 1 kilogram) and brain maturation, which make viability possible. By full term, all the organs function well in the 35- to 40-week newborn, who weighs about 7 pounds (about 3,200 grams).

>> Birth

About 38 weeks (266 days) after conception, when the fetus weighs 6 to 8 pounds (3,000 to 4,000 grams), the fetal brain signals the release of hormones, specifically *oxytocin,* which prepares the fetus for delivery and starts labor. The average baby is born after 12 hours of active labor for first births and 7 hours for subsequent births (Moore & Persaud, 2003), although labor may take twice or half as long. The definition of "active" labor varies, which is one reason some women believe they are in active labor for days and others say 10 minutes.

Women's birthing positions also vary—sitting, squatting, lying down. Some women give birth while immersed in warm water, which helps the woman relax (the fetus continues to get oxygen via the umbilical cord). However, some physicians believe water births increase the rate of infection, and the final emergence of the head is difficult for the medical team to monitor (Tracy, 2009). Preferences and opinions on positions are partly cultural and partly personal. In general,

FIGURE 4.3

Prenatal Growth of the Brain Just 25 days after conception *(a)*, the central nervous system is already evident. The brain looks distinctly human by day 100 *(c)*. By the 28th week of gestation *(e)*, at the very time brain activity begins, the various sections of the brain are recognizable. When the fetus is full term *(f)*, all the parts of the brain, including the cortex (the outer layers), are formed, folding over one another and becoming more convoluted, or wrinkled, as the number of brain cells increases.

FIGURE 4.4

A Normal, Uncomplicated Birth *(a)* The baby's position as the birth process begins. *(b)* The first stage of labor: The cervix dilates to allow passage of the baby's head. *(c)* Transition: The baby's head moves into the "birth canal," the vagina. *(d)* The second stage of labor: The baby's head moves through the opening of the vagina ("crowns") and *(e)* emerges completely. *(f)* The third stage of labor is the expulsion of the placenta. This usually occurs naturally, but it is crucial that the whole placenta be expelled, so birth attendants check carefully. In some cultures, the placenta is ceremonially buried, to commemorate the life-giving role it plays.

Observation Quiz In drawing *(e)*, what is the birth attendant doing as the baby's head emerges? (see answer, page 102)

Apgar scale A quick assessment of a newborn's health. The baby's color, heart rate, reflexes, muscle tone, and respiratory effort are given a score of 0, 1, or 2 twice—at one minute and five minutes after birth—and each time the total of all five scores is compared with the maximum score of 10 (rarely attained).

physicians find it easier to see the head emerge if the woman lies on her back and many women find it easier to push the fetus out if they sit up, but these generalities do not hold for every individual. Figure 4.4 shows the universal stages of birth.

The Newborn's First Minutes

Newborns usually breathe and cry on their own. Between spontaneous cries, the first breaths of air bring oxygen to the lungs and blood, and the infant's color changes from bluish to pinkish. (Pinkish refers to blood color, visible beneath the skin, and applies to newborns of all hues.) Eyes open wide; tiny fingers grab; even tinier toes stretch and retract. The newborn is instantly, zestfully, ready for life.

Nevertheless, there is much to be done. Mucus in the baby's throat is removed, especially if the first breaths seem shallow or strained. The umbilical cord is cut to detach the placenta, leaving an inch or so of the cord, which dries up and falls off to leave the belly button. The infant is examined, weighed, and given to the mother to preserve its body heat and to breast-feed a first meal of colostrum, a thick substance that helps the newborn's digestive and immune systems.

One widely used assessment of infant health is the **Apgar scale** (see Table 4.3), first developed by Dr. Virginia Apgar. When she graduated from Columbia medical school with her MD in 1933, Apgar wanted to work in a hospital but was told that only men did surgery. Consequently, she became an anesthesiologist. She saw that "delivery room doctors focused on mothers and paid little attention to babies. Those who were small and struggling were often left to die" (M. Beck, 2009, p. D-1). To save those young lives, Apgar developed a simple rating scale of five vital signs—color, heart rate, cry, muscle tone, and breathing—to alert doctors

TABLE 4.3	**Criteria and Scoring of the Apgar Scale**				
	Five Vital Signs				
Score	Color	Heartbeat	Reflex Irritability	Muscle Tone	Respiratory Effort
0	Blue, pale	Absent	No response	Flaccid, limp	Absent
1	Body pink, extremities blue	Slow (below 100)	Grimace	Weak, inactive	Irregular, slow
2	Entirely pink	Rapid (over 100)	Coughing, sneezing, crying	Strong, active	Good; baby is crying

Source: Apgar, 1953.

to newborn health. Since 1950, birth attendants worldwide have used the Apgar (often using the name as an acronym: Appearance, Pulse, Grimace, Activity, and Respiration) at one minute and again at five minutes after birth, assigning each vital sign a score of 0, 1, or 2.

If the five-minute Apgar is 7 or higher, all is well. If the five-minute total is below 7, the infant needs help. If the score is below 4, a neonatal pediatrician is summoned to the delivery room (the hospital loudspeaker may say "paging Dr. Apgar").

Medical Assistance

How closely any particular birth matches the foregoing depends on the parents' preparation, the position and size of the fetus, and the customs of the culture. In developed nations, births almost always include sterile procedures, electronic monitoring, and drugs to dull pain or speed contractions.

Surgery

Midwives are as skilled at delivering babies as physicians, but only medical doctors are licensed to perform surgery. More than one-third of U.S. births occur via **cesarean section (c-section,** or simply *section*), whereby the fetus is removed through incisions in the mother's abdomen. Cesareans are controversial: The World Health Organization suggests that c-sections are medically indicated in only 15 percent of births.

Culture and cohort affect the rates: Most nations have fewer cesareans than the United States, but some—especially in Latin America—have more (see Figure 4.5). In every nation, both the safety and the incidence of cesareans have increased over the past two decades, with the most dramatic increases in China. In that nation, rates were 5 percent in 1991, 20 percent by 2001, and 46 percent in 2008 (Guo et al., 2007; Juan, 2010). In the United States, the rate rose every year between 1996 and 2008 (from 21 percent to 34 percent). Cesareans are usually safe for mother and baby and have many advantages for hospitals (easier to schedule, quicker, and more expensive than vaginal deliveries), but they also bring more complications after birth and reduce breast-feeding (Malloy, 2009).

Less studied is the *epidural*, an injection in a particular part of the spine of the laboring woman to alleviate pain. Epidurals are often used in hospital births, but they increase the rate of cesarean sections and decrease the readiness of newborn infants to suck immediately after birth (Bell et al., 2010). Another medical

Modern Intervention He was born by C-Section, as are more than half of all Brazilian babies, especially those born to poor young women like this 16-year-old indigenous mother. At least she is breast feeding, a traditional practice likely to be better for him than formula.

cesarean section (c-section) A surgical birth, in which incisions through the mother's abdomen and uterus allow the fetus to be removed quickly, instead of being delivered through the vagina. (Also called simply *section*.)

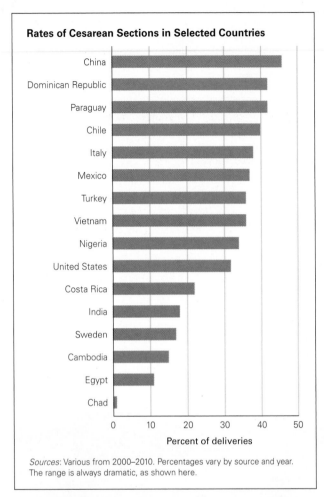

Rates of Cesarean Sections in Selected Countries

China
Dominican Republic
Paraguay
Chile
Italy
Mexico
Turkey
Vietnam
Nigeria
United States
Costa Rica
India
Sweden
Cambodia
Egypt
Chad

0　　10　　20　　30　　40　　50
Percent of deliveries

Sources: Various from 2000–2010. Percentages vary by source and year. The range is always dramatic, as shown here.

FIGURE 4.5

Too Many Cesareans or Too Few? Rates of cesarean deliveries vary widely from nation to nation. Latin America has the highest rates in the world (note that 40 percent of all births in Chile are by cesarean), and sub-Saharan Africa has the lowest (the rate in Chad is less than half of 1 percent). The underlying issue is whether some women who should have cesareans do not get them, while other women have unnecessary cesareans.

>> Answer to Observation Quiz (from page 100) The birth attendant is turning the baby's head after it has emerged; doing this helps the shoulders come out more easily.

intervention is *induced labor,* in which labor is started, speeded, or strengthened with a drug. The rate of induced labor in the United States has tripled since 1990 and is now close to 20 percent.

Newborn Survival

Every year worldwide, obstetricians, midwives, and nurses save millions of lives. A century ago, at least 5 of every 100 newborns in the United States died (De Lee, 1938). Currently in the United States, newborn mortality is about 1 in 250—a statistic that includes very fragile newborns weighing only 1 pound. In advanced nations, fewer than 1 in 10,000 women die as a result of complications from abortion or birth; in poor nations, the rate is 100 times higher.

The primary reason birth is still hazardous in the least developed nations is the lack of medical attention. In sub-Saharan Africa, where only one-third of all births are attended by a doctor or trained midwife and the average mother has four children, about 1 in 16 women dies from complications of pregnancy or birth (Kruk et al., 2008). Worldwide, almost 2 million newborns die each year (Rajaratnam et al., 2010). The main cause of maternal death is uncontrolled bleeding, and the main cause of neonatal death is lack of oxygen and nutrition. Both are routinely prevented in hospitals.

Nonetheless, several aspects of hospital birth arise from custom or politics, not from necessity (Selin & Stone, 2009). A particular issue concerns attention lavished on "miracle babies" who require intensive care, microsurgery, and weeks in the hospital. Those who survive often—but not always—need special care all their lives. Only happy outcomes are published, but critics note the public expense of keeping them alive and then the lifelong burden borne by the parents.

The American Academy of Pediatrics recommends careful and honest counseling for parents of very preterm babies so that they understand the consequences of each medical measure. As an obstetrics team writes, "We should be frank with ourselves, with parents and with society, that there are gaps of knowledge concerning the management of infants born at very low gestational ages . . . including ethical decisions such as . . . when to provide intensive care and how extensive this should be" (Iacovidou et al., 2010, p. 133).

Alternatives to Hospital Technology

Questions of costs and benefits abound. For instance, c-section and epidural rates vary more by doctor, hospital, day of the week, and region than by the circumstances of the birth—even in Sweden, where obstetric care is paid for by the government (Schytt & Walderenström, 2010). A rare complication (uterine rupture), which sometimes happens when women give birth vaginally after a previous cesarean, has caused most doctors to insist that after one cesarean, subsequent births be cesarean. Juries blame doctors for inaction more than for action; to avoid lawsuits, doctors intervene.

Most U.S. births now take place in hospital labor rooms with high-tech operating rooms nearby. Another 5 percent of U.S. births occur in *birthing centers* (not in a hospital), and less than 1 percent occur at home (illegal in some jurisdictions). About half of the home births are planned and half not, because of unexpectedly rapid labor. The latter are hazardous if no one is nearby to rescue a newborn in distress (Tracy, 2009).

Home Births

Compared with the United States, planned home births are more common in many other developed nations (2 percent in England, 30 percent in the Netherlands), where midwives are paid by the government. In the Netherlands, special ambulances called *flying storks* speed mother and newborn to a hospital if needed. Dutch research finds home births better for mothers and no worse for infants than hospital births (de Jonge et al., 2009).

In the poorest nations, almost all babies are born at home: Doctors are called only for emergencies, often arriving too late. Many women avoid hospitals unless they think they are dying. The following describes a birth in Ghana:

> Huddled in a corner of the hut, she was lying on the floor. . . . She lay curled into a small ball on her left side, her pregnant and contracting uterus protruding from her thin frame. No sound came from her. No sound came from the midwife either. She was seated in the corner of the dark, hot hut, waiting. Suddenly, Emefa gave a low whimper and hauled herself into a sitting and then squatting position. The midwife crept over to her and gently supported Emefa's back as she bore down. No words, no commands, no yelling. . . . The baby's head appeared gradually, slowly making its progress into the world. How did the midwife know that it was time? . . . A soft whoosh and the baby's body was born into the steady and confident hands of the midwife. And still there was no sound. The baby did not cry, not because there was any problem, but because it was a gentle birth. The baby was breathing as he was handed to his mother.
>
> [Hillier, 2003, p. 3]

The idea of a "gentle birth" is appealing, but this newborn may have been lucky. The infant mortality rate in Ghana is at least 10 times higher than in North America. Some people wish gentle home births would become more common in the United States; others shudder at the thought. Two opposite risks are apparent. On the one hand, home births might become emergencies and taking an ambulance to the hospital would delay care; on the other hand, hospital births might cause needless intervention, harming the new family.

One crucial question is how supportive the medical professionals are. One committee of obstetricians decided that planned home births are acceptable because women have "a right to make a medically informed decision about delivery," but they also insisted that a trained midwife or doctor be present, that the woman not be high-risk (e.g., no previous cesarean), and that speedy transportation to a hospital be ready (American College of Obstetricians and Gynecologists Committee on Obstetric Practice, 2011).

Some studies in England, Canada, Sweden, and the United States report that home births entail risks for the baby: The stillborn and newborn death rate, although very low, is higher than for a delivery room birth (home birth advocates dispute these conclusions). Every study finds benefits for the mother: fewer medical interventions and quicker recovery, and thus stronger mother–infant bonds, more successful breast-feeding, and less maternal depression—all of which benefit fathers and other children as well.

Probably the crucial phrase from the U.S. obstetricians is "medically informed." Unfortunately, many people are uninformed and, consequently, either unduly suspicious or irrationally appreciative of every hospital procedure. As one review of home births concluded: "Contradictory professional and public policies reflect the polarization and politicization of the controversy surrounding this birth option" (Wax et al., 2010, p. 132). Instead of polarization, critical and informed thinking is needed.

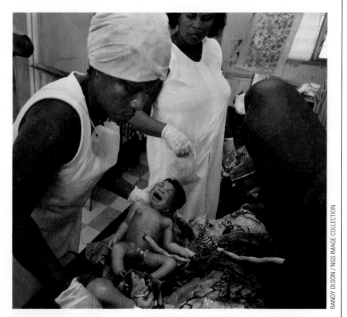

RANDY OLSON / NGS IMAGE COLLECTION

Celebration? The lusty cry of this infant is a good sign, as is his color (not bluish) and muscle tone. Moreover, this birth occurred in a clinic, which bodes well for the mother's recovery—unlike many other births in Ghana.

Observation Quiz Is this infant minutes, hours, or days old? (see answer, page 105)

The Same Situation, Many Miles Apart: Getting Ready There are many similarities here: Six adults and three fetuses on the left and six adults and two fetuses (twins) on the right. But the differences are tragic, evident in the face of the expectant mother on the right. The husbands in the Netherlands are learning how to help their wives give birth at home, as most Dutch couples do. The Afghan doctor on the right, however, is explaining why this woman's labor will be induced, with neither baby expected to survive—a devastating blow this woman has already faced, having twice lost a baby less than a week old.

doula A woman who helps with the birth process. Traditionally in Latin America, a doula was the only professional who attended childbirth. Now doulas are likely to arrive at the woman's home during early labor and later work alongside a hospital's staff.

In the first part of the twentieth century, in advanced nations, women in hospitals labored by themselves until birth was imminent; fathers and other family members were kept away. Almost everyone now agrees that a laboring woman should never be alone. However, family members may not know what to do, and professionals focus more on the medical than the psychological aspects of birth, so some women do not get the emotional support they need. To meet this need, more women now have a **doula,** a woman trained to support the laboring woman by timing contractions, doing massage, providing ice chips, or doing whatever else might be helpful.

Often doulas begin their work before active labor, and then, as the moment of birth approaches, they work beside the midwives or doctors. Many studies have

Pressure Point Many U.S. couples, like this one, benefit from a doula's gentle touch, strong pressure, and sensitive understanding —all of which make doula births less likely to include medical intervention.

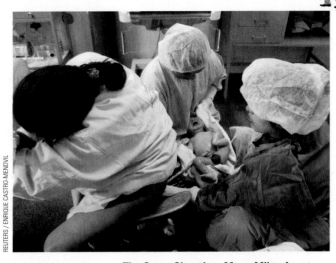

The Same Situation, Many Miles Apart: A Better Position The most obvious difference between these births in Chicago, Illinois (*left*), and Cuzco, Peru, is the mother's body position. In the United States, the horizontal position was designed to give doctors a better view when the head emerges (*left*). In Peru, women prefer "vertical births," and this maternity center boasts more patients as a result of its willingness—to perform them. Note other differences—the father present in Chicago, the protective head coverings in Cuzco. It is not so clear-cut which practices make better medical sense and which are simply social customs.

> ▶ **Research Design**

Scientists: Susan McGrath and John Kennell.

Publication: *Birth* (2008).

Participants: A total of 420 pregnant women, all healthy, middle class, and accompanied by their male partner when they arrived in labor at a major hospital in Cleveland, Ohio. They gave birth to their first baby, attended by their obstetrician or midwife.

Design: All 420 received the usual medical care as well as the support of their partners, but, on admission to the hospital, half were randomly assigned a doula. The doula stayed with the couple, providing physical care (e.g., massage), expertise, and reassurance until the birth. Mothers and their partners were questioned 24 hours and 6 weeks later.

Major conclusion: The doula births were less often cesareans (13 versus 25 percent) and involved fewer epidurals (65 versus 76 percent). More than 99 percent of the women and their partners rated the doula's help positively or very positively. The conclusion: "Continuous labor support by a doula is a risk-free obstetric technique that could benefit all laboring women" (p. 97).

Comments: Three factors in this design add confidence to the conclusion: (1) Random assignment avoided selection factors (women who choose doulas tend to be healthy and well-educated); (2) the fathers' presence for all women proved that not merely the presence of a support person caused the benefits; (3) the doula appeared only when the couple arrived at the hospital (avoiding the confounds of doula help in early labor).

---

found that doulas benefit low-income women with no partner, decreasing the disparity in birth outcomes between middle-class and poor women (Vonderheid et al., 2011). It is now believed that doulas benefit anyone giving birth, rich or poor, married or not. For example, in one study, 420 middle-class married women were randomly assigned a doula (McGrath & Kennell, 2008). Those with doulas needed less intervention (see the Research Design).

SUMMING UP

Most newborns score at least 7 out of 10 on the Apgar scale, and thrive without medical assistance. If necessary, neonatal surgery and intensive care save lives. Although modern medicine has reduced maternal and newborn deaths, many critics deplore treating birth as a medical crisis rather than a natural event. Responses to this critique include women choosing to give birth in hospital labor rooms rather than operating rooms, in birthing centers instead of hospitals, or even at home. The assistance of a doula is another recent practice that reduces medical intervention. ∎

>> Answer to Observation Quiz (from page 103) Probably ten minutes or less. His umbilical cord is still attached to the placenta, which is still inside the woman. Usually placentas are expelled with contractions a few minutes after birth.

>> Problems and Solutions

The early days of life place the developing person on the path toward health and success—or not. Fortunately, resilience is apparent from the beginning; healthy newborns are the norm, not the exception. However, if something is amiss, it is often part of a cascade that may become overwhelming.

Harmful Substances

teratogens Agents and conditions, including viruses, drugs, and chemicals, that can impair prenatal development and result in birth defects or even death.

Such a cascade begins before the woman realizes she is pregnant, as many toxins, illnesses, and experiences can harm a new pregnancy. Every week, scientists discover an unexpected **teratogen,** defined as anything—drugs, viruses, pollutants, malnutrition, stress, and more—that increases the risk of prenatal abnormalities. But do not be alarmed. Many abnormalities can be avoided, many potential teratogens do no harm, and much damage can be remedied. Thus, prenatal development is not a dangerous period to be feared as much as a natural process to be protected.

behavioral teratogens Agents and conditions that can harm the prenatal brain, impairing the future child's intellectual and emotional functioning.

Some teratogens cause no physical defects but affect the brain, making a child hyperactive, antisocial, or learning-disabled. These are **behavioral teratogens.** About 20 percent of all children have difficulties that *could* be connected to behavioral teratogens, although the link is not straightforward: The cascade is murky. One of my students described her little brother as follows:

> I was nine years old when my mother announced she was pregnant. I was the one who was most excited. . . . My mother was a heavy smoker, Colt 45 beer drinker. . . . I asked, "Why are you doing it?" She said, "I don't know."
> During this time I was in the fifth grade and we saw a film about birth defects. My biggest fear was that my mother was going to give birth to a fetal alcohol syndrome (FAS) infant. . . . My baby brother was born right on schedule. The doctors claimed a healthy newborn. . . . Once I heard healthy, I thought everything was going to be fine. I was wrong, then again I was just a child. . . . My baby brother never showed any interest in toys . . . he just cannot get the right words out of his mouth . . . he has no common sense . . .
>
> *[J., personal communication]*

My student asks, "Why hurt those who cannot defend themselves?" As you remember from Chapter 1, one case proves nothing, and as you just read, teratogens often cascade with murky connections. J. blames her mother for smoking and drinking beer, although genes, postnatal experiences, and lack of preventive information and services may be part of the cascade as well. Nonetheless, J. is right to wonder why her mother took a chance.

Behavioral teratogens can be subtle, and their effects may last a lifetime. That is one conclusion from research on pregnant women exposed to flu in 1918. Some miscarried; some babies were stillborn. Most survivors seemed unharmed and lived long lives—but not as long as the average baby born a year earlier. By middle age, the flu-exposed babies averaged less education, more unemployment, and lower income than their peers (Almond, 2006).

Risk Analysis

Life entails risks. *Risk analysis* discerns which chances are worth taking and how risks are minimized. To pick an easy example: Crossing the street is a risk, yet it would be worse to avoid all street crossing. Knowing this, we cross carefully, looking both ways.

Sixty years ago, no one applied risk analysis to prenatal development. It was assumed that the placenta screened out all harmful substances. Then two tragic episodes showed otherwise: (1) On an Australian military base, an increase in babies born blind was linked to a rubella (German measles) epidemic on the same base seven months earlier (Gregg, 1941, reprinted in Persaud et al., 1985), and (2) a sudden rise in British newborns with deformed limbs was traced to maternal use of thalidomide, a new drug for nausea that was widely prescribed in Europe in the late 1950s (Schardein, 1976). Thus began *teratology,* a science of risk analysis. Although all teratogens increase the *risk* of harm, none *always* cause damage. The impact of teratogens depends on the interplay of many factors, both destructive and protective, an example of the dynamic-systems perspective described in Chapter 1.

The Critical Time

One crucial factor is *timing*—the age of the developing organism when it is exposed to the teratogen (Sadler, 2009). Some teratogens cause damage only during a *critical period* (see Chapter 1) (see Figure 4.6). Obstetricians recommend that *before* pregnancy occurs, women should avoid drugs (especially alcohol), supplement a balanced diet with extra folic acid and iron, and update their immunizations. Indeed, preconception health is at least as important as health during pregnancy.

FIGURE 4.6

Critical Periods in Human Development
The most serious damage from teratogens (green bars) is likely to occur early in prenatal development. However, significant damage (purple bars) to many vital parts of the body, including the brain, eyes, and genitals, can occur during the last months of pregnancy as well.

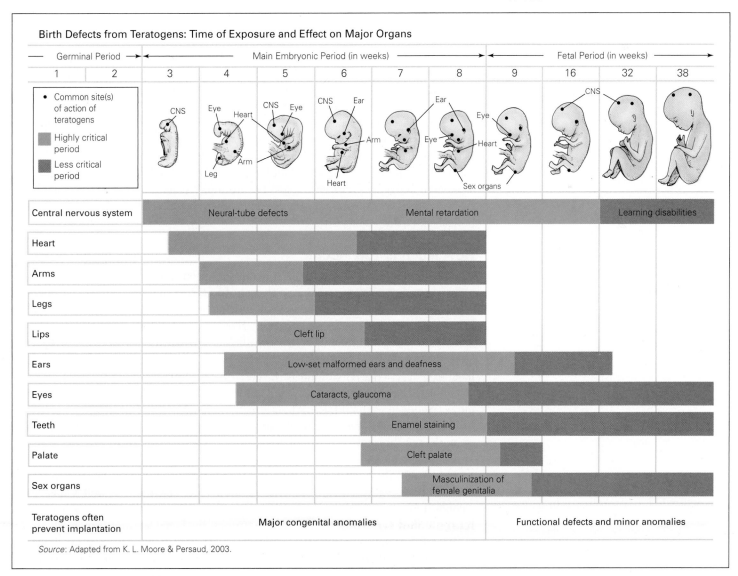

Birth Defects from Teratogens: Time of Exposure and Effect on Major Organs

Source: Adapted from K. L. Moore & Persaud, 2003.

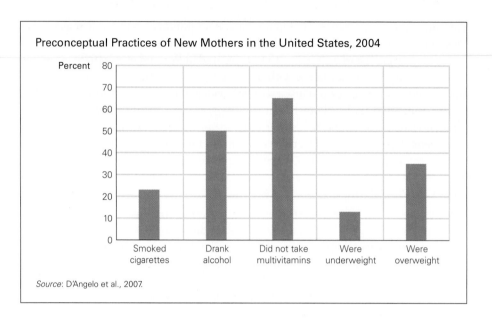

Preconceptual Practices of New Mothers in the United States, 2004

Source: D'Angelo et al., 2007.

FIGURE 4.7

No One is Perfect Blaming pregnant women is easy, but almost no one avoids all drugs and stresses, sleeps and eats well, weighs just the right amount, exercises at least an hour each day, and completely avoids fried or salty foods. If you are the exception, could you keep it up for a year, while gaining 35 pounds; sometimes feeling nauseous; coping with stares and the questions of friends, relatives, and strangers; and going to the doctor every few weeks?

threshold effect In prenatal development, when a teratogen is relatively harmless in small doses but becomes harmful once exposure reaches a certain level (the threshold).

fetal alcohol syndrome (FAS) A cluster of birth defects, including abnormal facial characteristics, slow physical growth, and retarded mental development, that may occur in the fetus of a woman who drinks alcohol while pregnant.

Unfortunately, almost half the births in the United States are unplanned, often to women who are not in the best of health before conception (D'Angelo et al., 2007) (see Figure 4.7).

The first days and weeks after conception (the germinal and embryonic periods) are critical for body formation, but health during the entire fetal period affects the brain. Some teratogens that cause preterm birth or low birthweight are particularly harmful in the second half of pregnancy. Indeed, one study found that, although smoking cigarettes throughout prenatal development can be lethal for the fetus, smokers who quit in the first weeks of pregnancy had no higher risks of birth complications than did women who never smoked (McCowan et al., 2009).

Timing may be important in another way. When pregnancy occurs soon after a previous pregnancy, risk increases. For example, second-born children may be twice as likely to be autistic if they are born within a year of the first-born child (Cheslack-Postava et al., 2011).

How Much Is Too Much?

A second factor affecting the harm from any teratogen is the dose and/or frequency of exposure. Some teratogens have a **threshold effect;** they are virtually harmless until exposure reaches a certain level, at which point they "cross the threshold" and become damaging. This threshold is not a fixed boundary: dose, timing, frequency, and other teratogens affect when the threshold is crossed (O'Leary et al., 2010).

A few substances are beneficial in small amounts but fiercely teratogenic in large quantities. One is vitamin A, essential for healthy development but a cause of abnormalities if the dose is 50,000 units per day or higher (obtained only in pills) (Naudé et al., 2007). Experts are reluctant to specify thresholds, partly because the presence of one teratogen may intensify the effects of another. For example, the threshold for alcohol, tobacco, and marijuana is lower when all three are combined.

Thresholds are controversial. It is known that high doses of psychoactive drugs are harmful, but it is not known if small amounts are teratogenic as well. Consider alcohol. Early in pregnancy, an embryo exposed to heavy drinking can develop **fetal alcohol syndrome (FAS),** which distorts the facial features (especially the eyes, ears, and upper lip). Later in pregnancy, alcohol is a behaviorial teratogen, the cause of *fetal alcohol effects (FAE),* leading to hyperactivity, poor concentration, impaired spatial reasoning, and slow learning (Niccols, 2007; Streissguth & Connor, 2001).

However, some pregnant women drink alcohol in moderation with no evident harm to the fetus. If occasional drinking during pregnancy always caused FAS, almost everyone born in Europe before 1980 would be affected. As for FAE, hyperactivity and slow learning are so common that FAE cannot be blamed for every case. Currently, pregnant women are advised to avoid all alcohol, but women in the United Kingdom receive conflicting advice about drinking a glass of wine a day or two a week (Raymond et al., 2009), and French women are told to abstain but many do not seem to have heard that message (Toutain, 2010). Total abstinence requires that all women who might become pregnant avoid a legal substance that most adults use routinely. Wise? Probably. Necessary?

Innate Vulnerability

Genes influence the effects of teratogens. When a woman carrying dizygotic twins drinks alcohol, for example, the twins' blood alcohol levels are equal; yet one twin may be more severely affected than the other because their alleles for the enzyme that metabolizes alcohol differ. Genetic vulnerability is suspected for many birth defects (Sadler et al., 2010). (Remember differential sensitivity.)

One particular chromosome, the Y, may be crucial. Male fetuses are more likely to be spontaneously aborted and, if born, more likely to have been affected by teratogens than female fetuses. Are those extra genes on the second X chromosome protective, or does the Y chromosome carry genes that increase vulnerability? Scientists do not know.

Genes are important in another way, in that the mother's genes affect the prenatal environment she provides. One maternal allele results in low levels of folic acid during pregnancy, which can produce *neural-tube defects*—either *spina bifida,* in which the tail of the spine is not enclosed properly (in healthy embryos, enclosure occurs at about week 7), or *anencephaly,* when part of the brain is missing. Neural-tube defects are more common in certain ethnic groups (Irish, English, and Egyptian) than in others (most Asian and African groups) because that maternal allele is rare among Asians and Africans (Mills et al., 1995).

A U.S. law required that, beginning in 1998, folic acid be added to packaged cereal. That initiative is credited with reducing neural-tube defects by 26 percent (MMWR, September 13, 2002). But some women rarely eat cereal and do not take vitamins. In 2010, in the Appalachian region of the United States (parts of West Virginia, Tennessee, and Kentucky), about 1 newborn in 1000 had a neural-tube defect.

Applying the Research

Risk analysis cannot precisely predict the results of teratogenic exposure in individual cases. However, much is known about destructive and damaging teratogens and what individuals, family members, and society can do to reduce the risks. Table 4.4 on pages 110–111 lists some teratogens and their possible effects, as well as preventive measures.

Remember that the effects of teratogens vary. Many fetuses are exposed with no evident harm. The opposite occurs as well: About 20 percent of all serious defects occur for reasons unknown. Women are advised to maintain good nutrition and avoid teratogens, especially drugs and chemicals (pesticides, cleaning fluids, and many cosmetics contain teratogenic chemicals). Some medications are necessary (e.g., for women who have epilepsy, diabetes, severe depression) and should continue, but caution should begin *before* pregnancy is confirmed (Haas et al., 2011).

Swing High and Low Adopted by loving parents but born with fetal alcohol syndrome, Philip, shown here at age 11, sometimes threatens to kill his family members. His parents sent him to this residential ranch in Eureka, Montana, a temporary home (nonprofit, tuition $3,500 a month) for children like him. This moment during recess is a happy one; it is not known whether he learned to control his fury.

Especially for Nutritionists Is it beneficial that most breakfast cereals are fortified with vitamins and minerals? (see response, page 111)

Sadly, the cascade of teratogens is most likely to begin with women who are already vulnerable. For example, cigarette smokers are more often drinkers (as was J.'s mother); those whose jobs involve chemicals and pesticides are more often malnourished (Ahmed & Jaakkola, 2007; Hougaard & Hansen, 2007).

Advice From Doctors

While prenatal care can be helpful to women who need to know how to protect the developing person, even doctors are not always as careful as they could or should be. According to a massive study of 152,000 new mothers in eight health maintenance organizations (HMOs) in the United States, doctors wrote an average of three prescriptions per pregnant woman, including drugs that had not been

TABLE 4.4 Teratogens: Effects of Exposure and Prevention of Damage

Teratogens	Effects of Exposure	To Prevent Harm
Diseases		
Rubella (German measles)	In embryonic period, causes blindness and deafness; in fetal period, brain damage.	Immunization before pregnancy.
Toxoplasmosis	Causes brain damage, loss of vision, mental retardation.	Avoid eating undercooked meat and handling cat feces, garden dirt.
Measles, chicken pox, influenza	May impair brain functioning.	Immunization before pregnancy; avoid infections during pregnancy (wash hands).
Syphilis	Baby born with syphilis; may damage brain and bones; eventual death.	Get early prenatal diagnosis and treatment with antibiotics.
HIV/AIDS	Baby may catch the virus during birth. If so, drugs may prevent illness and death.	Prenatal drugs and cesarean birth limit HIV transmission.
Other sexual infections, such as gonorrhea	Not harmful prenatally but may cause blindness and infections after vaginal birth.	Get early diagnosis and treatment; if necessary, cesarean section, treatment of newborn.
Infections, including infections of urinary tract, gums, teeth	May cause premature labor, which increases vulnerability to brain damage.	Get infection treated, preferably before pregnancy.
Pollutants		
Lead, mercury, PCBs, dioxin, pesticides, cleaning compounds	May cause spontaneous abortion, preterm labor, and brain damage.	Most substances are harmless in small doses. Avoid unwashed fruits, toxic chemicals, fish from polluted waters.
Radiation		
Massive or repeated exposure to radiation, as in medical X-rays	Early in pregnancy, may cause small head (microcephaly), retardation; late, may damage brain.	Get ultrasounds, not X-rays; reassignment suggested for women who work directly with radiation
Social/Behavioral		
Very high stress	Early in pregnancy, may cause cleft lip or cleft palate, spontaneous abortion. Later may cause preterm labor.	Adequate relaxation, rest, and sleep; reduce hours of employment; get help with housework and child care.
Malnutrition	When severe, interferes with conception, implantation, fetal development, and birthweight.	Consume balanced diet, extra folic acid, and iron; women with normal weight, gain 25–35 lbs (10–15 kg) during pregnancy.
Excessive, exhausting exercise	Can affect fetal development when it interferes with woman's sleep or digestion.	Maintain regular, moderate exercise.

declared safe during pregnancy (prescribed for 40 percent) and drugs with proven risks to fetuses (prescribed for 2 percent) (Andrade et al., 2004). Perhaps these doctors did not know their patients were pregnant and perhaps these women did not take the medications, but even a few pills early in pregnancy may be harmful.

Another problem is that not every doctor takes the time to understand the woman's life patterns, some of which may be harmful. For example, one Maryland study found that almost one-third of pregnant women were not asked and counseled about their alcohol use (Cheng et al., 2011). Those who were over age 35 and college-educated were least likely to be counseled, perhaps because their doctors assumed they knew the dangers, but in this study at least, they were also most likely to drink during pregnancy.

>> **Response for Nutritionists** (from page 109) Useful, yes; optimal, no. Some essential vitamins are missing (too expensive), and individual needs differ, depending on age, sex, health, genes, and eating habits. The reduction in neural-tube defects is good, but many women don't eat cereal or take vitamin supplements before becoming pregnant.

Teratogens	Effects of Exposure	To Prevent Harm
Medicinal Drugs		
Lithium	Can cause heart abnormalities.	Avoid all medicines, whether prescription or over-the-counter, unless essential and approved by a medical professional who understands recent research.
Tetracycline	Can harm the teeth.	
Retinoic acid	Can cause limb deformities.	
Streptomycin	Can cause deafness.	
ACE inhibitors	Can harm digestive organs.	
Phenobarbital	Can affect brain development.	
Thalidomide	Halts ear and limb formation.	
Psychoactive Drugs		
Caffeine	Normal use poses no problem.	Avoid excessive use: Limit beverages containing caffeine (coffee, tea, cola, cocoa).
Alcohol	May cause fetal alcohol syndrome (FAS) or fetal alcohol effects (FAE).	Stop or severely limit alcohol consumption during pregnancy; binge drinking is dangerous.
Tobacco	Decreases birthweight. May harm lungs, heart, urinary tract.	Stop smoking. If not, severely limit consumption.
Marijuana	Heavy exposure may affect the central nervous system; may hinder fetal growth.	Avoid or strictly limit use of marijuana.
Heroin	Slows fetal growth, starts preterm labor; addicted newborns require treatment to prevent convulsions.	Stop before pregnancy; if already pregnant, gradual methadone withdrawal is better than sudden abstinence.
Cocaine	May cause slow fetal growth, preterm birth, slow learning in infancy and childhood.	Stop before pregnancy; children may need special medical and educational attention
Inhaled solvents (glue or aerosol)	May cause abnormally small head, crossed eyes, and other indications of brain damage.	Stop sniffing before pregnancy; serious damage occurs during first weeks after conception.
Antipsychotic drugs (e.g., Haldol, Risperdal)	May cause movement abnormalities or withdrawal symptoms in newborns.	Caution needed. Sudden stopping is harmful; such drugs may make the woman a better prospective mother.

Note: This table includes only relatively common teratogens. As the text makes clear, many individual factors interact to determine harm. Some of these generalities will change with new research. Pregnant women should consult with their physicians.

Sources: Briggs et al., 2008; R. D. Mann & Andrews, 2007; Sadler, 2009; U.S. Food and Drug Administration, 2011.

Advice from Scientists

Scientists interpret the research in contradictory ways. For instance, pregnant women in the United States are told to eat less fish, but those in the United Kingdom are told to increase fish consumption. The reason for these opposite messages is that fish contains both mercury (a teratogen) and DHA (an omega-3 fatty acid needed for fetal brain development) (Oken & Bellinger, 2008; Ramón et al., 2009). Scientists in the two nations weigh the benefits and risks of fish differently, and few women can assess each mouthful, which would require them to know each kind of fish and where it swam.

Another dispute involves bisphenol A (commonly used in plastics), banned in Canada but allowed in the United States. The effect of bisphenol A is disputed because research on mice, not humans, finds it teratogenic. Should people be guided by mouse studies? Undisputed epidemiological research on humans is logistically difficult because exposure must be measured at several different time points, including early gestation, but the outcome may not be manifest for many years. No doubt pregnant women are more exposed to bisphenol A than they were a decade ago, and perhaps exposure correlates with hyperactive 2-year-olds, but those facts can be interpreted in at least a dozen ways (Braun & Hauser, 2011; Diamanti-Kandarakis et al., 2009).

No one doubts that prenatal teratogens can cause behavioral problems, reproductive impairment, and several diseases many years after birth. Almost every common disease, almost every food additive, most prescription and nonprescription drugs (even caffeine and aspirin), many trace minerals in the air and water, emotional stress, exhaustion, and poor nutrition *might* impair prenatal development—but only at some times, in some amounts, in some mammals. Most research is with mice; harm to humans is rarely proven to everyone's satisfaction, and even when it is, the proper response can be controversial.

Some people worry that research is misapplied, making every woman worry and causing evident harm to a few. For example, since 1998, five states (Minnesota, North Dakota, Oklahoma, South Dakota, and Wisconsin) have authorized "involuntary commitment" (jail or forced residential treatment) for pregnant women who drink alcohol or use other psychoactive drugs. The legal basis is that the fetus is a future child and that therefore drinking during pregnancy is child abuse.

If a baby is stillborn, women who took drugs during pregnancy can be convicted of second-degree murder, as occurred for an Oklahoma woman, Theresa Hernandez, who took methamphetamines while pregnant and was sentenced to 15 years (Fentiman, 2009). Advocates for women consider such laws discriminatory, especially since women who are poor or American Indian are most likely to be imprisoned (Schroedel & Fiber, 2001). The threat of jail may cause women who most need prenatal care to avoid it altogether.

Prenatal Diagnosis

The benefits of early prenatal care are many: Women can be told which substances to avoid, they can learn what to eat and what to do, and they may be diagnosed and treated for some conditions (syphilis and HIV among them) that harm the fetus only if early treatment does not occur. Prenatal tests (of blood, urine, and fetal heart rate as well as ultrasound) reassure the parents long before fetal movement is apparent.

In general, early care protects fetal growth, makes birth easier, and renders parents better able to cope. When complications (such as twins, gestational diabetes, infections) arise, early recognition increases the chance of a healthy birth. Unfortunately, about 20 percent of early pregnancy tests *raise* anxiety instead of reducing

Especially for Social Workers When is it most important to convince women to be tested for HIV: before pregnancy, after conception, or immediately after birth? (see response, page 114)

it. For instance, the level of alpha-fetoprotein (AFP) may be too high or too low, or ultrasound may indicate multiple fetuses, abnormal growth, Down syndrome, or a mother's narrow pelvis. Many such warnings are **false positives,** which means they falsely suggest a problem that does not exist. Any warning, whether false or true, requires further testing but also leads to worry and soul-searching. Some choose to abort, some not, with neither option being what the parents assumed before prenatal testing. Consider the following.

false positive The result of a laboratory test that reports something as true when in fact it is not true. This can occur for pregnancy tests, when a woman might not be pregnant even though the test says she is, or during pregnancy when a problem is reported that actually does not exist.

A CASE TO STUDY

"What Do People Live to Do?"

John and Martha, both under age 35, were expecting their second child. Martha's initial prenatal screening revealed low alpha-fetoprotein, which could indicate Down syndrome.

Another blood test was scheduled. . . . John asked:

"What exactly is the problem?" . . .

"We've got a one in eight hundred and ninety-five shot at a retarded baby."

John smiled, "I can live with those odds."

"I'm still a little scared."

He reached across the table for my hand. "Sure," he said, "that's understandable. But even if there is a problem, we've caught it in time. . . . The worst case scenario is that you might have to have an abortion, and that's a long shot. Everything's going to be fine." . . .

"I might *have to have* an abortion?" The chill inside me was gone. Instead I could feel my face flushing hot with anger. "Since when do you decide what I *have* to do with my body?"

John looked surprised. "I never said I was going to decide anything," he protested. "It's just that if the tests show something wrong with the baby, of course we'll abort. We've talked about this."

"What we've talked about," I told John in a low, dangerous voice, "is that I am pro-choice. That means I decide whether or not I'd abort a baby with a birth defect. . . . I'm not so sure of this."

"You used to be," said John.

"I know I used to be." I rubbed my eyes. I felt terribly confused. "But now . . . look, John, it's not as though we're deciding whether or not to have a baby. We're deciding what *kind* of baby we're willing to accept. If it's perfect in every way, we keep it. If it doesn't fit the right specifications, whoosh! Out it goes.". . .

John was looking more and more confused. "Martha, why are you on this soapbox? What's your point?"

"My point is," I said, "that I'm trying to get you to tell me what you think constitutes a 'defective' baby. What about . . . oh, I don't know, a hyperactive baby? Or an ugly one?"

"They can't test for those things and—"

"Well, what if they could?" I said. "Medicine can do all kinds of magical tricks these days. Pretty soon we're going to be aborting babies because they have the gene for alcoholism, or homosexuality, or manic depression. . . . Did you know that in China they abort a lot of fetuses just because they're female?" I growled. "Is being a girl 'defective' enough for you?"

"Look," he said, "I know I can't always see things from your perspective. And I'm sorry about that. But the way I see it, if a baby is going to be deformed or something, abortion is a way to keep everyone from suffering—especially the baby. It's like shooting a horse that's broken its leg. . . . A lame horse dies slowly, you know? . . . It dies in terrible pain. And it can't run anymore. So it can't enjoy life even if it doesn't die. Horses live to run; that's what they do. If a baby is born not being able to do what other people do, I think it's better not to prolong its suffering."

". . . And what is it," I said softly, more to myself than to John, "what is it that people do? What do we live to do, the way a horse lives to run?"

[M. N. Beck, 1999, pp. 132–133, 135]

The second AFP test was in the normal range, "meaning there was no reason to fear . . . Down syndrome" (p. 137).

COURTESY KAREN GERDES

As you read in Chapter 3, genetic counselors help couples discuss their choices *before* becoming pregnant. John and Martha had had no counseling because the pregnancy was unplanned and their risk for Down syndrome was low. The opposite of a false positive is a false negative, a mistaken assurance that all is well. Amniocentesis later revealed that the second AFP was a false negative. Their fetus had Down syndrome after all. Martha decided against abortion.

Happy Boy Martha Beck not only loves her son Adam (shown here), but she also writes about the special experiences he has brought into the whole family's life—hers, John's, and their other children's. She is "pro-choice"; he was a chosen child.

Low Birthweight

Some newborns are small and immature. With modern hospital care, tiny infants usually survive, but it would be better for everyone—mother, father, baby, and society—if all newborns were in the womb for at least 35 weeks and weighed more than 2,500 grams (5½ pounds). (Usually, this text gives pounds before grams, but hospitals worldwide report birthweight using the metric system, so grams precede pounds and ounces here.)

Low birthweight (LBW) is defined by the World Health Organization as under 2,500 grams. LBW babies are further grouped into **very low birthweight (VLBW),** under 1,500 grams (3 pounds, 5 ounces), and **extremely low birthweight (ELBW),** under 1,000 grams (2 pounds, 3 ounces).

Maternal Behavior and Low Birthweight

Remember that fetal weight normally more than doubles in the last trimester of pregnancy, with 900 grams (about 2 pounds) of that gain occurring in the final three weeks. Thus, a baby born **preterm** (three or more weeks early; no longer called *premature*) is usually, but not always, LBW. Preterm birth correlates with many of the teratogens already mentioned, an example of the cascade that leads to newborns with evident problems. When the environment of the womb is harmful, the hormones of the fetus may begin birth early.

Early birth is only one cause of low birthweight. Some fetuses gain weight slowly throughout pregnancy and are *small-for-dates,* or **small for gestational age (SGA).** A full-term baby weighing only 2,500 grams and a 30-week-old fetus weighing only 1,000 grams are both SGA, even though the first is not quite low birthweight. Maternal or fetal illness might cause SGA, but maternal drug use is a more common cause. Every psychoactive drug slows fetal growth, with tobacco implicated in 25 percent of all low-birthweight births worldwide.

Another common reason for slow fetal growth is maternal malnutrition. Women who begin pregnancy underweight, who eat poorly during pregnancy, or who gain less than 3 pounds (1.3 kilograms) per month in the last six months are more likely to have an underweight infant. Malnutrition (not age) is the primary reason teenagers often have small babies. Unfortunately, many of the risk factors just mentioned—underweight, undereating, underage, and smoking—tend to occur together.

What About the Father?

The causes just mentioned of low birthweight focus on the pregnant woman: If she takes drugs or is undernourished, her fetus suffers. However, the more we learn about birth problems, the more important fathers—and grandmothers, neighbors, and communities—are discovered to be. As an editorial in a journal for obstetricians explains: "Fathers' attitudes regarding the pregnancy, fathers' behaviors during the prenatal period, and the relationship between fathers and mothers . . . may indirectly influence risk for adverse birth outcomes" (Misra et al., 2010, p. 99).

As already explained in Chapter 1, each person is embedded in an ecosystem of other people who influence every action. Since the future mother's behavior impacts the fetus, everyone who affects her also affects the future baby. For instance, one correlate of low birthweight is whether the pregnancy was intended (Shah et al., 2011). Obviously, a mother's intentions are in her mind, not her body. Just as obviously, her intentions are affected by the father, and his intentions as well as hers affect her diet, drug abstinence, prenatal care, and so on.

Not only fathers, but the entire social network and culture are crucial influences (Lewallen, 2011). This is most apparent in what has been called the *Hispanic paradox.* In general, low socioeconomic status (SES) correlates with low birthweight.

---

low birthweight (LBW) A body weight at birth of less than 5½ pounds (2,500 grams).

very low birthweight (VLBW) A body weight at birth of less than 3 pounds, 5 ounces (1,500 grams).

extremely low birthweight (ELBW) A body weight at birth of less than 2 pounds, 3 ounces (1,000 grams).

preterm A birth that occurs 3 or more weeks before the full 38 weeks of the typical pregnancy—that is, at 35 or fewer weeks after conception.

small for gestational age (SGA) A term for a baby whose birthweight is significantly lower than expected, given the time since conception. For example, a 5-pound (2,265-gram) newborn is considered SGA if born on time but not SGA if born two months early. (Also called *small-for-dates.*)

>> Response for Social Workers (from page 112) Testing and then treatment are useful at any time because women who know they are HIV-positive are more likely to get treatment, reduce the risk of transmission, or avoid pregnancy. If pregnancy does occur, early diagnosis is best. Getting tested after birth is too late for the baby.

Immigrants average lower SES than the native-born, and low-SES babies are often small. But, paradoxically, newborns born in the United States to immigrants are generally healthier in every way, including in birthweight, than are newborns of American-born women of the same ethnicity. Thus, although Hispanic Americans born in Mexico or South America average lower SES than Hispanics born in the United States, their pregnancies and newborns have fewer problems because their husbands, their mothers, and their culture keep them healthy.

Consequences of Low Birthweight

You have already read that life itself is uncertain for the smallest newborns. Ranking worse than most developed nations—and similar to Poland and Malaysia—the U.S. infant mortality rate (death in the first year) is about 7 per 1000, primarily because of low birthweight. When compared with newborns conceived at the same time but born later, very-low-birthweight infants are later to smile, to hold a bottle, to walk, and to communicate.

As months go by, cognitive difficulties as well as visual and hearing impairments emerge. Survivors who were high-risk newborns become infants and children who cry more, pay attention less, disobey, and experience language delays (Aarnoudse-Moens et al., 2009; Spinillo et al., 2009). Longitudinal research studies find that, compared with the average child in middle childhood, formerly SGA children have smaller brain volume, and those who were preterm have lower IQs (van Soelen et al., 2010). Even in adulthood, risks persist: Adults who were LBW are more likely to have heart disease and diabetes.

Longitudinal data provide both hope and caution. Remember that risk analysis gives odds, not certainties—averages that are not true in every case. Some ELBW infants, by age 4, are normal in brain development and overall (Claas et al., 2011; Spittle et al., 2009).

Comparing Nations

In some northern European nations, only 4 percent of newborns weigh under 2,500 grams; in several South Asian nations, more than 20 percent do. Worldwide, far fewer low-birthweight babies are born than 20 years ago, and neonatal deaths have been reduced by one-third as a result (Rajaratnam et al., 2010). Some nations, China and Chile among them, have shown dramatic improvement. In 1970, about half of Chinese newborns were LBW; recent estimates put that number at 3 percent (UNICEF, 2011). By contrast, in other nations, notably in sub-Saharan Africa, the LBW rate is steady or rising because global warming, AIDS, food shortages, wars, and other problems affect pregnancy.

Another nation with a rising LBW rate is the United States, where the rate fell steadily throughout most of the twentieth century, reaching a low of 7.0 percent in 1990. But then it rose again, with the 2008 rate at 8.2 percent—higher than that of virtually every other developed nation (see Figure 4.8 for a sampling).

Many scientists have developed hypotheses to explain the rising U.S. rates. One logical possibility is assisted reproduction, since ART often leads to low-birthweight twins and triplets (and other multiples). However, LBW rates are rising even for naturally

FIGURE 4.8

Getting Better Some public health experts consider the rate of low birthweight to be indicative of national health, since both are affected by the same causes. If that is true, the world is getting healthier, since the estimated LBW world average was 28 percent in 1980 but is now 15 percent. When all nations are included, 47 report LBW at 6 per 1000 or lower, which suggests that many nations (including the United States and United Kingdom) could improve.

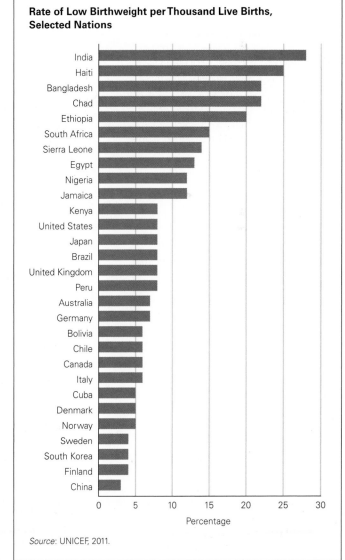

Rate of Low Birthweight per Thousand Live Births, Selected Nations

Source: UNICEF, 2011.

A Growing Trend The rate of first births to women in their 40s tripled from 1990 to 2008, although most newborns (96%) have mothers under age 40. Nonetheless, prenatal testing and medical advances have made late motherhood less risky than it was, with some happy results. This mother is 42.

cerebral palsy A disorder that results from damage to the brain's motor centers. People with cerebral palsy have difficulty with muscle control, so their speech and/ or body movements are impaired.

anoxia A lack of oxygen that, if prolonged, can cause brain damage or death.

conceived babies (Pinborg et al., 2004), so the ART hypothesis cannot be the only explanation. Added to the puzzle is the fact that several changes in maternal ethnicity, age, and health since 1990 should have decreased LBW, not increased it.

For example, African Americans have LBW newborns twice as often as the national average (almost 14 percent compared with 7 percent), and younger teenagers have smaller babies than do women in their 20s. However, the birth rate among African Americans and young teens was much lower in 2010 than it was in 1990. Furthermore, maternal obesity and diabetes are increasing; both lead to heavier babies.

Something must be amiss. One possibility is nutrition. Nations with many small newborns are also nations where hunger is prevalent, and increasing hunger correlates with increasing LBW. In both Chile and China, LBW fell as nutrition improved. As for the United States, the Department of Agriculture found an increase in *food insecurity* (measured by skipped meals, use of food stamps, and outright hunger) between 2000 and 2007. Food insecurity directly affects LBW, and it also increases chronic illness, which itself correlates with LBW (Seligman & Schillinger, 2010). In 2008, about 15 percent of U.S. households were considered food insecure, with rates higher among women in their prime reproductive years than among middle-aged women or men of any age. These rates increased with the economic recession of 2008–2010; if this hypothesis is accurate, rates of LBW will continue to increase.

Another possibility is drug use. As you will see in Chapter 16, the rate of smoking, drinking, and other drug use among high school girls reached a low in 1992, then increased, then decreased. Most U.S. women now giving birth are in a cohort that experienced rising drug use; they may still suffer the effects. If that is the reason, the current decrease in drug use will mean that LBW should fall again in the United States. Sadly, in developing nations, more young women are smoking and drinking than a decade ago, including in China, where LBW decreased dramatically. Will rates rise in China soon?

Complications During Birth

When a fetus is at risk because of low birthweight, preterm birth, genetic abnormality, or teratogen exposure, or when a mother is unusually young, old, small, or ill, birth complications become likely. As an example, **cerebral palsy** (difficulties with movement control resulting from brain damage) was once thought to be caused solely by birth procedures (excessive medication, slow breech birth, or use of forceps to pull the fetal head through the birth canal). However, we now know that birth procedures are not the sole cause: Cerebral palsy results from genetic vulnerability, teratogens, and maternal infection (J. R. Mann et al., 2009), worsened by insufficient oxygen to the fetal brain.

A lack of oxygen is **anoxia**, which often occurs for a second or two during birth, indicated by a slower fetal heart rate. To prevent prolonged anoxia, the fetal heart rate is monitored during labor and the Apgar is used immediately after birth. How long anoxia can continue without harming the brain depends on genes, birthweight, gestational age, drugs in the bloodstream (either taken by the mother before birth or given during birth), and many other factors. Thus, anoxia is part of a cascade that may cause cerebral palsy.

SUMMING UP

Risk analysis is a complex but necessary aspect of prenatal development because the placenta does not protect the fetus from all teratogens. Many factors reduce risk, including the mother's health and nourishment before pregnancy, her early prenatal care (to diagnose and treat problems and to teach the woman how to protect her fetus), and the father's protection. The timing of exposure to teratogens, the amount of toxin ingested, and the genes of the mother and fetus may be crucial. Low birthweight, slow growth, and preterm birth increase vulnerability: Maternal illness, drug use, and malnutrition are among the most common causes of these complications. The birth process can add to the problems of the vulnerable infant, especially if anoxia lasts more than a moment or two. ◼

>> The New Family

Humans are social creatures, seeking interaction with their families and their societies. Each person is affected by every other person, particularly within each family. We have already seen how this is true in fetal development; if anything, social interactions become even more important once the child is born.

The Newborn

Before birth, developing humans already contribute to their families via fetal movements and hormones that cause protective impulses in the mother early in pregnancy and nurturing impulses at the end. The appearance of the newborn (big hairless head, tiny feet, and so on) stirs the human heart, evident in adults' brain activity and heart rate when they see a baby. Fathers are often enraptured by their scraggly newborn and protective of the exhausted mothers, who may appreciate their husbands more than at other times.

Newborns are responsive social creatures in the first hours of life. They listen, stare, cry, stop crying, and cuddle. In the first day or two, a professional might administer the **Brazelton Neonatal Behavioral Assessment Scale (NBAS),** which records 46 behaviors, including 20 reflexes. Parents who watch their infant perform on the NBAS are amazed at the newborn's responses—and this fosters early parent–child connection (Hawthorne, 2009).

Technically, a **reflex** is an involuntary response to a particular stimulus. That definition makes reflexes seem automatic, with the new person having no role. Actually, the strength of reflexes varies from one newborn to the next, an early indication that each person is unique. Humans of every age instinctively seek to protect themselves (the eyeblink is an example). Newborns do this also, with three sets of reflexes (12 are cited here in italics) that protect them:

- *Reflexes that maintain oxygen supply.* The *breathing reflex* begins even before the umbilical cord, with its supply of oxygen, is cut. Additional reflexes that maintain oxygen are reflexive *hiccups* and *sneezes,* as well as *thrashing* (moving the arms and legs about) to escape something that covers the face.
- *Reflexes that maintain constant body temperature.* When infants are cold, they *cry, shiver,* and *tuck their legs* close to their bodies. When they are hot, they try to *push away* blankets and then stay still.
- *Reflexes that manage feeding.* The *sucking reflex* causes newborns to suck anything that touches their lips—fingers, toes, blankets, and rattles, as well as natural and artificial nipples of various textures and shapes. The *rooting reflex* causes babies to turn their mouths toward anything that brushes against their cheeks—a reflexive search for a nipple—and start to suck. *Swallowing* is another reflex that aids feeding, as are *crying* when the stomach is empty and *spitting up* when too much has been swallowed quickly.

Other reflexes are not necessary for survival but signify the state of brain and body functions. Among them are the following five:

Brazelton Neonatal Behavioral Assessment Scale (NBAS) A test often administered to newborns that measures responsiveness and records 46 behaviors, including 20 reflexes.

reflex An unlearned, involuntary action or movement in response to a stimulus. A reflex occurs without conscious thought.

Never Underestimate the Power of a Reflex For developmentalists, newborn reflexes are mechanisms for survival, indicators of brain maturation, and vestiges of evolutionary history. For parents, they are mostly delightful and sometimes amazing. Both of these viewpoints are demonstrated by three star performers: a newborn boy sucking peacefully on the doctor's finger, a newborn grasping so tightly that his legs dangle in space, and a 1-day-old girl stepping eagerly forward on legs too tiny to support her body.

- *Babinski reflex.* When a newborn's feet are stroked, the toes fan upward.
- *Stepping reflex.* When newborns are held upright, feet touching a flat surface, they move their legs as if to walk.
- *Swimming reflex.* When held horizontally on their stomachs, newborns stretch out their arms and legs.
- *Palmar grasping reflex.* When something touches newborns' palms, they grip it tightly.
- *Moro reflex.* When someone bangs on the table they are lying on, newborns fling their arms outward and then bring them together on their chests, crying with wide-open eyes.

These reflexes are responses to experiences, not unlike an adult's sudden fear, or lust, or anger. The senses are also responsive: New babies listen more to voices than to traffic, for instance. Thus, in many ways newborns connect with the people of their world, who usually respond. If the baby performing these actions on the Brazelton were your own, you would be proud and amazed; that is part of being human.

Especially for Scientists Research with animals can benefit people, but it is sometimes wrongly used to support conclusions about people. When does that happen? (see response, page 120)

New Fathers

Fathers affect a newborn's development. As we have seen, fathers-to-be help mothers-to-be stay healthy, nourished, and drug-free. The father's role in birth may also be crucial.

Father Presence

At birth, the father's presence reduces complications, in part because his presence helps his wife. I observed this with my own daughter, whose anxiety rose when the doctor and midwife discussed a possible cesarean without asking her opinion. Her husband told her, "All you need to do is relax between contractions and push when a contraction comes. I will do the rest." Elissa listened. No cesarean.

The father's actual presence is helpful, but present or not, his legal acceptance of the birth is important to the newborn. A study of all live single births in Milwaukee from 1993 to 2006 (151,869 babies!) found that medical complications correlated

Especially for Nurses in Obstetrics Can the father be of any practical help in the birth process? (see response, page 120)

with several expected variables (e.g., maternal cigarette smoking) and one unexpected one—no father listed on the birth record. This was especially apparent for European American births: When the mother did not list the father, she was more likely to have long labor, a cesarean section, or other complications (Ngui et al., 2009).

Currently, about 40 percent of all U. S. women are not married when their baby is born (U.S. Bureau of the Census, 2010), but fathers may still be on the birth certificate. Apparently, when fathers acknowledge their paternity, birth is better for mother and baby.

Couvade

Pregnancy and birth may be biologically (not just psychologically) experienced by fathers. For example, levels of the stress hormone cortisol correlate between expectant fathers and mothers, probably because they make each other anxious or relaxed (Berg & Wynne-Edwards, 2002). Beyond that, many fathers experience symptoms of pregnancy and birth, including weight gain and indigestion during pregnancy and pain during labor. Indeed, among some Latin American Indians, fathers go through the motions of labor when their wives do, to help ensure an easy birth.

Paternal experiences of pregnancy and birth are called **couvade,** expected in some cultures, a normal variation in many, and considered pathological in others (M. Sloan, 2009). In developed nations, couvade is unnoticed and unstudied, but researchers find that fathers are often intensely involved with pregnancy and birth (Brennan et al., 2007).

Parental Alliance

Remember John and Martha, the young couple whose amniocentesis revealed that their fetus had trisomy-21 (Down syndrome)? One night at 3:00 A.M., after about seven months of pregnancy, Martha was crying uncontrollably. She told John she was scared.

> "Scared of what?" he said. "Of a little baby who's not as perfect as you think he ought to be?"
>
> "I didn't say I wanted him to be perfect," I said. "I just want him to be normal. That's all I want. Just normal."
>
> "That is total bullshit. . . . You don't want this baby to be normal. You'd throw him in a dumpster if he just turned out to be normal. What you really want is for him to be superhuman."
>
> "For your information," I said in my most acid tone, "I was the one who decided to keep this baby, even though he's got Down's. You were the one who wanted to throw him in a dumpster."
>
> "How would you know?" John's voice was still gaining volume. "You never asked me what I wanted, did you? No. You never even asked me."
>
> [M. N. Beck, 1999, p. 255]

This episode ended well, with a long, warm, and honest conversation between the two prospective parents. Each learned what their fetus meant to the other, a taboo topic until that night. Adam, their future son, became an important part of their relationship. Their lack of communication up to this point, and the sudden eruption of unexpressed emotions, is not unusual, because pregnancy itself raises memories from childhood and fears about the future. Yet honest and intimate communication is crucial throughout pregnancy,

Paternal Pride Twins mean trouble—less sleep, less money, more worry. Yet, like most parents of newborns, no matter what special complications they entail, this father is enraptured with his 1-day-old sons.

couvade Symptoms of pregnancy and birth experienced by fathers.

A Good Beginning The apparent joy and bonding between this expectant couple and their unborn child is a wonderful sign. Although this couple in Germany may experience social discrimination—one reason the divorce rate is higher among multiracial couples than monoracial ones—their own parental alliance is crucial for their child. Many multiracial children become adults with higher achievement, greater self-understanding, and more tolerance than others.

parental alliance Cooperation between a mother and a father based on their mutual commitment to their children. In a parental alliance, the parents support each other in their shared parental roles.

birth, and child rearing, helping to create the foundation for a **parental alliance,** a commitment by both parents to cooperate in raising the child.

The parental alliance is especially beneficial when the infant is physically vulnerable, such as having a low birthweight. The converse is also true: Family conflict when a newborn needs extra care increases the risk of child maladjustment and parental divorce (Whiteside-Mansell et al., 2009).

New Mothers

About half of all women experience physical problems after birth, such as healing from a c-section, or painfully sore nipples, or problems with urination (Danel et al., 2003). However, worse than any physical problems are psychological ones. When the birth hormones decrease, between 8 and 15 percent of women experience **postpartum depression,** a sense of inadequacy and sadness (called *baby blues* in the mild version and *postpartum psychosis* in the most severe form) (Perfetti et al., 2004). With postpartum depression, baby care (feeding, diapering, bathing) feels very burdensome, babies are not always comforted, and the mother may have thoughts of neglecting or abusing the infant.

postpartum depression A new mother's feelings of inadequacy and sadness in the days and weeks after giving birth.

Sometimes the first sign that something is amiss is that the mother is euphoric after birth. She cannot sleep, or stop talking, or keep from worrying about the newborn. Some of this is normal, but family members and medical personnel need to be supportive yet alert to the mother's moods. Maternal depression can have a long-term impact on the child, one of the many reasons that postpartum depression should be quickly recognized and treated. Fathers are usually the first responders; they may be instrumental in getting the help the mother and baby need (Cuijpers et al., 2010; Goodman & Gotlib, 2002). This is easier said than done: Fathers may become depressed as well; in such cases, other people need to help.

From a developmental perspective, some causes of postpartum depression (such as financial stress or marital problems) predate the pregnancy; others occur during pregnancy; others correlate with birth (especially if the mother is unprepared or alone or if she fantasized a very different birth process than actually occurred); and still others are specific to the particular infant (health, feeding, or sleeping problems). Successful breast-feeding mitigates maternal depression, one of the many reasons a lactation consultant is an important part of the new mother's support team.

>> Response for Scientists (from page 118) Animal research should not, by itself, confirm an assertion that has popular appeal but no scientific evidence. This occurred in the social construction that physical contact was crucial for parent–infant bonding.

Bonding

parent–infant bond The strong, loving connection that forms as parents hold, examine, and feed their newborn.

To what extent are the first hours crucial for the **parent–infant bond,** the strong, loving connection that forms as parents hold, examine, and feed their newborn? It has been claimed that this bond develops in the first hours after birth when a mother touches her naked baby, just as sheep and goats must immediately smell and nuzzle their newborns if they are to nurture them (Klaus & Kennell, 1976).

Although the concept of bonding has been used to argue against the impersonal medicalization of birth, research does not find that early skin-to-skin contact is essential for humans (Eyer, 1992; Lamb, 1982). Unlike sheep and goats, most mammals do not need immediate contact for parents to nurture their offspring. In fact, substantial research on monkeys begins with *cross-fostering,* a strategy in which newborns are removed from their biological mothers in the first days of life and raised by another female or even a male. A strong and beneficial relationship sometimes develops (Suomi, 2002).

>> Response for Nurses in Obstetrics (from page 118) Usually not, unless he is experienced, well taught, or has expert guidance. But his presence provides emotional support for the woman, which makes the birth process easier and healthier for mother and baby.

However, although mother–infant contact is not essential for bonding, the active involvement of both parents in pregnancy, birth, and newborn care nonetheless benefits them and their baby. Factors that encourage parents (biological

Beginning Well Newborns in Manila are more often low-weight and fragile than babies born in wealthier nations, but they do have one advantage, shown here: Kangaroo care is standard practice.

or adoptive) to nurture their newborns have lifelong benefits, proven with mice, monkeys, and humans (Champagne & Curley, 2010).

The role of early maternal care has recently become apparent with **kangaroo care,** when the newborn lies between the mother's breasts, skin-to-skin, listening to her heartbeat and feeling her body heat. Many studies find that kangaroo-care newborns sleep more deeply, gain weight more quickly, and spend more time alert than do infants with standard care (Feldman et al., 2002; Ferber & Makhoul, 2004; Gathwala et al., 2008).

Kangaroo care was first used with low-birthweight newborns and resulted in faster weight gain and fewer medical complications. Recently, it has also been successful with healthy newborns and with fathers providing the care—evidence that the entire new family is affected by early contact (Thomas, 2008). All the research finds that kangaroo care benefits babies, not only in the hospital but months later, either because of improved infant adjustment to life outside the womb or because of increased parental sensitivity and effectiveness. Which of these two is the explanation? Probably both.

Implementation of many strategies, especially for fragile infants and their parents, is especially needed in developing nations, where kangaroo care and other measures could reduce infant deaths by 20 to 40 percent (Bhutta et al., 2008). From a developmental perspective, the most difficult time for high-risk infants occurs when they leave the hospital, in the days and weeks after birth. At this time, measures to involve parents in early care are crucial. As we will see in later chapters, the relationship between parent and child is mutual, developing over months, not merely hours. Birth is one step of a lifelong journey.

kangaroo care A form of newborn care in which mothers (and sometimes fathers) rest their babies on their naked chests, like kangaroo mothers that carry their immature newborns in a pouch on their abdomen.

SUMMING UP

Every member of the new family contributes to their shared connection, enabling them all to thrive. The new baby has responsive senses and many reflexes. Close observation and reflection reveal how much the new baby can do. Father support of the new family is crucial, sometimes being the reason for a healthy, happy newborn and mother. Postpartum depression is not rare; factors before and after birth affect how serious and long-lasting it is. Family relationships begin before conception, may be strengthened throughout pregnancy and birth, and continue throughout the life span. ∎

A Teenage Mother This week-old baby, born in a poor village in Myanmar (Burma), has a better chance of survival than he might otherwise have had because his 18-year-old mother has bonded with him.

SUMMARY

Prenatal Growth

1. The first two weeks of prenatal growth are called the germinal period. During this time, the single-celled zygote multiplies into more than 100 cells that will eventually form both the placenta and the embryo. The growing organism may travel down the fallopian tube and implant.

2. The period from the third through the eighth week after conception is called the embryonic period. The heart begins to beat, and the eyes, ears, nose, and mouth form. By the eighth week, the embryo has the basic organs and features of a human, with the exception of the sex organs.

3. The fetal period extends from the ninth week until birth. In the ninth week, the sexual organs develop. By the end of the third month, all the organs and body structures have formed. The fetus attains viability at 22 weeks, when the brain is sufficiently mature to regulate basic body functions. Babies born before the 26th week are at high risk of death or disability.

4. The average fetus gains approximately 5 pounds (2,268 grams) during the last three months of pregnancy and weighs 7½ pounds (3,400 grams) at birth. Maturation of brain, lungs, and heart ensures survival of more than 99 percent of all full-term babies born in developed nations.

Birth

5. Birth typically begins with contractions that push the fetus out of the uterus and then through the vagina. The Apgar scale, which rates the neonate's vital signs at one minute and again at five minutes after birth, provides a quick evaluation of the infant's health.

6. Medical assistance can speed contractions, dull pain, and save lives. However, many aspects of medicalized birth have been criticized as impersonal and unnecessary, including about half the cesareans performed in the United States. Contemporary birthing practices are aimed at finding a balance, protecting the baby but also allowing more parental involvement and control.

Problems and Solutions

7. Some teratogens (diseases, drugs, and pollutants) cause physical impairment. Others, called behavioral teratogens, harm the brain and therefore impair cognitive abilities and affect personality traits.

8. Whether a teratogen harms an embryo or fetus depends on timing of exposure, amount of exposure, and genetic vulnerability. To protect against prenatal complications, good public and personal health practices are strongly recommended. Some specifics are debatable, but it is always the case that fathers and other family members affect the pregnant woman's health.

9. Doctors differ in the advice they give to pregnant women about avoiding teratogens, partly because they interpret the research differently and partly because of culture.

10. Low birthweight (under 5½ pounds, or 2,500 grams) may arise from multiple births, placental problems, maternal illness, malnutrition, smoking, drinking, drug use, and age. Compared with full-term newborns, preterm and underweight babies experience more medical difficulties. Fetuses that grow slowly (small for gestational age, or SGA) are especially vulnerable.

11. Birth complications, such as unusually long and stressful labor that includes anoxia (a lack of oxygen to the fetus), have many causes. Long-term handicaps, such as cerebral palsy, are not inevitable for such children, but careful nurturing from their parents may be needed.

The New Family

12. Humans are social animals. Newborns respond to others in many ways. The Brazelton Neonatal Behavioral Assessment Scale measures 46 newborn behaviors, 20 of which are reflexes.

13. Fathers can be supportive during pregnancy as well as helpful in birth; such support correlates with shorter labor and fewer complications. Some fathers become so involved with the pregnancy and birth that they experience couvade.

14. Many women feel unhappy, incompetent, or unwell after giving birth. Postpartum depression gradually disappears with appropriate help; fathers are crucial to the well-being of mother and child. Ideally, a parental alliance supports the child's well-being from birth on.

15. Kangaroo care is especially beneficial when the newborn is of low birthweight. Mother–newborn interaction should be encouraged, although the parent–infant bond depends on many factors in addition to birth practices.

KEY TERMS

germinal period (p. 94)
embryonic period (p. 94)
fetal period (p. 94)
implantation (p. 94)
embryo (p. 94)
fetus (p. 96)
ultrasound (p. 96)
age of viability (p. 97)
Apgar scale (p. 100)

cesarean section (c-section) (p. 101)
doula (p. 104)
teratogens (p. 106)
behavioral teratogens (p. 106)
threshold effect (p. 108)
fetal alcohol syndrome (FAS) (p. 108)
false positive (p. 113)
low birthweight (LBW) (p. 114)

very low birthweight (VLBW) (p. 114)
extremely low birthweight (ELBW) (p. 114)
preterm (p. 114)
small for gestational age (SGA) (p. 114)
cerebral palsy (p. 116)
anoxia (p. 116)

Brazelton Neonatal Behavioral Assessment Scale (NBAS) (p. 117)
reflex (p. 117)
couvade (p. 119)
parental alliance (p. 120)
postpartum depression (p. 120)
parent–infant bond (p. 120)
kangaroo care (p. 121)

WHAT HAVE YOU LEARNED?

Prenatal Growth

1. What are three major developments in the germinal period?

2. What body parts develop during the embryonic period?

3. What major milestone is reached about halfway through the fetal period?

4. What are three major reasons for why pregnancy continues months after the fetus could live outside the uterus?

Birth

5. Why has the Apgar scale increased newborns' survival rate?

6. Why has the rate of cesarean sections increased?

7. Why are developmentalists concerned that surgery is often part of birth?

8. Why is the newborn mortality rate much higher in some countries than in others?

9. What are the differences among a doula, a midwife, and a doctor?

Problems and Solutions

10. What teratogens harm the developing body structure?

11. Why is it difficult to establish the impact of behavioral teratogens?

12. How does timing affect the risk of harm to the fetus?

13. Why does risk analysis not predict precise damage to a fetus?

14. What factors increase or decrease the risk of spina bifida?

15. What are the potential consequences of drinking alcohol during pregnancy?

16. What are the differences among LBW, VLBW, and ELBW?

17. List at least four reasons why a baby might be born LBW.

18. How have U.S. LBW rates changed in the past decade?

19. What is the long-term prediction for a very tiny or vulnerable newborn who survives?

20. How do culture and customs affect one's exposure to teratogens?

The New Family

21. What do newborns do to aid their survival?

22. What impact do fathers have during and after birth?

23. How do fathers experience pregnancy?

24. What are the signs of postpartum depression?

25. What affects the parent–infant bond?

26. What are the results of kangaroo care?

APPLICATIONS

1. Go to a nearby greeting-card store and analyze the cards about pregnancy and birth. Do you see any cultural attitudes (e.g., variations depending on the sex of the newborn or of the parent)? If possible, compare those cards with cards from a store that caters to another economic or ethnic group.

2. Interview three mothers of varied backgrounds about their birth experiences. Make your interviews open-ended—let them choose what to tell you, as long as they give at least a 10-minute description. Then compare and contrast the three accounts, noting especially any influences of culture, personality, circumstances, and cohort.

3. People sometimes wonder how any pregnant woman could jeopardize the health of her fetus. Consider your own health-related behavior in the past month—exercise, sleep, nutrition, drug use, medical and dental care, disease avoidance, and so on. Would you change your behavior if you were pregnant? Would it make a difference if you, your family, and your partner did not want a baby?

>>ONLINE CONNECTIONS

To accompany your textbook, you have access to a number of online resources, including quizzes for every chapter of the book, flashcards (in English and Spanish), critical thinking questions, and case studies. For access to any of these links, go to www.worthpublishers.com/bergerca9e. In addition to these free resources, you'll also find links to podcasts, video clips, diagnostic quizzing with personalized study advice, and an ebook. Some of the videos and activities available online include:

- *Brain Development: In the Beginning.* Three-dimensional animation follows brain development from the formation of the neural tube until birth. Animations of microscopic changes in the brain include synaptic pruning.

- *Periods of Prenatal Development.* A series of detailed animations show the stages of prenatal development from fertilization to birth.

II

the first two years

Adults don't change much in a year or two. Their hair might grow longer, grayer, or thinner; they might gain or lose weight; they might learn something new. But if you saw friends you hadn't seen for two years, you'd recognize them immediately.

By contrast, if you cared for a newborn 24 hours a day for a month, traveled for two years, and came back, you might not recognize him or her. The baby would have quadrupled in weight, grown a foot taller, and sprouted a new head of hair. Behavior and emotions would have changed, too—less crying, but new laughter and fear—including fear of you.

A year or two is not much compared with the 70 to 85 years of the average life. However, in those first two years humans reach half their adult height, start to talk in sentences, and begin to express almost every emotion—not just joy and fear but also love, jealousy, and shame. The next three chapters describe these radical and awesome changes.

The First Two Years: Biosocial Development

WHAT WILL YOU KNOW?

1. How can you tell if a baby is growing normally in the first year of life?

2. Does brain wiring in the first two years depend on genes or experience?

3. When do babies see clearly, hear well, and walk on their own?

4. Why did more than half the newborns die a century ago, and almost all thrive now?

Our first child, Bethany, was born when I was in graduate school. I studiously memorized developmental norms, including sitting at 6 months, walking and talking at 12. At 14 months, though, Bethany spoke a dozen words but had not yet taken her first step. Instead of worrying, I decided genes were more influential than anything I did. I also read that French babies are among the latest walkers in the world, and my grandmother was French. My speculation was confirmed when our next two children, Rachel and Elissa, were also slow to walk.

Fourteen years later, when Sarah was born, I could afford a full-time caregiver, Mrs. Todd, from Jamaica. I cautioned her that Berger children walk late.

"Sarah will be walking by one year," Mrs. Todd told me. "My daughter Gillian walked at 10 months."

"We'll see," I replied, confident of my genetic explanation.

I underestimated Sarah and Mrs. Todd, who bounced my baby on her lap, day after day, and spent hours giving her "walking practice"—to Sarah's great delight. My fourth child took her first step at 12 months, late for a Todd baby, early for a Berger, and a humbling lesson for me.

This chapter describes physical development in the first two years of life, emphasizing changes in the body and brain, including cortex maturation, perceptions, and muscle control. All these changes make toddlers quite different from newborns. Individual variations in development abound, some genetic and some contextual, including, as I now believe, many resulting from cultures and caregivers. This chapter is titled *biosocial*, not merely biological or physical, because biological development is closely connected to the social context.

>> Body Changes

In infancy, growth is so rapid and the consequences of neglect are so severe that gains are closely monitored. Medical checkups, including measurement of height, weight, and head circumference, occur often in developed nations because those measurements provide the first clues as to whether an infant is progressing as expected—or not.

Body Size

Exactly how rapidly does growth usually occur? Infants typically double their birthweight by the fourth month and triple it by age 1. For example, a 7-pound newborn might weigh 14 pounds at 4 months and 21 pounds at 12 months (from 3,250 to 6,500 to 9,750 grams). Physical growth then slows somewhat, but it is still rapid. By 24 months, most children weigh almost 28 pounds (13 kilograms) and have grown from about 20 inches at birth to about 34 inches tall (51 to 86 centimeters). This means that 2-year-olds are half their adult height and about a fifth of their adult weight, four times heavier than they were at birth (see Figure 5.1).

Much of the weight increase in the early months is fat. Often, in the *birth catch-up*, small babies experience extra gain to catch up to the norm. Baby fat is

FIGURE 5.1

Eat and Sleep The rate of increasing weight in the first weeks of life makes it obvious why new babies need to be fed, day and night.

stored to keep the brain nourished if teething or the sniffles interfere with sucking. If nutrition is temporarily inadequate, the body stops growing but not the brain—a phenomenon called **head-sparing.** (Chronic malnutrition is discussed later in this chapter.)

These norms are averages; individuals vary. Ethnic differences are common: Babies of South Asian ancestry tend to be somewhat smaller than babies from Africa if both groups of babies are well nourished (Nightingale et al., 2011). Of course, those are generalities: There are dozens of ethnic groups in South Asia and Africa, and even within groups, genes vary. A better predictor of expected growth for a particular infant is the average growth of both parents and all siblings. Even so, each infant shares only half of the genes of any one of these family members; some well-nourished children differ not only from their ethnic group but also from their relatives.

To decide whether a particular baby is growing well, it is best to know that infant's **percentile,** a number that indicates rank compared to other similar people of the same age. Percentiles range from zero to 100. Thus, a child of average weight would be close to the 50th percentile. Some children would be heavy (above the 75th percentile) and some quite light (below the 25th). Although half of all babies would weigh below the 25th or above the 75th percentile, most of them would be fine if they always ranked relatively high or low.

Percentiles allow a given child to be compared not only to others the same age but also to his or her own past growth. Thus, 6-month-olds whose weight *and* height are at the 90th percentile are quite normal if their newborn weight and height were also at the 90th percentile. Also growing normally is the child who is consistently at the 20th percentile.

Percentiles alert professionals and parents when something is amiss. If a newborn is at the 50th percentile in height and weight but 6 months later is at the 40th percentile in height but the 80th percentile in weight, that infant may be getting too heavy. Neither the 40th nor the 80th percentile is worrisome alone, but the combination and the change are warning signs. Losing weight compared to one's former percentile is also worrisome, as is being markedly underweight throughout the first two years. That is worse than being born underweight, since many small newborns catch up. Continual underweight in infancy correlates with becoming a short adult and, for females, with becoming overweight (Wang et al., 2010).

head-sparing A biological mechanism that protects the brain when malnutrition affects body growth. The brain is the last part of the body to be damaged by malnutrition.

percentile A point on a ranking scale of 0 to 100. The 50th percentile is the midpoint; half the people in the population being studied rank higher and half rank lower.

Same Boy, Much Changed All three photos show Conor, first at 3 months, then at 12 months, and finally at 24 months. Note the rapid growth in the first two years, not only in hair and expression, but also in cognition—from a focus on sucking to a fantasy as a caped crusader.

CECILIA VARAS

PETER SOLNESS / LONELY PLANET IMAGES

Protective Sleeping It matters little what infants sleep in—bassinet, cradle, crib, or Billum bag made from local plants in Papua New Guinea, as shown here. In fact, this kind of bag is very useful since babies can easily be carried in it. It can also be used for carrying food, tools, and much else. What does matter is the infant's sleeping position—always on the back, like this healthy infant.

REM sleep Rapid eye movement sleep, a stage of sleep characterized by flickering eyes behind closed lids, dreaming, and rapid brain waves.

FIGURE 5.2

Good Night, Moon Average sleep per 24-hour period is given in percentiles because there is much variation in how many hours a young child normally sleeps. Other charts from this study show nighttime sleep and daytime napping. Most 1-year-olds sleep about 10 hours a night, with about 2 hours of napping, but some sleep much less; by age 3, about 10 percent have given up naps altogether. Note that these data are drawn from reports by U.S. parents, based on an Internet questionnaire. Actual sleep monitors or reports by a more diverse group of parents would probably show even more variation.

Sleep

Newborns spend most of their time sleeping, about 15 to 17 hours a day. Hours of sleep decrease rapidly with maturity: The norm per day for the first 2 months is 14¼ hours; for the next 3 months, 13¼ hours; for 6 to 17 months, 12¾ hours. Variation is particularly apparent in the early weeks: One new baby in 20 sleeps nine hours or fewer per day and one in 20 sleeps 19 hours or more, according to parents' reports (Sadeh et al., 2009) (see Figure 5.2).

Sleep specifics vary not only because of biology (age and genes) but also because of the social environment. With responsive parents, full-term newborns who are well-fed sleep more than low-birthweight newborns, who need to eat every two hours. Babies who are fed cow's milk and cereal sleep more soundly—easier for parents but not necessarily good for the baby. Social environment matters more directly: If parents respond to predawn cries with food and play, babies learn to wake up early night after night, which is not necessarily good for anyone (Sadeh et al., 2009).

Throughout childhood, regular and ample sleep correlates with normal brain maturation, learning, emotional regulation, academic success, and psychological adjustment (Mindell & Owens, 2010). Children who wake up frequently and sleep too little often have other physical or psychological problems. Lifelong, sleep deprivation can cause poor health, and vice versa (Murphy & Delanty, 2007).

Over the first months, the relative amount of time spent in each type or stage of sleep changes. Babies born preterm may always seem to be dozing. Full-term newborns dream a lot; about half their sleep is **REM sleep** (rapid eye movement sleep), with flickering eyes and rapid brain waves. That indicates dreaming. REM sleep declines over the early weeks, as does "transitional sleep," the dozing, half-awake stage. At 3 or 4 months, quiet sleep (also called *slow-wave sleep*) increases markedly.

By about 3 months, all the various states of waking and sleeping become more evident. Thus, although newborns often seem half asleep, neither in deep sleep nor wide awake, by 3 months most babies have periods of alertness (when they are neither hungry nor sleepy) and periods of deep sleep (when noises do not rouse them).

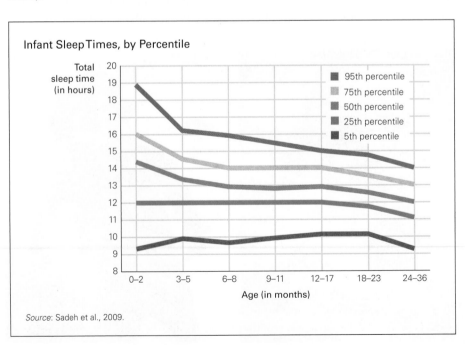

Infant Sleep Times, by Percentile

Total sleep time (in hours)

- 95th percentile
- 75th percentile
- 50th percentile
- 25th percentile
- 5th percentile

Age (in months): 0–2, 3–5, 6–8, 9–11, 12–17, 18–23, 24–36

Source: Sadeh et al., 2009.

First-born infants typically "receive more attention" (Bornstein, 2002, p. 28), which may be why they have more sleep problems than do later-borns. Overall, an Internet study of more than 5,000 North American children under age 3 found that, according to their parents, sleep was a problem for 25 percent (Sadeh et al., 2009). Of course, sleep problems are more troubling for parents than for infants. This does not render them insignificant; overtired parents may be less patient and responsive (Bayer et al., 2007).

Developmentalists agree that insisting that infants conform to the parents' sleep–wake schedule can be frustrating to the parents and difficult for infants, whose brain patterns and digestion are not ready for a long night's sleep. However, when children frequently interrupt the adults' sleep, parents suffer. Parent reactions to infant sleep shape the baby's sleep patterns, which in turn affect the parents (Sadeh et al., 2010), as the following explains. Ideally, families interact and adapt until everyone's needs are met.

Especially for New Parents You are aware of cultural differences in sleeping practices, and this raises a very practical issue: Should your newborn sleep in bed with you? (see response, page 132)

co-sleeping A custom in which parents and their children (usually infants) sleep together in the same room.

THINKING CRITICALLY

Where Should Babies Sleep?

Traditionally, most Western infants slept in cribs in their own rooms; it was thought that they might be traumatized by the parents' sexual interactions. By contrast, traditional parents in Asia, Africa, and Latin America slept beside their infants, a practice called **co-sleeping.** They thought that parent–child separation at night was cruel. Even today, Asian and African mothers worry more about separation, and European and North American mothers worry more about sex. A recent study in 19 nations confirms those differences: The extremes were 82 percent of babies in Vietnam sleeping with their parents compared to 6 percent in New Zealand (Mindell et al., 2010).

Co-sleeping is becoming more common among Western parents, although reports differ as to the rates. About half of a group of British parents slept with their infants some of the time (Blair & Ball, 2004). A North American Internet survey found that 20 percent of the youngest babies were put to sleep in the parents' bed, as were 18 percent of the toddlers (Sadeh et al., 2009). Those parents who did not begin the night with their babies in the same room were asked, "What do you do if your infant wakes during the night?" "Bring child to parents' bed," answered 21 percent.

Both those who advocate co-sleeping and those who oppose it cite evidence (Hormann, 2007). With co-sleeping, breast-feeding is easier and more common. But so is sudden infant death (Gettler & McKenna, 2010; Ruys et al., 2007). For both these statistics, co-sleeping sometimes means *bed-sharing,* and that may be one reason the controversy

rages. Everyone agrees that sharing a bed with a newborn is dangerous if the adult is drugged or drunk—and thus in danger of "overlying" the baby. It may be that co-sleeping is beneficial but bed-sharing is not, partly because adult beds, unlike cribs, are often soft, with comforters, mattresses, and pillows that increase a baby's risk of suffocation (Alm, 2007). (In cultures where bed-sharing is the norm, most people sleep on the floor.) Manufacturers, noting this dilemma, have designed "co-sleepers," which fit on the side of a bed, allowing newborns to be safe but also next to parents.

Obviously, culture affects sleep customs (in many cultures, husbands and wives do not share a bed). In addition, adults are influenced by their past experiences as infants, a phenomenon called *ghosts in the nursery* because the parents bring decades-old memories into the bedrooms of their children. One study found that, compared to Israeli adults who had slept near their parents as infants, those who had slept communally with other infants (as sometimes occurred on a kibbutz) were more likely to interpret their own infants' nighttime cries as distress, requiring comfort (Tikotzky et al., 2010).

Developmentalists hesitate to declare any particular pattern best (Tamis-Lemonda et al., 2008) because the issue is "tricky and

STEPHEN CHANG / JUPITER IMAGES

Danger or Safety? Will Susan roll over on newborn Anisa as they sleep? Some physicians fear that co-sleeping poses a risk of suffocation, but others believe that it is protective.

complex" (Gettler & McKenna, 2010, p. 77). Sleeping alone may encourage a child's independence and individuality—traits appreciated in some cultures, abhorred in others. Past experiences—the ghosts in the nursery—affect adult thinking; developmentalists do not want to welcome some ghosts while dismissing others.

A crucial issue is sleep deprivation. A videotape analysis found that, although co-sleeping infants awakened twice as often as solo-sleeping infants (six versus three times a night), co-sleeping babies got as much sleep as solo sleepers because they went back to sleep more quickly (Mao et al., 2004). One of the main reasons parents opt for co-sleeping—and a powerful argument for it—is that adults are less exhausted if they can stay in bed all night, simply reaching over to give a nighttime feeding.

This choice may backfire, however: If children become accustomed to co-sleeping, they may continue to crawl into their parents' bed when they are long past infancy. Thus, in the long run parents might lose sleep for years because they wanted more sleep when their babies were small. Of course, that concern reflects a cultural norm as well. According to an ethnographic study, by the time Mexican Mayan children are 5 years old, they choose "when, how long, and with whom to sleep" (Gaskins, 1999, p. 40), a practice that bewilders many other North Americans.

Logical arguments on both sides are many, but they are usually overwhelmed by cultural practices and personal ghosts. Whatever you think best, do your conclusions reflect values and emotions that are disconnected from developmental considerations?

>> **Response for New Parents** (from page 131) From the psychological and cultural perspectives, babies can sleep anywhere as long as the parents can hear them if they cry. The main consideration is safety: Infants should not sleep on a mattress that is too soft, nor should a baby sleep beside an adult who is drunk or drugged or sleeps very soundly. Otherwise, the family should decide for itself where its members would sleep best.

SUMMING UP

Birthweight doubles, triples, and quadruples by 4 months, 12 months, and 24 months, respectively. Height increases by about a foot (about 30 centimeters) in the first two years. Such norms are useful as general guidelines, but personal percentile rankings over time indicate whether a particular infant is growing appropriately, with brain growth more critical than body growth. With maturation, sleep becomes regular, dreaming becomes less common, and distinct sleep–wake patterns develop. The youngest infants sleep more hours in total but for less time at a stretch; by age 1, most babies sleep longer at night, with a nap or two during the day. Cultural and caregiving practices influence norms, schedules, and expectations. ■

In Just the First Two Years . . .

Percentage of adult size

FIGURE 5.3

Growing Up Two-year-olds are barely talking and are totally dependent on adults, but they have already reached half their adult height and three-fourths of their adult brain size. This is dramatic evidence that biosocial growth is the foundation for cognitive and social maturity.

neurons The billions of nerve cells in the central nervous system, especially the brain.

>> Brain Development

Recall that the newborn's skull is disproportionately large. That's because it must be big enough to hold the brain, which at birth is already 25 percent of its adult weight. The neonate's body, by comparison, is about 5 percent of adult weight. The brain continues to grow very rapidly in the first years of life. By age 2, it is almost 75 percent of adult brain weight (see Figure 5.3).

Connections in the Brain

Head circumference provides a rough idea of how the brain is growing, which is why medical checkups include measurement of skull circumference. The distance around the head typically increases about 35 percent (from 13 to 18 inches, or from 33 to 46 centimeters) in the first year. Much more significant (although harder to measure) are changes in the brain's communication system. To understand this, we review the basics of neurological development (see Figure 5.4).

Communication within the central nervous system (CNS)—the brain and spinal cord—begins with nerve cells, called **neurons.** Most neurons are created before birth, at a peak production rate of 250,000 new cells per minute in mid-pregnancy (Purves et al., 2004). In infancy, the human brain has billions of neurons. Some are deep inside the brain in a region called the *brain stem,* which controls automatic responses such as heartbeat, breathing, temperature, and arousal. Others are in the

Frontal cortex The front part of the cortex assists in planning, self-control, and self-regulation. It is very immature in the newborn.

Cortex The crinkled outer layer of the brain (colored here in pink, tan, purple, and blue) is the cortex.

Auditory cortex Hearing is quite acute at birth, the result of months of eavesdropping during the fetal period.

Visual cortex Vision is the least mature sense at birth because the fetus has nothing to see while in the womb.

FIGURE 5.4

The Developing Cortex The infant's cortex consists of four to six thin layers of tissue that cover the brain. It contains virtually all the neurons that make conscious thought possible. Some areas of the cortex, such as those devoted to the basic senses, mature relatively early. Others, such as the frontal cortex, mature quite late, after age 20.

midbrain, in areas that affect emotions and memory. And most neurons (about 70 percent) are in the **cortex,** the brain's six outer layers (sometimes called the *neocortex*). The cortex is crucial: Most thinking, feeling, and sensing occur in the cortex, although parts of the midbrain join in (Johnson, 2011).

The last part of the brain to mature is the **prefrontal cortex,** the area for anticipation, planning, and impulse control. It is virtually inactive in the first months of infancy and gradually becomes more efficient in childhood and adolescence (Wahlstrom et al., 2010). (The prefrontal cortex is discussed in later chapters.) Various areas of the cortex specialize. For instance, there is a visual cortex, an auditory cortex, and an area dedicated to the sense of touch for each body part—including for each finger of a person or each whisker of a rat (Barnett et al., 2006).

Dendrites Sprouting

Within and between areas of the central nervous system, neurons are connected to other neurons by intricate networks of nerve fibers called **axons** and **dendrites** (see Figure 5.5). Each neuron has a single axon and numerous dendrites, which spread out like the branches of a tree. The axon of one neuron meets the dendrites of other neurons at intersections called **synapses,** which are critical communication links within the brain.

To be more specific, neurons communicate by sending electrochemical impulses through their axons to synapses, to be picked up by the dendrites of other neurons. The dendrites bring the message to the cell bodies of their neurons, which, in turn, convey the message via their axons to the dendrites of other neurons.

Axons and dendrites do not touch at synapses. Instead, the electrical impulses in axons typically cause the release of chemicals called *neurotransmitters,* which carry information from the axon of the sending neuron, across the *synaptic gap,* to the dendrites of the receiving neuron, a process speeded up by myelination (described in Chapter 8).

cortex The outer layers of the brain in humans and other mammals. Most thinking, feeling, and sensing involve the cortex. (Sometimes called the *neocortex*.)

prefrontal cortex The area of cortex at the front of the brain that specializes in anticipation, planning, and impulse control.

axon A fiber that extends from a neuron and transmits electrochemical impulses from that neuron to the dendrites of other neurons.

dendrite A fiber that extends from a neuron and receives electrochemical impulses transmitted from other neurons via their axons.

synapse The intersection between the axon of one neuron and the dendrites of other neurons.

FIGURE 5.5

How Two Neurons Communicate The link between one neuron and another is shown in the simplified diagram at right. The infant brain actually contains billions of neurons, each with one axon and many dendrites. Every electrochemical message to or from the brain causes thousands of neurons to fire, each transmitting the message across the synapse to neighboring neurons. The electron micrograph directly above shows neurons greatly magnified, with their tangled but highly organized and well-coordinated sets of dendrites and axons.

In the synapse, or intersection between an axon and dendrite, neurotransmitters carry information from one neuron to another.

transient exuberance The great but temporary increase in the number of dendrites that develop in an infant's brain during the first two years of life.

pruning When applied to brain development, the process by which unused connections in the brain atrophy and die.

Exuberance and Pruning

At birth, the brain contains at least 100 billion neurons, more than a person needs. By contrast, the newborn's brain has far fewer dendrites and synapses than the person will eventually possess. During the first months and years, rapid growth and refinement in axons, dendrites, and synapses occur, especially in the cortex. Dendrite growth is the major reason that brain weight triples from birth to age 2 (Johnson, 2011).

An estimated fivefold increase in dendrites in the cortex occurs in the 24 months after birth, with about 100 trillion synapses being present at age 2. This extensive postnatal brain growth is highly unusual for mammals. It is biologically necessary, given the large human brain and the relatively small human pelvis, but it also requires lengthy protection and feeding from adults, not needed by other animals (Konner, 2010). This early dendrite growth is called **transient exuberance**: *exuberant* because it is so rapid and *transient* because some of it is temporary. The expansive growth of dendrites is followed by **pruning** (see Figure 5.6), in which unused connections atrophy and die (Stiles & Jernigan, 2010), just as a gardener might prune a rose bush by cutting away parts to enable more, or more beautiful, roses to bloom.

Transient exuberance enables neurons to connect to, and communicate with, a greatly expanding number of other neurons within the brain. Synapses, dendrites, and probably neurons continue to form and die throughout life, more rapidly in infancy than at any other postnatal time (Stiles & Jernigan, 2010). Thinking and learning require connections among many parts of the brain. For example, to understand any sentence in this text, you need to know the letters, the words, the surrounding text, the ideas they convey, and how they relate to your other thoughts and experiences. Baby brains have the same requirements—no wonder it takes years to learn to read (see the Thinking Critically feature in Chapter 6).

Experience Shapes the Brain

The specifics of brain structure and growth depend on genes and maturation but even more on experience (Stiles & Jernigan, 2010). Infant brain organization itself depends partly on input, and some dendrites wither away because they are never used—that is, no experiences have caused them to send a message to other neurons. Expansion and pruning of dendrites occur for every aspect of early experience, from noticing musical rhythms to understanding emotions (Scott et al., 2007).

Strangely enough, this loss of dendrites increases brainpower. The space between neurons in the human brain—especially in regions for advanced, abstract thought—is far greater than the space in chimpanzee brains (Miller, 2010). It may seem logical that the more densely packed neurons of chimps would make them smarter than people, but the opposite is true. The probable explanation is that having more space for dendrite formation allows more connections as well as more pruning, thus fostering complex thinking. Further evidence of the benefit of cell death comes from one of the sad symptoms of fragile X syndrome (described in Chapter 3), "a persistent failure of normal synapse pruning" (Irwin et al., 2002, p. 194). Affected children become mentally retarded without this pruning; their dendrites are too dense and long, making thinking difficult.

Thus, pruning is essential. Normally, as brains mature, the process of extending and eliminating dendrites is exquisitely attuned to experience, as the appropriate links in the brain are established, protected, and strengthened. As with the rose bush, pruning needs to be done carefully, allowing further growth. Without certain experiences, some pruning may occur that limits later thought rather than aiding it. One group of scientists speculates that "lack of normative experiences may lead to overpruning of neurons and synapses, both of which may lead to reduction of brain activity" (Moulson et al., 2009, p. 1051).

Necessary and Possible Experiences

What are those needed "normative experiences"? A scientist named William Greenough identified two experience-related aspects of brain development (Greenough et al., 1987):

- **Experience-expectant brain function.** Certain functions require basic experiences in order to develop, just as a tree requires water. Those experiences are part of almost every infant's life, and thus almost every human brain grows as human genes direct. Brains need and expect such experiences; development would suffer without them.
- **Experience-dependent brain function.** Some brain functions depend on particular experiences. These specific experiences are not essential: They happen to infants in some families and cultures but not in others. Because of experience-dependent experiences, humans can be quite different from one another, yet all fully human.

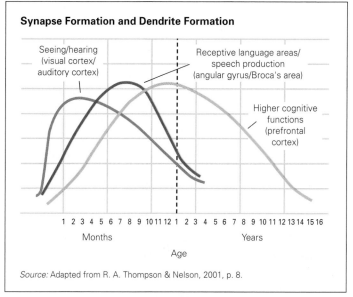

Synapse Formation and Dendrite Formation

Seeing/hearing (visual cortex/auditory cortex)

Receptive language areas/speech production (angular gyrus/Broca's area)

Higher cognitive functions (prefrontal cortex)

1 2 3 4 5 6 7 8 9 10 11 12   1   2   3   4   5   6   7   8   9   10 11 12 13 14 15 16

Months   Years

Age

Source: Adapted from R. A. Thompson & Nelson, 2001, p. 8.

FIGURE 5.6

Brain Growth in Response to Experience These curves show the rapid rate of experience-dependent synapse formation for three functions of the brain (senses, language, and analysis). After the initial increase, the underused neurons are gradually pruned, or inactivated, as no functioning dendrites are formed from them.

Observation Quiz Why do both "12 months" and "1 year" appear on the "Age" line? (see answer, page 137)

experience-expectant brain functions Brain functions that require certain basic common experiences (which an infant can be expected to have) in order to develop normally.

experience-dependent brain functions Brain functions that depend on particular, variable experiences and that therefore may or may not develop in a particular infant.

The basic, expected experiences *must* happen for normal brain maturation to occur, and they almost always do. For example, in deserts and in the Arctic, on isolated farms and in crowded cities, almost all babies have things to see, objects to manipulate, and people to love them. Babies everywhere welcome such experiences: They look around, they grab for objects, they smile at people. As a result, baby brains develop.

In contrast, dependent experiences *might* happen; because of them, one brain differs from another. Experiences vary, such as which language babies hear, what faces they see, whether curiosity is encouraged, or how their mother reacts to frustration. *Depending* on those particulars, infant brains are structured and connected one way or another; some dendrites grow and some neurons thrive while others die (Stiles & Jernigan, 2010). Consequently, experience-expectant events make all people similar, yet everyone is unique because each undergoes particular experience-dependent experiences as well.

One of the conclusions from research using twins to ascertain the effect of socioeconomic status (SES) and intelligence is that early on, until about 10 months, experience-expectant circumstances (things to see, people to love) are as likely to be provided—or not—in families of every income level. After that age, however, babies from high-SES families are more likely to be encouraged to explore, talk, and play. Consequently, for them, genetics, which vary more than context (which is adequate for all high-SES twins) causes intellectual differences between one twin and another.

However, some low-SES families encourage cognition and some do not, differences that may emerge especially when the families have toddler twins to raise. Because of wide variations among low-income families, the family context is a more powerful influence than genes on the IQ of low-income toddlers. In other words, all 1-year-olds need some basic stimulation and attention to develop their full genetic capacity, and those basic requirements are usually met by wealthy families (who can afford individualized child care, even with twins) but not necessarily by poorer families (perhaps especially those with twins) (Tucker-Drob et al., 2011). (See the Research Design.)

Examples from Bird Brains

The distinction between essential and variable input to the brain's networks can be made for all mammals. Some of the most persuasive research has been done with songbirds. All male songbirds have a brain region dedicated to listening and reproducing sounds (experience-expectant), but birds of the same species that

---

▶ **Research Design**

Scientists: Elliot M. Tucker-Drob, Mijke Rhemtulla, K. Paige Harden, Eric Turkheimer, and David Fask.

Publication: *Psychological Science* (2011).

Participants: The data for this study came from 750 pairs of twins (about one-fourth of them monozygotic) who were part of the Early Childhood Longitudinal Study, which began with 14,000 newborns from throughout the United States who were chosen to be representative of all economic levels and ethnicities. As you remember from Chapter 3, comparing monozygotic and dizygotic twins enables researchers to track genetic similarities and differences.

Design: Mothers and fathers were asked about their education, occupation, and income, and SES was calculated on a continuum from very low (e.g., no more than a sixth-grade education, both parents) to very high (e.g., professional degrees, both parents). Infants were tested on the Bayley Scales (tests developed by Nancy Bayley to measure development in the first years of life) at 10 months and again at 24 months. The mental scores (such as whether the infant could pull a string to ring a bell, could put three cubes in a cup on demand), not the motor scores (such as whether the infant could walk and run), were used to calculate intelligence.

Results: All the infants were much more capable at 24 months than at 10 months, as expected. Average intelligence did not correlate with SES at 10 months, but it did at 24 months. The variances in mental ability (i.e., the differences between one infant and another) at 10 months of age were traced primarily to the family environment (called a *shared environment,* the same for both twins), no matter what the SES; however, by 24 months of age, genetic differences were an important source of variance among high-SES but not among low-SES families. For them, environmental influences remained pivotal.

Comments: Remember from Chapter 3 that genetic differences emerge when basic needs are met, since a certain foundation is necessary before a child's genes can be fully expressed. (For example, genetic differences in height are obvious when every child is well fed.) This research suggests that, between 10 and 24 months, some low-income families do not provide the expected experiences for both twins that would enable all the brain growth that the genes allow.

As with conclusions from any one study, caution is needed. This research may overestimate SES similarities and differences for two reasons: (1) Intellectual tests are less reliable at 10 months than later in childhood, and (2) all families are challenged by twins, so low-income families may provide "expected experiences" for the brains of single-born toddlers, even if not for twins.

Nonetheless, the basic conclusion—that genes are more influential on the intellectual growth of advantaged children and environment is more crucial for the intellectual growth of low-income children—may be valid. Research on older children also finds notable variability in low-income households in opportunities for intellectual growth (Harden et al., 2007; Turkheimer et al., 2003). Might some low-SES children, born to become intellectual stars, never reach their potential? That is a conclusion reached by many experts on gifted children (Dai, 2010).

happen to live in different locations produce slightly different songs (experience-dependent) (Konner, 2010). This is not unlike regional accents, as with English-speaking adults who grew up in Kingston or Kansas, or, for that matter, one neighborhood of Boston or another.

Birds inherit genes that produce the brain cells they need, which might be neurons dedicated to learning new songs (canaries) or to finding hidden seeds (chickadees). For the dendrites and neurons to connect, birds depend on specific experiences with song-learning or seed-finding (Barinaga, 2003). A human example comes from face recognition: All infants need to see faces (experience-expectant), but which particular face differences they learn to notice depends on who they see (experience-dependent), as the following explains.

>> **Answer to Observation Quiz** (from page 135) "One year" signifies the entire year, from day 365 to day 729, and that is indicated by its location between "12 months" and "2 years."

A VIEW FROM SCIENCE

Face Recognition

If you were in an unfamiliar city, walking down a strange street with thousands of other people, and you chanced to see a close friend from your hometown, would you recognize him or her? Of course (unless you are one of those unfortunate few who have an impairment called prosopagnosia, or face blindness). A part of the brain is astonishingly adept at face recognition, and past experiences trigger immediate recognition, as in this example when an adult sees a friend.

The *fusiform face area* is that crucial part of the brain, both experience-expectant and experience-dependent. The specifics are fascinating, which is why "face perception remains one of the most intensively researched areas in psychology" (Slater et al., 2010, p. 205). Most research has occurred in the past decade, as scientists try to figure out why a person would recognize a friend (one in 7 billion humans who might be on that street)—an awesome, taken-for-granted ability.

We now know that the fusiform face area of the brain is active in newborns, who respond to monkey faces as well as human ones and to visual stimuli (e.g., photos and toys with faces) as well as live faces. Soon, experiences refine face perception (de Heering et al., 2010). For example, 2-month-olds recognize their mothers and fathers, 3-month-olds pay close attention to faces they have never seen before, 6-month-olds ignore details of monkey faces because they have learned not to care (M. H. Johnson, 2005). (Researchers have learned all this by showing infants several faces and timing how long they look at each one.)

Before their first birthday, infants more readily notice differences among faces from their own species and their own ethnic group (called *own-race effect*) than among faces of other species and groups, and most distinguish female faces more readily than male ones (Slater et al., 2010). The own-race effect persists throughout life, handicapping adults who have always known people of one ethnicity if they try to recognize individuals from

another group or even to read facial expressions of joy or anger in people from an unfamiliar culture.

Research finds that the own-race effect is the result of limited multiethnic experience, not innate prejudice against those who look different from oneself. One study found that genetic Koreans who were adopted early in life by European Americans were better at distinguishing non-Asian faces than Korean ones (Sangrigoli et al., 2005). Many adoptive parents now seek out members of their children's ethnic group, to help their children with ethnic identity later on. That may explain the result of a recent study of Asian adoptees: It was found that they were adept at distinguishing faces of both their native and adopted ethnic groups, unlike people who had been raised in communities that included only one ethnic group (de Heering et al., 2010).

The importance of early experience is also evident in two more studies. In one (Scott & Monesson, 2010), infants from 6 to 9 months were repeatedly (more than 30 times) shown a book of pictures of six monkey faces, each with a name written on the page (see photo). For one-third of the babies, the parents were told to read the names as they showed the pictures; another one-third of the parents were told to say only "monkey" as they showed each page; and for the final one-third, no verbal label was given. At 9 months, all the infants were shown pictures of six other monkeys, and their gaze patterns were closely tracked. Those infants who were repeatedly exposed to named monkeys were better at distinguishing one new monkey from another than were the infants who saw the same picture book but did not hear each monkey's name.

The second example begins with the fact that many children and adults fail to notice the individuality of newborns. Some even claim that "all babies look alike." However, one study found that 3-year-olds with younger siblings were much better at recognizing differences between photos of unfamiliar newborns than were 3-year-olds with no younger brothers or sisters (Cassia et al., 2009). Experience mattered.

Dario   Boris   Anice

Iona   Flora   Louis

REPRINTED FROM NEUROPSYCHOLOGIA, FIG. 1. EXPERIENCE-DEPENDENT NEURAL SPECIALIZATION

Iona Is Not Flora If you heard that Dario was quite different from Louis or Boris, would you stare at unfamiliar monkey faces more closely in the future? For 6-month-olds, the answer is yes.

The ability to differentiate faces improves with age—you are now quicker to recognize your best friend than you were as a child. Distinguishing individual faces is best learned via early exposure, but adults can learn to recognize individuals of other ethnic groups or even individual animals of the same species or breed. This recognition takes slightly longer without early experience involving dozens of named individuals from that group, but it is never too late to learn. Infancy is a sensitive period, but plasticity is lifelong.

Harming the Infant Brain

Thus far, we have focused on the many normal variations that families offer babies; most infants develop well within their culture. For brain development, it does not matter whether a person learns French or Farsi, or expresses emotions dramatically or subtly (e.g., throwing themselves to the floor or merely pursing their lips, a cultural difference). However, the research has also found that infant brains do not develop well if they do not have the basic experiences that all humans need.

Lack of Stimulation

To begin with, infants need stimulation. Playing with a young baby, allowing varied sensations, and encouraging movement (arm waving in the early months, walking later on) are all fodder for brain connections. Severe lack of stimulation stunts the brain, as has been shown many times, not only with mice but also with humans. As one review explains, "enrichment and deprivation studies provide powerful evidence of . . . widespread effects of experience on the complexity and function of the developing system" (Stiles & Jernigan, 2010, p. 345).

This does not mean that babies require spinning, buzzing, multitextured and multicolored toys. In fact, infants can be overstimulated as well; they usually cry or go to sleep when that happens, as a way of avoiding the bombardment. Perhaps for that reason, there is no evidence that overstimulation harms the brain. It may, however, be wasted time and money; an infant can be fascinated by a simple object, intrigued by a smiling face.

Stress and the Brain

In addition to lack of stimulation, some specific experiences are particularly harmful, especially in the first six months (Jansen et al., 2010). If the brain produces an overabundance of stress hormones early in life (as when an infant is frequently terrified, or when the whole family experiences a massive earthquake and flood), sometimes that damages the brain's later functioning. The brain might produce either too many stress hormones, making the child and then the adult hypervigilant (always on the alert), or too few, making the person emotionally flat (never happy, sad, or angry). Note that this is an emotional response, not necessarily caused by physical pain: An infant might be terrified (by yelling, frightening faces, witnessed abuse) without directly being hurt.

Exactly how and when this happens is not yet clear; research finds conflicting conclusions (Jansen et al., 2010). Some stress seems part of every infant's life: It may even be experience-expectant. But there is a limit to how much stress an infant can accommodate. Years later, a kindergarten teacher might notice that one child becomes furious or terrified at a slight provocation and another child seems indifferent to everything. Why? In both cases, the underlying cause could be excessive stress-hormone production in infancy, changing how that child's brain responds to stress. It is also possible, with differential sensitivity, that some infants are unharmed by a stressful early life—but, of course, no infant should experience that risk (Sapienza & Masten, 2011).

Shaken Baby Syndrome

Another example is much more direct, the consequence of adults who do not understand the immaturity of the infant brain. Because the prefrontal cortex has not yet developed, telling infants to stop crying is pointless because they cannot *decide* to stop crying. Such decisions require brain maturity not yet present. Some adults react by shaking a baby. This can cause **shaken baby syndrome,** a life-threatening condition that occurs when infants are shaken back and forth sharply and quickly. Shaking stops the crying because blood vessels in the brain rupture and neural connections break. Pediatricians consider shaken baby syndrome an example of *abusive head trauma* (Christian et al., 2009).

Not every infant who has neurological symptoms of head trauma is the victim of abuse. Nonetheless, in the United States, brain scans show that more than one in five of all children hospitalized for maltreatment (broken bones, burns, and so on) also suffers from shaken baby syndrome (Rovi et al., 2004).

shaken baby syndrome A life-threatening injury that occurs when an infant is forcefully shaken back and forth, a motion that ruptures blood vessels in the brain and breaks neural connections.

Severe Social Deprivation

The developmental community was stunned and saddened by the discovery of a girl named Genie, born in 1957. Genie spent most of her childhood tied to a chair, never hearing human speech (her father barked and growled at her) or feeling love, because her parents were severely disturbed. After being rescued at age 13, she eventually responded to affection and learned to speak, but she never developed normally. Most developmentalists concluded that her normal experiences came too late; her brain had already passed the sensitive period for development of many abilities.

But Genie was just one person, and as you remember from Chapter 1, one case is not proof of any general principle. Perhaps Genie had been born brain-damaged. Or perhaps her early care after the rescue was itself traumatic (Rymer, 1993).

More research, with more participants, was needed but would be unethical to perform with humans. Consequently, Marion Diamond, William Greenough, and their colleagues studied some "deprived" rats (raised alone in small, barren cages) and compared them with "enriched" rats (raised in large cages with other rats as well as toys). At autopsy, the brains of the enriched rats were larger and heavier, with more dendrites (M. Diamond, 1988; Greenough & Volkmar, 1973). Much

A Fortunate Pair Elaine Himelfarb (shown in the background), of San Diego, California, is shown here in Bucharest to adopt 22-month-old Maria. This joyous moment may be repeated through Maria's childhood—or maybe not.

research with other mammals confirms that isolation and sensory deprivation harm the developing brain, including social and emotional development. This is further explored with longitudinal studies of orphans from Romania, as described in Chapter 7.

Intervention

The fact that infant brains respond to their circumstances suggests that waiting until a young child is evidently mistreated is waiting too long. In the first months of life, babies adjust to their world, becoming withdrawn and quiet if their care-givers are depressed or becoming loud and demanding if that is the only way they get fed. Such adjustments help babies survive but set patterns that are destruc-tive later on. Thus, understanding development as dynamic and interactive means helping caregivers from the start, not waiting until destructive patterns are estab-lished (Tronick & Beegly, 2011).

A program to do this, beginning with high-risk mothers *before* any evidence of problems arose and including individualized support that did not require the mothers to leave their homes, resulted in less stress for the mothers and improved language development in the infants (Lowell et al., 2011). Developmentalists want this for every infant, either formally as in this program, or informally as when a relative or a neighbor helps a new mother with whatever she needs.

Implications for Caregivers

Developmental discoveries about early brain development have many implications for loving, low-risk caregivers as well as those at high risk. First, since each brain region follows a sequence of growing, connecting, and pruning, it helps to know which developmental events are experience-expectant and when those expecta-tions arise.

For example, proliferation and pruning begin at about 4 months in the visual and auditory cortexes, which explains why very young infants are attentive to sights and sounds. Consequently, remedies for blind or deaf infants should occur early in life to prevent atrophy of those brain regions that expect sights and sounds. Hearing-impaired infants whose difficulties are recognized and remediated with cochlear implants become more adept at understanding and expressing language than those with the same losses but later implants. Brain expectancy is the reason (Kennedy et al., 2006).

The language areas of the brain develop most rapidly between the ages of 6 and 24 months; that is when infants need to hear speech in order to talk fluently. In fact, speech heard between 6 and 12 months helps infants recognize the characteristics of their local language long before they utter a word (Saffran et al., 2006). On the other hand, some stimulation is meaningless before the brain is ready. A 6-month-old might be uninterested in looking at a book, but a few months later book-reading may be a favorite activity. Infants respond to whatever their brains need; that's why musical mobiles, cars on the street, and, best of all, animated caregivers are fascinating.

This preference reflects **self-righting,** the inborn drive to remedy deficits. Infants with few toys develop their brains by using whatever is available. They do not need the latest educational playthings—their brains expect human interaction and whatever objects their parents find that interest them. Human brains are designed to grow and adapt; plasticity is apparent from the beginning of life (Tomalski & Johnson, 2010).

Thus, how people respond to infants echoes lifelong. This means that caressing a newborn, talking to a preverbal infant, and showing affection toward a toddler may be essential to developing the child's full potential. If such experiences are missing, lifelong brain damage may result.

self-righting The inborn drive to remedy a developmental deficit; literally, to return to sitting or standing upright, after being tipped over. People of all ages have self-righting impulses, for emotional as well as physical imbalance.

SUMMING UP

Brain growth is rapid during the first months of life, when dendrites and the synapses within the cortex increase exponentially. By age 2, the brain already weighs three-fourths of its adult weight. Pruning of underused and unconnected dendrites begins in the sensory and motor areas and then occurs in other areas. Although some brain development is maturational, experience is also essential—both the universal experiences that almost every infant has (experience-expectant brain development) and the particular experiences that reflect the child's family or culture (experience-dependent brain development). Infant brains need stimulation—though not so much as to become overwhelming—for the dendrites to grow and neurological connections to proliferate. ■

>> Sensation and Movement

You learned in Chapter 2 that Piaget called the first period of intelligence the *sensorimotor* stage, emphasizing that cognition develops from the senses and motor skills. The same concept—that infant brain development depends on sensory experiences and early activity—underlies the discussion you have just read. Experience molds the brain, and the brain allows sensory and motor experiences to occur (Fox et al., 2010).

The Senses

Every sense functions at birth. Human newborns have open eyes; sensitive ears; and responsive noses, tongues, and skin. Throughout their first year, infants use the senses to sort and classify everything they experience. Indeed, "infants spend the better part of their first year merely looking around" (Rovee-Collier, 2001, p. 35). As they look, they also listen, smell, taste, and touch anything they can, seeming to attend to everything without much focus or judgment. For instance,

sensation The response of a sensory system (eyes, ears, skin, tongue, nose) when it detects a stimulus.

perception The mental processing of sensory information when the brain interprets a sensation. Perception occurs in the cortex.

Especially for Parents of Grown Children
Suppose you realize that you seldom talked to your children until they talked to you and that you never used a stroller or a walker but put them in cribs and playpens. Did you limit their brain growth and their sensory capacity? (see response, page 145)

in the first months of life, they smile at strangers and put almost anything in their mouths (Adolph & Berger, 2005).

Why are they not more selective? Because sensation precedes perception. **Sensation** occurs when a sensory system detects a stimulus, as when the inner ear reverberates with sound or the retina and pupil of the eye intercept light. Thus, sensations begin when an outer organ (eye, ear, nose, tongue, or skin) meets anything that can be seen, heard, smelled, tasted, or touched. But what appear to be simple responses to every stimulus actually show some selection: Even newborns are attracted to social stimuli, preferring sensations from people over sensations from objects (Lloyd-Fox et al., 2009). They would rather suck your finger than a scrap of cloth; they settle for cloth when no finger is available.

Perception occurs when the brain notices and processes a sensation. This happens in the cortex, usually as the result of a message from one of the sensing organs. That message connects with past experience to suggest that a particular sensation might be worth interpreting (M. E. Diamond, 2007).

Some sensations are beyond comprehension at first. A newborn has no idea that the letters on a page might have significance, that Mother's face should be distinguished from Father's, or that the smells of roses and garlic have different connotations. Perceptions require experience, either direct experience or messages from other people.

Infants' brains are especially attuned to their own repeated social experiences. Thus, a newborn named Emily has no concept that *Emily* is her name, but she has the brain and auditory capacity to hear sounds in the usual speech range (not the high sounds that only dogs can hear) and an inborn preference for repeated patterns and human speech, so she attends to people saying her name. At about 4 months, when her auditory cortex is rapidly creating and pruning dendrites, the repeated word *Emily* is perceived as well as sensed, especially because that sound emanates from the people Emily has learned to love (Saffran et al., 2006). Before 6 months, Emily may open her eyes and turn her head when her name is called. It will take many more months before she tries to say "Emmy" and still longer before she knows that *Emily* is indeed her name.

Thus, perception follows sensation, when senses are noticed by the brain. Then cognition follows perception, when people think about what they have perceived. (Later, cognition no longer requires sensation: People imagine, fantasize, hypothesize.) The sequence from sensation to perception to cognition requires that an infant's sense organs function. No wonder the parts of the cortex dedicated to the senses develop rapidly: That is the prerequisite for human intellect. Now some details.

Hearing

The sense of hearing develops during the last trimester of pregnancy and is already quite acute at birth, when certain sounds trigger reflexes, even without conscious perception. Sudden noises startle newborns, making them cry; rhythmic sounds, such as a lullaby or a heartbeat, soothe them and put them to sleep.

A newborn's hearing can be checked with advanced equipment, routine at most hospitals in North America and Europe, since early remediation benefits deaf infants. Screening is needed later as well because some infants develop hearing losses in the early months (Harlor & Bower, 2009). Normally, even in the first days of life, infants turn their heads at a sound. Soon they can pinpoint the actual source of the noise.

Because of maturation of the language areas of the cortex, even 4-month-old infants particularly attend to voices, developing expectations of the rhythm, segmentation, and cadence of spoken words long before comprehension (Minagawa-

Kawai et al., 2011). As time goes on, sensitive hearing combines with the maturing brain to distinguish patterns of sounds and syllables. Infants become accustomed to the rules of their native language, such as which syllable is stressed (various dialects have different rules), whether changing inflection matters (as in Chinese), whether certain sound combinations are repeated, and so on. All this is based on very careful listening to human speech, even speech not directed toward them with words they do not yet understand.

Seeing

Vision is the least mature sense at birth. Although the eyes open in mid-pregnancy and are sensitive to bright light (if the pregnant woman is sunbathing in a bikini, for instance), the fetus has nothing much to see. Newborns are legally blind; they focus only on things between 4 and 30 inches (10 and 75 centimeters) away (Bornstein et al., 2005).

Almost immediately, experience combines with maturation of the visual cortex to improve the ability to see shapes and then notice details, with vision improving so rapidly that researchers are hard-pressed to describe the day-by-day improvements (Dobson et al., 2009). By 2 months, infants look intently at a human face and, tentatively and fleetingly, smile at the person. (Smiling can occur earlier, but not as a direct response to something the baby sees.) Soon visual scanning becomes organized and more efficient, centered on important points. Thus, 3-month-olds look closely at the eyes and mouth, the parts of a face that contain the most information, and they prefer photos of faces with features over photos of faces with the features blanked out. They pay attention to patterns, colors, and motion (Kellman & Arterberry, 2006).

Binocular vision is the ability to coordinate the two eyes to see one image. Because using both eyes together is impossible in the womb (nothing is far enough away to need two eyes), many newborns seem to focus with one eye or the other, or to use their two eyes independently, momentarily appearing wall-eyed or cross-eyed. At about 14 weeks, the underlying brain mechanisms are activated, allowing binocular vision, with both eyes focused on a single thing (Atkinson & Braddick, 2003).

Smelling and Tasting

As with vision and hearing, the senses of smell and taste function at birth and rapidly adapt to the social world. Infants learn to appreciate whatever their mothers eat, first through the breast milk and then through smells and spoonfuls of whatever the family has for dinner. Some herbs and plants contain natural substances that are medicinal. The foods of a particular culture may aid survival: Bitter foods seem to provide some defense against malaria, spicy ones preserve food and thus work against food poisoning, and so on (Krebs, 2009). Thus, an infant's preference for whatever foods the family eats may be life-saving.

Families who eat foods that protected their community pass on those preferences to their children throughout childhood. Taste preferences endure when a person migrates to another culture or when historical circumstances change so that a particular food that was once protective is no longer so. Indeed, one reason for the obesity epidemic may be that when starvation was a threat, families sought high-fat foods; now their descendants still enjoy French fries, whipped cream, bacon, and so on.

Similar adaptation occurs for the sense of smell. As babies learn to recognize each person's scent, they prefer to sleep next to their caregivers, and they nuzzle

Before Leaving the Hospital As mandated by a 2004 Ohio law, 1-day-old Henry has his hearing tested via vibrations of the inner ear in response to various tones. The computer interprets the data and signals any need for more tests—as is the case for about 1 baby in 100. Normal newborns hear quite well; Henry's hearing was fine.

binocular vision The ability to focus the two eyes in a coordinated manner in order to see one image. This ability is absent at birth.

Learning About a Lime As with every other normal infant, Jacqueline's curiosity leads to taste and then to a slow reaction, from puzzlement to tongue-out disgust. Jacqueline's responses demonstrate that the sense of taste is acute in infancy and that quick brain reactions are still to come.

into their caregivers' chests—especially when the adults are shirtless. One way to help infants who are frightened of being given a bath (some love bathing, some hate it at first) is to take the baby into the bath with the parent. The smells of the adult's body mix with the smell of soap, making the experience comforting.

Touch and Pain

The sense of touch is acute in infants, with wrapping, rubbing, and cradling all soothing to many new babies. Some infants relax when held by their familiar caregiver, even when their eyes are closed. The ability to be comforted by touch is one of the important skills tested in the Brazelton Neonatal Behavioral Assessment Scale (NBAS, described in Chapter 4). Although almost all newborns respond to being securely held, over time they perceive what each touch communicates. Caressing, swaddling, kissing, massaging, tickling, bouncing, and rocking are each comforting to some infants, all involving the sense of touch as well as motion.

Pain is not usually considered one of the five senses, but it is often connected to touch. Some babies cry when being changed because cold on their skin is distressing, and some are upset when they need clean diapers, not because wetness itself is distressing but because a diaper rash is sensitive. Scientists are not certain about when and why infants feel pain. Certainly some things that are painful to adults (circumcision, setting a broken bone) seem much less so to newborns. For many medical procedures, from a pin-prick to minor surgery, a taste of sugar syrup right before the event is anesthetic: Infants typically cry lustily when their heel is pricked (routine after birth), but some remain calm if they have had a drop of sucrose (Harrison et al., 2010).

Basic Infant Care In many cultures, infant massage is considered an essential part of daily care, no less important than diapering or feeding. In other cultures, mothers attend classes to learn how best to touch their infants—firmly on the stomach, as shown here, or rhythmically moving the arms and legs, as these mothers will soon practice.

Some people argue that even the fetus can feel pain; others say that the sense of pain does not mature until months or years after birth. Many young infants cry for 10 minutes or more, with no obvious reason or effective consolation: Digestive pain is the usual explanation. Many infants seem distressed and in pain before their first tooth erupts: Teething is the explanation. That is difficult to ascertain, however, because crying may not reliably indicate pain. Certainly it does not in adults.

Many physiological measures, including stress hormones in the bloodstream and erratic beating of the heart, are being explored to measure infant pain. Recent research has focused on brain patterns as indicators of pain in premature infants, who typically experience numerous procedures that would be painful to an adult (Holsti et al., 2011). Some argue that infants should be given anesthetics; others say this would slow down breathing, a needless risk. We know from developmental studies that infants are unlike adults in many ways: It is a mistake to assume that they never feel pain, and it is equally wrong to assume that they feel pain as an adult might.

Dynamic Sensory Systems

The entire package of sensations furthers two goals: social interaction (to respond to familiar caregivers) and comfort (to be soothed amid the disturbances of infant life). The most important experiences are perceived with interacting senses, in dynamic systems (see Chapter 1). Breast milk, for instance, is a mild sedative, so the newborn literally feels happier at mother's breast, connecting that pleasure with taste, touch, smell, and sight. Young human infants are, physiologically, an unusual combination of immaturity (they cannot walk) and sensitivity (their senses function at birth, unlike the many animals who are born with eyes closed). This combination aids social connections between infants and adults (Konner, 2010).

Infants respond to motion as well as to sights and sounds. Many new parents soothe their baby's distress by rocking, carrying, or even driving (with the baby in a safety seat) while crooning a lullaby; here again, infant comfort is connected with social interaction. Massage is especially calming when infants realize that the touch comes from a familiar caregiver who simultaneously provides auditory and visual stimulation. Even vacuuming the carpet with the baby in a sling may quiet a fussy baby because steady noise, changing sights, and carrying combine to soothe distress.

By 6 months, infants have learned to coordinate the senses, expecting lip movements to synchronize with speech, for instance (Lewkowicz, 2010). In sum, infant senses are immature, but each is part of a dynamic system of stimulation, functioning together as babies join the human family.

Motor Skills

We now come to the most visible and dramatic advances of infancy, those that ultimately allow the child to "stand tall and walk proud." Thanks to ongoing changes in size and proportion and to increasing brain maturation, infants markedly improve their **motor skills,** the movement abilities that are needed to control actions.

Gross Motor Skills

Deliberate actions that coordinate many parts of the body, producing large movements, are called **gross motor skills.** These emerge directly from reflexes (discussed in Chapter 4) and proceed in a cephalocaudal and proximodistal direction. Infants first control their heads, lifting them up to look around or turning them from one side to another. Then they control their upper bodies, their arms, and finally their legs and feet.

Crawling is one example. As you remember from Chapter 4, when placed on their stomachs, many newborns reflexively lift their heads and move their arms and legs as if they were swimming. As they gain muscle strength, infants wiggle, attempting to move forward by pushing their arms, shoulders, and upper bodies against whatever surface they are lying on. Usually by 5 months or so, they become able to use their arms, and then legs, to inch forward (or sometimes backward) on their bellies. That is a gross motor skill.

Between 8 and 10 months after birth, most infants become able to lift their midsections and crawl (or *creep,* as the British call it) on "all fours," coordinating

>> Response for Parents of Grown Children (from page 142) Probably not. Experience-expectant brain development is programmed to occur for all infants, requiring only the stimulation that virtually all families provide—warmth, reassuring touch, overheard conversation, facial expressions, movement. Extras such as baby talk, music, exercise, mobiles, and massage may be beneficial but are not essential.

motor skills The learned abilities to move some part of the body, in actions ranging from a large leap to a flicker of the eyelid. (The word *motor* here refers to movement of muscles.)

gross motor skills Physical abilities involving large body movements, such as walking and jumping. (The word *gross* here means "big.")

Young Expert This infant is an adept crawler. Note the coordination between hands and knees as well as the arm and leg strength needed to support the body in this early version of push-ups. This boy will probably become an expert walker and runner, as do many babies who bypass the crawling phase altogether.

the movements of their hands and knees in a smooth, balanced manner. Crawling is experience-dependent. Some normal babies never do it, especially if the floor is cold, hot, or rough, or if they have always lain on their backs (Pin et al., 2007). It is not true that babies *must* crawl to develop normally. All babies figure out some way to move before they can walk (inching, bear-walking, scooting, creeping, or crawling), but many resist "tummy time" by rolling over and fussing (Adolph & Berger, 2005). Overweight babies master gross motor skills later than thinner babies do (Slining et al., 2010).

Sitting also develops gradually, a matter of developing the muscles to steady the top half of the body. By 3 months, babies have sufficient muscle control to be lap-sitters if the lap's owner provides supportive arms. By 6 months, they can usually sit unsupported. Walking progresses from reflexive, hesitant, adult-supported stepping to a smooth, coordinated gait. Some children step while holding on at 9 months, stand alone momentarily at 10 months, and walk well, unassisted, at 12 months. Three factors combine to allow toddlers to walk (Adolph et al., 2003):

1. *Muscle strength.* Newborns with skinny legs and infants buoyed by water make stepping movements, but 6-month-olds on dry land do not; their legs are too chubby for their underdeveloped muscles.
2. *Brain maturation within the motor cortex.* The first leg movements—kicking (alternating legs at birth and then kicking both legs together or one leg repeatedly at about 3 months)—occur without much thought or aim. As the brain matures, deliberate leg action becomes possible.
3. *Practice.* Unbalanced, wide-legged, short strides become a steady, smooth gait after hours of practice.

Once the first two developments have made walking possible, infants become passionate walkers, logging those needed hours of practice. They take steps on many surfaces, barefoot or wearing socks, slippers, or shoes. They resist being pushed in their strollers when they can walk.

Bossa Nova Baby? This boy in Brazil demonstrates his joy at acquiring the gross motor skill of walking, which quickly becomes dancing whenever music plays.

> Walking infants practice keeping balance in upright stance and locomotion for more than 6 accumulated hours per day. They average between 500 and 1,500 walking steps per hour so that by the end of each day, they have taken 9,000 walking steps and traveled the length of 29 football fields.
>
> [Adolph et al., 2003, p. 494]

Fine Motor Skills

fine motor skills Physical abilities involving small body movements, especially of the hands and fingers, such as drawing and picking up a coin. (The word *fine* here means "small.")

Small body movements are called **fine motor skills.** Finger movements are fine motor skills, enabling humans to write, draw, type, tie, and so on. Movements of the tongue, jaw, lips, and toes are fine movements, too.

Actually, mouth skills precede finger skills by many months, and skillful grabbing with the toes sometimes precedes grabbing with the hands (Adolph & Berger, 2005). However, hand skills are more valued by society. Every culture encourages finger dexterity, so children practice finger movements. By contrast, skilled spitting or chewing is not praised; even mastery of blowing bubble gum is admired only by other children.

CATHARINA VAN DEN DIKKENBERG / ISTOCKPHOTO

RICK GOMEZ / MASTERFILE

Regarding finger skills, newborns have a strong reflexive grasp but lack hand and finger control. During their first 2 months, babies excitedly stare and wave their arms at objects dangling within reach. By 3 months, they can usually touch such objects, but they cannot yet grab and hold on unless an object is placed in their hands, partly because their eye–hand coordination is limited.

By 4 months, infants sometimes grab, but their timing is off: They close their hands too early or too late. Finally, by 6 months, with a concentrated, deliberate stare, most babies can reach for, grab at, and hold almost any object that is of the right size. Some can even transfer an object from one hand to the other. Almost all can hold a bottle, shake a rattle, and yank a sister's braids. Once grabbing is possible, babies practice it enthusiastically: "from 6 to 9 months, reaching appears as a quite compulsive behaviour for small objects presented within arm's reach" (Atkinson & Braddick, 2003, p. 58).

Toward the end of the first year and throughout the second, finger skills improve, as babies master the pincer movement (using thumb and forefinger to pick up tiny objects) and self-feeding (first with hands, then fingers, then utensils) (Ho, 2010). In the second year, grabbing becomes more selective. Toddlers learn when *not* to pull at a sister's braids, or Mommy's earrings, or Daddy's glasses. However, as you will learn in Chapter 6, the curiosity of the "little scientist" may overwhelm this inhibition.

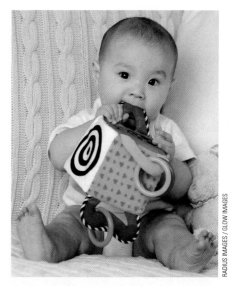

Sensory Exuberance Human animals are unusual in that all the senses function at birth, but motor skills develop slowly. This Toronto boy loves to taste and bite the toy designed for looking (that bull's eye) and grabbing (those plastic rings), even though he cannot yet sit up unsupported.

Cultural Variations

All healthy infants develop skills in the same sequence, but the age of acquisition varies. At About This Time shows age norms for gross motor skills, based on a large, representative, multiethnic sample of U.S. infants. When infants are grouped by ethnicity, generally African Americans are ahead of Latinos, who are ahead of babies of European descent. Internationally, the earliest walkers are in Africa, where many well-nourished and healthy babies walk at 10 months. The latest walkers may be in France.

What accounts for this variation? The power of genes is suggested not only by ethnic differences but also by identical twins, who begin to walk on the same day more often than fraternal twins do. Striking individual differences are apparent in infants' strategies, effort, and concentration in mastering motor skills, again suggesting something inborn (Thelen & Corbetta, 2002).

But much more than genes contribute to variations, as the example that opened this chapter shows. Cultural patterns affect acquisition of every sensory and motor skill. For instance, early reflexes may not fade if culture and conditions allow extensive practice. This has been demonstrated with legs (the stepping reflex), hands (the grasping reflex), and crawling (the swimming reflex). Senses and motor skills are part of a complex and dynamic system in which practice counts (Thelen & Corbetta, 2002). Nutrition makes a difference as well: Both malnourished and overweight children are slower to develop motor skills.

AT ABOUT THIS TIME
Age Norms (in Months) for Gross Motor Skills

Skill	When 50% of All Babies Master the Skill (months)	When 95% of All Babies Master the Skill (months)
Sit, head steady	3	4
Sit, unsupported	6	7
Pull to stand (holding on)	9	10
Stand alone	12	14
Walk well	13	15
Walk backward	15	17
Run	18	20
Jump up	26	29

Note: As the text explains, age norms are affected by culture and cohort. These are U.S. norms, mostly for European Americans. Mastering skills a few weeks earlier or later does not indicate health or intelligence. Being very late, however, is a cause for concern.

Source: Coovadia & Wittenberg, 2004; based on Denver II (Frankenburg et al., 1992).

Observation Quiz Which of these skills has the greatest variation in age of acquisition? Why? (see answer, page 148)

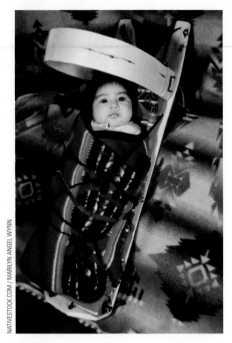

NATIVESTOCK.COM / MARILYN ANGEL WYNN

Modern Equipment A cradle board is designed to keep infants safe, warm, and near their parents—a more mobile piece of baby furniture than the crib or playpen.

>> **Answer to Observation Quiz** (from page 147) Jumping up, with a three-month age range for acquisition. The reason is that the older an infant is, the more impact culture has.

Cross-cultural research finds that some caregivers (including Jamaican ones like Mrs. Todd, who cared for my youngest daughter) provide rhythmic stretching exercises for their infants as part of daily care; their infants are among the world's youngest walkers (Adolph & Berger, 2005). Other cultures discourage or even prevent infants from crawling or walking. The people of Bali, Indonesia, never let their infants crawl, because babies are considered divine and crawling is for animals (Diener, 2000). Similar reasoning appeared in colonial America, where "standing stools" were designed for children so they could strengthen their legs without sitting or crawling (Calvert, 2003).

By contrast, the Beng people of the Ivory Coast are proud when their babies start to crawl but do not let them walk until at least 1 year. Although the Beng do not recognize the connection, one reason for this prohibition may be birth control: Beng mothers do not resume sexual relations until their baby takes a first step (Gottlieb, 2000).

Although variation in the timing of the development of motor skills is normal, slow development relative to the norm within an infant's ethnic group suggests that attention should be paid: Early visual, auditory, and motor difficulties are much easier to remedy than the same problems discovered later in childhood. Remember the dynamic systems of senses and motor skills: If one aspect of the system lags behind, the other parts may as well. On the other hand, early walkers are thrilled to have within reach dozens of objects they were unable to explore before—caregivers beware.

SUMMING UP

The five senses (seeing, hearing, smelling, tasting, touching) function at birth, although hearing is far superior to vision, probably because of experience: The fetus has much more to hear than to see. After birth, vision develops rapidly, leading to binocular vision at about the 14th week. The sense of pain seems less acute in newborns than in adults, with sugar often an effective analgesic. More research is needed to measure infant pain—and to relieve it. By one year, infants heed stimuli from all the sense organs; sensitive perception and preferences for the familiar are evident. The senses work together and are particularly attuned to human interaction.

Motor skills begin with reflexes but quickly expand to include various body movements. Infants lift their heads, then sit, then stand, then walk and run. Sensory and motor skills interact in dynamic systems, with each ability affecting all the others. Skills follow a genetic and maturational timetable, but they are also powerfully influenced by experiences, guided by caregivers and culture, and by practice, which infants do as much as their immature and top-heavy bodies allow. Fine motor skills, especially hand skills, mature over the first two years, although many more years of practice and maturation are needed before children can do the simple actions that adults take for granted. ■

>> Surviving in Good Health

Although precise worldwide statistics are unavailable, at least 10 billion children were born between 1950 and 2010. More than 2 billion of them died before age 5. Although 2 billion is far too many, twice as many would have died without recent public health measures. As best we know, in earlier centuries more than half of all newborns died in infancy.

In the twenty-first century, most people live to adulthood. In the healthiest nations, 99.9 percent who survive the first month (when the sickest and smallest newborns may die) live to age 15, and most live for decades more. Even in the poorest nations, where a few decades ago half the children died, now about three-fourths live (see Table 5.1).

The world death rate in the first five years of life has dropped about 2 percent per year since 1990 (Rajaratnam et al., 2010). Improvements in public health measures (clean water, nourishing food, immunization) are the main reason for increased survival, which in turn has led to many other benefits—lower birth rates, less starvation, and more education worldwide. Further reductions would occur if there were more doctors and nurses in underserved parts of the world: That would reduce infant deaths by 15 percent immediately (primarily because of healthier births and increased immunization) and by 50 percent over a few decades (primarily because of society-wide improvements in disease prevention) (Farahani et al., 2009).

One particular medical treatment, oral rehydration therapy (giving restorative liquids to sick children who have diarrhea), is now widely used, saving 3 million young children *per year*. Most such children are in developing nations, but oral rehydration saves lives in developed nations as well (Spandorfer et al., 2005).

Every year in Africa, 1 million people die of malaria, most of them undernourished children. Immediate drug treatment can save lives, but many victims live far from medical help. Furthermore, some anti-malaria drugs are no longer effective (Kun et al., 2010). One innovation has cut the malaria death rate in half: bed nets treated with insect repellant that drape over sleeping areas (Roberts, 2007). Better drugs are also urgently needed.

Immunization

No immunization is yet available for malaria. However, measles, mumps, whooping cough, smallpox, pneumonia, polio, and rotavirus no longer kill hundreds of thousands of children each year, because targeted **immunization** primes the body's immune system to resist a specific contagious disease. Immunization (also called *vaccination*) is said to have had "a greater impact on human mortality reduction and population growth than any other public health intervention besides clean water" (J. P. Baker, 2000, p. 199).

When people catch a contagious disease, their immune system produces antibodies to prevent recurrence. In a healthy person who has not had the disease, a vaccine—a small dose of inactive virus (often via a "shot" in the arm)—stimulates the same antibodies. (Immunization schedules, with U.S. recommendations, appear in Appendix A, page A-4. Most of the vaccines listed are advised for infants in every nation. However, specifics vary; caregivers need to consult local public health authorities.)

Dramatic Successes

Stunning successes in immunization include the following:

- Smallpox, the most lethal disease for children in the past, was eradicated worldwide as of 1971. Vaccination against smallpox is no longer needed.
- Polio, a crippling and sometimes fatal disease, is rare. Widespread vaccination, begun in 1955, eliminated polio in the Americas. Only 784 cases were reported anywhere in the world in 2003. In the same year, rumors halted immunization in northern Nigeria. Polio reappeared, sickening 1,948 people in 2005, almost all in West Africa. Then public health workers and community

TABLE 5.1	Deaths of Children Under Age 5 in Selected Countries
Country	**Number of Deaths per 1,000**
Singapore	3**
Iceland	3**
Sweden	3**
Japan	3**
Italy	4**
Spain	4**
Australia	5*
United Kingdom	6*
Canada	6*
New Zealand	6*
United States	8*
Russia	12*
Vietnam	24**
Mexico	17**
China	19**
Brazil	21**
Philippines	33**
India	66**
Nigeria	138*
Sierra Leone	192*
Afghanistan	199

*Reduced by at least one-third since 1990.
**Reduced by half or more since 1990.
Source: You et al., 2010.

This table shows the number of deaths per 1,000 children under age 5 for 21 of the 192 members of the United Nations. Most nations have improved markedly on this measure since 1990. Only when war destroys families and interferes with public health measures (as it has in Afghanistan) are nations not improving this statistic.

immunization The process of protecting a person against a disease, via antibodies. Immunization can happen naturally, when someone survives a disease, or medically, usually via a small dose of the virus that stimulates the production of antibodies and thus renders a person immune. (Also called *vaccination*.)

SCOTT EELLS / THE NEW YORK TIMES / REDUX

A Religious Experience Buddha taught that life is suffering, but this young Buddhist monk might prefer to avoid it. He lives in a remote region of Nepal, where, until recently, measles was a fatal disease. Fortunately, a UNICEF porter carried the vaccine over mountain trails for two days so that this boy—and his whole community—could be immunized.

leaders campaigned to increase immunization and Nigeria's polio rate plummeted. Meanwhile, poverty and new conflicts in South Asia prevented immunization: 1,606 worldwide cases were reported in 2009, primarily in Afghanistan, India, and Pakistan (MMWR, May 14, 2010). (See Figure 5.7.)

■ Measles (rubeola, not rubella) is disappearing, thanks to a vaccine developed in 1963. Prior to that time, 3 to 4 million cases occurred each year in the United States alone (Centers for Disease Control and Prevention, 2007). In 2010, in the United States, only 61 people had measles, most of them born in nations without widespread immunization (MMWR, January 7, 2011).

■ In 2006, a vaccine was introduced against rotavirus, which causes severe diarrhea. Before the vaccine, about 35 children died from rotavirus each year in the United States, but that rate is dropping (Pitzer et al., 2009). For technical and economic reasons (the vaccine is relatively expensive, about 30 cents per dose), it is not yet widely used in developing nations. Annually, more than half a million children die of rotovirus (Santosham, 2010).

Immunization protects children not only from temporary sickness but also from serious complications, including deafness, blindness, sterility, and meningitis. Sometimes the damage from illness is not apparent until decades later. Childhood mumps, for instance, can cause sterility and doubles the risk of schizophrenia (Dalman et al., 2008).

Furthermore, each vaccinated child stops the spread of the disease and thus protects others, a phenomenon called *herd immunity*. Some people cannot be safely immunized, including: (1) embryos exposed to rubella (German measles), who may be born blind, deaf, and brain-damaged; (2) newborns, who may die from a disease that is mild in children; (3) people with impaired immune systems (HIV-positive, aged, or undergoing chemotherapy). All these are protected if they are part of a community (a herd) in which 90 percent of the people are immunized, because then the disease does not spread to those who are vulnerable. Without herd immunity, adults can die of a "childhood" disease.

FIGURE 5.7

Not Yet Zero Many public health advocates hope polio will be the next infectious disease to be eliminated worldwide, as is the case in almost all of North America. However, this graph shows a discouraging increase in polio rates from 2003 to 2005.

Observation Quiz Was the polio rate cut in half between 1989 and 2003? (see answer, page 152)

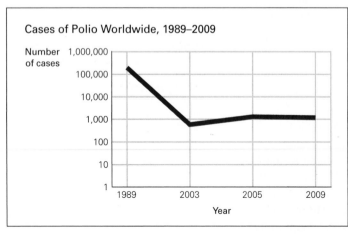

Cases of Polio Worldwide, 1989–2009

Number of cases

1,000,000
100,000
10,000
1,000
100
10
1

1989   2003   2005   2009

Year

Problems with Immunization

Some infants react to immunization by being irritable or even feverish for a day or so, to the distress of their parents. However, parents do not notice if their child does *not* get seriously ill. One doctor laments, "No one notices when things go right" (Bortz, 2005, p. 389). Before the varicella (chicken pox) vaccine, more than 100 people in the United States died each year from that disease and 1 million were itchy and feverish for a week. Now almost no one dies, and far fewer get chicken pox.

Many parents are concerned about potential side effects; the rate of missed vaccinations has been rising over the past decade. This frightens public health workers and most developmentalists, as the specter of an epidemic is more terrifying to them than to parents who want to avoid the distress after each round of shots. Developmentalists, taking a longitudinal and society-wide perspective, consider the risks of the diseases far greater than the risks from immunization.

Doctors agree that vaccines "are one of the most cost-effective, successful interventions in the history of public health" and lament that that success has made parents, physicians, and governments less vigilant (Hannan et al., 2009, p. S571). A hypothesis that the MMR (measles-mumps-rubella) vaccine causes autism has been repeatedly disproved (Mrozek-Budzyn et al., 2010; Shattuck, 2006). (More on autism in Chapter 11.)

The biggest problem with immunization is that no effective vaccine has been found for AIDS, malaria, cholera, typhoid, and shigellosis—all devastating diseases in the developing world. Another problem is that public health measures have not reached many rural areas of the world: About 2 to 3 million children die each year from diphtheria, tetanus, and measles because they have not been immunized (Mahmoud, 2004). This problem can occur in every nation. Late and inadequate immunization is blamed for a spike in infant whooping cough deaths in California in 2010, especially among farm families, prompting California to declare an epidemic (McKinley, 2010). Failure to immunize infants constitutes medical neglect.

Nutrition

Infant mortality worldwide has plummeted in recent years. Several reasons have already been mentioned: fewer sudden infant deaths (explained in Chapter 1), advances in prenatal and newborn care (explained in Chapter 4), and, as you just read, immunization. One more measure would make a huge difference: better nutrition.

Breast Is Best

Ideally, nutrition starts with *colostrum,* a thick, high-calorie fluid secreted by the mother's breasts at birth. After about three days, the breasts begin to produce milk. Compared with formula based on cow's milk, human milk is sterile; always at body temperature; and rich in iron, vitamins, and other newly discovered nutrients for brain and body (Drover et al., 2009).

Babies who are exclusively breast-fed are less often sick. This is true in infancy because breast milk provides antibodies against any disease to which the mother is immune and decreases the risk of allergies and asthma. Disease protection continues lifelong, because breast-fed babies are less likely to become obese adults and are thus less likely to suffer from diabetes and heart disease.

Breast milk is especially protective for preterm babies; if a preterm baby's mother cannot provide breast milk, physicians recommend milk from another woman (Schanler, 2011). (Once a woman has given birth, her breasts produce milk if they continue to be stimulated; women can therefore produce breast milk for years after giving birth.)

TABLE 5.2	The Benefits of Breast-Feeding	

For the Baby	For the Mother
Balance of nutrition (fat, protein, etc.) adjusts to age of baby	Easier bonding with baby
Breast milk has micronutrients not found in formula	Reduced risk of breast cancer and osteoporosis
Less infant illness, including allergies, ear infections, stomach upsets	Natural contraception (with exclusive breast-feeding, for several months)
Less childhood asthma	Pleasure of breast stimulation
Better childhood vision	Satisfaction of meeting infant's basic need
Less adult illness, including diabetes, cancer, heart disease	No formula to prepare; no sterilization
Protection against childhood diseases, since breast milk contains antibodies	Easier travel with the baby
Stronger jaws, fewer cavities, advanced breathing reflexes (less SIDS)	**For the Family**
Higher IQ, less likely to drop out of school, more likely to attend college	Increased survival of other children (because of spacing of births)
Later puberty, less teenage pregnancy	Increased family income (because formula and medical care are expensive)
Less likely to become obese or hypertensive by age 12	Less stress on father, especially at night

Sources: Beilin & Huang, 2008; Riordan & Wambach, 2009; Schanler, 2011; U.S. Department of Health and Human Services, 2011.

The specific fats and sugars in breast milk make it more digestible and better for the brain than any formula (Drover et al., 2009; Riordan, 2005). The composition of breast milk adjusts to the age of the baby, with breast milk for premature babies distinct from breast milk for older infants. Quantity increases to meet the demand: Twins and even triplets can grow strong while being exclusively breast-fed for months. In fact, breast milk appears to have so many advantages over formula (see Table 5.2) that one might question the validity of the research. Are breast-feeding mothers better in some other, non-measured, ways that lead to such positive outcomes?

In the United States, parents of breast-fed babies are more likely to be married, college graduates, and/or immigrants (Gibson-Davis & Brooks-Gunn, 2006). Could one of those variables account for the advantages of breast-feeding? Perhaps somewhat, but the evidence in favor of breast-feeding seems overwhelming.

Formula-feeding is preferable only in unusual cases, such as when the mother is HIV-positive or uses toxic or addictive drugs. Even then, however, breast milk without supplementation may be advised. In some African nations, HIV-positive women are encouraged to breast-feed because their infants' risk of catching HIV from their mothers is lower than the risk of dying from infections, diarrhea, or malnutrition as a result of bottle-feeding (Cohen, 2007; Kuhn et al., 2009). Pediatricians agree that it "is clear and incontrovertible that human milk is the best nutritive substance for infants during the first year" (Wagner et al., 2008, p. 1148).

>> **Answer to Observation Quiz** (from page 150) No, much better than that. Note that this graph is on a log scale. The 2003 rate is less than one percent of the 1989 rate.

The Same Situation, Many Miles Apart: Breast-Feeding Breast-feeding is universal. None of us would exist if our foremothers had not successfully breast-fed their babies for millennia. Currently, breast-feeding is practiced worldwide, but it is no longer the only way to feed infants, and each culture has particular practices.

Observation Quiz (see answer, page 154) What three differences do you see between these two breast-feeding women—one in the United States and one in Laos?

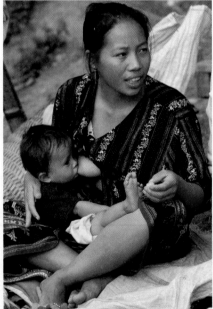

JENNIE HART / ALAMY

ALAIN EVRARD / ROBERT HARDING

For all these reasons, doctors worldwide recommend exclusive breast-feeding, with the only dispute being whether other foods should be added at about 4 months or 6 months (Fewtrell et al., 2011). Successful breast-feeding involves some learning (how to latch on and off, for instance) and often some pain (cracked nipples) in the early weeks. Encouragement from family members, especially new fathers, is crucial.

Breast milk should remain in the diet for a year or more, according to the World Health Organization, although other easily digested foods should be added by at least 6 months. Some supplemental vitamins may also be needed, as the following explains.

A CASE TO STUDY

Breast-Fed Kiana, Close to Death

Thinking his 10-month old daughter, Kiana, had a bad case of flu, Ian Barrow took her to the emergency room earlier this year. Doctors immediately noticed something more serious: soft bones, an enlarged heart, and organs close to shutting down. The diagnosis was a shock: rickets. Barrow, a technician at the National Cancer Institute, says, "Rickets is something that has supposedly disappeared."

[Stokstad, 2003, p. 1886]

Rickets is caused by severe deficiency of vitamin D, a vitamin naturally produced by the body in response to sunshine. For light-skinned adults, even a few minutes of direct sun exposure three days a week is enough to make adequate vitamin D. Rickets was once common in children who rarely played outside; that is why vitamin D is added to milk. Although almost no older children get rickets, the disease has not disappeared: Exclusively breast-fed babies, aged 6 to 18 months, are at highest risk. Rickets is the worst consequence, but people of all ages may suffer from inadequate vitamin D, resulting in reduced immunity and less energy (Wagner et al., 2008).

Many modern mothers prevent the exposure of even an inch of infant skin to direct sunlight in order to avoid later cancer. Many also believe that breast milk provides complete nutrition. But if this latter belief prevents infants from getting vitamin D (88 percent of U.S. mothers do not give vitamin D to their babies), serious deficiencies may occur (J. A. Taylor et al., 2010).

Some researchers "blame public health experts who have urged women to breast feed without emphasizing the need for supplements. And they're even more angry at those who recommend that infants under 6 months avoid all sunlight to reduce cancer risks" (Stokstad, 2003, p. 1887). Many pediatricians do not prescribe vitamin D for breast-fed babies, and, even if they do, about half of their breast-feeding mothers do not follow that advice. Actually, only a blood test reveals how much vitamin D an infant has; many babies need no extra dose, but others do—rickets should never occur.

Remember how shocked Ian Barrow was. He knew that his child should be breast-fed, and he was proud of his wife for doing so. However, he did not know that rickets was still possible or that Kiana's dark skin meant that more sunlight was needed. Fortunately, this case ended well, because an alert father noticed that something was wrong and took his daughter to doctors who diagnosed her quickly and provided vitamin D immediately. Kiana not only survived; she thrived.

Experts are still debating how much vitamin D a person needs. In 2008, the American Academy of Pediatrics doubled its recommendation (from 200 to 400 IU a day) (Wagner et al., 2008). Not every doctor or parent agrees (J. A. Taylor et al., 2010), but "Ian Barrow, for one, says that he's making sure that Kiana and her brothers spend more time outside" (Stokstad, 2003, p. 1888). No expert doubts that breast is best, but that does not mean that breast-fed children always have every nutrient they need.

Cloudy, Cold, and Dangerous Weather The danger is not from the temperature, but from the sun which can burn a baby's skin even on a cloudy day. This lad has a hat and long sleeves—he should be okay. But is he getting enough vitamin D?

SOULSURFING · JASON SWAIN

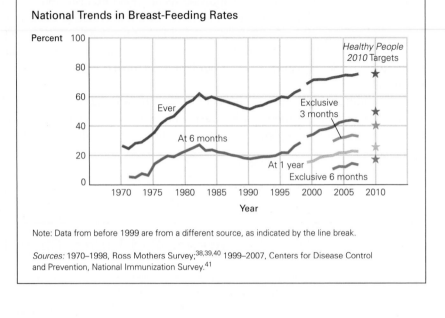

National Trends in Breast-Feeding Rates

Note: Data from before 1999 are from a different source, as indicated by the line break.

Sources: 1970–1998, Ross Mothers Survey;[38,39,40] 1999–2007, Centers for Disease Control and Prevention, National Immunization Survey.[41]

FIGURE 5.8

A Smart Choice In 1970, educated women were taught that formula was the smart, modern way to provide nutrition—but no longer. Today, more education for women correlates with more breast milk for babies. About half of U.S. women with college degrees now manage three months of *exclusive* breastfeeding—no juice, no water, and certainly no cereal.

protein-calorie malnutrition A condition in which a person does not consume sufficient food of any kind. This deprivation can result in several illnesses, severe weight loss, and even death.

stunting The failure of children to grow to a normal height for their age due to severe and chronic malnutrition.

wasting The tendency for children to be severely underweight for their age as a result of malnutrition.

>> **Answer to Observation Quiz** (from page 152) The babies' ages, the settings, and the mothers' apparent attitudes. The U.S. mother *(left)* is indoors in a hospital and seems attentive to whether she is feeding her infant the right way. The mother in Laos *(right)* seems confident and content as she feeds her older baby in a public place, enjoying the social scene.

Breast-feeding dramatically reduces infant disease and death. In the United States 75 percent of infants are breast-fed at birth, 46 percent at six months (most with other food as well), and 22 percent at a year (virtually all with other food and drink) (see Figure 5.8). Developmentalists and public health workers wish all these percentages were higher (U.S. Department of Health and Human Services, 2011). Worldwide, about half of all 2-year-olds are still nursing, usually at night.

How long a mother breast-feeds is strongly affected by her experiences in the first week, when encouragement and practical help are most needed (DiGirolamo et al., 2005). Ideally, nurses visit new parents weekly at home; such visits (routine in some nations, rare in others) increase the likelihood that breast-feeding will continue.

Malnutrition

Protein-calorie malnutrition occurs when a person does not consume sufficient food to sustain normal growth. That form of malnutrition occurs for roughly a third of the world's children in developing nations: They suffer from **stunting,** being very short for their age because chronic malnutrition kept them from growing (World Bank, 2010). Stunting is most common in the poorest nations (see Figure 5.9).

An even worse indicator of severe malnutrition is **wasting,** when children are severely underweight for their age and height (2 or more standard deviations below average). Many nations, especially in East Asia, Latin America, and central Europe, have seen improvement in child nutrition in the past decades; but in some other nations, primarily in Africa, wasting has increased since 2000. Several nations in South Asia also have high rates of malnutrition, with about half the children over age 5 stunted and almost half the children under age 5 wasted, at least for a year (World Bank, 2010).

One common way to measure a particular child's nutritional status is to compare weight and height with the detailed norms presented in Figure 5.10 and Appendix A, pages A-6 and A-7. Remember that percentiles may be more indicative of underweight than absolute numbers. A child may simply be genetically short or thin, but a decline in percentile ranking during the first two years is an ominous sign—and being in the bottom 3 percent is almost always a sign of malnutrition.

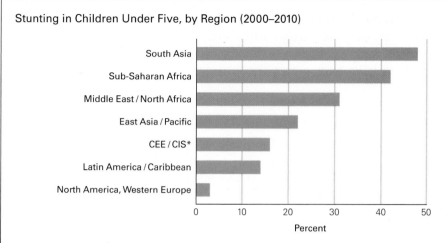

Stunting in Children Under Five, by Region (2000–2010)

*Refer to Central and Eastern Europe Fund (CEE) and Commonwealth of Independent States (CIS), which together comprise the countries of central Europe as well as those that made up the former Soviet Union.

Source: UNICEF, 2011.

FIGURE 5.9

Genetic? The data show that basic nutrition is still unavailable to many children in the developing world. Some critics contend that Asian children are genetically small and therefore that Western norms make it appear as if India and Africa have more stunted children than they really do. However, children of Asian and African descent born and nurtured in North America are as tall as those of European descent. Thus, malnutrition, not genes, accounts for most stunting worldwide.

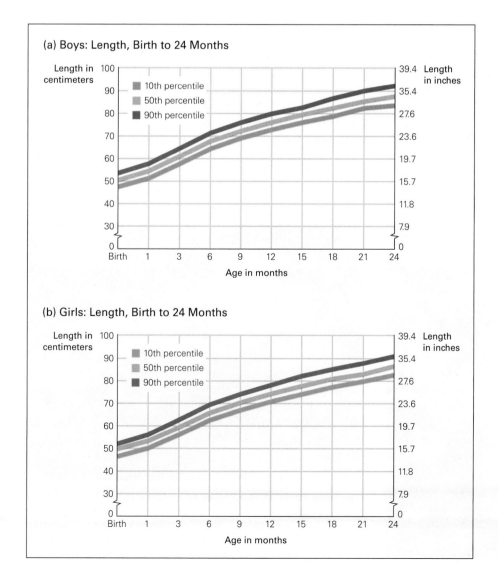

FIGURE 5.10

Gender Differences Boys and girls grow at almost the same rate throughout childhood—until age 11 or so, when girls temporarily grow faster than boys. Compare these graphs to the ones on weight, and note that already by age 2, genetic growth patterns are disturbed by overfeeding and underfeeding.

Also remember that there are ethnic differences among children. The average height in India, for instance, is several inches shorter than the average height in northern Europe, which suggests that some "stunted" children may not be malnourished. However, children born in North America whose parents were immigrants from India often grow taller than their parents—a sign that the parents were underfed.

Chronically malnourished infants and children suffer in three ways (World Bank, 2010):

1. Their brains may not develop normally. If malnutrition has continued long enough to affect height, it may also have affected the brain.
2. Malnourished children have no body reserves to protect them against common diseases. About half of all childhood deaths occur because malnutrition makes a childhood disease lethal.
3. Some diseases result directly from malnutrition.

marasmus A disease of severe protein-calorie malnutrition during early infancy, in which growth stops, body tissues waste away, and the infant eventually dies.

The worst disease directly caused by malnutrition is **marasmus.** Growth stops, body tissues waste away, and an infant victim dies. Prevention of marasmus begins long before birth, with good nutrition for the woman before and while she is pregnant. Then breast-feeding on demand (10 or more times a day) and frequent checkups to monitor the baby's weight prevent marasmus. Infants who show signs of "failure to thrive" (they do not gain weight) can be hospitalized and treated before brain damage occurs.

kwashiorkor A disease of chronic malnutrition during childhood, in which a protein deficiency makes the child more vulnerable to other diseases, such as measles, diarrhea, and influenza.

Malnutrition after age 1 may cause **kwashiorkor.** Ironically, *kwashiorkor* means "a disease of the older child when a new baby arrives"—signifying cessation of breast-feeding and less maternal attention. Although it may be that lack of protein is not the sole cause, the symptoms of kwashiorkor are unmistakable: Growth slows down; the liver is damaged; the immune system is weakened; the face, legs, and abdomen swell with fluid (edema); energy is reduced (malnourished children play less); hair becomes thin, brittle, and colorless; skin becomes blotchy (Osorio, 2011).

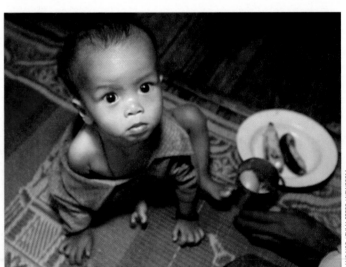

The Same Situation, Many Miles Apart: Children Still Malnourished
Infant malnutrition is common in nations at war (like Afghanistan, at right) or with crop failure (like Niger, at left). UNICEF relief programs reach only half the children in either nation. The children in these photographs are among the lucky ones who are being fed.

Normal   Extreme Neglect

BRUCE D. PERRY / THE CHILD TRAUMA ACADEMY

Lifelong Deprivation These images illustrate the negative impact of neglect on the developing brain. The CT scans on the left are from healthy 3-year-old children with an average head size (FOC: 50th percentile). The image on the right is from a series of three 3-year-old children following severe sensory-deprivation neglect in early childhood. Each deprived child's brain is significantly smaller than average and each has abnormal development of cortex (cortical atrophy) and other abnormalities suggesting abnormal development of the brain.

Treatment includes providing protein that the body has long lacked. However, perhaps because the bodies of children with kwashiorkor have become less efficient at digestion, or perhaps because some other toxins or viruses have taken hold as the immune system has slowed down, when children are hospitalized with kwashiorkor they have a higher death rate than those hospitalized with marasmus (Badaloo et al., 2006; Osorio, 2011).

Prevention, more than treatment, stops childhood malnutrition. Prenatal nutrition defends against marasmus after birth; breast-feeding protects against marasmus in infancy; ongoing breast-feeding and ample food with iron and vitamin A prevent kwashiorkor in childhood. A study of two poor African nations (Niger and Gambia) found several specific factors that reduced the likelihood of wasting and stunting: breast-feeding, both parents at home, water piped to the house, a tile (not dirt) floor, a toilet, electricity, immunization (for measles, polio, and several other diseases), a radio, and the mother's secondary education (Oyekale & Oyekale, 2009).

Several items on this list are taken for granted by readers of this book. However, two themes apply to everyone at any age: (1) Prevention is better than treatment, and (2) people with some knowledge are more likely to protect their health and that of their loved ones. The next chapters continue these themes.

SUMMING UP

Many public health practices save millions of infants each year. Immunizing children and breast-feeding are simple yet life-saving steps. These are called public health measures rather than parental practices because they are affected by culture and national policies.

An underlying theme of this chapter is that healthy biological growth is the result not simply of genes and nutrition but also of a social environment that provides opportunities for growth: lullabies and mobiles for stimulating the infant's senses, encouragement for developing the first motor skills, and protection against disease. Each aspect of development is linked to every other aspect, and each developing person is linked to family, community, and the world.

SUMMARY

Body Changes

1. In the first two years of life, infants grow taller, gain weight, and increase in head circumference—all indicative of development. The norm at birth is 7½ pounds in weight, 20 inches in length (about 3,400 grams, 51 centimeters). Birthweight doubles by 4 months, triples by 1 year, and quadruples by 2 years, when toddlers weigh about 30 pounds (13½ kilograms). Even if babies are temporarily slow to gain overall, brain weight continues to increase.

2. Sleep gradually decreases over the first two years. As with all areas of development, variations in sleep patterns are normal, caused by both nature and nurture. In developed nations, co-sleeping is increasingly common for very young infants, and many (but not all) developmentalists consider it a harmless, or even beneficial, practice.

Brain Development

3. The brain increases dramatically in size, from about 25 to 75 percent of adult weight, in the first two years. Complexity increases as well, with cell growth, development of dendrites, and formation of synapses. Both growth and pruning aid cognition.

4. Experience is vital for dendrites and synapses to link neurons. In the first year, the parts of the cortex dedicated to the senses and motor skills mature. If neurons are unused, they atrophy, and the brain regions are rededicated to processing other sensations. Normal stimulation, which almost all infants obtain, fosters experience-expectant maturation.

5. Most experience-dependent brain growth reflects the varied, culture-specific experiences of the infant. Therefore, one person's brain differs from another's. However, in the basic capacities that humans share—emotional, linguistic, and sensory—all normal infants are equally capable.

6. Infant brains are designed to grow and mature, but deprivation, excessive stress, physical shaking, and lack of stimulation can all harm an infant brain, with impairment evident lifelong.

Sensation and Movement

7. At birth, the senses already respond to stimuli. Prenatal experience makes hearing the most mature sense. Vision is the least mature sense at birth, but it improves quickly, including onset of binocular vision at about 14 weeks. Infants use all their senses to strengthen their early social interactions.

8. The senses of taste, touch, smell, and motion are all apparent in young infants, and all are affected by the social context. Babies' sense of pain is controversial.

9. Infants gradually improve their motor skills as they begin to grow and brain maturation increases. Gross motor skills are soon evident, from rolling over to sitting up (at about 6 months), from standing to walking (at about 1 year), from climbing to running (before age 2). Practice and cultural encouragement affect development of gross motor skills.

10. Fine motor skills are difficult for infants, but babies gradually develop the hand and finger control needed to grab, aim, and manipulate almost anything within reach. Experience, time, and motivation allow infants to advance in fine motor skills.

Surviving in Good Health

11. About 2 billion infant deaths have been prevented in the past half-century because of improved health care worldwide, including relatively simple measures such as oral rehydration therapy and insect-repellant bed nets. More medical professionals are needed to prevent, diagnose, and treat the diseases that still cause many infant deaths.

12. Immunization has eradicated smallpox and virtually eliminated polio and measles in developed nations. In recent years, some parents worry about potential side effects of immunization, but the social benefits have consistently been shown to greatly outweigh any risks.

13. Breast-feeding is best for infants, partly because breast milk helps them resist disease and promotes growth of every kind. Most babies are breast-fed at birth, but not all are exclusively breast-fed for six months, as many doctors worldwide recommend. Supplemental food and vitamins are needed as well.

14. Severe malnutrition stunts growth and can cause death, directly through marasmus or kwashiorkor and indirectly through vulnerability if a child catches measles, an intestinal disorder, or some other illness. Malnourished infants become shorter (stunted) children than their genes would have otherwise programmed them to be.

KEY TERMS

head-sparing (p. 129)
percentile (p. 129)
REM sleep (p. 130)
co-sleeping (p. 131)
neurons (p. 132)
cortex (p. 133)
prefrontal cortex (p. 133)
axon (p. 133)

dendrite (p. 133)
synapse (p. 133)
transient exuberance (p. 134)
pruning (p. 134)
experience-expectant brain
   functions (p. 135)
experience-dependent brain
   functions (p. 135)

shaken baby syndrome (p. 139)
self-righting (p. 141)
sensation (p. 142)
perception (p. 142)
binocular vision (p. 143)
motor skills (p. 145)
gross motor skills (p. 145)
fine motor skills (p. 146)

immunization (p. 149)
protein-calorie malnutrition
  (p. 154)
stunting (p. 154)
wasting (p. 154)
marasmus (p. 156)
kwashiorkor (p. 156)

WHAT HAVE YOU LEARNED?

Body Changes

1. What specific facts indicate that infants grow rapidly in the first year?

2. Why is it OK for an infant to be consistently at the 20th percentile in height and weight?

3. How much do newborns usually sleep and dream?

4. What are the reasons for and against co-sleeping?

Brain Development

5. What is the difference between the cortex and the rest of the brain?

6. How does the brain change from birth to age 2?

7. What factors increase the accuracy of perception in the fusiform face area?

8. How can pruning increase brain potential?

9. What is the difference between experience-expectant and experience-dependent brain function?

10. What is the effect of stress hormones on early brain development?

11. What should caregivers remember about brain development when an infant cries?

Sensation and Movement

12. What is the relationship between perception and sensation?

13. What particular sounds and patterns do infants pay attention to?

14. How does an infant's vision change over the first year?

15. What suggests that infants experience less pain than adults?

16. What is universal and what is cultural in the development of gross motor skills in infancy?

17. Which fine motor skills are developed in infancy?

Surviving in Good Health

18. Why do public health doctors wish that all infants worldwide would get immunized?

19. What are the reasons for and against breast-feeding until a child is at least 1 year old?

20. What is the relationship between malnutrition and disease?

21. As an indication of malnutrition, which is better, stunting or wasting? Why?

APPLICATIONS

1. Immunization regulations and practices vary, partly for social and political reasons. Ask at least two faculty or administrative staff members what immunizations students at your college must have and why. If you hear, "It's a law," ask why that law is in place.

2. Observe three infants (whom you do not know) in public places such as a store, playground, or bus. Look closely at body size and motor skills, especially how much control each baby has over legs and hands. From that, estimate the age in months and

then ask the caregiver how old the infant is. (Most caregivers know the infant's exact age and are happy to tell you.)

3. *This project can be done alone, but it is more informative if several students pool responses.* Ask 3 to 10 adults whether they were bottle-fed or breast-fed and, if breast-fed, for how long. If anyone does not know, or if anyone expresses embarrassment about how long they were breast-fed, that itself is worth noting. Do you see any correlation between adult body size and infant feeding?

>>ONLINE CONNECTIONS

To accompany your textbook, you have access to a number of online resources, including quizzes for every chapter of the book, flashcards (in English and Spanish), critical thinking questions, and case studies. For access to any of these links, go to www.worthpublishers.com/bergerca9e. In addition to these free resources, you'll also find links to podcasts, video clips, diagnostic quizzing with personalized study advice, and an ebook. Some of the videos and activities available online include:

- *Infant Reflexes.* Watch video clips of some of the most common infant reflexes, from the Babinski to the Moro.

- *Nutritional Needs of Infants and Children.* Including video footage from UNICEF of children around the world, this activity provides an overview of the nutritional needs and challenges children face in both developed and developing countries.

The First Two Years: Cognitive Development

WHAT WILL YOU KNOW?

1. Why isn't Piaget's theory of sensorimotor intelligence universally recognized as insightful?
2. What factors influence whether infants remember what happens to them before they can talk?
3. When and how do infants learn to talk?

My aunt Anna's husband, Uncle Henry, boasted that he did nothing with his three children—all boys—until they were smart enough to talk. He may have found an excuse to avoid diapering, burping, and bathing, but he was wrong about infant cognition. Babies are smart from the first days of life; they think about people and things, communicating long before they say their first words. His sons grew up to be devoted to their mother and much more interactive with their own infants than Uncle Henry had been with them, a marked improvement in fathering. The research presented in this chapter explains why.

Newborns seem to know nothing. Two years later they can make a wish, say it out loud, and blow out their birthday candles. Thousands of developmentalists have traced this rapid progression. We begin with Piaget's six stages of intellectual progression over the first two years and his overall understanding of early cognition. We then describe another approach (information processing) with some intriguing research, using habituation and brain scans, that reveals preverbal memory and communication. The most dramatic evidence of early intellectual growth—the talking that Uncle Henry waited for—is then described. The final topic of this chapter may be the most important one: How do early cognitive accomplishments, particularly language, occur? The implications for caregivers are many—none of which Uncle Henry knew.

>> Sensorimotor Intelligence

As you remember from Chapter 2, Jean Piaget was a Swiss scientist, born in 1896. He was "arguably the most influential researcher of all times within the area of cognitive developmental psychology" (Birney et al., 2005, p. 328). When Piaget was growing up, most scientists thought infants were capable of only eating, crying, and sleeping, not learning and exploring. Contrary to conventional wisdom (including that of Uncle Henry), Piaget realized that infants are active learners, adapting to experience. That realization, with scientific observation to support it, has earned Piaget the admiration of developmentalists.

Adaptation, according to Piaget, is the core of intelligence. Piaget described four distinct periods of cognition, ending with formal operational thought at adolescence. The first period lasts until about 24 months, when words and thoughts become symbols, not merely labels.

sensorimotor intelligence Piaget's term for the way infants think—by using their senses and motor skills—during the first period of cognitive development.

primary circular reactions The first of three types of feedback loops in sensorimotor intelligence, this one involving the infant's own body. The infant senses motion, sucking, noise, and other stimuli and tries to understand them.

Time for Adaptation Sucking is a reflex at first, but adaptation begins as soon as an infant differentiates a pacifier from her mother's breast or realizes that her hand has grown too big to fit into her mouth. This infant's expression of concentration suggests that she is about to make that adaptation and suck just her thumb from now on.

Piaget called cognition in the first two years **sensorimotor intelligence** because infants learn through the senses and motor skills that were developing before birth and continue to develop throughout infancy, as described in Chapters 4 and 5. Sensorimotor intelligence is subdivided into six stages (see Table 6.1).

Stages One and Two: Primary Circular Reactions

In every aspect of sensorimotor intelligence, the brain and the senses interact with experiences, each shaping the other as part of a dynamic system (Ambady & Bharucha, 2009). Piaget described this interaction of sensation, perception, and cognition as *circular reactions,* emphasizing that, like a circle, there is no beginning and no end (see Figure 6.1). The first two stages of sensorimotor intelligence are **primary circular reactions,** involving the infant's own body.

Stage one, called the *stage of reflexes,* lasts only a month. It includes senses as well as motor reflexes, the foundations of infant thought. The newborn's reflexes evoke some brain reactions, and soon reflexes become deliberate; sensation leads to perception, perception leads to cognition, and then cognition leads back to sensation. Sensorimotor intelligence begins.

As reflexes adjust to whatever responses they elicit, stage two, *first acquired adaptations* (also called the *stage of first habits*), begins, usually at about 1 month. Adaptation is cognitive; it includes both assimilation and accommodation (see page 47), which people use to understand their experience. Infants adapt their reflexes as repeated responses provide information about what the body does and how each action feels.

TABLE 6.1	The Six Stages of Sensorimotor Intelligence
For an overview of the stages of sensorimotor thought, it helps to group the six stages into pairs. The first two stages involve the infant's responses to its own body.	
Primary Circular Reactions	
Stage One (birth to 1 month)	*Reflexes:* sucking, grasping, staring, listening
Stage Two (1–4 months)	*The first acquired adaptations:* accommodation and coordination of reflexes *Examples:* sucking a pacifier differently from a nipple; grabbing a bottle to suck it
The next two stages involve the infant's responses to objects and people.	
Secondary Circular Reactions	
Stage Three (4–8 months)	*Making interesting sights last:* responding to people and objects *Example:* clapping hands when mother says "patty-cake"
Stage Four (8–12 months)	*New adaptation and anticipation:* becoming more deliberate and purposeful in responding to people and objects *Example:* putting mother's hands together in order to make her start playing patty-cake
The last two stages are the most creative, first with action and then with ideas.	
Tertiary Circular Reactions	
Stage Five (12–18 months)	*New means through active experimentation:* experimentation and creativity in the actions of the "little scientist" *Example:* putting a teddy bear in the toilet and flushing it
Stage Six (18–24 months)	*New means through mental combinations:* considering before doing, which provides the child with new ways of achieving a goal without resorting to trial-and-error experiments *Example:* before flushing, remembering that the toilet overflowed and mother was angry the last time, and hesitating

FSTOP / PUNCHSTOCK

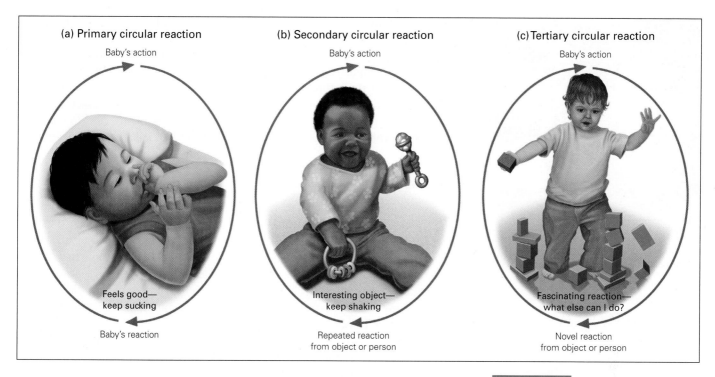

(a) Primary circular reaction

Baby's action

Feels good—
keep sucking

Baby's reaction

(b) Secondary circular reaction

Baby's action

Interesting object—
keep shaking

Repeated reaction
from object or person

(c) Tertiary circular reaction

Baby's action

Fascinating reaction—
what else can I do?

Novel reaction
from object or person

FIGURE 6.1

Never Ending Circular reactions keep going because each action produces pleasure that encourages more action.

Especially for Parents When should parents decide whether to feed their baby only by breast, only by bottle, or using some combination? When should they decide whether or not to let their baby use a pacifier? (see response, page 164)

Here is one example. In a powerful reflex, full-term newborns suck anything that touches their lips. By about 1 month, infants adapt this reflex to bottles or breasts, pacifiers or fingers, each requiring specific types of tongue pushing. This adaptation is a sign that infants have begun to interpret their perceptions; as they accommodate to pacifiers, they are "thinking."

During stage two, which Piaget pegged from about 1 to 4 months of age, additional adaptation of the sucking reflex is evident. Infant cognition leads babies to suck in some ways for hunger, in other ways for comfort—and not to suck fuzzy blankets or large balls. Once adaptation is successful, it sticks. For instance, breast-fed babies may reject milk from the nipple of a bottle (one reason breast-feeding mothers should offer breast-milk in a bottle occasionally in the early months). Likewise, if parents of a 6-month-old thumb-sucker decide that a pacifier would be better, they may be too late. The infant may refuse to adapt, spitting out the pacifier and finding the thumb instead. Piaget believed that people of all ages tend to be stuck in their ways for cognitive reasons; the adaptation of the young infant is one example.

Stages Three and Four: Secondary Circular Reactions

In stages three and four, development advances from primary to **secondary circular reactions.** Those reactions are no longer confined to the infant's body; they are an *interaction* between the baby and something else. One explanation for this advance is neurological; it seems that mirror neurons begin to function, as infants observe closely whatever they see someone do.

During stage three (4 to 8 months), infants attempt to produce exciting experiences, *making interesting events last.* Realizing that rattles make noise, for example, they wave their arms and laugh whenever someone puts a rattle in their hand. The sight of something delightful—a favorite book, a smiling parent—can trigger active efforts for interaction.

secondary circular reactions The second of three types of feedback loops in sensorimotor intelligence, this one involving people and objects. Infants respond to other people, to toys, and to any other object they can touch or move.

Intelligence in Action At four months, he has already learned that every sense and motor skill connects with Daddy—or is it the other way around?

Next comes stage four (8 months to 1 year), *new adaptation and anticipation,* also called the *means to the end* because babies have goals that they try to reach. Often they ask for help (fussing, pointing, gesturing) to accomplish what they want. Thinking is more innovative in stage four than in stage three because adaptation is more complex. For instance, instead of always smiling at Daddy, an infant might first assess Daddy's mood and then try to engage. Stage-three babies know how to continue an experience; stage-four babies initiate and anticipate.

Pursuing a Goal

A 10-month-old girl might crawl over to her mother, bringing a bar of soap as a signal to start her bath, and then remove her clothes to make her wishes crystal clear—finally squealing with delight when the bath water is turned on. Similarly, if a 10-month-old boy sees his mother putting on her coat to leave, he might drag over his own jacket to signal that he wants to go along.

At that age, babies learn to indicate that they are hungry—and learn to keep their mouths firmly shut if the food on the spoon is something they do not like. If the caregivers have been using sign language, 10-month-olds gesture that they want food or are finished eating.

These examples reveal *goal-directed behavior*—that is, purposeful action. Neurological maturation makes this possible. The baby's obvious goal seeking stems from (1) an enhanced awareness of cause and effect, (2) memory for actions already completed, and (3) understanding of other people's intentions (Behne et al., 2005; Brandone & Wellman, 2009; Willatts, 1999). These cognitive advances benefit from new motor skills (e.g., crawling, grabbing), skills which themselves are the result of brain maturation—dynamic systems again.

Object Permanence

object permanence The realization that objects (including people) still exist when they can no longer be seen, touched, or heard.

Piaget thought that, at about 8 months, babies first understand the concept of **object permanence,** the realization that objects or people continue to exist when they are no longer in sight. As Piaget predicted, not until about 8 months do infants search for toys that have fallen from the crib, rolled under a couch, or disappeared under a blanket. Blind babies also acquire object permanence toward the end of their first year, reaching for an object that they hear nearby (Fazzi et al., 2011).

As they grow older, toddlers become better at seeking hidden objects, which Piaget again considered symptomatic of their advanced levels of sensorimotor intelligence. Piaget developed a basic experiment to measure object permanence: An adult shows an infant an interesting toy, covers it with a lightweight cloth, and observes the response. The results:

- Infants younger than 8 months do not search for the object (by removing the cloth).
- At about 8 months, infants search immediately (removing the cloth) after the object is covered but not if they have to wait a few seconds.
- By 2 years, children fully understand object permanence, progressing through several stages of ever-advanced cognition (Piaget, 1954).

>> Response for Parents (from page 163) Both decisions should be made within the first month, during the stage of reflexes. If parents wait until the infant is 4 months or older, they may discover that they are too late. It is difficult to introduce a bottle to a 4-month-old who has been exclusively breast-fed or a pacifier to a baby who has already adapted the sucking reflex to a thumb.

This research provides many practical suggestions. If very young infants fuss because they want something they see but cannot have (keys, a cigarette, candy), the solution is to put that coveted object out of sight. Fussing stops. By contrast, for toddlers, merely hiding a forbidden object is not enough. It must be securely locked up or discarded, lest the child later retrieve it, climbing onto the kitchen counter or under the bathroom sink. The fact that object permanence develops

Peek-a-Boo The best hidden object is Mom under an easily moved blanket, as 7-month-old Elias has discovered. Peek-a-boo is fun from about 7 to 12 months. In another month, Elias will search for more conventionally hidden objects. In a year or two, his surprise and delight at finding Mom will fade.

gradually lets caregivers know that games such as peek-a-boo and hide-and-seek are too advanced in the first months but are fun once infants understand object permanence. For older children, peek-a-boo is boring, but hide-and-seek becomes more complex (longer waiting, more imaginative hiding) as children's comprehension of hidden objects matures.

Piaget believed that an infant's failure to search before 8 months of age was evidence that the baby had no concept of object permanence—that "out of sight" literally means "out of mind." That belief has been questioned. As one researcher points out, "Amid his acute observation and brilliant theorizing, Piaget . . . mistook infants' motor incompetence for conceptual incompetence" (Mandler, 2004, p. 17). A series of clever experiments in which objects seemed to disappear behind a screen while researchers traced babies' eye movements and brain activity revealed that long before 8 months, infants are surprised if an object vanishes (Baillargeon & DeVos, 1991; Spelke, 1993).

The idea that such surprise indicates object permanence is accepted by some scientists, who believe that "infants as young as 2 and 3 months of age can represent fully hidden objects" (Cohen & Cashon, 2006, p. 224). Other scientists are not convinced (Kagan, 2008). Perhaps an eager researcher too quickly interprets shifts and pauses in infant eye gaze as evidence of thought.

Further research on object permanence continues to raise questions and produce surprises. For instance, many other creatures (cats, monkeys, dogs, birds) develop object permanence at younger ages than Piaget found. Does this reflect slower development of the human brain or simply slower maturation of motor skills (Bruce & Muhammad, 2009)?

Stages Five and Six: Tertiary Circular Reactions

In their second year, infants start experimenting in thought and deed—or, rather, in the opposite sequence, deed and thought. They act first (stage five) and think later (stage six). **Tertiary circular reactions** begin when 1-year-olds take independent actions to discover the properties of other people, animals, and things. Infants no longer respond only to their own bodies (primary reactions) or to other people or objects (secondary reactions). Their cognitive pattern is more like a spiral than a closed circle, increasingly creative with each new discovery.

The first stage of tertiary circular reactions, Piaget's stage five (ages 12 to 18 months), is called *new means through active experimentation,* which builds on the accomplishments of stage four. Now goal-directed and purposeful activities become more expansive and creative. Toddlers delight in squeezing all the toothpaste out of the tube, taking apart an iPod, or uncovering an anthill, activities they

tertiary circular reactions The third of three types of feedback loops in sensorimotor intelligence, this one involving active exploration and experimentation. Infants explore a range of new activities, varying their responses as a way of learning about the world.

Especially for Parents One parent wants to put all the breakable or dangerous objects away because a toddler is now able to move around independently. The other parent says that the baby should learn not to touch certain things. Who is right? (see response, page 167)

"little scientist" The stage-five toddler (age 12 to 18 months) who experiments without anticipating the results, using trial and error in active and creative exploration.

Exploration at 15 Months One of the best ways to investigate food is to squish it in your hands, observing any changes in color and texture and listening for any sounds. Taste and smell are primary senses for adults when eating, but it looks as if Jonathan has already had his fill of those.

deferred imitation A sequence in which an infant first perceives something done by someone else and then performs the same action hours or even days later.

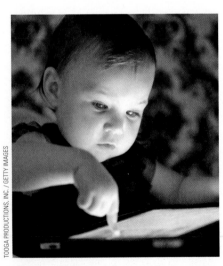

No More Playpens Much has changed since Jacqueline watched a temper tantrum in a playpen. "Little scientists" still "experiment in order to see," but this 14-month-old uses a digital tablet and might protest if it is taken away.

have never seen an adult do. Piaget referred to the stage-five toddler as a **"little scientist"** who "experiments in order to see." Their scientific method is trial and error. Their devotion to discovery is familiar to every adult scientist—and to every parent.

Finally, on reaching the sixth stage (ages 18 to 24 months), toddlers begin to anticipate and solve simple problems by using *mental combinations*, intellectual experimentation via imagination that sometimes supersedes the active experimentation of stage five. Thankfully, the stage-six sequence may begin with thought (especially if the toddler remembers that something was forbidden) and then move on to action. Of course, the urge to explore may overtake memories of prohibition: Things that are truly dangerous (poisons, swimming pools, open windows) need to be locked and gated, not simply forbidden.

Another major cognitive accomplishment at the sixth stage is that toddlers can pretend. For instance, they know that a doll is not a real baby, but they can strap it into a stroller and take it for a walk. If an adult pretends to eat imaginary food (my nephew enjoyed giving me "shoe ice cream"), they may laugh—unlike older children, who no longer find that funny because they are long past stage six.

Evidence of an advance in cognition at about 18 months occurs in language as well: Instead of just uttering one word at a time, the stage-six child can combine two words to express more complex thoughts, an impressive intellectual accomplishment discussed later in this chapter. Because they combine ideas, stage-six toddlers think about consequences, hesitating a moment before yanking the cat's tail or dropping a raw egg on the floor. Of course, their strong drive to discover may overwhelm reflection; they do not always choose wisely.

Piaget describes another stage-six intellectual accomplishment, involving both thinking and memory. **Deferred imitation** occurs when infants copy behavior they noticed hours or even days earlier (Piaget, 1945/1962). A classic example is Piaget's daughter, Jacqueline, who observed another child

> who got into a terrible temper. He screamed as he tried to get out of a playpen and pushed it backward, stamping his feet. Jacqueline stood watching him in amazement, never having witnessed such a scene before. The next day, she herself screamed in her playpen and tried to move it, stamping her foot lightly several times in succession.
>
> *[Piaget, 1945/1962, p. 63]*

Piaget and Modern Research

As detailed by hundreds of developmentalists, many infants reach the stages of sensorimotor intelligence earlier than Piaget predicted (Oakes et al., 2011). Not only do 5-month-olds show surprise when objects seem to disappear (evidence of object permanence before 8 months, as described earlier), but also some babies younger than 1 year pretend and defer imitation (both stage-six abilities, according to Piaget) (Bauer, 2006; Fagard & Lockman, 2010; Hayne & Simcock, 2009; Meltzoff & Moore, 1999). How could a gifted scientist be so wrong? There are at least three reasons.

Sample Too Small

First, Piaget's original insights were based on his own infants. Direct observation of three children is a start, and Piaget was an extraordinarily meticulous and creative observer, but no contemporary researcher would stop there. Given the immaturity and variability of babies, dozens of infants must be studied. For instance, as evidence for early object permanence, Baillargeon (2000) listed 30 studies involving more than a thousand infants younger than 6 months old.

Methods Too Simple

Second, infants are not easy to study; there are problems with "fidelity and credibility" (Bornstein et al., 2005, p. 287). To overcome these problems, modern researchers use innovative statistics, research designs, sample sizes, and strategies that were not available to Piaget—often finding that object permanence, deferred imitation, and other sensorimotor accomplishments occur earlier, and with more variation, than Piaget had assumed (Hartmann & Pelzel, 2005; Kolling et al., 2009). For instance, if an infant looks a few milliseconds longer when an object seems to have vanished, is that evidence of object permanence? Many researchers believe the answer is yes—but only advanced measurement can prove it.

One particular research method has been a boon to scientists, confirming the powerful curiosity of very young babies. That research method is called **habituation** (from the word *habit*). Habituation refers to getting accustomed to an experience after repeated exposure, as when the school cafeteria serves macaroni day after day or when infants repeatedly encounter the same sound, sight, toy, or so on. Evidence of habituation is loss of interest (or, for macaroni, loss of appetite).

Using habituation as a research strategy with infants involves repeating one stimulus until babies lose interest and then presenting another, slightly different stimulus (a new sound, sight, or other sensation). Babies indicate that they detect a difference between the two stimuli with a longer or more focused gaze; a faster or slower heart rate; more or less muscle tension around the lips; a change in the rate, rhythm, or pressure of suction on a nipple. Such subtle indicators are recorded by technology that was unavailable to Piaget (such as eye-gaze cameras and heart monitors).

By inducing habituation and then presenting a new stimulus, scientists have learned that even 1-month-olds can detect the difference between a *pah* sound and a *bah* sound, between a circle with two dots inside it and a circle without any dots, and much more. Babies younger than 6 months perceive far more than Piaget imagined.

Brain Activity Unseen

Third, several ways of measuring brain activity now allow scientists to record infant cognition long before any observable evidence is found (see Table 6.2) (M. H. Johnson, 2011). In functional magnetic resonance imaging, or **fMRI,** a burst of electrical activity measured by blood flow within the brain is recorded, indicating that neurons are firing. This leads researchers to conclude that a particular stimulus has been noticed and processed. As time goes on, changes in the blood flow indicate that habituation has occurred. Based on such advanced methods, scientists are convinced that infants have memories, goals, deferred imitation, and even mental combinations well in advance of Piaget's stages (Bauer et al., 2010; Morasch & Bell, 2009).

Brain imagery of normal children is not only difficult and expensive to acquire, but CT scans in particular raise questions about long-term effects (Schenkman, 2011). Brain scans may be essential if an infant is ill or injured, but many parents are cautious about allowing such measures with healthy infants. Such caution is understandable, even admirable, but it slows down neurological confirmation of infant cognition.

As detailed in Chapter 5, it is known that early brain growth is rapid and wide-ranging: Dendrites proliferate, and pruning is extensive. The first months and years of life are filled with mental activity, prime time for cognitive development (M. H. Johnson, 2011), although, of course, neurological maturation and cognitive advances continue long past infancy. Despite many valid criticisms of Piaget's work, he was correct in many ways. For instance, significant new connections

habituation The process of becoming accustomed to an object or event through repeated exposure to it, and thus becoming less interested in it.

fMRI Functional magnetic resonance imaging, a measuring technique in which the brain's electrical excitement indicates activation anywhere in the brain; fMRI helps researchers locate neurological responses to stimuli.

>> Response for Parents (from page 165) It is easier and safer to babyproof the house because toddlers, being "little scientists," want to explore. However, it is important for both parents to encourage and guide the baby, so it is preferable to leave out a few untouchable items if that will help prevent a major conflict between husband and wife.

TABLE 6.2	**Some Techniques Used by Neuroscientists to Understand Brain Function**

EEG, normal brain

Technique
EEG (electroencephalogram)

Use
Measures electrical activity in the top layers of the brain, where the cortex is.

Limitations
Especially in infancy, much brain activity of interest occurs below the cortex.

ERP when listening

Technique
ERP (event-related potential)

Use
Notes the amplitude and frequency of electrical activity (as shown by brain waves) in specific parts of the cortex in reaction to various stimuli.

Limitations
Reaction within the cortex signifies perception, but interpretation of the amplitude and timing of brain waves is not straightforward.

fMRI when talking

Technique
fMRI (functional magnetic resonance imaging)

Use
Measures changes in blood flow anywhere in the brain (not just the outer layers).

Limitations
Signifies brain activity, but infants are notoriously active, which can make fMRIs useless.

PET scan of sleep

Technique
PET (positron emission tomography)

Use
Also (like fMRI) reveals activity in various parts of the brain. Locations can be pinpointed with precision, but PET requires injection of radioactive dye to light up the active parts of the brain.

Limitations
Many parents and researchers hesitate to inject radioactive dye into an infant's brain unless a serious abnormality is suspected.

For both practical and ethical reasons, these techniques have not been used with large, representative samples of normal infants. One of the challenges of neuroscience is to develop methods that are harmless, easy to use, and comprehensive for the study of normal children. A more immediate challenge is to depict the data in ways that are easy to interpret and understand.

in brain networks and functions seem to occur at years 2, 4, 6, and throughout puberty (Kagan, 2008)—all ages when Piaget described cognitive growth. Furthermore, there is "ample data to suggest that learning and memory are correlated with changes in the brain at multiple levels" (Nelson, de Haan et al., 2006, p. 17). Piaget was also correct to describe babies as avid learners. His main mistake was underestimating how rapidly their learning occurs.

SUMMING UP

Piaget discovered, studied, and then celebrated active infant learning, which he described in six stages of sensorimotor intelligence. Babies use their senses and motor skills to gain an understanding of their world, first with reflexes and then by adapting through assimilation and accommodation. Piaget's description of active infant learning was a welcome contrast to earlier assumptions that babies did not think until they could talk.

We now know that object permanence, pursuit of goals, and deferred imitation all develop before the time Piaget assigned to his stages. The infant is a "little scientist" not only at 1 year, as Piaget described, but months earlier. Thinking develops before infants have the motor skills to demonstrate their thoughts; eye movements and brain scans find that babies have active minds.

>> Information Processing

As explained in Chapter 2, Piaget's sweeping overview of four periods of cognition contrasts with **information-processing theory,** a perspective originally modeled after computer functioning, including input, memory, programs, calculation, and output. For infants, the output might be moving a hand to uncover a toy (object permanence), saying a word to signify recognition (e.g., *mama*), or simply glancing at one photo longer than another (habituation). As you remember, sensation leads to perception, which may lead to cognition.

For example, instead of the newborn's reflexive cry in response to the sensation of hunger, a slightly older hungry infant might perceive a bottle, grab, and then suck, or see Mother coming, reach to be picked up, and then nuzzle at her breast. Each step of this process requires information to be processed; older infants are much more thoughtful and effective than newborns because of more advanced information processing. Researchers have demonstrated that these advances occur week by week or even day by day in the first year, contrary to Piaget's notion of six discrete stages (Cohen & Cashon, 2006).

With the aid of the sensitive technology just described, information-processing research has found impressive intellectual capacities: Concepts and categories seem to develop in infants' brains by about 6 months (Mandler, 2007; Quinn, 2004). Research inspired by information processing finds detailed sequences in number sense. For instance, habituation and brain scans reveal that 6-month-olds can detect the difference between a display of 8 dots and one of 16 dots but not the difference between 8 and 12 dots. This number sense advances within the next 3 months, so that by 9 months of age, babies can distinguish a display of 8 dots from one of 12 dots (Lipton & Spelke, 2003). It will be years before they can count, and even longer before they can add, subtract, and so on, but some number sense may appear as early as 3 months (Libertus & Brannon, 2009).

Knowing the incremental details of such cognitive development has many practical implications. For example, information processing pinpoints ways to avoid the later intellectual deficits many preterm children experience (Rose et al., 2008). The information-processing perspective helps tie together many aspects of infant cognition. We review two of these now: affordances and memory. Affordances concern perception or, by analogy, input. Memory concerns brain organization and output—that is, information storage and retrieval.

Affordances

Perception, remember, is mental processing of information that arrives at the brain from the sensory organs. It is the first step of information processing. One puzzle of development is that two people can have discrepant perceptions of the same situation, not only interpreting it differently but actually observing it differently.

Decades of thought and research led Eleanor and James Gibson to conclude that perception is far from automatic (E. J. Gibson, 1969; J. J. Gibson, 1979). Perception—for infants, as for the rest of us—is a cognitive accomplishment that requires selectivity: "Perceiving is active, a process of obtaining information about the world. . . . We don't simply see, we look" (E. J. Gibson, 1988, p. 5). Or, as one neuroscientist said, "You see what you expect or are trained to see, not what is there" (Freeman, quoted in Bower, 2007, p. 106).

The Gibsons contend that the environment (people, places, and objects) *affords,* or offers, many opportunities for interaction with what is perceived (E. J. Gibson, 1997). Each of these opportunities is called an **affordance.** Which particular affordance is perceived and acted on depends on four factors: sensory awareness,

information-processing theory A perspective that compares human thinking processes, by analogy, to computer analysis of data, including sensory input, connections, stored memories, and output.

Especially for Computer Experts In what way is the human mind not like a computer? (see response, page 171)

affordance An opportunity for perception and interaction that is offered by a person, place, or object in the environment.

Chewable? Motivation is crucial for affordances. This baby's toy was designed to afford pulling, but he is teething, so he is motivated to recognize that it also affords chewing.

Depth Perception This toddler in a laboratory in Berkeley, California, is crawling on the experimental apparatus called a visual cliff. She stops at the edge of what she perceives as a drop-off.

visual cliff An experimental apparatus that gives the illusion of a sudden drop-off between one horizontal surface and another.

Especially for Parents of Infants When should you be particularly worried that your baby will fall off the bed or down the stairs? (see response, page 172)

dynamic perception Perception that is primed to focus on movement and change.

immediate motivation, current development, and past experience. As an example, imagine that you are lost in an unfamiliar city. Whom will you ask for directions? Not usually the first person you see: You will look for someone who seems knowledgeable and approachable. Both avoiding one person and choosing another are affordances, connected to the strangers' expressions, body language, gender, dress, and more (Miles, 2009).

Age affects the affordances a person perceives. Toddlers enjoy running as soon as their motor skills enable it. Then they seek places to run: a meadow, a long hallway in an apartment building, or a road. To an adult eye, the degree to which these places afford running may be restricted by such factors as a bull grazing in the meadow, neighbors behind the hallway doors, or traffic on the road. Adults may restrict the toddler for those reasons. Furthermore, they are unlikely to start running themselves because motivation is pivotal in affordances: Many adults prefer to stay put.

Selective perception of affordances is characteristic not only of every age but also of every culture. Just as a baby might be oblivious to something adults consider crucial—or vice versa—an American in, say, Thailand might miss an important sign of the social network. In every nation, foreigners are considered rude because of their thoughtless behavior, but that rudeness may simply be evidence that their affordances are not what the native people perceive. That applies within cultures as well. Residents of Manhattan complain that tourists walk too slowly: Natives see sidewalks as affording rapid progress, not views of architecture.

Research on Early Affordances

The fact that experience affects which affordances are perceived is quite apparent in studies of depth perception. Research that demonstrates this fact began with an apparatus called the **visual cliff,** designed to provide the illusion of a sudden drop-off between one horizontal surface and another. Mothers were able to urge their 6-month-olds to wiggle toward them over the supposed edge of the cliff, but even with their mothers urging them on, 10-month-olds fearfully refused to budge (E. J. Gibson & Walk, 1960).

Scientists once thought that a visual deficit—specifically, inadequate depth perception—prevented the 6-month-olds from seeing the drop. According to this hypothesis, as the visual cortex matured, 10-month-olds could see that crawling into the gap afforded falling. Later research (using more advanced technology) disproved that interpretation. Even 3-month-olds notice a drop: Their heart rate slows and their eyes open wide when they are placed over the cliff. But until they can crawl, they do not realize that crawling over an edge affords falling, perhaps with a frightening and painful consequence.

The infant's awareness of the affordance of the visual cliff depends on past experience. The difference is in processing, not input; in affordance, not mere stimulus. Further research on affordances of the visual cliff included the social context, with the tone of the mother's encouragement being a significant indicator of whether the cliff affords crawling or not (Kim et al., 2010). The same sequence happens with walking: Novice walkers are fearless and reckless; experienced walkers are more cautious and deliberate (Adolph & Berger, 2005).

Movement and People

Despite the variations from one infant to another in the particular affordances they perceive, all babies are attracted to two kinds of affordances. Babies pay close attention to things that move and to people. **Dynamic perception** focuses on movement and change. Infants love motion. As soon as they can, they move their bodies—grabbing, scooting, crawling, walking. To their delight, such motion changes what the world affords them. As a result, infants work hard to master the next motor accomplishment (Adolph & Berger, 2005). They also look at things that move—passing cars, flickering images on a screen, mobiles.

Other creatures that move, especially an infant's own caregivers, are among the main sources of pleasure, again because of dynamic perception. It's almost impossible to teach a baby not to chase and grab any moving creature, including a dog, a cat, or even a cockroach. Infants' interest in motion was the inspiration for another experiment that sought to learn what affordances were perceived by babies too young to talk or walk (van Hof et al., 2008). A ball was moved at various speeds in front of infants aged 3 to 9 months. Most tried to touch or catch the ball as it passed within reach. However, marked differences appeared in their perception of the affordance of "catchableness."

Sometimes younger infants did not reach for slow-moving balls yet tried to grasp the faster balls. They tried but failed, touching the ball only about 20 percent of the time. By contrast, the 9-month-olds knew when a ball afforded catching. They grabbed the slower balls and did not try to catch the fastest ones; their success rate was almost 100 percent. This "follows directly from one of the key concepts of ecological psychology, that animals perceive the environment in terms of action possibilities or affordances" (van Hof et al., 2008, p. 193).

The other universal principle of infant perception is **people preference.** This is in accord with another key principle of evolutionary psychology: that over the centuries, humans of all ages survived by learning to attend to, and rely on, one another. You just read that the affordance of the visual cliff depends partly on the tone of the mother's voice (Kim et al., 2010). Infants soon recognize their caregivers and expect certain affordances (comfort, food, entertainment) from them.

Very young babies are particularly interested in emotional affordances, using their limited perceptual abilities and intellectual understanding to respond to smiles, shouts, and so on. Infants connect facial expressions with tone of voice long before they understand language. This ability led to an interesting hypothesis:

> Given that infants are frequently exposed to their caregivers' emotional displays and further presented with opportunities to view the affordances (Gibson, 1959, 1979) of those emotional expressions, we propose that the expressions of familiar persons are meaningful to infants very early in life.
>
> [*Kahana-Kalman & Walker-Andrews, 2001, p. 366*]

Building on earlier studies, these researchers tested their hypothesis by presenting infants with two moving images side by side on one video screen (Kahana-Kalman & Walker-Andrews, 2001). Both images were of a woman, two views each of either the infant's own mother or of a stranger. In one image, the woman was joyful; in the other, sad. Each presentation was accompanied by an audiotape of that woman's happy *or* sad talk.

Previous studies had found that 7-month-olds could match emotional words with facial expressions, but younger babies could not. At 7 months, but not earlier, infants looked longer at strangers whose voice matched the emotion shown on their face and less at strangers whose facial expression did not match the tone they heard.

These researchers first replicated the earlier experiments, again finding that 3½-month-old babies could not match a stranger's voice and facial expression. However, when the 3½-month-olds saw two images of their *own* mother and heard

MARINA RAITH / PHOTOLIBRARY

The Next Move These infants are intrigued by things and people, as would be expected. However, they have much to learn about how to grab a ball or play with a friend. It would not be surprising if, a minute later, the ball rolled away, one child cried, and the wide-eyed redhead hit her playmate.

people preference A universal principle of infant perception, specifically an innate attraction to other humans, evident in visual, auditory, and other preferences.

>> Response for Computer Experts (from page 169) In dozens of ways, including speed of calculation, ability to network across the world, and vulnerability to viruses. In at least one crucial way, the human mind is better: Computers wear out within a few years, while human minds keep advancing for decades.

Especially for Parents This research on early affordances suggests a crucial lesson about how many babysitters an infant should have. What is it? (see response, page 173)

>> Response for Parents of Infants (from page 170) Constant vigilance is necessary for the first few years of a child's life, but the most dangerous age is from about 4 to 8 months, when infants can move but do not yet fear falling over an edge.

her happy or her sad voice, they correctly matched visual and vocal emotions. They looked longest when their smiling mother talked happily; but when their mother sounded sad, they stared more at the video of their sad-faced mother than at the video of their happy mother—thus connecting sound and sight, presumably based on their past experience with that person.

The researchers noticed something else as well. When infants saw and heard their happy mothers, they smiled twice as fast, seven times as long, and much more brightly (cheeks raised and lips upturned) than for the happy strangers. Experience had taught them that a smiling mother affords joy. The affordances of a smiling stranger are more difficult to judge.

Memory

Both a certain amount of experience and a certain amount of brain maturation are required in order to process and remember anything (Bauer et al., 2010). Infants have difficulty storing new memories in their first year, and older children are often unable to describe events that occurred when they were younger. Many adults have what Freud called "childhood amnesia"—they forget experiences, people, and even languages they knew when they were young. One reason is linguistic: People use words to store (and sometimes distort) memories, so preverbal children have difficulty with recall (Richardson & Hayne, 2007) while adults cannot access early memories because they did not have words to solidify them.

Calvin & Hobbes

Selective Amnesia As we grow older, we forget about spitting up, nursing, crying, and almost everything else from our early years. However, strong emotions (love, fear, mistrust) may leave lifelong traces.

However, a series of experiments reveals that very young infants *can* remember, even if they cannot later put memories into words. Memories are particularly evident in these circumstances:

- Experimental conditions are similar to those of real life.
- Motivation is high.
- Retrieval is strengthened by reminders and repetition.

The most dramatic evidence for infant memory comes from innovative experiments in which 3-month-olds were taught to make a mobile move by kicking their legs (Rovee-Collier, 1987, 1990). The infants lay on their backs, in their own cribs, connected to a mobile by means of a ribbon tied to one foot (see photograph on the next page). Virtually all the infants began making some occasional kicks (as well as random arm movements and noises) and realized, after a while, that kicking made the mobile move. They then kicked more vigorously and frequently, sometimes laughing at their accomplishment. So far, this is no surprise—self-activated movement is highly reinforcing to infants, a part of dynamic perception.

When some infants had the mobile-and-ribbon apparatus reinstalled in their cribs *one week later,* most started to kick immediately. Their reaction indicated that they remembered their previous experience. But when other 3-month-old infants were retested *two weeks later,* they began with only random kicks. Apparently they had forgotten what they had learned—evidence that memory is fragile early in life. But that conclusion needs revision, or at least qualification.

Reminders and Repetition

The lead researcher, Carolyn Rovee-Collier, developed another experiment that demonstrated that 3-month-old infants *could* remember after two weeks *if* they had a brief reminder session before being retested (Rovee-Collier & Hayne, 1987). A **reminder session** is any experience that helps people recollect an idea, a thing, or an event.

In this particular reminder session, two weeks after the initial training the infants watched the mobile move but were *not* tied to it and were positioned so that they could *not* kick. The next day, when they were again connected to the mobile and positioned so that they *could* move their legs, they kicked as they had learned to do two weeks earlier. Apparently, watching the mobile move on the previous day had revived their faded memory. The information about making the mobile move was stored in their brains, but they needed processing time to retrieve it. The reminder session provided that time.

Other research finds that repeated reminders are more powerful than single reminders and that context is crucial, especially for infants younger than 9 months of age: Being tested in the same room as the initial experience aids memory (Rovee-Collier & Cuevas, 2009a). Six-month-old infants, who went through only two half-hour sessions with a novel puppet on one day, remembered the experience four weeks later—an amazing feat (Giles & Rovee-Collier, 2011). Many other studies have found that infant memory is fragile but that reminders, repetition, and retrieval cues may help very young infants remember (S. P. Johnson & Shuwairi, 2009).

A Little Older, a Little More Memory

After about 6 months of age, infants retain information for a longer time than younger babies do, with less training or reminding. Toward the end of the first year, many kinds of memory are apparent. For example, suppose a 9-month-old watches someone playing with a toy he or she has never seen. The next day, if given the toy, the 9-month-old will play with it in the same way as he or she had observed. Younger infants will not.

Many experiments show that toddlers can transfer learning from one object or experience to another and that they learn from various people and events—from parents and strangers, from other babies and older siblings, from picture books and family photographs (Hayne & Simcock, 2009). The dendrites and neurons of the brain change to reflect their experiences and memories even in the first years of life.

In one series of experiments, 15-month-old infants were shown a toy, with an adult acting on it in a particular way. A day later, they were given another toy they had never seen, and they tried to act on it in the same way they remembered from the day before. This was true even if they had merely watched the action and if nothing had happened as a result of the action; it was even more true, though, if the action had produced a reaction (e.g., a noise), especially if the baby had also been allowed to manipulate the toy (Yang et al., 2010).

TEK IMAGE / PHOTO RESEARCHERS, INC.

He Remembers! In Rovee-Collier's experiment, a young infant immediately remembers how to make the familiar mobile move. (Unfamiliar mobiles do not provoke the same reaction.) He kicks his right leg and flails both arms, just as he learned to do several weeks ago.

Observation Quiz How and why is this mobile unlike those usually sold for babies? (see answer, page 175)

reminder session A perceptual experience that helps a person recollect an idea, a thing, or an experience.

>> **Response for Parents** (from page 171) It is important that infants have time for repeated exposure to each caregiver, because infants adjust their behavior to maximize whatever each particular caregiver affords in the way of play, emotions, and vocalization. Parents should find one steady babysitter rather than several.

Note that these experiments are further evidence of several facts already mentioned: Babies observe affordances carefully; they are especially attuned to actions and people; and deferred imitation is possible before 18 months, when Piaget's stage six begins.

Aspects of Memory

Brain activity patterns shown on fMRI and PET scans indicate that one region of the brain (the fusiform face area, explained in Chapter 5) is devoted to memory for faces, another to memory for sounds, another to memory for sights. While memories for many specific kinds of things are located in particular clusters of neurons, several additional brain regions also participate in these various memories: Particularly early in life, brain organization varies depending on the particular experiences to be remembered (Rovee-Collier & Cuevas, 2009b). An infant could lose one part of the brain yet still remember things that supposedly were stored there. As the brain matures and dendrites are formed, some kinds of memories are consolidated more than others. Again, memory for movement and for people is particularly strong.

Memories need not be of any specific object or experience but may instead be general notions of how the world works. In one experiment, 11-month-olds viewed a jumble of blocks, then some saw a face and some saw a ball, and then they all viewed the same blocks they'd seen earlier, except this time stacked in some order. The length of time they looked at the third view suggested that they realized that a person (the face) could organize blocks but an inanimate ball could not (Newman et al., 2010).

Many other studies show that infants not only remember specific events but also develop memories for patterns (Keil, 2011). Some examples come from research, such as what syllables and rhythms are heard and how objects move in relation to others; additional examples arise from close observations of babies at home, such as what behaviors are expected from Mommy as compared to Daddy or what details indicate it is time to go to sleep (e.g., a particular blanket, book, or crib). All this is evidence that every day of their young lives, infants are processing information and storing conclusions.

One reason earlier scientists underestimated memory is that they failed to distinguish between **implicit memory,** which is memory that remains hidden until a particular stimulus brings it to mind (like the mobile reminder session), and **explicit memory,** which is memory that can be recalled on demand. Explicit memories are usually verbal, and therefore "although explicit memory *emerges* sometime between 6 and 12 months, it is far from fully developed" (Nelson, de Haan et al., 2006, p. 23). The particular part of the brain on which explicit memory depends is the hippocampus (explained in Chapter 8), present at birth but very immature until about age 5 or 6. It is no surprise that this timing coincides with the beginning of formal education, because children are much better at memorizing at that age.

Implicit memories, by contrast, begin in infancy or perhaps even before birth. Implicit memories are evident in all the examples just mentioned, when evidence of memory comes from the situation, not from the answer to a spoken question. For instance, adults who knew a language in childhood often have no explicit memory of it: They claim to have forgotten all the Spanish, French, Chinese, or whatever they knew. When asked the word for a common object such as table or apple in that language, they quite honestly reply that they do not know (Bowers et al., 2009). Moreover, when first tested, such adults do no better than those who never knew that language.

However, repeated exposure reveals implicit memories from infancy. For example, a student who has forgotten all the Spanish he ever knew seems to catch

NANCY SHEEHAN / PHOTOEDIT

Memory Aid Personal motivation and action are crucial to early memory, which is why Noel has no trouble remembering which shape covers the photograph of herself as a baby.

implicit memory Unconscious or automatic memory that is usually stored via habits, emotional responses, routine procedures, and various sensations.

explicit memory Memory that is easy to retrieve on demand (as in a specific test). Most explicit memory involves consciously learned words, data, and concepts.

Especially for Teachers People of every age remember best when they are active learners. If you must teach fractions to a class of 8-year-olds, how would you do it? (see response, page 177) on much more quickly in Spanish class than does the student who never heard Spanish as an infant. Apparently, the first weeks of Spanish class served as a reminder session. Reminders may also explain the phenomenon of déjà vu; people, places, and smells sometimes seem familiar or emotionally evocative, even if never experienced before, because something very similar occurred in infancy and was stored implicitly.

Infants probably store in their brains many emotions and sensations that they cannot readily retrieve. The information-processing approach finds that infant memory is crucial for later development—far more so than are other components of early thought, such as attention and processing speed (Rose et al., 2009). Extensive research finds that memories help in early word learning, and those words in turn help encode later memories (Richardson & Hayne, 2007).

SUMMING UP

Infant cognition can be studied using the information-processing perspective. Information processing analyzes each component of how thoughts begin; how they are organized, remembered, and expressed; and how cognition builds, day by day. Infants' perception is powerfully influenced by particular experiences and motivation; affordances perceived by one infant differ from those perceived by another. Memory depends on brain maturation and on experience. For that reason, memory is fragile in the first year (although it can be triggered by dynamic perception and reminders) and becomes more evident, although still fragile, in the second year. ∎

>> Language: What Develops in the First Two Years?

No other species has anything approaching the neurons and networks that support the 6,000 or so human languages. The human ability to communicate, even at age 2, far surpasses that of full-grown adults from every other species, including dolphins and chimpanzees, both of which have much better communication mechanisms than was formerly believed. Here we describe the specific steps in early language learning and then raise the crucial question: How do babies do it?

The Universal Sequence

The timing of language acquisition varies; the most advanced 10 percent of 2-year-olds speak more than 550 words, and the least advanced 10 percent speak fewer than 100 words—a fivefold difference (Merriman, 1999). But, although timing varies, the sequence is the same worldwide (see At About This Time on page 177). Even deaf children who become able to hear before age 3 (thanks to cochlear implants) follow the sequence. If they could not hear for the first months, their first words appear later, but they often catch up to their age-mates within a year or so (Ertmer et al., 2007). If they learn sign language, they also follow the sequence of word by word, then sentences of increasing length and complexity.

Listening and Responding

Infants begin learning language before birth, via brain organization and hearing. Habituation to noises has been demonstrated in

>> **Answer to Observation Quiz** (from page 173) It is black and white, with larger objects—designed to be particularly attractive to infants, not to adult shoppers.

Who Is Babbling? Probably both the 6-month-old and the 27-year-old. During every day of infancy, mothers and babies communicate with noises, movements (notice the hands), and expressions.

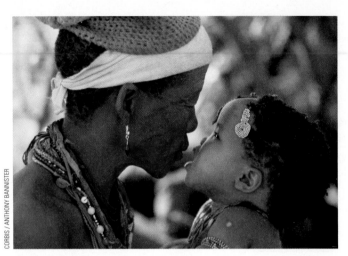

Too Young for Language? No. The early stages of language involve communication through noises, gestures, and facial expressions, very evident here between this !Kung grandmother and granddaughter.

fetuses several weeks before birth, which suggests that listening and remembering are inborn, basic to being human (Dirix et al., 2009). They even learn to prefer the language their mother speaks over an unheard language, with newborns of bilingual mothers preferring both languages and differentiating between them (Byers-Heinlein et al., 2010). (See the Research Design.)

Newborns look closely at facial expressions and prefer to hear speech over other sounds, a preference that is evident by 4 months (Minagawa-Kawai et al., 2011). By 6 months of age, infants can distinguish, just by looking at someone's mouth movements (no sound), whether that person is speaking their native language or not (Weikum et al., 2007). In fact, infants' ability to distinguish sounds and gestures in the language, or languages, most often heard improves over the first year, whereas the ability to hear sounds never spoken in their native language deteriorates (Narayan et al., 2010).

Careful analysis has found that adult communication with babies is distinct from communication with other adults (Falk, 2004). For instance, adults use higher pitch, simpler words, repetition, varied speeds, and exaggerated emotional tones when they speak to infants (Bryant & Barrett, 2007). This special language form is sometimes called *baby talk*, since it is talk directed to babies, and sometimes called *motherese*, since mothers universally speak it. Non-mothers speak it

---

▶ Research Design

Scientists: Krista Byers-Heinlein, Tracey C. Burns, and Janet Werker.

Publication: *Psychological Science* (2010).

Participants: In three experiments, data were collected from 94 newborns (0–5 days old) in a large hospital in Vancouver, Canada. Half were born to mothers who spoke both English and Tagalog (the native language of Filipinos), one-third to mothers who spoke only English, and one-sixth to mothers who spoke English and Chinese.

Design: The infants sucked as they listened to 10 minutes of recorded sentences matched for pitch, duration, and number of syllables, alternating each minute in English or Tagalog. When they sucked at "high amplitude" (predetermined for each infant), the recording played. More frequent sucking was taken as a preference for one language or the other. The total number of intense sucks for English was subtracted from the Tagalog sucks.

Major conclusion: Most of the bilingual newborns preferred Tagalog, whereas the monolinguals preferred English. The Chinese bilinguals (who had not heard Tagalog in utero) were tested to rule out alternate explanations. As you see in the figure, newborn preferences were affected by language heard before birth. The researchers believe it is the rhythm of the language that becomes familiar, and they note that the rhythm of Chinese is somewhat similar to that of Tagalog, leading to the results of the Chinese bilinguals.

Comments: Other research had already shown that the fetus responds to the language spoken by the mother; this study suggests that some children begin to become bilingual before they are born. One advantage of this study is that all the participants were born in a large Canadian hospital, and thus all probably had adequate prenatal nutrition, health care, and birth experiences. More details, controls, and replication would help confirm the results. For example, although

the bilingual mothers said they spoke both languages, with the less common one spoken at least 30 percent of the time, direct observation may have found otherwise. Until these results are replicated with other bilingual infants, it is possible that these results are related to something specific in Tagalog or English or are related to when and how much the mothers spoke each language, such as at work or at home. Nonetheless, this study confirms and extends a conclusion from thousands of studies: Infants have an amazing ability to learn languages, evident long before their first spoken word.

AT ABOUT THIS TIME
The Development of Spoken Language in the First Two Years

Age*	Means of Communication
Newborn	Reflexive communication—cries, movements, facial expressions.
2 months	A range of meaningful noises—cooing, fussing, crying, laughing.
3–6 months	New sounds, including squeals, growls, croons, trills, vowel sounds.
6–10 months	Babbling, including both consonant and vowel sounds repeated in syllables.
10–12 months	Comprehension of simple words; speechlike intonations; specific vocalizations that have meaning to those who know the infant well. Deaf babies express their first signs; hearing babies also use specific gestures (e.g., pointing) to communicate.
12 months	First spoken words that are recognizably part of the native language.
13–18 months	Slow growth of vocabulary, up to about 50 words.
18 months	Naming explosion—three or more words learned per day. Much variation: Some toddlers do not yet speak.
21 months	First two-word sentence.
24 months	Multiword sentences. Half the toddler's utterances are two or more words long.

*The ages of accomplishment in this table reflect norms. Many healthy children with normal intelligence attain these steps in language development earlier or later than indicated here.

Sources: Bloom, 1993, 1998; Fenson et al., 2000; Lenneberg, 1967.

as well. In fact, both "baby talk" and "motherese" may be misleading terms; scientists prefer the more formal designation, **child-directed speech.**

No matter what term is used, child-directed speech fosters learning. Even at 7 months of age, infants begin to recognize words that are highly distinctive (Singh, 2008): *Bottle, dog,* and *mama,* for instance, might be distinguished from one another before words that sound alike (such as *baby, Bobbie,* and *Barbie*). Infants respond vocally to adult noises and expressions (as well as to their own internal pleasures and pains) in many ways—with crying, cooing, and a variety of other sounds. Their responses gradually become more varied. By 4 months, most babies squeal, growl, gurgle, grunt, croon, and yell, telling everyone what is on their minds.

Also within the first months, infants' listening becomes more selective. Not only do infants prefer child-directed speech, they like alliteration, rhymes, repetition, rhythm, and varied pitch (Hayes & Slater, 2008; Schön et al., 2008). Think of your favorite lullaby (itself an alliterative word); obviously, babies prefer sounds over content.

Babbling

Between 6 and 9 months of age, babies begin to repeat certain syllables (*ma-ma-ma, da-da-da, ba-ba-ba*), a phenomenon referred to as **babbling** because of the way it sounds. Babbling is experience-expectant; all babies do it, even deaf ones. Responses from other people encourage babbling (this is the age of "making interesting events last"). Deaf babies stop babbling because they cannot hear responses; hearing babies continue.

All babies make rhythmic gestures, again in response to the actions of others (Iverson & Fagan, 2004). Toward the end of the first year, babbling begins to sound like the infant's native language; infants imitate what they hear in accents,

child-directed speech The high-pitched, simplified, and repetitive way adults speak to infants and children. (Also called *baby talk* or *motherese*.)

>> Response for Teachers (from page 174) Remember the three principles of infant memory: real life, motivation, and repetition. Find something children already enjoy that involves fractions—even if they don't realize it. Perhaps get a pizza and ask them to divide it in half, quarters, eighths, sixteenths, and so on.

babbling An infant's repetition of certain syllables, such as *ba-ba-ba,* that begins when babies are between 6 and 9 months old.

Especially for Nurses and Pediatricians
The parents of a 6-month-old have just been told that their child is deaf. They don't believe it because, as they tell you, the baby babbles as much as their other children did. What do you tell them? (see response, page 178)

Happy Talk Ty's mother and the teacher demonstrate the sign for "more" in a sign language class at the public library in Hudson, Florida. Ty takes the lesson very seriously: Learning language in any form is crucial for 1-year-olds.

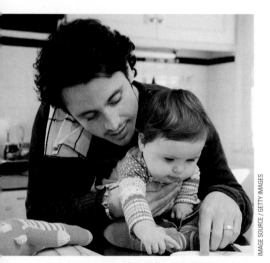

Show Me Where Pointing is one of the earliest forms of communication, emerging at about 10 months.

>> Response for Nurses and Pediatricians (from page 177) Urge the parents to begin learning sign language immediately and investigate the possibility of cochlear implants. Babbling has a biological basis and begins at a specified time, in deaf as well as hearing babies. However, deaf babies eventually begin to use gestures more and to vocalize less than hearing babies. If their infant can hear, sign language does no harm. If the child is deaf, however, noncommunication may be devastating.

cadence, consonants, and so on. Videotapes of deaf infants whose parents sign to them show that 10-month-olds use about a dozen distinct hand gestures in a repetitive manner similar to babbling. All babies express concepts with gestures sooner than with speech (Goldin-Meadow, 2006). Many caregivers, recognizing the power of gestures, teach "baby signs" to their 6- to 12-month-olds, allowing them to communicate with hand signs months before the infants master the fine motor skill of moving tongue, lips, and jaws to make specific words (Pizer et al., 2007).

One early gesture is pointing, typical in human babies at 10 months. Pointing is an advanced social gesture that requires understanding another person's perspective. Most animals cannot interpret pointing; most 10-month-old humans can look toward the place another person is pointing and can point themselves, even at the place where an object should be but no longer is (Liszkowski et al., 2009). Pointing with the index finger is a different and more advanced signal than doing so with a full hand, as if reaching (Liszkowski & Tomasello, 2011).

First Words

Finally, at about 1 year of age, the average hearing baby utters a few words. Caregivers usually understand the first words before strangers do, which makes it hard for researchers to pinpoint exactly what a 12-month-old can say. For example, at 13 months, Kyle knew standard words such as *mama,* but he also knew *da, ba, tam, opma,* and *daes,* which his parents knew to be, respectively, "downstairs," "bottle," "tummy," "oatmeal," and "starfish" (yes, that's what *daes* meant!) (Lewis et al., 1999).

Gradual Beginnings

In the first months of the second year, spoken vocabulary increases gradually (perhaps one new word a week). However, 6- to 15-month-olds learn meanings rapidly; they understand about 10 times more words than they can say (Schafer, 2005; Snow, 2006). Initially, the first words are merely labels for familiar things (*mama* and *dada* are common), but some early words are soon accompanied by gestures, facial expressions, and nuances of tone, loudness, and cadence that are precursors of the first appearance of grammar (Saxton, 2010). A single word can convey various messages. Imagine meaningful sentences encapsulated in "Dada!" "Dada?" and "Dada." Each is a **holophrase,** a single word that expresses an entire thought.

Intonation (variations of tone and pitch) is extensive in early babbling and again in holophrases, with a temporary reduction in the range of intonation at about 12 months. Apparently, at 1 year of age infants reorganize their vocalization from universal to language-specific (Snow, 2006). They are no longer just singing and talking to themselves; they are trying to communicate in a specific language. Uttering meaningful words takes all their attention—none left over for intonation.

Careful tracing of early language from the information-processing perspective finds other times when vocalization seems to slow down before a burst of new talking, as perception and action are interdependent (Pulvermüller & Fadiga, 2010). That means that sometimes, with a new perceptual understanding, it takes time for verbal output to reflect that neurological advance. This slowdown before a language spurt is not evident in every infant, but many seem temporarily quieter before a burst of new words (Parladé & Iverson, 2011).

The Naming Explosion

Once vocabulary reaches about 50 *expressed* words (understood words are far more extensive), it builds rapidly, at a rate of 50 to 100 words per month, with 21-month-olds saying twice as many words as 18-month-olds (Adamson & Bakeman, 2006). This language spurt is called the **naming explosion** because many early words are nouns, although the word *noun* is a linguistic category, not an infant's preference (Waxman & Lidz, 2006).

In almost every language, the name of each significant caregiver (often *dada, mama, nana, papa, baba, tata*) and sibling (and sometimes each pet) is learned between 12 and 18 months (Bloom, 1998). (See Appendix A, page A-4.) Other frequently uttered words refer to the child's favorite foods (*nana* can mean "banana" as well as "grandma") and to elimination (*pee-pee, wee-wee, poo-poo, ka-ka, doo-doo*). No doubt you notice that all these words have two identical syllables, each a consonant followed by a vowel. Many more words follow that pattern—not just *baba* but also *bobo, bebe, bubu, bibi.* Other early words are only slightly more complicated—*ma-me, ama,* and so on.

Cultural Differences

Cultures and families vary a great deal in how much child-directed speech children hear. Some parents read to their infants, teach them signs that communicate, and respond to every noise, including a burp or a fart, as if it is an attempt to talk. Others are much less verbal, using gestures, touch, and tone, saying "hush" and "no" instead of trying to teach vocabulary. As young as 5 months of age, babies prefer adults who often engage in child-directed speech, revealing their preferences even if, for the moment, those adults are silent. Apparently, just as infants seek to master physical skills as soon as they can, they seek to learn language from the best teachers available (Schachner & Hannon, 2011).

The idea that children should be "seen but not heard" is contrary to the emphasis on communication in most American families; however, an emphasis on listening respectfully, not talking, is common in other families, including many Latino ones (Cabrera et al., 2006), and among many fathers, especially those of low socioeconomic status (SES). Nonetheless, all infants listen to whatever they can and appreciate the sounds of their culture. Even musical tempo is culture-specific: 4- to 8-month-olds seem to like their own native music best (Soley & Hannon, 2010).

holophrase A single word that is used to express a complete, meaningful thought.

naming explosion A sudden increase in an infant's vocabulary, especially in the number of nouns, that begins at about 18 months of age.

Especially for Caregivers A toddler calls two people "Mama." Is this a sign of confusion? (see response, page 180)

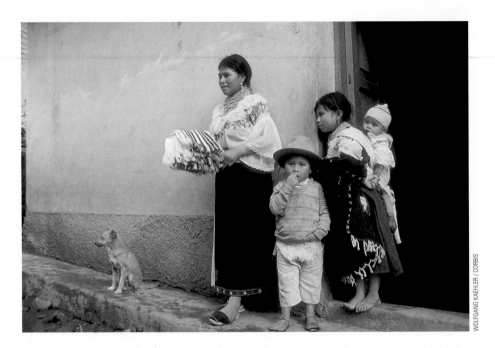

WOLFGANG KAEHLER / CORBIS

Cultural Values If they are typical of most families in the relatively taciturn Otavalo culture of Ecuador, these three children hear significantly less conversation than children elsewhere. In most Western cultures, that might be called maltreatment. However, each culture encourages the qualities it values, and verbal fluency is not a priority in this community. In fact, people who talk too much are ostracized and those who keep secrets are valued, so encouragement of talking may constitute maltreatment in the Otavalo culture.

Parts of Speech

Although all new talkers say names, use similar sounds, and say more nouns than any other parts of speech, the ratio of nouns to verbs and adjectives varies from place to place. For example, by 18 months, English-speaking infants use relatively more nouns but fewer verbs than Chinese or Korean infants do. Why?

One explanation goes back to the language itself. Mandarin and Korean are "verb-friendly" in that verbs are placed at the beginning or end of sentences, which makes them easier to learn. In English, verbs occur in various positions within sentences, and their forms change in illogical ways (e.g., *go, gone, will go, went*). This irregularity makes English verbs harder to learn than nouns.

An alternative explanation considers the entire social context: Playing with a variety of toys and learning about dozens of objects are crucial in North American culture, whereas East Asian cultures emphasize human interactions—specifically, how one person responds to another. Accordingly, North American infants are expected to name many objects, whereas Asian infants are expected to act on objects (as explained in Chapter 1) and respond to people. Thus, Chinese toddlers might learn the equivalent of *come, play, love, carry, run,* and so on before Canadian ones. (This is the result of experience, not genes. A toddler of Chinese ancestry, growing up in an English-speaking Canadian home, has the learning patterns of other English toddlers.)

A simpler explanation is that young children are sensitive to the sounds of words, with some sounds more salient than others. Verbs are learned more easily if they sound like the action (Imai et al., 2008), and such verbs may be more common in some languages than others. In English, most verbs are not onomatopoeic, although perhaps *jump, kiss,* and *poop*—all learned relatively early on—are exceptions. The infant preference for sounds may be one reason why many English-speaking toddlers who have never been on a farm nonetheless know that a cow says "moo" and a duck says "quack."

Every language has some words and concepts that are difficult. English-speaking infants confuse *before* and *after*; Dutch-speaking infants misuse *out* when it refers to taking off clothes; Korean infants need to learn two meanings of *in* (Mandler, 2004). Learning adjectives is easier in Italian and Spanish than

>> Response for Caregivers (from page 179) Not at all. Toddlers hear several people called "Mama" (their own mother, their grandmothers, their cousins' and friends' mothers) and experience mothering from several people, so it is not surprising if they use "Mama" too broadly. They will eventually narrow the label down to one person.

in English or French because of patterns in those languages (Waxman & Lidz, 2006). Specifically, adjectives can stand by themselves without the nouns. If I want a blue cup from a group of multicolored cups, I would ask for "a blue cup" or "a blue one" in English but simply "uno azul" (a blue) in Spanish. Despite such variations, in every language infants demonstrate impressive speed and efficiency in acquiring both vocabulary and grammar.

Putting Words Together

Grammar includes all the methods that languages use to communicate meaning. Word order, prefixes, suffixes, intonation, verb forms, pronouns and negations, prepositions and articles—all of these are aspects of grammar. Grammar can be discerned in holophrases but becomes obvious between 18 and 24 months, when two-word combinations begin (Hollich, 2010).

For example, "Baby cry" and "More juice" follow the proper English word order rather than the reverse. No child asks, "Juice more," and by age 2 children know that "cry baby" has an entirely different meaning. Soon the child combines three words, usually in subject–verb–object order in English (for example, "Mommy read book"), rather than any of the five other possible sequences of those words.

Children's grammar correlates with the size of their vocabulary (Snow, 2006). The child who says "Baby is crying" is advanced in language development compared with the child who says "Baby crying" or simply the holophrase "Baby." Comprehension advances as well. Their expanding knowledge of both vocabulary and grammar helps toddlers understand what others are saying (Kedar et al., 2006).

Young children can master two languages, not just one. The crucial variable is how much speech in both languages the child hears. Listening to two languages does not necessarily slow down the acquisition of grammar, but "development in each language proceeds separately and in a language specific manner" (Conboy & Thal, 2006, p. 727). Indeed, some evidence suggests that children are statisticians: They implicitly track the number of words and phrases and learn those expressed most often. That is certainly the case when children are learning their mother tongue; it is probably also true for knowing which sounds are most often

grammar All the methods—word order, verb forms, and so on—that languages use to communicate meaning, apart from the words themselves.

GETTY IMAGES

Look Who's Talking Men have a reputation for being strong and silent, but these three are more typical of today's men—sharing the joys and tribulations of fatherhood. Such conversations are distinctly human; other animals communicate, but only people use language so extensively.

Observation Quiz Which of these three prams is best for encouraging infant language? (see answer, page 182)

>> Answer to Observation Quiz (from page 181) The one on the left, which allows the baby to listen, watch, and talk to the father. One-on-one interaction is pivotal for learning language no matter which theory is right—reinforcement, social interaction, or brain maturation.

Especially for Nurses and Pediatricians
Bob and Joan have been reading about language development in children. They are convinced that because language is "hardwired" they need not talk to their 6-month-old son. How do you respond? (see response, page 184)

combined in two or three languages (Johnson & Tyler, 2010). Bilingual toddlers soon realize differences between languages, adjusting tone, cadence, as well as vocabulary when speaking to a monolingual person. Most bilingual children have parents who are also bilingual; hence, these children mix languages because they expect their parents to understand.

Theories of Language Learning

Worldwide, people who are not yet 2 years old already speak their native tongue. They continue to learn rapidly: Some teenagers compose lyrics or deliver orations that move thousands of their co-linguists. How is language learned so easily and so well?

Answers come from three schools of thought, each connected to a theory (behaviorism, sociocultural theory, and evolutionary psychology). The first says that infants are directly taught, the second that social impulses propel infants to communicate, and the third that infants understand language because of brain advances thousands of years ago that allowed survival of our species.

Theory One: Infants Need to Be Taught

The seeds of the first perspective were planted more than 50 years ago, when the dominant theory in North American psychology was behaviorism, or learning theory. The essential idea was that all learning is acquired, step by step, through association and reinforcement. Just as Pavlov's dogs learned to associate the sound of a tone with the presentation of food (see Chapter 2), behaviorists believe that infants associate objects with words they have heard often, especially if reinforcement occurs.

B. F. Skinner (1957) noticed that spontaneous babbling is usually reinforced. Typically, every time the baby says "ma-ma-ma-ma," a grinning mother appears, repeating the sound as well as showering the baby with attention, praise, and perhaps food. These affordances are exactly what infants want, so babies repeat "ma-ma-ma-ma"; via operant conditioning, talking begins.

Skinner believed that most parents are excellent instructors, replying to their infants' gestures and sounds, thus reinforcing speech (Saxton, 2010). Even in preliterate societies, parents use child-directed speech, responding quickly with high pitch, short sentences, stressed nouns, and simple grammar—exactly the techniques that behaviorists would recommend.

The core ideas of this theory are the following:

- Parents are expert teachers, although other caregivers help.
- Frequent repetition is instructive, especially when linked to daily life.
- Well-taught infants become well-spoken children.

Behaviorists note that some 3-year-olds converse in elaborate sentences; others just barely put one simple word with another. Such variations correlate with the amount of language each child has heard. Parents of the most verbal children teach language throughout infancy—singing, explaining, listening, responding, and reading to them every day, even before age 1 (Forget-Dubois et al., 2009).

In one detailed U.S. study, researchers analyzed the language that mothers used with their 9-month-old infants (Tamis-LeMonda et al., 2001). Although all the mothers were middle class, from the same nation (to control for cultural and SES factors), in 10 minutes one mother never imitated her infant's babbling; another mother imitated 21 times, babbling back in conversation. All mothers described things or actions (e.g., "That is a spoon you are holding—spoon"), but one mother offered only 4 descriptions while another gave 33.

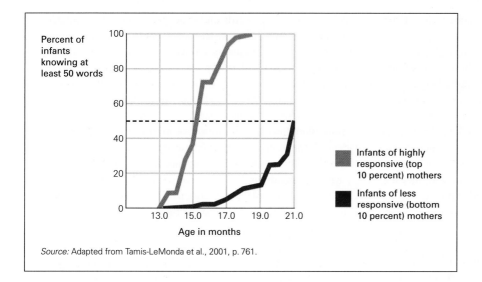

Source: Adapted from Tamis-LeMonda et al., 2001, p. 761.

FIGURE 6.2

Maternal Responsiveness and Infants' Language Acquisition Learning the first 50 words is a milestone in early language acquisition, as it predicts the arrival of the naming explosion and the multiword sentence a few weeks later. Researchers found that the 9-month-old infants of highly responsive mothers (top 10 percent) reached this milestone as early as 15 months. The infants of nonresponsive mothers (bottom 10 percent) lagged significantly behind.

Observation Quiz Why does the blue line end at 18 months? (see answer, page 185)

The frequency of maternal responsiveness at 9 months predicted language acquisition at 17 months (see Figure 6.2). It was not that noisy infants, whose genes would soon make them verbal, elicited more talk. Some quiet infants had mothers who frequently suggested play activities, described things, and asked questions. Quiet infants with talkative mothers usually became talkative later on. Those results are found in many nations. For example, in one large study in Australia, parents who provided extensive language to their preverbal infants had children who spoke early and well (Reilly et al., 2006).

According to behaviorists, if adults want children who speak, understand, and (later) read well, they must talk to their infants. A recent application of this theory comes from commercial videos, designed to advance toddlers' vocabulary. Typically, such videos use repetition and attention-grabbing measures (sound, tone, color) to encourage babies to learn new words (Vaala et al., 2010). Such videos, and Skinner's theories, have come under attack from many developmentalists, as explained in the following.

THINKING CRITICALLY

My Baby Can Read?

Toddlers can learn to swim in the ocean, throw a ball into a basket, walk on a narrow path beside a precipice, dial a phone, cut a melon with a sharp knife, play a guitar, say whatever word is on a flashcard, and much else—if provided appropriate opportunity, tools, encouragement, and practice. Indeed, toddlers in some parts of the world do each of these things—often to the dismay, disapproval, and even shock of adults in other cultures. Infants attempt to do what they see others doing, a trait that fosters rapid learning. The same trait challenges caregivers, who find it is not easy to keep "little scientists" safe.

In the past decade, many commercial companies have recognized this learning and have packaged videos, toys, and instructions for parents to teach babies to sort objects by shape, to recognize colors, or to say a word when they see a particular sign. Parents buy such products in order to accomplish two goals: to keep the baby safely entertained and to foster learning. The commercial products are expensive, advertised with testimonials, and named to appeal to parents, such as *Baby Einstein, Brainy Baby,* and *My Baby Can Read.* Contemporary toddlers are impressive learners. Is this because of educational videos? Probably not.

The learning abilities and accomplishments of toddlers have always been astonishing. Piaget is acclaimed for recognizing that; ignoring that made Uncle Henry a fool. Remember from Chapter 5 the face recognition skills that develop over the first year? A 1½-year-old can see another child on one occasion, hear his or her name, and then call that child by name a week later. Astonishing. Could you call that reading?

Similarly, 1-year-olds can reproduce actions demonstrated only once, can use a new toy in ways they have seen similar toys being used, can remember things that adults have forgotten. They are fascinated by dynamic activity, especially when it includes movement, sound, and people. This explains the popularity of child-directed videos—"like crack for babies," as one mother said (DeLoache et al., 2010, p. 1572). Not only are 1-year-olds "little scientists," experimenting with everything they can to reach conclusions about the natural world, they are also little linguists, mastering words at a rapid clip by age 2.

Thus, the abilities of toddlers have always been impressive. Since computers, talking toys, and commercial videos are pervasive in Western culture, and since many parents believe that their child's eventual achievement rests on what they do, many adults buy programs that are supposed to advance knowledge. Once people spend money and time on something, they tend to believe it works: Parents buy learning tools and then are impressed by their toddler's advances.

A rebuttal comes from research, which finds that the more video exposure a 6-month-old has, the slower the infant's cognitive and linguistic development (Tomopoulos et al., 2010). This study was not explicitly about "educational" videos, but there is no evidence that videos designed for infants improve later intellectual achievement. Before age 3, children's visual, auditory, symbolic, and conceptual skills render them less likely to learn with a video than without it—unless the video is a prop for parental involvement, in the same way a book or a trip to the store might be (Richert et al., 2011). In that case, learning would occur as well or better *without* the video (DeLoache et al., 2010). The crucial factor for intellectual growth seems to be caregiver responsiveness and encouragement.

Many developmentalists fear that advertisements take advantage of parents' wish to do everything they can for their child's future success (Yang et al., 2010). If toddlers exposed to a video express new words and concepts, parents tend to attribute that accomplishment to the video, not to the typical, amazing cognitive advances just described.

If a particular toddler does *not* master new skills at the advertised rate, few parents ask for a refund or complain of false advertising, instead blaming themselves or their baby. In 2009, developmentalists, pediatricians, and parents won a lawsuit against *Baby Einstein*, the source of most of the child-directed videos. As a result, *Baby Einstein* advertisements can no longer claim that their products are educational (Lewin, 2009).

Much depends on how a video is used (Courage & Setliff, 2010). Scientists might not criticize the parent who wrote a comment about the lawsuit against *Baby Einstein*:

> It's not a substitute for parental interaction or being read to, it's just a good way to spend 30 minutes in a long day being a baby. The more experiences babies have and the more things they see and hear, the more of a framework they have on which to hang further learning. Walks down the block, playing with parents, being read to, being spoken to, playing at anything, and yes, watching a TV screen that shows something that your child finds engaging, all contribute to that framework of experience, knowledge and understanding the world.
>
> My daughter, whom we adopted from China, had not been bathed in a bathtub in her orphanage. She did *not* like baths, or swimming pools (held by mommy or daddy) *at all*. One day we were watching Baby Neptune together. She was about 18 months old. After one scene with a kid playing in water, she got off of my lap (video still playing) and marched right into the bathroom, up her step stool, turned on the water in the sink and started to play in the water. Since that moment, she has turned into a true fish, loving baths, the sprinkler, her kiddie pool and now, at 8, she loves to swim all day. Not that she wouldn't have eventually found her love for water, but I saw the light go on!
>
> [comment on Lewin, 2009]

This seems to be a battle between most experts and many businesses, with parents on both sides and infants caught in the middle. Which side are you on? More important, why?

>> **Response for Nurses and Pediatricians** (from page 182) While much of language development is indeed hardwired, many experts assert that exposure to language is required. You don't need to convince Bob and Joan of this point, though—just convince them that their baby will be happier if they talk to him.

Especially for Educators An infant day-care center has a new child whose parents speak a language other than the one the teachers speak. Should the teachers learn basic words in the new language, or should they expect the baby to learn the majority language? (see response, page 186)

Theory Two: Social Impulses Foster Infant Language

The second theory is called *social-pragmatic*. It arises from the sociocultural reason for language: communication. According to this perspective, infants communicate because humans are social beings, dependent on one another for survival and joy. Each culture has practices that further social interaction; talking is one of those practices.

It is the emotional messages of speech, not the words, that are the focus of early communication, according to this perspective. In one study, people who had never heard English (Shuar hunter-gatherers living in isolation near the Andes Mountains) listened to tapes of North American mothers talking to their babies. The Shuar successfully distinguished speech conveying comfort, approval, attention, and prohibition, without knowing any of the words (Bryant & Barrett, 2007). Thus, the social content of speech is universal, which is why babies learn whatever specifics their culture provides.

Suppose an 18-month-old is playing with an unnamed toy and an adult utters a word. Does the child connect that word to the toy? A behaviorist, learning-by-association prediction would be yes, but the answer is no. In an experiment, when toddlers played with a fascinating toy and adults said a word, the toddlers looked up, figured out what the adult was looking at, and assigned the new word to that, not to the fascinating toy (Baldwin, 1993). This supports theory two: The toddlers wanted to know what the adults intended.

Another study also suggests social learning. Many 1-year-olds enjoy watching television and videos, but the evidence implies that they learn from it only when adults are actively involved in teaching (see Thinking Critically). In a controlled experiment, 1-year-olds learned vocabulary much better when someone directly taught them than when the same person taught on a video (Roseberry et al., 2009). This suggests personal, social, language acquisition, not impersonal learning.

According to theory two, then, social impulses, not explicit teaching, lead infants to learn language "as part of the package of being a human social animal" (Hollich et al., 2000). Those same impulses are evident in all the ways infants learn: According to this theory, people differ from the great apes in that they are social, driven to communicate. Thus, every infant (and no chimpanzee) masters words and grammar to join the social world in which he or she finds himself or herself (Tomasello & Herrmann, 2010).

Theory Three: Infants Teach Themselves

A third theory holds that language learning is innate; adults need not teach it, nor is it simply a by-product of social interaction. It arises from the universal human impulse to imitate. As already explained in the research on memory, infants and toddlers observe what they see and apply it—not slavishly but according to their own concepts and intentions. According to theory three, this is exactly what they do with the language they hear as well (Saxton, 2010).

The seeds of this perspective were planted soon after Skinner proposed his theory of verbal learning. Noam Chomsky (1968, 1980) and his followers felt that language is too complex to be mastered merely through step-by-step conditioning. Although behaviorists focus on variations among children in vocabulary size, Chomsky focused on similarities in language acquisition—the universals (see Chapter 2), not the differences.

Noting that all young children master basic grammar at about the same age, Chomsky cited this *universal grammar* as evidence that humans are born with a mental structure that prepares them to seek some elements of human language—for example, the use of a raised tone at the end of an utterance to indicate a question. Chomsky labeled this hypothesized mental structure the **language acquisition device (LAD).** The LAD enables children to derive the rules of grammar quickly and effectively from the speech they hear every day, regardless of whether their native language is English, Thai, or Urdu.

Other scholars agree with Chomsky that infants are innately ready to use their minds to understand and speak whatever language is offered. All babies are eager learners, and language may be considered one more aspect of neurological maturation (Wagner & Lakusta, 2008). This idea does not strip languages and cultures of their differences in sounds, grammar, and almost everything else, but the basic idea is that "language is a window on human nature, exposing deep and universal features of our thoughts and feelings" (Pinker, 2007, p. 148).

College Grad, Class of '33? Reading to an infant correlates with talking at age 1, reading at age 5, and college graduation at age 21. Of course, correlation is not causation, but in any case, this shared joy bodes well for the future.

>> **Answer to Observation Quiz** (from page 183) By 18 months, every one of the infants of highly responsive mothers (top 10 percent) knows 50 words. Not until 30 months do all the infants with quiet mothers reach the naming explosion.

language acquisition device (LAD)
Chomsky's term for a hypothesized mental structure that enables humans to learn language, including the basic aspects of grammar, vocabulary, and intonation.

The various languages of the world are all logical, coherent, and systematic. Infants are primed to grasp the particular language they are exposed to, making caregiver speech "not a 'trigger' but a 'nutrient'" (Slobin, 2001, p. 438). There is no need for a trigger, according to theory three, because words are expected by the developing brain, which quickly and efficiently connects neurons to support whichever language the infant hears. Thus, language itself is experience-expectant, although obviously the specific language is experience-dependent.

Research supports this perspective as well. As you remember, newborns are primed to listen to speech (Vouloumanos & Werker, 2007), and all infants babble *ma-ma* and *da-da* sounds (not yet referring to mother or father). No reinforcement or teaching is required; all infants need is for dendrites to grow, mouth muscles to strengthen, neurons to connect, and speech to be heard.

Nature even provides for deaf infants. All 6-month-olds, hearing or not, prefer to look at sign language over nonlinguistic pantomime. For hearing infants, this preference disappears by 10 months because their affinity for gestural language is not necessary for communication (Krentz & Corina, 2008). Deaf infants are signing by then.

A Hybrid Theory

Which of these three perspectives is correct? Perhaps all of them. In one monograph that included details and results of 12 experiments, the authors presented a hybrid (which literally means "a new creature, formed by combining other living things") of previous theories (Hollich et al., 2000). Since infants learn language to do numerous things—indicate intention, call objects by name, put words together, talk to family members, sing to themselves, express their wishes, remember the past, and much more—some aspects of language learning may be best explained by one theory at one age and other aspects by another theory at another age. Although originally developed to explain acquisition of first words, mostly nouns, this theory also explains learning verbs: Perceptual, social, and linguistic abilities combine to make that possible (Golinkoff & Hirsh-Pasek, 2008).

One study supporting the hybrid theory began, as did the study previously mentioned, with infants looking at pairs of objects that they had never seen and never heard named. One of each pair was fascinating to babies and the other was boring, specifically "a blue sparkle wand . . . [paired with] a white cabinet latch . . . a red, green, and pink party clacker . . . [paired with] a beige bottle opener" (Pruden et al., 2006, p. 267). The experimenter said a made-up name (not an actual word), and then the infants were tested to see whether they assigned the new word to the object that had the experimenter's attention (the dull one) or to the one that was interesting to them.

Unlike the previous study, which involved 18-month-olds, the participants in this one were 10-month-olds. The results differed from those involving older infants: The 10-month-olds seemed to assign the word to the fascinating object, not the dull one. These researchers' interpretation was that *how* language is learned depends on the age of the child as well as on the particular circumstances. Behaviorism may work for young children, social learning for slightly older ones: "The perceptually driven 10-month-old becomes the socially aware 19-month-old" (Pruden et al., 2006, p. 278).

After intensive study, another group of scientists also endorsed a hybrid theory, concluding that "multiple attentional, social and linguistic cues" contribute to early language (Tsao et al., 2004, p. 1081). It makes logical and practical sense for nature to provide several paths toward language learning and for various theorists

>> **Response for Educators** (from page 184) Probably both. Infants love to communicate, and they seek every possible way to do so. Therefore, the teachers should try to understand the baby, and the baby's parents, but should also start teaching the baby the majority language of the school.

to emphasize one or another of them (Sebastián-Gallés, 2007). It also seems that not only are some aspects of language learned in one way or another at certain ages, but also that each child learns differently; that is, some children learn better one way, and others, another way (Goodman et al., 2008). Parents need to talk often to their infants (theory one), encourage social interaction (theory two), and appreciate the innate abilities of the child (theory three).

As one expert concludes:

> In the current view, our best hope for unraveling some of the mysteries of language acquisition rests with approaches that incorporate multiple factors, that is, with approaches that incorporate not only some explicit linguistic model, but also the full range of biological, cultural, and psycholinguistic processes involved.
>
> *[Tomasello, 2006, pp. 292–293]*

The idea that every theory is correct in some way may seem almost idealistic. However, a similar conclusion was arrived at by scientists extending and interpreting research on language acquisition. They contend that language learning is neither the direct product of repeated input (behaviorism) nor the result of a specific human neurological capacity (LAD). Rather, from an evolutionary perspective, "different elements of the language apparatus may have evolved in different ways," and thus a "piecemeal and empirical" approach is needed (Marcus & Rabagliati, 2009, p. 281). In other words, a single theory that explains how babies learn language does not reflect the data: Humans accomplish this feat in many ways.

What conclusion can we draw from all this? That infants are active learners, not only of language, concepts, objects, and goals as explained in this chapter but also of the motor skills detailed in Chapter 5 and the social understanding to be described in Chapter 7.

Now back to Uncle Henry: My cousins loved their mother because she knew instinctively that her infant boys were ready to learn. When they grew up they realized, as developmentalists all recognize, that even in the first weeks of life, every caregiver—fathers as well as mothers—can be the first, and perhaps the best, teacher.

SUMMING UP

From the first days of life, babies attend to words and expressions, responding as well as their limited abilities allow—crying, cooing, and soon babbling. Before age 1, they understand simple words and communicate with gestures. At 1 year, most infants speak. Vocabulary accumulates slowly at first, but then more rapidly with the naming explosion and with the emergence of the holophrase and the two-word sentence.

The impressive language learning of the first two years can be explained in many ways: that caregivers must teach language, that infants learn because they are social beings, that inborn cognitive capacity propels infants to acquire language as soon as maturation makes that possible. Because infants vary in culture, learning style, and social context, a hybrid theory contends that each theory may be valid for some aspects of language learning and at different ages.

SUMMARY

Sensorimotor Intelligence

1. Piaget realized that very young infants are active learners, seeking to understand their complex observations and experiences. Sensorimotor intelligence, the first of Piaget's four periods of cognitive development, involves early adaption to experience.

2. Sensorimotor intelligence develops in six stages, beginning with reflexes and ending with mental combinations. The six stages occur in pairs, with each pair characterized by a circular reaction, or feedback loop, as infants first react to their own bodies (primary), then respond to other people and things (secondary). Finally, in the stage of tertiary circular reactions, infants become more goal-oriented, creative, and experimental as "little scientists."

3. Infants gradually develop an understanding of objects. As shown in Piaget's classic experiments, infants understand object permanence and begin to search for hidden objects at about 8 months. Other research, using brain scans and other new methods, finds that Piaget underestimated infant cognition, in object permanence and many other ways.

Information Processing

4. Another approach to understanding infant cognition involves information-processing theory, which looks at each step of the thinking process, from input to output. The perceptions of a young infant are attuned to the particular affordances, or opportunities for action, that are present in the infant's world.

5. Objects that move are particularly interesting to infants, as are other humans. Objects as well as people afford many possibilities for interaction and perception, and therefore these affordances enhance early cognition.

6. Infant memory is fragile but not completely absent. Reminder sessions help trigger memories, and young brains learn motor sequences long before they can remember with words. Memory is multifaceted; explicit memories are rare in infancy.

Language: What Develops in the First Two Years?

7. Language learning may be the most impressive cognitive accomplishment of infants, distinguishing the human species from other animals. The universal sequence of early language development is well known; there are alternative explanations for how early language is learned.

8. Eager attempts to communicate are apparent in the first weeks and months. Infants babble at about 6 to 9 months, understand words and gestures by 10 months, and speak their first words at about 1 year. Deaf infants make their first signs even before a year.

9. Vocabulary begins to build very slowly until the infant knows approximately 50 words. Then the naming explosion begins. Toward the end of the second year, toddlers put words together in short sentences, evidence that that they understand basic grammar.

10. Various theories explain how infants learn language as quickly as they do. The three main theories emphasize different aspects of early language learning: that infants must be taught, that their social impulses foster language learning, and that their brains are genetically attuned to language.

11. Each theory of language learning is confirmed by some research. The challenge for developmental scientists has been to formulate a hybrid theory that uses all the insights and research on early language learning. The challenge for caregivers is to respond to the infant's early attempts to communicate, expecting neither too much nor too little.

KEY TERMS

sensorimotor intelligence (p. 162)
primary circular reactions (p. 162)
secondary circular reactions (p. 163)
object permanence (p. 164)

tertiary circular reactions (p. 165)
"little scientist" (p. 166)
deferred imitation (p. 166)
habituation (p. 167)
fMRI (p. 167)
information-processing theory (p. 169)

affordance (p. 169)
visual cliff (p. 170)
dynamic perception (p. 170)
people preference (p. 171)
reminder session (p. 173)
implicit memory (p. 174)
explicit memory (p. 174)

child-directed speech (p. 177)
babbling (p. 177)
holophrase (p. 177)
naming explosion (p. 179)
grammar (p. 181)
language acquisition device (LAD) (p. 185)

WHAT HAVE YOU LEARNED?

Sensorimotor Intelligence

1. Why did Piaget call his first stage of cognition *sensorimotor* intelligence?

2. How do the first two sensorimotor stages illustrate primary circular reactions?

3. If a parent speaks and a baby babbles in response, how does that illustrate stage three of sensorimotor intelligence?

4. How is object permanence an example of stage four of sensorimotor intelligence?

5. In sensorimotor intelligence, what is the difference between stages five and six?

6. What steps of the scientific method does the "little scientist" follow?

7. Why is becoming bored a sign of infant cognitive development?

8. Why did Piaget underestimate how rapidly early cognition occurs?

Information Processing

9. How do the affordances of this book, for example, differ at age 1 month, 12 months, and 20 years?

10. What are several hypotheses to explain why infants refuse to crawl over visual cliffs?

11. What two preferences show that infants are selective in early perception?

12. What conditions help 3-month-olds remember something?

13. What is the crucial difference between implicit and explicit memory?

14. Why is explicit memory difficult for babies under age 2?

Language: What Develops in the First Two Years?

15. What communication abilities do infants have at 6 months?

16. What aspects of early language development are universal, apparent in babies of every culture and family?

17. What is typical of the rate and nature of the first words that infants speak?

18. What have developmentalists discovered about the way adults talk to babies?

19. What are the early signs of grammar in infant speech?

20. According to behaviorism, how do adults teach infants to talk?

21. According to sociocultural theory, why do infants try to communicate?

22. What does the idea that child speech results from brain maturation imply for caregivers?

23. How does the hybrid theory of language development compare to the eclectic approach to developmental study described in Chapter 2?

APPLICATIONS

1. Elicit vocalizations from an infant—babbling if the baby is under age 1, using words if older. Write down all the baby says for 10 minutes. Then ask the primary caregiver to elicit vocalizations for 10 minutes, and write these down. What differences are apparent between the baby's two attempts at communication? Compare your findings with the norms described in the chapter.

2. Piaget's definition of intelligence is adaptation. Others consider a good memory or an extensive vocabulary to be a sign of intelligence. How would you define intelligence? Give examples.

3. Many educators recommend that parents read to babies even before the babies begin talking. What theory of language development does this reflect?

4. Test an infant's ability to search for a hidden object. Ideally, the infant should be about 7 or 8 months old, and you should retest over a period of weeks. If the infant can immediately find the object, make the task harder by pausing between the hiding and the searching or by secretly moving the object from one hiding place to another.

The First Two Years: Psychosocial Development

WHAT WILL YOU KNOW?

1. How do smiles and tears change from birth to age 2, and what difference does it make?

2. How much do various theories and cultures differ in their perceptions of infant emotions?

3. What are the signs of the parent–infant bond in infancy?

My 1-week-old grandson cried. Often. Again and again. Day and night. For a long time. Again. He and his parents were living with me while they looked for an apartment. I was the dog walker and cook, not caregiver, so I didn't mind for myself. But I did mind for my sleep-deprived daughter.

"Give him a pacifier," I told her.

"No, that causes 'nipple confusion,'" she said.

"I never heard of that. What have you been reading? Give him a pacifier."

My daughter knows that I value research and evidence, not hearsay or anecdote. She replied, "The American Academy of Pediatrics says no pacifiers for breast-fed babies in the first month. Here it is on their Web site."

That quieted me, but in the next few months I developed another worry—that my son-in-law would resent fatherhood. He spent many hours, day and night, carrying my unhappy grandson while my daughter slept.

"It seems to me that you do most of the baby comforting," I told him.

"That's because Elissa does most of the breast-feeding," he answered with a smile.

I learned a good deal in those months. In the decades since my children were infants, pediatricians have made new recommendations and fathers have become more active partners.

This chapter opens by tracing infants' emotions as their brains mature and their experiences accumulate, noting temperamental and cultural differences. Then we apply each of the five theories introduced in Chapter 2. Infant feeding and ethnotheories are included when we compare theories, as many practices are applications of general assumptions. This leads to an exploration of caregiver–infant interaction, particularly *synchrony, attachment,* and *social referencing.* For every aspect of caregiving, fathers as well as mothers are included.

We then consider infant day care, paying special attention to its impact on psychosocial development. The chapter ends with practical suggestions, reflecting what I have learned from my experiences, old and new, as well as from thousands of researchers, parents, and infants. Many specifics vary depending on culture and cohort, but some universal psychosocial needs are apparent. With or without pacifiers or patient fathers, most infants (including my now-happy grandson) thrive, as long as their basic emotional needs are met.

>> Emotional Development

Within the first two years, infants progress from reactive pain and pleasure to complex patterns of social awareness (see At About This Time) (Lewis, 2010). This is a period of "high emotional responsiveness" (Izard et al., 2002, p. 767), expressed in speedy, uncensored reactions—crying, startling, laughing, raging—and, by toddlerhood, in complex responses, from self-satisfied grins to mournful pouts.

CHRISTOPHER HERWIG / LONELY PLANET IMAGES

Smiles All Around Joy is universal when an infant smiles at her beaming grandparents—a smile made even better when the tongue joins in. This particular scene takes place in Kazakhstan in central Asia, an independent nation only since 1991.

social smile A smile evoked by a human face, normally evident in infants about six weeks after birth.

As always, culture and experience influence the norms of development. This is especially true for emotional development after the first eight months.

Infants' Emotions

At first, there is pleasure and pain. Newborns look happy and relaxed when fed and drifting off to sleep. They cry when they are hurt or hungry, tired or frightened (as by a loud noise or a sudden loss of support). About one-third of infants have bouts of uncontrollable crying, called *colic*—probably the result of immature digestion.

Smiling and Laughing

Soon, additional emotions become recognizable (Lavelli & Fogel, 2005). Curiosity is evident as infants (and people of all ages) respond to objects and experiences that are new but not too novel. Happiness is expressed by the **social smile,** evoked by a human face at about 6 weeks. Preterm babies are later to smile at people because the social smile is affected by age since conception.

Infants worldwide express social joy, even laughter, between 2 and 4 months (Konner, 2007; Lewis, 2010). Among the Navajo, whoever brings forth that first laugh gives a feast to celebrate the baby's becoming a person (Rogoff, 2003). Laughter builds as curiosity does; a typical 6-month-old laughs loudly upon discovering new things, particularly social experiences that have the right balance between familiarity and surprise, such as Daddy making a funny face.

Anger and Sadness

The positive emotions of joy and contentment are soon joined by negative emotions, more frequent in infancy than later on (Izard, 2009). Anger is evident at 6 months, usually triggered by frustration. Anger is obvious when infants are prevented from grabbing an object they want or from moving as they wish. For instance, when researchers wanted to see how infants responded to frustration, they "crouched behind the child and gently restrained his or her arms for 2 minutes or until 20 seconds of hard crying ensued" (Mills-Koonce et al., 2011, p. 390). "Hard crying" was not infrequent: Infants hate to be strapped in, caged in, closed in, or even just held tightly when they want to explore.

Anger in infancy is a healthy response to frustration, unlike sadness, which also appears in the first months. Sadness indicates withdrawal and is accompanied by an increase in the body's production of *cortisol*, the primary stress hormone. In a series of experiments, 4-month-olds were taught to pull a string to see a picture, which they enjoyed—not unlike the leg kicking that made the mobiles move, discussed in Chapter 6. Then the string no longer made the picture appear—and most of the babies reacted by angrily pulling the string. Some babies, how-

AT ABOUT THIS TIME	
Ages When Emotions Emerge	
Birth	Crying; contentment
6 weeks	Social smile
3 months	Laughter; curiosity
4 months	Full, responsive smiles
4–8 months	Anger
9–14 months	Fear of social events (strangers, separation from caregiver)
12 months	Fear of unexpected sights and sounds
18 months	Self-awareness; pride; shame; embarrassment

ever, quit trying and looked sad (Lewis & Ramsay, 2005); they were the ones for whom cortisol increased. This suggests that anger relieves stress, but some babies had learned, to their sorrow, that anger was not appropriate.

Since, in this study and others, sadness is shown to be accompanied by stress, sorrow is probably not a superficial emotion. Many researchers believe that the infant brain is shaped by the early social emotions, particularly sadness and fear (Fries & Pollak, 2007; S. C. Johnson, 2010).

Fear

Fully formed fear in response to some person, thing, or situation (not just distress at a surprise) emerges at about 9 months and then rapidly becomes more frequent as well as more apparent (Witherington et al., 2004). Two kinds of social fear are obvious:

- **Stranger wariness,** evident when an infant no longer smiles at any friendly face but cries if an unfamiliar person moves too close, too quickly
- **Separation anxiety,** expressed in tears, dismay, or anger when a familiar caregiver leaves

Separation anxiety is normal at age 1, intensifies by age 2, and usually subsides after that. If it remains strong after age 3, it is considered an emotional disorder (Silverman & Dick-Niederhauser, 2004). Fear of separation may interfere with infant sleep; for example, if infants have learned to expect the presence of familiar objects and people when they go to sleep, they may wake up terrified if they are alone (Sadeh et al., 2010). Unless the parents also are fearful of their child sleeping alone, eventually children learn to do so.

Many 1-year-olds fear not only strangers but also anything unexpected, from the flush of a toilet to the pop of a jack-in-the-box, from the closing of elevator doors to the tail-wagging approach of a dog. With repeated experiences and caregiver reassurance, older infants might themselves enjoy flushing the toilet (again and again) or calling the dog (crying if the dog does *not* come).

Toddlers' Emotions

Emotions take on new strength during toddlerhood (Izard, 2009). For example, throughout the second year and beyond, anger and fear become less frequent but more focused, targeted toward infuriating or terrifying experiences. Similarly, laughing and crying become louder and more discriminating.

New emotions appear: pride, shame, embarrassment, disgust, and guilt (Stevenson et al., 2010; Thompson, 2006). These emotions require social awareness, which emerges from family interactions and is influenced by the culture (Mesquita & Leu, 2007). For example, North American parents encourage pride in their toddlers (saying, "You did it yourself"—even when that is untrue), but Asian families discourage pride and cultivate modesty and shame (Rogoff, 2003). Disgust is strongly influenced by other people: Many 18-month-olds (but not younger infants) express disgust at touching a dead animal, but none are yet disgusted when a teenager curses at an elderly person, something that parents and older children may find disgusting (Stevenson et al., 2010).

By age 2, children can display the entire spectrum of emotional reactions. They have been taught what is acceptable in their family and culture—sometimes fear, sometimes boldness (Saarni et al., 2006). For example, if a toddler hides his face in his mother's skirt when a friendly dog approaches, the mother could hastily pick the child up or enthusiastically pet the dog, teaching fear or welcome the next time a dog appears.

stranger wariness An infant's expression of concern—a quiet stare, clinging to a familiar person, or sadness—when a stranger appears.

separation anxiety An infant's distress when a familiar caregiver leaves, most obvious between 9 and 14 months.

Stranger Wariness Becomes Santa Terror For toddlers, even a friendly stranger is cause for alarm, especially if Mom's protective arms are withdrawn. The most frightening strangers are men who are unusually dressed and who act as if they might take the child away. Ironically, therefore, Santa Claus remains terrifying until children are about 3 years old.

Especially for Nurses and Pediatricians Parents come to you concerned that their 1-year-old hides her face and holds onto them tightly whenever a stranger appears. What do you tell them? (see response, page 195)

self-awareness A person's realization that he or she is a distinct individual, whose body, mind, and actions are separate from those of other people.

Self-Awareness

In addition to social awareness, another foundation for emotional growth is **self-awareness,** the realization that one's body, mind, and activities are separate from those of other people (Kopp, 2011). Closely following the new mobility that results from walking, at about age 1 an emerging sense of "me" and "mine" leads to a new consciousness of others.

Very young infants have no sense of self—at least of *self* as most people define it (Harter, 2006). In fact, a prominent psychoanalyst, Margaret Mahler, theorized that for the first 4 months infants see themselves as part of their mothers. They "hatch" at about 5 months and spend the next several months developing their sense of self (Mahler et al., 1975).

Some aspects of selfhood emerge even before age 1, but

> more complex self-representations are reflected [in] . . . self-referential emotions . . . . By the end of the second year and increasingly in the third [ages 1 and 2] the simple joy of success becomes accompanied by looking and smiling to an adult and calling attention to the feat; the simple sadness of failure becomes accompanied either by avoidance of eye contact with the adult and turning away or by reparative activity and confession . . .
>
> *[Thompson, 2006, p. 79]*

In a classic experiment (M. Lewis & Brooks, 1978), babies aged 9 to 24 months looked into a mirror after a dot of rouge had been surreptitiously put on their noses. If the babies reacted by touching their noses, that meant they knew the mirror showed their own faces. None of the babies younger than 12 months old reacted as if they recognized themselves (they sometimes smiled and touched the dot on the "other" baby in the mirror). However, between 15 and 24 months, babies usually showed self-awareness, touching their own noses with curiosity and puzzlement.

Self-recognition in the mirror/rouge test (as well as in photographs) usually emerges at about 18 months, along with two other advances: pretending and using first-person pronouns (I, *me, mine, myself, my*) (Lewis, 2010). Therefore, some developmentalists connect self-recognition in the mirror with self-understanding, although "the interpretation of this seemingly simple task is plagued by controversy" (Nielsen et al., 2006, p. 176).

For example, one study found that self-recognition in the mirror/rouge test *negatively* correlated with embarrassment when a doll's leg fell off (it had been rigged to do so) as each toddler played with it (Barrett, 2005). Many 17-month-olds who recognized themselves, particularly boys, were *less* embarrassed at this mishap and more likely to tell the examiner about it. Does a sense of self diminish shame as it increases pride? Perhaps. Pride may be linked to the maturing self-concept, not necessarily to other people's opinions (Barrett, 2005).

Who Is That? At 18 months, he is at the beginning of self-awareness, testing to see whether his mirror image will meet his finger.

ANTOINE JULIETTE / AGE FOTOSTOCK

Brain Maturation and the Emotions

Brain maturation is involved in all the emotional developments just described. There is no doubt that varied experiences, as well as good nutrition, promote both brain growth and emotional development. Nor is there any doubt that emotional reactions begin with neurons connecting to other neurons (M. H. Johnson, 2011).

Social Impulses

Many specific aspects of brain maturation support social emotions (Lloyd-Fox et al., 2009). For instance, most developmentalists agree that the social smile and the first laughter appear as the cortex matures (Konner, 2007). The same is probably true for nonreflexive fear, self-awareness, and anger. The maturation of a particular part of the cortex (the anterior cingulate gyrus) is directly connected to emotional self-regulation, which allows a child to moderate these emotions (Posner et al., 2007). (Several other parts of the brain comprise the limbic system, where many emotions originate. This is described in Chapter 8.)

One aspect of the infant's emotional development is that particular people (typically those the infant sees most often) arouse specific emotions. This is the result not only of past experience but also of neurological maturation, as a sequence of neurons that fire together become more closely and quickly connected in the brain. In the first weeks after birth, babies are content to be cared for by any competent person—a biological relative or a stranger. Soon preferences form, which is one reason adopted children are, ideally, placed with their new parents in the first days of life—unlike 100 years ago, when adoptions began after age 1.

All emotional reactions, particularly those connected to self-awareness, depend partly on memory (Harter, 2006; Lewis, 2010). As already explained in Chapter 6, memory is fragile at first and gradually improves as dendrites and axons connect. No wonder children over age 1 are more quickly angered than younger children when teased by an older sibling or are more obviously reluctant to enter the doctor's office. Toddlers remember the previous time a sibling frustrated them or the doctor gave them a shot. (As already noted, anger appears earlier when an infant is restricted or frustrated—not much memory needed for that.)

Stress

Chapter 5 suggested that excessive stress impairs the brain, particularly in areas associated with emotions (Adam et al., 2007). Brain imagery and cortisol measurements suggest that the hypothalamus (part of the brain that regulates bodily functions and hormone production, discussed further in Chapter 8) grows more slowly if an infant is often stressed.

The brain damage from abuse in infancy is difficult to prove experimentally, for obvious ethical reasons. However, brain scans of maltreated children reveal abnormal activation in response not only to stress and other emotions but even to photographs of frightened people (Gordis et al., 2008; Masten et al., 2008). Such abnormal neurological responses are likely caused by early abuse.

As first mentioned in Chapter 5, this research has important biosocial applications. Here we focus on the psychosocial aspects, which show how the social context relates to infant emotions. Since infants are learning emotional responses from the beginning of life, it is crucial that new parents be supported by the community so that they can respond consistently and lovingly to the newborn.

One study found a cascade of stress throughout development: Fathers affect mothers' stress levels, and, if a mother is highly stressed, that stress can harm their child (Talge et al., 2007). Contemporary fathers also directly affect infants' stress: If they are intrusive and critical caregivers, already by 7 months their babies have higher cortisol levels in response to challenges, such as the restraint described above (Mills-Koonce et al., 2011).

Synesthesia

Brain maturation may affect an infant's ability to differentiate emotions—for instance, distinguishing between fear and joy. Some infants seem to cry at everything. Early emotional confusion seems similar to *synesthesia*, a phenomenon in which one sense triggers another in the brain. For older children and adults, the most common form of synesthesia is when a number or letter evokes a vivid color. Among adults, synesthesia is unusual; often, it is partly genetic and indicates artistic creativity (K. J. Barnett et al., 2008).

>> Response for Nurses and Pediatricians (from page 193) Stranger wariness is normal up to about 14 months. This baby's behavior actually sounds like secure attachment!

On Top of His World This boy's blissful expression is evidence that fathers can prevent or relieve stress in infants, protecting a baby's brain and promoting the mother's peace of mind.

Synesthesia seems more common in infants because the boundaries between the sensory parts of the cortex are still forming (Walker et al., 2010). Textures seem associated with vision, sounds with smells, and the infant's own body seems connected to the bodies of others. The sensory connections are called *cross-modal perception;* the interpersonal connections may become the basis for early social understanding (Meltzoff, 2007).

The tendency of one part of the brain to activate another may also occur for emotions. An infant's cry can be triggered by pain, fear, tiredness, surprise, or excitement; laughter can turn to tears. Discrete emotions during early infancy are more difficult to recognize, differentiate, or predict than the same emotions in adulthood; infant emotions erupt, increase, or disappear for unknown reasons (Camras & Shutter, 2010). Brain immaturity is a likely explanation.

Temperament

Every human emotion is influenced by a person's genotype. Thus, an infant might be happy or fearful not only because of maturation but also because of the combination of various alleles on many genes. Among each person's genetic predispositions are traits of **temperament,** defined as the "biologically based core of individual differences in style of approach and response to the environment that is stable across time and situations" (van den Akker et al., 2010, p. 485). "Biologically based" means that these traits originate with nature (genes). Confirmation that temperament is constitutionally, not experientially, based comes from an analysis of newborn cries after the hepatitis B inoculation: Cry variations correlated with later temperament (Jong et al., 2010).

temperament Inborn differences between one person and another in emotions, activity, and self-regulation. Temperament is epigenetic, originating in genes but affected by child-rearing practices.

Temperament may overlap with personality, but the two terms are not synonymous. Personality traits (e.g., honesty and humility) are thought to be primarily learned, whereas temperamental traits (e.g., shyness and aggression) are considered primarily genetic. Of course, even though temperament originates with the genes, the actual expression of the traits is modified by experience—the result of child-rearing methods, culture, and learning (Rothbart & Bates, 2006).

The New York Longitudinal Study

In laboratory studies of temperament, infants are exposed to events that are frightening. Four-month-olds might see spinning mobiles or hear unusual sounds. Older babies might confront a noisy, moving robot or a clown who quickly moves close. At such experiences, some children laugh (and are classified as "easy"), some cry ("difficult"), and some are quiet ("slow to warm up"). These three categories come from the *New York Longitudinal Study* (NYLS). Begun in the 1960s, the NYLS was the first among many large studies to recognize that each newborn has distinct inborn traits (Thomas & Chess, 1977).

According to the NYLS, by 3 months, infants manifested nine temperamental traits that could be clustered into four categories (the three described above and a fourth category of infants who are "hard to classify"). The proportion of infants in each category was as follows:

- Easy (40 percent)
- Difficult (10 percent)
- Slow to warm up (15 percent)
- Hard to classify (35 percent)

Later research has confirmed that newborns differ in temperament and that some babies are unusually difficult. However, although the NYLS began a rich research endeavor, the nine dimensions of the NYLS have not held up to later research (Caspi & Shiner, 2006; Zentner & Bates, 2008). Generally, only three (not nine) dimensions of temperament are clearly present in early childhood (Else-Quest et al., 2006; van den Akker et al., 2010). Although each study of infant temperament uses somewhat different terms, the overall conclusions are similar, and the following three dimensions are apparent:

- Effortful control (able to regulate attention, balanced)
- Negative mood (fearful, angry, unhappy)
- Surgency (active, social, not shy, exuberant)

Especially for Nurses Parents come to you with their fussy 3-month-old. They say they have read that temperament is "fixed" before birth, and they are worried that their child will always be difficult. What do you tell them? (see response, page 198)

A VIEW FROM SCIENCE

Still Frightened?

One longitudinal study (Fox et al., 2001) identified three distinct types among 4-month-olds—exuberant, negative, and inhibited (fearful). We report this study in detail partly because these researchers used many methods to measure infant emotions: experiments within a laboratory, measures that varied depending on the age of the babies, detailed reports from the mothers, and brain scans. Moreover, they studied the same children at 4, 9, 14, 24, and 48 months and also followed up years later (Williams et al., 2010).

In the original study, half of the participants did not change much from 4 months to 4 years, reacting the same way and having similar brain-wave patterns when confronted with frightening experiences every time they were tested. The other half exhibited altered responses as they grew older. Inhibited, fearful infants were most likely to change and exuberant infants, least likely (see Figure 7.1). That speaks to the influence of child-rearing methods: Adults coax frightened children to be brave and encourage exuberant children to stay happy. The

longitudinal research also speaks to the influence of culture: The formerly inhibited boys, as teenagers, were more likely to use drugs, but the inhibited girls were less likely to do so (Williams et al., 2010).

Similar results were found in another study that described temperament using three traits (typical, fearful, and expressive). Continuity was common, but the fearful children (already only 14 percent at age 2½) were most likely to change. By age 3, only 5 percent of the 3-year-olds were classified as fearful (van den Akker et al., 2010). Parental attitudes and actions were likely to cause the changes.

Other longitudinal studies of the relationship between infant temperament and adolescent personality (especially antisocial traits) again confirm these results: Continuity is evident, but so is the effect of family and culture, which sometimes diminish difficult or negative traits (Kagan et al., 2007; Zentner & Bates, 2008). Science repeatedly finds that many factors, both nature and nurture, underlie every trait of temperament or personality.

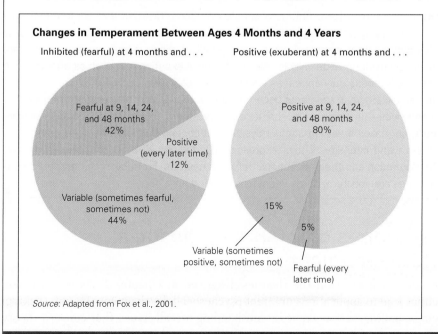

Changes in Temperament Between Ages 4 Months and 4 Years

Source: Adapted from Fox et al., 2001.

FIGURE 7.1

Do Babies' Temperaments Change? The data suggest that fearful babies are not necessarily fated to remain that way. Adults who are reassuring and do not act frightened themselves can help children overcome an innate fearfulness. Some fearful children do not change, however, and it is not known whether that's because their parents are not sufficiently reassuring (nurture) or because they are temperamentally more fearful (nature).

Observation Quiz Out of 100 4-month-olds who react positively to noises and other experiences, how many are fearful at later times in early childhood? (see answer, page 198)

goodness of fit A similarity of temperament and values that produces a smooth interaction between an individual and his or her social context, including family, school, and community.

Goodness of Fit

All the research finds that traces of childhood temperament endure, blossoming into adult personality, but all the research also confirms that innate tendencies are only part of the story. Context always shapes behavior. Ideally, parents find a **goodness of fit**—that is, an adjustment that allows smooth infant–caregiver interaction. With a good fit, parents of difficult babies build a close and affectionate relationship; parents of exuberant infants learn to protect them from harm; parents of slow-to-warm-up toddlers encourage them while giving them time to adjust. Parents must do most of the accommodating, evident in this father and daughter episode:

> Kevin is a very active, outgoing person who loves to try new things. Today he takes his 11-month-old daughter, Tyra, to the park for the first time. Tyra is playing alone in the sandbox, when a group of toddlers joins her. At first, Tyra smiles and eagerly watches them play. But as the toddlers become more active and noisy, Tyra's smiles turn quickly to tears. She . . . reaches for Kevin, who picks her up and comforts her. But then Kevin goes a step further. After Tyra calms down, Kevin gently encourages her to play near the other children. He sits at her side, talking and playing with her. Soon Tyra is slowly creeping closer to the group of toddlers, curiously watching their moves.
>
> *[Lerner & Dombro, 2004, p. 42]*

>> Response for Nurses (from page 197) It's too soon to tell. Temperament is not truly "fixed" but variable, especially in the first few months. Many "difficult" infants become happy, successful adolescents and adults, especially if their parents are supportive.

Tyra needed Kevin. In general, anxious, difficult children are more affected by their parents' responsiveness than are easygoing children (Belsky & Pluess, 2009; Leerkes et al., 2009; Pauli-Pott et al., 2004). Ineffective or harsh parenting *combined with* a negative temperament creates antisocial, destructive children (Cicchetti et al., 2007).

Childhood temperament is linked to the parents' genes and their personality, which often is assessed using five dimensions, called the **Big Five**—openness, conscientiousness, extroversion, agreeableness, and neuroticism. Adults who are high in extroversion (surgency), high in agreeableness (effortful control), and low in neuroticism (negative mood) tend to be warmer and more competent parents (de Haan et al., 2009).

Big Five The five basic clusters of personality traits that remain quite stable throughout life: openness, conscientiousness, extroversion, agreeableness, and neuroticism.

SUMMING UP

Newborns seem to have only two simple emotions, distress and contentment, expressed by crying or looking peaceful. Very soon curiosity and obvious joy, with social smiles and laughter, appear. By the second half of the first year, anger and fear are increasingly evident, especially in reaction to social experiences, such as encountering a stranger. Sadness may appear as well.

In the second year, as infants become self-aware, they express emotions connected to themselves—including pride, shame, embarrassment, and guilt—and to other people. Maturation makes these emotions possible, but context and learning affect the timing, frequency, and intensity of their expression. Underlying all emotional development is brain maturation and the connections between neurons. From birth on, temperamental differences are apparent; some infants are easier than others. ▪

>> Answer to Observation Quiz (from page 197) Out of 100 4-month-olds who react positively, 20 are fearful at least occasionally later in childhood, but only 5 are consistently fearful.

>> Theories of Infant Psychosocial Development

We now consider again the theories discussed in Chapter 2. As you will see, theories lead to applications in infant psychosocial development. Thumb sucking, crying, spoiling, self-awareness, and bonding are all issues that concern theory and practice.

Psychoanalytic Theory

Psychoanalytic theory connects biosocial and psychosocial development. Both major psychoanalytic theorists, Sigmund Freud and Erik Erikson, described two distinct stages of early development. Freud (1935, 1940/1964) wrote about the *oral stage* and the *anal stage.* Erikson (1963) called his first stages *trust versus mistrust* and *autonomy versus shame and doubt.*

Freud: Oral and Anal Stages

According to Freud (1935), the first year of life is the *oral stage,* so named because the mouth is the young infant's primary source of gratification. In the second year, with the *anal stage,* the infant's main pleasure comes from the anus—particularly from the sensual pleasure of bowel movements and, eventually, the psychological pleasure of controlling them.

Freud believed that the oral and anal stages are fraught with potential conflicts that have long-term consequences. If a mother frustrates her infant's urge to suck—weaning the infant too early, for example, or preventing thumb and finger sucking—the child may become distressed and anxious, eventually becoming an adult with an *oral fixation.* Such a person is stuck (fixated) at the oral stage and therefore eats, drinks, chews, bites, or talks excessively, in quest of the mouth-related pleasure denied in infancy.

Similarly, if toilet training is overly strict or if it begins before the infant is mature enough, parent and infant may become locked into a conflict over the toddler's refusal, or inability, to comply. The child develops an anal personality—as an adult, seeking self-control with an unusually strong need for regularity in all aspects of life. Most developmentalists no longer agree with this part of Freud's theory, although diverse opinions flourish about the optimal timing and method of toilet training, as you remember from Chapter 2.

Erikson: Trust and Autonomy

According to Erikson, the first crisis of life is **trust versus mistrust,** when infants learn whether the world can be trusted to satisfy basic needs. Babies feel secure when food and comfort are provided with "consistency, continuity, and sameness of experience" (Erikson, 1963, p. 247). If social interaction inspires trust and security, the child (and later the adult) confidently explores the social world.

The second crisis is **autonomy versus shame and doubt,** beginning at about 18 months, when self-awareness emerges. Toddlers want autonomy (self-rule) over their own actions and bodies. Without it, they feel ashamed and doubtful. Like Freud, Erikson believed that problems in early infancy could last a lifetime, creating adults who are suspicious and pessimistic (mistrusting) or easily shamed (lacking autonomy).

Erikson was aware of cultural variations. He knew that mistrust or shame could be destructive or not, depending on norms and expectations. Some cultures encourage independence and autonomy; in others (e.g., China), "shame is a normative emotion that develops as parents use explicit shaming techniques" to encourage children's loyalty and harmony within their families (Mascolo et al., 2003, p. 402). Westerners expect toddlers to go through the stubborn and defiant "terrible twos"; parents elsewhere expect toddlers to be docile and obedient. Autonomy may be prized among North Americans, but it is considered immature by many other peoples (Morelli & Rothbaum, 2007).

Especially for Nursing Mothers You have heard that if you wean your child too early, he or she will overeat or become an alcoholic. Is it true? (see response, page 200)

trust versus mistrust Erikson's first psychosocial crisis. Infants learn basic trust if their basic needs (for food, comfort, attention, and so on) are met.

autonomy versus shame and doubt Erikson's second crisis of psychosocial development. Toddlers either succeed or fail in gaining a sense of self-rule over their own actions and bodies.

A Mother's Dilemma Infants are wonderfully curious, as this little boy demonstrates. Parents, however, must guide as well as encourage the drive toward autonomy. Notice this mother's expression as she makes sure her son does not crush or eat the flower.

>> Response for Nursing Mothers (from page 199) Freud thought so, but there is no experimental evidence that weaning, even when ill timed, has such dire long-term effects.

Behaviorism

From the perspective of behaviorism, emotions and personality are molded as parents reinforce or punish a child's spontaneous behaviors. Behaviorists believe that parents who smile and pick up their infant at every glimmer of a grin will have children with a sunny disposition. The opposite is also true, according to behaviorist John Watson:

> Failure to bring up a happy child, a well-adjusted child—assuming bodily health—falls squarely upon the parents' shoulders. [By the time the child is 3] parents have already determined . . . [whether the child] is to grow into a happy person, wholesome and good-natured, whether he is to be a whining, complaining neurotic, an anger-driven, vindictive, over-bearing slave driver, or one whose every move in life is definitely controlled by fear.
>
> *[Watson, 1928, pp. 7, 45]*

social learning Learning that is accomplished by observing others.

Later behaviorists recognized that infants also experience **social learning.** Albert Bandura conducted a classic experiment: Children watched an adult hitting a rubber Bobo clown with a mallet and then treated the doll the same way (Bandura, 1977). In this experiment, those children had good reason to follow the example; they were frustrated by being told they could not play with some attractive toys and were then left alone with a mallet and the Bobo doll, having just seen an adult hit the doll. Both boys and girls pounded and kicked Bobo.

Hammering Bobo These images are stills from the film of Bandura's original study of social learning, in which frustrated 4-year-olds imitated the behavior they had observed an adult perform. The children used the same weapon as the adult, with the same intent—whether that involved hitting the doll with a hammer, shooting it with a toy gun, or throwing a large ball at it.

Since that experiment, developmentalists have demonstrated that social learning occurs throughout life (Morris et al., 2007; Nielsen, 2006), a theme expressed many times in the latter half of this chapter. In many families, toddlers express emotions in various ways—from giggling to cursing—just as they have seen their parents or older siblings do. A boy might develop a hot temper, for instance, if his father's outbursts seem to win his mother's respect. Social learning theory acknowledges inborn temperament but stresses parental example: Shyness may be inborn, for instance, but parents who model social interaction will help a withdrawn child become more outgoing (Rubin et al., 2009).

Cognitive Theory

Cognitive theory holds that thoughts and values determine a person's perspective. Early experiences are important because beliefs, perceptions, and memories make them so, not because they are buried in the unconscious (psychoanalytic theory) or burned into the brain's patterns (behaviorism). Early relationships help infants develop a **working model,** a set of assumptions that become a frame of reference for later life (S. C. Johnson et al., 2010). It is a "model" because these early relationships are a prototype, or blueprint, for later relationships; it is "working" because, although it is used, it is not necessarily fixed or final.

working model In cognitive theory, a set of assumptions that the individual uses to organize perceptions and experiences. For example, a person might assume that other people are always trustworthy and be surprised when this working model of human behavior is proven inadequate.

Ideally, infants develop "a working model of the self as valued, loved, and competent" and "a working model of parents as emotionally available, loving, sensitive and supportive" (Harter, 2006, p. 519). However, reality does not always conform to this ideal. A 1-year-old girl might develop a model, based on her parents' inconsistent responses to her, that people are unpredictable. She will continue to apply that model to everyone: Her childhood friendships will be insecure and her adult relationships will be guarded.

To use Piaget's terminology, such a girl develops a cognitive *schema* to organize her perceptions. According to cognitive theory, an infant's early experiences themselves are not necessarily crucial, but the interpretation of those experiences is (Olson & Dweck, 2009). Remembered childhood echoes lifelong. A hopeful message from cognitive theory is that people can rethink and reorganize their thoughts, developing new models. Our mistrustful girl might marry a faithful and loving man and gradually develop a new model. Plasticity applies to cognition.

Sociocultural Theory

No one doubts that "human development occurs in a cultural context" (Kagitcibasi, 2003, p. 166). The crucial question is *how much* influence culture has. Sociocultural theorists argue that the influence is substantial, that the entire social and cultural context shapes infant emotional development.

Ethnotheories

An **ethnotheory** is a theory that is embedded in a particular culture or ethnic group. Although people are rarely aware of it—as you have already seen with breast-feeding, co-sleeping, child-directed speech, and toilet training—many child-rearing practices arise from ethnotheories (H. Keller et al., 2006). The motor skill and language timetables detailed in the previous chapters may be a result of parental encouragement, based on their ethnotheories. For example, part of the ethnotheory of the Kokwet in Kenya is that mothers should

Stranger Danger Some parents teach their children to be respectful of any adult; others teach them to fear any stranger. No matter what their culture or parents say, each of these two sisters in Nepal reacts according to her inborn temperament.

ethnotheory A theory that underlies the values and practices of a culture but is not usually apparent to the people within the culture.

> teach their babies to sit, stand, and walk. What would happen, they were asked, if a mother somewhere, for some reason, did not teach these things. The common answer, after a moment to assimilate such an outrageous idea, was that the child would not learn them.
>
> *[Super & Harkness, 2009, p. 93]*

Ethnotheories are apparent with emotional development. A simple example comes whenever an infant cries: Is the baby expressing pain, anger, or just normal activity? Adults interpret it through their own culture's lens (Holodynski & Friedlmeier, 2010), with some adults rushing to comfort a crying baby and others believing the baby should "cry it out" to strengthen lungs and independence.

A more elaborate ethnotheory arises from cultures that believe that ancestors are reincarnated in the younger generation. In such a case, "children are not expected to show respect for adults, but adults [are expected to show respect] for their reborn ancestors." Consequently, children are allowed to express many emotions. Such cultures favor indulgent child rearing with no harsh punishment, a practice that "Western people perceive as extremely lenient" (Dasen, 2003, pp. 149–150).

Remember from Chapter 1 that cultures change when circumstances do. This was found in a study of the values of grandmothers and mothers of 3-month-olds (Lamm et al., 2008). The grandmother–mother pairs were from four contexts: urban Germany, urban India, and urban and rural West Africa. Women in each locale held ethnotheories unlike women living elsewhere. In all four cultures, generational differences were apparent, with the mothers valuing children's autonomy more than the grandmothers did.

The generation gap was smallest, however, in the two cultures that were most different from each other. Among urban Germans, grandmothers tended to agree with mothers in valuing autonomy; among rural Africans, mothers tended to agree with grandmothers in valuing obedience. The greatest mother–grandmother gap was in urban Africa, probably because dramatic social change meant that the grandmothers' traditions were quite unlike those learned by their daughters (Lamm et al., 2008).

Personal Theories

Parents are influenced not only by the theories of their ethnic group, but also by personal theories that arose from their own family or personal history. For instance, some parents blame their infants for crying, not realizing that young infants have no control over their crying or much else. As you just read, expressions such as crying and smiling, and emotions such as anger and fear, first arise because of maturation, not because of how the infant feels about the caregiver. Caregivers can respond to such emotions, but they cannot eliminate them.

Since theories of development are open to change, parents who are tempted to be abusive—either because of their own stresses or because their infants are difficult—can reframe their perceptions. They can stop blaming the infant and instead become more responsive, as cognitive theory would hope (Bugental & Schwartz, 2009). That is exactly the goal of the NBAS (Brazelton Neonatal Behavioral Assessment Scale, described in Chapter 4), in which the parents watch as a clinician encourages a baby to respond to sights, sounds, and people.

For example, Lucas was born with one foot that turned out. His parents were distant and dismayed, perhaps going by the theory that they were being punished through his deformity. The clinician demonstrated to them how they could listen and react better to Lucas. Soon Lucas looked at his mother when she spoke, which "elicited intense emotion in his mother, who took him in her arms and looked at him as if she had never realized until that moment that, behind his deformed foot, there was a little guy eager for her attention and her care" (Bruschweiler-Stern, 2009, p. 76).

Proximal and Distal Parenting

Another example of ethnotheory involves a culture's ideas about how frequently parents should carry and cuddle their babies. **Proximal parenting** involves being physically close to a baby, often holding and touching. **Distal parenting** involves keeping some distance—providing toys, feeding by putting finger food within reach, and talking face-to-face instead of communicating by touch. Caregivers who believe that one of these is better are usually unaware that they are expressing an ethnotheory, but such differences begin to emerge early in life, when the infant is about 2 months old (Kärtner et al., 2010).

A longitudinal study comparing child-rearing methods of the Nso people of Cameroon with those of Greeks in Athens found marked differences in proximal and distal parenting (H. Keller et al., 2004). The researchers videotaped 78 mothers as they played with their 3-month-olds. Coders (who did not know the study's hypothesis) counted frequency of proximal play (e.g., carrying, swinging, caressing, exercising the child's body) and distal play (e.g., face-to-face talking) (see Table 7.1). The Nso mothers were proximal, holding their babies all the time and almost never using toys or bottles. The Greek mothers were relatively distal, using objects almost half the time.

Especially for Linguists and Writers U.S. culture has given rise to the term *empty nest,* signifying an ethnotheory about mothers whose children have grown up and moved out of the family home. What cultural values are expressed by that term? (see response, page 204)

proximal parenting Caregiving practices that involve being physically close to a baby, with frequent holding and touching.

distal parenting Caregiving practices that involve remaining distant from a baby, providing toys, food, and face-to-face communication with minimal holding and touching.

TABLE 7.1	Infants in Rural Cameroon and Urban Greece	
	Cameroon	Athens, Greece
I. Infant–mother play at 3 months		
Percent of time held by mother	100%	31%
Percent of time playing with objects	3%	40%
II. Toddler behavior at 18 months		
Self-recognition	3%	68%
Immediate compliance with request	72%	2%

Source: Adapted from Keller et al., 2004.

The researchers hypothesized that proximal parenting would result in toddlers who were less self-aware but more compliant—traits needed in an interdependent and cooperative society such as that of rural Cameroon. By contrast, distal parenting might produce children who were self-aware but less obedient, as needed when a culture values independence and self-reliance. The predictions were accurate. At 18 months, the same infants were tested on self-awareness (via the mirror/rouge test) and obedience to their parents. The African toddlers didn't recognize themselves in the mirror but were compliant; the opposite was true of the Greek toddlers.

Replicating their own work, these researchers studied a dozen mother–infant pairs in Costa Rica. In that Central American nation, caregiver–infant distance was midway between the Nso and the Greeks, as was later toddler behavior. The researchers reanalyzed all their data, child by child. They found that, even apart from culture, proximal or distal play at 3 months was highly predictive: Greek mothers who, unlike most of their peers, held a personal theory that they should hold their infants often (they were proximal parents) had more obedient toddlers (H. Keller et al., 2004) (see the Research Design). Research with German father–infant pairs replicated these results (Borke et al., 2007).

Every aspect of early emotional development interacts with cultural beliefs, expressed in parental actions. Other research has found more separation anxiety in Japan than in Germany because Japanese infants "have very few experiences with separation from the mother," whereas in Germany "infants are frequently left alone outside of stores or supermarkets" while their mothers shop (Saarni et al., 2006, p. 237).

Still other research has found that Italian mothers and infants seem more intensely responsive to each other compared to U.S. and Argentinean mother–infant pairs and that rural mothers are more intrusive in that they are likely to stop an infant from exploring something in order to get him or her to do something else (Bornstein, Putnick et al., 2011). Despite such differences, no culture anywhere encourages caregivers to be indifferent to infant emotions: If such a culture existed, it probably would not endure for more than a generation. Babies everywhere need responsive adults.

Especially for Pediatricians A mother complains that her child refuses to stay in the car seat, spits out disliked foods, and almost never does what she says. How should you respond? (see response, page 205)

▶ **Research Design**

Scientists: A team of six from three nations (Germany, Greece, Costa Rica): Heidi Keller, Relindis Yovsi, Joern Borke, Joscha Kärtner, Henning Jensen, and Zaira Papaligoura.

Publication: *Child Development* (2004).

Participants: A total of 90 mothers participated when their babies were 3 months old and again when they were 18 months old (32 from Cameroon, 46 from Greece, 12 from Costa Rica). In Greece and Costa Rica, researchers recruited mothers in hospitals. In Cameroon, permission was first sought from the local leader, and then announcements were made among local people.

Design: First, mothers played with their 3-month-olds, and that play was videotaped and coded for particular behaviors by researchers who did not know the hypothesis. Fifteen months later, the toddlers' self-recognition was assessed with the mirror/rouge test, and compliance with preset maternal commands was measured. The mother's frequency of eye contact and body contact with the infant at 3 months was compared with the toddler's self-awareness and compliance at 18 months.

Major conclusion: Toddlers with proximal mothers were more obedient but less self-aware; toddlers with distal mothers tended to show the opposite pattern.

Comments: This is a good comparison study of child-rearing practices in various cultures in that it is longitudinal, using the same measures in each nation. However, with only three locations and relatively few mother–infant pairs (12 in Costa Rica), it is possible that factors unrelated to proximal/distal parenting affected the results. For example, the mothers in Athens were wealthier and more urbanized than the ones in Cameroon. However, if wealthier urban parents are also more distal parents, that itself would be a cultural difference.

>> Response for Linguists and Writers
(from page 202) The implication is that human mothers are like sad birds, bereft of their fledglings, who have flown away.

Cultural differences may become encoded in the infant brain, called "a cultural sponge" by one group of scientists (Ambady & Bharucha, 2009, p. 342). It is difficult to measure how infant brains are molded by their context, but one study of adults born either in the United States or in China found that in both groups, a particular area of the brain (the medial prefrontal cortex) was activated when the adults judged whether certain adjectives applied to them. However, only in the Chinese was that area also activated when they were asked whether those adjectives applied to their mothers. The researchers consider this to be "neuro-imaging evidence that culture shapes the functional anatomy of self-representation" (Zhu et al., 2007, p. 1310) and speculate that the Chinese learned, as babies, that they are closely aligned with their mothers, whereas the Americans learned to be independent.

From the beginning of life, families dampen some emotions and fuel others. Another cross-cultural study found that culture affected how mothers in Germany and in India talked to their 3-month-olds, but even when a particular mother was unlike others in her community, all mothers tended to be quite stable in their responses as their infants grew: Their specific practices changed by age, but the underlying ethnotheories remained (Keller et al., 2010).

We noted earlier that infants become angry when they are restrained. Some Western parents rarely hold their infants *except* to restrain them (and the purpose of the restraint is often to enforce parent–infant separation). Parents strap protesting toddlers into strollers, buckle them into car seats, put them in cribs or behind gates that they cannot climb over—all examples of distal parenting. If toddlers do not passively allow diapers to be changed (and few do), some parents simply hold the protesting child down to get the task done. Compare this approach to that of Roberto's parents, who used nursing (very proximal) and the threat of separation to get their son diapered and dressed.

A CASE TO STUDY

"Let's Go to Grandma's"

Mayan parents from Mexico and Guatemala hold the ethnotheory that children should not be forced to obey their parents. Roberto, at 18 months, was playing with a ball and did not want to wear a diaper or put on his pants.

> "Let's put on your diaper . . . Let's go to Grandma's . . . We're going to do an errand." This did not work, and the mother invited Roberto to nurse, as she swiftly slipped the diaper on him with the father's assistance. The father announced, "It's over."

Roberto's mother felt

> increasing exasperation that the child was wiggling and not standing to facilitate putting on his pants. Her voice softened as Roberto became interested in the ball, and she increased the stakes: "Do you want another toy?" They [father and mother] continued to try to talk Roberto into cooperating, and handed him various objects, which Roberto enjoyed. But still he stubbornly refused to cooperate with dressing. They left him alone for a while. When his father asked if he was ready, Roberto pouted "nono!"
>
> After a bit, the mother told Roberto that she was leaving and waved goodbye. "Are you going with me?" Roberto sat quietly with a worried look. "Then put on your pants, put on your pants to go up the hill." Roberto stared into space, seeming to consider the alternatives. His mother started to walk away, "OK then, I'm going. Goodbye." Roberto started to cry, and his father persuaded, "Put on your pants then!" and his mother asked, "Are you going with me?"
>
> Roberto looked down worriedly, one arm outstretched in half a take-me gesture.
>
> "Come on, then," his mother offered the pants and Roberto let his father lift him to a stand and cooperated in putting his legs into the pants and in standing to have them fastened. His mother did not intend to leave; instead she suggested that Roberto dance for the audience. Roberto did a baby version of a traditional dance.

[Rogoff, 2003, p. 204]

This is an example of an ethnotheory that "elders protect and guide rather than giving orders or dominating" (Rogoff, 2003, p. 205). A second ethnotheory is apparent as well: The parents readily used deception to get their child to do what they wanted.

© SHEHZAD NOORANI

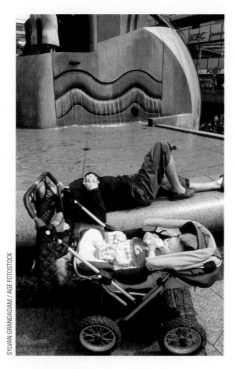

SYLVAN GRANDADAM / AGE FOTOSTOCK

The Same Situation, Many Miles Apart: Intimate Parenting Some parents are proximal, encouraging mutual touch, as shown by this pair in the Sudan *(left)*; other parents are distal, as shown by this father in Germany *(right)*. Each is part of a cultural pattern that teaches values essential to that society—in this case, intimate family interdependence or individual self-sufficiency.

SUMMING UP

Theories differ in their explanations of the origins of early emotions and personality. Psychoanalytic theory stresses a mother's responses to an infant's need for food and elimination (Freud) or for security and independence (Erikson). Behaviorism also stresses caregiving—especially as parents reinforce the behaviors they want their baby to learn or as they thoughtlessly teach unwanted behaviors.

Cognitive theory highlights the child's concept, or working model, of the world. Sociocultural theory emphasizes that the diversity of nurture explains much of the diversity of emotions. According to sociocultural theory, child-rearing practices arise from ethnotheories, implicit and unexpressed but very powerful. ∎

>> **Response for Pediatricians** (from page 203) Remember the origins of the misbehavior—probably a combination of the child's inborn temperament and the mother's distal parenting. Blended with ethnotheory, all contribute to the child's being stubborn and independent. Acceptance is more warranted than anger. On the other hand, this mother may be expressing hostility toward the child—a sign that intervention may be needed. Find out.

>> The Development of Social Bonds

You surely have noticed that the fifth theory was omitted from the preceding discussion. It is evident, however, in the following discussion, as both humanism and evolutionary theory stress the social interaction of infant and parent. Both the "love and belonging" and "unconditional positive regard" in humanism, and the urgency of species survival central to evolutionary psychology, are best explained within the context of social bonds.

Synchrony

Synchrony is a coordinated interaction between caregiver and infant, an exchange in which they respond to each other with split-second timing, evident in the first three months and then more frequently and elaborately as the infant matures (Feldman, 2007). Parents and infants average about an hour a day in face-to-face play. That is an average: Some parents play several hours a day, and others rarely play.

synchrony A coordinated, rapid, and smooth exchange of responses between a caregiver and an infant.

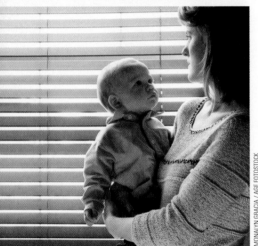

Learning from Mother Lessons in emotion endure longer than do intellectual ones. The 9-month-old *(top)* knows she can make her mother laugh, and the 12-month-old *(bottom)* knows he should sometimes worry, although he does not know why.

still-face technique An experimental practice in which an adult keeps his or her face unmoving and expressionless in face-to-face interaction with an infant.

Mutual Responding

Detailed research reveals the mutuality of the interaction: Adults rarely smile at newborns until the infants smile at them, at which point adults grin broadly and talk animatedly (Lavelli & Fogel, 2005). Infants are more sensitive than mothers to the specific timing of their interactions, which makes synchrony especially important (Henning & Striano, 2011). Synchrony is evident not only through careful observation but also via computer calculation of the timing of smiles, arched eyebrows, and so on (Messinger et al., 2009). Via synchrony, infants learn to read others' emotions and to develop the skills of social interaction, such as taking turns and paying attention.

Although infants imitate adults, synchrony usually begins with parents imitating infants (Lavelli & Fogel, 2005). Careful research finds that they do so not only with split-second timing but also with tone and rhythm (Van Puyvelde et al., 2010). It is not surprising that the metaphors for synchrony often are musical: Synchrony has been called a dance, a duet, and improvised jazz. When parents detect an emotion from an infant's facial expressions and body motions and then respond, the infant learns to connect an internal state with an external expression. Such responsive parenting is particularly apparent in Asian cultures, perhaps because interpersonal sensitivity is crucial, and thus very young infants begin to learn it (Morelli & Rothbaum, 2007).

In Western cultures as well, parents become partners to their infants. This is especially important when the infant is at medical risk and the parent may ignore psychosocial needs because of urgent and time-consuming biological needs (Newnham et al., 2009). A study of emotional responsiveness among U.S. parents and infants found that those mothers who spent more time to bathe, feed, diaper, and so on were also those mothers who were most responsive. Apparently, some parents combine caregiving with emotional play, which takes longer but also provides more synchrony. Note that synchrony is exactly what Maslow and the other humanists would recommend. If basic needs (safety, food) are satisfied, people need love and belonging (responsiveness) without conditions, judgment, or rejection. That is synchrony.

When Synchrony Disappears

Is synchrony necessary? If no one plays with an infant, what will happen? Experiments using the **still-face technique** have addressed these questions (Tronick, 1989; Tronick & Weinberg, 1997). An infant is placed facing an adult, who responds normally while video cameras record each partner's reactions. Frame-by-frame analysis typically reveals that parents instinctively synchronize their responses to the infants' movements, with exaggerated tone and expression. Babies reciprocate with smiles and moving limbs. Long before they can actually reach out and grab an object, they respond by waving their arms—and are delighted if the adult moves in such a way that the waving arm touches the face or, even better, the hand grabs the hair.

In the still-face experiments, on cue, the adult erases all facial expression and stares with a "still face" for a minute or two. Sometimes by 2 months, and clearly by 6 months, babies are very upset by the still face, especially from their parents (less so from strangers). Babies frown, fuss, drool, look away, kick, cry, or suck their fingers. By 5 months, they also increase their babbling, as if to say, "Pay attention to me" (Goldstein et al., 2009).

Many research studies such as those using the still face lead to the same conclusion: Responsiveness to an infant aids development, measured both psychosocially and biologically—by heart rate, weight gain, and brain maturation (Moore & Calkins, 2004; Newnham et al., 2009). Particularly in the first year of life (more than later on), if a mother is depressed, her child suffers. Fathers, other relatives, and day-care providers need to help (Bagner et al., 2010). Young brains need social interaction—an essential, expected stimulant—to develop to their fullest.

Attachment

Toward the end of the first year, face-to-face play almost disappears. Once infants can move around, they are no longer content to respond to adult facial expressions and vocalizations. Another connection, called *attachment,* overtakes synchrony.

Attachment is a lasting emotional bond between people. It begins before birth, solidifies by age 1, and influences relationships throughout life (see At About This Time). Adults' attachment to their parents, formed decades earlier, affects their behavior with their own children as well as their relationship with their partners (Grossmann et al., 2005; Kline, 2008; Simpson & Rholes, 2010; Sroufe et al., 2005).

Infants show their attachment through *proximity-seeking* (such as approaching and following their caregivers) and through *contact-maintaining* (such as touching, talking, snuggling, and holding). Contact can be visual or verbal: A securely

attachment According to Ainsworth, an affectional tie that an infant forms with a caregiver—a tie that binds them together in space and endures over time.

AT ABOUT THIS TIME

Stages of Attachment

Birth to 6 weeks	*Preattachment.* Newborns signal, via crying and body movements, that they need others. When people respond positively, the newborn is comforted and learns to seek more interaction. Newborns are also primed by brain patterns to recognize familiar voices and faces.
6 weeks to 8 months	*Attachment in the making.* Infants respond preferentially to familiar people by smiling, laughing, babbling. Their caregivers' voices, touch, expressions, and gestures are comforting, often overriding the infant's impulse to cry. Trust (Erikson) develops.
8 months to 2 years	*Classic secure attachment.* Infants greet the primary caregiver, show separation anxiety when the caregiver leaves, play happily when the caregiver is present. Both infant and caregiver seek to be close to each other (proximity) and frequently look at each other (contact). In many caregiver–infant pairs, physical touch (patting, holding, caressing) is frequent.
2 to 6 years	*Attachment as launching pad.* Young children seek their caregiver's praise and reassurance as their social world expands. Interactive conversations and games (hide-and-seek, object play, reading, pretending) are common. Children expect caregivers to comfort and entertain.
6 to 12 years	*Mutual attachment.* Children seek to make their caregivers proud by learning whatever adults want them to learn, and adults reciprocate. In concrete operational thought (Piaget), specific accomplishments are valued by adults and children.
12 to 18 years	*New attachment figures.* Teenagers explore and make friendships on their own, using their working models of earlier attachments as a base. With more advanced, formal operational thinking (Piaget), physical contact is less important; shared ideals and goals are more influential.
18 years on	*Attachment revisited.* Adults develop relationships with others, especially relationships with romantic partners and children, influenced by earlier attachment patterns. Past insecure attachments from childhood can be repaired rather than repeated, although this does not always happen.

Source: Adapted from Grobman, 2008.

attached toddler is curious and eager to explore but maintains contact by occasionally looking back at the caregiver, or calling, "Mama?" Caregivers show attachment as well. They keep a watchful eye on their baby and maintain contact by initiating and responding to expressions, gestures, and vocalizations ("Here I am"). Many parents, awakening in the middle of the night, tiptoe to the crib to gaze at their sleeping infant, evidence of proximity-seeking. During the day, in contact-maintaining, they may absent-mindedly smooth their toddler's hair or caress the child's hands.

Attachment is a reflection of a universal trait, as expressed in evolutionary theory. Over humanity's history, proximity-seeking and contact-maintaining fostered the survival of the species by keeping toddlers near their caregivers and the caregivers vigilant. All of us inherited these impulses from our great-great- . . . grandparents, who would have died without them (Hrdy, 2009).

Although this evolutionary explanation of attachment rings true, we should also note that psychoanalytic and sociocultural theories are evident here as well. The original concept of attachment was developed by John Bowlby (1969, 1973, 1988), a British developmentalist influenced by both psychoanalytic theory and *ethology,* the study of animals. His thinking on mother–infant bonding inspired Mary Ainsworth, then a young graduate student, who spent more than a year in Uganda and wrote the first book on attachment based on her African research (Ainsworth, 1967).

Since then, research on attachment has taken place in dozens of nations. Attachment seems to be universal, but not everyone expresses it in the same way. Specific manifestations of attachment vary by culture (e.g., Ugandan mothers never kiss their infants but often massage them, contrary to Western custom), and some scholars believe that Ainsworth's descriptions are not equally relevant in every culture (Molitor & Hsu, 2011). Keep that in mind as you read about secure and insecure attachment.

Secure and Insecure Attachment

Most scholars now agree that attachment can be classified into four types, labeled A, B, C, and D (see Table 7.2). Infants with **secure attachment** (type B) feel comfortable and confident. The caregiver becomes a *base for exploration,* providing assurance that enables exploration. A toddler might, for example, scramble down from the caregiver's lap to play with an intriguing toy but periodically look back, vocalize a few syllables, or return for a hug.

On the other hand, insecure attachment (types A and C) is characterized by fear, anxiety, anger, or indifference. Some insecure children play independently without maintaining contact with the caregiver; this is **insecure-avoidant attachment** (type A). By contrast, another insecure child might be unwilling to leave the caregiver's lap; this is **insecure-resistant/ambivalent attachment** (type C). Ainsworth's original schema differentiated only A, B, and C, but later researchers discovered a fourth category (type D), **disorganized attachment.** Type D infants may shift from hitting to kissing their mothers, from staring blankly to crying hysterically, from pinching themselves to freezing in place.

In developed nations, almost two-thirds of all infants are secure (type B). Their mothers' presence gives them courage to explore. A caregiver's departure causes distress; the caregiver's return elicits positive social contact (such as smiling or hugging) and then more playing. A balanced reaction, being concerned but not overwhelmed by comings and goings, is an indication of secure attachment.

In those same nations, about one-third of infants are insecure, either indifferent (type A) or unduly anxious (type C). As already mentioned, although type B

secure attachment A relationship (type B) in which an infant obtains both comfort and confidence from the presence of his or her caregiver.

insecure-avoidant attachment A pattern of attachment (type A) in which an infant avoids connection with the caregiver, as when the infant seems not to care about the caregiver's presence, departure, or return.

insecure-resistant/ambivalent attachment A pattern of attachment (type C) in which anxiety and uncertainty are evident, as when an infant becomes very upset at separation from the caregiver and both resists and seeks contact on reunion.

disorganized attachment A type of attachment (type D) that is marked by an infant's inconsistent reactions to the caregiver's departure and return.

Type	Name of Pattern	In Play Room	Mother Leaves	Mother Returns	Toddlers in Category (%)
TABLE 7.2	**Patterns of Infant Attachment**				
A	Insecure-avoidant	Child plays happily.	Child continues playing.	Child ignores her.	10–20
B	Secure	Child plays happily.	Child pauses, is not as happy.	Child welcomes her, returns to play.	50–70
C	Insecure-resistant/ ambivalent	Child clings, is preoccupied with mother.	Child is unhappy, may stop playing.	Child is angry; may cry, hit mother, cling.	10–20
D	Disorganized	Child is cautious.	Child may stare or yell; looks scared, confused.	Child acts oddly— may scream, hit self, throw things.	5–10

predominates in almost every published study of normal children, in some regions, the insecure infants are usually type A while in others, they are type C.

About 5 to 10 percent of infants fit into none of these categories and are classified as disorganized (type D). Disorganization prevents them from developing a strategy for social interaction (even an avoidant or resistant one, type A or C). Sometimes they become hostile and aggressive, difficult for anyone to relate to (Lyons-Ruth et al., 1999). This is evident in observational studies of the emotional reactions of type D children and also in hormonal assays. Unlike the first three types, disorganized infants have elevated levels of cortisol in reaction to stress (Bernard & Dozier, 2010).

Measuring Attachment

Ainsworth (1973) developed a now-classic laboratory procedure called the **Strange Situation** to measure attachment. In a well-equipped playroom, an infant is closely observed for eight episodes, each lasting three minutes. First, the caregiver and child are together. Then, according to a set sequence, the caregiver and a stranger come and go. Infants' responses indicate which type of attachment they have formed to their caregivers. (Reactions to the caregiver indicate attachment; reactions to the stranger are influenced more by temperament than by attachment.)

Researchers are trained and certified as able to distinguish types A, B, C, and D. They focus on the following:

- *Exploration of the toys.* A secure toddler plays happily.
- *Reaction to the caregiver's departure.* A secure toddler notices when the caregiver leaves and shows some sign of missing him or her. Depending on the child's temperament and past experiences, this sign may be loud crying or merely a pause in playing.
- *Reaction to the caregiver's return.* A secure toddler welcomes the caregiver's reappearance, usually seeking contact, and then plays again.

Attachment is not always measured via the Strange Situation, especially when researchers want to study a large number of people (Andreassen & West, 2007). Instead, surveys and interviews are used. Sometimes parents sort out 90 questions about their children's characteristics, and sometimes adults are interviewed extensively (according to a detailed protocol) about their relationships with their own parents, again with various specific measurements (Fortuna & Roisman, 2008).

Research measuring attachment has revealed that some behaviors that might seem normal are, in fact, a sign of insecurity. For instance, an infant who clings to

Strange Situation A laboratory procedure for measuring attachment by evoking infants' reactions to stress in eight episodes of three minutes each.

The Attachment Experiment In this episode of the Strange Situation, this little girl shows every sign of secure attachment. *(a)* She explores the playroom happily when her mother is present; *(b)* she cries when her mother leaves; and *(c)* she is readily comforted when her mother returns.

the caregiver and refuses to explore the toys in the new playroom might be type A, not the secure type B. Likewise, adults who say their childhood was happy and their mother was a saint, especially if they provide few specific memories, might be insecure. And young children who are too friendly to strangers may never have formed a secure attachment to one familiar person (Tarullo et al., 2011). A new diagnostic category in DSM-5, reactive attachment disorder, recognizes also that some children never form an attachment at all, even an insecure one.

Insecure Attachment and Social Setting

At first, developmentalists expected secure attachment to "predict all the outcomes reasonably expected from a well-functioning personality" (R. A. Thompson & Raikes, 2003, p. 708). But this expectation turned out to be invalid.

Securely attached infants *are* more likely to become secure toddlers, socially competent preschoolers, high-achieving schoolchildren, and capable parents (R. A. Thompson, 2006) (see Table 7.3). Some researchers find that secure attachment affects early brain development, one reason these later outcomes occur (Diamond & Fagundes, 2010). However, attachment status may shift with family circumstances as children grow older and parents change. Furthermore, harsh contexts,

TABLE 7.3	Predictors of Attachment Type

Secure attachment (type B) is more likely if:

- The parent is usually sensitive and responsive to the infant's needs.
- The infant–parent relationship is high in synchrony.
- The infant's temperament is "easy."
- The parents are not stressed about income, other children, or their marriage.
- The parents have a working model of secure attachment to their own parents.

Insecure attachment is more likely if:

- The parent mistreats the child. (Neglect increases type A; abuse increases types C and D.)
- The mother is mentally ill. (Paranoia increases type D; depression increases type C.)
- The parents are highly stressed about income, other children, or their marriage. (Parental stress increases types A and D.)
- The parents are intrusive and controlling. (Parental domination increases type A.)
- The parents are active alcoholics. (Alcoholic father increases type A; alcoholic mother increases type D.)
- The child's temperament is "difficult." (Difficult children tend to be type C.)
- The child's temperament is "slow to warm up." (This correlates with type A.)

especially the stress of poverty, make secure attachment less likely (Seifer et al., 2004; van IJzendoorn & Bakermans-Kranenburg, 2010), which means that later problems can be blamed on socioeconomic status (SES), not specifically on attachment. The underlying concept of attachment—that responsive parenting early in life leads to a secure parent–child relationship that buffers later stress and encourages later exploration—provides important insights into early psychosocial development, but exceptions may occur.

Insights from Romania

No scholar doubts that close human relationships ideally begin in the first year of life. Unfortunately, this has now been proven by thousands of children born in Romania. When Romanian dictator Nicolae Ceausesçu forbade birth control and abortions in the 1980s, illegal abortions became the leading cause of death for Romanian women aged 15 to 45 (Verona, 2003), and more than 100,000 children were abandoned to crowded, impersonal, state-run orphanages. The children experienced severe deprivation, including virtually no normal interaction, play, or conversation (Rutter et al., 2007).

In the two years after Ceausesçu was ousted in 1989, thousands of these children were adopted by American and western European families. Those who were adopted before 6 months of age fared best; most of them developed normally. For those adopted after age 1, early signs were encouraging: Skinny infants gained weight and grew faster than other 1-year-olds, developing motor skills they had lacked (Park et al., 2010). However, for many, but not all, of those who had been adopted *after* they were 6 months old, deprivation was evident in emotional and cognitive abilities. At age 11, they scored an average of only 85 on a standard IQ test (the WISC, described in Chapter 11), 15 points below normal (Rutter et al., 2010). Many were overly friendly to strangers throughout childhood, a sign that early attachment to a caregiver did not occur (Tarullo et al., 2011).

These children are now approaching adulthood, and ongoing research finds that most of them have emotional or conduct problems as they navigate adolescence and emerging adulthood. Initially it was thought that many of their problems resulted from malnutrition—that their brains as well as their bodies were deprived. The recent research, sadly, disputes this. Even those who were relatively well nourished, or who caught up to normal growth once they were adopted, nonetheless have had psychosocial problems in adolescence. The research question now is: What can modify or remedy early deprivation? Answers are not yet known (Rutter et al., 2010).

Romanian infants are no longer available for international adoption, but some are still abandoned by their parents. Research on them confirms that early experience, not genetics, is the main problem. Romanian infants develop best in their own families, second best in foster families, and much worse in institutions (Nelson et al., 2007). Research on institutionalized toddlers from many nations of eastern Europe, Asia, Africa, and South America who were adopted by western European or North American families still finds that they have a higher rate of emotional problems, especially evident at puberty. However, more recent adoptees develop better than those severely deprived Romanian orphans (Merz & McCall, 2010).

All infants need basic love and stimulation; all seek attachment—secure if possible, insecure if not. Without this sort of support, an infant becomes disorganized and adrift, emotionally troubled because extreme early social deprivation is very difficult to overcome.

Given that synchrony and attachment develop over the first year, and given that some parents have difficulty establishing secure attachments with their children, many developmentalists now seek to discover what impairs the parents and what can be done. It is apparent that secure attachment is more elusive when the parents were abused as children, the families are socially isolated, or the infants are unusually difficult (Berlin et al., 2011).

The most effective prevention must begin before problems start. Success has been reported by having skilled professionals come to the home to help build secure relationships between infant and caregiver (Lowell et al., 2011). In fact, if a professional helps parents in the first days after birth, perhaps by using the NBAS (first mentioned in Chapter 4) to encourage bonding, that can stop problems before they start (e.g., Nugent et al., 2009).

Social Referencing

social referencing Seeking information about how to react to an unfamiliar or ambiguous object or event by observing someone else's expressions and reactions. That other person becomes a social reference.

At every age, people want to know what other people feel about the experiences they themselves encounter. **Social referencing** refers to seeking appropriate emotional responses or information from other people, much as a student might consult a dictionary or other reference work. A glance of reassurance or words of caution or an expression of alarm, pleasure, or dismay—each becomes a social reference.

After age 1, when infants reach the stage of active exploration (Piaget) and the crisis of autonomy versus shame and doubt (Erikson), the need to consult others becomes urgent. Toddlers search for clues in gazes and facial expressions, paying close attention to emotions and intentions to understand what people do. Toddlers are selective in their social referencing: Even 16-month-olds notice which strangers are reliable references and which are not (Poulin-Dubois & Chow, 2009).

Social referencing has many practical applications. Consider mealtime. Caregivers the world over smack their lips, pretend to taste, and say "yum-yum," encouraging toddlers to eat and enjoy their first beets, liver, or spinach. For their part, toddlers become astute at reading expressions, insisting on the foods that the adults *really* like. Through this process, children in some cultures develop a taste for raw fish or curried goat or smelly cheese—foods that children in other cultures refuse. Similarly, toddlers are able to use their mothers' cues to understand the difference between real and pretend eating (Nishida & Lillard, 2007).

Who to Believe? Logically, the doctor is the one to watch: He has the stethoscope. But this baby references her mother, as any securely attached baby would.

Fathers as Social Partners

In most nations and ethnic groups, fathers spend much less time with infants than mothers do (Parke & Buriel, 2006; Tudge, 2008). Ethnotheories often limit father–child involvement, with some mothers believing that child care is the special domain of women (Gaertner et al., 2007) and some fathers thinking it unmanly to dote on an infant. That is not true everywhere. In Denmark, for instance, researchers report that 97 percent of fathers are present at the delivery of their babies; and, in a survey when the infants were 5 months old, 98 percent played with their infants every day, 83 percent changed diapers every day, and 61 percent fed the baby every day (Munck, 2009).

In many nations, ethnotheories about fathers are changing. One obvious example is Latino fathers, who were said to be less involved with their infants than many other fathers. Research refutes this assumption (Cabrera et al., 2006; Tamis-LeMonda et al., 2009). In the United States, many fathers of Mexican, Cuban, and Dominican heritage are active caregivers for their infants. Similar findings occur worldwide: Brazilian fathers seem to spend more time caring for their infants than do fathers in any other nation (Tudge, 2008). Among low-income families in the United States, the best predictor of a father's involvement with his infant is his relationship with the mother, and young Latina mothers are more likely to be married to their baby's father than are other young mothers of the same SES. Thus, many Latino infants begin life with a very involved male caregiver.

The normative involvement of Latino fathers has an unfortunate downside. If a biological Hispanic American father is absent, single Latinas seem to demand more from and respond less to their infants than do other single mothers (Cooper et al., 2009). Similar findings come from rural Mexico, where most infants are born to married parents, with fathers helping with infant care. However, when fathers are absent (usually because they have migrated to the United States to alleviate family poverty), infants are significantly more likely to become sick—a sign that the mothers find infant care more difficult when the fathers are gone (Schmeer, 2009).

Comparing Fathers and Mothers

Fathers enhance their children's social and emotional development in many ways (Lamb, 2010). Synchrony, attachment, and social referencing are all apparent with fathers. Indeed, fathers are more likely to elicit smiles and laughter from their infants than mothers are. Close father–infant relationships can teach infants (especially boys) appropriate expressions of emotion (Boyce et al., 2006), particularly anger.

The results of father–infant care may endure: Teenagers are less likely to lash out at friends and authorities if, as infants, they experienced a warm, responsive relationship with their father (Trautmann-Villalba et al., 2006). Close relationships with infants help the men, too, reducing the risk of depression (Borke et al., 2007; Bronte-Tinkew et al., 2007).

Contemporary fathers feed, diaper, and bathe infants, but typically "mothers engage in more caregiving and comforting, and fathers in more high intensity play" (Kochanska et al., 2008, p. 41), such as moving their infant's limbs in imitation of walking, kicking, or climbing, or swinging the baby through the air, sideways, or even upside down. Fathers provide excitement; mothers caress, read, or sing.

Research on father–infant care has focused on three different questions over the past two decades (Bretherton, 2010; Lamb, 2010). The first and second questions were: Can fathers provide the same care as mothers? Is father–infant interaction different from mother–infant interaction? As you just read, many studies found that the answer to both questions was yes.

The third question is: How do fathers and mothers interact to provide infant care? The answer seems to be that, in a well-functioning family, they cooperate and complement each other, each giving the infant what the other does not (Bretherton, 2010). Mothers are the usual caregivers and fathers are usually the best playmates, but not always—each set of parents, given their circumstances (which might include being immigrant, gay, low-income, or having a premature or disabled infant), finds their own way to make sure their infant thrives (Lamb, 2010).

HILL STREET STUDIOS / AGE FOTOSTOCK

Up, Up, and Away! The vigorous play typical of fathers is likely to help in the infant's mastery of motor skills and the development of muscle control. (Of course, fathers must be careful not to harm fragile bones and developing brains.)

Infant Day Care

About 134 million babies were born worldwide in 2011. Most of them are cared for exclusively by their mothers over the first two years, with the rest usually cared for by relatives, typically fathers in the United States and grandmothers in most other nations (Leach, 2009). Worldwide, only about 15 percent of infants receive regular care from a nonrelative who is both paid and trained to provide it. Statistics on the precise incidence and consequences of such care in each nation are difficult to interpret because "informal in-family arrangements speak to the ingenuity of parents trying to cope but bedevil child care statistics" (Leach, 2009, p. 44).

International Comparisons

It is known that the proportion of infants in nonrelative care varies markedly from nation to nation (Leach, 2009; Melhuish & Petrogiannis, 2006). Center-based care is common in France, Israel, China, and Sweden, where it is heavily subsidized by the government, and scarce in South Asia, Africa, and Latin America, where it is not. North America is in between these extremes, but variation from place to place is apparent.

Involvement of relatives other than mothers in infant care also varies. Worldwide, fathers are increasingly involved in baby care, but this varies by culture. Most nations do not yet have policies in place to facilitate father care. Some nations provide paid leave for new fathers as well as mothers; several nations provide paid family leave that can be taken by either parent or shared between them; some nations mandate that a job be kept available when mothers take an unpaid maternity leave; and most nations in the developing world provide limited paid leave for mothers (India does not allow women to be employed in the first six weeks after birth) but not fathers.

Some employers are more generous than the laws require. To help you grasp the variations in paid paternal leave, here is a list of policies in a few nations:

- Canada: 50 weeks of shared leave (either parent), at about three-fourths pay.
- Sweden: 16 months, close to full pay, shared (e.g., both parents can take 8 months) but at least 2 months is reserved for the father.
- Denmark: 52 weeks, shared, full pay; at least 2 weeks is reserved for the father and at least 18 weeks for the mother.
- Bulgaria: 52 weeks, full pay; shared by mother, father, and grandmother.
- Brazil: 5 days for the father and 120 days for the mother at full pay.
- Kenya: 2 weeks for the father and 2 months for the mother at full pay.
- Indonesia: 2 days for the father and 3 months for the mother at full pay.
- Lebanon: 1 day for the father and 7 weeks for the mother at full pay.
- Australia: 18 weeks for the father and 18 weeks for the mother at minimal wage.

In the United States, marked variations are apparent by state and by employer, although paid paternal leave is rare. Federal policy mandates that a job be held for a parent who takes unpaid leave of up to 12 weeks, unless the company has fewer than 50 employees. The U.S. military allows 10 days of paid paternal leave.

Cultures vary a great deal, as one would expect from the variations in ethnotheories. In some places, mothers of young children are discouraged from working; in others, they are refused public benefits unless they work. In England, many mothers return to work after 6 months, and day care is relatively common: One British survey found that only 9 percent of 4-month-olds were in regular nonmaternal care but 48 percent of 1-year-olds were (Leach, 2009).

In Germany, few mothers of young children are employed, not only because the ethnotheory discourages it but also because for decades a federal law mandated store closings (even for grocery, drug, and convenience stores) by 6:30 P.M. on weekdays, by 3:00 P.M. on Saturdays, and all day Sunday, which meant that an

TABLE 7.4	Percentage of U.S. Wives in the Labor Market by Ethnicity and Age of Child: 2008			
	Ethnic Background			
Age of Child	European	African	Asian	Latina
Birth to 24 months	59	62	58	45
24 to 36 months	59	64	58	46
3 to 6 years	65	81	61	53
6 to 13 years	74	83	70	66
14 to 17 years	79	82	80	66

Source: U.S. Bureau of the Census, 2010.

Culture or Economy? Note that this table includes only married women. In most cases, their husbands are employed, which means that these are families who have two incomes. Obviously, economic necessity is not the only reason most U.S. mothers are in the labor force. Latino families tend to have relatively low income, but many Latina mothers stay home until the youngest child enters school.

Observation Quiz In which ethnic group does it make a difference whether the youngest child is in primary school or secondary school? (see answer, page 217)

adult family member (usually the mother) had to shop during the day. That law was changed in 2006, and now stores in many places are allowed to stay open longer, but the culture still expects mothers of infants to care for them 24/7.

In the United States, paid leave depends on the employer and is scarce and short; unpaid leave is legally mandated for mothers whose employers have more than 50 workers. Fifty-nine percent of married mothers of babies younger than 12 months old are in the labor force (rates are higher for mothers who are not married or who have slightly older infants) (U.S. Bureau of the Census, 2010). (See Table 7.4.)

Of course, paid leave is not the only factor; some unemployed mothers take time for themselves or for volunteer work. Father, grandmother, and paid caregivers are common: In the United States, only 20 percent of infants are cared for *exclusively* by their mothers (no other relatives or babysitters) throughout their first year. By contrast, in Canada (similar in ethnic diversity but with lower rates of maternal employment), 70 percent of Canadian infants are in exclusive maternal care (Côté et al., 2008). Obviously, these national differences are affected by ethnotheory more than by essential psychosocial needs of babies and parents.

Types of Nonmaternal Care

Most North American mothers who want someone else to help with infant care prefer that the caregiver be the baby's father. Many parents coordinate their work schedules so one or the other parent is always present, an arrangement that may help the infant and the budget but not the marriage, as parents have much less time together (Meteyer & Perry-Jenkins, 2010). Grandmothers are also often caregivers in the first year, less so in the second as infants become more mobile and social (Leach, 2009).

When parents turn to paid nonrelatives, wealthier families may hire someone to come to the home, but most parents find **family day care,** in which the caregiver looks after a small group of young children in her (almost never his) home. The quality of family day care varies; if ages vary, infants and toddlers may get less attention than older children, who resent them (Kryzer et al., 2007). As you know, providing physical care and ensuring safety are only the beginning of quality caretaking; ideally, the caregiver spends many hours each day talking to and playing with each baby.

A better option than family day care may be **center day care,** in which licensed and educated adults care for several infants in a place designed especially for children. Most centers separate infants from older children. Ideally, the center has ample safe space, appropriate equipment, trained providers, and two adults

family day care Child care that occurs in the home of someone to whom the child is not related and who usually cares for several children of various ages.

center day care Child care that occurs in a place especially designed for the purpose, where several paid adults care for many children. Usually the children are grouped by age, the day-care center is licensed, and providers are trained and certified in child development.

TABLE 7.5	**High-Quality Day Care**

High-quality day care during infancy has five essential characteristics:

1. *Adequate attention to each infant.* A small group of infants (no more than five) needs two reliable, familiar, loving caregivers. Continuity of care is crucial.

2. *Encouragement of language and sensorimotor development.* Infants need language—songs, conversations, and positive talk—and easily manipulated toys.

3. *Attention to health and safety.* Cleanliness routines (e.g., handwashing), accident prevention (e.g., no small objects), and safe areas to explore are essential.

4. *Professional caregivers.* Caregivers should have experience and degrees/certificates in early-childhood education. Turnover should be low, morale high, and enthusiasm evident.

5. *Warm and responsive caregivers.* Providers should engage the children in active play and guide them in problem solving. Quiet, obedient children may indicate unresponsive care.

for a group of five or fewer infants (de Schipper et al., 2006) (see Table 7.5). Such a setting advances cognitive and social skills: Toddlers are intrigued by other toddlers, and they learn from interaction. No matter what form of day care is chosen, responsive, individualized care with stable caregivers seems best (Morrissey, 2009). Caregiving change is difficult for babies, because each infant gesture or sound not only merits individualized response but also requires interpretation by someone who knows that baby well.

The Effects of Infant Day Care

The evidence is overwhelming that good preschool education (discussed in Chapter 9) benefits young children, especially in cognition. However, when it comes to infants, "disagreements about the wisdom (indeed, the morality) of non-maternal child care for the very young remain" (NICHD Early Child Care Research Network, 2005, p. xiv). A major problem is that quality varies a great deal. Some caregivers with no training look after many infants, and the result is inadequate care.

The consequences of nonmaternal care are a subject of debate. The concern is that infants with extensive nonmaternal care tend to become more aggressive later on (Jacob, 2009), although some babies seem far more affected than others (Phillips et al., 2011; Pluess & Belsky, 2009). As one review explained: "This evidence now indicates that early nonparental care environments sometimes pose risks to young children and sometimes confer benefits" (Phillips et al., 2011). Differential effects are evident: For genetic and familial reasons, the choice about how best to care for an infant varies from case to case.

Consider some of this "evidence" in detail. In England, one study found that infants who were not exclusively in their mothers' care were less advanced emotionally (Fergusson et al., 2008). Proof? No. Most of those infants were cared for by grandmothers, especially when the mothers were young and poor. As you know from your understanding of correlation, SES accounts for several variables in addition to nonmaternal care. In this case, the relevant variables probably include the grandmothers' low education, the mothers' immaturity, and the households' financial stress. Any of those could be the reason for emotional immaturity.

A large study in Canada found that when children were cared for by someone other than their mothers (usually relatives) in their first year, girls seemed to develop equally well in various care arrangements. However, boys from high-income families whose mothers were not their only caregivers fared less well than similar boys in exclusive maternal care: By age 4, they were slightly more assertive or aggressive and had more emotional problems (e.g., a teacher might note that a boy "seems unhappy"). The opposite was true for boys from low-income families: On average, they benefited from nonmaternal care, again according to teacher reports. The researchers insist that no policy implications can be derived from this study, partly because care varied so much in quality, location, and provider (Côté et al., 2008).

Research in the United States on low-income families also finds that center care is beneficial (Peng & Robins, 2010). For less impoverished children, an ongoing longitudinal study by the Early Child Care Network of the National Institute of Child Health and Human Development (NICHD) has followed the development of more than 1,300 children from birth to age 11. It has found many cognitive benefits of early day care, especially in language development.

The social consequences are less clear (Loeb et al., 2005). Most analyses find that secure attachment to the mother was as common among infants in center care as among infants cared for at home. Like other, smaller studies, the NICHD research confirms that the mother–child relationship is pivotal. The NICHD study and the consensus of other research in the United States is that infant day care, even for 40 hours a week before age 1, has much less influence on child development than does the warmth of the mother–infant relationship (Phillips et al., 2011).

The NICHD study has also found that infant day care seems detrimental when the mother is insensitive *and* the infant spends more than 20 hours a week in a poor-quality program with too many children per group (McCartney et al., 2010). Again, boys sometimes become more quarrelsome, having more conflicts with their teachers than did the girls or other boys with a different mix of maternal traits and day-care experiences.

As you see, the research does not provide a simple answer about nonmaternal care. Each study is complex: International variations, uncertainty about quality and extent of care (both at home and elsewhere), and the fact that choices are not random make it hard to draw general conclusions. Family income, culture, and education affect choice of care, and those same variables affect child development. The fact that boys are more affected than girls may indicate something about biological sex, but it simply may be that difficult boys are more often in day care because mothers do not want exclusive care of their active, difficult sons. That selection effect may explain why the average 5-year-old boy who was in family or center care at age 1 is slightly more aggressive than his classmate who had full-time maternal care in his early years.

>> Answer to Observation Quiz (from page 215) Asian Americans. One of every four Asian American wives who were unemployed when their children were of school age enters the labor market when the children become teenagers.

Especially for Day-Care Providers A mother who brings her child to you for day care says that she knows she is harming her baby but must work out of economic necessity. What do you say? (see response, page 218)

The Same Situation, Many Miles Apart: Universal Day Care? Casper, Wyoming *(left)*, is on the opposite side of the earth from Dhaka, Bangladesh *(right)*, but day care is needed in both places, as shown here.

Observation Quiz What three cultural differences do you see? (see answer, page 218)

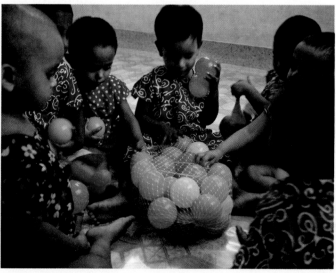

>> Response for Day-Care Providers
(from page 217) Reassure the mother that you will keep her baby safe and will help to develop the baby's mind and social skills by fostering synchrony and attachment. Also tell her that the quality of mother–infant interaction at home is more important than anything else for psychosocial development; mothers who are employed full time usually have wonderful, secure relationships with their infants. If the mother wishes, you can discuss ways in which she can be a more responsive mother.

>> Answer to Observation Quiz (from page 217) The Bangladeshi children are dressed alike, are the same age, and are all seated around toy balls in a net—there's not a book in sight, unlike the Wyoming setting.

A careful summary of the longitudinal outcomes of nonmaternal infant care finds that "externalizing behavior is predicted from a constellation of variables in multiple contexts . . . and no study has found that children of employed mothers develop serious emotional or other problems *solely* because their mothers are working outside the home" (McCartney et al., 2010, pp. 1, 16).

Another complication in the United States is that children generally benefit if their mothers are employed (Goldberg et al., 2008), in part because maternal income reduces parental depression and increases family wealth, both of which correlate with happier and more successful children. Many employed mothers make infant care their top priority, sometimes at the expense of their own self-care or marriage.

A time-use study found that mothers who worked full time outside the home spent almost as much time playing with their babies (14½ hours a week) as did mothers with no outside jobs (16 hours a week) (Huston & Aronson, 2005). To make more time for their babies, they spent half as much time on housework, less time with their husbands, and almost no time on leisure. The study concludes:

> There was no evidence that mothers' time at work interfered with the quality of their relationship with their infants, the quality of the home environment, or children's development. In fact, the results suggest the opposite. Mothers who spent more time at work provided slightly higher quality home environments.
>
> [Huston & Aronson, 2005, p. 479]

That is a comforting conclusion for working mothers, but again other interpretations are possible. It may be that the women who were able to find worthwhile work were more capable of providing a "quality home environment" than the women who were unemployed. Every study reflects several possible variables and consequently researchers find mixed evidence on infant day care. Many factors are relevant: infant sex and temperament, family income and education, and especially the quality of care at home and elsewhere.

As with many topics in child development, questions remain. What is definitive is that each infant needs personal responsiveness from at least one person—ideally from both mother and father—who is the infant's partner in the synchrony duet, the base for secure attachment, and then the social reference who encourages exploration. If the baby has that, development should go well.

SUMMING UP

Infants seek social bonds, which they develop with one or several people. Synchrony begins in the early months: Infants and caregivers interact face-to-face, making split-second adjustments in their emotional responses to each other. Synchrony evolves into attachment, an emotional connection. Secure attachment allows infants to learn; insecure infants are less confident and may develop emotional impairments. As infants become more curious and encounter new toys, people, and events, they use social referencing to learn whether such new things are fearsome or fun.

The emotional connections evident in synchrony, attachment, and social referencing may occur with mothers, fathers, other relatives, and day-care providers. Nations and families vary in how much nonmaternal infant care they use, as well as in the quality of that care. Consequences also vary, with neither exclusive maternal care, family day care, nor center care necessarily best. Problems with later development may occur if an infant receives unresponsive care (as when one caregiver has too many infants or a depressed mother is the sole caregiver). Quality and continuity of care matter. ▪

SUMMARY

Emotional Development

1. Two emotions, contentment and distress, appear as soon as an infant is born. Smiles and laughter are evident in the early months. Anger emerges with restriction and frustration, between 4 and 8 months of age, and becomes stronger by age 1.

2. Reflexive fear is apparent in very young infants. Fear of something specific, including fear of strangers and of separation, appears toward the end of the first year.

3. In the second year, social awareness produces more selective fear, anger, and joy. As infants become increasingly self-aware, emotions emerge that encourage an interface between the self and others—specifically, pride, shame, and affection.

4. Brain maturation has an obvious impact on emotional development, although specifics are not yet known. Synesthesia (when a sense or emotion in one part of the brain spreads to other parts) is apparent early in life. Self-recognition (on the mirror/rouge test) emerges at about 18 months.

5. Stress impedes early brain and emotional development. Some infants are particularly vulnerable to the effects of early mistreatment.

6. Temperament is a set of genetic traits whose expression is influenced by the context. Inborn temperament is linked to later personality, although plasticity is also evident.

7. Parental practices inhibit and guide a child's emotions. Ideally, a good fit develops between the parents' actions and the child's personality.

Theories of Infant Psychosocial Development

8. According to all major theories, caregiver behavior is especially influential in the first two years. Freud stressed the mother's impact on oral and anal pleasure; Erikson emphasized trust and autonomy.

9. Behaviorists focus on learning; parents teach their babies many things, including when to be fearful or joyful. Cognitive theory holds that infants develop working models based on their experiences.

10. The sociocultural approach notes the impact of social and cultural factors on the parent–infant relationship. Ethnotheories shape infant emotions and traits so that they fit well within the culture. Some cultures encourage proximal parenting (more physical touch); others, distal parenting (more talk and object play). Personal theories also affect how parents respond to infants.

The Development of Social Bonds

11. Sometimes by 2 months, and clearly by 6 months, infants become more responsive and social, and synchrony begins. Synchrony involves moment-by-moment interaction. Infants are disturbed by a still face because they expect and need social interaction.

12. Attachment, measured by the baby's reaction to the caregiver's presence, departure, and return in the Strange Situation, is crucial. Some infants seem indifferent (type A attachment—insecure-avoidant) or overly dependent (type C—insecure-resistant/ambivalent), instead of secure (type B). Disorganized attachment (type D) is the most worrisome. Some children never form an attachment at all, even an insecure one.

13. Secure attachment provides encouragement for infant exploration. As they play, toddlers engage in social referencing, looking to other people's facial expressions to detect what is frightening and what is fun.

14. Fathers are wonderful playmates for infants, who frequently use them as social references, learning about emotions and exploration. If a man thinks that infant care is unmanly, or a woman thinks only women can care for babies, that may inhibit father involvement. Many modern fathers, however, complement the mother's infant care—and babies are happier because of it.

15. The impact of non-maternal care depends on many factors; it varies from one nation to another and probably from one child to another. Quality of care (responsive, individualized) is crucial, no matter who provides that care.

KEY TERMS

social smile (p. 192)
stranger wariness (p. 193)
separation anxiety (p. 193)
self-awareness (p. 194)
temperament (p. 196)
goodness of fit (p. 198)
Big Five (p. 198)

trust versus mistrust (p. 199)
autonomy versus shame and doubt (p. 199)
social learning (p. 200)
working model (p. 200)
ethnotheory (p. 201)
proximal parenting (p. 202)

distal parenting (p. 202)
synchrony (p. 205)
still-face technique (p. 206)
attachment (p. 207)
secure attachment (p. 208)
insecure-avoidant attachment (p. 208)

insecure-resistant/ambivalent attachment (p. 208)
disorganized attachment (p. 208)
Strange Situation (p. 209)
social referencing (p. 212)
family day care (p. 215)
center day care (p. 215)

WHAT HAVE YOU LEARNED?

Emotional Development

1. What are the first emotions to appear in very young infants?

2. What are 1-year-olds afraid of?

3. How do the emotions of the second year of life differ from those of the first year?

4. How does stress during infancy affect brain development?

5. Why does synesthesia seem to be more common in infants than in adults?

6. Why are temperamental traits more apparent in some people than others?

Theories of Infant Psychosocial Development

7. What are the similarities and differences between the oral stage and the trust stage?

8. What are the similarities and differences between the anal stage and the autonomy stage?

9. How would behaviorists explain family and cultural patterns of personality traits?

10. Why does "working model" arise from cognitive theory instead of the other theories?

11. What would be the beliefs of an ethnotheory that supports proximal parenting?

12. What would be the beliefs of an ethnotheory that supports distal parenting?

The Development of Social Bonds

13. How does synchrony help infants learn about emotions?

14. Is it possible to overemphasize the importance of secure attachment? Why or why not?

15. In what circumstances would an infant develop type A attachment?

16. In what circumstances would an infant develop type C attachment?

17. In what circumstances would an infant develop type D attachment?

18. For infants, how is father care different from, and similar to, mother care?

19. Why are most infants, in most nations, cared for exclusively by their mothers?

20. What are the differences between grandmother care, family day care, and center day care?

21. For which infants does early day care correlate with aggression in kindergarten?

22. Why is it difficult to draw definite conclusions about infant day care?

APPLICATIONS

1. One cultural factor influencing infant development is how infants are carried from place to place. Ask four mothers whose infants were born in each of the past four decades how they transported them—front or back carriers, facing out or in, strollers or carriages, car seats or on mother's laps, and so on. Why did they choose the mode(s) they chose? What are their opinions and yours on how that cultural practice might affect infants' development?

2. Observe synchrony for three minutes. Ideally, ask the parent of an infant under 8 months of age to play with the infant. If no infant is available, observe a pair of lovers as they converse. Note the sequence and timing of every facial expression, sound, and gesture of both partners.

3. Telephone several day-care centers to try to assess the quality of care they provide. Ask about such factors as adult–child ratio, group size, and training for caregivers of children of various ages. Is there a minimum age? If so, why was that age chosen? Analyze the answers, using Table 7.3 as a guide.

≫ONLINE CONNECTIONS

To accompany your textbook, you have access to a number of online resources, including quizzes for every chapter of the book, flashcards (in English and Spanish), critical thinking questions, and case studies. For access to any of these links, go to www.worthpublishers.com/bergerca9e. In addition to these free resources, you'll also find links to podcasts, video clips, diagnostic quizzing with personalized study advice, and an ebook. Some of the videos and activities available online include:

- *Attachment Behaviors in the Strange Situation.* You'll get a chance to watch—and take your best guess about attachment states—as some infants are left in the company of strangers.

- *Child Care.* A variety of videos showcase different types of early child care and different strategies for best practices.

The First Two Years

BIOSOCIAL

Body Changes Over the first two years, body weight quadruples and brain weight triples. Connections between brain cells grow dense, with complex networks of dendrites and axons. Neurons become coated with myelin, sending messages more efficiently. Experiences that are universal (experience-expectant) and culture-bound (experience-dependent) aid brain growth, partly by pruning unused connections between neurons.

Senses and Motor Skills Brain maturation underlies the development of all the senses. Seeing, hearing, and mobility progress from reflexes to coordinated voluntary actions, including focusing, grasping, and walking. Culture is evident in sensory and motor development, as brain networks respond to the particulars of each infant's life.

Public Health Infant health depends on immunization, parental practices (including "back to sleep"), and nutrition. Breast milk protects health and has so many other benefits that the World Health Organization recommends exclusive breast-feeding for the first six months. Survival rates are much higher today than even a few decades ago, yet in some regions, infant growth is still stunted because of malnutrition.

COGNITIVE

Sensorimotor Intelligence and Information Processing As Piaget describes it, in the first two years, infants progress from knowing their world through immediate sensory experiences to "experimenting" on that world through actions and mental images. Information-processing theory stresses the links between sensory experiences and perception. Infants develop their own ideas regarding the possibilities offered by the objects and events of the world. Research over the past two decades finds traces of memory at 3 months, of object permanence at 4 months, and of deferred imitation at 9 months—all much younger ages than Piaget described.

Language Interaction with responsive adults exposes infants to the structures of communication and language. By age 1, infants usually speak a word or two; by age 2, language has exploded—toddlers talk in short sentences and add vocabulary each day. Language develops through reinforcement, neurological maturation, and social motivation; all three processes combine to create a very conversational toddler.

PSYCHOSOCIAL

Emotions and Theories Emotions develop from newborn reactions to complex, self-conscious responses. Infants' self-awareness and independence are shaped by parents, in a transition explained by Freud's oral and anal stages, by Erikson's crises of trust versus mistrust and autonomy versus shame and doubt, by behaviorism's focus on parental responses, and by cognitive theory's working models. Much of basic temperament is inborn and apparent throughout life. Sociocultural theory stresses cultural norms, evident in parents' ethnotheories in raising their infants; some parents are more proximal (encouraging touch), others more distal (encouraging cognition).

The Development of Social Bonds Parents and infants respond to each other by synchronizing their behavior. Toward the end of the first year, secure attachment to the parent sets the stage for the child's increasingly independent exploration of the world. Insecure attachment—avoidant, resistant, or disorganized—signifies a parent–child relationship that hinders learning. Infants actively participate socially, using social referencing to interpret their experiences. Mothers, fathers, and day-care providers encourage infants' social confidence.

III

early childhood

From age 2 to age 6, children spend most of their waking hours discovering, creating, laughing, and imagining, as they acquire the skills they need. They chase each other and attempt new challenges (developing their bodies); they play with sounds, words, and ideas (developing their minds); they invent games and dramatize fantasies (learning social skills and morals).

These years have been called the *preschool years,* but that has become a misnomer. School no longer means sitting at desks in rows. Many 2- to 6-year-olds are in "school," learning and playing. These years have also been called the *play years*. The young child's delight in play seems magical—whether quietly tracking a beetle through the grass or riotously turning a bedroom into a shambles. Young children's minds seem playful, too; they explain that "a bald man has a barefoot head" or that "the sun shines so children can go outside to play." But people of all ages play, so these are not the only play years.

Therefore, these three chapters are called *early childhood*, the traditional term for this period. Early childhood is a period of extraordinary growth, learning, and play, joyful not only for young children but also for anyone who knows them, a time for impressive growth in every domain.

Early Childhood: Biosocial Development

WHAT WILL YOU KNOW?

1. Do children eat too much, too little, or both?
2. How does brain maturation affect emotional development in early childhood?
3. What do children need for their gross motor skills to develop?
4. When and how should child abuse be prevented

When I was 4, I jumped off the back of our couch again and again, trying to fly. I did it many times because I tried it with and without a cape, with and without flapping my arms. My laughing mother wondered whether she had made a mistake in letting me see *Peter Pan*. An older woman warned that jumping would hurt my uterus. I didn't know what a uterus was, I didn't heed that lady, and I didn't stop until I decided I could not fly because I had no pixie dust.

When you were 4, I hope you also wanted to fly and someone laughed while keeping you safe. Protection, appreciation, and fantasy are all needed in early childhood. Do you remember trying to skip, climb a tree, or write your name? Young children try, fail, and try again. They become skilled and wise, eventually understanding some of life's limitations, including that humans have no wings. Advances in body and brain, and the need for adult protection, are themes of this chapter. Amazing growth, unexpected injury, and sobering maltreatment are all described.

>> Body Changes

In early childhood as in infancy, the body and brain develop according to powerful epigenetic forces, biologically driven and socially guided, experience-expectant and experience-dependent (as explained in Chapter 5). Bodies and brains mature in size and function.

Growth Patterns

Just comparing a toddling, unsteady 1-year-old with a cartwheeling 6-year-old makes some differences obvious. During early childhood, children slim down as the lower body lengthens and fat turns to muscle. In fact, the average body mass index (BMI, the ratio of weight to height) is lower at ages 5 and 6 than at any other time of life. Gone are the toddler's protruding belly, round face, short limbs, and large head. The center of gravity moves from the breast to the belly, enabling cartwheels, somersaults, and many other motor skills. The joys of dancing, gymnastics, and pumping a swing become possible; changing body proportions enable new achievements year by year. Toddlers often tumble, unbalanced: It is fortunate they are close to the floor. Kindergartners race and rarely fall.

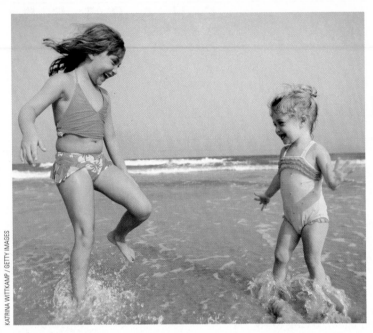

KATRINA WITTKAMP / GETTY IMAGES

Size and Balance These cousins are only four years apart, but note the doubling in leg length and marked improvement in balance. The 2-year-old needs to plant both legs on the sand, while the 6-year-old cavorts on one foot.

Increases in weight and height accompany this growth. Over each year of early childhood, well-nourished children gain about 4½ pounds (2 kilograms) and grow almost 3 inches (about 7 centimeters). By age 6, the average child in a developed nation:

- Weighs between 40 and 50 pounds (between 18 and 22 kilograms)
- Is at least 3½ feet tall (more than 100 centimeters)
- Looks lean, not chubby (ages 5 to 6 are lowest in body fat)
- Has adultlike body proportions (legs constitute about half the total height)

When many ethnic groups live together in a nation with abundant food and adequate medical care, children of African descent tend to be tallest, followed by those of European descent, then Asians, and then Latinos. However, height differences are greater *within* ethnic groups than *between* groups.

Nutrition

Although they rarely die of malnutrition, preschool children may be at greater nutritional risk than children of any other age, primarily because it is easy to satisfy their small appetites with unhealthy foods, leaving no room for the nutrition they need. Over the centuries, low-income families encouraged their children to eat, protecting them against famine. This saved lives. Even today in the poorest nations, malnutrition beginning in infancy and continuing through early childhood contributes to one-third of all child deaths (UNICEF, 2008) and slows later growth, including growth of the brain. For instance, according to a study of hungry young children in Ghana, many became depressed or mentally impaired adolescents, although few became delinquents—perhaps they lacked the energy (Appoh, 2004; Appoh & Krekling, 2004).

Unfortunately, the well-intentioned tradition of encouraging young children to eat becomes destructive when food is abundant. This is true in many nations: In Brazil 30 years ago, the most common nutritional problem was undernutrition; now it is overnutrition (Monteiro et al., 2004), with low-income Brazilians particularly vulnerable (Monteiro et al., 2007).

A study of 2- to 4-year-olds in low-income families in New York City found many overweight children: Weight increased as family income fell (J. A. Nelson et al., 2004) and as children grew older (14 percent at age 2; 27 percent at age 4). This age pattern suggests that eating habits, not genes, were the cause. In that study, overweight children were more often Latino (27 percent) or Asian American (22 percent) rather than of African (14 percent) or European (11 percent) descent.

One explanation for these ethnic differences is that many of these children lived with grandparents who knew firsthand the dangers of malnutrition. This possibility is supported by generational data: Latino and Asian American grandparents are unlikely to be obese themselves but often have overweight grandchildren (Bates et al., 2008). Of course, this varies depending on the background, culture, and community of the particular grandparents, but for every group children's nutritional needs have changed faster than customs have.

An epidemic of heart disease and diabetes is spreading worldwide as overfed children become overweight adults (Gluckman & Hanson, 2006). An article in

The Lancet (the leading medical journal in England) predicted that by 2020, 228 million adults worldwide will have diabetes (more in India than in any other nation) as a result of unhealthy eating habits acquired in childhood. This article suggests that measures to reduce childhood overeating in the United States have been inadequate and that "U.S. children could become the first generation in more than a century to have shorter life spans than their parents if current trends of excessive weight and obesity continue" (Devi, 2008, p. 105).

Appetite decreases between ages 2 and 6 because, compared with infants, young children need fewer calories per pound. This is especially true for the current generation since children get much less exercise than their parents or grandparents did. They do not feed the animals, walk miles to school, or even go outside often to play. However, instead of accepting this generational change, many parents foolishly fret, threaten, and cajole their children to overeat ("Eat all your dinner and you can have ice cream"). Pediatricians have found that most parents of infants, toddlers, and preschoolers believe that relatively thin children are less healthy than relatively heavy ones, a false belief that leads to overfeeding (Laraway et al., 2010).

Nutritional Deficiencies

Although most children in developed nations consume more than enough calories, they do not always obtain adequate iron, zinc, and calcium. For example, children now drink less milk than formerly, which means less calcium and weaker bones later on.

Another problem is sugar. Many customs entice children to eat sweets—in birthday cake, holiday candy, desserts, and other treats. Sweetened cereals and drinks (advertised as containing 100 percent of daily vitamins) are a poor substitute for a balanced, varied diet, partly because some nutrients have not yet been identified, much less listed on food labels. This means that eating a wide variety of foods may be essential for optimal health.

Compared with the average child, those preschoolers who eat more dark-green and orange vegetables and less fried food benefit in many ways. They gain bone mass but not fat, according to a study that controlled for other factors that might correlate with body fat, such as gender (girls have more), ethnicity (people of some ethnic groups are genetically thinner), and income (poor children have worse diets) (Wosje et al., 2010).

An added complication is that an estimated 3 to 8 percent of all young children are allergic to a specific food—almost always a common, healthy one: Cow's milk, eggs, peanuts, tree nuts, soy, wheat, fish, and shellfish are the usual culprits. Diagnostic standards vary (which explains the range of estimates) and treatment varies even more (Chafen et al., 2010). Some experts advocate total avoidance of the offending food—there are peanut-free schools, where no one is ever allowed to pack a peanut butter sandwich for lunch—but others suggest that tolerance to the offending food should be built up, beginning by giving babies a tiny bit of peanut butter (Reche et al., 2011). Fortunately, many childhood food allergies are outgrown, but since young children are already at nutritional risk, allergies make it even harder to achieve a balanced diet.

Oral Health

Too much sugar and too little fiber cause tooth decay, the most common disease of young children in developed nations, affecting more than one-third of all U.S. children under age 6 (Brickhouse

Victory! Well, maybe not quite yet, but he's on his way. This boy participates in a British effort to combat childhood obesity; mother and son exercising in Liverpool Park is part of the solution. Harder to implement are dietary changes—many parents let children eat as much as they want.

HOWARD BARLOW / ALAMY

Healthy Eating Children eat the way their culture teaches them to-about ⅓ with hands, ⅓ with forks, and ⅓ with chopsticks. They also eat whatever their community presents, establishing lifelong tastes that might predict their health as well. This boy in Beijing may be fortunate: Traditional Chinese cuisine (brown rice and many vegetables) is among the healthiest in the world. However, with rising income, more meat and more obesity have become a trend in China. Has it reached this preschool?

ELLEN B. SENISI

et al., 2008). Sugary fruit drinks and soda are prime causes; even diet soda contains acid that makes decay more likely (Holtzman, 2009).

Fortunately, "baby" teeth are replaced naturally at about ages 6 to 10. The schedule is primarily genetic, with girls averaging a few months ahead of boys. However, tooth care should not be postponed until the permanent teeth erupt. Severe tooth decay in early childhood harms those permanent teeth (which form below the first teeth) and can cause jaw malformation, chewing difficulties, and speech problems. Teeth are affected by diet and illness, which means that the state of a young child's teeth can alert adults to other health problems.

Most preschoolers visit the dentist if they have U.S.-born, middle-class parents—but not if their parents were born elsewhere. A study in San Francisco found that fear of the dentist was common among immigrants from China, who were unlikely to take their young children for an oral health checkup (Hilton et al., 2007). Young parents (below age 22 at the child's birth) of every ethnicity are more likely to have poor oral health habits themselves, and their children more often have cavities (Niji et al., 2010).

Of course, many low-income parents of all ethnic groups are overwhelmed with work and child care and do not realize that tooth brushing is a vital habit, best learned early in life (Mofidi et al., 2009). But in many countries, ignorance is not the problem; access is. In the United States, free dentistry is not available to most poor parents, who "want to do better" for their children's teeth than they did for their own (Lewis et al., 2010).

Hazards of "Just Right"

Many young children are compulsive about their daily routines, insisting that bedtime be preceded by tooth brushing, a book, and prayers—or by a snack, sitting on the toilet, and a song. Whatever the routine, children expect it and are upset if someone puts them to bed without it. Similarly, mealtime can become a time for certain foods, prepared and placed in a particular way, on a specific plate. This rigidity, known as the "just right" or "just so" phenomenon, might be a sign of a pathological obsessive-compulsive disorder in older children and adults. However, a wish for continuity and sameness is normal and widespread among young children (Evans et al., 2006; Pietrefesa & Evans, 2007). For example:

> Whereas parents may insist that the child eat his vegetables at dinner, the child may insist that the potatoes be placed only in a certain part of the plate and must not touch any other food; should the potatoes land outside of this area, the child may seem to experience a sense of near-contamination, setting off a tirade of fussiness for which many 2- and 3-year-olds are notorious.
>
> [Evans et al., 1997, p. 59]

Most children's food preferences and rituals are far from ideal. (One 3-year-old I know wanted to eat only cream cheese sandwiches on white bread; one 4-year-old, only fast-food chicken nuggets.) According to a survey of 1,500 parents of 1- to 6-year-olds (Evans et al., 1997), the "just right" phase peaked at about age 3, when children:

- Preferred to have things done in a particular order or in a certain way
- Had a strong preference to wear (or not wear) certain articles of clothing
- Prepared for bedtime by engaging in a special activity, routine, or ritual
- Had strong preferences for certain foods

By age 6, this rigidity faded somewhat (see Figure 8.1). Another team of experts put it this way: "Most, if not all, children exhibit normal age-dependent obsessive-compulsive behaviors [that are] usually gone by middle childhood" (March et al.,

Especially for Nutritionists A parent complains that she prepares a variety of vegetables and fruits, but her 4-year-old wants only French fries and cake. What should you advise? (see response, page 231)

VAHAN SHIRVANIAN / CARTOONSTOCK

"I'm not hungry. I ate with Rover."

Eat Your Veggies On their own, children do not always eat wisely.

2004, p. 216). The best reaction may be patience: A young child's insistence on a particular routine, a preferred pair of shoes, or a favorite cup can be accommodated for a year or two. After all, adults also have preferred routines, keeping their obsessions in check with rational thinking (Evans & Leckman, 2006). For preschool teachers, this means that routines need to be simple, clear, and followed by all the children—otherwise, every child will want to be an exception.

Childhood Overeating

Overeating can become a serious problem: Indulgence and patience—necessary for "just right"—may be destructive if the result is an overweight child. Our major discussion of childhood obesity occurs in Chapter 11 because the problem is most obvious in middle childhood, but the origins are found in early childhood.

As already mentioned, many adults entice young children to eat more than their small bellies want, developing habits and appetites that are destructive decades later. Caregivers are not the only ones at fault. The social context of early childhood (television commercials, store displays, other children's eating habits) encourages overconsumption, yet childhood obesity leads to later illness.

Pediatricians need to provide parents of 2- to 5-year-olds with "anticipatory guidance" (Collins et al., 2004), since prevention is better than putting a 6-year-old on a diet (as some pediatricians do). Preschool educators (sometimes via guidelines for parents or requests to food providers) can also influence children's nutritional intake, affording them more opportunities to expand their knowledge and experience—and ensuring that they have nutritious food (no candy).

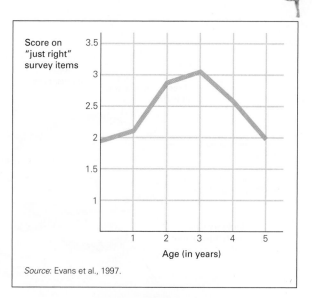

Source: Evans et al., 1997.

FIGURE 8.1

Young Children's Insistence on Routine
This chart shows the average scores of children (who are rated by their parents) on a survey indicating the child's desire to have certain things—including food selection and preparation—done "just right." Such strong preferences for rigid routines tend to fade by age 6.

SUMMING UP

Between ages 2 and 6, children grow taller and proportionately thinner, with variations depending on genes, nutrition, income, and ethnicity. Nutrition and oral health are serious concerns, as many children eat unhealthy foods, developing cavities and too much body fat. Young children usually have small appetites and picky eating habits. Unfortunately, many adults encourage overeating, not realizing that overweight leads to life-threatening illness.

>> Brain Development

Brains grow rapidly before birth and throughout infancy, as you saw in Chapter 5. By age 2, most neurons have connected to other neurons and substantial pruning has occurred. The 2-year-old's brain already weighs 75 percent of what it will weigh in adulthood. (The major structures of the brain are diagrammed in Figure 8.2).

Since most of the brain is already present and functioning by age 2, what remains to develop? The most important parts! Although the brains and bodies of other primates seem better than humans in some ways (they climb trees better, walk faster, and so on), and although many animals have abilities humans lack (dogs' sense of smell, for instance), humans have intellectual capacities far beyond those of any other animal. Considered from an evolutionary perspective, because of our brains, the human species developed "a mode of living built on social cohesion, cooperation and efficient planning . . . survival of the smartest" seems more accurate than survival of the fittest (Corballis, 2011, p. 194).

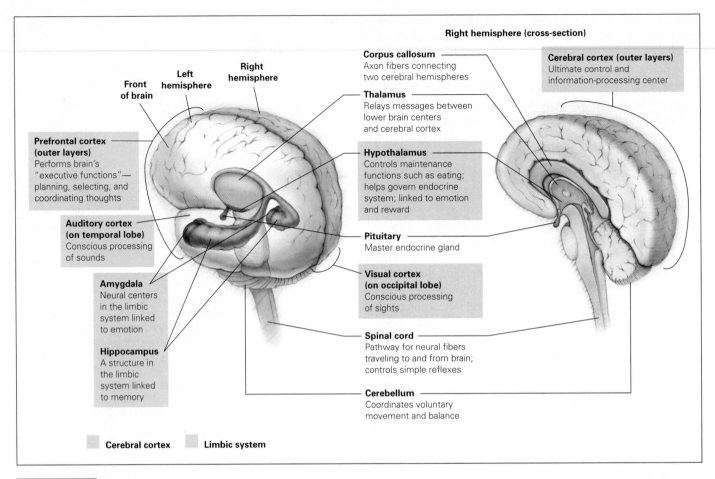

Right hemisphere (cross-section)

Corpus callosum
Axon fibers connecting
two cerebral hemispheres

Cerebral cortex (outer layers)
Ultimate control and
information-processing center

Front of brain — Left hemisphere — Right hemisphere

Prefrontal cortex (outer layers)
Performs brain's "executive functions"—planning, selecting, and coordinating thoughts

Thalamus
Relays messages between lower brain centers and cerebral cortex

Hypothalamus
Controls maintenance functions such as eating; helps govern endocrine system; linked to emotion and reward

Auditory cortex (on temporal lobe)
Conscious processing of sounds

Pituitary
Master endocrine gland

Amygdala
Neural centers in the limbic system linked to emotion

Visual cortex (on occipital lobe)
Conscious processing of sights

Hippocampus
A structure in the limbic system linked to memory

Spinal cord
Pathway for neural fibers traveling to and from brain; controls simple reflexes

Cerebellum
Coordinates voluntary movement and balance

Cerebral cortex   Limbic system

FIGURE 8.2

Connections A few of the dozens of named parts of the brain are shown here. Although each area has particular functions, the entire brain is interconnected. The processing of emotions, for example, occurs primarily in the limbic system, but many other brain areas are involved.

Especially for Early-Childhood Teachers You know you should be patient, but you feel your frustration rising when your young charges dawdle on the walk to the playground a block away. What should you do? (see response, page 232)

myelination The process by which axons become coated with myelin, a fatty substance that speeds the transmission of nerve impulses from neuron to neuron.

Those functions of the brain that make us human, not merely apes, begin in infancy but develop notably after age 2, enabling quicker, better-coordinated, and more reflective thought (Johnson, 2005; Kagan & Herschkowitz, 2005). Between ages 2 and 6, the brain grows from 75 percent to 90 percent of its adult weight, with increases particularly in the areas that allow advanced language and social understanding. The size of the cortex—brain regions where planning, thinking, and language occur—is a crucial difference between humans and other animals. Elephants, crows, chimpanzees, and dolphins have all recently surprised researchers with their intelligence, but none come close to *Homo sapiens* in the relative size of their cortex and their social understanding (Corballis, 2011).

For example, a careful series of tests given to 106 chimpanzees, 32 orangutans, and 105 human 2½-year-olds found that young children were "equivalent . . . to chimpanzees on tasks of physical cognition but far outstripped both chimpanzees and orangutans on tasks of social cognition" such as pointing or following someone's gaze (Herrmann et al., 2007, p. 1365).

Speed of Thought

After infancy, some brain growth is the result of proliferation of the communication pathways (dendrites and axons). However, most increased brain weight occurs because of **myelination.** *Myelin* (sometimes called the *white matter* of the brain) is a fatty coating on the axons that speeds signals between neurons (see Figure 8.3). Although myelination continues throughout childhood and adolescence, the effects of myelination are especially apparent in early childhood (Silk & Wood,

2011), partly because the areas of the brain that show greatest early myelination are the motor and sensory areas (Kolb & Whishaw, 2008).

Speed of thought from axon to neuron becomes pivotal when several thoughts must occur in rapid succession. By age 6, most children can see an object and immediately name it, catch a ball and throw it, write their ABCs in proper sequence, and so on. In fact, rapid naming of letters and objects—possible only when myelination is extensive—is a crucial indicator of later reading ability (Shanahan & Lonigan, 2010). Of course, adults must be patient when listening to young children talk, helping them get dressed, or watching them write each letter of their names. Everything is done more slowly by 6-year-olds than by 16-year-olds because the younger children's brains have less myelination, which slows information processing. However, thanks to myelination, older preschoolers are much quicker than toddlers, who sometimes forget what they were doing before they finish.

Connecting the Brain's Hemispheres

One part of the brain that grows and myelinates rapidly during early childhood is the **corpus callosum,** a long, thick band of nerve fibers that connects the left and right sides of the brain. Growth of the corpus callosum makes communication between the hemispheres more efficient, allowing children to coordinate the two sides of the brain or body. Failure of the corpus callosum to develop results in serious disorders: This is one of several possible causes of autism (Frazier & Hardan, 2009).

To understand the significance of the corpus callosum, note that the two sides of the body and of the brain are not identical. Each side specializes, being dominant for certain functions—the result of **lateralization,** literally, "sidedness." The entire human body is lateralized, apparent not only in right- or left-handedness but also in the feet, the eyes, the ears, and the brain itself. Genes, prenatal hormones, and early experiences all affect which side does what. Lateralization advances with development of the corpus callosum (Boles et al., 2008).

Left-handed people tend to have thicker corpus callosa than right-handed people do, perhaps because they need to readjust the interaction between the two sides of their bodies, depending on the task. For example, most left-handed people brush their teeth with their left hand because using their dominant hand is more natural, but they shake hands with their right hand because that is what the social convention requires.

Some research a decade ago found that, relatively speaking, the corpus callosum was thicker in females than in males, a finding that led to speculation about women's superior emotional understanding. However, research using more advanced techniques now finds that this sex difference is far from universal. Some individual males and females have notably thicker corpus callosa than others, but gender does not seem relevant (Savic-Berglund, 2010). Much brain research, including data on the corpus callosum, has led some scientists to jump to conclusions—conclusions that are later proved wrong. Another male–female difference is that male brains are bigger and heavier. However, researchers are understandably cautious about interpreting this difference.

The Left-Handed Child

Infants and toddlers usually prefer one hand over the other for grabbing spoons and rattles, and by age 2 most children have a dominant hand used for scribbling and throwing. Preschool teachers notice that about 1 child in 10 prefers the left

DR. DAVID FURNESS, KEELE UNIVERSITY / PHOTO RESEARCHERS, INC.

FIGURE 8.3

Faster and Faster Myelination is a lifelong process. Shown here is a cross section of an axon (dark middle) coated with many layers of Schwann cells, as more and more myelin wraps around the axon throughout childhood. Age-related slowdowns in adulthood are caused by gradual disappearance of myelin layers.

corpus callosum A long, thick band of nerve fibers that connects the left and right hemispheres of the brain and allows communication between them.

lateralization Literally, sidedness, referring to the specialization in certain functions by each side of the brain, with one side dominant for each activity. The left side of the brain controls the right side of the body, and vice versa.

>> Response for Nutritionists (from page 228) The nutritionally wise advice would be to offer only fruits, vegetables, and other nourishing, low-fat foods, counting on the child's eventual hunger to drive him or her to eat them. However, centuries of cultural custom make it almost impossible for parents to be wise in such cases. A physical checkup, with a blood test, may be warranted to make sure the child is healthy.

No Correction Needed The teacher in this preschool does not correct the left-handed children, one of whom happily draws beside her friends. Why does the word *correct* literally mean "to make right"?

hand. Handedness is partly genetic (Goymer, 2007), but many cultures have tried to make everyone right-handed, with some success. When left-handed children were forced to use their right hands, most learned to write right-handedly. However, neurological success was incomplete: Their brains were only partly reprogrammed (Klöppel et al., 2007).

Even today, many cultures endorse the belief that being right-handed is best, an example of the *difference-equals-deficit error*, explained in Chapter 1. Consider language. In English, a "left-handed compliment" is insincere, and no one wants to have "two left feet" or to be "out in left field." In Latin, *dexter* (as in *dexterity*) means "right" and *sinister* means "left" (and also "evil"). *Gauche,* the French word for *left,* means "socially awkward" in English. Many languages are written from left to right, which is easier for right-handed people.

The design of doorknobs, scissors, baseball mitts, instrument panels, and other objects favor the right hand. (Some manufacturers have special versions for lefties, but few young children know to ask for them.) In many Asian and African cultures, the left hand is used only for wiping after defecation; it is an insult to give someone anything with that "dirty" hand.

Developmentalists advise against switching a child's handedness, not only because this causes adult–child conflicts and may create confusion in the brain but also because left lateralization is an advantage in some professions, especially those involving creativity and split-second actions. A disproportionate number of artists, musicians, and sports stars were/are left-handed, including Michelangelo, Seal, Jimi Hendrix, Paul McCartney, Larry Bird, and Sandy Koufax. Four of the past six presidents of the United States were/are lefties: Ronald Reagan, Jimmy Carter, Bill Clinton, and Barack Obama (John McCain is also left-handed).

Acceptance of left-handedness is more widespread now than a century ago. That might explain why more adults in Great Britain and the United States claim to be left-handed today (about 10 percent) than in 1900 (about 3 percent) (McManus et al., 2010). There also seem to be more left-handed men than women, as well as more left-handers in North America than elsewhere.

The Whole Brain

Astonishing studies of humans whose corpus callosa are severed in a procedure that relieves severe epilepsy, as well as research on humans and other vertebrates with intact corpus callosa, have revealed how the brain's hemispheres specialize. Typically, the brain's left half controls the body's right side as well as areas dedicated to logical reasoning, detailed analysis, and the basics of language; the brain's right half controls the body's left side and areas dedicated to emotional and creative impulses, including appreciation of music, art, and poetry. Thus, the left side notices details and the right side grasps the big picture—a distinction that provides a clue in interpreting Figure 8.4.

This left–right distinction has been exaggerated, especially when broadly applied to people (Hugdahl & Westerhausen, 2010). No one is exclusively left-brained or right-brained (except severely brain-damaged individuals); moreover, the brain is flexible, especially in childhood, so a lost function of one hemisphere is sometimes replaced in the other hemisphere.

For most people, both sides of the brain are involved in almost every skill. That is why the corpus callosum is crucial: It connects the left and right hemispheres. As myelination of the corpus callosum progresses, signals between the two hemispheres become quicker and clearer, enabling children to become better thinkers

>> Response for Early-Childhood Teachers (from page 230) One solution is to remind yourself that the children's brains are not yet myelinated enough to enable them to quickly walk, talk, or even button their jackets. Maturation has a major effect, as you will observe if you can schedule excursions in September and again in April. Progress, while still slow, will be a few seconds faster in April than it was in September.

and less clumsy. To pick an easy example: No 2-year-old has the balance to hop on one foot, but most 6-year-olds can do it—an example of brain balancing. Many songs, dances, and games that young children love involve moving their bodies in some coordinated way—difficult, but fun because of that.

Planning and Analyzing

You learned in Chapter 5 that the *prefrontal cortex* (sometimes called the *frontal cortex* or *frontal lobe*) is an area in the front part of the brain's outer layers (the cortex), just behind the forehead. The prefrontal cortex is crucial; it is called the *executive* of the brain because the planning, prioritizing, and reflection that occur in the prefrontal cortex govern the rest of the brain.

For example, someone might feel anxious on meeting a new person whose friendship could be valuable. The prefrontal cortex can calculate and plan, not letting the anxious feelings ruin the interaction. Young children are much less adept than adults at social understanding and planning because their prefrontal cortexes are immature (Kolb & Whishaw, 2008). For example, when a stranger greets them, many 2-year-olds are speechless, hiding behind their mothers if possible; adults may feel equally shy, but they bravely respond.

Brain maturation is partly genetic, but early experience matters (Lenroot & Giedd, 2008). Control of anxiety, for instance, depends not only on age and temperament but also on caregiver patience and guidance. Brain scans of the prefrontal cortex and amygdala (soon described) taken at age 18 may show inhibition, but most inhibited adults no longer act in extremely anxious ways (Schwartz et al., 2010). Emotional regulation is further discussed in Chapter 10.

Maturation of the Prefrontal Cortex

The frontal lobe continues to develop for many years after early childhood; dendrite density and myelination continue to increase in emerging adulthood (Johnson, 2005). Nonetheless, advances in neurological control between ages 2 and 6 are evident in several ways:

- Sleep becomes more regular.
- Emotions become more nuanced and responsive.
- Temper tantrums subside.
- Uncontrollable laughter and tears are less common.

One example of the maturing prefrontal cortex is how children play the game Simon Says. Players are supposed to follow the leader *only* when orders are preceded by the words "Simon says." Thus, if leaders touch their noses and say, "Simon says touch your nose," players are supposed to touch their noses; but when leaders touch their noses and say, "Touch your nose," no one is supposed to follow the example. Young children quickly lose at this game because they impulsively do what they see and hear. Older children can think before acting. The prefrontal cortex works!

Such advances can be observed in every child. Might experience rather than brain maturation be the reason? A convincing demonstration that something neurological, not experiential, is the primary reason for these changes comes from a series of experiments in which 3-year-olds consistently make a stunning mistake that disappears by age 5. Children are given a set of cards with clear outlines of trucks or flowers, some red and some blue. They are asked to "play the shape game," putting trucks in one pile and flowers in another. Three-year-olds (and even some 2-year-olds) can do this correctly.

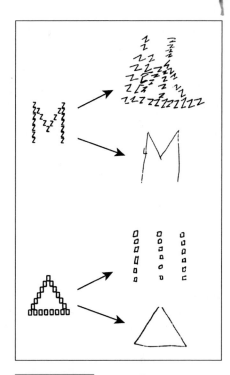

FIGURE 8.4

Copy What You See Brain-damaged adults were asked to copy the leftmost figure in each panel. One person drew the top set; another, the set at the bottom.

Observation Quiz Which set was drawn by someone with left-side damage and which set by someone with right-side damage? (see answer, page 234)

Then children are asked to "play the color game," sorting the cards by color. Most children under age 4 fail. Instead they sort by shape, as they had done before. This basic test has been replicated in many nations; 3-year-olds usually get stuck in their initial sorting pattern. Most older children make the switch.

When this result was first obtained, experimenters thought perhaps the children didn't know their colors; so the scientists switched the order, first playing "the color game." Most 3-year-olds did that correctly. Then, when they were asked to play "the shape game," they still sorted by color. Even with a new set of cards, such as yellow and green or rabbits and boats, 3-year-olds still tend to sort however they did originally, either by color or shape.

Researchers are looking into many possible explanations for this result (Marcovitch et al., 2010; Müller et al., 2006; Yerys & Munakata, 2006). All agree, however, that something in the cortex must mature before children are able to switch from one way of sorting objects to another. (Maturation of the prefrontal cortex is also discussed in Chapters 5, 11, and 14.)

Impulsiveness and Perseveration

Neurons have only two kinds of impulses: on–off, or activate–inhibit. Each is signaled by biochemical messages from dendrites to axons to neurons. Both activation and inhibition are necessary for thoughtful adults, who neither leap too quickly nor hesitate too long. (A balanced brain is most effective throughout life: One explanation of cognitive loss in late adulthood is that older people are too cautious or too impulsive.)

Many young children have not yet found the balance. They are impulsive, flitting from one activity to another. That explains why many 3-year-olds cannot stay quietly on one task, even in "circle time" in an early-childhood preschool, where each child is supposed to sit in place, not talking or touching anyone else. In another example, some young children want a toy that another child has but then lose interest when the toy becomes available. Few 3-year-olds are capable of the sustained attention that is required in most primary schools.

During the same age period, some children play with a single toy for hours. **Perseveration** refers to the tendency to persevere in, or stick to, one thought or action—evident in the card-sorting study just described (Hanania, 2010). Although many explanations are plausible, the fact that young children sometimes perseverate is apparent to anyone who hears a young child repeat one phrase or question again and again or who witnesses a tantrum when a child is told to stop something he or she was doing. (Wise teachers give a warning—"Cleanup in five minutes"—which sometimes helps.) The tantrum itself may perseverate. Crying may become uncontrollable; the child seems stuck in the emotion that triggered the tantrum.

Impulsiveness and perseveration are opposite manifestations of the same underlying cause: immaturity of the prefrontal cortex. No young child is perfect at regulating attention; impulsiveness and perseveration are evident in every 2-year-old (Else-Quest et al., 2006).

Over the years of childhood, from ages 2 to 12, brain maturation (innate) and emotional regulation (learned) increase: Most children become able to pay attention and switch activities as needed. By early adolescence, children change tasks at the sound of the bell—no perseveration allowed. Exceptions include children diagnosed with attention-deficit/hyperactivity disorder (ADHD), who are too impulsive for their age as well as too resistant to change. An imbalance between the left and right sides of the prefrontal cortex and abnormal growth of the corpus callosum seem to underlie (and perhaps cause) ADHD (Gilliam et al., 2011).

perseveration The tendency to persevere in, or stick to, one thought or action for a long time.

>> **Answer to Observation Quiz** (from page 233) In each pair, the copy on the top, with its careful details, reflects damage to the right half of the brain, where overall impressions are formed. The person with left-brain damage produced the copies that were just an M or a △, without the details of the tiny z's and rectangles. With a whole functioning brain, people can see both "the forest and the trees."

As with all biological maturation, some of this is related to culture—hence the reason this chapter is called *biosocial development*, not simply *physical development*. A study of Korean preschoolers found that they had earlier attention control and less perseveration than a comparable group of English children (Oh & Lewis, 2008). This study included the shape–color task: Of the 3-year-olds, 40 percent of Korean children but only 14 percent of British children successfully shifted from sorting by shape to sorting by color. The researchers explored many possible explanations, including genes, but concluded that "a cultural explanation is more likely" (Oh & Lewis, 2008, p. 96).

Emotions and the Brain

Now that we have considered the prefrontal cortex, we turn to another region of the brain, sometimes called the *limbic system,* the major region for emotions. Emotional expression and emotional regulation advance during early childhood (more about that in Chapter 10). Crucial to that advance are three major areas of the limbic system—the amygdala, the hippocampus, and the hypothalamus.

Three Brain Parts

The **amygdala** is a tiny structure deep in the brain, named after an almond because it is about the same shape and size. It registers emotions, both positive and negative, especially fear (Kolb & Whishaw, 2008). Increased amygdala activity is one reason some young children have terrifying nightmares or sudden terrors, overwhelming the prefrontal cortex and disrupting reason. A child may refuse to enter an elevator or hide when it thunders. The amygdala responds to comfort but not to logic. If a child is terrified of, say, a lion in the closet, an adult should not laugh but might open the closet door and command the lion to go home.

Another structure in the brain's limbic system, the **hippocampus,** is located right next to the amygdala. A central processor of memory, especially memory for locations, the hippocampus responds to the anxieties of the amygdala by summoning memory. A child can remember, for instance, whether previous elevator riding was scary or fun. Memories of location are fragile in early childhood because the hippocampus is still developing. Nonetheless, deep emotional memories from early childhood can interfere with expressed, rational thinking: An adult might have a panic attack but not know why.

The interaction of the amygdala and the hippocampus is sometimes helpful, sometimes not; fear can be constructive or destructive (LaBar, 2007). Studies performed on some animals show that when the amygdala is surgically removed, the animals are fearless in situations that should scare them; for instance, a cat will stroll nonchalantly past monkeys—something no normal cat would do (Kolb & Whishaw, 2008).

A third part of the limbic system, the **hypothalamus,** responds to signals from the amygdala (arousing) and to signals from the hippocampus (usually dampening) by producing cortisol and other hormones that activate parts of the brain and body (see Figure 8.5). Ideally, this hormone production occurs in moderation (Tarullo & Gunnar, 2006).

As the limbic system develops, young children watch their parents' emotions closely. If a parent looks worried when entering an elevator, the child may fearfully cling to the parent when the elevator moves. If this sequence recurs often

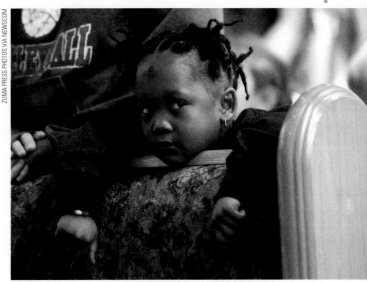

Ashes to Ashes, Dust to Dust Many religious rituals have sustained humans of all ages for centuries, including listening quietly in church on Ash Wednesday—as Nailah Pierre tries to do. This is developmentally difficult for young children, but for three reasons she probably will succeed: (1) gender (girls mature earlier than boys), (2) experience (she has been in church many times), and (3) social context (she is one of 750 students in her school attending a special service at Nativity Catholic church).

amygdala A tiny brain structure that registers emotions, particularly fear and anxiety.

hippocampus A brain structure that is a central processor of memory, especially memory for locations.

Especially for Neurologists Why do many experts think the limbic system is an oversimplification? (see response, page 237)

hypothalamus A brain area that responds to the amygdala and the hippocampus to produce hormones that activate other parts of the brain and body.

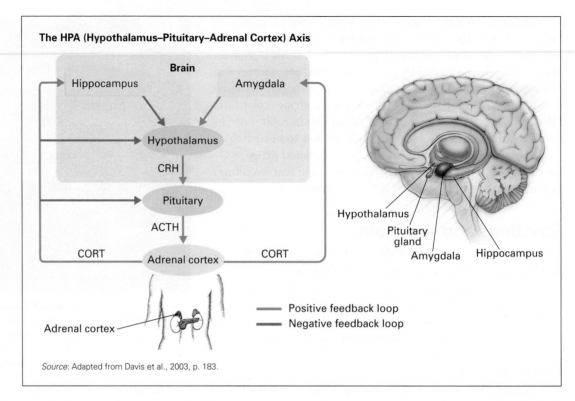

The HPA (Hypothalamus–Pituitary–Adrenal Cortex) Axis

Source: Adapted from Davis et al., 2003, p. 183.

FIGURE 8.5

A Hormonal Feedback Loop This diagram simplifies a hormonal linkage, the HPA (hypothalamus–pituitary–adrenal) axis. Both the hippocampus and the amygdala stimulate the hypothalamus to produce CRH (corticotropin-releasing hormone), which in turn signals the pituitary gland to produce ACTH (adrenocorticotropic hormone). ACTH then triggers the production of CORT (glucocorticoids) by the adrenal cortex (the outer layers of the adrenal glands, atop the kidneys). Fear may either build or disappear, depending on other factors, including how the various parts of the brain interpret that first alert from the amygdala.

enough, the child's amygdala may become hypersensitive to elevators, as fear joins the hippocampus in remembering a specific location, and the result is increased cortisol. If, instead, the parent seems calm and makes elevator riding fun (letting the child push the buttons, for instance), the child will overcome initial feelings of fear, and the limbic system will be aroused to enjoy elevators—even when there is no need to go from floor to floor.

Knowing the varieties of fears and joys is helpful when a teacher takes a group of young children on a trip. To stick with the elevator example, one child might be terrified while another child might rush forward, pushing the close button before the teacher enters. Every experience (elevators, fire engines, animals at the zoo, a police officer) is likely to trigger a range of emotions, without much reflection, in a group of 3-year-olds: A field trip requires several adults, ready to respond to whatever the experience evokes.

Stress and the Limbic System

As you remember from previous chapters, excessive cortisol (the primary stress hormone) may flood the brain and destroy part of the hippocampus. Permanent deficits in learning and memory may result as "children exposed to traumatic or stressful events have an increased probability of developing major depression, post-traumatic stress disorder, and attention-deficit/hyperactivity" (Garcia-Segura, 2009, p. 169).

Yet stress may be helpful instead of harmful. Ongoing research seeks to discover exactly how and when stress harms the human brain (Loman et al., 2010). Emotionally arousing experiences—meeting new friends, entering school, visiting a strange place—seem beneficial if a young child has someone or something to moderate the stress.

In an experiment, brain scans and hormone measurements were taken of 4- to 6-year-olds immediately after a fire alarm. Some children were upset; some not, as measured by their levels of cortisol. Two weeks later, either a friendly or a stern adult questioned them about the event. Those with higher cortisol reactions to the alarm remembered more details than did those with less stress, which suggests that some stress aided memory. Another finding was that, for all the children, memory was better with a friendly interviewer (Quas et al., 2004).

Other research also finds that preschoolers remember experiences better when an interviewer is warm and attentive (Bruck et al., 2006). Context is crucial: Stress can facilitate memory and cognitive growth if adults are reassuring.

However, because developing brains are fragile, "prolonged physiological responses to stress and challenge put children at risk for a variety of problems in childhood, including physical and mental disorders, poor emotional regulation, and cognitive impairments" (Quas et al., 2004, p. 797). Such problems originating in early development of the limbic system may impair health decades later (Shonkoff et al., 2009).

Studies of children who have been maltreated suggest that excessive stress hormones in early childhood may permanently damage the limbic system, blunting or accelerating emotional responses lifelong (Wilson et al., 2011). But this research is not definitive because, as you remember from Chapter 1, correlation does not prove causation. Ethics precludes experiments that severely stress children. However, research with mice suggests that the relationship between early stress and abnormal brain development is causal, not merely correlational.

Sadly, this topic leads again to research on those adopted Romanian children mentioned in Chapter 7. When they saw pictures of happy, sad, frightened, or angry faces, their limbic systems were less reactive than were those of Romanian children living with their biological parents. Their brains were also less lateralized, suggesting less specialized, less efficient thinking (Parker & Nelson, 2005). Thus, early stress had probably damaged their brains.

Romania no longer permits wholesale international adoptions. Nonetheless, there are still many Romanian children in institutions. In one study, some were randomly assigned to foster homes at about age 2 whereas others were not. By age 4, those in foster homes were smarter (by about 10 IQ points) than those who remained institutionalized (Nelson et al., 2007). This research suggests that ages 2 to 4 may be a sensitive time for the brain, at least for the brain growth that is measured by IQ tests, primarily language and memory.

"I would share, but I'm not there developmentally."

Good Excuse It is true that emotional control of selfish instincts is difficult for young children because the prefrontal cortex is not yet mature enough to regulate some emotions. However, family practices can advance social understanding.

SUMMING UP

The brain continues to mature during early childhood. Myelination is notable in several crucial areas. One is the corpus callosum, which connects the left and right sides of the brain and therefore the right and left sides of the body. Increased myelination speeds up bodily actions and reactions. Furthermore, the prefrontal cortex enables a balance between action and inhibition, allowing children to think before they act as well as to stop one action in order to begin another. As impulsiveness and perseveration decrease, children become better able to learn.

Several key areas of the brain—including the amygdala, the hippocampus, and the hypothalamus—make up the limbic system, which matures from ages 2 to 6, aiding emotional expression and control. Children whose early experiences were highly stressful and who lacked nurturing caregivers may have impaired limbic systems. ∎

>> **Response for Neurologists** (from page 235) The more we discover about the brain, the more complex we realize it is. Each part has specific functions and is connected to every other part.

The Joy of Climbing Would you delight in climbing on an unsteady rope swing, like this 6-year-old in Japan (and almost all his contemporaries worldwide)? Each age has special sources of pleasure.

DIGITAL VISION / PUNCHSTOCK

>> Improved Motor Skills

Maturation of the prefrontal cortex improves impulse control, while myelination of the corpus callosum and lateralization of the brain permit better physical coordination. No wonder children move with greater speed and grace as they age from 2 to 6, becoming better able to direct and refine their actions. (At About This Time lists approximate ages for the acquisition of various motor skills in early childhood.)

Mastery of gross and fine motor skills is one result of the extensive, active play of young children, true everywhere. A study in Brazil, Kenya, and the United States tracked how young children spend their time. Some cultural variations and differences based on socioeconomic status (SES) emerged—for example, compared to their peers, middle-class European American children did the most talk-

AT ABOUT THIS TIME
Motor Skills at Ages 2–6*

Approximate Age	Skill or Achievement
2 years	Run for pleasure without falling (but bumping into things) Climb chairs, tables, beds, out of cribs Walk up stairs Feed self with spoon Draw lines, spirals
3 years	Kick and throw a ball Jump with both feet off the floor Pedal a tricycle Copy simple shapes (e.g., circle, rectangle) Walk down stairs Climb ladders
4 years	Catch a ball (not too small or thrown too fast) Use scissors to cut Hop on either foot Feed self with fork Dress self (no tiny buttons, no ties) Copy most letters Pour juice without spilling Brush teeth
5 years	Skip and gallop in rhythm Clap, bang, sing in rhythm Copy difficult shapes and letters (e.g., diamond shape, letter *S*) Climb trees, jump over things Use knife to cut Tie a bow Throw a ball Wash face, comb hair
6 years	Draw and paint with preferred hand Write simple words Scan a page of print, moving the eyes systematically in the appropriate direction Ride a bicycle Do a cartwheel Tie shoes Catch a ball

*Context and culture are crucial for acquisition of all these skills. For example, many 6-year-olds cannot tie shoelaces because they have no shoes with laces.

ing with adults, and working-class Kenyan children did the most chores. But at every income level in all three nations, children spent more time playing than doing anything else—chores, lessons, or conversations with adults (Tudge et al., 2006).

Gross Motor Skills

Gross motor skills improve dramatically during early childhood. When playing, many 2-year-olds fall down and bump clumsily into each other, but some 5-year-olds are skilled and graceful, performing coordinated dance steps or sports moves.

Specific Skills

Most North American 5-year-olds can ride a tricycle, climb a ladder, and pump a swing, as well as throw, catch, and kick a ball. Some can skate, ski, dive, and ride a bicycle—activities that demand balance and coordination of both brain hemispheres. In some nations, 5-year-olds swim in oceans or climb cliffs. Brain maturation, motivation, and guided practice make these skills possible.

Adults need to make sure children have safe spaces, time, and playmates; skills will follow. According to sociocultural theory, children learn best from peers who demonstrate whatever skills the child is ready to try—from catching a ball to climbing a tree. Of course, culture and locale influence which skills children display—some small children learn to ski, others to sail.

Recent urbanization concerns many developmentalists. Compared with a century ago, when almost all children played together in empty lots or fields without adult supervision, half the world's children now live in cities. Many of these are "megacities . . . overwhelmed with burgeoning slums and environmental problems" (Ash et al., 2008, p. 739). Crowded, violent streets not only impede development of gross motor skills but also add to the natural fears of the immature limbic system.

The next generation of young children may have few older playmates and no safe space to practice motor skills. Gone are the days when parents told their children to go out and play, expecting them safely back when hunger, weather, or nightfall brought them home. Now parents fear strangers, cars, trucks, and stray animals and therefore keep their 3- to 5-year-olds inside, perhaps watching television or playing video games but not developing gross motor skills (Taylor et al., 2009). Preschool programs have many things to recommend them: Motor-skill development is one.

Environmental Hazards

Pollutants do more harm to young, growing brains and bodies than to older, more developed ones; they are of particular concern for urban young children. Much depends on local regulations. For example, in India, one city of 14 million (Kolkata, formerly Calcutta) has such extensive air pollution that childhood asthma rates are soaring and lung damage is prevalent. In another Indian city (Mumbai, formerly Bombay), air pollution has been reduced and children's health improved through

CHIEN-MIN CHUNG/ GETTY IMAGES

Could Your Child Do This? Perhaps. If acrobatics was your family's passion, you might encourage your child to practice, and years later, your child could stretch like Bola, a young girl from Kovd, Mongolia. Everywhere, young children try to do whatever their parents do.

Observation Quiz Was this photo taken in the United States? (see answer, page 241)

Exploring the Great Outdoors Two children climb over a rock outcrop in Shenandoah National Park in Virginia. Such outdoor play is important for the development of motor skills, even though many parents are tempted to try to keep their children safer by keeping them indoors.

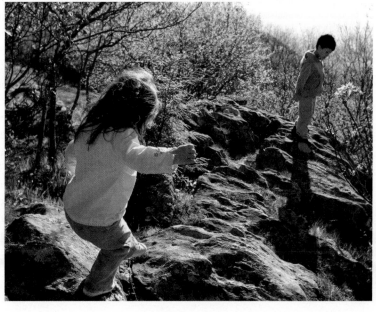

JEFF GREENBERG / THE IMAGE WORKS

several measures, including an extensive system of public buses that are required to use clean fuels (Bhattacharjee, 2008).

Asthma has many causes, and, once it occurs, attacks can be precipitated by several substances and circumstances that almost every child experiences, from dust to cold weather. Causes and consequences of childhood asthma are discussed in detail in Chapter 11, but connecting asthma and pollution in India requires mention of the complexity of pinpointing the effects of pollution on health. One major complication is that children from low-SES families are more likely to live in areas of high pollution—in cities with smog, near major highways or industrial plants, and so on. If they are in poor health, or slow to talk, or low in school achievement, that could be the direct result of air pollution on their bodies and brains, or it could be the result of several other circumstances that are more common in low-SES families.

Scientists have grappled with this complication and found that environmental substances cause as well as correlate with health problems in young children of families at every SES level. For example, one study in British Columbia, where pollution is relatively low and universal public health care and birth records allow solid research, found that air pollution from traffic and industry early in life was a cause, not just a correlate, of asthma during the preschool years (Clark et al., 2010). (See the Research Design.)

One complication is that the particles in the air that harm health are not necessarily the particles that people consider to be pollution. For example, burning wood makes smoke that is easy to see and smell, but according to that British Columbia study, wood smoke did not increase asthma. Of course, this conclusion may apply only to the particular kind of wood that is burned in western Canada—another research complication.

Respiratory problems are not the only early-childhood complications that may be caused by pollution. Research on lower animals suggests that hundreds of substances in the air, food, and water affect the brain and thus impede balance, finger dexterity, and motivation. The data are not clear-cut, leading one research team to implore that "developmental researchers direct basic and applied research about the effects of pollutant exposures and ways to reduce children's pollutant burdens" (Dilworth-Bart & Moore, 2006, p. 264). These researchers particularly stress the need to examine the effects of low doses of lead and pesticides on children of low-income and ethnic-minority families, as such children are most likely to be exposed as well as most vulnerable for a host of reasons.

Some substances—including lead in the water and air, pesticides in the soil or on clothing, bisphenol A (BPA) in plastic, and secondhand cigarette smoke—are already proven to be harmful to any child. Lead has been thoroughly researched at high exposure and has been found to reduce intelligence and increase behavior problems in young children.

Over the past 20 years, U.S. regulations have reduced the amount of lead in paint, gasoline, and manufacturing, and

---

▶ Research Design

Scientists: Nina Annika Clark, Paul A. Demers, Catherine J. Karr, Mieke Koehoorn, Cornel Lencar, Lillian Tamburic, and Michael Brauer.

Publication: *Environmental Health Perspectives* (2010).

Participants: This study began with all births in southwest British Columbia (which includes Vancouver) in 1999 and 2000, a total of 59,917 babies. After excluding newborns with characteristics known to increase asthma risk (e.g., low birthweight) and those without sufficient data, 37,401 newborns were studied for three years. Among those, the researchers found 3,482 who, by age 4, had been hospitalized for asthma at least once, or had been diagnosed with asthma at least twice by a physician. As part of the research, each of those 3,482 was matched by SES, gender, and so on with five other children from the same cohort.

Design: Exposure to air pollution was measured by detailing the air pollution on the particular block where each child with asthma and his or her five matches lived. Many pollutants were included: carbon monoxide (CO), nitrogen oxides (nitric oxide [NO] and nitrogen dioxide [NO_2]), particulate matter ($\leq$ 10 micrometers and $\leq$ 2.5 micrometers in aerodynamic diameter [PM_{10} and $PM_{2.5}$]), ozone (O_3), sulfur dioxide (SO_2), black carbon, and wood smoke. Researchers also noted whether the mother smoked cigarettes as well as how close the residence was to major roads and factories that released pollutants in the air. The exposure of the children with asthma was compared with the exposure of the matched controls.

Major conclusion: Every subgroup category (such as high, middle, or low SES; breast- or formula-fed; ethnic background) had some children with asthma, although rates varied. For example, high-SES, breast-fed girls had lower rates of asthma than did low-SES, formula-fed boys. However, no matter what a particular child's background, air pollution, particularly from cars and trucks, increased the incidence of asthma. The extensive controls and matching in this study also revealed that some factors hypothesized to increase asthma did not do so, among them proximity to highways, birth to a First Nations family, birth to a mother not born in Canada, exposure to wood smoke, and having a mother who smoked. (On exposure to cigarette smoke, the researchers note that, unlike most of the measures, the only indicator of maternal smoking was the mother's admission.)

Comments: Strengths of this study include the conscientious and detailed measures, including air pollution block by block, wood smoke by season, an entire cohort with government health and population records, and the matched-control design. This raises a question: What results would be found in a region with higher pollution? Perhaps genes protect most children, even in high pollution areas, or perhaps the advantages of being a girl or being breast-fed disappear if pollution reaches a certain level. Further research is needed.

children's blood lead levels have dropped sharply—in some states (e.g., Colorado and Wyoming) the average is now close to zero. In other states (e.g., Michigan and Ohio) average lead levels are still too high, defined as above 10 micrograms per deciliter of blood among children under age 6 (MMWR, May 27, 2005). Some sources of lead remain unregulated, including lead in city water (from old pipes), in manufacturing, and in jet fuel. It is not known precisely how high blood levels of lead must be before harm occurs, but some scientists are convinced that even 5 micrograms per deciliter is probably too much (Cole & Winsler, 2010).

Lead must be reduced by laws and policies, but parents can take action as well. Specifics include increasing children's consumption of calcium, wiping window ledges clean of dust, testing drinking water, and making sure the child never eats peeling chips of lead-based paint (still found in old buildings) (Dilworth-Bart & Moore, 2006). Although scientists, laws, and parents have raised awareness about the dangers of lead exposure for young brains, the administrator of environmental public health for the state of Oregon says, "We simply do not know—as scientists, as regulators, as health professionals—the health impacts of the soup of chemicals to which we expose human beings" (Shibley, quoted in Johnson, 2011). Whether you think Shibley is needlessly alarmist or stating the obvious depends on your own perspective.

Fine Motor Skills

Fine motor skills, especially small movements of the hands and fingers, are harder to master than gross motor skills. Pouring juice into a glass, cutting food with a knife and fork, and achieving anything more artful than a scribble with a pencil all require a level of muscular control, patience, and judgment that are beyond most 2-year-olds.

Many fine motor skills involve two hands and thus both sides of the brain: The fork stabs the meat while the knife cuts it; one hand steadies the paper while the other writes; tying shoes, buttoning shirts, cutting paper, and zipping zippers require both hands. An immature corpus callosum and prefrontal cortex may be the underlying reason that shoelaces get knotted, paper gets ripped, and zippers get stuck. Short, stubby fingers add to the problem. As with gross motor skills, practice and maturation are key; thus, making things with glue, markers, and scraps of cloth are part of the curriculum for preschools. Puzzles—with large pieces of splinter-proof wood—are essential supplies.

Traditional academic learning also depends on fine motor skills and body control. Writing requires finger control, reading a line of print requires eye control, sitting for hours at a desk requires bladder control, and so on. These are beyond most young children, so even the brightest 3-year-old is not allowed in first grade, and some slower-developing 6-year-olds are frustrated if their teachers expect them to write neatly and cut straight.

Fine motor skills—like many other biological characteristics, such as bones, brains, and teeth—typically mature about six months earlier in girls than in boys. This may be one reason why girls typically outperform boys on elementary school tests of school achievement and many young girls consider boys "stupid." Some educators suggest waiting until a child is "ready" for school; others suggest that school expectations should adjust to the immaturity of the child, a controversy explored in Chapter 9.

>> Answer to Observation Quiz (from page 239) No—not because of ethnicity (many U.S. citizens are of Indian descent) but because of child labor laws. This duo is part of a circus (note the rigging), and no child in North America is allowed to perform such feats for pay.

Especially for Immigrant Parents You and your family eat with chopsticks at home, but you want your children to feel comfortable in Western culture. Should you change your family's eating customs? (see response, page 243)

Admirable Skill Lenny feeds herself with knife and fork, using carefully placed fingers. This fine motor skill is achieved by 5-year-olds worldwide if their culture encourages it and if they have time to practice and observe (as Willy does).

Observation Quiz How can you tell that this does not depict American culture? (see answer, page 243)

AP PHOTO / MATTHIAS RIETSCHE

Careful Cutting For a left-handed 5-year-old with poor vision, is this task necessary practice or needless frustration?

Singing or Screaming Don't judge a picture by what you see, judge it by the intent of the artist. This 4-year-old's smiling pride and the heart-shaped head suggest a happy picture.

Artistic Expression

Young children are imaginative, creative, and not yet self-critical. They love to express themselves, especially if their parents applaud their performances, display their artwork, and otherwise communicate approval. The fact that their fine motor skills are immature, and that their drawings thus lack precision, is not yet important. Perhaps the immaturity of the prefrontal cortex is a blessing: It allows creativity without anxiety (an older child might say, "I can't draw" or "I am horrible at dancing").

All forms of artistic expression blossom during early childhood. Psychologists disagree as to whether drawings reflect children's emotions (Burkitt, 2004). But there is no doubt that 2- to 6-year-olds love to dance around the room, build an elaborate tower of blocks, make music by pounding in rhythm, and put bright marks on shiny paper. In every artistic domain, skill gradually comes with practice and maturation. For example, when drawing a person, 2- to 3-year-olds usually draw a "tadpole"—a circle head, dots for eyes, sometimes a smiling mouth, and then a line or two beneath to indicate the rest of the body. Gradually, tadpoles get bodies, limbs, hair, and so on.

Cultural and cohort differences are apparent. For the most part, Chinese culture incorporates the idea that drawing benefits from instruction, so young children are guided in how best to draw a person, a house, and—most important for the Chinese—a word. By age 9, Chinese children draw more advanced pictures than children of other cultures, where artistic guidance is uncommon. Adult encouragement, child practice, and developing technical skill correlate with more mature, creative drawings a few years later (Chan & Zhao, 2010; Huntsinger et al., 2011).

SUMMING UP

Maturation of the brain leads to better hand and body control. Gross motor skills advance every year as long as young children have space to play, older children to emulate, and freedom from environmental toxins. Pollution and fear of strangers reduce the opportunity many contemporary children have to develop gross motor skills. Children also develop their fine motor skills, which prepares them for the many requirements of formal education. They love to dance, draw, and build, which help in the gradual mastery of finger movements, which will in turn be essential when they start to write. ■

>> Injuries and Abuse

In almost all families of every income, ethnicity, and nation, parents want to protect their children while fostering their growth. Yet more children die of violence—either accidental or deliberate—than from any specific disease.

The contrast is most obvious in developed nations, where medical prevention, diagnosis, and treatment make fatal illness rare until late adulthood. In the United States in 2007, out of every 100,000 1- to 4-year-olds, only 2.2 died of cancer (the leading fatal disease at this age), but 9.6 died accidentally and 2.5 were murdered (National Center for Health Statistics, 2011). Some nations have fewer violent deaths than the United States. In Canada, the comparable rates for 1- to 4-year-olds were 2.6 (cancer), 5.2 (accidents), and 0.5 (murder) (Statistics Canada, 2011). In every nation, more young children die from accidents than from any other specific cause.

Avoidable Injury

Worldwide, injuries cause millions of premature deaths among adults as well as children: Not until age 40 does any specific disease overtake accidents as a cause of mortality, and worldwide 14 percent of all life-years lost are caused by injury (World Health Organization, 2010). In some nations, malnutrition, malaria, and other infectious diseases *combined* cause more infant and child deaths than injuries do, but everywhere children die from preventable accidents.

Nations with high rates of child disease also have high rates of child injury: India, for example, has one of the highest rates worldwide of child motor-vehicle deaths; most children who die in such accidents are pedestrians (Naci et al., 2009). Everywhere, 2- to 6-year-olds are at even greater risk than slightly older children. In the United States, for instance, children are twice as likely to be seriously hurt in early childhood as in middle childhood (Safe Kids USA, 2008).

Age-Related Dangers

Why are 2- to 6-year-olds so vulnerable? Some of the reasons have just been explained. Immaturity of the prefrontal cortex makes young children impulsive; they plunge into danger. Unlike infants, their motor skills allow them to run, leap, scramble, and grab in a flash. Their curiosity is boundless; their impulses are uninhibited; if they do something forbidden, such as playing with matches and causing a fire, their limbic systems might cause them to hide instead of getting help.

Age-related trends are apparent in particulars. Falls are more often fatal for the very young (under 24 months) and very old (over 80 years); motor-vehicle deaths peak from ages 15 to 25. In developed nations, safety seats are required for children in cars, helmets protect bike riders, and cities have sidewalks, but fatal accidents in early childhood often involve poison, fire, or drowning (Safe Kids USA, 2008).

Injury Control

Instead of using the term *accident prevention*, public health experts prefer **injury control** (or **harm reduction**). Consider the implications of this terminology. *Accident* implies that an injury is a random, unpredictable event; if anyone is at fault, it's a careless parent or an accident-prone child. This is called the "accident paradigm"—as if "injuries will occur despite our best efforts," allowing the public to feel blameless (Benjamin, 2004, p. 521).

A better phrase is *injury control*, which implies that harm can be minimized with appropriate controls. Minor mishaps (scratches and bruises) are bound to occur, but serious injury is unlikely if a child falls on a safety surface instead of on concrete, if a car seat protects the body in a crash, if a bicycle helmet cracks instead of a skull, if swallowed pills come from a tiny bottle.

Only half as many 1- to 5-year-olds in the United States were fatally injured in 2005 as in 1985, thanks to laws that govern poisons, fires, and cars. Control has not yet caught up with some newer hazards, however. For instance, as more homes in California, Florida, Texas, and Arizona have swimming pools, drowning has become a leading cause of unintentional death among young children (Safe Kids USA, 2008).

Prevention

Prevention begins long before any particular child, parent, or politician does something foolish. Unfortunately, no one notices the injuries and deaths that did not happen. For developmentalists, two types of analysis are useful to uncover the primary causes of injuries.

>> **Response for Immigrant Parents** (from page 241) Children develop the motor skills that they see and practice. They will soon learn to use forks, spoons, and knives. Do not abandon chopsticks completely, because young children can learn several ways of doing things, and the ability to eat with chopsticks is a social asset.

>> **Answer to Observation Quiz** (from page 241) Lenny is using the fork with her left hand, as all good Germans do. This school is in Dresden.

injury control/harm reduction Practices that are aimed at anticipating, controlling, and preventing dangerous activities; these practices reflect the beliefs that accidents are not random and that injuries can be made less harmful if proper controls are in place.

One is called an *accident autopsy*. When a child is seriously injured, analysis can find causes in the microsystem and exosystem as well as in the macrosystem. For example, when a child is hit by a car, an autopsy might point to parental neglect (microsystem), but it might also note that there were no nearby parks, that cars drove too fast and traffic lights were absent, that sidewalks were too narrow and curbs too low (exosystem), or that the entire nation valued speedy vehicles more than slow pedestrians (macrosystem).

The second way to analyze is to look at statistics. For example, the rate of childhood poisoning has decreased since pill manufacturers adopted bottles with safety caps that are difficult for 2-year-olds to open—a statistic which supports that regulation when anyone complains about the cost and inconvenience. Some adults say that children today are overprotected, with fewer swings and jungle gyms, more safety surfaces and mandated car seats, and so on. Statistics, not anecdotes and memories ("I loved the metal playground equipment, and I am still alive"), can quiet such complaints.

Levels of Prevention

Three levels of prevention apply to every childhood health and safety issue, including injuries, neglect, and abuse.

- In **primary prevention,** the overall situation is structured to make harm less likely. Primary prevention fosters conditions that reduce everyone's chance of injury.
- **Secondary prevention** is more specific, averting harm in high-risk situations or for vulnerable individuals.
- **Tertiary prevention** begins after an injury has already occurred, limiting the damage it might cause.

In general, tertiary prevention is most visible, but primary prevention is most effective (Cohen et al., 2010). A good example of this comes from data on pedestrian deaths. Fewer people in the United States die after being hit by a motor vehicle than did 25 years ago (see Figure 8.6). How does each level of prevention contribute?

primary prevention Actions that change overall background conditions to prevent some unwanted event or circumstance, such as injury, disease, or abuse.

secondary prevention Actions that avert harm in a high-risk situation, such as stopping a car before it hits a pedestrian.

tertiary prevention Actions, such as immediate and effective medical treatment, that are taken after an adverse event (such as illness or injury) occurs and that are aimed at reducing the harm or preventing disability.

FIGURE 8.6

While the Population Grew This chart shows dramatic evidence that prevention measures are succeeding in the United States. Over the same time period, the total population has increased by about one-third, making these results even more impressive.

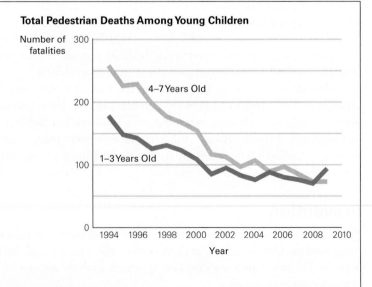

Source: United States Department of Transportation, 2010.

Primary prevention includes sidewalks, speed bumps, pedestrian overpasses, streetlights, and traffic circles (Retting et al., 2003; Tester et al., 2004). Cars have been redesigned (e.g., better headlights, bumpers, and brakes), and drivers' competence has improved (e.g., with stronger drunk-driving penalties and tougher licensing exams). If congestion is reduced via traffic regulations and improved mass transit, that is additional primary prevention.

Secondary prevention reduces danger in high-risk situations. Teachers know that they must hold the hand of a particular child when the group goes near the street. Flashing lights on stopped school buses and school-crossing guards are also secondary prevention. Salt on icy roads, warning signs before blind curves, and walk signals at busy intersections are also examples of secondary prevention because each is a high-risk situation that has special intervention.

Finally, *tertiary prevention* reduces damage after crashes, such as laws against hit-and-run drivers. Speedy ambulances, efficient emergency rooms, and effective rehabilitation are also tertiary. Medical personnel speak of the *golden hour* following an accident, when a victim should get to emergency care. Of course, there is nothing magical about 60 minutes in contrast to 61 minutes, but the faster an

Especially for Urban Planners Describe a neighborhood park that would benefit 2- to 5-year-olds. (see response, page 247)

(a)

(b)

(c)

And If He Falls . . . These could all be considered secondary prevention, as children need playgrounds away from cars *(a)*, five-point buckles in infant seats *(b)*, and adult supervision when they cross the street *(c)*. Furthermore, the children in photos *(b)* and *(c)* are well-protected—the Russian child wears a snowsuit, and the French teacher blocks traffic as the schoolchildren cross. But the U.S. child in photo *(a)* is climbing a seemingly rusted metal ladder, which could do serious injury. Fortunately, more current playground equipment is plastic.

Especially for Economists In the feature below, how did Kathleen Berger's SES protect Bethany from serious harm? (see response, page 248)

injury victim reaches a trauma center, the better the chance of survival (Bansal et al., 2009). Speed becomes part of tertiary prevention, reducing permanent harm, but primary and secondary prevention halt harm before it occurs.

A CASE TO STUDY

"My Baby Swallowed Poison"

The first strategy that most people think of to prevent injury to young children is to educate the parents. However, public health research finds that laws that apply to everyone are more effective than education, especially if parents are so overwhelmed by the daily demands of child care and money management that they do not realize they need to learn.

For example, infant car seats have saved thousands of lives. However, use of car seats is much less common when it is voluntary than when it is mandated. For that reason, car seats are now legally required.

Parents often consider safety a lower priority than everyday concerns. That explains two findings from the research: (1) The best time to convince parents to use a car seat is before they take their newborn home from the hospital, and (2) the best way to make sure a car seat is correctly used is to have an expert show the parent how it works—not simply tell them or make them watch a video (Tessier, 2010).

Motivation is key, yet "too often, we design our physical environment for smart people who are highly motivated" (S. P. Baker, 2000). But in real life, everyone has moments of foolish indifference, when automatic safety measures save lives.

I know this firsthand. Our daughter Bethany, at age 2, climbed onto the kitchen counter to find, open, and swallow most of a bottle of baby aspirin. Where was I? A few feet away, nursing our second child and watching television. I did not notice what Bethany was doing until I checked on her during a commercial.

Bethany is alive and well today, protected not by her foolish mother but by all three levels of prevention. Primary prevention included laws limiting the number of baby aspirin per container, secondary prevention included my pediatrician's written directions when Bethany was a week old to buy syrup of ipecac, and tertiary prevention was my phone call to Poison Control.

I told the helpful stranger who answered the phone, "My baby swallowed poison." He calmly asked me a few questions and then advised me to give Bethany ipecac to make her throw up. I did, and she did. I still blame myself, but I am grateful for all three levels of prevention that protected my child. I am also well aware that my SES helped avert a tragedy. I had chosen a wise pediatrician and I followed his advice; I had a phone and knew who to call. As I remember all the mistakes I made in parenting (only a few of them detailed in this book), I am grateful for every level of prevention.

Culture and Injury Prevention: Baby on the Plane

I once was the director of a small preschool, and I was struck by the diverse fears and prevention measures of the parents, some helpful and some not. Some were thrilled that our children painted, but others were worried about the ingredients of the paint, for instance. I know that all children need to grab, run, and explore to develop their motor skills as well as their minds, yet they also need to be prevented from falling down stairs, eating pebbles, or running into the street—as many are inclined to do. Adults may not know the best strategies to prevent injury. Consider what one mother wrote about her flight from Australia to California:

> I travelled with my 10-month-old daughter and was absolutely and thoroughly disappointed in the treatment we received from the flight crew captain at the time. I was told or more like instructed that I was to "restrain" my child for the whole flight, which was 13 hours.
>
> I said that other people were able to move around the plane freely, why wasn't she? I was told that due to turbulence she would have to be restrained for the whole trip. On several occasions the flight crew captain would make a point of going out of his way to almost scold me for not listening to him when I would put her down to crawl around.

[Retrieved April 3, 2011, from Complaints.com]

This same mother praised her treatment on other long flights, specifically on Asian airlines, when her child was allowed to move more freely and the crew was helpful. Which culture is better at protecting children without needlessly restraining them?

My sympathies were with the mother, and I had praise for the Asian crew, until I read this response:

> Consider the laws in the U.S. regarding child safety in an automobile. Nobody thinks a child should be free to crawl around in a car. No parent thinks their rights have been violated because their child is prevented from free flight inside a car when it impacts. Why not just put the child in the bed of a truck and drive around? . . . Her child could get stepped on, slammed against a seat leg, wedged under a seat, fallen on, etc.

Both sides in this dispute make sense, yet both cannot be right. The data prove that safety seats in cars save lives, but "impact" in planes is unlike that in a car crash. Statistical analysis is needed, or at least a case study of injured children on airplanes. Do passengers on planes step on crawling children? If so, is that controllable harm or a serious hazard?

Child Maltreatment

The next time you read headlines about some horribly neglected or abused child, think of these words from a leading researcher in child maltreatment:

> Make no mistake—those who abuse children are fully responsible for their actions. However, creating an information system that perpetuates the message that offenders are the only ones to blame may be misleading. . . . We all contribute to the conditions that allow perpetrators to succeed.
>
> *[Daro, 2002, p. 1133]*

"We all contribute" in the sense that the causes of child maltreatment are multifaceted, involving not only the parents but also the neighbors, the teachers, the medical community, the culture, and even the maltreated children themselves. Difficult infants (fragile, needing frequent feeding, crying often) are at greatest risk of being maltreated, especially if their mothers are depressed and feel they have no control over their lives. Family financial stress adds to the risk (Bugental & Happaney, 2004). Each of these factors could be mitigated or prevented by the community, through laws, practices, or direct help.

Maltreatment Noticed and Defined

Noticing is the first step. Until about 1960, people thought child maltreatment was rare and consisted of a sudden attack by a disturbed stranger. Today we know better, thanks to a pioneering study based on careful observation in one Boston hospital (Kempe & Kempe, 1978): Maltreatment is neither rare nor sudden, and 80 percent of the perpetrators are one or both of the child's own parents (Children's Bureau, 2010a). That makes the situation much worse: Ongoing maltreatment, with no protector, is much more damaging than a single incident, however injurious.

With this recognition came a broader definition: **Child maltreatment** now refers to all intentional harm to, or avoidable endangerment of, anyone under 18 years of age. Thus, child maltreatment includes both **child abuse,** which is deliberate action that is harmful to a child's physical, emotional, or sexual well-being,

>> **Response for Urban Planners** (from page 245): The adult idea of a park—a large, grassy open place—is not best for young children. For them, you would design an enclosed area, small enough and with adequate seating to allow caregivers to socialize while watching their children. The playground surface would have to be protective (since young children are clumsy), with equipment that encourages both gross motor skills (such as climbing) and fine motor skills (such as sandbox play). Swings are not beneficial, since they do not develop many motor skills. Teenagers and dogs should have their own designated area, far from the youngest children.

MISHAWAKA POLICE DEPARTMENT / GETTY IMAGES

Nobody Watching? Madelyn Gorman Toogood looks around to make sure no one is watching before she slaps and shakes her 4-year-old daughter, Martha, who is in a car seat inside the vehicle. A security camera recorded this incident in an Indiana department store parking lot. A week later, after the videotape was repeatedly broadcast nationwide, Toogood was recognized and arrested. The haunting question is: How much child abuse takes place that is not witnessed?

child maltreatment Intentional harm to or avoidable endangerment of anyone under 18 years of age.

child abuse Deliberate action that is harmful to a child's physical, emotional, or sexual well-being.

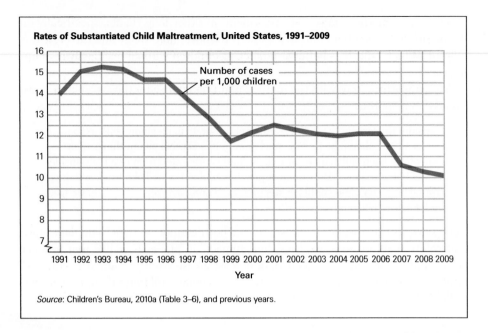

Rates of Substantiated Child Maltreatment, United States, 1991–2009

Number of cases per 1,000 children

Year

Source: Children's Bureau, 2010a (Table 3–6), and previous years.

FIGURE 8.7

Still Far Too Many The number of reported and substantiated cases of maltreatment of children under age 18 in the United States is too high, but there is some good news: The rate has declined significantly from its peak in 1993.

Observation Quiz The data point for 2009 is close to the bottom of the graph. Does that mean it is close to zero? (see answer, page 251)

child neglect Failure to meet a child's basic physical, educational, or emotional needs.

reported maltreatment Harm or endangerment about which someone has notified the authorities.

substantiated maltreatment Harm or endangerment that has been reported, investigated, and verified.

and **child neglect,** which is failure to meet a child's basic physical or emotional needs. The more that researchers study the long-term harm of child maltreatment, the worse neglect seems to be, especially in early childhood.

Reported maltreatment means that the authorities have been informed. Since 1993, the number of *reported* cases of maltreatment in the United States has ranged from about 2.7 million to 3.5 million a year (Children's Bureau, 2010b). **Substantiated maltreatment** means that a reported case has been investigated and verified (see Figure 8.7). With the exception of sexual abuse (discussed in Chapter 14), most victims are under age 6. The substantiated annual maltreatment rate in early childhood is about 1 maltreated child in every 80; the reported rate is triple that (U.S. Bureau of the Census, 2009).

The overall ratio of 3-to-1 for reported versus substantiated cases can be attributed to three factors:

1. Each child is counted once, even if repeated maltreatment is reported. Thus, five reports that are verified can lead to one substantiated case.
2. Substantiation requires proof in the form of unmistakable injuries, severe malnutrition, or a witness willing to testify. Such evidence is not always available.
3. A report may be deliberately false (though few are) (Kohl et al., 2009) or may describe a circumstance that was not the result of maltreatment.

Frequency of Maltreatment

How often does maltreatment occur? No one knows. Not all cases are noticed; not all are reported; not all reports are substantiated. Similar issues apply in every nation, city, and town, with marked variations in reports and confirmations. Reports have increased since 1950, but that does not mean that abuse has increased. U.S. laws now require teachers to report suspected maltreatment—reports have increased because of those laws. Official U.S. statistics find that substantiated child maltreatment increased from about 1960 to 1990 but decreased by 18 percent between 2000 and 2009 (see Figure 8.8). During those years, physical and sexual abuse declined but neglect increased. Other sources also report declines over the past two decades.

>> Response for Economists (from page 246) Children from families at all income levels have accidents, but Kathleen Berger's SES allowed her to have a private pediatrician as well as the income to buy ipecac "just in case." She also had a working phone and the education to know about Poison Control.

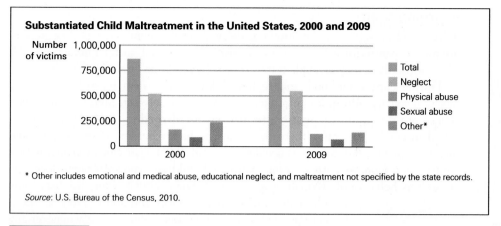

Substantiated Child Maltreatment in the United States, 2000 and 2009

Number of victims

Legend:
- Total
- Neglect
- Physical abuse
- Sexual abuse
- Other*

* Other includes emotional and medical abuse, educational neglect, and maltreatment not specified by the state records.

Source: U.S. Bureau of the Census, 2010.

FIGURE 8.8

Getting Better? As you can see, the number of victims of child maltreatment in the United States has declined in the past decade. The legal and social-work response to serious maltreatment has improved over these years, which is a likely explanation for the decline. Other, less sanguine, explanations are possible, however.

Observation Quiz Have all types of maltreatment declined since 2000? (see answer, page 251)

That is good news, but unfortunately official reports leave room for doubt. For example, Pennsylvania and Maine reported almost identical numbers of substantiated incidents of maltreatment in 2009 (4,084 and 4,073), but the child population of Pennsylvania is ten times that of Maine (U.S. Bureau of the Census, 2010). No one thinks that Maine children suffer ten times more than Pennsylvania ones; something in the reporting and substantiating process must differ between those two states. Furthermore, whether or not a person reports maltreatment is powerfully influenced by culture (one of my students asked, "When is a child too old to be beaten?") and in personal willingness to report. The United States has become more culturally diverse in the past decade—could that be why the rate of reported abuse has declined?

Finally, some professionals are more likely to notice and report maltreatment than others. The most marked variation occurs for teachers. The percent of maltreatment reports from educators is 10 times higher in Minnesota than in North Carolina (24 percent versus 2.5 percent) (Children's Bureau, 2010). There are many plausible reasons for why teachers in North Carolina report less often, but no one thinks Minnesota schoolchildren are much more often abused.

In a confidential nationwide survey of young adults in the United States, 1 in 4 said they had been physically abused ("slapped, hit, or kicked" by a parent or other adult caregiver) before sixth grade, and 1 in 22 had been sexually abused ("touched or forced to touch someone else in a sexual way") (Hussey et al., 2006). Almost never had their abuse been reported. The authors of this study think these rates are *underestimates* (Hussey et al., 2006)!

One reason for these high rates of unreported abuse may be that the respondents were asked if they had *ever* been mistreated by someone who was caring for them; most other sources report annual rates. Another reason is that few children report their own abuse; many do not know that they are mistreated until later, when they compare their experiences with those of their friends. Indeed, some adults who were slapped, hit, or kicked in childhood do not think they were abused. Reinterpretation of childhood experiences is controversial: Some memories are false and others are accurate, finally recognized as abuse (McNally & Geraerts, 2009).

Especially for Criminal Justice Professionals Over the past decade, the rate of sexual abuse has gone down by almost 20 percent. What are three possible explanations? (see response, page 252)

post-traumatic stress disorder (PTSD)
An anxiety disorder that develops as a delayed reaction to having experienced or witnessed a profoundly shocking or frightening event, such as rape, severe beating, war, or natural disaster. Its symptoms may include flashbacks to the event, hyperactivity and hypervigilance, displaced anger, sleeplessness, nightmares, sudden terror or anxiety, and confusion between fantasy and reality.

Abuse or Athletics? Four-year-old Budhia Singh ran 40 miles in 7 hours with adult marathoners. He says he likes to run, but his mother (a widow who allowed his trainer to "adopt" him because she could not feed him) has charged the trainer with physical abuse. The government of India has declared that Singh cannot race again until he is fully grown. If a child, the parent, and the community approve of some activity, can it still be maltreatment?

Especially for Nurses While weighing a 4-year-old, you notice several bruises on the child's legs. When you ask about them, the child says nothing and the parent says the child bumps into things. What should you do? (see response, page 253)

Warning Signs

Often the first sign of maltreatment is delayed development, such as slow growth, immature communication, lack of curiosity, or unusual social interactions. All these difficulties may be evident even at age 1 (Valentino et al., 2006).

During early childhood, maltreated children may seem fearful, startled by noise, defensive and quick to attack, and confused between fantasy and reality. These are symptoms of **post-traumatic stress disorder (PTSD),** first identified in combat veterans, then in adults who had experienced some emotional injury or shock (after a serious accident, natural disaster, or violent crime, for example), and more recently in some maltreated children, who suffer neurologically as well as behaviorally (Neigh et al., 2009; Yehuda, 2006). Table 8.1 lists signs of child maltreatment, both neglect and abuse. None of these signs are proof that a child has been abused, but whenever any of them occurs, it signifies trouble.

Consequences of Maltreatment

The impact of any child-rearing practice is affected by the cultural context. Certain customs (such as circumcision, pierced ears, and spanking) are considered abusive in some cultures but not in others; their effects on children vary accordingly. Children suffer if their parents seem to love them less than most parents in their neighborhood. If a parent forbids something other children have (from candy to cell phones) or punishes more severely or not at all, children might feel unloved. However, although culture is always relevant, the more longitudinal research is published, the more widespread and long-lasting the impact of maltreatment is found to be.

TABLE 8.1	Signs of Maltreatment in Children Aged 2 to 10
Injuries that do not fit an "accidental" explanation, such as bruises on both sides of the face or body; burns with a clear line between burned and unburned skin; "falls" that result in cuts, not scrapes	
Repeated injuries, especially broken bones not properly tended (visible on X-ray)	
Fantasy play, with dominant themes of violence or sexual knowledge	
Slow physical growth, especially with unusual appetite or lack of appetite	
Ongoing physical complaints, such as stomachaches, headaches, genital pain, sleepiness	
Reluctance to talk, to play, or to move, especially if development is slow	
No close friendships; hostility toward others; bullying of smaller children	
Hypervigilance, with quick, impulsive reactions, such as cringing, startling, or hitting	
Frequent absence from school	
Frequent changes of address	
Turnover in caregivers who pick up child or caregiver who comes late, seems high	
Expressions of fear rather than joy on seeing the caregiver	

REUTERS / SANJIB MUKHERJEE

A VIEW FROM SCIENCE

Emotions Are Hard to Heal

The biological and academic impairment from maltreatment is substantial and thus relatively easy to notice—the teacher sees that a child is bruised, broken, or failing despite ability. However, when researchers follow maltreated children over the years, enduring deficits in social skills seem more crippling. Children continue to hate themselves, and they hate everyone else, too.

To be specific, many studies have found that mistreated children typically regard other people as hostile and exploitative; hence, they are less friendly, more aggressive, and more isolated than other children. The earlier abuse starts and the longer it continues, the worse their peer relationships are (Scannapieco & Connell-Carrick, 2005). Neglected children may have greater social deficits than abused ones, because they were unable to relate to their parents (Stevenson, 2007). The best cure is a warm and enduring friendship, but maltreatment makes this unlikely.

Deficits are lifelong. Maltreated children may become bullies or victims or both, not only in childhood and adolescence but also in adulthood (Dietrich, 2008). They tend to dissociate, that is, to disconnect their memories from their understanding of themselves (Valentino et al., 2008). Adults who were severely maltreated (physically, sexually, or emotionally) often abuse drugs or alcohol, enter unsupportive relationships, become victims or aggressors, sabotage their own careers, eat too much or too little, and engage in other self-destructive behavior (M. G. Smith & Fong, 2004). They also have a much higher risk of emotional disorders and suicide attempts, even after other risk factors (e.g., poverty) are considered (Afifi et al., 2008).

In the current economic climate, finding and keeping a job is a critical aspect of adult well-being; adults who were maltreated suffer in this way as well. One study carefully matched 807 children who had experienced substantiated abuse with other children who were of the same sex, ethnicity, and family SES. About 35 years later, the employment rates of those who had been mistreated were 14 percent lower than the rates of those who had not been abused. The researchers concluded that "abused and neglected children experience large and enduring economic consequences" (Currie & Widom, 2010, p. 111). In this study, the women were more impaired than the men: It may be that self-esteem, emotional stability, and social skills are even more important for female than for male workers.

This is just one of hundreds of longitudinal studies, all of which find that maltreatment affects children decades after the broken bones, or skinny bodies, or medical neglect disappear. Some people feel sorry for mistreated children; others blame parents, or poverty, or racism. But an emotion more universal than sympathy or anger may be enough. If our instinct for self-preservation leads to thoughts about our future, we might prevent child maltreatment. The health of the entire society a few decades from now depends on every child.

Three Levels of Prevention, Again

Just as with injury control, there are three levels of prevention of maltreatment. The ultimate goal is *primary prevention* that focuses on the macrosystem and exosystem (see Chapter 1). Examples of primary-prevention include increasing stable neighborhoods and family cohesion, and decreasing financial instability, family isolation, and teenage parenthood.

Secondary prevention involves spotting warning signs and intervening to keep a risky situation from getting worse (Giardino & Alexander, 2011). For example, insecure attachment, especially of the disorganized type (described in Chapter 7), is a sign of a disrupted parent–child relationship. Someone needs to help repair that interaction. Secondary prevention includes home visits by helpful nurses or social workers, as well as high-quality day care that gives vulnerable parents a break while teaching children how to make friends and resolve conflicts. Secondary prevention notes that families with several young children are at risk, especially when the family head is a single parent with money problems. If a nation has free health care for everyone, vulnerable children can be protected before serious harm occurs.

>> **Answer to Observation Quiz** (from page 248) No. The number is actually 10.1 per 1,000. Note the little squiggle on the graph's vertical axis below the number 10. This means that numbers between 0 and 9 are not shown.

>> **Answer to Observation Quiz** (from page 249) Most types of abuse are declining, but not neglect. This kind of maltreatment may be the most harmful because the psychological wounds last for decades.

The Same Situation, Many Miles Apart: Fun with Grandpa Grandfathers, like those shown here in Japan and Sweden, often delight their grandchildren. Sometimes, however, they protect them—either in kinship care, when parents are designated as neglectful, or as secondary prevention before harm is evident. (The grandparents in Sweden are refugees from Iraq.)

permanency planning An effort by child-welfare authorities to find a long-term living situation that will provide stability and support for a maltreated child. A goal is to avoid repeated changes of caregiver or school, which can be particularly harmful to the child.

foster care A legal, publicly supported system in which a maltreated child is removed from the parents' custody and entrusted to another adult or family, which is reimbursed for expenses incurred in meeting the child's needs.

kinship care A form of foster care in which a relative of a maltreated child, usually a grandparent, becomes the approved caregiver.

>> Response for Criminal Justice Professionals (from page 249) Hopefully, more adults or children are aware of sexual abuse and stop it before it starts. A second possibility is that sexual abuse is less often reported and substantiated because the culture is more accepting of teenage sex (most victims of sexual abuse are between ages 10 and 18). A third possible explanation is that the increase in single mothers means that fathers have less access to children (fathers are the most frequent sexual abusers).

Tertiary prevention includes everything that limits harm after maltreatment has already occurred. Reporting and substantiating abuse are only the first steps. Often the caregiver needs help to provide better care. Sometimes the child needs another home. If hospitalization is required, that signifies failure: Intervention should have begun much earlier. At that point, treatment is very expensive, harm has already been done, and hospitalization itself further strains the parent–child bond (Rovi et al., 2004).

Children need caregivers they trust, in safe and stable homes, whether they live with their biological parents, a foster family, or an adoptive family. Whenever a child is legally removed from an abusive or neglectful home and placed in foster care, **permanency planning** must begin, to find a family to nurture the child until adulthood. This is a complex task, requiring cooperation among social workers, judges, and psychologists as well as the caregivers themselves (Edwards, 2007). Sometimes the child's original family can become better; sometimes a relative can be found who will provide good care; sometimes a stranger is the best caregiver.

In **foster care,** children are officially removed from their parents' custody and entrusted to another adult or family; foster parents are reimbursed for the expenses they incur in meeting the children's needs. In every year from 2000 to 2009, about half a million children in the United States were in foster care. More than half of them were in a special version of foster care called **kinship care,** in which a relative—usually a grandparent—becomes the caregiver. This estimate is for official kinship care; three times as many children are unofficially cared for by relatives.

In every nation, most foster children are from low-income, ethnic-minority families, a statistic that should alert everyone to problems in the macrosystem as well as the microsystem. In the United States, children officially in foster care often have a history of severe maltreatment and multiple physical, intellectual, and emotional problems (Pew Commission on Children in Foster Care, 2004). Despite these problems, most develop better in foster care (including kinship care) than with their original abusive families if a supervising agency screens foster families effectively and provides ongoing financial support and counseling (MacMillan et al., 2009; Oosterman et al., 2007).

Adequate support is not typical, however. One obvious failing is that many children move from one foster home to another for reasons that are unrelated to the child's behavior or wishes. Foster children average three placements before permanent placement is achieved (Pew Commission on Children in Foster Care, 2004). Each move increases the risk of a poor outcome (Oosterman et al., 2007). Another

A Missing Piece This British couple was told they would not be able to adopt a non-White British child, so they traveled to Mexico to find their new family. Some adoptive parents bond with their children, no matter what the differences. This mother said that when she first saw her daughter, "A piece of me that was missing suddenly clicked into place."

problem is that kinship care is sometimes used as an easy, less expensive solution. Kinship care may be better than stranger care, but supportive services are especially needed since the grandparent who gets the child is also the parent of the abusive adult (Edwards, 2010; Fechter-Leggett & O'Brien, 2010).

Adoption (when an adult or couple unrelated to the child is legally granted parenthood) is the preferred permanent option when a child should not be returned to a relative, but adoption is difficult for many reasons. Among those reasons: Judges and biological parents are reluctant to release children for adoption; most adoptive parents prefer infants; some agencies screen out families not headed by a heterosexual married couple; some professionals insist that adoptive parents be of the same ethnicity and religion as the child.

As detailed many times in this chapter, caring for young children—from making sure they brush their teeth to keeping them safe and active—is not easy. Parents shoulder most of the burden, and their love and protection usually result in strong and happy children. Teachers can be crucial during these years, working closely with the parents. The benefit to the entire community of having well-nurtured children is obvious; the ways to achieve that seem less clear.

adoption A legal proceeding in which an adult or couple unrelated to a child is granted the joys and obligations of being that child's parent(s).

>> Response for Nurses (from page 250) Any suspicion of child maltreatment must be reported, and these bruises are suspicious. Someone in authority must find out what is happening so that the parent as well as the child can be helped.

SUMMING UP

As they move with more speed and agility, young children encounter new dangers and are seriously injured more often than older children. They are also more often mistreated, either deliberately (abuse) or because essential care is not provided (neglect). Three levels of prevention are needed. Laws and customs can protect everyone (primary prevention); supervision, forethought, and protective care can prevent harm to those at risk (secondary prevention); and when injury or maltreatment occurs, quick and effective medical and psychosocial intervention, as well as prevention of further harm, are needed (tertiary prevention). Putting an end to maltreatment of all kinds is urgent but complex because the sources are often the family, the culture, the community, and the laws.

SUMMARY

Body Changes

1. Children continue to gain weight and add height during early childhood. One reason this occurs is that many adults overfeed children, not realizing that young children are naturally quite thin.

2. Culture, income, and family customs all affect children's growth. In contrast to past decades, children of low-income families are twice as likely to be overweight as their wealthier counterparts. Worldwide, an increasing number of children are eating too much, risking heart disease and diabetes.

3. Many young children consume too much sugar and too little calcium and other nutrients. One consequence is poor oral health. Children need to brush their teeth and visit the dentist years before the permanent teeth erupt.

Brain Development

4. The brain continues to grow in early childhood, reaching 75 percent of its adult weight at age 2 and 90 percent by age 5.

5. Myelination is substantial during early childhood, speeding messages from one part of the brain to another. The corpus callosum becomes thicker and functions much better. The prefrontal cortex, known as the executive of the brain, is strengthened as well.

6. Brain changes enable more reflective, coordinated thought and memory, better planning, and quicker responses. Left–right specialization is apparent in the brain as well as in the body, although the entire brain and the entire body work together for most skills.

7. The expression and regulation of emotions are fostered by several brain areas, including the amygdala, the hippocampus, and the hypothalamus. Childhood abuse may cause overactivity in the amygdala and hippocampus, creating a flood of stress hormones that interfere with learning. Some stress aids learning if reassurance is also present.

Improved Motor Skills

8. Gross motor skills continue to develop; clumsy 2-year-olds become 6-year-olds who move their bodies well, guided by their cul-

ture. Play is their main activity. By playing with other children in safe places, they practice the skills needed for formal education.

9. Urbanization and chemical pollutants hamper development. More research is needed, but it is already apparent that high lead levels in the blood can impair the brain and that opportunities to develop gross motor skills are restricted when play space is scarce.

10. Fine motor skills are difficult to master during early childhood. Young children enjoy expressing themselves artistically, developing their body and finger control as well as self-expression. Fortunately, self-criticism is not yet strong.

Injuries and Abuse

11. Accidents cause more child deaths than diseases, with young children more likely to suffer a serious injury or premature death than older children. Close supervision and public safeguards can protect young children from their own eager, impulsive curiosity.

12. Injury control occurs on many levels, including long before and immediately after each harmful incident. Primary prevention protects everyone. Secondary and tertiary prevention also save lives.

13. Child maltreatment includes ongoing abuse and neglect, usually by a child's own parents. Each year, about 3 million cases of child maltreatment are reported in the United States; less than 1 million are substantiated.

14. Physical abuse is the most obvious form of maltreatment, but neglect is more common and may be more harmful. Health, learning, and social skills are all impeded by abuse and neglect, not only during childhood but also decades later.

15. Tertiary prevention may include placement of a child in foster care, including kinship care. Adoption is much less common, although often the best solution for the child. Permanency planning is required because frequent changes are harmful to children. Primary and secondary prevention help parents care for their children and reduce the need for tertiary prevention.

KEY TERMS

myelination (p. 230)
corpus callosum (p. 231)
lateralization (p. 231)
perseveration (p. 234)
amygdala (p. 235)
hippocampus (p. 235)

hypothalamus (p. 235)
injury control/harm reduction (p. 243)
primary prevention (p. 244)
secondary prevention (p. 244)
tertiary prevention (p. 244)

child maltreatment (p. 247)
child abuse (p. 247)
child neglect (p. 248)
reported maltreatment (p. 248)
substantiated maltreatment (p. 248)

post-traumatic stress disorder (PTSD) (p. 250)
permanency planning (p. 252)
foster care (p. 252)
kinship care (p. 252)
adoption (p. 253)

WHAT HAVE YOU LEARNED?

Body Changes

1. About how much does a well-nourished child grow in height and weight from ages 2 to 6?

2. Why do many parents overfeed their children?

3. The incidence of what adult diseases increases with childhood obesity?

4. What specific measures should be part of oral health in early childhood?

5. When is it normal for children to be picky about eating and other daily routines?

Brain Development

6. How much does the brain grow from ages 2 to 6?

7. Why is *myelination* important for thinking and motor skills?

8. What is the function of the corpus callosum?

9. What should parents do if their toddler seems left-handed?

10. How does the prefrontal cortex affect impulsivity and perseveration?

11. What are the functions of three areas of the brain that are part of the limbic system?

12. Is stress beneficial or harmful to young children? Explain why.

Improved Motor Skills

13. What factors help children develop their motor skills?

14. What is known and unknown about the effects on young children of chemicals in food, air, and water?

15. How does brain and body maturation affect children's artistic expression?

Injuries and Abuse

16. Why is the term *injury control* preferred over the term *accident prevention*?

17. What primary measures prevent childhood injury, abuse, and neglect?

18. What secondary measures prevent childhood injury, abuse, and neglect?

19. What tertiary measures prevent further childhood injury, abuse, and neglect?

20. Why did few people recognize childhood maltreatment 50 years ago?

21. Why is neglect in childhood considered more harmful, in the long term, than abuse?

22. Why is it difficult to know exactly how often childhood maltreatment occurs?

23. What are the signs that a child may be mistreated?

24. What are the long-term consequences of childhood maltreatment?

25. Why would a child be placed in foster care?

APPLICATIONS

1. Keep a food diary for 24 hours, writing down what you eat, how much, when, how, and why. Then think about nutrition and eating habits in early childhood. Do you see any evidence in yourself of imbalance (e.g., not enough fruits and vegetables, too much sugar or fat, eating when you are not really hungry)? Did your food habits originate in early childhood, in adolescence, or at some other time?

2. Go to a playground or other place where young children play. Note the motor skills that the children demonstrate, including abilities and inabilities, and keep track of age and sex. What differences do you see among the children?

3. Ask several parents to describe each accidental injury of each of their children, particularly how it happened and what the consequences were. What primary, secondary, or tertiary prevention measures would have made a difference?

4. Think back to your childhood and the friends you had at that time. Was there any maltreatment? Considering what you have learned in this chapter, why or why not?

>>ONLINE CONNECTIONS

To accompany your textbook, you have access to a number of online resources, including quizzes for every chapter of the book, flashcards (in English and Spanish), critical thinking questions, and case studies. For access to any of these links, go to www.worthpublishers.com/bergerca9e. In addition to these free resources, you'll also find links to podcasts, video clips, diagnostic quizzing with personalized study advice, and an ebook. Some of the videos and activities available online include:

- *Brain Development in Early Childhood.* Animations illustrate the macroscopic and microscopic changes as children's brains grow.

- *Stolen Childhoods.* Some children, because of poverty or abuse, never have the opportunities for schooling and nurture that many of us take for granted. Children in a variety of difficult circumstances, from sex work to work in carpet factories, tell their stories in a variety of video clips.

Early Childhood: Cognitive Development

WHAT WILL YOU KNOW?

1. Are 2- to 6-year-olds focused mostly on their own perspective (egocentric) or are they strongly influenced by others?
2. Why is it much easier to fool a 3-year-old than a 5-year-old?
3. Are children confused if they hear two languages?
4. Are there important differences between one preschool program and another?

I was one of dozens of subway riders who were captivated by a little girl, about age 3, with sparkling eyes and many braids. She sat beside a large man, her legs straight out in front of her. Her mother was standing about 6 feet away, on the other side of the man. The little girl repeatedly ducked her head behind him, saying, "You can't see me, Mama," unaware that her legs (in colorful striped stockings) were constantly visible to her mother.

Like that little girl, every young child has much to learn. Young children are sometimes *egocentric,* understanding only their own perspective. Among their developing ideas is a *theory of mind,* an understanding of how minds work (as in knowing that your mother would never lose sight of you on a subway).

Early childhood is a time of prodigious new learning. Examples abound. Toddlers' simple block towers become elaborate cities, with tunnels, bridges, and houses designed and built by kindergartners. The youngest children are easy to fool; by age 5, they do the fooling. The halting, simple sentences of a typical 2-year-old become the nonstop, complex outpourings of a talkative 6-year-old.

How does such rapid cognitive development happen? How much comes from maturation and how much from education? Many young children are now taught, not merely babysat (as if adults ever merely sat) or simply cared for (as in day care or home care). This chapter describes thinking and learning from ages 2 to 6, including advances in thought, language, and education, and explores how all this develops.

>> Piaget and Vygotsky

Jean Piaget and Lev Vygotsky are justly famous for their descriptions of cognition. Their theories are "intertwined" (Fox & Riconscente, 2008, p. 373), especially when they describe young children. As you read, look for the commonalities.

Piaget: Preoperational Thought

Early childhood is the second of Piaget's four stages of cognition. He called cognitive development between about 2 and 6 years **preoperational intelligence,** a time for symbolic thought, especially language and imagination. He called this period of intelligence *pre*operational in that children do not yet use logical operations

preoperational intelligence Piaget's term for cognitive development between the ages of about 2 and 6; it includes language and imagination (which involve symbolic thought), but logical, operational thinking is not yet possible at this stage.

(reasoning processes), but they are no longer limited to senses and motor skills (sensorimotor) (Inhelder & Piaget, 1964).

Piaget lauded the development of **symbolic thought,** a major accomplishment of preoperational intelligence. When a child can think symbolically, he or she becomes much more adept at pretending, and words can refer to things not seen. "Dog" can be a dog once seen, or a dog that might be seen, or an imagined dog never seen—all examples that the word *dog* has become a symbol, not simply the name of a creature within sight. Symbolic thought allows the language explosion, detailed later in this chapter, as children can talk about what they think, imagine, and remember.

Research on U.S. children of several cultural backgrounds (European, Japanese, South American) found that all infants tend to spontaneously explore objects and, as they grow older, to engage in symbolic play, as Piaget described (Cote & Bornstein, 2009). This study did not trace developmental paths from ages 2 to 6, but other scientists suggest that all children switch from sensorimotor to symbolic thinking as the result of brain maturation (experience-expectant) and social interactions (experience-dependent) (Mundy & Jarrold, 2010).

Obstacles to Logical Operations

Although symbolic thought and language are typical advances for young children everywhere, Piaget described four limitations of preoperational thought that make logic difficult until about age 6: centration, focus on appearance, static reasoning, and irreversibility.

Centration is the tendency to focus on one aspect of a situation to the exclusion of all others. Young children may, for example, insist that lions and tigers seen at the zoo or in picture books cannot be cats, because the children "center" on the house-pet aspect of the cats they know. Or they may insist that Daddy is a father, not a brother, because they center on the role that each family member fills for them.

The daddy example illustrates a particular type of centration that Piaget called **egocentrism**—literally, "self-centeredness." Egocentric children contemplate the world exclusively from their personal perspective, as the little girl on the subway did. Egocentrism is not selfishness. Consider, for example, a 3-year-old who chose to buy a model car as a birthday present for his mother: His "behavior was not selfish or greedy; he carefully wrapped the present and gave it to his mother with an expression that clearly showed that he expected her to love it" (Crain, 2005, p. 108).

A second characteristic of preoperational thought is a **focus on appearance** to the exclusion of other attributes. A girl given a short haircut might worry that she has turned into a boy; a tall child is thought to be older. In preoperational thought, a thing is whatever it appears to be—evident in the joy young children have in wearing the hats or shoes of someone else.

Third, preoperational children use **static reasoning,** believing that the world is unchanging, always in the state in which they currently encounter it. A young boy might want a live television show turned off while he goes to the bathroom and be furious and unbelieving when his parents tell him a particular program cannot be paused. Similarly, many children cannot imagine that their own parents were once children. Once they grasp that, they still do not understand developmental change. One preschooler told his grandmother to tell his mother to stop spanking him, because "she has to do what her mother says."

The fourth characteristic of preoperational thought is **irreversibility.** Preoperational thinkers fail to recognize that reversing a process sometimes restores whatever existed before. A young child might cry because her mother put lettuce

---

symbolic thought A major accomplishment of preoperational intelligence that allows a child to think symbolically, including understanding that words can refer to things not seen and that an item, such as a flag, can symbolize something else (in this case, for instance, a country).

centration A characteristic of preoperational thought in which a young child focuses (centers) on one idea, excluding all others.

egocentrism Piaget's term for children's tendency to think about the world entirely from their own personal perspective.

focus on appearance A characteristic of preoperational thought in which a young child ignores all attributes that are not apparent.

static reasoning A characteristic of preoperational thought in which a young child thinks that nothing changes. Whatever is now has always been and always will be.

irreversibility A characteristic of preoperational thought in which a young child thinks that nothing can be undone. A thing cannot be restored to the way it was before a change occurred.

on her sandwich. Overwhelmed by her desire to have things "just right" (explained in Chapter 8), she might reject the food even after the lettuce is removed because she believes that what is done cannot be undone.

Conservation and Logic

Piaget highlighted the many ways in which preoperational intelligence overlooks logic. A famous set of experiments involved **conservation,** the notion that the amount of something remains the same (is conserved) despite changes in its appearance.

Suppose two identical glasses contain the same amount of liquid, and the liquid from one of these glasses is poured into a taller, narrower glass. If young children are asked whether one glass contains more liquid or both glasses contain the same amount, they will insist that the narrower glass (in which the liquid level is higher) has more.

All four characteristics of preoperational thought are evident in this mistake. Young children fail to understand conservation of liquids because they focus (*center*) on what they see (*appearance*), noticing only the immediate (*static*) condition. It does not occur to them that they could reverse the process and re-create the liquid's level of a moment earlier (*irreversibility*). (See Figure 9.1 for other examples.)

This research has many practical implications. For example, when teachers give a snack to preschoolers, all the cups should be the same size, and children will be happier with two very small crackers than one bigger one. Similarly, in a grocery store, children may be fooled by what they see, unaware that packaging is deceptive (Gaumer & Arnone, 2010).

Animism in Preoperational Thought

A final aspect of preoperational thought is called **animism,** the belief that natural objects and phenomena are alive (Piaget, 1929). Egocentric reasoning leads many children to believe that clouds, mountains, and trees have feelings, goals, and capabilities. A child might talk to a tree and ask for its protection from the rain, for instance.

Closely related to animism is treating nonhuman animals as similar to humans. For example, a dead bird discovered by a child might bring forth tears and require a burial ceremony. A dog might be told wishes and worries by a child who believes that the pet understands and sympathizes. Many children's stories—in books, cartoons, or fairy tales—include animals or objects that talk and help people. Consider the three bears, or the Pooh stories, or Teletubbies.

Especially for Nutritionists How can Piaget's theory help you encourage children to eat healthy foods? (see response, page 261)

conservation The principle that the amount of a substance remains the same (i.e., is conserved) even when its appearance changes.

animism The belief that natural objects and phenomena are alive.

Easy Question; Obvious Answer
(A) Sadie, age 5, carefully makes sure both glasses contain the same amount. (B) When one glass of pink lemonade is poured into a wide jar, she triumphantly points to the tall glass as having more. Sadie is like all 5-year-olds—only a development psychologist or a 7-year-old child knows better.

Tests of Various Types of Conservation

Type of Conservation	Initial Presentation	Transformation	Question	Preoperational Child's Answer
Volume	Two equal glasses of liquid.	Pour one into a taller, narrower glass.	Which glass contains more?	The taller one.
Number	Two equal lines of checkers.	Increase spacing of checkers in one line.	Which line has more checkers?	The longer one.
Matter	Two equal balls of clay.	Squeeze one ball into a long, thin shape.	Which piece has more clay?	The long one.
Length	Two sticks of equal length.	Move one stick.	Which stick is longer?	The one that is farther to the right.

FIGURE 9.1

Conservation, Please According to Piaget, until children grasp the concept of conservation at (he believed) about age 6 or 7, they cannot understand that the transformations shown here do not change the total amount of liquid, checkers, clay, and wood.

Attempts to measure children's animism find that many children simultaneously hold rational and irrational ideas (Meshcheryakov, 2005). Magical happenings and sayings are common. Wishing on a star or an eyelash, saying "Cross my heart and hope to die," holding one's breath when passing a cemetery, and much more are frequent behaviors, even if parents belittle them.

Like Piaget, adults may underestimate children and their superstitions. Many religions and cultural myths have talking animals, and most adults encourage children's faith in Santa Claus, the Tooth Fairy, and so on (Barrett, 2008). If preschoolers are cute and foolish to believe such things, what are adults who talk to their dogs?

Limitations of Piaget's Research

Notice that Piaget's original tests of conservation require the child's words, not actions or brain scans. Later research has found that when the tests of logic are simplified, young children may succeed. In many ways, children indicate that they know something via eye movements or gestures before they can say it in words (Goldin-Meadow, 2009).

Furthermore, even when words are the measure, some young children demonstrate conservation and other logical ideas in a gamelike setting, although not in Piaget's experiments (Donaldson, 1963/2003). For example, if a "naughty bear" lengthens a row of checkers, 4-year-olds say that the new row has the same number as before. That's conservation of number, a concept Piaget did not expect children to grasp until age 6.

Researchers now believe that Piaget underestimated cognition during early childhood, just as he had during infancy (Halford & Andrews, 2006). He relied on words spoken in an experimental setting rather than on nonverbal signs in a play context.

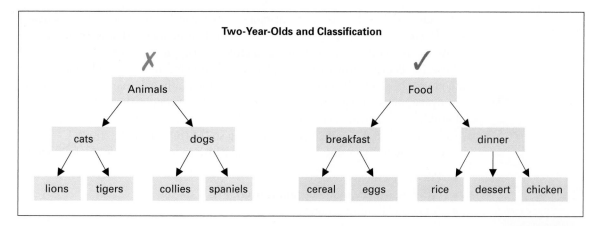

FIGURE 9.2

Everyday Categories Experience is the best teacher, especially for 2-year-olds. Many know that eating can mean a snack, or breakfast, or dinner and that particular foods belong in each of these categories. However, few know or care that tigers and lions are both cats. By the same token, humans and baboons are both primates, a subcategory of animals—something even a few adults forget.

Other experiments to distinguish preoperational thought from Piaget's next stage (concrete operational thought) show the same results. Mastery of the concept of *classification* is another example: Piaget thought that preoperational children cannot classify objects properly, that they do not firmly grasp that dogs, cats, and cows are all categories of animals. This is not necessarily accurate.

It is easy to understand why Piaget reached this conclusion. Children are confused about the relationship between superordinate categories (such as animals), subcategories (such as dogs), and further subcategories (such as collies). (Classification is discussed further in Chapter 12.) However, even 3-year-olds can classify things if the categories are ones they often use, such as that cereal and toast are part of breakfast or that ice cream and cake both belong to the dessert category (Nguyen & Murphy, 2003). (See Figure 9.2.)

Piaget was right that young children are not as logical as older children, but he did not realize how much they understand. One reason is that he did not have available the brain scans that developmentalists now use. Scans show much more early intellectual activity than was previously imagined, although they also show that Piaget was quite perceptive about early cognitive growth (Crone & Ridderinkhof, 2011).

Vygotsky: Social Learning

For decades, the magical, illogical, and self-centered aspects of early-childhood cognition dominated research; scientists were understandably awed by Piaget. His description of egocentrism was confirmed daily by anecdotes of young children's behavior. Vygotsky was the first leading developmentalist to emphasize another side of early cognition—that the thinking of young children, instead of being egocentric, is shaped by the wishes and emotions of others. He emphasized the sociocultural aspects of young children's cognition, in contrast to Piaget's emphasis on the individual.

That led Vygotsky to seek to understand cultural differences, acknowledging that "the culturally specific nature of experience is an integral part of how the person thinks and acts," as a contemporary team of developmentalists explain (Gauvain et al., 2011).

Children and Mentors

Vygotsky believed that every aspect of children's cognitive development is embedded in a social context (Vygotsky, 1934/1987). Children are curious and observant. They ask questions—about how machines work, why weather changes, where the

>> Response for Nutritionists (from page 259) Take each of the four characteristics of preoperational thought into account. Because of egocentrism, having a special place and plate might assure the child that this food is exclusively his or hers. Since appearance is important, food should look tasty. Since static thinking dominates, if something healthy is added (e.g., grate carrots into the cake, add milk to the soup), do it before the food is given to the child. In the reversibility example in the text, the lettuce should be removed out of the child's sight and the "new" hamburger presented.

sky ends—and seek answers from more knowledgeable mentors. These answers are affected by the mentors' perceptions and ethnotheories—that is, their culture.

As you remember from Chapter 2, a child is an *apprentice in thinking,* someone whose intellectual growth is stimulated and directed by older and more skilled members of society. Parents are the first mentors, although many teachers, other family members, and peers are mentors as well. For example, the verbal proficiency of children in day-care centers is affected by the language of their playmates, who teach vocabulary without consciously doing so (Mashburn et al., 2009).

According to Vygotsky, children learn because their mentors do the following:

- Present challenges
- Offer assistance (without taking over)
- Add crucial information
- Encourage motivation

guided participation The process by which people learn from others who guide their experiences and explorations.

Thinking occurs as the mentor and the child join in **guided participation,** sharing social experiences and explorations. For example, imagine a group of children learning to draw or write or dance. A teacher might perform some action first. Then the children follow the teacher but also copy one another. A child who is copied does not resent it but appreciates that someone else follows his or her lead.

Indeed, one sign of a socially attuned 3-year-old is that, when another child copies, the first child smiles and soon reciprocates, copying something the copier did. Shared joy is the result of this social interaction. Overall, the ability to learn from mentors indicates intelligence, according to Vygotsky: "What children can do with the assistance of others might be in some sense even more indicative of their mental development than what they can do alone" (1934/1987, p. 5).

Scaffolding

Vygotsky believed that each individual has a **zone of proximal development (ZPD).** The zone of proximal development, first described in Chapter 2, is reiterated here because ZPD is crucial for early-childhood learning. *Proximal* means "near," so the ZPD includes the ideas children are close to understanding and skills they are close to attaining but not yet able to master independently. How and when children learn depends, in part, on the wisdom and willingness of mentors to provide **scaffolding,** or temporary sensitive support, to help them within their developmental zone.

Words, Don't Fail Me Now Could you describe how to tie shoes? The limitations of verbal tests of cognitive understanding are apparent in many skills.

Observation Quiz What three sociocultural factors make it likely that this child will learn? (see answer, page 264)

Good mentors provide plenty of scaffolding, encouraging children to look both ways before crossing the street (while holding the child's hand) or letting them stir the cake batter (perhaps the adult's hand covers the child's hand on the spoon handle, in guided participation). A preschool teacher sets up each activity in advance, with the appropriate scaffolds, and then guides each child. Scaffolding is crucial for cognitive experiences—that is, experiences that will produce better understanding of words and ideas.

zone of proximal development (ZPD) Vygotsky's term for the skills—cognitive as well as physical—that a person can exercise only with assistance, not yet independently.

scaffolding Temporary support that is tailored to a learner's needs and abilities and aimed at helping the learner master the next task in a given learning process.

The particulars of scaffolding vary by culture. Consider book-reading, for instance. In many North American families, when an adult reads to a child, the adult scaffolds—explaining, pointing, listening—within the child's zone of development. A sensitive adult reader does not tell the child to be quiet but might instead prolong the session by expanding on the child's questions and the pictures in the book.

By contrast, book-reading in middle-class Peruvian families includes teaching the child to listen when adults talk, so that a 2-year-old who interrupts is lovingly taught to be quiet (Melzi & Caspe, 2005). Obviously, scaffolded behaviors and processes in Peru differ because the goal is a respectful child, not a talkative one. Nonetheless, everywhere adults guide children to master the ideas, skills, and behaviors of the culture.

Vygotsky Applied

Motivation is crucial in early education—one reason why sensitive social interaction is so powerful. The social learning emphasized by Vygotsky is transmitted in every culture through scaffolding (Gauvain, 2005). Toys, clothes, playground equipment, eating routines, social interactions—everything scaffolds certain skills and behaviors that children learn. Although objects help—some 2-year-olds have toy guitars, others toy brooms, others toy guns—the critical role is observation: Every child watches other people and tries to do what they do. Notice 2-year-olds who try to play the guitar: Their body movements and facial expressions copy what they have seen.

This is obvious in the research as well. For instance, a program introduced 2- and 3-year-olds to science in the sandbox: Teachers helped children experiment with sand and water. Later these children did more sandbox exploration on their own than children who did not have this apprenticeship (van Schijndel et al., 2010).

Even in conversation, scaffolding is possible and helpful. North American adults often answer young children's questions not with a simple answer but with a response that builds vocabulary and understanding (Chouinard, 2007). If a child asks, "What is that?" a teacher, instead of simply saying, "That is a truck," might say, "That is a kind of t-r-r . . ." (guiding the child to respond "truck") or "That is a garbage truck. What do you think it has inside?" Older siblings can be excellent mentors, too.

The power of scaffolding is demonstrated when 2- to 6-year-olds imitate adult actions that are irrelevant, time-consuming, and inefficient. This is called **overimitation,** evident in children from many cultures but not in other animals. Overimitation is thought to be a way that children learn from older members of their community, allowing "rapid, high-fidelity intergenerational transmission of cultural forms" (Nielsen & Tomaselli, 2010, p. 735). (See the Research Design.)

Language as a Tool

Although all the objects of a culture guide children, Vygotsky believed that words are especially pivotal. Empirical research finds this to be the case, in every culture and with children of every ability (e.g., Baker et al., 2007; Philips & Tolmie, 2007; Schick & Melzi, 2010). Just as a builder needs tools to construct a house, the mind needs language. Talking, listening, reading, and writing are tools to advance thought, and informal scaffolding leads to advances in language and cognition.

Especially for Driving Instructors Sometimes your students cry, curse, or quit. How would Vygotsky advise you to proceed? (see response, page 265)

overimitation When a person imitates an action that is not a relevant part of the behavior to be learned. Overimitation is common among 2- to 6-year-olds when they imitate adult actions that are irrelevant and inefficient.

> ### ▶ Research Design
>
> **Scientists:** Mark Nielsen and Keyan Tomaselli.
>
> **Publication:** *Psychological Science* (2010).
>
> **Participants:** Sixty-one 2- to 6-year-olds from Bushman communities in South Africa and Botswana; 16 young children from Brisbane, Australia; and 17 older Bushman children. The reason for these three groups of participants is that overimitation (that is, imitating unnecessary actions) has been repeatedly demonstrated among Western children, but Bushman adults rarely explicitly teach children how to use objects. Thus, if apprenticeship in learning occurs only in cultures with deliberate training, the children raised in the Bushman culture would not overimitate.
>
> **Design:** Experimenters tested the children, one by one, on overimitation of irrelevant and inefficient ways to open three boxes. For example, a blue box could be easily opened by pulling a knob, but in the experimental condition, an adult (sometimes a Western scientist, sometimes a member of the local community) waved a red stick above the box three times and then used that stick to push down the knob to open the box. The children were given the stick and the box, and their actions were noted.
>
> In the control condition, the children were simply given the stick and the box with no demonstration; again, their actions were noted. In an extension of this basic design, some of the control-group participants were shown the stick-waving demonstration after they had discovered on their own how to open the box the easy way.
>
> **Major conclusion:** No matter who tested them, children of every age and culture performed the irrelevant and inefficient actions they saw, even if they had already opened the box the easy way. Apparently, children are universally predisposed to learn from mentors. If their culture does not rely on deliberate apprenticeship, then they learn via observation without adult verbal explanation. Thus, scaffolding can occur when children learn whatever routines and procedures they witness. Across cultures, "similarity of performance is profound" (p. 734). (Soon you will read applications to preschool education: Young children learn what adults encourage—imaginative play, artistic activities, social cooperation, or writing the alphabet.)
>
> **Comments:** Originally, the researchers hypothesized that overimitation resulted from the practice in Western cultures whereby adults explicitly teach young children, explaining as they demonstrate. The scientists were surprised that the Bushman children imitated as often as Western children did. Such cross-cultural research discovers which aspects of cognitive development are part of Western culture and which are universal. Other developmentalists have found that a child may be selective (less likely to imitate untrustworthy adults or accidental acts). More research will "determine when children will do precisely as others have done and when they instead choose their own actions" (p. 735).

private speech The internal dialogue that occurs when people talk to themselves (either silently or out loud).

Language advances thinking in two ways, according to Vygotsky (Fernyhough, 2010). The first way is with internal dialogue, or **private speech,** in which people talk to themselves (Vygotsky, 1934/1987). Young children use private speech often, although they do not realize it (Manfra & Winsler, 2006). They talk aloud to review, decide, and explain events to themselves (and, incidentally, to anyone else within earshot).

Older preschoolers are more selective, effective, and circumspect, sometimes whispering. Audible or not, private speech aids cognition and self-reflection; adults should encourage it (Perels et al., 2009; Winsler et al., 2007). Many people of all ages talk to themselves when alone or write down ideas to help them think. That is private speech as well. Preschool curricula based on Vygotsky's ideas use games, play, social interaction, and private speech to develop executive functioning (Diamond et al., 2007).

social mediation Human interaction that expands and advances understanding, often through words that one person uses to explain something to another.

The second way in which language advances thinking, according to Vygotsky, is by mediating the social interaction that is vital to learning. This **social mediation** function of speech occurs during both formal instruction (when teachers explain things) and casual conversation. Words entice people into the zone of proximal development, as mentors guide children to learn numbers, recall memories, and follow routines.

Words, Cultures, and Math

Learning about numbers begins very early in life. Apparently, even babies have a sense of whether one, two, or three objects are in a display, although exactly what infants understand about numbers is controversial (Varga et al., 2010). However, there is no doubt that words are tools that enable many children between ages 2 and 6 to do the following:

>> Answer to Observation Quiz
(from page 262) Motivation (in Spain, yellow running shoes are popular); human relationships (note the physical touching of father and son); and materials (the long laces make tying them easier).

- Count objects, with one number per item (called *one-to-one correspondence*)
- Remember times and dates (bedtime at 8 P.M., a child is 4 years old, and so on).
- Understand sequence (first child wins, last child loses)

Dozens of the cognitive accomplishments of young children—in numbers, memory, logic, and much more—have been the subject of extensive research: Mentoring and language are always found to be pivotal. What would happen if the language learned by a child had no words for numbers? Anthropologists have found a few languages in South America that lack many counting words: They use "many" for numbers higher than 2. When children and adults are tested in those languages, they have a much more difficult time with simple math examples (Gordon, 2004). By contrast, children whose parents often count out loud often become early counters and, in school, math whizzes.

Culture may affect language and therefore math knowledge, even when the language has words for trillions of numbers. English-speaking and Chinese-speaking preschoolers seem equal in their understanding of the numbers 1 to 10, but the Chinese are ahead in their understanding of 11 to 19. There are many possible explanations for this, but one is directly verbal: In Chinese, those numbers are logical and direct, the equivalent of ten-one, ten-two, ten-three, and so on. This may be easier for young children to understand than eleven, twelve, thirteen, and so on (Miller et al., 1995).

German-speaking children have an additional problem with numbers from 20 to 99, since they say the equivalent of one-and-twenty, two-and-twenty, and so on, not twenty-one, twenty-two, and so on. German 3-year-olds may become very proficient at 1 to 9, but not at 20 to 99. In these and many other ways, language and culture affect young children's understanding of math (Göbel et al., 2011).

By age 3 or 4, children's brains are mature enough to comprehend numbers, store memories, and recognize routines. Whether or not children actually demonstrate such understanding depends on what they hear and how they participate in various activities within their families, schools, and cultures. Some 2-year-olds hear sentences such as "One, two, three, takeoff," and "Here are two cookies," and "Dinner in five minutes" several times a day. Others do not—and they have a harder time with math when they reach first grade. Words are the mediator between brain potential and comprehension.

>> Response for Driving Instructors (from page 263) Use guided participation and scaffold the instruction so your students are not overwhelmed. Be sure to provide lots of praise and days of practice. If emotion erupts, do not take it as an attack on you.

A VIEW FROM SCIENCE

Witness to a Crime

One application of early cognitive competency has received attention among lawyers and judges. Some children are the only witnesses to crimes, especially of sexual abuse or domestic violence. Can a young child's words be trusted? Adults have gone to both extremes in answering this question. As one legal discussion begins:

> Perhaps as a result of the collective guilt caused by disbelieving the true victims of this abuse, in recent years the pendulum has swung in the opposite direction, to an unwavering conviction that a young child is incapable of fabricating a story of abuse, even when the tale of mistreatment is inherently incredible.
>
> *[Shanks, 2011]*

To find the right balance, the answer to the question "Is child testimony accurate?" is "sometimes." In recent years, psychologists have shown that people of all ages misremember (Frenda et al., 2011; Lyons et al., 2010) and that each age group misremembers in particular ways. Younger children, not yet imbued with stereotypes, are sometimes more accurate than older witnesses who are influenced by prejudice (Brainerd et al., 2008). However, young children want to please adults and themselves, and they may lie to do so. Even in elementary school, some children do not realize that words and memories might be false (London et al., 2011) or that enjoyable fantasies are simply imaginary and might conflict with verified facts.

Words and expressions can plant false ideas in young children, either deliberately (as an abuser might) or inadvertently (as a fearful parent might). Children's shaky grasp of reality makes them vulnerable to scaffolding memories that are imagined, not experienced (Bruck et al., 2006). This happened tragically 35 years ago in many jurisdictions, when adults suddenly realized that small children could be sexually abused and then decided that sexual abuse was rampant in preschools. For instance, 3-year-olds at Wee Care nursery school in New Jersey convinced a judge that a teacher had sexually abused them in bizarre ways (including making them lick peanut butter off her genitals) (Ceci & Bruck, 1995). In retrospect, one wonders why any adult believed what they said. Since that time, much has been learned about witnesses of all ages.

Young children are not necessarily worse than adults at recounting experiences if they are interviewed with open-ended questions by someone who does not indicate what the preferred answers are (Brainerd et al., 2008; Feltis et al., 2010). Children who have already learned to tell coherent narratives provide more accurate accounts of what happened (Kulkofsky & Klemfuss, 2008). Whether or not a child understands the difference between truth and falsehood is irrelevant to accuracy; the crucial factor is whether the interviewer is straightforward or suggestive (Lyon et al., 2008).

Guided participation can be destructive, since the guidance might lead in the wrong direction. Remember the children in the Research Design who waved the red stick before they opened the box? As Vygotsky noted, children are acutely sensitive to the culture around them, particularly to what they observe in adults. That is both a strength and a liability.

With sexual abuse in particular, a child might believe that some lewd act is OK if an adult says so. Only years later does the victim realize that it was abuse. Research on adult memory finds that sometimes adults reinterpret what happened to them, concluding only later that they were indeed abused, with genuine memories of experiences that were criminal. However, some people of all ages can be led to believe that an event, including sexual abuse, occurred when it did not (Geraerts et al., 2009).

This knowledge provides guidelines for police officers, social workers, judges, teachers, and parents. When children are witnesses, they should simply be asked to tell what happened, perhaps with eyes closed to reduce their natural attempt to please. If, instead, an adult says, "Did he touch you there?" a child might say "yes" if he thinks that is what the adult wants to hear. Preschool cognition is a mix of egocentric fantasy, social influence, and innocent honesty—care must be taken to neither automatically believe nor disbelieve what children say.

SUMMING UP

Cognition develops rapidly from ages 2 to 6. Children's active search for understanding was first recognized by Piaget, who believed that young children are generally incapable of performing logical operations (hence *pre*operational intelligence). Piaget thought that egocentrism limits understanding, as young children center on only one thing at a time, focusing on appearance. Their thinking is magical and animistic.

Vygotsky emphasized the social and cultural aspects of children's cognition. He believed that children are guided as apprentices, within their zones of proximal development. Other people are mentors, providing the scaffolding that helps children master various skills and concepts. Language is a crucial learning tool, in private speech and social mediation, a point made by Vygotsky and confirmed by recent research. ▪

>> Children's Theories

Piaget and Vygotsky realized that children actively work to understand their world. No developmental scientist or teacher doubts that. The question then becomes exactly when and how does children's knowledge develop? One discovery is that children do not simply learn words and ideas—they develop theories.

Theory-Theory

theory-theory The idea that children attempt to explain everything they see and hear by constructing theories.

Humans of all ages try to explain whatever happens. The term **theory-theory** refers to the idea that children naturally construct theories to explain whatever they see and hear. In other words, the theory about how children learn is that children develop a theory:

> More than any animal, we search for causal regularities in the world around us. We are perpetually driven to look for deeper explanations of our experience, and broader and more reliable predictions about it. . . . Children seem, quite literally, to be born with . . . the desire to understand the world and the desire to discover how to behave in it.
>
> *[Gopnik, 2001, p. 66]*

According to theory-theory, the best explanation for cognition in young children is that humans always seek reasons, causes, and underlying principles to make sense of their experience. That requires displaying a lot of curiosity and thinking, which is what young children do.

Exactly how are explanations sought in early childhood? In one study, Mexican American mothers kept detailed diaries of every question their 3- to 5-year-olds asked and how they themselves responded (Kelemen et al., 2005). Most of the questions were about human behavior and characteristics (see Figure 9.3); for example, "Why do you give my mother a kiss?" "Why is my brother bad?" "Why do women have breasts?" "Why are there Black kids?" Fewer questions were about nonliving things ("Why does it rain?") or objects ("Why is my daddy's car white?").

Questions were often about the underlying purpose of whatever the child observed, although parents usually responded as if children were asking about science instead. An adult might interpret a child's one-word question "Why?" to mean "What causes *X* to happen?" when the child intended "Why?" to mean "I want to know more about *X*" (Leach, 1997). For example, if a child asks why women have breasts, the response might be about hormones and maturation, but a child-centered explanation would be that breasts are for feeding babies. From a child's egocentric perspective, any query includes "How does this relate to me?"

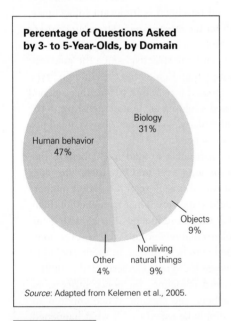

Percentage of Questions Asked by 3- to 5-Year-Olds, by Domain

Biology 31%

Human behavior 47%

Objects 9%

Nonliving natural things 9%

Other 4%

Source: Adapted from Kelemen et al., 2005.

FIGURE 9.3

Questions, Questions Parents found that most of their children's questions were about human behavior—especially the parents' behavior toward the child. Children seek to develop a theory to explain things, so the question "Why can't I have some candy?" is not satisfactorily answered by "It's almost dinnertime."

Accordingly, an adult might add that the child got his or her first nourishment from the mother's breast.

A series of experiments that explored when and how 3-year-olds imitate others provides some support for theory-theory (Williamson et al., 2008). Children seem to figure out *why* adults act as they do before deciding to copy those actions. If an adult intended to accomplish something and succeeded, a child is likely to follow the example, but if the same action and result seemed inadvertent or accidental, the child is less likely to copy it.

Indeed, even when asked to repeat something ungrammatical that an adult says, children are likely to correct the grammar based on their theory that the adult intended to speak grammatically but failed to do so (Over & Gattis, 2010). This is another example of a general principle: Children develop theories about intentions before they employ their impressive ability to imitate; they do not mind-lessly copy whatever they observe. For instance, in the example in which the adult deliberately waved the stick before opening the box, the children theorized that stick-waving was somehow important.

Theory of Mind

Human mental processes—thoughts, emotions, beliefs, motives, and intentions—are among the most complicated and puzzling phenomena that we encounter every day. Adults wonder why people fall in love with the particular persons they do, or why they vote for the candidates they choose, or why they make foolish choices—from taking on a huge mortgage to buying an overripe cucumber. Children are puzzled about a playmate's unexpected anger, a sibling's generosity, or an aunt's too-wet kiss.

To know what goes on in another's mind, people develop a *folk psychology,* which includes a set of ideas about other people's thinking called **theory of mind.** Theory of mind is an emergent ability, slow to develop but typically beginning in most children at about age 4 (Sterck & Begeer, 2010).

Belief and Reality: Understanding the Difference

The idea that thoughts may not reflect reality is beyond very young children, but then it occurs to each child rather suddenly sometime after age 3. This idea leads to the realization that people can be deliberately deceived or fooled—an idea that requires some theory of mind, beyond almost every 2-year-old and most 3-year-olds.

In one of several false-belief tests that researchers have developed, a child watches a doll named Max put a puppy in a red box. Then Max leaves and the child sees the puppy taken out of the red box and put in a blue box. When Max returns, the child is asked, "Where will Max look for the puppy?" Most 3-year-olds confidently say, "In the blue box"; most 6-year-olds correctly say, "In the red box," a pattern found in a dozen nations (Wellman et al., 2001).

Indeed, 3-year-olds almost always confuse what they recently learned with what they once thought and what someone else might think. Another way of describing this is to say that they are "cursed" by their own knowledge (Birch & Bloom, 2003), too egocentric to grasp others' perspectives.

Telling a Lie

The development of theory of mind can be seen in everyday life: Young children are notoriously bad at deception. They play hide-and-seek by hiding in the same place time after time, or their facial expression betrays them when they tell a fib. Parents sometimes say, "I know when you are lying," and, to the consternation of

theory of mind A person's theory of what other people might be thinking. In order to have a theory of mind, children must realize that other people are not necessarily thinking the same thoughts that they themselves are. That realization seldom occurs before age 4.

Especially for Social Scientists Can you think of any connection between Piaget's theory of preoperational thought and 3-year-olds' errors in this theory-of-mind task? (see response, page 269)

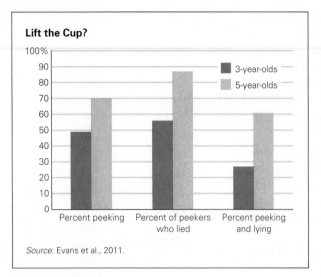

Lift the Cup?

Source: Evans et al., 2011.

FIGURE 9.4

Better with Age? Could an obedient and honest 3-year-old become a disobedient and lying 5-year-old? Apparently, yes, as the proportion of peekers and liars in this study more than doubled over those 2 years. Does maturation make children more able to think for themselves or less trustworthy?

most 3-year-olds, parents are usually right. (This is not true at older ages because children become better at fooling their parents; knowing this, parents may be suspicious of the truth as well as of a lie.)

The development of the ability to lie was demonstrated in an experiment in which 247 children, aged 3 to 5, were left alone in a room with a cup that covered dozens of candies (Evans et al., 2011). The children were told not to peek, but 142 (75 percent) did. When they lifted the cup, the candies spilled out onto the table, and it was impossible for the children to hide the evidence before the examiner returned to ask the children how the candies got on the table. Only one-fourth of the participants (more often the younger ones) told the truth, but the lies told by the 3-year-olds were often hopeless (e.g., "The candies got out by themselves"); those told by the 4-year-olds seemed possible but unlikely (e.g., "Other children came in and knocked over the cup"). By age 5, however, most of the lies were logical and plausible (e.g. "My elbow knocked over the cup accidentally").

This particular study was done in Beijing, China, but the results seem universal: Older children are more likely to lie and they are more plausible liars. Beyond the age differences, the experimenters found that the better liars were also more advanced in theory of mind (Evans et al., 2011) (see Figure 9.4).

Closely related to young children's trouble with lying are their belief in fantasy (the magical thinking noted earlier) and their static reasoning (characteristic of preoperational thought), which make it difficult for them to change their minds. This is another example of the perseveration explained in Chapter 8.

Brain and Context

Developmentalists wonder what, precisely, strengthens theory of mind at about age 4. Is this change more nature or nurture, brain maturation or experience? There is firm evidence for nature. Age-related maturation of the prefrontal cortex seems crucial, according to brain scans of 4-, 5-, and 6-year-olds and of adults as they figured out theory-of-mind puzzles (Liu et al., 2009) (see photo). Children with autism are deficient in social understanding, particularly theory of mind: Brain imaging finds this to be neurological, not a matter of experience (Mar, 2011).

Brains at Work Neuroscience confirms the critical role of the prefrontal cortex for development of theory of mind. Adults and 4- to 6-year-olds were questioned on 40 theory-of-mind examples. The adults answered correctly, as did some 4- to 6-year-olds (passers), though not all (failers). The leftmost images are brain-wave patterns; the middle ones represent brain activity (fMRI), and the rightmost trio contrasts mental activity when distinguishing reality and belief. Adult brain waves show quick answers, and the contrast *(right)* shows that they answered quickly with little effort; but the child passers needed to think longer before they answered. The authors concluded that "social cognition and the brain develop together" (Liu et al., 2009, pp. 318, 325).

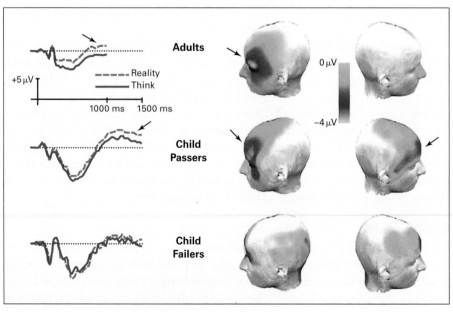

LIU, D., ET AL. (2009), NEURAL CORRELATES OF CHILDREN'S THEORY OF MIND DEVELOPMENT. *CHILD DEVELOPMENT*, 80: 318–326. JOHN WILEY & SONS, INC.

Other evidence also suggests that the prefrontal cortex is crucial. The study of lying among Chinese preschoolers also tested the children's ability to say "day" when they saw a picture of the moon and "night" when they saw a picture of the sun. This is a measure of mental flexibility, which indicates the *executive function* that occurs with maturation of the prefrontal cortex. The results confirm the importance of the brain: Children who failed the day–night tests typically told impossible lies, whereas the lies of children the same age who were high in executive function were plausible (Evans et al., 2011).

Does the crucial role of brain maturation make context irrelevant? Not at all (Sterck & Begeer, 2010). Language development is significant, especially if mother–child conversations involve thoughts and wishes (Ontai & Thompson, 2008).

Furthermore, in developing theory of mind, one expert explains, "Two older siblings are worth about a year of chronological age" (Perner, 2000, p. 383). As brothers and sisters argue, agree, compete, and cooperate, and as older siblings fool younger ones, it dawns on 3-year-olds that not everyone thinks as they do. By age 5, their theory of mind is well established: They know how to gain parental sympathy to protect themselves against their older siblings, as well as how to persuade their younger brothers and sisters to give them a toy.

Finally, culture matters. A meta-analysis of 254 studies done in China and North America found that Chinese children were about six months ahead of U.S. children (Liu et al., 2008). Another study comparing theory of mind among young children in preschools in Canada, India, Peru, Samoa, and Thailand found that the Canadian 5-year-olds were slightly more advanced and the Samoan 5-year-olds were slightly slower in passing tests of executive function (Callaghan et al., 2005). Particular aspects of culture seem relevant: In Canada, children who were often read to were more advanced than average in theory of mind compared with similar Canadian children who often watched children's television (Mar et al., 2010).

SUMMING UP

Scholars have recently noted that children develop theories to explain whatever they observe and that those theories do not necessarily spring from explanations given to them by adults. Children are interested in the underlying purpose of events; adults are more focused on scientific causes. Many researchers have explored the development of theory of mind, which is the realization at about age 4 that other people's thoughts and ideas might differ from one's own. Neurological maturation, linguistic competence, family context, and culture all affect the attainment of theory of mind. ∎

>> Language Learning

Language is more than an example of symbolic thought (Piaget) and a tool for learning (Vygotsky); it is the premier cognitive accomplishment of early childhood. Two-year-olds use short, telegraphic sentences, but 6-year-olds seem able to understand and discuss almost anything (see At About This Time).

Brain maturation, myelination, scaffolding, and social interaction make early childhood the ideal time for learning language. As you remember from Chapter 1, scientists once thought that early childhood was a *critical period* for language learning—the *only* time when a first language could be mastered and the best time for learning a second or third language. It is true that the young child's brain organizes words and sounds into meaning (theory-theory), and for that reason teachers and parents should speak and listen to children many hours each day.

Ready to Learn When 2-year-olds quarrel, they grab toys and, if expedient, push and kick. Such fights between siblings seem to advance theory of mind: By age 4, these two may use deception to get what they want.

>> Response for Social Scientists (from page 267) According to Piaget, preschool children focus on appearance and on static conditions (so they cannot mentally reverse a process). Furthermore, they are egocentric, believing that everyone shares their point of view. No wonder they believe that they had always known the puppy was in the blue box and that Max would know that, too.

A Shared Pleasure As they read stories to young children, many adults express exaggerated surprise, excitement, worry, and relief. They realize that words are better understood and remembered when they are connected to emotions.

AT ABOUT THIS TIME
Language in Early Childhood

Approximate Age	Characteristic or Achievement in First Language
2 years	*Vocabulary:* 100–2,000 words *Sentence length:* 2–6 words *Grammar:* Plurals; pronouns; many nouns, verbs, adjectives *Questions:* Many "What's that?" questions
3 years	*Vocabulary:* 1,000–5,000 words *Sentence length:* 3–8 words *Grammar:* Conjunctions, adverbs, articles *Questions:* Many "Why?" questions
4 years	*Vocabulary:* 3,000–10,000 words *Sentence length:* 5–20 words *Grammar:* Dependent clauses, tags at sentence end ("... didn't I?" "... won't you?") *Questions:* Peak of "Why?" questions; many "How?" and "When?" questions
5 years	*Vocabulary:* 5,000–20,000 words *Sentence length:* Some seem unending ("... and ... who ... and ... that ... and ...") *Grammar:* Complex, depending on what the child has heard. Some children correctly use the passive voice ("Man bitten by dog") and subjunctive ("If I were ..."). *Questions:* Some about social differences (male–female, old–young, rich–poor) and many other issues

fast-mapping The speedy and sometimes imprecise way in which children learn new words by tentatively placing them in mental categories according to their perceived meaning.

However, millions of people have learned languages after age 6; the critical-period hypothesis is false (Singleton & Munoz, 2011).

Instead, early childhood is a *sensitive period* for language learning—for rapidly and easily mastering vocabulary, grammar, and pronunciation. Young children are called "language sponges" because they soak up every drop of language they encounter. Language learning is an example of dynamic systems, in that every part of the developmental process influences every other part. To be specific, there are "multiple sensitive periods . . . auditory, phonological, semantic, syntactic, and motor systems, along with the developmental interactions among these components" (Thomas & Johnson, 2008, p. 2), all of which facilitate language learning early in life.

One of the valuable (and sometimes frustrating) traits of young children is that they talk a lot—to adults, to each other, to themselves, to their toys—unfazed by misuse, mispronunciation, stuttering, or other impediments to fluency. Language comes easily partly because young children are less self-conscious about what they say. Egocentrism has advantages; this is one of them.

The Vocabulary Explosion

Children add new words to their vocabulary rapidly. The average child knows about 500 words at age 2 and more than 10,000 at age 6 (Herschensohn, 2007). Precise estimates of vocabulary size vary because contexts are diverse; some children learn four times as many words as others. For every young child, however, vocabulary builds quickly and language potential is greater than is apparent; comprehension is more extensive than speech. Every child could become fluently bilingual given the proper circumstances.

Fast-Mapping

How does the vocabulary explosion occur? After painstakingly learning one word at a time at 12 to 18 months, children develop an interconnected set of categories for words, a kind of grid or mental map, which makes speedy vocabulary acquisition possible. The process is called **fast-mapping** (Woodward & Markman, 1998) because, rather than figuring out the exact definition after hearing a word used in several contexts, children hear a word once and quickly stick it into one of the categories in their mental language grid. That quick-sticking is fast-mapping.

Like more conventional mental mapping, language mapping is not always precise. For example, if asked where Cameroon is, most adults can locate it approximately ("It's in Africa"), but few can name the six countries that border it (Nigeria, Chad, Central African Republic, Equatorial Guinea, Gabon, Congo). Similarly, children quickly map new animal names close to already-known animal names, without knowing all the precise details. Thus, *tiger* is easy to map if you know *lion*. A trip to the zoo facilitates fast-mapping of dozens of animal words, especially since zoos scaffold learning by placing similar animals near each other.

Egocentrism is an asset here—children say "tiger" for any animal that is fast-mapped in that category, from cheetah to jaguar. They do not worry that they might be wrong; they center on their own concept. Adults, however, might be silent if they cannot distinguish a lynx from an ocelot; that slows down their learning.

Fast-mapping is evident even before age 2, and it accelerates as new words are learned because each word makes it easier to map other words (Gershkoff-Stowe & Hahn, 2007). Generally, the more linguistic clues children already have, the better their fast-mapping is (Mintz, 2005). One set of experiments in vocabulary learning began in cultures whose languages had only a few counting words: the equivalents of *one, two,* and *many.* As already explained, people in such cultures were much worse at estimating quantity because they did not have the words to guide them (Gordon, 2004). Mapping and understanding a new number word, such as *nineteen,* is easier if one already knows a related word, such as *nine.*

An experiment in teaching the names of parts of objects (e.g., the spigot of a faucet) found that children learned much better if the adults named the object that had the part and then spoke of the object in the possessive (e.g., "See this butterfly? Look, this is the butterfly's thorax") (Saylor & Sabbagh, 2004). This finding shows that it is easier to map a new word when it is connected to a familiar one.

Words and the Limits of Logic

Closely related to fast-mapping is a phenomenon called *logical extension:* After learning a word, children use it to describe other objects in the same category. One child told her father she had seen some "Dalmatian cows" on a school trip to a farm. He understood because he remembered that she had petted a Dalmatian dog the weekend before. Bilingual children might insert a word from another language if they don't know the word in the language they are speaking, although soon they separate one language from the other and know who speaks which—and stick to one language when speaking to a monolingual person.

Some words are particularly difficult—*who/whom, have been/had been, here/there, yesterday/tomorrow.* More than one child has awakened on Christmas morning and asked, "Is it tomorrow yet?" A child told to "stay there" or "come here" may not follow instructions because the terms are confusing. Extensive study of children's language abilities finds that fast-mapping is only one of many techniques that children use to learn language: When a word does not refer to an object on the mental map, children use other ways to master it (Carey, 2010).

Listening and Talking

Because literacy is considered crucial in the United States, a national study analyzed which activities in early childhood aided reading a few years later in elementary school. Overall, language development was found to be crucial, with both vocabulary and attention to the sounds of words (phonics) predictive of fluent reading. Based on data from about 300 published studies, five intervention efforts were discovered to be effective:

1. *Code-focused teaching.* In order for children to learn to read, they must "break the code" from the written word to the spoken word. Teaching children to recognize the letters of the alphabet and to know the sounds each makes (e.g., "A, Alligators all around" or, more conventionally, "C is for cat") is important.
2. *Book-reading.* Vocabulary as well as print familiarity build when adults read to children. It seems better when the reading includes the child asking and answering questions, not quietly listening.
3. *Parent education.* When teachers and other professionals teach parents how to stimulate cognition (as in the book-reading of #2), that predicts later literacy.

Horse or Dromedary? These children might fast-map and call it a horse since it is horse-sized, horse-colored, and has a horse-like head and legs. Fast-mapping is misleading. However, if you think this is a dromedary, you made a similar mistake. All dromedaries are camels, but not all camels are dromedaries. This one is not.

Observation Quiz Is this scene set in the United States or some other country? (see answer, page 273)

Student and Teachers Children at the Lawrence, Massachusetts, YWCA show Rashon McCloud of the Boston Celtics how they use a computer to learn reading. They are participating in an NBA-sponsored program called Read to Achieve. Children are often faster than adults to catch on to technological innovations.

overregularization The application of rules of grammar even when exceptions occur, making the language seem more "regular" than it actually is.

4. *Language enhancement.* Within each child's zone of proximal development (not too easy, not too hard) adults need to build vocabulary and grammar, expanding on what the child already knows.

5. *Preschool programs.* Children benefit from spending some time with a teacher and other children (further discussed later in this chapter).

These five measures helped children of all incomes, ages, and ethnicities. The child's age was relevant for only one item: 2- and 3-year-olds may benefit more from language-enhancement activities than 4- and 5-year-olds. Ideally, however, all young children experience all five (Shanahan & Lonigan, 2010).

Acquiring Basic Grammar

We noted in Chapter 6 that the *grammar* of language includes the structures, techniques, and rules that are used to communicate meaning. Word order and word repetition, prefixes and suffixes, intonation and emphasis—all are part of grammar.

By age 3, children understand the basics. For example, English-speaking 3-year-olds know word order (subject/verb/object), saying, "I eat the apple," not any of the 23 other sequences of those four words. They use plurals; tenses (past, present, and future); and nominative, objective, and possessive pronouns (*I/me/mine* or *my*). Some even use articles (*the, a, an*) correctly, although article use in English is bewilderingly complex (as adults learning English know all too well).

Each aspect of language (grammar, vocabulary, pronunciation, etc.) follows a particular developmental path, partly because parts of the brain myelinate at specific rates and every language has both easy and difficult constructions. In general, genes affect *expressive* (spoken or written) language more than *receptive* (heard or read) language. Thus, some children are relatively talkative or quiet because they inherit that tendency, but experience (not genes) determines which words and grammatical constructions they understand (Kovas et al., 2005). Not only do they understand most of what they hear, they believe they know more than they do (Marazita & Merriman, 2011).

Sometimes children apply the rules of grammar when they should not, an error called **overregularization.** For example, English-speaking children learn to add an *s* to form the plural: Toddlers follow that rule when they ask for two *cookies* or more *blocks.* They apply this to nonsense words: If they are shown a drawing of an abstract shape, are told it is called a *wug,* and are then shown two of these shapes, they say there are two *wugs.*

However, many young children overregularize that final *s,* talking about *foots, tooths,* and *mouses.* This is evidence of increasing knowledge: Many children first say words correctly because they repeat what they have heard; later, when they grasp the grammar and try to apply it, they overregularize. Repeated exposure to exceptions is needed: At first, children assume that irregular constructions follow the regular path (Ramscar & Dye, 2011).

Learning Two Languages

Language-minority children (those who speak a language that is not the dominant language of their nation) suffer if they do not speak the majority language well. In the United States, those who are not proficient in English tend to have lower school achievement, diminished self-esteem, and inadequate employment, as well as many other problems. Fluency in English can erase these liabilities, and then fluency in another language is an asset.

In the United States in 2010, 21 percent of schoolchildren spoke a language other than English at home, with most of them (75 percent) also speaking English well. The percentage of bilingual children has been rising in the United States, but it is higher in other nations: In Canada and many African, Asian, and European nations, by sixth grade most children are at least bilingual, sometimes trilingual. When should additional languages be learned? Generally, younger is quicker.

What Is the Goal?

In thinking about learning languages, we need to clarify the goal. Is national unity crucial, and will speaking one and only one language achieve that? Is international understanding important, and will speaking several languages accomplish that? Is a nation better off with one language or with more than one official language (Switzerland has three, Canada has two)? Do individuals who speak more than one language gain in cognitive as well as linguistic development, or do they become confused?

Some say that young children need to become proficient in one, and only one, language and that children taught two languages might become semilingual, not bilingual, "at risk for delayed, incomplete, and possibly even impaired language development" (Genesee, 2008, p. 17). Others say that it is better for everyone to speak at least two languages and that "there is absolutely no evidence that children get confused if they learn two languages" (Genesee, 2008, p. 18). This second position has more research support: Soon after the vocabulary explosion, children who have heard two languages since birth usually master two distinct sets of words and grammar, along with each language's characteristic pauses, pronunciations, intonations, and even gestures (Genesee & Nicoladis, 2007).

No doubt early childhood is the best time to learn language, whether it is one, two, or three languages. Neuroscience finds that young bilingual children site both languages in the same areas of their brains yet manage to keep them separate. This separation allows them to activate one language and temporarily inhibit the other, experiencing no confusion when they speak to a monolingual person (Crinion et al., 2006). They may be a millisecond slower to respond if they must switch languages, but their brains overall function better and may even have some resistance to Alzheimer dementia in old age (Bialystok et al., 2009).

Neurological studies show that people who learn a second language in adulthood usually show different activation sites for each language and are slowed down—especially if they silently translate as they listen and speak. A few fortunate adults who learn a second language after puberty activate the same brain area for both; they tend to be unusually skilled bilingualists (Thomas & Johnson, 2008).

Pronunciation is particularly hard to master after childhood, in any language. However, do not mistake pronunciation for comprehension. From infancy on, hearing is more acute than vocalization. Almost all children have pronunciation difficulties in their first language, but they are blithely unaware of their mistakes and gradually learn to speak clearly with whatever accent they hear. Children who have spoken English all their lives, for instance, may speak with a southern accent, or a West Indian one, or a Canadian one—accents that are hard to erase when people leave their childhood home in adulthood.

In early childhood, children transpose sounds (*magazine* becomes *mazagine*), drop consonants (*truck* becomes *ruck*), and convert difficult sounds to easier ones (*father* becomes *fadder*). Mispronunciation does not impair fluency primarily because young children are more receptive than expressive—they hear better than they talk. When 4-year-old Rachel asked for a "yeyo yayipop," her father repeated, "You want a yeyo yayipop?" She replied, "Daddy, sometimes you talk funny."

To speak well, young children need to be "bathed in language," as some early-childhood educators express it. The emphasis is on hearing and speaking in every

>> **Answer to Observation Quiz** (from page 271) It is not in the United States. Some clues are the boys' haircuts, the girl's headscarf, and the clothes on all three—each possible in the United States, but unlikely on three U.S. children together. Another clue is that camels with two humps are rare in U.S. zoos. But one thing is definitive: the fence. By law and custom, no U.S. zoos have fences children can crawl through. Is this cultural scaffolding, leading U.S. preschoolers to fear camels more than these Italians do?

situation, just as a person taking a bath is surrounded by water. Television is a poor teacher because children need personalized, responsive instruction in the zone of proximal development. In fact, young children who watch the most television tend to be delayed in language learning (Harrison & McLeod, 2010).

Language Loss

Schools in all nations stress the dominant language, and language-minority parents fear that their children will make a *language shift,* becoming more fluent in the school language than in their home language. This is a valid fear: Language shift occurs everywhere—some language-minority children in Mexico shift to Spanish (Messing, 2007), some children from the First Nations in Canada shift to English (Allen, 2007), as do some Chinese-speaking children in the United States—but not always (Zhang, 2010). Crucial are the attitudes of the parents and the larger society about the native language.

Children may shift in talking but not in comprehending. Many 5-year-olds understand their parents' language but refuse to speak it. Nor is it unusual for immigrant adults to use a child as spokesperson and interpreter when they deal with monolingual bureaucrats. This may be a practical necessity, but the role reversal widens the generational gap between child and parent. It also reinforces the language shift, because children realize that the majority language is preferred outside the home.

Language shift and role reversal are unfortunate, not only for the cognition and mental health of the child but also for the family and society (Toppelberg et al., 2010). Having many fluently bilingual citizens is a national strength, and respect for family traditions moderates adolescent rebellion. Yet remember that young children are preoperational: They center on the immediate status of the "foreign" language, not on its global usefulness; on appearances more than history; on parental dress and customs, not on traditions and wisdom; on the present more than the past. No wonder many shift toward the dominant culture. Since language is integral to culture, if a child is to become fluently bilingual, everyone who speaks with the child should show evident appreciation of both cultures (Pearson, 2008; Snow & Kang, 2006).

Language Gains

Becoming a **balanced bilingual,** speaking two languages so well that no audible hint suggests the other language, is accomplished by millions of young children in many nations, to their cognitive and linguistic benefit (Bialystok & Viswanathan, 2009; Pearson, 2008). Yet millions of other children either abandon their first language or do not learn the second as well as they might. Although skills in one language can be transferred to benefit acquisition of another, "transfer is neither automatic nor inevitable" (Snow & Kang, 2006, p. 97). Scaffolding is needed.

The basics of language learning—the naming and vocabulary explosions, fast-mapping, overregularization, extensive practice—apply to every language a young child learns. Young children's vocabulary in two languages is directly connected to how much language they hear; for a child to become a balanced bilingual, adults need to expose that child to twice as much talk as usual (Hammer et al., 2011). The same practices can make a child fluently trilingual, as some 5 year-olds are. One parent might read to a child in French, for instance, and another in English, while the child attends a Spanish-speaking preschool. Thanks to theory of mind, by the time children are 5, they can understand that a particular language is understood by one person but not another, and speak accordingly.

MARY KNOX MERRILL / THE CHRISTIAN SCIENCE MONITOR / GETTY IMAGES

Smiling Faces, Usually Everyone in this group is an immigrant, born far from his current home in Burlington, Vermont. Jean Luc Dushime escaped the 1994 genocide in Rwanda, central Africa, when he was 14. He eventually adapted to his new language, climate, surroundings, and culture. Today he helps immigrant children make the same transition.

balanced bilingual A person who is fluent in two languages, not favoring one over the other.

Especially for Immigrant Parents You want your children to be fluent in the language of your family's new country, even though you do not speak that language well. Should you speak to your children in your native tongue or in the new language? (see response, page 276)

SUMMING UP

Children aged 2 to 6 have impressive linguistic talents. They explode into speech, from about a hundred words at 24 months to thousands at 6 years, from halting baby talk to rapid, bilingual fluency. Fast-mapping and grammar are among the sophisticated devices they use, although both can backfire: Many young children misuse words or assume grammar regularities that do not exist. No other time in the entire life span is as sensitive for language learning, especially for mastering pronunciation.

Extensive exposure to two languages, with strong encouragement and repeated practice, can result in children being balanced bilinguals, which confers not only fluency but also cognitive and social benefits. ∎

>> Early-Childhood Education

A hundred years ago, children had no formal education until first grade, which is why it was called "first" and why young children were "*pre*schoolers." Today, many 3- to 6-year-olds are in school (see Figure 9.5 for U.S. trends) not only because of changing family patterns but also because research "documents the rapid development and great learning potential of the early years" (Hyson et al., 2006, p. 6). Especially by age 3 or 4, children learn best if they have extensive practice in hearing and speaking, in fine and gross motor skills, and in literacy and numeracy, all of which most preschools provide.

Homes and Schools

A key research conclusion is that the quality of both the home and the school matter. If the home educational environment is poor, a good preschool program is especially beneficial (Hindman et al., 2010). A preschool with an inadequate curriculum is less destructive if the family provides learning opportunities and

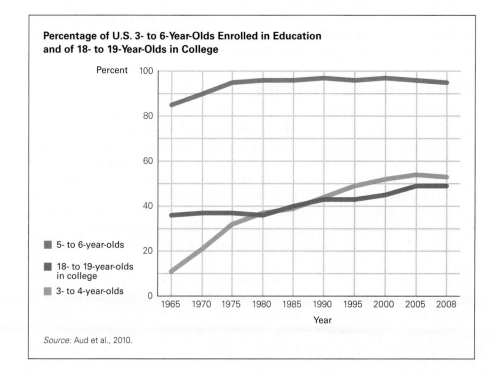

Source: Aud et al., 2010.

FIGURE 9.5

Changing Times As research increasingly finds that preschool education provides a foundation for later learning, most young children are enrolled in educational programs. Note the contrast with 18- to 19-year-olds in college (not shown are the 18- to 19-year-olds still in high school—about 15 percent).

Observation Quiz At what point did the percentage of 3- to 4-year-olds in school exceed that of 18- to 19-year-olds in college? (see answer, page 277)

"We teach them that the world can be an unpredictable, dangerous, and sometimes frightening place, while being careful not to spoil their lovely innocence. It's tricky."

Tricky Indeed Young children are omnivorous learners, picking up habits, curses, and attitudes that adults would rather not transmit. Deciding what to teach—by actions more than words—is essential.

>> Response for Immigrant Parents
(from page 274) Children learn by listening, so it is important to speak with them often. Depending on how comfortable you are with the new language, you might prefer to read to your children, sing to them, and converse with them primarily in your native language and find a good preschool where they will learn the new language. The worst thing you could do would be to restrict speech in either tongue.

Especially for Unemployed Early-Childhood Teachers You are offered a job in a program that has 10 children for every 1 adult. You know that is too many, but you want a job. What should you do? (see response, page 279)

encouragement every afternoon, evening, and weekend. Ideally, each child has both, partly because no home or preschool is always within the child's zone of proximal development.

It is difficult to judge both homes and schools in the United States because of the "stunning variability and fragmentation" of public and private schools (Pianta et al., 2009, p. 50). Overall, preschools foster cognition, but some programs are very weak and parents might do better in that realm. However, families do not choose home education as often as they settle for it: Access to a quality preschool is particularly difficult for middle-class families, although in some places low-income families are shut out as well.

When early-education programs are compared, the most important variables are teachers who know how to respond to the needs of young children and have time to do so. This is achieved via a combination of teacher education and experience, as well as relatively few children per teacher.

Some specific characteristics of quality day care were described in Chapter 7: safety, adequate space and equipment, a low child/adult ratio, positive social interactions among children and adults, and trained staff who stay year after year. When comparing options, one question that parents might ask is, "How long has each staff member worked here?" Even more important is to assess how effective the teachers are at implementing a curriculum that responds to the needs of each child—an assessment difficult to make even with direct observation but almost impossible for distant regulators (Pianta et al., 2009).

Educational institutions for young children are referred to by various names (preschool, nursery school, day care, pre-primary, pre-K) or structures (public, private, center, family), but these labels are not reliable indicators of the quality of an institution (Fuligni et al., 2009). Each early-childhood educational program (and sometimes each teacher) emphasizes different skills, goals, and methods (Chambers et al., 2010; Walsh & Petty, 2007). We will now consider three general categories: child-centered, teacher-directed, and intervention programs. Remember, however, that the quality of the home and the effectiveness of the teachers have more impact on young children than does the label of the program.

Child-Centered Programs

Many programs are called *developmental,* or *child-centered,* because they stress children's development and growth. Teachers in such programs believe children need to follow their own interests rather than adult directions, for example, endorsing the idea that "children should be allowed to select many of their own activities from a variety of learning areas that the teacher has prepared" (Lara-Cinisomo et al., 2011). Children are allowed to discover ideas at their own pace. The physical space and the materials (such as dress-up clothing, art supplies, puzzles, blocks of many sizes, and other toys) are arranged to allow self-paced exploration.

Most child-centered programs encourage artistic expression (Lim, 2004). Some educators argue that young children "are all poets" in that they are gifted in seeing the world more imaginatively than older people do. According to advocates of child-centered programs, this peak of creative vision should be encouraged; children are given many opportunities to tell stories, draw pictures, dance, and make music for their own delight.

Child-centered programs are often influenced by Piaget, who emphasized that each child will discover new ideas, and by Vygotsky, who thought that children learn from other children, with adult guidance (Bodrova & Leong, 2005). Teachers are crucial: A child-centered program requires teachers to organize the classroom with developmentally appropriate activities for each child and then guide each child toward the activities that will advance learning (Dominguez et al., 2010).

Although children make their own choices, some aspects of the program entice children to learn words, numbers, and social skills. For example, to promote numeracy, children play games that include math (counting objects, keeping score) and follow routines that use measurements (daily calendars, schedules). Teachers also use numbers as part of managing the children (only three children in the block corner, two volunteers to get the juice).

Montessori Schools

One type of child-centered school began a hundred years ago, when Maria Montessori opened nursery schools for poor children in Rome. She believed that children needed structured, individualized projects to give them a sense of accomplishment. They completed puzzles, used sponges and water to clean tables, traced shapes, and so on.

Like Piaget (her contemporary), Montessori (1870–1952) realized that children's thoughts and needs differ from those of adults. In her schools, children learned from activities that might seem like play. Teachers gave each child tasks that dovetailed with his or her cognitive eagerness. For example, because they have a need for order, for language learning, and for using all their senses, Montessori children are given systematic exercises that allow them to explore—such as cinnamon sticks in a paper bag, to be first smelled, then touched, then tasted. In many ways, the child's own curiosity and joy in developing and practicing various motor skills is used to aid learning.

Today's **Montessori schools** still emphasize individual pride and achievement, presenting many literacy-related tasks (such as outlining letters and looking at books) to young children (Lillard, 2005). Specific materials differ from those that Montessori developed, but the underlying philosophy is the same. Children seek out learning tasks and are not made to sit quietly while a teacher instructs them. That is what makes Montessori programs child-centered, although traditional

>> **Answer to Observation Quiz** (from page 275) Between 1985 and 1990. The exact year (not shown) was 1988.

Montessori schools Schools that offer early-childhood education based on the philosophy of Maria Montessori, which emphasizes careful work and tasks that each young child can do.

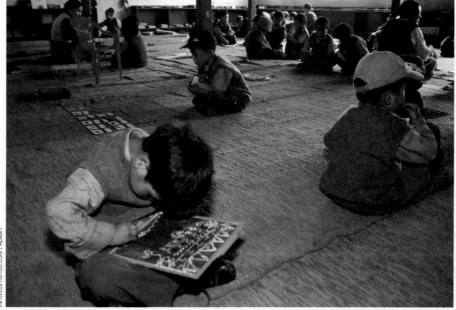

Tibet, China, India, and . . . Italy? Over the past half-century, as China increased its control of Tibet, thousands of refugees fled to northern India. Tibet traditionally had no preschools, but young children adapt quickly, as here in Ladakh, India. This Tibetan boy is working a classic Montessori board.

Montessori schools exclude some activities that children enjoy (dress-up play, for example).

The goal is for all children to feel proud of themselves and engage in learning. Many aspects of Montessori's philosophy are in accord with current developmental research. That is one reason this kind of school remains popular. A study of 5-year-olds in inner-city Milwaukee who were chosen by lottery to attend Montessori programs found that the children became better at prereading and early math tasks, as well as at developing a theory of mind, than their peers in other schools (Lillard & Else-Quest, 2006). The probable explanation: Their gains in self-confidence, curiosity, and exploration transferred into more academic tasks.

Reggio Emilia

Reggio Emilia A program of early-childhood education that originated in the town of Reggio Emilia, Italy, and that encourages each child's creativity in a carefully designed setting.

Another form of early-childhood education is called **Reggio Emilia** because it began in the Italian town of that name, where virtually every young child attends preschool. In Reggio Emilia, children are encouraged to master skills that are not usually taught in North American schools until age 7 or so, such as writing and using tools. There is no large-group instruction, with formal lessons in, say, forming letters or cutting paper. Instead, "Every child is a creative child, full of potential" (Gandini et al., 2005, p. 1), with personal learning needs and artistic drive. Measurement of achievements, such as testing to see whether children have learned their letters, is not part of the core belief that each child should explore and learn in his or her own way (Lewin-Benham, 2008).

Appreciation of the arts is evident. Every Reggio Emilia school has a studio and an artist who encourages the children to be creative. The space also fosters creativity. Reggio Emilia schools have a large central room where children gather, children's art is displayed on white walls and hung from high ceilings, and floor-to-ceiling windows open to a spacious, plant-filled playground. Big mirrors are part of the school's décor—again, with the idea of fostering individuality. Reggio Emilia programs have a low child/teacher ratio, ample space, and abundant materials for creative expression.

ELIZABETH FLORES KRT / NEWSCOM

Child-Centered Pride How can Rachel Koepke, a 3-year-old from a Wisconsin town called Pleasant Prairie, seem so pleased that her hands (and cuffs) are blue? The answer arises from northern Italy—Rachel attends a Reggio Emilia preschool that encourages creative expression.

One distinctive feature of the curriculum is that a small group of children become engaged in long-term projects of their choosing. Such projects foster the children's pride in their accomplishments (which are displayed for all to admire) while teaching them to plan and work together. Children are also encouraged to investigate their physical world—plants, insects, and much more. Outdoor play space, with greenery of many kinds, is also part of the Reggio Emilio plan.

As detailed in later chapters, many nations currently emphasize children's need to learn the basics of science and math in their early years. This means a familiarity with numbers and an enthusiasm for inquiry, both of which are fostered in Reggio Emilia programs. One analysis of Reggio Emilia classrooms in the United States found "a science-rich context that triggered and supported preschoolers' inquiries, and effectively engaged preschoolers' hands, heads, and hearts with science" (Inan et al., 2010, p. 1186).

Reggio Emilia teachers are encouraged to collaborate. For six hours each week, they work without the children: planning activities, having group discussions, and talking to parents. Parents collaborate as well, teaching special subjects and learning about their child with individualized reports that include photographs, artwork, and detailed observations written by the teachers.

Teacher-Directed Programs

Unlike child-centered programs, teacher-directed preschools stress academics, usually taught by one adult to the entire group. The curriculum includes learning the names of letters, numbers, shapes, and colors according to a set timetable; every child naps, snacks, and goes to the bathroom on schedule as well. Children are taught to sit quietly and listen to the teacher. Praise and other reinforcements are given for good behavior, and time-outs (brief separation from activities) are imposed to punish misbehavior.

In teacher-directed programs, the serious work of schooling is distinguished from the unstructured play of home. Teachers endorse several ideas that indicate a teacher-directed focus, one being that children should form letters correctly before they are allowed to create a story (Lara-Cinisomo et al., 2011). Such programs occur in many nations. As one young German boy explained:

> So home is home and kindergarten is kindergarten. Here is my work and at home is off-time, understand? My mum says work is me learning something. Learning is when you drive your head, and off-time is when the head slows down.

> [quoted in Griebel & Niesel, 2002, p. 67]

The teachers' goal is to make all children "ready to learn" when they enter elementary school by teaching basic skills, including precursors to reading, writing, and arithmetic, perhaps via teachers asking questions that children answer together. Children practice forming letters, sounding out words, counting objects, and writing their names. If a 4-year-old learns to read, that is success. (In a child-centered program, early reading might arouse suspicion that the child had too little time to play or socialize.) Note that these preschools do not stress social skills, which require more informal interaction between the children. Perhaps the definition of "readiness" is too narrow (Winter, 2011).

Many teacher-directed programs were inspired by behaviorism, which emphasizes step-by-step learning and repetition. Another inspiration comes from research indicating that children who have not learned basic vocabulary and learning strategies before kindergarten often fall behind in primary school. Many state legislatures mandate that all children learn particular concepts in preschool; such specifics are best fostered by teacher-directed learning (Bracken & Crawford, 2010).

The contrast between child-centered and teacher-directed philosophies is evident not only in lessons but also in attitudes and expectations. For instance, if one child bothers another child, should the second child tell the teacher, or should the two children work it out by themselves? If one child bites another, should the biter be isolated, counseled, admonished, punished, or—as sometimes happens—should the victim be told to bite back? Preschools need rules for such situations, and rules vary because of contrasting philosophies. In a child-centered program, the offender might be asked to think of the effect of his or her actions; in a teacher-directed program, punishment might be immediate.

It may seem easier for each teacher to do whatever he or she believes is best, resulting in a happy hodgepodge of strategies, but this may confuse children and parents. According to a detailed study of early-childhood staff in the Netherlands, differences are notable among adults raised in diverse cultures. In this study, the native-born Dutch teachers emphasized individual achievement more than the adults from the Caribbean or Mediterranean, who stressed sharing and group learning (Huijbregts et al., 2009). Thus, the Dutch teachers were more child-centered, while the immigrant teachers were more teacher-directed.

>> **Response for Unemployed Early-Childhood Teachers** (from page 276) It would be best for you to wait for a job in a program where children learn well, organized along the lines explained in this chapter. You would be happier, as well as learn more, in a workplace that is good for children. Realistically, though, you might feel compelled to take the 10-children-to-1-adult job. If you do, change the child/adult ratio—find a helper, perhaps a college intern or a volunteer grandmother. But choose carefully—some adults are not helpful at all. Before you take the job, remember that children need continuity: You can't leave simply because you find something better.

PAUL CHESLEY / STONE / GETTY IMAGES

Learning from One Another Every nation creates its own version of early education. In this scene at a nursery school in Kuala Lumpur, Malaysia, note the head coverings, uniforms, bare feet, and absence of boys. None of these elements would be found in most early-childhood-education classrooms in North America or Europe.

Observation Quiz What seemingly universal aspects of childhood are visible in this photograph? (see answer, page 282)

Especially for Teachers In trying to find a preschool program, what should parents look for? (see response, page 283)

New teachers in those schools (and probably in all schools) were likely to believe their way was best; teachers who had worked together for years were more similar in their beliefs and practices than those who had not (Huijbregts et al., 2009). One probable reason is that they had learned from one another.

This study highlights the complexities that can result when parents, teachers, and aides are from different backgrounds, as is often the case in North American programs. As many studies have shown, children can learn whatever academic and social skills are taught to them; those who attended preschool are usually advanced in cognitive skills over those who did not (Camilli et al., 2010; Chambers et al., 2010). However, all young children need personal attention, consistency, and continuity: It does not help when each adult applies different rules and routines.

Intervention Programs

Many nations try to narrow the learning gap evident between the most and least proficient kindergartner by offering early education to everyone (e.g., China, France, Italy, and Sweden). Public support for the early education of children as an intervention measure varies by cohort and culture.

First let's look at China, in some ways the opposite of the United States. When China's new regime took over in 1949, it wanted to increase national coherence and pride—not an easy task after a civil war and with a population of a billion people of many ethnicities. Accordingly, China opened thousands of preschools, emphasizing teacher-directed "collectivity and discipline," not play and individuality. Forty years later, in 1989, as educators became more influenced by Piaget and Vygotsky, the central government again imposed a curriculum, but this time it mandated a more child-centered curriculum (Xu, 2011, p. 151). The success of this curriculum is debatable, depending on what goals and standards should be measured. However, as detailed in later chapters, Chinese children have catapulted to the top in terms of scores on international achievement tests.

In Western nations, the reason for intervention has primarily been to help low-income children do better in school. By that measure, such intervention has been successful. In England, Canada, Australia, and the United States, numerous studies find that early education helps disadvantaged children (Camilli et al., 2010; Coghlan et al., 2009). Now we look at more specifics in the United States, in part to show the impact of changing policies over the decades.

Head Start

In the United States, since 1965, millions of young children were thought to need a "head start" on their formal education, to help foster better health and cognition before first grade. Consequently, the federal government funded a massive program for 4-year-olds called **Head Start.**

The first wave of research found dramatic improvement in children's intelligence and language; the first follow-up found that the early advances faded by second grade. Then, just as the funding was about to vanish because of diminishing returns, a third wave of research found that former Head Start students were more likely to graduate from high school and have jobs than those who had never had preschool education (Zigler & Styfco, 2004). Funding has continued: In 2009–2010, nearly a million children attended Head Start programs.

The intent of Head Start has changed over the decades, from lifting families out of poverty to promoting literacy, from providing dental care and immunizations to teaching standard English, from teaching parents better discipline methods to teaching children to solve their own conflicts. As more children speak a language other than English, literacy has become increasingly stressed; as the United States seems to fall behind other nations in science, children are encouraged to enjoy math and exploration.

Some Head Start teachers practice child-centered education while others prefer a teacher-directed approach; some consider parents to be a problem whereas others regard parents as allies (D. R. Powell, 2006). Some programs enroll only children of citizens; others allow all young children to attend.

These variations have immediate impact on children and families because young children are great learners, but what they learn depends on quite specific educational experiences. For example, many low-income 3- and 4-year-olds in the United States are not normally exposed to math. One Head Start program engaged children in a board game with numbers; their mathematical understanding advanced significantly (Siegler, 2009). Early Head Start, for children aged 3 and younger, is particularly effective for children of teenage parents of low socioeconomic status (SES). The program is thought to be effective not only because of the direct teaching in school but also because relieving some of the parents' stress allows them to provide more cognitive stimulation for their children (Ayoub et al., 2011).

Now to the present day. A recent congressional authorization of funding for Head Start included a requirement for extensive evaluation to answer two questions:

1. What difference does Head Start make to key outcomes of development and learning (in particular, school readiness) for low-income children? How does Head Start affect parental practices?
2. Under what circumstances and for whom does Head Start achieve the greatest impact?

The answers were not as dramatic as either advocates or detractors had hoped (U.S. Department of Health and Human Services, 2010). Head Start did improve children's literacy and math skills while they were in the program; their oral health

Head Start A federally funded early-childhood intervention program for low-income children of preschool age.

Disaster Recovery The success of Head Start led to Early Head Start, for children such as this 2-year-old in Biloxi, Mississippi. When Hurricane Katrina destroyed most of the community, it was the first program to reemerge there. Small children recover from disasters more easily if their parents can reestablish a normal life— which is why this Head Start program is helping entire families.

>> **Answer to Observation Quiz** (from page 280) Three aspects are readily apparent: These girls enjoy their friendships; they are playing a hand-clapping game, some version of which is found in every culture; and, most important, they have begun the formal education that their families want for them.

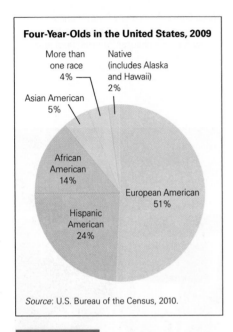

Four-Year-Olds in the United States, 2009

More than one race 4%

Native (includes Alaska and Hawaii) 2%

Asian American 5%

African American 14%

European American 51%

Hispanic American 24%

Source: U.S. Bureau of the Census, 2010.

FIGURE 9.6

Only Six Categories? Diversity in the United States is far greater than these statistics from the U.S. Census indicate. For instance, more than 50 distinct languages are spoken in U.S. homes. However, this pie chart reflects at least one cohort change: Children are more diverse than elders. Of those over age 75, 83 percent are European American.

All Together Now Socialization is part of every early-education program, in ways almost impossible for children who stay at home to benefit from. In this intervention program in Washington, D.C., children learn Spanish and English culture, with the help of a Peruvian American foster grandparent. All four are also learning computer skills—best mastered as one person shows another.

and their parents' responsiveness also improved. However, many benefits faded by first grade. One reason might be that many of the non–Head Start children in the comparison group were enrolled in other early-childhood programs—sometimes excellent ones, sometimes not.

Certain children benefited from Head Start more than others did, with benefits most apparent for children with the lowest family incomes, or those living in rural areas, or those with disabilities (U.S. Department of Health and Human Services, 2010). These were also the children least likely to find other sources of early education, which supports the notion that Head Start is better than no program at all. The strongest overall benefits were advances in language and social skills during early childhood, but those advances did not endure past kindergarten, with one exception—vocabulary. It is likely that more results will be found with long-term follow-up, a possibility shown by several small studies, reviewed now.

Bilingual Education

One type of early intervention program that does seem effective is bilingual education. This is increasingly necessary worldwide, as global migration results in millions of young children speaking a language at home that is not the language of instruction in school. International research on young children who need to learn another language is limited, but results from many nations suggest that successful strategies vary depending on the child, the home background, and national values. As one review concludes, "It is highly unlikely that one approach will be equally effective for all DLLs [dual language learners]" (Hammer et al., 2011).

In the United States, the parents of about one-third of all preschoolers speak a language other than English. Most often that language is Spanish, but about 2 percent of all 4-year-olds are of Chinese background, and immigrants from other countries—especially India, Russia, the Philippines, and Korea—are also likely to speak their original language at home. Some of the parents speak English as well, and some young children are enrolled in English preschools. As a result, many 4-year-olds are fluent in more than one language.

Research has focused on the approximately 24 percent of young children of Hispanic heritage (see Figure 9.6). In general, programs that combine English

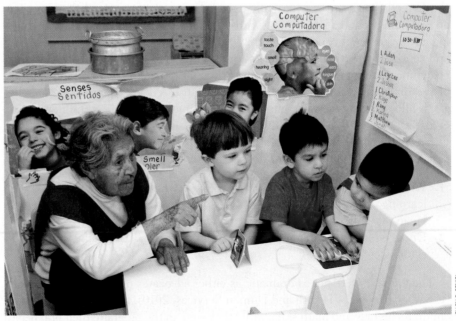

and Spanish instruction, sometimes with half a day for each, are more successful at teaching English while advancing Spanish than are programs that simply immerse the Spanish-speaking children in an English-only setting (Barnett et al., 2007). The various approaches to teaching a second language are further described in Chapter 12.

Unfortunately, for political and cultural reasons, the young children who are least likely to attend preschool in the United States are those from Spanish-speaking homes—less than half are in preschool (see Figure 9.7). These data are for 4-year-olds; the proportions of 3-year-olds from Spanish-speaking homes who are in preschools is even lower, perhaps 15 percent. Learning a second language is easiest before age 4: Most Spanish-speaking children do not have that opportunity.

As you see, the contrast between European and Hispanic Americans is most dramatic for center-based care, which includes private and state-funded preschools. The federal program, Head Start, requires that children be from low-income families, but even among such families, Hispanic children are less likely to be enrolled. One reason is fear of deportation if any member of the family is undocumented. Another reason is custom: The evidence that young children need preschool is familiar to most middle-class Americans, but not to most immigrants. An added problem is that many Head Start programs are limited to three hours a day, which limits language learning.

These data include only children who are U.S. citizens, thus excluding young children who were born in other nations and who are now living in the United States. Almost none of them are in preschool, although all of them are eligible for public education once they reach age 6. Each year, almost a million U.S. children enter first grade with poor English skills.

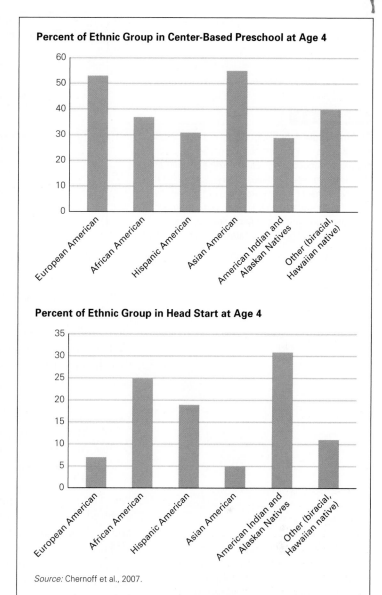

Source: Chernoff et al., 2007.

FIGURE 9.7

The Other Half Many research studies find that 4-year-olds who attend preschool are more competent in kindergarten—they have better language skills and are more likely to make friends. However, it is not known why almost half of all 4-year-olds are not in pre-kindergarten programs of any kind.

>> Response for Teachers (from page 280) Tell parents to look at the people more than the program. Parents should see the children in action and note whether the teachers show warmth and respect for each child.

Long-Term Gains from Intensive Programs

Based on longitudinal evaluation, most developmentalists are convinced that early intervention can make a difference if it is sufficiently intense with effective teachers. The evidence comes from three specific programs that enrolled children full time for years, sometimes beginning with home visits in infancy, sometimes continuing in after-school programs through first grade. One program, called Perry (or High/Scope), was spearheaded in Michigan (Schweinhart & Weikart, 1997); another, called Abecedarian, got its start in North Carolina (Campbell et al., 2001); a third, called Child–Parent Centers, began in Chicago (Reynolds, 2000).

All three programs compared experimental groups of children with matched control groups, and all reached the same conclusion: Early education can have substantial long-term benefits that become most apparent when the children are in the third grade or later. Children in these three programs scored higher on math and reading achievement tests at age 10 than did other children from the same backgrounds, schools, and neighborhoods. They were less likely to be placed in special classes for slow or disruptive children or to repeat a year of school compared with other children from the same neighborhoods.

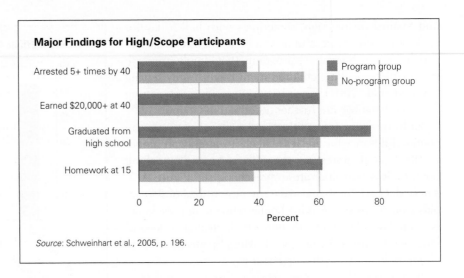

Major Findings for High/Scope Participants

Source: Schweinhart et al., 2005, p. 196.

FIGURE 9.8

And in Middle Age Longitudinal research found that two years in the intensive High/Scope preschool program changed the lives of dozens of children from impoverished families. The program had a positive impact on many aspects of their education, early adulthood, and middle age. (This graph does not illustrate another intriguing finding: The girls who attended High/Scope fared much better than the boys.)

Benefits continued. In adolescence, the children who had undergone intensive preschool education had higher aspirations, possessed a greater sense of achievement, and were less likely to have been abused. As young adults, they were more likely to attend college and less likely to go to jail, more often paying taxes rather than being on welfare (Reynolds & Ou, 2011; Schweinhart et al., 2005). Early education affected every aspect of their adult life, as "early cognitive and scholastic advantages lead to social and motivational gains that culminate in enhanced well-being" (Reynolds & Ou, 2011, p. 578) (see Figure 9.8).

All three research projects found that providing direct cognitive training (rather than simply letting children play), with specific instruction in various school-readiness skills, was useful as long as each child's needs and talents were considered—a circumstance made possible because the child/adult ratio was low. The curricular approach was a combination of child-centered and teacher-directed. Teachers were encouraged to involve parents in their child's education, and each program included strategies to ensure this home–school connection.

These programs were expensive (ranging from $5,000 to $17,000 annually per young child in 2010 dollars). From a developmental perspective, the decreased need for special education and other social services eventually made such programs a wise investment, perhaps saving $4 for every dollar spent (Barnett, 2007). The benefits to society over the child's lifetime, including increased employment and reduced crime, are much more than that.

In fact, the greatest lifetime return came from boys from high-poverty neighborhoods in the Chicago preschool program, with a social benefit over the boys' lifetime more than 12 times the cost (Reynolds et al., 2011). The problem is that the costs are immediate and the benefits long term. Without a developmental perspective, few legislators or voters are willing to fund expensive intervention programs that do not pay off until a decade or more later. An additional problem with all successful programs is scale: Success with a small program is difficult to translate into success for a million children.

State Programs

Inspired by these intensive programs as well as by other research on young children, many U.S. developmentalists advocate early education for every child, at least by age 3. Unfortunately, in the United States overall, only about half of 3- and

4-year-olds are enrolled in preschool, which reduces the "chance for success" in elementary school for the other half (*Education Week,* January 14, 2010).

This may be changing: 40 states sponsor public education for young children—although usually only for low-income 4-year-olds. In 2009–2010, more than a million children (1,292,310) attended state-sponsored preschools—more than double the number a decade earlier (Barnett et al., 2010). Since more than 4 million (4,268,000) children were born in 2006, that is about one-fourth of the entire cohort.

From a developmental perspective, the leading state is Oklahoma, which provides full-day kindergarten and preschool education for all children. Attendance is voluntary, but most children are enrolled. The data on the children's learning showed more gains than in Head Start or other state programs (Gormley et al., 2008). The curriculum emphasizes literacy and math; benefits are particularly strong for children whose home language is Spanish (Phillips et al., 2009).

For the 40 states that sponsor early education, the average funding is less than $5,000 per year per student. That is obviously not enough for a program with a low child/adult ratio, teachers who have college degrees, and professional mentoring in a safe, well-equipped space. The best programs include at least two adults per group, additional adults for special needs (such as an artist in Reggio Emilia or a nurse-educator in some U.S. programs), and a director who guides the program.

Only four states (Alabama, Alaska, North Carolina, and Rhode Island) have programs that developmentalists consider to be of high quality, and none of those four states have extensive programs (Barnett et al., 2010). Developmentalists agree that increasing the number of participants and improving the quality of preschool programs are prime goals; the problem is convincing legislators and the public that it must be done.

SUMMING UP

Research, particularly on preschool programs for children in low-income families, has proven that high-quality early education benefits children by improving language learning, social skills, and prospects for the future. Many different programs, including child-centered (Montessori and Reggio Emilia) and teacher-directed programs, are available—although sometimes very expensive. Massive intervention programs—such as Head Start and state-sponsored pre-kindergarten, as well as smaller ones such as High/Scope, Abecedarian, and Chicago's Child–Parent Centers—seem to improve the life course of low-income children who attend them. Nations, states, and parents differ in what they seek from early education for their children, and programs vary in teacher preparation, curriculum, physical space, and child/adult ratios. Quality matters. ∎

SUMMARY

Piaget and Vygotsky

1. Piaget stressed the egocentric and illogical aspects of thought during the play years. He called this stage preoperational thought because young children often cannot yet use logical operations to think about their observations and experiences.

2. Young children, according to Piaget, sometimes focus on only one thing (centration) and see things only from their own viewpoint (egocentrism), remaining stuck on appearances and current reality. They may believe that living spirits reside in inanimate objects, a belief called animism.

3. Vygotsky stressed the social aspects of childhood cognition, noting that children learn by participating in various experiences, guided by more knowledgeable adults or peers. Such guidance assists learning within the zone of proximal development, which encompasses the knowledge and skills that the child has the potential to learn.

4. According to Vygotsky, the best teachers use various hints, guidelines, and other tools to provide the child with a scaffold for new learning. Language is a bridge that provides social mediation between the knowledge that the child already has and the learning that the society hopes to impart. For Vygotsky, words are a tool for learning.

Children's Theories

5. Children develop theories, especially to explain the purpose of life and their role in it. In fact, one theory about children's thinking is called "theory-theory"—the hypothesis that children develop theories because all humans innately seek explanations for everything they observe.

6. One example of the developmental theory is called theory of mind—an understanding of what others may be thinking.

Notable advances in theory of mind occur at around age 4. Theory of mind is partly the result of brain maturation, but culture and experiences also have an impact.

Language Learning

7. Language develops rapidly during early childhood, a sensitive period but not a critical one for language learning. Vocabulary increases dramatically, with thousands of words added between ages 2 and 6. In addition, basic grammar is mastered.

8. Many children learn to speak more than one language, gaining cognitive as well as social advantages. Ideally, children become balanced bilinguals, equally proficient in two languages, by age 6.

Early-Childhood Education

9. Organized educational programs during early childhood advance cognitive and social skills, although specifics vary a great deal. Montessori and Reggio Emilia are two child-centered programs that began in Italy and are now offered in many nations. Behaviorist principles led to many specific practices of teacher-directed programs.

10. Head Start is a U.S. federal government program primarily for low-income children. Longitudinal research finds that early-childhood education reduces the risk of later problems, such as needing special education. High-quality programs increase the likelihood that a child will become a law-abiding, gainfully employed adult.

11. Many types of preschool programs are successful. It is the quality of early education that matters. Children learn best if teachers follow a defined curriculum and if the child/adult ratio is low. The training, warmth, and continuity of early-childhood teachers benefit the children in many ways.

KEY TERMS

preoperational intelligence (p. 257)
symbolic thought (p. 258)
centration (p. 258)
egocentrism (p. 258)
focus on appearance (p. 258)
static reasoning (p. 258)

irreversibility (p. 258)
conservation (p. 259)
animism (p. 259)
guided participation (p. 262)
zone of proximal development (ZPD) (p. 262)
scaffolding (p. 262)

overimitation (p. 263)
private speech (p. 263)
social mediation (p. 264)
theory-theory (p. 266)
theory of mind (p. 267)
fast-mapping (p. 270)
overregularization (p. 272)

balanced bilingual (p. 274)
Montessori schools (p. 277)
Reggio Emilia (p. 278)
Head Start (p. 281)

WHAT HAVE YOU LEARNED?

Piaget and Vygotsky

1. What are the strengths and weaknesses of preoperational thought?

2. What is the difference between egocentrism in a child and selfishness in an adult?

3. How does the animism of young children differ from the animism of adults?

4. How do the toys given to young children scaffold particular behaviors and values?

5. How does guided participation increase a child's zone of proximal development?

6. Why did Vygotsky think that talking to yourself is not a sign of illness but an aid to cognition?

Children's Theories

7. Is theory-theory as valid for adults as for children?

8. Why does a child's development of theory of mind make it more difficult to fool him or her?

9. What factors spur the development of theory of mind?

Language Learning

10. What is the evidence that early childhood is a sensitive time for learning language?

11. How does fast-mapping aid the language explosion?

12. How does overregularization signify a cognitive advance?

13. What evidence in language learning shows the limitations of logic in early childhood?

14. What are the advantages of teaching a child two languages?

15. How can language loss be avoided?

Early-Childhood Education

16. What do most preschools provide for children that most homes do not?

17. In child-centered programs, what do the teachers do?

18. What makes the Reggio Emilia program different from most other preschool programs?

19. Why are Montessori schools still functioning, 100 years after the first such schools opened?

20. What are the advantages and disadvantages of teacher-directed preschools?

21. What are the goals of Head Start?

22. Why have various evaluations of Head Start reached different conclusions?

23. What are the long-term results of intervention preschools?

APPLICATIONS

The best way to understand thinking in early childhood is to listen to a child, as applications 1 and 2 require. If some students have no access to children, they should do application 3 or 4.

1. Replicate one of Piaget's conservation experiments. The easiest one is conservation of liquids (Figure 9.1). Work with a child under age 5 who tells you that two identically shaped glasses contain the same amount of liquid. Then carefully pour one glass of liquid into a narrower, taller glass. Ask the child if one glass now contains more or if the glasses contain the same amount.

2. To demonstrate how rapidly language is learned, show a preschool child several objects and label one with a nonsense word the child has never heard. (*Toma* is often used; so is *wug*.) Or choose a word the child does not know, such as *wrench, spatula,* or the name of a coin from another nation. Test the child's fast-mapping.

3. Theory of mind emerges at about age 4, but many adults still have trouble understanding other people's thoughts and motives. Ask several people why someone in the news did whatever he or she did (e.g., a scandal, a crime, a heroic act). Then ask your informants how sure they are of their explanation. Compare and analyze the reasons as well as the degrees of certainty. (One person may be sure of an explanation that someone else thinks is impossible.)

4. Think about an experience in which you learned something that was initially difficult. To what extent do Vygotsky's concepts (guided participation, language mediation, apprenticeship, zone of proximal development) explain the experience? Write a detailed, step-by-step account of your learning process as Vygotsky would have described it.

>>ONLINE CONNECTIONS

To accompany your textbook, you have access to a number of online resources, including quizzes for every chapter of the book, flashcards (in English and Spanish), critical thinking questions, and case studies. For access to any of these links, go to www.worthpublishers.com/bergerca9e. In addition to these free resources, you'll also find links to podcasts, video clips, diagnostic quizzing with personalized study advice, and an ebook. Some of the videos and activities available online include:

- *Theory of Mind.* Watch a variety of children challenged by false-belief tasks.

- *Early-Childhood Language Development.* Six-year-olds can tell jokes and 3-year-olds engage in private speech. A variety of video clips showcase the development of children's speech through early childhood.

Early Childhood: Psychosocial Development

WHAT WILL YOU KNOW?

1. Should children be rewarded for doing what adults want them to do?
2. What do children learn from playing with other children?
3. Should caregivers let children watch television?
4. What is the best way to teach children right from wrong?
5. Why do young children exaggerate the differences between boys and girls?

My daughter Bethany, at about age 5, challenged one of my students to a fight.

"Girls don't fight," he said, laughing.

"*Nobody* fights," I corrected him.

We were both teaching Bethany how to express emotions. She learned well; by age 6, she no longer challenged young men to fight.

I remember this incident because I am troubled by what I said. "Nobody" refers to both sexes, but would I have said the same thing if I were male? Was I teaching Bethany to be passive? Should I have asked my student to play-fight with her, as men do with young boys? Or should I have allowed him to express gender norms?

Emotional control, rough play, parenting, morality, and sex differences are all discussed in this chapter. On some aspects experts agree. For instance, no developmentalist doubts that play teaches social understanding, that parents should guide and discipline their children, that bullies should be stopped. However, other aspects are controversial. "Nobody fights" may have been wrong . . . or right.

>> Emotional Development

Children gradually learn when and how to express emotions, becoming more capable in every aspect of their lives (Buckley & Saarni, 2009; Denham et al., 2003; Morrison et al., 2010). Controlling the expression of emotions, called **emotional regulation,** is the preeminent psychosocial accomplishment between ages 2 and 6 (N. Eisenberg et al., 2004). Such regulation is virtually impossible in infancy, but when the emotional hot spots of the limbic system connect to the maturing prefrontal cortex, children become more aware of their reactions. With emotional regulation, children learn how to be angry but not explosive, frightened but not terrified, sad but not inconsolable, anxious but not withdrawn, proud but not boastful, and so on.

Initiative Versus Guilt

During Erikson's third developmental stage, **initiative versus guilt,** pride emerges from the acquisition of the skills and competencies described in the previous two chapters. "Initiative" is saying something new, extending a skill, beginning

emotional regulation The ability to control when and how emotions are expressed.

initiative versus guilt Erikson's third psychosocial crisis, in which children undertake new skills and activities and feel guilty when they do not succeed at them.

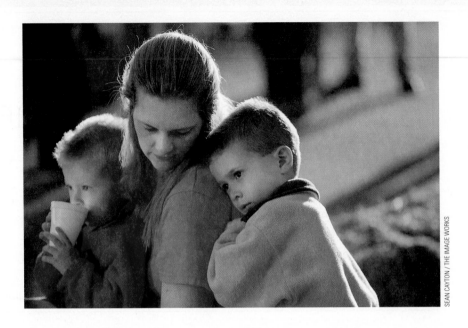

Close Connection Unfamiliar events often bring developmental tendencies to the surface, as with the curious boy and his worried brother, who are attending Colorado's Pikes Peak or Bust Rodeo breakfast. Their attentive mother keeps the livelier boy calm and reassures the shy one.

Observation Quiz Mother is obviously a secure base for both boys, who share the same family and half the same genes but are different ages: One is 2 and the other is 4. Can you tell which boy is younger? (see answer, page 292)

self-concept A person's understanding of who he or she is, in relation to self-esteem, appearance, personality, and various traits.

A Poet and We Know It She is the proud winner of a national poetry contest. Is she as surprised, humbled, and thankful as an adult winner would be?

a project. Depending on the outcome (including the parents' response), children feel the emotions of pride or guilt. Usually, North American parents encourage the natural enthusiasm, effort, and pride of their 3- to 6-year-olds. If, instead, parents dismiss rather than guide a child's emotions—fear, anger, or any other feeling—that child may not learn emotional regulation (Morris et al., 2007).

Protective Optimism

Children's beliefs about their worth are connected to parental confirmation, especially when parents remind their children of their positive accomplishments (Reese et al., 2007). ("You helped Daddy sweep the sidewalk? You made it very clean.") Remember that Erikson described *autonomy* at age 2, often expressed as stubbornness, nicknamed the terrible twos. By age 3, that trait is better regulated and directed and soon becomes *initiative,* as children are eager to learn new skills (Rubin et al., 2009). In the process, a child forms a **self-concept,** an understanding of the self, which usually includes gender and size. Girls are usually happy to be girls, boys to be boys, and both are glad they aren't babies. "Crybaby" is a major insult; praise for being "a big boy" or "a big girl" is welcomed.

Erikson recognized that young children are more proud than realistic. They believe that they are strong, smart, and good-looking—and thus that any goal is achievable. Whatever they are (self-concept) is thought to be good. For instance, they believe that their nation and religion are best; they feel sorry for children who do not belong to their country or church. But don't be too critical of such narrowness: Each of Erikson's stages is appropriate for development at each age. During early childhood, a positivity bias is beneficial; it encourages children to try unfamiliar activities, make friends, begin school, and so on (Boseovski, 2010).

Research finds that many young children are confident that their good qualities will endure but that bad qualities (even biological traits such as poor eyesight) will disappear (Lockhart et al., 2002). This "protective optimism" begins at about age 3, continues through childhood, and often disappears during adolescence (Boseovski, 2010). This seems true in many nations. Modesty is valued in Asian nations, but that does not necessarily diminish children's optimism: Many Japanese children believe they could become better if they just tried hard enough (Lockhart et al., 2008).

Brain Maturation

The new initiative that Erikson describes benefits from myelination of the limbic system, growth of the prefrontal cortex, and a longer attention span, all made possible by the neurological maturation described in Chapter 8. Concentrated attention aids social competence (Murphy et al., 2007) as children practice and then master various skills. They learn to pour juice, zip pants, or climb trees, undeterred by overflowing juice, stuck zippers, or a perch too high to climb down from. Faith in themselves helps them persist.

Erikson believed that as children develop self-awareness, some begin to feel guilt if they realize their own mistakes. Many people believe that guilt is a more mature emotion than shame (as in Erikson's autonomy versus shame and doubt) because guilt is internalized (Kochanska et al., 2002; Tangney et al., 2007). Guilt comes from within the person, whereas shame comes from outside and depends on other people's opinions. Unlike guilt, shame can be based on social prejudices regarding gender, ethnicity, or background.

To counter social prejudice, many parents of minority kindergartners (Mexican American, African American, or American Indian among others) encourage ethnic pride in their children (Brown et al., 2007; Lesane-Brown et al., 2010). Although very young children raised exclusively in one ethnic group begin to prefer faces that look familiar, they do not categorize ethnicity as adults do. At about age 4, however, social awareness and self-concept become stronger, and children tend to notice categories. That is when minority families typically teach children racial pride. Meanwhile, all children begin to develop moral values via pride and guilt, not shame and doubt—discussed later in this chapter.

Motivation

The idea that guilt comes from within the child highlights the distinction between *intrinsic motivation* and *extrinsic motivation*. **Intrinsic motivation** occurs when people do something for the joy of doing it: A musician might enjoy making music, even when no one else hears. **Extrinsic motivation** comes from outside, when people do something to gain praise (or some other reinforcement): A musician who plays for the reward of applause is an example. Knowing the difference is crucial in teaching young children (Cheng & Yeh, 2009).

For the most part, preschool children are intrinsically motivated. They enjoy learning, playing, and practicing whether or not someone else wants them to. Praise and prizes might be appreciated, but they are not the reason why children work at what they do. When playing a game, they might not keep score; the fun is in playing, not winning.

Intrinsic motivation is seen when children invent dialogues for their toys, concentrate on creating a work of art or architecture, and converse with **imaginary friends** who exist only in the child's imagination. The latter are rarely encouraged by adults (so the child has no extrinsic motivation to create them), but imaginary friends are nonetheless increasingly common as initiative builds from ages 3 through 7. They combat loneliness and aid emotional regulation. Children realize their imaginary friends are invisible and pretend, but conjuring them up nevertheless meets some of the child's psychosocial needs (Taylor et al., 2009).

Some imaginary friends are useful, as children need to control their tears and temper, to have a friend to provide comfort and reassurance, to learn how to share their toys, and so on (Taylor et al., 2009). Such friends have various characteristics, depending on what is needed. One girl's imaginary friend named Elephant was "7 inches tall, grey color, black eyes, wears tank top and shorts . . . sometimes

Glad to be Navajo These sisters are about to join the procession for the annual Inter-tribal Indian Ceremonial in Gallup, New Mexico. More important, they are gaining pride in their ancestry, a key aspect of childhood emotional development.

intrinsic motivation A drive, or reason to pursue a goal, that comes from inside a person, such as the need to feel smart or competent.

extrinsic motivation A drive, or reason to pursue a goal, that arises from the need to have one's achievements rewarded from outside, perhaps by receiving material possessions or another person's esteem.

imaginary friends Make-believe friends who exist only in a child's imagination; increasingly common from ages 3 through 7, they combat loneliness and aid emotional regulation.

Especially for Teachers One of your students tells you about playing, sleeping, and talking with an imaginary friend. Does this mean that that child is emotionally disturbed? (see response, page 293) is mean" (Taylor et al., 2004, p. 1178). By having an imaginary friend who is "sometimes mean," this girl was developing strategies to deal with mean people.

An Experiment in Motivation

In a classic experiment, preschool children were given markers and paper and assigned to one of three groups who received, respectively: (1) no award, (2) an expected award (they were told *before* they had drawn anything that they would get a certificate), and (3) an unexpected award (*after* they had drawn something, they heard, "You were a big help," and got a certificate) (Lepper et al., 1973). Later, observers noted how often children in each group chose to draw on their own. Those who received the expected award were less likely to draw later than those who were unexpectedly rewarded. The interpretation was that extrinsic motivation (condition 2) undercut intrinsic motivation.

This research triggered a flood of studies seeking to understand whether, when, and how positive reinforcement should be given. The consensus is that praising or paying a person after an accomplishment sometimes encourages that behavior. However, if payment is promised in advance, that extrinsic reinforcement may backfire (Cameron & Pierce, 2002; Deci et al., 1999; Gottfried et al., 2009).

Culture and Emotional Control

Cultures differ in what emotions they expect children to regulate, and children try to follow the norms of their culture. Some research finds that specific cultures emphasize control of particular emotions and behaviors (Harkness et al., 2011; J. G. Miller, 2004; Stubben, 2001):

- Fear (United States)
- Anger (Puerto Rico)
- Pride (China)
- Selfishness (Japan)
- Impatience (many Native American communities)
- Disobedience (Mexico)
- Erratic behavior (the Netherlands)

Cultures differ in control strategies as well (Matsumoto, 2004). Shame is used when a family's reputation is a priority. Indeed, in some cultures, "pride goeth before a fall" and people who "have no shame" are considered mentally ill (Stein, 2006). Cultural differences are also apparent in emotional expression: Children may be encouraged to express their feelings, or they may be taught that emotions are best kept to oneself (Kim et al., 2008).

Of course, cultures change, parents do not always follow cultural norms, and a child's temperament may not conform to cultural expectations. Not everyone from a particular background regulates emotions in a particular way, since "cultures are inevitably more complicated than the framework that is supposed to explain them" (Harkness et al., 2011, p. 92). Sometimes Asian versus North American or other Western cultures are assumed to endorse one value over another (cooperation versus independence is often cited), but once groups within those regions are compared, many differences emerge.

There are some universals, however. In every culture, parents encourage emotional regulation, and children of depressed parents are less able to regulate their emotions (Kovacs et al., 2008). As for impulsive children, everywhere neglectful or inconsistent caregivers make their emotional problems worse, whereas nurturing caregivers guide them to be *more* competent than other children (Belsky et al., 2007; Hane & Fox, 2006).

Especially for College Students Is extrinsic or intrinsic motivation more influential in your study efforts? (see response, page 294)

Especially for Teachers of Young Children Should you put gold stars on children's work? (see response, page 294)

>> Answer to Observation Quiz (from page 290) Size is not much help, since children grow slowly during these years and the heads of these two boys appear about the same size. However, emotional development is apparent. Most 2-year-olds, like the one at the right, still cling to their mothers; most 4-year-olds are sufficiently mature, secure, and curious to watch the excitement as they drink their juice.

Seeking Emotional Balance

In every culture and cohort, and at every age, developmentalists seek to prevent **psychopathology,** an illness or disorder (*-pathology*) of the mind (*psycho-*). Although symptoms and diagnoses are influenced by culture—rebellion might be alarming in some cultures but appreciated in others—impaired emotional regulation universally signals pathology. Parents are expected to guide their young children toward cultural norms (Trommsdorff & Cole, 2011).

psychopathology An illness or disorder of the mind.

Externalizing and Internalizing Problems

Without adequate regulation, emotions are overpowering. Intense reactions occur in two seemingly opposite ways.

Some people have **externalizing problems:** Their powerful feelings burst out (exit) uncontrollably. They may externalize a feeling of rage, for example, by lashing out at other people or breaking things. Without emotional regulation, an angry child might flail at another person or lie down screaming and kicking. That externalized reaction might be accepted in a 2-year-old's temper tantrum, but 5-year-olds should have more self-control, perhaps pouting or cursing, not hitting and screaming.

externalizing problems Difficulty with emotional regulation that involves expressing powerful feelings through uncontrolled physical or verbal outbursts, as by lashing out at other people or breaking things.

Other people have **internalizing problems:** They are fearful and withdrawn, turning distress inward. Again, with maturity, the extreme fears of some 2-year-olds (e.g., terror of the bathtub drain, of an imagined tidal wave, of a stranger on crutches) diminish. They may still be afraid of the first day of kindergarten, for instance, but they bravely let go of their mother's hand. One manifestation of internalizing problems is physical illness: A child might have headaches or stomachaches. Although the cause may be psychological, the ache is real. The worst reaction would be to blame the child for the symptom: That might make internalizing worse.

internalizing problems Difficulty with emotional regulation that involves turning one's emotional distress inward, as by feeling excessively guilty, ashamed, or worthless.

Neither externalizing nor internalizing children regulate their emotions very well—or, more precisely, they do not regulate the *expression* of emotions. Either they have too little self-control or they control themselves too much (Caspi & Shiner, 2006; Hart et al., 2003). If emotional regulation is not learned in early childhood, children are likely to develop externalizing or internalizing problems in middle childhood—particularly if the emotion they never learned to regulate is anger (Morris et al., 2010). Problems get worse in adolescence, with some internalizing young children becoming externalizing teenagers.

Who's Chicken? Genes and good parenting have made this boy neither too fearful nor too bold. Appropriate caution is probably the best approach to meeting a chicken.

Sex Differences in Emotional Regulation

Girls usually develop emotional regulation ahead of boys. This difference is especially evident with externalizing emotions; it is apparent in childhood, and then continues in adolescence, with some externalizing boys becoming violent. However, girls also increase their rate of psychopathology: As detailed in Chapter 16, teenage girls are more often depressed than teenage boys, a manifestation of internalized emotions.

One study traced internalizing and externalizing emotions from early to middle childhood. Researchers gave 5-year-olds toy figures and told them the beginning of a story (Zahn-Waxler et al., 2008). Two children (named Mark and Scott for the boys, Mary and Sarah for the girls) were said to start yelling at each other, and the 5-year-olds were asked to show what happened next.

>> **Response for Teachers** (from page 291) No. In fact, imaginary friends are quite common, especially among creative children. The child may be somewhat lonely, though; you could help him or her find a friend.

>> **Response for College Students** (from page 292) Both are important. Extrinsic motivation includes parental pressure and the need to get a good job after graduation. Intrinsic motivation includes the joy of learning. Have you ever taken a course that was not required and was said to be difficult? That was intrinsic motivation.

>> **Response for Teachers of Young Children** (from page 292) Perhaps, but only after the work is completed and if the child has put genuine effort into it. You do not want to undercut intrinsic motivation, as happens with older students who know a particular course will be an "easy A."

Learning Emotional Regulation Like this girl in Hong Kong, all 2-year-olds burst into tears when something upsets them—a toy breaks, a pet refuses to play, or it's time to go home. A mother who comforts them and helps them calm down is teaching them to regulate their emotions.

Many boys had Mark and Scott hitting and kicking each other. Boys whose behavior problems worsened between ages 5 and 9 (as rated by their teachers and parents) were the most likely to show such externalizing play-acting at age 5. By contrast, 5-year-old girls often had Mary and Sarah talk about their conflict or change the subject. Curiously, those girls whose behavior problems worsened from age 5 to 9 were more likely than the other children to engage in "reparative be-havior," such as Mary hugging Sarah and saying, "I'm sorry." This response may indicate internalized guilt or shame. The authors explain:

> Gender-role stereotypes or exaggerations of masculine qualities (e.g., impulsive, aggressive, uncaring) and feminine qualities (submissive, unassertive, socially sensitive) are reflected not only in the types of problems males and females tend to develop but also in different forms of expression.
>
> [*Zahn-Waxler et al., 2008, p. 114*]

These researchers suggest that, for both sexes, extreme externalization or extreme internalization predicts future psychopathology.

The Brains of Boys and Girls

For both sexes, emotional regulation requires thinking before acting (deciding whether and how to display joy, anger, fear, or any other emotion). Such thinking occurs in the prefrontal cortex, the executive area of the brain. As you remember from Chapter 8, the prefrontal cortex regulates the limbic system (especially the amygdala), where powerful emotions form.

Normally, neurological advances in the prefrontal cortex at about age 4 or 5 make children less likely to throw a temper tantrum, provoke a physical attack, or burst into giggles during prayer (Kagan & Herschkowitz, 2005). Throughout early childhood, violent outbursts, uncontrolled crying, and terrifying phobias (irrational, crippling fears) diminish. The capacity for self-control—such as not opening a present immediately if asked to wait and not expressing disappointment at an undesirable gift—becomes more evident (Carlson, 2003; Grolnick et al., 2006).

Children of both sexes learn emotional regulation and avoid extremes of emotional imbalance, guided by their families (Grusec, 2011). However, when a family mistreats their children, emotions are dysregulated. Because of gender differences in the brain and in hormones, mistreated boys are more likely to externalize and mistreated girls to internalize. This gender difference is found in every culture and thus is probably genetic—the result of the XX or XY chromosomes—although culture and family have an impact. Neurological impairments compound the problem. For many reasons, then, by age 5, maltreated boys with immature emotional regulation are likely to throw things and vulnerable girls are likely to sob uncontrollably.

Parents are obviously crucial in helping children regulate their emotions, but preschool teachers are important as well. A program that helped Head Start teachers in 18 classrooms encourage emotional control was effective in promoting reading and math skills without changing the curriculum. The teachers learned how to set clear rules and routines and to redirect negative behavior (e.g., when one child began to hit another to get a toy, the teacher helped the first child use words to express the problem and implement turn-taking). That meant less impulsive behavior and fewer teacher–child confrontations. A control group of 17 teachers used the same curriculum, but their students did not advance as much in naming letters and understanding numbers as the students of the teachers who learned and practiced techniques to regulate emotions (Raver et al., 2011).

Erikson and many others find that pride, purpose, and initiative are integral components of the self-concept of young children, who want to try new activities. Children who have difficulty with emotional regulation may develop internalizing or externalizing problems, which may be early signs of psychopathology. Many factors—including genes, gender, brain development, culture, and hormones—influence emotional regulation. Parents and teachers can help children with emotional maturation, and this affects later school achievement.

>> Play

Play is timeless and universal—apparent in every part of the world for thousands of years. Many developmentalists believe that play is the most productive as well as most enjoyable activity that children undertake (Elkind, 2007; Frost, 2009), although whether play is critical or merely fun is controversial. Some educators want to reduce playtime so children will focus on reading and math skills; others predict both emotional and academic problems for children who play too rarely (Hirsh-Pasek et al., 2009; Pellegrini, 2009; Rubin et al., 2009).

Playmates

Young children play best with *peers,* that is, people of about the same age and social status. Two-year-olds are intrigued by peers but are not yet good playmates: They might throw a ball and expect another child to throw it back rather than hold it. By contrast, most 6-year-olds are quite skilled: They can gain entry to a peer group, manage conflict, take turns, find friends, and keep playmates. Over those years, peers provide practice in emotional regulation, empathy, and social understanding (Cohen, 2006).

There is an obvious task for parents: Find playmates, ideally of the same age and sex. Even the most playful parent is outmatched by another child at negotiating the rules of tag, at wrestling on the grass, at pretending to be sick, at killing a dragon. Although the specifics vary, "social play with peers is one of the most important areas in which children develop positive social skills" (Xu, 2010, p. 496).

Cultural Differences in Play

All young children play, whether they are on Arctic ice or desert sand. Children create dramas that reflect their culture and play games that have been passed down from older generations. Because play varies by culture, gender, and age, it teaches children values and skills required in their particular context (Sutton-Smith, 1997). Chinese children fly kites, Alaskan natives tell dreams and stories, Lapp children pretend to be reindeer, Cameroon children hunt mice, and so on. Although play is thought to be universal, not only do specifics differ but so do frequency and playmates: When adults are concerned with basic survival, they rarely play with their children. Children play with each other instead (Kalliala, 2006; Roopnarine, 2011).

As children grow older, play becomes more social, influenced not only by the availability of playmates

Play Ball! In every nation, young children play with balls, but the specific games they play vary with the culture. Soccer is the favorite game in many countries, including Brazil, where these children are practicing their dribbling on Copacabana Beach in Rio de Janeiro.

REUTERS / SERGIO MORAES

but also by the physical setting (a small playroom, a large park, a wild hillside). One developmentalist bemoans the twenty-first century's "swift and pervasive rise of electronic media" and modern adults who lean "more toward control than freedom," while lauding children who find places to play independently and "conspire ways to elude adult management" (Chudacoff, 2007, p. 98). Many young children incorporate plots and characters that originated on television into their play, including dramas that indicate sexual awareness by age 6 (Kalliala, 2006). Not long ago, such early knowledge of sex was a sign of abuse; now it may simply mean too much television.

Before the electronic age, young children played outside with other children, often of both sexes and several ages. The youngest children learned from the older ones. The development of social play from ages 1 to 6 was described by American sociologist Mildred Parten (1932). She distinguished five kinds of play, each more interactive than the previous one:

1. *Solitary play:* A child plays alone, unaware of any other children playing nearby.
2. *Onlooker play:* A child watches other children play.
3. *Parallel play:* Children play with similar toys in similar ways, but not together.
4. *Associative play:* Children interact, observing one another and sharing material, but their play is not yet mutual and reciprocal.
5. *Cooperative play:* Children play together, creating dramas or taking turns.

As already mentioned, play is affected by culture and context, and these have changed since Parten's day. Many Asian parents teach 3-year-olds to take turns, share, and otherwise cooperate—and they do. On the other hand, many North American children, at age 6 and older, still engage in parallel play. Given all the social and economic changes over the past century, this may be developmentally appropriate (Xu, 2010).

Active Play

Children need physical activity to develop muscle strength and control. Peers provide an audience, role models, and sometimes competition. For instance, running skills develop best when children chase or race each other, not when a child runs alone. Gross motor play is favored among young children, who enjoy climbing, kicking, and tumbling (Case-Smith & Kuhaneck, 2008).

Active social play—not solitary play—correlates with peer acceptance and a healthy self-concept (Nelson et al., 2008) and may help regulate emotions (Sutton-Smith, 2011)—something adults might remember when they prefer young children to be quiet. Among nonhuman primates, deprivation of social play warps later life, rendering some monkeys unable to mate, to make friends, even to survive with other monkeys (Herman et al., 2011; Suomi, 2004).

Rough-and-Tumble Play

rough-and-tumble play Play that mimics aggression through wrestling, chasing, or hitting, but in which there is no intent to harm.

The most common form of active play is called **rough-and-tumble** because it looks quite rough and because the children seem to tumble over one another. The term was coined by British scientists who studied primates in East Africa (Blurton-Jones, 1976). They noticed that monkeys often chased, attacked, rolled over in the dirt, and wrestled quite roughly, but without hurting one another. If a young monkey wanted to play, all it had to do was come close, catch the eye of a peer, and then run a few feet, looking back. This invitation was almost always accepted, with the other monkey responding with a *play face* rather than an angry one. Puppies, kittens, and young chimpanzees similarly invite rough-and-tumble play.

When the scientists returned to their own children, they saw that human youngsters, like baby monkeys, also enjoy rough-and-tumble play (Pellegrini & Smith, 2005). They chase, wrestle, and grab each other, developing games like tag and cops-and-robbers, with play faces, lots of chasing, and various conventions, expressions, and gestures that children use to signify "just pretend."

Rough-and-tumble play appears everywhere (although cops-and-robbers can be robots-and-humans or many other iterations), particularly among young males (human and otherwise) when they are allowed to play freely with ample space and minimal supervision (Berenbaum et al., 2008; Hassett et al., 2008). Many scientists think that rough-and-tumble play helps the prefrontal cortex to develop, as children learn to regulate emotions, practice social skills, and strengthen their bodies (Pellegrini et al., 2007; Pellis & Pellis, 2011). Indeed, some believe that play in childhood, especially rough-and-tumble play between boys and their fathers, not only teaches regulation of aggression but may also prevent antisocial behavior (even murder) later on (Wenner, 2009).

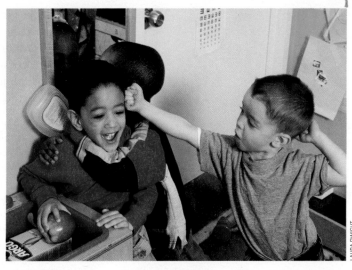

Male Bonding Sometimes the only way to distinguish aggression from rough-and-tumble play is to look at the faces. The hitter is not scowling, the hittee is laughing, and the hugger is just joining in the fun. Another clue that this is rough-and-tumble play comes from gender and context. These boys are in a Head Start program, where they are learning social skills, such as how to avoid fighting.

sociodramatic play Pretend play in which children act out various roles and themes in stories that they create.

Drama and Pretending

Another major type of active play is **sociodramatic play,** in which children act out various roles and plots, taking on "any identity, role, or activity that they choose. They can be mothers, babies, Cinderella, or Captain Hook. They can make tea or fly to the moon. Or they can fight, hurt others, or kill or imprison someone" (Dunn & Hughes, 2001, p. 491).

Sociodramatic play allows children to do the following:

- Explore and rehearse social roles
- Learn how to explain their ideas and convince playmates to agree
- Practice emotional regulation by pretending to be afraid, angry, brave, and so on
- Develop self-concept in a nonthreatening context

Sociodramatic play builds on pretending and social interest, both of which emerge in toddlerhood. But preschool children do more than pretend; they combine their own imagination with that of others, advancing in theory of mind (see Chapter 9) as they do so (Kavanaugh, 2011). The beginnings of sociodramatic play are illustrated by this pair, a 3-year-old girl and a 2-year-old boy. The girl wanted to act out the role of a baby, and she persuaded the boy to play a parent.

Boy: Not good. You bad.
Girl: Why?
Boy: 'Cause you spill your milk.
Girl: No. 'Cause I bit somebody.
Boy: Yes, you did.
Girl: Say, "Go to sleep. Put your head down."
Boy: Put your head down.
Girl: No.
Boy: Yes.
Girl: No.
Boy: Yes. Okay, I will spank you. Bad boy. [*Spanks her, not hard*]
Girl: No. My head is up. [*Giggles*] I want my teddy bear.
Boy: No. Your teddy bear go away.
  [*At this point she asked if he was really going to take the teddy bear away.*]

  [*from Garvey, reported in Cohen, 2006, p. 72*]

Note that the girl not only directed the play but also played her part, sometimes accepting what the boy said and sometimes not. The boy took direction yet also made up his own dialogue and actions ("Bad boy").

Compare their simple plot to the play of four boys, about age 5, in a day-care center in Finland. Joni plays the role of the evil one who menaces the other boys; Tuomas directs the drama and acts in it as well.

> **Tuomas:** And now he *[Joni]* would take me and would hang me. . . . This would be the end of all of me.
> **Joni:** Hands behind.
> **Tuomas:** I can't help it. I have to. *[The two other boys follow his example.]*
> **Joni:** I would put fire all around them.
> *[All three brave boys lie on the floor with hands tied behind their backs. Joni piles mattresses on them, and pretends to light a fire, which crackles closer and closer.]*
> **Tuomas:** Everything is lost.
> *[One boy starts to laugh.]*
> **Petterl:** Better not to laugh, soon we will all be dead. . . . I am saying my last words.
> **Tuomas:** Now you can say your last wish. . . . And now I say I wish we can be terribly strong.
> *[At that point, the three boys suddenly gain extraordinary strength, pushing off the mattresses and extinguishing the fire. Good triumphs over evil, but not until the last moment, because, as one boy explains, "Otherwise this playing is not exciting at all."]*
>
> [adapted from Kalliala, 2006, p. 83]

Good versus evil is a favorite theme of boys' sociodramatic play. In contrast, girls often act out domestic scenes. Such gender differences are found in many cultures. In the same day-care center where Joni piles mattresses on his playmates, the girls say their play is "more beautiful and peaceful . . . [but] boys play all kinds of violent games" (Kalliala, 2006, p. 110). Although gender differences in sociodramatic play are found universally, prevalence varies. Some cultures find it frivolous and discourage it: In those places, sociodramatic play still occurs, but less often. Other cultures encourage it; parents teach toddlers to be pretend lions, or space creatures, or ladies drinking tea, and then children develop more elaborate and extensive play with each other (Kavanaugh, 2011).

A Toy Machine Gun These boys in Liberia are doing what young children everywhere do—following adult example. Whenever countries are at war, children play soldiers, rebels, heroes, or spies. From their perspective, there is only one problem with such play—no one wants to be the enemy.

MIKE GOLDWATER / ALAMY

SUMMING UP

Playing with other children is a boon for children's emotional regulation, as they learn how to get along with one another. Although play is universal, the particular form it takes varies not only by age but also by gender and culture. Many forms of play, including rough-and-tumble and sociodramatic, require social understanding and compromise. Younger children chase each other and act out simple dramas; older children have more nuanced and elaborate rules and scripts. ∎

>> Challenges for Adults

We have seen that young children's emotions and actions are affected by many factors, including brain maturation, culture, and peers. Now we focus on another primary influence on young children: their parents and teachers.

Caregiving Styles

Although thousands of researchers have traced the effects of parenting on child development, the work of one person, 40 years ago, continues to be influential. Teachers can also be categorized in the styles identified here (Ertesvåg, 2011). In her original research, Diana Baumrind (1967, 1971) studied 100 preschool children, all from California, almost all middle-class European Americans. (The cohort and cultural limitations of this sample were not obvious at the time.)

Baumrind found that parents differed on four important dimensions:

1. *Expressions of warmth.* Some parents are warm and affectionate; others, cold and critical.
2. *Strategies for discipline.* Parents vary in whether and how they explain, criticize, persuade, ignore, and punish.
3. *Communication.* Some parents listen patiently; others demand silence.
4. *Expectations for maturity.* Parents vary in the degree of responsibility and self-control they expect from their children.

Baumrind's Three Styles of Caregiving

On the basis of the dimensions listed above, Baumrind identified three parenting styles (summarized in Table 10.1).

- **Authoritarian parenting.** The authoritarian parent's word is law, not to be questioned. Misconduct brings strict punishment, usually physical (but not so harsh as to be abusive). Authoritarian parents set down clear rules and hold high standards. They do not expect children to offer opinions; discussion about emotions is especially rare. (One adult from such a family said that "How do you feel?" had only two possible answers: "Fine" and "Tired.") Authoritarian parents love their children, but they seem cold, rarely showing affection.
- **Permissive parenting.** Permissive parents (also called *indulgent*) make few demands, hiding any impatience they feel. Discipline is lax, partly because permissive parents have low expectations for maturity. Instead, permissive parents are nurturing and accepting, listening to whatever their offspring say. They try to be helpful, but they do not feel responsible for shaping their children.
- **Authoritative parenting.** Authoritative parents set limits and enforce rules, yet they also listen to their children. They encourage maturity, but they usually forgive (not punish) if the child falls short. They consider themselves

authoritarian parenting An approach to child rearing that is characterized by high behavioral standards, strict punishment of misconduct, and little communication.

permissive parenting An approach to child rearing that is characterized by high nurturance and communication but little discipline, guidance, or control. (Also called *indulgent parenting*.)

authoritative parenting An approach to child rearing in which the parents set limits but listen to the child and are flexible.

"He's just doing that to get attention."

one could be hurt). The researchers explain that these Mexican American families do not fit any of Baumrind's categories; respect for adult authority is rarely accompanied by a hostile mother–child relationship. Instead, the relationship shows evident *cariono* (caring) (Livas-Dlott et al., 2010).

In general, multicultural and international research has found that particular discipline methods and family rules are less important than warmth, support, and concern. Children from every ethnic group and every country benefit if they believe that they are appreciated; children everywhere suffer if they feel rejected and unwanted (Khaleque & Rohner, 2002; Maccoby, 2000).

Socioeconomic factors may be crucial. Authoritarian practices increase as income falls, perhaps because low-income families tend to be larger and thus cannot individualize their attention as authoritative families might, or perhaps because the adults want to raise obedient children who will not challenge police or employers later on. Every culture has ethnotheories about child rearing that relate to adult expectations within that society and that may differ from those of the culture of the original families Baumrind studied, as she herself acknowledges (Baumrind, 2005).

Given a multicultural perspective, developmentalists hesitate to recommend any particular parenting style (Dishion & Bullock, 2002; J. G. Miller, 2004). That does not mean that all families function equally well—far from it. Signs of trouble, including overcontrol, undercontrol, and inability to play with others, appear in children's behavior. Adults who are ineffective or uninvolved are one cause of these problems, but not the only one.

What About the Teachers?

Cohort patterns alert us to an obvious change. When Baumrind did her original research, most young children were cared for, almost exclusively, by their parents. Now most children in the United States and in many other nations have nonparental caregivers as well, who can be authoritative, authoritarian, permissive, or neglectful. Although some babysitters fall under the last two of these four styles, almost never is a preschool teacher permissive or neglectful because allowing a group of children to do whatever they want results in chaos, conflict, and perhaps even danger. Young children are not sufficiently adept at emotional regulation that they can play together, unsupervised, for long.

However, teachers can be authoritarian, setting down the law with no exceptions, or authoritative, setting guidelines that can change with discussion. Teachers with more education tend to be more authoritative, responding to each child, listening and encouraging language, and so on. This fosters more capable children, which is one reason colleges are encouraged to offer degrees for students who want to teach young children and one reason teacher education is one of the criteria used to measure program excellence (Barnett et al., 2010; Norris, 2010).

In general, young children learn more from authoritative teachers because the teachers are perceived as warmer and more loving. In fact, one study found that, compared with children who had authoritarian teachers, those children whose teachers were child-centered, noncontrolling, and very supportive scored higher on school-readiness measures (Barbarin et al., 2010). This is another example illustrating how preschool teachers who attend to the emotional climate of the classroom

>> Response for Political Scientists
(from page 300) There are many parenting styles, and it is difficult to determine each one's impact on children's personalities. At this point, attempts to connect early child rearing with later political outlook are speculative.

are more successful at teaching academic skills. In this study, children learned the most if all their caregivers were authoritative, but if their parents were authoritarian and their teachers authoritative (a mismatch more likely for the African American children), that was better than having authoritarian teachers.

This result was unexpected, since usually a mismatch creates stress. Why didn't it in this case? Perhaps young children, with their preoperational focus on appearance instead of logic, feel personally rejected (recall egocentrism) if their teacher harshly punishes them—especially if the teacher is of another ethnic group. In this study, the African American children with authoritarian parents may have recognized their parents' affection within an authoritarian style, but they did not see warmth in their strict teachers.

The New Media

New challenges confront each generation. One of today's great challenges is the influence of electronic media on children. All media—television, the Internet, electronic games, and so on—can be harmful, especially when the content is violent (Anderson et al., 2007, 2008; Bailey et al., 2010; Gentile et al., 2007; Smyth, 2007).

However, most young children in the United States spend more than three hours each day using one electronic medium or another. Almost every North American family owns at least two televisions, and most preschoolers watch apart from their parents, often in their own rooms. Many children in child-care programs watch videos, play games on computers, and so on.

Electronic media are not always harmful, a topic discussed further in later chapters. During early childhood, some children may learn basic literacy from educational programs, especially if adults watch with them and reinforce the lessons. However, children rarely select educational programs over fast-paced cartoons, in which everyone hits, shoots, and kicks. Unfortunately, although many parents, teachers, and politicians are rightly concerned about children's eating and health habits, they seem oblivious to children's media diet. As a result, even health suffers: For example, in one study, one-third of the 5-year-olds were too heavy for their age and height, and hours spent watching television correlated with overweight (Kimbro et al., 2011).

"Why don't you get off the computer and watch some TV?"

Hoping Are electronic devices destructive in early childhood? Not if the girl's family are just moving into their new home, soon to turn this unfurnished room into a living or dining area and setting up the TV in the basement. And not if the boys intend to take turns playing the video game—both of which are unlikely.

Research Design

Scientists: Heather L. Kirkorian, Tiffany A. Pempek, Lauren A. Murphy, Marie E. Schmidt, and Daniel R. Anderson, all at the University of Massachusetts.

Publication: *Child Development* (2009).

Participants: Fifty-one parents and their 1- to 3-year olds, mostly middle-class European Americans.

Design: Children and parents were videotaped in a well-equipped playroom for an hour, with a television in the corner showing an adult program (chosen by the parent) for half of the time. Magazines were also available for the adults to read. Parents were asked to relax, interacting with their child as they would at home. Observations of interaction were noted every 10 seconds (360 segments per parent–child dyad) and tallied for language and parental involvement by coders blind to the hypothesis of the study.

Major conclusion: Most (not all) parents interacted and spoke less when the television was on. This was true for adults of both sexes (two fathers were included), all ethnicities, and with children of all ages, especially the 2-year-olds, as shown in Figure 10.1.

Comments: This study has many strengths: detailed observation (every 10 seconds) by "blind" coders, each dyad exposed to both conditions (thus controlling for individual differences in interaction patterns), and inclusion of very young children (most earlier research assumed 1-year-olds were not affected by television). However, only 51 parent–child dyads were studied, all from one region of the United States and almost all middle class, even though background television is more prevalent in low-income families. Furthermore, the researchers were all from one university. Do any of these factors limit this study?

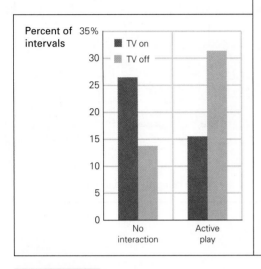

FIGURE 10.1

Don't Bother Me For dyads of 2-year-olds and their parents, having a TV on in the background reduced play by half. The effect was not as dramatic (although still evident) for 1-year-olds. Have 2-year-olds learned to be quiet when the television is on?

Good choices are particularly hard for adults to enforce because people of all ages are currently more engaged with electronic media (television, texting, e-mail, social networking) than with direct interaction. Young children learn from that example. Even when they are too young to understand television dialogue and television is merely background noise, children play less and interaction is markedly reduced when the TV is on (Kirkorian et al., 2009; Schmidt et al., 2008). Yet language development depends on conversation that is individualized to each child, and emotional regulation depends on personal guidance. (See the Research Design.)

Thus, the problem is not only that violent media teach destructive behavior but also that all media take time from constructive interactions. According to the *displacement hypothesis,* whatever time children devote to electronic media reduces time spent in social and educational activities—a hypothesis proven in school-age children and likely true in younger children as well (Weis & Cerankosky, 2010).

SUMMING UP

Over the past 40 years, Diana Baumrind and most other developmentalists have found that authoritative caregiving (warm, with guidance) is more effective than either authoritarian (very strict) or permissive (very lenient) styles. Other researchers have found that uninvolved caregivers are the least effective of all. In any culture, children thrive when their caregivers appreciate them and care about their accomplishments. The children of parents who are uninvolved, uncaring, or abusive seldom become happy, well-adjusted, and high-achieving adults.

Good caregiving is not achieved by following any one simple rule; children's temperaments vary, and so do cultural patterns. Teachers of young children are most effective when they are warm and responsive. For all adults, the media pose a particular challenge worldwide because children are attracted to colorful, fast-paced images; but violent TV programs in particular lead to more aggressive behavior. Educational television and computer games may be instructive, but all media reduce direct, one-on-one interaction, which is particularly needed when children are young.

■

>> Moral Development

Children develop increasingly complex moral values, judgments, and behaviors as they mature. The social bonds described in Chapter 7, the theory of mind described in Chapter 9, and the emotional development and social awareness described in this chapter are the foundation for morality. Piaget thought that moral development began when children learned games with rules, which he connected with concrete operational thought at about age 7 (Piaget, 1932/1997). We now know that Piaget underestimated young children: Games with rules and moral development are both evident during early childhood. Indeed, some researchers see moral judgment beginning in infancy (Narvaez & Lapsley, 2009).

Many developmentalists believe that children's attachment to their parents, and then to others, is the beginning of morality. According to evolutionary theory, humans protect, cooperate, and even sacrifice for one another precisely because social groups evolved to encourage such prosocial behavior (Krebs, 2008). With maturity and adult guidance, children develop guilt (as Erikson explained) and self-control, and that helps them behave in ethical ways (Kochanska et al., 2009; Konner, 2010).

Nature and Nurture

Debate rages over how children internalize standards, develop virtues, and avoid vices. Conflicting perspectives are taken by theories and scholars of psychology, philosophy, theology, and sociology. This conflict reflects the primal debate in developmental study—nature versus nurture:

- The "nature" perspective suggests that morality is genetic, an outgrowth of natural bonding, attachment, and cognitive maturation. That would explain why young children help and defend their parents, no matter what the parents do, and punish other children who violate moral rules.
- The "nurture" perspective contends that culture is crucial, as children learn the values of their community. Some children believe that people who eat raw fish, or hamburgers, or bacon, or crickets are immoral.

Both nature and nurture are always important, but developmentalists disagree about which is more important for morality (Killen & Smetana, 2007; Krebs, 2008; Narvaez & Lapsley, 2009; Turiel, 2006). That debate cannot be settled here, but it does seem that parents and teachers are crucial. Our discussion centers on two moral issues that arise from age 2 to age 6: First, prosocial and antisocial behavior (especially aggression), and second, the moral lessons inherent in discipline.

Empathy and Antipathy

Two moral emotions are evident as children play with one another. With increasing social experiences and decreasing egocentrism, they develop **empathy,** an understanding of other people's feelings and concerns, and **antipathy,** dislike or even hatred.

Empathy is not the same as sympathy, which means feeling sorry *for* someone. Rather, empathy means feeling sorry *with* someone, experiencing the other person's pain or sadness as if it were one's own. This recalls the research with mirror neurons (see Chapter 1), which suggests that observing someone else's behavior activates the same areas in the brain of the observer as in the person performing the action. Scientists studying young humans and other primates report spontaneous efforts to help others who are hurt, crying, or in need of help: That is evidence of empathy (Warneken & Tomasello, 2009).

empathy The ability to understand the emotions and concerns of another person, especially when they differ from one's own.

antipathy Feelings of dislike or even hatred for another person.

prosocial behavior Actions that are helpful and kind but are of no obvious benefit to oneself.

Empathy leads to **prosocial behavior,** extending helpfulness and kindness without any obvious benefit to oneself. Prosocial behavior seems to be more a result of empathy than cognition, more emotional understanding than theory of mind (Eggum et al., 2011). Expressing concern, offering to share food or a toy, and including a shy child in a game or conversation are examples of prosocial behavior among young children. Jack, age 3, showed empathy when he

> refused to bring snacks with peanuts to school because another boy had to sit alone during snack because he was allergic to nuts. Jack wanted to sit with him.
>
> *[Lovecky, 2009, p. 161]*

antisocial behavior Actions that are deliberately hurtful or destructive to another person.

Antipathy can lead to **antisocial behavior,** deliberate hurtfulness or destructiveness aimed at another person, including people who have not actually harmed the antisocial person. Antisocial actions include verbal insults, social exclusion, and physical assaults (Calkins & Keane, 2009). An antisocial 4-year-old might look another child in the eye, scowl, and then kick him hard without provocation.

Toddlers may hit, grab, pull hair, and so on, seemingly unaware that they are hurting someone. By age 4 or 5—as a result of brain maturation, theory of mind, emotional regulation, and interactions with caregivers—children can be deliberately prosocial or antisocial. When children are antisocial, adults sometimes assume that the other child's tears will make the mean child feel guilty. This is not necessarily true: Brain scans show that adults who want to punish others do so with pleasure, even if it means some loss (of money, time, or effort) to themselves (Takahashi et al., 2009). Children need to *learn* to control their aggression; most do, but this is not inevitable.

Emotional regulation, moral development, and the emergence of empathy are nowhere more apparent than in the way children learn to deal with their aggressive impulses. The gradual control of aggression is evident on close observation of rough-and-tumble play; in the fantasies of domination and submission acted out in sociodramatic play; in the increase in self-control from ages 2 to 6; and in the sharing of art supplies, construction materials, and toys (Peterson & Flanders, 2005; Utendale & Hastings, 2011).

Not surprisingly, given the moral sensibilities of young children, 5-year-olds already judge whether another child's aggression is justified or not (Etchu, 2007). As with adults, self-defense is more readily forgiven than is a deliberate, unprovoked attack. However, do not assume that bullies realize when they are wrong: At every age, aggressors feel they had a reason to do what they did.

instrumental aggression Behavior that hurts someone else because the aggressor wants to get or keep a possession or a privilege.

Researchers recognize four general types of aggression. **Instrumental aggression** is common among 2-year-olds, who often want something they do not have and who try, without thinking, to get it. The reaction of another child—crying and resisting the grab of the instrumentally aggressive child—is also more typical at age 2 than earlier or later.

reactive aggression An impulsive retaliation for another person's intentional or accidental action, verbal or physical.

Reactive aggression is common among young children as well; almost every child responds in some way when attacked by another child, with the specific response becoming better controlled as emotional regulation increases. In fact, children are less likely to react with physical aggression as they develop emotional control and theory of mind (Olson et al., 2011).

relational aggression Nonphysical acts, such as insults or social rejection, aimed at harming the social connection between the victim and other people.

Relational aggression (usually verbal) destroys another child's self-esteem and disrupts the victim's social networks, becoming more hurtful as children mature. A young child might tell another, "You can't be my friend" or "You are fat," hurting another's feelings. That is relational aggression.

The fourth and most ominous type is **bullying aggression,** done to dominate someone else. It is not rare among young children but should be stopped before school age, when it becomes particularly destructive for both victims and bullies (see Chapter 13). All forms of aggression should become less common over the years of early childhood, as the brain matures and empathy increases. Parents, peers, and preschool teachers are all pivotal mentors in this process.

Discipline

A particular issue for many developmentalists is discipline, administered when children violate a norm of their family and culture. Adult values and experiences affect when and how they discipline. Of course, values depend partly on culture. Discipline does as well.

Ideally, adults anticipate misbehavior and guide children toward patterns of behavior and internalized standards of morality, taking developmental immaturity into account, as shown in Table 10.2. However, misbehavior cannot always be prevented. In case any reader imagines that children can be cajoled to always be good, consider the results of a study of mothers and 3-year-olds during late afternoon (a stressful time). Conflicts (including verbal disagreements) arose about every two minutes (Laible et al., 2008). Here is one example:

> **Child:** I want my other shoes.
> **Mother:** You don't need your other shoes. You wear your Pooh sandals when we go for a walk.
> **Child:** Noooooo.
> **Mother:** [Child's name]! You don't need your other shoes.
> **Child:** [Cries loudly]
> **Mother:** No, you don't need your other shoes. You wear your Pooh sandals when we go for a walk.
> **Child:** Ahhhh. Want pretty dress. [Crying]
> **Mother:** Your pretty dress.
> **Child:** Yeah.
> **Mother:** You can wear them some other day.
> **Child:** Noooooo. [Crying]
>
> [quoted in Laible et al., 2008, pp. 442–443]

In this study of 64 young children and their mothers, securely attached children had as many conflicts as insecurely attached ones. However, unlike in the dialogue above, the mothers of the securely attached children were more likely to compromise and explain (Laible et al., 2008). Was that the best response? Consider the alternatives.

Physical Punishment

In the United States, young children are slapped, spanked, or beaten more often than are infants or older children. Many adults remember receiving such punishment and think it works. Physical punishment (called *corporal punishment* because it hurts the body) succeeds at the moment—spanking stops misbehavior—but longitudinal research finds that children who are physically punished are more likely to become bullies, delinquents, and then abusive adults, as well as slower to learn in school (Straus & Paschall, 2009).

In some nations (New Zealand is the most recent example), corporal punishment is illegal; in other nations, it is the norm. In the United States, it is illegal

bullying aggression Unprovoked, repeated physical or verbal attack, especially on victims who are unlikely to defend themselves.

TABLE 10.2	Discipline and Children's Thinking

1. *Remember theory of mind.* Young children gradually come to understand things from other viewpoints. Encouraging empathy ("How would you feel if someone did that to you?") increases prosocial behavior and decreases antisocial behavior by age 5.

2. *Remember egocentrism.* Young children are developing a sense of who they are. Adults might protect that emerging self by, for example, not insisting on sharing.

3. *Remember fast-mapping.* Young children are eager to talk and think, but they say more than they understand. A child who "doesn't listen" may have not understood.

4. *Remember that young children are not logical.* Before age 5, children confuse lies and wishes, and forget why they are punished.

Many developmentalists study how children's thinking affects behavior. Here are four reminders from Chapter 9 that apply to disciplining young children. Often children believe their parents' anger, not their own misdeeds, cause punishment.

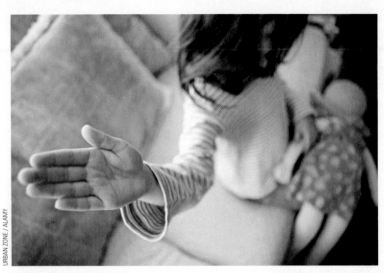

URBAN ZONE / ALAMY

Smack Will the doll learn never to disobey her mother again?

(although sometimes used anyway) in most schools, especially schools for young children. Although adults might believe that physical punishment will "teach a lesson" of obedience, the lesson that children often learn is that "might makes right." When they become bigger and stronger, they'll use corporal punishment on others.

Of course, children who are spanked do not always become violent adults. Some experts believe that the correlations are merely correlations—not causes. For example, teenage mothers are more likely to spank their children, who are more likely to become delinquents who fail in school, but this does not prove that spanking is causal. Spanking may increase the risk of school failure and crime, but other factors that correlate with teen parenthood (poverty, low education, and impulsive, antisocial personality) are stronger influences.

Nonetheless, many developmentalists wonder why parents would take the chance. The only argument in favor of spanking is that alternative measures are no better, either in controlling bad behavior or increasing moral values (Larzelere et al., 2010). Before reaching that conclusion yourself, however, consider the alternatives again.

Psychological Control

psychological control A disciplinary technique that involves threatening to withdraw love and support and that relies on a child's feelings of guilt and gratitude to the parents.

Another method of discipline is called **psychological control,** in which children's shame, guilt, and gratitude are used to control their behavior (Barber, 2002). Psychological control may reduce academic achievement, just as spanking does.

Consider the results of a study of an entire cohort (the best way to obtain an unbiased sample) of children born in Finland (Aunola & Nurmi, 2004). Their parents were asked 20 questions about their approach to child rearing. The following four items, which the parents rated from 1 ("Not at all like me") to 5 ("Very much like me"), measured psychological control:

1. "My child should be aware of how much I have done for him/her."
2. "I let my child see how disappointed and shamed I am if he/she misbehaves."
3. "My child should be aware of how much I sacrifice for him/her."
4. "I expect my child to be grateful and appreciate all the advantages he/she has."

The higher the parents scored on these four measures of psychological control, the lower the children's math scores—and this connection grew stronger over time. Surprisingly, math achievement suffered most if parents were also high in affection (e.g., they frequently hugged their children), perhaps because that increased the child's guilt when the parent was disappointed (Aunola & Nurmi, 2004).

Other research finds that psychological control can depress children's achievement, creativity, and social acceptance (Soenens & Vansteenkiste, 2010). Compared to corporal punishment, children punished with psychological control seem less likely to be physical bullies but more likely to be relationally aggressive (Kuppens et al., 2009), depressed, and anxious (Gershoff et al., 2010).

Exclusion and Conversation

time-out A disciplinary technique in which a child is separated from other people for a specified time.

The disciplinary technique most often used in North America is the **time-out,** whereby an adult requires the misbehaving child to sit quietly, without toys or playmates, for a short time (Barkin et al., 2007). Time-out is favored by many experts in North American education. For example, in the large, longitudinal evaluation of Head Start highlighted in Chapter 9, an increase in use of time-out and a decrease in use of spanking were considered signs of improved parental discipline (U.S. Department of Health and Human Services, 2010).

However, research on the effectiveness of time-out is confounded by the many ways it is used. Some parents angrily put the child in a corner, yelling at him or her to stay there until the parent is no longer angry. The effect is similar to corporal punishment: The child feels rejected. To be effective, time-out must be brief; one minute for each year of the child's age is suggested.

Another alternative to physical punishment and psychological control is *induction,* in which the parents talk extensively with the offending child, getting the child to understand why his or her behavior was wrong. Conversation helps children internalize standards, but induction takes time and patience. Since 3-year-olds confuse causes with consequences, they cannot answer an angry "Why did you do that?" or appreciate a lengthy explanation. Simple induction ("You made him sad") may be more appropriate.

Induction may be best used before the child has seriously offended. In a study of parents and older siblings responding to a young child violating various norms and risking danger, the parents were more likely to talk to the child and encourage alternate behavior, while the siblings waited until the child was clearly offending and then yelled "time-out."

In general, induction is recommended if the goal is an internalized standard of right and wrong (Turiel, 2006). An interesting example comes from Japan, where physical punishment is rare and a close and protective mother–child bond is the norm: The rate of homicide is one-tenth that of the United States and one-one-hundredth that of Jamaica. Some developmentalists think inductive discipline is the reason (Guerra et al., 2011), although, again, there are dozens of explanations for this correlation.

Bad Boy or Bad Parent? For some children and cultures, sitting alone is an effective form of punishment; for others, it produces an angry child.

No Simple Answer

Methods of discipline vary in consequences and effectiveness, depending on temperament, culture, and the adult–child relationship. For example, time-out is effective *if* the child prefers to be with other people and *if* it is delivered without anger. As explained in Chapter 2, one version of time-out for older children is suspension from school. However, if a child hates school, suspension amounts to reinforcement, not punishment.

In every nation and family, adults vary in their expectations for proper behavior and in their response to transgressions. What is "rude" or "nasty" in one community is accepted, even encouraged, in another. Even family conflicts (such as between a child and an adult) are thought to require understanding and negotiation in some homes, including many in the United States, but are completely unacceptable in others.

Parents are often unaware of their ethnotheories—no wonder they do not explain them and no wonder their children disagree, disobey, and disappoint (Harkness et al., 2011). When the two parents have different childhood backgrounds or when the school culture differs from that of the home, the children are more likely to be considered disobedient and disrespectful—and indeed they are, without realizing it.

Given all this, adults might be tempted to give up and let the child alone. But remember that children need guidance in order to develop the emotional regulation and other advances

Cruel and Unusual? The PBS series *Antiques Roadshow* is popular among adults, but for a child whose sense of the finer things in life is still developing, it might be an apt punishment.

SHE USED TO HAVE 'TIME OUT' IN HER BEDROOM BUT WE FIND MAKING HER WATCH RERUNS OF THE 'ANTIQUES ROADSHOW' IS **FAR** MORE EFFECTIVE!

that occur during early childhood: Permissive or uninvolved caregivers have unhappy children.

All adults agree that moral development is important, and all developmentalists agree that the cognitive and emotional characteristics of young children make early childhood a critical time for teaching moral behavior. However, exactly what morals are crucial and how to achieve them is not obvious, as explained in the following. No wonder punishment is not a simple issue. One young child who was disciplined for fighting protested, "Sometimes the fight just crawls out of me." Ideally, punishment won't "just crawl out" of the adult.

A VIEW FROM SCIENCE

Culture and Punishment

Worldwide, cultural differences in child discipline are apparent. For example, only half as many Canadian parents as U.S. parents slap, pinch, or smack their children (Oldershaw, 2002). Although many U.S. school districts forbid corporal punishment in schools, the U.S. Supreme Court decided in 2004 that teachers and parents could use "reasonable force" to punish children (Bugental & Grusec, 2006). Physical punishment by anyone—parent, teacher, sibling, stranger—is illegal in many other developed nations (including Austria, Croatia, Cyprus, Denmark, Finland, Germany, Israel, Italy, Norway, New Zealand, and Sweden) because it is considered a violation of human rights (Bitensky, 2006).

Perhaps the United States has more authoritarian parents than other nations do. However, cultural differences are evident by region and income even within the United States (Giles-Sims & Lockhart, 2005). Parents in the southern states and parents in low-income families do more spanking than do parents in New England and in wealthier families.

Cultural differences may lie behind a controversy that recently arose in the United States over a recommendation by some evangelical Christians to put a drop of hot sauce (which burns) on a child's tongue as punishment for forbidden speech. This method is included in a book titled *Creative Correction* (Whelchel, 2005). Most evangelical parents as well as developmentalists consider this practice abusive. Yet opinions are strongly divided. For example, most comments (posted on Amazon.com in 2011) regarding this book were either highly favorable (90 readers rated it at 5) or highly unfavorable (66 readers rated it at 1), with only 30 in between (at 2, 3, or 4).

One woman wrote:

> Putting hot sauce on your child's tongue? I bet the author wouldn't ever dare to do that to herself & look at all the hate spewing out of her mouth. As a born-again believer & mother, I'd never follow anything in this book. It's so unchristlike that it's sickening. There's nothing "creative" about her correction ideas—it's just plain mean & a newer version of old abuse tactics that our parents used to do.

A woman who highly recommended the book wrote:

> I haven't had the need for the Tabasco trick yet, but I'm not above using it. It would make a strong impression and wouldn't require a repeat dose, I'm quite sure. Child abuse? Hardly. Giving a child free reign over the TV, internet and the house IS child abuse. Ask any elementary school teacher who her problem child is and it'll be the kid with no discipline at home. A well-behaved child grows into a well-behaved adult. This world certainly needs more of those.

Remember the study of Latino mothers and their 4-year-olds (Livas-Dlott et al., 2010)? Induction was rare and time-out was almost never used: The implicit belief was that the connection between child and mother should not be broken, even in discipline. In those Mexican American families, disobedient children needed to listen to their mothers; if they didn't comply, the child

Laughing? Pulling an ear is physical punishment—and this would be considered abuse in some cultures. Here, however, no one seems upset.

might be moved from the scene of the forbidden action or told the social reason to obey (one mother got her son to help tidy the living room by saying that she should not be the only one cleaning up). In only 3 percent of the disobedient instances did the mother lay hands on the child.

As for international comparisons, most Americans consider Japanese mothers too permissive. The Japanese almost never punish children younger than 6. Instead, they use reason, empathy, and expressions of disappointment. They might be considered permissive parents. However, although U.S. children in permissive families tend to be immature and unhappy, Japanese children raised in a permissive home usually develop well. The reason may be summed up in the word *amae*, which refers to the strong and affectionate bond that is typical of Japanese mother–child relationships (Rothbaum et al., 2000). For many Japanese children, their mother's approval is so important that no punishment is needed. Six-year-olds who, to a Western eye, might appear overly dependent on and affectionate toward their indulgent mothers seem quite normal in Japan.

The parents' underlying attitude may be crucial. One study of African American mothers found that if they disapproved of spanking but did it nonetheless, their children were likely to be depressed; however, their children were OK if spanking mothers were convinced that spanking was what they should do (McLoyd et al., 2007). Similarly, Chinese American parents who used physical punishment and shame raised children who were relatively happy and well adjusted *if* the parents used those methods because they agreed with the Chinese ideology that led to them (Fung & Lau, 2009).

Do all these observations lead to any general conclusions? Perhaps only that a multicultural understanding makes it difficult to judge which tactic is best, but that long-term as well as immediate consequences need to be considered. All children need guidance; there are many ways to provide it.

Especially for Parents Suppose you agree that spanking is destructive, but you sometimes get so angry at your child's behavior that you hit him or her. Is your reaction appropriate? (see response, page 313)

SUMMING UP

Moral development occurs throughout childhood and adolescence. During early childhood, the most powerful moral lessons—particularly the need to be appropriately prosocial, with aggression controlled—are learned. Ideally, children learn to be good friends to each other, particularly avoiding unprovoked aggression. Parents discipline their children in many ways, with each method teaching lessons about right and wrong. Induction seems most likely to lead to internalized standards of morality.

>> Becoming Boys and Girls

Biology determines whether a child is male or female. As you know from Chapters 3 and 4, at about 8 weeks after conception, the SRY gene on the Y chromosome directs the reproductive organs to develop externally, and then male hormones exert subtle internal control over the brain, body, and later behavior. Without that SRY gene, the fetus develops female organs, which produce other hormones, again beginning in prenatal development and affecting the brain.

However, sexual identity is more than biology, and it is during early childhood that patterns and preferences become apparent. Children become more gender conscious with every year of childhood (Ruble et al., 2006). Even 2-year-olds apply gender labels (*Mrs., Mr., lady, man*) consistently. By age 4, children are convinced that certain toys (such as dolls or trucks) are appropriate for one sex but not the other and that certain roles (not just Daddy or Mommy, but also nurse, teacher, police officer, soldier) are best for one sex or the other.

Sex and Gender

Scientists distinguish **sex differences,** which are biological differences between males and females, from **gender differences,** which are culturally prescribed roles and behaviors. In theory, this seems like a straightforward separation, but, as with every nature–nurture distinction, the interaction between sex and gender makes it hard to separate the two (Hines, 2004).

sex differences Biological differences between males and females, in organs, hormones, and body type.

gender differences Differences in the roles and behaviors of males and females that are prescribed by the culture.

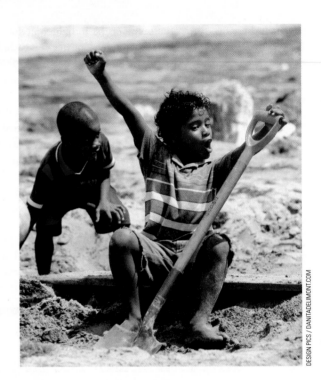

Playing in the Sand What do you need at the beach? Depending on gender, either a man-sized shovel or a flowery raincoat. Already by age 4, girls are more likely to hold hands and boys much more likely to use construction tools.

Young children are particularly confused about gender and sex, partly because culture emphasizes gender. One little girl said she would grow a penis when she got older, and one little boy offered to buy his mother one. Ignorance about biology and sex was demonstrated by a 3-year-old who went with his father to see a neighbor's newborn kittens. Returning home, the child told his mother that there were three girl kittens and two boy kittens. "How do you know?" she asked. "Daddy picked them up and read what was written on their tummies," he replied.

In recent years, sex and gender issues have become increasingly complex as cultural acceptance of varied sexual orientations has increased—to the outrage of some and the joy of others. Adults may be lesbian, gay, bi, trans, "mostly straight," or totally heterosexual (Thompson & Morgan, 2008, p. 15). Despite the increasing acceptance of sexual diversity, at around age 5 many children become quite rigid in their ideas of sex and gender. If 5-year-old boys need new shoes, but the only ones that fit them are pink, most would rather go barefoot. In fact, by age 3 boys reject pink toys and girls prefer them (LoBue & DeLoache, 2011).

Theories of Gender-Role Development

There are many theories to explain the reasons why boys and girls, and men and women, see the sexes as they do. A dynamic-systems approach reminds us that the attitudes, the roles, and even the biology of gender differences and similarities change from one developmental period to the next; the theories about how and why this occurs change as well (Martin & Ruble, 2010).

Biologically, the differences may seem minor—a matter of only one of the 46 chromosomes. Yet that chromosome seems to affect almost everything (e.g., rough-and-tumble play, emotional regulation, parental reactions to misbehavior, to name just a few), although it determines very little, at least until puberty. For instance, the fact that boys are more likely to chase and catch each other in rough-and-tumble play does not keep millions of little girls from chasing and catching.

Nonetheless, if given many playmates to choose from, as when a child is in preschool with a dozen peers, girls usually prefer to play with the girls and boys with the boys. Despite their parents' and teachers' wishes, children of either sex might say, "No girls [or boys] allowed." Even teenagers see ethnic discrimination as more wrong than sex discrimination (Møller & Tenenbaum, 2011). How can this be explained?

Psychoanalytic Theory

Freud (1938) called the period from about ages 3 to 6 the **phallic stage** because he believed its central focus is the *phallus*, or penis. At about 3 or 4 years of age, said Freud, the process of maturation makes a boy aware of his male sexual organ. He begins to masturbate, to fear castration, and to develop sexual feelings toward his mother.

These feelings make every young boy jealous of his father—so jealous, according to Freud, that every son wants to replace his dad. Freud called this the **Oedipus complex,** after Oedipus, son of a king in Greek mythology. Abandoned as an infant and raised in a distant kingdom, Oedipus later returned to his birthplace and, not realizing who they were, killed his father and married his mother. When he discovered what he had done, he blinded himself in a spasm of guilt.

Freud believed that this ancient drama has been replayed in the Greek classic *Oedipus Rex* over two millennia because it dramatizes emotions that all boys feel about their parents—both love and hate. Every male feels guilty about the incestuous and murderous impulses that are buried in his unconscious. In self-defense, boys develop a powerful conscience called the **superego,** which is quick to judge and punish. That marks the beginning of morality, according to psychoanalytic theory, which contends that a young boy's fascination with superheroes, guns, kung fu, and the like arises from his unconscious impulse to kill his father. An adult man's homosexuality, homophobia, or obsession with punishment might be explained by an imperfectly resolved phallic stage. Later psychoanalytic theorists agree that morality originates from the clash between unconscious wishes and parental prohibitions in childhood (Hughes, 2007).

Freud offered several descriptions of the phallic stage in girls. One centers on the **Electra complex** (also named after a figure in classical mythology). The Electra complex is similar to the Oedipus complex in that the little girl wants to eliminate the same-sex parent (her mother) and become intimate with the opposite-sex parent (her father). Girls may also develop a superego, although Freud thought it weaker than in boys.

According to psychoanalytic theory, children of both sexes cope with their guilt and fear through **identification;** that is, they try to become like the same-sex parent. Consequently, young boys copy their father's mannerisms, opinions, actions, and so on, and girls copy their mother's. Both sexes exaggerate the male or female role. Since the superego arises from the phallic stage, and since Freud believed that sexual identity and expression were crucial for mental health, his theory suggests parents should encourage boys and girls to follow appropriate sex roles, with every child accepting his or her sexual identity.

Many social scientists from the mid-twentieth century onward have believed that Freud's explanation of sexual and moral development "flies in the face of sociological and historical evidence" (David et al., 2004, p. 139). In graduate school, I learned that Freud was unscientific. However, as explained in Chapter 1, developmental scientists seek to connect research, theory, and experience. My own experience has made me rethink my rejection of Freud, as the following explains.

phallic stage Freud's third stage of development, when the penis becomes the focus of concern and pleasure.

Oedipus complex The unconscious desire of young boys to replace their father and win their mother's romantic love.

superego In psychoanalytic theory, the judgmental part of the personality that internalizes the moral standards of the parents.

Electra complex The unconscious desire of girls to replace their mother and win their father's romantic love.

identification An attempt to defend one's self-concept by taking on the behaviors and attitudes of someone else.

>> Response for Parents (from page 311) No. The worst time to spank a child is when you are angry. You might seriously hurt the child, and the child will associate anger with violence. You would do better to learn to control your anger and develop other strategies for discipline and for prevention of misbehavior.

THINKING CRITICALLY

Berger and Freud

My family's first "Electra episode" occurred in a conversation with my eldest daughter, Bethany, when she was about 4 years old:

> **Bethany:** When I grow up, I'm going to marry Daddy.
> **Mother:** But Daddy's married to me.
> **Bethany:** That's all right. When I grow up, you'll probably be dead.
> **Mother:** *[Determined to stick up for myself]* Daddy's older than me, so when I'm dead, he'll probably be dead, too.
> **Bethany:** That's OK. I'll marry him when he gets born again.

At this point, I couldn't think of a good reply. I had no idea where she had gotten the concept of reincarnation. Bethany saw my face fall, and she took pity on me:

> **Bethany:** Don't worry, Mommy. After you get born again, you can be our baby.

The second episode was a conversation I had with Rachel when she was about 5:

> **Rachel:** When I get married, I'm going to marry Daddy.
> **Mother:** Daddy's already married to me.
> **Rachel:** *[With the joy of having discovered a wonderful solution]* Then we can have a double wedding!

The third episode was considerably more graphic. It took the form of a "valentine" left on my husband's pillow by my daughter Elissa, who was about 8 years old at the time. It is reproduced here.

Finally, when my youngest daughter, Sarah, turned 5, she also expressed the desire to marry my husband. When I told her she couldn't, because he was married to me, her response revealed one more hazard of watching TV: "Oh, yes, a man can have two wives. I saw it on television."

I am not the only feminist developmentalist to be taken aback by her own children's words. Nancy Datan (1986) wrote about the Oedipal conflict: "I have a son who was once five

years old. From that day to this, I have never thought Freud mistaken." As you remember from Chapter 1, however, a single example (or four daughters from another family) does not prove that Freud was correct. A behaviorist explanation would be that my daughters wanted to model themselves after me and thus naively thought that marrying my husband would do it. Cohort changes, which my two infant grandsons remind me of daily, may mean that my grandsons (no granddaughters yet) may seek someone quite unlike their mothers—or may choose to avoid marriage completely.

Or they may make me change my mind again. You have your own theories and experiences, and I still think Freud was wrong on many counts. But his description of the phallic stage seems less bizarre than I once thought.

Pillow Talk Elissa placed this artwork on my husband's pillow. My pillow, beside it, had a less colorful, less elaborate note—an afterthought. It read "Dear Mom, I love you too."

Behaviorism

In contrast to psychoanalytic theorists, behaviorists believe that virtually all roles, values, and morals are learned. To behaviorists, gender distinctions are the product of ongoing reinforcement and punishment, as well as social learning.

Some evidence supports learning theory as an explanation of gendered roles. Parents, peers, and teachers all reward behavior that is "gender appropriate" more than behavior that is "gender inappropriate" (Berenbaum et al., 2008). For example, "adults compliment a girl when she wears a dress but not when she wears pants" (Ruble et al., 2006, p. 897). According to social learning theory, children notice the ways men and women behave, and children are punished when they act inappropriately (usually not physically but with shaming words, such as "Boys don't cry" or "Be a good girl"). They internalize the standards they observe, becoming proud of themselves when they act like a "little man" or a "little lady" (Bandura & Bussey, 2004; Bussey & Bandura, 1999).

Interestingly, sex roles seem more significant for males than for females (Banerjee & Lintern, 2000; David et al., 2004). Boys are criticized for being sissies more than girls are for being tomboys. Fathers, particularly, expect their daughters to be sweet and their sons to be tough.

Behaviorists believe children learn about proper behavior not only directly (as by receiving a gender-appropriate toy or an adult's praise) but also indirectly, through *social learning.* Children model their behavior after people they perceive to be nurturing, powerful, and yet similar to themselves. For young children, those people are their parents, and men and women are usually the most sex-typed of their entire lives when they are raising young children. For instance, if ever an adult woman quits work to become a housewife, she does so when she has young children; the children do not realize that their family's arrangement, with their mother doing domestic work and their father working outside the home, is a temporary aberration.

Cognitive Theory

Cognitive theory offers an alternative explanation for the strong gender identity that becomes apparent at about age 5. Remember that cognitive theorists focus on how children understand various ideas. Children develop concepts about their experiences. In this case, a **gender schema** is the child's understanding of sex differences (Kohlberg et al., 1983; Martin et al., 2002; Renk et al., 2006).

Young children have many gender-related experiences but not much cognitive depth. They tend to see the world in simple terms. For this reason, they categorize male and female as opposites, even when evidence contradicts such a sexist view. Nuances, complexities, exceptions, and gradations about gender (as well as about everything else) are beyond the preoperational child. Furthermore, as they try to make sense of their culture, they encounter numerous customs, taboos, and terminologies that enforce the gender norms. Remember that for preoperational children, appearance is crucial and static thinking makes them believe that whatever is has always been and is irreversible.

In addition, the need to develop a self-concept leads young children to categorize themselves as male or female and then to behave in a way that fits their concept. For that reason, cognitive theorists see "Jill's claim that she is a girl because

gender schema A cognitive concept or general belief based on one's experiences—in this case, a child's understanding of sex differences.

Toy Guns for Boys, Cinderella for Girls
Young boys throughout the world are the ones who aim toy guns, while young girls imagine themselves as Cinderella, admiring the glass slipper. The question is why: Are these young monks in Laos and these young girls in Virginia responding to biology or culture?

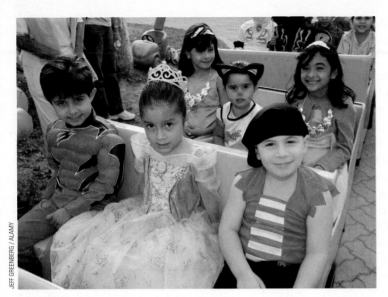

JEFF GREENBERG / ALAMY

Imagine Halloween is a time for fantasy. Can you imagine these two boys dressed like the girl while she wore a pirate's outfit? If you can, you are not stuck in cultural norms, but you probably also realize that none of these children would be smiling if their costumes violated gender norms.

she is wearing her new frilly socks as a genuine expression of her gender identity" (David et al., 2004, p. 147). Similarly, a 3½-year-old boy whose aunt called him *cute* insisted that he should be called *handsome* instead (Powlishta, 2004). Obviously, he had developed gender-based categories, and he wanted others to see him as he conceptualized himself.

Gender and Universal Social Order

As you can see, the three grand theories differ in how they explain the young child's understanding of male and female. The newer theories have other explanations, and new research continues to find that the traditional theories themselves must change (Martin & Ruble, 2010). Evolutionary theory holds that sexual attraction is crucial for humankind's most basic urge, to reproduce; thus, males and females try to look attractive to the other sex, taking on many behaviors to do so. Sociocultural theory holds that sexual behavior depends on the culture (men holding hands with men is taboo or expected, depending on local customs) and that some of the distinctions are tied to general patterns of social organization. Therefore, evolutionary theory would encourage male–female differences and sociocultural theory would conclude that sex differences are changeable if they interfere with other values.

The theories all raise a question: What gender patterns *should* children learn? Should everyone combine the best of both sexes (called *androgyny*), and should gender stereotypes disappear with age (like Santa Claus and the Tooth Fairy)? Or should male–female distinctions be encouraged as essential for the human family? Answers vary among developmentalists as well as among mothers, fathers, and cultures. Was I right or wrong to stop my student who told Bethany, "Girls don't fight"?

SUMMING UP

Gender stereotypes are held most forcefully at about age 6. Each theory, each discipline, and probably each parent has an explanation for this phenomenon: Freud described unconscious incestuous urges; behaviorists highlight social reinforcement; cognitive theorists describe immature categorization. Moreover, people differ as to the moral response—from considering gender identification as the bedrock of morality to seeing gender stereotypes as childish and destructive. ■

SUMMARY

Emotional Development

1. Learning to regulate and control emotions is crucial during early childhood. Emotional regulation is made possible by maturation of the brain, particularly of the prefrontal cortex, as well as by experiences with parents and peers.

2. In Erikson's psychosocial theory, the crisis of initiative versus guilt occurs during early childhood. Children normally feel pride, sometimes mixed with feelings of guilt. Shame is also evident, particularly in some cultures.

3. Both externalizing and internalizing problems indicate impaired self-control. Some emotional problems that indicate psychopathology are first evident during these years.

4. Boys more often manifest externalizing behaviors and girls, internalizing behaviors. For both sexes, brain maturation and the quality of early caregiving affect emotional control.

Play

5. All young children enjoy playing—with other children of the same sex (preferably), alone, or with parents. Rough-and-tumble play teaches many social skills and occurs everywhere, especially among boys who have space to run and chase.

6. Sociodramatic play allows development of emotions and roles within a safe setting. Both sexes engage in dramatic play, with girls preferring more domestic, less violent themes.

Challenges for Adults

7. Three classic styles of parenting have been identified: authoritarian, permissive, and authoritative. Generally, children are more successful and happy when their parents express warmth and set guidelines.

8. A fourth style of parenting, uninvolved, is always harmful. The particulars of parenting reflect the culture as well as the temperament of the child.

9. Children are prime consumers of many kinds of media, usually for several hours a day and often without their parents' involvement. Content is crucial. The problems that arise from media exposure include increased aggression and less creative play.

Moral Development

10. The sense of self and the social awareness of the young child become the foundation for morality. This is evident in both prosocial and antisocial behavior.

11. There are four types of aggression: instrumental, reactive, relational, and bullying. Instrumental aggression is used by all children but becomes less common with age. Unprovoked injury (bullying) is considered wrong by children as well as by adults.

12. Parents' choice of punishment can have long-term consequences. Physical punishment may teach lessons that parents do not want their children to learn. Other forms of punishment have long-term consequences as well.

Becoming Boys and Girls

13. Even 2-year-olds correctly use sex-specific labels. Young children become aware of gender differences in clothes, toys, future careers, and playmates.

14. Freud emphasized that children are attracted to the opposite-sex parent and eventually seek to identify, or align themselves, with the same-sex parent. Behaviorists hold that gender-related behaviors are learned through reinforcement and punishment (especially for males) and social modeling.

15. Cognitive theorists note that simplistic preoperational thinking leads to gender schema and therefore stereotypes. Sociocultural theorists point to the many male–female distinctions that are apparent in every society and are taught to children.

16. Evolutionary theory contends that sex and gender differences are crucial for the survival and reproduction of the species.

KEY TERMS

emotional regulation (p. 289)
initiative versus guilt (p. 289)
self-concept (p. 290)
intrinsic motivation (p. 291)
extrinsic motivation (p. 291)
imaginary friends (p. 291)
psychopathology (p. 293)
externalizing problems (p. 293)
internalizing problems (p. 293)

rough-and-tumble play (p. 296)
sociodramatic play (p. 297)
authoritarian parenting (p. 299)
permissive parenting (p. 299)
authoritative parenting (p. 299)
neglectful/uninvolved parenting (p. 300)
empathy (p. 305)
antipathy (p. 305)

prosocial behavior (p. 306)
antisocial behavior (p. 306)
instrumental aggression (p. 306)
reactive aggression (p. 306)
relational aggression (p. 306)
bullying aggression (p. 307)
psychological control (p. 308)
time-out (p. 308)
sex differences (p. 311)

gender differences (p. 311)
phallic stage (p. 313)
Oedipus complex (p. 313)
superego (p. 313)
Electra complex (p. 313)
identification (p. 313)
gender schema (p. 315)

WHAT HAVE YOU LEARNED?

Emotional Development

1. What aspects of brain development aid emotional regulation?

2. What are the differences between shame and guilt?

3. How is initiative different from autonomy (Erikson's third and second stages, respectively)?

4. What is the connection between psychopathology and emotional regulation?

5. What emotions are hard for people to regulate and why?

6. How do children learn emotional regulation?

7. What would be an example of intrinsic versus extrinsic motivation for reading a book?

Play

8. What do children learn from rough-and-tumble play?

9. Why do children prefer to play with peers rather than adults?

10. How is the development of social play affected by culture?

11. What does sociodramatic play help children learn?

12. What are the differences in the typical play of young boys and young girls?

Challenges for Adults

13. In Baumrind's three parenting styles, how do parents differ in expectations?

14. Why are children of permissive parents often unhappy?

15. Why do many non–European American parents seem stricter than other parents?

16. What do most American child professionals advise about television and young children?

17. What is likely to be displaced when young children are using electronic media?

Moral Development

18. What did Piaget believe about the moral development of children?

19. What is the nature perspective on how people develop morals?

20. What are the differences among sympathy, empathy, and antipathy?

21. What are the advantages and disadvantages of prosocial behavior?

22. What are the similarities and differences of the four kinds of aggression?

23. Why do developmentalists hope that parents will discuss discipline with each other before their child needs it?

24. What are the advantages and disadvantages of physical punishment?

25. Why have many nations made corporal punishment illegal?

26. When is time-out an effective punishment and when is it not?

27. What are the advantages and disadvantages of using induction as punishment?

Becoming Boys and Girls

28. How and when do children learn about sex differences between males and females?

29. How and when do children learn about gender differences between boys and girls?

30. Why do many social scientists dispute Freud's theory of sex-role development?

31. What would be easy and what difficult for society if gender roles changed?

APPLICATIONS

1. Observe the interactions of two or more young children. Sort your observations into four categories: emotions, reasons, results, and emotional regulation. Note every observable emotion (expressed by laughter, tears, etc.), the reason for it, the consequences, and whether or not emotional regulation was likely. For example: "Anger: Friend grabbed toy; child suggested sharing; emotional regulation probable."

2. Ask three parents about punishment, including their preferred type, at what age, for what misdeeds, and by whom. Ask your three informants how they were punished as children and how that affected them. If your sources agree, find a parent (or a classmate) who has a different view.

3. Children's television programming has been accused of stereotyping ethnicity, gender, and morality. Watch an hour of children's TV, especially on a Saturday morning, and describe the content of both the programs and the commercials. Draw conclusions about stereotyping, citing specific evidence (rather than merely reporting your impressions).

4. Gender indicators often go unnoticed. Go to a public place (park, restaurant, busy street) and spend an hour recording and quantifying examples of gender differentiation, such as articles of clothing, mannerisms, interaction patterns, and activities.

>>ONLINE CONNECTIONS

To accompany your textbook, you have access to a number of online resources, including quizzes for every chapter of the book, flashcards (in English and Spanish), critical thinking questions, and case studies. For access to any of these links, go to www.worthpublishers.com/bergerca9e. In addition to these free resources, you'll also find links to podcasts, video clips, diagnostic quizzing with personalized study advice, and an ebook. Some of the videos and activities available online include:

■ *Children at Play.* Watch video clips of children at play, identify the types of play you see, and review how each type contributes to children's development.

■ *Bullying.* With video clips of bullying, this activity covers physical and relational aggression, gender differences in bullying, and the impact on victims. It presents causes and preventive measures.

PART III

The Developing Person So Far:

Early Childhood

BIOSOCIAL

Body Changes Children continue to grow from ages 2 to 6, but at a slower rate. Normally, the BMI (body mass index) is lower at about ages 5 and 6 than at any other time of life. Children often eat too much unhealthy food and refuse to eat certain other foods altogether, insisting that food and other routines be "just right."

Brain Development The proliferation of neural pathways and myelination continue. Parts of the brain (e.g., the corpus callosum, prefrontal cortex, amygdala, hippocampus, and hypothalamus) connect, which allows lateralization of the brain's left and right hemispheres and better coordination of the left and right sides of the body; it also leads to a decline in impulsivity and perseveration. Gross motor skills slowly develop.

Injuries and Maltreatment Injury control is particularly necessary in these years, since far more children worldwide die of avoidable accidents than of diseases. Child abuse and neglect can occur in any family but are especially likely in homes with many children and few resources.

COGNITIVE

Piaget and Vygotsky Piaget stressed the young child's egocentric, illogical perspective, which prevents the child from grasping concepts such as conservation. Vygotsky stressed the cultural context, noting that children learn from mentors—which include parents, teachers, peers—and from the social context. Children develop their own theories, including a theory of mind, as they realize that not everyone thinks as they do.

Language Language develops rapidly. By age 6, the average child knows 10,000 words and demonstrates extensive grammatical knowledge. Young children can become balanced bilinguals during these years if their social context is encouraging.

Early-Childhood Education Young children are avid learners. Child-centered, teacher-directed, and intervention programs can all nurture learning; the outcome depends on the skill of teachers, as well as on the specifics of the curriculum.

PSYCHOSOCIAL

Emotional Development Self-esteem is usually high during early childhood. Self-concept emerges in Erikson's stage of initiative versus guilt, as does the ability to regulate emotions. Externalizing problems may be the result of too little emotional regulation; internalizing problems may result from too much control.

Parents A parenting style that is warm and encouraging, with good communication as well as high expectations (called authoritative), is most effective in promoting the child's self-esteem, autonomy, and self-control. The authoritarian and permissive styles are less beneficial. Extensive use of television and other media by children can disrupt family life.

Moral Development There is no consensus about how much of moral development is innate and how much is learned, but it is apparent that morality becomes more evident during early childhood. Empathy produces prosocial behavior; antipathy leads to antisocial actions. Aggression takes many forms; bullying aggression is ominous. Every method of parental discipline has consequences.

Becoming Boys and Girls Children develop stereotypic concepts of sex (biological) and gender (cultural). Current theories give contradictory explanations.

IV

middle childhood

Every age has joys and sorrows, gains and losses. But if you were pushed to choose one best time, you might select ages 6 to 11, when many children experience good health and steady growth as they master new athletic skills, learn thousands of words, become less dependent on families. Usually, they appreciate their parents, make new friends, and proudly learn about their nation and religion. Life is safe and happy; the dangers of adolescence (drugs, sex, violence) are not yet on the horizon.

Yet some adults remember these years as the worst, not the best. Some children hate school; some live in destructive families; some have no permanent home; some contend with obesity, asthma, learning disabilities, or bullies. The next three chapters celebrate the joys and acknowledge the difficulties of ages 6 to 11.

Middle Childhood: Biosocial Development

WHAT WILL YOU KNOW?

1. What would happen if more parents let their children "go out and play"?

2. Should the epidemic of childhood obesity be blamed on parents, schools, or policies?

3. Why are IQ tests not used as often as they were a few decades ago?

4. If every child is abnormal in some way, why is early diagnosis of special needs helpful?

In the middle of the second grade, my family and I moved a thousand miles. I entered a new school where my accent was odd; I was self-conscious and lonely. Cynthia had a friendly smile, freckles, and red hair. More important, she talked to me; I asked her to be my friend.

"We cannot be friends," she said, "because I am a Democrat."

"So am I," I answered. (I knew my family believed in democracy.)

"No, you're not. You are a Republican," she said.

I was stunned and sad. We never became friends.

Neither Cynthia nor I realized that all children are unusual in some way (perhaps because of appearance, culture, or family) and yet capable of friendship with children unlike themselves. Cynthia and I could have been good friends, but neither of us knew it. Her parents had told her something about my parents' politics that I did not understand. Cynthia left the school later that year, friendless; I made other friends.

This chapter describes not only the similarities among all school-age children but also differences that may become significant—in size, health, learning ability, and more. At the end of this chapter, we focus on children with special needs—who need friends but have trouble finding them.

>> A Healthy Time

Genetic and environmental factors safeguard **middle childhood** (about age 6 to 11), the period after early childhood and before adolescence. One explanation comes from the evolutionary perspective. A death during middle childhood would mean that the effort to nurture the young child was in vain (Konner, 2010). For whatever reason, few fatal diseases or accidents occur during these years. Contemporary schoolchildren have two added protections: education about risks and several doses of vaccine. All in all, middle childhood is the healthiest period of the entire life span (see Figure 11.1).

middle childhood The period between early childhood and early adolescence, approximately from ages 6 to 11.

Slower Growth, Greater Strength

Unlike infants or adolescents, school-age children's growth is slow and steady. Self-care is easy—from brushing their new adult teeth to dressing themselves, from making their own lunch to walking with friends to school. Once at school,

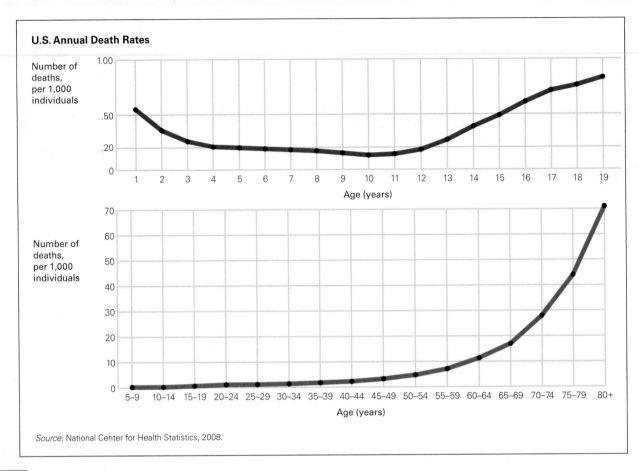

U.S. Annual Death Rates

Source: National Center for Health Statistics, 2008.

FIGURE 11.1

Death at an Early Age? Almost Never!
Schoolchildren are remarkably hardy, as measured in many ways. These charts show that death rates for 6- to 11-year olds are lower than those for children under 6 or over 11 and about 100 times lower than for adults

Observation Quiz From the bottom graph, it looks as if ages 9 and 19 are equally healthy, but they are dramatically different in the top graph. What is the explanation for this? (see answer, page 326)

they can sit at their desks or tables and do their work without breaking their pencils, tearing their papers, or elbowing their classmates. In these middle years, children are quite capable and self-sufficient and are not yet buffeted by adolescent body changes and impulses.

Muscles become stronger. For example, the average 10-year-old can throw a ball twice as far as a 6-year-old can. Hearts and lungs are muscles, too, increasing in strength and capacity. Consequently, with each passing year, children run faster and exercise longer (Malina et al., 2004). Some sports valued by adults (such as basketball and football) require taller, bigger bodies than school-age children possess, but these children are far superior to their younger selves in every athletic skill.

Few are severely undernourished. As long as their entire community is not starving, school-age children feed themselves. As the "just right" obsession fades, they try new foods, especially if they are eating at a friend's house. As discussed in Chapter 8, earlier malnutrition becomes evident in height, not weight. By middle childhood, children from the poorest nations are several inches shorter than those from richer ones, with some of the short ones overweight, on the road to poor health later on (Worthman et al., 2010).

Physical Activity

Children often play joyfully, "fully and totally immersed" (Loland, 2002, p. 139). Beyond the sheer fun of playing, the benefits of physical activity—especially games with rules, which school-age children are now able to follow—can last a lifetime.

These benefits include the following:

- Better overall health
- Less obesity
- Appreciation of cooperation and fair play
- Improved problem-solving abilities
- Respect for teammates and opponents of many ethnicities and nationalities

However, there are hazards as well:

- Loss of self-esteem (teammates and coaches are sometimes cruel)
- Injuries (the infamous "Little League elbow" is one example)
- Reinforcement of prejudices (especially against the other sex)
- Increased stress (evidenced by altered hormone levels, insomnia)

Where can children reap the benefits and avoid the hazards of active play? There are three possibilities: neighborhoods, schools, and sports leagues.

Neighborhood Games

Neighborhood play is flexible. Rules and boundaries are adapted to the context (out of bounds is "past the tree" or "behind the parked truck"). Stickball, touch football, tag, hide-and-seek, and dozens of other running and catching games go on forever—or at least until dark. The play is active, interactive, and inclusive—ideal for children. It also teaches ethics. As one scholar notes:

> Children play tag, hide and seek, or pickup basketball. They compete with one another but always according to rules, and rules that they enforce themselves without recourse to an impartial judge. The penalty for not playing by the rules is not playing, that is, social exclusion . . .
>
> *[Gillespie, 2010, p. 398]*

For school-age children, "social exclusion" is a steep price to pay for insisting on their own way. Instead, they learn to cooperate. Unfortunately, this lesson may not be learned by the current cohort of children because modern life undercuts informal neighborhood games. Vacant lots and empty fields have largely disappeared.

A century ago, 90 percent of the world's children lived in rural areas; now the majority live in cities or in shantytowns at the city's edge. The cities that have exploded most rapidly are in developing nations, where playgrounds and parks are particularly rare, but even in the slower-growing developed nations, population increases are notable. For instance, in 1990 slightly fewer than 4 million people lived in metropolitan Dallas, Texas; in 2010, nearly 7 million did.

An additional problem, especially for city children, is that their parents keep them at home because of "stranger danger"—although one expert writes that "there is a much greater chance that your child is going to be dangerously overweight from staying inside than that he is going to be abducted" (quoted in Layden, 2004, p. 86). Indoor activities like homework, television, and video games compete with outdoor play in every nation, perhaps especially in the United States. According to an Australian scholar:

> Australian children are lucky. Here the dominant view is that children's after school time is leisure time. In the United States, it seems that leisure time is available to fewer and fewer children. If a child performs poorly in school, recreation time rapidly becomes remediation time. For high achievers, after school time is often spent in academic enrichment.
>
> *[Vered, 2008, p. 170]*

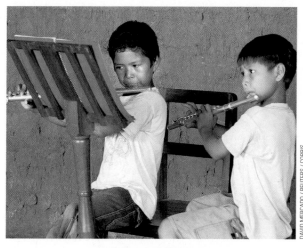

Expert Eye–Hand Coordination The specifics of motor-skill development in middle childhood depend on the culture. These flute players are carrying on the European Baroque musical tradition that thrives among the poor, remote Guarayo people of Bolivia.

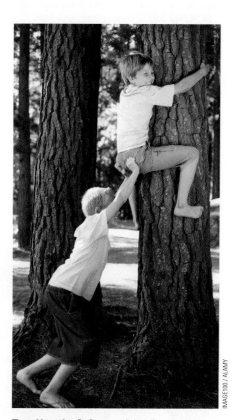

Tree Hugging? Some adults disparage other adults who seek to preserve nature, but for children worldwide, climbing trees is a joy. Not every child has this opportunity. These fortunate boys are playing on a South African estate.

"Just remember, son, it doesn't matter whether you win or lose—unless you want Daddy's love."

>> Answer to Observation Quiz (from page 324) Look at the vertical axes. From age 1 to 20, the annual death rate is less than 1 in 1,000.

Why Helmets? Sports organized by adults, such as this football team of 7- to 8-year-old boys sponsored by the Lyons and Police Athletic League of Detroit, may be harmful to children. The best games are those that require lots of running and teamwork—but no pushing or shoving.

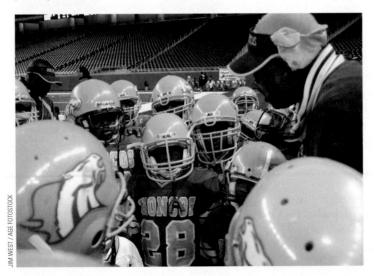

Exercise in School

When opportunities for neighborhood play are scarce, physical education in school is a logical alternative. However, because schools are pressured to increase reading and math time (see Chapter 12), time for physical education and recess has declined. A study of Texas elementary schools found that 24 percent had no recess at all, and only 1 percent had recess several times a day (W. Zhu et al., 2010).

A much larger study of a U.S. cross section of more than 10,000 third-graders found that about two-thirds of all children have at least 15 minutes of recess each day. Unfortunately, those children least likely to have recess are those most likely to need it—city-dwellers who live in poor neighborhoods, where fearful parents do not let them go outside to play (Barros et al., 2009) (see the Research Design and Figure 11.2 on the next page). Many schools are required to have gym, but those classes are often too large for active play.

Not only has school time for recess and for physical education declined, but during gym class some children spend more time sitting and waiting than moving. Paradoxically, school exercise may improve academic achievement (Carlson et al., 2008). The Centers for Disease Control recommends that children be active at least half of the time in required physical education classes (Khan et al., 2009). These are minimal goals; many schools do not meet them.

Athletic Clubs and Leagues

Private or nonprofit clubs and organizations offer additional opportunities for children to play. Culture and family affect the specifics: Some children learn golf, others tennis, others boxing. Cricket and rugby are common in England and in former British colonies such as India, Australia, and Jamaica; baseball is common in Japan, the United States, Cuba, Panama, and the Dominican Republic; soccer is central in many European, African, and Latin American nations.

The best-known organized recreation program for children is Little League. When it began in 1939, Little League had only three baseball teams of boys aged 9 to12. Now it includes girls, younger and older children, and 22,000 children with disabilities, with an annual total of 2.7 million children playing baseball or softball on more than 180,000 teams in 100 nations. Coaches are usually parent volunteers, who are not necessarily adept at encouraging every child. Nonetheless, most children enjoy it. One adult confesses:

> I was a lousy Little League player. Uncoordinated, small, and clueless are the accurate adjectives I'd use if someone asked politely. . . . What I did possess, though, was enthusiasm. Wearing the uniform—cheesy mesh cap, scratchy polyester shirt, old-school beltless pants, uncomfortable cleats and stirrups that never stayed up—gave me a sort of pride. It felt special and made me think that I was part of something important.
>
> [Ryan, 2005]

Being "part of something important" raises a problem: Many children are left out (Collins, 2003). Not all parents can pay for after-school sports or can afford the time to transport children to practices and games; many do not have the energy to cheer on the teams, much less coach them. Children from low-SES families, or those who are not well coordinated, or those who have disabilities rarely

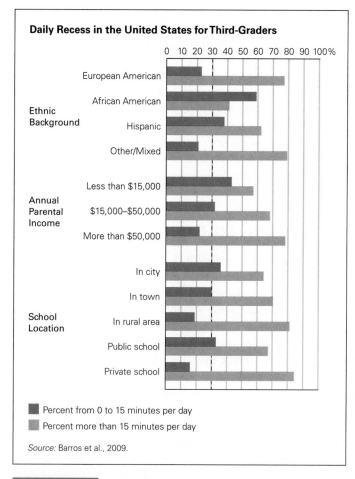

Daily Recess in the United States for Third-Graders

■ Percent from 0 to 15 minutes per day
■ Percent more than 15 minutes per day

Source: Barros et al., 2009.

FIGURE 11.2

Time for Recess Although many studies find that children learn better if they have recess every day and although recess decreases obesity and increases social skills, about one-third of all children in the United States have less than 15 minutes a day of recess. This includes many schools that have no recess at all.

Observation Quiz If a child is African American, is of low SES, and attends a public school in a large city in the South, what is that child's chance of having less than 15 minutes a day of recess? (see answer, page 328)

▶ **Research Design**

Scientists: Romina M. Barros, Ellen J. Silver, and Ruth E. K. Stein.

Publication: *Pediatrics* (2009).

Participants: Participants were about 11,000 8-year-olds from one part of the Early Childhood Longitudinal Study. This study began with kindergartners from many U.S. regions, of many ethnicities, and with many different levels of family income. The scientists analyzed data reported on these children in third grade. Not included were children who repeated a grade, who were immigrants, or who entered school after kindergarten. Parents and teachers were also queried.

Design: Teachers reported how much recess (unstructured play time) the children had each day. The lowest option was 0–15 minutes, chosen by 30 percent. That variable was compared to class behavior, class size, boy/girl ratio, frequency of gym class, parents' SES, and school type and location.

Results: Many significant differences were found. Less recess correlated with lower SES, classes that were "hard to manage," public schools, cities, southern states, and fewer physical education periods. Variables not associated with length of recess included class size and boy/girl ratio.

Major conclusion: Given the correlation between recess and class behavior, as well as other research on childhood learning, attention, and obesity, these researchers suggest that all children benefit from at least 20 minutes of recess each day. This is particularly important for children who have difficulty paying attention. The researchers worry that students who most need recess are least likely to have it, because "many children from disadvantaged backgrounds are not free to roam their neighborhoods or even their own yards unless they are accompanied by adults. For many of these children, recess periods may be the only opportunity for them to practice their social skills with other children" (p. 434).

These authors also note that 40 percent of U.S. schools have cut back on recess in order to spend more time on reading and math, although schools in Asia, with the highest scores on international tests of achievement, have several recess breaks totaling more than an hour each day.

Comments: Given the large, representative sample, with participants queried independently (thus avoiding the danger of researcher bias influencing results), the data reported here are probably reliable. Many adults mistakenly believe that children who misbehave and who have academic difficulties need less free play and more academic work. This study suggests the opposite—that recess not only provides exercise, it may increase academic learning.

belong to athletic clubs—yet those are the very children who could benefit most from the strength, activity, and teamwork that organized play provides.

Indeed, especially for low-income children, participation in structured sports activities correlates with academic achievement; one Canadian study found that academic performance improved for 6- and 7-year-olds who felt victimized but played sports (Perron et al., 2011). (Academic performance decreased for victimized children who did not play sports, as well as for nonvictimized sports players). Although participation in extracurricular activities, especially sports, benefits low-income children more than others, such children are less likely to join even when available after-school activities are free. The reasons are many; the consequences, sad (Dearing et al., 2009).

Especially for Physical Education Teachers A group of parents of fourth- and fifth-graders has asked for your help in persuading the school administration to sponsor a competitive sports team. How should you advise the group to proceed? (see response, page 328)

>> Answer to Observation Quiz (from page 327) The graph doesn't explicitly calculate that statistic, but since the child is in the lowest percentage of each category, any estimate between 75 and 95 percent is probably correct.

>> Response for Physical Education Teachers (from page 327) Discuss with the parents their reasons for wanting the team. Children need physical activity, but some aspects of competitive sports are better suited to adults than to children.

BMI (body mass index) A person's weight in kilograms divided by the square of height in meters.

overweight In a child, having a BMI above the 85th percentile, according to the U.S. Centers for Disease Control's 1980 standards for children of a given age.

obesity In a child, having a BMI above the 95th percentile, according to the U.S. Centers for Disease Control's 1980 standards for children of a given age.

SUMMING UP

School-age children are usually healthy, strong, and capable. Genes as well as immunization protect them against contagious diseases, and medical care has improved over the past decades. Moreover, children's developmental advances add strength, understanding, and coordination and enable them to undertake self-care, providing a foundation that allows them to learn effectively in school as well as to have a healthy adulthood. Specific habits, and exercise overall, aid learning. Although neighborhood play, school physical education, and community sports leagues all provide needed activity, energetic play is much more likely for some children than for others; unfortunately, those who need it most are the least likely to have access to it. ▪

>> Health Problems in Middle Childhood

Chronic conditions may become more troubling if they interfere with school, play, and friendship. Some worsen during the school years, including Tourette syndrome, stuttering, and allergies. Even minor problems—wearing glasses, repeatedly coughing or blowing one's nose, or having a visible birthmark—make children self-conscious.

For children with chronic conditions, learning good health habits is especially vital before adolescence: Teenagers might dye their hair green or get a tattoo, but hopefully they still take their medication and see the doctor. If adolescent rebellion includes medical noncompliance, those with serious, chronic conditions (including diabetes, phenylketonuria [PKU], epilepsy, cancer, asthma, and sickle-cell anemia) often ignore special diets, pills, and so on and get sicker (Dean et al., 2010; Suris et al., 2008). To prevent this, elementary schoolchildren need to take charge of their health, developing habits that will sustain them lifelong.

Researchers increasingly recognize that every physical and psychological problem is affected by the social context and, in turn, affects that context (Jackson & Tester, 2008). Parents and children are not merely reactive: In a dynamic-systems manner (see Chapter 1), individuals and contexts influence each other. We now focus on two examples: obesity and asthma.

Childhood Obesity

Of any age group, 5- and 6-year-olds have the least body fat and lowest **BMI (body mass index).** Yet many young children are too heavy. Childhood **overweight** is defined as having a BMI above the 85th percentile for age; childhood **obesity** is defined as having a BMI above the 95th percentile (Barlow et al., 2007). Both percentiles are measured against children's growth norms published by the U.S. Centers for Disease Control in 1980, which explains why more than 5 percent can be above the 95th percentile.

Childhood obesity in all three nations of North America (Mexico, the United States, and Canada) has more than doubled since 1980. The latest U.S. data suggest the increases have stopped—but at a high level. In the United States in 2005, one-third (32 percent) of children under age 18 were overweight, half of them (16 percent) were obese and 11 percent of those obese children were extremely obese (Ogden et al., 2008). Using the same standards, 28 percent of Canadian 2- to 17-year-olds were overweight, with increases particularly in middle childhood (Shields & Tremblay, 2010).

Overweight children more often have asthma, high blood pressure, and elevated cholesterol (especially LDL, the "bad" form of cholesterol). Furthermore, on average, as excessive weight builds, school achievement decreases, self-esteem falls, and loneliness rises. This has been studied most often in the United States, where schoolchildren are more likely to reject their obese classmates, who often hate school (Zeller et al., 2008). Over time, it gets worse: If they stay heavy, obese children risk diabetes, heart disease, and strokes and are less likely to marry, to find jobs, and to live to old age. Because of obesity, today's children may be the first generation to die at younger ages than their parents did (Devi, 2008; Yajnik, 2004).

What Causes Overweight in Children?

To halt the epidemic of childhood obesity, many people search for the cause. The problem is that there is no single cause. There are "hundreds if not thousands of contributing factors" (Harrison et al., 2011, p. 51).

First, some people are genetically predisposed to high proportions of body fat. More than 200 genes affect weight by influencing activity level, food preference, body type, and metabolism (Gluckman & Hanson, 2006). Having two copies of an allele called FTO (inherited by 16 percent of all European Americans) increases the likelihood of both obesity and diabetes (Frayling et al., 2007). However, genes change little from one generation to the next and thus cannot have caused the marked increase in obesity (Harrison et al., 2011). Factors around those genes may exacerbate them—embryos that gain too little are likely to become children who weigh too much, but that seems more a matter of child rearing than of genes. One critic notes that "fat runs in families but so do frying pans" (S. Jones, 2006, p. 1879).

Second, in many ways, parenting practices *have* changed for the worse. Obesity is more common in infants who are not breast-fed, in preschoolers who watch TV and drink soda, and in school-age children who are driven to school and rarely play outside (Institute of Medicine, 2006; Patrick et al., 2004; Rhee, 2008). Parents are crucial in all these, but during middle childhood, children themselves can change family patterns. An important factor is called "pester power"—the ability of the child to nag the parent. Usually, children pester their parents to provide calorie-dense food, but some children pester their parents in the opposite way—to play ball with them, to let them join a sports team, and so on. School health education can convince children to advocate for better diets.

A third source of childhood obesity is "embedded in social policies" (Branca et al., 2007). Communities and nations determine the quality of school lunches; the presence of snack vending machines; the prevalence of parks, bike paths, and sidewalks; and the subsidies for corn oil but not fresh vegetables. One report lists 24 specific strategies that local governments could employ to reduce overweight (Khan et al., 2009).

Particularly potent for children is food advertising. In the United States, billions of dollars are spent on ads that entice children to eat unhealthy foods. Parents rarely realize how many of those ads their children see (Linn & Novosat, 2008). Such advertising is illegal in some nations, limited in others, and unrestricted in still others—and a country's rate of childhood obesity correlates with how often children see food commercials on television (Lobstein & Dibb, 2005).

Since all three factors—genes, parents, and policies—are relevant, it is not surprising that parents blame genes or policies, while others (medical professionals, political leaders) blame parents, and the media claim that they advertise what

Especially for Teachers A child in your class is overweight, but you are hesitant to say anything to the parents, who are also overweight, because you do not want to insult them. What should you do? (see response, page 331)

A Happy Meal A close look at this photograph reveals that this scene is a McDonald's in Switzerland—one of hundreds of fast-food chain branches in Europe, where many normal-weight 6-year-olds become overweight 12-year-olds.

GAETAN BALLY / KEYSTONE / CORBIS

the highest bidder wants as part of freedom of speech or capitalism. Everyone may be right: It is unclear which particular measures would markedly reduce obesity.

For instance, childhood weight correlates with hours of TV watched per day (Philipsen & Brooks-Gunn, 2008)—but remember that correlation does not prove cause. If families that allow unlimited television are also likely to allow unlimited snacking, then the snacking, not the TV, might be the problem. Or maybe content is crucial: One study found that neither educational television nor commercial-free videos correlated with childhood obesity but that commercials for calorie-dense foods did (Zimmerman & Bell, 2010). As with many other aspects of child development, experimental research on children cannot *prove* that television makes children fat because we cannot compare a TV-free group with an equal group who watch several hours each day. Rather than trying to zero in on any single factor, a dynamic-systems approach is needed: Many factors, over time, make a child overweight (Harrison et al., 2011).

Asthma

Asthma is a chronic inflammatory disorder of the airways that makes breathing difficult. Although asthma affects people of every age, rates are highest among school-age children, with marked increases worldwide (Cruz et al., 2010). In the United States, asthma rates among every age group of children have tripled since 1980. Parents report that 10 percent of U.S. 5- to 9-year-olds currently have asthma, with 6 percent of them having had an attack within the past year.

Ethnicity matters, either because of genes or culture (probably both). Of all U.S. children under age 18, 14 percent have been diagnosed at least once with asthma. The rate for Puerto Rican children is 26 percent; African American, 21 percent; Mexican American, 10 percent; European American, 13 percent (Bloom et al., 2009; National Center for Health Statistics, 2011).

Causes of Asthma

Many researchers seek the causes of asthma. A few alleles have been identified as potential factors, but asthma has many genetic roots, none of which act in isolation (Bossé & Hudson, 2007). Environment combined with genes is crucial (Akinbami et al., 2010). Air pollution, especially that caused by traffic congestion, increases the prevalence of asthma among vulnerable children (Gilliland, 2009).

Several aspects of modern life—carpets, pets inside the home, airtight windows, less outdoor play—also contribute to the increased rates of asthma (Tamay et al., 2007). Many allergens (pet dander, cigarette smoke, dust mites, cockroaches, and mold among them) that trigger attacks are concentrated in today's well-insulated homes.

Some experts suggest a *hygiene hypothesis,* proposing that contemporary children are kept too hygienic, overprotected from viruses and bacteria, which means they do not contract minor infections and diseases that would actually strengthen their immune systems (Busse & Lemanske, 2005; Tedeschi & Airaghi, 2006). This hypothesis is supported by data showing that (1) first-born children are more likely to develop asthma than are later-born ones and (2) farm children have much lower rates of asthma and allergies than do other children.

Especially for Parents Suppose that you always serve dinner with the television on, tuned to a news broadcast. Your hope is that your children will learn about the world as they eat. Can this practice be harmful? (see response, page 332)

asthma A chronic disease of the respiratory system in which inflammation narrows the airways from the nose and mouth to the lungs, causing difficulty in breathing. Signs and symptoms include wheezing, shortness of breath, chest tightness, and coughing.

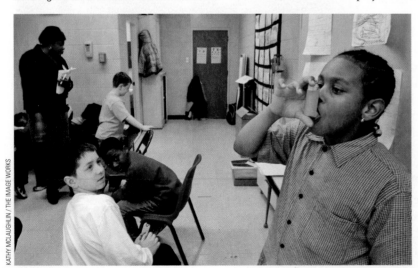

Pride and Prejudice In some city schools, asthma is so common that using an inhaler is a sign of prestige, as suggested by the facial expressions of these two boys. The "prejudice" is more apparent beyond the walls of this school nurse's room, in a society that allows high rates of childhood asthma to occur.

KATHY MCLAUGHLIN / THE IMAGE WORKS

However, the lower rates for farm children do not *prove* the hygiene hypothesis. Other possibilities include certain genetic factors or drinking unpasteurized milk (von Mutius & Vercelli, 2010). Surprisingly, children born by c-section have higher rates of asthma—perhaps because their birth was too sterile? One review of the hygiene hypothesis notes that "the picture can be dishearteningly complex" (Couzin-Frankel, 2010, p. 1168). The incidence of asthma seems to increase as nations get richer; at least that is dramatically true in Brazil and China. Better hygiene is one explanation, but so is increasing urbanization—which correlates with more cars, more pollution, and smaller families (Cruz et al., 2010).

Prevention of Asthma

The three levels of prevention (discussed in Chapter 8) apply to every health problem.

Primary prevention requires changes in the entire society. Better ventilation of schools and homes, less pollution, fewer cockroaches, fewer antibiotics, fewer c-sections, and more outdoor play would benefit everyone while reducing asthma.

Secondary prevention decreases asthma attacks among high-risk children. If asthma runs in the family, then prolonged breast-feeding, less dust and smoke, and no cats or cockroaches cut the onset of asthma in half (Elliott et al., 2007; Gdalevich et al., 2001).

Finally, *tertiary prevention* includes the prompt use of injections and inhalers. Using hypoallergenic materials (e.g., for mattress covers) also reduces asthma attacks—but not by much, probably because it occurs too late (MMWR, January 14, 2005). But even if tertiary prevention does not halt asthma, it can help asthmatic children, as the following illustrates.

>> **Response for Teachers** (from page 329) Speak to the parents, not accusingly (because you know that genes and culture have a major influence on body weight) but helpfully. Alert them to the potential social and health problems their child's weight poses. Most parents are very concerned about their child's well-being and will work with you to improve the child's snacks and exercise level.

A CASE TO STUDY

Asthma in Two Active 8-Year-Olds

A team of social scientists analyzed statistics and interviewed individuals to produce *The Measure of America,* a book comparing development in the United States and elsewhere (Burd-Sharps et al., 2008). Among their case studies were those of Sophie and Alexa, two 8-year-olds with asthma.

Sophie is a vibrant eight-year-old who was diagnosed with severe asthma when she was two. She lives in a house in a New York City suburb with a park down the street and fresh air outside—an environment with few asthma triggers.

Her family has private health insurance, a benefit of her father's job, with extensive provisions for preventative care and patient education. Her parents' jobs have personal and sick days that give them time off from work to take her to the doctor. After some early difficulty finding a suitable medication regime, she has settled into a routine of daily-inhaled medication (at a cost of $500 per month, fully covered by insurance), annual flu shots, and a special medication she takes only when she is sick with a cold. Sophie sees her pediatrician regularly and a top-flight asthma specialist yearly, to monitor her progress; has a nebulizer for quick relief in case of a serious attack; and can rely on nebulizers in her school and after-school program as well.

Sophie has never had to go to the emergency room for an attack, almost always participates in gym, and misses about two or three days of school a year due to asthma-related problems.

Alexa is also an active eight-year-old, first diagnosed with severe asthma at age three. She lives with her mother in a Brooklyn apartment three blocks from a waste transfer station that receives, sorts, and dispatches thirteen thousand tons of garbage each weekday. In addition to the acrid smell of garbage, the cockroaches that frequent her apartment also trigger Alexa's asthma attacks through allergens in their droppings. Her mother works at a minimum-wage job; she loses income when she takes Alexa to the doctor, fills emergency prescriptions, or stays home with Alexa when she is sick.

Alexa's mother could qualify for SCHIP, which would provide health insurance for Alexa, but she has never heard of it. Instead, Alexa is officially listed as living with her grandmother, whose Medicaid coverage extends to Alexa. Alexa sees a doctor annually, though her grandmother fears Alexa is not benefitting from the latest advances in asthma care.

Alexa misses twelve to fifteen days of school each year, does not participate in gym, and spends up to eight fearful nights each year in a hospital emergency room. When she misses consecutive days of school, she struggles with schoolwork. She wishes she could run around like her classmates.

[Burd-Sharps et al., 2008, p. 67]

These cases were originally published to highlight economic disparities. Few families can afford the excellent care Sophie receives, and programs such as SCHIP do not reach every low-income child like Alexa. However, as with obesity, severe asthma in childhood can be blamed on genes, parents, schools, doctors, and neighborhoods, as well as on public policies regarding poverty and health care. Who to blame is a hotly disputed political question, but everyone agrees that Alexa should not spend "eight fearful nights" in the hospital each year. Someone, or perhaps everyone, should help her.

>> **Response for Parents** (from page 330) Habitual TV watching correlates with obesity, so you may be damaging your children's health rather than improving their intellect. Your children would probably profit more if you were to make dinner a time for family conversation about world events.

The increase in childhood asthma is disheartening. But improvement is possible. One hundred and thirty-three Latino (primarily Puerto Rican) adult smokers, who were caregivers for children with asthma, agreed to allow a Spanish-speaking counselor to come repeatedly to their homes (Borrelli et al., 2010). The counselor placed a smoke monitor in the child's room and a week later told the caregiver how much smoke exposure the child had experienced. Then, in three sessions, she provided specific counseling on quitting, based on the best research on addiction, with particular sensitivity to Latino values.

Three months later, one-fourth of the caregivers had quit smoking completely. Many of the rest had cut down. The average child's exposure to smoke was cut in half, and asthma problems diminished (Borrelli et al., 2010). Note that knowledge and encouragement were needed—which not all parents have. Most parents want to provide good care (many wonder how).

SUMMING UP

Some children have chronic health problems that interfere with school and friendship. Among these are obesity and asthma, both increasing in every nation and both having genetic and environmental causes. Childhood obesity may seem harmless, but it leads to social problems among classmates and severe health problems later on. Asthma's harm is more immediate: Asthmatic children often miss school and are rushed to emergency rooms, gasping for air. Family practices and lifestyle are part of the reason for increases in obesity and asthma, and many society-wide policies and cultural customs make the problems worse.

■

© SCIENCE PHOTO LIBRARY / AGE FOTOSTOCK

Finger Math Some teachers forbid counting with hands and fingers, yet "embodied cognition" has been part of human thought since prehistoric times. Math knowledge advanced when humans realized that counting by tens was the natural way, as this boy demonstrates.

>> Brain Development

Recall that emotional regulation, theory of mind, and left–right coordination emerge in early childhood. The maturing corpus callosum connects the hemispheres of the brain, enabling balance and two-handed coordination, while myelination speeds up thoughts and behavior. The prefrontal cortex—the executive part of the brain—begins to plan, monitor, and evaluate. All of these neurological developments continue in middle childhood and beyond. We now look at additional advances in middle childhood.

Coordinating Connections

Increasing maturation results "by 7 or 8 years of age, in a massively interconnected brain" (Kagan & Herschkowitz, 2005, p. 220). Such connections are crucial for the complex tasks that children must master (M. H. Johnson et al., 2009). One example is learning to read, perhaps the most important intellectual accomplishment of the school-age child. Reading is not instinctual: Our ancestors never did it, and until recent centuries only a few scribes and scholars were expected to make sense of those marks on paper. Consequently, the brain has no areas dedicated to reading, the way it does for talking or gesturing (Gabrieli, 2009).

How do humans read without brain-specific structures? The answer is "massive interconnections." The connections are among brain structures already described in Chapter 8, with white matter (myelination) increasing particularly in the prefrontal cortex and the corpus callosum. Those connections increase executive functioning, which in turn makes all forms of education more possible, with literacy a much-studied example.

Reading uses several parts of the brain—one for sounds, another for recognizing letters, another for sequencing, another for comprehension, and so on (Booth, 2007). Those massive interconnections are needed for many social skills as well—deciding whom to trust, figuring out what is fair, interpreting ambiguous gestures and expressions. Younger children are not proficient at interpreting social cues (that's why they are told, "Don't talk to strangers"). During middle childhood, various parts of the brain connect to allow social decision making (Crone & Westenberg, 2009). Indeed, for many activities, children use more parts of their brains than adults do, thus requiring more connections (M. H. Johnson et al., 2009).

A crucial measure of better brain coordination is the ability of the prefrontal cortex to control various impulses, as already described in the chapters on early childhood. Advances in the "mental control processes that enable self-control" (Verté et al., 2005, p. 415) allow planning for the future, which is beyond the ability of the impatient younger child. School-age children can analyze possible consequences before they lash out in anger or dissolve in tears, and they can figure out when a curse word seems advisable (on the playground to a bully, perhaps) and when it is not (in the classroom or at home). Planning for the future means they can count the days until summer vacation.

The prefrontal cortex takes decades to mature. For children who want to be rocket scientists, billionaire stock analysts, or brain surgeons, connecting those distant goals with current behavior or social reality is not yet possible. Nonetheless, connections between one part of the brain and another may be crucial because some neuroscientists believe that "social or linguistic disorders could be caused by disruptions in the pathways" of brain connections, not in the neurons themselves (Minogue, 2010, p. 747).

"The path to becoming an astronaut is rougher than I thought."

Think Quick; Too Slow

Advance planning and impulse control are aided by faster **reaction time,** which is how long it takes to respond to a stimulus. Thus, reaction time indicates speed of thought as an impulse travels from one neuron to another, and increasing myelination speeds reaction time every year from birth until about age 16.

A simple example is being able to kick a speeding soccer ball toward a teammate; a more complex example is being able to calculate when to utter a witty remark and when to stay quiet. Young children find both impossible; fast-thinking older children sometimes succeed; few adults can beat a teenager at a quick-paced video game.

Pay Attention

Neurological advances allow children not only to process information quickly but also to pay special heed to the most important elements of their environment. **Selective attention,** the ability to concentrate on some stimuli while ignoring

reaction time The time it takes to respond to a stimulus, either physically (with a reflexive movement such as an eyeblink) or cognitively (with a thought).

selective attention The ability to concentrate on some stimuli while ignoring others.

others, improves markedly at about age 7. School-age children not only notice various stimuli (which is one form of attention) but also select appropriate responses when several possibilities conflict (Rueda et al., 2007).

In the classroom, selective attention allows children to listen, take concise notes, and ignore distractions (all difficult at age 6, easier by age 10). In the din of the cafeteria, children can understand one another's gestures and expressions and react. On the baseball diamond, older batters ignore the other team's attempts to distract them, and older fielders start moving into position as soon as a ball is hit their way. Indeed, selective attention underlies all the abilities that gradually mature during the school years. "Networks of collaborating cortical regions" (M. H. Johnson et al., 2009, p. 151) are required because attention involves not just one brain function but three: alerting, orienting, and executive control (Posner et al., 2007).

Automatic

One final advance in brain function in middle childhood is **automatization,** the process by which a sequence of thoughts and actions is repeated until it becomes automatic, or routine. At first, almost all behaviors under conscious control require careful and slow thought. After many repetitions, as neurons fire in sequence, actions become automatic and patterned. Less thinking is needed because the firing of one neuron sets off a chain reaction: That is automatization.

Consider again learning to read. At first, eyes (sometimes aided by a guiding finger) focus intensely, painstakingly making out letters and sounding out each one. This leads to the perception of syllables and then words. Eventually, the process becomes so automatic that, for instance, as you read this text, automatization allows you to concentrate on concepts without thinking about the letters. Automatization aids every skill. Learning to speak a second language, to recite the multiplication tables, and to write one's name are all slow at first but gradually become automatic.

Measuring the Mind

In ancient times, if an adult was strong and fertile, that was enough, worthy of admiration. By the twentieth century, however, cognitive abilities had become important; a stupid person, even if strong and fertile, was not admired. Because the mind became increasingly significant, many ways to measure intellect were developed.

Aptitude, Achievement, and IQ

In theory, **aptitude** is the potential to master a specific skill or to learn a certain body of knowledge. Intellectual aptitude is often measured by **IQ tests.** Originally, an IQ score was literally an intelligence quotient: Mental age (the age of a typical child who had reached a particular intellectual level) was divided by a child's chronological age, and the result of that division (the quotient) was multiplied by 100. The current method of calculating IQ is more complicated, but an IQ of 100 is still considered average (see Figure 11.3).

In theory, achievement is actual learning, not learning potential (aptitude). **Achievement tests** in school (see Chapter 12) compare scores to norms established for each grade. For example, third-grade students whose reading is typical of all third-grade students (achievement tests have national norms) would be at the third-grade level in reading achievement. Note, however, that third-graders

Brains at Work Like all 10-year-olds, Luna and Carlotta love games. Playing games frequently makes some brain connections automatic, allowing players to concentrate on the most challenging aspects. Unlike the pastimes of 10-year-olds in previous generations, however, today's games usually involve small gadgets rather than big balls.

automatization A process in which repetition of a sequence of thoughts and actions makes the sequence routine, so that it no longer requires conscious thought.

aptitude The potential to master a specific skill or to learn a certain body of knowledge.

IQ test A test designed to measure intellectual aptitude, or ability to learn in school. Originally, intelligence was defined as mental age divided by chronological age, times 100—hence the term *intelligence quotient,* or *IQ.*

achievement test A measure of mastery or proficiency in reading, mathematics, writing, science, or some other subject.

Theoretical Distribution of IQ Scores

Moderate to severe retardation — 0.14%

Mild retardation —

Slow learner —

Average

Superior

Gifted

Genius — 0.14%

2.13%   13.6%   68.26%   13.6%   2.13%

40   55   70   85   100   115   130   145   160

IQ Score

FIGURE 11.3

In Theory, Most People Are Average Almost 70 percent of IQ scores fall within the normal range. Note, however, that this is a norm-referenced test. In fact, actual IQ scores have risen in many nations; 100 is no longer exactly the midpoint. Furthermore, in practice, scores below 50 are slightly more frequent than indicated by the normal curve shown here because severe retardation is the result not of normal distribution but of genetic and prenatal factors.

Observation Quiz If a person's IQ is 110, what category is he or she in? (see answer, page 337)

who are 7, 8, or 9 years old might all be reading on grade level—achievement tests do not reflect age. The words *in theory* precede the definitions of aptitude and achievement because, although potential and accomplishment are supposed to be distinct, IQ and achievement scores are strongly correlated for individuals, for groups of children, and for nations (Lynn & Mikk, 2007).

It was once assumed that aptitude was a fixed characteristic, present at birth. Longitudinal data show that this is not the case. Children with a low IQ can become above average, or even gifted, like my nephew David (discussed in Chapter 1). Indeed, the average IQ scores of entire nations have risen substantially—a phenomenon called the **Flynn effect,** named after the researcher who first described it (Flynn, 1999, 2007).

A professor of psychology begins his attack on the hereditary view of intelligence with his personal experience:

> I began having trouble with arithmetic in the fifth grade, after I missed school for a week just when my class took up fractions. For the rest of elementary school, I never quite recovered from that setback. My parents were sympathetic, telling me that people in our family had never been very good at math. They viewed math skills as something you either had or not, for reasons having mostly to do with heredity.

[*Nisbett, 2009, p. 1*]

Nisbett believes that his parents were wrong. He has gathered evidence that parents, schools, and cultures can raise a child's IQ substantially. Not every social scientist agrees with him. However, all agree that the IQ score is only a snapshot, a static view of a dynamic, developing brain.

Criticisms of Testing

Beyond the fact that scores change, a more fundamental question is whether any single test can measure the complexities of the human brain. This criticism has been targeted particularly at IQ tests when the underlying assumption is that there is one general thing called *intelligence* (often referred to as *g*, for general intelligence). Children may instead inherit a set of abilities, some high and some low, rather than a general intellectual ability (e.g., Q. Zhu et al., 2010). Leading developmentalists are among those who believe that humans have **multiple intelligences,** not just one.

Howard Gardner originally described seven intelligences: linguistic, logical-mathematical, musical, spatial, bodily-kinesthetic (movement), interpersonal (social

Trial and Understanding This youngster completes one of the five performance tests of the Wechsler Intelligence Scale for Children (WISC). If her score is high, is that because of superior innate intelligence? ["Wechsler Intelligence Scale for Children" and "WISC" are trademarks, in the U.S. and/or other countries, of Pearson Education, Inc. or its affiliate(s).]

Flynn effect The rise in average IQ scores that has occurred over the decades in many nations.

multiple intelligences The idea that human intelligence is comprised of a varied set of abilities rather than a single, all-encompassing one.

High IQ? No. These three are not geniuses according to IQ tests, but they are each brilliant in their own way. *(a)* Rachel Trezise is a prize-winning Welsh novelist, *(b)* Carmelo Anthony is a star for the New York Knicks, and *(c)* Taboo is a lead singer for the Black Eyed Peas. Each excels in one of Gardner's nine multiple intelligences (respectively, linguistic, kinesthetic, and musical), but in other ways, each is simply average.

Genius at Work Ten-year-old Kishan Shrikanth is a Bollywood director, shown here shooting his first full-length feature film (about street children in India). He excels at some intelligences (spatial, interpersonal) but not others (kinesthetic, naturalistic). Such variations may be much more common than traditional IQ tests measure.

understanding), and intrapersonal (self-understanding), each associated with a particular brain region (Gardner, 1983). He subsequently added an eighth intelligence (naturalistic: understanding nature, as in biology, zoology, or farming) and a ninth (existential: thinking about life and death) (Gardner, 1999, 2006; Gardner & Moran, 2006). (See photos.)

Although every normal person has at least a little of all nine intelligences, Gardner believes each individual excels in some more than others. For example, someone might be gifted spatially but not linguistically (a visual artist who cannot describe her work) or might have interpersonal but not naturalistic intelligence (an astute clinical psychologist whose houseplants die).

Gardner's theory has been influential in education, especially the education of children (e.g., Armstrong, 2009; Rettig, 2005), as teachers allow children to demonstrate knowledge in their own ways—illustrating history with a drawing rather than an essay, for instance. Some children may learn by listening, others by looking, others by doing—an idea that led to research on learning styles.

Brain Scans

One way to measure the mind might be to measure the brain directly, avoiding the pitfalls of written exams or individual questions. Yet even with such measures, interpretations of brain scans, especially those of normal children, are controversial. Although it seems logical that less activation of the brain would mean less intelligence, such a conclusion would be a mistake.

In fact, many areas of a young child's brain are activated simultaneously and then, with practice, automatization reduces the need for brain activity, so the smartest children might have less active brains in some circumstances. Similarly, some research finds that a thick cortex correlates with higher ability and also that thickness develops more slowly in gifted children (Karama et al., 2009; Miller, 2006). This gifted pattern is puzzling—but so is much brain research.

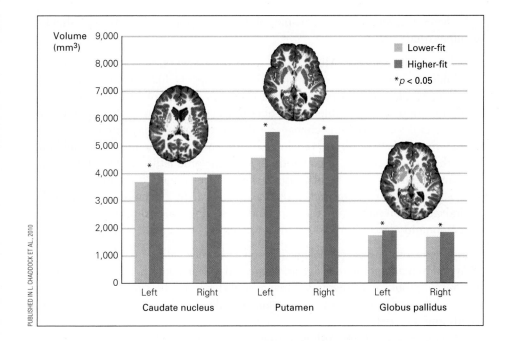

PUBLISHED IN L. CHADDOCK ET AL., 2010

Brain Fitness Aerobic fitness was measured (by VO$_2$—volume of oxygen expelled after exercise) in 59 children (average age 10, none of whom had ADHD or were pubescent); then the children's brains were scanned. Overall brain size did not correlate with fitness—genes and early nutrition are more important for that. However, the volume of crucial areas for cognitive control (attention, contextualizing, planning) was significantly greater in the children who were in better shape. This is one more reason to go biking, running, or swimming with your child.

>> **Answer to Observation Quiz** (from page 335) He or she is average. Anyone with a score between 85 and 115 is of average IQ.

Neuroscientists agree, however, on three conclusions:

1. Brain development depends on a person's specific experiences because "brain, body, and environment are . . . dynamically coupled" (Marshall, 2009, p. 119), and thus any brain scan is accurate only for the moment it is done.
2. Brain development continues throughout life. Middle childhood is crucial, but so are developments before and after these years.
3. Children with disorders often have unusual brain patterns, and training their brains may help. However, brain complexity means that no neuroscience remediation always succeeds.

This leads to the final topic of this chapter, children with special needs.

SUMMING UP

During middle childhood, neurological maturation allows faster, more automatic reactions. Selective attention enables focused concentration in school and in play. Aptitude tests, including IQ tests, compare mental age to chronological age, while actual learning is measured by achievement tests. IQ scores change much more than was originally imagined, as children and cultures adapt to changing contexts. The concept that an IQ score measures one underlying aptitude is challenged by Howard Gardner and others, who believe that people have not just one type of intelligence but many. Neuroscientists see that brain activity does not reliably correlate with IQ scores. ∎

Especially for Teachers What are the advantages and disadvantages of using Gardner's nine intelligences to guide your classroom curriculum? (see response, page 338)

>> Children with Special Needs

Developmental psychopathology links the study of typical development with the study of disorders (Cicchetti & Toth, 2009). Every topic already described including "genetics, neuroscience, developmental psychology . . . must be combined to understand how psychopathology develops and can be prevented" (Dodge, 2009, p. 413).

developmental psychopathology The field that uses insights into typical development to understand and remediate developmental disorders.

comorbid Refers to the presence of two or more unrelated disease conditions at the same time in the same person.

>> **Response for Teachers** (from page 337) The advantages are that all the children learn more aspects of human knowledge and that many children can develop their talents. Art, music, and sports should be an integral part of education, not just a break from academics. The disadvantage is that they take time and attention away from reading and math, which might lead to less proficiency in those subjects on standard tests and thus to criticism from parents and supervisors.

multifinality A basic principle of developmental psychopathology that holds that one cause can have many (multiple) final manifestations.

equifinality A basic principle of developmental psychopathology that holds that one symptom can have many causes.

attention-deficit/hyperactivity disorder (ADHD) A condition in which a person not only has great difficulty concentrating for more than a few moments but also is inattentive, impulsive, and overactive.

At the outset, four general principles of developmental psychopathology should be emphasized.

1. *Abnormality is normal.* Most children sometimes act oddly. At the same time, children with serious disorders are, in many respects, like everyone else.
2. *Disability changes year by year.* Most disorders are **comorbid,** which means that more than one problem is evident in the same person. Which particular disorder is most disabling changes, as does the degree of impairment.
3. *Life may be better or worse in adulthood.* Prognosis is difficult. Many children with severe disabilities (e.g., blindness) become productive adults. Conversely, some conditions (e.g., bipolar disorder) may become more disabling.
4. *Diagnosis and treatment reflect the social context.* In a dynamic system, each individual interacts with the surrounding setting—including family, school, community, and culture—to modify, worsen, or even create psychopathology.

Developmental psychopathology is especially relevant in middle childhood, when children are grouped by age and expected to learn on schedule. Those practices reveal problems in many children who differ from their peers. Fortunately, middle childhood is also a time when some disorders can be mitigated if treatment is early and targeted.

Therein lies a problem: Although treatment is more likely to succeed the earlier it begins, accurate diagnosis is more difficult the younger a child is, not only because many disorders are comorbid but also because symptoms differ by age. There is no simple link between cause and effect, which means that a specific behavior might be normal for children or might be an early sign of serious problems. As you remember, difference is not necessarily deficit—but this does not mean that differences are necessarily benign.

Two basic principles of developmental psychopathology are *multifinality* and *equifinality,* which lead to caution in diagnosis and treatment (Cicchetti & Toth, 2009). **Multifinality** means that one cause can have many (multiple) final manifestations (as when a child who has been flooded with stress hormones in infancy may be either hypervigilant or unusually calm, may be either easily angered or quick to cry, or may not be affected at all because of differential vulnerability). **Equifinality** (equal in final form) means that one symptom can have many causes (for instance, a 6-year-old who does not talk may be autistic, hard of hearing, mentally retarded, or electively mute).

We focus here on only three topics (attention-deficit and bipolar disorders, learning disabilities, and autism spectrum disorder), each with many permutations. These three clusters illustrate the general principles of childhood psychopathology. (Readers interested in any specific condition are urged to read some of the extensive relevant research).

Attention-Deficit/Hyperactivity, Bipolar, and Disruptive Mood Dysregulation Disorders

Attention-deficit/hyperactivity disorder and bipolar disorder are discussed together here because they are often comorbid and confused with each other (Miklowitz & Cicchetti, 2010). Disruptive mood dysregulation disorder is a new diagnosis that helps to resolve this confusion.

Attention-Deficit/Hyperactivity Disorder

Perhaps 10 percent of all young children have an **attention-deficit/hyperactivity disorder (ADHD),** which means they have difficulty paying attention and may also be filled with uncontrollable urges to be active or to act out impulsively. Children with ADHD can be inattentive, impulsive, and overactive and are thus disruptive when adults want them to be still (Barkley, 2006). About twice as many boys as girls have ADHD: Current estimates for children in middle childhood in the United States are 12 percent of boys and 6 percent of girls (National Center for Health Statistics, 2011).

A typical child with ADHD, when sitting down to do homework, might look up, ask questions, think about playing, get a drink, fidget, squirm, tap the table, jiggle his or her legs, and go to the bathroom—and then start the whole sequence again. Not surprisingly, such children tend to have academic difficulties; they are less likely to graduate from high school and college (Loe & Feldman, 2007).

The number of children diagnosed with ADHD has increased in the United States from about 5 percent in 1980 to about 10 percent currently. Rates are affected by ethnicity: More European American children than Latino ones are thought to have ADHD—at least as measured by medication use. The rate has also doubled in Europe (e.g., Hsia & Maclennan, 2009; van den Ban et al., 2010).

Almost Impossible The concentration needed to do homework is almost beyond Clint, age 11, who takes medication for ADHD. Note his furrowed brow, resting head, and sad face.

Observation Quiz Will he complete his homework on his own? (see answer, page 340)

bipolar disorder A condition characterized by extreme mood swings, from euphoria to deep depression, not caused by outside experiences.

Bipolar Disorder

Bipolar disorder is characterized by extreme mood swings, from euphoria to deep depression. Children with bipolar disorder experience at least one episode of grandiosity. They might believe, for instance, that they are the smartest person in the school, a genius destined to save the entire world. At other times, that child might be severely depressed, unwilling or unable to read, play with friends, or go to school (Miklowitz & Cicchetti, 2010).

One U.S. study reported that medical visits for youth under age 18 with a primary diagnosis of bipolar disorder increased 40-fold between 1995 and 2003, a period when adult diagnoses of bipolar merely doubled (Moreno et al, 2007). Such a rapid increase suggested to critics that childhood bipolar disorder was a diagnosis in the mind of the observer, not in the moods of the child. Others suggested that the rapid increase in diagnosis was the result of earlier misdiagnosis, not current overdiagnosis (Markowitz& Chicetti, 2010; Santosh & Congraman, 2008).

Disruptive Mood Dysregulation Disorder (DMDD)

None of these critics doubted, however, that there were many children who were brought to pediatricians and psychologists by parents (or referred by teachers) because they were too often rageful and irritable, even on their best days. These weren't just children going through a difficult phase, but children who were chronically angry, and their behavior was occurring at home, at school, and for months on end. In the new edition of the DSM-5, a new type of depressive disorder is included, **disruptive mood dysregulation disorder (DMDD),** to describe the behavior of these children. These are children who may scream over a dropped ice cream cone, or throw a remote control across the room rather than share it—and who look sad or angry when they are not losing their temper. These behaviors may not be precursers of adult bipolar disorder but may instead predict later anxiety and depressive disorders, now apparent in a storm of unregulated feeling.

Go Team Remember that abnormality is normal. Which of these boys has been diagnosed with a serious disability? Michael, second from the right, has bipolar disorder.

disruptive mood dysregulation disorder (DMDD) A condition in which a child has chronic irritability and anger that culminates in frequent tantrums that are inappropriate to the circumstances and to the child's age.

Distinguishing Between Disorders

Bipolar disorder "remains notoriously difficult to differentiate from other psychiatric illnesses in youth" (Phillips, 2010, p. 4). Many children diagnosed with either ADHD or bipolar disorder may be more accurately diagnosed with the other. Some symptoms are the same: Children with either disorder tend to be irritable,

>> Answer to Observation Quiz (from page 339) No. His mother is writing the answers for him.

Especially for Health Workers Parents ask that some medication be prescribed for their kindergarten child, who they say is much too active for them to handle. How do you respond? (see response, page 342)

even rageful, when adults demand that they behave normally. Most with either condition have trouble sleeping, are sometimes notably active, and at other times are depressed.

Both disorders are more common in children whose parents have a disorder, which strongly suggests a genetic link. However, the specifics of parental disability differ. Parents of children with ADHD often have learning disabilities, whereas parents of children with bipolar disorder are likely to have mood disturbances, including depression or eating disorders (also equifinal, in that not all eating disorders are related to emotional problems but many are).

Both disorders in children are also linked to unusual brain patterns, either in structures or activity, although, again, some differences may be apparent (Riccio et al., 2010; Santosh & Canagaratnam, 2008). In one study, children's brain activity was measured while they observed pictures of faces. Children with either disorder were less able to differentiate emotions than were the control-group children, but different parts of the amygdala were aroused in children with ADHD and in those with bipolar disorder (Brotman et al., 2008, 2010). There is not yet any definitive biological or neurological sign of either disorder, however. It is hoped that the new DMDD diagnosis will result in more accurate diagnosis and effective treatment.

A VIEW FROM SCIENCE

Drugs for Children

In the United States, more than 2 million children and adolescents under age 18 take prescription drugs to regulate their emotions and behavior. The rate has leveled off in recent years but remains high, with about 1 in 20 children taking psychoactive drugs in middle childhood, usually for ADHD (Scheffler et al., 2009; Vitiello et al., 2006; Zuvekas et al., 2006). In many other nations, drug use in middle childhood has recently increased (e.g., Hsia & Maclennan, 2009; van den Ban et al., 2010).

The most commonly prescribed drug is Ritalin for ADHD, but at least 20 other psychoactive drugs treat depression, anxiety, developmental delay, autism, bipolar disorder, and many other conditions in middle childhood. Younger children (ages 2 to 5) are taking these drugs at increasing rates, although their rates (about 1 child in 600) are far lower than for older children (Olfson et al., 2010). Because they have been inadequately tested for children, many drugs are prescribed "off label"—they have not been approved for patients of that age or condition. The incidence, ages, rates, and off-label uses all raise questions. Much of the American public is suspicious of any childhood psychiatric medicine (dosReis & Myers, 2008; McLeod et al., 2004; Rose, 2008).

Many child psychologists believe that drugs can be helpful, but they raise additional issues (Mayes et al., 2009). They find that some parents punish their children instead of seeking help, and developmentalists know that, for every child, finding the best drug at the right strength is difficult. Moreover, since children's weight and metabolism change, the right dose at one time is wrong at another.

Underdosing and overdosing are especially destructive when brains and habits are developing, yet only about half of all 2- to 5-year-olds who take psychoactive drugs are evaluated and monitored by a mental health professional (Olfson et al., 2010), and only half of the children diagnosed with ADHD take medication of any kind for it (National Center for Health Statistics, 2011).

Most professionals are convinced by research that finds that medication helps schoolchildren with emotional problems, particularly ADHD (Epstein et al., 2010; King et al., 2009; Scheffler et al., 2009). Some professionals also believe that contextual interventions (instructing parents and teachers on how best to manage such children) should be tried before any drug (Daley et al., 2009; Pelham & Fabiano, 2008).

By contrast, parents are less sure. One study of parents whose children were diagnosed with ADHD found that about 20 percent believed drugs should *never* be used for children, and about 29 percent believed that drugs were *necessary to* treat illnesses. The other 51 percent were in neither camp (dosReis et al., 2009). That was a small study (48 families), but a large-scale study found that only about half (56 percent) of the parents of U.S. children who are diagnosed with ADHD give them medication every day (Scheffler et al., 2009). African American children have more ADHD symptoms but are less often medicated, for reasons that include fragmented medical care and distrust of doctors (Miller et al., 2009).

The result of the discrepancy between public attitudes and research data is that some children who would benefit are never given medication, other children are given medication without the necessary monitoring, and still other children are given medication only until their symptoms subside. A group of children with ADHD from many cities in the United States and Canada were given appropriate medication, carefully calibrated. Their symptoms improved. However, eight years later, many had stopped taking their medicine. At this follow-up, both those who were still on medication and those who had stopped were likely to have learning difficulties and lower grades in school (Molina et al., 2009). Thus, the drug did not erase the problems.

What about long-term effects of taking medication? Much remains to be learned, and opinions are divided. However, two concerns—that children who take drugs in childhood will become adolescent addicts and that their growth will be stunted—seem invalid. In fact, longitudinal research comparing nonmedicated and medicated children with ADHD finds the opposite: Childhood medication reduces the risk of illegal drug use in adolescence and does not seem to adversely affect growth (Biederman et al., 2010; Faraone et al., 2003).

When appropriately used, drugs may help children make friends, learn in school, feel happier, and behave better. However, as the longitudinal study of ADHD children found, problems do not disappear: Adolescents who had childhood emotional problems were less successful academically and personally, whether or not they were medicated (Geller et al., 2008; Loe & Feldman, 2007; Molina et al., 2009). When children have special needs, parents and teachers need support and training. Drugs may help, but they are not the solution.

Treatment involves (1) counseling and training for the family and the child, (2) showing teachers how to help the children learn, and (3) medication to stabilize moods for bipolar children and to quiet ADHD children. Ongoing monitoring is crucial because stimulants may help children with ADHD but harm bipolar ones. Even with accurate diagnosis, each child responds differently to each drug, and responses change with time. Psychoactive medication for children raises many issues, as the following explains.

Learning Disabilities

The DSM-5 diagnosis of **specific learning disorder** now combines diagnoses of deficits in the perception or processing of information; such difficulty is commonly referred to as a **learning disability.** Many people have some specific learning disorder that leads to difficulty in mastering a particular skill that most other people acquire easily. Indeed, according to Gardner's view of multiple intelligences, almost everyone has a specific inadequacy or two. Perhaps one person is clumsy (low in kinesthetic intelligence), while another sings loudly but off key (low in musical intelligence).

Most such learning disabilities are not debilitating (the off-key singer learns to be quiet in chorus), but every schoolchild is expected to learn reading and math. Disabilities in either of these two subjects often undercut academic achievement and make a child feel inadequate, ashamed, and stupid. Hopefully, such children find (or are taught) ways to compensate: They learn coping strategies, and in adulthood their other abilities shine. Winston Churchill, Albert Einstein, and Hans Christian Andersen are all said to have had learning disabilities as children.

Dyslexia

The most commonly diagnosed learning disability is **dyslexia,** unusual difficulty with reading. No single test accurately diagnoses dyslexia (or any learning disability) because every academic achievement involves many specifics (Riccio & Rodriguez, 2007). One child with a reading disability might have trouble sounding out words but might excel in comprehension and memory of printed text; another child might have the opposite problem. Dozens of types and causes of dyslexia have been identified.

specific learning disorder (learning disability) A marked deficit in a particular area of learning that is not caused by an apparent physical disability, by intellectual disability, or by an unusually stressful home environment.

dyslexia Unusual difficulty with reading; thought to be the result of some neurological underdevelopment.

Say Ooo Most children teach themselves to talk clearly, but some need special help—as this 5-year-old does. Mirrors, mentoring, and manipulation may all be part of speech therapy.

© LAURENT / GLUCK

Early theories hypothesized that visual difficulties—for example, reversals of letters (reading *was* instead of *saw*) and mirror writing (*b* instead of *d*)—were the cause of dyslexia, but we now know that dyslexia often originates with speech and hearing difficulties (Gabrieli, 2009). An early warning occurs if a 3-year-old does not talk clearly or has not exhibited a naming explosion (see Chapter 6). Early speech therapy might reduce or prevent later dyslexia.

Dyscalculia

Similar suggestions apply to learning disabilities in math, called *dyscalculia*. Early help with numbers and concepts (long before first grade) can help prevent the emotional anxiety that occurs if a child is made to feel stupid (Butterworth et al., 2011). Remember that in early childhood, maybe even in infancy, most children can look at a series of dots and estimate how many there are. This basic number sense is deficient in children with dyscalculia, which provides a clue for early remediation (Piazza et al., 2010).

When a young child has trouble performing tasks that other children can do easily, such problems can be spotted in brain scans. For example, a second-grader, when asked to estimate the height of a normal room, might answer "200 feet" or, when asked whether the 5 or the 8 of hearts is higher, correctly answer 8—but only after counting the number of hearts on each card (Butterworth et al., 2011). Some success has occurred using computers to train children with dyscalculia to improve in number understanding, but—remember equifinality—this does not help every child.

Autism Spectrum Disorder

Of all the special-needs children, those with autism are probably the most troubling, not only because their problems are severe but also because the causes of and treatments for autism are hotly disputed. Most children with autism can be spotted in the first year of life, but some seem quite normal at first and then deteriorate later on.

Parents' responses vary, from irrational hope to deep despair, from blaming doctors and public policy to feeling guilty. Developmentalists generally believe that genes are one factor in autism but that parents are not to blame. Parents and teachers can be very helpful, however, if they cooperate while the child is young.

Symptoms

autism spectrum disorder A developmental disorder marked by difficulty with social communication and interaction—including difficulty seeing things from another person's point of view—and restricted, repetitive patterns of behavior, interests, or activities.

Autism spectrum disorder is characterized by inadequate social skills and restricted, repetitive patterns of behavior, interests, or acitivities. Half a century ago, it was considered a single, rare disorder affecting fewer than 1 in 1,000 children with "an extreme aloneness that, whenever possible, disregards, ignores, shuts out anything . . . from the outside" (Kanner, 1943). Children who developed slowly but were not so withdrawn were diagnosed as being intellectually disabled or as having a "pervasive developmental disorder."

Much has changed in the past decades. Now many children who would have been considered intellectually disabled are said to have autism spectrum disorder, which characterizes about 1 in every 110 children (three times as many boys as girls and more European Americans than Latino, Asian, or African Americans) (Lord & Bishop, 2010). Many of these children do not seem intellectually disabled at all.

As mentioned above, there are two signs of autism spectrum disorder: (1) problems in social interaction and the social use of language, and (2) restricted, repetitive patterns of behavior. Underlying these is a kind of emotional blindness (Scambler et al., 2007). Children with any form of autism find it difficult to understand the emotions of others, which makes them feel alien, like "an anthropologist on Mars," as Temple Grandin, an educator and writer with autism, expressed it (quoted in Sacks, 1995). Consequently, many do not want to talk, play, or otherwise interact with anyone, and they are especially delayed in developing a theory of mind (Senju et al., 2010).

Autism spectrum disorder includes many symptoms of varied severity. Some children never speak, rarely smile, and often play for hours with one object (such as a spinning top or a toy train). Others are called "high-functioning"—they are extremely talented in some specialized area, such as drawing or geometry. Such high-functioning children are still said by some to have Asperger syndrome, but most clinicians and the DSM-5 consider this a part of the autism spectrum. Many are brilliant in unusual ways (Dawson et al., 2007), including Grandin, a well-respected expert on animal care (Grandin & Johnson, 2009). However, social interaction is always impaired. Grandin was bewildered by romantic love.

Far more children have autism spectrum disorder now than in 1990, either because the incidence of this disorder has increased or because more children receive that diagnosis. You read earlier that currently about 1 child in 110 is autistic. This figure is based on careful assessment, but other research puts the number even higher—perhaps 1 child in 40. Underlying that estimate is the reality that no definitive measure diagnoses autism: Many people are socially inept and poor at communication—are they all somewhat autistic? No; for a diagnosis of autism spectrum disorder a person's symptoms must be severe enough to significantly impact their ability to function.

The hypothesis that the diagnosis, not the disorder, is more common is supported by a detailed study in Texas showing that in the wealthiest school districts, the number of children diagnosed with autism tripled over six years, but the number did not change in the poorest districts (Palmer et al., 2005; see the Research Design).

Treatment

Equifinality certainly applies to autism: A child can have autistic symptoms for many reasons, which makes selecting effective treatment difficult. An intervention that seems to help one child proves worthless for another. Biology is crucial (genes, birth complications, prenatal injury, or perhaps chemicals) and brain patterns are unusual; autism is not caused by family nurture (G. Dawson, 2010). One family factor may be influential, however: having one baby soon after another. Children born less than a year after a previous birth are more than twice as often diagnosed as autistic compared with children born 3 or more years apart (Cheslack-Postava et al., 2011).

A vast number of treatments have been used for children with autism spectrum disorder, none of them completely successful. Some parents are convinced that a particular treatment helped their child, whereas other parents say that same treatment failed. Scientists disagree as well. For instance, one popular treatment is putting the child in a hyperbaric chamber to breathe more concentrated oxygen than is found in everyday air. Two studies of hyperbaric treatments—both randomized in participant selection and both with control groups—reported contradictory results, either benefits (Rossignol et al., 2009) or no effect (Granpeesheh et al., 2010). Part of the problem may be multifinality and equifinality: Children with autism spectrum disorder have core symptoms in common, but they also differ in the cause and consequence of those symptoms.

Research Design

Scientists: Raymond Palmer, Stephen Blanchard, and David Mandall designed the study, and C. R. Jean provided critical interpretation.

Publication: *American Journal of Public Health (2005).*

Participants: All 1,040 school districts in Texas over six school years, 1994 to 2001.

Design: The school districts were sorted into tenths according to wealth—a composite of average income, salaries, proportion of disadvantaged students, and so on. Within each tenth, the number of students designated as autistic was tallied each year.

Major conclusion: Increases in diagnosis of students with autism spectrum disorder correlated with wealth, from an increase of 300 percent in districts in the top two-tenths to no change in the bottom tenth. For every 10,000 children, 21 in the top districts and 3 in the bottom districts were designated as having autism.

Comments: These findings, covering an entire state, suggest that increases in the incidence of autism are caused by better diagnosis, more available physicians, advanced special education, and perhaps parental insistence on diagnosis and treatment.

PHANIE / PHOTO RESEARCHERS, INC.

Precious Gifts Many children with autism are gifted artists. This boy attends a school in Montmoreau, France, that features workshops in which children with autism develop social, play, and learning skills.

All Together Now Kiemel Lamb (top center) leads autistic children in song, a major accomplishment. For many of them, music is soothing, words are difficult, and hand-holding in a group is almost impossible.

An added problem is the gap between parents and professionals. One example concerns thimerosal, an antiseptic containing mercury that was once used in childhood immunizations. Many parents first noticed their infants' impairments after their vaccinations and believe thimerosal was the cause. No scientist who examines the evidence agrees: Extensive research has disproven the immunization hypothesis many times (Offit, 2008). Thimerosal was removed from vaccines a decade ago, but the rates of autism are still rising. Many doctors fear that parents who cling to this hypothesis are harming millions of children who suffer needless illnesses because some parents fear immunization.

Some children with autism are on special diets, take vitamin supplements, or are on medication. One drug in particular, risperidone, relieves some symptoms (although research finds side effects, including weight gain), but no treatment has proven successful at relieving the basic condition. As you already know, all medication use is controversial: Whether or not a child takes risperidone depends on many factors other than symptoms (Arnold et al., 2010; Rosenberg et al., 2010).

Many behavioral methods to improve talking and socialization have also been tried, again with mixed results (Granpeesheh et al., 2009; Hayward et al., 2009; Howlin et al., 2009). Many clinicians use a mix of behavior analysis, sensory play, and communication therapy to help children with ASD develop imaginative play, cognitive flexibility, and an understanding of the feelings of others. Early and individualized education of both the child and the parents has had some success, although the connection between disorder and special education is an uncertain one, as you will now see.

Special Education

The overlap of the biosocial, cognitive, and psychosocial domains is evident to developmentalists, who see each child's growth in every area affected by every other area. However, whether or not a child is designated as needing special education is not straightforward, nor is it closely related to specific special needs. Here, we discuss education as it pertains to developmental psychopathology, but the link between disorder and education is problematic. (Education is also discussed in every chapter on cognitive development, including the next one.)

Changing Laws and Practices

In the United States, recognition that the distinction between normal and abnormal is not clear-cut (the first principle of developmental psychopathology) led to a series of reforms in the treatment and education of children with special needs. According to the 1975 Education of All Handicapped Children Act, children with special needs must be educated in the **least restrictive environment (LRE).**

least restrictive environment (LRE) A legal requirement that children with special needs be assigned to the most general educational context in which they can be expected to learn.

Most of the time, LRE has meant educating children with special needs with other children in a regular class, sometimes called *mainstreaming,* rather than in a special classroom or school. Sometimes a child is sent to a *resource room,* with a teacher who provides targeted tutoring. Sometimes a class is an *inclusion class,* which means that children with special needs are "included" in the general classroom, with "appropriate aids and services" (usually from a trained teacher who works with the regular teacher) (Kalambouka et al., 2007).

The latest educational strategy in the United States is called **response to intervention (RTI)** (Fletcher & Vaughn, 2009; Shapiro et al., 2011). All children in the early grades who are below average in achievement (which may be half the class) are given some special intervention. Most of them respond by improving their achievement, but for those who do not, more intervention occurs. If there is no response to repeated intervention, the child is referred for testing and observation to diagnose the problem.

Professionals use a battery of tests (not just IQ or achievement tests) to reach their diagnosis and develop recommendations. If they find that a child has special needs, they discuss an **individual education plan (IEP)** with the parents, to specify educational goals for the child.

> **response to intervention (RTI)** An educational strategy intended to help children in early grades who demonstrate below-average achievement by means of special intervention.

> **individual education plan (IEP)** A document that specifies educational goals and plans for a child with special needs.

Cohort and Culture

Looking at Table 11.1, you can see cohort effects. More than one in four of the children with special needs in 1977 were called "mentally retarded," a category now called "intellectually disabled"; currently, of those needing special education, only about one child in 14 is designated as intellectually disabled. However, in 2010, of the special needs children, about 5 percent were designated as autistic and almost 6 percent were designated developmentally delayed (Snyder & Dillow, 2011). Neither of those two categories existed in 1977. Apparently, some children who were considered mentally retarded in the 1970s would have been called autistic or developmentally delayed if they had been diagnosed today. Labels change more quickly with the times than symptoms do.

Looking internationally, the connection between special needs and education varies for cultural reasons, not child-related ones. In many African and Latin American nations, no children are designated as having special needs; in many Asian nations, the diagnosis of special needs refers primarily to the physically disabled. As a result, in Taiwan, for example, less than 1 percent of the students receive special education of any kind (Tzeng, 2007).

TABLE 11.1	**Proportion of Children with Special Education Needs by Specific Designation* (percent of children)**					
	1977		**1997**		**2007**	
Learning disabilities	21.5	(1.8**)	46	(5.9)	39	(5.2)
Speech impairment	35.2	(2.9)	17	(2.3)	22	(3.0)
Mentally retarded	28	(2.2)	10.0	(1.3)	7.6	(1.0)
Emotionally disturbed	7.7	(0.6)	7.7	(1.0)	6.7	(0.9)
Deafness and hearing loss	2.4	(0.2)	1.2	(0.2)	1.2	(0.2)
Blindness and low vision	1	(0.1)	0.4	(0.1)	0.4	(0.1)
Developmental delay	—	—			5.4	(0.7)
Autism spectrum	—		0.7	(0.1)	4.5	(0.6)
Orthopedic handicap	2.4	(0.2)	1.2	(0.1)	1.0	(0.1)
Other health problems***	2.8	(0.3)	3.2	(0.5)	9.7	(1.3)

*Based on evaluation by U.S. public school professionals.

**Numbers in parentheses are percentages of all public school children.

***Limited strength, vitality, or alertness due to chronic health problems, such as asthma, sickle-cell anemia, and diabetes.

Source: Snyder & Dillow (2010).

Gifted and Talented

Children who are unusually gifted are often thought to have special needs as well, yet they are not covered by the federal laws for the disabled. Each state of the United States selects and educates gifted and talented children, but the specifics not only vary—they are also hotly debated. A scholar writes: "The term gifted . . . has never been more problematic than it is today" (Dai, 2011, p. 8). Educators, political leaders, scientists, and everyone else argue about who is gifted and what should be done about them. Are gifted children unusually intelligent, or talented, or creative? Should they be skipped, segregated, enriched, included, or left alone?

A hundred years ago, the definition of gifted was simple: high IQ. A famous longitudinal study followed a thousand "genius" children, all of whom scored about 140 on the Stanford-Binet IQ test (Terman, 1925). Even today, some school systems define gifted as having an IQ of 130 or above (attained by 1 child in 50), or sometimes as 145 and above (1 child in 1,000).

acceleration Educating gifted children alongside other children of the same mental, not chronological, age.

A hundred years ago, the educational solution was simple, too: Educate them with children who were their mental age, not their chronological age, a practice called **acceleration.** Today this is rarely done because many of those accelerated children were bullied, unhappy, and never learned proper social skills. As one woman remembers:

> Nine-year-old little girls are so cruel to younger girls. I was much smaller than them, of course, and would have done anything to have a friend. Although I could cope with the academic work very easily, emotionally I wasn't up to it. Maybe it was my fault and I was asking to be picked on. I was a weed at the edge of the playground.
>
> [Rachel, quoted in Freeman, 2010, p. 27]

Weeds grow no matter where they are planted, and research on thousands of children has found that while the gifted learn differently from other children, they are neither more nor less likely to need emotional and social education. Educating the whole child, not just the mind, is required (Winner, 1996).

There is a related type of special child, often called talented instead of gifted, who is precocious in one of Gardner's nine intelligences. Mozart was such a child, composing music at age 3; so was Pablo Picasso, creating works of art at age 4. Historically, many famous musicians, artists, and scientists were child prodigies whose fathers recognized their talent (often because the father himself was in the same field) and provided special education. Mozart's father transcribed his son's earliest creations and toured Europe with his gifted son. Picasso's father removed him from school in second grade so he could create all day (Pablo said he never learned to read or write).

Although such intense early education nourished talent, neither Mozart nor Picasso had happy adult lives. Similar patterns are still apparent, as exemplified by gifted athletes (e.g., Tiger Woods and Steffi Graf) as well as those in more erudite specialties. One recent example:

> Sufiah Yusof started her maths degree at Oxford [the leading University in England] in 2000, at the age of 13. She too had been dominated and taught by her father. But she ran away the day after her final exam. She was found by police but refused to go home, demanding of her father in an email: "Has it ever crossed your mind that the reason I left home was because I've finally had enough of 15 years of physical and emotional abuse?" Her father claimed she'd been abducted and brainwashed. She refuses to communicate with him. She is now a very happy, high-class, high-earning prostitute.
>
> [Freeman, 2010, p. 286]

Fourth Grade Challenge How much weight can a bridge hold? Thirty-three students in gifted classes at an Idaho elementary school designed and built toothpick bridges and then tested them. David Stubbens (shown here) added 61 pounds to the bucket before his bridge collapsed.

A third kind of child who might need special education is the unusually creative one (Sternberg et al., 2011). They are *divergent thinkers,* finding many solutions and even more questions for every problem. Such students joke in class, dodge drudgery, resist repetition, and bedevil their teachers. They may become innovators, inventors, and creative forces of the future.

Creative children do not conform to social standards. They are not *convergent thinkers,* who choose the correct answer on school exams. One such person was Charles Darwin, whose "school reports complained unendingly that he wasn't interested in studying, only shooting, riding, and beetle-collecting" (Freeman, 2010, p. 283). Other creative geniuses who were poor students were Einstein, Freud, Newton, and almost every contemporary innovator.

Since both acceleration and intense parental tutoring have led to later problems, a third method of educating the gifted has become popular, at least in the United States. A group of children who are bright, talented, and/or creative—all the same age but each with special abilities—are taught as a group. Ideally, such children are neither bored nor lonely; each is challenged and appreciated.

Neuroscience has recently discovered another advantage: brain development. Many studies have found that children who are allowed to practice their musical talents develop brain structures that enhance their talent. Specialized brain growth is also likely for child athletes and mathematicians, suggesting that neurological specialization in childhood may occur for every form of giftedness. As you know, a child's brain is quite plastic, and all children learn whatever their context teaches. Thus, talents may be developed, not wasted, with special education.

THINKING CRITICALLY

Fair and Reasonable Grounds?

How can a school system know which children will be geniuses? Is the class clown a creative soul who needs to be cherished or a disruptive child who needs to be disciplined? Tests of creativity have been developed, but such tests are imperfect at distinguishing the "schoolhouse gifted" from the "creative-productive gifted"; both kinds of giftedness may need specialized education, but the specifics would differ (Renzulli, 2009). Indeed, identification and then education is imperfect for all gifted children (Dai, 2010). If a child is above average (say, an IQ of 120), eventual success may depend more on motivation, personality, and good fortune than on teaching and test scores.

Furthermore, how can we be sure that the designation is valid and fair? Gifted children of lower-SES families, or those from less privileged ethnic groups, may be unfairly excluded. Bias against girls, or boys, may be problematic as well.

This concern is not abstract. Consider data from the United States in 2006 (Snyder & Dillow, 2011). Of every 150 schoolchildren, 23 in Kentucky are designated gifted and talented; only 1 in Massachusetts is designated as such. Obviously, something in the culture or politics of those states, not in the nature of the children, influences this determination.

Most states have 10 percent more girls than boys in gifted classes (sexist or biological?), yet three states (Kansas, New Mexico, and South Dakota) have about 10 percent more boys than girls in such classes (fair?). In most states, the percent of White children in gifted-and-talented classes is twice as high as the number of children from minority groups (politics or biology?), but rates are almost equal in Utah (fair?). In most states, higher proportions of African Americans than Hispanics are designated as gifted, but the opposite is true in Texas (politics or biology?).

A leading U.S. educator suggests that we scrap all designations of gifted or talented children and

> give up the notions of the "the normal," "the disabled," and "the gifted" as they are typically applied in schools, especially for the purposes of classification and grouping, and simply accept difference as the rule.
>
> [Borland, 2003, p. 121]

All developmentalists now see that there are many valid ways to designate and educate gifted and talented children and that the best solution reflects the cultural context. But the specifics of that best solution are far from obvious.

SUMMING UP

Many children have special learning needs that originate with problems in the development of their brains. Developmental psychopathologists emphasize that no one is typical in every way; the passage of time sometimes brings improvement to children with special needs and sometimes not. Children with attention-deficit disorders, learning disabilities, and autism spectrum disorders may function adequately or may have lifelong problems, depending on many variables such as the severity of the problem; family, school, and cultural environments; and the presence of comorbid conditions. Specifics of diagnosis, prognosis, medication, and education are debatable; no child learns or behaves exactly like another, and no educational strategy is entirely successful with every child.

SUMMARY

A Healthy Time

1. Middle childhood is a time of steady growth and few serious illnesses. Increasing independence and self-care allow most school-age children to be relatively happy and competent.

2. Advances in medical care have reduced childhood sickness and death. Immunization is effective, fewer children are exposed to toxins, and early diagnosis and treatment have mitigated many conditions.

3. Physical activity aids health and joy in many ways. However, current social and environmental conditions make informal neighborhood play scarce, school physical education less prevalent, and sports leagues less welcoming for some school-age children.

Health Problems in Middle Childhood

4. Childhood obesity is a worldwide epidemic. Although genes are part of the problem, less exercise and the greater availability of unhealthy foods are the main reasons today's youth are heavier than their counterparts 50 years ago. Parents and policies share the blame.

5. The incidence of asthma is increasing overall, with notable ethnic differences. The origins of asthma are genetic; the triggers are specific environmental allergens. Preventive measures include longer breast-feeding, increased outdoor play, and less air pollution, particularly from cars.

Brain Development

6. Brain development continues during middle childhood, enhancing every aspect of development. Notable are advances in reaction time and automatization, allowing faster and better coordination of many parts of the brain.

7. IQ tests quantify intellectual aptitude. Most such tests emphasize language and logical ability and predict school achievement. IQ scores sometimes change over time, partly because of maturation but primarily because of experience.

8. Achievement tests measure accomplishment, often in specific academic areas. Aptitude and achievement are correlated, both for individuals and for nations.

9. Critics contend that intelligence is manifested in multiple ways that conventional IQ tests are too limited to measure. Multiple intelligences include creative and practical abilities as well as many skills not usually valued in typical North American schools.

Children with Special Needs

10. Developmental psychopathology uses an understanding of normal development to inform the study of unusual development. Four general lessons have emerged: Abnormality is normal; disability changes over time; adolescence and adulthood may make a condition better or worse; and diagnosis depends on context.

11. Children with attention-deficit/hyperactivity disorder (ADHD) have potential problems in three areas: inattention, impulsiveness, and overactivity. Stimulant medication often helps children with ADHD to learn, but any drug use by children must be carefully monitored.

12. Children with bipolar disorder have marked mood swings, from grandiosity to depression. This disorder is often mistaken for attention-deficit/hyperactivity disorder.

13. People with a specific learning disorder have unusual difficulty in mastering a specific skill that other people learn easily. The most common learning disability that manifests itself during the school years is dyslexia, unusual difficulty disorder.

14. Children with autism spectrum disorder typically show impaired social interaction and communication as well as restricted, repetitive patterns of behavior, interests, or activities. Many causes are hypothesized. Autism is partly genetic; no one now views autism as primarily the result of inadequate parenting. Treatments are diverse: All are controversial and none are certain to help.

15. About 13 percent of all school-age children in the United States receive special education services. These services begin with an IEP (individual education plan) and assignment to the least restrictive environment (LRE), usually the regular classroom.

KEY TERMS

middle childhood (p. 323)
BMI (body mass index) (p. 328)
overweight (p. 328)
obesity (p. 328)
asthma (p. 330)
reaction time (p. 333)
selective attention (p. 333)
automatization (p. 334)
aptitude (p. 334)

IQ test (p. 334)
achievement test (p. 334)
Flynn effect (p. 335)
multiple intelligences (p. 335)
developmental psychopathology (p. 337)
comorbid (p. 338)
multifinality (p. 338)
equifinality (p. 338)

attention-deficit/hyperactivity disorder (ADHD) (p. 338)
bipolar disorder (p. 339)
disruptive mood dysregulation disorder (DMDD) (p. 339)
specific learning disorder (learning disability) (p. 341)
dyslexia (p. 341)
autism spectrum disorder (p. 342)

least restrictive environment (LRE) (p. 344)
response to intervention (RTI) (p. 345)
individual education plan (IEP) (p. 345)
acceleration (p. 346)

WHAT HAVE YOU LEARNED?

A Healthy Time

1. What physical abilities emerge from age 6 to age 11?

2. How do childhood health habits affect adult health?

3. What are the main advantages and disadvantages of physical play during middle childhood?

4. How do children benefit from physical education in school?

5. How do SES, gender, and culture affect after-school activities?

Health Problems in Middle Childhood

6. What are the national and cohort differences in childhood obesity?

7. Why does a thin 6-year-old not need to fatten up?

8. What roles do nature and nurture play in childhood asthma?

9. What would be primary prevention for childhood obesity?

10. Why does good tertiary prevention for childhood asthma not reach every child who needs it?

Brain Development

11. Why does quicker reaction time improve the ability to learn?

12. How do changes in brain functioning make it easier for a child to sit in a classroom?

13. When would a teacher give an aptitude test instead of an achievement test?

14. If the theory of multiple intelligences is correct, should IQ tests be discarded? Why or why not?

15. Why are some intellectual abilities valued more than others? Give examples.

16. Should brain scans replace traditional intelligence tests? Why or why not?

Children with Special Needs

17. What would be normal child behavior in one culture but not in another?

18. What examples illustrate the difference between multifinality and equifinality?

19. Why is medication recommended for children with ADHD?

20. Why might parents ask a doctor to prescribe Ritalin for their child?

21. Why is bipolar disorder hard to diagnose in children?

22. What is the difference between bipolar disorder in children and in adults?

23. What specific learning disabilities are not recognized in the United States currently?

24. How could an adult have a learning disability that has never been diagnosed?

25. If a successful adult has high-functioning autism, what kind of profession and what sort of family life would you expect him or her to have?

26. Why does the frequency of some kinds of developmental psychopathology increase while that of others decreases?

27. What are the signs of autism spectrum disorders?

APPLICATIONS

1. Compare play spaces for children in different neighborhoods—ideally, urban, suburban, and rural areas. Note size, safety, and use. How might children's weight and motor skills be affected by differences you observe?

2. Developmental psychologists believe that every teacher should be skilled at teaching children with a wide variety of needs. Does the teacher-training curriculum at your college or university reflect this goal? Should all teachers take the same courses, or should some teachers be specialized? Give reasons for your opinions.

3. Internet sources vary in quality on any topic, but this may be particularly true of Web sites designed for parents of children with special needs. Pick one childhood disability or disease and find several Web sources devoted to that condition. How might parents evaluate the information provided?

4. Special education teachers are in great demand. In your local public school, what is the ratio of regular to special education teachers? How many are in self-contained classrooms, resource rooms, and inclusion classrooms? What do your data reveal about the education of children with special needs in your community?

>>ONLINE CONNECTIONS

To accompany your textbook, you have access to a number of online resources, including quizzes for every chapter of the book, flashcards (in English and Spanish), critical thinking questions, and case studies. For access to any of these links, go to www.worthpublishers.com/bergerca9e. In addition to these free resources, you'll also find links to podcasts, video clips, diagnostic quizzing with personalized study advice, and an ebook. Some of the videos and activities available online include:

- *Autism.* This activity explores the symptoms of autism and the importance of early diagnosis. Video clips give a glimpse into the world of parents and autistic children.

- *Educating the Girls of the World.* Girls around the world talk about the challenges that hinder their enrollment in all levels of education. Highlights initiatives for change.

Middle Childhood: Cognitive Development

WHAT WILL YOU KNOW?

1. Is it better to let children learn from experience or to teach them what they need to know?

2. Why do children change vocabulary, grammar, tone, and gestures, depending on their audience?

3. What is the best kind of school for children age 6 to 11?

At age 9, I wanted a puppy. My parents said no—we already had Dusty, our family dog. I dashed off a poem, promising "to brush his hair as smooth as silk" and "to feed him milk." (Wrong, of course: Puppies should not have cow's milk.) My father praised my poem; I got Taffy, a blonde cocker spaniel.

At age 10, my daughter Sarah wanted her ears pierced. I said no—it wouldn't be fair to her three older sisters, who had had to wait until they were teenagers before ear-piercing. Sarah wrote an affidavit and persuaded her sisters to sign it, saying that they had no objection. She got gold posts.

Sarah and I were typical, although our wishes differed by cohort and our strategies by family. Sarah knew I wouldn't budge for doggerel but that I respect signed documents. All school-age children master whatever their context presents: dividing fractions, surfing the Web, memorizing rap songs, loading rifles, or persuading parents.

This chapter describes that impressive cognitive development. We begin by examining how Piaget, Vygotsky, and information-processing theory describe cognition in middle childhood. Then we discuss applications of those theories to language, as well as the many disputes about how and what children should learn in school.

>> Building on Theory

Learning is rapid in childhood. Some children, by age 11, beat their elders at chess, play music that adults pay to hear, publish poems, win trophies. Others live on the streets or fight in civil wars, learning lessons that no child should know. How do they learn so quickly?

Piaget and School-Age Children

Piaget called the cognition of middle childhood **concrete operational thought,** characterized by concepts that enable children to use logic. *Operational* comes from the Latin word *operare,* "to work; to produce." By calling this period operational, Piaget emphasized productive thinking. The school-age child, no longer limited by egocentrism, performs logical operations. Children apply their new reasoning skills to *concrete* situations—that is, situations with visible, tangible, real

concrete operational thought Piaget's term for the ability to reason logically about direct experiences and perceptions.

AP PHOTO / THE AUGUSTA CHRONICLE CHRIS THELEN

His Science Project Concrete operational 10-year-olds like Daniel, shown here with some of his family's dairy cows, can be logical about anything they see, hear, or touch. Daniel's science experiment, on the effect of music on milk production, won first place in a Georgia regional science fair.

classification The logical principle that things can be organized into groups (or categories or classes) according to some characteristic they have in common.

transitive inference The ability to figure out the unspoken link between one fact and another.

things (not abstractions). Children become more systematic, objective, scientific—and educable.

A Hierarchy of Categories

One logical concept is **classification,** the organization of things into groups (or *categories* or *classes*) according to some characteristic that they share. For example, *family* includes parents, siblings, and cousins. Other common classes are people, animals, toys, and food. Each class includes some elements and excludes others, and each is part of a hierarchy.

Food, for instance, is a category, with the next-lower level of that hierarchy being meat, grains, fruits, and so on. Most subclasses can be further divided: Meat includes poultry, beef, and pork, each of which can be divided again. Adults realize that items at the bottom of a classification hierarchy belong to every higher level: Bacon is always pork, meat, and food. Younger children may know that bacon is pork, but they cannot perform the mental operation of moving up and down the hierarchy.

Piaget devised many experiments to reveal children's understanding of classification. For example, an examiner shows a child a bunch of nine flowers—seven yellow daisies and two white roses (revised and published in Piaget et al., 2001). The examiner makes sure the child knows the words *flowers, daisies,* and *roses.* Then comes the pivotal question: "Are there more daisies or more flowers?" Until about age 7, most children say, "More daisies." Younger children can offer no justification for their answers, but some 6- or 7-year-olds explain that "there are more yellow ones than white ones" or that "because daisies are daisies, they aren't flowers" (Piaget et al., 2001). By age 8, most children can classify: "More flowers than daisies," they say.

Other Logical Concepts

Another example of logic is the ability to grasp connections that are implied, not stated. Piaget studied **transitive inference,** the ability to figure out (infer) the unspoken link (transfer) between one fact and another. For example, "John is taller than Jim. Jim is taller than David. Who is taller, John or David?" Preoperational children are stumped. They cannot do this simple transitive inference because they know only what they have been told directly, not implications. By contrast, school-age children infer relationships.

Later research connects transitive inference to the maturation of the hippocampus, which reaches a critical point at about age 7, making inferences and other kinds of mental logic possible (DeVito et al., 2010; Zalesak & Heckers, 2009). This may seem to confirm Piaget's findings, but neurological and comparative research finds that transitive inference is both simpler and more complex than Piaget imagined (Goodwin & Johnson-Laird, 2008), with some nonhuman animals succeeding at simple versions of it.

Nonetheless, transitive inference is related to another logical concept that Piaget called *seriation,* the knowledge that things can be arranged in a logical series. Seriation is crucial for using (not merely memorizing) the alphabet or for understanding the number sequence. By age 5, most children can count up to 100, but they cannot correctly estimate where any particular two-digit number would be placed on a line that starts at 0 and ends at 100. Generally, this is possible by age 8 (Meadows, 2006).

The logical abilities of school-age children may allow them to understand arithmetic. For example, children need to understand that 12 plus 3 equals 3 plus 12 and that 15 is always 15 no matter how it was reached (conservation). Reversibility eventually allows the realization that if 5 times 7 equals 35, then 35 divided by 5 must be 7. Seriation and classification abilities correlate with math skills in primary school, although many other factors contribute to math achievement (Desoete et al., 2009).

The Significance of Piaget's Findings

Although logic connects to math concepts, researchers have found more continuity than discontinuity in number skills. Thus, Piaget was mistaken: There is no sudden shift between preoperational and concrete operational logic. In fact, some children learn logic via math, not vice versa. As explained in Chapter 9, the ability to classify appears long before middle childhood (Halford & Andrews, 2006), and you have just read that transitive inference is not unique to humans.

Nonetheless, Piaget's experiments revealed something important. School-age children can use mental categories and subcategories more flexibly, inductively, and simultaneously than younger children can (Meadows, 2006). They are more advanced thinkers, intellectually capable in ways that younger children are not.

After "Gee Whiz!" After he sees the magnified image that his classmate expects will amaze him, will he analyze his observations? Ideally, concrete operational thought enables children to use their new logic to interpret their experiences.

Vygotsky and School-Age Children

Like Piaget, Vygotsky felt that educators should consider children's thought processes, not just the outcomes. He recognized that younger children are confused by some concepts that older children understand. Children are curious, creative learners. For that reason, Vygotsky believed that an educational system based on rote memorization rendered the child "helpless in the face of any sensible attempt to apply any of this acquired knowledge" (Vygotsky, 1934/1994, pp. 356–357).

The Role of Instruction

Unlike Piaget, Vygotsky regarded instruction as crucial. He thought that peers and teachers provide the bridge between developmental potential and needed skills and knowledge, via guided participation, scaffolding, and the zone of proximal development (see Chapters 2 and 9).

Confirmation of the role of social interaction and instruction comes from children who, because of their school's entry-date cutoff, are either relatively old kindergartners or quite young first-graders. At the end of the school year, achievement scores of 6-year-old first-graders far exceed those of kindergarten 6-year-olds who are only one month younger (Lincove & Painter, 2006; NICHD, 2007). Obviously, they had learned a great deal from the first-grade teachers.

Remember that Vygotsky believed education occurs everywhere, not only in school. Children mentor one another as they play together. They learn from television, dinner with their families, people they see on the street, and every other daily experience. This education accumulates from infancy on.

For instance, a study of the reading and math achievement of more than a thousand third- and fifth-grade children from ten U.S. cities found that high-scoring primary schoolchildren were likely to have had extensive cognitive stimulation. There were three main sources of intellectual activity: their families (e.g., parents

Especially for Teachers How might Piaget's and Vygotsky's ideas help in teaching geography to a class of third-graders? (see response, page 354)

read to them daily when they were toddlers), preschool programs (e.g., a variety of learning activities), and the first grade (e.g., literacy emphasis with individual evaluation). Although children from families of low socioeconomic status (SES) were least likely to have been highly stimulated in all three contexts, achievement scores of those low-SES children who had all three influences showed even more advances than did scores of the high-SES children (Crosnoe et al., 2010).

International Contexts

In general, Vygotsky's emphasis on sociocultural contexts contrasts with Piaget's maturational, self-discovery approach. Vygotsky believed that cultures (tools, customs, and mentors) teach. For example, a child who is surrounded by adults reading for pleasure, by full bookcases, by daily newspapers, and by street signs will read better than a child who has had little exposure to print, even if both are in the same classroom. Of course, classroom experiences matter as well, with some teachers showering children with words, spoken and written, and encouraging writing and talking from every student, whereas other teachers stress safety and silence.

The most detailed international example of the influence of context on learning comes from Brazil, where street children sell fruit, candy, and other products. Many never attend school and consequently score poorly on standard math achievement tests. This is no surprise to developmentalists, who have data from numerous nations showing that unschooled children score lower in every academic area (Rogoff et al., 2005).

However, some young Brazilian peddlers are skilled at pricing their wares and making change. Some cannot read, but they use colors and pictures to identify how many *reals* each bill is worth (Saxe, 2004). They may recalibrate selling prices daily in response to inflation, wholesale costs, and customer demand, calculating "complex markup computations . . . by using procedures that were widespread in their practice but not known to children in school" (Saxe, 1999, p. 255). Ratios and fractions, not usually taught until the end of middle childhood, are understood by young street sellers. They learn math from the following:

- The social context
- Other sellers (especially older children)
- Daily experience

None of this would surprise Vygotsky, who believed that peers are good mentors. Much other research shows that children's understanding of arithmetic depends on context: If they learn math in school, they are proficient at school math; if they learn math out of school, they are adept at problems encountered in similar situations (Abreu, 2008).

Another example of knowledge acquired from the social context comes from children in the northeast Indian district of Varanasi, many of whom have an extraordinary sense of spatial orientation—such as knowing whether they are facing north or south, even when they are inside a room with no windows. In one experiment, after children were blindfolded, spun around, and led to a second room, many of them still knew which way they were now facing (Mishra et al., 2009). This skill was learned during childhood, as adults and peers in that culture refer to the compass orientation to name the location of objects and so on. (Although the specifics differ from those of Western culture, the equivalent might be to say not that the dog is sleeping by the door but that the dog is sleeping southeast.)

This transfer of knowledge from one context to another is not automatic. The blindfolded children retained their excellent sense of direction, but a child from

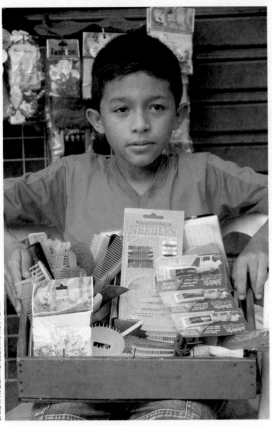

DAVID R. FRAZIER PHOTOLIBRARY, INC. / ALAMY

He Knows His Stuff Many child vendors, like this boy selling combs and other grooming aids on the streets of Manaus, Brazil, understand basic math and the give-and-take of social interaction. But, deprived of formal education, they know little or nothing about history and literature.

>> Response for Teachers (from page 353) Here are two of the most obvious ways. (1) Use logic. Once children can grasp classification and class inclusion, they can understand cities within states, states within nations, and nations within continents. Organize your instruction to make logical categorization easier. (2) Make use of children's need for concrete and personal involvement. You might have the children learn first about their own location, then about the places where relatives and friends live, and finally about places beyond their personal experience (via books, photographs, videos, and guest speakers).

Varanasi might become disoriented in the tangle of mega-city streets—still knowing where north is, but not knowing how to get downtown.

Culture affects the methods of learning, not just the content. This was evident in a study of 80 children in California (Silva et al., 2010). All were Mexican American, similar in genetic background, but half were from families where indigenous Indian learning was the norm: Children from that culture are expected to learn by watching others and to help each other if need be. The other half were from families more acculturated to U.S. norms; the children were accustomed to direct instruction, not observational learning. They expected to work on their own, not collaboratively with their peers.

In the first session of this study, each child was shown how to make a toy while his or her sibling sat nearby. First, the younger sibling waited while the older sibling made a toy mouse and then the older sibling waited while the younger sibling made a toy frog. Each child's behavior while awaiting his or her turn was videotaped and coded every five seconds as *sustained attention* (alert and focused on the sibling's activity), as *glancing (sporadic interest, but primary focus on something else)*, or as *not attending* (looking elsewhere). (See Figure 12.1 and the Research Design.)

Unexpectedly, a week later, each child was individually given the materials to make the toy his or her sibling had made but was not told how to do so (as the sibling had been told a week earlier) unless the child needed help. Children from indigenous backgrounds were more attentive in the first session and needed less help a week later (Silva et al., 2010).

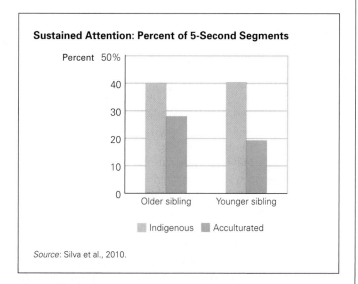

Sustained Attention: Percent of 5-Second Segments

Source: Silva et al., 2010.

FIGURE 12.1

Watch Your Brother! When a brother (or sister) is learning how to make a toy, do you focus your attention on that, or do you look elsewhere? Apparently, it depends partly on what your mother has taught you, not directly but in the way she expects you to learn.

Observation Quiz Among those children accustomed to U.S. styles of learning, were older or younger siblings more likely to pay attention to their siblings? Why? (see answer, page 356)

▶ **Research Design**

Scientists: Katie G. Silva, Maricela Correa-Chávez, and Barbara Rogoff.

Publication: *Child Development* (2010).

Participants: Forty 5- to 11-year-old pairs of siblings, living in southern California and attending public school. All were Mexican American, most born in the United States to families originally from rural areas in the state of Michoacán. They were divided into two groups, one closer to native Indian culture and the other more urban. For instance, the groups differed in maternal education: Some mothers were high school graduates, an accomplishment that signified more acculturation to U.S. ways of learning, while other mothers averaged six years of schooling (range 0–9) and were more indigenous (Indian) in their ways. Other indicators also showed that the two groups were different: family size (2.4 versus 3.3 children) and fathers' birthplace (half in the United States in one group versus almost all in Mexico in the other).

Design: A Spanish-speaking "toy lady" showed each child how to make a toy, with the younger sibling waiting while the older child made a mouse, and then the older child waiting while the younger child made a frog. The children were allowed to keep their toys. A week later, each child individually was given the materials to make the toy that his or her sibling had made. The toy lady ostensibly was involved in paperwork, giving hints about toy construction only when needed. Coders noted the waiting children's attention during the first session and the number of hints needed during the second. The coders and the toy ladies did not know the hypothesis, nor did they know the background of the children, who had been rated as more or less acculturated before the first session with the toy lady.

Results: Virtually none of the children were disruptive; most simply waited their turn. As they waited, the children from the indigenous backgrounds were more likely to pay close attention to the instructions and actions of their siblings; they did so in 40.4 percent of the five-second segments versus 23.6 percent for the acculturated group. Some of the indigenous siblings tried to help their brother or sister, but virtually none of the acculturated children did so. Moreover, the indigenous children remembered what they saw: A week later, they needed an average of 37 percent of the possible hints versus 47 percent for the other pairs.

Major conclusion: Even when children currently live in the same settings and attend the same schools, they follow family cultural traditions in how they learn. This is reflected in their achievement, in this case remembering how to make a toy.

Comments: This was a well-designed study. Several aspects helped all the children feel comfortable (sibling nearby, Spanish-speaking toy lady), and several measures made the data detailed and objective (videotapes, "blind" coders, five-second segments). These features suggest that the conclusion—that children from rural, lower-SES backgrounds learn better under some conditions than similar children who ordinarily are better students—is probably valid. This is useful information for all teachers and parents: Children reflect cultural ways of gathering information, and thus to teach children it is useful to know the specific ways in which they learn best.

>> **Answer to Observation Quiz** (from page 355) Older siblings were more attentive. The reasons are speculative—whatever reason you thought of, does it reflect your own sibling experience or your cultural values?

Information Processing

Today's educators and psychologists regard both Piaget and Vygotsky as insightful; international research confirms the merits of their theories. Piaget described universal changes; Vygotsky noted cultural impact.

A third, and more recent, approach to understanding cognition adds crucial insight. As you learned in Chapter 2, the *information-processing perspective* benefits from technology that allows much more detailed data and analysis than was possible 50 years ago. Thousands of researchers who study cognition can be said to use the information-processing approach. Not all of them would identify themselves that way, however, because "information processing is not a single theory but, rather, a framework characterizing a large number of research programs" (Miller, 2011, p. 266).

Like computers, people sense and perceive large amounts of information. They then: (1) seek specific units of information (as a search engine does), (2) analyze (as software programs do), and (3) express their conclusions so another person can understand (as a networked computer or a printout might do). By tracing the paths and links of each of these functions, scientists better understand the process of learning. This approach has become particularly useful in educating children with learning disabilities, whose processing of information is often impaired. Dyslexia or dyscalculia may be symptoms, not causes, of a learning disability (Waber, 2010), the result of some neurological roadblock in the path between input and output.

The brain's gradual growth confirms the information-processing perspective. So do data on children's school achievement: Absences, vacations, new schools, and even new teachers sometimes hinder a child's achievement because each day's learning builds on that of the previous day. Ongoing brain connections and pathways are forged from repeated experiences, allowing advances in processing. For many schoolchildren, teachers are the best facilitators, encouraging practice of exactly the next skill to be mastered. Without that, fragile connections between neurons break.

One of the leaders of the information-processing perspective is Robert Siegler (Siegler & Chen, 2008), who has studied the day-by-day details of children's cognition in math. Apparently, children do not suddenly grasp the number system, as might be expected when they reach Piaget's concrete operational stage. Instead, number understanding accrues gradually, with new and better strategies for calculation tried, ignored, half-used, abandoned, and finally adopted. Siegler compared the acquisition of knowledge to waves on a beach when the tide is rising. There is substantial ebb and flow, although eventually a new level is reached.

One specific example is children's ability to estimate where a number might fall on a number line, such as where 53 would be placed on a line from 0 to 100. U.S. kindergartners are usually lost with this task (Chinese kindergartners are somewhat better [Siegler & Mu, 2008]), but first- through third-graders gradually become more proficient. They tend to place the 53 decidedly off-center at first but then put it just above the middle on an imagined linear scale. This ability improves gradually over middle childhood and correlates with memory for numbers (such as a phone number). This has led many information-processing experts to advocate giving children practice with number lines in order to help them with other math concepts.

Memory

Many scientists who study memory take an information-processing approach. They have learned that various methods of input, storage, and retrieval affect the increasing cognitive ability of the schoolchild. Each of the three major steps in the

sensory memory The component of the information-processing system in which incoming stimulus information is stored for a split second to allow it to be processed. (Also called the *sensory register.*)

working memory The component of the information-processing system in which current conscious mental activity occurs. (Formerly called *short-term memory.*)

memory process—sensory memory, working memory, and long-term memory—is affected by maturation and experience.

Sensory memory (also called the *sensory register*) is the first component of the human information-processing system. It stores incoming stimuli for a split second after they are received, with sounds retained slightly longer than sights. To use terms explained in Chapter 5, *sensations* are retained for a moment, and then some become *perceptions*. This first step of sensory awareness is already quite good in early childhood, improves slightly until about age 10, and remains adequate until late adulthood.

Once some sensations become perceptions, the brain selects those perceptions that are meaningful and transfers them to working memory for further analysis. It is in **working memory** (formerly called *short-term memory*) that current, conscious mental activity occurs. Working memory improves steadily and significantly every year from about age 4 to age 15 (Gathercole et al., 2004) as the brain matures and experiences accumulate (Baddeley, 2007). Especially significant is increased myelination and dendrite formation in the prefrontal cortex, allowing the "massive interconnections" described in Chapter 11.

Processing, not mere exposure, is essential to getting information into working memory, which is why working memory improves markedly in middle childhood (Cowan & Alloway, 2009). Improvement in working memory during the school years includes advances in two crucial areas—one called the *phonological loop*, which stores sounds, and one called the *visual–spatial sketchpad*, which stores sights (Meadows, 2006). As the brain matures, schoolchildren use memory strategies that are not accessible to younger children (see Table 12.1).

As Siegler's metaphor of waves of cognition suggests, these strategies do not appear suddenly. Gradual improvement occurs from toddlerhood through adolescence (Schneider & Lockl, 2008), with school-age children finally knowing how to increase their working memory (Camos & Barrouillet, 2011).

Verbs and Adverbs Erin, Ally, Paige, and Sabrina perform rap lyrics they wrote to review key concepts for an upcoming assessment test. Such mnemonic devices are beyond younger children but may be very helpful in middle childhood.

TABLE 12.1	Advances in Memory from Infancy to Age 11
Child's Age	**Memory Capabilities**
Under 2 years	Infants remember actions and routines that involve them. Memory is implicit, triggered by sights and sounds (an interactive toy, a caregiver's voice).
2–5 years	Words are now used to encode and retrieve memories. Explicit memory begins, although children do not yet use memory strategies. Children remember things by rote (their phone number, nursery rhymes) without truly understanding them.
5–7 years	Children realize that some things should be remembered, and they begin to use simple strategies, primarily rehearsal (repeating an item again and again). This is not a very efficient strategy, but with enough repetition, automatization occurs.
7–9 years	Children use new strategies if they are taught them. Children use visual clues (remembering how a particular spelling word looks) and auditory hints (rhymes, letters), evidence of the visual–spatial sketchpad and phonological loop. Children now benefit from the organization of things to be remembered.
9–11 years	Memory becomes more adaptive and strategic as children become able to learn various memory techniques from teachers and other children. They can organize material themselves, developing their own memory aids.

Source: Based on Meadows, 2006.

The relationship among strategy, classification, and working memory was demonstrated by an experiment in which 7- and 9-year-olds memorized two lists of 10 items each (M. L. Howe, 2004). Some children had one list of toys and another of vehicles; others had the same 20 items in two mixed lists, with toys and vehicles in both. A day later, each child was asked to remember one of the two lists. Having had separate lists of toys and vehicles helped the 7-year-olds somewhat but benefited the 9-year-olds more. Those older children used the topical lists well: Not only did they surpass all the 7-year-olds, they also remembered much more than the other 9-year-olds who had mixed lists.

Older children's ability to use memory strategies is evident in other research, too. For instance, another experiment, also involving memory of lists, found that 10-year-olds did much better than 8-year-olds because fewer of them relied on rote item-by-item memory; more of them used active memory, repeating a string of items as they memorized them (Lehmann & Hasselhorn, 2010). (Stringing is similar to another way of grouping items, called *chunking*, except that in stringing, a group of items are learned in sequence). School-age children who realize this have better memories than those who do not (Cowan, 2010).

Finally, information from working memory may be transferred to **long-term memory,** to store it for minutes, hours, days, months, or years. The capacity of long-term memory—how much can be crammed into one brain—is very large by the end of middle childhood. Together with sensory memory and working memory, long-term memory organizes ideas and reactions. Crucial to long-term memory is not merely *storage* (how much material has been deposited) but also *retrieval* (how readily past learning can be brought into working memory). For everyone, at every age, retrieval is easier for some memories (especially memories of vivid, highly emotional experiences) than for others. And for everyone, long-term memory is imperfect: We all forget and distort memories.

Knowledge

According to information-processing research, the more people know, the more they learn. Having an extensive **knowledge base,** or a broad body of knowledge in a particular subject, makes it easier to master related new information.

Three factors facilitate increases in the knowledge base: past experience, current opportunity, and personal motivation. Children's knowledge base, however, is not always what their parents or teachers would like it to be. Some schoolchildren memorize words and rhythms of hit songs, know plots and characters of television programs, and can recite the names and histories of football players—yet they may not know whether World War I occurred in the nineteenth or twentieth century, or whether Afghanistan is in Asia or Africa. Motivation provides a clue for teachers: New concepts are learned best if they are connected to personal and emotional experiences (Schneider & Lockl, 2008; Wittrock, 1974/2010).

Control Processes

The mechanisms that pull memory, processing speed, and the knowledge base together are **control processes;** they regulate the analysis and flow of information within the system. Control processes include *emotional regulation* and *selective attention*, explained in Chapters 10 and 11. Equally important is **metacognition,** sometimes defined as "thinking about thinking." Metacognition is the ultimate control process because it allows a person to evaluate a cognitive task, determine how to accomplish it, monitor performance, and then make adjustments.

Control processes require the brain to organize, prioritize, and direct mental operations, as the CEO (chief executive officer) of a business does. For that reason, control processes are also called *executive processes,* evident whenever people

---

long-term memory The component of the information-processing system in which virtually limitless amounts of information can be stored indefinitely.

Especially for Teachers How might your understanding of memory help you teach a 2,000-word vocabulary list to a class of fourth-graders? (see response, page 360)

knowledge base A body of knowledge in a particular area that makes it easier to master new information in that area.

control processes Mechanisms (including selective attention, metacognition, and emotional regulation) that combine memory, processing speed, and knowledge to regulate the analysis and flow of information within the information-processing system. (Also called *executive processes*.)

metacognition "Thinking about thinking," or the ability to evaluate a cognitive task in order to determine how best to accomplish it, and then to monitor and adjust one's performance on that task.

concentrate on only the relevant parts of a task, using their knowledge base to connect new information or apply memory strategies. Such control is more evident among 10-year-olds than among 4- or 6-year-olds (Bjorklund et al., 2009). Fourth-grade students can listen to the teacher talk about the river Nile, ignoring classmates who are chewing gum or passing notes. That's control.

Both metacognition and control processes improve with age and experience. For instance, in one study, children took a fill-in-the-blanks test and indicated how confident they were of each answer. Then they were allowed to delete some questions, thus making the remaining ones count more. Already by age 9, the children were able to estimate correctness; by age 11, they were skilled at knowing what to delete (Roebers et al., 2009). Sometimes experience is not directly related but nonetheless has an impact. This seems to be true for fluently bilingual children, who must learn to inhibit one language while using another. They are advanced in control processes, obviously in language but also in more abstract measures of control (Bialystok, 2010).

THINKING CRITICALLY

Balls Rolling Down

Should metacognition be taught, or should children develop it spontaneously when they are old enough? This question has been the focus of decades of research (Orlich et al., 2009; Pressley & Hilden, 2006), much of which has looked at both "discovery" learning (inspired by Piaget) and explicit teaching (from an information-processing perspective), always with awareness of cultural differences (as Vygotsky stressed).

The answer depends partly on the goals and methods of the culture. Some cultures value single-minded concentration, others multitasking; some stress explicit instruction, others implicit learning from observation. The latter is not necessarily inefficient, for as one commentator explained, "Simultaneous attention may be important when learning relies on observation

of ongoing events" (Correa-Chavez et al., 2005, p. 665), a point made by the research cited earlier on toy-making (Silva et al., 2010).

To illustrate the impact of instruction, one study wanted children to learn that a valid scientific experiment controls all the relevant variables and measures one at a time (Klahr & Nigam, 2004). The researchers showed 112 third- and fourth-graders two balls that could roll down several ramps (see Figure 12.2). There were four variables: golf or rubber ball, steep or shallow slope, smooth or rough ramp, long or short downhill run.

First, the children were asked to design four experiments on their own: two to determine the effect of distance and two to determine the effect of steepness. Only 8 of the 112 children

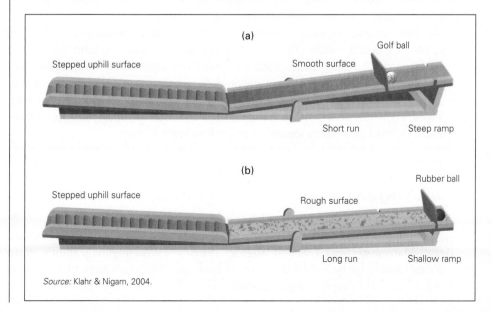

Source: Klahr & Nigam, 2004.

FIGURE 12.2

Design for a Confounded Experiment
On each of these two ramps, children could vary the steepness, surface, and length of the ramp as well as the type of ball. The confounded experiment depicted here contrasts *(a)* a golf ball on a steep, smooth, short ramp with *(b)* a rubber ball on a shallow, rough, long ramp.

designed experiments that controlled the variables. Unless the variables were controlled, the results would be confounded (inappropriately combined). Thus, for example, a child might confound the conclusions by comparing one trial with the golf ball on a shallow ramp to a second trial with the rubber ball on a steep ramp.

The 104 children who did not spontaneously control the variables were then divided into two groups. Half were told to create their own experiments; the other half received explicit instruction by watching an experimenter create pairs of demonstrations. For that half, the experimenter asked the children whether a demonstrated pair allowed them to "tell for sure" how a particular variable affected the distance traveled by the ball. After each response, the experimenter explained the correct answer and emphasized the importance of testing a single variable at a time.

Then all 104 children were asked to design four experiments, as before. Far more children who received direct instruction (40 of 52) correctly isolated the variables than did children who explored on their own (12 of 52). A week later, to assess whether the children had really learned the importance of controlling variables, those children who seemed to understand (the 40 and the 12) were asked to examine two science posters ostensibly created by 11-year-olds. The researcher requested suggestions to make the posters "good enough to enter in a state science fair." The 40 children who had been instructed were virtually

as perceptive in their critiques of the posters as the 12 who had learned through discovery. This study suggests that strategy can be taught—if the teacher actively engages the students. That is exactly what information-processing theory would predict.

Of course, scientific understanding is about more than understanding variables: It is about questioning conclusions and realizing that answers can and do change. How children develop this ability—whether by discovery and experience, as Piaget might expect, or whether by explicit instruction, as information-processing theory suggests—is a matter of intense concern to educators. Furthermore, a logical and skeptical approach to life is pivotal for scientists, but that itself may be culturally determined: Questions, critiques, and doubts may be handicapping in some communities. An understanding of human development can be helpful here. As one expert explains:

> The developmentalist can contribute knowledge of what needs to develop, sketch its course, and hopefully even gain insight into the mechanisms involved. Developmentalists and educators in collaboration can seek to identify the kinds of experiences that make it more likely to happen.
>
> *[Kuhn, 2009, p. 115]*

What experiences help children learn? Answers vary. Whatever you think about teaching metacognitive skills, Vygotsky would ask, "How does your personal experience and cultural heritage affect your answer?"

>> Response for Teachers (from page 358) Children this age can be taught strategies for remembering by forming links between working memory and long-term memory. You might break down the vocabulary list into word clusters, grouped according to root words, connections to the children's existing knowledge, applications, or (as a last resort) first letters or rhymes. Active, social learning is useful; perhaps in groups the students could write a story each day that incorporates 15 new words. Each group could read its story aloud to the class.

SUMMING UP

Every theory of cognitive development recognizes that school-age children are avid learners who actively build on the knowledge they already have. Piaget emphasized children's own logical thinking, as they come to understand classification and develop transitive inference during concrete operational thought. Research inspired by Vygotsky and the sociocultural perspective reveals that cultural differences can be powerful and that specific instruction and practical experience vary from one context to another. Therefore, each child learns different skills, guided by local culture.

An information-processing analysis highlights the many components of thinking that advance during middle childhood. Although sensory and long-term memory do not change much during these years, the speed and efficiency of working memory improve dramatically, making school-age children better thinkers as well as more strategic learners as they mature. Another advantage for older children is that they develop a greater knowledge base. As control processes and metacognition advance, children are able to direct their minds toward whatever they want to learn. ▪

>> Language

As you remember, many aspects of language advance during early childhood. By age 6, children have mastered the basic vocabulary and grammar of their first language. Many also speak a second language fluently. Those linguistic abilities form a strong knowledge base, enabling some school-age children to learn up to 20 new words a day and to apply complex grammar rules. Here are some specifics.

Vocabulary

By age 6, children know the names of thousands of objects, and they use many parts of speech—adjectives and adverbs as well as nouns and verbs. As Piaget stressed, they soon become more flexible and logical; they can understand prefixes, suffixes, compound words, phrases, and figures of speech. For example, 2-year-olds know *egg,* but 10-year-olds also know *egg salad, egg-drop soup, last one in is a rotten egg.* They know that each of these expressions is connected to *egg* but is distinct from the eggs in the refrigerator.

Understanding Metaphors

Metaphors, jokes, and puns are finally comprehended. Some jokes ("What is black and white and red all over?" "Why did the chicken cross the road?") are funny only during middle childhood. Younger children don't understand why they provoke laughter, and teenagers find them lame and stale, but 6- to 11-year-olds enjoy puns, unexpected answers to normal questions, and metaphors because their new cognitive flexibility and social awareness make them funny. Indeed, a lack of metaphorical understanding, even if a child has a large vocabulary, signifies cognitive problems (Thomas et al., 2010). Humor can be a diagnostic tool.

Many adults do not realize how difficult it is for young children or adults who are learning a new language to grasp figures of speech. The humorist James Thurber remembered:

> the enchanted private world of my early boyhood. . . . In this world, businessmen who phoned their wives to say they were tied up at the office sat roped to their swivel chairs, and probably gagged, unable to move or speak except somehow, miraculously, to telephone. . . . Then there was the man who left town under a cloud. Sometimes I saw him all wrapped up in the cloud and invisible. . . . At other times it floated, about the size of a sofa, above him wherever he went. . . . [I remember]the old lady who was always up in the air, the husband who did not seem able to put his foot down, the man who lost his head during a fire but was still able to run out of the house yelling.
>
> [Thurber, 1999, p. 40]

Part of the problem is that metaphors are context-specific. A book written by an American who has lived in China for decades discusses dozens of cultural differences, including basic phrases having to do with baseball that U.S. children learn but that children from other cultures do not—"dropped the ball," "on the ball," "to play ball," "to throw a curve," "to strike out" (Davis, 1999). If a teacher wants a class to pay attention and says, "Keep your eye on the ball," some immigrant children might be lost.

Adjusting Vocabulary to the Context

One aspect of language that advances markedly in middle childhood is **pragmatics,** the practical use of language, which includes the ability to adjust expressions to communicate with varied audiences in different contexts. This ability is obvious to linguists when they compare how children talk informally with friends (the last to arrive can be a *rotten* egg or worse) to how they talk formally with teachers (never calling them a *rotten egg*). As children master pragmatics, they become more adept. Shy 6-year-olds cope far better with the social pressures of school if they use pragmatics well (Coplan & Weeks, 2009).

Mastery of pragmatics allows children to change styles of speech, or "codes," depending on their audience. Each code includes many aspects of language—tone, pronunciation, gestures, sentence length, idioms, vocabulary, and grammar.

RADIUS IMAGES / PHOTOLIBRARY

Homework Despite first appearances, this is not teacher and student but father and daughter, as Dad becomes excited about his 7-year-old's science project. Actually, if she is as intrigued as she appears to be, he is teacher as well as father. Children learn most of their vocabulary with friends and family, not in class.

pragmatics The practical use of language that includes the ability to adjust language communication according to audience and context.

Especially for Parents You've had an exhausting day but are setting out to buy groceries. Your 7-year-old son wants to go with you. Should you explain that you are so tired that you want to make a quick solo trip to the supermarket this time? (see response, page 362)

CAREY KIRKELLA / GETTY IMAGES

A Good Message If he is skilled at text messaging, he understands the basics of written language. That makes learning the formal code easier, if he has a teacher who appreciates his ability.

ELLs (English Language Learners) Children in the United States whose proficiency in English is low—usually below a cutoff score on an oral or written test. This term replaces *ESL* (English as a Second Language) because many children who primarily speak a non-English language at home are also capable in English; they are *not* ELLs.

>> Response for Parents (from page 361) Your son would understand your explanation, but you should take him along if you can do so without losing patience. You wouldn't ignore his need for food or medicine; don't ignore his need for learning. While shopping, you can teach vocabulary (does he know *pimientos, pepperoni, polenta*?), categories ("root vegetables," "freshwater fish"), and math (which size box of cereal is cheaper?). Explain in advance that you need him to help you find items and carry them and that he can choose only one item that you wouldn't normally buy. Seven-year-olds can understand rules, and they enjoy being helpful.

Sometimes the switch is between *formal code* (used in academic contexts) and *informal code* (used with friends); sometimes it is between standard (or proper) speech and dialect or vernacular (used on the street). Many children use code in text messaging, with numbers (411), abbreviations (LOL), and emoticons (:-D).

Code changes are obvious when children speak one language at home and another at school. Every nation includes many such children; most of the world's 6,000 languages are not school languages. For instance, English is the language of instruction in Australia, but 17 percent of the children speak one of 246 other languages at home (Centre for Community Child Health, 2009). In the United States, an estimated one school-age child in five speaks a language other than English at home; half of them also speak English well (Passel, 2011). In addition, some children speak a dialect of English at home that is quite different from the pronunciation and grammar taught at school. All these alternate codes have distinct patterns of timing and emphasis as well as vocabulary.

Some children of every ethnicity are called **ELLs,** or **English Language Learners,** based on their proficiency in English. Among U.S. children of Hispanic heritage, those who speak English well are much better at reading than those who do not, but even they are less adept at reading than the average European American child (Garcia & Miller, 2008). Culture may be the reason, as their learning style may not be the same as their teachers', even though they are proficient in English.

Differences in Language Learning

Learning to speak, read, and write the school language is pivotal for academic achievement, the foundation of all primary school education. Children differ widely in how well they use the school language. Some differences may be innate: A child with a language disability has trouble with both the school and the home language. However, most of the language gap between one child and another is the result of the social context, specifically of two factors: family income and adult expectations.

Family Poverty

Decades of research throughout the world have found a strong correlation between academic achievement and socioeconomic status. Language is a major reason. Not only do children from low-SES families usually have smaller vocabularies, but their grammar is simpler (fewer compound sentences, dependent clauses, and conditional verbs) and their sentences are shorter (Hart & Risley, 1995; E. Hoff, 2006). They fall behind their peers in talking, in reading, and then in other subjects, and even their brains signal linguistic weaknesses (Hackman & Farah, 2009).

The information-processing perspective focuses on specifics that might affect the brain and thus the ability to learn. Possibilities abound—inadequate prenatal care, exposure to lead, no breakfast, overcrowded households, few books at home, teenage parents, authoritarian child rearing, inexperienced teachers . . . The list could go on and on. All of these correlate with low SES and less learning, but none have been proven to be a major cause (not merely a correlate) of low achievement during primary school.

Three factors, however, *do* appear causal. One is limited early exposure to words. Unlike parents who attended college, many less educated parents do not provide varied and extensive language to their infants and young children. Daily book-reading to 2-year-olds, for instance, occurs for 24 percent of the children of mothers with less than a high school education as opposed to 70 percent of the children of mothers with at least a BA (National Center for Education Statistics, 2009) (see Figure 12.3).

As you remember from Chapter 1, book-reading is not the only way to increase language exposure in children (some families never read books to their children but may engage them in conversation about the interesting sights around them), but in the United States it often indicates how much verbal input a child is given. Another way to increase language exposure is to sing to a child, not only simple songs, but dozens of songs. Ideally, parents read and sing to each child every day, as well as provide extensive vocabulary about various activities (e.g., for a young child, "Here we are on the bumpy cobblestones. See the wilted rose, is it red or magenta or maroon? Look at the truck with six huge tires—why does it have so many tires?").

Expectations

A second cause of low achievement in middle childhood is teachers' and parents' expectations, as found in many nations (Melhuish et al., 2008; Phillipson & Phillipson, 2007; Rosenthal, 1991; Rubie-Davies, 2007). Expectations are related to another factor: whether or not a child is taught advanced words and concepts, especially the vocabulary words that are the foundation for later learning, such as *negotiate, evolve, respire, allegation, deficit* (Snow et al., 2007).

International achievement test scores (soon to be discussed) indicate that the income gap, and consequent variation in school resources and student achievement, is much greater in some nations than in others. One of the largest spreads is in the United States, where the fourth-grade reading scores among the schools with the most low-income children are 35 points below the national average. That is more than the average of 23 points in the 40 nations studied and much more than in most European nations (e.g., 11 points in France). The reason is thought to be that school systems expect too little of children from some communities, so they emphasize discipline, not academic challenge.

One of the exceptions to the SES trends is E. P. Jones, who grew up in a poor family, headed by an illiterate single mother who had high expectations for her son. Jones writes:

> For as many Sundays as I can remember, perhaps even Sundays when I was in the womb, my mother has pointed across "I" street to Seaton [school] as we come and go to Mt. Carmel [church].
> "You gonna go there and learn about the whole world."
>
> *[E. P. Jones, 1992/2003, p. 29]*

He did "learn about the whole world" (although he did not attend that particular school because his mother did not understand the school zones), and he won the 2004 Pulitzer Prize for his novel *The Known World* (2003).

The process works in reverse as well. Low expectations lead to low achievement, as demonstrated by Yolanda and Paul in the following.

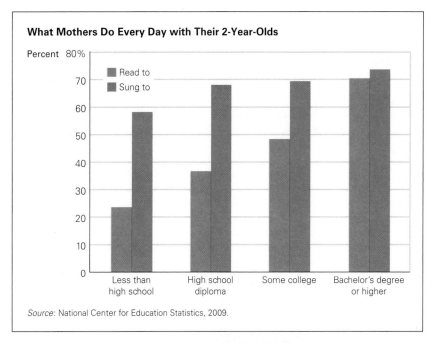

What Mothers Do Every Day with Their 2-Year-Olds

Source: National Center for Education Statistics, 2009.

FIGURE 12.3

Red Fish, Blue Fish As you can see, most mothers sing to their little children, but the college-educated mothers are much more likely to know that book-reading is important. Simply knowing how to turn a page or hearing new word combinations (fish with a little car?) correlates with reading ability later on.

The Best of Both Worlds These Inupiat children are learning via computer in Northern California. The fact that they are together suggests group learning, a pedagogical method common in Eskimo culture that is now recognized as effective for all children.

A   C A S E   T O   S T U D Y

Two Immigrants

Two children, both Mexican American, describe their experiences in their local public school in California.

Yolanda:

When I got here [from Mexico at age 7], I didn't want to stay here, 'cause I didn't like the school. And after a little while, in third grade, I started getting the hint of it and everything and I tried real hard in it. I really got along with the teachers. . . . They would start talking to me, or they kinda like pulled me up some grades, or moved me to other classes, or took me somewhere. And they were always congratulating me.

Paul:

I grew up . . . ditching school, just getting in trouble, trying to make a dollar, that's it, you know? Just go to school, steal from the store, and go sell candies at school. And that's what I was doing in the third or fourth grade. . . . I was always getting in the principal's office, suspended, kicked out, everything, starting from the third grade.

My fifth grade teacher, Ms. Nelson . . . she put me in a play and that like tripped me out. Like, why do you want me in a play? Me, I'm just a mess-up. Still, you know, she put me in a play. And in the fifth grade, I think that was the best year out of the whole six years. I learned a lot about the Revolutionary War. . . .

Had good friends. . . . We had a project we were involved in. Ms. Nelson . . . just involved everyone. We made books, this and that. And I used to write, and wrote two, three books. Was in a book fair. . . . She got real deep into you. Just, you know, "Come on now, you can do it." That was a good year for me, fifth grade.

[quoted in Nieto, 2000, pp. 220, 249]

Note that initially Yolanda didn't like the United States because of school, but her teachers "kinda like pulled me up." By third grade, she was beginning to get "the hint of it." For Paul, school was where he sold stolen candy and where his third-grade teacher sent him to the principal, who suspended him. Ms. Nelson's fifth grade was "a good year," but it was too late—he had already learned he was "just a mess-up." Paul was later sent to a special school, and the text implies (but does not verify) that he was arrested and jailed by age 18. Yolanda became a successful young woman, fluently bilingual.

It would be easy to conclude that the difference was gender, since girls generally do better in school than boys. But that is too simple: Some Mexican-born boys do well in California schools—which raises the question of how teachers impact children: What could the third-grade teacher have done for Paul?

SUMMING UP

Children continue to learn language rapidly during the school years. They become more flexible, logical, and knowledgeable, figuring out the meanings of new words and grasping metaphors, jokes, and compound words. Many converse with friends using informal speech and master a more formal code to use in school. They learn whatever grammar and vocabulary they are taught, and they succeed at pragmatics, the practical task of adjusting their language to friends, teachers, or family. Millions become proficient in a second language, a process facilitated by teachers and peers. For academic achievement during middle childhood, both past exposure to language and adult expectations are influential. ■

>> Teaching and Learning

As we have just described, school-age children are great learners, developing strategies, accumulating knowledge, expanding language, and using logic. Throughout history and worldwide, children are given new responsibility and instruction in middle childhood because that is when the human body and brain are ready. Traditionally, this occurred at home, but now more than 95 percent of the world's 7-year-olds are in school; that is where their parents and political leaders want them to be (Cohen & Malin, 2010). In 2010, for instance, India passed a law providing free education (no more school fees) to all 6- to 14-year olds, regardless of caste or income. India now has over 100 million children in primary school.

Parents rate their own children's schools more favorably than do nonparents in the same community. In one example, a U.S. survey found that nationwide people grade schools overall lower (C–) than their local schools (C+), while parents of public school children rate their local schools higher still (B–) (Snyder & Dillow, 2011). No matter what schooling children are given, parents are usually satisfied with their choice. However, educators and developmentalists are not as satisfied, as you will now see.

International Schooling

Everywhere in the world, children are taught to read, write, and do arithmetic. There are some age-based goals: Because of brain maturation and the necessity of learning in sequence, no nation teaches 6-year-olds to multiply three-digit numbers or read paragraphs fluently out loud, but every nation expects 10-year-olds to do so. Some of the sequences for reading and math that are recognized universally are listed in the accompanying At About This Time tables. Nations also want their children to be good citizens, although there is no consensus as to what that means or what developmental paths (a specific curriculum? at what age?) should be followed (Cohen & Malin, 2010).

Differences by Nation

Although literacy and numeracy (reading and math) are valued everywhere, many specifics of curriculum vary by nation, by community, and by school subject. These variations

AT ABOUT THIS TIME
Math

Age	Norms and Expectations
4–5 years	▪ Count to 20. ▪ Understand one-to-one correspondence of objects and numbers. ▪ Understand *more* and *less*. ▪ Recognize and name shapes.
6 years	▪ Count to 100. ▪ Understand *bigger* and *smaller*. ▪ Add and subtract one-digit numbers.
8 years	▪ Add and subtract two-digit numbers. ▪ Understand simple multiplication and division. ▪ Understand word problems with two variables.
10 years	▪ Add, subtract, multiply, and divide multidigit numbers. ▪ Understand simple fractions, percents, area, and perimeter of shapes. ▪ Understand word problems with three variables.
12 years	▪ Begin to use abstract concepts, such as formulas, algebra.

Math learning depends heavily on direct instruction and repeated practice, which means that some children advance more quickly than others. This list is only a rough guide, to illustrate the importance of sequence.

AT ABOUT THIS TIME
Reading

Age	Norms and Expectations
4–5 years	▪ Understand basic book concepts. For instance, children learning English and many other languages understand that books are written from front to back, with print from left to right, and that letters make words that describe pictures. ▪ Recognize letters—name the letters on sight. ▪ Recognize and spell own name.
6–7 years	▪ Know the sounds of the consonants and vowels, including those that have two sounds (e.g., *c, g, o*). ▪ Use sounds to figure out words. ▪ Read simple words, such as *cat, sit, ball, jump.*
8 years	▪ Read simple sentences out loud, 50 words per minute, including words of two syllables. ▪ Understand basic punctuation, consonant–vowel blends. ▪ Comprehend what is read.
9–10 years	▪ Read and understand paragraphs and chapters, including those with advanced punctuation (e.g., the colon). ▪ Answer comprehension questions about concepts as well as facts. ▪ Read polysyllabic words (e.g., *vegetarian, population, multiplication*).
11–12 years	▪ Demonstrate rapid and fluent oral reading (more than 100 words per minute). ▪ Vocabulary includes words that have specialized meaning in various fields. For example, in civics, *liberties, federal, parliament,* and *environment* all have special meanings. ▪ Comprehend paragraphs about unfamiliar topics. ▪ Sound out new words, figuring out meaning using cognates and context. ▪ Read for pleasure.
13+ years	▪ Continue to build vocabulary, with emphasis more on comprehension than on speech. Understand textbooks.

Reading is a complex mix of skills, dependent on brain maturation, education, and culture. The sequence given here is approximate; it should not be taken as a standard to measure any particular child.

are evident in the results of international tests; in the mix of school subjects; and in the relative power of parents, educators, and political leaders.

For example, as alluded to in Chapter 11, daily physical activity is mandated in some schools, absent in others. Many schools in Japan have swimming pools; virtually no schools in Africa or Latin America do. Geography, music, and art are essential in some places, not in others.

hidden curriculum The unofficial, unstated, or implicit rules and priorities that influence the academic curriculum and every other aspect of learning in a school.

Variation from nation to nation is even greater in aspects of the **hidden curriculum,** which refers to implicit values and assumptions evident in course selection, schedules, tracking, teacher characteristics, discipline, teaching methods, sports competition, student government, extracurricular activities, and so on. For example, if teachers differ from their students in gender, ethnicity, or economic background, the hidden message may be that education is irrelevant for these children's daily lives. If some students are in gifted classes, the message is that they are more capable of learning and that less is expected of the other students (see Chapter 11). A message regarding social values is expressed in the school's physical setting, which might include spacious classrooms, wide hallways, and large, grassy playgrounds—or cramped, poorly equipped rooms and cement play yards or play streets. In some nations, school is outdoors, with no chairs, desks, or books; school is cancelled in severe rain.

AP PHOTO / DANIEL SHANKEN

All the Same These five children all speak a language other than English at home and are now learning English as a new language at school. Although such classes should ideally be taught to true ELLs, children who already speak English are sometimes mistakenly included in such classes (like 8-year-old Elana, from Mexico).

Learning a Second Language

The questions of when, how, to whom, and whether schools should provide second-language instruction are answered in different ways from nation to nation. Some nations teach two or more languages throughout elementary school, while others punish children who utter any word in any language except the majority one.

Almost every European child speaks two languages by age 10, as does almost every Canadian child. Those African children who are talented and fortunate enough to reach high school often speak three languages. In the United States, less than 5 percent of children under age 11 study a language other than English in school (Robelen, 2011). (In secondary school, almost every U. S. student takes a year or two of a language other than English, but cognitive theory suggests that is too late for efficient learning).

immersion A strategy in which instruction in all school subjects occurs in the second (usually the majority) language that a child is learning.

bilingual schooling A strategy in which school subjects are taught in both the learner's original language and the second (majority) language.

Teaching approaches range from **immersion,** in which instruction occurs entirely in the new language (the traditional approach in the United States for children who do not already speak English), to the opposite, in which children are taught in their first language until the second language can be taught as a "foreign" tongue (a strategy rare in the United States, but common in many other nations). Between these extremes lie **bilingual schooling,** with instruction in two languages, and, in North America, ELL (formerly known as ESL, English as a Second Language) in which all non-English speakers are grouped together to be taught intensively and exclusively in English to prepare them for regular classes.

Methods for teaching a second language sometimes succeed and sometimes fail, with the research not yet clear as to which approach is best (Gandara & Rumberger, 2009). The success of any method seems to depend on the literacy of the home environment (frequent reading, writing, and listening in any language helps); the national culture; and the warmth, training, and skill of the teacher. In some schools, every teacher is bilingual; in other schools, none are—and children quickly understand the hidden curriculum. Some react to the school culture by underachieving or dropping out.

Although cognitive research leaves no doubt that school-age children *can* learn a second language if taught logically, step by step, and that they *can* maintain their original language, whether they do so is affected by factors beyond cognitive research: SES, family ethnotheories, expectations, and national policies.

International Testing

Over the past two decades, more than 50 nations have participated in at least one massive international test of educational achievement. Longitudinal data find that, if achievement rises, the national economy advances—a sequence that seems causal, not merely correlational (Hanushek & Woessmann, 2009). The probable reason is that better-educated adults become more productive workers. We focus here on results for fourth-graders, usually the youngest children tested.

Science and math achievement are tested in the **Trends in Math and Science Study (TIMSS).** East Asian nations are always at the top. Indeed, among 10-year-olds, the *average* Singapore student scores higher than the top 5 percent of U.S. students (Mullis et al., 2008).

The primary test of reading is the **Progress in International Reading Literacy Study (PIRLS).** In the most recent published study (Mullis et al., 2007), Canadian children from the western provinces were close to the top, and the United States ranked 15th out of 45 groups (most groups are nations, but some, as with the provinces of Canada, are not). Russia scored first in the PIRLS, up from 16th only five years earlier, probably because of extensive changes in education in the early grades. Only two East Asian groups took the PIRLS, Hong Kong and Singapore, where instruction is in English; they scored second and fourth among the groups. Africa and Middle Eastern groups scored low; their reading skills are, overall, no match for those of the Asians.

Problems with International Benchmarks

Elaborate and extensive measures are in place to make the PIRLS and the TIMSS valid. Test items are carefully designed to be fair and culture-free; participant children are of both sexes, many incomes, many regions, and so on, to represent the entire child population of the nation. Children are compared with other schoolchildren of the same age. Consequently, these results are respected by most social scientists worldwide. However, researchers also realize that absolute equivalency is impossible, given cultural and historical differences.

Designing test items is difficult. For example, should fourth-graders be expected to understand fractions, graphs, and simple geometry, or should the test focus only on basic operations with whole numbers? Once those general questions are decided, specific items may inadvertently be culturally biased. One item testing fourth-grade math was the following:

> Al wanted to find out how much his cat weighed. He weighed himself and noted that the scale read 57 kg. He then stepped on the scale holding his cat and found that it read 62 kg. What was the weight of the cat in kilograms?
> Answer: _____ kilograms

This item requires simple subtraction. However, 40 percent of U.S. fourth-graders got it wrong. Were they unable to subtract 57 from 62, or did they not understand the example, or did the abbreviation for kilograms confuse them because—unlike children in most nations—they are more familiar with pounds? On this item, children from Yemen were at the bottom, with

Trends in Math and Science Study (TIMSS) An international assessment of the math and science skills of fourth- and eighth-graders. Although the TIMSS is very useful, different countries' scores are not always comparable because sample selection, test administration, and content validity are hard to keep uniform.

Progress in International Reading Literacy Study (PIRLS) Inaugurated in 2001, a planned five-year cycle of international trend studies in the reading ability of fourth-graders.

"Big deal, an A in math. That would be a D in any other country."

Catching Up with the West These Iranian girls are acting out a poem they have memorized from their third-grade textbook. They attend school in a UNICEF-supported Global Education pilot project. Their child-centered classes encourage maximum participation.

No Child Left Behind Act A U.S. law enacted in 2001 that was intended to increase accountability in education by requiring states to qualify for federal educational funding by administering standardized tests to measure school achievement.

How Many Fingers? It looks as if teacher Alvin Yardley and fourth-grader Matthew are fully engaged in figuring out a math problem. However, U.S. fourth-graders score far below those in East Asia. Some critics blame the teachers, some the students, others the schools, and still others the culture.

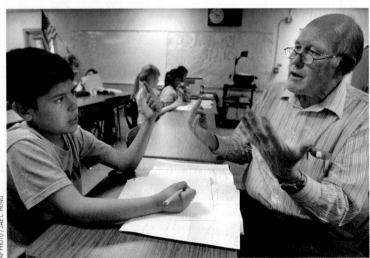

95 percent of them failing. Is that because few of them have cats for pets or weigh themselves on a scale?

Gender Differences in School Performance

In addition to marked national, ethnic, and economic differences, gender differences in achievement scores are reported. The PIRLS finds girls ahead of boys in verbal skills in every nation. Traditionally, boys are ahead of girls in math and science.

The most recent TIMSS finds that gender differences in math have narrowed or disappeared. Boys were slightly (10 points) higher than girls overall, but the differences were even smaller (6 points) in the United States, and girls scored higher than boys in four nations (Russia, Singapore, Algeria, and Iran) (Gonzales et al., 2009). Such results lead to a *gender-similarities hypothesis* that males and females are similar on most test measures, with "trivial" exceptions (Hyde et al., 2008, p. 494).

Classroom performance also shows gender differences in almost every nation. Girls have higher grades overall, including in math and science. Then, at puberty, girls' grades dip, especially in science. Many reasons for this drop have been suggested. One is that, since girls are ahead in physiological maturation, it is easier for young girls to sit at their desks and concentrate. Then, when they reach puberty earlier than boys, they may underachieve because they think boys will like them better if they are not too smart.

An alternate explanation is that social prejudice favors young girls but not young women. Since most elementary school teachers are women, girls in the early grades may feel (or be) more encouraged. Then, when girls begin to prepare for adult roles, they seek the skills and jobs that characterize people of their sex, perhaps office assistants instead of engineers or physicists (Weisgram et al., 2010). For that reason, their motivation may falter in science classes.

In the United States

Although some national tests find improvements in achievement for U.S. children, when compared with other nations they have not improved much in reading or math from 1990 to 2010. Furthermore, among fourth-graders, the ethnic gap between European Americans and their Latino and African American peers is as wide as it was years ago (see Table 12.2), to the consternation of many political and educational leaders.

National Standards

International comparisons and disparities within the nation led to the **No Child Left Behind Act** of 2001 (NCLB), a federal law promoting high national standards for public schools. One controversial aspect of the law is the requirement for frequent testing to measure whether standards are being met. Low-scoring schools lose funding and may close. An unfortunate result is that children of middling achievement are pushed to make sure they meet the benchmark, but children far above it are ignored because they will do well enough without help. Children far below may be ignored as well because they will never attain the benchmark.

Most parents and teachers agree with the goals of NCLB (accountability and higher achievement) but not with the strategies. Strong opinions on opposite sides are common—such as those expressed in the very same issue of *Science* (Hanushek, 2009; Koretz, 2009). NCLB troubles those who value the arts, social studies, or physical education because those subjects are often squeezed out when reading and math achievement is the priority. The tests, and testing, are controversial.

Many states have created achievement tests that allow most of their schools to progress (and thus get federal funds). Federally sponsored tests called the **National Assessment of Educational Progress (NAEP)** measure achievement in reading, mathematics, and other subjects. Many critics believe that the NAEP is better than state tests (Applegate et al., 2009), a conclusion reached because fewer children are labeled proficient on the NAEP (see Figure 12.4).

Disagreement about state tests and standards led the governors of all 50 states to designate a group of experts to develop a Common Core of standards, finalized in 2010, for use nationwide. The standards, higher than most state standards, are quite explicit, with half a dozen or more specific expectations for achievement in each subject for each grade (Table 12.3 provides a sample of the specific standards). As of 2011, 45 states have adopted this Common Core.

Reading Wars, Math Wars, and Cognitive Theory

To help you understand why educators seek a common standard, consider the recent disputes about teaching reading and math. It could be that educators now have battle fatigue; they no longer want to fight over specifics of curriculum.

Clashes over teaching reading led to "serious, sometimes acrimonious debate, fueling the well-named 'reading wars'" (Keogh, 2004, p. 93). The dispute pitted advocates of the **phonics approach** (teaching letter–sound correspondence) versus advocates of the **whole-language approach** (which encourages all language—talking, listening, reading, and writing).

TABLE 12.2	TIMSS Ranking and Average Scores of Math Achievement for Fourth-Graders, 2007	
Rank*	Country	Score
1.	Hong Kong	667
2.	Singapore	599
3.	China/Taipei	576
4.	Japan	568
5.	Kazakhstan	549
6.	Russian Federation	544
7.	England	541
8.	Latvia	537
9.	Netherlands	535
10.	United States	531
11.	Lithuania	530
12.	Germany	525
	Denmark	523
	Canada/Quebec	519
	Australia	516
	Hungary	516
	Canada/Ontario	512
	Italy	507
	New Zealand	492
	Iran	402
	Colombia	355
	Yemen	224

*The top 12 groups are listed in order, but after that not all the jurisdictions that took the test are listed. Some nations have improved over the past 15 years (notably, Hong Kong, England) and some have declined (Austria, Netherlands), but most continue about where they have always been.

Source: TIMSS 2007 International Mathematics Report (Mullis et al., 2008).

National Assessment of Educational Progress (NAEP) An ongoing and nationally representative measure of U.S. children's achievement in reading, mathematics, and other subjects over time; nicknamed "the Nation's Report Card."

phonics approach Teaching reading by first teaching the sounds of each letter and of various letter combinations.

whole-language approach Teaching reading by encouraging early use of all language skills—talking and listening, reading and writing.

FIGURE 12.4

Local Standards Each state sets its own level of proficiency, which helps states in which children score low on the NAEP to obtain more federal money for education. That practice may undercut high standards for student learning in all the green and especially the purple states.

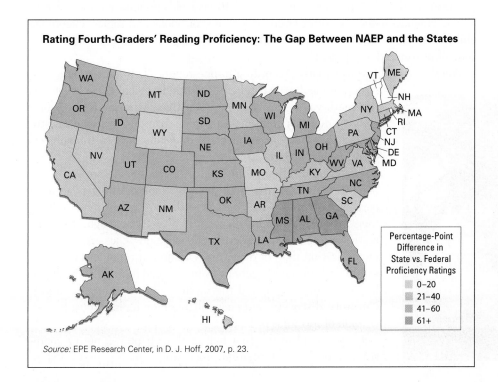

Rating Fourth-Graders' Reading Proficiency: The Gap Between NAEP and the States

Percentage-Point Difference in State vs. Federal Proficiency Ratings
- 0–20
- 21–40
- 41–60
- 61+

Source: EPE Research Center, in D. J. Hoff, 2007, p. 23.

TABLE 12.3	The Common Core: Sample Items for Each Grade	
Grade	**Reading and Writing**	**Math**
Kindergarten	Pronounce the primary sound for each consonant	Know number names and the count sequence
First	Decode regularly spelled one-syllable words	Relate counting to addition and subtraction (e.g., by counting 2 more to add 2)
Second	Decode words with common prefixes and suffixes	Measure the length of an object twice, using different units of length for the two measurements; describe how the two measurements relate to the size of the unit chosen
Third	Decode multisyllabic words	Understand division as an unknown-factor problem; for example, find 32 × 8 by finding the number that makes 32 when multiplied by 8
Fourth	Use combined knowledge of all letter–sound correspondences, syllable patterns, and morphology (e.g., roots and affixes) to read accurately unfamiliar multisyllabic words in context and out of context	Apply and extend previous understandings of multiplication to multiply a fraction by a whole number
Fifth	With guidance and support from peers and adults, develop and strengthen writing as needed by planning, revising, editing, rewriting, or trying a new approach	Graph points on the coordinate plane to solve real-world and mathematical problems

Source: National Governor's Association, 2010.

All This and More This is a small sample of the elements in the Common Core, but it is enough for you to see that the grade-by-grade standards are explicit and not easy. Teachers are encouraged to make sure all the children in each grade achieve the skills and knowledge listed for that grade.

Collaborative Learning Japanese children learn mathematics in a more structured and socially interactive way than are their North American counterparts.

RUSSELL D. CURTIS / PHOTO RESEARCHERS, INC.

Phonics proponents believe that decoding letters and sounds is essential to reading and that, without it, children will flounder, become frustrated, and fail. This is particularly likely if families have not prepared their children for reading. One critic said a "child-centered anti-academic" approach did not teach the basics of reading, rendering children helpless without explicit standards and foundations (Hirsch, 2008, p. 9). Basics include phonics, some educators contend.

The whole-language proponents are proud to be "child-centered." They counter that drilling children with phonics destroys motivation, reduces comprehension, and leads to the "fourth-grade slump," when 10-year-olds no longer want to learn. Whole-language educators offer children a choice of books and topics, encourage children to read their own stories to each other, and guide learners within their zone of proximal development.

Another battle involves math. According to one report, "U.S. mathematics instruction has been scorched in the pedagogical blaze known as the 'math wars'—a divide between those who see a need for a greater emphasis on basic skills in math and others who say students lack a broader, conceptual understanding of the subject" (Cavanagh, 2005, p. 1).

Historically, children in the United States memorized number facts, such as the multiplication tables, filling page after page of workbooks. In reaction to this approach, many educators, inspired again by Piaget and Vygotsky, sought to make math instruction more active and engaging—less a matter of memorization than of discovery. Children used blocks or marks to add and subtract; algebra was introduced in middle childhood because children enjoyed the mystery of an unknown *x* and *y*. Curiosity, discovery, and peer collaboration replace most memorization of formulas or facts.

As you read in the first half of this chapter, a newer cognitive approach is information processing, which stresses a step-

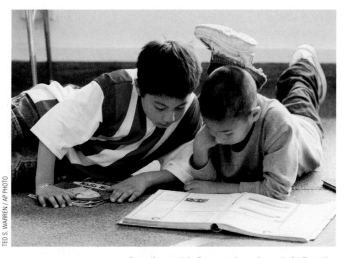

NAM Y. HUH / AP PHOTO

TED S. WARREN / AP PHOTO

by-step sequence in learning. That might seem to support explicit, sequenced standards such as phonics and number facts. The emphasis on national and international tests and on Common Core standards can also be seen as an outcome of the information-processing approach. However, before deciding that current cognitive theory supports one side or the other of these wars, you need to remember that all children are great learners, each with particular learning needs.

Who Determines Educational Practice?

An underlying issue for both wars, for the hidden curriculum, and for international variations is the role of parental choice. In most nations, matters regarding public education—including curriculum, funding, teacher training, and so on—are set by the central government. In the United States, by contrast, local jurisdictions provide most of the funds and guidelines. Parents affect education by communicating with their child's teacher, by becoming active in parent–teacher associations (PTAs), by moving to a particular school zone. Moreover, while most U.S. parents send their children to the local zoned public school, almost one-third do not. An increasing number choose a public charter school, a private school, or home schooling (see Figure 12.5).

Reading with Comprehension *(left)* Reading and math scores in third-grader Monica's Illinois elementary school showed improvement under the standards set by the No Child Left Behind Act. However, the principal noted a cost for this success in less time spent on social studies and other subjects. *(right)* Some experts believe that children should have their own books and be able to read them wherever and however they want. This strategy seems to be working with Josue and Cristo, two 8-year-olds who were given books through their after-school program in Rochester, Washington.

Especially for School Administrators
Children who wear uniforms in school tend to score higher on reading tests. Why? (see response, page 373)

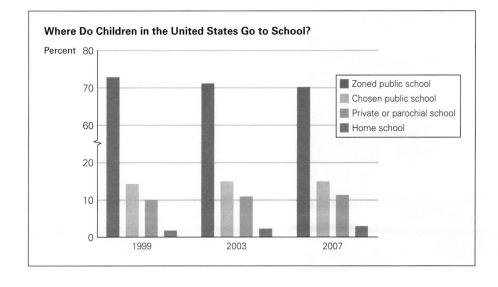

Where Do Children in the United States Go to School?

Percent
- Zoned public school
- Chosen public school
- Private or parochial school
- Home school

1999   2003   2007

FIGURE 12.5

Where'd You Go to School? Note that although home schooling is still the least-chosen option, the number of home-schooled children is increasing, while the number of children attending zoned public schools is slightly decreasing. More detailed data indicate that, while any child might be home-schooled, the typical home-schooled child is a 7-year-old European American girl living in a rural area of the South with two parents (only one of whom is employed).

charter school A public school with its own set of standards that is funded and licensed by the state or local district in which it is located.

private school A school funded by tuition charges, endowments, and often religious or other non-profit sponsors. .

voucher Public subsidy for tuition payment at a non-public school. Vouchers vary a great deal from place to place, not only in amount and availability, but in restrictions as to who gets them and what schools accept them.

home schooling Education in which children are taught at home, usually by their parents.

Chance or Design? These third-graders are using dice to play a game that may teach them multiplication.

Observation Quiz This is a charter school in New Jersey. What three signs are visible here that few typical public schools share? (see answer, page 373)

Charter schools are public schools, free to students and funded and licensed by states or local districts. Typically, they also have private money and sponsors. They are exempt from some regulations, especially those stipulated in contracts negotiated by unions, and they have some control over admissions and expulsions. For that reason, they often are more racially segregated and have fewer children with special needs. Typically, teachers are younger and work longer hours, and school size is smaller than that of traditional public schools.

Some charter schools are remarkably successful; others are not. A major criticism is that not every child who enters a charter school stays to graduate—one scholar says "the dropout rate for African-American males is shocking" (Miron, quoted in Zehr, 2011, p. 24). Overall, children and teachers leave charter schools more often than they leave zoned public schools, but since teachers and parents have chosen charter schools, they may be more likely to choose again, leaving if their expectations are not met.

Private schools are funded by tuition charges, endowments, and church sponsors. Traditionally in the United States, most private schools were organized by the Catholic Church, to educate students in religion. Tuition was relatively low since many teachers were nuns who earned little pay. In the past decades, many Catholic schools have closed, but the number of independent schools has increased.

Some U.S. jurisdictions issue pay **vouchers,** with which parents may pay some or all of the tuition at a private school. This practice is controversial, not only because it decreases public school funding and enrollment but also because some families choose church-sponsored schools, which may violate separation of church and state. Proponents say that vouchers increase competition and may improve all schools, public and private.

Home schooling occurs when parents decide to avoid both public and private schools and instead educate their children at home. As Figure 12.5 shows, this solution is becoming more common, but still only a tiny minority of children are home-schooled, about 1 child in 35. Home schooling is illegal in some nations but not in the United States, where authorities set standards for what a child must learn but allow families to decide curriculum, schedules, and discipline. The major problem with home schooling is not academic (some children score high on achievement tests) but social, since children miss out on the social interactions of the classroom. To compensate, many home-schooling parents plan social activities with other home-schooling families.

On some issues, research clashes with parental emotions. For example, small class sizes and nightly homework can be more attractive to parents than beneficial to children. Nations whose children score high on international tests sometimes have large student/teacher ratios (Korea's average is 28 to 1) and sometimes small (Finland's is 14 to 1, as is that of the United States); and fourth-graders with no homework sometimes have higher achievement scores than those with homework (Snyder & Dillow, 2010). These data suggest that class size and homework are not the crucial variables in how much a child learns; rather, other interpretations are possible.

Underlying many disputes is another question: Who should decide what children should learn and how? Every developmental theory can lead to suggestions for teaching and learning

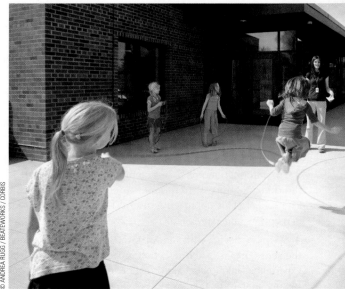

Coming and Going Two U.S. elementary schools—one in Modesto, California *(left)*, the other in Wayzata, Minnesota *(right)*—illustrate differences in hidden curriculum. Political leaders and taxpayers often disagree with parents and teachers as to whether this affects classroom learning.

(Farrar & Al-Qatawneh, 2010), but none endorse one curriculum or method to the exclusion of all others. Parents, politicians, and developmental experts all agree that some children learn much more than others and that some teachers are more skilled than others, but adults vehemently disagree on curriculum—hidden or overt.

More quantitative and qualitative research is needed. A 19-member panel of experts seeking the best math curricula for the United States examined 16,000 studies but "found a serious lack of studies with adequate scale and design for us to reach conclusions" (Faulkner, quoted in Mervis, 2008, p. 1605). Similarly, a review of home schooling, charter schools, and vouchers complains of "the difficulty of interpreting the research literature on this topic, most of which is biased and far from approaching balanced social science" (Boyd, 2007, p. 7). The same complaint could apply to research on the reading and math wars, controversies about testing and standards, and mixed results on class size and homework: All would benefit from large-scale, controlled studies.

Fortunately, some such research is under way, and compared to even a decade ago, much more national and international interest and data are evident. School-age children are great learners: Once the strengths and weaknesses of scientific study are understood, parents and everyone else may know how best to teach them.

SUMMING UP

Societies throughout the world recognize that school-age children are avid learners and that educated citizens are essential to economic development, which has led to increased enrollment: More than 95 percent of the world's children are in school of some sort, at least for a few years. Schools differ in what and how children are taught, and international tests find some nations are far more successful than others in educating their young. Test scores, as well as the nature and content of education, raise ideological and political passions: Examples are found in the reading wars, the math wars, and many other aspects of the overt and the hidden curricula. Research finds that direct instruction (in phonics; in mathematical symbols and procedures; in the vocabulary, grammar, and syntax of second languages) is useful. Also crucial are motivation, pride, and social interaction. School-age children are great learners, but they cannot learn everything. Adults must decide the specifics.
■

>> Response for School Administrators
(from page 371) The relationship reflects correlation, not causation. Wearing uniforms is more common when the culture of the school emphasizes achievement and study, with strict discipline in class and a policy of expelling disruptive students.

>> Answer to Observation Quiz (from page 372) Carpets and rugs, students lying down to do schoolwork, clipboards and dice—all are highly unusual for traditional schools.

SUMMARY

Building on Theory

1. According to Piaget, middle childhood is the time of concrete operational thought, when egocentrism diminishes and logical thinking begins. School-age children can understand classification and conservation, and they develop transitive inference.

2. Vygotsky stressed the social context of learning, including the specific lessons of school and learning from peers and adults. Culture affects not only what children learn but also how they learn.

3. An information-processing approach examines each step of the thinking process, from input to output, using the computer as a model. This approach is useful for understanding memory, perception, and expression.

4. Memory begins with information that reaches the brain from the sense organs. Then selection processes, benefiting from past experience, allow some information to reach working memory. Finally, long-term memory stores images and ideas indefinitely, retrieving parts when needed.

5. A broader knowledge base, logical strategies for retrieval, and faster processing advance every aspect of memory and cognition. Control processes are crucial. Children become better at controlling and directing their thinking as the prefrontal cortex matures. Metacognition improves over the years of middle childhood and beyond.

Language

6. Language learning advances in many practical ways, including expanded vocabulary as words are logically linked together and as an understanding of metaphors begins.

7. Children excel at pragmatics during middle childhood, often using one code with their friends and another in school. Many children become fluent in the school language while speaking their first language at home.

8. Children of low SES are usually lower in linguistic skills, primarily because they hear less language and because adult expectations for their learning are low. This is not inevitable for low-SES families, however.

Teaching and Learning

9. Nations and experts agree that education is critical during middle childhood. Almost all the world's children now attend primary school. Schools differ in what and how they teach, especially with regard to religion, languages, and the arts.

10. International assessments are useful as comparisons, partly because few objective measures of learning are available. Reading is assessed with the PIRLS, math and science with the TIMSS. On both measures, children in East Asia excel and children in the United States are middling.

11. In the United States, the No Child Left Behind Act and the National Assessment of Educational Progress (NAEP) attempt to raise the standard of education, with mixed success. The Common Core, developed with the sponsorship of the governors of the 50 states, is an effort to raise national standards and improve accountability.

12. The reading wars pitted advocates of phonics against advocates of the whole-language approach. A truce has been reached, however. Research finds that both methods may be needed, as children require both basic skills and more advanced thinking.

13. Disagreements about education are frequent; some parents choose charter schools, others prefer private schools, and still others opt for home schooling. However, parents value some aspects (class size, homework) more than do educators, and nations differ in how much national control they seek for public education. More research is needed to discover the best way for children to learn.

KEY TERMS

concrete operational thought (p. 351)
classification (p. 352)
transitive inference (p. 352)
sensory memory (p. 357)
working memory (p. 357)
long-term memory (p. 358)
knowledge base (p. 358)
control processes (p. 358)

metacognition (p. 358)
pragmatics (p. 361)
ELLs (English Language Learners) (p. 362)
hidden curriculum (p. 366)
immersion (p. 366)
bilingual schooling (p. 366)
Trends in Math and Science Study (TIMSS) (p. 367)

Progress in International Reading Literacy Study (PIRLS) (p. 367)
No Child Left Behind Act (p. 368)
National Assessment of Educational Progress (NAEP) (p. 369)

phonics approach (p. 369)
whole-language approach (p. 369)
charter school (p. 372)
private school (p. 372)
voucher (p. 372)
home schooling (p. 372)

WHAT HAVE YOU LEARNED?

Building on Theory

1. Why did Piaget call cognition in middle childhood *concrete operational* thought?

2. How would you express classification in categories of transportation or plants?

3. How is transitive inference the result of logic, not experience?

4. How do Vygotsky and Piaget differ in their explanation of cognitive advances in middle childhood?

5. According to Vygotsky, where and how does cognitive development occur?

6. What have developmentalists learned from child vendors in Brazil?

7. How does information processing differ from traditional theories of cognitive development?

8. According to information processing, how do children learn math concepts?

9. What aspects of memory improve markedly during middle childhood?

10. How might metacognitive skills help a student?

Language

11. How does the process of learning language differ between age 3 and age 10?

12. How is the understanding of metaphors and jokes affected by a child's age?

13. Why are prefixes and suffixes useful in expanding vocabulary?

14. Why would a child's linguistic code be criticized by teachers but admired by friends?

15. Which factors affect a child's ability to learn grammar and advanced vocabulary?

16. How and why does SES affect language learning?

Teaching and Learning

17. What do all nations have in common regarding education in middle childhood?

18. What is the difference between the overt curriculum and the hidden curriculum?

19. What are the differences in the ways that nations teach the language of the school?

20. What are the similarities and differences between the two most common international tests of achievement?

21. What are the main goals and criticisms of No Child Left Behind?

22. What gender differences are found in educational tests and school grades?

23. What problems does the Common Core attempt to solve?

24. Why are some disagreements about education called "wars," not merely differences?

25. What are the differences among charter schools, private schools, and home schooling?

26. What are the advantages and disadvantages of parental choice in how children are educated?

APPLICATIONS

1. Visit a local elementary school and look for the hidden curriculum. For example, do the children line up? Why or why not, when and how? Does gender, age, ability, or talent affect the grouping of children or the selection of staff? What is on the walls? Are parents involved? If so, how? For everything you observe, speculate about the underlying assumptions.

2. Interview a 7- to 11-year-old child to find out what he or she knows *and understands* about mathematics. Relate both correct and incorrect responses to the logic of concrete operational thought.

3. What do you remember about how you learned to read? Compare your memories with those of two other people, one at least 10 years older and the other at least 5 years younger than you are. Can you draw any conclusions about effective reading instruction? If so, what are they? If not, why not?

4. Talk to two parents of primary school children. What do they think are the best and worst parts of their children's education? Ask specific questions and analyze the results.

>>ONLINE CONNECTIONS

To accompany your textbook, you have access to a number of online resources, including quizzes for every chapter of the book, flashcards (in English and Spanish), critical thinking questions, and case studies. For access to any of these links, go to www.worthpublishers.com/bergerca9e. In addition to these free resources, you'll also find links to podcasts, video clips, diagnostic quizzing with personalized study advice, and an ebook. Some of the videos and activities available online include:

- *Conservation.* Half empty or half full? Watch as children of different ages perform the Piagetian conservation-of-liquid task and note the differences as they explain their reasoning.

- *Motivation and Learning.* Are children really "little scientists," as Piaget believed? Explores intrinsic motivation and classroom strategies that inspire it.

Middle Childhood: Psychosocial Development

WHAT WILL YOU KNOW?

1. What helps some children thrive in difficult family or neighborhood conditions?

2. Is it better for parents to marry, risking divorce, or to avoid marriage and thus avoid divorce?

3. What can be done to stop a bully?

4. When would children lie to adults to protect a friend?

A student of mine drove to a gas station to get a flat tire fixed. She wrote:

> As I pulled up, I saw a very short boy sitting at the garage door. I imagined him to be about 8 or 9 years old and wondered why he was sitting there by himself. He directed me to park, and summoned a man who looked at my tire and spoke to the boy in a language I did not understand. This little boy then lifted my car with a jack, removed all the bolts, and fixed the flat. I was in shock. When I paid the man (who was his father), I asked how long his son had been doing this. He said about three years.
>
> [adapted from Tiffany, personal communication, March 15, 2008]

Adults like Tiffany are shocked to learn that many of the world's children are forced to work, in defiance of the United Nations' declaration that children have the right

> to be protected from economic exploitation and from performing any work that is likely to be hazardous or to interfere with the child's education, or to be harmful to the child's health or physical, mental, spiritual, moral, or social development.
>
> [Convention on the Rights of the Child]

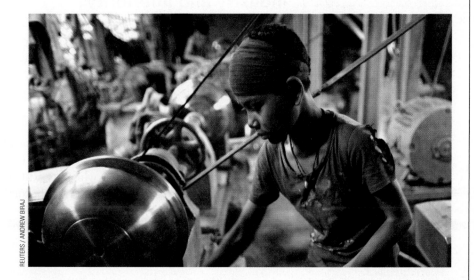

REUTERS / ANDREW BIRAJ

"To Be Protected" Shaheen, age 10, is one of two dozen children, most of whom work 12 hours a day, employed in this aluminum factory in Dhaka, Bangladesh. Who is to blame for this "economic exploitation"—family, factory, nation, or all of us? None of them is protecting Shaheen at this moment.

The International Labour Organization (ILO) of the United Nations (Diallo et al., 2010) estimated that this right was violated for 153 million 5- to 14-year-olds worldwide, with 115 million of them (4.3 percent of all children) engaged in hazardous work.

Changing tires is not defined as hazardous, but did the work "interfere with the child's education" or was the boy harmed in any way? The answer is not obvious. With almost every aspect of middle childhood, specific details are crucial.

All children need friends, families, and skills, but some peers are destructive, some families are dysfunctional, and some skills should not be learned. This chapter describes some of the many circumstances that affect a child's "physical, mental, spiritual, moral, or social development." You will learn when child labor, peer culture, bullying, single-parent families, poverty, divorce, and so on are harmful. We begin with the children themselves and then discuss families, peers, and morality.

>> The Nature of the Child

As explained in the previous two chapters, steady growth, brain maturation, and intellectual advances make middle childhood a time when children gain independence and autonomy (see At About This Time). They acquire an "increasing ability to regulate themselves, to take responsibility, and to exercise self-control"—all strengths that make this a period of positive growth (Huston & Ripke, 2006, p. 9).

One result is that school-age children can finally care for themselves. They not only feed themselves but also make their own dinner, not only dress themselves but also pack their own suitcases, not only walk to school but also organize games with friends on the playground. They venture outdoors alone. Boys are especially likely to put some distance between themselves and their home, engaging in activities without their parents' awareness or approval (Munroe & Romney, 2006). This budding independence fosters growth.

AT ABOUT THIS TIME

Signs of Psychosocial Maturation over the Years of Middle Childhood

Children have specific chores to perform.
Children make decisions about a weekly allowance.
Children can tell time, and they have set times for various activities.
Children have homework, including some assignments over several days.
Children are less often punished physically than in early childhood.
Children try to conform to peers in clothes, language, and so on.
Children voice preferences about their after-school care, lessons, and activities.
Children use media (TV, computers, video games) without adult supervision.
Children are responsible for younger children, pets, and, in some places, work.
Children strive for independence from parents.

Industry and Inferiority

One particular characteristic of school-age children, throughout the centuries and in every culture, is that they are industrious. They busily and actively master whatever skills their culture values. Their mind and body maturation, described in the previous two chapters, makes such activity possible.

Erikson's Insights

industry versus inferiority The fourth of Erikson's eight psychosocial crises, during which children attempt to master many skills, developing a sense of themselves as either industrious or inferior, competent or incompetent.

The tension between productivity and incompetence is the fourth psychosocial crisis, **industry versus inferiority,** as described by Erik Erikson. He noted that during these years the child "must forget past hopes and wishes, while his exuberant imagination is tamed and harnessed to the laws of impersonal things," becoming "ready to apply himself to given skills and tasks" (Erikson, 1963, pp. 258, 259).

Think of learning to read and add—painstaking and boring tasks. For instance, slowly sounding out "Jane has a dog" or writing "3 + 4 = 7" for the hundredth time are not very exciting. Yet school-age children busily practice reading and math: They are intrinsically motivated to read a page, finish a worksheet, memorize a spelling word, color a map, and so on. Similarly, they enjoy collecting, categorizing, and counting whatever they accumulate—perhaps stamps, stickers, stones, or seashells. That is industry.

Overall, children judge themselves as either *industrious* or *inferior*—deciding whether they are competent or incompetent, productive or useless, winners or losers. Being productive is intrinsically joyous, and it fosters the self-control that is a crucial defense against emotional problems (Bradley & Corwyn, 2005).

A sense of industry may be a defense against early substance use as well. In a study of 509 third- and fourth-graders in Arizona over a five-month period, an increasing number said that they had tried, or were expecting to try, alcohol (from 58 percent at the start of the study to 72 percent at the end) and cigarettes (from 18 to 23 percent). Those most likely to show such upturns were the children who increasingly felt inferior, not industrious (Jones, 2011). For example, they did not agree that they "stick with things until they are finished" and they were not proud of what they did.

Freud on Latency

Sigmund Freud described this period as **latency,** a time when emotional drives are quiet and unconscious sexual conflicts are submerged. Some experts complain that "middle childhood has been neglected at least since Freud relegated these years to the status of an uninteresting 'latency period'" (Huston & Ripke, 2006, p. 7).

But in one sense, at least, Freud was correct: Sexual impulses are quiet. Even when children were betrothed before age 12 (rare today, but not uncommon in earlier centuries), the young husband and wife had little interaction. Everywhere, boys and girls typically choose to be with others of their own sex. Indeed, boys who write "Girls stay out!" and girls who complain that "boys stink" are quite typical. Parents sometimes worry about sexual predators. However, school-age children are not very sexual; strangers rarely attempt to seduce children who have yet to reach puberty (Wolak et al., 2008).

Self-Concept

As children mature, they develop their *self-concept*, which is their idea about themselves, including their intelligence, personality, abilities, gender, and ethnic background. As you remember, the very notion that they are individuals is a discovery in toddlerhood, and a positive, global self-concept is typical in early childhood. Not so in middle childhood. The self-concept gradually becomes more specific and logical, as one might expect, given increases in cognitive development and social awareness. As one group explains, "The cognitive ability to combine specific behavioral features of the self (I can run fast and throw far) into higher order generalizations . . . (I am athletic) appears in middle childhood . . ." (Pfeifer et al., 2010, p. 144).

As the self-concept becomes more specific and logical, it also becomes less optimistic, incorporating influences from peers and the overall society. For example, some 6-year-olds from minority ethnic groups are refreshingly unaware of prejudice

Celebrating Spring No matter where they live, 7- to 11-year-olds seek to understand and develop whatever skills are valued by their culture. They do so in active, industrious ways, as described in every theory. This is illustrated here, as four friends in Assam, northeastern India, usher in spring with a Bihu celebration. Soon they will be given sweets and tea, which is the sociocultural validation of their energy, independence, and skill.

latency Freud's term for middle childhood, during which children's emotional drives and psychosexual needs are quiet (latent). Freud thought that sexual conflicts from earlier stages are only temporarily submerged, bursting forth again at puberty.

against their group; by age 11, they are aware, usually taking pride in their self-concept as Latino, or whatever, in defense (García Coll & Marks, 2009).

Ideally, "children develop feelings of self-esteem, competence, and individuality during middle childhood as they begin comparing themselves with peers" (Ripke et al., 2006, p. 261). Research in many nations has found that teaching anxious children to confide in friends as well as to understand their own emotions helps them develop a better self-concept (Siu, 2007). After-school activities, particularly sports, can provide a foundation for friendship and realistic self-esteem.

Academic and social competence are aided by realistic self-perception. Unrealistically high self-esteem reduces **effortful control** (deliberately modifying one's impulses and emotions). A reduction of effortful control leads to lower achievement and increased aggression. The same consequences occur if self-esteem is unrealistically low, so obviously the goal is to find a middle ground—not easy, since children may be too self-critical or not self-critical enough and since cultures differ on what that middle ground is.

High self-esteem is not universally valued or universally criticized (Yamaguchi et al., 2007). Many cultures expect children to be modest, not prideful. For example, Australians say that "tall poppies" are cut down, and the Japanese discourage social comparison aimed at making oneself feel superior.

Although Japanese children often excel at mathematics on international tests, only 17 percent have a high opinion of their math ability. In the United States, 53 percent of the students taking the TIMSS (Trends in Math and Science Study) are very confident of their math ability, yet they score significantly lower than the Japanese do (Snyder & Dillow, 2010). In Estonia, low self-esteem correlates with high academic achievement (Pullmann & Allik, 2008).

Often in the United States, children's successes are praised and teachers are wary of being too critical, especially in middle childhood. For example, some schools issue report cards with grades ranging from "Excellent" to "Needs improvement" instead of from A to F. An opposite trend is found in the national reforms of education explained in Chapter 12, which rate some schools as failing. Obviously culture, cohort, and age all influence self-concept, with the long-term effects debatable (Heine, 2007).

Resilience and Stress

In infancy and early childhood, children depend on their immediate families for food, learning, and life itself. Then "experiences in middle childhood can sustain, magnify, or reverse the advantages or disadvantages that children acquire in the preschool years" (Huston & Ripke, 2006, p. 2). Supportive families continue to be protective, but children may escape destructive family influences by finding their own niche in the larger world.

Surprisingly, some children seem unscathed by early experiences. They have been called "resilient" or even "invincible." Current thinking about resilience (see Table 13.1), with insights from dynamic-systems theory, makes it clear that, although some children cope better than others, none are impervious to their past history or current context (Jenson & Fraser, 2006; Luthar et al., 2003). Differential sensitivity is apparent, not only for genetic reasons but also because early child rearing, preschool education, and sociocultural values may strengthen children. Some children are hardy, more like dandelions than orchids, but all are influenced by their situation (Ellis & Boyce, 2008).

Resilience has been defined as "a dynamic process encompassing positive adaptation within the context of significant adversity" (Luthar et al., 2000, p. 543). Note the three parts of this definition:

effortful control The ability to regulate one's emotions and actions through effort, not simply through natural inclination.

Not Easy Newspapers aren't the only thing being recycled here. Family values are transmitted from one generation to the next. It is easier for adults to take out the trash themselves, but having a 7-year-old do it, as shown here, develops social commitment, responsibility, and pride.

resilience The capacity to adapt well to significant adversity and to overcome serious stress.

- Resilience is *dynamic,* not a stable trait. That means a given person may be resilient at some periods but not others.
- Resilience is a *positive adaptation* to stress. For example, if parental rejection leads a child to a closer relationship with another adult, that is positive adaptation, not mere passive endurance. That child is resilient.
- Adversity must be *significant.* Some adversities are comparatively minor (large class size, poor vision), and some are major (victimization, neglect). Children need to cope with all kinds of adversities, but not all coping qualifies them as resilient.

Cumulative Stress

One important discovery is that accumulated stresses over time, including minor ones (called "daily hassles"), are more devastating than an isolated major stress. Almost every child can withstand one stressful event, but repeated stresses make resilience difficult (Jaffee et al., 2007). One example comes from research on children in New Orleans who survived Hurricane Katrina. Years after the hurricane, about half were resilient but the other half (especially those in middle childhood) were still traumatized. Their risk of developing serious psychological problems was affected not so much by the hurricane itself as by ongoing problems—frequent moves, changes in caregivers, disruption of schooling, and so on (Kronenberg et al., 2010; Viadero, 2007).

TABLE 13.1	Dominant Ideas about Challenges and Coping in Children, 1965–Present
1965	All children have the same needs for healthy development.
1970	Some conditions or circumstances—such as "absent father," "teenage mother," "working mom," and "day care"—are harmful for every child.
1975	All children are *not* the same. Some children are resilient, coping easily with stressors that cause harm in other children.
1980	Nothing inevitably causes harm. Indeed, both maternal employment and preschool education, once thought to be risk factors, usually benefit children.
1985	Factors beyond the family, both in the child (low birthweight, prenatal alcohol exposure, aggressive temperament) and in the community (poverty, violence), can be very risky for children.
1990	Risk–benefit analysis finds that some children seem to be "invulnerable" to, or even to benefit from, circumstances that destroy others. (Some do well in school despite extreme poverty, for example.)
1995	No child is invincibly resilient. Risks are always harmful—if not in educational achievement, then in emotions.
2000	Risk–benefit analysis involves the interplay among all three domains (biosocial, cognitive, and psychosocial), including factors within the child (genes, intelligence, temperament), the family (function as well as structure), and the community (including neighborhood, school, church, and culture).
2008	The focus is on strengths, not risks. Assets in the child (intelligence, personality), the family (secure attachment, warmth), the community (good schools, after-school programs), and the nation (income support, health care) must be nurtured.
2010	Strengths vary by culture and national values. Both universal ideals and local variations must be recognized and respected.
2011	Genes as well as cultural practices can be either strengths or weaknesses, with the same stress being beneficial to one child and harmful to another.

Similarly, it is a major stress for children to see their father beating their mother, but the damage to the children occurs when that stress is repeated. One study of children witnessing such abuse found that 20 percent of them were resilient, especially if their mother left the abuser, found a better life, and was not herself depressed (Graham-Bermann et al., 2009).

An international example comes from Sri Lanka, where many children were exposed to war, the 2004 tsunami, poverty, deaths of relatives, and relocation. The accumulated stresses, more than any single problem, increased pathology and decreased achievement. The authors point to "the importance of multiple contextual, past, and current factors in influencing children's adaptation" (Catani et al., 2010, p. 1188).

Coping measures reduce the impact of repeated stress. One factor is the child's own interpretation. Cortisol (the stress hormone) increased in low-income children *if* they interpreted events connected to their family's poverty as a personal threat and *if* the family lacked order and routines (thus increasing daily hassles) (E. Chen et al., 2010). When low-income children did not take things personally and their family was not chaotic, they were more resilient. Many adults who, by income standards, were poor in childhood did not consider themselves poor; thus, they were less affected by it.

In general, a child's interpretation of a family situation (poverty, divorce, and so on) determines how that situation affects him or her (Olson & Dweck, 2008). Some children consider the family they were born into a temporary hardship; they look forward to the day when they can leave childhood behind. Other children experience *parentification*: They act as parents, trying to take care of everyone, including their actual parents (Byng-Hall, 2008). Children who endured Katrina were affected by their thoughts, both positive and negative, even more than by factors one might expect, such as the distress of their caregivers (Kilmer & Gil-Rivas, 2010).

Some children develop their own friends, activities, and skills, blossoming once they are old enough, becoming "increasingly autonomous and industrious" (Pagani et al., 2006, p. 132). Many activities, from 4-H to midnight basketball, from choir to Little League, help children develop a view of themselves as industrious, not

Healing Time Children who survived Hurricane Katrina participate in a fire drill at their new charter school, Lafayette Academy in New Orleans. The resumption of school routines helps them overcome the stress they experienced in the chaos of the deadly storm.

TIM MUELLER / THE NEW YORK TIMES / REDUX

inferior. Teachers and other adult leaders can help children develop those positive self-concepts.

A 40-year study in Hawaii began with children born into poverty, often to parents who were alcoholic or mentally ill. Not surprisingly, many of these children showed signs of deprivation when they were infants (low weight, medical problems, and so on). Experts at the time predicted a troubled future for them. But that did not necessarily happen.

One such infant was Michael, born preterm, weighing less than 5 pounds. His parents were low-income teenagers; his father was absent for the first two years of his life, returning later only to impregnate Michael's mother again and again and again. When Michael was 8, both parents left him and three younger siblings with his grandparents. Yet Michael ultimately became a successful, happy, loving adult (E. Werner, 1979).

Michael was not the only resilient one. Amazingly, about one-third of the high-risk Hawaiian babies coped well. By middle childhood, they had discovered ways to avoid family stresses, to achieve in school, to make good friends, and to find adult mentors. As adults, they left family problems behind (many moved far away) and established their own healthy relationships (E. Werner & Smith, 1992, 2001).

As was true for many of these children, school and then college can be an escape. An easygoing temperament and a high IQ help (Curtis & Cicchetti, 2003), but they are not essential. In the Hawaiian study, "a realistic goal orientation, persistence, and 'learned creativity' enabled . . . a remarkable degree of personal, social, and occupational success," even for children with evident learning disabilities (E. Werner & Smith, 2001, p. 140).

Grandmother Knows Best About 20,000 grandmothers in Connecticut are caregivers for their grandchildren. This 15-year-old boy and his 17-year-old sister came to live with their grandmother in New Haven after their mother died several years ago. This type of family can help children cope with stress, especially when the grandmother is relatively young and has her own house, as is the case here.

Social Support and Religious Faith

Social support is a major factor that strengthens the ability to deal with stress. Compared with the homebound lives of younger children, the expanding social world of school-age children allows new possibilities (Morris & Kalil, 2006). Relatives, teachers, peers, pets, community programs (even free libraries and concerts) all help children cope with stress (Bryant & Donnellan, 2007). One study concludes:

> When children attempt to seek out experiences that will help them overcome adversity, it is critical that resources, in the form of supportive adults or learning opportunities, be made available to them so that their own self-righting potential can be fulfilled.

> [Kim-Cohen et al., 2004, p. 664]

A specific example is children's use of religion, which often provides support via adults from the same faith group (P. E. King & Furrow, 2004, p. 709). Church involvement particularly helps African American children in communities rife with social stress and racial prejudice (Akiba & García Coll, 2004). Faith is psychologically protective when it helps children reinterpret their experiences (Crawford et al., 2006).

Prayer may also foster resilience. In one study, adults were required to pray for a specific person for several weeks. Their attitude about that person changed (Lambert et al., 2010). Ethics precludes such an experiment with children, but it is known that children often pray, expecting that prayer will make them feel better, especially when they are sad or angry (Bamford & Lagattuta, 2010). As already explained, expectations and interpretations can be powerful.

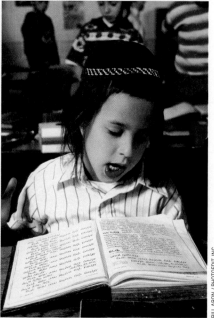

Become Like a Child Although the particulars vary a great deal, school-age children's impulses toward industriousness, stability, and dedication place them among the most devout members of every religious faith.

SUMMING UP

Children gain in maturity and responsibility during the school years. According to Erikson, the crisis of industry versus inferiority generates feelings of confidence or self-doubt. Freud thought latency enables children to master new skills. Often children develop more realistic self-concepts, with the help of their families. Resilience to major adversity is apparent in some children in middle childhood, especially if the stress is temporary and coping measures are available. Children cope with stresses not only through their own interpretations but also by becoming more independent. They use school achievement, after-school activities, supportive adults, and religious beliefs to help them overcome whatever problems they face.

>> Families and Children

No one doubts that genes affect personality as well as ability, that peers are vital, and that schools and cultures influence what, and how much, children learn. It has been suggested that genes, peers, and communities have so much influence that parenting has little impact—unless it is grossly abusive (Harris, 1998, 2002; McLeod et al., 2007). This suggestion arose from studies about the impact of the environment on child development.

Shared and Nonshared Environments

Many studies have found that children are much less affected by *shared environment* (influences that arise from being in the same environment, such as for two siblings living in one home, raised by their parents) than by *nonshared environment* (e.g., the different experiences of two siblings). Careful research finds that most personality traits and intellectual characteristics can be traced to genes and nonshared environments, with little left over for the shared influence of being raised by the same parents.

Even psychopathology (Burt, 2009) and sexual orientation (Långström et al., 2010) arise primarily from genes and nonshared environment. Might parents be merely caretakers, providing basic care (food, shelter) but inconsequential no matter what rules, routines, or responses they provide?

More recent findings, however, reassert parent power. The analysis of shared and nonshared influences was correct, but the conclusion was based on a false assumption. Siblings raised together do *not* share the same environment. For example, if relocation, divorce, unemployment, or a new job occurs in a family, the impact on each child depends on each child's age, genes, resilience, and gender. Moving to another town might disturb a school-age child more than an infant, divorce harms boys more than girls, poverty may hurt the preschoolers the most, and so on.

The age and gender variations above do not apply for all siblings: Differential sensitivity means that one child is more affected, for better or worse, than another (Pluess & Belsky, 2010). Even if siblings are raised together, the mix of parental personality, genes, and gender may lead one child to become antisocial, another to have a personality disorder, and a third to be resilient, capable, and strong (Beauchaine et al., 2009).

Family Unity Thinking about any family—even a happy, wealthy family like this one—makes it apparent that each child's family experiences differ. For instance, would you expect the 5-year-old boy to be treated the same way as his two older sisters? And how about each child's feelings toward the parents? Even though the 12-year-olds are twins, one may favor her mother while the other favors her father.

MASTERFILE / RADIUS IMAGES

In addition, some nonshared influences, such as school, neighborhood, after-school activity, and peers, are affected by the parents (Simpkins et al., 2006). For example, a nonshared difference would be the oldest child having attended the zoned public school and the youngest having attended a private school 10 miles away—the result of parental decisions and family income. Even identical twins, who share genes, age, sex, and home, may not share environment, as the following illustrates.

Especially for Scientists How would you determine whether or not parents treat all their children the same? (see response, page 386)

A VIEW FROM SCIENCE

"I Always Dressed One in Blue Stuff . . ."

An expert team of scientists compared 1,000 sets of mono-zygotic twins reared by their biological parents (Caspi et al., 2004). Obviously, the pairs were identical in genes, sex, and age. The researchers assessed each child's temperament by asking the mothers and teachers to fill out a detailed, standardized checklist. They also asked every mother to describe each twin. Maternal attitudes ranged from very positive ("my ray of sunshine") to very negative ("I wish I never had her. . . . She's a cow, I hate her") (quoted in Caspi et al., 2004, p. 153). Many mothers described personality differences between their twins. For example, one mother spoke of her identical-twin daughters:

> Susan can be very sweet. She loves babies . . . she can be insecure . . . she flutters and dances around. . . . There's not much between her ears. . . . She's exceptionally vain, more so than Ann. Ann loves any game involving a ball, very sporty, climbs trees, very much a tomboy. One is a serious tomboy and one's a serious girlie girl. Even when they were babies I always dressed one in blue stuff and one in pink stuff.

[quoted in Caspi et al., 2004, p. 156]

Some mothers were much more cold and rejecting toward one twin than toward the other:

He was in the hospital and everyone was all "poor Jeff, poor Jeff" and I started thinking, "Well, what about me? I'm the one's just had twins. I'm the one's going through this, he's a seven-week-old baby and doesn't know a thing about it" . . . I sort of detached and plowed my emotions into Mike.

[quoted in Caspi et al., 2004, p. 156]

This mother blamed Jeff for favoring his father: "Jeff would do anything for Don but he wouldn't for me, and no matter what I did for either of them [Don or Jeff] it wouldn't be right" (p. 157). She said Mike was much more lovable.

In this longitudinal study, the researchers measured personality at age 5 (assessing, among other things, antisocial behavior as reported by kindergarten teachers) and then measured each twin's personality two years later. They found that if the mothers were more negative toward one of their twins, that twin *became* more antisocial than the co-twin. The rejected twins were more likely to fight, steal, and hurt others at age 7 than at age 5, after all background factors were taken into account.

These researchers acknowledge that many other nonshared factors—peers, teachers, and so on—are significant. But this difference in monozygotic twins confirms that parents matter. As every sibling knows, each child's family experiences are unique.

Family Function and Family Structure

The data reaffirm that parents are crucial, which raises the next question: What family structures make it likely (or unlikely) that families will function well? **Family structure** refers to the legal and genetic connections among related people living in the same household. **Family function** refers to how a family cares for its members.

Function is more important than structure in every developmental period. No matter what the structure, people need family love and encouragement. The ideal manifestations of that love vary by age. Infants need responsive caregiving and social interaction; teenagers need freedom and guidance; young adults need peace and privacy; the aged need respect and appreciation. But everyone needs affection in some form.

family structure The legal and genetic relationships among relatives living in the same home; includes nuclear family, extended family, stepfamily, and so on.

family function The way a family works to meet the needs of its members. Children need families to provide basic material necessities, to encourage learning, to help them develop self-respect, to nurture friendships, and to foster harmony and stability.

Family Function in Middle Childhood

What specific forms of love and encouragement do school-age children need?

1. *Physical necessities.* Although children in middle childhood eat, dress, and go to sleep without help, families furnish food, clothing, and shelter.
2. *Learning.* These are prime learning years: Families can support, encourage, and guide education.
3. *Self-respect.* Because children at about age 6 become much more self-critical and socially aware, families can praise accomplishments and provide opportunities for success (in sports, the arts, or specific skills if academic success is difficult).
4. *Peer relationships.* Families can foster friendships, via play dates, group activities, and so on.
5. *Harmony and stability.* Families can provide protective, predictable routines with a home that is a safe haven for everyone.

No family always functions perfectly, but children worldwide fare better in families than they do in other structures (such as group residences). The final item on the list above is especially crucial in middle childhood, when children like continuity, not change.

Ironically, many parents move from one neighborhood or school to another during these years, thinking they are securing a better life for their children. To be specific, in one year (2008), 17 percent of U.S. 5- to 9-year-olds moved from one home to another, a rate four times that of adults over age 50 (U.S. Bureau of the Census, 2010). Since those data come from just one year, they suggest that over the six years from ages 5 to 11, the average child moved at least once. As with all quantitative data, some individual variations are lost. If one child moved every year (not uncommon for homeless children), the average must be balanced by five other children who stayed put. However, the basic point holds for all school-age children—change is difficult.

Lack of stability also seems to harm U.S. children in military families. Such children have several advantages: Enlisted parents tend to have higher incomes, better health care, and more education than do civilians from the same backgrounds. However, military parents repeatedly depart and return, and families typically relocate every few years (Titus, 2007). Military children (dubbed "military brats") have more emotional problems and lower school achievement than do other children of the same age and background. As one author explains:

> Military parents are continually leaving, returning, leaving again. School work suffers, more for boys than for girls, and . . . reports of depression and behavioral problems go up when a parent is deployed.
>
> [Hall, 2008, p. 52]

For exactly that reason, the U.S. military has instituted a special program to help children whose parents are deployed. Caregivers of such children are encouraged to avoid changes in the child's life: no new homes, new rules, or new schools (Lester et al., 2011).

Diversity of Structures

One of the many differences from one nation to another as well as one generation to another is the pattern of family structures. Worldwide, two factors—more single-parent households and fewer children per family—have changed childhood from what it was a few decades ago. The specifics vary from nation to nation (see Figure 13.1 on page 388). Most of our discussion here focuses on the United States in about 2010, partly because most of the research has been published in

What Must She Leave Behind? In every nation, children are uprooted from familiar places as a result of adult struggles and/or aspirations for a better life. This girl is leaving a settlement in the Gaza Strip, due to the Israeli–Palestinian conflict that has disrupted millions of lives. Worldwide, it's the children who suffer most from relocation.

AMIT SHABI / LAIF / REDUX

>> Response for Scientists (from page 385) Proof is very difficult when human interaction is the subject of investigation, since random assignment is impossible. Ideally, researchers would find identical twins being raised together and would then observe the parents' behavior over the years.

The Same Situation, Many Miles Apart: Happy Families The boys in both photos are about 4 years old. Roberto *(left)* lives with his single mother in Chicago. She pays $360 a month for her two children to attend a day-care center. The youngest child in the Balmedina family *(right)* lives with his nuclear family—no day care needed—in the Philippines. Which boy has the better life? The answer is not known; family function is more crucial than family structure.

that nation. Nevertheless, although the proportions differ across countries, the problems with each family structure are similar worldwide.

About two-thirds of all U.S. school-age children live in two-parent homes (see Table 13.2), most often with their biological parents—an arrangement called a **nuclear family.** In U.S. nuclear families, the parents are usually married, although in many other nations, nuclear families are headed by couples who are not legally wed. Other two-parent structures include adoptive parents, foster parents, grandparents but no parents, a biological parent with a stepparent, and same-sex couples.

In the United States, about 31 percent of all school-age children live in a **single-parent family.** Some observers may think that the single-parent percentage is actually higher than 31 percent because 40 percent of new births in the United States are to unmarried women. More than half of all contemporary U.S. children will live in a single-parent family before they reach age 18 for one of three reasons: (1) Their mother was neither married nor cohabiting when they were born, (2) their parents later separated or divorced, or (3) one parent died. However, at any given moment, less than one-third of 6-to 11-year-olds live with only one parent.

Two-parent and single-parent structures are often contrasted with the **extended family,** a three-generation family that usually includes grandparents and often aunts, uncles, and cousins. In 2010, about one in six U.S. families was an extended family—an increase from 1980 (one in eight) and a decrease from 1940 (one in five) (Pew Social Trends Staff, 2010). Such families are particularly common when children are small: By the time children reach puberty, most parents have separate households from their own parents.

Extended families are less costly and thus are more common among low-income households (the current economic picture has more poor families, which is one reason the rate of extended families is increasing). Other reasons are culture and convenience: Extended families share child care and are the norm in some other nations.

The distinction between one-parent, two-parent, and extended families is not as simple in practice as on paper. Many young parents live near relatives who provide meals, emotional support, money, and child care, functioning as an extended family. The opposite is true as well, especially in developing nations: Some families are considered extended because they share a household, but they create separate living quarters for each set of parents and children, making these units somewhat like nuclear families (Georgas et al., 2006).

In many nations, the **polygamous family** (one husband with two or more wives) is an acceptable family structure. Generally in polygamous families, income

nuclear family A family that consists of a father, a mother, and their biological children under age 18.

single-parent family A family that consists of only one parent and his or her biological children under age 18.

extended family A family of three or more generations living in one household.

polygamous family A family consisting of one man, several wives, and their children.

per child is reduced and education, especially for the girls, is limited (Omariba & Boyle, 2007). Polygamy is rare and illegal in the United States. Even in nations where it is allowed, polygamy is less common than it was 30 years ago. In Ghana, for example, men with several wives and a dozen children are now a rarity (Heaton & Darkwah, 2011).

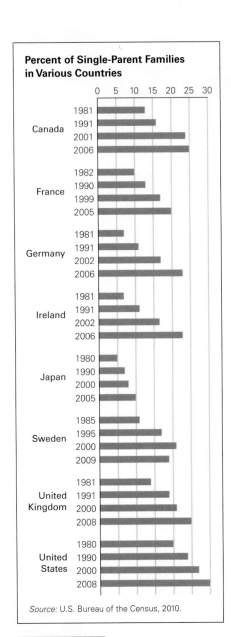

Percent of Single-Parent Families in Various Countries

Source: U.S. Bureau of the Census, 2010.

FIGURE 13.1

Single Parents Of all the households with children, a rising percent of them are headed by a single parent. In some countries, many households are headed by two unmarried parents, which is not shown here.

TABLE 13.2   Family Structures (with percent of U.S. 6- to 11-year-olds in each type)*

Two-Parent Families (69%)

1. **Nuclear family** (55%). Named after the nucleus (the tightly connected core particles of an atom), the nuclear family consists of a man and a woman and their biological offspring under 18 years of age. About half of all school-age children live in nuclear families. Although traditionally in nuclear families, no other adults are present, about 10 percent of families headed by two biological parents include a grandparent, and often an aunt or uncle, and hence are extended families.

2. **Stepparent family** (9%). Divorced fathers usually remarry; divorced mothers remarry about half the time. When children from a former relationship live with the new couple in their home, that makes a stepparent family. If the stepparent family includes children born to two or more couples (such as children from the spouses' previous marriages and/or children of the new couple), that is called a *blended family*.

3. **Adoptive family** (2%). Although as many as one-third of infertile married couples adopt children, few adoptable children are available and so most adoptive couples have only one or two children. Thus, the number of school-age children who are adopted is only 2 percent, although the overall percentage of adoptive families is higher than that.

4. **Grandparents alone** (2%). Grandparents take on parenting for some school-age children because the children's biological parents are absent (dead, imprisoned, sick, addicted, and so on). This is increasing, especially in communities where many parents have died of AIDS.

5. **Two same-sex parents** (1%). Some two-parent families are headed by a same-sex couple, whose legal status (married, step-, adoptive) varies.

Single-Parent Families (31%)

One-parent families are increasing, but they average fewer children than two-parent families, so the number of school-age children in such families is only 31%.

1. **Single mother, never married** (12%). Almost 40 percent of all U.S. births are to unmarried mothers, but some such mothers marry by the time the child is in school. Almost half of the single-mother families also include a grandparent, and hence are extended families.

2. **Single mother—divorced, separated, or widowed** (13%). Although many marriages end in divorce (almost half in the United States, fewer in other nations), many divorcing couples have no children. Others remarry. Thus, only 13 percent of school-age children currently live with single, formerly married mothers.

3. **Single father** (5%). About 1 in 20 fathers has physical custody of his children and raises them without their mother or a new wife. This category is increasing, especially for children in middle childhood, but it is still much less common than single mother.

4. **Grandparent alone** (1%). Sometimes a single grandparent (usually the grandmother) becomes the sole caregiving adult for a child.

More Than Two Adults (15%) [Also listed as two-parent or one-parent family]

1. **Extended family** (15%). Some school-age children live with a grandparent or other relatives, as well as with one (5%) or both of their parents (10%). This pattern is most common with infants (20%) but occurs in middle childhood as well.

2. **Polygamous family** (0%). In some nations (not the United States), men can legally have several wives. This family structure is more favored by adults than children. Everywhere, polyandry (one woman, several husbands) is rare.

* Less than 1 percent of school-age children in the United States live without any adults in a parental role; they are not included here.

Source: The percentages on this table are estimates, based on data in U.S. Bureau of the Census, 2010, *Statistical Abstract* and Current Population Reports, *America's Families and Living Arrangements,* 2011; and Pew Social Trends Staff, 2010. The category "extended family" is an estimate higher than the official statistics, since some families do not tell official authorities about relatives living with them.

Connecting Family Structure and Function

More important for the children is not the structure of their family, but how that family functions. The two are related; structure influences (but does not determine) function. The crucial question for schoolchildren is whether the structure makes it more or less likely that the five family functions mentioned earlier (necessities, learning, self-respect, friendship, harmony/stability) will be fulfilled.

Benefits of Nuclear Families

In general, nuclear families function best; children in the nuclear structure tend to achieve better in school with fewer psychological problems. A scholar who summarized dozens of studies concludes: "Children living with two biological married parents experience better educational, social, cognitive, and behavioral outcomes than do other children" (Brown, 2010, p. 1062). Why? Does this mean that parents should all marry and stay married? Not exactly: Some of the benefits are correlates, not causes.

Many advantages of nuclear families begin before the wedding because education, earning potential, and emotional maturity all make it more likely that people will marry, have children, and stay married. Thus, brides and grooms bring personal assets to their new family. In other words, there is a correlation between child success and married parents partly because of the people who marry, not the fact of marriage itself.

After the marriage, ideally, mutual affection encourages both partners to become wealthier and healthier than either would be alone. Research finds that this is often true—the selection effects noted in the previous paragraph are not the entire story (Amato, 2005; Brown, 2010). For children, the *parental alliance,* when mother and father support each other in their mutual commitment to the child (as first described in Chapter 4), is crucial. Shared parenting decreases the risk of maltreatment and makes it more likely that children have someone to read to them, check their homework, invite their friends over, buy them new clothes, and save for their education.

In fact, a broad survey of parental contributions to college tuition found that the highest contributions came from nuclear families. These results might be expected when two-parent families are compared with single and divorced parents because one-parent families average less income; but remarried parents, whose family income is comparable to that of nuclear parents, nonetheless contribute less, on average, to college tuition (Turley & Desmond, 2011). This and other research find that the benefits of nuclear families continue for decades, even after children are grown.

Other Two-Parent Families

The advantages of two-parent families are not limited to biological parents, whose genetic connections to their children might explain their commitment. Adoptive and same-sex parents typically function well for children, and single parents who then marry and thus create two-parent families often seek a new mate who will be a good stepfather or stepmother. Especially if the child is under age 2 and the stepparent forms a happy relationship with the biological parent, the children adapt to their family (Ganong et al., 2011). Of course, none of these two-parent families always function well, but the circumstances (genetic or chosen) provide a nudge in the right direction.

Considerable controversy has focused on how same-sex couples function for children. Only recently have male–male couples been

Surprising? It should be no surprise that happy two-parent families can be of any ethnicity. Some people, however, may be surprised that a married same-sex couple can provide a well-functioning home, as this family seems to enjoy.

A Comfortable Combination The blended family—husband, wife, and children from both spouses' previous marriages—often breeds resentment, depression, and rebellion in the children. That is apparently not the case for the family shown here, which provides cheerful evidence that any family structure is capable of functioning well.

able to marry and raise children; thus, longitudinal research on a large sample, with valid comparisons to male–female families of the same age and education, has not yet been published. However, research on female–female couples finds that their children develop well, emotionally and intellectually (Biblarz & Stacey, 2010). Same-sex relationships have problems similar to those of other-sex relationships, unless social prejudice disrupts family life.

The stepparent structure also has advantages and disadvantages. The primary advantage is financial, especially when compared with most single-parent families. The primary disadvantage is in meeting the fifth family function listed earlier—providing harmony and stability. Compared with other two-parent families, older stepchildren leave sooner than older biological children, new babies arrive, and marriages are more likely to dissolve (Teachman, 2008a). Harmony may also be absent, especially if the child's loyalty to both biological parents is attacked by ongoing disputes between them. A solid parental alliance is more difficult to form when it includes three adults—two of whom disliked each other enough to divorce, and a third who is a newcomer to the child's life.

Finally, when grandparents are the caretakers for children without parents present (called a *skipped-generation family*, the most common form of foster care), the hope is that grandparents provide excellent care since they are experienced, mature, and devoted to their grandchildren. Those characteristics may be present, but grandparent families average lower incomes, more health problems, and less stability than other two-parent families. They have particular difficulty obtaining adequate health care for the children, who often have special needs (such as attention-deficit/hyperactivity or learning disabilities) because of the very circumstances that led them to live with the grandparents in the first place. Thus, skipped-generation families need special help, but they are less likely to receive it (Baker & Mutchler, 2010).

Single-Parent Families

Overall, the single-parent structure functions less well for children because income and stability tend to be reduced. Most single parents fill many roles—including wage earner, daughter or son (single parents often depend on their own parents), and lover (many seek a new partner)—which makes it harder for them to provide steady emotional and academic support for their schoolchildren. If they are depressed (and many are), they are less available to meet their children's needs. Neesha is an example.

Especially for Single Parents You have heard that children raised in one-parent families will have difficulty in establishing intimate relationships as adolescents and adults. What can you do about this possibility? (see response, page 392)

BILL ARON / PHOTOEDIT, INC.

A CASE TO STUDY

How Hard Is It to Be a Kid?

Neesha's fourth-grade teacher referred her to the school guidance team because she often fell asleep in class, was late 51 days, and was absent for 15. The counselor did not have time to see Neesha at the end of the fourth grade, so she was held back and seen in the fall. Testing found Neesha at the seventh-grade level in reading and writing and at the fifth-grade level in math. Since learning was not the problem, something psychosocial might be amiss.

The counselor spoke to Tanya, Neesha's mother. Tanya was a single parent, depressed and worried about paying the rent on a tiny apartment where she had moved when Neesha's father left three years earlier to live with his girlfriend, now with a baby. Tanya said she had no problems with Neesha, who was "more like a little mother than a kid," unlike her 15-year-old son, Tyrone, who suffered from fetal alcohol effects and whose behavior worsened when his father left.

Tyrone was recently beaten up badly as part of a gang initiation, a group he considered "like a family." He was currently in juvenile detention, after being arrested for stealing bicycle parts. Note the nonshared environment here: Although the siblings grew up together and their father left them both, 12-year-old Tyrone became rebellious whereas 7-year-old Neesha became "a little mother."

Tanya said that she:

> often gets depressed, and when she isn't working evenings either she goes to bed early or cries herself to sleep. On these occasions, Neesha is very quiet and tries to comfort her mother. Tanya said that when she woke up the other morning, Neesha had placed a handmade card on her pillow. The card was decorated with hearts and bows and huge letters: "I love you, Mom. Neesha"

> *[Wilmhurst, 2011, pp. 150–151]*

The school counselor also spoke with Neesha.

> Neesha volunteered that she worried a lot about things and that sometimes when she worries she has a hard time falling asleep. . . . Last year she got in trouble for being late so many times, but it was hard to wake up. Her mom was sleeping late because she was working more nights cleaning the offices. Neesha said it was a very hard year. She was tired and cranky and just couldn't seem to concentrate on her work. She said

> she would read a page and then not remember what she had read. Neesha said she got so far behind that she just gave up. She was also having problems with the other girls in the class, who were starting to tease her about sleeping in class and not doing her work. She said they called her names like "Sleepy" and "Dummy." She said that at first it made her very sad, and then it made her very mad. That's when she started to hit them to make them stop.

> *[Wilmhurst, 2011, pp. 152–153]*

Neesha at age 10 is coping with poverty, a depressed mother, an absent father, a delinquent brother, and classmate bullying. The stress makes concentration difficult. Her response is parentification, hitting, and sleeping. She also shows signs of resilience—her academic achievement is impressive. Shortly after Neesha was interviewed,

> The school principal received a call from Neesha's mother, who asked that her daughter not be sent home from school because she was going to kill herself. She was holding a loaded gun in her hand and she had to do it, because she was not going to make this month's rent. She could not take it any longer, but she did not want Neesha to come home and find her dead. . . . While the guidance counselor continued to keep the mother talking, the school contacted the police, who apprehended mom while she was talking on her cell phone. . . . The loaded gun was on her lap. . . . The mother was taken to the local psychiatric facility.

> *[Wilmhurst, 2011, p. 154–155]*

Like many single mothers, Tanya is overwhelmed. If Neesha's father were involved, perhaps Tyrone would not need a gang family and perhaps Neesha would get to school on time. Whether Neesha's resilience will continue depends on her ability to find support beyond her mother. Social support might come from the school, but Neesha's fourth-grade teacher did not stop the bullying and failed Neesha. However, there is reason to hope:

> When asked if she would like to meet with the school psychologist once in a while, just to talk about her worries, Neesha said she would like that very much. After she left the office, she turned and thanked the psychologist for working with her, and added "You know, sometimes it's hard being a kid."

> *[Wilmhurst, 2011, p. 154]*

Community support for single parents makes a difference. For example, many French parents are unmarried and might be categorized as single parents in U.S. surveys, but they generally live together and share child rearing. French cohabiting parents separate less often than do married couples in the United States. Since separation and divorce are disruptive for children, this suggests that the cohabiting structure functions better in France than does the married structure in the

>> **Response for Single Parents** (from page 390) Do not get married mainly to provide a second parent for your child. If you were to do so, things would probably get worse rather than better. Do make an effort to have friends of both sexes with whom your child can interact.

United States. However, for U.S. children, the cohabiting structure is worse than marriage because cohabiting parents separate more often. This is one example of a general truth: Function within single-parent structures is affected by national mores (S. L. Brown, 2004).

Ethnic culture matters as well. Single parenthood is more accepted among African Americans (60 percent of African American 6- to 11-year-olds live with only one parent). In that culture, relatives and friends routinely help single parents, who might be more isolated and dysfunctional if they were of another ethnicity (Cain & Combs-Orme, 2005; Taylor et al., 2008). By contrast, only 14 percent of Asian American families are headed by single parents (U.S. Bureau of the Census, 2010). Consequently, most Asian American children have two parents to provide daily care, but those who do not may be more isolated.

All these are generalities: Contrary to the averages, thousands of nuclear families are destructive, thousands of stepparents provide excellent care, and thousands of single-parent families are wonderful. Structure and culture tend to protect or undercut healthy function, but many parents overcome structural problems to support their children.

A VIEW FROM SCIENCE

Divorce

Scientists try to provide analysis and insight, based on empirical data (of course), but the task goes far beyond reporting facts. Regarding divorce, thousands of studies and several opposing opinions need to be considered, analyzed, and combined—no easy challenge. One scholar who has done this is Andrew Cherlin. He has studied the family for over 35 years, publishing 13 books and over 200 articles since 1988.

Among the facts that need analysis are these three (Amato, 2005; Brown, 2010; Potter, 2010):

1. The United States leads the world in the rates of divorce, marriage, and remarriage. The ratio of marriage to divorce is slightly lower than it was 30 years ago, but still almost half of all marriages end in divorce. Why?

2. Single parents, cohabiting parents, and stepparent families sometimes provide the love and support children need, but, on average, children fare better in nuclear families with married parents. Why?

3. Virtually every study shows that, on average, divorce impairs children's academic achievement and psychosocial development for years, even decades. Why?

Cherlin (2009) has analyzed these facts. The problem, he contends, is that U.S. culture is conflicted: Marriage is idolized, but so is personal freedom. As a result, many people assert their independence by marrying without considering anyone else, such as their parents or community. Then, when they are overwhelmed by child care (freedom of the individual means the United States does not provide paid parental leave or extensive child care), the

marriage becomes strained, so they separate. Because marriage remains the ideal, they blame their former mate or their own poor decision, not the institution, and they are eager to remarry.

Consequently, they seek another partner and, if possible, another marriage—which may lead to another divorce. (Divorced people are more likely to remarry than are other single people their age, and second marriages fail more often than first marriages.) All this is in keeping with the culture's emphasis on individual freedom, but none of it benefits the children who suffer from repeated transitions.

From this perspective, the effort to persuade unmarried parents to wed is well intentioned but shortsighted because such marriages are at high risk of divorce (Brown, 2010). Indeed, at least one longitudinal study of unwed mothers found that those who married were eventually worse off than those who did not (Lichter et al., 2006). Research on unwed parents finds that many consider marriage a much riskier commitment than childbearing (Gibson-Davis, 2009).

This leads to a related insight. Cherlin suggests that the main reason children are harmed by divorce—as well as by cohabitation, single parenthood, and stepparenthood—is not the legal status of their parents but the lack of stability.

Scholars now describe divorce as a process, with transitions and conflicts before and after the formal event (Magnuson & Berger, 2009; Potter, 2010). As you remember, resilience is difficult when the child must contend with repeated changes and ongoing hassles—yet this is what divorce brings. Coping is particularly hard when children are at a developmental transition, such as entering first grade or beginning puberty.

Given all this, despite the U. S. effort to encourage marriage, many young adults are making the opposite choice, avoiding marriage in order to avoid divorce. This strategy is working—the age at first marriage is increasing, which is one reason the divorce rate is falling even faster than the marriage rate (Amato, 2010).

Beyond analysis and insight, the other task of developmental science is to provide practical suggestions. Most scholars would agree with the following four points:

1. Marriage commitments need to be made carefully, to minimize the risk of divorce.

2. Once married, couples need to work to keep the relationship strong. Often happiness dips after the birth of the first child, then again at adolescence. Knowing that, especially during these years, couples can plan to spend time together doing what they love—dancing, traveling, praying, clubbing, and so on.

3. If divorce occurs, adults need to minimize transitions and maintain a child's relationships with both parents.

4. In middle childhood, schools can provide vital support for children who are experiencing family change. Teachers can ensure that school is a haven of stability when the home is not.

This may sound idealistic. However, another scientist, who has spent her lifetime following the patterns of divorced families, writes:

> Although divorce leads to an increase in stressful life events, such as poverty, psychological and health problems in parents, and inept parenting, it also may be associated with escape from conflict, the building of new more harmonious fulfilling relationships, and the opportunity for personal growth and individuation.
>
> [Hetherington, 2006, p. 204]

Not every parent should marry, not every marriage should continue, and not every child is devastated by divorce. However, every child benefits from all five family functions, including a stable and harmonious home. Adults can provide that. Scientists hope they do.

Family Trouble

Two factors interfere with family function in every structure, ethnic group, and nation: low income and high conflict. Many families experience both, because financial stress increases conflict and vice versa (McLanahan, 2009).

Poverty

Suppose a 6-year-old boy spills his milk, as every 6-year-old sometimes does. In a well-functioning, financially stable family, one parent then guides him to mop up the spill while the other parent pours more milk, perhaps encouraging family harmony by saying, "Everyone has an accident sometimes."

What if the 6-year-old lives with a single parent struggling with overdue rent, unemployment, and an older child who wants money for a school trip? What if the last of the food stamps bought that milk? Shouting, crying, and accusations are almost inevitable (perhaps the sibling claims, "He did it on purpose," to which the 6-year-old responds, "You pushed me," and a visitor adds, "You should teach him to be careful"). As in this example, poverty makes anger spill over when the milk does.

Family income correlates with both function and structure. The effects of poverty are cumulative; low socioeconomic status (SES) may be especially damaging during middle childhood if it has continued from early childhood (Duncan et al., 2010).

Many researchers want to know exactly why income affects development. Several have developed the *family-stress model,* which holds that the crucial question about any risk factor (such as low income, divorce, single parenthood, unemployment) is whether it increases stress. Poverty is less stressful *if* low income is temporary and the family's net worth (home ownership, investments, and so on) buffers the strain (Yeung & Conley, 2008). However, if economic hardship is ongoing and parents have little education, that increases stress, making adults tense and hostile toward their partners and children (Conger et al., 2002; Parke et al., 2004). Thus, the *reaction* to poverty is crucial.

Reaction to wealth may cause problems, too. Children in high-income families develop more than their share of developmental problems. One reason may

▶ Research Design

Scientists: Greg J. Duncan, Kathleen M. Ziol-Guest, and Ariel Kalil.

Publication: *Child Development* (2010).

Participants: Individuals born between 1968 and 1975 to parents who were part of the Panel Study of Income Dynamics, a longitudinal study in the United States that traces the effect of income on families. Only people with repeated measures throughout childhood and adulthood (1,589 of them) were included. The goal of this study was to seek developmental outcomes, not merely correlates, of income.

Design: Data were collected at many stages of each person's life, incorporating detailed and repeated family economic indicators, including adult body mass index (BMI), health, education, arrests, income, employment, and psychological distress.

Major conclusion: Childhood poverty had a decided effect on adult functioning 20 and even 30 years later, particularly on work hours and earnings. This study controlled for many factors that vary with income, such as parents' education and family structure. Childhood poverty itself, especially during middle childhood, impaired well-being in adulthood.

Comments: Since low income correlates with large family size, single parenthood, low education, and so on, studies that simply link poverty to outcomes may reflect third variables. Because this study has longitudinal data on many individuals and variables, the conclusion —that childhood poverty itself impairs development—is probably valid.

be parental pressure on the children to excel, causing stress in middle childhood and creating externalizing and internalizing problems that lead to drug use, delinquency, and poor academic performance in high school (Ansary & Luthar, 2009).

Some intervention programs aim to teach parents to be more encouraging and patient (McLoyd et al., 2006). In low-income families, however, this focus may be misplaced. Poverty itself—with attendant problems such as inadequate schools, poor health, and the threat of homelessness—causes stress (see the Research Design).

Remember the dynamic-systems perspective described in Chapter 1? That perspective applies to poverty: Multigenerational research finds that poverty is both a cause and a symptom—parents with less education and immature emotional control are more likely to have difficulty finding employment and raising their children, and then low income adds to those difficulties (Schofield et al., 2011).

If that is so, more income means better family functioning. Some support for that possibility is that children in single-mother households do much better if their father pays child support, even if he is not actively involved in the child's daily life (Huang, 2009). Nations that subsidize single parents (e.g., Austria and Iceland) also have smaller achievement gaps between low- and middle-SES children on the TIMSS. This is suggestive, but controversial and value-laden. Some developmentalists report that raising income does *not*, by itself, improve parenting (L. M. Berger et al., 2009).

Conflict

There is no controversy about conflict. Every researcher agrees that family conflict harms children, particularly when adults fight about child rearing. Such fights are more common in stepfamilies, divorced families, and extended families. Of course, nuclear families are not immune: Children suffer especially if their parents abuse each other or if one parent walks out, leaving the other distraught.

Researchers are now trying to understand exactly which aspects of family conflict are harmful, as well as whether genetics has an impact. For example, according to Big Five personality research, genes make some people less agreeable and more neurotic than others. Their children may inherit those genes. Thus, if a child in a conflict-filled family has problems, the root cause could be vulnerability because of genes for neuroticism, not just the conflict.

The impact of genes on children's reaction to conflict was explored in a longitudinal study of 867 twin pairs in Sweden, all married with an adolescent child. Genetics as well as conflict could be studied, since 388 of the pairs were monozygotic and 479 were dizygotic. Each adolescent was compared to his or her cousin, the child of one parent's twin (Schermerhorn et al., 2011). The study had data from 5,202 individuals, one-third of them adult twins, one-third of them spouses of twins, and one-third of them adolescents. Conflict was assessed with a well-known questionnaire completed by all participants that included items such as, "We fight a lot in our family." The researchers found that although genes had some effect, conflict itself was the main influence on the child's well-being.

SUMMING UP

Parents influence child development. For school-age children, families serve five crucial functions: to supply basic necessities, to encourage learning, to develop self-respect, to nurture friendships, and to provide harmony and stability. Low income and family conflict interfere with these functions, no matter what the family structure.

The nuclear, two-parent family is the most common, but many families are headed by a single parent (including more than one-fourth of all families of school-age children in the United States). Families headed by two biological parents tend to provide more income, stability, and adult attention, all of which benefit children. Families that are extended, grandparent, one-parent, stepparent, same-sex parents, or adoptive sometimes raise successful children, although each type has vulnerabilities. No structure inevitably harms children, and none (even headed by married biological parents) guarantee optimal function. ■

>> The Peer Group

Peers become increasingly important in middle childhood. Younger children learn from their friends, but egocentrism buffers them from rejection. School-age children, in contrast, are painfully aware of their classmates' opinions, judgments, and accomplishments. Social comparison is one consequence of concrete operational thought.

The Culture of Children

Peer relationships, unlike adult–child relationships, involve partners who negotiate, compromise, share, and defend themselves as equals. Consequently, children learn social lessons from one another that grown-ups cannot teach them. Adults sometimes command obedience, sometimes are subservient, but they are always much older and bigger, with the values and experiences of their own cohort, not the child's.

Child culture includes the particular rules and behaviors that are passed down to younger children from slightly older ones; it includes not only fashions and gestures but also values and rituals. Jump-rope rhymes, insults, and superstitions are often part of the peer culture. Even nursery games echo child culture. For instance, "Ring around the rosy/Pocketful of posy/Ashes, ashes/We all fall down," originated with children coping with death (Kastenbaum, 2006). (*Rosy* is short for *rosary*.)

Throughout the world, the child culture encourages independence from adults. Classmates pity those (especially boys) whose parents kiss them ("mama's boy"), tease children who please the teachers ("teacher's pet," "suckup"), and despise those who betray children to adults ("tattletale," "grasser," "snitch," "rat"). Keeping secrets is part of the culture of children, even as parents want to know the details of their children's lives (Gillis, 2008). A clash may develop. For instance, many children reject clothes that parents buy as too loose, too tight, too long, too short, or wrong in color, style, brand, or some other aspect that adults do not notice.

The culture of children is not always benign. For example, because children seek to communicate with their peers, parents proudly note how quickly their children come to speak a second language, but, for the same reason, parents are distressed when their children spout their peers' curses, accents, and slang. Seeking independence from parents, children find friends who defy authority (J. Snyder et al., 2005), sometimes harmlessly (passing a note during class), sometimes not (shoplifting, cigarette smoking).

Attitudes are affected by friends. Remember Yolanda and Paul (Chapter 12)? Their friends guided their lives.

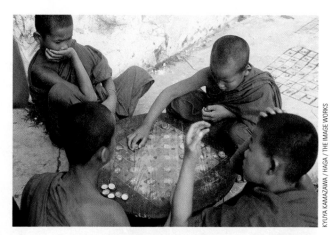

KYUYA KAMAZAWA / HAGA / THE IMAGE WORKS

The Rules of the Game These young monks in Myanmar (formerly Burma) are playing a board game that adults also play, but the children have some of their own refinements of the general rules. Children's peer groups often modify the norms of the dominant culture, as is evident in everything from superstitions to stickball.

child culture The particular habits, styles, and values that reflect the set of rules and rituals that characterize children as distinct from adult society.

How to Play Boys teach each other the rituals and rules of engagement. The bigger boy shown here could hurt the smaller one, but he won't; their culture forbids it in such situations.

GETTY IMAGES / BLEND IMAGES

Yolanda:

There's one friend . . . she's always been with me, in bad or good things. . . . She's always telling me, "Keep on going and your dreams are gonna come true."

Paul:

I think right now about going Christian, right? Just going Christian, trying to do good, you know? Stay away from drugs, everything. And every time it seems like I think about that, I think about the homeboys. And it's a trip because a lot of the homeboys are my family, too, you know?

[quoted in Nieto, 2000, pp. 220, 149]

Yolanda went to college; Paul went to jail.

Friendship and Social Acceptance

Children want to be liked; they learn faster as well as feel happier when they have friends. Indeed, if they had to choose between being friendless but popular (looked up to by many peers) or having close friends but being unpopular (ignored by peers), most would choose to have friends. This is particularly true in the first years of primary school, whereas in early adolescence popularity is sometimes the priority (LaFontana & Cillessen, 2010).

Friendships become more intense and intimate as social cognition and effortful control advance. Six-year-olds are usually friends with anyone of the same sex and age who is willing to play with them cooperatively. Comparatively, 10-year-olds demand more of their friends, change friends less often, become more upset when a friendship breaks up, and find it harder to make new friends. Gender differences persist in activities (girls converse more, whereas boys play more active games), but both boys and girls want best friends. Having no close friend at age 11 predicts depression at age 13 (Brendgen et al., 2010).

Most children learn during middle childhood how to be a good friend. For example, when fifth-graders were asked how they would react if other children teased their friend, almost all said they would ask their friend to do something fun with them and would reassure the friend that "things like that happen to everyone" (Rose & Asher, 2004).

Friends and Culture Like children everywhere, these children—two 7-year-olds and one 10-year-old, of the Surma people in southern Ethiopia—model their appearance after that of slightly older children, in this case adolescents who apply elaborate body paint for courtship and stick-fighting rituals.

Observation Quiz Are they boys or girls? (see answer, page 398)

CAROL BECKWITH & ANGELA FISHER / HAGA / THE IMAGE WORKS

Popular and Unpopular Children

It seems universally true that children seek close friends, yet it also is true that culture and cohort affect what makes a child well liked or not. In North American culture, shy children are not popular, but in 1990 in Shanghai, shy children were respected and often popular (X. Chen et al., 1992).

That is a cultural difference, but a cohort difference occurred over 12 years in Shanghai. As assertiveness became more valued in Chinese culture, a survey from the same schools found that shy children were less popular than their shy predecessors had been (X. Chen et al., 2005). A third study found that, in rural China, shyness was still valued and predicted adult adjustment (X. Chen et al., 2009). Obviously, cohort and context matter.

At least in the United States, over the years of middle childhood, two types of popular children and three types of unpopular children become apparent. Throughout childhood, children who are "kind, trustworthy, cooperative" are well liked. The second type of popular children appear around fifth grade, when children who are "athletic, cool, dominant, arrogant, and . . . aggressive" are sometimes popular (Cillessen & Mayeux, 2004a, p. 147; Rodkin & Roisman, 2010).

As for the three types of unpopular children, some are *neglected,* not rejected; ignored, but not shunned. The neglected child does not enjoy school but is psychologically unharmed, especially if the child has a supportive family and outstanding talent (in music or the arts, say) (Sandstrom & Zakriski, 2004).

The other two types of unpopular children are at increased risk of depression and uncontrolled anger over the years of middle childhood. One type is **aggressive-rejected,** disliked because they are antagonistic and confrontational; the other type is **withdrawn-rejected,** disliked because they are timid and anxious. Children of these two types have much in common, often misinterpreting social situations, lacking emotional regulation, and experiencing mistreatment at home. They may become bullies and victims, a topic now discussed.

Bullies and Victims

From a developmental perspective, childhood bullying is connected to many other aspects of aggression, including maltreatment and delinquency (discussed in Chapters 8, 11, and 16, respectively). Here we focus on bullies and victims in school.

Bullying is defined as repeated, systematic attacks intended to harm those who are unable or unlikely to defend themselves. It occurs in every nation, in every community, and in every kind of school (religious or secular, public or private, progressive or traditional, large or small). Although adults are often unaware of it, children recognize it as common. As one girl said, "There's a little bit of bully in everyone" (Guerra et al., 2011, p. 303).

Bullying may be of four types:

- *Physical* (hitting, pinching, or kicking)
- *Verbal* (teasing, taunting, or name-calling)
- *Relational* (destroying peer acceptance)
- *Cyberbullying* (using electronic means to harm another)

The first three are common in primary school and begin even earlier, in preschool. Cyberbullying is a particularly devastating form of relational bullying, more common in secondary school and college than in primary school, and thus it is discussed in Chapter 15.

A key word in the definition of bullying is *repeated.* Almost everyone experiences an isolated attack or is called a derogatory name at some point in middle childhood. Victims of bullying, however, endure shameful experiences again and again—being forced to hand over lunch money, laugh at insults, drink milk mixed with detergent, and so on—with no one defending them. Victims tend to be "cautious, sensitive, quiet . . . lonely and abandoned at school. As a rule, they do not have a single good friend in their class" (Olweus et al., 1999, p. 15). Although it is often thought that victims are particularly ugly or odd, this is not usually the case. Victims are chosen because of their emotional vulnerability and social isolation, not their appearance, although sometimes a distinctive feature becomes the focus of teasing.

As one boy said,

> You can get bullied because you are weak or annoying or because you are different. Kids with big ears get bullied. Dorks get bullied. You can also get bullied because you think too much of yourself and try to show off. Teacher's pet gets bullied. If you say the right answer too many times in class you can get bullied. There are lots of popular groups who bully each other and other groups, but you can get bullied within your group too. If you do not want to get bullied, you have to stay under the radar, but then you might feel sad because no one pays attention to you.

[quoted in Guerra et al., 2011, p. 306]

Pity the Teacher The culture of children encourages pranks, jokes, and the defiance of authorities at school. At the same time, as social cognition develops, many children secretly feel empathy for their teachers.

aggressive-rejected Rejected by peers because of antagonistic, confrontational behavior.

withdrawn-rejected Rejected by peers because of timid, withdrawn, and anxious behavior.

bullying Repeated, systematic efforts to inflict harm through physical, verbal, or social attack on a weaker person.

PETER TITMUSS / ALAMY

 HENRY KING / GETTY IMAGES

Who Suffers More? The 12-year-old girl and the 10-year-old boy are both bullying younger children, but their attacks differ. Some developmentalists think a verbal assault is more painful than a physical one because it lingers for years.

bully-victim Someone who attacks others and who is attacked as well. (Also called *provocative victims* because they do things that elicit bullying.)

>> **Answer to Observation Quiz** (from page 396) They are all girls. Boys would not be likely to stand so close together. Also, the two 7-year-olds have decorated their soon-to-be budding breasts.

Remember the three types of unpopular children? Neglected children are not victimized, they are ignored, "under the radar." If their family relationships are good, they suffer less from bullying—true for all children who are teased, but particularly true for neglected children (Bowes et al., 2010).

Rejected victims, however, often have trouble at home as well. Most of them are withdrawn-rejected, but some are aggressive-rejected. The latter are **bully-victims** (or *provocative victims*) (Unnever, 2005), "the most strongly disliked members of the peer group," with neither friends nor sympathizers (Sandstrom & Zakriski, 2004, p. 110). One study found that teachers tend to mistreat bully-victims, making their problems worse (Khoury-Kassabri, 2009). Bully-victims suffer the most, no matter what form the bullying takes (Dukes et al., 2009).

Unlike bully-victims, most bullies are *not* rejected. Although some have low self-esteem, others are proud; they bully because they are pleased with themselves and they find bullying cool (Guerra et al., 2011). Often, bullies have a few admiring friends. They may be socially perceptive, in that they pick their victims carefully, seeking out those who are already rejected by most classmates (Veenstra et al., 2010). Over the years of middle childhood, they become skilled at avoiding adult awareness, attacking victims who will not resist effectively. This seems to be as true for relational bullying as for physical and verbal bullying.

Boys bully more than girls, and during childhood most bullies pick on their own sex. Boy bullies are often big; they target smaller, weaker boys. Girl bullies are often sharp-tongued; they harass shyer, more soft-spoken girls. Boys tend to use force (physical aggression), while girls tend to mock, ridicule, or spread rumors (verbal aggression). Both sexes may also use relational aggression, especially cyberbullying, which becomes more common with age. Interestingly, in middle childhood, the gender divide extends to bullying: Girls who bully boys are rejected whereas younger boys can sometimes be accepted by other boys if they bully girls, but this does not hold as puberty begins (about age 11), when boys who bully girls are no longer admired (Veenstra et al., 2010).

Causes and Consequences of Bullying

Bullying may originate with a genetic predisposition or a brain abnormality, but when a toddler is aggressive, parents, teachers, and peers usually teach that child to rein in those impulses and develop emotional regulation and effortful control. However, the opposite may occur (Granic & Patterson, 2006). Young children become more aggressive if their families create insecure attachment, provide a stressful home life, are ineffective at discipline, or include hostile siblings.

Peers are influential as well. Some peer groups approve of relational bullying, and children in those groups entertain their classmates as they mock and insult each other (N. E. Werner & Hill, 2010). On the other hand, when students themselves disapprove of bullying, its incidence is reduced (Guerra & Williams, 2010).

The consequences of bullying can echo for years. Many victims become depressed; many bullies become increasingly cruel. However, this is not inevitable. Both bullies and victims can be identified in first grade and "need active guidance and remediation" before their behavior patterns become truly destructive (Leadbeater & Hoglund, 2009, p. 857). Unless bullies are deterred, they and their victims risk impaired social understanding, lower school achievement, and relationship difficulties (Ma et al., 2009; Pepler et al., 2004). Bystanders suffer, too, as do adults when bullies grow up (Monks & Coyne, 2011; Nishina & Juvonen, 2005; Rivers et al., 2009).

Can Bullying Be Stopped?

Most victimized children find ways to halt ongoing bullying—by ignoring, retaliating, defusing, or avoiding. A study of older children who were bullied in one year but not in the next indicated that finding new friends was crucial (P. K. Smith et al., 2004). Friendships help individual victims, but what can be done to halt bullying altogether?

We know what does *not* work: increasing students' awareness, instituting zero tolerance for fighting, or putting troubled students together in a therapy group or a classroom (Baldry & Farrington, 2007; Monks, & Coyne, 2011). This last measure tends to make daily life easier for some teachers, but it increases aggression.

The school community itself needs to change as a whole—teachers and bystanders, parents and aides, bullies and victims. In fact, the entire school can either increase the rate of bullying or decrease it. For example, a Colorado study of children with high self-esteem found that, when the overall school climate encouraged learning and cooperation, children with high self-esteem were unlikely to be bullies; yet when the school climate was hostile, those with high self-esteem were often bullies (Gendron et al., 2011).

Peers are crucial: If they simply notice bullying, becoming aware without doing anything, that is no help. However, if they empathize with victims and refuse to admire bullies, that reduces classroom aggression (Salmivalli, 2010). Dan Olweus, a pioneer in antibullying efforts, advocates involving everyone—teachers, parents, and peers—to reduce bullying (Olweus, 1993). Efforts to change the entire school are credited with recent successful efforts to decrease bullying in 29 schools in England (e.g., Cross et al., 2011), throughout Norway, in Finland (Kärnä et al., 2011), and often in the United States (Allen, 2010; Limber, 2011). A review of all research on successful ways to halt bullying (Berger, 2007) finds the following:

- Everyone in the school must change, not just the identified bullies.
- Intervention is more effective in the earlier grades.
- Evaluation is critical: Programs that appear to be good might actually be harmful.

Only an Act? Fifth-grade boys play passengers on a bus as they act out a scene in which three of them reject a fourth (at right). They are participating in a curriculum designed to increase empathy and reduce bullying.

Especially for Parents of an Accused Bully Another parent has told you that your child is a bully. Your child denies it and explains that the other child doesn't mind being teased. (see response, page 402)

This final point merits special emphasis. Longitudinal research on whole-school efforts finds that some programs make a difference and some do not, with variations depending on the age of the children and the indicators (peer report of bullying or victimization, teacher report of incidents reported, and so on). Objective follow-up efforts suggest that bullying can be reduced but not eliminated.

SUMMING UP

School-age children develop their own culture, with customs that encourage them to be loyal to one another. All 6- to 11-year-olds want and need social acceptance and close, mutual friendships to protect against loneliness and depression. Friendship is more valued than popularity; being rejected is painful.

Most children experience occasional peer rejection. However, some children are victims, repeatedly rejected and friendless, experiencing physical, verbal, or relational bullying. Bullies are sometimes admired in middle childhood and early adolescence, but they and their victims may suffer in adulthood because of behavior patterns established in childhood. Some efforts to reduce bullying succeed and some do not; a whole-school approach seems best, with the bystanders crucial to establishing an anti-bullying culture.

>> Children's Moral Values

Although the origins of morality are debatable (see Chapter 10), there is no doubt that middle childhood is prime time for moral development. Ages 7 to 11 are:

> years of eager, lively searching on the part of children . . . as they try to understand things, to figure them out, but also to weigh the rights and wrongs. . . This is the time for growth of the moral imagination, fueled constantly by the willingness, the eagerness of children to put themselves in the shoes of others.
>
> *[Coles, 1997, p. 99]*

That optimistic assessment seems validated by detailed research. In middle childhood, children are quite capable of making moral judgments, differentiating universal principles from mere conventional norms (Turiel, 2008). Empirical studies show that throughout middle childhood, children readily suggest moral arguments to distinguish right from wrong (Killen, 2007).

Many forces drive children's growing interest in moral issues. Three of them are (1) peer culture, (2) personal experience, and (3) empathy. As already explained, part of the culture of children involves moral values, such as being loyal to friends and protecting children from adults. A child's personal experiences also matter. For example, children in multiethnic schools are better able to argue against prejudice using moral values than are children who attend racially and ethnically homogeneous schools (Killen et al., 2006). Finally, empathy becomes stronger in middle childhood because children are more aware of one another.

This increasing perception can backfire, however. One example was just described: Bullies become adept at picking victims who are rejected by people the bullies admire (Veenstra et al., 2010). However, the increase in empathy during middle childhood at least allows the possibility of moral judgment that notices, and defends, children who are unfairly rejected.

Obviously, moral advances are not automatic. Children who are slow to develop theory of mind—which, as you remember from Chapter 9, is affected by family and culture—are also slow to develop empathy (Caravita et al., 2010). The authors of a study of 7-year-olds "conclude that moral *competence* may be a universal

Empathy Building Look at their facial expressions, not just their matching hats and gloves. For this 9-year-old sister and 7-year-old brother, moral development is apparent. This is not necessarily the case for all siblings, however; imagine the same behavior but with angry expressions.

JOHN ANTHONY RIZZO / UPPERCUT IMAGES / PHOTOLIBRARY

human characteristic, but that it takes a situation with specific demand characteristics to translate this competence into actual prosocial performance" (van IJzendoorn et al., 2010, p. 1). In other words, school-age children can think and act morally, but they do not always do so.

Moral Reasoning

Much of the developmental research on children's moral thinking began with Piaget's descriptions of the rules used by children as they play (Piaget, 1932/ 1997). This led to Lawrence Kohlberg's description of cognitive stages of morality (Kohlberg, 1963).

Kohlberg's Levels of Moral Thought

Kohlberg described three levels of moral reasoning and two stages at each level (see Table 13.3), with parallels to Piaget's stages of cognition.

- **Preconventional moral reasoning** is similar to preoperational thought in that it is egocentric, with children seeking their personal pleasure or avoiding pain more than focusing on social concerns.

- **Conventional moral reasoning** parallels concrete operational thought in that it relates to current, observable practices: Children watch what their parents, teachers, and friends do, and try to follow suit.

- **Postconventional moral reasoning** is similar to formal operational thought because it uses logic and abstractions, going beyond what is concretely observed in a particular society, willing to question "what is" in order to decide "what should be."

preconventional moral reasoning
Kohlberg's first level of moral reasoning, emphasizing rewards and punishments.

conventional moral reasoning Kohlberg's second level of moral reasoning, emphasizing social rules.

postconventional moral reasoning
Kohlberg's third level of moral reasoning, emphasizing moral principles.

According to Kohlberg, intellectual maturation advances moral thinking. During middle childhood, children's answers shift from being primarily preconventional to being more conventional: Concrete thought and peer experiences help children move past the first two stages (level I) to the next two (level II). Postconventional reasoning is not usually present until adolescence or adulthood.

Kohlberg posed moral dilemmas to school-age boys (and eventually girls, teenagers, and adults). The story of a poor man named Heinz, whose wife was dying, serves as an example. A local druggist had the only cure for the wife's illness, a drug that Heinz could not pay for and that sold for 10 times what it cost to make.

> Heinz went to everyone he knew to borrow the money, but he could only get together about half of what it cost. He told the druggist that his wife was dying and asked him to sell it cheaper or let him pay later. But the druggist said "no." The husband got desperate and broke into the man's store to steal the drug for his wife. Should the husband have done that? Why?
>
> *[Kohlberg, 1963, p. 19]*

The crucial element in Kohlberg's scheme is not the answer given but the *reasons* for it. For instance, someone might say that the husband should steal the drug because he needs his wife to care for him (preconventional), or because people will blame him if he lets his wife die (conventional), or because trying to save her life is more important than obeying the law (postconventional).

Criticisms of Kohlberg

Kohlberg has been criticized for not appreciating cultural or gender differences. His original participants were all boys, which may have led him to discount female values of nurturance and relationships (Gilligan, 1982). Kohlberg seemed to value

TABLE 13.3	Kohlberg's Three Levels and Six Stages of Moral Reasoning

Level I: Preconventional Moral Reasoning

The goal is to get rewards and avoid punishments; this is a self-centered level.

- *Stage one: Might makes right* (a punishment and obedience orientation). The most important value is to maintain the appearance of obedience to authority, avoiding punishment while still advancing self-interest. Don't get caught!

- *Stage two: Look out for number one* (an instrumental and relativist orientation). Each person tries to take care of his or her own needs. The reason to be nice to other people is so that they will be nice to you.

Level II: Conventional Moral Reasoning

Emphasis is placed on social rules; this is a community-centered level.

- *Stage three: "Good girl" and "nice boy."* Proper behavior is behavior that pleases other people. Social approval is more important than any specific reward.

- *Stage four: "Law and order."* Proper behavior means being a dutiful citizen and obeying the laws set down by society, even when no police are nearby.

Level III: Postconventional Moral Reasoning

Emphasis is placed on moral principles; this level is centered on ideals.

- *Stage five: Social contract.* Obey social rules because they benefit everyone and are established by mutual agreement. If the rules become destructive or if one party doesn't live up to the agreement, the contract is no longer binding. Under some circumstances, disobeying the law is moral.

- *Stage six: Universal ethical principles.* General, universally valid principles, not individual situations (level I) or community practices (level II), determine right and wrong. Ethical values (such as "life is sacred") are established by individual reflection and may contradict egocentric (level I) or social and community (level II) values.

abstract principles more than individual needs, but caring for people may be no less moral than impartial justice (Sherblom, 2008).

In one respect, however, Kohlberg was undeniably correct. Children use their intellectual abilities to justify their moral actions. This was shown in an experiment in which trios of children aged 8 to 18 had to decide how to divide a sum of money with another trio of children. Some groups chose to share equally; other groups were more selfish. There were no age differences in the actual decisions, but there were age differences in the arguments voiced. Older children suggested more complex rationalizations for their choices, both selfish and altruistic (Gummerum et al., 2008).

What Children Value

Many lines of research have shown that children develop their own morality, guided by peers, parents, and culture (Turiel, 2006). Some prosocial values are evident in early childhood. Among these are caring for close family members, cooperating with other children, and not hurting anyone intentionally (Eisenberg et al., 2006). Even very young children think stealing is wrong.

As children become more aware of themselves and others in middle childhood, they realize that one person's values may conflict with another's. Concrete operational cognition, which gives children the ability to observe and to use logic, propels them to think about morality and to try to behave ethically (Turiel, 2006). As part of growing up, children become conscious of immorality in their peers (Abrams et al., 2008) and, later, in their parents, themselves, and their culture.

Adults Versus Peers

When child culture conflicts with adult morality, children often align themselves with peers. A child might lie to protect a friend, for instance. On a broader level, one study found that 98 percent of a group of children believed that no child should be excluded from a sports team because of gender or race, even when adult society was less tolerant. Some of the same children, however, justified excluding another child from a friendship circle (Killen et al., 2002).

The conflict between the morality of children and that of adults is evident in the value that children place on education. Adults usually prize school, but children may encourage one another to play hooky, cheat on tests, or drop out. Peer morals sometimes outweigh adult values. Consider another comment from Paul:

> I try not to get influenced too much, pulled into what I don't want to be into. But mostly, it's hard. You don't want people to be saying you're stupid. "Why do you want to go to school and get a job? . . . Drop out."
>
> [quoted in Nieto, 2000, p. 252]

Not surprisingly, Paul later left school.

It is apparent that three common values among 6- to 11-year-olds are the following:

>> Response for Parents of an Accused Bully (from page 400) The future is ominous if the charges are true. Your child's denial is a sign that there is a problem. (An innocent child would be worried about the misperception instead of categorically denying that any problem exists.) You might ask the teacher what the school is doing about bullying. Family counseling might help. Because bullies often have friends who egg them on, you may need to monitor your child's friendships and perhaps befriend the victim. Talk matters over with your child. Ignoring the situation might lead to heartache later on.

- Protect your friends.
- Don't tell adults what is happening.
- Don't be too different from your peers.

These three values can explain both apparent boredom and overt defiance, as well as standards of dress that mystify adults (such as jeans so loose that they fall off or so tight that they impede digestion—both styles worn by my children, who grew up in different cohorts). Given what is known about middle childhood, it is no surprise that children do not echo adult morality.

Developing Moral Values

A detailed examination of the effect of peers on morality began with an update on one of Piaget's moral issues: whether punishment should seek *retribution* (hurting the transgressor) or *restitution* (restoring what was lost). Piaget believed the latter to be more advanced; he also found that between ages 8 and 10, children progress from retribution to restitution (Piaget, 1932/1997).

To learn how this occurs, researchers arranged for 133 9-year-olds to ponder the following:

> Late one afternoon there was a boy who was playing with a ball on his own in the garden. His dad saw him playing with it and asked him not to play with it so near the house because it might break a window. The boy didn't really listen to his dad, and carried on playing near the house. Then suddenly, the ball bounced up high and broke the window in the boy's room. His dad heard the noise and came to see what had happened. The father wonders what would be the fairest way to punish the boy. He thinks of two punishments. The first is to say: "Now, you didn't do as I asked. You will have to pay for the window to be mended, and I am going to take the money from your pocket money." The second is to say: "Now, you didn't do as I asked. As a punishment you have to go to your room and stay there for the rest of the evening." Which of these punishments do you think is the fairest?
>
> *[Leman & Björnberg, 2010, p. 962]*

The children were split equally in their answers. Then 48 of them were paired with a child who answered the other way, and each pair was asked to discuss the broken window event and try to reach agreement on the fairest punishment. As a control, the rest of the children were not paired and did not discuss the dilemma. Six pairs were boy–boy, six were boy–girl with the boy favoring restitution, six were boy–girl with the girl favoring restitution, and six were girl–girl. The conversations typically took only five minutes, and the retribution side was more often chosen—which Piaget would consider a moral backslide. However, all the children were queried again, two weeks and eight weeks later, and their responses changed toward the more advanced, restitution thinking (see Figure 13.2). This was particularly true for the children who engaged in conversation.

The main conclusion from this study was that children's "conversation on a topic may stimulate a process of individual reflection that triggers developmental advances" (Leman & Björnberg, 2010, p. 969). Parents and teachers take note: Raising moral issues, and letting children talk about them, may advance morality—not immediately, but soon.

The Morality of Child Labor

Now we are ready to reexamine the tire-changing boy from the opening vignette of this chapter. Child labor is deemed immoral by the United Nations, but that international body has had difficulty educating children about their rights and convincing nations to enforce child labor standards (Print et al., 2008). Some child labor

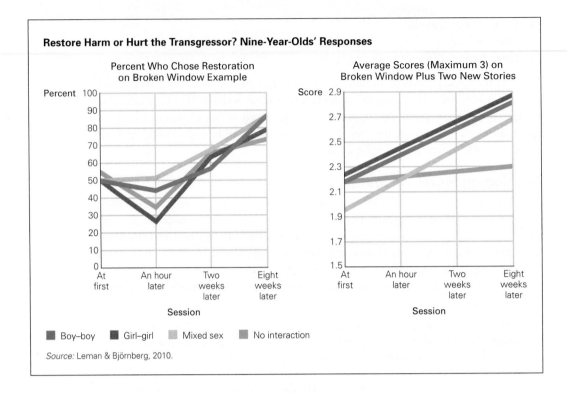

Restore Harm or Hurt the Transgressor? Nine-Year-Olds' Responses

Percent Who Chose Restoration on Broken Window Example

Average Scores (Maximum 3) on Broken Window Plus Two New Stories

■ Boy–boy   ■ Girl–girl   ■ Mixed sex   ■ No interaction

Source: Leman & Björnberg, 2010.

FIGURE 13.2

Benefits of Time and Talking The graph on the left shows that most children, immediately after their initial punitive response, became even more likely to seek punishment rather than to repair damage. However, after some time and reflection, they affirmed the response Piaget would consider more mature. The graph on the right indicates that children who had talked about the broken window example moved toward restorative justice even in examples they had not heard before, which was not true for those who had not talked about the first story.

is clearly hazardous, such as working in mines with cancer-causing pollutants or becoming sex workers with no opportunity for escape. Even for these examples, nations do not always protect children as they should (Diallo et al., 2010).

However, some work done by children is harder to judge. Morality is quite variable, not only among children but also among cultures. Thus, to decide whether that young boy should be helping his father would require finding out whether his life situation satisfies the five needs that are thought to be universal during middle childhood. Are his material needs met, is he learning in school, does he have friends, is he proud of himself, is his work keeping his family harmonious and stable? If the answer to all these questions is yes, then Tiffany's understandable shock, or the father's acceptance of child labor, may be more reflective of their respective cultures than of the boy's condition.

The moral lesson of this chapter, then, is that the psychosocial development of children needs to be carefully assessed, child by child. For example, married-couple families are usually good for children but not always; friends are helpful in protecting victims, but they may also encourage bullies; self-esteem is a positive attribute, but it may become too high. As with all of development, individual children, families, and cultures vary, and that must be taken into account before conclusions are drawn.

SUMMING UP

Moral issues are of great interest to school-age children, who are affected by their cultures, by their parents, and particularly by their peers. Kohlberg's stages of moral thought parallel Piaget's stages of development, suggesting that the highest level of morality goes beyond the norms of any particular nation. Children develop moral standards that they try to follow, although these may differ from adult morals. Maturation, reflection, and discussion all foster moral development.

SUMMARY

The Nature of the Child

1. All theories of development acknowledge that school-age children become more independent and capable in many ways. Erikson emphasized industry, when children busily strive to master various tasks. If they are unable to do so, they feel inferior. Freud described latency, when psychosexual needs are quiet.

2. Children develop their self-concept during these years, basing it on a more realistic assessment of their competence than they had in earlier years. High self-esteem may reduce effort and is not valued in every culture; low self-esteem is also harmful.

3. Both daily hassles and major stresses take a toll on children, with accumulated stresses more likely to impair development than any single event on its own. The child's interpretation of the situation and the availability of supportive adults and peers aid resilience.

Families and Children

4. Families influence children in many ways, as do genes and peers. Although most siblings share a childhood home and parents, each sibling experiences different (nonshared) circumstances within that family.

5. The five functions of a supportive family are to satisfy children's physical needs; to encourage learning; to support friendships; to protect self-respect; and to provide a safe, stable, and harmonious home.

6. The most common family structure worldwide is the nuclear family, usually with other relatives nearby and supportive. Other two-parent families include adoptive, same-sex, grandparent, and stepfamilies, each of which sometimes functions well for children. However, each also has vulnerabilities.

7. Generally, it seems better for children to live with two parents rather than one because a parental alliance can support their development. Single-parent families have higher rates of changes—for example, in where they live and who belongs to the family—and children are stressed by new circumstances and conditions, especially in middle childhood.

8. Income affects family function. Poor children are at greater risk for emotional and behavioral problems because the stresses that often accompany poverty hinder effective parenting. Instability and conflict are harmful.

The Peer Group

9. Peers are crucial for social development during middle childhood. Each cohort of children has a culture, passed down from slightly older children. Close friends are particularly helpful during these years.

10. Popular children may be cooperative and easy to get along with or may be competitive and aggressive. Much depends on the age and culture of the children.

11. Rejected children may be neglected, aggressive, or withdrawn. Aggressive and withdrawn children have difficulty with social cognition; their interpretation of the normal give-and-take of childhood is impaired.

12. Bullying is common among school-age children and has long-term consequences for both bullies and victims. Bullies themselves may be admired, which makes their behavior more difficult to stop. Overall, a multifaceted, long-term, whole-school approach, with parents, teachers, and bystanders working together, seems the best way to halt bullying.

Children's Moral Values

13. School-age children are very interested in differentiating right from wrong. Kohlberg described three levels of moral reasoning, each related to cognitive maturity. Although he has been criticized for focusing too much on abstractions and for ignoring cultural and gender differences in morality, it does seem that children advance in moral thinking as they mature.

14. When values conflict, children often choose loyalty to peers over adult standards of behavior. When children discuss moral issues with other children, they develop more thoughtful answers to moral questions.

KEY TERMS

industry versus inferiority (p. 378)
latency (p. 379)
effortful control (p. 380)
resilience (p. 380)
family structure (p. 385)

family function (p. 385)
nuclear family (p. 387)
single-parent family (p. 387)
extended family (p. 387)
polygamous family (p. 387)
child culture (p. 395)

aggressive-rejected (p. 397)
withdrawn-rejected (p. 397)
bullying (p. 397)
bully-victim (p. 398)
preconventional moral reasoning (p. 401)

conventional moral reasoning (p. 401)
postconventional moral reasoning (p. 401)

WHAT HAVE YOU LEARNED?

The Nature of the Child

1. How do Erikson's stages for school-age children and for preschool children differ?

2. Why is social comparison particularly powerful during middle childhood?

3. Why do cultures differ in how they value pride or modesty?

4. Why and when might minor stresses be more harmful than major stresses?

5. What factors help a child become resilient?

Families and Children

6. Why does research on nonshared environments *not* prove that parents are irrelevant?

7. Which of the five family functions is most difficult for divorcing parents to fulfill?

8. What is the difference between family function and family structure?

9. What are the advantages for children of the nuclear family structure?

10. What are the advantages and disadvantages of a stepparent family?

11. Why is a safe, harmonious home particularly important during middle childhood?

12. How can single parents fulfill the five desirable family functions for children?

13. What is the evidence that school-age children benefit from continuity?

14. What are the advantages and disadvantages for children in an extended family?

The Peer Group

15. How does the disapproval of tattletales affect bullies and victims?

16. How does what children wear reflect the culture of children?

17. How is a child's popularity affected by culture and the child's age?

18. What is the difference between being a bully and being a bully-victim?

19. Who is best able to stop a bully and why—victim, teacher, another child?

Children's Moral Values

20. What is the highest stage of morality, according to Kohlberg?

21. What are the main criticisms of Kohlberg's theory of moral development?

22. How does children's conversation impact their moral reasoning?

23. Why don't children always accept the moral standards of their parents?

APPLICATIONS

1. Go someplace where school-age children congregate (such as a schoolyard, a park, or a community center) and use naturalistic observation for at least half an hour. Describe what popular, average, withdrawn, and rejected children do. Note at least one potential conflict (bullying, rough-and-tumble play, etc.). Describe the sequence and the outcome.

2. Focusing on verbal bullying, describe at least two times when someone said something hurtful to you and two times when you

said something that might have been hurtful to someone else. What are the differences between the two types of situations?

3. How would your childhood have been different if your family structure had been different, such as if you had (or had not) lived with your grandparents, if your parents had (or had not) gotten divorced, if you had (or had not) been adopted?

>> ONLINE CONNECTIONS

To accompany your textbook, you have access to a number of online resources, including quizzes for every chapter of the book, flashcards (in English and Spanish), critical thinking questions, and case studies. For access to any of these links, go to www.worthpublishers.com/bergerca9e. In addition to these free resources, you'll also find links to podcasts, video clips, diagnostic quizzing with personalized study advice, and an ebook. Some of the videos and activities available online include:

■ *Moral Reasoning.* This activity reviews Kohlberg's theory of age-related changes in moral reasoning. Was he right? You can decide as you watch footage of people solving the famous Heinz dilemma.

■ *Effects of Divorce and Remarriage on Children.* Learn three factors that affect a child's adjustment and what parents can do to avoid potential problems.

Middle Childhood

BIOSOCIAL

A Healthy Time During middle childhood, children grow more slowly than they did earlier or than they will during adolescence. Physical play is crucial for health and happiness. Prevalent physical problems, including obesity and asthma, have genetic roots and psychosocial consequences.

Brain Development Brain maturation continues, leading to faster reactions and better self-control. Which specific skills are mastered depends largely on culture, gender, and inherited ability, all of which are reflected in intelligence tests. Children have multiple intellectual abilities, most of which are not reflected in standard IQ tests.

Special Needs Many children have special learning needs. Early recognition, targeted education, and psychological support can help them, including those with bipolar and attention-deficit disorders, specific learning disabilities, and the many disorders of the autism spectrum. Whether or not children with special needs should be educated with other children, a strategy called inclusion, is especially controversial for gifted children.

COGNITIVE

Building on Theory Piaget noted that, beginning at about age 7, children attain concrete operational thought, including the ability to understand the logical principles of classification and transitive inference. Vygotsky emphasized that children become more open to learning from mentors, both adults and peers. Information-processing abilities increase, including greater memory, knowledge, control, and metacognition.

Language Children's increasing ability to understand the structures and possibilities of language enable them to extend the range of their cognitive powers and to increase vocabulary. Children master various language codes, both formal and informal, and many become fluent in more than one language..

Education International comparisons reveal marked variations in the overt and hidden curricula, as well as in learning, between one nation and another. The emphasis in the United States on higher standards increases the importance of testing, a controversial practice. The reading and math wars pit traditional education against a more holistic approach to learning. Alternate school structures, including home schooling and charter schools, are an attempt to increase learning among U.S. schoolchildren.

PSYCHOSOCIAL

The Nature of the Child Theorists agree that many school-age children develop competencies, emotional control, and attitudes to defend against stress. Some children are resilient, coping well with problems and finding support in friends, family, school, religion, and community.

Families Parents continue to influence children, especially as they exacerbate or buffer problems in school and the community. During these years, families need to meet basic needs, encourage learning, foster self-respect, nurture friendship, and—most important—provide harmony and stability. Nuclear families often provide this, but one-parent, stepparent, same-sex, or grandparent families can also function well for children. No family structure guarantees optimal functioning. Adequate income, low conflict, and family stability benefit children of all ages, particularly in middle childhood.

Peers and Morals The peer group becomes increasingly important as children become less dependent on their parents and more dependent on friends for help, loyalty, and sharing of mutual interests. Peer rejection and bullying become serious problems. Moral development, influenced by peers, advances during these years.

V

Adolescence

One observer said adolescence is like "starting turbo-charged engines with an unskilled driver" (Dahl, 2004, p. 17). Would you ride with an unskilled driver? I did. When my daughter Bethany had her learner's permit, I sought to convey confidence. Not until a terrified "Mom! Help!" did I grab the wheel to avoid hitting a subway kiosk. I should have intervened sooner, but it is hard to know at what age, and in what situations, grown daughters need their mothers. Bethany was an adolescent, neither child nor adult, sometimes wanting independence, sometimes not.

A century ago, puberty began at age 15 or so. Soon after that, most girls married and most boys found work. It is said that *adolescence begins with biology and ends with culture.* If so, then a hundred years ago adolescence lasted a few months; now it lasts a decade or more. Currently, puberty starts earlier and adulthood later, with adult responsibilities often postponed until after the next stage of development, emerging adulthood.

In the next three chapters (covering ages 11 to 18), we begin with biology (this chapter) and move toward culture (in chapter 16). Understanding adolescence is more than an abstract challenge: Those turbo-charged engines need skilled guidance. Get ready to grab the wheel.

Adolescence: Biosocial Development

WHAT WILL YOU KNOW?

1. Since puberty normally begins anytime from age 8 to 14, is there any way to predict the onset for a particular child?

2. Why do some teenagers starve themselves and others overeat?

3. Since adolescent sexual impulses are powerful and inevitable, why is there so much variation in rates of teen pregnancy, child sexual abuse, and STIs?

I overheard a conversation among three teenagers, including my daughter Rachel, all past their awkward years, now becoming beautiful. They were discussing the imperfections of their bodies. One spoke of her fat stomach (what stomach? I could not see it), another of her long neck (hidden by her silky, shoulder-length hair). Rachel complained not only about her bent finger but also about her feet!

The reality that children grow into men and women is no shock to any adult. But for teenagers, heightened self-awareness often triggers surprise or even horror, joy or despair. Like these three, adolescents pay attention to details of their growth. This chapter describes some of those biosocial details of growing bodies and emerging sexuality. It all begins with hormones, but other invisible changes may be even more potent—such as the timing of neurological maturation that does not yet allow adolescents to realize that their minor imperfections are insignificant.

>> Puberty Begins

Puberty refers to the years of rapid physical growth and sexual maturation that end childhood, producing a person of adult size, shape, and sexuality. The forces of puberty are unleashed by a cascade of hormones that produce external growth and internal changes, including heightened emotions and sexual desires. This process normally starts between ages 8 and 14 and follows the sequence outlined in At About This Time. Most physical growth and maturation ends about four years after the first signs appear, although some individuals add height, weight, and muscle until age 20 or so.

For girls, the observable changes of puberty usually begin with nipple growth. Soon a few pubic hairs are visible, then peak growth spurt, widening of the hips, the first menstrual period (**menarche**), full pubic-hair pattern, and breast maturation (Susman et al., 2010). The average age of menarche among normal-weight girls is about 12 years, 8 months (Rosenfield et al., 2009), although variation in timing is quite normal.

For boys, the usual sequence is growth of the testes, initial pubic-hair growth, growth of the penis, first ejaculation of seminal fluid (**spermarche**), appearance of facial hair, peak growth spurt, deepening of the voice, and final pubic-hair growth (Biro et al., 2001; Herman-Giddens et al., 2001; Susman et al., 2010). The typical age of spermarche is just under 13 years, close to the age for menarche.

puberty The time between the first onrush of hormones and full adult physical development. Puberty usually lasts three to five years. Many more years are required to achieve psychosocial maturity.

menarche A girl's first menstrual period, signaling that she has begun ovulation. Pregnancy is biologically possible, but ovulation and menstruation are often irregular for years after menarche.

spermarche A boy's first ejaculation of sperm. Erections can occur as early as infancy, but ejaculation signals sperm production. Spermarche may occur during sleep (in a "wet dream") or via direct stimulation.

AT ABOUT THIS TIME		
The Sequence of Puberty		
Girls	Approximate Average Age*	Boys
Ovaries increase production of estrogen and progesterone**	9	
Uterus and vagina begin to grow larger	9½	Testes increase production of testosterone**
Breast "bud" stage	10	Testes and scrotum grow larger
Pubic hair begins to appear; weight spurt begins	11	
Peak height spurt	11½	Pubic hair begins to appear
Peak muscle and organ growth (also, hips become noticeably wider)	12	Penis growth begins
Menarche (first menstrual period)	12½	Spermarche (first ejaculation); weight spurt begins
First ovulation	13	Peak height spurt
Voice lowers	14	Peak muscle and organ growth (also, shoulders become noticeably broader)
Final pubic-hair pattern	15	Voice lowers; visible facial hair
Full breast growth	16	
	18	Final pubic-hair pattern

*Average ages are rough approximations, with many perfectly normal, healthy adolescents as much as three years ahead of or behind these ages.

**Estrogens and testosterone influence sexual characteristics, including reproduction. Charted here are the increases produced by the gonads (sex glands). The ovaries produce estrogens and the testes produce androgens, especially testosterone. Adrenal glands produce some of both kinds of hormones (not shown).

hormone An organic chemical substance that is produced by one body tissue and conveyed via the bloodstream to another to affect some physiological function.

pituitary A gland in the brain that responds to a signal from the hypothalamus by producing many hormones, including those that regulate growth and that control other glands, among them the adrenal and sex glands.

adrenal glands Two glands, located above the kidneys, that produce hormones (including the "stress hormones" epinephrine [adrenaline] and norepinephrine).

HPA (hypothalamus–pituitary–adrenal) axis A sequence of hormone production originating in the hypothalamus and moving to the pituitary and then to the adrenal glands.

Unseen Beginnings

Just described are the visible changes of puberty, but the entire process begins with an invisible event, a marked hormonal increase. **Hormones** are body chemicals that regulate hunger, sleep, moods, stress, sexual desire, immunity, reproduction, and many other bodily reactions, including puberty. Hormones start the process: Menarche or spermarche is "a very late event," long after hormonal beginnings (J. L. Cameron, 2004, p. 116). Throughout adolescence, hormone levels correlate with physiological changes and self-reported developments (Shirtcliff et al., 2009).

You learned in Chapter 8 that the production of many hormones is regulated deep within the brain, where biochemical signals from the hypothalamus signal another brain structure, the **pituitary,** to go into action. The pituitary produces hormones that stimulate the **adrenal glands,** located above the kidneys at either side of the lower back. The adrenal glands produce more hormones.

Many hormones that regulate puberty follow this route, known as the **HPA (hypothalamus–pituitary–adrenal) axis** (see Figure 14.1). Abnormalities of the HPA axis in adolescence are associated with eating disorders, anxiety, and

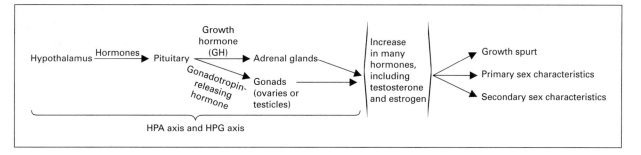

FIGURE 14.1

Biological Sequence of Puberty Puberty begins with a hormonal signal from the hypothalamus to the pituitary gland. The pituitary, in turn, signals the adrenal glands and the ovaries or testes to produce more of their hormones.

depression. These conditions and many other types of psychopathology, appearing for the first time or worsening at puberty, are connected to hormones (Dahl & Gunnar, 2009). Indeed, abnormalities of the HPA axis probably cause the sudden increases in clinical depression in early adolescence (Guerry & Hastings, 2011), and HPA disruptions are one harmful result of childhood sexual abuse (discussed later in this chapter) (Trickett et al., 2011b).

Sex Hormones

At adolescence, the pituitary activates not only the adrenal glands but also the **gonads,** or sex glands (ovaries in females; testes, or testicles, in males), following another sequence called the **HPG (hypothalamus–pituitary–gonad) axis.** One hormone in particular, GnRH (gonadotropin-releasing hormone), causes the gonads to enlarge and dramatically increase their production of sex hormones, chiefly **estradiol** in girls and **testosterone** in boys. These hormones affect the body's entire shape and functioning, including production of additional hormones that regulate stress and immunity (E. A. Young et al., 2008).

Estrogens (including estradiol) are female hormones and *androgens* (including testosterone) are male hormones, although the adrenal glands produce estrogens and androgens in everyone. The gonads, however, produce sex-specific hormones: The ovaries produce much more of the estrogens than of the androgens; the reverse is true of the testes. Testosterone skyrockets in boys—up to 20 times the prepubescent level (Roche & Sun, 2003). Estradiol increases to about 8 times a girl's childhood level (Malina et al., 2004).

The activated gonads eventually produce mature sperm or ova, released in spermarche or menarche. That signifies the potential for parenthood, although peak fertility occurs four to six years later. Hormonal increases and differences may underlie sex differences in psychopathology (Naninck et al., 2011; Steiner & Young, 2008); compared with their peers of the other sex, males are twice as likely to become schizophrenic and females are twice as likely to become depressed. For both sexes, hormones awaken and then increase interest in sex. The first sexual objects are usually unattainable—a film star, a teacher, someone's older sibling—but by mid-adolescence, fantasies may settle on another teen.

gonads The paired sex glands (ovaries in females, testicles in males). The gonads produce hormones and gametes.

HPG (hypothalamus–pituitary–gonad) axis A sequence of hormone production originating in the hypothalamus and moving to the pituitary and then to the gonads.

estradiol A sex hormone, considered the chief estrogen. Females produce much more estradiol than males do.

testosterone A sex hormone, the best known of the androgens (male hormones); secreted in far greater amounts by males than by females.

Primping, Bonding, or Both? Lip gloss and eyelash-curling have the full concentration of these three, as the two "older" girls (the one on the left is 13) work on the youngest one. Critics lament society's focus on superficial appearance, but this scene may be more biological than cultural, since similar moments have occurred throughout history and in every nation.

Observation Quiz This moment was captured fairly recently, in 2007. Are these girls North American? For a clue, look at their hair. (see answer, page 415)

Especially for Parents of Teenagers
Why would parents blame adolescent moods on hormones? (see response, page 417)

Not only are brain and body affected by hormones, but behavior is as well. Surges of emotions and sudden lustful impulses are partly hormonal, but thoughts *cause* physiological and neurological processes as well as result from them (Damasio, 2003). For example, when other people react to emerging breasts, beards, or body shapes, these reactions evoke thoughts and frustrations in the adolescent, which then raise hormone levels and produce emotional outbursts, each increasing the other.

Body Rhythms

The brain of every living creature responds to the environment with natural rhythms that rise and fall by the hours, days, and seasons. For example, body weight and height are affected by time of year (children grower taller in summer and heavier in winter—by a small amount that is apparent only when thousands of children are measured very precisely). Some *biorhythms* are on a day–night cycle of biological activity that occurs approximately every 24 hours, called the **circadian rhythm.** (*Circadian* means "about a day.") Puberty affects biorhythms.

circadian rhythm A day–night cycle of biological activity that occurs approximately every 24 hours (*circadian* means "about a day").

The hypothalamus and the pituitary regulate the hormones that affect patterns of stress, appetite, sleep, and so on. These hormones cause a *phase delay* in sleep–wake cycles, making many teens wide awake and hungry at midnight but half asleep, with little appetite or energy, all morning. By contrast, many older adults are naturally alert in the morning and sleepy at night because of their circadian rhythms.

Added to the adolescent day–night pattern, some individuals (especially males) are naturally more alert in the evening than in the morning, a genetic trait called *eveningness.* Exacerbated by the pubescent phase delay, eveningness puts adolescents at high risk for antisocial activities (Susman et al., 2007) because they are awake when adults are sound asleep. Another result is that "teenagers are notoriously sleep deprived" (Ruder, 2008, p. 10). Uneven sleep schedules (more sleep on weekends, erratic bedtimes) decrease well-being, as does sleep deprivation (Fuligni & Hardway, 2006; Holm et al., 2009).

Sleep deprivation and irregular sleep schedules lead to several specific dangers, including insomnia, nightmares, mood disorders (depression, conduct disorder, anxiety), and falling asleep while driving. Individuals who are sleep deprived do not think or learn as well as they might when rested. The implications of that fact may be ignored by adults, as the following explains.

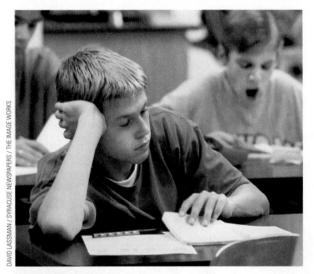

Too Early It is 8:00 A.M. on their first day of high school, and these freshmen are having trouble staying awake for orientation in their homeroom.

A VIEW FROM SCIENCE

Get Real

Some parents fight biology. They command their wide-awake teen to "go to sleep," they hang up on their child's classmates who phone after 10:00 P.M., they set curfews and stay awake until their teenagers come home, and they drag their offspring out of bed for school. (An opposite developmental clash occurs when parents tell their toddlers to stay in their cribs after dawn.) This parent–adolescent fight goes against the circadian rhythm, so sleep-deprived teenagers are likely to fall asleep in

school (see Figure 14.2), have poor relationships with their parents, and abuse substances (partly to wake up or go to sleep) (Mueller et al., 2011; Patrick & Schulenberg, 2011).

Data on the adolescent phase delay convinced social scientists at the University of Minnesota to ask 17 school districts to start high school at 8:30 A.M. or later. Few parents agreed. Many (42 percent) thought high school should begin before 8:00 A.M. Some (20 percent) wanted their teenagers out of the house by

7:15 A.M., as did only 1 percent of parents with younger children (Wahlstrom, 2002).

Workers in many occupations had their own reasons for believing school should begin early. Teachers generally thought that learning was more efficient early in the morning; bus drivers hated rush hour; cafeteria workers wanted to leave by midafternoon; police said teenagers should be home by 4:00 P.M.; coaches needed after-school sports events to end before dark; business owners wanted teens to staff the afternoon shift; community program directors liked to use school gyms for nonschool events in the late afternoon.

Only one school district experimented. In Edina, Minnesota, high school schedules changed to 8:30 A.M. to 3:10 P.M. instead of 7:25 A.M. to 2:05 P.M. After a trial year, most parents

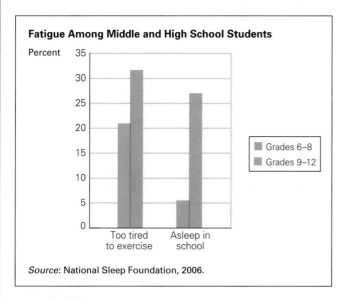

Fatigue Among Middle and High School Students

Source: National Sleep Foundation, 2006.

FIGURE 14.2

Dreaming and Learning? This graph shows the percentage of U.S. students who, once a week or more, fall asleep in class or are too tired to exercise. Not shown are those who are too tired overall (59 percent for high school students) or who doze in class "almost every day" (8 percent).

(93 percent) and virtually all students liked the new schedule. One student said, "I have only fallen asleep in school once this whole year, and last year I fell asleep about three times a week" (quoted in Wahlstrom, 2002, p. 190). The data showed fewer absent, late, disruptive, or sick students (the school nurse became an advocate) and higher grades.

Other school districts reconsidered. Minneapolis, which had started high school at 7:15 A.M., changed the starting time to 8:40 A.M. Again, attendance improved, as did the graduation rate. School boards in South Burlington (Vermont), West Des Moines (Iowa), Tulsa (Oklahoma), Arlington (Virginia), and Milwaukee (Wisconsin) voted in favor of later starting times, switching on average from 7:45 A.M. to 8:30 A.M. (Tonn, 2006), as did one private school in Rhode Island (Owens et al., 2010). Unexpected advantages appeared: financial savings (more efficient energy use), less adolescent depression, and, at least in Tulsa, unprecedented athletic championships.

But change is hard. Many school districts stick to their old schedules. From 2006 to 2009, the community of Fairfax (Virginia) argued, forming two opposing groups: SLEEP (Start Later for Excellence in Education Proposal) versus WAKE (Worried About Keeping Extra-Curriculars). One high school sports reporter argued:

> The later start would hinder teams without lighted practice fields. Hinder kids who work after-school jobs to save for college or to help support their families. Hinder teachers who work second jobs or take late-afternoon college classes. Hinder commuters who would get stopped behind more buses during peak traffic times. Hinder kids who might otherwise seek after-school academic help, or club or team affiliation. Hinder families that depend on high school children to watch younger siblings after school. Hinder community groups that use school and park facilities in the late afternoons and evenings.
>
> [Williams, 2009]

This writer wrote that science was on the side of change but reality was not. To developmentalists, of course, science *is* reality. However, the school board focused on the cost of school buses in rush hour. It voted to keep high school starting time at 7:20 A.M.

Age and Puberty

A practical question is: "When will adolescence begin?" Some fear *precocious puberty* (sexual development before age 8) or very late puberty (after age 16), but both are rare (Cesario & Hughes, 2007). Quite normal is hormonal activity beginning any time from age 8 to age 14, with visible signs appearing a year later. Many parents, teachers, and children want to know more precisely when puberty will occur: They want to be prepared, but not years before the events. Fortunately, genes, gender, body fat, and stress all aid in prediction.

Genes and Gender

About two-thirds of the variation in age of puberty is genetic, evident not only in families but also in ethnic groups (Ge et al., 2007; Susman et al., 2010; van den Berg

>> Answer to Observation Quiz (from page 413) This girlish behavior is universal, but the hairstyles are not. All three have braids; these girls are Argentinean.

SKJOLD PHOTOGRAPHS / THE IMAGE WORKS

Both 12 The ancestors of these two Minnesota 12-year-olds came from northern Europe and West Africa, respectively. Their genes have dictated some differences between them, including the timing of puberty, but these differences are irrelevant to their friendship.

secular trend The long-term upward or downward direction of a certain set of statistical measurements, as opposed to a smaller, shorter cyclical variation. As an example, over the last two centuries, because of improved nutrition and medical care, children have tended to reach their adult height earlier and their adult height has increased.

leptin A hormone that affects appetite and is believed to affect the onset of puberty. Leptin levels increase during childhood and peak at around age 12.

& Boomsma, 2007). African Americans reach puberty about seven months earlier than European or Hispanic Americans, while Chinese Americans average several months later. Ethnic differences are apparent on other continents as well. For instance, northern European girls reach menarche at 13 years, 4 months, on average; southern European girls do so at 12 years, 5 months (Alsaker & Flammer, 2006).

Genes on the sex chromosomes have a marked effect. In height, the average girl is about two years ahead of the average boy. However, the female height spurt occurs before menarche, whereas for boys, the increase in height is relatively late, occurring after spermarche. Thus, when it comes to hormonal and sexual changes, girls are only a few months ahead of boys (Hughes & Gore, 2007). Therefore, the sixth-grade boy with sexual fantasies about the taller girls in his class is neither perverted nor precocious; his hormones are simply ahead of his visible growth.

Body Fat

Another major influence on the onset of puberty is body fat, at least in girls. Heavy girls reach menarche years earlier than malnourished ones do. Most girls must weigh at least 100 pounds (45 kilograms) before they experience their first period (Berkey et al., 2000).

Worldwide, urban children are more often overfed and underexercised compared with rural children. That is probably why puberty starts earlier in the cities of India and China than it does in more remote villages, a year earlier in Warsaw than in rural Poland, and earlier in Athens than in other parts of Greece (Malina et al., 2004).

Body fat also explains why youth reach puberty at age 15 or later in some parts of Africa, although their genetic relatives in North America mature much earlier. Similarly, malnutrition may explain why puberty began at about age 17 in sixteenth-century Europe. Puberty has occurred at younger ages every century since then (an example of what is called the **secular trend**): nutrition and medicine have improved, allowing not only earlier puberty but also taller average height.

One curious bit of evidence of the secular trend is that U.S. presidents are taller in recent decades than they were earlier (James Madison, the fourth president, was shortest at 5 feet, 4 inches; Barack Obama is 6 feet, 1 inch tall). Over most of the twentieth century, each generation experienced puberty a few weeks earlier and grew a centimeter or so taller than did the preceding one (Floud et al., 2011). The secular trend has stopped in developed nations, perhaps because nutrition is now sufficient for everyone to attain their genetic potential. That means that, unlike their grandparents, young men are unlikely to look down at their short fathers, or girls at their little mothers, unless they are born in Asia or Africa, where the secular trend continues.

Hormones

Of course, hormones affect sex differences, height, and weight, but there may be additional effects directly on the age of puberty. Many scientists suspect that hormones in the food supply speed the onset of puberty. As evidence, they point to the steroids fed to cattle to increase bulk and milk supply, as well as to many other substances in meat and other foods consumed by children. Steriods affect appetite, body fat, and sex hormones (Wang et al., 2005).

One hormone in particular has been implicated in the onset of puberty: **leptin,** which stimulates the appetite. Leptin levels in the blood show a natural increase over childhood, peaking at puberty (Rutters et al., 2008). Curiously, leptin affects appetite in females more than it does in males (Geary & Lovejoy, 2008), and body fat is more closely connected to the onset of puberty in girls than in boys. In fact, the well-established finding that body fat precipitates puberty may not be true for boys in nations where malnutrition is rare: One study found that U.S. boys who are heavy in childhood reach puberty later, not earlier, than others (J. M. Lee et al., 2010).

It is not yet known for certain exactly what the effects of leptin are or what factors increase or decrease leptin in the bloodstream, although it is known that leptin, body fat, and puberty are connected somehow. Most of the research has been with lower animals, including mice, goats, and rabbits. Children with abnormally low levels of leptin are sometimes too thin, sometimes overweight, but often experience delayed puberty. For some, injections of leptin start puberty (Friedman, 2011), but far more research needs to occur before the effects are understood.

It also is not yet known precisely how the many chemicals in the air, water, or diet affect the human sexual-reproductive system. In general, more is known about female than male puberty, partly because menarche is easier to date than spermarche. Among adults, some toxins affect women more than men (Tomicic et al., 2011), and this may be true for adolescents as well. One conclusion is certain: For both sexes, childhood malnutrition slows growth, puberty, and reproduction. As for the specific impact and mechanisms of hormones and chemicals, many questions need answers.

Stress

There is uncertainty regarding the role of stress as well. Stress affects the sexual-reproductive system by making reproduction more difficult in adulthood and by *hastening* (not delaying) the hormonal onset of puberty. Thus, puberty arrives earlier if a child's parents are sick, addicted, or divorced or if the neighborhood is violent and impoverished.

A study of sexually abused girls found that they began puberty seven months earlier, on average, than did a matched comparison group (Trickett et al., 2011b). Puberty in some children seems unaffected by family stress, yet in children who are genetically sensitive to context, puberty comes early if their family context is stressful but late if their family is supportive (Ellis et al., 2011). Thus, specifics are influenced by the genes of the child as well as by the family situation, as differential sensitivity (explained in Chapter 1) would predict.

Corroboration comes from studies with other animals. Opossums experience earlier puberty if their environment is stressful (Warshofsky, 1999). Mice experience later puberty if their mother is highly nurturant, indicated by frequent licking and grooming during infancy, thus protecting mice against stress later on (N. M. Cameron et al., 2008).

Several longitudinal studies suggest that stress hormones directly cause early puberty. For example, one study followed 756 children from infancy to adolescence. For them, earlier puberty correlated with harsh parenting in childhood. Their parents were likely to demand quiet and respect, to spank often, and to rarely hug their children. Generally, parents punish sons more than daughters, but this study found that harsh parenting correlated with earlier puberty for daughters, not sons—especially if those daughters cried a lot as infants, which suggests that they were sensitive to stress (Belsky et al., 2007).

A further study of the same girls at age 15, controlled for genetic differences, found that harsh treatment in childhood increased sexual risk taking (e.g., more sex partners, pregnancies, diseases) but not other risks (e.g., drugs, crime) (Belsky et al., 2010). This suggests that stress targets sexual hormones more than factors that lead to overall rebellion.

>> Response for Parents of Teenagers (from page 414) If something causes adolescents to shout "I hate you," to slam doors, or to cry inconsolably, parents may decide that hormones are the problem. This makes it easy to disclaim personal responsibility for the teenager's anger. However, research on stress and hormones suggests that this comforting attribution is too simplistic.

Especially for Parents Worried About Early Puberty Suppose your cousin's 9-year-old daughter has just had her first period, and your cousin blames hormones in the food supply for this "precocious" puberty. Should you change your young daughter's diet? (see response, page 419)

Why would stress trigger puberty? Given what is known about optimal development, it makes more sense for stress to *delay* puberty. If puberty were delayed, then stressed young teens would still look and act childlike, and that might evoke adult protection, not lust or anger. Delayed puberty would be especially beneficial in conflicted or single-parent homes. But the opposite occurs. One explanation comes from evolutionary theory:

> Maturing quickly and breeding promiscuously would enhance reproductive fitness more than would delaying development, mating cautiously, and investing heavily in parenting. The latter strategy, in contrast, would make biological sense, for virtually the same reproductive-fitness-enhancing reasons, under conditions of contextual support and nurturance.
>
> [Belsky et al., 2010, p. 121]

In other words, in past stressful times, for species survival, stressed adolescents needed to replace themselves before they died. Of course, natural selection would postpone puberty during extreme famine (so that pregnant girls or their newborns would not die of malnutrition). But natural selection would also favor genes that hastened puberty when girls were well-fed but their families and tribes were in conflict, threatening the survival of the adolescents and adults. In that case, a new generation needed to be born before too many of the older generations went to war. By contrast, in more peaceful times and families, puberty could occur later, allowing children to benefit from years of nurturance from their parents and grandparents before having children of their own. Genes could evolve to respond differentially to war and peace.

Of course, this evolutionary rationale no longer applies. Today, early sexuality and reproduction are more likely to destroy societies than protect them. However, the genome has been shaped over millennia; timing takes centuries to change.

Too Early, Too Late

For most adolescents, this speculation about hormones and evolution is irrelevant. Only one aspect of pubertal timing is important: their friends' schedules. Puberty can enhance or diminish a person's status with peers. No one wants to be too early or too late.

Girls

Think about the early-maturing girl. If she has visible breasts at age 10, the boys her age tease her; they are distressed by the sexual creature in their midst. She must fit her developing body into a school chair designed for smaller children; she might hide her breasts in large T-shirts and bulky sweaters; she might refuse to undress for gym. Early-maturing girls tend to have lower self-esteem, more depression, and poorer body image than do other girls (Compian et al., 2009). They also exercise less than their classmates, which contributes to their difficulties with self-image (Davison et al., 2007).

Sometimes early-maturing girls have older boyfriends, who are attracted to their womanly shape and girlish innocence. Having an older boyfriend gains them status—but also increases their risk of drug and alcohol use (Weichold et al., 2003), relational bullying, and victimization of physical violence (from that same boyfriend) (Schreck et al., 2007). Early-maturing girls enter abusive relationships more often than other girls do, perhaps because they are lonely and their social judgment is immature. Depression and suicide are also risks for early-maturing girls, especially if they are genetically predisposed to eveningness and are sleep deprived (Negriff et al., 2011).

Not Yet a Woman She may look like an attractive woman, but she is really an early-maturing girl. Notice her long and sandy feet, her relatively short torso, her thin upper arms. Her body is changing—in a photo taken two years earlier or two years later, her shape would be different.

PHOTOLIBRARY.COM

Boys

Early maturation in girls has always seemed more harmful than helpful, but cohort seems crucial for boys. Early-maturing boys who were born around 1930 often became leaders in high school and more successful as adults (M. C. Jones, 1965; Taga et al., 2006). Since about 1960, however, the risks associated with early male maturation have outweighed the benefits. In the twenty-first century, early-maturing boys are more aggressive, law-breaking, and alcohol-abusing than are later-maturing boys (Biehl et al., 2007; Lynne et al., 2007) and thus are more likely to have trouble with parents, schools, and the police. For boys as well as girls, early puberty correlates with sexual activity and teenage parenthood, which in turn correlate with depression and other psychosocial problems (B. Brown, 2004; Siebenbruner et al., 2007). Not only is early puberty stressful, but speed of change is difficult as well: The boys most likely to become depressed are those for whom puberty was both early and quick (Mendle et al., 2010).

Late puberty may also be difficult, especially for boys. Slow-developing boys tend to be more anxious, depressed, and afraid of sex, at least according to research in Finland (Lindfors et al., 2007). In fact, every adolescent wants to hit puberty "on time." They are likely to overestimate or underestimate their maturation, or become depressed, if they are not average (Conley & Rudolph, 2009; Shirtcliff et al., 2009).

Ethnic Differences

Puberty that is late by world norms (age 14 or so) is not troubling if one's friends are late as well. Well-nourished Africans tend to experience puberty a few months earlier and Asians a few months later than Europeans, but they all develop well if their classmates are on the same schedule. However, variable timing may add to intergroup tensions in multiethnic schools. Peer approval is more important in adolescence than is approval from adults (Green et al., 2006).

For instance, in one New England high school, the shorter and thinner "quiet Asian boys" were teased, much to their dismay. When one larger Asian American fought back at an ethnic insult, he was a hero to his Asian peers, even though school authorities punished him (Lei, 2003). In a California high school, Samoan students were a small minority of the school population but advanced in puberty, which earned them respect from classmates of all backgrounds. They were accepted as peacemakers between the two more numerous groups, African and Mexican Americans (Staiger, 2006).

Size and maturation are important for many adolescents in every nation. For example, a study of more than 3,000 Australian students, primarily of English heritage, found that late developers had four times the rate of self-harm (cutting or poisoning themselves) as did other students. This is a marked indication of serious depression (Patton et al., 2007).

SUMMING UP

Puberty usually begins between ages 8 and 14 (typically around age 11) in response to a chain reaction of hormone production from the hypothalamus to the pituitary to the adrenal and sex glands. Hormones affect emotions as well as the body: Adolescent outbursts of sudden anger, sadness, and lust are caused by hormones combined with reactions from other people to the young person's changing body. Many factors, including genes, body fat, and stress, affect the onset of puberty, especially among girls. Early or late puberty is less desirable than puberty at the same age as one's peers; off-time maturation may lead to depression, drug abuse, and other problems. ∎

> **>> Response for Parents Worried About Early Puberty** (from page 417) Probably not. If she is overweight, her diet should change, but the hormone hypothesis is speculative. Genes are the main factor; she shares only one-eighth of her genes with her cousin.

>> Nutrition

All the changes of puberty depend on adequate nourishment, yet many adolescents do not consume enough vitamins or minerals. Teenagers often skip breakfast, eat at midnight, guzzle down soda, and munch on salty, processed snacks. One reason is that their hormones affect their diurnal rhythms, including their appetites. Another reason is that they seek independence, which may mean refusing to sit down to a family dinner.

Cohort and age are crucial. In the United States, each new generation eats less well than the previous one, and each 18-year-old tends to eat a less balanced diet than he or she did at age 10 (N. I. Larson et al., 2007). Most adolescents consume enough calories, but in 2009 only 14 percent of high school seniors ate the recommended three or more servings of vegetables a day (MMWR, June 4, 2010).

Come Here Often? Teenagers worldwide (like this group in Yangshuo, China) are attracted by fast-food restaurants because the cheap food and public setting of such places make them ideal for snacking and socializing. However, the food—usually high in fat and low in nutrition—contributes to overweight and undernourishment in many young customers.

Diet Deficiencies

Deficiencies of iron, calcium, zinc, and other minerals are especially common during adolescence. Because menstruation depletes iron, anemia is more likely among adolescent girls than among any other age group. This is true everywhere, especially in South Asia and sub-Saharan Africa, where teenage girls rarely eat iron-rich meat and green vegetables and most are thought to be anemic. Specific data on that population are unavailable because large-scale studies that include laboratory analysis of blood iron are rare in developing nations. However, research in Saudi Arabia of 18- to 23-year-old college women (usually in good health, never pregnant, and from wealthy families) found that, despite these advantages, 26 percent had insufficient iron and another 24 percent were clinically anemic (Al-Sayes et al., 2011).

Boys may also be iron-deficient if they push their bodies in physical labor or sports: Muscles need iron for growth and strength. The cutoff for anemia is lower for boys than for girls because boys naturally require more iron to be healthy (Morón & Viteri, 2009). Many adolescents of both sexes in every nation spurn iron-rich foods (green vegetables, eggs, and meat) in favor of iron-poor chips, sweets, and fries.

Similarly, although the daily recommended intake of calcium for teenagers is 1,300 milligrams, the average U. S. teen consumes less than 500 milligrams a day. About half of adult bone mass is acquired from ages 10 to 20, which means many contemporary teenagers will develop osteoporosis (fragile bones), a major cause of disability, injury, and death in late adulthood among people of European descent.

One reason for calcium deficiency is that milk drinking has declined. In 1959, most North American children drank at least three glasses (about ¾ liter) of milk each day, providing most (about 900 milligrams) of their daily calcium requirement; by 1999, only 18 percent of U.S. children drank three glasses of milk a day. A decade after that (2009), rates for twelfth-graders were only 8 percent for girls and 20 percent for boys (MMWR, June 4, 2010). In the twenty-first century, the beverage most often consumed by 2- to 18-year-olds is soda (U.S. Department of Agriculture and U.S. Department of Health and Human Services, 2011.)

Choices Made

Many economists advocate a "nudge" to encourage people to make better choices, not only in nutrition but in all aspects of their lives (Thaler & Sunstein,

2008). Teenagers are nudged in the wrong direction. Their nutritional deficiencies result from the food choices that young adolescents are allowed, even enticed, to make.

Fast-food establishments cluster around high schools, often with extra seating that encourages teenagers to eat and socialize. This is especially true for high schools with large Hispanic populations, the teens most at risk for obesity (Taber et al., 2011). Price influences food choices, especially for adolescents (Epstein et al., 2006), and healthy foods are more expensive than unhealthy ones. To cite one specific example: In New York City in 2010, a McDonald's salad cost five times more than a hamburger ($5.59 versus $1.09).

Furthermore, nutritional deficiencies increase when schools have vending machines that offer soda and snacks, especially for middle school students (Rovner et al., 2011). A constructive nudge of higher prices, less attractive placement, and healthier selections for in-school vending machines would improve adolescent nutrition.

A more drastic strategy would be to ban the purchase of unhealthy foods in schools altogether—a strategy used by 29 percent of U.S. high schools in 2002 and 69 percent in 2008. During the same years, obesity leveled off in the United States, although school policies are only a small part of the necessary changes. Experts call for "increased efforts" at schools, in communities, and among adolescents (MMWR, October 9, 2009).

Body Image

Another reason for poor nutrition among teenagers is anxiety about **body image**—that is, a person's idea of how his or her body looks. Few teenagers welcome every change in their bodies. Instead, they tend to focus on and exaggerate imperfections (as did the three girls in the anecdote that opens this chapter).

Girls diet because they want to be thinner, partly because boys tend to prefer dating thin girls (Halpern et al., 2005). Boys want to look taller and stronger, a concern that increases from ages 12 to 17, partly because girls value well-developed muscles in males (D. Jones & Crawford, 2005). Thus, as the hormones of puberty awaken sexual interest, both sexes become less happy with their own bodies and more superficial in their evaluation of the other sex. This is true worldwide. A longitudinal study in Korea found that, as in the West, body image dissatisfaction began in early adolescence and increased until age 15 or so. For 10-year-old girls and 15-year-old boys, body dissatisfaction increased depression and thoughts of suicide (Kim & Kim, 2009).

In many nations, the ideal body type and facial appearance is tall, thin, and Anglo-Saxon. This is striking in places far from England, where Anglo-Saxons originated. Now teenagers in every nation are bombarded by media images that differ markedly from those their mirrors reflect (see photo at right).

Of course, few Anglo-Saxon youth achieve the media ideal, either, but the discrepancy is particularly cruel far from England. A longitudinal study in China found that adolescents in that country had anxieties about weight gain similar to those of U.S. teenagers (Chen & Jackson, 2009). Everywhere, young adolescents wish their bodies looked different, and teenagers tend to lie about their bodies—adding 3 inches and subtracting 4 pounds on average, with the boys doing more adding and the girls more subtracting (Brener et al., 2003).

Cute? Teens of both sexes are intensely concerned with how peers view their appearance. Notice this boy's overly long bangs. He seems to be looking for an invisible blemish.

A. CHEDERROS / ONOKY / CORBIS

body image A person's idea of how his or her body looks.

African Fashion She is Anglo Saxon in almost every detail—nose, hair, eyebrows, facial shape, and body type—much like her tight-fitting strapless gown. However, she is modeling a designer dress during Africa Fashion Week in Johannesburg, South Africa, in 2010.

GABRIEL BOUYS / AFP / GETTY IMAGES

Girl or Woman? Hannah Hartney, here age 16, has been suffering from anorexia since she was 9. Some clinicians suggest that starving oneself is a way to avoid the womanly body that develops at puberty.

anorexia nervosa An eating disorder characterized by severe calorie restriction and the fear of being fat. Affected individuals undereat, or overeat and then overexercise or purge, depriving their vital organs of nutrition. Anorexia can be fatal.

bulimia nervosa An eating disorder characterized by binge eating and subsequent purging, usually by induced vomiting and/or use of laxatives.

Eating Disorders

One result of dissatisfaction with body image is that many teenagers, mostly girls, eat erratically or ingest drugs (especially diet pills) to lose weight; others, mostly boys, take steroids to increase muscle mass. Eating disorders are rare in childhood but increase dramatically at puberty, accompanied by distorted body image, food obsession, and depression (Bulik et al., 2008; Hrabosky & Thomas, 2008).

Individual adolescents sometimes switch from obsessive dieting to overeating to overexercising and back again. Obesity is a problem at every age, discussed in Chapters 8 and 11. Here we describe two other eating disorders that are common in adolescence.

Anorexia Nervosa

Some women (and occasionally men) suffer from **anorexia nervosa,** a disorder characterized by severe calorie restriction, or a cycle of bingeing followed by purging, that can lead to death by organ failure or suicide for between 5 and 20 percent of sufferers. If someone's body mass index (BMI) is 17 or lower, and if she (less often, he), has a fixation with their weight—believing themselves to be overweight despite all the evidence to the contrary—anorexia is suspected. According to DSM-5, anorexia is officially diagnosed when three symptoms are present:

1. Significantly low body weight for developmental stage (BMI of 17 or lower)
2. Intense fear of weight gain
3. Disturbed body perception and denial of the problem

The DSM-5 introduces a new diagnostic category, binge-eating disorder, in part to recognize that bingeing is sometimes associated with anorexia.

Although anorexia existed in earlier centuries, the disease was undiagnosed until about 1950, when some high-achieving, upper-class young women became so emaciated that they died. Soon anorexia became evident among younger women (the rate spikes at puberty and again in emerging adulthood), among men, and in every nation and ethnic group (Chao et al., 2008). Certain alleles increase the risk of anorexia (J. K. Young, 2010), as is evident from the higher rates among people who have a close relative, especially a monozygotic twin, with anorexia or severe depression. Probably many genes make a person more vulnerable to eating disorders, and certainly many people at genetic risk never develop anorexia: Context is pivotal.

Bulimia Nervosa

About three times as common as anorexia is **bulimia nervosa,** a disorder clinically present in 1 to 3 percent of female teenagers and young adults in the United States. The person with bulimia overeats compulsively, wolfing down thousands of calories within an hour or two, and then purges via vomiting or laxatives. Most are close to normal in weight and therefore unlikely to starve. However, they risk serious health problems, including damage to their gastrointestinal systems and cardiac arrest from electrolyte imbalance (Shannon, 2007).

Three things combine to warrant a clinical diagnosis of bulimia:

1. Bingeing and purging at least once a week for three months
2. Uncontrollable urges to overeat
3. Sense of self inordinately tied to body shape and weight

These symptoms and those for anorexia are from DSM-5, the fifth edition of the *Diagnostic and Statistical Manual of Mental Disorders*, published by the American Psychiatric Association. Many experts think that eating disorders are much more widespread among adolescents than these official statistics and listed symptoms portray. For instance, 6 percent of U.S. eleventh-grade girls and 3 percent of the boys vomited or took laxatives to lose weight in the month before a 2009 survey (MMWR, June 4, 2010). For all eating problems, treatment that begins in early adolescence has a better chance of halting the problem than treatment begun later on (Keel & Brown, 2010).

Origins of Disordered Eating

Many adolescents have unhealthy eating habits: They try new diets, go without food for 24 hours (as did 15 percent of U.S. high school girls and 7 percent of the boys in 2009), or take diet drugs (6 percent) (MMWR, June 4, 2010). Some become so hungry that they binge; some become anorexic; many eat oddly (e.g., only rice or only carrots) for awhile.

Each episode of bingeing, purging, or fasting makes the next one easier. A combination of causes leads to obesity, anorexia, or bulimia, with at least five general elements—cultural images, stress, puberty, hormones, and childhood patterns—all making disordered eating more likely (Shannon, 2007).

One family practice reduces the risk of adolescent eating disorders: eating together during childhood (Franko et al., 2008). It is not known whether family cohesion and routine are the protective factors or whether family meals directly encourage nutrition. Nonetheless, developmentalists agree that healthy eating begins with childhood habits and family routines. Some overweight or underweight infants never develop nutritional problems, but the older an overweight or underweight child is, the more likely an eating disorder will occur in adolescence.

SUMMING UP

All adolescents are vulnerable to poor nutrition; few are well nourished. Insufficient consumption of iron and calcium is particularly common, as fast food and nutrient-poor snacks often replace family meals. Both boys and girls often choose junk food instead of a balanced diet, in part because they are concerned about peer opinions regarding their appearance. The combination of nutritional deficiencies, peer culture, and anxiety about body image sometimes causes obesity, anorexia, or bulimia, influenced by heredity and childhood patterns. All adolescent nutrition problems have lifelong, potentially life-threatening, consequences.

≫ The Transformations of Puberty

Every body part changes during puberty. For simplicity, the study of this transformation from child to adult is traditionally divided into two parts: growth and sexuality. We will use that division here. We will also describe a third transformation—changes in the adolescent brain. All three relate to adolescent cognitive and psychosocial development, described in Chapters 15 and 16, making this chapter division somewhat artificial. However, it is useful to consider each major transformation separately.

Growing Bigger and Stronger

The first set of changes is called the **growth spurt**—a sudden, uneven jump in the size of almost every body part, turning children into adults. Growth proceeds from the extremities to the core (the opposite of the earlier proximodistal growth). Thus, fingers and toes lengthen before hands and feet, hands and feet before arms and legs, arms and legs before the torso. This growth is not always symmetrical: One foot, one breast, or even one ear may grow later than the other.

growth spurt The relatively sudden and rapid physical growth that occurs during puberty. Each body part increases in size on a schedule: Weight usually precedes height, and growth of the limbs precedes growth of the torso.

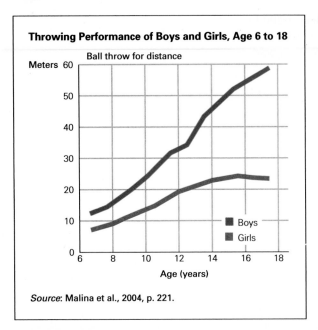

Throwing Performance of Boys and Girls, Age 6 to 18

Source: Malina et al., 2004, p. 221.

Big Difference All children experience an increase in muscles during puberty, but gender differences are much more apparent in some gross motor skills than in others. For instance, upper-arm strength increases dramatically only in boys.

Observation Quiz At what age does the rate of increase in the average boy's muscle strength accelerate? (see answer, page 427)

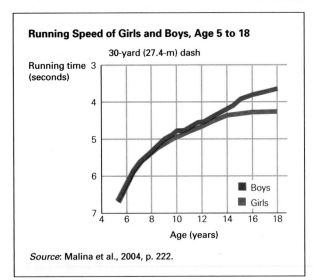

Running Speed of Girls and Boys, Age 5 to 18

Source: Malina et al., 2004, p. 222.

Little Difference Both sexes develop longer and stronger legs duing puberty.

Because the torso is the last body part to grow, many pubescent children are temporarily big-footed, long-legged, and short-waisted. If young teenagers complain that their jeans don't fit, they are probably correct, even if those same jeans fit when their parents bought them a month earlier. (At least the parents had advance warning when they had to buy their children's shoes in the adult section.)

Sequence: Weight, Height, Muscles

As the bones lengthen and harden (visible on X-rays) and the growth spurt begins, children eat more and gain weight. Exactly when, where, and how much weight they gain depends on heredity, hormones, diet, exercise, and gender. For instance, at age 17, the average girl has twice the percentage of body fat as her male classmate, whose increased weight is mostly muscle (Roche & Sun, 2003).

A height spurt follows the weight spurt, then a year or two later a muscle spurt occurs. Thus, the pudginess and clumsiness of early puberty are usually gone by late adolescence. (The young teenager who took nutritional supplements or lifted weights could have simply waited a year or two.)

Arm muscles develop more in boys. On average, a boy's arm muscles are twice as strong at age 18 as at age 8, enabling him to throw a ball four times as far (Malina et al., 2004) (see Figure 14.3). Other muscles are gender-neutral. For instance, both sexes run faster with each year of adolescence, with boys not much faster than girls (unless the girls choose to slow down) (see Figure 14.4).

Organ Growth

In both sexes, organs mature. Lungs triple in weight; consequently, adolescents breathe more deeply and slowly. The heart doubles in size as the heartbeat slows, decreasing the pulse rate while increasing blood pressure (Malina et al., 2004). Consequently, endurance improves: Some teenagers can run for miles or dance for hours. Red blood cells increase in both sexes, but dramatically more in boys, which aids oxygen transport during intense exercise. By age 18, the normal boy is less likely to become winded during a long race (Malina et al., 2004).

Both weight and height increase *before* muscles and internal organs: Athletic training and weight lifting should be tailored to an adolescent's size the previous year, to protect immature muscles and organs. Sports injuries are the most common school accidents, and they increase at puberty, partly because the height spurt precedes increases in bone mass, making young adolescents particularly vulnerable to fractures (Mathison & Agrawal, 2011).

Only one organ system, the lymphoid system (which includes the tonsils and adenoids), *decreases* in size, so teenagers are less susceptible to respiratory ailments. Mild asthma, for example, often switches off at puberty (Busse & Lemanske, 2005), and teenagers have fewer colds than younger children do. This is aided by growth of the larynx, which gives deeper voices to both sexes, dramatically noticeable in boys.

Another organ system, the skin, becomes oilier, sweatier, and more prone to acne. Hair also changes. During puberty, hair on the head and limbs becomes coarser and darker. New hair grows under arms, on faces, and over sex organs (pubic hair, from the same Latin root as *puberty*). Visible facial and chest hair is sometimes considered a sign of manliness, although hairiness in either sex depends on genes as well as on hormones. Girls pluck or dye any facial hair they see; boys proudly shave or grow sideburns, soul patches, chinstraps, moustaches, and so on—with specifics dependent on culture and cohort. Girls shave their legs and sometimes their pubic hair before wearing a bikini.

Although everyone's hair changes texture at puberty, many teenagers use their head hair to indicate gender and autonomy. Often teenagers cut, style, or grow their hair in ways their parents do not like, as a sign of independence. To become more attractive, many adolescents spend considerable time, money, and thought on their visible hair—growing, gelling, shaving, curling, straightening, highlighting, brushing, combing, styling, dyeing, wetting, drying . . . In many ways, hair is more than a growth characteristic; it becomes a display of sexuality.

Sexual Maturation

Now we turn to the physical changes that are universal, not cultural, transforming boys into men and girls into women.

Sexual Characteristics

The body characteristics that are directly involved in conception and pregnancy are called **primary sex characteristics.** During puberty, every primary sex organ (the ovaries, the uterus, the penis, and the testes) increases dramatically in size and matures in function. By the end of the process, reproduction is possible.

At the same time as maturation of the primary sex characteristics, secondary sex characteristics develop. **Secondary sex characteristics** are bodily features that do not directly affect fertility (hence they are secondary) but that signify masculinity or femininity. One such characteristic is shape. Young boys and girls have similar shapes, but at puberty, males widen at the shoulders and grow about 5 inches taller than females, while girls develop breasts and a wider pelvis. Breasts and broad hips are often considered signs of womanhood, but neither is required for conception; thus, they are secondary, not primary, sex characteristics.

The pattern of hair growth at the scalp line (widow's peak), the prominence of the larynx (Adam's apple), and several other anatomical features tend to differ for men and women—all secondary sex characteristics that few people notice. As just explained, facial hair increases in both sexes, but it is affected by sex hormones as well as genes and is a secondary sex characteristic.

Secondary sex characteristics are important psychologically, if not biologically. Consider breasts. Many adolescent girls buy "minimizer," "maximizer," "training," or "shaping" bras in the hope that they can conform their breasts to an idealized body image. During the same years, many boys are horrified to notice a swelling around their nipples—a normal and temporary result of the erratic hormones of early puberty. If a boy's breast growth is very disturbing, drugs can reduce the swelling, although many doctors prefer to let time, rather than tamoxifen, deal with the problem (Derman et al., 2003).

Sexual Activity

The primary and secondary sex characteristics just described are not the only manifestations of the sex hormones. Fantasizing, flirting, hand-holding, staring, standing, sitting, walking, displaying, and touching are all done in particular ways

primary sex characteristics The parts of the body that are directly involved in reproduction, including the vagina, uterus, ovaries, testicles, and penis.

secondary sex characteristics Physical traits that are not directly involved in reproduction but that indicate sexual maturity, such as a man's beard and a woman's breasts.

Competition Adolescent boys not only get arm muscles, they also have hormones that encourage them to compete—in sports, in body function, and in "scoring with girls."

to reflect gender, availability, and culture. As already explained, hormones trigger thoughts and emotions, but the social context shapes thoughts into enjoyable fantasies, shameful preoccupations, frightening impulses, or actual contact (see Figure 14.5).

FIGURE 14.5

Hormones → Sexual impulses → **CULTURE** → Opportunity → Action

A recent study on sexual behaviors such as hand-holding and cuddling among young adolescents found that biological maturation was only one factor in whether or not such activities occurred: Especially among young European Americans, those girls with lower self-esteem were more likely to engage in sexual intimacy (Hipwell et al., 2010).

Regarding sex-related impulses, some experts believe that boys are more influenced by hormones and girls by culture (Baumeister & Blackhart, 2007). Perhaps. If a relationship includes sexual intimacy, girls seem more concerned than boys are about the depth of the romance (Zani & Cicognani, 2006). Girls hope their partners say, "I'll love you forever"; boys like to hear, "I want you now."

However, everyone is influenced by both hormones and society, biology and culture. All adolescents have sexual interests they did not previously have (biology), which produce behaviors that teenagers in other nations would not do (culture) (Moore & Rosenthal, 2006). Since only girls can become pregnant, their wish for long-term commitment may be a consequence of biology, not culture. If this is so, the gender difference (girls' wanting love versus boys' seeking sex) may disappear as contraception makes unwanted pregnancy rare.

The gender gap in experience is narrowing. It has already reversed in some European nations, including Norway. In 1987, Norwegian boys averaged their first coitus almost a year younger than girls did; in 2002, girls were half a year younger than boys were at the time of first intercourse (Stigum et al., 2009).

It may seem that choosing sexual partners is a private and personal matter. Yet culture rules. For example, most North Americans find partners who are about the same age as they are (Zani & Cicognani, 2006), but in some nations girls' first partners are significantly older, and in other nations boys' first partners are older.

A Daughter's Promise At a "purity ball" in Colorado, a father reads the pledge signed by his 14-year-old daughter, in which she promises that she will abstain from sex until she marries. Young adolescents who take a virginity pledge are more likely than their peers to be celibate in high school. However, they are also more likely to become parents before they graduate from college.

Nature and Nurture These twin girls pray while holding hands with their godparents as part of their quinceañera, a coming-of-age celebration for 15-year-old Latinas. However, they share chronological age and Hispanic culture—but only half of their genes. Their biological, temperamental differences may explain why they wear their nearly identical dresses in quite different ways.

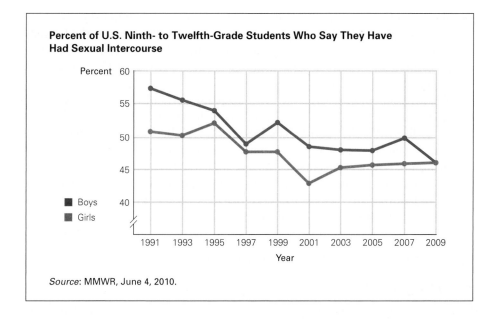

Percent of U.S. Ninth- to Twelfth-Grade Students Who Say They Have Had Sexual Intercourse

■ Boys
■ Girls

Source: MMWR, June 4, 2010.

FIGURE 14.6

Boys and Girls Together Boys tend to be somewhat more sexually experienced than girls during the high school years, but since the Youth Risk Behavior Survey began in 1991, the overall trend has been toward equality in rates of sexual activity.

>> Answer to Observation Quiz (from page 424) About age 13. This is most obvious in ball throwing (Figure 14.3), but it is also apparent in the 30-yard dash (Figure 14.4).

Cohort and culture affect sexual activity. For most of the twentieth century, surveys in North America reported sexual activity among adolescents at younger and younger ages. This trend reversed in the 1990s. In 1991, 62 percent of U.S. eleventh-graders said they had had intercourse, but in 2009 only 53 percent said so. Rates vary by state as well, from a low of 39 percent of Idaho high school students (ninth to twelfth grade) to a high of 61 percent in Mississippi (MMWR, June 4, 2010).

During the same time period, the double standard (with boys expected to be more sexually active than girls) decreased, and today boys and girls are quite similar in reported sexual activity (see Figure 14.6). These gender trends are apparent within every ethnic group, but the rates of both activity and change differ. For high school students between 1991 and 2009, rates of sexual experience among African Americans decreased 16 percentage points (from 81 to 65 percent); among European Americans, they were down 8 percentage points (from 50 to 42 percent); among Latinos, down 4 percentage points (from 53 to 49 percent) (MMWR, June 4, 2010).

All these examples demonstrate that a universal experience (rising hormones) that produces another universal experience (growth of primary and secondary sex characteristics) is powerfully influenced by cohort, gender, and culture. Other research finds that for any particular adolescent of any group, the sexual activity of his or her close friends is the most powerful influence.

Problems with Adolescent Sex

One of the changes in research on sexual activity is appreciation that adolescents are sexual beings. Sexual interest and interaction are normal, and researchers have found that healthy adult relationships are more likely when shame and fear do not haunt adolescent impulses (Tolman & McClelland, 2011). Teenage sexual impulses need to be channeled and guided, and reproduction controlled, but it is a mistake to make teenagers feel depraved or evil if they experience sexual urges. Before focusing specifically on hazards, we should note that several "problems" are less problematic now than in earlier decades. Here are three specifics:

Pin It on Him Boutonniere, corsage, formal shirt with matching tie, bare arms—all are common at U.S. high school proms, including here, at Notre Dame in Harper Woods, Michigan. Yet these sights are unknown to most 17-year-olds in other nations. Despite such cultural oddities and this once-in-a-lifetime moment, Mariel West and John Felczak are evidence of a worldwide phenomenon: sexual attraction in late adolescence.

JIM WEST

■ *Teen births have decreased in every nation.* For example, between 1960 and 2010, the adolescent birth rate in China was cut in half (reducing the United Nations' projections of the world's population in 2050 by about 1 billion). In the United States, in 1991, the birth rate per 1,000 girls aged 15 to 17 was 39; in 2009, it was 20.

■ *The use of "protection" has risen.* Contraception, particularly condom use among adolescent boys, has increased markedly in most nations since 1990 (Santelli & Melnikas, 2010). The U.S. Youth Risk Behavior Survey found that 70 percent of sexually active ninth-grade boys had used a condom during their most recent intercourse (MMWR, June 4, 2010).

■ *The teen abortion rate is down.* In the United States, the teen abortion rate is about half the rate 20 years earlier (for all girls aged 15 to 19, the rate was 15 per 1,000 in 2007) (MMWR, February 25, 2011).

Now we focus on biological problems that result from adolescent sexual activity—pregnancy and infections—and on sexual abuse.

Sex Too Soon

Sex can, of course, be thrilling and affirming, a bonding experience. However, compared to a century ago, adolescent sexual activity—especially if it results in birth—is more hazardous because four circumstances have changed:

1. Earlier puberty and weaker social taboos mean teens have sexual impulses and experiences at younger ages. Early sex correlates with depression and drug abuse.
2. Most teenage mothers have no husbands to help them. A century ago, teenage mothers were married; now, in the United States, 85 percent are unwed.
3. Raising a child has become more complex and expensive, and fewer mothers of teenagers are available to help (many are employed).
4. Sexually transmitted infections are more common and dangerous.

As you just read, teen births are declining, as are teen abortions. However, the U.S. rate of adolescent pregnancy is the highest of any developed nation (true among every ethnic group). If a pregnant girl is under 16 (most are not), she is more likely to experience complications—including spontaneous or induced abortion, high blood pressure, stillbirth, preterm birth, and a low-birthweight newborn—than are teenagers who are age 16 or older. The risks are reduced with age, but they do not disappear: Babies born to young parents (even as "old" as 17 or 18) have higher rates of medical, educational, and social problems lifelong.

There are many reasons in addition to maternal age for these hazards. Poverty and lack of education correlate with teenage pregnancy and with every problem just listed (Santelli & Melnikas, 2010). Beyond that, younger pregnant teenagers are often malnourished and postpone prenatal care (Borkowski et al., 2007). After birth, adolescents are less likely to be the responsive mothers that newborns need, so insecure attachment (see Chapter 7) is more common. These problems are not inevitable, but some are a direct consequence of chronological age: Immature bodies are less ready for pregnancy and birth, and it is harder to meet the nutritional needs for two growing people than for one.

Early intercourse also risks psychosocial problems later on. A study of 3,923 adult women in the United States found that those

Rosie Will Be Fine Monica, here with her dog Rosie, is a mom-to-be—as are 13 percent of her female classmates at Timkin High School in Canton, Ohio. She is one of the fortunate ones; already a senior, she will probably earn her diploma. Plus, she is six months past conception, so the fetus is likely to be healthy. Teenagers typically welcome their unplanned babies but tend to have trouble raising them. This child will reach puberty before Monica is 30; their mutual immaturity will increase the child's risk of depression, delinquency, and another teen pregnancy.

AP TONY DEJAK

who voluntarily had sex before age 16 were more likely to divorce later on, whether or not that early sex resulted in pregnancy and whether or not they later married that man. The same study found that adolescents of any age whose first sexual experience was unwanted (either "really didn't want" or "had mixed feelings about") were also more likely to later experience divorce (Paik, 2011). Forced sex is much worse, of course, as now explained.

Sexual Abuse

Teenage births are risky, but sexual abuse is devastating: It harms development lifelong. **Child sexual abuse** is defined as any sexual activity (including fondling) between a juvenile and an adult, with age 18 the usual demarcation (although legal age varies by state). The most common time for sexual abuse is when the first stirrings of puberty occur, with girls particularly vulnerable—although boys are also at risk. Puberty not only increases the odds for sexual abuse, it also makes the emotional consequences worse because young adolescents are typically confused about their own sexual urges and identity (Graber et al., 2010). Virtually every adolescent problem, including early pregnancy, drug abuse, eating disorders, and suicide, is more frequent in adolescents who have been sexually abused.

> **child sexual abuse** Any erotic activity that arouses an adult and excites, shames, or confuses a child, whether or not the victim protests and whether or not genital contact is involved.

This is true worldwide. The United Nations reports that millions of girls in their early teens are forced into marriage, genital surgery, or prostitution (often across national borders) each year (Pinheiro, 2006). Exact numbers are elusive. Almost every nation has laws against child sexual abuse, but these laws are rarely enforced, and sensationalism about a single horrific case often crowds out systemic efforts to prevent, monitor, and eliminate the problem (Davidson, 2005).

In the United States, rates of sex abuse are declining (see Table 14.1), perhaps because adolescents are becoming wiser about sexual activity (Finkelhor & Jones, 2004). Evidence of their wisdom is condom use (a sign that at least one member of the couple is sexually informed and acting responsibly). Teenagers and young adults are more likely to use condoms correctly than older adults are (see Figure 14.7). (Specifics of sex education are discussed in Chapter 16.)

TABLE 14.1	Age and Sex Abuse: United States, 2007	
Age	Number of Sex-Abuse Victims	Percent of Malreatment That Is Sex Abuse
Less than 1 year	315	0.3%
1–3	3,249	2.2
4–7	13,137	7.4
8–11	13,459	9.5
12–15	19,848	14.5
16–17	6,084	13.5

Source: U.S. Department of Health and Human Services, 2010.

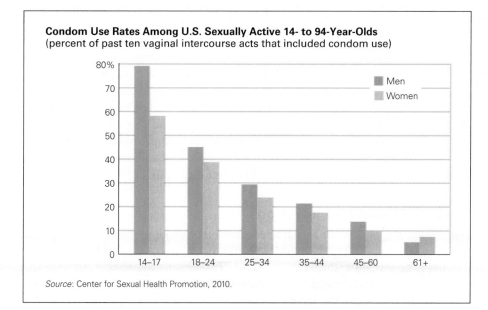

Condom Use Rates Among U.S. Sexually Active 14- to 94-Year-Olds
(percent of past ten vaginal intercourse acts that included condom use)

Source: Center for Sexual Health Promotion, 2010.

FIGURE 14.7

Pleasure and Protection Teenagers are much more likely to use condoms than are older adults, who probably never used them when they were young. This study found that sexual pleasure did not correlate with condom use. However, a negative correlation was found between condom use and having a steady partner—another reason for the age differences.

▶ **Research Design**

Scientists: Penelope K. Trickett, Jennie G. Noll, and Frank W. Putnam.

Publication: *Development and Psychopathology* (2011).

Participants: The Child Protection Service in Washington, D.C., referred 84 girls, ages 6 to 16, who had recently been sexually abused. Most (70 percent) had been vaginally or anally penetrated; the abuser was usually (60 percent of the time) their father or stepfather. The scientists found a comparison group from the same neighborhoods who had not been sexually abused (16 percent of the original comparison group were excluded after the first in-depth interview because they had been sexually abused but had not reported it). They also interviewed the caretakers of the girls. In later interviews, almost half of the original sample had had children, who became participants as well.

Design: Participants were interviewed six times over 23 years, with 96 percent of the sample interviewed at least once after age 18. (This retention rate is much higher than for most longitudinal samples; the scientists used many ways to find their participants, including searching MySpace and Facebook.) Interviews lasted three to four hours, were confidential, and assessed dozens of traits and characteristics. Caregivers and offspring were also interviewed, confidentially.

Results: Every trait examined showed a far higher incidence of problems in the victims than in their nonvictimized peers. That included attitudes directly related to sex abuse (e.g., most of those abused by their biological fathers thought of sex as dirty, shameful, dangerous) and behaviors seemingly unconnected (e.g., although their body weight was in the normal range in childhood, 42 percent were obese in their 20s). Cognitive development—school achievement as well as language use—was also impaired. Among the most troubling results were much higher rates of self-harm, aggression, and repeated victimization—both sexual and physical abuse.

The children of those who had been abused often experienced problems. In fact, 3 of their 78 children died in infancy, a much higher rate than usual, and 9 were permanently removed from their mothers.

Early in this chapter, we noted that the HPA system regulates puberty and many other physiological responses. Many of the victims had signs of a breakdown in the HPA regulatory system, altering their cortisol responses. That produced heightened stress reactions in early adolescence but then abnormally low stress responses in adulthood.

Major conclusion: Severe sexual abuse damages every aspect of development, affecting victims not only in childhood and adolescence but also in adulthood. Many become victims again as well as inadequate parents. None of this is inevitable, however; a few participants escaped these problems, especially if their own caretakers were wonderful (few were).

Comments: These scientists have made major contributions to our understanding of sexual abuse, which was once ignored or considered less harmful than physical abuse. This longitudinal research on a volatile group who move frequently, are isolated, and disappear for follow-up is commendable. Part of the researchers' success is attributable to their dedication, which included sending birthday and holiday cards to their participants even when funding temporarily disappeared. These results should lead to better long-term treatment of sex-abuse victims (hopefully better than the treatment these participants received—they averaged only four visits to a therapist). The researchers believe that effective treatment would markedly reduce the rate of rape, domestic violence, and child neglect.

However, many of the youngest adolescents remain ignorant, and almost all depend on adults to protect them. Few schools teach anything about sex until high school, and even then, the curriculum may be only about the biology of sex and disease. Meanwhile, peers brag and lie about their sexual exploits, and the teen media virtually never discuss healthy sexuality (Hust et al., 2008). That leaves youth to depend on their families—the worst possible source of information and protection for sexually abused adolescents, since the abusers are almost always family members. Relatives (including the abuser) sometimes blame the child. Many children trust their family members, which makes them doubly distressed later on, when they realize what happened (Clancy, 2010).

Abusers often isolate adolescents from their peers, depriving them of the friendships and romances that aid in developing a healthy and satisfying life. As with other types of maltreatment, the consequences extend far beyond the event. Young people who are sexually exploited tend to fear sexual relationships and to devalue themselves lifelong.

A longitudinal study of reported victims (all girls) of child sex abuse traced their development for 23 years (see the Research Design). The abuse of these girls began at age 7½, on average, and continued for two years, although some of them had experienced a briefer, usually violent, rape. (Slightly older girls and boys are more often abused, but their abuse is less often reported.) In order to isolate the effects of abuse, the researchers also traced the development of girls from the same backgrounds (SES, ethnicity, and so on) who were not sexually abused. They found that all the adolescent problems were more common in the victims and that impairment continued and even worsened in adulthood, including repeated physical and sexual abuse, severe depression, drug addiction, and obesity (Trickett et al., 2011a).

Sexually Transmitted Infections

Unlike teen pregnancy and sexual abuse, the other major problem of teenage sex shows no signs of abating. A **sexually transmitted infection (STI)** (sometimes referred to as sexually transmitted disease [STD] or venereal disease [VD]) is any infection transmitted through sexual contact. Worldwide, sexually active teenagers have higher rates of the most common STIs—gonorrhea, genital herpes, and

sexually transmitted infection (STI) A disease spread by sexual contact, including syphilis, gonorrhea, genital herpes, chlamydia, and HIV.

chlamydia—than do sexually active people of any other age group (World Health Organization, 2005). In the United States, 15- to 24-year-olds constitute only one-fourth of the sexually active population but account for half of all sexually transmitted infections. On average for urban U.S. teenagers, an STI is diagnosed only two years after intercourse begins (Tu et al., 2009).

Those who have sexual intercourse before age 16 are twice as likely to catch an infection as are those who begin sexual activity at age 20 (Ryan et al., 2008). One reason is biological. Fully developed women have some natural biological defenses against STIs; this is less true for pubescent girls, who are more likely to develop any STI they are exposed to, including HIV/AIDS (World Health Organization, 2005). In addition, if symptoms appear, sexually active teens hesitate to seek diagnosis or alert their partners. In cultures or families where teenage sex is forbidden, adolescents avoid treatment for STIs until pain requires it. Adolescents with same-sex partners are especially reluctant to find treatment if their community considers homosexuality shameful.

There are hundreds of STIs (James, 2007). *Chlamydia* is the most frequently reported one; it often begins without symptoms, yet it can cause permanent infertility. A laboratory test can detect chlamydia, and it can be treated and cured, but many young people avoid doctors. Worse is *human papillomavirus (HPV)*, which has no immediate consequences but, later in life, increases a female's risk of cervical cancer and death. Immunization before the first intercourse makes contracting HPV much less likely, but many parents hesitate to immunize their virginal 11- and 12-year-olds. The interested reader is encouraged to consult Appendix A, p. A-17, as well as other sources.

National variations in laws and rates of STIs are large, with rates among U.S. teenagers higher than in any other medically advanced nation. Internationally, a comparison of 30 nations found that French teenagers were among the most likely to use condoms, while those in the United States were least likely to do so (MMWR, June 4, 2010; Nic Gabhainn et al., 2009) (see Table 14.2). One reason may be that, by law, every French high school (including Catholic ones) is required to provide students with free, confidential medical care as well as condoms; by contrast, providing either medical care or condoms is illegal at many U.S. schools.

Especially for Health Practitioners How might you encourage adolescents to seek treatment for STIs? (see response, page 432)

No Safer? Educational posters and even intense educational programs have little proven effect on the incidence of AIDS among adolescents. This poster was displayed outside an HIV testing center in Windhoek, Namibia, a country that has one of the highest HIV infection rates in the world.

TABLE 14.2	Condom Use Among 15-Year-Olds (Tenth Grade)	
Country	Sexually Active (% of total)	Used Condom at Last Intercourse (% of those sexually active)
France	20	84
Israel	14	72
Canada	23	78
United States	41	68
England	29	83
Russia	33	75

Sources: MMWR, June 4, 2010; Nic Gabhainn et al., 2009.

Neurological Development

Like the other parts of the body, different parts of the brain grow at different rates (Blakemore, 2008). The limbic system, including the amygdala, where intense fear and excitement originate, matures before the prefrontal cortex, where planning, emotional regulation, and impulse control occur. Myelination and maturation continue in the entire brain but in sequence, proceeding from the inner brain to the cortex and from back to front (Sowell et al., 2007). The result is that

Right lateral and top views of the dynamic sequence of GM maturation over the cortical surface

NITIN GOGTAY ET AL. / NATIONAL ACADEMY OF SCIENCES, USA

Same People, But Not the Same Brain
These brain scans are part of a longitudinal study that repeatedly compares the proportion of gray matter from childhood through adolescence. Gray matter is reduced as white matter increases, in part because pruning during the teen years (the last two pairs of images here) allows intellectual connections to build. As the authors of one study that included this chart explain, teenagers may "look like an adult, but cognitively they are not there yet" (K. Powell, 2006, p. 865).

the instinctual and emotional areas of the adolescent brain develop ahead of the reflective, analytic areas. Furthermore, pubertal hormones target the amygdala directly, whereas the cortex responds more to age and experience than to hormones. As a consequence, early puberty means emotional rushes, unchecked by caution.

This is evident via brain scans. Emotional control, revealed by fMRI studies, is not fully developed until adulthood (Luna et al., 2010). When compared with 18- to 23-year-olds, 14- to 15-year-olds show heightened arousal in the brain's reward centers, making them seek excitement and pleasure (Van Leijenhorst et al., 2010).

Many types of psychopathology that originate in the brain increase at puberty. Most vulnerable are those who experience early puberty, because they must cope with the stresses of adolescence long before their prefrontal cortexes mature. As two experts explain, "The higher rates of psychopathology among early maturers are expected because their slow developing neurocognitive systems are mismatched with the fast-approaching social and affective challenges at the onset of puberty" (Ge & Natsuaki, 2009, p. 329).

Caution Needed

Adolescents are not the only ones who sometimes forget caution when excitement rises: Developmentalists, journalists, and the general public are vulnerable to the same problem. Scientists try to be careful: The same pair of researchers just quoted regarding prefrontal immaturity suggest other explanations as well (Ge & Natsuaki, 2009), although the uneven neurological maturity seems most plausible.

However, as noted in Chapter 6, the fMRI, the PET scan, and other measures of neurological activity are expensive and complex. Furthermore, "the images generated by such methods may have a power to captivate that reaches beyond their power to explain" (Miller, 2008, p. 1413). Reliable, longitudinal, multidisciplinary, replicated research on the brains of typical 10- to 17-year-olds is scarce. Probably the adolescent problem is an imbalance in the rate of growth in the various parts of the brain, not in immaturity of any one part (Casey et al., 2011).

Although caution is warranted, recent discoveries about the adolescent brain are exciting. The fact that the frontal lobes (prefrontal cortex) are the last to ma-

>> Response for Health Practitioners
(from page 431): Many adolescents are intensely concerned about privacy and fearful of adult interference. This means your first task is to convince the teenagers that you are nonjudgmental and that everything is confidential.

ture may explain something that has long bewildered adults: Many adolescents are driven by the excitement of new experiences, sensations, and peers—forgetting the caution that their parents have tried to instill (Steinberg, 2008). The following is one example.

"What Were You Thinking?"

Laurence Steinberg is a noted expert on adolescent thinking. He is also a father.

> When my son, Benjamin, was 14, he and three of his friends decided to sneak out of the house where they were spending the night and visit one of their girlfriends at around two in the morning. When they arrived at the girl's house, they positioned themselves under her bedroom window, threw pebbles against her windowpanes, and tried to scale the side of the house. Modern technology, unfortunately, has made it harder to play Romeo these days. The boys set off the house's burglar alarm, which activated a siren and simultaneously sent a direct notification to the local police station, which dispatched a patrol car. When the siren went off, the boys ran down the street and right smack into the police car, which was heading to the girl's home. Instead of stopping and explaining their activity, Ben and his friends scattered and ran off in different directions through the neighborhood. One of the boys was caught by the police and taken back to his home, where his parents were awakened and the boy questioned.
>
> I found out about this affair the following morning, when the girl's mother called our home to tell us what Ben had done. . . . After his near brush with the local police, Ben had returned to the house out of which he had snuck, where he slept soundly until I awakened him with an angry telephone call, telling him to gather his clothes and wait for me in front of his friend's house. On our drive home, after delivering a long lecture about what he had done and about the dangers of running from armed police in the dark when they believe they may have interrupted a burglary, I paused.
>
> "What were you thinking?" I asked.
>
> "That's the problem, Dad," Ben replied, "I wasn't."
>
> [Steinberg, 2004, pp. 51, 52]

Steinberg agrees with his son. As he expresses it, "The problem is not that Ben's decision-making was deficient. The problem is that it was nonexistent" (Steinberg, 2004, p. 52). In his analysis, Steinberg points out a characteristic of adolescent thought: When emotions are intense, especially when friends are nearby, the logical part of the brain shuts down. This shutdown is not reflected in questionnaires that require teenagers to respond to paper-and-pencil questions regarding hypothetical dilemmas. On those tests, most teenagers think carefully and answer correctly. They have been taught the risks of sex and drugs in biology or health classes in school. However,

> the prospect of visiting a hypothetical girl from class cannot possibly carry the excitement about the possibility of surprising someone you have a crush on with a visit in the middle of the night. It is easier to put on a hypothetical condom during an act of hypothetical sex than it is to put on a real one when one is in the throes of passion. It is easier to just say no to a hypothetical beer than it is to a cold frosty one on a summer night.
>
> [Steinberg, 2004, p. 53]

Ben reached adulthood safely. Some other teenagers, with less cautious police or less diligent parents, do not. Ideally, research on adolescent brains will help protect teens from their dangerous impulses (Monastersky, 2007). Brain immaturity is not the origin of every "troublesome adolescent behavior," but it is true that teenage brains have underdeveloped "response inhibition, emotional regulation, and organization" (Sowell et al., 2007, p. 59) because their prefrontal cortexes are immature.

The normal sequence of brain maturation (limbic system at puberty, then prefrontal cortex by the early 20s) combined with the early onset of puberty means that, for contemporary teenagers, emotions rule behavior for years (Blakemore, 2008; Compas, 2004). The limbic system, unchecked by the slower-maturing prefrontal cortex, makes powerful sensations—loud music, speeding cars, strong drugs—compelling.

It is not that the prefrontal cortex shuts down. In fact, it continues to mature throughout childhood and adolescence, and, when they think about it, adolescents are able to assess risks better than children are (Pfeifer et al., 2011). However, the thoughtful parts of the adolescent brain are less synchronized with the limbic system than they were earlier, and thus emotions from the amygdala are less

Not Me! A young woman jumps into the Pacific Ocean near Santa Cruz, California, while at a friend's birthday party. The jump is illegal, yet since 1975, 52 people have died taking that leap off these cliffs. Hundreds of young people each year decide that the thrill is worth the risk, aided by what they think are sensible precautions. (Note that she is wearing shoes. Also note that the dog has apparently decided against risking a jump.) As Chapter 17 explains, slightly older adolescents now jump into the Pacific off the California coast using parachutes—even riskier since sharks also live there.

modulated than they were (Pfeifer et al., 2011). It is the balance and coordination between the various parts of the brain that is off-kilter, not the brain itself (Casey et al., 2011).

When stress, arousal, passion, sensory bombardment, drug intoxication, or deprivation is extreme, the adolescent brain is flooded with impulses that might shame adults. As further explained regarding drug abuse in Chapter 16, teenagers brag about being so drunk they were "wasted," "bombed," "smashed"—a state most adults try to avoid and would be ashamed to admit. Also, unlike adults, some teenagers choose to spend a night without sleep, go through a day without eating, exercise in pain, play football after a mild concussion. The parts of the brain dedicated to analysis may be immature until years after the first hormonal rushes and sexual urges, while teenagers have access to fast cars, lethal weapons, and dangerous drugs. As one friend said to a next-door neighbor who had given his son a red convertible for high school graduation, "Why didn't you just give him a loaded gun?"

One example of the cautious part of the brain being overwhelmed by the emotions of the moment comes from teens sending text messages while they are driving. In a survey, 64 percent of U.S. 16- to 17-year-olds say they have been in a car when the driver was texting—a practice that occurs in every state and nation even though it is illegal in many of them (Madden & Lenhart, 2009). More generally, despite quick reflexes and better vision than at later ages, by far the most common cause of teenage death is motor-vehicle accidents. Thoughtless impulses and poor decisions are almost always to blame.

Every decision, from whether to eat a peach to when and where to enroll in college, requires balancing risk and reward, caution and attraction. For everyone, experiences, memories, emotions, and the prefrontal cortex help in choosing to avoid some actions and perform others. Neurological research finds that the reward parts of adolescents' brains (the parts that respond to excitement and pleasure) are far stronger than the inhibition parts (the parts that urge caution) (Van Leijenhorst et al., 2010). That may explain many adolescent actions that seem foolhardy to adults.

Benefits of Adolescent Brain Development

It is easy to be critical of adolescent behavior and then to blame it on hormones, or brains, or the media. Yet remember from Chapter 1 that difference is not always deficit and that gains as well as losses are part of every life development. Thus, the fact that the limbic system develops faster than the prefrontal cortex has benefits as well as hazards.

With increased myelination and slower inhibition, reactions become lightning fast; such speed is valuable in many aspects of life. For instance, adolescent athletes are potential superstars, not only quick but fearless as they steal a base, tackle a fullback, or race when their lungs feel about to burst. Ideally, coaches have the wisdom to channel such bravery. Furthermore, as the reward areas of the brain activate and the production of positive neurotransmitters increases, teenagers become happier. Reaction to a new love, or a first job, or even an A on a term paper can be ecstasy, a joy to be cherished in memory lifelong.

Adolescence is a good time to question tradition and learn new things. Before the brain becomes fully mature (at about age 25) and before another wave of pruning (at about age 18), "young brains have both fast-growing synapses and sections that remain unconnected" (Ruder, 2008, p. 8). This allows new connections to facilitate acquisition of new ideas, words, memories, personality patterns, and dance steps (Keating, 2004).

Synaptic growth enhances moral development as well. Adolescents question their elders and seek to forge their own standards. Values embraced during adolescence are more likely to endure than those acquired later, after brain connections are firmly established. This is an asset if values developed during adolescence are less self-centered than those of children or are more culturally attuned than those of older generations.

In short, several aspects of adolescent brain development can be positive. The fact that the prefrontal cortex is still developing "confers benefits as well as risks. It helps explain the creativity of adolescence and early adulthood, before the brain becomes set in its ways" (Monastersky, 2007, p. A17). The emotional intensity of adolescents "intertwines with the highest levels of human endeavor: passion for ideas and ideals, passion for beauty, passion to create music and art" (Dahl, 2004, p. 21). As a practical application, those who care about the next generation must attend to the life lessons that adolescents are learning. Adults should provide "scaffolding and monitoring" until adolescents' brains can function well on their own (Dahl, quoted in Monastersky, 2007, p. A18).

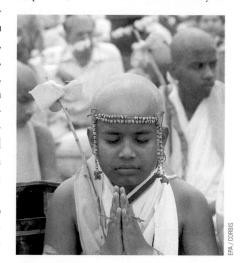

Sacred Thread Every religion has some ritual in which young people make a public commitment to their faith. These Hindu boys are receiving the jenoi, a sacred thread that they will wear all their lives. In this initiation ceremony, they shave their heads, wear new robes, and vow to pray three times a day and to study the Vedas, which are the scriptures of Hinduism.

By age 18, not only brains but also bodies can be strong and healthy, as described in this chapter. Most 18-year-olds are capable of hard physical work, problem-free reproduction, and peak athletic performance. Growth and sexual awakening, strength and speed, emotional intensity and hormonal rushes—all of these can be wonderful. Of course, adolescent minds and contexts are not always benign, as the following chapters describe. But before learning about alienation from school, or addiction to drugs, or juvenile delinquency, pause to appreciate the transformations just described.

SUMMING UP

Three transformations of puberty—the growth spurt, sexual differentiation, and brain maturation—are dramatic. Children become men or women, first in physical and sexual growth and then in brain maturation. Growth proceeds from the extremities to the center, so the limbs grow before the internal organs. Increase in weight precedes that in height, which precedes growth of the muscles and of the internal organs. Primary sex characteristics, which are connected to reproduction, and secondary sex characteristics, which signify masculinity or femininity, develop. Both boys and girls experience an increase in sexual interest as their bodies mature and their hormone levels rise. Adolescents' sexual behavior and thoughts are powerfully affected by culture.

The brain develops unevenly, with the limbic system ahead of the prefrontal cortex and the reward centers more active than the cautionary areas. As a result, adolescents are fast and fearless, qualities that may cause trouble or may benefit society. ∎

SUMMARY

Puberty Begins

1. Puberty refers to the various changes that transform a child's body into an adult one. Even before the teenage years, biochemical signals from the hypothalamus to the pituitary gland to the adrenal glands (the HPA axis) increase production of testosterone, estrogen, and various other hormones, which causes the body to develop.

2. Some emotional reactions, such as quick mood shifts and thoughts about sex, are directly caused by hormones. Others are caused by reactions (of others and then of the young person) to the physical changes of adolescence.

3. The body rhythms of life, both by the day and by the season, are regulated by hormones. In adolescence, these changes often result in sleep deprivation, partly because the natural circadian rhythm makes teenagers wide awake at night.

4. Puberty normally begins anytime from about age 8 to about age 14, most often between ages 10 and 13. The young person's sex, genetic background, body fat, and level of family stress all contribute to this variation in timing.

5. Girls generally begin and end the process of puberty before boys do, although the time gap in sexual maturity is much shorter than the two-year gender gap in reaching peak height.

6. Adolescents who reach puberty earlier or later than their friends experience additional stresses. Generally (depending on culture, community, and cohort), early-maturing girls and late-maturing boys have a particularly difficult time.

Nutrition

7. To sustain body growth, many adolescents consume large quantities of food, although they do not always make healthy choices. One reason for poor nutrition is the desire to lose (or, less often, gain) weight because of anxiety about body image.

8. Although eating disorders—overeating, anorexia, and bulimia—are not usually diagnosed until early adulthood, their precursors are evident during puberty. Many adolescents eat too much of the wrong foods or too little food overall.

The Transformations of Puberty

9. The growth spurt is an acceleration of growth in every part of the body. Peak weight usually precedes peak height, which is then followed by peak muscle growth. The lungs and the heart also increase in size and capacity.

10. Male–female differences become apparent at puberty. The maturation of primary sex characteristics means that by age 13 or so, after experiencing menarche or spermarche, teenagers are capable of reproducing.

11. Secondary sex characteristics are not directly involved in reproduction but signify that the child is becoming a man or a woman. Body shape, breasts, voice, body hair, and numerous other features differentiate males from females. Sexual activity is influenced more by culture than by physiology.

12. Among the problems that adolescents face is the tendency to become sexually active before their bodies and minds are truly ready. Pregnancy before age 16 takes a physical toll on a growing girl, and STIs at any age can lead to infertility and even death.

13. Sexual abuse, which includes any sexually provocative activity that involves a juvenile and an adult, is more likely to occur in early adolescence than at other ages. Girls are most often victims; the perpetrators are most often family members.

14. Various parts of the brain mature during puberty and the following decade. The regions dedicated to emotional arousal (including the amygdala) mature before those that regulate and rationalize emotional expression (the prefrontal cortex).

15. Because of the sequence of brain development, many adolescents seek intense emotional experiences, untempered by rational thought. For the same reasons, adolescents are quick to react, explore, and learn. As a result, adolescents take risks, bravely or foolishly, with potential for harm as well as for good.

KEY TERMS

puberty (p. 411)
menarche (p. 411)
spermarche (p. 411)
hormone (p. 412)
pituitary (p. 412)
adrenal glands (p. 412)

HPA (hypothalamus–pituitary–adrenal) axis (p. 412)
gonads (p. 413)
HPG (hypothalamus–pituitary–gonad) axis (p. 413)
estradiol (p. 413)
testosterone (p. 413)

circadian rhythm (p. 414)
secular trend (p. 416)
leptin (p. 416)
body image (p. 421)
anorexia nervosa (p. 422)
bulimia nervosa (p. 422)
growth spurt (p. 423)

primary sex characteristics (p. 425)
secondary sex characteristics (p. 425)
child sexual abuse (p. 429)
sexually transmitted infection (STI) (p. 430)

WHAT HAVE YOU LEARNED?

Puberty Begins

1. What are the first visible signs of puberty?

2. What body parts of a teenage boy or girl are the last to reach full growth?

3. How do hormones affect the physical and psychological aspects of puberty?

4. Why do adolescents have sudden, intense emotions, such as anger, ecstasy, or despair?

5. Why is the genetic trait of eveningness a particular problem during adolescence?

6. Why do parents and adolescents fight about bedtime?

7. What are the gender differences in the growth spurt?

8. What are the ethnic and cultural differences in the changes of puberty?

9. How would society be affected if puberty occurred for everyone a few years later?

10. Why is early puberty more difficult for girls than for boys?

11. Why is late puberty more difficult for boys than for girls?

Nutrition

12. Why would anyone voluntarily starve herself or himself to death?

13. Why would anyone make herself or himself throw up?

14. What problems might occur if adolescents do not get enough iron or calcium?

The Transformations of Puberty

15. Why are most adolescents unhappy with their appearance?

16. Why is body image often distorted in adolescence?

17. What are examples of the uneven growth patterns in adolescent bodies?

18. What problems result from the growth spurt sequence (weight/height/muscles)?

19. How do religion and culture affect adolescent sexual activity?

20. Among sexually active people, why do adolescents have more STIs than adults?

21. What are positive changes in adolescent sexuality over the past five decades?

22. Why is adolescent sexuality more hazardous now than it was five decades ago?

23. Why is it harmful for a young adolescent and an adult to have sex?

24. How might the timing of brain maturation during adolescence create problems?

25. In what ways is adolescent brain functioning better than adult brain functioning?

APPLICATIONS

1. Visit a fifth-, sixth-, or seventh-grade class. Note variations in the size and maturity of the students. Do you see any patterns related to gender, ethnicity, body fat, or self-confidence?

2. Interview two to four of your friends who are in their late teens or early 20s about their memories of menarche or spermarche, including their memories of others' reactions. Do their comments indicate that these events are, or are not, emotionally troubling for young people?

3. Talk with someone who became a parent before the age of 20. Were there any problems with the pregnancy, the birth, or the

first years of parenthood? Would the person recommend teen parenthood? What would have been different had the baby been born three years earlier or three years later?

4. Find two or three adults who, as adolescents, acted impulsively and did something that could have potentially caused great harm to themselves and/or other people. What do they recall about their thinking at the time of the incident? How would their actions differ now? What do their answers reveal about the adolescent mind?

>>ONLINE CONNECTIONS

To accompany your textbook, you have access to a number of online resources, including quizzes for every chapter of the book, flashcards (in English and Spanish), critical thinking questions, and case studies. For access to any of these links, go to www.worthpublishers.com/bergerca9e. In addition to these free resources, you'll also find links to podcasts, video clips, diagnostic quizzing with personalized study advice, and an ebook. Some of the videos and activities available online include:

- *Brain Development: Adolescence.* There's a lot going on in a teenager's brain! Animations and illustrations highlight that development and its effect on behavior.

- *The Timing of Puberty.* Too early? Too late? Teens tell their own stories about the impact of pubertal timing. The video also reviews physical changes and gender differences in maturation.

Adolescence: Cognitive Development

WHAT WILL YOU KNOW?

1. Why do some young adolescents think everyone else is focused on them?
2. Why don't adolescents use their new cognitive ability to think logically?
3. How do computers and cell phones affect adolescent learning?
4. Which adolescents (age and background) in which schools (size and type) are likely to feel lost and ignored?

I have taught child development to thousands of college students, at four universities. Most of the content is standard, and I know it well. That allows me to update, to add examples from current events, to figure out the best strategy for each session: lecture, discussion, show of hands, group work, demonstration, video clip, pair/share, written responses, quizzes, and so on. I adjust to each class; no group is exactly like the others. Each student is unique as well: Some need encouragement to express their ideas, others need to think before they speak, some laugh easily, some are impassive. Knowing who should learn what, when, and how is the challenge—and joy—of teaching.

A few years ago, I agreed to teach a college course to advanced high school students. I was pleased: They grasped concepts quickly, they studied for tests, they completed written assignments on time. But one day I was explaining Freud's stages.

> **Student:** I don't agree with that.
> **Me:** You don't have to agree, you just need to learn the terms and ideas.
> **Student:** Why should I do that?
> **Me:** You need to understand Freud, so you can then disagree.
> **Student:** But that's just Freud. I have my own ideas, and I like them better.

I was stunned. My college students were never so egocentric as to claim that their own ideas were so much better than Freud's that they didn't need to bother with him. Then I remembered; bright as they were, these students were adolescents.

This chapter describes adolescent cognition, sometimes impressively brilliant, sometimes surprisingly abstract, and sometimes amazingly egocentric. Taking into account the way adolescents think, we then describe how they are taught—in middle school, in high school, and around the world.

>> Logic and Self

Brain maturation, intense conversations, additional years of schooling, moral challenges, and increased independence all occur between ages 11 and 18. The combination propels impressive cognitive growth, from egocentrism to abstract logic.

Egocentrism

During puberty, young people center many of their thoughts on themselves, in part because maturation of the brain heightens self-consciousness (Sebastian et al., 2008). It is typical for young adolescents to try to understand their conflicting feelings about their parents, school, and classmates and to think deeply (but not always realistically) about their future. One reason adolescents spend so much time talking on the phone, e-mailing, and texting is that they like to ruminate about each nuance of everything they have done, are doing, and might do.

Thus, young adolescents think intensely about themselves and about what others think of them. Together these two aspects of thought are called **adolescent egocentrism,** first described by David Elkind (1967). Egocentrism is common in early adolescence among youth of both sexes and every ethnic group (Beaudoin & Schonert-Reichl, 2006). It continues throughout adolescence, especially in teenagers who have problems such as delinquency, aggression, and eating disorders, and it may increase again at the start of college (Schwartz et al., 2008).

In egocentrism, adolescents regard themselves as unique, special, and much more socially significant (that is, noticed by everyone) than they actually are. Accurately imagining someone else's perspective is difficult when egocentrism rules (Lapsley, 1993). For example, it seems unlikely that adolescent girls are especially attracted to boys with pimples and braces, but Edgar did not realize this, according to his older sister:

> Now in the 8th grade, Edgar has this idea that all the girls are looking at him in school. He got his first pimple about three months ago. I told him to wash it with my face soap but he refused, saying, "Not until I go to school to show it off." He called the dentist, begging him to approve his braces now instead of waiting for a year. The perfect gifts for him have changed from action figures to a bottle of cologne, a chain, and a fitted baseball hat like the rappers wear.
>
> *[adapted from Eva, personal communication, 2007]*

Egocentrism leads adolescents to interpret everyone else's behavior as if it were a judgment on them. A stranger's frown or a teacher's critique could make a teenager conclude that "No one likes me" and then deduce that "I am unlovable" or even claim that "I can't leave the house." More positive casual reactions—a smile from a sales clerk or an extra-big hug from a younger brother—could lead to "I am great" or "Everyone loves me," with similarly distorted self-perception. Given the rapid mood changes described in the previous chapter, such conclusions are usually short-lived, susceptible to reversal with another offhand remark.

As an aspect of egocentrism, acute self-consciousness about one's physical appearance is probably more prevalent between ages 10 and 14 than earlier or later (Rankin et al., 2004). Young adolescents would rather not stand out from their peers, hoping instead to blend in. They also believe that everyone is as egocentric as they are. As one girl said:

> I am a real worrier when it comes to other people's opinions. I care deeply about what they say, think and do. If people are very complimentary, it can give you a big confidence boost, but if people are always putting you down you feel less confident and people can tell. A lot of advice that is given is "Do what you want and don't listen to anyone else," but I don't know one person who can do that.
>
> *[quoted in J. H. Bell & Bromnick, 2003, p. 213]*

Fables

Elkind named several aspects of adolescent egocentrism, among them the **personal fable** and the **invincibility fable,** which often appear together. The

adolescent egocentrism A characteristic of adolescent thinking that leads young people (ages 10 to 13) to focus on themselves to the exclusion of others.

Every Detail Appearance has always been significant to young adolescents, but each cohort is distinct. Thin, waxed eyebrows, blue hair and nails, and a checkered shirt over stripes would all have been anathema to this girl's grandmother at age 15, who might have examined her rosy cheeks in a large, living room mirror.

personal fable An aspect of adolescent egocentrism characterized by an adolescent's belief that his or her thoughts, feelings, and experiences are unique, more wonderful or awful than anyone else's.

invincibility fable An adolescent's egocentric conviction that he or she cannot be overcome or even harmed by anything that might defeat a normal mortal, such as unprotected sex, drug abuse, or high-speed driving.

PICTURE PARTNERS / ALAMY

personal fable is the belief that one is unique, destined to have a heroic, fabled, even legendary life. Some 12-year-olds plan to star in the NBA, or become billionaires, or cure cancer. Another example is the belief that one is destined to die a young and tragic death; thus, habits that could lead to midlife lung cancer or heart disease are no problem. In some adolescent minds, there is no contradiction between the personal fable and *invincibility,* the idea that, unless fate wills it, they will not be hurt by fast driving, unprotected sex, or addictive drugs. If they take risks and survive without harm, they feel invincible, not grateful.

In every nation, those who volunteer for military service—knowing or even hoping that they will be sent into combat—are more likely to be under age 20 than over it. Young recruits take risks more often than older, more experienced soldiers (Killgore et al., 2006). Another example comes from online chat rooms. Young teenagers reveal personal information to electronic "friends," oblivious to the dangers that adults see in such revelations (McCarty et al., 2011).

Sometimes a jolting life experience punctures the illusion of invincibility, as happened to one Pennsylvania college student when his parents ended their 19-year marriage.

> I had read a lot of things about divorce affecting children at a young age, but I was a freshman in college and did not think there would be . . . downs and corkscrews that just sent my thoughts spiraling out of control. I, the invincible wrestler, the invincible college student, had finally found that kryptonite that would weaken me. . . . I did something that was not at all a sign of invincibility: I got help.
>
> *[Pikounis, 2010, p. 14]*

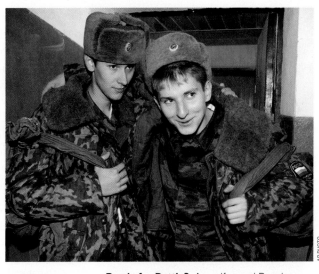

Ready for Battle? As uniformed Russian draftees, Yevgeny and Alexei might imagine that an audience sees them as tough men, but they would be mortified to know how boyishly naive they appear.

The Imaginary Audience

Egocentrism creates an **imaginary audience** in the minds of many adolescents. They believe they are at center stage, with all eyes on them, and they imagine how others might react to their appearance and behavior.

I witnessed this with my daughter Bethany at age 16. She was already a gifted artist. Perhaps that is why I agreed to go with her to the Metropolitan Museum of Art on a humid midsummer afternoon. When we emerged from the subway, we encountered a sudden downpour. Bethany stopped and became angry—at me!

imaginary audience The other people who, in an adolescent's egocentric belief, are watching and taking note of his or her appearance, ideas, and behavior. This belief makes many teenagers very self-conscious.

> **She:** You didn't bring an umbrella? You should have known.
> **Me:** It's OK—we'll walk quickly. It's a warm rain.
> **She:** But we'll get all wet.
> **Me:** No problem. We'll dry.
> **She:** But people will see us with our hair all wet.
> **Me:** Honey, no one cares how we look. And we won't see anyone we know.
> **She:** That's OK for you to say. You're already married.
> **Me:** *[incredulous]* Do you think you'll meet your future husband here?
> **She:** *[exasperated]* No, of course not. But people will look at me and think, "She'll never find a husband looking like that!"

The imaginary audience can cause teenagers to enter a crowded room as if they are the most attractive human beings alive. They might put studs in their lips or blast music for all to hear, calling attention to themselves. The reverse is also possible: Unlike Edgar, they might avoid scrutiny lest someone notice a blemish on their chin or make fun of their braces. Many a 12-year-old balks at going to school with a bad haircut or the wrong shoes.

Egocentrism Reassessed

After Elkind first described adolescent egocentrism, some psychologists blamed it for every teenage problem, from drug use to pregnancy (Eckstein et al., 1999). It is still a common explanation for the risk taking evident in adolescence (Leather, 2009). However, other research has found that some adolescents do not feel invincible; in fact, some have exaggerated perceptions of risks (Mills et al., 2008).

Some developmentalists now believe that egocentrism "may signal growth toward cognitive maturity" (Vartanian, 2001, p. 378), that egocentrism may be protective "each time an individual enters into a new environmental context or dramatically new life situation" (Schwartz et al., 2008, p. 447) as the adolescent responds to culture and cohort. For example, a 13-year-old who moved to Los Angeles from a small town recalled:

> When I got to school the first day, everyone looked at me like I was from outer space or something. It was like, "Who's that? Look at her hair. Look at what she's wearing." That's all anybody cares about around here; what you look like and what you wear. I felt like a total outcast. As soon as I got home, I locked myself in my room and cried for about an hour. I was so lonely.
>
> *[Tina, quoted in R. Bell, 1998, p. 78]*

The phrase "all anybody cares about around here" applies not only to Los Angeles. The same words could have been written by a young adolescent who moved from Los Angeles to a small town or by almost any adolescent new to a school. This girl's reaction was egocentric if she imagined more scrutiny than actually occurred, but young adolescents do sometimes reject peers who dress or act in unusual ways. Self-awareness and cultural sensitivity may be helpful.

Every year, thousands of new students in middle and high schools are harassed, especially if they differ from the norm in sexual behavior, accent, or clothing. In 2010, 15-year-old Phoebe Prince killed herself three months after she moved from a small town in Ireland to Massachusetts. At first, she thought she was a star—a senior boy was romantically involved with her. Then other students called her an Irish slut and taunted her—culminating in her suicide and the indictment of nine of them. The bullies were wrong, of course. But this tragedy could have been anticipated and halted by adults if they had understood adolescent egocentrism.

Lest you conclude that young adolescents are foolhardy to think they are invincible and the subject of others' attention, we should point out that there is a positive aspect to egocentrism. Young adolescents who feel psychologically invincible (not harmed by others' judgments) tend to be resilient, less likely to be depressed (Hill et al., 2011). Without that, tragedy might occur.

Formal Operational Thought

Adolescents move past concrete operational thinking and consider abstractions. Jean Piaget described a shift to what he called **formal operational thought,** including "assumptions that have no necessary relation to reality" (Piaget, 1972, p. 148).

formal operational thought In Piaget's theory, the fourth and final stage of cognitive development, characterized by more systematic logical thinking and by the ability to understand and systematically manipulate abstract concepts.

One way to distinguish formal from concrete thinking is to compare curricula in primary school and high school. Here are three examples:

1. *Math.* Younger children multiply real numbers, such as $4 \times 3 \times 8$; adolescents can multiply unreal numbers, such as $(2x)(3y)$ or even $(25xy^2)(3zy^3)$.
2. *Social studies.* Younger children study other cultures by considering daily life—drinking goat's milk or building an igloo, for instance. Adolescents can consider "gross national product" and "fertility rate" and how these affect global politics.
3. *Science.* Younger students water plants; adolescents test H_2O in the lab.

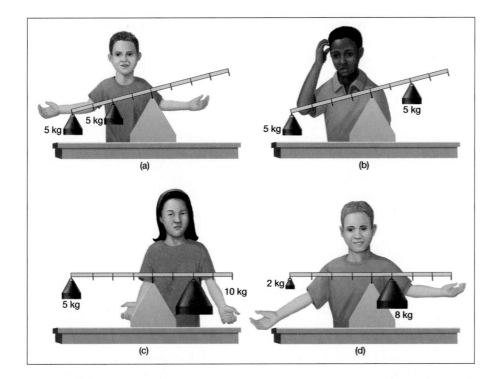

FIGURE 15.1

How to Balance a Scale Piaget's balance-scale test of formal reasoning, as it is attempted by *(a)* a 4-year-old, *(b)* a 7-year-old, *(c)* a 10-year-old, and *(d)* a 14-year-old. The key to balancing the scale is to make weight times distance from the center equal on both sides of the center; the realization of that principle requires formal operational thought.

Piaget's Experiments

Piaget and his colleagues devised a number of tasks to assess formal operational thought (Inhelder & Piaget, 1958); "in contrast to concrete operational children, formal operational adolescents imagine all possible determinants . . . [and] systematically vary the factors one by one, observe the results correctly, keep track of the results, and draw the appropriate conclusions" (P. H. Miller, 2011, p. 57).

In one experiment (diagrammed in Figure 15.1), children of many ages balance a scale by hooking weights onto the scale's arms. To master this task, they must realize that the weights' heaviness and distance from the center interact reciprocally to affect balance. Therefore, a heavier weight close to the center can be counterbalanced with a lighter weight far from the center. For example, a 12-gram weight placed 2 centimeters to the left of the center might balance a 6-gram weight placed 4 centimeters to the right.

This balancing concept was completely beyond the 3- to 5-year-olds. By age 7, children could balance the scale by putting the same amount of weight on each arm, but they didn't realize that the distance from the center mattered. By age 10, children thought about location but used trial and error, not logic. Finally, by about age 13 or 14, some children hypothesized and tested the reciprocal relationship between weight and distance and developed the correct formula (Piaget & Inhelder, 1969).

Hypothetical-Deductive Reasoning

One hallmark of formal operational thought is the capacity to think of possibility, not just reality. "Here and now" is only one of many alternatives, including "there and then," "long, long ago," "nowhere," "not yet," and "never." As Piaget said:

> The adolescent . . . thinks beyond the present and forms theories about everything, delighting especially in considerations of that which is not . . .

> *[Piaget, 1972, p. 148]*

hypothetical thought Reasoning that includes propositions and possibilities that may not reflect reality.

A Proud Teacher "Is it possible to train a cockroach?" This hypothetical question, an example of formal operational thought, was posed by 15-year-old Tristan Williams of New Mexico. In his award-winning science project, he succeeded in conditioning Madagascar cockroaches to hiss at the sight of a permanent marker. (His parents' logical reasoning about having 600 cockroaches living in their home is not known.)

deductive reasoning Reasoning from a general statement, premise, or principle, through logical steps, to figure out (deduce) specifics. (Also called *top-down reasoning.*)

inductive reasoning Reasoning from one or more specific experiences or facts to reach (induce) a general conclusion. (Also called *bottom-up reasoning.*)

Especially for Natural Scientists Some ideas that were once universally accepted, such as the belief that the sun moved around the Earth, have been disproved. Is it a failure of inductive or deductive reasoning that leads to false conclusions? (see response, page 446)

Adolescents are therefore primed to engage in **hypothetical thought,** reasoning about *if–then* propositions that do not reflect reality. For example, consider this question (adapted from De Neys & Van Gelder, 2009):

> If all mammals can walk,
> And whales are mammals,
> Can whales walk?

Younger adolescents often answer "No!" They know that whales swim, not walk, so the logic escapes them. Some adolescents answer "Yes." They understand the concept of *if.*

> *Possibility* no longer appears merely as an extension of an empirical situation or of action actually performed. Instead, it is *reality* that is now secondary to *possibility.*
>
> [*Inhelder & Piaget, 1958, p. 251; emphasis in original*]

Hypothetical thought transforms perceptions, not necessarily for the better. Adults sometimes become exasperated at the adolescent penchant for criticizing everything from the way their mother cooks spaghetti to why the Gregorian calendar, not the Chinese or Jewish one, is standard. They criticize what *is* precisely because of their hypothetical thinking about what might be. Adolescents' reflection about serious issues becomes complicated because they consider many possibilities, avoiding conclusions about the immediate issues (Moshman, 2005). They "naively underestimate the practical problems involved in achieving an ideal future for themselves or for society" (Miller, 2011, p. 59).

For example, a survey of U.S. teenagers' religious ideas found that most 13- to 17-year-olds considered themselves religious and thought that practicing their particular faith would help them avoid hell. However, they did not take the next logical step by trying to convince their friends to believe as they did and avoid hellfire. As one explained, "I can't speak for everybody, it's up to them. I know what's best for me, and I can't, I don't, preach" (quoted in C. Smith, 2005, p. 147).

Another said:

> I think every religion is important in its own respect. You know, if you're Muslim, then Islam is the way for you. If you are Jewish, well, that's great too. If you're Christian, well, good for you. It's just whatever makes you feel good about you.
>
> [*quoted in C. Smith, 2005, p. 163*]

In developing the capacity to think hypothetically, by age 14 or so adolescents become capable of **deductive reasoning,** or *top-down reasoning,* which begins with an abstract idea or premise and then uses logic to draw specific conclusions (Galotti, 2002; Keating, 2004). By contrast, **inductive reasoning,** or *bottom-up reasoning,* predominates during the school years, as children accumulate facts and personal experiences (the knowledge base) to aid their thought.

In essence, a child's reasoning goes like this: "This creature waddles and quacks. Ducks waddle and quack. Therefore, this must be a duck." This reasoning is inductive: It progresses from particulars ("waddles" and "quacks") to a general conclusion ("a duck"). By contrast, deduction progresses from the general to the specific: "If it's a duck, it will waddle and quack" (see Figure 15.2).

An example of the increase in deductive reasoning comes from the ways children, adolescents, and adults change in their support of anti-racist policies in the United States. By adolescence, almost everyone in the United States is aware that racism exists—and opposes it. As one might imagine, people who are directly harmed are more aware of racism than those who merely learn about it in history books. However, children tend to think the core problem is the prejudice of individuals. Using inductive reasoning, they think that the remedy is to reduce

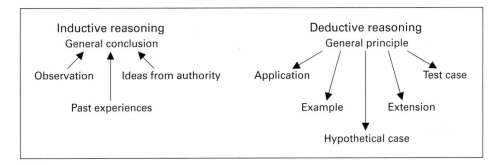

FIGURE 15.2

Bottom Up or Top Down? Children, as concrete operational thinkers, are likely to draw conclusions on the basis of their own experiences and what they have been told. This is called inductive, or bottom-up, reasoning. Adolescents can think deductively, from the top down.

racism among those people who express it, believing there will be less prejudice as individuals become more accepting of everyone. By contrast, older adolescents think, deductively, that racism is a society-wide problem that requires policy solutions.

This interpretation arises from a study of adolescent agreement or disagreement with policies to remedy racial discrimination (Hughes & Bigler, 2011). Not surprisingly, most (not all) students in an interracial U.S. high school recognized disparities between African and European Americans and believed that racism was a major cause. What was surprising to the researchers is that age made a difference. Among those who believed there were marked inequalities, older adolescents (age 16 to 17) were more likely to support systemic solutions (e.g., affirmative action and desegregation) than were younger adolescents (age 14 to 15). The authors suggest that "during adolescence, cognitive development facilitates the understanding that discrimination exists at the social-systemic level . . . racial awareness begins to inform views of race-conscious policies during middle adolescence" (Hughes & Bigler, 2011, p. 489).

Logical Fallacies

Many cognitive scientists study how people think, especially when logic fails. Failures are often apparent during adolescence (Albert & Steinberg, 2011).

One example is the **sunk cost fallacy.** In this fallacy, people who have spent money, time, or effort that cannot be recovered (a cost already "sunk") continue to try to achieve their desired goal because otherwise that previous effort is wasted. Sunk costs include not only monetary costs, but time and energy as well (Cunha & Caldieraro, 2009). People of all ages invest in repairing a "lemon" of a car, remaining in a class they are failing, continuing a destructive marriage, and so on.

Another common fallacy is **base rate neglect** (Barbey & Sloman, 2007). People ignore information about the frequency of a phenomenon and, influenced perhaps by a vivid experience, ignore the data. Egocentrism makes base rate neglect more likely. For instance, a teen might not wear a bicycle helmet, feeling invincible despite statistics, until a friend is brain-damaged in a biking accident. "When adolescents take unjustified risks, it is often because of the weakness of their analytic systems, which provide an inadequate check on impulsive or ill-considered decisions" (Sunstein, 2008, p. 145).

The prevalence of logical fallacies makes it apparent that formal operational thinking does not come to everyone at a certain developmental stage. On the contrary, research since Piaget has found marked variability: Some adolescents and adults still reason like concrete operational children. "No contemporary scholarly reviewer of research evidence endorses the emergence of a discrete new cognitive structure at adolescence that closely resembles . . . formal operations" (Kuhn & Franklin, 2006, p. 954).

Impressive Thinking "Correlating Genetic Signature with Surface Sugar Expression in Vibrio Vulnificus" is the title of Shilpa Argade's winning science project about a sometimes deadly bacteria. Like many of her peers in southern California, she is capable of deductive reasoning, but she does not always think that way.

sunk cost fallacy The mistaken belief that if money, time, or effort that cannot be recovered (a "sunk cost," in economic terms) has already been invested in some endeavor, then more should be invested in an effort to reach the goal. Because of this fallacy, people spend money trying to fix a "lemon" of a car or send more troops to fight a losing battle.

base rate neglect A common fallacy in which a person ignores the overall frequency of some behavior or characteristic (called the *base rate*) in making a decision. For example, a person might bet on a "lucky" lottery number without considering the odds that that number will be selected.

Piaget "launched the systematic study of adolescent cognitive development" (Keating, 2004, p. 45), but his description is not the final word. This is evident in the study just cited: Certainly adults disagree about the merits of affirmative action, for reasons that may be unrelated to whether they think inductively or deductively. Nonetheless, something shifts in cognition after puberty: Piaget was right that most older adolescents think differently than most children do.

SUMMING UP

Thinking reaches heightened self-consciousness at puberty, when adolescent egocentrism may be apparent. Some young adolescents have unrealistic notions about their place in the social world, as evidenced by the personal fable and the imaginary audience. They often imagine themselves as invincible, unique, and the center of attention. Adults often criticize this self-awareness, but it shows a cognitive advance and may be shaped by the social context.

Piaget thought the fourth and final stage of intelligence, called *formal operational thought,* begins in adolescence. He found that adolescents improve in deductive logic and hypothetical reasoning. Other scholars note logical lapses at every age and much more variability in adolescent thought than Piaget's description implies. ∎

>> Two Modes of Thinking

The fact that adolescents *can* use hypothetical-deductive reasoning does not necessarily mean that they *do* use it (Kuhn & Franklin, 2006). Adolescents find it much easier and quicker to forget about logic and instead to follow their impulses. Advanced logic in adolescence is counterbalanced by the increasing power of intuitive thinking. A **dual-process model** of adolescent cognition has been formulated (Albert & Steinberg, 2011).

dual-process model The notion that two networks exist within the human brain, one for emotional and one for analytical processing of stimuli.

Intuition Versus Analysis

For adults as well as adolescents, at least two modes characterize thought. Various scholars choose different terms and sometimes distinct definitions. These two modes of thought have been called: intuitive/analytic, implicit/explicit, creative/factual, contextualized/decontextualized, unconscious/conscious, gist/quantitative, hot/cold, emotional/intellectual, experiential/rational.

The thinking described by the first half of each pair is preferred in everyday life. Sometimes, however, circumstances compel the second mode, when deeper thought is demanded. The discussion in Chapter 14 about the discrepancy between the maturation of the limbic system and the prefrontal cortex reflects this duality. Research on adolescent cognition focuses on this intuitive/analytic pair (Gerrard et al., 2008).

intuitive thought Thought that arises from an emotion or a hunch, beyond rational explanation, and is influenced by past experiences and cultural assumptions.

analytic thought Thought that results from analysis, such as a systematic ranking of pros and cons, risks and consequences, possibilities and facts. Analytic thought depends on logic and rationality.

- **Intuitive thought** begins with a belief, assumption, or general rule (called a *heuristic*) rather than logic. Intuition is quick and powerful; it feels "right."
- **Analytic thought** is the formal, logical, hypothetical-deductive thinking described by Piaget. It involves rational analysis of many factors whose interactions must be calculated, as in the scale-balancing problem.

When the two modes of thinking conflict, people sometimes use one mode and sometimes the other. Experiences and role models influence the choice. For example, one study found that when adolescents enter a multicultural high school, some rely on old stereotypes and others consider new perspectives, depending on their specific experiences and on adult attitudes (Crisp & Turner, 2011). By adulthood, people try to coordinate intuitive and analytic thought, making sure that whatever feels right is also a wise move. As one scholar expresses it, there are "two systems but one reasoner" (De Neys, 2006, p. 428).

Comparing Intuition and Analysis

Paul Klaczynski has conducted dozens of studies comparing the thinking of children, young adolescents, and older adolescents (usually 9-, 12-, and 15-year-olds) (Holland & Klaczynski, 2009; Klaczynski, 2001, 2011; Klaczynski et al., 2009). In one, he presented 19 logical problems to children and adolescents. For example:

> Timothy is very good-looking, strong, and does not smoke. He likes hanging around with his male friends, watching sports on TV, and driving his Ford Mustang convertible. He's very concerned with how he looks and with being in good shape. He is a high school senior now and is trying to get a college scholarship.
>
> *Based on this [description], rank each statement in terms of how likely it is to be true. . . . The most likely statement should get a 1. The least likely statement should get a 6.*
>
> _____ Timothy has a girlfriend.
> _____ Timothy is an athlete.
> _____ Timothy is popular and an athlete.
> _____ Timothy is a teacher's pet and has a girlfriend.
> _____ Timothy is a teacher's pet.
> _____ Timothy is popular.

In ranking these statements, most adolescents (73 percent) made at least one analytic error, ranking a double statement (e.g., popular *and* an athlete) as more likely than a single statement included in it (popular *or* an athlete). They intuitively jumped to the more inclusive statement, rather than sticking to logic. Klaczynski found that almost all adolescents were analytical and logical on some of the 19 problems but not on others. Logical thinking improved with age and education, although not with IQ.

In other words, being smarter as measured by an intelligence test did not advance logic as much as did having more experience, in school and in life. Klaczynski (2001) concluded that, even though teenagers *can* use logic, "most adolescents do not demonstrate a level of performance commensurate with their abilities" (p. 854).

Preferring Emotions

What would motivate adolescents to use—or fail to use—their formal operational thinking? Klaczynski's participants had all learned the scientific method in school, and they knew that scientists use empirical evidence and deductive reasoning. But they did not always think like scientists. Why not?

Dozens of experiments and extensive theorizing have found some answers (Albert & Steinberg, 2011). Essentially, logic is more difficult than intuition, and it requires examination of comforting, familiar prejudices. Once people of any age reach an emotional conclusion (sometimes called a "gut feeling"), they resist changing their minds. As people gain experience in making decisions and thinking things through, they become better at knowing when analysis is needed (Milkman et al., 2009). For example, in contrast to younger students, when judging the legitimacy of a rule, older adolescents are more suspicious of authority and

Impressive Connections This robot is about to compete in the Robotics Competition in Atlanta, Georgia, but much more impressive are the brains of the Oregon high school team (including Melissa, shown here) who designed the robot.

AP PHOTO / GREGORY SMITH

more likely to consider mitigating circumstances (Klaczynski, 2011). Both suspicion of authority and awareness of context signify advances in reasoning, but both also complicate simple issues.

Rational judgment is difficult when egocentric emotions dominate. One psychologist discovered this firsthand when her teenage son phoned to be picked up from a party that had "gotten out of hand." The boy heard

> his frustrated father lament "drinking and trouble—haven't you figured out the connection?" Despite the late hour and his shaky state, the teenager advanced a lengthy argument to the effect that his father had the causality all wrong and the trouble should be attributed to other covariates, among them bad luck.
>
> [Kuhn & Franklin, 2006, p. 966]

Better Thinking

Sometimes adults conclude that more mature thought processes are wiser, since they lead to a more cautious approach (as in the father's connection between "trouble" and alcohol in the excerpt above). Adults are particularly critical when egocentrism leads an impulsive teenager to risk future addiction by experimenting with drugs or to risk pregnancy and AIDS by avoiding the awkwardness of using a condom.

But adults may themselves be egocentric in making such judgments because they assume that adolescents share their values. Parents want healthy, long-living children, and they conclude that adolescents use faulty reasoning when they risk their lives. Adolescents, however, value social warmth and friendship. A 15-year-old who is offered a cigarette might rationally choose social acceptance over the distant risk of cancer (Engels et al., 2006).

Research on how adults make complex decisions, such as whom to marry or which investment to make, finds that sometimes intuitive decisions are best and sometimes not (Dijksterhuis & Aarts, 2010). At every age, the best thinking may be "fast and frugal" (Gigerenzer, 2008). Weighing alternatives, and thinking of possibilities, could be paralyzing. The systematic, analytic thought that Piaget described is slow and costly, not fast and frugal, wasting precious time when a young person wants to act.

As the knowledge base increases and the brain matures, both modes of thought become more forceful. With maturity, adolescents avoid both extremes: They are neither paralyzed by too much analysis nor plummeted into danger via intuition. Logic increases from adolescence to adulthood (and then decreases somewhat in old age) (De Neys & Van Gelder, 2009).

Ideally, people use whatever combination of dual processing leads to good decisions (Gigerenzer, 2008). Adolescents may use formal, analytic thinking in science class and emotional, experiential thinking (which is quicker and more satisfying) for personal issues (Kuhn & Franklin, 2006).

Thinking About Religion

As you remember from Chapter 1, scientists build on previous research or theories, replicating, extending, or refuting the work of others. Scientists question assumptions, seeking empirical evidence to verify or criticize both new theories and old cultural myths. This is a formal operational approach.

Some impressionistic descriptions of teenagers and religion (e.g., Flory & Miller, 2000) emphasize cults and sects. As one observation reports, young congregants gather, "dressed as they are, piercings and all, and express their commitment by means of hip-hop and rap music, multimedia presentations, body modification, and anything else that can be infused with religious meaning" (Ream & Savin-Williams, 2003, p. 51).

This description evokes emotions—the quick, intuitive responses that judge piercings and rap to be the antithesis of religion. When another team of researchers began by "reading many published overview reports on adolescence . . . [they got] the distinct impression that American youth simply do not have religious or spiritual lives" (C. Smith, 2005, p. 4). Seeking evidence, not impressions, they surveyed 3,360 13- to 17-year-olds and their parents, tallied the quantitative results, and then added qualitative depth by interviewing 287 teenagers privately, in long, structured, conversations.

The researchers found that most adolescents (71 percent) felt close to God; believed in heaven, hell, and angels; and affirmed the same religion as their parents (78 percent Christian, 3 percent Jewish or Muslim, almost none Buddhist or Hindu). Some were agnostic (2 percent), and 16 percent said they were not religious—although many of those attended church and prayed. Less than 1 percent were "unconventional" (e.g., Wiccan). This was quite contrary to the impressionistic accounts the researchers had read.

They also found that adolescents' religious beliefs were often egocentric: Faith was a personal tool to be used in times of difficulty (e.g., while taking an exam). Many (82 percent) claimed their beliefs were important in daily life. One boy explained that religion kept him from doing "bad things, like murder or something," and one girl said:

> [Religion] influences me a lot with the people I choose not to be around. I would not hang with people that are, you know, devil worshipers because that's just not my thing. I could not deal with that negativity.
>
> *[quoted in C. Smith, 2005, p. 139]*

The researchers doubt that "socializing with Satanists is a real issue in this girl's life" or that this boy "struggles with murderous tendencies" (C. Smith, 2005, p. 139). They also noted that few adolescents (less than 1 percent) used theology to guide them in the actual issues of daily life, such as seeking justice or loving one's neighbor. For most, religious beliefs were intuitive, not analytic.

What does this imply for adults who hope to instill values in the next generation? In many ways, these data are encouraging: Most children and adolescents adhere to the faith and values of their parents. However, the authors wish that adults would encourage teenagers to discuss complex spiritual issues (e.g., stewardship of the environment, economic disparity, the implications of scriptures). This would require parents and church leaders to engage in the more difficult processes of cognition.

As good scientists, the researchers surveyed the same individuals three years later. They found a "shifting away from conventional religious beliefs" (Denton et al., 2008, p. 3). But, despite less certainty about God, angels, or an afterlife, these older adolescents tended to feel they had become more, not less, religious over the three-year period. One possible reason is that "as adolescents develop and mature, they take more ownership over their own beliefs and practices so that their religiosity feels stronger and more authentic" (Denton et al., 2008, p. 32). In other words, maturation, independence, and years of questioning thought may advance cognition.

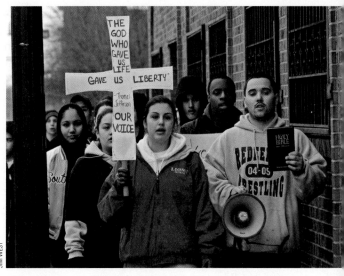

Living Their Faith? Theologians may separate faith from personal or political concerns, but few adolescents do. In a protest aimed at keeping their Catholic school open, one student leader carries a white cross with a quote from Thomas Jefferson (a deist who opposed clergy and religious doctrine); her classmate carries a bullhorn and a Bible. Secular concerns also affect adult religious thought: Despite community and student protests such as this one, the Detroit Archdiocese closed Holy Redeemer for financial reasons.

Dual Processing and the Brain

The brain maturation described in Chapter 14 seems directly related to the dual processes just explained (Steinberg, 2010). Because the limbic system is activated by puberty whereas the prefrontal cortex matures more gradually over time, it is easy to understand why adolescents are swayed by their intuition instead of logic.

New evidence for the power of impulses comes from more than 7,000 adolescents surveyed longitudinally five times between ages 12 and 24. The results were "consistent with neurobiological research indicating that cortical regions involved in impulse control and planning continue to mature through early adulthood [and that] subcortical regions that respond to emotional novelty and reward are more responsive in middle adolescence than in either children or adults" (Harden & Tucker-Drob, 2011, p. 743).

To be specific, this study traced the development of sensation seeking (e.g., "I enjoy new and exciting experiences"), which seems connected to the limbic system, maturing rapidly soon after puberty. Increases in sensation seeking were notable from ages 12 to 14 (see Figure 15.3). Sensation seeking can be seen as intuitive—direct from the gut to the brain. The researchers also studied impulsivity, as indicated by agreement with statements such as "I often get in a jam because I do things without thinking." A decline in impulsive actions can be considered an increase in analytic thinking—not the fast responses of intuitive thought (Harden & Tucker-Drob, 2011).

Impulsivity declined (and therefore analytic thinking increased) as adolescents matured over the twelve years of the study. The burst of sensation seeking at puberty and the decline of impulsivity over the years of adolescence were general trends. This could be interpreted as confirming the dual-process view because each of the two modes of thought followed a distinct trajectory. In other words, there was no significant correlation between changes in sensation seeking and changes in impulsivity within individuals—a person could have a faster decline in one than in the other, or vice versa.

Indicative of this lack of correlation is that there were marked individual differences in the patterns, as found in the many personal variations in biological changes during adolescence. However, over the years of adolescence, age trends were apparent: Both sensation seeking and impulsivity eventually declined.

Those age trends could be interpreted as another example of the overall pattern of maturation of the limbic system occurring ahead of advances in the prefrontal cortex. This led one neurologist to conclude:

> The teenage brain is not just an adult brain with fewer miles on it. It's a paradoxical time of development. These are people with very sharp brains, but they're not quite sure what to do with them.
>
> *[Jensen, quoted in Ruder, 2008, p. 8]*

Trends in Impulsivity and Sensation Seeking

Source: Harden & Tucker-Drob, 2011.

FIGURE 15.3

Look Before You Leap As you can see, as they mature, adolescents become less impulsive, but they still enjoy the thrill of a new sensation.

SUMMING UP

Current research recognizes that there are at least two modes of cognition: People sometimes use analytical thinking and other times prefer intuitive reasoning. This second kind of thinking is experiential, quicker, and more intense than formal operational thought. Both forms develop during adolescence, although sometimes intuitive processes crowd out logical ones. The logic necessary for impulse control may not increase rapidly enough when sensation seeking is strong, as the prefrontal cortex develops slowly. Each form of thinking is appropriate in some contexts. With neurological maturation, logical, reflective thinking becomes more possible, as is evident in thoughts about religion and about racism. Adolescents' impulsive and quick responses need to be guided until their logical processes can analyze and anticipate the impact of their actions. ▪

>> Technology and Cognition

Is technology beneficial or harmful for adolescent cognition? Both opinions are strongly expressed, and both have research to support them (Gentile, 2011b). Adults over age 40 grew up without the World Wide Web, instant messaging, Twitter, blogs, cell phones, iPods, iPads, BlackBerries, or digital cameras. Until 2006, only students at elite colleges could join Facebook. Yet today's teenagers are "digital natives." Since childhood they have been networking, texting, and clicking for definitions, directions, and data without realizing how alien that might be for their elders. Most adolescents have cell phones, iPods, and other mobile devices within reach, day and night.

The gap between those who did and did not have computers was bemoaned a decade ago; it divided boys from girls and rich from poor (Dijk, 2005; Norris, 2001). However, in many nations, that *digital divide* has virtually disappeared. Low-income children are somewhat less likely to have high-speed Internet at home, and Hispanic households lag behind others in technology, but those divides are rapidly narrowing. Virtually every secondary school and library in every developed nation is connected to the Internet, as are many in developing nations.

Thus, today's students take technology for granted. Many own computers; some get them free from their schools (Ash, 2009). The only significant digital divide is now age: Of those over age 65, less than half (42 percent) are online (see Figure 15.4). No wonder most critics of technology are older adults.

Learning via Electronic Technology

In many schools, teachers use computers and cell phones as tools for learning. In some states (e.g., Idaho) and some school districts, students must take at least one class completely online. Internet use and video games improve visual-spatial skills and vocabulary (Greenfield, 2009). Recall that research conducted before the technology explosion found that, with education, conversation, and experience, adolescents move past egocentric thought. Social networking may speed up this process, as teens communicate daily with dozens—perhaps even hundreds or thousands—of friends via e-mail, texting, and cell phones.

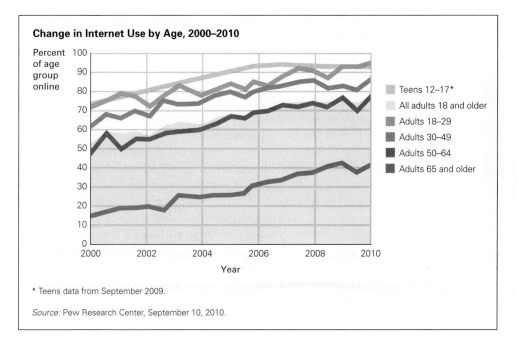

Change in Internet Use by Age, 2000–2010

Percent of age group online

Legend:
- Teens 12–17*
- All adults 18 and older
- Adults 18–29
- Adults 30–49
- Adults 50–64
- Adults 65 and older

* Teens data from September 2009.

Source: Pew Research Center, September 10, 2010.

FIGURE 15.4

Almost Every Teenager Most teenagers go online every day, more often for social reasons than academic ones. The challenge for American educators is no longer access (virtually every school has Internet capability) but guidance: Adolescents need to learn appropriate Web use, including how to identify and evaluate propaganda and how to avoid plagiarism.

The Same Situation, Many Miles Apart: Where Is the Teacher? Free laptops are provided for every middle school student in Maine *(left)* and at some public schools in Uruguay *(right)*. Benefits include more active learning, collaboration, and independence—or are these liabilities instead?

Online connections bring friends closer together and reduce social isolation (Valkenburg & Peter, 2009). Although most social networking is between friends who know each other well, the Internet may be a lifeline for teenagers who are isolated because of their sexual orientation, culture, religion, or native language. For everyone, the Internet allows contact with like-minded people thousands of miles away and enables individuals to expand their knowledge on virtually any subject. Most secondary students check facts, read explanations, view videos, and thus grasp concepts they would not have known if they had grown up a few years earlier.

Addiction and Technology

Adults worry about sexual abuse via the Internet. There is comforting research here: Although sexual predators lurk online, most teens avoid them, just as most adults avoid distasteful ads and pornography. Sexual abuse is a serious problem, but social networking does not increase the risk (Wolak et al., 2008).

There are some dangers, however. Technology encourages rapid shifts of attention, multitasking without reflection, visual learning instead of invisible analysis (Greenfield, 2009). Video games with violent content promote aggression (Gentile, 2011b). For some adolescents, chat rooms, video games, or Internet gambling can become addictive, taking time from needed play, schoolwork, and friendship (Shuler, 2009; Yen et al., 2008).

This is not mere speculation. A study using a representative sample of 8- to 18-year-olds in the United States found that one-third of the boys and one-eighth of the girls played video games every day (see the Research Design). Most of the rest played almost as often; only 3 percent of the boys and 21 percent of the girls never played. The *average* respondent played two hours a day. Those with symptoms of addiction (12 percent of the boys and 3 percent of the girls) played, on average, more than three hours a day, with some of them (about 10 percent) playing more than six hours a day (Gentile et al., 2011a). (See Figure 15.5 for time spent playing video games, by age group.)

In this study, many adolescents admitted that video games took time away from household chores and homework. Worse, one-fourth used video games to escape from problems, and one-fifth had "done poorly on a school assignment or test" because of spending too much time playing. The heaviest users

FIGURE 15.5

More Than Eating The average adolescent boy spends more time playing video games than reading, eating, doing homework, talking with friends, playing sports, or almost anything else except sleeping or sitting in class. Indeed, some skip school or postpone sleep to finish a game.

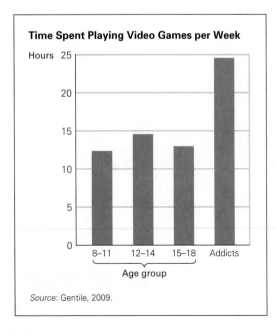

Time Spent Playing Video Games per Week

Source: Gentile, 2009.

got lower school grades and had more physical fights than did the average users. Sadly, the data from this study may underestimate the problem, since adolescents reported on themselves.

Addiction of any kind limits life experience, with the harm especially severe when the brain is still growing. Thus, adolescent video game addiction is a serious problem. This survey found that most game playing occurred at home, often in the child's own bedroom, and that only half of the parents had rules about their adolescents' play (Gentile, 2009). One conclusion is that if parents allow such games, then rule setting and monitoring are needed. As the next chapter explains, parents need to be careful: Especially with adolescents, overly restrictive parenting can backfire.

A simple solution is to ban technology from schools and bedrooms, but, as one critic writes, "Cell phones have the potential to be negative in schools. But we don't ban pencils and paper because students pass notes" (Shuler, 2009, p. 35). Some teachers confiscate computers and cell phones used in class; others include them in the curriculum.

Cyberdanger

When a person is bullied via electronic devices, usually via e-mail, text messages, or cell phone videos, that is **cyberbullying** (Tokunaga, 2010). The adolescents most involved are usually already bullies or victims or both, with bully-victims the most likely to engage in, and suffer from, cyberbullying. Technology does not create bullies per se, but it gives them another means and wider access. It enables relational bullying, not physical bullying, and thus girls seem to engage in cyberbullying as often as boys do.

A scholar who has studied bullying in all its forms finds that cyberbullying is similar to other forms of harassment (P. K. Smith et al., 2008), a conclusion reached by numerous other social scientists. For example, a study of 1,169 15-year-olds in New Zealand found that cyberbullying correlated with physical and relational bullying (Marsh et al., 2010).

This does not mean that cyberbullying is just like other forms. Relational bullying can be more harmful when done over the Internet, since rumors can "go viral" and insults can be transmitted day and night. The imaginary audience magnifies the shame (Englander et al., 2009). An added dimension of cyberbullying comes from cell phone photos: Some adolescents photograph another in a compromising position (such as drunk, naked, or crying) and then send it to a wide audience. While the causes of all forms of bullying seem similar, each form has its own sting, and the sting of cyberbullying is worse when the self-image is forming and impulsive thoughts precede analytic ones.

All forms of bullying are affected by the school climate. When students consider their school a good place to be—with supportive teachers, friendly students, opportunities for growth (clubs, sports, theater, music) and so on—those with high self-esteem are not only less likely to engage in cyberbullying, but they also disapprove of it. That reduces the incidence overall. However, when the school climate is negative, those with high self-esteem are often bullies themselves

---

▶ Research Design

Scientist: Douglas Gentile.

Publication: *Psychological Science* (2009).

Participants: All were part of a Harris interactive sample, selected to be representative of youth aged 8 to 18 in the United States. The 1,178 participants (about 100 at each age) were equally divided by gender and ethnically diverse (about half non-Hispanic White; about one-sixth each African American and Latino; and the remaining mixed, Asian or Native American, or declining to specify).

Design: The participants were asked questions, via computer, about their video game use, including frequency, parental policies, and signs of possible addiction.

Results: Almost all played video games many hours a week, with boys spending about twice the time on it as girls did. For both sexes, video game frequency peaked between ages 12 and 14. Younger students played slightly less often, and older students played for a longer time at a stretch. More than half of the boys had M-rated games (rated mature, with explicit violence or sex), almost always with their parents' permission. Video game playing correlated with lower achievement and more behavior problems, especially attention-deficit disorder.

Major conclusion: Many parents, teachers, and psychologists have worried that some teenagers are addicted to video games, curtailing important aspects of their lives and using games to avoid problems. Using criteria for addiction developed by psychiatrists for other addictions (gambling, drugs, and so on), this study found an answer: 12 percent of the boys and 3 percent of girls were addicted to playing video games. Their addiction decreased their family and school involvement.

Comments: These numbers are chillingly high. One hopes those in the sample are more likely than the average teenager to be game-addicted (they were all contacted via computer) or, since this study is correlational, that low school achievement leads to video game playing, rather than vice versa. However, a later controlled study began with children whose parents intended to buy them a video game system. Half of them were given the system, and the other half had to wait. Those 6- to 9-year-old boys who received the video game system had lower reading and writing achievement than did other boys from the same population with the same characteristics who had to wait four months (Weis & Cerankosky, 2010). (A similar study with adolescents would be enlightening, but most teenage boys whose parents allow video game systems already have them.)

---

cyberbullying Bullying that occurs when one person spreads insults or rumors about another by means of e-mails, text messages, or cell phone videos.

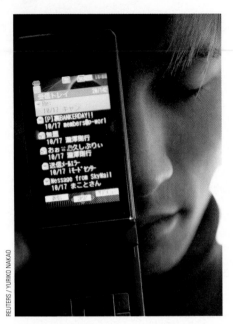

REUTERS / YURIKO NAKAO

Suicide Device High schooler Yuriko's cell phone capabilities drove him to thoughts of suicide. Fortunately, he got help to stop the mental torture he suffered from cyberbullying—a problem that may be worse in Japan because social reputation is crucial. For the same reason, young adolescents are particularly vulnerable.

cutting An addictive form of self-mutilation that is most prevalent among adolescent girls and that correlates with depression and drug abuse.

(Gendron et al., 2011). Some students believe that cyberbullying is unstoppable; however, not only schools but also some teens themselves use successful strategies, including deleting messages unread (Parris et al., 2011).

A complication is that the technology is trusted by most adolescents but misunderstood by many adults. As a result, parents and teachers are often unaware of cyberbullying, and few laws and policies are in place to prevent it. Adolescents are far more vulnerable than adults realize. This was tragically evident in the suicide of a Missouri 13-year old, Megan Meier, who believed a boy she never met named Josh Evans was her MySpace friend. When Josh turned on her, finally e-mailing that "the world would be a better place without you," she hung herself.

"Josh" was actually the mother of another girl who had been hurt by Megan. The mother was convicted of "computer fraud and abuse" in California (MySpace headquarters) but acquitted on appeal. This case is a dramatic example of a widespread problem: Electronic communication allows a dangerous mix of adult ignorance and adolescent egocentrism.

Another problem with electronic technology is less common but equally dangerous. Some teenagers use online connections to pursue a destructive action, such as extreme dieting, abusive prejudice, or self-harm. A European study of 700 adolescents in several nations found that those who were addicted to Internet use were also likely to be severely depressed (Durkee et al., 2011).

Let us look at one example in detail: self-mutilation, known as **cutting.** Over 400 Web sites are dedicated to cutting, an addictive activity (particularly among adolescent girls) that correlates with depression, drug abuse, and Internet misuse.

Analysis of a representative sample of 3,219 posts on cutting sites found that most were positive and helpful, allowing self-injuring adolescents to "establish interpersonal intimacy . . . [which is] especially difficult for young people struggling with intense shame, isolation, and distress" (Whitlock et al., 2006, p. 415). The most common theme of the messages was informal support (28 percent). Other posts described treatment (7 percent, usually positively) and emotional triggers (20 percent). Some posts, however, told how to conceal marks (9 percent) or described techniques of cutting (6 percent). Here is one exchange:

Poster 1: Does anyone know how to cut deep without having it sting and bleed too much?
Poster 2: I use box cutter blades. You have to pull the skin really tight and press the blade down really hard. You can also use a tourniquet to make it bleed more.
Poster 3: I've found that if you press your blade against the skin at the depth you want the cut to be and draw the blade really fast it doesn't hurt and there is blood galore. Be careful, though, 'cause you can go very deep without meaning to.

[quoted in Whitlock et al., 2006, p. 413]

Note that with both cyberbullying and cutting, the danger lies not in the computer but in the cognition of the person at the keyboard. Technology must be used with care. As with many aspects of adolescence (puberty, brain development, egocentric thought, and so on), context, adults, peers, and the adolescent's own personality and temperament "shape, mediate, and/or modify effects" of technology (Oakes, 2009, p. 1142). If a teen is intuitive, impulsive, and egocentric, he or she has difficulty analyzing the impact of whatever harmful remark is sent or limiting the emotional response to whatever destructive comment is read. Adults should know better, but all of us are sometimes illogical and emotional: It takes time and experience to use technology wisely.

SUMMING UP

In fostering adolescent cognition, technology seems to have many positive aspects: Computers are used as a tool for learning in many classrooms, and online connections can promote social cohesion and reduce isolation, especially for those who feel marginalized. Friends often connect via texting and e-mail, and social-networking sites expand the social circle. However, technology also has a dark side, evident in the frequency of cyberbullying and addiction to video games, which can interfere with education and friendship, rather than enhance them.   ■

>> Teaching and Learning

What does our knowledge of adolescent thought imply about school? Educators, developmentalists, political leaders, and parents wonder exactly which curricula and school structures are best for 11- to 18-year-olds. There are dozens of options: academic knowledge or practical skills, single sex or co-ed, competitive or cooperative, large or small, public or private—and more. To further complicate matters, adolescents differ from one another in many ways. As a result, "some students thrive at school, enjoying and benefiting from most of their experiences there; others muddle along and cope as best they can with the stress and demands of the moment; and still others find school an alienating and unpleasant place to be . . ." (Eccles & Roeser, 2011, p. 225).

Given all these variations, no one school structure or style of pedagogy seems best for everyone. Various scientists, nations, schools, and teachers try many strategies, some based on opposite, but logical, hypotheses. To analyze these, we present some definitions, facts, issues, and possibilities.

Definitions and Facts

Each year of schooling advances human potential, as recognized by leaders and scholars in every nation and discipline. Adolescents are capable of deep and wide-ranging thought, no longer limited by personal experience. Yet they are often egocentric, impulsive, and intuitive. The quality of education matters: A year can propel thinking forward or can have little impact (Hanushek & Woessmann, 2010).

Secondary education—traditionally grades 7 through 12—denotes the school years after elementary or grade school (known as *primary education*) and before college or university (known as *tertiary education*). Adults are healthier and wealthier if they complete primary education, learning to read and write, and then continue on through secondary and tertiary education.

Even such a seemingly unrelated condition as serious hearing loss in late adulthood is 40 percent more common among those who never graduated from high school as it is among high school graduates (National Center for Health Statistics, 2011). This statistic comes from the United States, but data on almost every ailment, from every nation and every ethnic group, confirm that high school graduation correlates with better health. Some of the reasons are only indirectly related to education (e.g., income and place of residence), but even when inadequate resources and toxic neighborhoods are taken into account, health improves with education.

Partly because political leaders recognize that educated adults advance national wealth and health, every nation is increasing the number of students in secondary schools. Education is compulsory until at least age 12 almost everywhere (UNESCO, 2010). Often, two levels of secondary education are provided.

secondary education Literally, the period after primary education (elementary or grade school) and before tertiary education (college). It usually occurs from about age 12 to 18, although there is some variation by school and by nation.

Traditionally, secondary education was divided into junior high (usually grades 7 and 8) and senior high (usually grades 9 through 12). As the average age of puberty declined over the past century (see Chapter 14) and younger adolescents became ready for more intellectual challenge, **middle schools** were created to educate 10- to 13-year-olds (grades 6, 7, and 8). In addition, some nations have added a precollege year after grade 12.

Middle School

Many developmentalists find middle schools to be "developmentally regressive" (Eccles & Roeser, 2010, p. 13)—they force children to step backward. Does this matter for later achievement? One team believes so: "Long-term academic trajectories—the choice to stay in school or to drop out and the selection in high school of academic college-prep courses versus basic-level courses—are strongly influenced by experience in grades 6–8" (Snow et al., 2007, p. 72).

For many reasons, compared to primary schools, high schools, or colleges, middle schools are the weakest link in the educational sequence, with many students feeling stressed, parents feeling worried, and teachers feeling ineffective (Meece & Eccles, 2010). The data validate such feelings. For example, a longitudinal study of 900 U.S. children, followed from birth through ninth grade, found that between grades 5 and 9 the rate of reading and math achievement was only half as rapid as between grades 3 and 5. This was true for all ethnic groups. Many explanations are possible, but less learning in middle school is one of the most likely (Hooper et al., 2010).

For many middle school students, as academic achievement slows down, behavioral problems rise. Puberty itself is part of the problem. At least for other animals, especially when under stress, learning slows down at puberty (McCormick et al., 2010).

However, many experts think that the biological or psychological stresses of puberty are *not* the main reasons learning suffers in early adolescence. Instead, the organizational structure of many middle schools may undermine adolescent thought (Meece & Eccles, 2010). However, the idea that young adolescents can be taught, not merely warehoused in middle school, is supported by the experience of China. At least one team of scholars connects the Chinese economic expansion in recent years to the massive expansion of middle school education two decades ago, when millions of students learned skills that now serve their nation well (Lamb et al., 2011).

What is amiss in the structure of middle schools in the West? One hypothesis is that middle schools reduce achievement because they undercut student–teacher relationships. Unlike the situation in primary school, where each teacher is responsible for one classroom of children, middle school teachers are not connected to any small group. Instead, they specialize in an academic subject, taught to hundreds of students each year. This makes them impersonal and distant: Their students learn less and risk more (Crosnoe et al., 2004).

Adolescents' relationships with their parents may change as well. Some parents feel unable to help their adult-size children. By contrast, high-achieving middle school children tend to have parents who encourage them (but do not directly help with homework) (Hill & Tyson, 2009). The particulars vary by nation. In Korea, for instance, many parents of middle school children hire tutors and keep a close watch on the tutoring process, which improves the children's school performance (Park et al., 2011). In other nations, parents are more likely to engage their children in nonacademic activities after school. If parents think that teenagers no longer need parental support and encouragement, that's a mistake. Consider James.

middle school A school for children in the grades between elementary and high school. Middle school usually begins with grade 6 and ends with grade 8.

Especially for Teachers You are stumped by a question your student asks. What do you do? (see response, page 458)

Especially for Middle School Teachers You think your lectures are interesting and you know you care about your students, yet many of them cut class, come late, or seem to sleep through it. What do you do? (see response, page 459)

A CASE TO STUDY

James, the High-Achieving Dropout

A longitudinal study in Massachusetts followed children from preschool through high school. James was one of the most promising. In his early school years, he was an excellent reader whose mother took great pride in him, her only child. Once James entered middle school, however, something changed:

> Although still performing well academically, James began acting out. At first his actions could be described as merely mischievous, but later he engaged in much more serious acts, such as drinking and fighting, which resulted in his being suspended from school.
>
> [*Snow et al., 2007, p. 59*]

Family problems increased at puberty. James and his father blamed each other for their poor relationship, and his mother was uninvolved in his schooling. She bragged "about how independent James was for being able to be left alone to fend for himself," while James "described himself as isolated and closed off" (Snow et al., 2007, p. 59).

James said, "The kids were definitely afraid of me but that didn't stop them" from associating with him (Snow et al., 2007, p. 59). James's experiences with other classmates are not unusual. Generally, aggressive and drug-using students are admired in middle school more than those who are conscientious and studious—a marked difference from elementary school (Allen et al., 2005; Mayeux & Cillessen, 2007). Students dislike those who are unlike them, which may mean general antipathy toward those who excel (Laursen et al., 2010). As a consequence, some of the brightest adolescents sacrifice academics rather than risk social exclusion.

This was verified in three nations (Germany, Canada, and Israel); mathematically gifted girls were particularly likely to underachieve (Boehnke, 2008). In general, many studies find that girls are more likely to attend class and become involved in various activities but are less competitive on achievement tests. Boys are more likely to disengage from school. Data on U.S. education for the past 150 years show that more boys than girls leave school before high school graduation (Snyder & Dillow, 2011).

Puberty awakens sexual concerns, with each sex wanting to appear masculine or feminine, as the case may be. Boys particularly fear becoming a "nerd" or teacher's pet. Perhaps that is why most (60 percent) of U.S. 18- to 19-year-olds who have not completed high school are male (Snyder & Dillow, 2011). James may have been one of many "boys who choose to emphasize their masculine identities [and] may thus actively avoid literacy activities and academic success" (Snow et al., 2007, p. 64). At the end of primary school, James planned to go to college; in middle school, he said he had "a complete lack of motivation"; in tenth grade, he left school.

As with James, the early signs of a future high school dropout are found in middle school. Those students who will leave without graduating tend to be boys from minority ethnic groups and of low income, yet almost no middle school has guidance counselors or teachers who are men from those groups. Given the egocentric and intuitive way that young adolescents think, it is not surprising that many stop trying to achieve in middle school. Young adolescents are not the only ones who think egocentrically: Many school systems count as dropouts only those who begin twelfth grade but never earn diplomas—a method that puts the dropout rate at about 10 percent, much lower than the actual rate. (See Table 15.1 on ways to calculate dropouts.)

Finding Acclaim

To pinpoint the developmental mismatch between students' needs and the middle school context, note that just when egocentrism leads young people to feelings of shame or fantasies of stardom (the imaginary audience), schools typically require them to change rooms, teachers, and classmates every 40 minutes or so. That makes public acclaim and personal recognition difficult.

Personal satisfaction via academic excellence is difficult as well, because middle school teachers mark more harshly and the effort that was earlier called "outstanding" is now "average." Acclaim may also be elusive after school, since few activities

TABLE 15.1	Measuring Dropout Rates

There are three commonly used ways to measure high school dropout rates.

1. Compare the number of students in the ninth grade with the number who graduate four years later. Students who transfer out, stop out and then return, or take more than four years to graduate are counted as dropouts. This is the most rigorous method, and it is used here.

2. Determine the percentage of 16- to 24-year-olds who are not in school and have no high school diploma. (These are called *status dropouts*.) One problem with this mode is that newly arrived young-adult immigrants who have not completed high school are considered drop-outs. Another problem is that General Education Diplomas are counted, although students with a GED may not have gone to high school.

3. Count only those students who formally register as school leavers, not those who simply stop coming to school. This method finds the lowest rates of dropouts but may be the least realistic.

>> **Response for Teachers** (from page 456) Praise a student by saying, "What a great question!" Egos are fragile, so it's best to always validate the question. Seek student engagement, perhaps asking whether any classmates know the answer or telling the student to discover the answer online. Whatever you do, don't fake it—if students lose faith in your credibility, you may lose them completely.

entity approach to intelligence An approach to understanding intelligence that sees ability as innate, a fixed quantity present at birth; those who hold this view do not believe that effort enhances achievement.

incremental approach to intelligence An approach to understanding intelligence that holds that intelligence can be directly increased by effort; those who subscribe to this view believe they can master whatever they seek to learn if they pay attention, participate in class, study, complete their homework, and so on.

treat 11- to 13-year-olds appropriately, neither like children nor like adults. Finally, athletic teams become competitive, so fragile egos avoid them.

Since public acclaim is elusive, many middle school students seek acceptance from their peers. Bullying increases, appearance becomes important, status symbols are displayed (from gang colors to expensive shoes), and sexual conquests are flaunted. Of course, much depends on the cultural context, but almost every middle school student seeks peer approval in ways that adults disapprove (Véronneau & Dishion, 2010).

Coping with Middle School

One way to cope with stress is directly cognitive, that is, thinking that other people—classmates, teachers, parents, governments—are to blame. This may explain the surprising results of a Los Angeles study: Students in schools that were *more* ethnically mixed felt safer and *less* lonely. They did not necessarily have friends from other groups, but students who felt rejected could "attribute their plight to the prejudice of other people" rather than blame themselves (Juvonen et al., 2006, p. 398). Furthermore, since each group was a minority, they accepted rather than attacked one another.

Some students prevent feelings of failure by simply avoiding effort—that way, they can blame a low grade on a lack of trying ("I didn't study") rather than on stupidity. Pivotal in this is students' understanding of their own potential and how to achieve what they wish. If they believe in the **entity approach to intelligence** (i.e., that ability is innate, a fixed quantity present at birth), then they do not believe that they can improve their own intellectual ability. All they can do is accept their deficiencies, such as low math, or writing, or memory ability. They are convinced that they are innately stupid in some ways and always will be. The entity belief reduces stress but also reduces achievement: It is hopeless to try very hard.

By contrast, if adolescents believe in the **incremental approach to intelligence** (i.e., that intelligence can increase if they try to master whatever they seek to learn), then they will pay attention, participate in class, study, complete their homework, and so on. That is called *mastery motivation,* an example of the intrinsic motivation explained in Chapter 10.

This is not just a hypothesis. In the first year of middle school, students with entity beliefs do not achieve much, whereas the achievement of those with mastery motivation improves (Blackwell et al., 2007). After one study confirmed this finding, some students in their first year of middle school were taught eight lessons designed to convey the idea that being smart was incremental; these lessons included ways to "grow your intelligence." Especially if they had formerly held the entity theory of intelligence, those students gained while students in other classes had lower grades (Blackwell et al., 2007).

Teachers themselves were surprised at the effect. Among the "typical comments" was a teacher explaining that a boy

> who never puts in any extra effort and doesn't turn in homework on time, actually stayed up late working for hours to finish an assignment early so I could review it and give him a chance to revise it. He earned a B+ . . . he had been getting C's and lower.

[quoted in Blackwell et al., 2007, p. 256]

The concept that skills and intelligence can be mastered motivates the learning of social skills as well as academic subjects (Olson & Dweck, 2008). This makes it particularly important in adolescence, when peers are so important.

The contrast between entity and incremental approaches is apparent not only for individual adolescents but also for teachers, parents, schools, and cultures. If a school is structured so that children individually compete with one another rather than being placed in cooperative groups, with each group striving for mastery, then individuals who score low are likely to cope by endorsing the entity theory (Eccles & Roeser, 2011).

According to international comparisons, educational systems that track students into higher or lower classes, expel students who are not learning, and allow competition between schools for the brightest students (all reflecting entity, not incremental, theory) also show lower average achievement and a larger gap between the scores of students at the highest and lowest score quartiles (OECD, 2010b).

The Transition to a New School

Changing schools during the growth spurt or the onset of sexual characteristics is stressful. Remember from Chapter 13 that ongoing minor stresses can become overwhelming, causing pathology if they are repeated day after day. One expert notes:

> A number of disorders and symptoms of psychopathology, including depression, self-injury behavior, substance abuse, eating disorders, bipolar disorder, and schizophrenia have striking developmental patterns corresponding to transitions in early and late adolescence.

[Masten, 2004, p. 310]

Of course, transitions are not the only cause of adolescent pathology; hormones, body changes, sexual experiences, family conflict, and cultural expectations also contribute. In addition, puberty may activate genes that predispose a person to mental disorders (Erath et al., 2009), and the sequence of brain development may cause emotional difficulties. Nonetheless, many schools try to make transitions easier, with special groupings or programs for entering classes.

Some transitions are particularly difficult. When students enter a new school with classmates and customs unlike those in their old school, minority students may feel alienated, fearing failure (Benner & Graham, 2007). It is not diversity per se that is difficult; it is suddenly finding oneself in the minority, in unfamiliar circumstances. That may cause *stereotype threat,* the anxiety-producing idea that other people are judging you in stereotyped ways. Students already at risk of emotional

>> Response for Middle School Teachers (from page 456) Students need both challenge and involvement; avoid lessons that are too easy or too passive. Create small groups; assign oral reports, debates, and role-plays; and so on. Remember that adolescents like to hear one another's thoughts and their own voices.

International Communication The Russian girl on the left was one of 300 middle schoolers who crossed the border to visit a school in China, where students learn Russian and English as well as Chinese. Adolescents learn from one another, either constructively when adults structure and plan the interaction (as shown here) or destructively when adults do not engage with them.

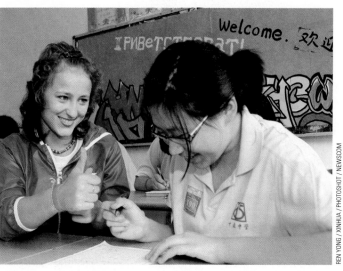

problems may be pushed over the edge by the transition; special nurturance can help them cope (Farmer et al., 2010).

Signs of stress—absenteeism, externalizing behavior, dropping out—are not inevitable, of course. For example, a program that helped parents and other students provide support to entering Mexican American middle schoolers (a vulnerable minority, since few teachers were from Mexico or spoke Spanish) had a significant impact: Fewer of them quit school than their peers without support (Gonzales et al., 2004).

Every transition is stressful. The most difficult times are the first year of middle school, the first year of high school, and the first year of college. The larger and less personal the new institution is and the more egocentric the student is, the more difficult the change. A study of the transition from middle to high school confirmed that personal relationships are crucial: Students are less likely to drop out if they have friends in the new school as well as teachers there who encourage learning. School policies (e.g., placement in classes) can facilitate such relationships (Langenkamp, 2010).

High School

As we have seen, adolescents can think abstractly, analytically, hypothetically, and logically—as well as personally, emotionally, intuitively, and experientially. The curriculum and teaching style in high school often require the former mode. Students who need more individualized, personal attention may be left out.

The College-Bound

From a developmental perspective, the fact that high schools emphasize formal thinking makes sense, since many older high schoolers are capable of abstract logic. High school teachers typically assume that their pupils have mastered formal thinking instead of teaching them how to do it (Kuhn & Franklin, 2006).

The United States is trying to raise standards so that all high school graduates will be ready for college. One way to accomplish this has been to increase the number of students who take classes that are assessed by externally scored exams, either the IB (International Baccalaureate) or the AP (Advanced Placement). Such classes have high standards and satisfy some college requirements.

Unfortunately, merely taking the class does not necessarily lead to college readiness (Sadler et al., 2010). Some students do not sign up for the external exams, and, although 17 percent of U.S. students took AP exams in 2010, about one-third

The Same Situation, Many Miles Apart: Top Students The New York girls just won a classroom history contest, and the Kenyan boys are studying physics, a subject available only to the brightest African students.

Observation Quiz Although the two groups of winners are thousands of miles apart, there are three evident similarities between them. What are they? (see answer, page 462)

of them failed. Far fewer take the IB exams, but, again, few receive the highest scores. In 2010, only one graduate in nine earned college credit based on an AP or IB exam—and that was an improvement over prior years (Gewertz, 2011a).

Of course, college credit is not the only measure of high school rigor. Another indicator is an increase in the requirements to receive an academic diploma. (In many U.S. schools, no one is allowed to earn a vocational or general diploma unless parents request it.) Graduation requirements usually include two years of math beyond algebra, two years of laboratory science, three years of history, and four years of English. Study of a language other than English is often required as well.

In 2011, in addition to these courses, 24 U.S. states required students to pass a **high-stakes test** in order to graduate. (Any exam for which the consequences of failing are severe is called a high-stakes test.) No state had such tests a decade ago; several additional states have scheduled them to begin soon. Because the more populous states are particularly likely to have high-stakes tests, 74 percent of U.S. high school students must take exit exams before graduation.

From 2000 to 2008, the percentage of students who pass high-stakes tests increased in some states and decreased in others (Zhang, 2009). The effect of such tests on education is in dispute. High school graduation rates in the United States are inching upward, with 72 percent of ninth-grade students staying in school to graduate four years later (see Figure 15.6) (Swanson, 2011).

The concern is that those who do not graduate are discouraged about education. According to the Center on Education Policy, high-stakes tests have "a negative impact on . . . low-performing students, students of color, or students from low-income families" (2010, p. 1). Even those who pass may be less excited about education. Overall, a panel of experts in education found that too much testing reduces learning rather than advancing it (Hout & Elliot, 2011).

As reviewed in Chapter 12, two international tests, the TIMSS and the PIRLS, show many nations ahead of the United States in achievement, with no dramatic change in the U.S. since the advent of high-stakes tests. Results at grade 4 were

Especially for High School Teachers You are much more interested in the nuances and controversies than in the basic facts of your subject, but you know that your students will take high-stakes tests on the basics and that their scores will have a major impact on their futures. What should you do? (see answer, page 462)

high-stakes test An evaluation that is critical in determining success or failure. If a single test determines whether a student will graduate or be promoted, it is a high-stakes test.

FIGURE 15.6

Graduation Rates on the Rebound The U.S. graduation rate has reached its highest point thus far. Every racial and ethnic group posted solid gains for the class of 2008, marking the second straight year of across-the-board improvements. These data are based on the most conservative and probably the most accurate estimate of graduation, that is, the percentage of new ninth-grade students who earn a diploma four years later. The gap between Asian/White and the three other groups is almost always the result of differences in socioeconomic status—that is, poor families live in communities with poor schools.

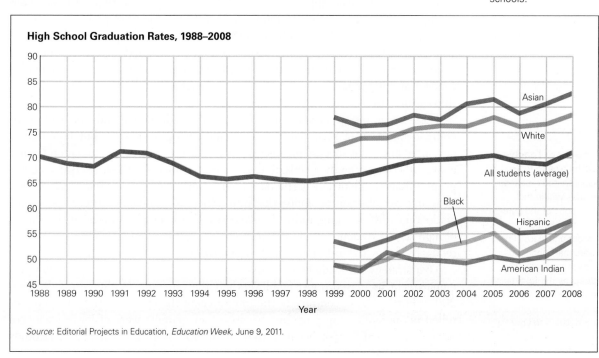

High School Graduation Rates, 1988–2008

Source: Editorial Projects in Education, *Education Week*, June 9, 2011.

>> **Answer to Observation Quiz** (from page 460) The similarities have to do with gender, uniforms, and cooperation. Sex segregation and similar garb are evident in both photographs, although they are voluntary in U.S. public schools and compulsory in many African secondary schools. Adolescents everywhere enjoy working collaboratively.

detailed in Chapter 12; the results at grade 8 are similar. Ironically, just when more U.S. schools are raising standards, tests, and requirements, many East Asian nations, including Korea, China, and Japan, are moving in the opposite direction.

Compared to a decade ago, Japan has fewer academic requirements, Japanese schools are open five days a week instead of six, and Japanese students have less "examination hell," as their high-stakes tests had been called. The science adviser to the prime minister of Japan recommends more flexibility in education in order to promote innovation. He wants students to "study whatever they are interested in" rather than to narrow their learning so as to score high on one final test (Normile, 2007).

Those Who Do Not Go to College

In the United States, one result of pushing an academic curriculum is that most students hope to attend college, most enroll, and . . . most leave without the bachelor's degree they sought. Many high school graduates (70 percent) enter college. However, only 22 percent of those entering public community colleges complete their program within three years (Adams, 2011), and almost half of those entering public or private four-year schools do not earn degrees. Even 10 years after the usual age for high school graduation, only 32 percent of U.S. young adults have earned a bachelor's degree (Snyder & Dillow, 2011).

These sobering statistics underlie a debate among educators. Should students be encouraged to "dream big" early in high school, aspiring for tertiary learning? This suggestion originates from studies finding a correlation between dreaming big in early adolescence and going to college years later (Domina et al., 2011a, 2011b). Others suggest that college is a "fairy tale dream" that may lead to low self-esteem (Rosenbaum, 2011). If adolescents fail academic classes, will they feel bored, stupid, and disengaged? Some school systems have noncollege options for such students in high school; others do not.

In the United States, some 2,500 *career academies* (small institutions of about 300 students each) prepare students for specific jobs. Seven years after graduation, students who were in career academies earn about $100 more a month than do other students who applied but could not enroll because there was no room (Kemple, 2008). They are also more likely to be married (38 percent versus 34 percent) and living with their children (51 percent versus 44 percent). In another example, in Italy, vocational education succeeded when the learning included hands-on practical education (rare in academic courses that prepare students for college) and a personal commitment of the teachers to their students (relationships again) (Bonica & Sappa, 2010).

These programs are available to relatively few high school students. More generally, completion of secondary school is increasing worldwide, but how that is measured and what success means vary dramatically from nation to nation (Lamb et al., 2011). Meeting the needs of all secondary students is the universal goal, but people disagree about the particulars as the world economy shifts. One solution is to arrange job-training apprenticeships, whereby students earn credits toward graduation while working in local businesses. Germany placed tens of thousands of high school students in apprenticeships during the 1980s, and all were guaranteed jobs if they did well. Japan had similar success in previous decades.

That strategy succeeded when businesses needed workers. However, when unemployment increased, most employers left the program (Grollmann & Rauner, 2007). Furthermore, contrary to the intentions of the creators, students were enrolled in apprenticeship programs because their parents were of lower socioeconomic status (SES), not because they themselves were less capable of rigorous

>> **Response for High School Teachers** (from page 461) It would be nice to follow your instincts, but the appropriate response depends partly on pressures within the school and on the expectations of the parents and administration. A comforting fact is that adolescents can think about and learn almost anything if they feel a personal connection to it. Look for ways to teach the facts your students need for the tests as the foundation for the exciting and innovative topics you want to teach. Everyone will learn more, and the tests will be less intimidating to your students.

academic work (Lehmann, 2004). In Japan, high school graduates are no longer coveted as new employees, in part because the economy is changing (Brinton & Tang, 2010).

Choosing Vocations

A crucial question for every adolescent is what job they hope to have in adulthood. Younger children tend to want work that fewer than one in a million of them will obtain—rock star, sports hero, U.S. president—and adults often encourage such fantasies. By the teen years, however, more practical concerns arise, specifically what employment is actually available and how enjoyable, remunerative, and demanding it is. For those concerns, adults are of little help. Parents usually know only their particular work, not what labor-market projections in the next decade will be. High school guidance counselors in the United States have an *average* caseload of 270 students a year, which includes many who want to apply to a dozen colleges as well as some who need time-consuming emotional support to prevent violence, suicide, or drug addiction. Often, counselors have neither the time nor the expertise for vocational guidance (Zehr, 2011).

Some ambitious adolescents begin to think about future careers on their own. One classic tool for doing so is developmentalist John Holland's 1997 description of six possible interests (see Figure 15.7). If students develop a vision of their future and realize how high school might advance their career, then they are likely to be motivated to study and learn. Given what we know about adolescent cognition, it is no surprise that few understand the eventual importance of critical analysis, articulate speech, fluent written expression, and interpersonal understanding. Furthermore, high-stakes tests rarely measure such skills.

Students are often told that they must graduate from high school and obtain a college degree if they hope to have a good job. Given the immediate, emotional response of many adolescents, that may seem abstract and irrelevant, especially if they know someone with a degree who cannot find work or someone without a degree who earns a good living.

In that case, the base rate fallacy described on page 445 needs to be countered with facts. The data in every nation show that adults with only a high school degree are likely to be unemployed or earn low wages, that most adults with some post–high school education do better in the job market, and that people with more advanced degrees have more income and responsibility (see Figure 15.8). They need to understand that a BA is not essential: In many occupations, most workers

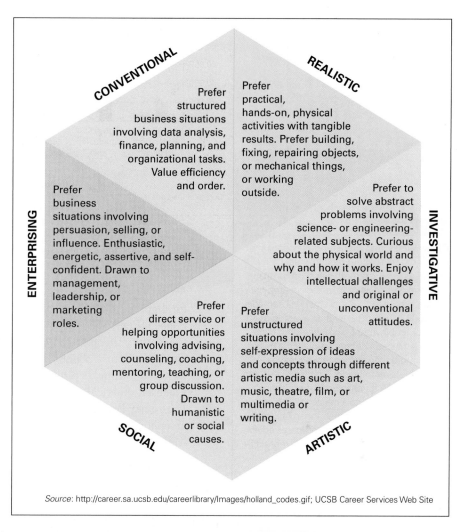

Source: http://career.sa.ucsb.edu/careerlibrary/Images/holland_codes.gif; UCSB Career Services Web Site

FIGURE 15.7

Happy at Work John Holland's six-part diagram is used to help adolescents realize that income and benefits are not the only goals of employment. Workers have healthier hearts and minds if their job fits their personal preferences.

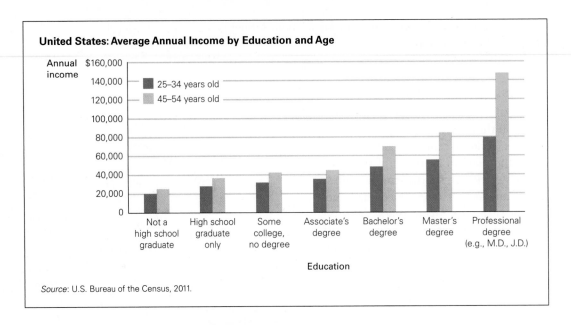

United States: Average Annual Income by Education and Age

Source: U.S. Bureau of the Census, 2011.

FIGURE 15.8

Older, Wiser, and Richer Adolescents find it easier to think about their immediate experiences (a boring math class) rather than their middle-age income, so some drop out of high school to take a job that will someday pay $500 a week. But over an average of 40 years of employment, someone who completes a master's degree earns half a million dollars more than someone who leaves school in eleventh grade. That translates into about $90,000 for each year of education from twelfth grade to a master's. The earnings gap is even wider than those numbers indicate because this chart compares adults who have jobs, yet finding work is more difficult for those with less education.

do not have advanced degrees (Swanson, 2011). Here are 10 such occupations, with average annual earnings:

> Air traffic controller, $70,000
> Firefighter, $60,000
> Police officer, $58,000
> Respiratory therapist, $49,000
> Dental hygienist, $44,000
> Payroll and timekeeping clerk, $33,000
> Licensed practical nurse, $33,000
> Data entry keyer, $25,000
> Telephone operator, $24,000
> Massage therapist, $18,000

These numbers are from 2009 in the United States as a whole: Variation is apparent not only in other nations but also in various regions of the United States. Although high school students need to know that college is not the only option, they also need to know that each of these occupations requires additional training that builds on skills mastered in high school. Understanding this may increase motivation.

Measuring Practical Cognition

Currently, employers in every nation provide on-the-job training (usually much more specific and current than high schools provide) and want their newly trained employees to know how to think, explain, write, concentrate, and get along with other people. Similar skills are necessary for the college-bound, especially if they hope to stay long enough to obtain a degree. Those skills are hard to measure on a high-stakes test or on the international tests explained in Chapter 12, the PIRLS and the TIMSS.

Another international test, the **PISA (Programme for International Student Assessment),** is designed to measure the kind of cognition needed in adult life. The PISA is taken by 15-year-olds in 50 nations, with that age picked deliberately because many students are close to the end of their formal school career. On this test, the questions are written to be practical, measuring knowledge that might apply at home or on the job. As a PISA report described it:

PISA (Programme for International Student Assessment) An international test taken by 15-year-olds in 50 nations that is designed to measure problem solving and cognition in daily life.

The tests are designed to generate measures of the extent to which students can make effective use of what they have learned in school to deal with various problems and challenges they are likely to experience in everyday life.

[PISA, 2009, p. 12]

For example, among the math questions is this one:

Robert's mother lets him pick one candy from a bag. He can't see the candies. The number of candies of each color in the bag is shown in the following graph.

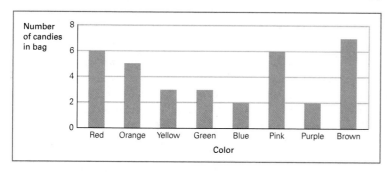

What is the probability that Robert will pick a red candy?

A. 10%   B. 20%   C. 25%   D. 50%

For that and the other questions on the PISA, the calculations are quite simple—most 10-year-olds can do them; no calculus or complex formulas are needed. However, the mathematical reasoning may be challenging, in part because of the *base rate neglect* fallacy described in the beginning of the chapter. On this question, only one-half of the students worldwide got it right (answer B), as did fewer than one-half of the students from the United States.

Overall, the U.S. students did worse on the PISA than on the PIRLS or TIMSS. On the PISA overall (reading, science, and math), China, Finland, and Korea were at the top, Canada close to the top, and the United States average in reading and science and below average in math (see Table 15.2). Analysis of nations and scores on the PISA finds four factors that correlate with high achievement (OECD, 2010b, p. 6):

- Leaders, parents, and citizens overall value education, with individualized approaches to learning so that all students learn what they need.
- Standards are high and clear, so every student knows what he or she must do, with a "focus on the acquisition of complex, higher order thinking skills."
- Teachers and administrators are valued, given "considerable discretion . . . in determining content" and sufficient salary as well as time for collaboration.
- Learning is prioritized "across the entire system," with high-quality teachers working in the most challenging environments.

Indications from the PISA and from international comparisons of high school dropout rates suggest that secondary education can be improved for those who do not go to college. The first step seems to be to keep students engaged in school, so they do not quit. How to do that requires critical thinking, as the following explains.

Not Geography The PISA is taken by 15-year-olds in many nations. Questions are designed to measure practical applications of school knowledge in science, reading, and math. National variations are more closely tied to educational practices and values at school and home, not to geography, genes, or immigration. For instance, Finland and Norway are close on the map but not in math achievement, and although most Asian nations do very well, note that Thailand scores low. Also note that nations with a higher proportion of immigrants than the United States (e.g., Canada) or very few immigrants (e.g., Japan) seem to do equally well.

TABLE 15.2	Math Scores on the PISA, 2006/2009		
Nation	Score	Nation	Score
Shanghai, China	—/600	Poland	495/495
Singapore	—/562	Hungary	491/490
Chinese Taipei	549/543	Norway	490/498
Finland	548/541	Spain	480/483
Hong Kong	547/555	Russia	476/468
South Korea	547/546	United States	474/487
Netherlands	531/526	Portugal	466/487
Switzerland	530/534	Italy	462/483
Canada	527/527	Greece	459/466
Japan	523/529	Israel	442/447
New Zealand	522/519	Uruguay	427/427
Belgium	520/515	Turkey	424/445
Australia	520/514	Thailand	417/419
Denmark	513/503	Romania	415/427
Czech Republic	510/493	Chile	411/421
Iceland	506/507	Mexico	406/419
Austria	505/496	Indonesia	391/371
Germany	504/513	Jordan	384/387
Sweden	502/494	Argentina	381/388
Ireland	501/487	Colombia	370/381
France	496/497	Brazil	370/386
United Kingdom	495/492	Tunisia	365/371
Source: PISA, 2009.			

THINKING CRITICALLY

Increasing Adolescent Engagement in School

What can be done to encourage adolescents to be engaged with school? There is no single, definitive answer. However, developmental research provides three suggestions:

- *Keep high schools small.* Schools educate best if 200 to 400 students are enrolled because many teachers and staff will know every student and almost every student will be involved in some sort of team or club. That fosters a sense of belonging to the school, more personal relationships, and more engagement with education. Unfortunately, in 2010 the *average* secondary school in eight U.S. states (Florida, California, Georgia, Hawaii, Maryland, Nevada, New Jersey, and Virginia) enrolled over a thousand students.

- *Encourage extracurricular activities.* There are "developmental benefits of participation in extracurricular activities for many high school adolescents" (Fredricks & Eccles, 2006, p. 712). Athletic teams elicit positive emotions and school bonding, for the athletes and everyone else. Even activities sponsored by nonschool groups help (Glanville et al., 2008). A North Carolina study found that high schools with more varied activities, and more students in them, had fewer dropouts and higher achievement. One reason for the correlation was SES: Students from wealthier families were more likely to go to schools with many activities. But the correlation held even when student and school SES were taken into account (Stearns & Glennie, 2010). Another study of students in extracurricular activities (sponsored by school, church, or community groups) found that engagement increased when students felt competent (e.g., in drama, dance) and had positive relationships with adults or peers (Dawes & Larson, 2011).

- *Reduce harassment.* School violence is decreasing in the United States, but fear of violence is increasing. Clear rules for student behavior, rewards for attendance, and more sporting events within (not just between) schools all reduce in-school crime, according to a survey of Texas middle and high schools (Cheurprakobkit & Bartsch,

2005). Cyberbullying is particularly difficult for school policy to forbid, but it is affected by school climate. Schools can foster adult cooperation, student friendships, and respect for learning, and the result is not only safety but engagement (Stewart, 2008).

Not everyone would agree with this list, which is why critical thinking is necessary. Furthermore, implementing each item would increase school costs. Ironically, every high school dropout saves money in the overall education budget. When taxpayers and political leaders set priorities, the education of secondary school students may not be among them, although the PISA results confirm that nations in which teachers are respected and well paid are also nations in which students achieve. A positive school climate "requires explicit, targeted, and aligned change efforts at the leverage points" (McGuigan, 2008, p. 112). To agree on those levers, and pull them, requires effort.

Bored or Attentive? This girl explains an aspect of history to her classmates at the small Manhattan International School. This public school's size (300 students) might increase student engagement, but the four-year graduation rate is only 60 percent, suggesting that factors beyond class size are important.

Surprisingly, students who are capable of passing their classes drop out as often as those who are less capable. Persistence, engagement, and motivation seem more crucial than intellectual ability (Archambault et al., 2009). One study that measured engagement and motivation reported that students were most motivated and engaged in primary school, somewhat engaged in college, but least engaged in secondary school (Martin, 2009).

Remember, however, that adolescents vary in every aspect and that the seriously troubled ones are a minority. A study of student emotional and academic engagement from the fifth to the eighth grade found that, as expected, the overall direction was less engagement; but a distinctive group (about 18 percent) were highly engaged throughout, and another distinctive group (about 5 percent) experienced precipitous disengagement year by year. The 5 percent who were most turned off were typically boys from low-income families (Li & Lerner, 2011). That is tragic, for society as well as for those boys.

Secondary school teachers are hired for their academic expertise, not for their ability to engage adolescents. They model formal operational thinking—answering questions about the intricacies of theoretical physics, advanced calculus, and iambic pentameter—but they may not connect with students or understand practical vocational requirements. Furthermore, the most qualified teachers tend to gravitate to schools with more able students (where salaries are higher and class sizes smaller); even within schools, the best teachers are often assigned classes of the elite college-bound. All students learn best when a master teacher guides active discussion, debate, and exposition, but those who most need such teaching are least likely to have it (Slavin et al., 2009).

Some nations provide equally qualified teachers for every school. The disparity in teacher quality between wealthy and impoverished schools is much greater in the United States than in nations that score high on the PISA (e.g., Finland and Canada) (Cavanagh, 2007).

A final question arises for all three of the groups discussed here: the college-bound, the students who quit after they earn their diploma, and those who drop out as soon as they can (legally age 16 in most U.S. states). That question is: Does learning during adolescence matter when considering the entire life span? For individuals, the answer is a resounding yes. Not only health but also almost every other indicator of a good life—high income, stable marriage, successful children, satisfying work—correlates with education.

Beyond the benefits to the individual, entire nations gain from the quality of secondary education. A detailed calculation found that if the U.S. average PISA score increased by a mere 25 points (up to the scores for France, Ireland, or Sweden; still far below those of Finland or South Korea), that would result in an increase of $40 *trillion* in the nation's GDP (gross domestic product, a number used by economists to measure national economic production) between 2010 and 2090 (Hanushek & Woessmann, 2010). How could this be?

The cognitive skills that boost economic development are creativity, flexibility, and analytic ability; they allow innovation and mastery of new technology. When nations raise their human capital by boasting more adults who possess those skills, their economies prosper (Cohen & Soto, 2007). Scores on the PISA and other tests predict later economic development (Hanushek & Woessmann, 2010).

The cognitive abilities that nations need in the twenty-first century are exactly what adolescents can develop—with proper education and guidance. As you have read, every scientist who studies adolescent cognition notes that the logical and creative potential of the adolescent mind is not always realized, but it can be. Does this chapter end on a hopeful note?

SUMMING UP

Middle schools tend to be less personal, less flexible, and more tightly regulated than elementary schools, which may contribute to a general finding: declining student achievement. School transitions are difficult but can be made less stressful. Ideally, secondary education advances thinking, although some measures that help students connect with their schools (such as sports) are too often undervalued. High school students who do not expect to attend college may be particularly unprepared for adult life. Guidance for careers is needed, but scarce.

SUMMARY

Logic and Self

1. Cognition in early adolescence may be egocentric, a kind of self-centered thinking. Adolescent egocentrism gives rise to the personal fable, the invincibility fable, and the imaginary audience.

2. *Formal operational thought* is Piaget's term for the last of his four periods of cognitive development. He tested and demonstrated formal operational thought with various problems that students in a high school science or math class might encounter.

3. Piaget realized that adolescents are no longer earthbound and concrete in their thinking; they imagine the possible, the probable, and even the impossible, instead of focusing on what is real. They develop hypotheses and explore, using deductive reasoning. However, few developmentalists find that adolescents move suddenly from concrete to formal thinking.

Two Modes of Thinking

4. Intuitive thinking becomes more forceful during adolescence. Few teenagers always use logic, although they are capable of doing so. Emotional, intuitive thinking is quicker and more satisfying, and sometimes better, than analytic thought.

5. Contrary to popular belief, research has found that a large majority of adolescents consider themselves to be religious, with most following the faith of their parents. With time, they move away from traditional practices, but they believe their deeper cognition results in stronger rather than weaker faith.

6. Neurological as well as survey research finds that adolescent thinking is characterized by more rapid development of the limbic system and slower development of the prefrontal cortex. This explains the imbalance evident in dual processing.

Technology and Cognition

7. Adolescents use technology, particularly the Internet, more than people of any other age group. They reap many educational benefits, but some technology is destructive, in video game addiction, cyberbullying, and support for pathology.

Teaching and Learning

8. Secondary education—after primary education (grade school) and before tertiary education (college)—correlates with the health and wealth of individuals and nations.

9. In middle school, many students tend to be bored, difficult to teach, and hurtful to one another. One reason may be that middle schools are not structured to accommodate egocentrism or intuitive thinking.

10. Many forms of psychopathology increase during the transitions to middle school, to high school, and to college. School changes may be particularly difficult in adolescence, when young people must also adjust to biological and family changes.

11. Education in high school emphasizes formal operational thinking. In the United States, the demand for more accountability has led to increased requirements for graduation as well as more Advanced Placement (AP) classes and high-stakes testing. The concern is that this may undermine creativity and innovation.

12. A sizable number of high school students do not graduate or go on to college, and many more leave college without a degree. Current high school education does not seem to meet their needs.

13. The PISA test taken by many 15-year-olds in 50 nations measures how well they can apply the knowledge they have been taught. Students in the United States seem to have particular difficulty with such tests.

KEY TERMS

adolescent egocentrism (p. 440)
personal fable (p. 440)
invincibility fable (p. 440)
imaginary audience (p. 441)
formal operational thought (p. 442)
hypothetical thought (p. 444)

deductive reasoning (p. 444)
inductive reasoning (p. 444)
sunk cost fallacy (p. 445)
base rate neglect (p. 445)
dual-process model (p. 446)
intuitive thought (p. 446)
analytic thought (p. 446)

cyberbullying (p. 453)
cutting (p. 454)
secondary education (p. 455)
middle school (p. 456)
entity approach to intelligence (p. 458)

incremental approach to intelligence (p. 459)
high-stakes test (p. 461)
PISA (Programme for International Student Assessment) (p. 464)

WHAT HAVE YOU LEARNED?

Logic and Self

1. How does adolescent egocentrism differ from early childhood egocentrism?

2. What are the two extreme perceptions that arise from the imaginary audience?

3. Why are the personal fable and the invincibility fable called "fables"?

4. How does formal operational thinking differ from concrete operational thinking?

5. What are the advantages and disadvantages of using induction rather than deduction?

6. How certain are contemporary developmentalists that Piaget accurately described adolescent cognition?

Two Modes of Thinking

7. When might intuition and analysis lead to contrasting conclusions?

8. What mode of thinking—intuitive or analytic—do most people prefer, and why?

9. How does personal experience increase the probability of base rate neglect?

10. How does egocentrism account for the clashing priorities of parents and adolescents?

11. When is intuitive thinking better than analytic thinking?

Technology and Cognition

12. What benefits come from adolescents' use of technology?

13. How do video games affect student learning?

14. Who is most and least likely to be involved in cyberbullying?

15. If an adolescent consults the Internet regarding cutting and/or other dangerous sites, what should adults do?

Teaching and Learning

16. Why have most junior high schools disappeared?

17. What characteristics of middle schools make them more difficult for students than elementary schools?

18. How does being a young adolescent affect a person's ability to learn?

19. Why are transitions a particular concern for educators?

20. Why is the first year of attending a new school more stressful than the second year?

21. How are educational standards changing in the United States?

22. What are the advantages and disadvantages of high-stakes testing?

23. Why is Germany's apprentice/vocational education system no longer prevalent?

24. How does the PISA differ from other international tests?

25. Why is high school achievement likely to advance the national economy?

APPLICATIONS

1. Describe a time when you overestimated how much other people were thinking about you. How was your mistake similar to and different from adolescent egocentrism?

2. Talk to a teenager about politics, families, school, religion, or any other topic that might reveal the way he or she thinks. Do you hear any adolescent egocentrism? Intuitive thinking? Systematic thought? Flexibility? Cite examples.

3. Think of a life-changing decision you have made. How did logic and emotion interact? What would have changed if you had given the matter more thought—or less?

4. Describe what happened and what you thought in the first year you attended a middle school or high school. What made it better or worse than later years in that school?

>> ONLINE CONNECTIONS

To accompany your textbook, you have access to a number of online resources, including quizzes for every chapter of the book, flashcards (in English and Spanish), critical thinking questions, and case studies. For access to any of these links, go to www.worthpublishers.com/bergerca9e. In addition to these free resources, you'll also find links to podcasts, video clips, diagnostic quizzing with personalized study advice, and an ebook. Some of the videos and activities available online include:

- *Child Soldiers and Child Peacemakers.* More than 150 wars since World War II! See the effects of armed conflict on children's development and hear how some young people take a stand for peace.

- *HIV/AIDS.* A brief history of the global spread of HIV and successful promotion of educational intervention in Sri Lanka. Videos let affected people tell their stories.

Adolescence: Psychosocial Development

"What does your mother do?" Emil, the head of Town Security, asked Bethany, whose summer job was as a security deputy.

"She writes books."

"How does she do that?"

"She spends a lot of time in the library, reading and writing."

"Oh, your poor mother!"

No need for pity. I enjoy my work. Each of us has our own preferences, habits, and interests, explored when we began to find our identity. Emil liked riding around town, responding to emergencies, searching for "perps." I would hate that. Even as a teenager, I enjoyed reading and writing, explaining ideas. I resented interruptions, such as those crackling on Emil's radio. I chose classes that let me figure things out with paper and pencil. Advanced math was a favorite, even though I was the only girl in the class.

In some ways, I was a rebel: I told my friends that I would never be a teacher (too conventional), and I refused the colleges my parents suggested (more of that in the epilogue). But in many ways, I was typical. For example, I was thrilled when Bill invited me to a college weekend. When his roommate said, "That's not the kind of girl you date, that's the kind of girl you marry," I was pleased. That was my plan for myself.

This chapter describes the search for identity, often a mixture of personal preferences, parental pressure, and teenage rebellion. Adults and peers influence each young person, and adolescents resist parts of their familial and cultural heritage while accepting other parts. One important topic is romance; many adolescents try to discern and express their gender identity via partners, aspirations, and sexuality. That college weekend was approved by my culture and cohort but would be less admired now. We also consider other forms of identity in this chapter, as well as dangers that threaten healthy growth.

A few adolescents plunge into despair and attempt suicide; most experiment with alcohol and minor lawbreaking—perhaps to be stopped by someone like Emil, who likes his job and would hate mine. All this is covered here, describing how 11- to 18-year-olds move through the psychosocial maze from childhood to adulthood.

>> Identity

Psychosocial development during adolescence is often understood as a search for a consistent understanding of oneself. Self-expression and self-concept become increasingly important at puberty, as the egocentrism described in Chapter 15 illustrates. Each young person wants to know, "Who am I?"

identity versus role confusion Erikson's term for the fifth stage of development, in which the person tries to figure out "Who am I?" but is confused as to which of many possible roles to adopt.

According to Erik Erikson, life's fifth psychosocial crisis is **identity versus role confusion:** The complexities of finding one's own identity are the primary task of adolescence (Erikson, 1968). He said this crisis is resolved with **identity achievement,** when adolescents have reconsidered the goals and values of their parents and culture, accepting some and discarding others, discerning their own identity.

identity achievement Erikson's term for the attainment of identity, or the point at which a person understands who he or she is as a unique individual, in accord with past experiences and future plans.

The result is neither wholesale rejection nor unquestioning acceptance of social norms (Côté, 2009). With their new autonomy, teenagers maintain continuity with the past so they can move to the future. Each person must achieve his or her own identity; the social context of each generation differs, and everyone must discover and adjust to a unique combination of genes and alleles.

Not Yet Achieved

Erikson's insights have inspired thousands of researchers. Notable among them was James Marcia, who described and measured four specific ways young people cope with this stage of life: (1) role confusion, (2) foreclosure, (3) moratorium, and finally (4) identity achievement (Marcia, 1966). Over the past half-century, major psychosocial shifts have lengthened the duration of adolescence and made identity achievement more complex (Côté, 2006; Kroger et al., 2010; Meeus, 2011). However, the three way stations on the road to identity achievement still seem evident.

role confusion A situation in which an adolescent does not seem to know or care what his or her identity is. (Sometimes called *identity* or *role diffusion*.)

Role confusion is the opposite of identity achievement. It is characterized by lack of commitment to any goals or values. Identity confusion is sometimes called *identity diffusion* instead of *role confusion*, to emphasize that some adolescents seem diffuse, unfocused, unconcerned about their future (Phillips & Pittman, 2007). Even the usual social demands—such as putting away clothes, making friends, completing school assignments, and thinking about college or career—are beyond role-confused adolescents. Instead, they might sleep too much, immerse themselves in video games or mind-numbing television, and turn from one flirtation to another. Their thinking is disorganized, they procrastinate, they avoid issues and actions (Côté, 2009).

foreclosure Erikson's term for premature identity formation, which occurs when an adolescent adopts parents' or society's roles and values wholesale, without questioning or analysis.

Identity **foreclosure** occurs when, in order to halt role confusion, young people accept traditional values (Marcia, 1966; Marcia et al., 1993). They might follow roles and customs transmitted from their parents or culture, never exploring alternatives. Or they might foreclose on an oppositional, negative identity—the direct opposite of whatever their parents want—again without thoughtful questioning. Foreclosure is comfortable. For many, it is a temporary shelter, a time for commitment to a particular identity, which will be followed by more exploration (Meeus, 2011).

moratorium An adolescent's choice of a socially acceptable way to postpone making identity-achievement decisions. Going to college is a common example.

A more mature shelter is **moratorium,** a time-out that includes some exploration, either in breadth (trying many things) or in depth (examining one path after making a tentative commitment) (Meeus, 2011). Societies provide many opportunities for moratoria, such as college or military service, that allow adolescents to postpone identity achievement. This identity status is most common at age 19, although it can occur earlier or later (Kroger et al., 2010). Many emerging adults are still in moratorium.

Several aspects of the search for identity, especially sexual and vocational identity, have become more arduous than they were when Erikson described them, and forging any personal identity is more difficult. Fifty years ago, the drive to become independent and autonomous was thought to be the "key normative psychosocial task of adolescence" (Zimmer-Gembeck & Collins, 2003, p. 177). Adolescents still struggle with identity, but now developmentalists believe that it is unusual for teenagers to resolve this crisis and reach identity achievement. Adolescents begin the search, but a review of longitudinal "studies among adults revealed that identity is a life-long process" (Meeus, 2011, p. 88).

Four Arenas of Identity Formation

Erikson (1968) highlighted four aspects of identity: religious, political, vocational, and sexual. Terminology and emphasis have changed for all four, as has timing. In fact, if an 18-year-old is no longer open to new possibilities in any of these four areas, that may indicate foreclosure, not achievement—and identity might shift again. (My own identity is one example: I did not marry Bill, or anyone, until my mid-20s, relatively late for my cohort. At age 23, I chose teaching as my vocation.)

None of these four identity statuses occurs in social isolation: Parents and peers are influential, as detailed later in this chapter, and the ever-changing chronosystem (historical context) makes identity dynamic. Nonetheless, each of these four arenas remains integral to adolescent development.

Religious Identity

For most adolescents, their *religious identity* is similar to that of their parents and community, as noted in Chapter 15. Few adolescents totally reject religion if they've grown up following a particular faith, partly because religion provides meaning as well as coping skills that are particularly useful during stressful times (King & Roeser, 2009).

Past parental practices influence adolescent religious identity, although some adolescents express that identity in ways that their parents did not anticipate: A Muslim girl might start to wear a headscarf, or a Catholic boy might study for the priesthood, or a Baptist teenager might join a Pentecostal youth group. Such new practices are relatively minor: Almost no young Muslim converts to Judaism, and almost no teenage Baptist becomes Hindu. Most adolescents accept the broad outlines of the religious identity of their parents and culture, questioning specific beliefs as their cognitive processes allow more reflective, less concrete assumptions, but without a crisis of faith unless unusual circumstances propel it (King & Roeser, 2009).

Political Identity

Parents are also influential for *political identity* in that most adolescents follow the political traditions of their parents. In the twenty-first century in the United States, party identification is weakening among adults, with more of them saying they are independent rather than Republican, Democratic, or of some other party (Pew Research Center, 2009). Their teenage children reflect this; some proudly say they do not care about politics, in which case their apolitical identity is likely to continue in adulthood (Côté, 2009).

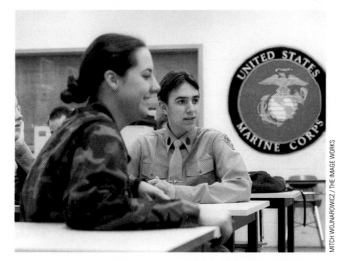

Not Just a Uniform Adolescents in moratorium adopt temporary roles to postpone achieving their final identity. High school students like these may sign up for an ROTC (Reserve Officers Training Corps) class, but few of them go on to enlist in the U.S. Marine Corps.

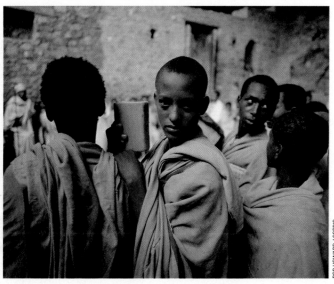

A Religious Life These young adolescents in Ethiopia are studying to be monks. Their monastery is a haven in the midst of civil strife. Will the rituals and beliefs also provide them with a way to achieve identity?

A word here about political terrorism and religious extremism. People who are relatively young (under age 30) are often on the front lines of terrorism or are converts to groups that their elders consider cults. Fanatical political and religious movements have much in common—age of new adherents is one of them (L. L. Dawson, 2010). However, adolescents are rarely drawn to these groups unless personal loneliness or family background (such as a parent's death caused by an opposing group) compels them. It is an adult myth that every teenager is potentially a suicide bomber or willing martyr.

This does not mean that adolescents ignore their ethnicity. Especially in a multicultural society such as the United States, most adolescents identify proudly with their ethnicity—or, often, ethnicities, claiming that several labels describe them (such as African, Black, and American). One study found that the typical adolescent endorsed three such labels, with bicultural adolescents considering ethnic identities more central to themselves than monocultural adolescents did (Marks et al., 2011).

Vocational Identity

Vocational identity originally meant envisioning oneself as a worker in a particular occupation. This made sense a century ago, when most girls became wives and mothers, not employees, and most men became farmers, small businessmen, or factory workers. Those few in professions were generalists (doctors were general practitioners, lawyers handled all kinds of cases, teachers were usually unmarried women who taught all subjects). Decades ago, adolescents sought a vocational identity so they could decide whether or not to stay in high school and aim for college.

Obviously, early vocational identity is no longer relevant. Secondary education is necessary for almost everyone; no one is ready for a particular lifetime job at age 16. Nor is any teenager prepared to choose among the tens of thousands of careers; most adults change vocations (not just employers) several times. One popular reference detailing possible careers is 4,128 pages long (Ferguson Publishing, 2010). As explained in Chapter 15, adolescents are more likely to be engaged in high school if they realize that the skills they are learning will be relevant for every job, even as they realize that a college degree is not the only post–high school training they need. However, almost no one finds work during adolescence that becomes a lifelong career. Vocational identity takes years to establish.

The Same Situation, Many Miles Apart: Learning in School For these two groups of Muslim girls, the distance between their schools in Dearborn, Michigan *(left)*, and Jammu, Kashmir *(right)*, is more than geographical. The schools' hidden curricula teach different lessons about the roles of women.

Observation Quiz What three differences are evident? (see answer, page 476)

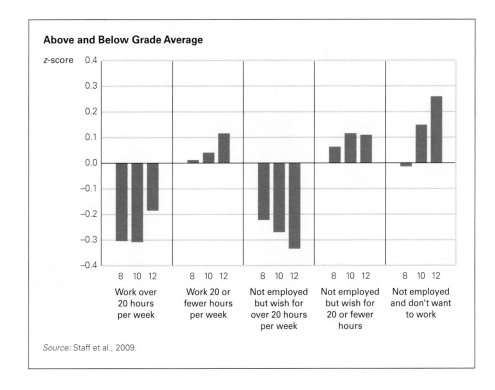

Above and Below Grade Average

FIGURE 16.1

Don't Think About It! There was a time when high school employment correlated with saving for college and lifetime success. No longer. The surprise is that even wanting a full-time job (and the extra income that would bring) reduces achievement—or is it the other way around?

Source: Staff et al., 2009.

Although some adults hope that part-time employment during high school will keep teenagers out of trouble, the opposite is more likely as adolescents develop their vocational identity (Staff & Schulenberg, 2010). Working over vacations or a few hours during the school week is harmless, but adolescents who work more than 20 hours a week during the school year tend to quit school, fight with parents, smoke cigarettes, and hate their jobs—both when they are teenagers and when they become adults. Typically, they spend their wages on clothes, cars, drugs, and concerts, not family support or college savings. Grades fall: Work hours interfere with homework, extra help, and school attendance (see Figure 16.1). Only a tiny and shrinking minority—alienated from school but appreciated, mentored, and promoted at work—benefit from intense teenage employment.

FIGURE 16.2

Young and Old Everyone knows that attitudes about same-sex relationships are changing. Less well known is that cohort differences are greater than the shift over the first decade of the twenty-first century.

Sexual Identity

Achieving *sexual identity* is also a lifelong task, in part because norms and attitudes keep changing (see Figure 16.2). Increasing numbers of young adults are single, gay, or cohabiting, providing teenagers with new role models and choices and thus making sexual identity more confusing. A half-century ago, Erikson and other theorists thought of the two sexes as opposites (P. Y. Miller & Simon, 1980). They assumed that adolescents who were confused about sexual identity would soon adopt "proper" male or female roles (Erikson, 1968; A. Freud, 1958/2000). Adolescence was once a time for "gender intensification," when people increasingly identified as male or female. No longer (Priess et al., 2009).

As you remember from Chapter 10, for social scientists *sex* and *sexual* refer to biological characteristics,

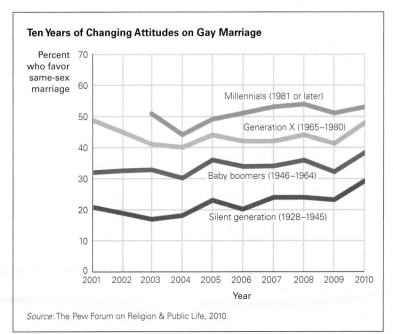

Ten Years of Changing Attitudes on Gay Marriage

Source: The Pew Forum on Religion & Public Life, 2010.

Who and Where? As Erikson explained in 1968, the pride of self-discovery is universal for adolescents: These could be teenagers anywhere. But a closer look reveals gay teenagers in Atlanta, Georgia, where this march could not have occurred 50 years ago.

gender identity A person's acceptance of the roles and behaviors that society associates with the biological categories of male and female.

whereas *gender* refers to cultural and social attributes that differentiate males and females. The distinction between biology and culture is not always clear-cut, since the body is affected by behavior and vice versa. Nonetheless, Erikson's term *sexual identity* has been replaced by **gender identity** (Denny & Pittman, 2007), which refers primarily to a person's self-definition as male or female. Gender identity often (not always) begins with the person's biological sex and leads to a gender role, which is a role that society considers appropriate for that gender.

Gender roles once meant that only men had jobs; they were *breadwinners* (good providers) and women were *housewives* (married to their houses). As women entered the labor market, gender roles expanded but were still apparent (nurse/doctor, secretary/businessman, pink collar/blue collar). All that continues to change today—with the degree, rate, and direction of change varying dramatically from culture to culture.

What has not changed is that adolescents experience strong sexual drives as hormones increase. As Erikson recognized, many are confused regarding when, how, and with whom to express those drives. That complicates achievement of gender identity (Baumeister & Blackhart, 2007; Gilchrist & Sullivan, 2006). Some adolescents foreclose by exaggerating male or female roles; others seek a moratorium by avoiding all sexual contact. Some of the complexities of gender-identity achievement are discussed later in this chapter, when we focus on romance.

SUMMING UP

Erikson's fifth psychosocial crisis, identity versus role confusion, was first described more than 50 years ago. Adolescence was characterized as a time to search for a personal identity in order to reach identity achievement by adulthood. The identity crisis still occurs; role confusion, foreclosure, and moratorium are apparent in religious, political, vocational, and gender identity. However, timing has changed. The identity crisis lasts much longer; fewer young people develop a firm sense of who they are and what path they will follow by age 18.

Specific aspects of identity—religious, political, vocational, and gender—have taken new forms, with complexities that Erikson did not anticipate. Settling early on an iden-

>> **Answer to Observation Quiz** (from page 474) Facial expressions, degree of adult supervision, and head covering. (Did you notice that the Kashmiri girls wear a tight-fitting cap under their one-piece white robes?)

tity may be a sign of foreclosure, not achievement. This is especially true for vocational identity: The vast array of possible jobs, and the training required for each one, means that adolescents need years of exploration and education. Likewise, adolescents are aware of many more possible religious, political, and gender identities than adults once recognized.

>> Relationships with Adults

Adolescence is often characterized as a period of waning adult influence, when children distance themselves from their elders. There is validity in this view, but it is not always accurate. In fact, some young people feel appreciated by their communities, trusted by teachers, and connected to parents or other adults; when they do, they usually avoid drugs, stay in school, and take good care of themselves.

Parents

The fact that parent–adolescent relationships are pivotal does not mean that they are peaceful (Eisenberg et al., 2008; Laursen & Collins, 2009). Disputes are common because the adolescent's drive for independence, arising from biological as well as psychological impulses, clashes with the parents' desire to maintain control.

Normally, parent–adolescent conflict peaks in early adolescence, especially between mothers and daughters. It usually manifests as **bickering**—repeated, petty arguments (more nagging than fighting) about routine, day-to-day concerns such as cleanliness, clothes, chores, and schedules (Eisenberg et al., 2008). One of the problems is that both generations misjudge the other: Parents think their offspring have more negative thoughts than the children have, and adolescents imagine much more intrusive control than the parents intend (Sillars et al., 2010).

Some bickering may indicate a healthy family, since close relationships almost always include conflict (Smetana et al., 2004). Both generations need to be more explicit—if the argument is only about the dirty socks on the floor, the teenager can put them in the laundry, but if it's about dictating personal habits, of course the child resists. With time, parents gradually grant more autonomy, and "friendship and positive affect [emotional state] typically rebound to preadolescent levels" (Collins & Laursen, 2004, p. 337). By age 18, many teenagers have reduced their impulsivity and egocentrism and can appreciate their parents, who have learned to accept less disclosure but improved communication as the young person matures (Masche, 2010).

In Chapter 10, you learned that authoritative parenting is usually best for children and that uninvolved parenting is worst. The same holds true for adolescents. Although teenagers may say they no longer need their parents, neglect is always destructive—as you saw with James in Chapter 15. Another example is Joy. When she was 16, her stepfather said: "Teens all around here [are] doing booze and doing drugs. . . . But my Joy here ain't into that stuff" (quoted in C. Smith, 2005, p. 10). In fact, however, Joy was smoking pot, drinking alcohol, and having sex with her boyfriend. She

> overdosed on a bunch of stuff once, pills or some prescription of my mom's—
> I took the whole bottle. It didn't work. I just went to sleep for a long time. . . .
> They never found out . . . pretty pitiful.
>
> *[quoted in C. Smith, 2005, p. 12]*

That suicide attempt was a clear indication that she was in far worse trouble than most "teens all around here."

bickering Petty, peevish arguing, usually repeated and ongoing.

What Next? Crying, cursing, quitting? Hopefully not. Every close relationship has moments of conflict, which ideally lead to mutual understanding, forgiveness, and even a new way of behaving.

ACE STOCK LIMITED / ALAMY

"So I blame you for everything—whose fault is that?"

Cultural Differences

Regarding parent–adolescent relationships, some cultures value harmony above all else, and in those places adolescents virtually never contradict their parents. Given that, some scholars wonder whether the adolescent rebellion they had taken for granted is actually a social construction (defined in Chapter 1) (Russell et al., 2010). Perhaps it is a middle-class Western assumption that adolescent rebellion is a psychosocial necessity. Or perhaps rebellion is a consequence of a competitive global economy, not a developmental universal (Larson & Wilson, 2004). This idea that rebellion is a cultural or cohort phenomenon is contrary to another idea, that bickering and the drive for autonomy are universal steps toward healthy adulthood.

More longitudinal research is needed before we can judge whether one side of this debate is more accurate than the other. But there is no doubt that culture affects the topics and methods of conflict. Because of globalization, adolescents who have never traveled far from home are aware of other ways of life, and they question why their parents do not act the same as others they have known or heard about.

Expectations vary by culture, as do justifications (Brown & Bakken, 2011). For example, Japanese youth expect autonomy in their musical choices but want parents to help them with romance (Hasebe et al., 2004), whereas U.S. teenagers resent parental interference in romance or friendship (Kakihara & Tilton-Weaver, 2009). In Chile, adolescents usually obey their parents even when they disagree, but if they do something their parents might not like, they keep it secret (Darling et al., 2008)—unlike many U.S. adolescents, who might provoke an argument by boldly announcing what they think (Cumsille et al., 2010). Filipino adolescents expect autonomy in daily choices but not in life goals: Parental advice is sought in the four aspects of identity explained earlier (Russell et al., 2010a).

Filial devotion (a child's feeling of obligation to his or her parents) is particularly strong in Asian cultures. That curbs adolescent rebellion. As a result, the independence and individuality expected for Western adolescents is not as apparent there (Russell et al., 2010b). The influence of culture was evident in a study that used language to discover prime cultural values: Hong Kong adolescents expressed more self-assertion when they spoke English than when they spoke Chinese (Wang et al., 2010). (See Figure 16.3 and the Research Design.) It was not the words themselves that mattered, of course, but rather the context evoked when a researcher spoke English or Chinese (e.g., Hong Kong's British heritage or the millennia of mainland Chinese culture).

Closeness Within the Family

More important than family conflict or independence may be family closeness, which has four aspects:

1. Communication (Do family members talk openly with one another?)
2. Support (Do they rely on one another?)
3. Connectedness (How emotionally close are they?)
4. Control (Do parents encourage or limit adolescent autonomy?)

No developmentalist doubts that the first two, communication and support, are helpful, perhaps essential. Patterns set in place during childhood continue, ideally buffering some of the turbulence of adolescence (Cleveland et al., 2005;

▶ Research Design

Scientists: Qi Wang, Yi Shao, and Yexin Jessica Li.

Publication: *Child Development* (2010).

Participants: A total of 125 children (aged 8, 10, 12, and 14) in Hong Kong, proficient in both Chinese and English (they spoke Chinese with their parents, but their education was in English). All the children were exposed to both cultures because, in the words of these researchers, "Hong Kong is a culturally dynamic place where Western and Chinese values intertwine and where modernity and tradition coexist" (p. 557).

Design: Trained bilingual researchers asked the children to speak about memories, themselves, and their values. Children were randomly assigned to be interviewed in Chinese or English. Among the data were statements in which the adolescents said something about themselves; their statements were judged by coders (who did not know the hypothesis) as being either about the individual alone (such as "I enjoy books," "My eyes are dark") or about the individual as one of a group or as a person connected to others (such as "I am a student," "My family loves me"). The ratio of individual to social descriptions was calculated.

Results: The descriptions of those interviewed in Chinese became more social at adolescence, while those interviewed in English were more likely to refer to themselves alone. This distinction was especially apparent at age 10, which is an age characterized by accelerating hormones and increasing egocentrism.

Major conclusion: The researchers interpreted these results to mean that, at adolescence, autonomy becomes less prominent in Chinese culture but not in English culture, presumably because of the divergent cultural emphases of China and Britain. The adolescents' self-concepts seemed influenced by the context—evoked by language.

Comments: Thousands of social scientists study culture, but it is difficult to determine whether their results are objective, unaffected by translation or by the perceptions and interpretations of the scientists. These researchers randomly assigned bilingual participants to be interviewed in one language or another, a clever way to evoke cultural context. However, this study was small (about 30 adolescents at each age, 125 in total, and only two cultures); replication is needed.

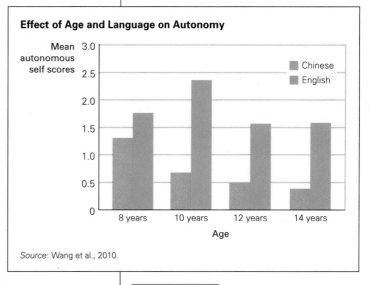

Effect of Age and Language on Autonomy

Source: Wang et al., 2010.

FIGURE 16.3

Words and Perceptions As they grew older, fluently bilingual students in Hong Kong who were interviewed in Chinese became less likely to refer to themselves as individuals distinct from their family and friends. By contrast, their classmates, who, by chance, were interviewed in English, were more self-focused—especially at age 10. Is that a shame? It depends on the culture (and maybe the language) of the observer.

Laursen & Collins, 2009). Regarding the next two, connectedness and control, consequences vary and observers differ in what they see. How do you react to this example, written by one of my students?

> I got pregnant when I was sixteen years old, and if it weren't for the support of my parents, I would probably not have my son. And if they hadn't taken care of him, I wouldn't have been able to finish high school or attend college. My parents also helped me overcome the shame that I felt when . . . my aunts, uncles, and especially my grandparents found out that I was pregnant.
>
> *[I., personal communication]*

My student is grateful to her parents, but others might wonder whether her early motherhood allowed her parents too much control and required her to remain dependent when she should have been seeking her own identity. Indeed, had they somehow allowed her to become pregnant? An added complexity is that my student's parents had emigrated from South America: Cultural expectations affected everyone's responses. A longitudinal study of nonimmigrant pregnant adolescents found that most (not all) young mothers and their children fared best if the teen's parents were supportive but did not take over child care (Borkowski et al., 2007). This may, or may not, be true for my student.

parental monitoring Parents' ongoing awareness of what their children are doing, where, and with whom.

A related issue is **parental monitoring**—that is, parental knowledge about each child's whereabouts, activities, and companions. When parental knowledge is the result of a warm, supportive relationship, children are likely to become confident, well-educated adults, avoiding drugs and risky sex (G. M. Barnes et al., 2006; Fletcher et al., 2004). That much is true, but the question broadcast to parents—"Do you know where your teenager is?"—is oversimplified.

The complication is that adolescents play an active role in their own monitoring: Some happily tell parents about their activities, whereas others are secretive (Vieno et al., 2009). Most disclose only part of the truth, selectively omitting things their parents would not approve of (Brown & Bakken, 2011). Thus, monitoring is a good sign if it indicates mutual, close interaction (Kerr et al., 2010). However, monitoring may be harmful when it derives from suspicion instead of from a warm connection.

Control is another aspect of parenting that can backfire. Adolescents expect parents to exert some control, especially over moral issues. However, overly restrictive and controlling parenting correlates with many adolescent problems, including depression (Brown & Bakken, 2011). Decreasing control over the years of adolescence is best, according to a longitudinal study of 12- to 14-year-olds in the suburbs of Chicago and Hong Kong. In both cultures, adolescents were given more autonomy over personal choices as they grew older, and in both cultures increased autonomy correlated with better emotional functioning (Qin et al., 2009).

Overall, parental reactions are crucial: Too much criticism and control might stop dialogue, not improve communication and behavior (Tilton-Weaver et al., 2010). An added complication is the personality of the adolescent and the context of the neighborhood. As one scholar who reviewed parental monitoring noted: "Some deft parental steering" is needed, but if "an adolescent is engaged in more than minor delinquent behavior, a much more structured and rule-based approach may be needed" (Capaldi, 2003, pp. 175–176).

A VIEW FROM SCIENCE

Parents, Genes, and Risks

Research on human development has practical applications. This was evident in a longitudinal study (first mentioned in Chapter 1) of African American families in rural Georgia that involved 611 parents and their 11-year-olds (Brody et al., 2009). Half of them were assigned to the control group, and the other half were invited to seven two-hour training sessions. Groups were small, and leaders were well prepared. Parents and their 11-year-olds were taught separately for an hour and then brought together.

The parents learned the following:

- The importance of being nurturing and involved
- The importance of conveying pride in being African American (called *racial socialization*)
- How monitoring and control benefit adolescents
- Why clear norms and expectations reduce substance use
- Strategies for communication about sex

The 11-year-olds learned the following:

- The importance of having household rules
- Adaptive behaviors when encountering racism
- The need for making plans for the future
- The differences between them and peers who use alcohol

After the hour during which parents and children were taught separately, the pairs were led in games, structured interactions, and modeling designed to improve family communication and cohesion. Three years later, both the experimental and control groups were reassessed regarding sex and alcohol/drug activity. The intervention helped, but the results were not dramatic.

Then, four years after the study began, the researchers read the new genetic research regarding the heightened risks for people with the short allele of the 5-HTTLPR gene. To see whether this applied to their African American teenagers, they collected and analyzed the DNA of 16-year-olds who had been, at age 11, in either the control or experimental groups. As Figure 16.4 shows, the training had no decided impact on those with the long allele, but it did have a major impact on those with the short one.

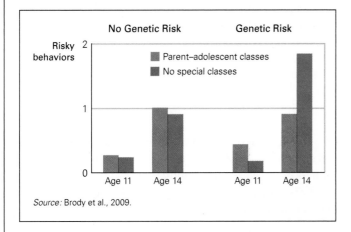

Source: Brody et al., 2009.

That only 14 hours or fewer of training (some families skipped sessions) had an impact is amazing, given all the other influences on these teenagers. However, since the parent–child relationship is crucial throughout adolescence, those seven sessions could have provided insights and connections that affected each vulnerable dyad from then on. Extensive research has found that postponing these three behaviors is beneficial to adolescent development in many ways, which makes these results particularly noteworthy.

FIGURE 16.4

Not Yet The risk score was a simple 0 to 3, with one point for each of the following: had drunk alcohol, had smoked marijuana, had had sex. As shown, most of the 11-year-olds had done none of these. By age 14, most had done one (usually had drunk beer or wine)—except for those at genetic risk who did not have the seven-session training. Some of them had done all three, and many had done at least two. As you see, for those youth without genetic risk, the usual parental advice was no better or worse than that of the special classes; the average 14-year-old had tried only one risky behavior. But for those at genetic risk, the special program made a decided difference.

Other Adults

Parents are important to adolescents, but so are many other adults—even those with no biological relationship to the young person (Chang et al., 2010; Scales et al., 2006). For instance, consider each of the four arenas of identity development (religion, politics, vocation, gender). A church or temple youth minister can affect a young person's faith and morality; a charismatic political leader can attract devotion (especially if the adolescent's own father is absent); a school counselor or adult friend can influence vocational direction; knowing an adult with a happy and satisfying opposite- or same-sex relationship allows appreciation of sexuality (Lerner & Steinberg, 2009).

These are all examples of nonrelatives affecting adolescents. For many youth, family members—older siblings, cousins, aunts and uncles, grandparents—are even more important. Sometimes parents delegate a sibling (the adolescent's aunt or uncle) to discuss taboo topics, such as sex or delinquency (Milardo, 2009). Links between the teenager and relatives are especially common in developing nations for two reasons: (1) Relatives often live together and (2) ethnotheories make family central.

For example, a Peruvian adolescent begins a narrative of his daily life with, "It was a very beautiful day, here in my house, with my friends, my family, my cousins, my aunts and uncles, my dad, my mom . . ." In that study, and many others, family members were sometimes harmful but more often helpful (Bayer et al., 2010). Especially when adolescents are impoverished, refugee, orphaned, mistreated, and so on, nonparent relatives aid resilience. Adolescents seek out relationships—and many of them seek family members.

Grandparents can be particularly crucial, whether the parents are single, married, or remarried (Attar-Schwartz et al., 2009). Although only about 10 percent of all U.S. children currently live with their grandparents (American Community

Survey, 2009), many more are affected by them. When Jim, age 21, was asked if he had any mentors, he replied:

> My mom's father—my grandfather. A very independent guy, but a very caring guy. They [grandparents] go down to Florida every winter. And our family often goes down to spend some time with them. My grandpa really loves swimming in the ocean. So he would go out floating on his back for hours at a time. . . . When I was younger, I used to stand on the shore and watch him float out. He would disappear and come back and ask me if I wanted to go out. I did once and people were worried because I was only ten. My parents and my grandma were concerned, "Oh, he's too small," even though I was with my grandpa. But what he said to me stuck. What he said was I need to know my own limits, my abilities. Other people are going to have their opinions and worries and concerns, but being independent is taking that stuff into consideration, but then also doing what you can.
>
> [cited in Pratt et al., 2010, p. 93]

As with many adults whom adolescents admire, this grandfather helped his grandson affirm his own abilities, even when his parents wanted to hold him back. Of course, if young Jim needed rescuing, his grandfather would have done it, but that is not what "stuck." For many teenagers struggling to know "my own limits, my abilities," adult mentors can be crucial.

SUMMING UP

Relationships with adults are essential during adolescence. Parents and adolescents often bicker over small things, especially in early adolescence, but parental guidance and ongoing communication promote adolescents' psychosocial health. Among the signs of a healthy parent–adolescent relationship are that parents know what their child is doing (parental monitoring) and that adolescents talk with their parents about their concerns; both these factors are affected by culture, by past relationships, and by the adolescent's maturity. Parental neglect or excessive parental control can foster adolescent rebellion; authoritative parenting continues to be effective. Other relatives and even strangers have an impact in guiding adolescents, especially when parental advice is limited.

>> Peer Power

Adolescents rely on peers to help them navigate the physical changes of puberty, the intellectual challenges of high school, and the social changes of leaving childhood. Friendships are important at every stage, but during early adolescence popularity is most coveted (LaFontana & Cillessen, 2010). Adults are sometimes unaware of adolescents' desire for respect from their contemporaries. I did not recognize this at the time with my own children:

- Our oldest daughter wore the same pair of jeans to tenth grade, day after day. She washed them each night by hand and asked me to put them in the dryer early each morning. My husband was bewildered. "Is this some weird female ritual?" he asked. Years later, she explained that she was afraid that if she wore different pants each day, her classmates would think she cared about her clothes and then criticize her choices.
- Our second daughter, at 16, pierced her ears for the third time. When I asked if this meant she would do drugs, she laughed at my ignorance. I later noticed that many of her friends had multiple holes in their ear lobes.

- At age 15, our third daughter was diagnosed with cancer. My husband and I weighed opinions from four physicians, each explaining how to minimize the risk of death. She had her own priorities: "I don't care what you choose, as long as I keep my hair." (Her hair fell out, but now her health is good—and her hair has grown back.)

- Our youngest, in sixth grade, refused to wear her jacket (it was new; she had chosen it) even in midwinter. Not until high school did she tell me she did it so that her middle school classmates would think she was tough.

In retrospect, I am amazed that I was unaware of the power of peers.

Sometimes adults conceptualize adolescence as a time when peers and parents are at odds, or worse, that peer influence overtakes parental influence. This is not true. Relationships with parents are the prototype for peer relationships: Healthy communication and support from parents make constructive peer relationships more likely. Parents and peers are often mutually reinforcing, although many adolescents downplay the influence of their parents and many parents are unaware of the influence of peers. Only when parents are harsh or neglectful does peer influence reign alone (Bakken & Brown, 2010).

Peer Pressure

For every adolescent, the judgment of peers is important, and having friends is vital. Friends are often a positive force in a young person's life. One high school boy said:

> A lot of times I wake up in the morning and I don't want to go to school, and then I'm like, you know, I have got this class and these friends are in it, and I am going to have fun. That is a big part of my day—my friends.

> *[quoted in Hamm & Faircloth, 2005, p. 72]*

Adults sometimes fear **peer pressure,** that is, that peers will push an adolescent to try drugs, break the law, or other things the child would never do alone. This fear ignores the fact that "friends generally encourage socially desirable behaviors" (Berndt & Murphy, 2002, p. 281), such as playing sports, studying, quitting cigarettes, applying to college. Peers are more helpful than harmful (Audrey et al., 2006; Nelson & DeBacker, 2008), especially in early adolescence, when biological and social stresses can be overwhelming. In later adolescence, teenagers are less susceptible to peer pressure, either positive or negative (Monahan et al., 2009).

Selecting Friends

The fact that peers are often beneficial does not mean that they always encourage the behaviors that adults value. Young people *can* lead one another into trouble. Collectively, peers sometimes provide **deviancy training,** whereby one person shows another how to rebel against social norms (Dishion et al., 2001). Especially if adolescents believe that the most popular, most admired peers are having sex, doing drugs, or ignoring homework, they become more likely to take up the destructive behavior themselves (Rodgers, 2003).

However, it is a myth that upstanding, innocent teens are routinely corrupted by deviant friends. Adolescents choose their friends and models—not always wisely, but never randomly. There is a developmental progression here: The combination of "problem behavior, school marginalization, and low academic performance" at age 11 leads to gang involvement two years later, deviancy training two years after that, and violent behavior at age 18 or 19 (Dishion et al., 2010, p. 603).

peer pressure Encouragement to conform to one's friends or contemporaries in behavior, dress, and attitude; usually considered a negative force, as when adolescent peers encourage one another to defy adult authority.

deviancy training Destructive peer support in which one person shows another how to rebel against authority or social norms.

Especially for Parents of a Teenager
Your 13-year-old comes home after a sleepover at a friend's house with a new, weird hairstyle—perhaps cut or colored in a bizarre manner. What do you say and do? (see response, page 487)

Beach Party These laughing barefoot girls, with the boys in the background displaying manly indifference, could be partying alongside any ocean and sandy shoreline—in California, Florida, New Jersey, or several other states and nations.

Observation Quiz This photo was taken in 2007. Is it set in the United States? (see answer, page 487)

Instant Connections Ignoring the rides at Coney Island, these two girls lean on each other; both have blue bracelets, tight jeans, sleeveless shirts, and, most important, texts to read and send. As with their use of the automobile and the telephone, teens have taken an adult invention (the Internet was originally developed for military use) and turned it into a tool for increasing peer support.

This cascade is not inevitable; adults can help disengaged 11-year-olds instead of blaming their friends years later.

To further understand the impact of peers, two concepts are helpful: *selection* and *facilitation*. Teenagers *select* a clique whose values and interests they share, abandoning former friends who follow other paths. Peers then *facilitate* destructive or constructive behaviors. It is easier to do the wrong thing ("Let's all skip school on Friday") or the right thing ("Let's study together for the chem exam") if close friends are doing it, too. Peer facilitation helps adolescents act in ways they are unlikely to act on their own.

Both selection and facilitation can work in any direction. One teenager joins a clique whose members smoke cigarettes and drink beer, and together they take the next step, perhaps sharing a joint at a party. Another teenager might choose friends who enjoy math puzzles, and, as demonstrated in this quote from Lindsay, they might all enroll in AP calculus together:

> [Companionship] makes me excited about calculus. That is a hard class, but when you need help with calculus, you go to your friends. You may think no one could be excited about calculus, but I am. Having friends in class with you definitely makes school more enjoyable.
>
> [quoted in Hamm & Faircloth, 2005, p. 72]

Thus, adolescents select and facilitate, choose and are chosen. Happy, energetic, and successful teens have close friends who themselves are high achievers, with no major emotional problems. The opposite also holds: Those who are drug users, sexually active, and alienated from school choose compatible friends and support one another in continuing on that path (Crosnoe & Needham, 2004).

A study of identical twins from ages 14 to 17 found that selection typically preceded facilitation, rather than the other way around. Young teenagers who were likely to rebel chose more lawbreaking friends than did their less externalizing twin (Burt et al., 2009). A study of teenage use of cigarettes and alcohol found that, contrary to the fear of peer pressure, selection was probably more important than facilitation, especially for smoking (Kiuru et al., 2010). Peers provide opportunity and encouragement for what the adolescent already wants to do.

Approval for Risk Taking

Remember that adolescents must grow up, finding their own identity within a context unlike the one their parents experienced. They cannot depend exclusively on their parents; peers must be influential as well.

An experiment in peer facilitation involved adolescents (ages 13 to 16), emerging adults (ages 18 to 22), and adults (over age 24) in a video driving game (Gardner & Steinberg, 2005). As each player drove, every so often the screen would flash a yellow light, indicating that soon (within one to several seconds) a wall would appear. The goal was to drive as long as possible but brake before crashing into the wall. Points were gained for travel time; a crash erased the points from that round.

The participants were randomly assigned to one of two conditions: playing alone or with two strangers of the same sex and age as themselves. When they played alone, adolescents, emerging adults, and adults all averaged one crash per 15-round session. That single crash was enough to make them wary.

Adults were equally cautious when playing with other adults. But when the adolescents were with peers, they became bolder, crashing three times on average (see Figure 16.5) (Gardner & Steinberg, 2005; Steinberg, 2007). They chose to lose points rather than to appear cautious. Foolish? Perhaps. But although crashes lost points, they also provided an emotional connection to a peer.

The same phenomenon is evident in daily life, with teenagers driving too fast, swimming too far, or challenging authority to gain approval from others. This is especially apparent when boys want girls to admire them (see photos).

Romance

Contemporary adolescents often have friends of the other sex who are not their lovers. Adults sometimes worry about that, assuming that teenagers will have intercourse if unchaperoned. However, many teenagers have close, even passionate, friendships with peers of both sexes, without romantic undertones. Disruptions of friendships (either same-sex or other-sex) can cause jealousy (e.g., if the friend befriends another person) or depression (e.g., if the friend moves away). Friendship precedes romance and may be pivotal in adolescence.

Nonetheless, romance often begins in the teen years. Decades ago, Dexter Dunphy (1963) described the sequence of male–female relationships during childhood and adolescence:

1. Groups of friends, exclusively one sex or the other
2. A loose association of girls and boys, with public interactions within a crowd
3. Small mixed-sex groups of the advanced members of the crowd
4. Formation of couples, with private intimacies

Culture affects the timing and manifestation, but subsequent research in many nations validates this sequence. Youth worldwide (and even the young of other primates) avoid the other sex in childhood and are attracted to them by adulthood. This universal pattern suggests that biology underlies this sequence.

The peer group is very much involved as well. Romantic partners, especially in early adolescence, are selected not primarily for their individual traits but for the traits that are accepted by peers. If leaders of a girls' clique pair with leaders of a

Video Game Risk Taking, by Age Group

Number of crashes — Adolescents, Young adults, Adults — Alone, With peers

Source: Adapted from Steinberg, 2007.

FIGURE 16.5

Admire Me Everyone wants to accumulate points in a game, earn high grades, and save money—unless one is a teenager and other teens are watching. Then a desire to obtain peer admiration by taking risks may overtake caution. In this game, teenage participants chose to lose points and increase crashes when other teens were present.

Watch Me Fall Adolescent boys in a skate park were videotaped in two circumstances: with an attractive female stranger sitting on a bench nearby and with no one watching. (The camera was hidden.) The boys took more risks, and fell more often, with the female observer present.

COURTESY RICHARD RONAY

The Same Situation, Many Miles Apart: Teenagers in Love No matter where in the world they are, teenage couples broadcast their love in universally recognized facial expressions and body positions. Samantha and Ryan *(top)*, visiting New York City from suburban Philadelphia, are similar in many ways to the teen couple *(bottom)* in Chicute, Mozambique, even though their social contexts are dramatically different.

sexual orientation A term that refers to whether a person is sexually and romantically attracted to others of the same sex, the opposite sex, or both sexes.

boys' clique, the unattached members of the two cliques are encouraged to pair with each other as well. That allows easy double or triple dating but also helps explain why adolescent romantic partners tend to have less in common, in personality and attitudes, than adult couples do (Zimmer-Gembeck & Ducat, 2010).

First Love

In modern developed nations, where puberty begins with hormones at about age 10 and marriage occurs much later if at all, each of Dunphy's four stages typically lasts several years. Early, exclusive romances are more often a sign of social trouble than of maturity, especially for girls (Eklund et al., 2010). Unlike the norm in earlier centuries, a long-lasting commitment to a life partner does not usually occur until adulthood.

The first romances appear in high school, rarely lasting more than a year, with girls having a steady partner more often than boys do. Exclusive commitment is desired, but "cheating," flirting, and disloyalty are rife. Breakups are common; so are unreciprocated crushes. All this can be devastating to the adolescent, in part because entire high school crowds are often witnesses (Schwartz, 2006). Adolescents may despair at rejection, contemplating revenge or suicide (Fisher, 2006). In such cases, peer support can be a lifesaver. Indeed, adolescents as well as adults rely on friends, who help them cope with romantic ups and downs (Mehta & Strough, 2009).

Contrary to adult fears, many teenage romances do not include sexual intercourse. In the United States in 2009, even though one-third of all high school students were sexually experienced by the tenth grade, another one-third were virgins at high school graduation (see Figure 16.6). Every survey finds that norms vary markedly from crowd to crowd, school to school, city to city, and nation to nation. For instance, twice as many high school students in Milwaukee as in Seattle say they have had intercourse (63 percent versus 29 percent) (MMWR, June 4, 2010).

Same-Sex Romances

Some adolescents are attracted to peers of the same sex. **Sexual orientation** refers to the direction of a person's erotic desires. One meaning of *orient* is to "turn toward"; thus, sexual orientation refers to whether a person is romantically attracted to (turned on by) people of the other sex, the same sex, or both sexes. It is not known how many adolescents are romantically oriented toward people of the same sex because sexual orientation can be strong, weak, acted upon, secretive, or unconscious. Thus, asking teenagers to indicate their sexual orientation is bound to underestimate prevalence.

Obviously, culture and cohort are powerful, not only in social acceptance but also in self-acceptance. In many nations of Africa and the Middle East, non-heterosexual orientation is considered criminal. Worldwide, many gay youth date members of the other sex to hide their orientation, and binge drinking and suicidal thoughts remain a danger. This may be less common among current cohorts in nations where same-sex partnerships are accepted: Recent research finds that gay and straight adolescents have many similar problems and similar strengths (Saewyc, 2011).

Another reason it is not known how many adolescents are gay, lesbian, bisexual, or asexual is that sexual orientation is fluid. Girls are particularly likely to wait until they have sexual experiences to decide their identity, and many lesbian women had other-sex relationships in adolescence (Saewyc, 2011). In the mid-1990s, one large study of high school students in Massachusetts found that 1 in 200 identified as gay or lesbian (Garofalo et al., 1999). More recently, a large

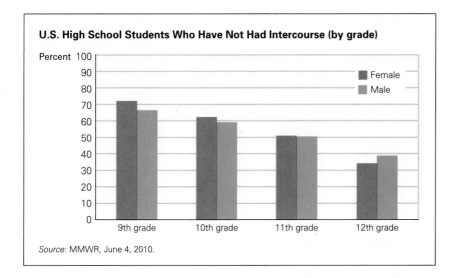

U.S. High School Students Who Have Not Had Intercourse (by grade)

Source: MMWR, June 4, 2010.

FIGURE 16.6

Many Virgins For 30 years, the Youth Risk Behavior Survey has asked high school students from all over the United States dozens of confidential questions about their behavior. As you can see, about one-third of all students have already had sex by the ninth grade, and about one-third have not yet had sex by their senior year, a group whose ranks have been increasing in recent years. Other research finds that sexual behaviors are influenced by peers, with some groups all sexually experienced by age 14 and others not until age 18 or later.

Dutch study of high school students found that 1 in 12 were attracted to people of their own sex (Bos et al., 2008).

Even more recently, among sexually active teenagers in New York City, 10 percent had had same-sex partners—but many of those individuals (38 percent) identified as straight (Pathela & Schillinger, 2010). In that study, those most at risk of sexual violence and sexually transmitted infections (STIs) were not those whose sexual experiences were exclusively same-sex or exclusively other-sex, but those who had partners of both sexes.

Sexual orientation should not be confused with gender identity. An increasing number of adolescents feel that they do not identify with their biological sex. In some places, it may be possible for these children to be treated as a member of the opposite sex by adopting different clothing and friends—or even, in adolescence, by trying hormone treatments. But others may not be able to transition to another gender as easily and may suffer from feeling they do not match their biological sex. These children may be diagnosed with gender dysphoria, a new DSM-5 diagnosis that describes the distress individuals may feel as a consequence of feeling that they are in "the wrong body."

These variations reflect culture, cohort, and the words used in the surveys. Adults who care about adolescent health are advised to ask about behavior—which may differ from gender identity or sexual orientation (Pathela & Schillinger, 2010). When and with whom a person becomes sexually active depends on a cascade of factors, including age at puberty, parenting practices, peer pressure, and dating relationships (Longmore et al., 2009).

Sex Education

Adults and peers both provide sex education, either explicit or implicit (through examples, expressions, silences). Many adolescents have strong sexual urges but minimal logic about pregnancy and disease, as might be expected with the differential maturation of the limbic system and prefrontal cortex or with the attraction of intuitive thought. One result is that millions of teenagers worry that they are oversexed, undersexed, or deviant, unaware that thousands, maybe millions, of people are just like them. As a result, "students seem to waffle their way through sexually relevant encounters driven both by the allure of reward and the fear of negative consequences" (Wagner, 2011, p. 193). Obviously, they have much to learn. Where do they learn it?

>> Response for Parents of a Teenager (from page 483) Remember: Communicate, do not control. Let your child talk about the meaning of the hairstyle. Remind yourself that a hairstyle in itself is harmless. Don't say "What will people think?" or "Are you on drugs?" or anything that might give your child reason to stop communicating.

>> Answer to Observation Quiz (from page 484) No. They are in Halong Bay, Vietnam. Beachgoing U.S. girls would be dressed differently.

From the Media

One source of sex information is the media. Sexual content appears almost seven times per hour on the TV shows most watched by teenagers (Steinberg & Monahan, 2011). That content is almost always alluring: Almost never does a television character develop an STI, deal with an unwanted pregnancy, or mention (much less use) a condom. At least one study found that men's magazines convince teenage boys that manliness means many sexual conquests (Ward et al., 2011).

There is controversy regarding sex on TV, in film, and in music (Collins et al., 2011; Steinberg & Monahan, 2011). Although there is a correlation between adolescent exposure to media sex and adolescent sexual initiation, that correlation may reflect selection, not cause. Perhaps teenagers watch sexy TV because they are sexually active, not vice versa. One analysis concludes that "the most important influences on adolescents' sexual behavior may be closer to home than Hollywood" (Steinberg & Monahan, 2011, p. 575).

From Parents and Peers

Home is where sex education begins. Every study finds that explicit parental communication is influential (Longmore et al., 2009). However, many parents wait too long to discuss sex, utter generalities, and know little about their adolescents' romances. Three studies of quite different groups illustrate the problem.

1. Mexican American mothers told their teenagers *cuidate*, "take care of yourself," which their teenagers interpreted as advice about health, not condoms. The teens became pregnant, and the mothers wondered why (Moncloa et al., 2010).

2. Parents of 12-year-old girls were asked whether their daughters had hugged or kissed a boy "for a long time" or hung out with older boys (signs that sex information is urgently needed). Only 5 percent of the parents said yes, as did 38 percent of the girls (O'Donnell et al., 2008).

3. African and Hmong American 14- to 19-year-olds rarely tell their parents about their romantic encounters. For example, one girl said she and her girlfriend were going to the movies (true) but omitted that their boyfriends were coming, too (Brown & Bakken, 2011).

What exactly should parents say? That is the wrong question, according to a longitudinal study of thousands of adolescents. Those teens who became sexually active and who were most likely to develop an STI had parents who had talked to them about sex, warning them to stay away from it. In contrast, adolescents were more likely to remain virgins if they had a warm relationship with their parents—specific information was less important, but open communication was necessary (Deptula et al., 2010).

Especially for Sex Educators Suppose adults in your community never talk to their children about sex or puberty. Is that a mistake? (see response, page 490)

Especially when parents are silent, forbidding, or vague, adolescent sexual behavior is strongly influenced by peers. Many younger adolescents discuss details of romance and sex with other members of their clique, seeking advice and approval (Laursen & Mooney, 2007). Often the boys brag and the girls worry. Specifics depend on the group: All members of a clique may be virgins or all may be sexually active. Once they acquire boyfriends or girlfriends, partners teach each other. However, their lessons are more about pleasure than consequences: Only about half of U.S. adolescent couples discuss pregnancy and disease before they have sex (Ryan et al., 2007).

From Teachers in School

Almost all U.S. parents want their adolescents to have up-to-date sex education, including details of safe sex and contraception. Developmentalists agree that sex education belongs in the schools as well as in parent–child conversations, since adolescents need to learn from trusted and informed adults rather than misinforming each other.

Sex education varies dramatically by nation. Most northern European schools begin sex education in elementary school, and by middle school students learn about sexual responsibility, masturbation, same-sex romance, oral and anal sex—subjects rarely covered in U.S. classes. Rates of teenage pregnancy in most European nations are less than half those in the United States; perhaps curriculum is the reason. On the other hand, in Russia, although most experts believe that sex education belongs in school, few schools include it—and yet the official rate of HIV and pregnancy is lower than in the United States (Gevorgyan et al., 2011). Obviously, school sex education does not act apart from the social context.

Within the United States, the timing and content of sex education vary by state and community. Some high schools provide comprehensive programs, free condoms, and medical treatment; others provide nothing. Some schools begin sex education in middle school; others wait until the end of high school. This makes a difference: Many sex-education programs delay the age at which adolescents become sexually active and increase their use of condoms. However, specific information and attitudes influence the success of the curriculum—some programs have no impact (Kirby & Laris, 2009).

One controversy is whether abstinence should be taught as the only sexual strategy for adolescents, as was U.S. federal policy until 2009. It is true, of course, that abstaining from sex (including oral sex) prevents sexually transmitted infections and pregnancy, but longitudinal data four to six years after adolescents had participated in abstinence-only programs revealed that the programs did not succeed. About half of students in both experimental (abstinence-only) and control groups had had sex by age 16. The number of partners and use of contraceptives were the same with and without the special curriculum (Trenholm et al., 2007). Students in the control groups knew slightly more about preventing disease and pregnancy, but that knowledge neither slowed nor hastened their sexual initiation.

"Smirking or Non-Smirking?"

SUMMING UP

Crowds, cliques, and friends are all part of adolescence. Contrary to what some adults may think, peer pressure can be positive. Many adolescents rely on friends of both sexes to help them with the concerns and troubles of the teen years. Romances are typical in high school, but early, exclusive, long-lasting romances are more often a sign of emotional trouble than of maturity. Some adolescents are romantically attracted to others of their own sex; it is not known how often this occurs.

Given the earlier onset of puberty and the later marriages today, adolescents spend a decade or more with intense sexual drives but no enduring partner. They need accurate information about all aspects of sexuality before they become sexually active themselves. Parents are influential role models, but few provide detailed and current information before adolescents begin experimenting with sex. Most adolescents learn from personal experience with peers. School instruction may increase condom use, but not every curriculum is equally effective, and schools vary dramatically in what they teach at what age.

>> **Response for Sex Educators** (from page 488) Yes, but forgive them. Ideally, parents should talk to their children about sex, presenting honest information and listening to the child's concerns. However, many parents find it very difficult to do this because they feel embarrassed and ignorant. You might schedule separate sessions for adults over 30, for emerging adults, and for adolescents.

>> Sadness and Anger

Adolescence is usually a wonderful time, perhaps better for current generations than for any generation before. Nonetheless, troubles plague about 20 percent of youth. Most of them are *comorbid*, with several problems occurring at once. Distinguishing between normal moodiness and pathology, between behavior that is merely unsettling to adults and behavior that is seriously troubled, is complex. Many adolescents are less happy and more angry than they were as children, at least at moments—many change emotions day to day (Neumann et al., 2011). For a few, negative emotions become intense, even deadly.

Depression

The general emotional trend from late childhood through adolescence is toward less confidence. A dip in self-esteem at puberty is found for children of every ethnicity and gender (Fredricks & Eccles, 2002; Greene & Way, 2005; Kutob et al., 2009). Some studies report rising self-esteem thereafter (especially for African American girls and European American boys), but variations are many, as are individual differences.

Self-esteem is, on average, lower in girls and higher in boys, lower in Asian Americans and higher in African Americans, lower in younger adolescents and higher in older adolescents (Bachman et al., 2011). Many studies report a gradual rise in self-esteem from early adolescence through at least age 30, but all find notable variability from one person to another. Seriously depressed adolescents cannot be promised "you'll feel better soon"—severe depression may lighten, but it rarely disappears (Huang, 2010).

All studies find that parents and peers affect self-esteem (Hall-Lande et al., 2007) and that some communities have lower rates of depression because they promote strong and supportive relationships between teenagers and adults. For some adolescents, family circumstances are crucial. One factor in an individual's level of self-esteem may be the adolescents' own neurological propensity, as one might expect from differential vulnerability, explained in Chapter 1. Some adolescent girls are likely to be depressed because their mothers are belligerent, disapproving, and contemptuous; other adolescents seem protected by their brains from such parenting (Whittle et al., 2011).

Specific cultural contexts are influential as well. For Latino American youth, self-esteem and ethnic pride rise after puberty, especially if familism is strong, because their new maturity enables them to contribute in meaningful ways to their families. However, if a Latino's family is characterized by fighting and fragmentation, that reduces self-esteem even more than do similar circumstances for non-Latino adolescents (Smokowski et al., 2010). For gay adolescents, family rejection increases the rate of suicide (Saewyc, 2011). Adolescents of any background with low self-esteem turn to drugs, sex, and dieting—all of which often make depression worse (Biro et al., 2006; Trzesniewski et al., 2006).

Clinical Depression

clinical depression Feelings of hopelessness, lethargy, and worthlessness that last two weeks or more.

Some adolescents sink into **clinical depression,** a deep sadness and hopelessness that disrupts all normal, regular activities. The causes, including genes and early care, predate adolescence. Then the onset of puberty—with its myriad physical and emotional ups and downs—pushes some vulnerable children, especially girls, into despair. The rate of clinical depression more than doubles during this time, to an estimated 15 percent, affecting about 1 in 5 girls and 1 in 10 boys.

It is not known whether the reasons for these gender differences are primarily biological, psychological, or social (Alloy & Abramson, 2007). Obviously, sex hormones differ, but girls also experience social pressures from their families, peers, and cultures that boys do not. Perhaps the combination of biological and psychosocial stress causes some to slide into depression. Genes are involved as well.

One study found that the short allele of the serotonin transporter promoter gene (5-HTTLPR) increased the rate of depression among girls everywhere but increased the rate of depression among boys only if they lived in low-SES communities (Uddin et al., 2010). It is not surprising that certain genes make depression more likely, but the gender-specific neighborhood correlation is puzzling. Maybe boys are particularly likely to be depressed if they see no job prospects, and that is more likely in poor neighborhoods.

Recently, a cognitive explanation has been offered for gender differences in depression. **Rumination**—talking about, remembering, and mentally replaying past experiences—is more common among girls than boys. If unpleasant incidents are replayed, rumination often leads to depression (Ayduk & Kross, 2008).

rumination Repeatedly thinking and talking about past experiences; can contribute to depression.

Suicide

Stress can lead to depression and thoughts of suicide. Serious, distressing thoughts about killing oneself (called **suicidal ideation**) are most common at about age 15. The 2009 Youth Risk Behavior Survey revealed that one-third (33.9 percent) of U.S. high school girls felt so hopeless that they stopped doing some usual activities for two weeks or more, and one-sixth (17.4 percent) seriously thought about suicide. The corresponding rates for boys were 19.1 percent and 10.5 percent (MMWR, June 4, 2010).

Suicidal ideation can lead to **parasuicide,** also called *attempted suicide* or *failed suicide.* Parasuicide includes any deliberate self-harm that could have been lethal. *Parasuicide* is the best word to use because "failed" implies that to die is to succeed (!); "attempt" is likewise misleading because, especially in adolescence, the difference between attempt and actual suicide is difficult to discern.

As you see in Table 16.1, parasuicide can be divided according to those who require medical attention (surgery, pumped stomachs, etc.) and those who do not, but any parasuicide needs to be taken seriously. Parasuicide is a flashing neon warning sign that, if there is a next time, the person may end up dead.

Internationally, rates of teenage parasuicide range between 6 and 20 percent. Among U.S. high school students in 2009, 7.9 percent of the girls and 4.6 percent of the boys said they had tried to kill themselves in the past year (MMWR, June 4, 2010; see Table 16.1).

While suicidal ideation during adolescence is common, completed suicides are not. The U.S. annual rate of completed suicide for people aged 15 to 19 (in school or not) is about 8 per 100,000, or 0.008 percent. Adolescents are *less* likely to kill

suicidal ideation Thinking about suicide, usually with some serious emotional and intellectual or cognitive overtones.

parasuicide Any potentially lethal action against the self that does not result in death. (Also called *attempted suicide* or *failed suicide.*)

TABLE 16.1		Suicidal Ideation and Parasuicide Among U.S. High School Students, 2009			
		Seriously Considered Suicide	Parasuicide (attempted suicide)	Parasuicide (w/medical attention)	Actual Suicide (ages 15–19)*
Overall		**13.8%**	**6.3%**	**1.9%**	Less than 0.01% (about 7.5 per 100,000)
Girls:	9th grade	20.3	10.3	2.8	
	10th grade	17.2	8.8	2.3	Girls: about 3.5 per 100,000
	11th grade	17.8	7.8	2.6	
	12th grade	13.6	4.6	1.0	
Boys:	9th grade	10.0	4.5	1.4	
	10th grade	10.0	5.2	2.0	Boys: about 11.5 per 100,000
	11th grade	11.4	4.7	1.7	
	12th grade	10.5	3.8	1.4	

*Actual suicide numbers are based on data for 2007.

Sources: MMWR, June 4, 2010; National Center for Health Statistics, 2010.

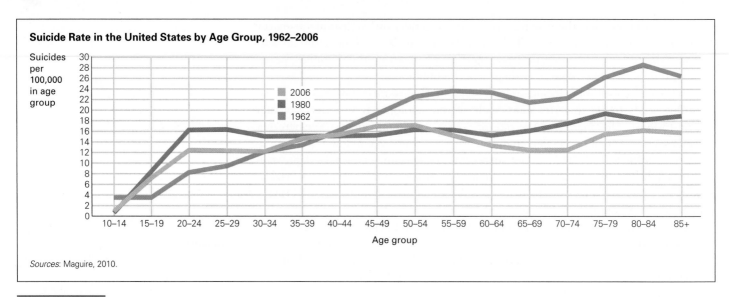

Suicide Rate in the United States by Age Group, 1962–2006

Sources: Maguire, 2010.

FIGURE 16.7

Much Depends on Age A historical look at U.S. suicide statistics reveals two trends, both of which were still apparent in 2009. First, older teenagers today are twice as likely to take their own lives as in 1960 but less likely to do so than in 1980. Second, suicide rates overall are down, but they continue to be high among elderly people.

themselves than adults are. Many people mistakenly think suicide is more frequent in adolescence for four reasons:

1. The rate, low as it is, is much higher than it appeared to be 50 years ago (see Figure 16.7).
2. Statistics on "youth" often include emerging adults aged 18 to 25, whose suicide rates are higher than those of adolescents.
3. Adolescent suicides capture media attention, and people of all ages make the logical error called base rate neglect (see Chapter 15).
4. Parasuicides may be more common in adolescence than later.

Gender differences in suicide are dramatic (see Table 16.1). Depression and parasuicide are more common among females, but completed suicide is higher for males (except in China). For instance, in the United States among 15- to 19-year-olds, boys kill themselves three times more often than girls (National Center for

Nothing to Do Compared with most other Americans, these three adolescents are at higher risk of diabetes, alcoholism, unemployment, and suicide. They live on the Rosebud Sioux Reservation in South Dakota. The suicide rate among Native American teenagers is more than three times as high as the rate for U.S. adolescents overall.

Health Statistics, 2010). A major reason is method: Males typically jump from high places or shoot themselves (immediately lethal), whereas females often swallow pills or cut their wrists (allowing intervention or second thoughts—common when the suicidal teen has a few minutes to reflect).

Another hypothesis is that girls talk about their emotions, allowing friends and families to get help for them. Rumination may increase depression but decrease suicide. Boys more often silently withdraw; their warning signs are less obvious. Furthermore, young men somehow think parasuicide is unmanly, so they choose deadly methods (Aseltine & DeMartino, 2004). Consider Bill.

A CASE TO STUDY

He Kept His Worries to Himself

A psychologist described an adolescent boy in these words:

> Bill is 17, a senior in high school. A good student, hard-working, some would say "driven," Bill has achieved well and is hoping to go to either Harvard or Stanford next year. He is also hopeful that his college career will lead him to medical school and a career as a surgeon like his father. Bill is a tall, handsome boy, attractive to girls but surprisingly shy among them. When he socializes, he prefers to hang out in groups rather than date; in these groups, he is likely to be seen deep in introspective discussion with one girl or another. Introspection has no place on the school football team, where this past season Bill led all receivers in pass catches. Nor does he appear at all the quiet type in his new sports car, a gift from his parents on his 17th birthday. The elder of two sons, Bill has always been close to his parents, and a "good son." Perhaps for these reasons, he has been increasingly preoccupied as verbalized threats of separation and divorce become common in his parents' increasingly frequent conflicts. These worries he has kept largely to himself.
>
> *[Berman et al., 2006, pp. 43–44]*

If you were Bill's friend, would you realize he needed professional help and make sure he got it? Unfortunately, Bill had no friends who heeded his warning signs. Even his parents did not realize he was troubled until

> Bill's body was brought to the local medical examiner's office; he put his father's .22-caliber handgun to his head and ended his life in an instant.
>
> *[Berman et al., 2006, p. 44]*

The report does not mention whether Bill's body was tested for drugs. About one-third of all U.S. suicides occur when a person has been drinking or drugging, behaviors that most high school seniors such as Bill do.

In retrospect, Bill had several risk factors and had shown danger signs—no close friends, male or female; his parents' conflicts; his foreclosure on his father's profession; his drive for perfection (Harvard or Stanford, football star); no older siblings to advise and comfort him. Did the gift of a sports car signify a problem—perhaps that Bill's parents provided material possessions instead of emotional closeness? Did his shyness around girls suggest worries about his sexuality? Had he been rejected from one of his college choices? Why did his father have a handgun, loaded and accessible?

Because they are not logical and analytical, adolescents are particularly affected when they hear about a suicide, either via media reports or from peers (Insel & Gould, 2008). That makes them susceptible to **cluster suicides,** a term for the occurrence of several suicides within a group over a brief span of time—a few weeks or months. If a high school student's "tragic end" is sentimentalized, that elicits suicidal ideation among his or her peers. Media attention increases the risk.

Wealth and education decrease the incidence of many disorders, but *not* of suicide—quite the opposite. The reason may be news reports that typically highlight the lost potential of a suicidal adolescent (e.g., "Honor Student Kills Self"). This may encourage cluster suicides among, say, other honor students. Or adolescents from high-SES families may not know how to cope with a failing grade or a broken relationship.

Since 1990, rates of adolescent suicide have fallen, especially among high-SES teenagers. One reason may be that parents spot problems and find psychotherapy,

cluster suicides Several suicides committed by members of a group within a brief period of time.

Especially for Journalists You just heard that a teenage cheerleader jumped off a tall building and died. How should you report the story? (see response, page 494)

>> Response for Journalists (from page 493) Since teenagers seek admiration from their peers, be careful not to glorify the victim's life or death. Facts are needed, as is, perhaps, inclusion of warning signs that were missed or cautions about alcohol abuse. Avoid prominent headlines or anything that might encourage another teenager to do the same thing.

which often includes antidepressants—which evidently relieve the desperate sadness that some adolescents feel (Gentile, 2010). A British study suggested that antidepressants might *increase* suicidal ideation (not suicide). However, an analysis of 27 controlled clinical trials (similar to experiments, except participants have a particular illness or disorder) found that antidepressants, especially combined with cognitive-behavioral therapy, were far more likely to relieve depression than to increase suicide (Bridge et al., 2007).

Delinquency and Disobedience

Like low self-esteem and suicidal ideation, bouts of anger are common in adolescence. In fact, the moody adolescent could be both depressed and delinquent because externalizing and internalizing behavior are more closely connected in adolescence than at any other age (Loeber & Burke, 2011). That is why teenagers jailed for assault (externalizing) are suicide risks (internalizing).

Externalizing actions are obvious. Many adolescents slam doors, defy parents, and tell friends exactly how badly other teenagers (or siblings or teachers) have behaved. Some teenagers—particularly boys—"act out" by breaking laws. They steal, damage property, or injure others.

Is such behavior normal? Some developmentalists answer yes. One was Anna Freud (Sigmund's daughter, herself a prominent psychoanalyst), who wrote that adolescent resistance to parental authority was "welcome . . . beneficial . . . inevitable." She explained:

> We all know individual children who, as late as the ages of fourteen, fifteen or sixteen, show no such outer evidence of inner unrest. They remain, as they have been during the latency period, "good" children, wrapped up in their family relationships, considerate sons of their mothers, submissive to their fathers, in accord with the atmosphere, idea and ideal of their childhood background. Convenient as this may be, it signifies a delay of their normal development and is, as such, a sign to be taken seriously.
>
> *[A. Freud, 1958/2000, p. 263]*

Contrary to Freud, many psychologists, most teachers, and almost all parents are quite happy with well-behaved, considerate teenagers. Which view is valid? Both. Adolescents vary; understanding the implications helps all of them.

Hope and Anger Adolescents and young adults everywhere demonstrate against adult authority, with varied strategies and results. In Cairo's Tahrir Square *(left)*, this young man flashes the peace sign hours before President Mubarak's resignation, but the 2011 "Arab Spring" in other nations was not as successful. French students *(right)* protested cuts in high school staff, but their demands were resisted by the government. Worldwide, social change is fueled by youthful aspirations—sometimes leading to victory, sometimes to despair.

Most teenagers usually obey the law, and their lawfulness does not predict a later explosion or breakdown. In fact, according to the 30-year New Zealand study first mentioned in Chapter 1, by age 26 men who had never been arrested usually earned degrees, "held high-status jobs, and expressed optimism about their own futures" (Moffitt, 2003, p. 61). Dozens of other longitudinal studies confirm that increased anger during puberty is normal but that most adolescents express their anger in acceptable ways. They yell at their parents, curse at their peers, complain about school. For a minority, anger explodes, and they break something or hurt someone. And a minority of that minority have been aggressive throughout childhood. They are the ones to be worried about.

Breaking the Law

Both the prevalence (how widespread) and the incidence (how frequent) of criminal actions are more common during adolescence. Arrest statistics in every nation reflect this, and confidential self-reports reveal that virtually every adolescent breaks the law at least once before age 20. Only about one-fourth of young lawbreakers are caught, and most of those are warned and released (Dodge et al., 2006).

In one study of 1,559 urban seventh-graders (both sexes, all races, from parochial as well as public schools), more than three-fourths had committed at least one offense (stolen something, damaged property, or hurt someone physically). Usually, however, adolescents are not chronic offenders: In the same study, less than one-third had committed five or more such acts (Nichols et al., 2006).

Some Want Her Dead But Florida law did not allow 15-year-old Morgan Leppert to be executed for murdering a 63-year-old man when she and her 22-year-old boyfriend, Toby, stole the man's car. Instead, she was sentenced to life in prison without parole. Developmentalists agree that teenage criminals are not like adult ones, but they also wonder why Morgan's mother let Toby sleep in Morgan's bedroom when she was just 14.

Causes of Delinquency

Two clusters of factors, one from childhood (primarily brain-based) and one from adolescence (primarily contextual), predict delinquency. The first of these clusters includes a short attention span, hyperactivity, inadequate emotional regulation, slow language development, low intelligence, early and severe malnutrition, autistic tendencies, maternal cigarette smoking, and being the victim of severe child abuse. Most of these factors are more common among boys than girls, which may be one reason for the gender difference in delinquency. Neurological impairment (either inborn or caused by early experiences) increases the risk that a child will become a **life-course-persistent offender** (Moffitt et al., 2001), someone who breaks the law before and after adolescence as well as during it.

life-course-persistent offender A person whose criminal activity typically begins in early adolescence and continues throughout life; a career criminal.

The second cluster of factors that predict delinquency encompasses risk factors that are primarily psychosocial. They include having deviant friends; having few connections to school; living in a crowded, violent, unstable neighborhood; not having a job; using drugs and alcohol; and having close relatives (especially older siblings) in jail. These factors are more prevalent among low-income, urban adolescents, but adolescents at all income levels who experience them risk becoming an **adolescence-limited offender,** someone whose criminal activity stops by age 21 (Moffitt, 2003). They break the law with their friends, facilitated by their chosen antisocial clique. More boys than girls are in this group, but some lawbreaking cliques include both sexes (the gender gap in lawbreaking is narrower in late adolescence than earlier) (Moffitt et al., 2001).

adolescence-limited offender A person whose criminal activity stops by age 21.

Especially for Police Officers You see some 15-year-olds drinking beer in a local park when they belong in school. What do you do? (see response, page 498)

The criminal records of both types of teenagers may be similar. However, if adolescence-limited delinquents can be protected from various snares (such as quitting school, entering prison, drug addiction, early parenthood), they may outgrow their criminal behavior. This is confirmed by other research: Few delinquent youth who are not imprisoned continue lawbreaking in early adulthood (Monahan et al., 2009).

Of course, adolescence-limited lawbreaking is neither inevitable nor insignificant. Antisocial behavior is always dangerous, especially to other adolescents, who are victimized three times as often as adults (Baum, 2005). But maturation puts an end to adolescence-limited lawbreaking. By contrast, life-course-persistent offending begins in childhood and correlates in adulthood with more crime, less education, lower income, unhappy marriages, disobedient children, and continued violence (Huesmann et al., 2009).

Another way to analyze adolescent crime is to consider earlier patterns and stop delinquency before it reaches the point at which the police become involved. Three pathways to dire consequences can be seen:

1. Stubbornness can lead to defiance, which can lead to running away—runaways are often victims as well as criminals (e.g., prostitutes, petty thieves).
2. Shoplifting can lead to arson and burglary.
3. Bullying can lead to assault, rape, and murder.

Each of these pathways demands a different response. The rebelliousness of the first can be channeled or limited until more maturation and less impulsive anger prevail. Those on the second pathway require stronger human relationships and moral education. Those on the third present the most serious problem, with the danger of becoming more like a life-course offender than someone whose crime is adolescence-limited. For the adolescent bullies, intense treatment may deflect the pattern; if it does not, then serious penalties may be needed, with jail eventually. In all cases, early warning signs are present, and intervention is more effective earlier than later (Loeber & Burke, 2011).

Only half as many juveniles under age 18 are currently arrested for murder than was true in 1990. Although the data are solid, the explanations are not. Many possibilities have been suggested: fewer high school dropouts (more education means less crime); wiser judges (who now have community service as an option); better policing (arrests for misdemeanors are up, which may warn parents); smaller families (parents are more attentive to each of two children than each of twelve); better contraception and legal abortion (wanted children are less likely to become criminals); stricter drug laws (binge drinking and crack use increase crime); more immigrants (who are more law abiding); and more.

SUMMING UP

Compared with people of other ages, many adolescents experience sudden and extreme emotions that lead to powerful sadness and explosive anger. Supportive families, friendships, neighborhoods, and cultures usually contain and channel such feelings. For some teenagers, however, emotions are unchecked or intensified by their social contexts. This situation can lead to parasuicide (especially for girls), to minor lawbreaking (for both sexes), and, less often, to completed suicide and arrests (especially for boys). Delinquents can be adolescence-limited or life-course-persistent, a distinction that may help the justice system target the best response. Pathways to crime can be seen in childhood and early adolescence: intervention is most effective then as well.

>> Drug Use and Abuse

Adolescents enjoy doing something forbidden, and their hormonal surges and cognitive immaturity may cause them to be attracted to the sensations produced by drugs. But their immature bodies and brains make drug use particularly hazardous, with lifelong damage.

Variations in Drug Use

Most teenagers try *psychoactive drugs*. To a developmentalist (but not to a police officer), cigarettes, alcohol, and many prescription medicines are as addictive and damaging as illegal drugs like marijuana, cocaine, and heroin. Both prevalence and incidence of drug use increase from about ages 10 to 25 and then decrease, with use before age 18 being the best predictor of later abuse.

The one exception to this developmental increase is inhalants (fumes from aerosol containers, cleaning fluid, etc.), which are used more by younger adolescents, partly because they can be easily purchased. Sadly, the youngest adolescents are least able, cognitively, to analyze risks, and parents rarely suspect a drug problem until their child dies from breathing toxic vapors.

Variations by Place

Nations vary markedly in drug use. Consider the most common drugs: alcohol and tobacco. In most European nations, alcohol is widely used, even by children. In much of the Middle East, alcohol use is illegal, and teenagers almost never drink. In many Asian nations, anyone may smoke anywhere; in the United States, smoking is often forbidden; in Canada, cigarette advertising is outlawed. (Not surprisingly, fewer teens in Canada smoke.)

Variations within nations are marked as well. In the United States, most high school students have tried alcohol, and almost half have smoked cigarettes and marijuana—but a significant minority (about 20 percent) never use any drugs. Regional differences are apparent. For instance, 26.1 percent of high school students in Kentucky have smoked at least one cigarette in the past month, but only 14.8 New York students have (MMWR, June 4, 2010).

Variations by Generation and Gender

Cohorts vary, sometimes dramatically, as shown by a longitudinal study called Monitoring the Future that has asked thousands of young people, diverse in every way, about their recent and lifetime drug use. Use of most drugs has decreased in the United States since 1976 (as Figure 16.8 shows), but adolescent abuse of synthetic narcotics and prescription drugs has increased. During 2009, 10 percent of U.S. high school seniors used Vicodin and 6 percent used OxyContin (Johnston et al., 2010), both highly addictive and neither known to teenagers two decades ago.

With some exceptions, adolescent boys use more drugs, and use them more often, than girls do, especially outside the United States. An international survey of 13- to 15-year-olds in 131 nations found that more boys are smokers (except in a few European nations), including three times as many boys as girls in Southeast Asia (Warren et al., 2006). According to another international survey of 31 nations, almost twice as many boys as girls have tried marijuana (26 versus 15 percent) (ter Bogt et al., 2006).

These gender differences are reinforced by social constructions about proper male and female behavior. In Indonesia, for instance, 38 percent of the boys smoke

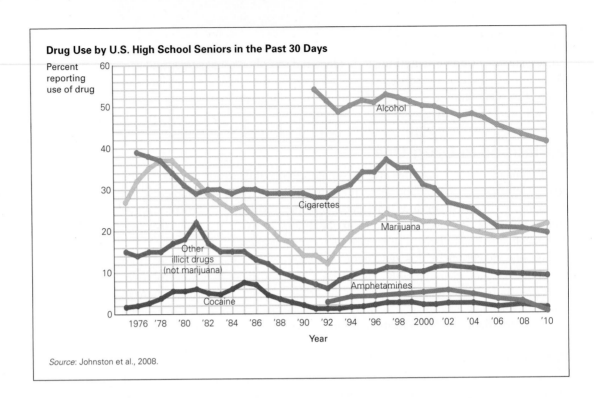

Drug Use by U.S. High School Seniors in the Past 30 Days

Source: Johnston et al., 2008.

FIGURE 16.8

Rise and Fall By asking the same questions year after year, the Monitoring the Future study shows notable historical effects. It is encouraging that something in society, not in the adolescent, makes drug use increase and decrease and that the most recent data show a decline. However, as Chapter 1 emphasized, survey research cannot prove what causes change.

>> Response for Police Officers (from page 496) Avoid both extremes: Don't let them think this situation is either harmless or serious. You might take them to the police station and call their parents. These adolescents are probably not life-course-persistent offenders; jailing them or grouping them with other lawbreakers might encourage more crime.

Especially for Parents Who Drink Socially You have heard that parents should allow their children to drink at home, to teach them to drink responsibly and not get drunk elsewhere. Is that wise? (see response, page 500)

cigarettes, but only 5 percent of the girls do. One Indonesian boy explained, "If I don't smoke, I'm not a real man" (quoted in Ng et al., 2007). These worldwide gender differences are not evident in the United States, where more girls than boys smoked in the 1990s. Recent statistics show that girls smoke less than boys but are younger when they start drinking alcohol, with eighth-grade girls having notably higher rates than boys (Johnston et al., 2010). The most notable gender difference in the United States is that steroids are used by more boys and diet drugs by more girls—both a reflection of gender roles.

Harm from Drugs

Many teenagers believe that adults exaggerate the evils of drug use. That may be, but developmentalists see both immediate and long-term harm. Addiction and brain damage are among "the deleterious consequences of drug use [that] appear to be more pronounced in adolescents than in adults, a difference that has been linked to brain maturation" (Moffitt et al., 2006, p. 12). Few adolescents notice when they move past *use* (experimenting) to *abuse* (experiencing harm) and then to *addiction* (needing the drug to avoid feeling nervous, anxious, or in pain).

An obvious negative effect of *tobacco* is that it impairs digestion and nutrition, slowing down growth. This is true for bidis, cigars, pipes, and chewing tobacco as well as for cigarettes. In India, widespread tobacco use is one reason for chronic undernutrition (Warren et al., 2006). Since internal organs continue to mature after the height spurt, drug-using teenagers who appear full-grown may damage their developing hearts, lungs, brains, and reproductive systems.

Alcohol is the most frequently abused drug in North America. Heavy drinking impairs memory and self-control by damaging the hippocampus and the prefrontal cortex, perhaps distorting the reward circuits of the brain lifelong (Guerri & Pascual, 2010). Although some specifics of the impact of alcohol on the adolescent brain are still to be discovered, there is no doubt that alcohol affects adolescents more than adults because of their brain immaturity (Chin et al., 2009).

Like many other drugs, alcohol allows momentary denial of problems; worries seem to disappear when a person is under the influence. When problems get worse because they have been ignored, more alcohol is needed—a vicious cycle that often leads to addiction. Denial is a problem for all alcoholics, but particularly for teenagers who have not yet learned that they cannot drive, write, or even think after several drinks.

Marijuana affects memory, language proficiency, and motivation (Lane et al., 2005)—all of which are especially crucial during adolescence. An Australian study found that even occasional marijuana use (once a week) before age 20 affected development up to 10 years later (Degenhardt et al., 2010).

Those are correlations, which, as you know, do not reveal causation. Is it possible that adolescents who are not particularly clever or ambitious choose to smoke marijuana, rather than vice versa? Is some third variable (such as hostile parents) the cause of both the academic problems and the drug use, rendering the correlation deceptive? This seemed plausible because drug-using adolescents often distrust their parents, injure themselves, hate their schools, and break many laws.

These questions led to the hypothesis that the psychic strains of adolescence lead to drug use. In fact, however, longitudinal research suggests that drug use *causes* more problems than it solves, often *preceding* anxiety disorders, depression, and rebellion (Chassin et al., 2009; Meririnne et al., 2010). Marijuana use is particularly common among wealthier adolescents, who then become less motivated to achieve in school and more likely to develop other problems (Ansary & Luthar, 2009). Rather than lack of ambition leading to marijuana use, marijuana itself destroys ambition.

Preventing Drug Abuse: What Works?

Drug use is a progression, beginning with a social occasion and ending alone. The first use usually occurs with friends, which leads adolescents to believe that occasional use is an expression of friendship or generational solidarity. Few adolescent drug users are addicts, and, for those who are, usually they and their friends are unaware of it.

However, the Monitoring the Future study found the following: 25 percent of high school seniors report having had five drinks in a row in the past two weeks, 11 percent are daily cigarette smokers, and 5 percent are daily marijuana users (Johnston et al., 2010). These figures are ominous, suggesting that addiction is the next step. The younger a person is when beginning drug use, the more likely addiction will occur.

That may not persuade adolescents, who, as you remember, think they are exceptions to any rule. However, every psychoactive drug excites the limbic system and interferes with the prefrontal cortex. Drug users are thus more emotional (specifics vary, from ecstasy to terror, paranoia to rage) than they otherwise would be, as well as less reflective. Every hazard of adolescence—including car crashes, unsafe sex, and suicide—is more common among teens who have taken a psychoactive drug.

With harmful drugs, as with many other aspects of life, each generation prefers to learn things for themselves. A common phenomenon is **generational forgetting,** the idea that each new generation forgets what the previous generation learned (Chassin et al., 2009; Johnston et al., 2010). Mistrust of the older generation, added to loyalty to one's peers, leads not only to generational forgetting but also to a backlash. If adults say something is forbidden, that may be an incentive to try it!

generational forgetting The idea that each new generation forgets what the previous generation learned. As used here, the term refers to knowledge about the harm drugs can do.

A Man Now This boy in Tibet is proud to be a smoker—in many Asian nations, smoking is considered manly.

>> **Response for Parents Who Drink Socially** (from page 498) No. Alcohol is particularly harmful for young brains. It is best to drink only when your children are not around. Children who are encouraged to drink with their parents are more likely to drink when no adults are present. It is true that adolescents are rebellious, and they may drink even if you forbid it. But if you allow alcohol, they might rebel with other drugs.

Some antidrug curricula and advertisements using scare tactics (such as the one that showed eggs being broken into a hot frying pan while an announcer intoned, "This is your brain on drugs") have the opposite effect from that intended, increasing rather than decreasing drug use. One reason may be that such advertisements make drugs seem exciting; another may be that adolescents recognize the exaggeration. Antismoking announcements produced by cigarette companies (such as one that showed a clean-cut young person advising viewers to think before they started smoking) actually increase use (Strasburger et al., 2008).

An added problem is that many parents do not know about their children's drug use, so their educational efforts may be too late, too general, or too ignorant. For instance, in one U.S. study, less than 1 percent of parents of sixth-graders thought their children had ever had alcohol, but 22 percent of the children said they had (O'Donnell et al., 2008). In general, adolescents follow their parents' example more than their advice.

This does not mean that trying to halt early drug use is hopeless. Massive ad campaigns in Florida and California cut adolescent smoking almost in half, in part because the publicity appealed to the young (Wakefield et al., 2003). A particularly effective ad depicted young people dumping 1,200 body bags in front of the corporate headquarters of a tobacco company to highlight the number of smoking-related deaths that occur in the United States each day (Farrelly et al., 2005). The anti-corporation message, with dramatic black-and-white footage (as if a teen had shot it a decade ago), had an impact.

Changing the social context is also helpful. Throughout the United States, higher prices, targeted warnings, and better law enforcement have led to a marked decline in cigarette smoking among younger adolescents. In 2009, only 6.5 percent of eighth-graders had smoked cigarettes in the past month, compared with 21 percent 10 years earlier (Johnston et al., 2010).

All the research confirms that parents continue to be influential on adolescent drug use. When parents forbid smoking in their homes, fewer adolescents smoke (Messer et al., 2008); when parents are careful with their own drinking, fewer teenagers abuse alcohol (Van Zundert et al., 2006). When parents provide guidance about drinking, teenagers not only drink less but use fewer other substances (Miller & Plant, 2010). Growing up with two married parents reduces cigarette and alcohol use, even when other influences (such as parental smoking and family income) are taken into account (Brown & Rinelli, 2010).

Looking broadly at the past three chapters and past 40 years in the United States, it is apparent that the universal biological processes do not lead to universal psychosocial problems. Sharply declining rates of teenage births and abortions (Chapter 14), increasing numbers graduating from high school (Chapter 15), and less use of legal and illegal drugs (Chapter 16) are apparent in many nations. Human growth starts with biology, that single sperm penetrating that single ovum, but the outcome depends on many social forces.

SUMMING UP

Most adolescents worldwide experiment with drugs, usually cigarettes and alcohol. Variations in adolescent drug use and abuse related to age, culture, cohort, and gender are evident. Drug use in adolescence is especially risky, since many drugs reduce learning and growth as well as smooth the path to addiction and abuse. Generational forgetting is one reason each cohort has distinctive drug-use patterns, and many efforts to stop drug use have failed, but the overall trend is positive: Drug use is lower in the United States and in many other places than it was a few decades ago. ▪

SUMMARY

Identity

1. Adolescence is a time for self-discovery. According to Erikson, adolescents seek their own identity, sorting through the traditions of their families and cultures.

2. Many young adolescents foreclose on their options without exploring possibilities, experience role confusion, or reach moratorium. Identity achievement takes longer for contemporary adolescents than it did half a century ago, when Erikson first described it.

3. Identity achievement occurs in many domains, including religion, politics, vocation, and sex. Each of these remains important over the life span, but timing, contexts, and often terminology have changed since Erikson and Marcia first described them.

Relationships with Adults

4. Parents continue to influence their growing children, despite bickering over minor issues. Ideally, communication and warmth remain high within the family, while parental control decreases and adolescents develop autonomy.

5. There are cultural differences in the timing of conflicts and particulars of parental monitoring. Too much parental control, with psychological intrusiveness, is harmful, as is neglect. Parents need to find a balance between granting freedom and providing guidance.

6. Adults who are not parents sometimes provide important mentoring and modeling for adolescents. Grandparents can be particularly influential.

Peer Power

7. Peers and peer pressure can be beneficial or harmful, depending on particular friends, cliques, and crowds. Adolescents select their friends, including friends of the other sex, who then facilitate constructive and/or destructive behavior.

8. Adolescents seek the approval of their peers, sometimes engaging in risky behavior for that reason.

9. Like adults, adolescents experience diverse sexual needs and may be involved in short-term or long-term romances, depending in part on their peer culture. This is a long process; early, exclusive sexual relationships are a sign of emotional immaturity.

10. The sexual orientation of some youth is toward same-sex romances. Depending on the culture and cohort, they may have a more difficult adolescence than others.

11. Most parents want schools to teach adolescents about sex, although such education often comes later than the personal experiences of the teen. No curriculum (including abstinence-only programs) markedly changes the age at which adolescents become sexually active, although some reduce pregnancy and STIs.

Sadness and Anger

12. Almost all adolescents become self-conscious and self-critical. A few become chronically sad and depressed. Many adolescents (especially girls) think about suicide, and some attempt it. Few adolescents actually kill themselves; most who do so are boys.

13. At least in Western societies, almost all adolescents become more independent and angry as part of growing up, although most still respect their parents. Lawbreaking as well as momentary rage are common; boys are more likely to be arrested for violent offenses than are girls.

14. Adolescence-limited delinquents should be prevented from hurting themselves or others; their criminal behavior will disappear with maturation. Life-course-persistent offenders are aggressive in childhood and may continue to be so in adulthood.

Drug Use and Abuse

15. Most adolescents experiment with drugs, especially alcohol and tobacco, although such substances impair growth of the body and the brain. National culture has a powerful influence on which specific drugs are used as well as on frequency of use. Age, gender, community, and parental factors are also influential.

16. Prevention and moderation of adolescent drug use and abuse are possible. Antidrug programs and messages need to be carefully designed to avoid a backlash or generational forgetting.

KEY TERMS

identity versus role confusion (p. 472)
identity achievement (p. 472)
role confusion (p. 472)
foreclosure (p. 472)
moratorium (p. 472)

gender identity (p. 476)
bickering (p. 477)
parental monitoring (p. 480)
peer pressure (p. 483)
deviancy training (p. 483)
sexual orientation (p. 486)

clinical depression (p. 490)
rumination (p. 491)
suicidal ideation (p. 491)
parasuicide (p. 491)
cluster suicides (p. 493)

life-course-persistent offender (p. 495)
adolescence-limited offender (p. 495)
generational forgetting (p. 499)

WHAT HAVE YOU LEARNED?

Identity

1. What is the relationship between the identity crisis and the past and future?

2. How does identity confusion differ from identity moratorium?

3. Why is foreclosure considered less mature than identity achievement?

4. Why is it premature for adolescents today to achieve their vocational identity?

5. What role do parents play in religious and political identity?

6. What assumptions did most adults hold 50 years ago about sexual identity?

Relationships with Adults

7. Why do parents and adolescents often bicker?

8. When is parental monitoring a sign of a healthy parent–adolescent relationship and when is it not?

9. What are the differences between the influence of parents and that of nonparent adults on adolescents?

Peer Power

10. What are the differences between the influence of peers and the influence of parents?

11. Why do many adults misunderstand the role of peer pressure?

12. What are the similarities and differences in crowds and cliques?

13. What is the role of parents, peers, and society in helping an adolescent develop an ethnic identity?

14. What are the differences in friendship during adolescence and in adulthood?

15. When is an adolescent romance healthy and when is it not?

16. How does culture affect the development of sexual orientation?

17. Where and from whom do adolescents usually learn about sex?

18. What are the variations in sex education in schools, and how does this affect adolescent sexual behavior?

Sadness and Anger

19. What is the difference between adolescent sadness and clinical depression?

20. Why do many adults think adolescent suicide is more common than it is?

21. How can rumination contribute to gender differences in depression and suicide?

22. Why are cluster suicides more common in adolescence than later?

23. What are the similarities between life-course-persistent and adolescence-limited delinquents?

24. What are the differences between life-course-persistent and adolescence-limited delinquents?

Drug Use and Abuse

25. Why are psychoactive drugs particularly attractive in adolescence?

26. Why are psychoactive drugs particularly destructive in adolescence?

27. What are the implications of national differences in drug use during adolescence?

28. What works and doesn't work in reducing adolescent drug use?

APPLICATIONS

1. Teenage cliques and crowds may be more important in large U.S. high schools than elsewhere. Interview people who spent their teenage years in U.S. schools of various sizes, or in another nation, about the peer relationships in their high schools. Describe and discuss any differences you find.

2. Locate a news article about a teenager who committed suicide. Can you find evidence in the article that there were warning signs that were ignored? Does the report inadvertently encourage cluster suicides?

3. Research suggests that most adolescents have broken the law but that few have been arrested or incarcerated. Ask 10 of your fellow students whether they broke the law when they were under 18 and, if so, how often, in what ways, and with what consequences. (Assure them of confidentiality.) What hypothesis arises about lawbreaking in your cohort?

4. Cultures have different standards for drug use among children, adolescents, and adults. Interview three people from different cultures (not necessarily from different nations; each occupation, generation, or religion can be said to have a culture) about their culture's drug-use standards. Ask your respondents to explain the reasons for any differences.

>>ONLINE CONNECTIONS

To accompany your textbook, you have access to a number of online resources, including quizzes for every chapter of the book, flashcards (in English and Spanish), critical thinking questions, and case studies. For access to any of these links, go to www.worthpublishers.com/bergerca9e. In addition to these free resources, you'll also find links to podcasts, video clips, diagnostic quizzing with personalized study advice, and an ebook. Some of the videos and activities available online include:

■ *Who Am I?* The video reviews pathways to identity achievement and Marcia's dimensions of exploration and commitment. Teens talk about identity. The embedded questionnaire lets you gauge your progress in identity formation.

■ *Interview with Anne Petersen.* This expert talks about the role of parents in adolescence and the need for solid community services.

Adolescence

BIOSOCIAL

Puberty Puberty begins adolescence, as the child's body becomes much bigger (the growth spurt) and more sexual. Both sexes experience increased hormones, reproductive potential, and primary as well as secondary sexual characteristics. Brain growth, hormones, and social contexts combine to make every adolescent more interested in sexual activities, with possible hazards of early pregnancy and sexual abuse.

Nutrition The growth spurt requires adequate nutrition. Many teens do not get enough iron or calcium, since they often consume fast food and soda instead of family meals and milk. Some suffer from serious eating disorders like anorexia and bulimia.

Brain Neurological growth continues through adolescence; the limbic system typically matures faster than the prefrontal cortex. As a result, adolescents act impulsively.

COGNITIVE

Adolescent Thinking Adolescents think differently than younger children do. Piaget stressed the new ability to use abstract logic (part of formal operational thought). Adolescents think hypothetically and deductively, as they are taught to do in school. Elkind recognized adolescent egocentrism; younger teens think they are invincible or that everyone notices what they do. Intuitive thought also increases during adolescence, with emotional and experiential thinking overcoming logic at times.

Teaching and Learning Secondary education promotes individual and national success. Nations vary in how many adolescents graduate from high school. Particularly in the United States, middle schools have been considered the "low ebb" of education: Grades and achievement fall, bullying increases, and teachers and students become disenchanted with learning. International tests find marked differences in achievement. In the United States, high-stakes tests and more rigorous course requirements before high school graduation are intended to improve standards of learning.

PSYCHOSOCIAL

Identity Adolescent development includes a search for identity, as Erikson described. Adolescents combine childhood experiences, cultural values, and their unique aspirations. The contexts of identity are religion, politics/ethnicity, vocation, and sex/gender. Few adolescents achieve identity; role confusion and foreclosure are more likely.

Relationships Families continue to be influential, despite rebellion and bickering. Adolescents seek autonomy but also rely on parental support. Friends and peers of both sexes are increasingly important. Romances often begin in adolescence. About half of all U.S. teens become sexually active. Among developed nations, the United States has higher rates of teen pregnancy and less comprehensive sex education.

Sadness and Anger Depression and rebellion become serious problems for a minority of adolescents. This troubled group is at some risk of suicide (rates are lower than for adults) and violent criminality (rates are higher than for adults). Many adolescents break the law, but their delinquency is adolescence-limited; they eventually become law-abiding adults. Some, however, are life-course-persistent delinquents.

Drugs Adolescents are attracted to psychoactive drugs. Specifics of use and legality vary by nation and culture. In North America, drug use is illegal for teenagers, but most adolescents drink alcohol, and many try cigarettes and marijuana.

Emerging Adulthood

WHAT WILL YOU KNOW?

1. How can the sex drive in emerging adulthood be both a joy and a disaster?
2. Does college teach older adolescents to think like adults?
3. How do personality traits and emotional needs change between child-hood and adulthood?

Consider this a review and a preview. Throughout the entire life span, genetic, prenatal, and early experiences have an impact. In this Epilogue, you will see many familiar themes—echoes of early relationships, differences among cultures, contextual and cohort effects. **Emerging adulthood** is a time of life when 18- to 25-year-olds continue their education and exploration, postponing marriage, parenthood, and career (see At About This Time).

It is not surprising that I experienced this path myself. Between ages 18 and 25, I attended four colleges or universities, changed majors five times, rejected marriage offers from four young men, lived in ten different places, and started several jobs—none lasting more than 18 months. Following that period of rapid change, I stayed put—one husband, one neighborhood, one job. What is surprising may be that similar patterns have become apparent everywhere: Young people in every nation are gaining more education and marrying later than their parents did (not always as late as I did). Emerging adulthood is a stage, or a process, worldwide (Arnett et al., 2011).

emerging adulthood The period of life between the ages of 18 and 25. Emerging adulthood is now widely thought of as a separate developmental stage.

AT ABOUT THIS TIME

Following Certain Patterns, by Average Age (U.S., 2010)

Age 17–18—Graduate from high school (about 25 percent do not do so)

Age 18–19—Enroll in college (about 30 percent of high school graduates do not)

Age 22—Earn college degree (about half of those who enter college)

Age 25—Steady employment in chosen field (rate fluctuates, depends on economy)

Age 25—Women's first birth* (for those who will have children; about 20 percent will not)

Age 26—Women's first marriage (about 18 percent never marry)

Age 28—Men's first marriage (about 25 percent never marry)

*By ethnicity: Age 23—African American or Hispanic; age 26—European American; age 29—Asian American
Source: U.S. Bureau of the Census, 2011 and previous years.

These are norms, which convey the median age for these events, each traditionally considered signs of adulthood. Note that most people do *not* achieve college graduation and that the median age for family commitment is at the end of emerging adulthood. Furthermore, many people do not follow this normative path.

>> Biosocial Development

Biologically, the years from ages 18 to 25 are prime time for hard physical work and safe reproduction. However, the fact that young adults can carry rocks, plow fields, or haul water better than older adults is no longer admired, nor is their fertility. If a contemporary young couple had a baby every year, their neighbors would be more appalled than approving. Now, during emerging adulthood, societies, families, and young adults themselves expect more education, later marriage, and fewer children than was the norm as recently as 50 years ago.

Strong and Active Bodies

Health has not changed, except maybe to improve. As always, every body system—including the digestive, respiratory, circulatory, and sexual-reproductive systems—functions optimally at the beginning of adulthood (Aspinall, 2003). Serious diseases are not yet apparent, and some childhood ailments are outgrown. For example, childhood asthma disappears as often as it continues. In a mammoth survey, 95.8 percent of young adults (aged 18 to 29) in the United States rated their health as good, very good, or excellent (National Center for Health Statistics, 2010).

However, health problems from childhood may continue. In the same survey in which only 4 percent of young adults rated their health as less than good, 15 percent said they had been told they had a chronic disease—often asthma, arthritis, or high blood pressure (National Center for Health Statistics, 2010). A comprehensive review of many studies finds that low birthweight, undernutrition in infancy, and rapid weight gain in early childhood tend to result in shorter height, reduced body functioning, and higher risk of disease (Victora et al., 2008).

Fortunately, these health problems are usually kept in check during these years. The immune system is strong, fighting off everything from the sniffles to cancer and responding well to vaccines (Grubeck-Loebenstein, 2010). Usually, teeth have no new cavities, heart rate is steady, the brain functions well, and lung capacity is sufficient. Many diagnostic tests, such as PSA (for prostate cancer), mammograms (for breast cancer), and colonoscopies (for colon cancer), are not usually recommended until age 40 or later. Death from disease is unusual (see Table EP.1).

Fertility, Then and Now

As already mentioned, the sexual-reproductive system is at its strongest during emerging adulthood. Thanks to nature's wonderful mechanism for preserving the human species, young adults experience great joy from sexual interactions. During these years, orgasms are frequent; the sex drive is powerful; fertility is optimal; miscarriage is less common; serious birth complications are relatively rare. Historically, most couples had their first child when they were under age 25, and often a second and third as well.

Premarital Sex

These physiological strengths may have become liabilities. The bodies of emerging adults want sex but their minds know they are not ready for parenthood (Lefkowitz & Gillen, 2006). For many, the solution to this dilemma is sex without pregnancy, made possible by modern contraception.

According to a poll at the beginning of the twenty-first century, most U.S. 18- to 24-year-olds say premarital sex is "not wrong at all"; only 18 percent of those over age 65 agree (T. W. Smith, 2005). Those sentiments may be even stronger

TABLE EP.1	U.S. Deaths from the Top Three Causes (Heart Disease, Stroke, Cancer)
Age Group	Annual Rate per 100,000
15–24	7
25–34	18
35–44	65
45–54	219
55–64	561
65–74	1,313
75–84	2,971
85+	7,126

Source: National Center for Health Statistics, 2010.

Young and Healthy Young adults rarely die of diseases, including the top four: heart disease, cancer, stroke, and obstructive pulmonary disease. These are annual rates, which means that for each person, the chance of death in that decade is 10 times the yearly rate. Thus, a 15-year-old has less than 1 chance in 1,000 of dying of disease before age 25; a 75-year-old has more than 1 chance in 3 of dying of disease before age 85. (As reported later in this chapter, nondisease deaths show a different pattern.)

Observation Quiz How likely is a 90-year-old person to die in the next year? What about a 19-year-old? (see answer, page 508)

among the current cohort of emerging adults: Few young adults (27 percent) think living together before marriage is bad for society, although most older adults (64 percent) think it is (Pew Research Center, 2010). Even compared with young adults in 1997, fewer young adults in 2010 are married but more hope to become good parents (Wang & Taylor, 2011). (See Figure EP.1.)

Although they accept *pre*marital sex, many emerging adults (80 percent) believe that *extra*marital sex is "always wrong" (T. W. Smith, 2005). For child development, this is good news: Children fare better if they are wanted, if their parents are emotionally ready for child rearing, and if their parents are committed to each other.

The Bad News

The sexual freedom of emerging adults has a serious downside, however. Globalization accelerates every contagious disease, including sexually transmitted infections (STIs) (Herring & Swedlund, 2010). In earlier times, prostitution was local, which kept STIs local as well. Now, with international travel, an STI caught from an infected sex worker in one place quickly spreads.

This proliferation is particularly tragic with HIV/AIDS, first reported among gay men in two or three U.S. cities and then among injection drug users who shared needles. Within 30 years, primarily because of the sexual activities of young adults, HIV has become a worldwide epidemic, with more female than male victims (Davis & Squire, 2010). In nations where HIV is not yet prevalent, such as Croatia, the sexual risk taking of 18- to 25-year-olds means that many may soon become infected (Štulhofer et al., 2009). Worldwide, young adults remain the prime STI vectors (those who spread disease) as well as the new victims.

Anywhere In some ways, life in China is radically different from life elsewhere, but universals are also apparent. This emerging-adult couple pose in front of the Beijing stadium.

Observation Quiz One detail in the young man's hands suggests that the setting is Asia, not North America. What is it? (see answer, page 509)

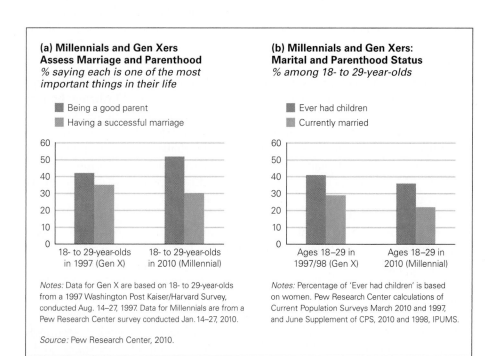

(a) Millennials and Gen Xers Assess Marriage and Parenthood
% saying each is one of the most important things in their life

- Being a good parent
- Having a successful marriage

(b) Millennials and Gen Xers: Marital and Parenthood Status
% among 18- to 29-year-olds

- Ever had children
- Currently married

Notes: Data for Gen X are based on 18- to 29-year-olds from a 1997 Washington Post Kaiser/Harvard Survey, conducted Aug. 14–27, 1997. Data for Millennials are from a Pew Research Center survey conducted Jan. 14–27, 2010.

Source: Pew Research Center, 2010.

Notes: Percentage of 'Ever had children' is based on women. Pew Research Center calculations of Current Population Surveys March 2010 and 1997, and June Supplement of CPS, 2010 and 1998, IPUMS.

FIGURE EP.1

Children before Partners Many young adults consider parenthood more important than partnerhood. At least for previous cohorts, however, children were more likely to thrive if their parents were happily married.

Do They Talk? This couple in Schenectady, New York, are in a "long-term relationship," probably years from marriage. We hope they agree about what they would do if she got pregnant, or if he found someone else, or if either was offered a great job or university scholarship in another state. Few emerging adults discuss such matters until they actually happen.

Taking Risks

Remember that each age group has its own gains and losses, characteristics that can be a blessing or a burden. This is apparent with risk taking. Some emerging adults bravely, or foolishly, take risks—a behavior that is gender- and age-related, as well as genetic and hormonal. Those who are genetically impulsive *and* male *and* emerging adults are most likely to be brave and foolish.

Societies as well as individuals benefit because emerging adults take chances. Enrolling in college, moving to a new state or nation, getting married, having a baby—all these endeavors are risky. So is starting a business, filming a documentary, entering an athletic contest, enlisting in the military, and joining the Peace Corps.

Yet risk taking is often destructive. Although their bodies are strong and their reactions quick, emerging adults nonetheless have more accidents that land them in emergency rooms than do people of any other age. The low rate of serious disease between ages 18 and 25 is counterbalanced by a high rate of serious injuries (see Figure EP.2, leftmost data) and violent deaths.

Destructive risks that are more common in emerging adulthood include unprotected sex with a new partner, driving fast without a seat belt, carrying a loaded gun, abusing drugs, and problem gambling—all done partly for an addictive rush of adrenaline (Cosgrave, 2010). Accidents, homicides, and suicides are leading causes of death among young adults—killing more young adults than all diseases combined, even where infectious diseases and malnutrition are rampant. The only exception is South Africa, where AIDS kills more young adults than suicide (but AIDS results from risk taking).

Risky Sports

Many young adults seek the rush of risk in recreation, as they climb mountains, swim in oceans, run in pain, play past exhaustion, and so on. Skydiving, bungee jumping, pond swooping, parkour, potholing (in caves), waterfall kayaking, and many more activities have been invented to satisfy the joy of risk—not that serious injury is the goal, but that high risk adds to the challenge, making preparation crucial (Brymer, 2010). Competitive **extreme sports** (such as *motocross*—motorcycle jumping off a ramp into "big air," doing tricks during the fall, and hoping to land upright) are new thrills for some emerging adults, who find golf, bowling, and so on too tame (Breivik, 2010).

This is clearer with an example. Travis Pastrana won the 2006 X Games motocross competition at age 22 with a double backflip because, as he explained, "The two main things are that I've been healthy and able to train at my fullest, and a lot of guys have had major crashes this year" (quoted in Higgins, 2006, p. D-7). Four years later, he set a new record for leaping through big air in an automobile, as he drove over the ocean from a ramp on the California shoreline to a barge more than 250 feet out. He crashed into a barrier on the boat but emerged, seemingly ecstatic and unhurt, to the thunderous cheers of thousands of other young adults on the shore (Roberts, 2010).

Drug Abuse

The same impulse that is admired in extreme sports can also lead to behaviors that are clearly destructive, not only for individuals but for the community. The

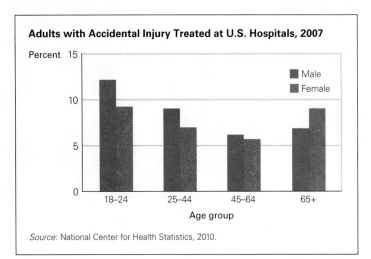

Adults with Accidental Injury Treated at U.S. Hospitals, 2007

Source: National Center for Health Statistics, 2010.

FIGURE EP.2

Send Them Home Accidents, homicides, and suicides occur more frequently during emerging adulthood than later. Note that the age range of more patients falls within the six years of emerging adulthood than within the 20 years of adulthood. Fewer young adults *stay* in the hospital, however. They are usually stitched, bandaged, injected, and sent home.

extreme sports Forms of recreation that include apparent risk of injury or death and that are attractive and thrilling as a result.

>> **Answer to Observation Quiz** (from page 506) Note that the rates are per 100,000 for the three leading diseases. This means that 1 out of every 14 90-year-olds and 1 out of every 14,000 19-year-olds will die of these diseases each year. However, people die from other causes as well. At age 90 in the United States, the rate of death doubles, meaning that a 90-year-old has about 1 chance in 7 of dying within a year. For emerging adults, the overall death rates are about 10 times higher, primarily because of violent deaths; 19-year-olds thus have an annual death rate of 1 per 1,400.

JOE RAEDLE / GETTY IMAGES

>> **Answer to Observation Quiz** (from page 507) The cigarette, not the camera. Most young men in Canada and the United States do not smoke, especially publicly and casually, as this man does.

Higher Education College provides many benefits, but it also seems to encourage some risky behavior. Some of these students on Spring Break in Miami Beach seem to be encouraging each other's drinking.

most studied of these is drug abuse (Reith, 2005), which can involve dozens of substances—from the perfectly legal to the extremely illegal.

By definition, **drug abuse** occurs whenever drug use harms physical, cognitive, or psychosocial well-being. Even occasional smoking or illegal drug use can be abuse, as can bingeing on alcohol (four or five drinks on one occasion). From an emerging-adult perspective, the potential for abuse is part of the attraction of drugs, especially if some authority figure disapproves: There is a special thrill in buying, carrying, and using an illegal drug, knowing that arrest is possible. Illegal drug use peaks at about age 20 and declines sharply with age (see Figure EP.3). The thrill is gone.

Surprisingly, drug abuse is more common among college students than among their peers who are not in college. For instance, college students are most likely to engage in extreme drinking, with 25 percent of young men and 5 percent of young women reporting that they consumed 10 or more drinks in a row at least once in the previous two weeks (Johnston et al., 2009). Such extremes arise from the same drive as extreme sports or other risks—with the same possible consequence: death.

drug abuse The ingestion of a drug to the extent that it impairs the user's biological or psychological well-being.

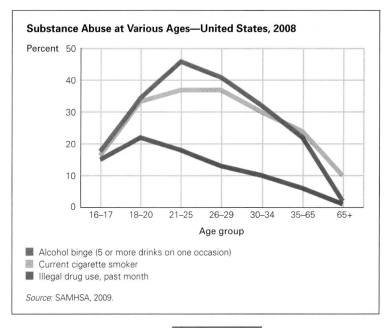

Source: SAMHSA, 2009.

FIGURE EP.3

Too Old for That As you can see, emerging adults are the biggest substance abusers, but illegal drug use drops much faster than do cigarette use or binge drinking.

Especially for Substance Abuse Counselors Can you think of three possible explanations for the more precipitous drop in the use of illegal drug compared to legal ones? (see response, page 510)

SUMMING UP

Emerging adults are physiologically at their prime, with strong and healthy bodies. One strength is the sexual-reproductive system, which pushes many contemporary young adults to engage in premarital sex. The thrill of risk taking can become a problem, since it leads emerging adults to extreme sports, unprotected sex, drug abuse, and serious injuries. Accidents, homicide, and suicide are leading causes of death among young adults worldwide. ∎

>> Response for Substance Abuse Counselors (from page 509) Legal drugs could be more addictive, or the thrill of illegality may diminish with age, or the fear of arrest may increase. In any case, treatment for young-adult substance abusers may need to differ from that for older ones.

postformal thought A proposed adult stage of cognitive development, following Piaget's four stages. Postformal thought goes beyond adolescent thinking by being more practical, more flexible, and more dialectical (i.e., more capable of combining contradictory elements into a comprehensive whole).

Especially for Someone Who Has to Make an Important Decision Which is better: to go with your gut feelings or to consider pros and cons as objectively as you can? (see response, page 512)

>> Cognitive Development

You remember that each of the four periods of child and adolescent development is characterized by major advances in cognition, with each advance representing a new stage, according to Piaget. Adult thinking also differs from earlier thinking: It is more practical, more flexible, and better able to coordinate objective and subjective perspectives. This may constitute a major advance, combining a new "ordering of formal operations" with a "necessary subjectivity" (Sinnott, 1998, p. 24).

Postformal Thought and Brain Development

Many developmentalists believe that Piaget's fourth stage, formal operational thought, is inadequate to describe adult thinking. Some proposed a fifth stage, called **postformal thought,** characterized by "problem finding" not just "problem solving," wherein a person is more open to ideas and less concerned with absolute right and wrong (Yan & Arlin, 1995). As one group of scholars explained, in postformal thought, "one can conceive of multiple logics, choices, or perceptions . . . in order to better understand the complexities and inherent biases in 'truth'" (Griffin et al., 2009, p. 173).

As you remember from Chapter 15, adolescents use two modes of thought (dual processing), but they have difficulty combining them. They use formal analysis to learn science, distill principles, develop arguments, and resolve the world's problems; or, alternatively, they think spontaneously and emotionally. Rarely, however, do they coordinate both modes. They prefer quick reactions, only later realizing the consequences.

Postformal thinkers are less impulsive. They do not wait for someone else to present a problem to solve. They take a more flexible and comprehensive approach, with forethought, noting difficulties and anticipating problems, not denying, avoiding, or procrastinating. As a result, postformal thinking is more practical as well as more creative and imaginative than was thinking in previous cognitive stages (Wu & Chiou, 2008).

Many scientists doubt Piaget's stage theory of child cognition. Many more question this fifth stage. Certainly, if *stage* is taken to mean attaining a new set of intellectual abilities (such as the language explosion that distinguishes sensorimotor from preoperational thought), then adulthood has no stages. However, the prefrontal cortex is not fully mature until one's early 20s, and new dendrites grow throughout adulthood. Apparently adults tend to think in ways that adolescents do not.

For instance, one study of people aged 13 to 45 found that logical skills improved from adolescence to emerging adulthood and then stayed steady, as might be expected as analytic thought becomes established. However, social understanding continued to advance beyond early adulthood (Demetriou & Bakracevic, 2009). (Social understanding includes knowing how best to interact with other people— making and keeping good friends, responding to social slights, helping others effectively, and so on.) As another lead researcher concluded, adult thinking "can be ordered in terms of increasing levels of complexity and integration" (Labouvie-Vief et al., 2009, p. 182).

This cognitive maturation is now thought to depend partly on the brain development that continues throughout adolescence and emerging adulthood. As you remember, the limbic system matures faster than the prefrontal cortex, and not until the early 20s is the brain typically ready to analyze, plan, and coordinate impulses with the maturity expected of adults. The brain is still quite plastic in adolescence—able to learn new ideas and embark on new adventures. In emerg-

(a)

(b)

Thinking Away from Home *(a)* Entering a residential college means experiencing new foods, new friends, and new neurons. A longitudinal study of 18-year-old students at the beginning and end of their first year in college (Dartmouth) found increases in the brain areas that integrate emotion and cognition—namely, the cingulate (blue and yellow), caudate (red), and insula (orange). Researchers also studied one-year changes in the brains of students over age 25 at the same college and found no dramatic growth. *(b)* Shown here are the areas of one person's brain changes from age 14 to 25. The frontal cortex (purple) demonstrated many changes in particular parts, as did the areas for processing speech (green and blue)—a crucial aspect of young adult learning. Areas for visual processing (yellow) showed less change.

Researchers now know that brains mature in many ways between adolescence and adulthood; scientists are not yet sure of the cognitive implications.

ing adulthood, the final consolidation of various brain regions occurs (Tanner & Arnett, 2011).

Overall, many scholars find that thinking changes both qualitatively and quantitatively during adulthood (Bosworth & Hertzog, 2009). The term *fifth stage* may be a misnomer, but emerging adults can and often do reach a new cognitive level when their brains and life circumstances allow it.

Countering Stereotypes

Cognitive flexibility, particularly the ability to change one's childhood assumptions, is needed to counter stereotypes. Young adults show many signs of such flexibility in daily life. The very fact that emerging adults marry and become parents later than previous generations did suggests that, couple by couple, their thinking processes are not determined by their own childhood experiences or by traditional norms. Of course, early experiences are influential, but for postformal thinkers they are not determinative.

Research on racial prejudice is one example. Many U.S. children and adults of every ethnic group harbor implicit bias against African Americans, detectable in slower reaction times when mentally processing photos of African Americans than when processing photos of European Americans (Baron & Banaji, 2006). However, most people believe that they are not racially prejudiced, and their behavior reveals no bias (at least in explicit tests in a research laboratory). Thus, many adults have both unconscious prejudice and rational nonprejudice—a combination that illustrates dual processing. Cognitive flexibility allows people to recognize their emotional biases and to change their behaviors—both difficult without openness and flexibility.

However, people are often unaware of their own stereotypes, even when their false beliefs harm them. One of the most pernicious of these beliefs is **stereotype threat,** the worry that other people assume that you yourself are stupid, lazy, oversexed, or worse because of your ethnicity, sex, age, or appearance. Even the *possibility* of being stereotyped arouses emotions and hijacks memory, disrupting cognition (Schmader, 2010), as illustrated in the following.

stereotype threat The possibility that one's appearance or behavior will be misread to confirm another person's oversimplified, prejudiced attitudes.

A VIEW FROM SCIENCE

Stereotype Threat

One statistic has troubled social scientists for decades: African American men have lower grades in high school and earn only half as many college degrees as their genetic peers, African American women, who themselves do less well than women of other ethnic groups. This disparity has many possible causes, with most scientists blaming the context and historical discrimination (Arnett & Brody, 2008).

One African American scholar thought of another possibility, which he labeled *stereotype threat,* a "threat in the air" if not in reality (Steele, 1997). When African American males are made aware of the stereotype that they are poor scholars, they might become anxious. That anxiety would reduce their ability to focus on academics. Then, if they underachieve, they might dismiss academics in order to protect their pride. That would lead to disengagement from studying and even lower achievement (Ogbu, 2008).

Two decades of research have demonstrated that downward trajectory, but African American men are not the only ones to experience it. Hundreds of studies show that almost all humans can be harmed by stereotype threat: Women underperform in math, older people are more forgetful, bilingual students stumble with English, and every member of a stigmatized minority in every nation performs less well. Even those sometimes thought to be on top—White men—do less well in math if they think they will be negatively compared with men of Asian descent, and they do

less well in some sports if they think they will be compared with men of African descent (Schmader et al., 2008). When athletes unexpectedly underperform because of stress (called choking), stereotype threat may be the cause (Hill et al., 2010).

Can stereotype threat be eliminated, or at least reduced? One group of researchers developed a hypothesis: that stereotype threat will decrease and achievement increase if African American college students *internalize* (believe wholeheartedly, not just intellectually) the idea that intelligence is plastic rather than the inalterable product of genes and gender. Using a clever combination of written material, mentoring, and video performing, these scientists convinced African Americans that their ability and hence their achievement depended on their personal efforts. That reduced stereotype threat and led to higher grades (Aronson et al., 2002).

This experiment intrigued thousands of researchers. They realized that this study required replication, since the participants were only 79 students at a highly selective university. Might other stereotyped groups respond differently? Soon thousands of other scientists replicated this study with many other groups, often targeting young adults since they may be most open to new ideas. The results confirmed, again and again, that stereotype threat is pervasive and debilitating but that it can be alleviated (Alter et al., 2010; Miyake et al., 2010; Rydell & Boucher, 2010).

>> Response for Someone Who Has to Make an Important Decision (from page 510) Both are necessary. Mature thinking requires a combination of emotions and logic. To make sure you use both, take your time (don't just act on your first impulse) and talk with people you trust. Ultimately, you will have to live with your decision, so do not ignore either intuitive or logical thought.

Especially for Those Considering Studying Abroad Given the effects of college, would it be better for a student to study abroad in the first year or last year of a college education? (see response, page 514)

The Effects of College

A major reason why emerging adulthood has become a new period of development, when people postpone the usual markers of adult life (marriage, a steady job), is that many older adolescents seek further education rather than taking on adult responsibilities. However, some aspects of the impact of that education are controversial.

Massification

There is no dispute about some consequences of tertiary education: It improves health and wealth. For those reasons, every nation has recently increased the number of students in college—a phenomenon called *massification*, the idea that college could benefit everyone (the masses) (Altbach et al., 2010). The United States was the first major nation to endorse massification, but it no longer leads in this regard.

More than half of all 25- to 34-year-olds in Canada, Korea, Russia, and Japan are college graduates; the United States ranks twelfth among major nations, with about 41 percent of people in this age group having college degrees (Montgomery & Williams, 2010; UNESCO, 2009). Although not every young adult enrolls in college, and even fewer graduate, U.S. census data and surveys of individuals still find that college education adds about $20,000 per year to a worker's salary (see Figure 15.9).

Massification has stalled in the United States, but not elsewhere (Altbach et al., 2010). In Asia and Africa, college enrollment has more than tripled (see Figure EP.4), and the wealthiest and most capable students from those nations continue to earn degrees in North America or Europe, often returning to developing nations to work as professors. A global shift is evident: Hundreds of new universities have opened in Asia, Africa, and the Middle East. As of 2010, more college students were enrolled in China than in the United States.

College and Cognition

For developmentalists interested in cognition, the crucial question is not about wealth, health, or numbers; it is about whether college education advances critical thinking and postformal thought. Past research has concluded that the answer is yes.

According to one classic study (Perry, 1981, 1999), thinking progresses through nine levels of complexity over the four years that lead to a bachelor's degree, moving from a simplistic dualism (right or wrong, yes or no, success or failure) to a relativism that recognizes a multiplicity of perspectives (see Table EP.2). Perry found that the college experience itself causes this progression: Peers, professors, books, and class discussion all

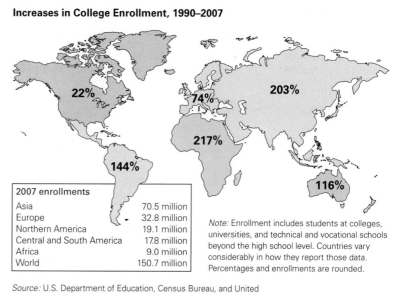

Increases in College Enrollment, 1990–2007

22%
74%
203%
217%
144%
116%

2007 enrollments	
Asia	70.5 million
Europe	32.8 million
Northern America	19.1 million
Central and South America	17.8 million
Africa	9.0 million
World	150.7 million

Note: Enrollment includes students at colleges, universities, and technical and vocational schools beyond the high school level. Countries vary considerably in how they report those data. Percentages and enrollments are rounded.

Source: U.S. Department of Education, Census Bureau, and United Nations Educational, Scientific and Cultural Organization (UNESCO).

FIGURE EP.4

Interpreting Data College-educated young adults know that maps combine facts with opinions. This map emphasizes that North America is lagging behind in college enrollment and that Africa is surging ahead, but the numbers suggest a more complex picture. Also note that eastern Europe and the Middle East are considered part of Asia and that Mexico is not included in North America. Nonetheless, one fact is obvious: Millions of students in developing nations are now attending college.

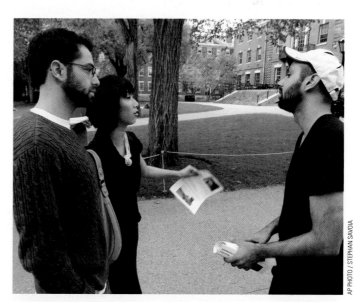

Education in Process These students, checking the Internet on the steps of San Miguel de Allende in Mexico *(left)* and discussing Pakistan on the quad at Brown University in the United States *(right)*, illustrate why some scholars claim that college students learn more from each other than from their professors.

TABLE EP.2	Perry's Scheme of Cognitive and Ethical Development During College		
Freshmen	Position 1	Authorities know, and if we work hard, read every word, and learn Right Answers, all will be well.
Dualism modified	Transition	But what about those Others I hear about? And different opinions? And Uncertainties? Some of our own Authorities disagree with each other or don't seem to know, and some give us problems instead of Answers
	Position 2	True Authorities must be Right; the others are frauds. We remain Right. Others must be different and Wrong. Good Authorities give us problems so we can learn to find the Right Answer by our own independent thought
	Transition	But even Good Authorities admit they don't know all the answers yet!
	Position 3	Then some uncertainties and different opinions are real and legitimate temporarily, even for Authorities. They're working on them to get to the Truth.
	Transition	But there are so many things they don't know the Answers to! And they won't for a long time
Relativism discovered	Position 4a	Where Authorities don't know the Right Answers, everyone has a right to his own opinion; no one is wrong!
	Transition	Then what right have They to grade us? About what?
	Position 4b	In certain courses, Authorities are not asking for the Right Answer. They want us to think about things in a certain way, supporting opinion with data. That's what they grade us on.
	Position 5	Then all thinking must be like this, even for Them. Everything is relative but not equally valid. You have to understand how each context works. Theories are not Truth but metaphors to interpret data with. You have to think about your thinking.
	Transition	But if everything is relative, am I relative, too? How can I know I'm making the Right Choice?
	Position 6	I see I'm going to have to make my own decisions in an uncertain world with no one to tell me I'm Right.
	Transition	I'm lost if I don't. When I decide on my career (or marriage or values), everything will straighten out.
Commitments in relativism developed	Position 7	Well, I've made my first Commitment!
	Transition	Why didn't that settle everything?
	Position 8	I've made several commitments. I've got to balance them—how many, how deep? How certain, how tentative?
	Transition	Things are getting contradictory. I can't make logical sense out of life's dilemmas.
Seniors	Position 9	This is how life will be. I must be wholehearted while tentative, fight for my values yet respect others, believe my deepest values are right yet be ready to learn. I see that I shall be retracing this whole journey over and over—but, I hope, more wisely.

Source: Perry, 1981, 1999.

>> **Response for Those Considering Studying Abroad** (from page 512) Since one result of college is that students become more open to other perspectives while developing their commitment to their own values, foreign study might be most beneficial after several years of college. If they study abroad too early, some students might be either too narrowly patriotic (they are not yet open) or too quick to reject everything about their national heritage (they have not yet developed their own commitments).

stimulate new questions and thoughts. Other research confirmed Perry's conclusions. In general, the more years of higher education a person has, the deeper and more postformal that person's reasoning becomes (Pascarella & Terenzini, 1991).

Which aspect of college is the primary catalyst for such growth? Is it the challenging academic work, professors' lectures, peer discussions, the new setting, living away from home? All are possible. Every scientist finds that social interaction and intellectual challenge advance thinking. College students expect classes and conversations to further their thinking—which is exactly what occurs (Kuh et al., 2005). This is not surprising, since colleges were designed to foster intellectual growth. Professors themselves can advance in their thinking, passing those advances on to their students, as is evident in the following.

A CASE TO STUDY

The Academic and the Personal

One of the leading thinkers in postformal thought is Jan Sinnott, a professor and now editor of the *Journal of Adult Development*. She describes the first course she taught:

> I did not think in a postformal way. . . . Teaching was good for passing information from the informed to the uninformed. . . . I decided to create a course in the psychology of aging . . . with a fellow graduate student. Being compulsive graduate students had paid off in our careers so far, so my colleague and I continued on that path. Articles and books and photocopies began to take over my house. And having found all this information, we seem to have unconsciously sworn to use all of it. . . .
>
> Each class day, my colleague and I would arrive with reams of notes and articles and lecture, lecture, lecture. Rapidly! . . . The discussion of death and dying came close to the end of the term (naturally). As I gave my usual jam-packed lecture, the sound of note taking was intense. But toward the end of the class . . . an extremely capable student burst into tears and said she had to drop the class. . . . Unknown to me, she had been the caretaker

of an older relative who had just died in the past few days. She had not said anything about this significant experience when we lectured on caretaking. . . . How could she? . . . We never stopped talking. "I wish I could tell people what it's really like," she said.

> *[Sinnott, 2008, pp. 54–55]*

Sinnott changed her lesson plan. In the next class, the student told her story.

> In the end, the students agreed that this was a class when they . . . synthesized material and analyzed research and theory critically.

> *[Sinnott, 2008, p. 56]*

Sinnott still lectures and gives multiple-choice exams, but she also includes personal stories. She combines analysis and emotion; she includes the experiences of her students. Her teaching became postformal, flexible, and responsive.

Current Contexts

But wait. You probably noticed that Perry's study was first published in 1981. Hundreds of other studies also found that college education deepens cognition, but most of that research occurred in the twentieth century. Since you know that cohort and culture are crucial influences on development, you may wonder whether those conclusions still hold.

Many recent books criticize college education on exactly those grounds. Notably, an impressive twenty-first-century longitudinal study of a cross section of U.S. college students found that students' growth in critical thinking, analysis, and communication over the four years of college was only half as much as among college students two decades ago (Arum et al., 2011). The same researchers published a detailed analysis of the first two years of college and reported that 45 percent of the students made no significant advances at all (Arum & Roksa, 2011).

The reasons were many: Students study less, professors expect less, and students avoid classes in which they must read at least 40 pages a week or write 20 pages a semester. Administrators and faculty still hope for intellectual growth, but rigorous classes are canceled or not required.

Motivation to Attend College

An underlying problem may be that people disagree about the purpose of a college education. Developmentalists, most professors, and many college graduates believe that the main purpose is "personal and intellectual growth." However, adults who have never attended college believe that "acquiring specific skills and knowledge" is more important (see Figure EP.5). In the Arum and Roksa report (2011), students majoring in business and other career fields were less likely to gain in critical thinking compared to those in the liberal arts (courses that demand more reading and writing).

Especially for High School Teachers
One of your brightest students doesn't want to go to college. She would rather keep waitressing in a restaurant, where she makes good money in tips. What do you say? (see response, page 517)

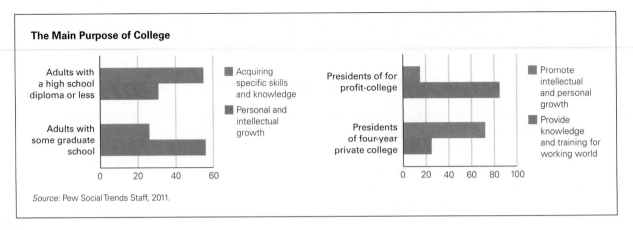

Source: Pew Social Trends Staff, 2011.

FIGURE EP.5

Intellectual or Practical Skills? As you see, people disagree as to whether a college education should foster intellectual growth or provide useful knowledge and skills. Presented here are the extremes—those with some college, and those who are leaders of community colleges, are in between these extremes.

FIGURE EP.6

Cohort Shift Students in 1980 thought new ideas and a philosophy of life were prime reasons to go to college—they were less interested in jobs, careers, and money than are students in 2010. If this thinking causes a conflict between student motivation and professor's goals, who should adjust?

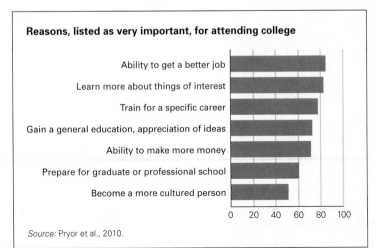

Source: Pryor et al., 2010.

Looking more closely at the U.S. college scene, it seems that students now attend college primarily for career reasons (see Figure EP.6). Furthermore, many select institutions for their job preparation, not their emphasis on reading and writing. Since tuition and government grants are major sources of income for colleges, institutions tend to meet the students' needs.

In 1955, most U.S. colleges were four-year institutions and most students majored in liberal arts. There were only 275 junior colleges. In 2010, there were almost 1,500 such colleges, now called community colleges, with some of them (19 in Florida) offering bachelor's degrees in careers in which jobs are available. Similarly, for-profit colleges were scarce until about 1980; now the United States has more than 1,300 of them (Chronicle of Higher Education, 2010). This is more than an increase in the number of various institutions; it signifies a shift in what people believe is the reason for college.

Students, parents, professors, and legislators disagree as to whether college should prepare people for jobs, expand their cultural understanding, or provide time and space for the development of advanced critical cognition. Depending on the goal, measurement of achievement and motivation to study will vary. No nation has reached consensus on the purpose of college.

Even in China, where the central government has fostered thousands of new institutions of higher learning, disagreement about the goals of college is evident. For instance, a new Chinese university (called South University of Science and Technology of China, SUSTC) is designed to encourage analysis and critical thinking, in deliberate contrast to the emphasis on knowledge and skills in other Chinese institutions. SUSTC does not require prospective students to take the national exam (*Gao Kao*); instead, "creativity and a passion for learning" are the admission criteria (Stone, 2011, p. 161). Faculty are supposed to nurture curiosity, not lecture. However, the Chinese government is not convinced about this educational approach: SUSTC is not yet officially accredited.

The Effects of Diversity

At least one characteristic of the twenty-first-century college scene in every nation bodes well for intellectual challenges—the diversity of the student body. The most obvious change is gender: In 1970, at least two-thirds of college students were male; now in every developed nation (except Germany), most are female; and most single-sex colleges have become co-ed, even in the sex-segregated societies of the Middle East. In addition, student ethnic, economic, religious, and cultural backgrounds are more varied. Compared to 1970, more students are parents, are older than age 24, are of non-European heritage, attend part time, and live and work off-campus—all true worldwide, although the modal student is still 18 to 22 years old and attends school full time.

Discussion among people of different backgrounds and varied perspectives leads to intellectual challenge and deeper thought. Thus, the increased diversity of the student body may enhance learning. Colleges that make use of their diversity—via curriculum, class assignments, discussions, cooperative education, learning communities, and so on—help students stretch their understanding, not only of differences and similarities among people but also of themselves (Nagda et al., 2005).

Skeptical readers might question the data that link college education to a wealthier, wiser, and happier adulthood. Such skepticism is warranted, since correlation does not equal causation: Student characteristics before college may be a third variable that explains these links. However, when selection is taken into account, college still seems to aid cognitive development (Pascarella, 2005). Even the critics agree that some students at every institution advance markedly in critical thinking and analysis because of their college experience (Arum & Roksa, 2011). Now each reader of this text can try to combine objective and subjective thought—does college advance your own postformal cognition?

>> **Response for High School Teachers** (from page 515) Even more than ability, motivation is crucial for college success, so don't insist that she attend college. Since your student has money and a steady job (prime goals for today's college-bound youth), she may not realize what she would be missing. Ask her what she hopes for herself, in work and lifestyle, over the many decades ahead.

SUMMING UP

Emerging adults often become more flexible, creative, and coordinated thinkers than they were as adolescents, an advancement sometimes described as postformal thought. College education brings health and wealth to graduates, and nations worldwide have increased the number of students in college. Research in earlier decades in the United States finds that college also advances cognition, helping students become more critical thinkers as well as more flexible. However, some find that those cognitive effects are less evident than they were previously, especially since many current students seek skills and knowledge, not intellectual challenge. Nonetheless, for many students college broadens their perspective, as the diversity of students and the opportunity to understand and debate new ideas lead to deeper, more flexible, postformal thought. ∎

>> Psychosocial Development

A theme of human development is that continuity and change are evident throughout life. In emerging adulthood, the legacy of early development is apparent amidst new achievement. Erikson recognized this ongoing process in his description of the fifth of his eight stages, identity versus role confusion. As you remember, the crisis of identity begins in adolescence, but it is not usually resolved then.

Identity Achieved

As already mentioned, Erikson believed that the outcome of earlier crises provides the foundation for each new stage of development. The identity crisis is an example (see Table EP.3). Worldwide, adults ponder all four arenas of identity—religious commitments, sex/gender roles, political/ethnic loyalties, and career options—trying to reconcile plans for the future with beliefs acquired in the past.

TABLE EP.3	Erikson's Eight Stages of Development	
Stage	Virtue/Pathology	Possible in Emerging Adulthood if Not Successfully Resolved
Trust vs. mistrust	Hope/withdrawal	Suspicious of others, making close relationships difficult
Autonomy vs. shame and doubt	Will/compulsion	Obsessively driven, single-minded, not socially responsive
Initiative vs. guilt	Purpose/inhibition	Fearful, regretful (e.g., very homesick in college)
Industry vs. inferiority	Competence/inertia	Self-critical of any endeavor, procrastinating, perfectionistic
Identity vs. role diffusion	Fidelity/repudiation	Uncertain and negative about values, lifestyle, friendships
Intimacy vs. isolation	Love/exclusivity	Anxious about close relationships, jealous, lonely
Generativity vs. stagnation	Care/rejection	[In the future] Fear of failure
Integrity vs. despair	Wisdom/disdain	[In the future] No "mindfulness," no life plan

Source: Erikson, 1982.

Past as Prologue In elaborating his eight stages of development, Erikson associated each stage with a particular virtue and a type of psychopathology, as shown here. He also thought that earlier crises could reemerge, taking a specific form at each stage. Listed are some possible problems (not directly from Erikson) that could occur in emerging adulthood if earlier crises were not resolved.

Now we will focus on the two identity areas that currently seem most fluid in emerging adulthood, ethnicity and vocation.

Ethnic Identity

High school senior Natasha Scott "just realized that my race is something I have to think about." Her mother is Asian and her father is African American, which had not been an issue as she was growing up. However, college applications (and the 2010 Census) required choices regarding ethnic identity (Saulny & Steinberg, 2011).

Natasha is not the only one. In the United States and Canada, almost half of 18- to 25-year-olds are of African, Asian, Latino, or Native American heritage, and many of them have ancestors of more than one ethnic group. Usually those ancestors are long dead, but an increasing number have living parents from two groups. In 2008, 15 percent of all U.S. marriages were interethnic, a statistic from the American Community Survey, which combined many groups into a single ethnicity (e.g., no matter where they were born, Black people who were from Africa, the Caribbean, and anywhere in the United States were considered one ethnicity; Asians from Pakistan and China were similarly considered one ethnic group. Obviously, if each bride and groom were asked whether they differed in ethnicity, far more than 15 percent would say yes).

Whether one's heritage is mixed or not, ethnicity is a significant aspect of American identity (Phinney, 2006). During late adolescence and early adulthood, people are more likely to be proud, or at least accepting, of their ethnic background than younger adolescents are (Worrell, 2008). There is no doubt that "identity development . . . from the teenage years to the early 20s, if not through adulthood, . . . has been extended to explain the development of ethnic and racial identity" (Whitbourne et al., 2009, p. 1328).

As they leave their childhood homes to enroll in colleges or to find work, emerging adults, more than any other age group, find friends and acquaintances of many backgrounds. Typically, they have "both positive and negative experiences" related to their ethnic background, developing "a strong sense of ethnic identity"—true for college students of every group (Syed & Azmitia, 2010, p. 218). It may be a mistake if they either assimilate (blend in) or become alienated (isolated and antagonistic), at least according to a study of Hispanic college students. Those who resisted both assimilation and alienation fared best: They were most likely to maintain their ethnic identity, deflect stereotype threat, and become good students (Rivas-Drake & Mooney, 2009).

College classes (especially in history, ethnic studies, and sociology) attract many emerging adults who want to learn more about their culture. In addition, extracurricular groups help solidify identity because students encounter others of similar backgrounds who confront the same issues.

When it comes to sexual intimacy, although most young adults are happy to know people of other groups and most approve of interethnic romance, a study in a large multiethnic university found that students tend to choose sexual partners (from hookups to marriage) within their own group (McClintock, 2010). The reason was not prejudice against others as much as bonding with co-ethnics. Thus, ethnic identity is an example of the emerging adult's ability to combine the personal and the political, the intuitive and the analytic. Young adults accept and appreciate interracial couples, even as they usually prefer mates like themselves.

Vocational Identity

Developmental psychologists influenced by Erikson and emerging adults themselves consider establishing a vocational identity to be part of growing up (Arnett, 2004). Many young adults go to college not only as a moratorium but also to prepare for work. Emerging adulthood is a "critical stage for the acquisition of resources"—including the education, skills, and experience needed for family and career success lifelong (Tanner et al., 2009, p. 34).

Just Like Me Emerging adults of every ethnicity take pride in their culture. In Japan, adulthood begins with a celebration at age 20, to the evident joy of these young women on Coming of Age Day, a national holiday.

Part of the preparation for lifetime work often includes taking temporary jobs. Between ages 18 and 27, the average U.S. worker holds eight jobs, with the college-educated changing jobs more than those who are less educated (U.S. Bureau of the Census, 2009). This illustrates the exploration that is part of the identity search, and it is also a sign that achievement has not yet occurred: The young worker is not yet climbing a particular vocational ladder, rung by rung. For most emerging adults, "the process of identifying with society's work ethic, the core of this issue [identity achievement] in Erikson's scheme, continues to evolve throughout early adulthood" (Whitbourne et al., 2009, p. 1329).

Many developmentalists wonder whether achieving a single vocational identity is still a worthy goal. Especially for young people, commitment to a particular career may limit rather than increase vocational success. Contemporary research finds that an economic recession (as apparent worldwide beginning roughly in 2008) makes vocational identity more difficult for adolescents and young adults to achieve. Research on older adults who came of age during past economic crises suggests that vocational problems may continue, affecting the current cohort when the financial picture improves (Johnson et al., 2011).

Personality in Emerging Adulthood

Continuity and change are evident in personality as well (McAdams & Olson, 2010). Of course, temperament and personality endure lifelong: The self-doubt, anxiety, depression, and so on that are present in childhood and adolescence are often still evident years later. Traits present at age 5 or 15 do not disappear by age 25.

Yet personality is not static. After adolescence, new characteristics may appear and negative traits may diminish. Emerging adults make choices that break with

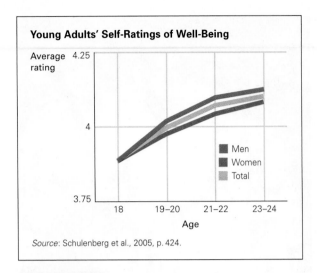

Young Adults' Self-Ratings of Well-Being

Source: Schulenberg et al., 2005, p. 424.

Worthy People This graph shows a steady increase in young adults' sense of well-being from age 18 to age 24, as measured by respondents' ratings of statements such as "I feel I am a person of worth." The ratings ranged from 1 (complete disagreement) to 5 (complete agreement). The average rating was already quite high at age 18, and it increased steadily over the years of emerging adulthood.

the past. This age period is now characterized by years of freedom from a settled lifestyle, which allows shifts in attitude and personality.

Rising Self-Esteem

Psychological research finds both continuity and improvement in attitudes. For example, one longitudinal study found that 17-year-olds who saw life in positive terms maintained their outlook as time went on, while those who were negative often changed for the better (Blonigen et al., 2008).

Another team of researchers traced 3,912 U.S. high school seniors until age 23 or 24. Those in college who lived away from home showed the largest gains in well-being, and those who had become single parents or who still lived with their own parents showed the least. Even the latter, however, tended to be happier than they had been in high school (see Figure EP.7; Schulenberg et al., 2005). Similarly, 404 young adults in western Canada, who were repeatedly questioned from ages 18 to 25, reported increasing self-esteem (Galambos et al., 2006).

This positive trend of increasing happiness has become more evident over recent decades, perhaps because young adults are more likely than adolescents to make their own life decisions (Twenge et al., 2008). Logically, the many stresses and transitions of emerging adulthood might reduce self-esteem, but that is not what the research finds. Psychopathology may increase and some emerging adults do develop serious disorders (Twenge et al., 2010), but most do not.

Worrisome Children Grow Up

The research just cited was conducted among North American youth, but similar conclusions come from a European longitudinal study that began with 4-year-olds who were at the extremes of either of two traits known to have strong genetic roots: extreme shyness and marked aggression. These children still tended to be shy or aggressive later in childhood (as one might expect, since genetic, familial, and cultural influences tend to be similar throughout childhood). However, by emerging adulthood most had changed for the better (Asendorpf et al., 2008).

Early traits were still evident. At age 25, those who had been aggressive 4-year-olds had more conflicts with their parents and friends and were more likely to have quit school and left jobs. (Two-thirds had dropped out of high school, as had only one-third of their nonaggressive peers.) By age 23, half had been arrested at least once, another sign of their aggressive personalities.

Yet, unexpectedly, these aggressive young adults had as many friends as their average peers did. They wanted more education, and they rated themselves as quite conscientious. They tended to be adolescence-limited offenders, and their crimes were usually minor: Only one had been sent to prison, and only one other had been arrested several times.

A closer examination of their school records found that their behavior, not their lack of ability, had caused their childhood teachers to fail them; as a result, many had repeated grades while their peers moved on. Since they were older than their classmates in high school, they quit because of the school restrictions and other peoples' assumptions, not because they hated learning. As emerging adults, most seemed to be developing well, putting their childhood problems behind them; some were employed and others had enrolled in college.

As for the emerging adults who had been inhibited as 4-year-olds, they were "cautious, reserved adults" but "with few signs of internalizing problems" (Asendorpf et al., 2008, p. 1007). They were slower than average to secure a job, choose a career, or find a romance (at age 23, two-thirds had no current partner). However, they were no more anxious or depressed than their peers, and their self-esteem was equally good. They had many friends and saw them often. Their delayed employment and later marriage were not unlike the patterns of the most successful of the emerging adults. Thus, the shyness that was considered to be a handicap in their childhood may have become an asset.

Plasticity

In the research just discussed and in other research as well, plasticity is evident. Personality is not fixed by age 5, or 15, or 20, as it was once thought to be. Emerging adults are open to new experiences (a reflection of their adventuresome spirit), and this allows personality shifts as well as eagerness for more education (McAdams & Olson, 2010; Tanner et al., 2009). The trend is toward less depression and more joy, along with more insight into the self (Galambos et al., 2006; McAdams et al., 2006).

Going to college, leaving home, paying one's way, stopping drug abuse, moving to a new city, finding satisfying work and performing it well, making new friends, committing to a partner—each of these might alter a person's life course. The feeling of self-efficacy builds with each successful accomplishment, giving people the confidence and courage to modify whatever destructive traits they may have.

Total transformation does not occur since genes, childhood experiences, and family circumstances affect people lifelong. Nor do new experiences always result in desirable changes. Indeed, it is possible that the rising self-esteem found in longitudinal research reflected historical improvements at the end of the twentieth century and that current conditions (health, the job market, the economy) may soon cause self-esteem to fall. But there is no doubt that personality *can* shift after adolescence.

Increased well-being and maturation may be the reasons for another shift: Emerging adults seem to become less self-centered and more caring of others (Eisenberg et al., 2005; Padilla-Walker et al., 2008). This can be seen as the foundation of the next psychosocial stage of development.

Intimacy

In Erikson's theory, after achieving identity, people experience the sixth crisis of development, **intimacy versus isolation.** This crisis arises from the powerful desire to share one's personal life with someone else. Without intimacy, adults suffer from loneliness and isolation. Erikson (1963) explains:

> The young adult, emerging from the search for and the insistence on identity, is eager and willing to fuse his identity with others. He is ready for intimacy, that is, the capacity to commit himself to concrete affiliations and partnerships and to develop the ethical strength to abide by such commitments, even though they call for significant sacrifices and compromises.
>
> *[p. 263]*

The urge for social connection is a powerful human impulse, one reason our species has thrived. Other theorists use different words (*affiliation, affection, interdependence, communion, belonging, love*) for the same human need. Attachment experienced in infancy may well be a precursor to adult intimacy (Simpson et al., 2007). There is no doubt that all adults seek to become friends, lovers, companions, and partners.

All intimate relationships (friendship, family ties, and romance) have much in common—in both the psychic needs they satisfy and in the behaviors they require

intimacy versus isolation The sixth of Erikson's eight stages of development. Adults seek someone with whom to share their lives in an enduring and self-sacrificing commitment. Without such commitment they risk profound loneliness and isolation.

(Reis & Collins, 2004). Intimacy progresses from attraction to close connection to ongoing commitment. Each relationship demands some personal sacrifice, including vulnerability that brings deeper self-understanding and shatters the isolation caused by too much self-protection. As Erikson (1963) explains, to establish intimacy, the emerging adult must

> face the fear of ego loss in situations which call for self-abandon: in the solidarity of close affiliations [and] sexual unions, in close friendship and in physical combat, in experiences of inspiration by teachers and of intuition from the recesses of the self. The avoidance of such experiences . . . may lead to a deep sense of isolation and consequent self-absorption.
>
> *[pp. 163–164]*

According to a more recent theory, an important aspect of close human connections is "self-expansion," the idea that each of us enlarges our understanding, our experiences, and our resources through our intimate friends and lovers (Aron et al., 2005).

Romantic Partners

Love, romance, and commitment are all of primary importance for emerging adults, although many specifics have changed. Most emerging adults are thought to be postponing, not abandoning, marriage. As one U.S. sociologist explains, "despite the culture of divorce, Americans remain optimistic about, and even eager to enter, marriages" (Hill, 2007, p. 295). One of the hottest political issues in 2011 was whether gay and lesbian couples should be allowed to marry. The very fact that gay couples want to marry, and that some other people are vehemently opposed and argue that marriage needs to be "defended," makes it clear that marriage is considered desirable.

The relationship between love and marriage depends on era and culture, with three distinct patterns evident (Georgas et al., 2006). In about one-third of the world's families, love does not lead to marriage because parents arrange marriages that will join two families together.

In another one-third of families, adolescents meet only a select group (single-sex schools keep them from meeting unsuitable mates). Parents supervise all male–female interactions. When young people decide to marry someone of that preselected group, then the young man asks the young woman's father for "her hand in marriage." Historically, if parental approval was not forthcoming, the teens parted sorrowfully or eloped—neither of which occurs as often today.

Suggesting "one-third" for each of these is a rough approximation. In former times, most marriages were of the first type; young people almost never met and married people unknown to their parents (Apostolou, 2007). Currently, in developing nations, practice often blends these two types. For example, in modern India most brides believe they have a choice, but many meet their future husbands shortly before the wedding via parental arrangement. The young man or woman can then veto the match, but usually they do not (Desai & Andrist, 2010).

The third pattern is relatively new, although familiar to most readers of this book. Young people socialize with hundreds of others and pair off but do not marry until they are able, financially and emotionally, to be independent. Their choices tilt toward personal qualities observable at the moment (physical appearance, personal hygiene, personality, sexuality, a sense of humor), not to qualities more important to parents, such as religion, ethnicity, or long-term stability—a person who has been married and divorced is seen much more negatively by parents than by unpartnered adults (Buunk et al., 2008).

For Western emerging adults, love is considered a prerequisite for marriage and then sexual exclusiveness is expected, as found in a survey of 14,121 people of many ethnic groups and orientations (Meier et al., 2009). They were asked to rate from 1 to 10 the importance of money, same racial background, long-term commitment, love, and faithfulness for a successful marriage or a serious, committed relationship. Faithfulness was the most important of all (rated 10 by 89 percent) and love was almost as high (rated 10 by 86 percent). Virtually all the rest thought faithfulness and love were very important (rated 9). By contrast, most thought being of the same race did not matter much (57 percent rated it 1, 2, or 3). Money, while important to many, was not nearly as crucial as love and fidelity.

This survey was conducted in North America, but emerging adults worldwide share many of the same values. Six thousand miles away, emerging adults in Kenya also reported that love was the primary reason for couples to connect and stay together; money was less important (Clark et al., 2010).

Finding Each Other

One major innovation of the current cohort of emerging adults is the use of social networks. Web sites such as Facebook allow individuals to post their photos and personal information on the Internet, sharing the details of their daily lives with thousands of others. Three-fourths of all 18- to 29-year-olds in the United States use social networking (Pew Research Center, 2010). Such sites often indicate whether an individual is or is not in a committed relationship. Many also use Internet matching sites to find potential partners.

One problem is that social networking may produce dozens of potential partners, increasing *choice overload* when too many options are available. Choice overload increases second thoughts after a choice is made (people wonder whether they would have been happier with another choice). Some people, overloaded with possibilities, refuse to make any selection (Iyengar & Lepper, 2000; Reutskaja & Hogarth, 2009).

Choice overload has been demonstrated with consumer goods—jams, chocolates, pens, restaurants—but it has not been proven for choosing a mate. Having many complex options that require weighing both present and future advantages and disadvantages (such trade-offs are inevitable in selecting a partner) makes choice overload likely, but more research is needed (Scheibehenne et al., 2010).

Living Together

A second major innovation among emerging adults is **cohabitation,** the term for living together in a romantic partnership without being married. Cohabitation was relatively unusual 40 years ago: In the United States, less than 1 percent of all households were comprised of a cohabiting man and woman; more recently, 5 percent are (see Figure EP.8). Many couples now married were earlier in that 5 percent.

Indeed, most 25-year-olds in the United States, Canada, northern Europe, England, and Australia have lived unmarried with a partner for at least a few months. Most adults in Sweden, France, Jamaica, and Puerto Rico live together and plan to stay together, never marrying. In most of the United States, committed same-sex couples are forced into this category, but not in Canada. In other nations—including Japan, Ireland, and Italy—fewer people cohabit, although the rate is rising everywhere.

Tradition—Not Both Alex Painter and Sarah Apgar love old tradition, which is why he wore a kilt and she wore a white dress for their wedding in 2011. But they would not have married even a few years earlier. The reason—they met online.

cohabitation An arrangement in which a couple live together in a committed romantic relationship but are not formally married.

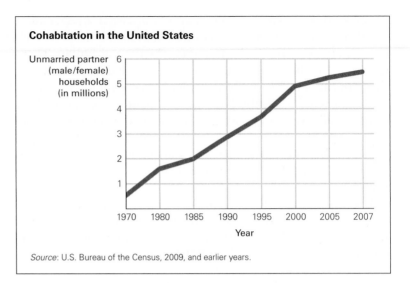

Cohabitation in the United States

Unmarried partner (male/female) households (in millions)

Source: U.S. Bureau of the Census, 2009, and earlier years.

FIGURE EP.8

More Together, Fewer Married As you see, the number of cohabiting male–female households in the United States has increased dramatically over the past decades. These numbers are an underestimate: Couples who do not tell the U.S. census takers that they are living together, or who cohabit within their parents' households, or who are same-sex couples (not tallied until 2000) are not included here. In addition, most emerging adults who are not now cohabiting may well be doing so within a few years.

Observation Quiz Did the rate of cohabitation increase faster before or after the year 2000? (see answer, page 526)

Research from 30 nations finds that acceptance of cohabitation within the nation affects the happiness of those who cohabit. Demographic differences within those 30 nations (such as education, income, age, and religion among the married and cohabitants) affect happiness as well (Soons & Kalmijn, 2009).

Research in the United States finds that people who cohabit and have children, or who cohabit and later marry (their cohabiting partner or someone else), have higher rates of separation and divorce. Furthermore, children born to cohabiting couples are more likely to have academic, health, or emotional difficulties (Schmeer, 2011; Stanley et al., 2006). Some factors—such as whether the couple is already engaged to marry before moving in together or having little or no financial stress (rare for most cohabiting couples)—mitigate such problems. However, although there are practical reasons for cohabitation—it saves money and postpones commitment—no longitudinal research has found that it improves psychosocial development. Thus, neither the popularity of cohabitation nor the immediate happiness of the participants prove that cohabitation is beneficial over the long term.

Love, Not Marriage Andrew and Jessica decided to raise their daughter together but not to marry. They live in White Bear, Minnesota, a relatively conservative area, but cohabiting couples are increasingly common everywhere.

RICHARD TSONG-TAATARII / MCT / NEWSCOM

Family Forces

It is hard to overestimate the importance of the family at any time of the life span. Although made up of individuals, a family is much more than the persons who belong to it: In dynamic synergy, children grow, adults find support, and everyone is part of an ethos that gives meaning to, and provides models for, personal aspirations and decisions.

Linked Lives

Emerging adults are said to set out independently, leaving their childhood home and parents behind. They strive for independence and avoid establishing their own families (Arnett, 2004). Thus, it might seem as if they no longer need family support and guidance. The data, however, show that parents continue to be crucial—perhaps even more so than for previous generations because many young people today rely on their parents: Compared with earlier cohorts, fewer contemporary young adults have finished their education or have started their own families and found high-paying jobs.

All members of each family have **linked lives,** meaning that the experiences and needs of family members at one stage of life are affected by those at other stages (Macmillan & Copher, 2005). We have seen this in earlier chapters: Children are affected by their parents' relationship, even if the children are not directly involved in domestic disputes, financial stresses, parental alliances, and so on. Likewise, each newborn affects every family member of every age.

The same historical conditions that gave rise to this stage called emerging adulthood may have an unanticipated benefit: stronger links between parents and their adult children. Because of demographic changes over the past few decades, most parents have small families, which allows them to attend to the financial and emotional needs of their emerging-adult children since they have no younger offspring. Parental concern is intensified by several factors: Young-adult children are usually not married, not parents, and almost never vocationally secure (long gone are the days when the young took over the family business).

Strong links between emerging adults and their parents may seem counterintuitive, as emerging adults are independent and cohort changes have occurred. Nonetheless, many studies have found congruence in attitudes between parents and their young-adult children. Political and religious loyalties often link the generations.

For instance, a detailed Dutch study found substantial agreement between parents and their adult children on issues that might, in theory, be contentious—such as cohabitation, same-sex partnerships, and divorce. Some generational differences appeared, but when parents were compared with their own children (not young adults in general), similar attitudes were apparent (Bucx et al., 2010). Adult children who still lived with their parents (about one-fourth of the sample) were more likely to agree with their parents than were adults who lived apart from them, but all groups showed "intergenerational convergence" (Bucx et al., 2010, p. 131).

Especially for Family Therapists More emerging-adult children today live with their parents than ever before, yet you have learned that families often function better when young adults live on their own. What would you advise? (see response, page 527)

linked lives Lives in which the success, health, and well-being of each family member are connected to those of other members, including members of another generation, as in the relationship between parents and children.

Brilliant, Unemployed, and Laughing This is not an unusual combination for contemporary college graduates. Melissa, in Missoula, Montana, graduated summa cum laude from George Washington University and is now one of the many college graduates who live with their parents. The arrangement provides many financial and family benefits, but it is not known who cooked dinner and who will wash the dishes.

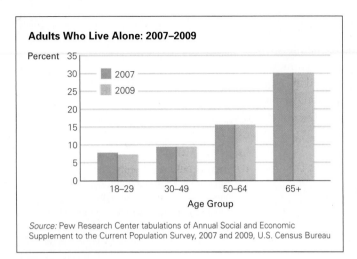

Adults Who Live Alone: 2007–2009

Source: Pew Research Center tabulations of Annual Social and Economic Supplement to the Current Population Survey, 2007 and 2009, U.S. Census Bureau

FIGURE EP.9

Not Lonely The assumption used to be that family affection led to multigenerational households, but that is not accurate. Financial struggle, not love, is what forces single adults to live with relatives. Young adults prefer to live with romantic partners or roommates, whereas widows and widowers favor independent households—if they can afford them.

>> Answer to Observation Quiz (from page 524) Before! The rate of increase from 2000 to 2005 was about 4/49, or 8 percent, whereas the rate from 1985 to 1990 was about 9/20, a 45 percent increase.

Worldwide, many emerging adults still live with their parents, though this varies from nation to nation. Almost all unmarried young adults in Italy and Japan stay in their childhood home, as do half of those in England (Manzi et al., 2006). Fewer do so in the United States if their parents can underwrite their young-adult children's independent living (Furstenberg, 2010), but the current economic downturn has increased the number of adult children living with their parents (see Figure EP. 9).

In many nations, researchers find a connection among early attachment, adult perceptions of their current relationships with their parents, as well as adult relationships with friends, lovers, and children (Grossmann et al., 2005; Mikulincer & Goodman, 2006; Sroufe et al., 2005). Securely attached infants are more likely to become happily married adults; avoidant infants may hesitate to marry. Young adults with good family relationships are more likely to establish supportive families of their own, although they are in no hurry to do so.

A Global Perspective

Looking at many cultures, it is apparent that families can be destructive as well as helpful to emerging adults. For example, a study of enmeshment (e.g., parents insisting on knowing what their emerging-adult children are doing and thinking) found that British emerging adults were less happy or successful if their parents were too intrusive. However, emerging adults in Italy seem able to remain closely connected with their parents without hindering their own development (Manzi et al., 2006). Enmeshment can be destructive, but not always.

Some Westerners believe that family dependence is more evident in developing nations. There is some truth in this. As explained earlier, familism is a strong value in many Latino cultures. In another example, many African young adults marry someone approved by their parents and work to support their many relatives—siblings, parents, cousins, uncles, and so on. Individuals sacrifice personal goals for family concerns, and "collectivism often takes precedence and overrides individual needs and interests," which makes "the family a source of both collective identity and tension" in Africa (Wilson & Ngige, 2006, p. 248).

In cultures with arranged marriages, parents not only provide practical support (such as child care) and emotional encouragement, they may also protect their child. If the relationship is a disaster (for instance, the husband severely beats the wife, the wife refuses sex, the husband never works, or the wife never cooks), then the parents intervene. Again, each family member within each culture judges such intervention differently: What is expected in, say, Cambodia, would be unacceptable in, say, Colombia. Chinese young adults expect their parents and friends to comment on their romantic partners and, compared with U.S. young adults, they are about twice as likely to say they might stop dating someone if their parents disapproved (Zhang & Kline, 2009).

There are developmental advantages to this family involvement. Each new baby is cared for by many people, so young adults are less burdened by child care. This may be one reason why parenthood begins much earlier in African nations. By contrast, parenthood in the United States is an impediment to education and career success (Osgood et al., 2005), and thus many emerging adults postpone it (Furstenberg, 2010).

Cultural differences aside, in every nation young adults are encouraged to do well in school and to get good jobs, partly to make their families proud, partly so they will be able to care for their relatives when necessary, and partly for their own future. Immigrant young adults tend to be highly motivated to learn and work, and they reciprocate their parents' support. These values help them to become more successful than many native-born young adults (Mollenkopf et al., 2005).

All Together Now

When we look at actual lives, not the cultural ideal of independence or interdependence, emerging adults worldwide have much in common, including close family connections and a new freedom from parental limits (Georgas et al., 2006). It is a mistake to assume that emerging adults in Western nations abandon their parents. Just the opposite: Some studies find that family relationships *improve* when young adults leave home (Graber & Brooks-Gunn, 1996; Smetana et al., 2004). Family members continue to feel obligated to one another no matter where they live. In fact, far from ignoring the needs of their elders, parents and adult children tend to expect their own generation to be more responsive to family needs than the other generation (Bucx et al., 2010).

As we think about the experiences of emerging adults overall, it is apparent that this stage of life has many pitfalls. These years may be crucial, as "decisions made during the transition to adulthood have a particularly long-lasting influence on the remainder of the life course because they set individuals on paths that are sometimes difficult to change" (Thornton et al., 2007, p. 13).

Fortunately, most emerging adults, like humans of all ages, have strengths as well as liabilities. Many survive risks, overcome substance abuse, combat loneliness, and deal with other problems through further education, friends, family, and maturation. If they postpone marriage, prevent parenthood, and avoid a set career (all characteristics of 18- to 25-year-olds) until their identity is firmly established and their education complete, they may be preparing for adult commitments and responsibilities.

As you read on the first page of Chapter 1, the science of human development is about how people change over time. As you learned from every chapter, development occurs as individuals are influenced, supported, and guided by other people. That is exactly what occurs as emerging adults continue to be influenced by their parents and their peers while they prepare for another cycle of growth. Erikson's seventh crisis is *generativity versus stagnation,* when adults care for the new generation. Back to babies: The cycle of human development is ongoing.

The Same Situation, Many Miles Apart: Dedication Is Universal It may seem as if the activities and clothing of the Fresno college student in the bookstore *(top)* could not differ more from those of the young mother in the doorway of her Rajastan, India, home *(bottom).* However, both are typical emerging adults: active, healthy, and working for their futures.

SUMMING UP

Patterns of psychosocial development in emerging adulthood evidence continuity and change. Personality traits endure, but improvement is often apparent as young adults experience rising self-esteem and self-efficacy. The need for social support is lifelong, but among young adults marriage is often postponed and, at least in contemporary North America, is more often a personal choice, not a family arrangement. Parental support is ongoing, with different particulars in various nations and cultures. ∎

>> Response for Family Therapists (from page 525) Remember that family function is more important than family structure. Sharing a home can work out well if contentious issues—like sexual privacy, money, and household chores—are clarified before resentments arise. You might offer a three-session preparation package, to explore assumptions and guidelines.

SUMMARY

Biosocial Development

1. Emerging adults usually have strong and healthy bodies. Death from disease is rare.

2. The sexual-reproductive system reaches a peak during these years. The sex drive is strong and orgasms frequent. Problem-free conception, pregnancy, and birth are more likely between ages 18 and 25 than earlier or later, although most current emerging adults postpone childbearing until age 25 or later.

3. Willingness to take risks is characteristic of emerging adults. This allows positive behaviors, such as entering college, meeting new people, volunteering for difficult tasks, finding new jobs. It also leads to destructive actions, such as unprotected sex and drug use.

4. Extreme sports are attractive to some emerging adults. Attempting to understand this, developmentalists posit that the risk of injury and even of death can be thrilling at this age and that boredom is to be avoided.

Cognitive Development

5. Adult thinking is more advanced than adolescent thought in that it is more flexible, better able to coordinate the objective and the subjective. Some scholars consider adult thinking a fifth stage of cognition called postformal thought.

6. The flexibility of young-adult thought allows people to reexamine stereotypes from their childhood. This is particularly important in decreasing stereotype threat, which may impair adult cognition if left unchecked.

7. Worldwide there are far more college students, especially in Asia and Africa, than there were a few decades ago. Everywhere the students' backgrounds and current situations are more diverse than formerly.

8. Although a college education has been shown to have health and income benefits, observers disagree as to how, or even whether, college improves cognition. Evidence suggests that it does, but perhaps not as much as in earlier generations.

Psychosocial Development

9. Identity continues to be worked out in emerging adulthood. Ethnic identity is particularly important in multiethnic cultures, not only for people of mixed and minority backgrounds, but also for those in the majority.

10. The current economic situation makes vocational identity even more problematic than it was a decade ago. The average emerging adult changes jobs several times.

11. Personality traits from childhood do not disappear in emerging adulthood, but many people learn to modify or compensate for whatever negative traits they have. New experiences—such as moving away from home and going to college—allow some plasticity in personality.

12. The need for social connections and relationships is lifelong. In earlier times, and in some cultures currently, emerging adults followed their parents' wishes in seeking marriage partners. Today's youth are more likely to choose their own partners and postpone marriage.

13. Cohabitation is the current norm for emerging adults in many nations. Some research finds that this increases marital and child-rearing problems later on.

14. Family members continue to be important to emerging adults. Parental support—financial as well as emotional—may be more crucial than in earlier times.

KEY TERMS

emerging adulthood (p. 505)
extreme sports (p. 508)
drug abuse (p. 509)

postformal thought (p. 510)
stereotype threat (p. 511)

intimacy versus isolation
 (p. 521)

cohabitation (p. 523)
linked lives (p. 525)

WHAT HAVE YOU LEARNED?

Biosocial Development

1. Why is maximum physical strength usually attained in emerging adulthood?

2. What has changed, and what has not changed, in the past decades regarding sexual and reproductive development?

3. Why are STIs more common currently than 50 years ago?

4. What are the social benefits of risk taking?

5. Why are some sports more attractive at some ages than others?

6. Why are serious accidents more common in emerging adulthood than later?

7. Why are college students more likely to abuse drugs than those not in college?

Cognitive Development

8. Why did scholars choose the term *postformal* to describe the fifth stage of cognition?

9. How does postformal thinking differ from typical adolescent thought?

10. How could the threat of a stereotype affect cognition?

11. Which groups of people are vulnerable to stereotype threat and why?

12. How do current college enrollment patterns differ from those 50 years ago?

13. Why do people disagree about the goals of a college education?

Psychosocial Development

14. How does ethnic pride change from early adolescence to adulthood?

15. Why might vocational identity be an "outdated social construction"?

16. What do emerging adults seek in a romantic partner?

17. How has the process of mate selection changed over the past decades?

18. Why do many emerging adults cohabit instead of marrying?

19. Why do people assume that emerging adults are not influenced by their parents?

20. What kinds of support do parents provide their young-adult children?

APPLICATIONS

1. Describe an incident during your emerging adulthood when taking a risk could have led to disaster. What were your feelings at the time? What would you do if you knew that a child of yours was about to do the same thing?

2. Read a biography or autobiography that includes information about the person's thinking from adolescence through adulthood. How did personal experiences, education, and maturation affect the person's thinking?

3. Statistics on cohort and culture in students and in colleges are fascinating, but only a few are reported here. Compare your nation, state, or province with another. Analyze the data and discuss causes and implications of differences.

4. Talk to three people you would expect to have contrasting views on love and marriage (differences in age, gender, upbringing, experience, and religion might affect attitudes). Ask each the same questions and then compare their answers.

>>ONLINE CONNECTIONS

To accompany your textbook, you have access to a number of online resources, including quizzes for every chapter of the book, flashcards (in English and Spanish), critical thinking questions, and case studies. For access to any of these links, go to www.worthpublishers.com/bergerca9e. In addition to these free resources, you'll also find links to podcasts, video clips, diagnostic quizzing with personalized study advice, and an ebook. Some of the videos and activities available online include:

- *Interview with Kurt Fischer.* This noted developmentalist discusses the influence of experience on brain development.

- *Transition to Parenthood.* Videos of couples in various stages of parenthood highlight the physical, emotional, social, household, and vocational changes that accompany this new responsibility.

- *Homosexuality: Genes Versus Environment.* What makes someone gay? This video shows how the nature–nurture debate plays out when applied to this question.

Appendix A

>> Supplemental Charts, Graphs, and Tables

Often, examining specific data is useful, even fascinating, to developmental researchers. The particular numbers reveal trends and nuances not apparent from a more general view. Each chart, graph, or table in this appendix contains information not generally known.

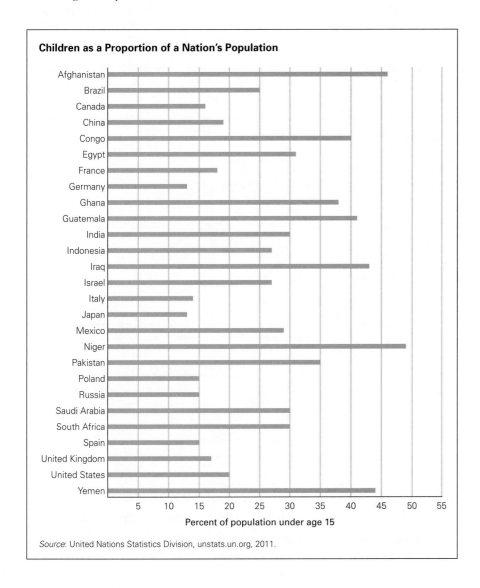

Children as a Proportion of a Nation's Population

Percent of population under age 15

Source: United Nations Statistics Division, unstats.un.org, 2011.

More Children, Worse Schools? (Chapter 1)

Nations that have high birth rates also have high death rates, short life spans, and more illiteracy. A systems approach suggests that these variables are connected: For example, the Montessori and Reggio Emilia early-childhood education programs, said to be the best in the world, originated in Italy, and Italy has one of the lowest proportions of children under 15.

Ethnic Composition of the U.S. Population (Chapter 2)

Thinking about the ethnic makeup of the U.S. population helps explain the rising importance of sociocultural theory. If you look only at the table, you will not see dramatic differences over the past 40 years: Whites are still the majority, Native Americans (Indians) are still a tiny minority, and African Americans are still about 12 percent of the population. However, if you look at the graph, you can see why every group feels that much has changed. Because the proportions of Hispanic Americans and Asian Americans have increased dramatically, European Americans see the current non-White population at almost one-third of the total, and African Americans see that Hispanics now outnumber them.

There are also interesting regional differences within the United States; for example, the Los Angeles metropolitan area has the largest number of Native Americans (125,000) and the largest number of Asians (1.8 million). Remember that racial categories (e.g., White, Black) are often rejected by social scientists but are used in the U.S. Census and other data sources. Also note that the terms for each group vary; some people prefer one term, some another.

Observation Quiz Which ethnic group is growing most rapidly since 1980 in rate of increase (not in numbers added)? (see answer, page A-4)

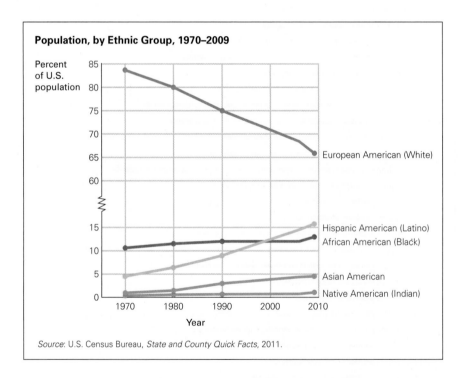

Population, by Ethnic Group, 1970–2009

Source: U.S. Census Bureau, *State and County Quick Facts*, 2011.

	Percent of U.S. population				
Ancestry	1970	1980	1990	2006	2009
European (White)	83.7	80	75	68.4	65.1
African (Black)	10.6	11.5	12	12	12.9
Hispanic (Latino)	4.5	6.4	9	14.5	15.8
Asian	1.0	1.5	3	4.3	4.6
Native American (Indian)	0.4	0.6	0.7	0.82	1.0

The Genetics of Blood Types (Chapter 3)

Blood types A and B are dominant traits, and type O is recessive. The percentages given in the first column of this chart represent the odds that a child born to the parents with the various combinations of genotypes will have the genotype given in the second column.

Genotypes of Parents*	Genotype of Offspring	Phenotype	Can Donate Blood to (Phenotype)	Can Receive Blood from (Phenotype)
AA + AA (100%) AA + AB (50%) AA + AO (50%) AB + AB (25%) AB + AO (25%) AO + AO (25%)	AA (inherits one A from each parent)	A	A or AB	A or O
AA + OO (100%) AB + OO (50%) AO + AO (50%) AO + OO (50%) AB + AO (25%) AB + BO (25%)	AO	A	A or AB	A or O
BB + BB (100%) AB + BB (50%) BB + BO (50%) AB + AB (25%) AB + BO (25%) BO + BO (25%)	BB	B	B or AB	B or O
BB + OO (100%) AB + OO (50%) BO + BO (50%) BO + OO (50%) AB + AO (25%) AB + BO (25%)	BO	B	B or AB	B or O
AA + BB (100%) AA + AB (50%) AA + BO (50%) AB + AB (50%) AB + BB (50%) AO + BB (50%) AB + BO (25%) AO + BO (25%)	AB	AB	AB only	A, B, AB, O ("universal recipient")
OO + OO (100%) AO + OO (50%) BO + OO (50%) AO + AO (25%) AO + BO (25%) BO + BO (25%)	OO	O	A, B, AB, O ("universal donor")	O only

*Blood type is not sex-linked because blood type comes equally from each parent.
Source: Adapted from Hartl & Jones, 1999.

Saving Young Lives: Childhood and Adolescent Immunizations (Chapter 5)

Recommended Childhood and Adolescent Immunization Schedule, United States, 2006

Age

Vaccine	Birth	1 Mo.	2 Mos.	4 Mos.	6 Mos.	12 Mos.	15 Mos.	18 Mos.	24 Mos.	4–6 Yrs.	11–12[†] Yrs.	13–18[†] Yrs.
Hepatitis B	Hep B #1	only if mother HBsAg (-)									Hep B series	
			Hep B #2			Hep B #3						
Influenza BCG*	X		Influenza (yearly)									
Diphtheria, tetanus, and pertussis			DTaP	DTaP	DTaP		DTaP			DTaP	Td	Td
Haemophilus influenzae type b			Hib	Hib	Hib	Hib						
Inactivated polio			IPV	IPV		IPV				IPV		
Measles, mumps, rubella						MMR #1				MMR #2	MMR #2	
Varicella (chicken pox)						Varicella					Varicella	
HPV (human papilloma virus)											HPV	
MCV4 (meningococcal conjugate vaccine)									MCV4			MCV4
Pneumococcal			PCV	PCV	PCV	PCV			PCV	PPV		

------ Vaccines below this line are for selected populations. ------

| Hepatitis A | | | | | | Hepatitis A series | | | | | | |

■ Range of recommended ages for vaccination
■ Catch-up immunization—age groups that warrant special effort to administer those vaccines not given previously
■ Preadolescent assessment

Note: For many diseases, repeated doses are recommended, as shown.
†See HPV, in Adult Immunizations table that follows.
*BCG vaccine is highly recommended in most nations, but is not required in the United States because the prevalence of tuberculosis is low.

Source: CDC Web site (http://cdc.gov/vaccines/pubs/acip-list.htm), December 15, 2009.

First Sounds and First Words: Similarities Among Many Languages (Chapter 6)

	Baby's word for:	
Language	Mother	Father
English	mama, mommy	dada, daddy
Spanish	mama	papa
French	maman, mama	papa
Italian	mamma	babbo, papa
Latvian	mama	te-te
Syrian Arabic	mama	baba
Bantu	ba-mama	taata
Swahili	mama	baba
Sanskrit	nana	tata
Hebrew	ema	abba
Korean	oma	apa

>> Answer to Observation Quiz (from page A-2)
Asian Americans, whose share of the U.S. population has quadrupled in the past 30 years. Latinos are increasing most rapidly in numbers, but not in proportion.

Breast-feeding in the United States (Chapter 7)

Differentiating excellent from destructive mothering is not easy, once the child's basic needs for food and protection are met. However, psychosocial development depends on responsive parent–infant relationships. Breast-feeding is one sign of intimacy between mother and infant.

Regions of the world differ dramatically in rates of breast-feeding. The highest rate is in Southeast Asia, where half of all 2-year-olds are still breast-fed. In the United States, factors that affect the likelihood of breast-feeding are ethnicity, maternal age, and education.

Breast-feeding in the United States					
Sociodemographic factors	Ever breast-feeding	Breast-feeding at 6 months	Breast-feeding at 12 months	Exclusive breast-feeding* at 3 months	Exclusive breast-feeding* at 6 months
U.S. National	74.6%	44.3%	23.8%	35.0%	14.8%
Sex of baby					
Male	75.4	42.6	22.0	33.1	12.9
Female	74.6	43.5	22.8	32.9	13.7
Birth order					
First born	74.5	44.1	23.7	33.4	13.8
Not first born	75.6	41.8	20.8	32.6	12.6
Ethnicity					
Native American (Indian)	73.8	42.4	20.7	27.6	13.2
Asian or Pacific Islander	83.0	56.4	32.8	34.1	14.5
Hispanic or Latino	80.6	46.0	24.7	32.4	13.2
African American (non-Hispanic)	59.7	27.9	12.9	22.7	8.2
European (non-Hispanic)	77.7	45.1	23.6	35.3	14.4
Mother's age					
Less than 20	59.7	22.2	10.7	18.1	7.9
20–29	69.7	33.4	16.1	28.8	10.2
More than 30	79.3	50.5	27.1	36.6	15.5
Mother's education					
Less than high school	67.0	37.0	21.9	33.7	9.2
High school	66.1	31.4	15.1	25.8	8.9
Some college	76.5	41.0	20.5	34.1	14.4
College graduate	88.3	59.9	31.1	45.9	19.6
Mother's marital status					
Married	81.7	51.6	27.5	39.0	16.7
Unmarried†	61.3	25.5	11.9	20.9	6.4
Residence					
Central city	75.5	43.9	24.4	32.8	13.3
Urban	77.9	45.3	22.3	34.9	13.9
Suburban and rural	66.4	35.0	17.4	28.8	11.8

*Exclusive breast-feeding is defined as only breast milk—no solids, no water, and no other liquids.
†Unmarried includes never married, widowed, separated, and divorced.
Source: National Immunization Survey, Centers for Disease Control and Prevention, Department of Health and Human Services, 2011.

Height Gains from Birth to Age 18 (Chapters 5, 8, 11)

The range of height (on this page) and weight (see page A-7) of children in the United States. The columns labeled "50th" (the fiftieth percentile) show the average; the columns labeled "90th" (the ninetieth percentile) show the size of children taller and heavier than 90 percent of their contemporaries; and the columns labeled "10th" (the tenth percentile) show the size of children who are taller than only 10 percent of their peers. Note that girls are slightly shorter, on average, than boys.

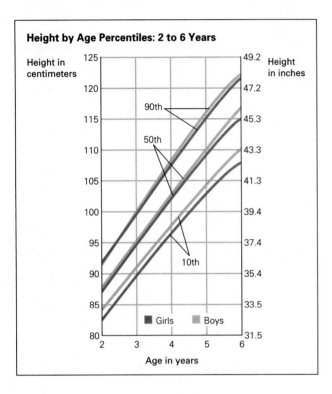

Height by Age Percentiles: 2 to 6 Years

Same Data, Different Form

The columns of numbers in the table at right provide detailed and precise information about height ranges for every year of childhood. The illustration above shows the same information in graphic form for ages 2–6. The same is done for weight ranges on page A-7. Ages 2–6 are singled out because that is the period during which a child's eating habits are set. Which form of data presentation do you think is easier to understand?

	Length in Centimeters (and Inches)					
	Boys: percentiles			**Girls: percentiles**		
AGE	**10th**	**50th**	**90th**	**10th**	**50th**	**90th**
Birth	47.5 (18¾)	50.5 (20)	53.5 (21)	46.5 (18¼)	49.9 (19¾)	52.0 (20½)
1 month	51.3 (20¼)	54.6 (21½)	57.7 (22¾)	50.2 (19¾)	53.5 (21)	56.1 (22)
3 months	57.7 (22¾)	61.1 (24)	64.5 (25½)	56.2 (22¼)	59.5 (23½)	62.7 (24¾)
6 months	64.4 (25¼)	67.8 (26¾)	71.3 (28)	62.6 (24¾)	65.9 (26)	69.4 (27¼)
9 months	69.1 (27¼)	72.3 (28½)	75.9 (30)	67.0 (26½)	70.4 (27¾)	74.0 (29¼)
12 months	72.8 (28¾)	76.1 (30)	79.8 (31½)	70.8 (27¾)	74.3 (29¼)	78.0 (30¾)
18 months	78.7 (31)	82.4 (32½)	86.6 (34)	77.2 (30½)	80.9 (31¾)	85.0 (33½)
24 months	83.5 (32¾)	87.6 (34½)	92.2 (36¼)	82.5 (32½)	86.5 (34)	90.8 (35¾)
3 years	90.3 (35½)	94.9 (37¼)	100.1 (39½)	89.3 (35¼)	94.1 (37)	99.0 (39)
4 years	97.3 (38¼)	102.9 (40½)	108.2 (42½)	96.4 (38)	101.6 (40)	106.6 (42)
5 years	103.7 (40¾)	109.9 (43¼)	115.4 (45½)	102.7 (40½)	108.4 (42¾)	113.8 (44¾)
6 years	109.6 (43¼)	116.1 (45¾)	121.9 (48)	108.4 (42¾)	114.6 (45)	120.8 (47½)
7 years	115.0 (45¼)	121.7 (48)	127.9 (50¼)	113.6 (44¾)	120.6 (47½)	127.6 (50¼)
8 years	120.2 (47¼)	127.0 (50)	133.6 (52½)	118.7 (46¾)	126.4 (49¾)	134.2 (52¾)
9 years	125.2 (49¼)	132.2 (52)	139.4 (55)	123.9 (48¾)	132.2 (52)	140.7 (55½)
10 years	130.1 (51¼)	137.5 (54¼)	145.5 (57¼)	129.5 (51)	138.3 (54½)	147.2 (58)
11 years	135.1 (53¼)	143.33 (56½)	152.1 (60)	135.6 (53½)	144.8 (57)	153.7 (60½)
12 years	140.3 (55¼)	149.7 (59)	159.4 (62¾)	142.3 (56)	151.5 (59¾)	160.0 (63)
13 years	145.8 (57½)	156.5 (61½)	167.0 (65¾)	148.0 (58¼)	157.1 (61¾)	165.3 (65)
14 years	151.8 (59¾)	63.1 (64¼)	173.8 (68½)	151.5 (59¾)	160.4 (63¼)	168.7 (66½)
15 years	158.2 (62¼)	169.0 (66½)	178.9 (70½)	153.2 (60¼)	161.8 (63¾)	170.5 (67¼)
16 years	163.9 (64½)	173.5 (68¼)	182.4 (71¾)	154.1 (60¾)	162.4 (64)	171.1 (67¼)
17 years	167.7 (66)	176.2 (69¼)	184.4 (72½)	155.1 (61)	163.1 (64¼)	171.2 (67½)
18 years	168.7 (66½)	176.8 (69½)	185.3 (73)	156.0 (61½)	163.7 (64½)	171.0 (67¼)

Source: These data are those of the National Center for Health Statistics (NCHS), Health Resources Administration, DHHS. They were based on studies of The Fels Research Institute, Yellow Springs, Ohio. These data were first made available with the help of William M. Moore, M.D., of Ross Laboratories, who supplied the conversion from metric measurements to approximate inches and pounds. This help is gratefully acknowledged.

Weight Gains from Birth to Age 18 (Chapters 5, 8, 11)

These height and weight charts present rough guidelines; a child might differ from these norms and be quite healthy and normal. However, if a particular child shows a discrepancy between height and weight (for instance, at the 90th percentile in height but only the 20th percentile in weight) or is much larger or smaller than most children the same age, a pediatrician should see whether disease, malnutrition, or genetic abnormality could be part of the reason.

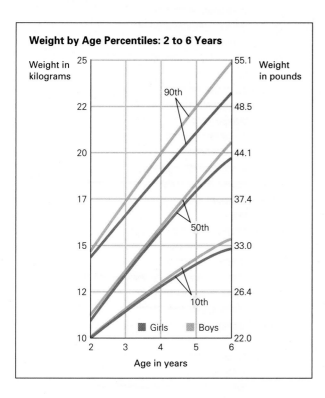

Weight by Age Percentiles: 2 to 6 Years

Comparisons

Notice that the height trajectories for boys and girls on page A-6 are much closer together than the weight trajectories shown above. By age 18, the height range amounts to only about 6 inches, but there is a difference of about 65 pounds between the 10th and the 90th percentiles.

Critical Thinking Question How can this discrepancy between height and weight ranges be explained? (see answer, page A-8)

	Weight in Kilograms (and Pounds)					
	Boys: percentiles			**Girls: percentiles**		
AGE	10th	50th	90th	10th	50th	90th
Birth	2.78 (6¼)	3.27 (7¼)	3.82 (8½)	2.58 (5¾)	3.23 (7)	3.64 (8)
1 month	3.43 (7½)	4.29 (9½)	5.14 (11¼)	3.22 (7)	3.98 (8¾)	4.65 (10¼)
3 months	4.78 (10½)	5.98 (13¼)	7.14 (15¾)	4.47 (9¾)	5.40 (12)	6.39 (14)
6 months	6.61 (14½)	7.85 (17¼)	9.10 (20)	6.12 (13½)	7.21 (16)	8.38 (18½)
9 months	7.95 (17½)	9.18 (20¼)	10.49 (23¼)	7.34 (16¼)	8.56 (18¾)	9.83 (21¾)
12 months	8.84 (19½)	10.15 (22½)	11.54 (25½)	8.19 (18)	9.53 (21)	10.87 (24)
18 months	9.92 (21¾)	11.47 (25¼)	13.05 (28¾)	9.30 (20½)	10.82 (23¾)	12.30 (27)
24 months	10.85 (24)	12.59 (27¾)	14.29 (31½)	10.26 (22½)	11.90 (26¼)	13.57 (30)
3 years	12.58 (27¾)	14.62 (32¼)	16.95 (37¼)	12.26 (27)	14.10 (31)	16.54 (36½)
4 years	14.24 (31½)	16.69 (36¾)	19.32 (42½)	13.84 (30½)	15.96 (35¼)	18.93 (41¾)
5 years	15.96 (35¼)	18.67 (41¼)	21.70 (47¾)	15.26 (33¾)	17.66 (39)	21.23 (46¾)
6 years	17.72 (39)	20.69 (45½)	24.31 (53½)	16.72 (36¾)	19.52 (43)	23.89 (52¾)
7 years	19.53 (43)	22.85 (50¼)	27.36 (60¼)	18.39 (40½)	21.84 (48¼)	27.39 (60½)
8 years	21.39 (47¼)	25.30 (55¾)	31.06 (68½)	20.45 (45)	24.84 (54¾)	32.04 (70¾)
9 years	23.33 (51½)	28.13 (62)	35.57 (78½)	22.92 (50½)	28.46 (62¾)	37.60 (83)
10 years	25.52 (56¼)	31.44 (69¼)	40.80 (90)	25.76 (56¾)	32.55 (71¾)	43.70 (96¼)
11 years	28.17 (62)	35.30 (77¾)	46.57 (102¾)	28.97 (63¾)	36.95 (81½)	49.96 (110¼)
12 years	31.46 (69¼)	39.78 (87¾)	52.73 (116¼)	32.53 (71¼)	41.53 (91½)	55.99 (123½)
13 years	35.60 (78½)	44.95 (99)	59.12 (130¼)	36.35 (80¼)	46.10 (101¾)	61.45 (135½)
14 years	40.64 (89½)	50.77 (112)	65.57 (144½)	40.11 (88½)	50.28 (110¾)	66.04 (145½)
15 years	46.06 (101½)	56.71 (125)	71.91 (158½)	43.38 (95¾)	53.68 (118¼)	69.64 (153¼)
16 years	51.16 (112¾)	62.10 (137)	77.97 (172)	45.78 (101)	55.89 (123¼)	71.68 (158)
17 years	55.28 (121¾)	66.31 (146¼)	83.58 (184¼)	47.04 (103¾)	56.69 (125)	72.38 (159½)
18 years	57.89 (127½)	68.88 (151¾)	88.41 (195)	47.47 (104¾)	56.62 (124¾)	72.25 (159¼)

Source: Data are those of the National Center for Health Statistics, Health Resources Administration, DHHS, collected in its Health Examination Surveys.

Children Are the Poorest Americans (Chapters 10, 11)

It probably comes as no surprise that the rate of poverty is twice as high in some states as in others. What is surprising is how much the rates vary between age groups within the same state.

Observation Quiz In which 13 states is the proportion of poor children more than twice as high as the proportion of poor people over age 65? (see answer page A-9)

>> **Answer to Critical Thinking Question** (from page A-7) Nutrition is generally adequate in the United States, and that is why height differences are small. But as a result of the strong influence that family and culture have on eating habits, almost half of all North Americans are overweight or obese.

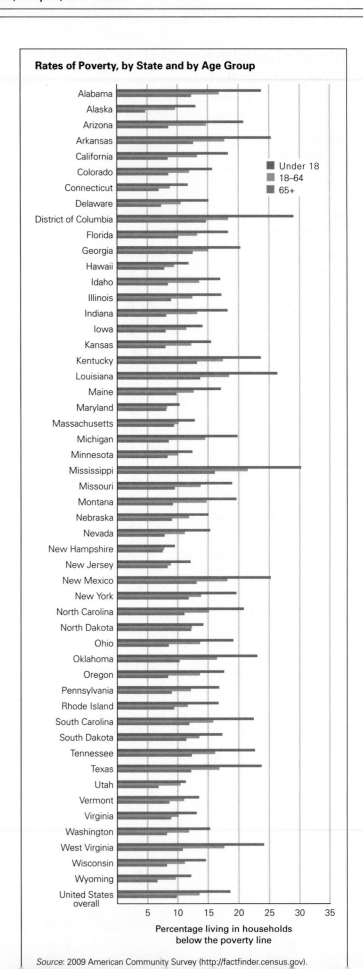

Rates of Poverty, by State and by Age Group

Legend: Under 18 / 18–64 / 65+

Percentage living in households below the poverty line

Source: 2009 American Community Survey (http://factfinder.census.gov).

Changes in the Average Weekly Amount of Time Spent by 6- to 11-Year-Olds in Various Activities (Chapter 12)

Facts are the bedrock of science, but facts can be presented in many ways, with many interpretations. Your opinions about these facts reflect your values, which may be quite different from those of the parents and teachers of these children.

Total Media Use	
Among all 8- to 18-year-olds, average amount of time spent with each medium in a typical day:	
	2009
TV content	4:29
Music/audio	2:31
Computer	1:29
Video games	1:13
Print	:38
Movies	:25
Total Media Exposure	10:45
Multitasking proportion	29%
Total Media Use	7:38

Source: Generation M2: Media in the Lives of 8- to 18-Year-Olds, A Kaiser Family Foundation Study, January 2010.

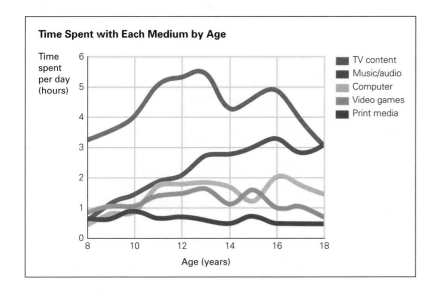

Time Spent with Each Medium by Age

Legend:
- TV content
- Music/audio
- Computer
- Video games
- Print media

Who Is Raising the Children? (Chapter 13)

Most children still live in households with a male/female couple, who may be the children's married or unmarried biological parents, grandparents, stepparents, foster parents, or adoptive parents. However, the proportion of households headed by single parents has risen—by 350 percent for single fathers and by almost 200 percent for single mothers. (In 2008, 66 percent of U.S. households had *no* children under age 18.)

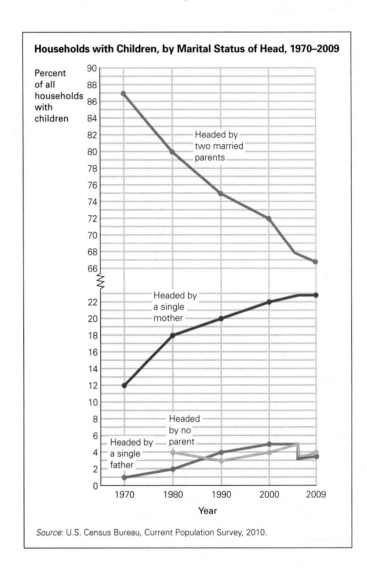

Households with Children, by Marital Status of Head, 1970–2009

Source: U.S. Census Bureau, Current Population Survey, 2010.

Major Sexually Transmitted Infections: Some Basics (Chapter 14)

These and other STIs, if left untreated, may lead to serious reproductive and other health problems or even, as with HIV/AIDS and syphilis, to death. STIs can be avoided by consistently using condoms, having sex only in a relationship with an uninfected partner, or abstaining from sex.

Sexually Transmitted Infection (and Cause)	Symptoms	Treatment
Chlamydia (bacterium)	The most frequently reported bacterial STI in the United States. In women, abnormal vaginal discharge or burning sensation when urinating; may be followed by pain in low abdomen or low back, nausea, fever, pain during intercourse, or bleeding between menstrual periods. In men, discharge from penis or burning sensation when urinating.	Antibiotics
Genital HPV infection (virus)	One of the most common STIs in the world. Causes no symptoms or health problems in most people, but certain types may cause genital warts and others can cause cervical cancer in women and other cancers of the genitals in both sexes.	A vaccine is now available and is recommended for 11- and 12-year-old girls who are not yet sexually active.
Genital herpes (virus)	Blisters on or around the genitals or rectum that break and leave sores, which may take 2 to 4 weeks to heal; some people may experience fever, swollen glands, and other flu-like symptoms. Later outbreaks are usually less severe and shorter. Many people never have sores and may take years to realize they are infected. May lead to potentially fatal infections in babies and makes infected person more susceptible to HIV infection.	There is no vaccine or cure, but antiviral medications can shorten and prevent outbreaks.
Gonorrhea (bacterium)	Some men and most women have no symptoms. In men, a burning sensation when urinating; a white, yellow, or green discharge from the penis; painful or swollen testicles. In women, symptoms—pain or burning during urination, increased vaginal discharge, vaginal bleeding between periods—may be so mild or nonspecific that they are mistaken for a bladder or vaginal infection. May cause pelvic inflammatory disease (PID) in women and infertility in both sexes. Infected person can more easily contract HIV.	Antibiotics
Pelvic inflammatory disease (PID) (various bacteria)	A common and serious complication in women who have certain other STIs, especially chlamydia and gonorrhea. Pain in lower abdomen, fever, unusual vaginal discharge that may have a foul odor, painful intercourse, painful urination, irregular menstrual bleeding, and (rarely) pain in the right upper abdomen. May lead to blocked fallopian tubes, causing infertility.	Administration of at least two antibiotics that are effective against a wide range of infectious agents. In severe cases, surgery.
HIV/AIDS (virus)	Infection with the human immunodeficiency virus (HIV) eventually leads to acquired immune deficiency syndrome (AIDS). Infection with other STIs increases a person's likelihood of both acquiring and transmitting HIV. Soon after exposure, some people have flu-like symptoms: fever, headache, tiredness, swollen lymph glands. Months or years later, when the virus has weakened the immune system, the person may experience lack of energy, weight loss, frequent fevers and sweats, yeast infections, skin rashes, short-term memory loss. Symptoms of full-blown AIDS include certain cancers (Kaposi's sarcoma and lymphomas), seizures, vision loss, and coma. A leading cause of death among young adults in many nations.	There is no vaccine or cure, but antiretroviral drugs can slow the growth of the virus; antibiotics can cure some secondary infections, and various treatments are available to relieve painful or unpleasant symptoms.
Syphilis (bacterium)	Symptoms may not appear for years. Primary stage: One or more sores (chancres) a few days or weeks after exposure. Secondary stage: Skin rash, lesions of mucous membranes, fever, swollen lymph glands, sore throat, patchy hair loss, headaches, weight loss, muscle aches, fatigue. Latent stage: Primary and secondary symptoms disappear, but infection remains in the body. Late stage (10 to 20 years after first infection): Damage to brain, nerves, eyes, heart, blood vessels, liver, bones, and joints, progressing to difficulty coordinating muscle movements, paralysis, numbness, blindness, dementia.	Penicillin injections will kill the syphilis bacterium and prevent further damage but cannot repair damage already done.
Trichomoniasis (Trichomonas *vaginalis,* *a single-celled* protozoan parasite)	Most men have no symptoms, but some may temporarily have an irritation inside the penis, mild discharge, or slight burning after urination or ejaculation. Women may have a frothy, yellow-green, strong-smelling vaginal discharge and may experience discomfort during intercourse and urination; irritation and itching of the genital area; and, rarely, lower abdominal pain.	A single oral dose of metronidazole or tinidazole

Source: Centers for Disease Control and Prevention, 2009, July 14.

Sexual Behaviors of U.S. High School Students, 2009 (Chapters 14)

These percentages, as high as they may seem, are actually lower than they were in the early 1990s. (States not listed did not participate fully in the survey.) The data in this table reflect responses from students in the 9th to 12th grades. When only high school seniors are surveyed, the percentages are higher: Nationwide, 62 percent of seniors have had sexual intercourse, and 21 percent have had four or more partners.

State	Ever had sexual intercourse (%)			Had first sexual intercourse before age 13 (%)			Has had four or more sex partners during lifetime (%)			Is currently sexually active (%)		
	Female	Male	Total	Female	Male	Total	Female	Male	Total	Female	Male	Total
Alabama	51.4	61.8	**56.6**	4.1	16.2	**10.1**	14.4	25.7	**19.9**	42.0	40.9	**41.5**
Alaska	42.9	44.0	**43.5**	2.6	7.1	**5.1**	10.7	12.1	**11.4**	31.1	29.6	**30.4**
Arizona	44.8	52.1	**48.6**	2.9	7.8	**5.5**	10.4	17.4	**14.1**	34.4	34.2	**34.5**
Arkansas	51.4	55.9	**53.6**	6.7	14.3	**10.3**	15.5	20.8	**18.0**	39.9	37.6	**38.9**
Colorado	36.2	43.7	**40.0**	2.7	6.4	**4.6**	11.0	16.5	**13.8**	25.6	29.1	**27.4**
Connecticut	38.0	42.9	**40.5**	2.8	6.1	**4.6**	8.4	12.5	**10.5**	30.3	28.9	**29.6**
Delaware	57.1	57.9	**57.5**	5.8	13.4	**9.7**	18.0	23.9	**21.1**	44.2	41.5	**42.9**
Florida	47.7	53.4	**50.6**	4.3	12.0	**8.3**	11.4	21.4	**16.6**	37.0	36.8	**37.0**
Hawaii	45.8	42.7	**44.3**	4.1	7.8	**6.0**	11.3	10.9	**11.1**	33.9	27.2	**30.5**
Idaho	39.2	38.8	**39.0**	3.4	4.9	**4.2**	—	—	—	—	—	—
Illinois	43.8	52.3	**48.1**	3.6	8.9	**6.3**	10.8	18.3	**14.5**	35.4	36.9	**36.2**
Indiana	52.8	45.5	**49.2**	2.8	6.3	**4.5**	13.7	13.5	**13.7**	41.3	31.9	**36.7**
Kansas	46.2	47.0	**46.6**	1.7	7.2	**4.5**	11.8	16.4	**14.2**	35.2	33.3	**34.2**
Kentucky	47.8	49.0	**48.3**	4.0	9.3	**6.7**	10.7	14.7	**12.7**	36.1	31.2	**33.6**
Maine	45.9	45.9	**46.0**	2.8	7.3	**5.0**	10.7	13.1	**11.9**	37.1	33.3	**35.3**
Massachusetts	44.6	48.0	**46.4**	3.0	8.0	**5.4**	10.6	15.2	**12.9**	36.0	33.1	**34.6**
Michigan	44.3	46.9	**45.6**	3.0	7.2	**5.1**	11.5	15.7	**13.6**	35.6	32.6	**34.1**
Mississippi	58.2	63.9	**61.0**	8.1	18.7	**13.4**	17.6	30.1	**23.7**	44.0	45.9	**44.9**
Missouri	47.3	50.2	**48.7**	3.4	7.9	**5.7**	13.6	18.3	**16.0**	36.3	34.9	**35.5**
Montana	47.0	48.1	**47.6**	3.7	7.7	**5.7**	14.7	17.3	**16.0**	33.6	30.8	**32.2**
Nevada	45.3	52.6	**49.0**	3.4	10.0	**6.7**	10.9	20.3	**15.7**	32.8	32.5	**32.7**
New Hampshire	46.2	46.1	**46.3**	1.9	6.4	**4.3**	10.9	11.6	**11.4**	39.5	32.3	**36.3**
New Jersey	43.6	49.0	**46.3**	1.5	6.7	**4.1**	8.8	16.3	**12.5**	33.7	33.5	**33.6**
New Mexico	—	—	—	4.7	10.1	**7.4**	12.4	17.8	**15.1**	33.5	31.8	**32.6**
New York	38.4	45.6	**42.0**	3.3	8.8	**6.1**	8.4	18.4	**13.4**	29.7	33.2	**31.5**
North Carolina	48.2	54.2	**51.1**	5.1	10.1	**7.5**	12.2	19.2	**15.7**	35.7	37.5	**36.6**
North Dakota	46.7	42.3	**44.6**	2.1	4.8	**3.5**	11.6	11.7	**11.7**	37.2	29.3	**33.3**
Oklahoma	50.7	51.2	**44.6**	3.4	6.0	**4.7**	15.2	20.1	**17.6**	40.3	39.5	**39.8**
Pennsylvania	51.0	45.8	**48.3**	3.6	7.9	**5.8**	13.2	17.7	**15.4**	39.6	34.3	**36.9**
Rhode Island	42.8	45.6	**44.2**	2.4	8.0	**5.2**	8.6	13.7	**11.2**	32.6	32.0	**32.3**
South Carolina	50.7	56.3	**53.4**	6.3	12.2	**9.2**	14.8	24.9	**19.7**	37.0	40.4	**38.6**
South Dakota	46.9	47.1	**47.0**	3.7	7.6	**5.7**	14.4	16.0	**15.2**	38.9	33.7	**36.3**
Tennessee	51.2	55.6	**53.4**	3.3	11.5	**7.5**	13.3	19.8	**16.6**	38.4	39.1	**38.8**
Texas	49.3	53.9	**51.6**	3.1	9.1	**6.1**	12.7	20.3	**16.5**	38.5	36.9	**37.7**
West Virginia	54.7	53.6	**54.1**	4.6	7.5	**6.0**	14.6	16.4	**15.5**	42.4	38.2	**40.3**
Wisconsin	41.1	40.7	**40.9**	2.5	4.4	**3.4**	8.7	11.0	**9.9**	31.7	26.9	**29.3**
Wyoming	51.6	49.6	**50.6**	3.0	8.8	**5.0**	16.8	19.0	**17.9**	40.4	35.0	**37.8**
U.S. median	**46.8**	**48.5**	**48.2**	**3.3**	**7.8**	**5.7**	**11.6**	**17.3**	**14.5**	**36.2**	**33.4**	**35.4**

Source: National Center for Chronic Disease Prevention and Health Promotion, Youth Risk Behavior Surveillance System, *MMWR*, June 6, 2011.

Demographic Changes (Chapter 14)

These numbers show dramatic shifts in family planning, with teenage births continuing to fall and births after age 30 rising again. These data come from the United States, but the same trends are apparent in almost every nation. Can you tell when contraception became widely available?

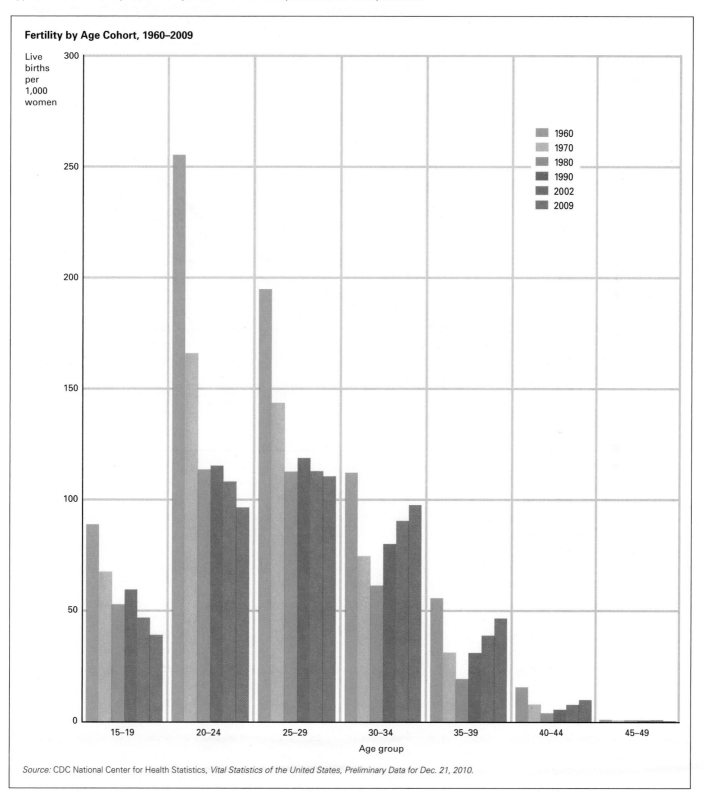

Fertility by Age Cohort, 1960–2009

Live births per 1,000 women

Legend: 1960, 1970, 1980, 1990, 2002, 2009

Age group: 15–19, 20–24, 25–29, 30–34, 35–39, 40–44, 45–49

Source: CDC National Center for Health Statistics, *Vital Statistics of the United States, Preliminary Data for Dec. 21, 2010.*

Education Affects Income (Chapter 15)

Although there is some debate about the cognitive benefits of college education, there is no doubt about the financial benefits. No matter what a person's ethnicity or gender is, an associate's degree more than doubles his or her income compared to that of someone who has not completed high school. These data are for the United States; similar trends, often with steeper increases, are found in other nations.

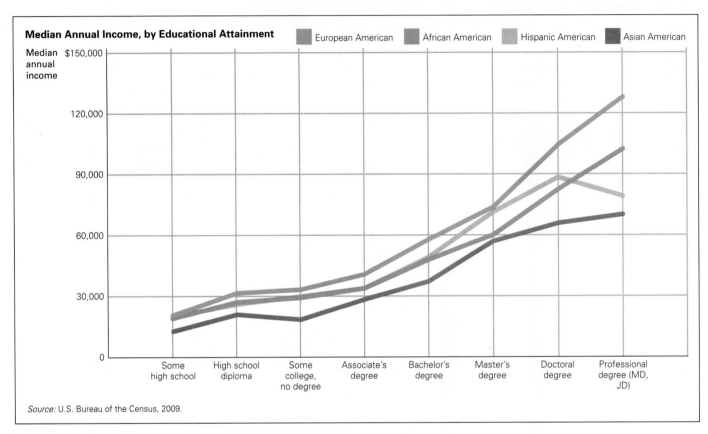

Median Annual Income, by Educational Attainment

Legend: European American, African American, Hispanic American, Asian American

Median annual income

y-axis: $150,000 / 120,000 / 90,000 / 60,000 / 30,000 / 0

x-axis: Some high school / High school diploma / Some college, no degree / Associate's degree / Bachelor's degree / Master's degree / Doctoral degree / Professional degree (MD, JD)

Source: U.S. Bureau of the Census, 2009.

U.S. Homicide Victim and Offender Rates, by Race and Gender, Ages 13–16 (Chapter 16)

Teenage boys are more often violent offenders than victims. The ratio of victimization to offense has varied for teenage girls over the years. The good news is that rates have decreased dramatically over the past 10 years for every category of adolescents—male and female, Black and White. (Similar declines are apparent for Asian and Hispanic Americans.) The bad news is that rates are far higher in the United States than in any other developed nation.

Number of Homicide Victims, Ages 13–16

Year	Total	Male	Female	White	Black
2001	390	291	99	190	182
2004	411	325	86	177	218
2005	467	426	41	176	272
2006	485	395	90	217	259
2007	487	380	107	206	265
2008	496	447	48	197	272
2009	400	319	81	190	199
2010	363	288	75	140	212

Source: U.S. Department of Justice—Federal Bureau of Investigation, 2011.

Number of Homicide Offenders, Ages 13–16

Year	Total	Male	Female	White	Black
2001	454	388	63	196	234
2004	480	440	39	210	256
2005	467	426	41	176	272
2006	610	560	47	213	377
2007	542	493	47	187	344
2008	496	447	48	197	272
2009	465	422	43	186	264
2010	437	395	42	153	265

Source: U.S. Department of Justice—Federal Bureau of Investigation, 2011.

The charts, graphs, and tables in this Appendix offer readers the opportunity to analyze raw data and draw their own conclusions. The same information may be presented in a variety of ways. On this page, you can create your own bar graph or line graph, depicting some noteworthy aspect of the data presented in the three tables. First, consider all the possibilities the tables offer by answering these five questions:

1. Are male or female teenagers more likely to be victims of homicide?
2. These are annual rates. How many African Americans in 1,000 were likely to commit homicide in 2010?
3. Which age group is *most* likely to commit homicide?
4. Which age group is *least* likely to be victims of homicide?
5. Of the four groups of adolescents, which has shown the greatest decline in rates of both victimization and perpetration of homicide over the past decade? Which has shown the least decline?

Answers: 1. Boys—at least 4 times as often. 2. Less than one. 3. 17–24. 4. 0–12. 5. Black males had the greatest decline, and White females had the least (but these two groups have always been highest and lowest, respectively, in every year).
Now—use the grid provided at right to make your own graph.

Overall Number of Homicides by Age, 2010, United States (Chapter 16)

Late adolescence and early adulthood are the peak times for murders—both for victims and offenders. The question for developmentalists is whether something changes before age 18 to decrease the rates in young adulthood.

Age group	Victims	Killers
0–12	627	11
13–16	363	437
17–24	3,487	4,121
25–34	3,505	2,753
35–49	2,792	1,384
50–64	1,666	651
Over 64	585	204

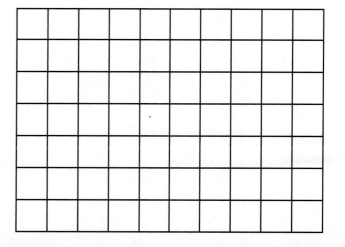

Smoking Behavior Among U.S. High School Students, 1991–2009 (Chapter 16)

The data in these two tables reveal many trends. For example, do you see that African American adolescents are much less likely to smoke than Hispanics or European Americans, but that this racial advantage is decreasing? Are you surprised to see that White females smoke more than White males?

Percentage of High School Students Who Reported Smoking Cigarettes							
Smoking Behavior	1991	1995	1999	2003	2005	2007	2009
Lifetime (ever smoked)	70.1	71.3	70.4	58.4	54.3	50.3	46.3
Current (smoked at least once in past 30 days)	27.5	34.8	34.8	21.9	23.0	20.0	19.5
Current frequent (smoked 20 or more times in past 30 days)	12.7	16.1	16.8	9.7	9.4	8.1	7.3

Percentage of High School Students Who Reported Current Smoking, by Sex, Ethnicity, and Grade							
Characteristic	1991	1995	1999	2003	2005	2007	2009
Sex							
Female	27.3	34.3	34.9	21.9	23.0	18.7	19.1
Male	27.6	35.4	34.7	21.8	22.9	21.3	19.8
Ethnicity							
White, non-Hispanic	30.9	38.3	38.6	24.9	25.9	23.2	22.5
Female	*31.7*	*39.8*	*39.1*	*26.6*	*27.0*	*22.5*	*22.8*
Male	*30.2*	*37.0*	*38.2*	*23.3*	*24.9*	*23.8*	*22.3*
Black, non-Hispanic	12.6	19.2	19.7	15.1	12.9	11.6	9.5
Female	*11.3*	*12.2*	*17.7*	*10.8*	*11.9*	*8.4*	*8.4*
Male	*14.1*	*27.8*	*21.8*	*19.3*	*14.0*	*14.9*	*10.7*
Hispanic	25.3	34.0	32.7	18.4	22.0	16.7	18.0
Female	*22.9*	*32.9*	*31.5*	*17.7*	*19.2*	*14.6*	*16.7*
Male	*27.9*	*34.9*	*34.0*	*19.1*	*24.8*	*18.7*	*19.4*
Grade							
9th	23.2	31.2	27.6	17.4	19.7	14.3	13.5
10th	25.2	33.1	34.7	21.8	21.4	19.6	18.3
11th	31.6	35.9	36.0	23.6	24.3	21.6	22.3
12th	30.1	38.2	42.8	26.2	27.6	26.5	25.2

Source: MMWR (2010, July 9).

Appendix B

>> Correlation of *The Developing Person Through Childhood and Adolescence, 9e* with NAEYC Standards

The following table provides an at-a-glance correlation between this text and the 2010 NAEYC Standards for Initial and Advanced Early Childhood Professional Preparation Programs. Key Elements of the Initial Standards are preceded by "(I)" and Key Elements of Advanced Standards are preceded by "(A)"; in cases in which a standard is the same for both Initial and Advanced programs, the standard is preceded by "(I and A)."

As might be expected for a textbook on child development, the strongest correlations are with Standard 1 (Promoting Child Development and Learning) and Standard 2 (Building Family and Community Relationships), which relate primarily to knowledge that an early-childhood-education candidate is required to master. There are also appropriate correlations between pertinent sections of the text and Key Elements 3a and 3b of Standard 3 (Observing, Documenting, and Assessing to Support Young Children and Families) and Key Elements 4a and 4b of Standard 4 (Using Developmentally Effective Approaches), although these standards relate more directly to the practical application of knowledge than to its acquisition.

Standard 3 (Key Elements 3c and 3d), Standard 4 (Key Elements 4c and 4d), Standard 5 (Using Content Knowledge to Build Meaningful Curriculum), Standard 6 (Becoming a Professional), and Standard 7 (Early Childhood Filed Experiences) relate to the early-childhood-education candidate's proficiency in applying knowledge and strategies and are therefore beyond the scope of a textbook to fulfill.

The NAEYC Standards were developed for educators of children up to 8 years of age. The correlations noted below apply to this age group although middle childhood is defined in the text as ages 6 to 11.

Standard 1 – Promoting Child Development and Learning	BIRTH TO AGE 2
Key Elements of Standard 1	**Chapter 2**
(I and A) 1: Knowing and understanding young children's characteristics and needs, from birth through age 8	■ Presents the "grand" theories of development: psychoanalytic, behaviorism/social learning, and cognitive/information processing. Includes a Thinking Critically feature on potential impact of toilet training methods.
(I and A) 1b: Knowing and understanding the multiple influences on early development and learning	■ Presents newer theories: Sociocultural (Vygotsky and beyond), humanism, and evolutionary theory.
	Chapter 3
(I and A) 1c: Using developmental knowledge to create healthy, respectful, supportive, and challenging learning environments for young children	■ Presents information about chromosomal and genetic variations that result in recognizable syndromes that effect children's biosocial, cognitive, and/or psychosocial development, including Down syndrome, hemophilia, fragile-X syndrome, sickle-cell anemia, cystic fibrosis, thalassemia.
	■ Includes a table of 20 common genetic diseases with a brief description of symptoms of each.
	Chapter 5
	■ Describes physical changes from birth to age 2.
	■ Discusses normal sleep patterns as well as sleep problems and their potential effects.

- Describes normal brain development over the first two years, including basic brain structures, formation of neuronal networks, and the impact of experience on brain development.

- Discusses the effect on brain development of lack of stimulation, stress, social deprivation, and shaken baby syndrome, as well as interventions for at-risk families.

- Discusses the development and role of the five senses; the difference between sensation and perception; maturation of the language areas of the cortex and its impact on language development; adaptation of the senses to the social world; the controversy over infants' perception of pain.

- Discusses development of gross and fine motor skills, including variations in the motor skills that are encouraged in different cultures.

- Discusses infants' nutritional needs, the benefits of breast-feeding, and the physical and cognitive effects of malnutrition.

Chapter 6

- Describes cognitive development in the first two years.

- Discusses Piaget's stages of sensorimotor intelligence.

- Discusses information-processing theory and aspects of infant memory.

- Describes language development in the first two years: the universal sequence of language acquisition, the naming explosion, and major theories of language learning.

Chapter 7

- Describes emotional development in infants and toddlers in the first two years.

- Discusses infants' emotions, including smiling and laughing, anger and sadness, fear (stranger wariness and separation anxiety). Discusses toddlers' emotions, including pride, shame, guilt, embarrassment, and the development of self-awareness.

- Discusses the role of brain maturation in supporting social impulses; abnormal brain development due to stress and the consequent negative impact on emotional development.

- Discusses the four types of temperament identified by the NYLS, the continuity and discontinuity of temperament, and the impact of temperament on caregiver–child relationships (including goodness of fit).

- Discusses theories of infant psychosocial development: psychoanalytic, behaviorism/social learning, cognitive (development of working models), sociocultural (ethnotheories and the impact of proximal and distal parenting).

- Discusses the development of social bonds, including synchrony, stages of attachment, types of attachment, and social referencing.

- Discusses types of nonmaternal day care, including characteristics of high-quality day care (adequate attention to each infant, encouragement of language and sensorimotor development, attention to health and safety, and warm and responsive professional caregivers; see also Table 7.3) and the effects of day care on infants and toddlers.

AGES 2 to 6

Chapter 8

- Describes typical growth patterns in early childhood, nutritional needs, the potential effects of nutritional problems (undernutrition, overweight, and obesity) on physical growth and cognitive functioning, and the importance of oral health.

- Discusses brain development, including a detailed diagram of the major brain structures (Figure 8.2).

- Discusses myelination, which speeds thought processes and reaction time.

- Discusses lateralization and the development of the corpus callosum; covers the difference-equals-deficit error in regard to left-handedness.

- Discusses ongoing maturation of the prefrontal cortex and resultant advances in neurological control; looks at cultural differences in impulsivity and perseveration.

- Discusses the maturing limbic system, with a detailed diagram of the HPA axis (Figure 8.5), practical advice for teachers regarding children's emotional reactions, and the effect of stress on the limbic system (excessive cortisol production and permanent deficits in learning and memory).

- Discusses improvement in motor skills in early childhood, with a table listing various skills or achievements and the approximate ages at which they normally develop; reflexes and activities that aid motor development; gender differences in timing of development of motor skills.

- Discusses environmental hazards that harm growing bodies and brains (pollution, lead, pesticides, BPA, cigarette smoke, and many others), impeding balance, finger dexterity, and motivation; discusses environmental risks in different cultural settings and notes the ties between risks and SES.

- Discusses three levels of prevention of avoidable injury, including provision of safe environments.

- Discusses the short- and long-term biosocial, cognitive, and psychosocial effects of child maltreatment, including sex abuse and neglect; notes warning signs of maltreatment.

Chapter 9

- Describes cognitive development from ages 2 to 6.

- Discusses characteristics of Piaget's preoperational thought (egocentrism, centration, focus on appearance, static reasoning, irreversibility, conservation, animism).

- Discusses elements of Vygotsky's theory of cognition (guided participation, zone of proximal development, scaffolding, private speech).

- Discusses pivotal importance of mentoring and language in a child's cognitive achievements, including accomplishments in understanding of numbers, logic, memory; influence of culture on proficiency with numbers.

- Discusses cognitive advances in early childhood, including theory-theory and theory of mind; the effects of brain maturation and culture on cognitive development.

- Describes language development from ages 2 to 6 (and the influences of brain maturation, myelination, scaffolding, and social interaction); vocabulary explosion, fast-mapping, acquisition of grammar, and learning two languages.

- Discusses the influence of culture and SES on language development.

- Early Childhood Education:

    - Discusses the influence on development of home and school environments; importance of the quality of home life and effectiveness of individual teachers.

    - Discusses characteristics of child-centered and teacher-directed programs, including the educational theories that underlie each approach and practical differences in children's daily experience in each type of environment.

    - Discusses the various intervention programs (Head Start and state-sponsored programs); cultural considerations in bilingual programs; and long-term gains from intensive programs.

Chapter 10

- Discusses children's achievement of emotional regulation.

- Discusses Erikson's stage of initiative versus guilt; protective optimism; aspects of the developing self-concept.

- Ties the emergence of initiative to brain maturation (specifically to myelination of the limbic system, growth of the prefrontal cortex, and longer attention span).

- Discusses intrinsic and extrinsic motivation and ways to encourage intrinsic motivation.

- Discusses cultural differences in which emotions children are expected to regulate as well as cultural differences in control strategies.

- A section on psychopathology discusses:

    - Internalizing and externalizing problems

    - Sex differences in emotional regulation

    - The impact of maltreatment on a child's ability to regulate emotions (and differences in the way boys and girls respond—boys by externalizing and girls by internalizing).

- A section on play discusses:

    - The importance of peer relationships in development of emotional regulation, empathy, and social understanding

- Cultural differences in play

- Parten's five types of play

- How active play advances planning and self-control; the theory that rough-and-tumble play advances development of the prefrontal cortex as children learn to practice social skills, regulate emotions, and strengthen their bodies.

- The benefits of sociodramatic play (children explore and rehearse social roles; learn how to explain their ideas and convince playmates to agree; practice emotional regulation by pretending to be afraid, angry brave, etc.; and develop self-concept in a non-threatening way.)

- Discusses Baumrind's caregiving styles and their characteristics as well as the impact of each style on the child; discusses cultural variations in caregiving styles and teachers' styles of interaction.

- Discusses pros and cons young children's exposure to electronic media.

- A section on moral development discusses:

  - Factors that result in development of empathy and antipathy, prosocial and antisocial behavior

  - The four major types of aggression

  - Disciplinary measures and their effects (physical punishment, psychological control, exclusion and conversation); cultural variations in discipline

- Discusses the distinction between sex differences and gender differences.

- Discusses major theories of gender-role development (psychoanalytic, behavioral, cognitive).

AGES 6 to 11

Chapter 11

- Describes normal growth pattern (slowdown in growth and increase in strength).

- Discusses improvements in medical care and the influence of children's health habits on development.

- Discusses benefits (and potential disadvantages) of physical activity; discusses physical, cognitive, and social impact of participation in neighborhood games, school exercise, and athletic clubs and leagues.

- A section on health problems discusses:

  - The increasing prevalence, causes, and consequences of childhood obesity (includes international and SES considerations)

  - Potential causes of asthmas; treatment and prevention

- A section on brain development discusses:

  - The "massively interconnected brain" that has developed by age 7 or 8

  - The results of this brain maturation, including increased speed of thought, faster reaction time (both mental and physical), longer attention span, and automatization of thoughts and actions

- A section on measurement of cognitive potential/abilities discusses:

  - The difference between aptitude and achievement

  - Assessment of aptitude and achievement through IQ and achievement tests, criticisms of testing (including cultural bias)

  - Gardner's nine types of intelligence

  - Brain scans and what they teach us about children's brain functioning

- A section on children with special needs discusses:

  - Four general principles of developmental psychopathology: (1) abnormality is normal, (2) disability changes year by year, (3) life may be better or worse in adulthood, and (4) diagnosis and treatment reflect the social context

  - Symptoms of ADHD and bipolar disorder; potential causes; treatments (including the controversy over drug therapy)

  - Diagnosis and treatment of learning disabilities (dyslexia, dyscalculia)

  - Symptoms, treatments, and impact of autism spectrum disorder

- Changing laws and practices with regard to special education
- Educating gifted and talented children

Chapter 12

- Discusses Piaget's concrete operational thought and the child's increasing ability to use logic in thinking; classification, transitive inference, and seriation.
- Discusses Vygotsky; the roles that social interaction and instruction play in children's cognitive development.
- Discusses the influence of culture and context on what, how, and when children learn.
- Discusses information-processing theory: sensory memory, working memory, and long-term memory (see Table 12.1 for advances in memory at different ages); the influence of children's knowledge base on their learning; development of control processes and metacognition.
- A section on language discusses:
  - Advances in vocabulary and grammatical constructions (use of prefixes, suffixes, compound words, phrases, figures of speech)
  - Understanding and use of metaphors
  - Pragmatics (the child's ability to adjust speech to the social context)
  - The effect of SES on a child's exposure to and acquisition of language
  - The impact of parents' and teachers' expectations on the child's acquisition of and proficiency with language
- A section on teaching and learning discusses:
  - Differences in curriculum by nation, by community, and by school subject (evident in the results of international tests; the mix of school subjects; and the relative power of parents, educators, and political leaders)
  - Benchmarks for achievement in math and reading at different ages (see At About This Time tables on p. 365)
  - The hidden curriculum (the implicit values and assumptions evident in course selection, schedules, tracking, teacher characteristics, discipline, teaching methods, sports competition, student government, extracurricular activities, etc.)
  - Learning a second language (immersion, bilingual education, ELL)
  - Gender differences in school performance
  - The phonics approach and the whole-language approach to reading
  - Determinants of educational practice (state governments, local jurisdictions, teachers, parents)
  - Types of schools in the U.S. (public, private, charter, home schooling) and characteristics of each

Chapter 13

- Discusses Erikson's fourth psychosocial crisis (industry versus inferiority) and the child's self-assessment as industrious or inferior; the relationship between productivity and self-control.
- Discusses Freud's latency period.
- Discusses ongoing development of self-concept (which includes children's ideas about their intelligence, personality, abilities, gender, and ethnic background) as self-concept becomes more specific and logical due to advances in cognitive development and social awareness.
- Discusses resilience and stress, and the effects of cumulative stress on all aspects of development (includes section on the importance of social support and the efficacy of religious faith).
- A section on moral reasoning discusses:
  - Kohlberg's levels of moral thought and criticisms of his research
  - The influence of peers, parents, and culture on children's development of moral values
  - Alignment with peers when peer values conflict with adult values
  - The morality of child labor

Standard 2. Building Family and Community Relationships

Key Elements of Standard 2

(I and A) 2a: Knowing about and understanding diverse family and community characteristics

(I and A) 2b: Supporting and engaging families and communities through respectful, reciprocal relationships

(I) 2c: Involving families and communities in young children's development and learning

- The importance of establishing and nurturing ties between the family and the community is evident throughout the text. Specific examples include the following.

Chapter 1

- Discusses Bronfenbrenner's ecological-systems approach and his insights about how elements of the overlapping systems affect development, and especially how elements of the microsystem—family, peer groups, classrooms, neighborhoods, houses of worship, etc.—interact to influence an individual's development.

Chapter 7

- Discusses the way in which early relationships help infants develop a working model, a set of assumptions about the world and how it works, that become a frame of reference for later life.

Chapter 8

- Discussion of prevention of avoidable injury includes measures that communities may take to ensure child safety.

Chapter 9

- Discusses the importance of good communication between school and home.

Chapter 10

- Discusses the role of communities in ensuring safe and adequate play spaces.

Chapter 11

- Discusses physical, cognitive, and social impact of participation in neighborhood games, school exercise, and athletic clubs and leagues.

- Discusses the connections between the state governments, local jurisdictions, teachers, and parents in determining what will be taught in schools and how it will be taught. Includes discussion of the variations by school district in identifying children with special needs (those who have difficulty learning as well as those who are gifted and talented) and providing appropriate educational environments for them.

Chapter 12

- Discusses Vygotsky; the roles of social interaction and instruction in children's cognitive development; the influence of culture and context on what, how, and when children learn; and the relative power of parents, educators, and political leaders in determining school curriculum.

- Discusses family and community influences on second-language learning and the effect that children's learning of a second language has on immigrant families.

Chapter 13

- Defines family structure and family function.

- Discusses the five major functions that families serve for children: (1) provide physical necessities, (2) support, encourage, and guide education, (3) provide opportunities for success that encourage children's self-respect, (4) foster friendships, and (5) provide harmony and stability in the home.

- Discusses the diversity of family structures (Table 13.2 describes family structures—Two-parent families: nuclear, extended, polygamous, step-parent, adoptive, grandparents alone, families of same-sex couples. Single-parent families: single mother, never married; single mother, divorced, separated, or widowed; single father; one grandparent alone).

- Discusses the ability/challenge of different structures in meeting the five family functions.

- Includes A View from Science feature on aspects of divorce and its potential effects on children.

- Discusses the effects of poverty on the family; explains the family stress model, including stresses experienced by children in low- and high-SES families.

- Discusses the effects of family conflict; includes a section on the importance of networks of social support and the efficacy of affiliation with religious institutions.

Standard 3. Observing, Documenting, and Assessing to Support Young Children and Families	▪ The importance of careful attention to a child's development in all three domains is evident throughout the text. The At About This Time tables, which appear in many chapters, highlight the ages at which children normally achieve certain physical, cognitive, and psychosocial benchmarks, providing a framework for assessment of individual children's progress in these areas.
Key Elements of Standard 3	**Chapter 12 (Academic performance)**
(I and A) 3a: Understanding the goals, benefits, and uses of assessment—including its use in development of appropriate goals, curriculum, and teaching strategies for young children	▪ This chapter discusses the following factors that affect assessment of individual students:
	▪ Differences in curriculum by nation, by community, and by school subject (evident in the results of international tests; the mix of school subjects; and the relative power of parents, educators, and political leaders)
(I) 3b: Knowing about assessment partnerships with families and with professional colleagues to build effective learning environments	▪ Benchmarks for achievement in math and reading at different ages (see At About This Time tables on p. 365)
	▪ The hidden curriculum (the implicit values and assumptions evident in course selection, schedules, tracking, teacher characteristics, discipline, teaching methods, sports competition, student government, extracurricular activities, etc.)
	▪ Learning a second language (immersion, bilingual education, ESL)
	▪ Gender differences in school performance
	▪ The phonics approach and the whole-language approach to reading
	▪ Determinants of educational practice (state governments, local jurisdictions, teachers, parents)
	▪ Types of schools in the U.S. (public, private, charter, home schooling) and characteristics of each
	▪ Discusses international standardized benchmarks of achievement in reading and mathematics for fourth-grade students (PIRLS and TIMMS, respectively).
	▪ Discusses goals and consequences of assessment under the No Child Left Behind Act of 2001.
	▪ Discusses the federally sponsored National Assessment of Educational Progress (NAEP) achievement tests in reading, mathematics, and other subjects.
Standard 4. Using Developmentally Effective Approaches	▪ The positive influence of warm, nurturing relationships and the negative influence of stressful relationships on every aspect of children's development are discussed throughout the text.
Key Elements of Standard 3	**Chapter 7**
(I and A) 4a: Understanding positive relationships and supportive interactions as the foundation of their work with young children	▪ Discusses sociocultural theory and the importance of culture and context on children's cognitive development.
(I and A) 4b: Knowing and understanding effective strategies and tools for early education, including appropriate uses of technology	**Chapter 9**
	▪ Discusses Vygotsky's theory of cognition, including the zone of proximal development and the efficacy of guided participation and scaffolding in supporting and encouraging children's learning.
	▪ Discusses pivotal importance of mentoring and language in a child's cognitive achievements, including accomplishments in understanding of numbers, logic, memory; influence of culture on proficiency with numbers.

Glossary

23rd pair The chromosome pair that, in humans, determines sex. The other 22 pairs are autosomes; inherited equally by males and females.

A

acceleration Educating gifted children alongside other children of the same mental, not chronological, age.

accommodation The restructuring of old ideas to include new experiences.

achievement test A measure of mastery or proficiency in reading, mathematics, writing, science, or some other subject.

adolescence-limited offender A person whose criminal activity stops by age 21.

adolescent egocentrism A characteristic of adolescent thinking that leads young people (ages 10 to 13) to focus on themselves to the exclusion of others.

adoption A legal proceeding in which an adult or couple unrelated to a child is granted the joys and obligations of being that child's parent(s).

adrenal glands Two glands, located above the kidneys, that produce hormones (including the "stress hormones" epinephrine [adrenaline] and norepinephrine).

affordance An opportunity for perception and interaction that is offered by a person, place, or object in the environment.

age of viability The age (about 22 weeks after conception) at which a fetus may survive outside the mother's uterus if specialized medical care is available.

aggressive-rejected Rejected by peers because of antagonistic, confrontational behavior.

allele A variation that makes a gene different in some way from other genes for the same characteristics. Many genes never vary; others have several possible alleles.

amygdala A tiny brain structure that registers emotions, particularly fear and anxiety.

analytic thought Thought that results from analysis, such as a systematic ranking of pros and cons, risks and consequences, possibilities and facts. Analytic thought depends on logic and rationality.

animism The belief that natural objects and phenomena are alive.

anorexia nervosa An eating disorder characterized by severe calorie restriction and the fear of being fat. Affected individuals undereat, or overeat and then overexercise or purge, depriving their vital organs of nutrition. Anorexia can be fatal.

anoxia A lack of oxygen that, if prolonged, can cause brain damage or death.

antipathy Feelings of dislike or even hatred for another person.

antisocial behavior Actions that are deliberately hurtful or destructive to another person.

Apgar scale A quick assessment of a newborn's health. The baby's color, heart rate, reflexes, muscle tone, and respiratory effort are given a score of 0, 1, or 2 twice—at one minute and five minutes after birth—and each time the total of all five scores is compared with the maximum score of 10 (rarely attained).

apprenticeship in thinking Vygotsky's term for how cognition is stimulated and developed in people by more skilled members of society.

aptitude The potential to master a specific skill or to learn a certain body of knowledge.

assimilation The reinterpretation of new experiences to fit into old ideas.

assisted reproductive technology (ART) A general term for the techniques designed to help infertile couples conceive and then sustain a pregnancy.

asthma A chronic disease of the respiratory system in which inflammation narrows the airways from the nose and mouth to the lungs, causing difficulty in breathing. Signs and symptoms include wheezing, shortness of breath, chest tightness, and coughing.

attachment According to Ainsworth, an affectional tie that an infant forms with a caregiver—a tie that binds them together in space and endures over time.

attention-deficit/hyperactivity disorder (ADHD) A condition characterized by a persistent pattern of inattention and/or by hyperactive or impulsive behaviors; ADHD interferes with a person's functioning or development.

authoritarian parenting An approach to child rearing that is characterized by high behavioral standards, strict punishment of misconduct, and little communication.

authoritative parenting An approach to child rearing in which the parents set limits but listen to the child and are flexible.

autism spectrum disorder A developmental disorder marked by difficulty with social communication and interaction—including difficulty seeing things from another person's point of view—and restricted, repetitive patterns of behavior, interests, or activities.

automatization A process in which repetition of a sequence of thoughts and actions makes the sequence routine, so that it no longer requires conscious thought.

autonomy versus shame and doubt Erikson's second crisis of psychosocial development. Toddlers either succeed or fail in gaining a sense of self-rule over their own actions and bodies.

axon A fiber that extends from a neuron and transmits electrochemical impulses from that neuron to the dendrites of other neurons.

B

babbling An infant's repetition of certain syllables, such as *ba-ba-ba*, that begins when babies are between 6 and 9 months old.

balanced bilingual A person who is fluent in two languages, not favoring one over the other.

base rate neglect A common fallacy in which a person ignores the overall frequency of some behavior or characteristic (called the *base rate*) in making a decision. For example, a person might bet on a "lucky" lottery number without considering the odds that that number will be selected.

behavioral teratogens Agents and conditions that can harm the prenatal brain, impairing the future child's intellectual and emotional functioning.

behaviorism A grand theory of human development that studies observable behavior. Behaviorism is also called *learning theory* because it describes the laws and processes by which behavior is learned.

bickering Petty, peevish arguing, usually repeated and ongoing.

Big Five The five basic clusters of personality traits that remain quite stable throughout life: openness, conscientiousness, extroversion, agreeableness, and neuroticism.

bilingual schooling A strategy in which school subjects are taught in both the learner's original language and the second (majority) language.

binocular vision The ability to focus the two eyes in a coordinated manner in order to see one image. This ability is absent at birth.

biopsychosocial A term emphasizing the interaction of the three developmental domains (biosocial, cognitive, and psychosocial). All development is biopsychosocial, although the domains are studied separately.

bipolar disorder A condition characterized by extreme mood swings, from euphoria to deep depression, not caused by outside experiences.

BMI (body mass index) A person's weight in kilograms divided by the square of height in meters.

body image A person's idea of how his or her body looks.

Brazelton Neonatal Behavioral Assessment Scale (NBAS) A test often administered to newborns that measures responsiveness and records 46 behaviors, including 20 reflexes.

bulimia nervosa An eating disorder characterized by binge eating and subsequent purging, usually by induced vomiting and/or use of laxatives.

bullying aggression Unprovoked, repeated physical or verbal attack, especially on victims who are unlikely to defend themselves.

bullying Repeated, systematic efforts to inflict harm through physical, verbal, or social attack on a weaker person.

bully-victim Someone who attacks others and who is attacked as well. (Also called *provocative victims* because they do things that elicit bullying.)

C

carrier A person whose genotype includes a gene that is not expressed in the phenotype. The carried gene occurs in half of the carrier's gametes and thus is passed on to half of the carrier's children. If such a gene is inherited from both parents, the characteristic appears in the phenotype.

center day care Child care that occurs in a place especially designed for the purpose, where several paid adults care for many children. Usually the children are grouped by age, the day-care center is licensed, and providers are trained and certified in child development.

centration A characteristic of preoperational thought in which a young child focuses (centers) on one idea, excluding all others.

cerebral palsy A disorder that results from damage to the brain's motor centers. People with cerebral palsy have difficulty with muscle control, so their speech and/or body movements are impaired.

cesarean section (c-section) A surgical birth, in which incisions through the mother's abdomen and uterus allow the fetus to be removed quickly, instead of being delivered through the vagina. (Also called simply *section*.)

charter school A public school with its own set of standards that is funded and licensed by the state or local district in which it is located.

child abuse Deliberate action that is harmful to a child's physical, emotional, or sexual well-being.

child culture The particular habits, styles, and values that reflect the set of rules and rituals that characterize children as distinct from adult society.

child maltreatment Intentional harm to or avoidable endangerment of anyone under 18 years of age.

child neglect Failure to meet a child's basic physical, educational, or emotional needs.

child sexual abuse Any erotic activity that arouses an adult and excites, shames, or confuses a child, whether or not the victim protests and whether or not genital contact is involved.

child-directed speech The high-pitched, simplified, and repetitive way adults speak to infants and children. (Also called *baby talk* or *motherese*.)

chromosome One of the 46 molecules of DNA (in 23 pairs) that virtually each cell of the human body contains and that, together, contain all the genes. Other species have more or fewer chromosomes.

circadian rhythm A day–night cycle of biological activity that occurs approximately every 24 hours (*circadian* means "about a day").

classical conditioning The learning process in which a meaningful stimulus (such as the smell of food to a hungry animal) is connected with a neutral stimulus (such as the sound of a tone) that had no special meaning before conditioning. (Also called *respondent conditioning*.)

classification The logical principle that things can be organized into groups (or categories or classes) according to some characteristic they have in common.

clinical depression Feelings of hopelessness, lethargy, and worthlessness that last two weeks or more.

cluster suicides Several suicides committed by members of a group within a brief period of time.

code of ethics A set of moral principles or guidelines that members of a profession or group are expected to follow.

cognitive equilibrium In cognitive theory, a state of mental balance in which people are not confused because they can use their existing thought processes to understand current experiences and ideas.

cognitive theory A grand theory of human development that focuses on changes in how people think over time. According to this theory, our thoughts shape our attitudes, beliefs, and behaviors.

cohabitation An arrangement in which a couple live together in a committed romantic relationship but are not formally married.

cohort People born within the same historical period who therefore move through life together, experiencing the same events, new technologies, and cultural shifts at the same ages. For example, the effect of the Internet varies depending on what cohort a person belongs to.

cohort-sequential research A research design in which researchers first study several groups of people of different ages (a cross-sectional approach) and then follow those groups over the years (a longitudinal approach). (Also called *cross-sequential research* or *time-sequential research*.)

comorbid Refers to the presence of two or more unrelated disease conditions at the same time in the same person.

concrete operational thought Piaget's term for the ability to reason logically about direct experiences and perceptions.

conditioning According to behaviorism, the processes by which responses become linked to particular stimuli and learning takes place. The word *conditioning* is used to emphasize the importance of repeated practice, as when an athlete conditions his or her body to perform well by training for a long time.

conservation The principle that the amount of a substance remains the same (i.e., is conserved) even when its appearance changes.

control processes Mechanisms (including selective attention, metacognition, and emotional regulation) that combine memory, processing speed, and knowledge to regulate the analysis and flow of information within the information-processing system. (Also called *executive processes*.)

conventional moral reasoning Kohlberg's second level of moral reasoning, emphasizing social rules.

copy number variations Genes with various repeats or deletions of base pairs.

corpus callosum A long, thick band of nerve fibers that connects the left and right hemispheres of the brain and allows communication between them.

correlation A number between +1.0 and −1.0 that indicates the degree of relationship between two variables, expressed in terms of the likelihood that one variable will (or will not) occur when the other variable does (or does not). A correlation indicates only that two variables are somehow related, not that one variable causes the other to occur.

cortex The outer layers of the brain in humans and other mammals. Most thinking, feeling, and sensing involve the cortex. (Sometimes called the *neocortex*.)

co-sleeping A custom in which parents and their children (usually infants) sleep together in the same room.

couvade Symptoms of pregnancy and birth experienced by fathers.

critical period A time when a particular type of developmental growth (in body or behavior) must happen for normal development to occur.

cross-sectional research A research design that compares groups of people who differ in age but are similar in other important characteristics.

culture A system of shared beliefs, norms, behaviors, and expectations that persist over time and prescribe social behavior and assumptions.

cutting An addictive form of self-mutilation that is most prevalent among adolescent girls and that correlates with depression and drug abuse.

cyberbullying Bullying that occurs when one person spreads insults or rumors about another by means of e-mails, text messages, or cell phone videos.

D

deductive reasoning Reasoning from a general statement, premise, or principle, through logical steps, to figure out (deduce) specifics. (Also called *top-down reasoning*.)

deferred imitation A sequence in which an infant first perceives something done by someone else and then performs the same action hours or even days later.

dendrite A fiber that extends from a neuron and receives electrochemical impulses transmitted from other neurons via their axons.

deoxyribonucleic acid (DNA) The chemical composition of the molecules that contain the genes, which are the chemical instructions for cells to manufacture various proteins.

dependent variable In an experiment, the variable that may change as a result of whatever new condition or situation the experimenter adds. In other words, the dependent variable *depends* on the independent variable.

developmental psychopathology The field that uses insights into typical development to understand and remediate developmental disorders.

developmental theory A group of ideas, assumptions, and generalizations that interpret and illuminate the thousands of observations that have been made about human growth. A developmental theory provides a framework for explaining the patterns and problems of development.

deviancy training Destructive peer support in which one person shows another how to rebel against authority or social norms.

difference-equals-deficit error The mistaken belief that a deviation from some norm is necessarily inferior to behavior or characteristics that meet the standard.

disorganized attachment A type of attachment (type D) that is marked by an infant's inconsistent reactions to the caregiver's departure and return.

disruptive mood dysregulation disorder (DMDD) A condition in which a child has chronic irritability and anger that culminates in frequent tantrums that are inappropriate to the circumstances and to the child's age.

distal parenting Caregiving practices that involve remaining distant from a baby, providing toys, food, and face-to-face communication with minimal holding and touching.

dizygotic (DZ) twins Twins who are formed when two separate ova are fertilized by two separate sperm at roughly the same time. (Also called *fraternal twins*.)

dominant–recessive pattern The interaction of a heterozygous pair of alleles in such a way that the phenotype reflects one allele (the dominant gene) more than the other (the recessive gene).

doula A woman who helps with the birth process. Traditionally in Latin America, a doula was the only professional who attended childbirth. Now doulas are likely to arrive at the woman's home during early labor and later work alongside a hospital's staff.

Down syndrome A condition in which a person has 47 chromosomes instead of the usual 46, with 3 rather than 2 chromosomes at the 21st site. People with Down syndrome typically have distinctive characteristics, including unusual facial features, heart abnormalities, and language difficulties. (Also called *trisomy-21*.)

drug abuse The ingestion of a drug to the extent that it impairs the user's biological or psychological well-being.

dual-process model The notion that two networks exist within the human brain, one for emotional and one for analytical processing of stimuli.

dynamic perception Perception that is primed to focus on movement and change.

dynamic systems A view of human development as an ongoing, ever-changing interaction between the physical, cognitive, and psychosocial influences. The crucial understanding is that development is never static but is always affected by, and affects, many systems of development.

dyslexia Unusual difficulty with reading; thought to be the result of some neurological underdevelopment.

E

eclectic perspective The approach taken by most developmentalists, in which they apply aspects of each of the various theories of development rather than adhering exclusively to one theory.

ecological-systems approach A perspective on human development that considers all the influences from the various contexts of development. (Later renamed *bioecological theory*.)

effortful control The ability to regulate one's emotions and actions through effort, not simply through natural inclination.

egocentrism Piaget's term for children's tendency to think about the world entirely from their own personal perspective.

Electra complex The unconscious desire of girls to replace their mother and win their father's romantic love.

ELLs (English Language Learners) Children in the United States whose proficiency in English is low—usually below a cut-off score on an oral or written test. This term replaces *ESL* (English as a Second Language) because many children who primarily speak a non-English language at home are also capable in English; they are *not* ELLs.

embryo The name for a developing human organism from about the third through the eighth week after conception.

embryonic period The stage of prenatal development from approximately the third through the eighth week after conception, during which the basic forms of all body structures, including internal organs, develop.

emerging adulthood The period of life between the ages of 18 and 25. Emerging adulthood is now widely thought of as a separate developmental stage.

emotional regulation The ability to control when and how emotions are expressed.

empathy The ability to understand the emotions and concerns of another person, especially when they differ from one's own.

empirical Based on observation, experience, or experiment; not theoretical.

entity approach to intelligence An approach to understanding intelligence that sees ability as innate, a fixed quantity present at birth; those who hold this view do not believe that effort enhances achievement.

epigenetic Referring to environmental factors that affect genes and genetic expression—enhancing, halting, shaping, or altering the expression of genes and resulting in a phenotype that may differ markedly from the genotype.

equifinality A basic principle of developmental psychopathology that holds that one symptom can have many causes.

estradiol A sex hormone, considered the chief estrogen. Females produce much more estradiol than males do.

ethnic group People whose ancestors were born in the same region and who often share a language, culture, and religion.

ethnotheory A theory that underlies the values and practices of a culture but is not usually apparent to the people within the culture.

experience-dependent brain functions Brain functions that depend on particular, variable experiences and that therefore may or may not develop in a particular infant.

experience-expectant brain functions Brain functions that require certain basic common experiences (which an infant can be expected to have) in order to develop normally.

explicit memory Memory that is easy to retrieve on demand (as in a specific test). Most explicit memory involves consciously learned words, data, and concepts.

extended family A family of three or more generations living in one household.

externalizing problems Difficulty with emotional regulation that involves expressing powerful feelings through uncontrolled physical or verbal outbursts, as by lashing out at other people or breaking things.

extreme sports Forms of recreation that include apparent risk of injury or death and that are attractive and thrilling as a result.

extremely low birthweight (ELBW) A body weight at birth of less than 2 pounds, 3 ounces (1,000 grams).

extrinsic motivation A drive, or reason to pursue a goal, that arises from the need to have one's achievements rewarded from outside, perhaps by receiving material possessions or another person's esteem.

F

false positive The result of a laboratory test that reports something as true when in fact it is not true. This can occur for pregnancy tests, when a woman might not be pregnant even though the test says she is, or during pregnancy when a problem is reported that actually does not exist.

family day care Child care that occurs in the home of someone to whom the child is not related and who usually cares for several children of various ages.

family function The way a family works to meet the needs of its members. Children need families to provide basic material necessities, to encourage learning, to help them develop self-respect, to nurture friendships, and to foster harmony and stability.

family structure The legal and genetic relationships among relatives living in the same home; includes nuclear family, extended family, stepfamily, and so on.

fast-mapping The speedy and sometimes imprecise way in which children learn new words by tentatively placing them in mental categories according to their perceived meaning.

fetal alcohol syndrome (FAS) A cluster of birth defects, including abnormal facial characteristics, slow physical growth, and retarded mental development, that may occur in the fetus of a woman who drinks alcohol while pregnant.

fetal period The stage of prenatal development from the ninth week after conception until birth, during which the fetus gains about 7 pounds (more than 3,000 grams) and organs become more mature, gradually able to function on their own.

fetus The name for a developing human organism from the start of the ninth week after conception until birth.

fine motor skills Physical abilities involving small body movements, especially of the hands and fingers, such as drawing and picking up a coin. (The word *fine* here means "small.")

Flynn effect The rise in average IQ scores that has occurred over the decades in many nations.

fMRI Functional magnetic resonance imaging, a measuring technique in which the brain's electrical excitement indicates activation anywhere in the brain; fMRI helps researchers locate neurological responses to stimuli.

focus on appearance A characteristic of preoperational thought in which a young child ignores all attributes that are not apparent.

foreclosure Erikson's term for premature identity formation, which occurs when an adolescent adopts parents' or society's roles and values wholesale, without questioning or analysis.

formal operational thought In Piaget's theory, the fourth and final stage of cognitive development, characterized by more systematic logical thinking and by the ability to understand and systematically manipulate abstract concepts.

foster care A legal, publicly supported system in which a maltreated child is removed from the parents' custody and entrusted to another adult or family, which is reimbursed for expenses incurred in meeting the child's needs.

fragile X syndrome A genetic disorder in which part of the X chromosome seems to be attached to the rest of it by a very thin string of molecules. The cause is a single gene that has more than 200 repetitions of one triplet.

G

gamete A reproductive cell; that is, a sperm or ovum that can produce a new individual if it combines with a gamete from the other sex to make a zygote.

gender differences Differences in the roles and behaviors of males and females that are prescribed by the culture.

gender identity A person's acceptance of the roles and behaviors that society associates with the biological categories of male and female.

gender schema A cognitive concept or general belief based on one's experiences—in this case, a child's understanding of sex differences.

gene A small section of a chromosome; the basic unit for the transmission of heredity. A gene consists of a string of chemicals that provide instructions for the cell to manufacture certain proteins.

generational forgetting The idea that each new generation forgets what the previous generation learned. As used here, the term refers to knowledge about the harm drugs can do.

genetic counseling Consultation and testing by trained experts that enable individuals to learn about their genetic heritage, including harmful conditions that they might pass along to any children they may conceive.

genome The full set of genes that are the instructions to make an individual member of a certain species.

genotype An organism's entire genetic inheritance, or genetic potential.

germinal period The first two weeks of prenatal development after conception, characterized by rapid cell division and the beginning of cell differentiation.

gonads The paired sex glands (ovaries in females, testicles in males). The gonads produce hormones and gametes.

goodness of fit A similarity of temperament and values that produces a smooth interaction between an individual and his or her social context, including family, school, and community.

grammar All the methods—word order, verb forms, and so on—that languages use to communicate meaning, apart from the words themselves.

gross motor skills Physical abilities involving large body movements, such as walking and jumping. (The word *gross* here means "big.")

growth spurt The relatively sudden and rapid physical growth that occurs during puberty. Each body part increases in size on a schedule: Weight usually precedes height, and growth of the limbs precedes growth of the torso.

guided participation The process by which people learn from others who guide their experiences and explorations.

H

habituation The process of becoming accustomed to an object or event through repeated exposure to it, and thus becoming less interested in it.

Head Start A federally funded early-childhood intervention program for low-income children of preschool age.

head-sparing A biological mechanism that protects the brain when malnutrition affects body growth. The brain is the last part of the body to be damaged by malnutrition.

heritability A statistic that indicates what percentage of the variation in a particular trait within a particular population, in a particular context and era, can be traced to genes.

heterozygous Referring to two genes of one pair that differ in some way. Typically one allele has only a few base pairs that differ from the other member of the pair.

hidden curriculum The unofficial, unstated, or implicit rules and priorities that influence the academic curriculum and every other aspect of learning in a school.

high-stakes test An evaluation that is critical in determining success or failure. If a single test determines whether a student will graduate or be promoted, it is a high-stakes test.

hippocampus A brain structure that is a central processor of memory, especially memory for locations.

holophrase A single word that is used to express a complete, meaningful thought.

home schooling Education in which children are taught at home, usually by their parents.

homozygous Referring to two genes of one pair that are exactly the same in every letter of their code. Most gene pairs are homozygous.

hormone An organic chemical substance that is produced by one body tissue and conveyed via the bloodstream to another to affect some physiological function.

HPA (hypothalamus–pituitary–adrenal) axis A sequence of hormone production originating in the hypothalamus and moving to the pituitary and then to the adrenal glands.

HPG (hypothalamus–pituitary–gonad) axis A sequence of hormone production originating in the hypothalamus and moving to the pituitary and then to the gonads.

Human Genome Project An international effort to map the complete human genetic code. This effort was essentially completed in 2001, though analysis is ongoing.

humanism A theory that stresses the potential of all humans for good and the belief that all people have the same basic needs, regardless of culture, gender, or background.

hypothalamus A brain area that responds to the amygdala and the hippocampus to produce hormones that activate other parts of the brain and body.

hypothesis A specific prediction that can be tested.

hypothetical thought Reasoning that includes propositions and possibilities that may not reflect reality.

I

identification An attempt to defend one's self-concept by taking on the behaviors and attitudes of someone else.

identity achievement Erikson's term for the attainment of identity, or the point at which a person understands who he or she is as a unique individual, in accord with past experiences and future plans.

identity versus role confusion Erikson's term for the fifth stage of development, in which the person tries to figure out "Who am I?" but is confused as to which of many possible roles to adopt.

imaginary audience The other people who, in an adolescent's egocentric belief, are watching and taking note of his or her appearance, ideas, and behavior. This belief makes many teenagers very self-conscious.

imaginary friends Make-believe friends who exist only in a child's imagination; increasingly common from ages 3 through 7, they combat loneliness and aid emotional regulation.

immersion A strategy in which instruction in all school subjects occurs in the second (usually the majority) language that a child is learning.

immunization The process of protecting a person against a disease, via antibodies. Immunization can happen naturally, when someone survives a disease, or medically, usually via a small dose of the virus that stimulates the production of antibodies and thus renders a person immune. (Also called *vaccination.*)

implantation The process, beginning about 10 days after conception, in which the developing organism burrows into the placenta that lines the uterus, where it can be nourished and protected as it continues to develop.

implicit memory Unconscious or automatic memory that is usually stored via habits, emotional responses, routine procedures, and various sensations.

in vitro fertilization (IVF) Fertilization that takes place outside a woman's body (as in a glass laboratory dish). The procedure involves mixing sperm with ova that have been surgically removed from the woman's ovary. If a zygote is produced, it is inserted into a woman's uterus, where it may implant and develop into a baby.

incremental approach to intelligence An approach to understanding intelligence that holds that intelligence can be directly increased by effort; those who subscribe to this view believe they can master whatever they seek to learn if they pay attention, participate in class, study, complete their homework, and so on.

independent variable In an experiment, the variable that is introduced to see what effect it has on the dependent variable. (Also called *experimental variable.*)

individual education plan (IEP) A document that specifies educational goals and plans for a child with special needs.

inductive reasoning Reasoning from one or more specific experiences or facts to reach (induce) a general conclusion. (Also called *bottom-up reasoning.*)

industry versus inferiority The fourth of Erikson's eight psychosocial crises, during which children attempt to master many skills, developing a sense of themselves as either industrious or inferior, competent or incompetent.

information-processing theory A perspective that compares human thinking processes, by analogy, to computer analysis of data, including sensory input, connections, stored memories, and output.

initiative versus guilt Erikson's third psychosocial crisis, in which children undertake new skills and activities and feel guilty when they do not succeed at them.

injury control/harm reduction Practices that are aimed at anticipating, controlling, and preventing dangerous activities; these practices reflect the beliefs that accidents are not random and that injuries can be made less harmful if proper controls are in place.

insecure-avoidant attachment A pattern of attachment (type A) in which an infant avoids connection with the caregiver, as when the infant seems not to care about the caregiver's presence, departure, or return.

insecure-resistant/ambivalent attachment A pattern of attachment (type C) in which anxiety and uncertainty are evident, as when an infant becomes very upset at separation from the caregiver and both resists and seeks contact on reunion.

Institutional Review Board (IRB) A group within most educational and medical institutions who ensure that research follows established ethical guidelines. Unlike in prior decades, most research in human development cannot begin without IRB approval.

instrumental aggression Behavior that hurts someone else because the aggressor wants to get or keep a possession or a privilege.

internalizing problems Difficulty with emotional regulation that involves turning one's emotional distress inward, as by feeling excessively guilty, ashamed, or worthless.

intimacy versus isolation The sixth of Erikson's eight stages of development. Adults seek someone with whom to share their lives in an enduring and self-sacrificing commitment. Without such commitment they risk profound loneliness and isolation.

intrinsic motivation A drive, or reason to pursue a goal, that comes from inside a person, such as the need to feel smart or competent.

intuitive thought Thought that arises from an emotion or a hunch, beyond rational explanation, and is influenced by past experiences and cultural assumptions.

invincibility fable An adolescent's egocentric conviction that he or she cannot be overcome or even harmed by anything that might defeat a normal mortal, such as unprotected sex, drug abuse, or high-speed driving.

IQ test A test designed to measure intellectual aptitude, or ability to learn in school. Originally, intelligence was defined as mental age divided by chronological age, times 100—hence the term *intelligence quotient, or IQ.*

irreversibility A characteristic of preoperational thought in which a young child thinks that nothing can be undone. A thing cannot be restored to the way it was before a change occurred.

K

kangaroo care A form of newborn care in which mothers (and sometimes fathers) rest their babies on their naked chests, like kangaroo mothers that carry their immature newborns in a pouch on their abdomen.

kinship care A form of foster care in which a relative of a maltreated child, usually a grandparent, becomes the approved caregiver.

knowledge base A body of knowledge in a particular area that makes it easier to master new information in that area.

kwashiorkor A disease of chronic malnutrition during childhood, in which a protein deficiency makes the child more vulnerable to other diseases, such as measles, diarrhea, and influenza.

L

language acquisition device (LAD) Chomsky's term for a hypothesized mental structure that enables humans to learn language, including the basic aspects of grammar, vocabulary, and intonation.

latency Freud's term for middle childhood, during which children's emotional drives and psychosexual needs are quiet (latent). Freud thought that sexual conflicts from earlier stages are only temporarily submerged, bursting forth again at puberty.

lateralization Literally, sidedness, referring to the specialization in certain functions by each side of the brain, with one side dominant for each activity. The left side of the brain controls the right side of the body, and vice versa.

learning disability (specific learning disorder) A marked deficit in a particular area of learning that is not caused by an apparent physical disability, by intellectual disability, or by an unusually stressful home environment.

least restrictive environment (LRE) A legal requirement that children with special needs be assigned to the most general educational context in which they can be expected to learn.

leptin A hormone that affects appetite and is believed to affect the onset of puberty. Leptin levels increase during childhood and peak at around age 12.

life-course-persistent offender A person whose criminal activity typically begins in early adolescence and continues throughout life; a career criminal.

linked lives Lives in which the success, health, and well-being of each family member are connected to those of other members, including members of another generation, as in the relationship between parents and children.

"little scientist" The stage-five toddler (age 12 to 18 months) who experiments without anticipating the results, using trial and error in active and creative exploration.

longitudinal research A research design in which the same individuals are followed over time, as their development is repeatedly assessed.

long-term memory The component of the information-processing system in which virtually limitless amounts of information can be stored indefinitely.

low birthweight (LBW) A body weight at birth of less than 5½ pounds (2,500 grams).

M

marasmus A disease of severe protein-calorie malnutrition during early infancy, in which growth stops, body tissues waste away, and the infant eventually dies.

menarche A girl's first menstrual period, signaling that she has begun ovulation. Pregnancy is biologically possible, but ovulation and menstruation are often irregular for years after menarche.

metacognition "Thinking about thinking," or the ability to evaluate a cognitive task in order to determine how best to accomplish it, and then to monitor and adjust one's performance on that task.

middle childhood The period between early childhood and early adolescence, approximately from ages 6 to 11.

middle school A school for children in the grades between elementary and high school. Middle school usually begins with grade 6 and ends with grade 8.

mirror neurons Cells in an observer's brain that are activated by watching an action performed by someone else as they would be if the observer had personally performed that action.

modeling The central process of social learning, by which a person observes the actions of others and then copies them.

monozygotic (MZ) twins Twins who originate from one zygote that splits apart very early in development. (Also called *identical twins*.) Other monozygotic multiple births (such as triplets and quadruplets) can occur as well.

Montessori schools Schools that offer early-childhood education based on the philosophy of Maria Montessori, which emphasizes careful work and tasks that each young child can do.

moratorium An adolescent's choice of a socially acceptable way to postpone making identity-achievement decisions. Going to college is a common example.

motor skills The learned abilities to move some part of the body, in actions ranging from a large leap to a flicker of the eyelid. (The word *motor* here refers to movement of muscles.)

multifactorial Referring to a trait that is affected by many factors, both genetic and environmental, that enhance, halt, shape, or alter the expression of genes, resulting in a phenotype that may differ markedly from the genotype.

multifinality A basic principle of developmental psychopathology that holds that one cause can have many (multiple) final manifestations.

multiple intelligences The idea that human intelligence is comprised of a varied set of abilities rather than a single, all-encompassing one.

myelination The process by which axons become coated with myelin, a fatty substance that speeds the transmission of nerve impulses from neuron to neuron.

N

naming explosion A sudden increase in an infant's vocabulary, especially in the number of nouns, that begins at about 18 months of age.

National Assessment of Educational Progress (NAEP) An ongoing and nationally representative measure of U.S. children's achievement in reading, mathematics, and other subjects over time; nicknamed "the Nation's Report Card."

nature In development, nature refers to the traits, capacities, and limitations that each individual inherits genetically from his or her parents at the moment of conception.

neglectful/uninvolved parenting An approach to child rearing in which the parents are indifferent toward their children and unaware of what is going on in their children's lives.

neurons The billions of nerve cells in the central nervous system, especially the brain.

No Child Left Behind Act A U.S. law enacted in 2001 that was intended to increase accountability in education by requiring states to qualify for federal educational funding by administering standardized tests to measure school achievement.

norm An average, or typical, standard of behavior or accomplishment, such as the norm for age of walking or the norm for greeting a stranger.

nuclear family A family that consists of a father, a mother, and their biological children under age 18.

nurture In development, nurture includes all the environmental influences that affect the individual after conception. This includes everything from the mother's nutrition while pregnant to the cultural influences in the nation.

O

obesity In a child, having a BMI above the 95th percentile, according to the U.S. Centers for Disease Control's 1980 standards for children of a given age.

object permanence The realization that objects (including people) still exist when they can no longer be seen, touched, or heard.

Oedipus complex The unconscious desire of young boys to replace their father and win their mother's romantic love.

operant conditioning The learning process by which a particular action is followed by something desired (which makes the person or animal more likely to repeat the action) or by something unwanted (which makes the action less likely to be repeated). (Also called *instrumental conditioning*.)

overimitation When a person imitates an action that is not a relevant part of the behavior to be learned. Overimitation is common among 2- to 6-year-olds when they imitate adult actions that are irrelevant and inefficient.

overregularization The application of rules of grammar even when exceptions occur, making the language seem more "regular" than it actually is.

overweight In a child, having a BMI above the 85th percentile, according to the U.S. Centers for Disease Control's 1980 standards for children of a given age.

P

parasuicide Any potentially lethal action against the self that does not result in death. (Also called *attempted suicide* or *failed suicide*.)

parental alliance Cooperation between a mother and a father based on their mutual commitment to their children. In a parental alliance, the parents support each other in their shared parental roles.

parental monitoring Parents' ongoing awareness of what their children are doing, where, and with whom.

parent–infant bond The strong, loving connection that forms as parents hold, examine, and feed their newborn.

peer pressure Encouragement to conform to one's friends or contemporaries in behavior, dress, and attitude; usually considered a negative force, as when adolescent peers encourage one another to defy adult authority.

people preference A universal principle of infant perception, specifically an innate attraction to other humans, evident in visual, auditory, and other preferences.

percentile A point on a ranking scale of 0 to 100. The 50th percentile is the midpoint; half the people in the population being studied rank higher and half rank lower.

perception The mental processing of sensory information when the brain interprets a sensation. Perception occurs in the cortex.

permanency planning An effort by child-welfare authorities to find a long-term living situation that will provide stability and support for a maltreated child. A goal is to avoid repeated changes of caregiver or school, which can be particularly harmful to the child.

permissive parenting An approach to child rearing that is characterized by high nurturance and communication but little discipline, guidance, or control. (Also called *indulgent parenting*.)

perseveration The tendency to persevere in, or stick to, one thought or action for a long time.

personal fable An aspect of adolescent egocentrism characterized by an adolescent's belief that his or her thoughts, feelings, and experiences are unique, more wonderful or awful than anyone else's.

phallic stage Freud's third stage of development, when the penis becomes the focus of concern and pleasure.

phenotype The observable characteristics of a person, including appearance, personality, intelligence, and all other traits.

phenylketonuria (PKU) A genetic disorder in which a child's body is unable to metabolize an amino acid called phenylalanine. Unless the infant immediately begins a special diet, the resulting buildup of phenylalanine in body fluids causes brain damage, progressive mental retardation, and other symptoms.

phonics approach Teaching reading by first teaching the sounds of each letter and of various letter combinations.

PISA (Programme for International Student Assessment) An international test taken by 15-year-olds in 50 nations that is designed to measure problem solving and cognition in daily life.

pituitary A gland in the brain that responds to a signal from the hypothalamus by producing many hormones, including those that regulate growth and that control other glands, among them the adrenal and sex glands.

plasticity The idea that abilities, personality, and other human characteristics can change over time. Plasticity is particularly evident during childhood, but even older adults are not always "set in their ways."

polygamous family A family consisting of one man, several wives, and their children.

polygenic Referring to a trait that is influenced by many genes.

postconventional moral reasoning Kohlberg's third level of moral reasoning, emphasizing moral principles.

postformal thought A proposed adult stage of cognitive development, following Piaget's four stages. Postformal thought goes beyond adolescent thinking by being more practical, more flexible, and more dialectical (i.e., more capable of combining contradictory elements into a comprehensive whole).

postpartum depression A new mother's feelings of inadequacy and sadness in the days and weeks after giving birth.

post-traumatic stress disorder (PTSD) An anxiety disorder that develops as a delayed reaction to having experienced or witnessed a profoundly shocking or frightening event, such as rape, severe beating, war, or natural disaster. Its symptoms may include flashbacks to the event, hyperactivity and hypervigilance, displaced anger, sleeplessness, nightmares, sudden terror or anxiety, and confusion between fantasy and reality.

pragmatics The practical use of language that includes the ability to adjust language communication according to audience and context.

preconventional moral reasoning Kohlberg's first level of moral reasoning, emphasizing rewards and punishments.

prefrontal cortex The area of cortex at the front of the brain that specializes in anticipation, planning, and impulse control.

preoperational intelligence Piaget's term for cognitive development between the ages of about 2 and 6; it includes language and imagination (which involve symbolic thought), but logical, operational thinking is not yet possible at this stage.

preterm A birth that occurs 3 or more weeks before the full 38 weeks of the typical pregnancy—that is, at 35 or fewer weeks after conception.

primary circular reactions The first of three types of feedback loops in sensorimotor intelligence, this one involving the infant's own body. The infant senses motion, sucking, noise, and other stimuli and tries to understand them.

primary prevention Actions that change overall background conditions to prevent some unwanted event or circumstance, such as injury, disease, or abuse.

primary sex characteristics The parts of the body that are directly involved in reproduction, including the vagina, uterus, ovaries, testicles, and penis.

private school A school funded by tuition charges, endowments, and often religious or other non-profit sponsors.

private speech The internal dialogue that occurs when people talk to themselves (either silently or out loud).

Progress in International Reading Literacy Study (PIRLS) Inaugurated in 2001, a planned five-year cycle of international trend studies in the reading ability of fourth-graders.

prosocial behavior Actions that are helpful and kind but are of no obvious benefit to oneself.

protein-calorie malnutrition A condition in which a person does not consume sufficient food of any kind. This deprivation can result in several illnesses, severe weight loss, and even death.

proximal parenting Caregiving practices that involve being physically close to a baby, with frequent holding and touching.

pruning When applied to brain development, the process by which unused connections in the brain atrophy and die.

psychoanalytic theory A grand theory of human development that holds that irrational, unconscious drives and motives, often originating in childhood, underlie human behavior.

psychological control A disciplinary technique that involves threatening to withdraw love and support and that relies on a child's feelings of guilt and gratitude to the parents.

psychopathology An illness or disorder of the mind.

puberty The time between the first onrush of hormones and full adult physical development. Puberty usually lasts three to five years. Many more years are required to achieve psychosocial maturity.

Q

qualitative research Research that considers qualities, not quantities. Narrative accounts and individual variations are often stressed in qualitative research.

quantitative research Research that provides data that can be expressed with numbers, such as ranks or scales.

R

race A group of people who are regarded by themselves or by others as distinct from other groups on the basis of physical appearance, typically skin color. Social scientists think race is a misleading concept, as biological differences are not signified by outward appearance.

reaction time The time it takes to respond to a stimulus, either physically (with a reflexive movement such as an eyeblink) or cognitively (with a thought).

reactive aggression An impulsive retaliation for another person's intentional or accidental action, verbal or physical.

reflex An unlearned, involuntary action or movement in response to a stimulus. A reflex occurs without conscious thought.

Reggio Emilia A program of early-childhood education that originated in the town of Reggio Emilia, Italy, and that encourages each child's creativity in a carefully designed setting.

reinforcement When a behavior is followed by something desired, such as food for a hungry animal or a welcoming smile for a lonely person.

relational aggression Nonphysical acts, such as insults or social rejection, aimed at harming the social connection between the victim and other people.

REM sleep Rapid eye movement sleep, a stage of sleep characterized by flickering eyes behind closed lids, dreaming, and rapid brain waves.

reminder session A perceptual experience that helps a person recollect an idea, a thing, or an experience.

replication Repeating a study, usually using different participants, perhaps of another age, SES, or culture.

reported maltreatment Harm or endangerment about which someone has notified the authorities.

resilience The capacity to adapt well to significant adversity and to overcome serious stress.

response to intervention (RTI) An educational strategy intended to help children in early grades who demonstrate below-average achievement by means of special intervention.

role confusion A situation in which an adolescent does not seem to know or care what his or her identity is. (Sometimes called *identity* or *role diffusion*.)

rough-and-tumble play Play that mimics aggression through wrestling, chasing, or hitting, but in which there is no intent to harm.

rumination Repeatedly thinking and talking about past experiences; can contribute to depression.

S

scaffolding Temporary support that is tailored to a learner's needs and abilities and aimed at helping the learner master the next task in a given learning process.

science of human development The science that seeks to understand how and why people of all ages and circumstances change or remain the same over time.

scientific method A way to answer questions using empirical research and data-based conclusions.

scientific observation A method of testing a hypothesis by unobtrusively watching and recording participants' behavior in a systematic and objective manner—in a natural setting, in a laboratory, or in searches of archival data.

secondary circular reactions The second of three types of feedback loops in sensorimotor intelligence, this one involving people and objects. Infants respond to other people, to toys, and to any other object they can touch or move.

secondary education Literally, the period after primary education (elementary or grade school) and before tertiary education (college). It usually occurs from about age 12 to 18, although there is some variation by school and by nation.

secondary prevention Actions that avert harm in a high-risk situation, such as stopping a car before it hits a pedestrian.

secondary sex characteristics Physical traits that are not directly involved in reproduction but that indicate sexual maturity, such as a man's beard and a woman's breasts.

secular trend The long-term upward or downward direction of a certain set of statistical measurements, as opposed to a smaller, shorter cyclical variation. As an example, over the last two centuries, because of improved nutrition and medical care, children have tended to reach their adult height earlier and their adult height has increased.

secure attachment A relationship (type B) in which an infant obtains both comfort and confidence from the presence of his or her caregiver.

selective adaptation The process by which living creatures (including people) adjust to their environment. Genes that enhance survival and reproductive ability are selected, over the generations, to become more prevalent.

selective attention The ability to concentrate on some stimuli while ignoring others.

self-awareness A person's realization that he or she is a distinct individual, whose body, mind, and actions are separate from those of other people.

self-concept A person's understanding of who he or she is, in relation to self-esteem, appearance, personality, and various traits.

self-efficacy In social learning theory, the belief of some people that they are able to change themselves and effectively alter the social context.

self-righting The inborn drive to remedy a developmental deficit; literally, to return to sitting or standing upright, after being tipped over. People of all ages have self-righting impulses, for emotional as well as physical imbalance.

sensation The response of a sensory system (eyes, ears, skin, tongue, nose) when it detects a stimulus.

sensitive period A time when a certain type of development is most likely, although it may still happen later with more difficulty. For example, early childhood is considered a sensitive period for language learning.

sensorimotor intelligence Piaget's term for the way infants think—by using their senses and motor skills—during the first period of cognitive development.

sensory memory The component of the information-processing system in which incoming stimulus information is stored for a split second to allow it to be processed. (Also called the *sensory register.*)

separation anxiety An infant's distress when a familiar caregiver leaves, most obvious between 9 and 14 months.

sex differences Biological differences between males and females, in organs, hormones, and body type.

sexual orientation A term that refers to whether a person is sexually and romantically attracted to others of the same sex, the opposite sex, or both sexes.

sexually transmitted infection (STI) A disease spread by sexual contact, including syphilis, gonorrhea, genital herpes, chlamydia, and HIV.

shaken baby syndrome A life-threatening injury that occurs when an infant is forcefully shaken back and forth, a motion that ruptures blood vessels in the brain and breaks neural connections.

single-parent family A family that consists of only one parent and his or her biological children under age 18.

small for gestational age (SGA) A term for a baby whose birthweight is significantly lower than expected, given the time since conception. For example, a 5-pound (2,265-gram) newborn is considered SGA if born on time but not SGA if born two months early. (Also called *small-for-dates.*)

social construction An idea that is built on shared perceptions, not on objective reality. Many age-related terms (such as *childhood, adolescence, yuppie,* and *senior citizen*) are social constructions, connected to biological traits but strongly influenced by social assumptions.

social learning Learning that is accomplished by observing others.

social learning theory An extension of behaviorism that emphasizes the influence that other people have over a person's behavior. Even without specific reinforcement, every individual learns many things through observation and imitation of other people. (Also called *observational learning.*)

social mediation Human interaction that expands and advances understanding, often through words that one person uses to explain something to another.

social referencing Seeking information about how to react to an unfamiliar or ambiguous object or event by observing someone else's expressions and reactions. That other person becomes a social reference.

social smile A smile evoked by a human face, normally evident in infants about six weeks after birth.

sociocultural theory A newer theory that holds that development results from the dynamic interaction of each person with the surrounding social and cultural forces.

sociodramatic play Pretend play in which children act out various roles and themes in stories that they create.

socioeconomic status (SES) A person's position in society as determined by income, occupation, education, and place of residence. (Sometimes called *social class.*)

specific learning disorder (learning disability) A marked deficit in a particular area of learning that is not caused by an apparent physical disability, by intellectual disability, or by an unusually stressful home environment.

spermarche A boy's first ejaculation of sperm. Erections can occur as early as infancy, but ejaculation signals sperm production. Spermarche may occur during sleep (in a "wet dream") or via direct stimulation.

static reasoning A characteristic of preoperational thought in which a young child thinks that nothing changes. Whatever is now has always been and always will be.

stem cells Cells from which any other specialized type of cell can form.

stereotype threat The possibility that one's appearance or behavior will be misread to confirm another person's oversimplified, prejudiced attitudes.

still-face technique An experimental practice in which an adult keeps his or her face unmoving and expressionless in face-to-face interaction with an infant.

Strange Situation A laboratory procedure for measuring attachment by evoking infants' reactions to stress in eight episodes of three minutes each.

stranger wariness An infant's expression of concern—a quiet stare, clinging to a familiar person, or sadness—when a stranger appears.

stunting The failure of children to grow to a normal height for their age due to severe and chronic malnutrition.

substantiated maltreatment Harm or endangerment that has been reported, investigated, and verified.

sudden infant death syndrome (SIDS) A situation in which a seemingly healthy infant, usually between 2 and 6 months old, suddenly stops breathing and dies unexpectedly while asleep.

suicidal ideation Thinking about suicide, usually with some serious emotional and intellectual or cognitive overtones.

sunk cost fallacy The mistaken belief that if money, time, or effort that cannot be recovered (a "sunk cost," in economic terms) has already been invested in some endeavor, then more should be invested in an effort to reach the goal. Because of this fallacy, people spend money trying to fix a "lemon" of a car or send more troops to fight a losing battle.

superego In psychoanalytic theory, the judgmental part of the personality that internalizes the moral standards of the parents.

survey A research method in which information is collected from a large number of people by interviews, written questionnaires, or some other means.

symbolic thought A major accomplishment of preoperational intelligence that allows a child to think symbolically, including understanding that words can refer to things not seen and that an item, such as a flag, can symbolize something else (in this case, for instance, a country).

synapse The intersection between the axon of one neuron and the dendrites of other neurons.

synchrony A coordinated, rapid, and smooth exchange of responses between a caregiver and an infant.

T

temperament Inborn differences between one person and another in emotions, activity, and self-regulation. Temperament is epigenetic, originating in genes but affected by child-rearing practices.

teratogens Agents and conditions, including viruses, drugs, and chemicals, that can impair prenatal development and result in birth defects or even death.

tertiary circular reactions The third of three types of feedback loops in sensorimotor intelligence, this one involving active exploration and experimentation. Infants explore a range of new activities, varying their responses as a way of learning about the world.

tertiary prevention Actions, such as immediate and effective medical treatment, that are taken after an adverse event (such as illness or injury) occurs and that are aimed at reducing the harm or preventing disability.

testosterone A sex hormone, the best known of the androgens (male hormones); secreted in far greater amounts by males than by females.

theory A comprehensive set of ideas.

theory of mind A person's theory of what other people might be thinking. In order to have a theory of mind, children must realize that other people are not necessarily thinking the same thoughts that they themselves are. That realization seldom occurs before age 4.

theory-theory The idea that children attempt to explain everything they see and hear by constructing theories.

threshold effect In prenatal development, when a teratogen is relatively harmless in small doses but becomes harmful once exposure reaches a certain level (the threshold).

time-out A disciplinary technique in which a child is separated from other people for a specified time.

transient exuberance The great but temporary increase in the number of dendrites that develop in an infant's brain during the first two years of life.

transitive inference The ability to figure out the unspoken link between one fact and another.

Trends in Math and Science Study (TIMSS) An international assessment of the math and science skills of fourth- and eighth-graders. Although the TIMSS is very useful, different countries' scores are not always comparable because sample selection, test administration, and content validity are hard to keep uniform.

trust versus mistrust Erikson's first psychosocial crisis. Infants learn basic trust if their basic needs (for food, comfort, attention, and so on) are met.

U

ultrasound An image of a fetus (or an internal organ) produced by using high-frequency sound waves. (Also called *sonogram.*)

V

very low birthweight (VLBW) A body weight at birth of less than 3 pounds, 5 ounces (1,500 grams).

visual cliff An experimental apparatus that gives the illusion of a sudden drop-off between one horizontal surface and another.

voucher Public subsidy for tuition payment at a non-public school. Vouchers vary a great deal from place to place, not only in amount and availability, but in restrictions as to who gets them and what schools accept them.

W

wasting The tendency for children to be severely underweight for their age as a result of malnutrition.

whole-language approach Teaching reading by encouraging early use of all language skills—talking and listening, reading and writing.

withdrawn-rejected Rejected by peers because of timid, withdrawn, and anxious behavior.

working memory The component of the information-processing system in which current conscious mental activity occurs. (Formerly called *short-term memory.*)

working model In cognitive theory, a set of assumptions that the individual uses to organize perceptions and experiences. For example, a person might assume that other people are always trustworthy and be surprised when this working model of human behavior is proven inadequate.

X

X-linked A gene carried on the X chromosome. If a male inherits an X-linked recessive trait from his mother, he expresses that trait because the Y from his father has no counteracting gene. Females are more likely to be carriers of X-linked traits but are less likely to express them.

XX A 23rd chromosome pair that consists of two X-shaped chromosomes, one each from the mother and the father. XX zygotes become females.

XY A 23rd chromosome pair that consists of an X-shaped chromosome from the mother and a Y-shaped chromosome from the father. XY zygotes become males.

Z

zone of proximal development In sociocultural theory, a metaphorical area, or "zone," surrounding a learner that includes all the skills, knowledge, and concepts that the person is close ("proximal") to acquiring but cannot yet master without help.

zygote The single cell formed from the union of two gametes, a sperm and an ovum.

References

Aarnoudse-Moens, Cornelieke S. H., Smidts, Diana P., Oosterlaan, Jaap, Duivenvoorden, Hugo J., & Weisglas-Kuperus, Nynke. (2009). Executive function in very preterm children at early school age. *Journal of Abnormal Child Psychology, 37,* 981–993.

Abrams, Dominic, Rutland, Adam, Ferrell, Jennifer M., & Pelletier, Joseph. (2008). Children's judgments of disloyal and immoral peer behavior: Subjective group dynamics in minimal intergroup contexts. *Child Development, 79,* 444–461.

Abreu, Guida de. (2008). From mathematics learning out-of-school to multicultural classrooms: A cultural psychology perspective. In Lyn D. English, Maria Bartolini Bussi, Graham A. Jones, Richard A. Lesh, & Bharath Sriraman (Eds.), *Handbook of international research in mathematics education* (2nd ed., pp. 323–353). New York, NY: Routledge.

Abrevaya, Jason. (2009). Are there missing girls in the United States? Evidence from birth data. *American Economic Journal: Applied Economics, 1,* 1–34.

Accardo, Pasquale. (2006). Who's training whom? *The Journal of Pediatrics, 149,* 151–152.

Ackerman, Joshua M., & Kenrick, Douglas T. (2009). Cooperative courtship: Helping friends raise and raze relationship barriers. *Personality and Social Psychology Bulletin, 35,* 1285–1300.

Adam, Emma K., Klimes-Dougan, Bonnie, & Gunnar, Megan R. (2007). Social regulation of the adrenocortical response to stress in infants, children, and adolescents: Implications for psychopathology and education. In Donna Coch, Geraldine Dawson, & Kurt W. Fischer (Eds.), *Human behavior, learning, and the developing brain: Atypical development* (pp. 264–304). New York, NY: Guilford Press.

Adams, Caralee J. (2011, June 9). Popularity offers challenges for community colleges. *Education Week,* pp. 14–17.

Adamson, Lauren B., & Bakeman, Roger. (2006). Development of displaced speech in early mother-child conversations. *Child Development, 77,* 186–200.

Adolph, Karen E., & Berger, Sarah E. (2005). Physical and motor development. In Marc H. Bornstein & Michael E. Lamb (Eds.), *Developmental science: An advanced textbook* (5th ed., pp. 223–281). Mahwah, NJ: Erlbaum.

Adolph, Karen E., Vereijken, Beatrix, & Shrout, Patrick E. (2003). What changes in infant walking and why. *Child Development, 74,* 475–497.

Afifi, Tracie O., Enns, Murray W., Cox, Brian J., Asmundson, Gordon J. G., Stein, Murray B., & Sareen, Jitender. (2008). Population attributable fractions of psychiatric disorders and suicide ideation and attempts associated with adverse childhood experiences. *American Journal of Public Health, 98,* 946–952.

Ahmed, Parvez, & Jaakkola, Jouni J. K. (2007). Maternal occupation and adverse pregnancy outcomes: A Finnish population-based study. *Occupational Medicine, 57,* 417–423.

Ainsworth, Mary D. Salter. (1973). The development of infant-mother attachment. In Bettye M. Caldwell & Henry N. Ricciuti (Eds.), *Review of child development research* (Vol. 3, pp. 1–94). Chicago, IL: University of Chicago Press.

Akiba, Daisuke, & García Coll, Cynthia. (2004). Effective interventions with children of color and their families: A contextual developmental approach. In Timothy B. Smith (Ed.), *Practicing multiculturalism: Affirming diversity in counseling and psychology* (pp. 123–144). Boston, MA: Pearson/Allyn and Bacon.

Akinbami, Lara J., Lynch, Courtney D., Parker, Jennifer D., & Woodruff, Tracey J. (2010). The association between childhood asthma prevalence and monitored air pollutants in metropolitan areas, United States, 2001–2004. *Environmental Research, 110,* 294–301.

Al-Sayes, Fatin, Gari, Mamdooh, Qusti, Safaa, Bagatian, Nadiah, & Abuzenadah, Adel. (2011). Prevalence of iron deficiency and iron deficiency anemia among females at university stage. *Journal of Medical Laboratory and Diagnosis, 2,* 5–11.

Albert, Dustin, & Steinberg, Laurence. (2011). Judgment and decision making in adolescence. *Journal of Research on Adolescence, 21,* 211–224.

Alexander, Robin. (2000). *Culture and pedagogy: International comparisons in primary education.* Malden, MA: Blackwell.

Allen, Elizabeth, Bonell, Chris, Strange, Vicki, Copas, Andrew, Stephenson, Judith, Johnson, Anne, et al. (2007). Does the UK government's teenage pregnancy strategy deal with the correct risk factors? Findings from a secondary analysis of data from a randomised trial of sex education and their implications for policy. *Journal of Epidemiology & Community Health, 61,* 20–27.

Allen, Joseph P., Porter, Maryfrances R., McFarland, F. Christy, Marsh, Penny, & McElhaney, Kathleen Boykin. (2005). The two faces of adolescents' success with peers: Adolescent popularity, social adaptation, and deviant behavior. *Child Development, 76,* 747–760.

Allen, Kathleen P. (2010). A bullying intervention system in high school: A two-year school-wide follow-up. *Studies In Educational Evaluation, 36,* 83–92.

Allen, Nicholas J. (2008). *Early human kinship: From sex to social reproduction.* Malden, MA: Blackwell.

Allen, Shanley. (2007). The future of Inuktitut in the face of majority languages: Bilingualism or language shift? *Applied Psycholinguistics, 28,* 515–536.

Alloy, Lauren B., & Abramson, Lyn Y. (2007). The adolescent surge in depression and emergence of gender differences: A biocognitive vulnerability-stress model in developmental context. In Daniel Romer & Elaine F. Walker (Eds.), *Adolescent psychopathology and the developing brain: Integrating brain and prevention science* (pp. 284–312). New York, NY: Oxford University Press.

Alm, Bernt. (2007). To co-sleep or not to sleep. *Acta Pædiatrica, 96,* 1385–1386.

Almond, Douglas. (2006). Is the 1918 influenza pandemic over? Long-term effects of in utero influenza exposure in the post-1940 U.S. population. *Journal of Political Economy, 114,* 672–712.

Alsaker, Françoise D., & Flammer, August. (2006). Pubertal development. In Sandy Jackson & Luc Goossens (Eds.), *Handbook of adolescent development* (pp. 30–50). Hove, East Sussex, UK: Psychology Press.

Altbach, Philip G., Reisberg, Liz, & Rumbley, Laura E. (2010, March/April). Tracking a global academic revolution. *Change: The Magazine of Higher Learning, 42,* 30–39.

Alter, Adam L., Aronson, Joshua, Darley, John M., Rodriguez, Cordaro, & Ruble, Diane N. (2010). Rising to the threat: Reducing stereotype threat by reframing the threat as a challenge. *Journal of Experimental Social Psychology, 46,* 166–171.

Amato, Paul R. (2005). The impact of family formation change on the cognitive, social, and emotional well-being of the next generation. *Future of Children, 15*(2), 75–96.

Amato, Paul R. (2010). Research on divorce: Continuing trends and new developments. *Journal of Marriage and Family, 72,* 650–666.

Ambady, Nalini, & Bharucha, Jamshed. (2009). Culture and the brain. *Current Directions in Psychological Science, 18,* 342–345.

American Community Survey. (2009). *2005–2009 American Community Survey 5-year estimates: S1002. Grandparents.* Retrieved from http://www.factfinder.census.gov/servlet/STTable?_bm=y&-geo_id=01000US&-qr_name=ACS_2009_5YR_G00_S1002&-ds_name=ACS_2009_5YR_G00_&-_lang=en&-_caller=geoselect&-state=st&-format=

American Psychological Association. (2010). *Ethical principles of psychologists and code of conduct 2002: 2010 amendments.* Retrieved from http://www.apa.org/ethics/code/index.aspx

Anderson, Craig A., Gentile, Douglas A., & Buckley, Katherine E. (2007). *Violent video game effects on children and adolescents: Theory, research, and public policy.* New York, NY: Oxford University Press.

Anderson, Craig A., Sakamoto, Akira, Gentile, Douglas A., Ihori, Nobuko, Shibuya, Akiko, Yukawa, Shintaro, et al. (2008). Longitudinal effects of violent video games on aggression in Japan and the United States. *Pediatrics, 122,* e1067–1072. doi:10.1542/peds.2008–1425

Andrade, Susan E., Gurwitz, Jerry H., Davis, Robert L., Chan, K. Arnold, Finkelstein, Jonathan A., Fortman, Kris, et al. (2004). Prescription drug use in pregnancy. *American Journal of Obstetrics and Gynecology, 191,* 398–407.

Andreassen, Carol, & West, Jerry. (2007). Measuring socioemotional functioning in a national birth cohort study. *Infant Mental Health Journal, 28,* 627–646.

Ansary, Nadia S., & Luthar, Suniya S. (2009). Distress and academic achievement among adolescents of affluence: A study of externalizing and internalizing problem behaviors and school performance. *Development and Psychopathology, 21,* 319–341.

Apgar, Virginia. (1953). A proposal for a new method of evaluation of the newborn infant. *Current Researches in Anesthesia and Analgesia, 32,* 260–267.

Apostolou, Menelaos. (2007). Sexual selection under parental choice: The role of parents in the evolution of human mating. *Evolution and Human Behavior, 28,* 403–409.

Applegate, Anthony J., Applegate, Mary DeKonty, McGeehan, Catherine M., Pinto, Catherine M., & Kong, Ailing. (2009). The assessment of thoughtful literacy in NAEP: Why the states aren't measuring up. *Reading Teacher, 62,* 372–381.

Appoh, Lily Yaa. (2004). Consequences of early malnutrition for subsequent social and emotional behaviour of children in Ghana. *Journal of Psychology in Africa, 14,* 87–94.

Appoh, Lily Yaa, & Krekling, Sturla. (2004). Effects of early childhood malnutrition on cognitive performance of Ghanaian children. *Journal of Psychology in Africa: South of the Sahara, the Caribbean, and Afro-Latin America, 14,* 1–7.

Archambault, Isabelle, Janosz, Michel, Fallu, Jean-Sebastien, & Pagani, Linda S. (2009). Student engagement and its relationship with early high school dropout. *Journal of Adolescence, 32,* 651–670.

Armstrong, Thomas. (2009). *Multiple intelligences in the classroom* (3rd ed.). Alexandria, VA: Association of Supervision and Curriculum Development.

Arnett, Jeffrey Jensen. (2004). *Emerging adulthood: The winding road from the late teens through the twenties.* New York, NY: Oxford University Press.

Arnett, Jeffrey Jensen, & Brody, Gene H. (2008). A fraught passage: The identity challenges of African American emerging adults. *Human Development, 51,* 291–293.

Arnett, Jeffrey Jensen, Kloep, Marion, Hendry, Leo B., & Tanner, Jennifer L. (2011). *Debating emerging adulthood: Stage or process?* New York, NY: Oxford University Press.

Arnold, L. Eugene, Farmer, Cristan, Kraemer, Helena Chmura, Davies, Mark, Witwer, Andrea, Chuang, Shirley, et al. (2010). Moderators, mediators, and other predictors of risperidone response in children with autistic disorder and irritability. *Journal of Child and Adolescent Psychopharmacology, 20,* 83–93.

Aron, Arthur. (2010). Behavior, the brain, and the social psychology of close relationships. In Christopher R. Agnew, Donald E. Carlston, William G. Graziano, & Janice R. Kelly (Eds.), *Then a miracle occurs: Focusing on behavior in social psychological theory and research* (pp. 283–298). New York, NY: Oxford University Press.

Aronson, Joshua, Fried, Carrie B., & Good, Catherine. (2002). Reducing the effects of stereotype threat on African American college students by shaping theories of intelligence. *Journal of Experimental Social Psychology, 38,* 113–125.

Arum, Richard, & Roksa, Josipa. (2011). *Academically adrift: Limited learning on college campuses.* Chicago, IL: University of Chicago Press.

Arum, Richard, Roksa, Josipa, & Cho, Esther. (2011). *Improving undergraduate learning: Findings and policy recommendations from the SSRC-CLA Longitudinal Project.* New York, NY: Social Science Research Council.

Aseltine, Robert H., Jr., & DeMartino, Robert. (2004). An outcome evaluation of the SOS suicide prevention program. *American Journal of Public Health, 94,* 446–451.

Asendorpf, Jens B., Denissen, Jaap J. A., & van Aken, Marcel A. G. (2008). Inhibited and aggressive preschool children at 23 years of age: Personality and social transitions into adulthood. *Developmental Psychology, 44,* 997–1011.

Ash, Caroline, Jasny, Barbara R., Roberts, Leslie, Stone, Richard, & Sugden, Andrew M. (2008, February 8). Reimagining cities. *Science, 319,* 739.

Ash, Katie. (2009, October 21). Maine 1–to-1 effort moves forward: Student laptop program expands into high schools *Education Week's Digital Directions, 3,* 14–15.

Aspinall, Richard J. (2003). *Aging of organs and systems.* Boston, MA: Kluwer Academic.

Asscheman, Henk. (2009). Gender identity disorder in adolescents. *Sexologies, 18,* 105–108.

Atkinson, Janette, & Braddick, Oliver. (2003). Neurobiological models of normal and abnormal visual development. In Michelle De Haan & Mark H. Johnson (Eds.), *The cognitive neuroscience of development* (pp. 43–71). New York, NY: Psychology Press.

Attar-Schwartz, Shalhevet, Tan, Jo-Pei, Buchanan, Ann, Flouri, Eirini, & Griggs, Julia. (2009). Grandparenting and adolescent adjustment in two-parent biological, lone-parent, and step-families. *Journal of Family Psychology, 23,* 67–75.

Aud, Susan, Hussar, William, Planty, Michael, Snyder, Thomas, Bianco, Kevin, Fox, Mary Ann, et al. (2010). *The condition of education 2010.* Washington, DC: National Center for Education Statistics, Institute of Education Sciences, U.S. Department of Education.

Audrey, Suzanne, Holliday, Jo, & Campbell, Rona. (2006). It's good to talk: Adolescent perspectives of an informal, peer-led intervention to reduce smoking. *Social Science & Medicine, 63,* 320–334.

Aunola, Kaisa, & Nurmi, Jari-Erik. (2004). Maternal affection moderates the impact of psychological control on a child's mathematical performance. *Developmental Psychology, 40,* 965–978.

Austad, Steven N. (2010). Methusaleh's zoo: How nature provides us with clues for extending human health span. *Journal of Comparative Pathology, 142*(Suppl. 1), S10–21.

Ayduk, Özlem, & Kross, Ethan. (2008). Enhancing the pace of recovery. *Psychological Science, 19,* 229–231.

Ayoub, Catherine, Vallotton, Claire D., & Mastergeorge, Ann M. (2011). Developmental pathways to integrated social skills: The roles of parenting and early intervention. *Child Development, 82,* 583–600.

Azrin, Nathan H., & Foxx, Richard M. (1974). *Toilet training in less than a day.* New York, NY: Simon and Schuster.

Bachman, Jerald G., O'Malley, Patrick M., Freedman-Doan, Peter, Trzesniewski, Kali H., & Donnellan, M. Brent. (2010). Adolescent self-esteem: Differences by race/ethnicity, gender, and age. *Self and Identity.* Advance online publication. doi:10.1080/15298861003794538

Badaloo, Asha V., Forrester, Terrence, Reid, Marvin, & Jahoor, Farook. (2006). Lipid kinetic differences between children with kwashiorkor and those with marasmus. *American Journal of Clinical Nutrition, 83,* 1283–1288.

Baddeley, Alan D. (2007). *Working memory, thought, and action.* New York, NY: Oxford University Press.

Bagner, Daniel M., Pettit, Jeremy W., Lewinsohn, Peter M., & Seeley, John R. (2010). Effect of maternal depression on child behavior: A sensitive period? *Journal of the American Academy of Child and Adolescent Psychiatry, 49,* 699–707.

Bailey, Kira, West, Robert, & Anderson, Craig A. (2010). A negative association between video game experience and proactive cognitive control. *Psychophysiology, 47,* 34–42.

Baillargeon, Renée. (2000). How do infants learn about the physical world? In Darwin Muir & Alan Slater (Eds.), *Infant development: The essential readings* (pp. 195–212). Malden, MA: Blackwell.

Baillargeon, Renée, & DeVos, Julie. (1991). Object permanence in young infants: Further evidence. *Child Development, 62,* 1227–1246.

Baker, Jason K., Fenning, Rachel M., Crnic, Keith A., Baker, Bruce L., & Blacher, Jan. (2007). Prediction of social skills in 6-year-old children with and without developmental delays: Contributions of early regulation and maternal scaffolding. *American Journal on Mental Retardation, 112,* 375–391.

Baker, Jeffrey P. (2000). Immunization and the American way: 4 childhood vaccines. *American Journal of Public Health, 90,* 199–207.

Baker, Lindsey A., & Mutchler, Jan E. (2010). Poverty and material hardship in grandparent-headed households. *Journal of Marriage and Family, 72,* 947–962.

Baker, Susan P. (2000). Where have we been and where are we going with injury control? In Dinesh Mohan & Geetam Tiwari (Eds.), *Injury prevention and control* (pp. 19–26). London, England: Taylor & Francis.

Bakken, Jeremy P., & Brown, B. Bradford. (2010). Adolescent secretive behavior: African American and Hmong adolescents' strategies and justifications for managing parents' knowledge about peers. *Journal of Research on Adolescence, 20,* 359–388.

Baldry, Anna C., & Farrington, David P. (2007). Effectiveness of programs to prevent school bullying. *Victims & Offenders, 2,* 183–204.

Baldwin, Dare A. (1993). Infants' ability to consult the speaker for clues to word reference. *Journal of Child Language, 20,* 395–418.

Bamford, Christi, & Lagattuta, Kristin Hansen. (2010). A new look at children's understanding of mind and emotion: The case of prayer. *Developmental Psychology, 46,* 78–92.

Bandura, Albert. (1977). *Social-learning theory.* Englewood Cliffs, NJ: Prentice-Hall.

Bandura, Albert. (1986). *Social foundations of thought and action: A social cognitive theory.* Englewood Cliffs, NJ: Prentice-Hall.

Bandura, Albert. (1997). The anatomy of stages of change. *American Journal of Health Promotion, 12,* 8–10.

Bandura, Albert. (2006). Toward a psychology of human agency. *Perspectives on Psychological Science, 1,* 164–180.

Bandura, Albert, Barbaranelli, Claudio, Caprara, Gian Vittorio, & Pastorelli, Concetta. (2001). Self-efficacy beliefs as shapers of children's aspirations and career trajectories. *Child Development, 72,* 187–206.

Bandura, Albert, & Bussey, Kay. (2004). On broadening the cognitive, motivational, and sociostructural scope of theorizing about gender development and functioning: Comment on Martin, Ruble, and Szkrybalo (2002). *Psychological Bulletin, 130,* 691–701.

Banerjee, Robin, & Lintern, Vicki. (2000). Boys will be boys: The effect of social evaluation concerns on gender-typing. *Social Development, 9,* 397–408.

Bansal, Vishal, Fortlage, Dale, Lee, Jeanne, Costantini, Todd, Potenza, Bruce, & Coimbra, Raul. (2009). Hemorrhage is more prevalent than brain injury in early trauma deaths: The golden six hours. *European Journal of Trauma and Emergency Surgery, 35,* 26–30.

Barbarin, Oscar, Downer, Jason T., Head, Darlene, & Odom, Erica. (2010). Home-school differences in beliefs, support, and control during public pre-kindergarten and their link to children's kindergarten readiness. *Early Childhood Research Quarterly, 25,* 358–372.

Barber, Brian K. (Ed.). (2002). *Intrusive parenting: How psychological control affects children and adolescents.* Washington, DC: American Psychological Association.

Barbey, Aron K., & Sloman, Steven A. (2007). Base-rate respect: From ecological rationality to dual processes. *Behavioral and Brain Sciences, 30,* 241–254.

Barinaga, Marcia. (2003, January 3). Newborn neurons search for meaning. *Science, 299,* 32–34.

Barkin, Shari, Scheindlin, Benjamin, Ip, Edward H., Richardson, Irma, & Finch, Stacia. (2007). Determinants of parental discipline practices: A national sample from primary care practices. *Clinical Pediatrics, 46,* 64–69.

Barkley, Russell A. (2006). *Attention-deficit hyperactivity disorder: A handbook for diagnosis and treatment* (3rd ed.). New York, NY: Guilford Press.

Barlow, Sarah E., & the Expert Committee. (2007). Expert Committee recommendations regarding the prevention, assessment, and treatment of child and adolescent overweight and obesity: Summary report. *Pediatrics, 120*(Suppl. 4), S164–S192.

Barnes, Grace M., Hoffman, Joseph H., Welte, John W., Farrell, Michael P., & Dintcheff, Barbara A. (2006). Effects of parental monitoring and peer deviance on substance use and delinquency. *Journal of Marriage and Family, 68,* 1084–1104.

Barnett, Kylie J., Finucane, Ciara, Asher, Julian E., Bargary, Gary, Corvin, Aiden P., Newell, Fiona N., et al. (2008). Familial patterns and the origins of individual differences in synaesthesia. *Cognition, 106,* 871–893.

Barnett, Mark, Watson, Ruth, & Kind, Peter. (2006). Pathways to barrel development. In Reha Erzurumlu, William Guido, & Zoltán Molnár (Eds.), *Development and plasticity in sensory thalamus and cortex* (pp. 138–157). New York, NY: Springer.

Barnett, W. Steven. (2007). The importance of demographic, social, and political context for estimating policy impacts: Comment on "Implementing New York's universal pre-kindergarten program." *Early Education and Development, 18,* 609–616.

Barnett, W. Steven, Epstein, Dale J., Carolan, Megan E., Fitzgerald, Jen, Ackerman, Debra J., & Friedman, Allison H. (2010). *The state of preschool 2010.* New Brunswick, NJ: National Institute for Early Education Research.

Barnett, W. Steven, Yarosz, Donald J., Thomas, Jessica, Jung, Kwanghee, & Blanco, Dulce. (2007). Two-way and monolingual English immersion in preschool education: An experimental comparison. *Early Childhood Research Quarterly, 22,* 277–293.

Baron, Andrew Scott, & Banaji, Mahzarin R. (2006). The development of implicit attitudes: Evidence of race evaluations from ages 6 and 10 and adulthood. *Psychological Science, 17,* 53–58.

Barrett, Justin L. (2008). Why Santa Claus is not a god. *Journal of Cognition and Culture, 8,* 149–161.

Barrett, Karen Caplovitz. (2005). The origins of social emotions and self-regulation in toddlerhood: New evidence. *Cognition & Emotion, 19,* 953–979.

Barry, Patrick. (2007, September 8). Genome 2.0: Mountains of new data are challenging old views. *Science News, 172,* 154.

Bates, Gillian, Harper, Peter S., & Jones, Lesley (Eds.). (2002). *Huntington's disease* (3rd ed.). Oxford, UK: Oxford University Press.

Bates, Lisa M., Acevedo-Garcia, Dolores, Alegria, Margarita, & Krieger, Nancy. (2008). Immigration and generational trends in body mass index and obesity in the United States: Results of the National Latino and Asian American Survey, 2002–2003. *American Journal of Public Health, 98,* 70–77.

Bateson, Patrick. (2005, February 4). Desirable scientific conduct. *Science, 307,* 645.

Bauer, Patricia J. (2006). Event memory. In William Damon & Richard M. Lerner (Series Eds.) & Deanna Kuhn & Robert S. Siegler (Vol. Eds.), *Handbook of child psychology: Vol. 2. Cognition, perception, and language* (6th ed., pp. 373–425). Hoboken, NJ: Wiley.

Bauer, Patricia J., San Souci, Priscilla, & Pathman, Thanujeni. (2010). Infant memory. *Wiley Interdisciplinary Reviews: Cognitive Science, 1,* 267–277.

Baum, Katrina. (2005). *Juvenile victimization and offending, 1993–2003* (NCJ 209468). Washington, DC: U.S. Department of Justice, Office of Justice Programs.

Baumeister, Roy F., & Blackhart, Ginnette C. (2007). Three perspectives on gender differences in adolescent sexual development. In Rutger C. M. E. Engels, Margaret Kerr, & Håkan Stattin (Eds.), *Friends, lovers, and groups: Key relationships in adolescence* (pp. 93–104). Hoboken, NJ: Wiley.

Baumrind, Diana. (1967). Child care practices anteceding three patterns of preschool behavior. *Genetic Psychology Monographs, 75,* 43–88.

Baumrind, Diana. (1971). Current patterns of parental authority. *Developmental Psychology, 4*(1, Pt. 2), 1–103.

Baumrind, Diana. (2005). Patterns of parental authority and adolescent autonomy. *New Directions for Child and Adolescent Development, 2005,* 61–69.

Baumrind, Diana, Larzelere, Robert E., & Owens, Elizabeth B. (2010). Effects of preschool parents' power assertive patterns and practices on adolescent development. *Parenting, 10,* 157–201.

Bayer, Angela M., Gilman, Robert H., Tsui, Amy O., & Hindin, Michelle J. (2010). What is adolescence?: Adolescents narrate their lives in Lima, Peru. *Journal of Adolescence, 33,* 509–520.

Bayer, Jordana K., Hiscock, Harriet, Hampton, Anne, & Wake, Melissa. (2007). Sleep problems in young infants and maternal mental and physical health. *Journal of Paediatrics and Child Health, 43,* 66–73.

Beal, Susan. (1988). Sleeping position and sudden infant death syndrome. *Medical Journal of Australia, 149,* 562.

Beauchaine, Theodore P., Klein, Daniel N., Crowell, Sheila E., Derbidge, Christina, & Gatzke-Kopp, Lisa. (2009). Multifinality in the development of personality disorders: A Biology × Sex × Environment interaction model of antisocial and borderline traits. *Development and Psychopathology, 21,* 735–770.

Beaudoin, Kathleen M., & Schonert-Reichl, Kimberly A. (2006). Epistemic reasoning and adolescent egocentrism: Relations to internalizing and externalizing symptoms in problem youth. *Journal of Youth and Adolescence, 35,* 999–1014.

Beck, Melinda. (2009, May 26). How's your baby? Recalling the Apgar score's namesake. Wall Street Journal, pp. D-1.

Beck, Martha Nibley. (1999). *Expecting Adam: A true story of birth, rebirth, and everyday magic.* New York, NY: Times Books.

Begos, Kevin. (2010, Winter). A wounded hero. *CR, 5,* 30–35, 62–63.

Behne, Tanya, Carpenter, Malinda, Call, Josep, & Tomasello, Michael. (2005). Unwilling versus unable: Infants' understanding of intentional action. *Developmental Psychology, 41,* 328–337.

Beilin, Lawrence, & Huang, Rae-Chi. (2008). Childhood obesity, hypertension, the metabolic syndrome and adult cardiovascular disease. *Clinical and Experimental Pharmacology and Physiology, 35,* 409–411.

Belfield, Clive R., Nores, Milagros, Barnett, Steve, & Schweinhart, Lawrence. (2006). The High/Scope Perry Preschool Program: Cost benefit analysis using data from the age-40 followup. *Journal of Human Resources, 41,* 162–190.

Bell, Aleeca F., White-Traut, Rosemary, & Medoff-Cooper, Barbara. (2010). Neonatal neurobehavioral organization after exposure to maternal epidural analgesia in labor. *Journal of Obstetric, Gynecologic, & Neonatal Nursing, 39,* 178–190.

Bell, Joanna H., & Bromnick, Rachel D. (2003). The social reality of the imaginary audience: A ground theory approach. *Adolescence, 38,* 205–219.

Bell, Ruth. (1998). *Changing bodies, changing lives: A book for teens on sex and relationships* (Expanded 3rd ed.). New York, NY: Times Books.

Belsky, Jay. (2011). The determinants of parenting in GxE perspective: A case of differential susceptibility? In Alan Booth, Susan M. McHale, & Nancy S. Landale (Eds.), *Biosocial foundations of family processes* (pp. 61–68). New York, NY: Springer Science + Business Media.

Belsky, Jay, Bakermans-Kranenburg, Marian J., & Van IJzendoorn, Marinus H. (2007). For better and for worse: Differential susceptibility to environmental influences. *Current Directions in Psychological Science, 16,* 300–304.

Belsky, Jay, & Pluess, Michael. (2009). The nature (and nurture?) of plasticity in early human development. *Perspectives on Psychological Science, 4,* 345–351.

Belsky, Jay, Steinberg, Laurence, Houts, Renate M., Halpern-Felsher, Bonnie L., & The NICHD Early Child Care Research Network. (2010). The development of reproductive strategy in females: Early maternal harshness → earlier menarche → increased sexual risk taking. *Developmental Psychology, 46,* 120–128.

Benacerraf, Beryl R. (2007). *Ultrasound of fetal syndromes* (2nd ed.). Philadelphia, PA: Churchill Livingstone/Elsevier.

Benjamin, Georges C. (2004). The solution is injury prevention. *American Journal of Public Health, 94,* 521.

Benner, Aprile D., & Graham, Sandra. (2007). Navigating the transition to multi-ethnic urban high schools: Changing ethnic congruence and adolescents' school-related affect. *Journal of Research on Adolescence, 17,* 207–220.

Bentley, Gillian R., & Mascie-Taylor, C. G. Nicholas. (2000). Introduction. In Gillian R. Bentley & C. G. Nicholas Mascie-Taylor (Eds.), *Infertility in the modern world: Present and future prospects* (pp. 1–13). Cambridge, England: Cambridge University Press.

Berenbaum, Sheri A., Martin, Carol Lynn, Hanish, Laura D., Briggs, Phillip T., & Fabes, Richard A. (2008). Sex differences in children's play. In Jill B. Becker, Karen J. Berkley, Nori Geary, Elizabeth Hampson, James P. Herman, & Elizabeth Young (Eds.), *Sex differences in the brain: From genes to behavior* (pp. 275–290). New York, NY: Oxford University Press.

Berg, Sandra J., & Wynne-Edwards, Katherine E. (2002). Salivary hormone concentrations in mothers and fathers becoming parents are not correlated. *Hormones & Behavior, 42,* 424–436.

Berger, Kathleen Stassen. (2007). Update on bullying at school: Science forgotten? *Developmental Review, 27,* 90–126.

Berger, Lawrence M., Paxson, Christina, & Waldfogel, Jane. (2009). Income and child development. *Children and Youth Services Review, 31,* 978–989.

Berkey, Catherine S., Gardner, Jane D., Frazier, A. Lindsay, & Colditz, Graham A. (2000). Relation of childhood diet and body size to menarche and adolescent growth in girls. *American Journal of Epidemiology, 152,* 446–452.

Berlin, Lisa J., Appleyard, Karen, & Dodge, Kenneth A. (2011). Intergenerational continuity in child maltreatment: Mediating mechanisms and implications for prevention. *Child Development, 82,* 162–176.

Berman, Alan L., Jobes, David A., & Silverman, Morton M. (2006). *Adolescent suicide: Assessment and intervention* (2nd ed.). Washington, DC: American Psychological Association.

Bernard, Kristin, & Dozier, Mary. (2010). Examining infants' cortisol responses to laboratory tasks among children varying in attachment disor-ganization: Stress reactivity or return to baseline? *Developmental Psychology, 46,* 1771–1778.

Berndt, Thomas J., & Murphy, Lonna M. (2002). Influences of friends and friendships: Myths, truths, and research recommendations. In Robert V. Kail (Ed.), *Advances in child development and behavior* (Vol. 30, pp. 275–310). San Diego, CA: Academic Press.

Bernstein, Mary. (2005). Identity politics. *Annual Review of Sociology, 31,* 47–74.

Bhattacharjee, Yudhijit. (2008, February 8). Choking on fumes, Kolkata faces a noxious future. *Science, 319,* 749.

Bhutta, Zulfiqar A., Ali, Samana, Cousens, Simon, Ali, Talaha M., Haider, Batool Azra, Rizvi, Arjumand, et al. (2008). Interventions to address maternal, newborn, and child survival: What difference can integrated primary health care strategies make? *Lancet, 372,* 972–989.

Bialystok, Ellen. (2010). Global-local and trail-making tasks by monolingual and bilingual children: Beyond inhibition. *Developmental Psychology, 46,* 93–105.

Bialystok, Ellen, & Viswanathan, Mythili. (2009). Components of executive control with advantages for bilingual children in two cultures. *Cognition, 112,* 494–500.

Biblarz, Timothy J., & Stacey, Judith. (2010). How does the gender of parents matter? *Journal of Marriage and Family, 72,* 3–22.

Biederman, Joseph, Spencer, Thomas J., Monuteaux, Michael C., & Faraone, Stephen V. (2010). A naturalistic 10-year prospective study of height and weight in children with attention-deficit hyperactivity disorder grown up: Sex and treatment effects. *The Journal of Pediatrics, 157,* 635–640.e1.

Biehl, Michael C., Natsuaki, Misaki N., & Ge, Xiaojia. (2007). The influence of pubertal timing on alcohol use and heavy drinking trajectories. *Journal of Youth and Adolescence, 36,* 153–167.

Bienvenu, Thierry. (2005). Rett syndrome. In Merlin Gene Butler & F. John Meaney (Eds.), *Genetics of developmental disabilities* (pp. 477–519). Boca Raton, FL: Taylor & Francis.

Bijou, Sidney W., & Baer, Donald M. (1978). *Behavior analysis of child development.* Englewood Cliffs, NJ: Prentice-Hall.

Birch, Susan A. J., & Bloom, Paul. (2003). Children are cursed: An asymmetric bias in mental-state attribution. *Psychological Science, 14,* 283–286.

Birdsong, David. (2006). Age and second language acquisition and processing: A selective overview. *Language Learning, 56*(Suppl. 1), 9–49.

Birney, Damian P., Citron-Pousty, Jill H., Lutz, Donna J., & Sternberg, Robert J. (2005). The development of cognitive and intellectual abilities. In Marc H. Bornstein & Michael E. Lamb (Eds.), *Developmental science: An advanced textbook* (5th ed., pp. 327–358). Mahwah, NJ: Erlbaum.

Biro, Frank M., McMahon, Robert P., Striegel-Moore, Ruth, Crawford, Patricia B., Obarzanek, Eva, Morrison, John A., et al. (2001). Impact of timing of pubertal maturation on growth in black and white female adolescents: The National Heart, Lung, and Blood Institute Growth and Health Study. *Journal of Pediatrics, 138,* 636–643.

Biro, Frank M., Striegel-Moore, Ruth H., Franko, Debra L., Padgett, Justina, & Bean, Judy A. (2006). Self-esteem in adolescent females. *Journal of Adolescent Health, 39,* 501–507.

Bisiacchi, Patrizia Silvia, Mento, Giovanni, & Suppiej, Agnese. (2009). Cortical auditory processing in preterm newborns: An ERP study. *Biological Psychology, 82,* 176–185.

Bitensky, Susan H. (2006). *Corporal punishment of children: A human rights violation.* Boston, MA: Brill.

Bjorklund, David F., Dukes, Charles, & Brown, Rhonda Douglas. (2009). The development of memory strategies. In Mary L. Courage & Nelson Cowan (Eds.), *The development of memory in infancy and childhood* (2nd ed., pp. 145–175). New York, NY: Psychology Press.

Blackwell, Lisa S., Trzesniewski, Kali H., & Dweck, Carol Sorich. (2007). Implicit theories of intelligence predict achievement across an adolescent transition: A longitudinal study and an intervention. *Child Development, 78,* 246–263.

Blair, Peter S., & Ball, Helen L. (2004). The prevalence and characteristics associated with parent-infant bed-sharing in England. *Archives of Disease in Childhood, 89,* 1106–1110.

Blakemore, Sarah-Jayne. (2008). Development of the social brain during adolescence. *The Quarterly Journal of Experimental Psychology, 61,* 40–49.

Blandon, Alysia Y., Calkins, Susan D., & Keane, Susan P. (2010). Predicting emotional and social competence during early childhood from toddler risk and maternal behavior. *Development and Psychopathology, 22,* 119–132.

Blonigen, Daniel M., Carlson, Marie D., Hicks, Brian M., Krueger, Robert F., & Iacono, William G. (2008). Stability and change in personality traits from late adolescence to early adulthood: A longitudinal twin study. *Journal of Personality, 76,* 229–266.

Bloom, Barbara, Cohen, Robin A., & Freeman, Gulnur. (2009). Summary health statistics for U.S. children: National Health Interview Survey, 2008. *Vital and Health Statistics, 10*(244).

Bloom, Lois. (1993). *The transition from infancy to language: Acquiring the power of expression.* New York, NY: Cambridge University Press.

Bloom, Lois. (1998). Language acquisition in its developmental context. In William Damon (Series Ed.) & Deanna Kuhn & Robert S. Siegler (Vol. Eds.), *Handbook of child psychology: Vol. 2. Cognition, perception, and language* (5th ed., pp. 309–370). New York, NY: Wiley.

Blum, Deborah. (2002). *Love at Goon Park: Harry Harlow and the science of affection.* Cambridge, MA: Perseus.

Blum, Nathan J., Taubman, Bruce, & Nemeth, Nicole. (2003). Relationship between age at initiation of toilet training and duration of training: A prospective study. *Pediatrics, 111*(4, Pt. 1), 810–814.

Blurton-Jones, Nicholas G. (1976). Rough-and-tumble play among nursery school children. In Jerome S. Bruner, Alison Jolly, & Kathy Sylva (Eds.), *Play: Its role in development and evolution* (pp. 352–363). New York, NY: Basic Books.

Bodrova, Elena, & Leong, Deborah J. (2005). High quality preschool programs: What would Vygotsky say? *Early Education and Development, 16,* 435–444.

Boehnke, Klaus. (2008). Peer pressure: A cause of scholastic underachievement? A cross-cultural study of mathematical achievement among German, Canadian, and Israeli middle school students. *Social Psychology of Education, 11,* 149–160.

Boles, David B., Barth, Joan M., & Merrill, Edward C. (2008). Asymmetry and performance: Toward a neurodevelopmental theory. *Brain and Cognition, 66,* 124–139.

Bonica, Laura, & Sappa, Viviana. (2010). Early school-leavers' microtransitions: Towards a competent self. *Education + Training, 52,* 368–380.

Booth, James R. (2007). Brain bases of learning and development of language and reading. In Donna Coch, Kurt W. Fischer, & Geraldine Dawson (Eds.), *Human behavior, learning, and the developing brain: Typical development* (pp. 279–300). New York, NY: Guilford.

Borke, Jörn, Lamm, Bettina, Eickhorst, Andreas, & Keller, Heidi. (2007). Father-infant interaction, paternal ideas about early child care, and their consequences for the development of children's self-recognition. *Journal of Genetic Psychology, 168,* 365–379.

Borkowski, John G., Farris, Jaelyn Renee, Whitman, Thomas L., Carothers, Shannon S., Weed, Keri, & Keogh, Deborah A. (2007). *Risk and resilience: Adolescent mothers and their children grow up.* Mahwah, NJ: Erlbaum.

Bornstein, Marc H. (2002). Parenting infants. In Marc H. Bornstein (Ed.), *Handbook of parenting: Vol. 1. Children and parenting* (2nd ed., pp. 3–43). Mahwah, NJ: Erlbaum.

Bornstein, Marc H. (2006). Parenting science and practice. In William Damon & Richard M. Lerner (Series Eds.) & K. Ann Renninger & Irving E. Sigel (Vol. Eds.), *Handbook of child psychology: Vol. 4. Child psychology in practice* (6th ed., pp. 893–949). Hoboken, NJ: Wiley.

Bornstein, Marc H., Arterberry, Martha E., & Mash, Clay. (2005). Perceptual development. In Marc H. Bornstein & Michael E. Lamb (Eds.), *Developmental science: An advanced textbook* (5th ed., pp. 283–325). Mahwah, NJ: Erlbaum.

Bornstein, Marc H., Mortimer, Jeylan T., Lutfey, Karen, & Bradley, Robert. (2011). Theories and processes in life-span socialization. In Karen Fingerman, Cynthia Berg, Jacqui Smith, & Toni Antonucci (Eds.), *Handbook of life-span development* (pp. 27–56). New York, NY: Springer.

Bornstein, Marc H., Putnick, Diane L., Suwalsky, Joan T. D., Venuti, Paola, de Falco, Simona, Galperín, Celia Zingman de, et al. (2010). Emotional relationships in mothers and infants: Culture-common and community-specific characteristics of dyads from rural and metropolitan settings in Argentina, Italy, and the United States. *Journal of Cross-Cultural Psychology.* Advance online publication. doi:10.1177/0022022110388563

Borrelli, Belinda, McQuaid, Elizabeth L., Novak, Scott P., Hammond, S. Katharine, & Becker, Bruce. (2010). Motivating Latino caregivers of children with asthma to quit smoking: A randomized trial. *Journal of Consulting and Clinical Psychology, 78,* 34–43.

Bortz, Walter M. (2005). Biological basis of determinants of health. *American Journal of Public Health, 95,* 389–392.

Bos, Henny M. W., Sandfort, Theo G. M., de Bruyn, Eddy H., & Hakvoort, Esther M. (2008). Same-sex attraction, social relationships, psychosocial functioning, and school performance in early adolescence. *Developmental Psychology, 44,* 59–68.

Boseovski, Janet J. (2010). Evidence for "rose-colored glasses": An examination of the positivity bias in young children's personality judgments. *Child Development Perspectives, 4,* 212–218.

Bossé, Yohan, & Hudson, Thomas J. (2007). Toward a comprehensive set of asthma susceptibility genes. *Annual Review of Medicine, 58,* 171–184.

Bosworth, Hayden B., & Hertzog, Christopher. (2009). *Aging and cognition: Research methodologies and empirical advances.* Washington, DC: American Psychological Association.

Bower, Bruce. (2007, February 17). Net heads. *Science News, 171,* 104–106.

Bowers, Jeffrey S., Mattys, Sven L., & Gage, Suzanne H. (2009). Preserved implicit knowledge of a forgotten childhood language. *Psychological Science, 20,* 1064–1069.

Bowes, Lucy, Maughan, Barbara, Caspi, Avshalom, Moffitt, Terrie E., & Arseneault, Louise. (2010). Families promote emotional and behavioural resilience to bullying: Evidence of an environmental effect. *Journal of Child Psychology and Psychiatry, 51,* 809–817.

Bowlby, John. (1969). *Attachment and loss: Vol. 1. Attachment.* New York, NY: Basic Books.

Bowlby, John. (1973). *Attachment and loss: Vol. 2. Separation: Anxiety and anger.* New York, NY: Basic Books.

Bowlby, John. (1988). *A secure base: Clinical applications of attachment theory.* London, England: Routledge.

Boyce, W. Thomas, Essex, Marilyn J., Alkon, Abbey, Goldsmith, H. Hill, Kraemer, Helena C., & Kupfer, David J. (2006). Early father involvement moderates biobehavioral susceptibility to mental health problems in middle childhood. *Journal of the American Academy of Child and Adolescent Psychiatry, 45,* 1510–1520.

Boyd, William L. (2007). The politics of privatization in American education. *Educational Policy, 21,* 7–14.

Bracken, Bruce A., & Crawford, Elizabeth. (2010). Basic concepts in early childhood educational standards: A 50–state review. *Early Childhood Education Journal, 37,* 421–430.

Bradley, Robert H., & Corwyn, Robert F. (2005). Productive activity and the prevention of behavior problems. *Developmental Psychology, 41,* 89–98.

Brainerd, Charles J., Reyna, Valerie F., & Ceci, Stephen J. (2008). Developmental reversals in false memory: A review of data and theory. *Psychological Bulletin, 134,* 343–382.

Branca, Francesco, Nikogosian, Haik, & Lobstein, Tim (Eds.). (2007). *The challenge of obesity in the WHO European Region and the strategies for response.* Copenhagen, Denmark: WHO Regional Office for Europe.

Brandone, Amanda C., & Wellman, Henry M. (2009). You can't always get what you want. *Psychological Science, 20,* 85–91.

Braun, Joe M, & Hauser, Russ. (2011). Bisphenol A and children's health. *Current Opinion in Pediatrics, 23,* 233–239.

Brazelton, T. Berry, & Sparrow, Joshua D. (2006). *Touchpoints: Birth to 3: Your child's emotional and behavioral development* (2nd ed.). Cambridge, MA: Da Capo Press.

Breivik, Gunnar. (2010). Trends in adventure sports in a post-modern society. *Sport in Society: Cultures, Commerce, Media, Politics, 13,* 260–273.

Brendgen, Mara, Lamarche, Véronique, Wanner, Brigitte, & Vitaro, Frank. (2010). Links between friendship relations and early adolescents' trajectories of depressed mood. *Developmental Psychology, 46,* 491–501.

Brener, Nancy D., McManus, Tim, Galuska, Deborah A., Lowry, Richard, & Wechsler, Howell. (2003). Reliability and validity of self-reported height and weight among high school students. *The Journal of Adolescent Health : Official Publication of the Society for Adolescent Medicine, 32,* 281–287.

Brennan, Arthur, Ayers, Susan, Ahmed, Hafez, & Marshall-Lucette, Sylvie. (2007). A critical review of the Couvade syndrome: The pregnant male. *Journal of Reproductive and Infant Psychology, 25,* 173–189.

Bretherton, Inge. (2010). Fathers in attachment theory and research: A review. *Early Child Development and Care, 180,* 9–23.

Brickhouse, Tegwyn H., Rozier, R. Gary, & Slade, Gary D. (2008). Effects of enrollment in Medicaid versus the State Children's Health Insurance Program on kindergarten children's untreated dental caries. *American Journal of Public Health, 98,* 876–881.

Bridge, Jeffrey A., Iyengar, Satish, Salary, Cheryl B., Barbe, Remy P., Birmaher, Boris, Pincus, Harold Alan, et al. (2007). Clinical response and risk for reported suicidal ideation and suicide attempts in pediatric antidepressant treatment: A meta-analysis of randomized controlled trials. *Journal of the American Medical Association, 297,* 1683–1696.

Briggs, Gerald G., Freeman, Roger K., & Yaffe, Sumner J. (2008). *Drugs in pregnancy and lactation: A reference guide to fetal and neonatal risk* (8th ed.). Philadelphia, PA: Lippincott Williams & Wilkins.

Brinton, Mary C., & Tang, Zun. (2010). School–work systems in postindustrial societies: Evidence from Japan. *Research in Social Stratification and Mobility, 28,* 215–232.

Brody, Gene H., Beach, Steven R. H., Philibert, Robert A., Chen, Yi-fu, & Murry, Velma McBride. (2009). Prevention effects moderate the association of 5–HTTLPR and youth risk behavior initiation: Gene × environment hypotheses tested via a randomized prevention design. *Child Development, 80,* 645–661.

Bronfenbrenner, Urie. (1977). Toward an experimental ecology of human development. *American Psychologist, 32,* 513–531.

Bronfenbrenner, Urie, & Morris, Pamela A. (2006). The bioecological model of human development. In William Damon & Richard M. Lerner (Series Eds.) & Richard M. Lerner (Vol. Ed.), *Handbook of child psychology: Vol. 1. Theoretical models of human development* (6th ed., pp. 793–828). Hoboken, NJ: Wiley.

Bronte-Tinkew, Jacinta, Moore, Kristin A., Matthews, Gregory, & Carrano, Jennifer. (2007). Symptoms of major depression in a sample of fathers of infants: Sociodemographic correlates and links to father involvement. *Journal of Family Issues, 28,* 61–99.

Brooker, Robert J. (2009). *Genetics: Analysis & principles* (3rd ed.). New York, NY: McGraw-Hill.

Brotman, Melissa A., Guyer, Amanda E., Lawson, Evin S., Horsey, Sarah E., Rich, Brendan A., Dickstein, Daniel P., et al. (2008). Facial emotion labeling deficits in children and adolescents at risk for bipolar disorder. *American Journal of Psychiatry, 165,* 385–389.

Brotman, Melissa A., Rich, Brendan A., Guyer, Amanda E., Lunsford, Jessica R., Horsey, Sarah E., Reising, Michelle M., et al. (2010). Amygdala activation during emotion processing of neutral faces in children with severe mood dysregulation versus ADHD or bipolar disorder. *American Journal of Psychiatry, 167,* 61–69.

Brown, B. Bradford. (2004). Adolescents' relationships with peers. In Richard M. Lerner & Laurence D. Steinberg (Eds.), *Handbook of adolescent psychology* (2nd ed., pp. 363–394). Hoboken, NJ: Wiley.

Brown, B. Bradford, & Bakken, Jeremy P. (2011). Parenting and peer relationships: Reinvigorating research on family–peer linkages in adolescence. *Journal of Research on Adolescence, 21,* 153–165.

Brown, B. Bradford, & Larson, James. (2009). Peer relationships in adolescence, *Handbook of adolescent psychology: Vol. 2. Contextual influences on adolescent development* (3rd ed., pp. 74–103). Hoboken, NJ: Wiley.

Brown, Christia Spears, Alabi, Basirat O., Huynh, Virginia W., & Masten, Carrie L. (2011). Ethnicity and gender in late childhood and early adolescence: Group identity and awareness of bias. *Developmental Psychology, 47,* 463–471.

Brown, Christia Spears, & Bigler, Rebecca S. (2005). Children's perceptions of discrimination: A developmental model. *Child Development, 76,* 533–553.

Brown, Susan L. (2004). Family structure and child well-being: The significance of parental cohabitation. *Journal of Marriage and Family, 66,* 351–367.

Brown, Susan L. (2010). Marriage and child well-being: Research and policy perspectives. *Journal of Marriage and Family, 72,* 1059–1077.

Brown, Susan L., & Rinelli, Lauren N. (2010). Family structure, family processes, and adolescent smoking and drinking. *Journal of Research on Adolescence, 20,* 259–273.

Brown, Tony N., Tanner-Smith, Emily E., Lesane-Brown, Chase L., & Ezell, Michael E. (2007). Child, parent, and situational correlates of familial ethnic/race socialization. *Journal of Marriage and Family, 69,* 14–25.

Bruce, Susan, & Muhammad, Zayyad. (2009). The development of object permanence in children with intellectual disability, physical disability, autism, and blindness. *International Journal of Disability, Development and Education, 56,* 229–246.

Bruck, Maggie, Ceci, Stephen J., & Principe, Gabrielle F. (2006). The child and the law. In William Damon & Richard M. Lerner (Series Eds.) & K. Ann Renninger & Irving E. Sigel (Vol. Eds.), *Handbook of child psychology: Vol. 4. Child psychology in practice* (6th ed., pp. 776–816). Hoboken, NJ: Wiley.

Bruschweiler-Stern, Nadia. (2009). Moments of meeting: Pivotal moments in mother, infant, father bonding: Switzerland. In Kevin J. Nugent, Bonnie J. Petrauskas, & T. Berry Brazelton (Eds.), *The newborn as a person: Enabling healthy infant development worldwide* (pp. 70–84). Hoboken, NJ: Wiley.

Bryant, Brenda K., & Donnellan, M. Brent. (2007). The relation between socio-economic status concerns and angry peer conflict resolution is moderated by pet provisions of support. *Anthrozoös, 20,* 213–223.

Bryant, Gregory A., & Barrett, H. Clark. (2007). Recognizing intentions in infant-directed speech: Evidence for universals. *Psychological Science, 18,* 746–751.

Brymer, Eric. (2010). Risk and extreme sports: A phenomenological perspective. *Annals of Leisure Research, 13,* 218–239.

Buccino, Giovanni, & Amore, Mario. (2008). Mirror neurons and the understanding of behavioural symptoms in psychiatric disorders. *Current Opinion in Psychiatry, 21,* 281–285.

Buckhalt, Joseph A., El-Sheikh, Mona, & Keller, Peggy. (2007). Children's sleep and cognitive functioning: Race and socioeconomic status as moderators of effects. *Child Development, 78,* 213–231.

Buckley, Kristi A., & Tobey, Emily A. (2011). Cross-modal plasticity and speech perception in pre- and postlingually deaf cochlear implant users. *Ear and Hearing, 32,* 2–15.

Buckley, Maureen, & Saarni, Carolyn. (2009). Emotion regulation: Implications for positive youth development. In Rich Gilman, E. Scott Huebner, & Michael J. Furlong (Eds.), *Handbook of positive psychology in schools* (pp. 107–118). New York, NY: Routledge/Taylor & Francis.

Bucx, Freek, Raaijmakers, Quinten, & van Wel, Frits. (2010). Life course stage in young adulthood and intergenerational congruence in family attitudes. *Journal of Marriage and Family, 72,* 117–134.

Bugental, Daphne Blunt, & Grusec, Joan E. (2006). Socialization theory. In William Damon & Richard M. Lerner (Series Eds.) & Nancy Eisenberg (Vol. Ed.), *Handbook of child psychology: Vol. 3. Social, emotional, and personality development* (6th ed., pp. 366–428). Hoboken, NJ: Wiley.

Bugental, Daphne Blunt, & Happaney, Keith. (2004). Predicting infant maltreatment in low-income families: The interactive effects of maternal attributions and child status at birth. *Developmental Psychology, 40,* 234–243.

Bugental, Daphne Blunt, & Schwartz, Alex. (2009). A cognitive approach to child mistreatment prevention among medically at-risk infants. *Developmental Psychology, 45,* 284–288.

Bulbulia, Joseph A. (2007). Evolution of religion. In R. I. M. Dunbar & Louise Barrett (Eds.), *Oxford handbook of evolutionary psychology* (pp. 621–636). New York, NY: Oxford University Press.

Bulik, Cynthia M., Thornton, Laura, Pinheiro, Andréa Poyastro, Plotnicov, Katherine, Klump, Kelly L., Brandt, Harry, et al. (2008). Suicide attempts in anorexia nervosa. *Psychosomatic Medicine, 70,* 378–383.

Burd-Sharps, Sarah, Lewis, Kristen, & Martins, Eduardo Borges. (2008). *The measure of America: American human development report, 2008–2009.* New York, NY: Columbia University Press.

Burkitt, Esther. (2004). Drawing conclusions from children's art. *The Psychologist, 17,* 566–568.

Burt, S. Alexandra. (2009). Rethinking environmental contributions to child and adolescent psychopathology: A meta-analysis of shared environmental influences. *Psychological Bulletin, 135,* 608–637.

Burt, S. Alexandra, McGue, Matt, & Iacono, William G. (2009). Nonshared environmental mediation of the association between deviant peer affiliation and adolescent externalizing behaviors over time: Results from a cross-lagged monozygotic twin differences design. *Developmental Psychology, 45,* 1752–1760.

Buss, David M. (2003). *The evolution of desire: Strategies of human mating* (Revised ed.). New York, NY: Basic Books.

Buss, David M., Haselton, Martie G., Shackelford, Todd K., Bleske, April L., & Wakefield, Jerome C. (1998). Adaptations, exaptations, and spandrels. *American Psychologist, 53,* 533–548.

Busse, William W., & Lemanske, Robert F. (Eds.). (2005). *Lung biology in health and disease: Vol. 195. Asthma prevention.* Boca Raton, FL: Taylor & Francis.

Bussey, Kay, & Bandura, Albert. (1999). Social cognitive theory of gender development and differentiation. *Psychological Review, 106,* 676–713.

Butler, Merlin Gene, & Meaney, F. John. (2005). *Genetics of developmental disabilities.* Boca Raton, FL: Taylor & Francis.

Butterworth, Brian, Reeve, R., & Reynolds, F. (2011). Using mental representations of space when words are unavailable: Studies of enumeration and arithmetic in indigenous Australia. *Journal of Cross-Cultural Psychology, 42*(4), 630–638.

Buunk, Abraham P., Park, Justin H., & Dubbs, Shelli L. (2008). Parent-offspring conflict in mate preferences. *Review of General Psychology, 12,* 47–62.

Byers-Heinlein, Krista, Burns, Tracey C., & Werker, Janet F. (2010). The roots of bilingualism in newborns. *Psychological Science, 21,* 343–348.

Byng-Hall, John. (2008). The significance of children fulfilling parental roles: Implications for family therapy. *Journal of Family Therapy, 30,* 147–162.

Cabrera, Natasha J., Shannon, Jacqueline D., West, Jerry, & Brooks-Gunn, Jeanne. (2006). Parental interactions with Latino infants: Variation by country of origin and English proficiency. *Child Development, 77,* 1190–1207.

Cain, Daphne S., & Combs-Orme, Terri. (2005). Family structure effects on parenting stress and practices in the African American family. *Journal of Sociology & Social Welfare, 32,* 19–40.

Calkins, Susan D., & Keane, Susan P. (2009). Developmental origins of early antisocial behavior. *Development and Psychopathology, 21,* 1095–1109.

Callaghan, Tara, Rochat, Philippe, Lillard, Angeline, Claux, Mary Louise, Odden, Hal, Itakura, Shoji, et al. (2005). Synchrony in the onset of mental-state reasoning: Evidence from five cultures. *Psychological Science, 16,* 378–384.

Calvert, Karin. (2003). Patterns of childrearing in America. In Willem Koops & Michael Zuckerman (Eds.), *Beyond the century of the child: Cultural history and developmental psychology* (pp. 62–81). Baltimore, MD: University of Pennsylvania Press.

Cameron, Judy, & Pierce, W. David. (2002). *Rewards and intrinsic motivation: Resolving the controversy.* Westport, CT: Bergin & Garvey.

Cameron, Judy L. (2004). Interrelationships between hormones, behavior, and affect during adolescence: Understanding hormonal, physical, and brain changes occurring in association with pubertal activation of the reproductive axis. Introduction to Part III. In Ronald E. Dahl & Linda Patia Spear (Eds.), *Adolescent brain development: Vulnerabilities and opportunities* (Vol. 1021, pp. 110–123). New York, NY: New York Academy of Sciences.

Cameron, Nicole M., Fish, Eric W., & Meaney, Michael J. (2008). Maternal influences on the sexual behavior and reproductive success of the female rat. *Hormones and Behavior, 54,* 178–184.

Camilli, Gregory, Vargas, Sadako, Ryan, Sharon, & Barnett, W. Steven. (2010). Meta-analysis of the effects of early education interventions on cognitive and social development. *Teachers College Record, 112,* 579–620.

Camos, Valérie, & Barrouillet, Pierre. (2011). Developmental change in working memory strategies: From passive maintenance to active refreshing. *Developmental Psychology, 47,* 898–904.

Campbell, Frances A., Pungello, Elizabeth P., Miller-Johnson, Shari, Burchinal, Margaret, & Ramey, Craig T. (2001). The development of cognitive and academic abilities: Growth curves from an early childhood educational experiment. *Developmental Psychology, 37,* 231–242.

Camras, Linda A., & Shutter, Jennifer M. (2010). Emotional facial expressions in infancy. *Emotion Review, 2,* 120–129.

Capaldi, Deborah M. (2003). Parental monitoring: A person-environment interaction perspective on this key parenting skill. In Ann C. Crouter & Alan Booth (Eds.), *Children's influence on family dynamics: The neglected side of family relationships* (pp. 171–179). Mahwah, NJ: Lawrence Erlbaum.

Caravita, Simona C. S., Di Blasio, Paola, & Salmivalli, Christina. (2010). Early adolescents' participation in bullying: Is ToM involved? *The Journal of Early Adolescence, 30,* 138–170.

Carey, Susan. (2010). Beyond fast mapping. *Language Learning and Development, 6,* 184–205.

Carlson, Susan A., Fulton, Janet E., Lee, Sarah M., Maynard, L. Michele, Brown, David R., Kohl, Harold W., III, et al. (2008). Physical education and academic achievement in elementary school: Data from the early childhood longitudinal study. *American Journal of Public Health, 98,* 721–727.

Carlson, Stephanie M. (2003). Executive function in context: Development, measurement, theory and experience. *Monographs of the Society for Research in Child Development, 68*(3, Serial No. 274), 138–151.

Carpendale, Jeremy I. M., & Lewis, Charlie. (2004). Constructing an understanding of mind: The development of children's social understanding within social interaction. *Behavioral and Brain Sciences, 27,* 79–96.

Case-Smith, Jane, & Kuhaneck, Heather Miller. (2008). Play preferences of typically developing children and children with developmental delays between ages 3 and 7 years. *OTJR: Occupation, Participation and Health, 28,* 19–29.

Casey, B. J., Jones, Rebecca M., & Somerville, Leah H. (2011). Braking and accelerating of the adolescent brain. *Journal of Research on Adolescence, 21,* 21–33.

Caspi, Avshalom, McClay, Joseph, Moffitt, Terrie, Mill, Jonathan, Martin, Judy, Craig, Ian W., et al. (2002, August 2). Role of genotype in the cycle of violence in maltreated children. *Science, 297,* 851–854.

Caspi, Avshalom, Moffitt, Terrie E., Morgan, Julia, Rutter, Michael, Taylor, Alan, Arseneault, Louise, et al. (2004). Maternal expressed emotion predicts children's antisocial behavior problems: Using monozygotic-twin differences to identify environmental effects on behavioral development. *Developmental Psychology, 40,* 149–161.

Caspi, Avshalom, & Shiner, Rebecca L. (2006). Personality development. In William Damon & Richard M. Lerner (Series Eds.) & Nancy Eisenberg (Vol. Ed.), *Handbook of child psychology: Vol. 3. Social, emotional, and personality development* (6th ed., pp. 300–365). Hoboken, NJ: Wiley.

Cassia, Viola Macchi, Kuefner, Dana, Picozzi, Marta, & Vescovo, Elena. (2009). Early experience predicts later plasticity for face processing: Evidence for the reactivation of dormant effects. *Psychological Science, 20,* 853–859.

Castle, David J., & Morgan, Vera. (2008). Epidemiology. In Kim T. Mueser & Dilip V. Jeste (Eds.), *Clinical handbook of schizophrenia* (pp. 14–24). New York, NY: Guilford Press.

Catani, Claudia, Gewirtz, Abigail H., Wieling, Elizabeth, Schauer, Elizabeth, Elbert, Thomas, & Neuner, Frank. (2010). Tsunami, war, and cumulative risk in the lives of Sri Lankan schoolchildren. *Child Development, 81,* 1176–1191.

Cavanagh, Sean. (2005, January 5). Poor math scores on world stage trouble U.S. *Education Week,* pp. 1, 18.

Cavanagh, Sean. (2007, December 13). Poverty's effect on U.S. scores greater than for other nations. *Education Week, 27,* 1, 13.

CBS News. (2005, Feb 8). *World's smallest baby goes home: Cellphone-sized baby is discharged from hospital.* Retrieved from http://www.cbsnews.com/stories/2005/02/08/health/main672488.shtml

CDC (Centers for Disease Control and Prevention) (Ed.). (2007). *Epidemiology and prevention of vaccine-preventable diseases* (10th ed.). Washington, DC: Public Health Foundation.

Ceci, Stephen J., & Bruck, Maggie. (1995). *Jeopardy in the courtroom: A scientific analysis of children's testimony.* Washington, DC: American Psychological Association.

Center for Sexual Health Promotion. (2010). *National Survey of Sexual Health and Behavior (NSSHB).* Retrieved from http://nationalsexstudy.indiana.edu/

Center on Education Policy. (2010). *State high school tests: Exit exams and other assessments.* Washington, DC: Author.

Centre for Community Child Health and Telethon Institute for Child Health Research. (2009). *A snapshot of early childhood development in Australia: Australian Early Development Index (AEDI) national report 2009.* Retrieved from Australian

Government Department of Education website: http://www.rch.org.au/aedi/media/Snapshot_of_Early_Childhood_DevelopmentinAustralia_AEDI_National_Report.pdf

Cesario, Sandra K., & Hughes, Lisa A. (2007). Precocious puberty: A comprehensive review of literature. *Journal of Obstetric, Gynecologic, & Neonatal Nursing, 36,* 263–274.

Chaddock, Laura, Erickson, Kirk I., Prakash, Ruchika Shaurya, VanPatter, Matt, Voss, Michelle W., Pontifex, Matthew B., et al. (2010). Basal ganglia volume is associated with aerobic fitness in preadolescent children. *Developmental Neuroscience, 32,* 249–256.

Chafen, Jennifer J. Schneider, Newberry, Sydne J., Riedl, Marc A., Bravata, Dena M., Maglione, Margaret, Suttorp, Marika J., et al. (2010). Diagnosing and managing common food allergies. *Journal of the American Medical Association, 303,* 1848–1856.

Chaignat, Evelyne, Yahya-Graison, Emilie Aït, Henrichsen, Charlotte N., Chrast, Jacqueline, Schütz, Frédéric, Pradervand, Sylvain, et al. (2011). Copy number variation modifies expression time courses. *Genome Research, 21,* 106–113.

Chambers, Bette, Cheung, Alan C., Slavin, Robert E., Smith, Dewi, & Laurenzano, Mary. (2010). *Effective early childhood education programs: A systematic review.* Baltimore, MD: Johns Hopkins University, Center for Research and Reform in Education.

Champagne, Frances A., & Curley, James P. (2010). Maternal care as a modulating influence on infant development. In Mark S. Blumberg, John H. Freeman, & Scott R. Robinson (Eds.), *Oxford handbook of developmental behavioral neuroscience* (pp. 323–341). New York, NY: Oxford University Press.

Chan, Cheri C. Y., Brandone, Amanda C., & Tardif, Twila. (2009). Culture, context, or behavioral control? English- and Mandarin-speaking mothers' use of nouns and verbs in joint book reading. *Journal of Cross-Cultural Psychology, 40,* 584–602.

Chan, David W., & Zhao, Yongjun. (2010). The relationship between drawing skill and artistic creativity: Do age and artistic involvement make a difference? *Creativity Research Journal, 22,* 27–36.

Chan, Siu Mui, Bowes, Jennifer, & Wyver, Shirley. (2009). Parenting style as a context for emotion socialization. *Early Education & Development, 20,* 631–656.

Chan, Tak Wing, & Koo, Anita. (2010). Parenting style and youth outcomes in the UK. *European Sociological Review.* Advance online publication. doi:10.1093/esr/jcq013

Chang, Esther S., Greenberger, Ellen, Chen, Chuansheng, Heckhausen, Jutta, & Farruggia, Susan P. (2010). Nonparental adults as social resources in the transition to adulthood. *Journal of Research on Adolescence, 20,* 1065–1082.

Chao, Ruth K. (2001). Extending research on the consequences of parenting style for Chinese

Americans and European Americans. *Child Development, 72,* 1832–1843.

Chao, Y. May, Pisetsky, Emily M., Dierker, Lisa C., Dohm, Faith-Anne, Rosselli, Francine, May, Alexis M., et al. (2008). Ethnic differences in weight control practices among U.S. adolescents from 1995 to 2005. *International Journal of Eating Disorders, 41,* 124–133.

Chaplin, Lan Nguyen, & John, Deborah Roedder. (2007). Growing up in a material world: Age differences in materialism in children and adolescents. *Journal of Consumer Research, 34,* 480–493.

Chassin, Laurie, Hussong, Andrea, Barrera, Manuel, Jr., Molina, Brooke S. G., Trim, Ryan, & Ritter, Jennifer. (2004). Adolescent substance use. In Richard M. Lerner & Laurence D. Steinberg (Eds.), *Handbook of adolescent psychology* (2nd ed., pp. 665–696). Hoboken, NJ: Wiley.

Chassin, Laurie, Hussong, Andrea, & Beltran, Iris. (2009). Adolescent substance use. In Richard M. Lerner & Laurence Steinberg (Eds.), *Handbook of adolescent psychology: Individual bases of adolescent development* (3rd ed., pp. 723–763). Hoboken, NJ: Wiley.

Chattopadhyay, Amit. (2008). Oral health disparities in the United States. *Dental Clinics of North America, 52,* 297–318.

Chein, Isidor. (2008). *The science of behavior and the image of man.* New Brunswick, NJ: Transaction.

Chen, Edith, Cohen, Sheldon, & Miller, Gregory E. (2010). How low socioeconomic status affects 2-year hormonal trajectories in children. *Psychological Science, 21,* 31–37.

Chen, Hong, & Jackson, Todd. (2009). Predictors of changes in weight esteem among mainland Chinese adolescents: A longitudinal analysis. *Developmental Psychology, 45,* 1618–1629.

Chen, Xinyin, Cen, Guozhen, Li, Dan, & He, Yunfeng. (2005). Social functioning and adjustment in Chinese children: The imprint of historical time. *Child Development, 76,* 182–195.

Chen, Xinyin, Wang, Li, & Wang, Zhengyan. (2009). Shyness-sensitivity and social, school, and psychological adjustment in rural migrant and urban children in China. *Child Development, 80,* 1499–1513.

Cheng, Diana, Kettinger, Laurie, Uduhiri, Kelechi, & Hurt, Lee. (2011). Alcohol consumption during pregnancy: Prevalence and provider assessment. *Obstetrics & Gynecology, 117,* 212–217.

Cheng, Yi-Chia, & Yeh, Hsin-Te. (2009). From concepts of motivation to its application in instructional design: Reconsidering motivation from an instructional design perspective. *British Journal of Educational Technology, 40,* 597–605.

Cherlin, Andrew J. (2009). *The marriage-go-round: The state of marriage and the family in America today.* New York, NY: Knopf.

Chernoff, Jodi Jacobson, Flanagan, Kristin Denton, McPhee, Cameron, & Park, Jennifer. (2007). *Preschool: First findings from the preschool follow-up of the Early Childhood Longitudinal Study, Birth Cohort (ECLS-B)* (NCES 2008–025). Washington, DC: National Center for Education Statistics.

Cheslack-Postava, Keely, Liu, Kayuet, & Bearman, Peter S. (2011). Closely spaced pregnancies are associated with increased odds of autism in California sibling births. *Pediatrics, 127,* 246–253.

Cheung, Benjamin Y., Chudek, Maciej, & Heine, Steven J. (2011). Evidence for a sensitive period for acculturation. *Psychological Science, 22,* 147–152.

Cheurprakobkit, Sutham, & Bartsch, Robert A. (2005). Security measures on school crime in Texas middle and high schools. *Educational Research, 47,* 235–250.

Chiao, Joan Y., & Blizinsky, Katherine D. (2010). Culture-gene coevolution of individualism-collectivism and the serotonin transporter gene. *Proceedings of the Royal Society B: Biological Sciences, 277,* 529–537.

Children's Bureau. (2010). *Child maltreatment 2008.* Washington, DC: U.S. Department of Health and Human Services, Administration for Children and Families, Administration on Children, Youth and Families.

Chin, Vivien S., Skike, Candice E. Van, & Matthews, Douglas B. (2010). Effects of ethanol on hippocampal function during adolescence: A look at the past and thoughts on the future. *Alcohol, 44,* 3–14.

Chomsky, Noam. (1968). *Language and mind.* New York, NY: Harcourt Brace & World.

Chomsky, Noam. (1980). *Rules and representations.* New York, NY: Columbia University Press.

Chouinard, Michelle M. (2007). Children's questions: A mechanism for cognitive development. *Monographs of the Society for Research in Child Development, 72*(1, Serial No. 286), vii–112.

Christian, Cindy W., Block, Robert, & and the Committee on Child Abuse and Neglect. (2009). Abusive head trauma in infants and children. *Pediatrics, 123,* 1409–1411.

Chronicle of Higher Education. (2010). *Almanac of higher education 2010–2011.* Washington, DC: Author.

Chua, Amy. (2011). *Battle hymn of the tiger mother.* New York, NY: Penguin.

Chudacoff, Howard P. (2007). *Children at play: An American history.* New York: New York University Press.

Cicchetti, Dante, Rogosch, Fred A., & Sturge-Apple, Melissa L. (2007). Interactions of child maltreatment and serotonin transporter and monoamine oxidase A polymorphisms: Depressive symptomatology among adolescents from low socioeconomic status backgrounds. *Development and Psychopathology, 19,* 1161–1180.

Cicchetti, Dante, & Toth, Sheree L. (2009). The past achievements and future promises of developmental psychopathology: The coming of age of a discipline. *Journal of Child Psychology and Psychiatry, 50,* 16–25.

Cillessen, Antonius H. N., & Mayeux, Lara. (2004). From censure to reinforcement: Developmental changes in the association between aggression and social status. *Child Development, 75,* 147–163.

Cipriano, Elizabeth A., & Stifter, Cynthia A. (2010). Predicting preschool effortful control from toddler temperament and parenting behavior. *Journal of Applied Developmental Psychology, 31,* 221–230.

Claas, Marieke J., de Vries, Linda S., Bruinse, Hein W., van Haastert, Ingrid C., Uniken Venema, Monica M. A., Peelen, Linda M., et al. (2011). Neurodevelopmental outcome over time of preterm born children ≤750g at birth. *Early Human Development, 87,* 183–191.

Clancy, Susan A. (2010). *The trauma myth: The truth about the sexual abuse of children—and its aftermath.* New York, NY: Basic Books.

Clark, Nina Annika, Demers, Paul A., Karr, Catherine J., Koehoorn, Mieke, Lencar, Cornel, Tamburic, Lillian, et al. (2009). Effect of early life exposure to air pollution on development of childhood asthma. *Environmental Health Perspectives, 118,* 284–290.

Clark, Shelley, Kabiru, Caroline, & Mathur, Rohini. (2010). Relationship transitions among youth in urban Kenya. *Journal of Marriage and Family, 72,* 73–88.

Cleland, Verity, Timperio, Anna, Salmon, Jo, Hume, Clare, Telford, Amanda, & Crawford, David. (2011). A longitudinal study of the family physical activity environment and physical activity among youth. *American Journal of Health Promotion, 25,* 159–167.

Cleveland, Michael J., Gibbons, Frederick X., Gerrard, Meg, Pomery, Elizabeth A., & Brody, Gene H. (2005). The impact of parenting on risk cognitions and risk behavior: A study of mediation and moderation in a panel of African American adolescents. *Child Development, 76,* 900–916.

Coghlan, Misia, Bergeron, Caroline, White, Karen, Sharp, Caroline, Morris, Marian, & Rutt, Simon. (2009). *Narrowing the gap in outcomes for young children through effective practices in the early years.* London, England: Centre for Excellence and Outcomes in Children and Young People's Services.

Cohen, David. (2006). *The development of play* (3rd ed.). New York, NY: Routledge.

Cohen, David. (2010). Probabilistic epigenesis: An alternative causal model for conduct disorders in children and adolescents. *Neuroscience & Biobehavioral Reviews, 34,* 119–129.

Cohen, Daniel, & Soto, Marcelo. (2007). Growth and human capital: Good data, good results. *Journal of Economic Growth, 12,* 51–76.

Cohen, Jon. (2007, September 7). DNA duplications and deletions help determine health. *Science, 317,* 1315–1317.

Cohen, Jon. (2007, March 9). Hope on new AIDS drugs, but breast-feeding strategy backfires. *Science, 315,* 1357.

Cohen, Joel E., & Malin, Martin B. (Eds.). (2010). *International perspectives on the goals of universal basic and secondary education.* New York, NY: Routledge.

Cohen, Larry, Chávez, Vivian, & Chehimi, Sana. (2007). *Prevention is primary: Strategies for community well-being.* San Francisco, CA: Jossey-Bass.

Cohen, Leslie B., & Cashon, Cara H. (2006). Infant cognition. In William Damon & Richard M. Lerner (Series Eds.) & Deanna Kuhn & Robert S. Siegler (Vol. Eds.), *Handbook of child psychology: Vol. 2. Cognition, perception, and language* (6th ed., pp. 214–251). Hoboken, NJ: Wiley.

Cole, Claire, & Winsler, Adam. (2010). Protecting children from exposure to lead: Old problem, new data, and new policy needs. *Social Policy Report, 24,* 3–29.

Coles, Robert. (1997). *The moral intelligence of children: How to raise a moral child.* New York, NY: Random House.

Collins, Juliet, Johnson, Susan L., & Krebs, Nancy F. (2004). Screen for and treat overweight in 2- to 5-year-olds? Yes! *Contemporary Pediatrics, 21,* 60–74.

Collins, Michael F. (with Kay, Tess). (2003). *Sport and social exclusion.* London, England: Routledge.

Collins, W. Andrew, & Laursen, Brett. (2004). Parent-adolescent relationships and influences. In Richard M. Lerner & Laurence D. Steinberg (Eds.), *Handbook of adolescent psychology* (2nd ed., pp. 331–361). Hoboken, NJ: Wiley.

Compas, Bruce E. (2004). Processes of risk and resilience during adolescence: Linking contexts and individuals. In Richard M. Lerner & Laurence D. Steinberg (Eds.), *Handbook of adolescent psychology* (2nd ed., pp. 263–296). Hoboken, NJ: Wiley.

Compian, Laura J., Gowen, L. Kris, & Hayward, Chris. (2009). The interactive effects of puberty and peer victimization on weight concerns and depression symptoms among early adolescent girls. *The Journal of Early Adolescence, 29,* 357–375.

Conboy, Barbara T., & Thal, Donna J. (2006). Ties between the lexicon and grammar: Cross-sectional and longitudinal studies of bilingual toddlers. *Child Development, 77,* 712–735.

Conger, John J. (1975). Proceedings of the American Psychological Association, Incorporated, for the year 1974: Minutes of the annual meeting of the Council of Representatives. *American Psychologist, 30,* 620–651.

Conger, Rand D., Wallace, Lora Ebert, Sun, Yumei, Simons, Ronald L., McLoyd, Vonnie C., & Brody, Gene H. (2002). Economic pressure in African American families: A replication and extension of the family stress model. *Developmental Psychology, 38,* 179–193.

Conley, Colleen S., & Rudolph, Karen D. (2009). The emerging sex difference in adolescent depression: Interacting contributions of puberty and peer stress. *Development and Psychopathology, 21,* 593–620.

Conley, Dalton, & Glauber, Rebecca. (2008). All in the family? Family composition, resources, and sibling similarity in socioeconomic status.

Research in Social Stratification and Mobility, 26, 297–306.

Cooper, Carey E., McLanahan, Sara S., Meadows, Sarah O., & Brooks-Gunn, Jeanne. (2009). Family structure transitions and maternal parenting stress. *Journal of Marriage and Family, 71,* 558–574.

Coovadia, Hoosen M., & Wittenberg, Dankwart F. (Eds.). (2004). *Paediatrics and child health: A manual for health professionals in developing countries* (5th ed.). New York, NY: Oxford University Press.

Coplan, Robert J., & Weeks, Murray. (2009). Shy and soft-spoken: Shyness, pragmatic language, and socio-emotional adjustment in early childhood. *Infant and Child Development, 18,* 238–254.

Corballis, Michael C. (2010). Mirror neurons and the evolution of language. *Brain and Language, 112,* 25–35.

Corballis, Michael C. (2011). *The recursive mind: The origins of human language, thought, and civilization.* Princeton, NJ: Princeton University Press.

Correa-Chavez, Maricela, Rogoff, Barbara, & Arauz, Rebeca Mejia. (2005). Cultural patterns in attending to two events at once. *Child Development, 76,* 664–678.

Cosgrave, James F. (2010). Embedded addiction: The social production of gambling knowledge and the development of gambling markets. *Canadian Journal of Sociology, 35,* 113–134.

Côté, James E. (2006). Emerging adulthood as an institutionalized moratorium: Risks and benefits to identity formation. In Jeffrey Jensen Arnett & Jennifer Lynn Tanner (Eds.), *Emerging adults in America: Coming of age in the 21st century* (pp. 85–116). Washington, DC: American Psychological Association.

Côté, James E. (2009). Identity formation and self-development in adolescence. In Richard M. Lerner & Laurence Steinberg (Eds.), *Handbook of adolescent psychology: Vol. 1. Individual bases of adolescent development* (3rd ed., pp. 266–304). Hoboken, NJ: Wiley.

Cote, Linda R., & Bornstein, Marc H. (2009). Child and mother play in three U.S. cultural groups: Comparisons and associations. *Journal of Family Psychology, 23,* 355–363.

Côté, Sylvana M., Borge, Anne I., Geoffroy, Marie-Claude, Rutter, Michael, & Tremblay, Richard E. (2008). Nonmaternal care in infancy and emotional/behavioral difficulties at 4 years old: Moderation by family risk characteristics. *Developmental Psychology, 44,* 155–168.

Courage, Mary L., & Setliff, Alissa E. (2010). When babies watch television: Attention-getting, attention-holding, and the implications for learning from video material. *Developmental Review, 30,* 220–238.

Couzin-Frankel, Jennifer. (2011, February 11). What would you do? *Science, 331,* 662–665.

Cowan, Nelson. (Ed.). (1997). *The development of memory in childhood.* Hove, East Sussex, UK: Psychology Press.

Cowan, Nelson. (2010). The magical mystery four. *Current Directions in Psychological Science, 19,* 51–57.

Cowan, Nelson, & Alloway, Tracy. (2009). Development of working memory in childhood. In Mary L. Courage & Nelson Cowan (Eds.), *The development of memory in infancy and childhood* (2nd ed., pp. 303–342). New York, NY: Psychology Press.

Coward, Fiona. (2008, March 14). Standing on the shoulders of giants. *Science, 319,* 1493–1495.

Cramer, Robert, Lipinski, Ryan, Bowman, Ashley, & Carollo, Tanner. (2009). Subjective distress to violations of trust in Mexican American close relationships conforms to evolutionary principles. *Current Psychology, 28,* 1–11.

Crawford, Emily, Wright, Margaret O'Dougherty, & Masten, Ann S. (2006). Resilience and spirituality in youth. In Eugene C. Roehlkepartain, Pamela Ebstyne King, Linda Wagener, & Peter L. Benson (Eds.), *The handbook of spiritual development in childhood and adolescence* (pp. 355–370). Thousand Oaks, CA: Sage Publications.

Crinion, Jenny, Turner, R., Grogan, Alice, Hanakawa, Takashi, Noppeney, Uta, Devlin, Joseph T., et al. (2006, June 9). Language control in the bilingual brain. *Science, 312,* 1537–1540.

Crisp, Richard J., & Turner, Rhiannon N. (2011). Cognitive adaptation to the experience of social and cultural diversity. *Psychological Bulletin, 137,* 242–266.

Crone, Eveline A., & Ridderinkhof, K. Richard. (2011). The developing brain: From theory to neuroimaging and back. *Developmental Cognitive Neuroscience, 1,* 101–109.

Crone, Eveline A., & Westenberg, P. Michiel. (2009). A brain-based account of developmental changes in social decision making. In Michelle de Haan & Megan R. Gunnar (Eds.), *Handbook of developmental social neuroscience* (pp. 378–396). New York, NY: Guilford.

Crosnoe, Robert, Johnson, Monica Kirkpatrick, & Elder, Glen H., Jr. (2004). Intergenerational bonding in school: The behavioral and contextual correlates of student-teacher relationships. *Sociology of Education, 77,* 60–81.

Crosnoe, Robert, Leventhal, Tama, Wirth, Robert John, Pierce, Kim M., Pianta, Robert C., & NICHD Early Child Care Research Network. (2010). Family socioeconomic status and consistent environmental stimulation in early childhood. *Child Development, 81,* 972–987.

Crosnoe, Robert, & Needham, Belinda. (2004). Holism, contextual variability, and the study of friendships in adolescent development. *Child Development, 75,* 264–279.

Cross, Donna, Monks, Helen, Hall, Marg, Shaw, Thérèse, Pintabona, Yolanda, Erceg, Erin, et al. (2010). Three-year results of the Friendly Schools whole-of-school intervention on children's bullying behaviour. *British Educational Research Journal, 37,* 105–129.

Cowan, Nelson. (2010). The magical mystery four. *Current Directions in Psychological Science, 19,* 51–57.

Cruz, Alvaro A., Bateman, Eric D., & Bousquet, Jean. (2010). The social determinants of asthma. *European Respiratory Journal, 35,* 239–242.

Cruz-Inigo, Andres E., Ladizinski, Barry, & Sethi, Aisha. (2011). Albinism in Africa: Stigma, slaughter and awareness campaigns. *Dermatologic Clinics, 29,* 79–87.

Cuijpers, Pim, Brännmark, Jessica G., & van Straten, Annemieke. (2008). Psychological treatment of postpartum depression: A meta-analysis. *Journal of Clinical Psychology, 64,* 103–118.

Cumsille, Patricio, Darling, Nancy, & Martínez, M. Loreto. (2010). Shading the truth: The patterning of adolescents' decisions to avoid issues, disclose, or lie to parents. *Journal of Adolescence, 33,* 285–296.

Cunha, Marcus, Jr., & Caldieraro, Fabio. (2009). Sunk-cost effects on purely behavioral investments. *Cognitive Science, 33,* 105–113.

Currie, Janet, & Widom, Cathy Spatz. (2010). Long-term consequences of child abuse and neglect on adult economic well-being. *Child Maltreatment, 15,* 111–120.

Curtis, W. John, & Cicchetti, Dante. (2003). Moving research on resilience into the 21st century: Theoretical and methodological considerations in examining the biological contributors to resilience. *Development & Psychopathology, 15,* 773–810.

D'Angelo, Denise, Williams, Letitia, Morrow, Brian, Cox, Shanna, Harris, Norma, Harrison, Leslie, et al. (2007). Preconception and interconception health status of women who recently gave birth to a live-born infant—Pregnancy Risk Assessment Monitoring System (PRAMS), United States, 26 reporting areas, 2004. *MMWR Surveillance Summaries, 56*(SS10), 1–35.

Daddis, Christopher. (2010). Adolescent peer crowds and patterns of belief in the boundaries of personal authority. *Journal of Adolescence, 33,* 699–708.

Dahl, Ronald E. (2004). Adolescent brain development: A period of vulnerabilities and opportunities. Keynote address. In Ronald E. Dahl & Linda Patia Spear (Eds.), *Adolescent brain development: Vulnerabilities and opportunities* (Vol. 1021, pp. 1–22). New York, NY: New York Academy of Sciences.

Dahl, Ronald E., & Gunnar, Megan R. (2009). Heightened stress responsiveness and emotional reactivity during pubertal maturation: Implications for psychopathology. *Development and Psychopathology, 21,* 1–6.

Dai, David Yun. (2010). *The nature and nurture of giftedness: A new framework for understanding gifted education.* New York, NY: Teachers College Press.

Daley, Dave, Jones, Karen, Hutchings, Judy, & Thompson, Margaret. (2009). Attention deficit hyperactivity disorder in pre-school children: Current findings, recommended interventions and future directions. *Child: Care, Health and Development, 35,* 754–766.

Dalman, Christina, Allebeck, Peter, Gunnell, David, Harrison, Glyn, Kristensson, Krister, Lewis, Glyn, et al. (2008). Infections in the

CNS during childhood and the risk of subsequent psychotic illness: A cohort study of more than one million Swedish subjects. *American Journal of Psychiatry, 165,* 59–65.

Damasio, Antonio R. (2003). *Looking for Spinoza: Joy, sorrow, and the feeling brain.* Orlando, FL: Harcourt.

Damasio, Antonio R. (2010). *Self comes to mind: Constructing the conscious brain.* New York, NY: Pantheon Books.

Danel, Isabella, Berg, Cynthia, Johnson, Christopher H., & Atrash, Hani. (2003). Magnitude of maternal morbidity during labor and delivery: United States, 1993–1997. *American Journal of Public Health, 93,* 631–634.

Darling, Nancy, Cumsille, Patricio, & Martinez, M. Loreto. (2008). Individual differences in adolescents' beliefs about the legitimacy of parental authority and their own obligation to obey: A longitudinal investigation. *Child Development, 79,* 1103–1118.

Daro, Deborah. (2002). Public perception of child sexual abuse: Who is to blame? *Child Abuse & Neglect, 26,* 1131–1133.

Darwin, Charles. (1859). *On the origin of species by means of natural selection.* London, England: J. Murray.

Dasen, Pierre R. (2003). Theoretical frameworks in cross-cultural developmental psychology: An attempt at integration. In T. S. Saraswati (Ed.), *Cross-cultural perspectives in human development: Theory, research, and applications* (pp. 128–165). New Delhi, India: Sage.

Datan, Nancy. (1986). Oedipal conflict, platonic love: Centrifugal forces in intergenerational relations. In Nancy Datan, Anita L. Greene, & Hayne W. Reese (Eds.), *Life-span developmental psychology: Intergenerational relations* (pp. 29–50). Hillsdale, NJ: Erlbaum.

David, Barbara, Grace, Diane, & Ryan, Michelle K. (2004). The gender wars: A self-categorization perspective on the development of gender identity. In Mark Bennett & Fabio Sani (Eds.), *The development of the social self* (pp. 135–157). Hove, East Sussex, England: Psychology Press.

Davidson, Julia O'Connell. (2005). *Children in the global sex trade.* Malden, MA: Polity.

Davis, Elysia Poggi, Parker, Susan Whitmore, Tottenham, Nim, & Gunnar, Megan R. (2003). Emotion, cognition, and the hypothalamic-pituitary-adrenocortical axis: A developmental perspective. In Michelle de Haan & Mark H. Johnson (Eds.), *The cognitive neuroscience of development* (pp. 181–206). New York, NY: Psychology Press.

Davis, Linell (1999). *Doing culture: Cross-cultural communication in action.* Beijing, China: Foreign Language Teaching & Research Press.

Davis, Mark, & Squire, Corinne (Eds.). (2010). *HIV treatment and prevention technologies in international perspective.* New York, NY: Palgrave Macmillan.

Davis-Kean, Pamela E., Jager, Justin, & Collins, W. Andrew (2009). The self in action:

An emerging link between self-beliefs and behaviors in middle childhood. *Child Development Perspectives, 3,* 184–188.

Davison, Kirsten Krahnstoever, Werder, Jessica L., Trost, Stewart G., Baker, Birgitta L., & Birch, Leann L. (2007). Why are early maturing girls less active? Links between pubertal development, psychological well-being, and physical activity among girls at ages 11 and 13. *Social Science & Medicine, 64,* 2391–2404.

Dawes, Nickki Pearce, & Larson, Reed. (2011). How youth get engaged: Grounded-theory research on motivational development in organized youth programs. *Developmental Psychology, 47,* 259–269.

Dawson, Geraldine. (2010). Recent advances in research on early detection, causes, biology, and treatment of autism spectrum disorders. *Current Opinion in Neurology, 23,* 95–96.

Dawson, Lorne L. (2010). The study of new religious movements and the radicalization of home-grown terrorists: Opening a dialogue. *Terrorism and Political Violence, 22,* 1–21.

Dawson, Michelle, Soulières, Isabelle, Gernsbacher, Morton Ann, & Mottron, Laurent. (2007). The level and nature of autistic intelligence. *Psychological Science, 18,* 657–662.

De Dreu, Carsten K. W., Nijstad, Bernard A., & van Knippenberg, Daan. (2008). Motivated information processing in group judgment and decision making. *Personality and Social Psychology Review, 22,* 49.

de Haan, Amaranta D., Prinzie, Peter, & Dekovic, Maja. (2009). Mothers' and fathers' personality and parenting: The mediating role of sense of competence. *Developmental Psychology, 45,* 1695–1707.

de Heering, Adelaide, de Liedekerke, Claire, Deboni, Malorie, & Rossion, Bruno. (2010). The role of experience during childhood in shaping the other-race effect. *Developmental Science, 13,* 181–187.

de Jonge, Ank, van der Goes, Birgit Y., Ravelli, Anita C. J., Amelink-Verburg, Marianne P., Mol, Ben Willem, Nijhuis, Jan G., et al. (2009). Perinatal mortality and morbidity in a nationwide cohort of 529,688 low-risk planned home and hospital births. *BJOG: An International Journal of Obstetrics & Gynaecology, 116,* 1177–1184.

De Lee, Joseph Bolivar. (1938). *The principles and practice of obstetrics* (7th ed.). Philadelphia, PA: Saunders.

De Neys, Wim. (2006). Dual processing in reasoning: Two systems but one reasoner. *Psychological Science, 17,* 428–433.

De Neys, Wim, & Van Gelder, Elke. (2009). Logic and belief across the lifespan: The rise and fall of belief inhibition during syllogistic reasoning. *Developmental Science, 12,* 123–130.

de Schipper, Elles J., Riksen-Walraven, J. Marianne, & Geurts, Sabine A. E. (2006). Effects of child-caregiver ratio on the interactions between caregivers and children in child-care centers: An experimental study. *Child Development, 77,* 861–874.

Dean, Angela J, Walters, Julie, & Hall, Anthony. (2010). A systematic review of interventions to enhance medication adherence in children and adolescents with chronic illness. *Archives of Disease in Childhood, 95,* 717–723.

Dearing, Eric, Wimer, Christopher, Simpkins, Sandra D., Lund, Terese, Bouffard, Suzanne M., Caronongan, Pia, et al. (2009). Do neighborhood and home contexts help explain why low-income children miss opportunities to participate in activities outside of school? *Developmental Psychology, 45,* 1545–1562.

Decety, Jean. (2011). Dissecting the neural mechanisms mediating empathy. *Emotion Review, 3,* 92–108.

Deci, Edward L., Koestner, Richard, & Ryan, Richard M. (1999). A meta-analytic review of experiments examining the effects of extrinsic rewards on intrinsic motivation. *Psychological Bulletin, 125,* 627–668.

Degenhardt, Louisa, Coffey, Carolyn, Carlin, John B., Swift, Wendy, Moore, Elya, & Patton, George C. (2010). Outcomes of occasional cannabis use in adolescence: 10-year follow-up study in Victoria, Australia. *The British Journal of Psychiatry, 196,* 290–295.

DeLoache, Judy S., Chiong, Cynthia, Sherman, Kathleen, Islam, Nadia, Vanderborght, Mieke, Troseth, Georgene L., et al. (2010). Do babies learn from baby media? *Psychological Science, 21,* 1570–1574.

Demetriou, Andreas, & Bakracevic, Karin. (2009). Reasoning and self-awareness from adolescence to middle age: Organization and development as a function of education. *Learning and Individual Differences, 19,* 181–194.

Denham, Susanne A., Blair, Kimberly A., DeMulder, Elizabeth, Levitas, Jennifer, Sawyer, Katherine, Auerbach-Major, Sharon, et al. (2003). Preschool emotional competence: Pathway to social competence. *Child Development, 74,* 238–256.

Denny, Dallas, & Pittman, Cathy. (2007). Gender identity: From dualism to diversity. In Mitchell S. Tepper & Annette Fuglsang Owens (Eds.), *Sexual health: Vol. 1. Psychological foundations* (pp. 205–229). Westport, CT: Praeger/Greenwood.

Denton, Melinda Lundquist, Pearce, Lisa D., & Smith, Christian. (2008). *Religion and spirituality on the path through adolescence* (Research Report Number 8). Chapel Hill, NC: National Study of Youth and Religion, University of North Carolina at Chapel Hill.

Deptula, Daneen P., Henry, David B., & Schoeny, Michael E. (2010). How can parents make a difference? Longitudinal associations with adolescent sexual behavior. *Journal of Family Psychology, 24,* 731–739.

Desai, Sonalde, & Andrist, Lester. (2010). Gender scripts and age at marriage in India. *Demography, 47,* 667–687.

DesJardin, Jean L., Ambrose, Sophie E., & Eisenberg, Laurie S. (2009). Literacy skills in children with cochlear implants: The importance of early oral language and joint storybook reading. *Journal of Deaf Studies and Deaf Education, 14,* 22–43.

Desoete, Annemie, Stock, Pieter, Schepens, Annemie, Baeyens, Dieter, & Roeyers, Herbert. (2009). Classification, seriation, and counting in grades 1, 2, and 3 as two-year longitudinal predictors for low achieving in numerical facility and arithmetical achievement? *Journal of Psychoeducational Assessment, 27,* 252–264.

Devi, Sharmila. (2008). Progress on childhood obesity patchy in the USA. *Lancet, 371,* 105–106.

DeVito, Loren M., Kanter, Benjamin R., & Eichenbaum, Howard. (2010). The hippocampus contributes to memory expression during transitive inference in mice. *Hippocampus, 20,* 208–217.

Diallo, Yacouba, Hagemann, Frank, Etienne, Alex, Gurbuzer, Yonca, & Mehran, Farhad (2010). *Global child labour developments: Measuring trends from 2004 to 2008.* Geneva, Switzerland: International Labour Office, International Programme on the Elimination of Child Labour.

Diamanti-Kandarakis, Evanthia, Bourguignon, Jean-Pierre, Giudice, Linda C., Hauser, Russ, Prins, Gail S., Soto, Ana M., et al. (2009). Endocrine-disrupting chemicals: An endocrine society scientific statement. *Endocrine Society, 30,* 293–342.

Diamond, Adele, & Amso, Dima. (2008). Contributions of neuroscience to our understanding of cognitive development. *Current Directions in Psychological Science, 17,* 136–141.

Diamond, Adele, Barnett, W. Steven, Thomas, Jessica, & Munro, Sarah. (2007, November 30). Preschool program improves cognitive control. *Science, 318,* 1387–1388.

Diamond, David M., Dunwiddie, Thomas V., & Rose, Gregory M. (1988). Characteristics of hippocampal primed burst potentiation in vitro and in the awake rat. *Journal of Neuroscience, 8,* 4079–4088.

Diamond, Lisa M., & Fagundes, Christopher P. (2010). Psychobiological research on attachment. *Journal of Social and Personal Relationships, 27,* 218–225.

Diamond, Mathew E. (2007). Neuronal basis of perceptual intelligence. In Flavia Santoianni & Claudia Sabatano (Eds.), *Brain development in learning environments: Embodied and perceptual advancements* (pp. 98–108). Newcastle, UK: Cambridge Scholars.

Diener, Marissa. (2000). Gift from the gods: A Balinese guide to early child rearing. In Judy S. DeLoache & Alma Gottlieb (Eds.), *A world of babies: Imagined childcare guides for seven societies* (pp. 96–116). New York, NY: Cambridge University Press.

Dietrich, Anne. (2008). *When the hurting continues: Revictimization and perpetration in the lives of childhood maltreatment survivors.* Saarbrücken, Germany: VDM Verlag.

DiGirolamo, Ann, Thompson, Nancy, Martorell, Reynaldo, Fein, Sara, & Grummer-Strawn, Laurence. (2005). Intention

or experience? Predictors of continued breastfeeding. *Health Education & Behavior, 32,* 208–226.

Dijk, Jan A. G. M. van. (2005). *The deepening divide: Inequality in the information society.* Thousand Oaks, CA: Sage.

Dijksterhuis, Ap, & Aarts, Henk. (2010). Goals, attention, and (un)consciousness. *Annual Review of Psychology, 61,* 467–490.

Dilworth-Bart, Janean E., & Moore, Colleen F. (2006). Mercy mercy me: Social injustice and the prevention of environmental pollutant exposures among ethnic minority and poor children. *Child Development, 77,* 247–265.

DiPietro, Janet A., Hilton, Sterling C., Hawkins, Melissa, Costigan, Kathleen A., & Pressman, Eva K. (2002). Maternal stress and affect influence fetal neurobehavioral development. *Developmental Psychology, 38,* 659–668.

Dirix, Chantal E. H., Nijhuis, Jan G., Jongsma, Henk W., & Hornstra, Gerard. (2009). Aspects of fetal learning and memory. *Child Development, 80,* 1251–1258.

Dishion, Thomas J., & Bullock, Bernadette Marie. (2002). Parenting and adolescent problem behavior: An ecological analysis of the nurturance hypothesis. In John G. Borkowski, Sharon Landesman Ramey, & Marie Bristol-Power (Eds.), *Parenting and the child's world: Influences on academic, intellectual, and social-emotional development* (pp. 231–249). Mahwah, NJ: Erlbaum.

Dishion, Thomas J., Poulin, François, & Burraston, Bert. (2001). Peer group dynamics associated with iatrogenic effects in group interventions with high-risk young adolescents. In William Damon (Series Ed.) & Douglas W. Nangle & Cynthia A. Erdley (Vol. Eds.), *New Directions for Child and Adolescent Development: No. 91. The role of friendship in psychological adjustment* (pp. 79–92). San Francisco, CA: Jossey-Bass.

Dishion, Thomas J., Véronneau, Marie-Hélène, & Myers, Michael W. (2010). Cascading peer dynamics underlying the progression from problem behavior to violence in early to late adolescence. *Development and Psychopathology, 22,* 603–619.

Dobson, Velma, Candy, T. Rowan, Hartmann, E. Eugenie, Mayer, D. Luisa, Miller, Joseph M., & Quinn, Graham E. (2009). Infant and child vision research: Present status and future directions. *Optometry & Vision Science, 86,* 559–560.

Dodge, Kenneth A. (2009). Mechanisms of gene–environment interaction effects in the development of conduct disorder. *Perspectives on Psychological Science, 4,* 408–414.

Dodge, Kenneth A., Coie, John D., & Lynam, Donald R. (2006). Aggression and antisocial behavior in youth. In William Damon & Richard M. Lerner (Series Eds.) & Nancy Eisenberg (Vol. Ed.), *Handbook of child psychology: Vol. 3. Social, emotional, and personality development* (6th ed., pp. 719–788). New York, NY: Wiley.

Domina, Thurston, Conley, AnneMarie, & Farkas, George. (2011a). The case for dreaming big. *Sociology of Education, 84,* 118–121.

Domina, Thurston, Conley, AnneMarie, & Farkas, George. (2011b). The link between educational expectations and effort in the college-for-all era. *Sociology of Education, 84,* 93–112.

Dominguez, Ximena, Vitiello, Virginia E., Maier, Michelle F., & Greenfield, Daryl B. (2010). A longitudinal examination of young children's learning behavior: Child-level and classroom-level predictors of change throughout the preschool year. *School Psychology Review, 39,* 29–47.

Donaldson, Margaret C. (2003). *A study of children's thinking.* New York, NY: Routledge. (Original work published 1963)

dosReis, Susan, Mychailyszyn, Matthew P., Evans-Lacko, Sara E., Beltran, Alicia, Riley, Anne W., & Myers, Mary Anne. (2009). The meaning of attention-deficit/hyperactivity disorder medication and parents' initiation and continuity of treatment for their child. *Journal of Child and Adolescent Psychopharmacology, 19,* 377–383.

dosReis, Susan, & Myers, Mary Anne. (2008). Parental attitudes and involvement in psychopharmacological treatment for ADHD: A conceptual model. *International Review of Psychiatry, 20,* 135–141.

Dowling, John E. (2004). *The great brain debate: Nature or nurture?* Washington, DC: Joseph Henry Press.

Drover, James, Hoffman, Dennis R., Castañeda, Yolanda S., Morale, Sarah E., & Birch, Eileen E. (2009). Three randomized controlled trials of early long-chain polyunsaturated fatty acid supplementation on means-end problem solving in 9-month-olds. *Child Development, 80,* 1376–1384.

Dukes, Richard L., Stein, Judith A., & Zane, Jazmin I. (2009). Effect of relational bullying on attitudes, behavior and injury among adolescent bullies, victims and bully-victims. *The Social Science Journal, 46,* 671–688.

Duncan, Greg J., Ziol-Guest, Kathleen M., & Kalil, Ariel. (2010). Early-childhood poverty and adult attainment, behavior, and health. *Child Development, 81,* 306–325.

Duncan, Jhodie R., Paterson, David S., Hoffman, Jill M., Mokler, David J., Borenstein, Natalia S., Belliveau, Richard A., et al. (2010). Brainstem serotonergic deficiency in sudden infant death syndrome. *Journal of the American Medical Association, 303,* 430–437.

Dunn, Judy, & Hughes, Claire. (2001). "I got some swords and you're dead!": Violent fantasy, antisocial behavior, friendship, and moral sensibility in young children. *Child Development, 72,* 491–505.

Dunphy, Dexter C. (1963). The social structure of urban adolescent peer groups. *Sociometry, 26,* 230–246.

Durkee, Tony, Kaess, Michael, Floderus, Birgitta, Carli, Vladimir, & Wasserman, Danuta. (2011). Adolescent internet behavior and its correlation to depression, self-harm and suicidal behavior in European pupils. *European Psychiatry, 26*(Suppl. 1), 1863.

Dweck, Carol S. (2007). Is math a gift? Beliefs that put females at risk. In Stephen J. Ceci & Wendy M. Williams (Eds.), *Why aren't* *more women in science: Top researchers debate the evidence* (pp. 47–55). Washington, DC: American Psychological Association.

Eccles, Jacquelynne. (2011). Gendered educational and occupational choices: Applying the Eccles et al. model of achievement-related choices. *International Journal of Behavioral Development, 35*, 195–201.

Eccles, Jacquelynne C., & Roeser, Robert W. (2010). An ecological view of schools and development. In Judith L. Meece & Jacquelynne S. Eccles (Eds.), *Handbook of research on schools, schooling, and human development* (pp. 6–22). New York, NY: Routledge.

Eccles, Jacquelynne S., & Roeser, Robert W. (2011). Schools as developmental contexts during adolescence. *Journal of Research on Adolescence, 21*, 225–241.

Eckstein, Daniel G., Rasmussen, Paul R., & Wittschen, Lori. (1999). Understanding and dealing with adolescents. *Journal of Individual Psychology, 55*, 31–50.

Education Week. (2010, January 14). *Chance for success* [Table]. Retrieved from http://www.edweek.org/media/ew/qc/2010/17sos.h29.chance.pdf

Edwards, Judge Leonard. (2010). Relative placement in child protection cases: A judicial perspective. *Juvenile and Family Court Journal, 61*, 1–44.

Eggum, Natalie D., Eisenberg, Nancy, Kao, Karen, Spinrad, Tracy L., Bolnick, Rebecca, Hofer, Claire, et al. (2011). Emotion understanding, theory of mind, and prosocial orientation: Relations over time in early childhood. *The Journal of Positive Psychology, 6*, 4–16.

Eisenberg, Nancy, Cumberland, Amanda, Guthrie, Ivanna K., Murphy, Bridget C., & Shepard, Stephanie A. (2005). Age changes in prosocial responding and moral reasoning in adolescence and early adulthood. *Journal of Research on Adolescence, 15*, 235–260.

Eisenberg, Nancy, Fabes, Richard A., & Spinrad, Tracy L. (2006). Prosocial development. In William Damon & Richard M. Lerner (Series Eds.) & Nancy Eisenberg (Vol. Ed.), *Handbook of child psychology: Vol. 3. Social, emotional, and personality development* (6th ed., pp. 646–718). Hoboken, NJ: Wiley.

Eisenberg, Nancy, Hofer, Claire, Spinrad, Tracy L., Gershoff, Elizabeth T., Valiente, Carlos, Losoya, Sandra, et al. (2008). Understanding mother-adolescent conflict discussions: Concurrent and across-time prediction from youths' dispositions and parenting. *Monographs of the Society for Research in Child Development, 73*(2, Serial No. 290), vii–viii, 1–160.

Eisenberg, Nancy, Spinrad, Tracy L., Fabes, Richard A., Reiser, Mark, Cumberland, Amanda, Shepard, Stephanie A., et al. (2004). The relations of effortful control and impulsivity to children's resiliency and adjustment. *Child Development, 75*, 25–46.

Eklund, Jenny M., Kerr, Margaret, & Stattin, Håkan. (2010). Romantic relationships and delinquent behaviour in adolescence: The moder-

ating role of delinquency propensity. *Journal of Adolescence, 33*, 377–386.

Elder, Glen H., Jr,, & Shanahan, Michael J. (2006). The life course and human development. In William Damon & Richard M. Lerner (Series Eds.) & Richard M. Lerner (Vol. Ed.), *Handbook of child psychology: Vol. 1. Theoretical models of human development* (6th ed., pp. 665–715). Hoboken, NJ: Wiley.

Elia, Josephine, & Vetter, Victoria L. (2010). Cardiovascular effects of medications for the treatment of attention-deficit hyperactivity disorder: What is known and how should it influence prescribing in children? *Pediatric Drugs, 12*, 165–175.

Elkind, David. (1967). Egocentrism in adolescence. *Child Development, 38*, 1025–1034.

Elkind, David. (2007). *The power of play: How spontaneous, imaginative activities lead to happier, healthier children*. Cambridge, MA: Da Capo Press.

Elliott, Leslie, Arbes, Samuel J., Jr., Harvey, Eric S., Lee, Robert C., Salo, Päivi M., Cohn, Richard D., et al. (2007). Dust weight and asthma prevalence in the National Survey of Lead and Allergens in Housing (NSLAH). *Environmental Health Perspectives, 115*, 215–220.

Ellis, Bruce J., & Boyce, W. Thomas. (2008). Biological sensitivity to context. *Current Directions in Psychological Science, 17*, 183–187.

Ellis, Bruce J., Shirtcliff, Elizabeth A., Boyce, W. Thomas, Deardorff, Julianna, & Essex, Marilyn J. (2011). Quality of early family relationships and the timing and tempo of puberty: Effects depend on biological sensitivity to context. *Development and Psychopathology, 23*, 85–99.

Else-Quest, Nicole M., Hyde, Janet Shibley, Goldsmith, H. Hill, & Van Hulle, Carol A. (2006). Gender differences in temperament: A meta-analysis. *Psychological Bulletin, 132*, 33–72.

Engelberts, Adèle C., & de Jonge, Guus A. (1990). Choice of sleeping position for infants: Possible association with cot death. *Archives of Disease in Childhood, 65*, 462–467.

Engels, Rutger C. M. E., Scholte, Ron H. J., van Lieshout, Cornelis F. M., de Kemp, Raymond, & Overbeek, Geertjan. (2006). Peer group reputation and smoking and alcohol consumption in early adolescence. *Addictive Behaviors, 31*, 440–449.

Englander, Elizabeth, Mills, Elizabeth, & McCoy, Meghan. (2009). Cyberbullying and information exposure: User-generated content in post-secondary education. *International Journal of Contemporary Sociology, 46*, 213–230.

Enserink, Martin. (2011, February 18). Can this DNA sleuth help catch criminals? *Science, 331*, 838–840.

Epps, Chad, & Holt, Lynn. (2011). The genetic basis of addiction and relevant cellular mechanisms. *International Anesthesiology Clinics, 49*, 3–14.

Epstein, Jeffery N., Langberg, Joshua M., Lichtenstein, Philip K., Altaye, Mekibib, Brinkman, William B., House, Katherine, et

al. (2010). Attention-deficit/hyperactivity disorder outcomes for children treated in community-based pediatric settings. *Archives of Pediatrics & Adolescent Medicine, 164*, 160–165.

Epstein, Leonard H., Handley, Elizabeth A., Dearing, Kelly K., Cho, David D., Roemmich, James N., Paluch, Rocco A., et al. (2006). Purchases of food in youth: Influence of price and income. *Psychological Science, 17*, 82–89.

Erath, Stephen A., Keiley, Margaret K., Pettit, Gregory S., Lansford, Jennifer E., Dodge, Kenneth A., & Bates, John E. (2009). Behavioral predictors of mental health service utilization in childhood through adolescence. *Journal of Developmental & Behavioral Pediatrics, 30*, 481–488.

Erikson, Erik H. (1963). *Childhood and society* (2nd ed.). New York, NY: Norton.

Erikson, Erik H. (1968). *Identity: Youth and crisis*. New York, NY: Norton.

Erikson, Erik H. (1969). *Gandhi's truth: On the origins of militant nonviolence*. New York, NY: Norton.

Erikson, Erik H. (1982). *The life cycle completed: A review*. New York, NY: Norton.

Ertesvåg, Sigrun K. (2011). Measuring authoritative teaching. *Teaching and Teacher Education, 27*, 51–61.

Ertmer, David J., Young, Nancy M., & Nathani, Suneeti. (2007). Profiles of vocal development in young cochlear implant recipients. *Journal of Speech, Language, and Hearing Research, 50*, 393–407.

Etchu, Koji. (2007). Social context and preschoolers' judgments about aggressive behavior: Social domain theory. *Japanese Journal of Educational Psychology, 55*, 219–230.

Evans, Angela D., Xu, Fen, & Lee, Kang. (2011). When all signs point to you: Lies told in the face of evidence. *Developmental Psychology, 47*, 39–49.

Evans, David W., & Leckman, James F. (2006). Origins of obsessive-compulsive disorder: Developmental and evolutionary perspectives. In Dante Cicchetti & Donald J. Cohen (Eds.), *Developmental psychopathology: Vol. 3. Risk, disorder, and adaptation* (2nd ed., pp. 404–435). Hoboken, NJ: Wiley.

Evans, David W., Leckman, James F., Carter, Alice, Reznick, J. Steven, Henshaw, Desiree, King, Robert A., et al. (1997). Ritual, habit, and perfectionism: The prevalence and development of compulsive-like behavior in normal young children. *Child Development, 68*, 58–68.

Eyer, Diane E. (1992). *Mother-infant bonding: A scientific fiction*. New Haven, CT: Yale University Press.

Fagard, Jacqueline, & Lockman, Jeffrey J. (2010). Change in imitation for object manipulation between 10 and 12 months of age. *Developmental Psychobiology, 52*, 90–99.

Falbo, Toni, Kim, Sunghun, & Chen, Kuan-yi. (2009). Alternate models of sibling status effects on health in later life. *Developmental Psychology, 45,* 677–687.

Falk, Dean. (2004). Prelinguistic evolution in early hominins: Whence motherese? *Behavioral and Brain Sciences, 27,* 491–503.

Farahani, Mansour, Subramanian, S. V., & Canning, David. (2009). The effect of changes in health sector resources on infant mortality in the short-run and the long-run: A longitudinal econometric analysis. *Social Science & Medicine, 68,* 1918–1925.

Faraone, Stephen V., Sergeant, Joseph, Gillberg, Christopher, & Biederman, Joseph. (2003). The worldwide prevalence of ADHD: Is it an American condition? *World Psychiatry, 2,* 104–113.

Farmer, Thomas W., Hamm, Jill V., Petrin, Robert A., Robertson, Dylan, Murray, Robert A., Meece, Judith L., et al. (2010). Supporting early adolescent learning and social strengths: Promoting productive contexts for students at-risk for EBD during the transition to middle school. *Exceptionality, 18,* 94–106.

Farrar, Ruth D., & Al-Qatawneh, Khalil S. (2010). Interdisciplinary theoretical foundations for literacy teaching and learning. *European Journal of Social Sciences, 13,* 56–66.

Farrelly, Matthew C., Davis, Kevin C., Haviland, M. Lyndon, Messeri, Peter, & Healton, Cheryl G. (2005). Evidence of a dose-response relationship between "truth" antismoking ads and youth smoking prevalence. *American Journal of Public Health, 95,* 425–431.

Fazzi, Elisa, Signorini, Sabrina Giovanna, Bomba, Monica, Luparia, Antonella, Lanners, Josée, & Balottin, Umberto. (2011). Reach on sound: A key to object permanence in visually impaired children. *Early Human Development, 87,* 289–296.

Fechter-Leggett, Molly O., & O'Brien, Kirk. (2010). The effects of kinship care on adult mental health outcomes of alumni of foster care. *Children and Youth Services Review, 32,* 206–213.

Feldman, Ruth. (2007). Parent-infant synchrony and the construction of shared timing; Physiological precursors, developmental outcomes, and risk conditions. *Journal of Child Psychology and Psychiatry, 48,* 329–354.

Feldman, Ruth, & Eidelman, Arthur I. (2004). Parent-infant synchrony and the social-emotional development of triplets. *Developmental Psychology, 40,* 1133–1147.

Feldman, Ruth, Weller, Aron, Sirota, Lea, & Eidelman, Arthur I. (2002). Skin-to-skin contact (kangaroo care) promotes self-regulation in premature infants: Sleep-wake cyclicity, arousal modulation, and sustained exploration. *Developmental Psychology, 38,* 194–207.

Feltis, Brooke B., Powell, Martine B., Snow, Pamela C., & Hughes-Scholes, Carolyn H. (2010). An examination of the association between interviewer question type and story-grammar detail in child witness interviews about abuse. *Child Abuse & Neglect: The International Journal, 34,* 407–413.

Fenson, Larry, Bates, Elizabeth, Dale, Philip, Goodman, Judith, Reznick, J. Steven, & Thal, Donna. (2000). Measuring variability in early child language: Don't shoot the messenger. *Child Development, 71,* 323–328.

Fentiman, Linda C. (2009). Pursuing the perfect mother: Why America's criminalization of maternal substance abuse is not the answer—A comparative legal analysis. *Michigan Journal of Gender & Law, 15.*

Ferber, Sari Goldstein, & Makhoul, Imad R. (2004). The effect of skin-to-skin contact (kangaroo care) shortly after birth on the neurobehavioral responses of the term newborn: A randomized, controlled trial. *Pediatrics, 113,* 858–865.

Ferguson Publishing. (2007). *Encyclopedia of careers and vocational guidance* (14th ed.). New York, NY: Author.

Fernyhough, Charles. (2010). Vygotsky, Luria, and the social brain. In Bryan W. Sokol, Ulrich Müller, Jeremy I. M. Carpendale, Arlene R. Young, & Grace Iarocci (Eds.), *Self and social regulation: Social interaction and the development of social understanding and executive functions* (pp. 56–79). New York, NY: Oxford University Press.

Fewtrell, Mary, Wilson, David C., Booth, Ian, & Lucas, Alan. (2011). Six months of exclusive breast feeding: How good is the evidence? *British Medical Journal, 342,* c5955. doi:10.1136/bmj.c5955

Finkelhor, David, & Jones, Lisa M. (2004). *Explanations for the decline in child sexual abuse cases.* Retrieved from Office of Juvenile Justice and Delinquency Prevention website: http://www.ncjrs.gov/html/ojjdp/199298/contents.html

Fisher, Helen E. (2006). Broken hearts: The nature and risks of romantic rejection. In Ann C. Crouter & Alan Booth (Eds.), *Romance and sex in adolescence and emerging adulthood: Risks and opportunities* (pp. 3–28). Mahwah, NJ: Erlbaum.

Fletcher, Anne C., Steinberg, Laurence, & Williams-Wheeler, Meeshay. (2004). Parental influences on adolescent problem behavior: Revisiting Stattin and Kerr. *Child Development, 75,* 781–796.

Fletcher, Jack M., & Vaughn, Sharon. (2009). Response to intervention: Preventing and remediating academic difficulties. *Child Development Perspectives, 3,* 30–37.

Flory, Richard W., & Miller, Donald E. (2000). *GenX religion.* New York, NY: Routledge.

Floud, Roderick, Fogel, Robert W., Harris, Bernard, & Hong, Sok Chul. (2011). *An overview of the changing body: Health, nutrition, and human development in the Western world since 1700.* Cambridge, MA: Cambridge University Press.

Floud, Roderick, Fogel, Robert W., Harris, Bernard, & Hong, Sok Chul. (2011). *The changing body: Health, nutrition, and human development in the western world since 1700.* Cambridge, UK: Cambridge University Press.

Flynn, James R. (1999). Searching for justice: The discovery of IQ gains over time. *American Psychologist, 54,* 5–20.

Flynn, James R. (2007). *What is intelligence? Beyond the Flynn effect.* New York, NY: Cambridge University Press.

Forget-Dubois, Nadine, Dionne, Ginette, Lemelin, Jean-Pascal, Pérusse, Daniel, Tremblay, Richard E., & Boivin, Michel. (2009). Early child language mediates the relation between home environment and school readiness. *Child Development, 80,* 736–749.

Fortuna, Keren, & Roisman, Glenn I. (2008). Insecurity, stress, and symptoms of psychopathology: Contrasting results from self-reports versus interviews of adult attachment. *Attachment & Human Development, 10,* 11–28.

Foster, Eugene A., Jobling, M. A., Taylor, P. G., Donnelly, P., de Knijff, P., Mieremet, Rene, et al. (1998, November 5). Jefferson fathered slave's last child. *Nature, 396,* 27–28.

Fox, Emily, & Riconscente, Michelle. (2008). Metacognition and self-regulation in James, Piaget, and Vygotsky. *Educational Psychology Review, 20,* 373–389.

Fox, Nathan A., Henderson, Heather A., Rubin, Kenneth H., Calkins, Susan D., & Schmidt, Louis A. (2001). Continuity and discontinuity of behavioral inhibition and exuberance: Psychophysiological and behavioral influences across the first four years of life. *Child Development, 72,* 1–21.

Fox, Sharon E., Levitt, Pat, & Nelson, Charles A., III. (2010). How the timing and quality of early experiences influence the development of brain architecture. *Child Development, 81,* 28–40.

Fragouli, Elpida, & Wells, Dagan. (2011). Aneuploidy in the human blastocyst. *Cytogenetic and Genome Research, 133,* 149–159.

Frankenburg, William K., Dodds, Josiah, Archer, Philip, Shapiro, Howard, & Bresnick, Beverly. (1992). The Denver II: A major revision and restandardization of the Denver Developmental Screening Test. *Pediatrics, 89,* 91–97.

Franko, Debra L., Thompson, Douglas, Affenito, Sandra G., Barton, Bruce A., & Striegel-Moore, Ruth H. (2008). What mediates the relationship between family meals and adolescent health issues. *Health Psychology, 27*(Suppl. 2), S109–S117.

Franks, Paul W., Hanson, Robert L., Knowler, William C., Sievers, Maurice L., Bennett, Peter H., & Looker, Helen C. (2010). Childhood obesity, other cardiovascular risk factors, and premature death. *New England Journal of Medicine, 362,* 485–493.

Frayling, Timothy M., Timpson, Nicholas J., Weedon, Michael N., Zeggini, Eleftheria, Freathy, Rachel M., Lindgren, Cecilia M., et al. (2007, May 11). A common variant in the FTO gene is associated with body mass index and predisposes to childhood and adult obesity. *Science, 316,* 889–894.

Frazier, Thomas W., & Hardan, Antonio Y. (2009). A meta-analysis of the corpus callosum in autism. *Biological psychiatry, 66,* 935–941.

Fredricks, Jennifer A., & Eccles, Jacquelynne S. (2002). Children's competence and value beliefs from childhood through adolescence: Growth trajectories in two male-sex-typed domains. *Developmental Psychology, 38,* 519–533.

Fredricks, Jennifer A., & Eccles, Jacquelynne S. (2006). Is extracurricular participation associated with beneficial outcomes? Concurrent and longitudinal relations. *Developmental Psychology, 42,* 698–713.

Freeman, Elisabeth. (2010). *Run for your life* (Book Three). Time to Heal Ministries Publishing.

Frenda, Steven J., Nichols, Rebecca M., & Loftus, Elizabeth F. (2011). Current issues and advances in misinformation research. *Current Directions in Psychological Science, 20,* 20–23.

Freud, Anna. (2000). Adolescence. In James B. McCarthy (Ed.), *Adolescent development and psychopathology* (Vol. 13, pp. 29–52). Lanham, MD: University Press of America. (Reprinted from *Psychoanalytic Study of the Child,* pp. 255–278, 1958, New Haven, CT: Yale University Press)

Freud, Sigmund. (1935). *A general introduction to psychoanalysis* (Joan Riviere, Trans.). New York, NY: Liveright.

Freud, Sigmund. (1938). *The basic writings of Sigmund Freud* (A. A. Brill, Ed. and Trans.). New York, NY: Modern Library.

Freud, Sigmund. (1949). *An outline of psychoanalysis* (James Strachey, Trans.). New York, NY: W. W. Norton. (Original work published 1940)

Freud, Sigmund. (1964). An outline of psychoanalysis. In James Strachey (Ed. and Trans.), *The standard edition of the complete psychological works of Sigmund Freud* (Vol. 23, pp. 144–207). London, England: Hogarth Press. (Original work published 1940)

Friedman, Jeffrey M. (2011). Leptin and the regulation of body weight. *Keio Journal of Medicine, 60,* 1–9.

Fries, Alison B. Wismer, & Pollak, Seth D. (2007). Emotion processing and the developing brain. In Donna Coch, Kurt W. Fischer, & Geraldine Dawson (Eds.), *Human behavior, learning, and the developing brain. Typical development* (pp. 329–361). New York, NY: Guilford Press.

Frost, Joe L. (2009). *A history of children's play and play environments: Toward a contemporary child-saving movement.* New York, NY: Routledge.

Fuligni, Andrew J., & Hardway, Christina. (2006). Daily variation in adolescents' sleep, activities, and psychological well-being. *Journal of Research on Adolescence, 16,* 353–378.

Fuligni, Andrew J., Hughes, Diane L., & Way, Niobe. (2009). Ethnicity and immigration. In Richard M. Lerner & Laurence Steinberg (Eds.), *Handbook of adolescent psychology: Vol. 2. Contextual influences on adolescent development* (3rd ed., pp. 527–569). Hoboken, NJ: Wiley.

Fuligni, Allison Sidle, Howes, Carollee, Lara-Cinisomo, Sandraluz, & Karoly, Lynn A. (2009). Diverse pathways in early childhood professional development: An exploration of early educators in public preschools, private preschools, and family child care homes. *Early Education and Development, 20,* 507–526.

Fung, Joey J., & Lau, Anna S. (2009). Punitive discipline and child behavior problems in Chinese-American immigrant families: The moderating effects of indigenous child-rearing ideologies. *International Journal of Behavioral Development, 33,* 520–530.

Furstenberg, Frank F., Jr. (2010). On a new schedule: Transitions to adulthood and family change. *Future of Children, 20,* 67–87.

Gabrieli, John D. E. (2009, July 17). Dyslexia: A new synergy between education and cognitive neuroscience. *Science, 325,* 280–283.

Gaertner, Bridget M., Spinrad, Tracy L., Eisenberg, Nancy, & Greving, Karissa A. (2007). Parental childrearing attitudes as correlates of father involvement during infancy. *Journal of Marriage and Family, 69,* 962–976.

Galambos, Nancy L., Barker, Erin T., & Krahn, Harvey J. (2006). Depression, self-esteem, and anger in emerging adulthood: Seven-year trajectories. *Developmental Psychology, 42,* 350–365.

Gallese, Vittorio, Fadiga, Luciano, Fogassi, Leonardo, & Rizzolatti, Giacomo. (1996). Action recognition in the premotor cortex. *Brain, 119,* 593–609.

Galotti, Kathleen M. (2002). *Making decisions that matter: How people face important life choices.* Mahwah, NJ: Erlbaum.

Gandara, Patricia, & Rumberger, Russell W. (2009). Immigration, language, and education: How does language policy structure opportunity? *Teachers College Record, 111,* 750–782.

Gandini, Leila, Hill, Lynn, Cadwell, Louise, & Schwall, Charles (Eds.). (2005). *In the spirit of the studio: Learning from the atelier of Reggio Emilia.* New York, NY: Teachers College Press.

Gangestad, Steven W., & Simpson, Jeffry A. (2007). *The evolution of mind: Fundamental questions and controversies.* New York, NY: Guilford Press.

Ganong, Lawrence H., Coleman, Marilyn, & Jamison, Tyler. (2011). Patterns of stepchild–stepparent relationship development. *Journal of Marriage and Family, 73,* 396–413.

García Coll, Cynthia T., & Marks, Amy Kerivan. (2009). *Immigrant stories: Ethnicity and academics in middle childhood.* New York, NY: Oxford University Press.

Garcia, Eugene E., & Miller, L. Scott. (2008). Findings and recommendations of the National Task Force on Early Childhood Education for Hispanics. *Child Development Perspectives, 2,* 53–58.

García, Fernando, & Gracia, Enrique. (2009). Is always authoritative the optimum parenting style? Evidence from Spanish families. *Adolescence, 44,* 101–131.

Garcia-Segura, Luis Miguel. (2009). *Hormones and brain plasticity.* New York, NY: Oxford University Press.

Gardner, Howard. (1983). *Frames of mind: The theory of multiple intelligences.* New York, NY: Basic Books.

Gardner, Howard. (1999). Are there additional intelligences? The case for naturalist, spiritual, and existential intelligences. In Jeffrey Kane (Ed.), *Education, information, and transformation: Essays on learning and thinking* (pp. 111–131). Upper Saddle River, NJ: Merrill.

Gardner, Howard. (2006). *Multiple intelligences: New horizons in theory and practice* (Completely rev. and updated ed.). New York, NY: Basic Books.

Gardner, Howard, & Moran, Seana. (2006). The science of multiple intelligences theory: A response to Lynn Waterhouse. *Educational Psychologist, 41,* 227–232.

Gardner, Margo, & Steinberg, Laurence. (2005). Peer influence on risk taking, risk preference, and risky decision making in adolescence and adulthood: An experimental study. *Developmental Psychology, 41,* 625–635.

Garofalo, Robert, Wolf, R. Cameron, Wissow, Lawrence S., Woods, Elizabeth R., & Goodman, Elizabeth. (1999). Sexual orientation and risk of suicide attempts among a representative sample of youth. *Archives of Pediatrics & Adolescent Medicine, 153,* 487–493.

Gaskins, Suzanne. (1999). Children's daily lives in a Mayan village: A case study of culturally constructed roles and activities. In Artin Goncu (Ed.), *Children's engagement in the world: Sociocultural perspectives* (pp. 25–60). New York, NY: Cambridge University Press.

Gathercole, Susan E., Pickering, Susan J., Ambridge, Benjamin, & Wearing, Hannah. (2004). The structure of working memory from 4 to 15 years of age. *Developmental Psychology, 40,* 177–190.

Gathwala, Geeta, Singh, Bir, & Balhara, Bharti. (2008). KMC facilitates mother baby attachment in low birth weight infants. *The Indian Journal of Pediatrics, 75,* 43–47.

Gaumer, Carol J., & Arnone, Carol. (2009). Grocery store observation: Parent-child interaction in family purchases. *Journal of Food Products Marketing, 16,* 1–18.

Gauvain, Mary. (2005). Scaffolding in socialization. *New Ideas in Psychology, 23,* 129–139.

Gauvain, Mary, Beebe, Heidi, & Zhao, Shuheng. (2011). Applying the cultural approach to cognitive development. *Journal of Cognition and Development, 12,* 121–133.

Gdalevich, Michael, Mimouni, Daniel, & Mimouni, Marc. (2001). Breast-feeding and the risk of bronchial asthma in childhood: A systematic review with meta-analysis of prospective studies. *Journal of Pediatrics, 139,* 261–266.

Ge, Xiaojia, & Natsuaki, Misaki N. (2009). In search of explanations for early pubertal timing effects on developmental psychopathology. *Current Directions in Psychological Science, 18,* 327–331.

Ge, Xiaojia, Natsuaki, Misaki N., Neiderhiser, Jenae M., & Reiss, David. (2007). Genetic and environmental influences on pubertal timing: Results from two national sibling studies. *Journal of Research on Adolescence, 17,* 767–788.

Geary, Nori, & Lovejoy, Jennifer. (2008). Sex differences in energy metabolism, obesity, and eating behavior. In Jill B. Becker, Karen J. Berkley, Nori Geary, Elizabeth Hampson, James P. Herman, & Elizabeth Young (Eds.), *Sex differences in the brain: From genes to behavior* (pp. 253–274). New York, NY: Oxford University Press.

Geller, Barbara, Tillman, Rebecca, Bolhofner, Kristine, & Zimerman, Betsy. (2008). Child bipolar I disorder: Prospective continuity with adult bipolar I disorder; characteristics of second and third episodes; predictors of 8-year outcome. *Archives of General Psychiatry, 65,* 1125–1133.

Gendron, Brian P., Williams, Kirk R., & Guerra, Nancy G. (2011). An analysis of bullying among students within schools: Estimating the effects of individual normative beliefs, self-esteem, and school climate. *Journal of School Violence, 10,* 150–164.

Genesee, Fred. (2008). Early dual language learning. *Zero to Three, 29,* 17–23.

Genesee, Fred, & Nicoladis, Elena. (2007). Bilingual first language acquisition. In Erika Hoff & Marilyn Shatz (Eds.), *Blackwell handbook of language development* (pp. 324–342). Malden, MA: Blackwell.

Gentile, Douglas. (2009). Pathological video-game use among youth ages 8 to 18. *Psychological Science, 20,* 594–602.

Gentile, Douglas A. (2011b). The multiple dimensions of video game effects. *Child Development Perspectives, 5,* 75–81.

Gentile, Douglas A., Choo, Hyekyung, Liau, Albert, Sim, Timothy, Li, Dongdong, Fung, Daniel, et al. (2011a). Pathological video game use among youths: A two-year longitudinal study. *Pediatrics.* Advance online publication. doi:10.1542/peds.2010–1353

Gentile, Douglas A., Saleem, Muniba, & Anderson, Craig A. (2007). Public policy and the effects of media violence on children. *Social Issues and Policy Review, 1,* 15–61.

Gentile, Salvatore. (2010). Antidepressant use in children and adolescents diagnosed with major depressive disorder: What can we learn from published data? *Reviews on Recent Clinical Trials 5,* 63–75.

Georgas, James, Berry, John W., van de Vijver, Fons J. R., Kagitçibasi, Çigdem, & Poortinga, Ype H. (2006). *Families across cultures: A 30–nation psychological study.* Cambridge, UK: Cambridge University Press.

Geraerts, Elke, Lindsay, D. Stephen, Merckelbach, Harald, Jelicic, Marko, Raymaekers, Linsey, Arnold, Michelle M., et al. (2009). Cognitive mechanisms underlying recovered-memory experiences of childhood sexual abuse. *Psychological Science, 20,* 92–98.

Gernsbacher, Morton Ann. (2010). Stigma from psychological science: Group differences, not deficits—Introduction to stigma special section. *Perspectives on Psychological Science, 5,* 687.

Gerrard, Meg, Gibbons, Frederick X., Houlihan, Amy E., Stock, Michelle L., & Pomery, Elizabeth A. (2008). A dual-process approach to health risk decision making: The pro-

totype willingness model. *Developmental Review, 28,* 29–61.

Gershkoff-Stowe, Lisa, & Hahn, Erin R. (2007). Fast mapping skills in the developing lexicon. *Journal of Speech, Language, and Hearing Research, 50,* 682–696.

Gershoff, Elizabeth T., Grogan-Kaylor, Andrew, Lansford, Jennifer E., Chang, Lei, Zelli, Arnaldo, Deater-Deckard, Kirby, et al. (2010). Parent discipline practices in an international sample: Associations with child behaviors and moderation by perceived normativeness. *Child Development, 81,* 487–502.

Gettler, Lee T., & McKenna, James J. (2010). Never sleep with baby? Or keep me close but keep me safe: Eliminating inappropriate safe infant sleep rhetoric in the United States. *Current Pediatric Reviews, 6,* 71–77.

Gevorgyan, Ruzanna, Schmidt, Elena, Wall, Martin, Garnett, Geoffrey, Atun, Rifat, Maksimova, Svetlana, et al. (2011). Does Russia need sex education? The views of stakeholders in three Russian regions. *Sex Education, 11,* 213–226.

Gewertz, Catherine. (2011a, February 22). AP passing rates rose for last year's seniors. *Education Week,* p. 5.

Gewertz, Catherine. (2011b, June 9). 'College for all' reconsidered: Are four-year degrees for all? *Education Week,* pp. 6–8.

Giardino, Angelo P., & Alexander, Randell. (2011). *Child maltreatment* (4th ed.). St. Louis, MO: G. W. Medical.

Gibson, Eleanor J. (1969). *Principles of perceptual learning and development.* New York, NY: Appleton-Century-Crofts.

Gibson, Eleanor J. (1988). Exploratory behavior in the development of perceiving, acting, and the acquiring of knowledge. *Annual Review of Psychology, 39,* 1–42.

Gibson, Eleanor J. (1997). An ecological psychologist's prolegomena for perceptual development: A functional approach. In Cathy Dent-Read & Patricia Zukow-Goldring (Eds.), *Evolving explanations of development: Ecological approaches to organism-environment systems* (pp. 23–54). Washington, DC: American Psychological Association.

Gibson, Eleanor J., & Walk, Richard D. (1960). The "visual cliff." *Scientific American, 202,* 64–71.

Gibson, James Jerome. (1979). *The ecological approach to visual perception.* Boston, MA: Houghton Mifflin.

Gibson-Davis, Christina M. (2009). Money, marriage, and children: Testing the financial expectations and family formation theory. *Journal of Marriage and Family, 71,* 146–160.

Gibson-Davis, Christina M., & Brooks-Gunn, Jeanne. (2006). Couples' immigration status and ethnicity as determinants of breastfeeding. *American Journal of Public Health, 96,* 641–646.

Gigerenzer, Gerd. (2008). Why heuristics work. *Perspectives on Psychological Science, 3,* 20–29.

Gilchrist, Heidi, & Sullivan, Gerard. (2006). The role of gender and sexual relations for young people in identity construction and youth suicide. *Culture, Health & Sexuality, 8,* 195–209.

Giles, Amy, & Rovee-Collier, Carolyn. (2011). Infant long-term memory for associations formed during mere exposure. *Infant Behavior and Development, 34,* 327–338.

Giles-Sims, Jean, & Lockhart, Charles. (2005). Culturally shaped patterns of disciplining children. *Journal of Family Issues, 26,* 196–218.

Gillespie, Michael Allen. (2010). Players and spectators: Sports and ethical training in the American university. In Elizabeth Kiss & J. Peter Euben (Eds.), *Debating moral education: Rethinking the role of the modern university* (pp. 293–316). Durham, NC: Duke University Press.

Gilliam, Mary, Stockman, Michael, Malek, Meaghan, Sharp, Wendy, Greenstein, Deanna, Lalonde, Francois, et al. (2011). Developmental trajectories of the corpus callosum in attention-deficit/hyperactivity disorder. *Biological Psychiatry, 69,* 839–846.

Gilligan, Carol. (1982). *In a different voice: Psychological theory and women's development.* Cambridge, MA: Harvard University Press.

Gilliland, Frank D. (2009). Outdoor air pollution, genetic susceptibility, and asthma management: Opportunities for intervention to reduce the burden of asthma. *Pediatrics, 123*(Suppl. 3), S168–173.

Gillis, John R. (2008). The islanding of children: Reshaping the mythical landscapes of childhood. In Marta Gutman & Ning De Coninck-Smith (Eds.), *Designing modern childhoods: History, space, and the material culture of children* (pp. 316–329). New Brunswick, NJ: Rutgers University Press.

Gintis, Herb, Bowles, Samuel, Boyd, Robert, & Fehr, Ernst. (2007). Explaining altruistic behaviour in humans. In R. I. M. Dunbar & Louise Barrett (Eds.), *Oxford handbook of evolutionary psychology* (pp. 605–620). New York, NY: Oxford University Press.

Glanville, Jennifer L., Sikkink, David, & Hernández, Edwin I. (2008). Religious involvement and educational outcomes: The role of social capital and extracurricular participation. *Sociological Quarterly, 49,* 105–137.

Gluckman, Peter D., & Hanson, Mark A. (2006). *Developmental origins of health and disease.* Cambridge, England: Cambridge University Press.

Göbel, Silke M., Shaki, Samuel, & Fischer, Martin H. (2011). The cultural number line: A review of cultural and linguistic influences on the development of number processing. *Journal of Cross-Cultural Psychology, 42,* 543–565.

Goldberg, Wendy A., Prause, JoAnn, Lucas-Thompson, Rachel, & Himsel, Amy. (2008). Maternal employment and children's achievement in context: A meta-analysis of four decades of research. *Psychological Bulletin, 134,* 77–108.

Goldin-Meadow, Susan. (2006). Nonverbal communication: The hand's role in talking and thinking. In William Damon & Richard M. Lerner (Series Eds.) & Deanna Kuhn & Robert S. Siegler (Vol. Eds.), *Handbook of child psychology: Vol.*

2. Cognition, perception, and language (6th ed., pp. 336–369). Hoboken, NJ: Wiley.

Goldin-Meadow, Susan. (2009). How gesture promotes learning throughout childhood. *Child Development Perspectives, 3,* 106–111.

Goldstein, Michael H., Schwade, Jennifer A., & Bornstein, Marc H. (2009). The value of vocalizing: Five-month-old infants associate their own noncry vocalizations with responses from caregivers. *Child Development, 80,* 636–644.

Goldston, David B., Molock, Sherry Davis, Whitbeck, Leslie B., Murakami, Jessica L., Zayas, Luis H., & Hall, Gordon C. Nagayama. (2008). Cultural considerations in adolescent suicide prevention and psychosocial treatment. *American Psychologist, 63,* 14–31.

Golinkoff, Roberta Michnick, & Hirsh-Pasek, Kathy. (2008). How toddlers begin to learn verbs. *Trends in Cognitive Sciences, 12,* 397–403.

Gonzales, Nancy A., Dumka, Larry E., Deardorff, Julianna, Carter, Sara Jacobs, & McCray, Adam. (2004). Preventing poor mental health and school dropout of Mexican American adolescents following the transition to junior high school. *Journal of Adolescent Research, 19,* 113–131.

Gonzales, Patrick, Williams, Trevor, Jocelyn, Leslie, Roey, Stephen, Kastberg, David, & Brenwald, Summer. (2009). *Highlights from TIMSS 2007: Mathematics and science achievement of U.S. fourth- and eighth-grade students in an international context.* Washington, DC: National Center for Education Statistics, U.S. Department of Education.

Goodman, Judith C., Dale, Philip S., & Li, Ping. (2008). Does frequency count? Parental input and the acquisition of vocabulary. *Journal of Child Language, 35,* 515–531.

Goodman, Sherryl H., & Gotlib, Ian H. (2002). *Children of depressed parents: Mechanisms of risk and implications for treatment.* Washington, DC: American Psychological Association.

Goodwin, Geoffrey P., & Johnson-Laird, Philip. N. (2008). Transitive and pseudo-transitive inferences. *Cognition, 108,* 320–352.

Gopnik, Alison. (2001). Theories, language, and culture: Whorf without wincing. In Melissa Bowerman & Stephen C. Levinson (Eds.), *Language acquisition and conceptual development* (pp. 45–69). Cambridge, UK: Cambridge University Press.

Gopnik, Alison, & Schulz, Laura. (2007). *Causal learning: Psychology, philosophy, and computation.* New York, NY: Oxford University Press.

Gordis, Elana B., Granger, Douglas A., Susman, Elizabeth J., & Trickett, Penelope K. (2008). Salivary alpha amylase-cortisol asymmetry in maltreated youth. *Hormones and Behavior, 53,* 96–103.

Gordon, Peter. (2004, August 19). Numerical cognition without words: Evidence from Amazonia. *Science, 306,* 496–499.

Gormley, William T., Jr., Phillips, Deborah, & Gayer, Ted. (2008, June 27). Preschool programs can boost school readiness. *Science, 320,* 1723–1724.

Gottesman, Irving I., Laursen, Thomas Munk, Bertelsen, Aksel, & Mortensen, Preben Bo. (2010). Severe mental disorders in offspring with 2 psychiatrically ill parents. *Archives of General Psychiatry, 67,* 252–257.

Gottfried, Adele Eskeles, Marcoulides, George A., Gottfried, Allen W., & Oliver, Pamella H. (2009). A latent curve model of parental motivational practices and developmental decline in math and science academic intrinsic motivation. *Journal of Educational Psychology, 101,* 729–739.

Gottlieb, Alma. (2000). Luring your child into this life: A Beng path for infant care. In Judy S. DeLoache & Alma Gottlieb (Eds.), *A world of babies: Imagined childcare guides for seven societies* (pp. 55–90). New York, NY: Cambridge University Press.

Gottlieb, Gilbert. (2002). *Individual development and evolution: The genesis of novel behavior.* Mahwah, NJ: Erlbaum. (Original work published 1992)

Gottlieb, Gilbert. (2007). Probabilistic epigenesis. *Developmental Science, 10,* 1–11.

Gottlieb, Gilbert. (2010). Normally occurring environmental and behavioral influences on gene activity. In Kathryn E. Hood, Carolyn Tucker Halpern, Gary Greenberg, & Richard M. Lerner (Eds.), *Handbook of developmental science, behavior, and genetics* (pp. 13–37). Malden, MA: Wiley-Blackwell.

Goymer, Patrick. (2007). Genes know their left from their right. *Nature Reviews Genetics, 8,* 652.

Graber, Julia A., & Brooks-Gunn, Jeanne. (1996). Expectations for and precursors to leaving home in young women. In Julia A. Graber & Judith Semon Dubas (Eds.), *Leaving home: Understanding the transition to adulthood* (pp. 21–38). San Francisco, CA: Jossey-Bass.

Graber, Julia A., Nichols, Tracy R., & Brooks-Gunn, Jeanne. (2010). Putting pubertal timing in developmental context: implications for prevention. *Developmental psychobiology, 52,* 254–262.

Graham-Bermann, Sandra A., Gruber, Gabrielle, Howell, Kathryn H., & Girz, Laura. (2009). Factors discriminating among profiles of resilience and psychopathology in children exposed to intimate partner violence (IPV). *Child Abuse & Neglect: The International Journal, 33,* 648–660.

Grandin, Temple, & Johnson, Catherine. (2009). *Animals make us human: Creating the best life for animals.* Boston, MA: Houghton Mifflin Harcourt.

Granic, Isabela, & Patterson, Gerald R. (2006). Toward a comprehensive model of antisocial development: A dynamic systems approach. *Psychological Review, 113,* 101–131.

Granpeesheh, Doreen, Tarbox, Jonathan, & Dixon, Dennis R. (2009). Applied behavior analytic interventions for children with autism: A description and review of treatment research. *Annals of Clinical Psychiatry, 21,* 162–173.

Granpeesheh, Doreen, Tarbox, Jonathan, Dixon, Dennis R., Wilke, Arthur E., Allen, Michael S., & Bradstreet, James Jeffrey. (2010). Randomized trial of hyperbaric oxygen therapy for children with autism. *Research in Autism Spectrum Disorders, 4,* 268–275.

Gray, John. (2004). *Men are from Mars, women are from Venus: A practical guide for improving communication and getting what you want in your relationships* (Paperback ed.). New York, NY: HarperCollins. (Original work published 1992)

Gray, John. (2010). *Venus on fire, Mars on ice: Hormonal balance—The key to life, love and energy.* Coquitlam, British Columbia, Canada: Mind.

Greely, Henry T. (2011, January 20). Get ready for the flood of fetal gene screening. *Nature, 469,* 289–291.

Green, Melinda A., Scott, Norman A., DeVilder, Elizabeth L., Zeiger, Amanda, & Darr, Stacy. (2006). Relational-interdependent self-construal as a function of bulimic symptomatology. *Journal of Clinical Psychology, 62,* 943–951.

Greene, Melissa L., & Way, Niobe. (2005). Self-esteem trajectories among ethnic minority adolescents: A growth curve analysis of the patterns and predictors of change. *Journal of Research on Adolescence, 15,* 151–178.

Greenfield, Patricia M. (2009, January 2). Technology and informal education: What is taught, what is learned. *Science, 323,* 69–71.

Greenhalgh, Susan. (2008). *Just one child: Science and policy in Deng's China.* Berkeley, CA: University of California Press.

Greenough, William T., & Volkmar, Fred R. (1973). Pattern of dendritic branching in occipital cortex of rats reared in complex environments. *Experimental Neurology, 40,* 491–504.

Greenwood, Charles R., Thiemann-Bourque, Kathy, Walker, Dale, Buzhardt, Jay, & Gilkerson, Jill. (2010). Assessing children's home language environments using automatic speech recognition technology. *Communication Disorders Quarterly.*

Gregg, Christopher. (2010, November 5). Parental control over the brain. *Science, 330,* 770–771.

Griebel, Wilfried, & Niesel, Renate. (2002). Co-constructing transition into kindergarten and school by children, parents, and teachers. In Hilary Fabian & Aline-Wendy Dunlop (Eds.), *Transitions in the early years: Debating continuity and progression for young children in early education* (pp. 64–75). New York, NY: RoutledgeFalmer.

Griffin, James, Gooding, Sarah, Semesky, Michael, Farmer, Brittany, Mannchen, Garrett, & Sinnott, Jan. (2009). Four brief studies of relations between postformal thought and non-cognitive factors: Personality, concepts of God, political opinions, and social attitudes. *Journal of Adult Development, 16,* 173–182.

Grobman, Kevin H. (2008). *Learning & teaching developmental psychology: Attachment theory, infancy, & infant memory development.* Retrieved from DevPsy.Org website: http://www.devpsy.org/questions/attachment_theory_memory.html

Grollmann, Philipp, & Rauner, Felix. (2007). Exploring innovative apprenticeship: Quality and costs. *Education + Training, 49,* 431–446.

Grolnick, Wendy S., McMenamy, Jannette M., & Kurowski, Carolyn O. (2006). Emotional self-regulation in infancy and toddlerhood. In Lawrence Balter & Catherine S. Tamis-LeMonda (Eds.), *Child psychology: A handbook of contemporary issues* (2nd ed., pp. 3–25). New York, NY: Psychology Press.

Grossmann, Klaus E., Grossmann, Karin, & Waters, Everett (Eds.). (2005). *Attachment from infancy to adulthood: The major longitudinal studies.* New York, NY: Guilford Press.

Grosvenor, Theodore. (2003). Why is there an epidemic of myopia? *Clinical and Experimental Optometry, 86,* 273–275.

Grubeck-Loebenstein, Beatrix. (2010). Fading immune protection in old age: Vaccination in the elderly. *Journal of Comparative Pathology, 142*(Suppl. 1), S116–S119.

Grusec, Joan E. (2011). Socialization processes in the family: Social and emotional development. *Annual Review of Psychology, 62,* 243–269.

Guerra, Nancy G., Graham, Sandra, & Tolan, Patrick H. (2011). Raising healthy children: Translating child development research into practice. *Child Development, 82,* 7–16.

Guerra, Nancy G., & Williams, Kirk R. (2010). Implementing bullying prevention in diverse settings: Geographic, economic, and cultural influences. In Eric M. Vernberg & Bridget K. Biggs (Eds.), *Preventing and treating bullying and victimization* (pp. 319–336). New York, NY: Oxford University Press.

Guerra, Nancy G., Williams, Kirk R., & Sadek, Shelly. (2011). Understanding bullying and victimization during childhood and adolescence: A mixed methods study. *Child Development, 82,* 295–310.

Guerri, Consuelo, & Pascual, María. (2010). Mechanisms involved in the neurotoxic, cognitive, and neurobehavioral effects of alcohol consumption during adolescence. *Alcohol, 44,* 15–26.

Guerry, John, & Hastings, Paul. (2011). In search of HPA axis dysregulation in child and adolescent depression. *Clinical Child and Family Psychology Review, 14,* 135–160.

Gummerum, Michaela, Keller, Monika, Takezawa, Masanori, & Mata, Jutta. (2008). To give or not to give: Children's and adolescents' sharing and moral negotiations in economic decision situations. *Child Development, 79,* 562–576.

Guo, Sufang, Padmadas, Sabu S., Zhao, Fengmin, Brown, James J., & Stones, R. William. (2007). Delivery settings and caesarean section rates in China. *Bulletin of the World Health Organization, 85,* 755–762.

Haas, David M., Gallauresi, Beverly, Shields, Kristine, Zeitlin, Deborah, Clark, Shannon M., Hebert, Mary F., et al. (2011). Pharmacotherapy and pregnancy: Highlights from the Third International Conference for Individualized Pharmacotherapy in Pregnancy. *Clinical and Translational Science, 4,* 204–209.

Hackman, Daniel A., & Farah, Martha J. (2009). Socioeconomic status and the developing brain. *Trends in Cognitive Sciences, 13,* 65–73.

Haden, Catherine A. (2010). Talking about science in museums. *Child Development Perspectives, 4,* 62–67.

Halford, Graeme S., & Andrews, Glenda. (2006). Reasoning and problem solving. In William Damon & Richard M. Lerner (Series Eds.) & Deanna Kuhn & Robert S. Siegler (Vol. Eds.), *Handbook of child psychology: Vol. 2. Cognition, perception, and language* (6th ed., pp. 557–608). Hoboken, NJ: Wiley.

Hall, Lynn K. (2008). *Counseling military families: What mental health professionals need to know.* New York, NY: Taylor and Francis.

Hall-Lande, Jennifer A., Eisenberg, Marla E., Christenson, Sandra L., & Neumark-Sztainer, Dianne. (2007). Social isolation, psychological health, and protective factors in adolescence. *Adolescence, 42,* 265–286.

Halpern, Carolyn Tucker, King, Rosalind Berkowitz, Oslak, Selene G., & Udry, J. Richard. (2005). Body mass index, dieting, romance, and sexual activity in adolescent girls: Relationships over time. *Journal of Research on Adolescence, 15,* 535–559.

Hamerton, John L., & Evans, Jane A. (2005). Sex chromosome anomalies. In Merlin Gene Butler & F. John Meaney (Eds.), *Genetics of developmental disabilities* (pp. 585–650). Boca Raton, FL: Taylor & Francis.

Hamm, Jill V., & Faircloth, Beverly S. (2005). The role of friendship in adolescents' sense of school belonging. *New Directions for Child and Adolescent Development, 107,* 61–78.

Hammer, Carol Scheffner, Jia, Gisela, & Uchikoshi, Yuuko. (2011). Language and literacy development of dual language learners growing up in the United States: A call for research. *Child Development Perspectives, 5,* 4–9.

Hammond, Christopher J., Andrew, Toby, Mak, Ying Tat, & Spector, Tim D. (2004). A susceptibility locus for myopia in the normal population is linked to the PAX6 gene region on chromosome 11: A genomewide scan of dizygotic twins. *American Journal of Human Genetics, 75,* 294–304.

Hanania, Rima. (2010). Two types of perseveration in the dimension change card sort task. *Journal of Experimental Child Psychology, 107,* 325–336.

Hane, Amie Ashley, & Fox, Nathan A. (2006). Ordinary variations in maternal caregiving influence human infants' stress reactivity. *Psychological Science, 17,* 550–556.

Hannan, Claire, Buchanan, Anna DeBlois, & Monroe, Judy. (2009). Maintaining the vaccine safety net. *Pediatrics, 124*(Suppl. 5), S571–S572.

Hanoch, Yaniv, Miron-Shatz, Talya, & Himmelstein, Mary. (2010). Genetic testing and risk interpretation: How do women understand lifetime risk results? *Judgment and Decision Making, 5,* 116–123.

Hanushek, Eric A. (2009, November 6). Building on No Child Left Behind. *Science, 326,* 802–803.

Hanushek, Eric A., & Woessmann, Ludger. (2009). *Do better schools lead to more growth? Cognitive skills, economic outcomes, and causation* (IZA Discussion Paper 4575). Bonn, Germany: Institute for the Study of Labor.

Hanushek, Eric A., & Woessmann, Ludger. (2010). *The high cost of low educational performance: The long-run economic impact of improving PISA outcomes.* Paris, France: Organisation for Economic Co-operation and Development.

Harden, K. Paige, & Tucker-Drob, Elliot M. (2011). Individual differences in the development of sensation seeking and impulsivity during adolescence: Further evidence for a dual systems model. *Developmental Psychology, 47,* 739–746.

Harden, K. Paige, Turkheimer, Eric, & Loehlin, John. (2007). Genotype by environment interaction in adolescents' cognitive aptitude. *Behavior Genetics, 37,* 273–283.

Hare, Kelly M., & Cree, Alison. (2010). Incidence, causes and consequences of pregnancy failure in viviparous lizards: Implications for research and conservation settings. *Reproduction, Fertility and Development, 22,* 761.

Harjes, Carlos E., Rocheford, Torbert R., Bai, Ling, Brutnell, Thomas P., Kandianis, Catherine Bermudez, Sowinski, Stephen G., et al. (2008, January 18). Natural genetic variation in Lycopene Epsilon Cyclase tapped for maize biofortification. *Science, 319,* 330–333.

Harkness, Sara, Super, Charles M., & Mavridis, Caroline Johnston. (2011). Parental ethnotheories about children's socioemotional development, *Socioemotional development in cultural context* (pp. 73–98). New York, NY: Guilford Press.

Harlor, Allen D. Buz, Jr., & Bower, Charles. (2009). Hearing assessment in infants and children: Recommendations beyond neonatal screening. *Pediatrics, 124,* 1252–1263.

Harris, Judith Rich. (1998). *The nurture assumption: Why children turn out the way they do.* New York, NY: Free Press.

Harris, Judith Rich. (2002). Beyond the nurture assumption: Testing hypotheses about the child's environment. In John G. Borkowski, Sharon Landesman Ramey, & Marie Bristol-Power (Eds.), *Parenting and the child's world: Influences on academic, intellectual, and social-emotional development* (pp. 3–20). Mahwah, NJ: Erlbaum.

Harrison, Denise, Bueno, Mariana, Yamada, Janet, Adams-Webber, Thomasin, & Stevens, Bonnie. (2010). Analgesic effects of sweet-tasting solutions for infants: Current state of equipoise. *Pediatrics, 126,* 894–902.

Harrison, Kristen, Bost, Kelly K., McBride, Brent A., Donovan, Sharon M., Grigsby-Toussaint, Diana S., Kim, Juhee, et al. (2011). Toward a developmental conceptualization of contributors to overweight and obesity in childhood: The Six-Cs model. *Child Development Perspectives, 5,* 50–58.

Harrison, Linda J., & McLeod, Sharynne. (2010). Risk and protective factors associated with speech and language impairment in a nationally representative sample of 4- to 5-year-old children. *Journal of Speech, Language, and Hearing Research,* 53, 508–529.

Hart, Betty, & Risley, Todd R. (1995). *Meaningful differences in the everyday experience of young American children.* Baltimore, MD: Brookes.

Hart, Daniel, Atkins, Robert, & Fegley, Suzanne. (2003). Personality and development in childhood: A person-centered approach. *Monographs of the Society for Research in Child Development,* 68(Serial No. 272), vii–109.

Harter, Susan. (2006). The self. In William Damon & Richard M. Lerner (Series Eds.) & Nancy Eisenberg (Vol. Ed.), *Handbook of child psychology: Vol. 3. Social, emotional, and personality development* (6th ed., pp. 505–570). Hoboken, NJ: Wiley.

Hartmann, Donald P., & Pelzel, Kelly E. (2005). Design, measurement, and analysis in developmental research. In Marc H. Bornstein & Michael E. Lamb (Eds.), *Developmental science: An advanced textbook* (5th ed., pp. 103–184). Mahwah, NJ: Erlbaum.

Hasebe, Yuki, Nucci, Larry, & Nucci, Maria S. (2004). Parental control of the personal domain and adolescent symptoms of psychopathology: A cross-national study in the United States and Japan. *Child Development,* 75, 815–828.

Hassett, Janice M., Siebert, Erin R., & Wallen, Kim. (2008). Sex differences in rhesus monkey toy preferences parallel those of children. *Hormones and Behavior,* 54, 359–364.

Hastie, Peter A. (2004). Problem-solving in teaching sports. In Jan Wright, Lisette Burrows, & Doune MacDonald (Eds.), *Critical inquiry and problem-solving in physical education* (pp. 62–73). London, UK: Routledge.

Hawthorne, Joanna. (2009). Promoting development of the early parent-infant relationship using the Neonatal Behavioural Assessment Scale. In Jane Barlow & P. O. Svanberg (Eds.), *Keeping the baby in mind: Infant mental health in practice* (pp. 39–51). New York, NY: Routledge/Taylor & Francis Group.

Haydon, Jo. (2007). *Genetics in practice: A clinical approach for healthcare practitioners.* Hoboken, NJ: Wiley.

Hayes, Rachel A., & Slater, Alan. (2008). Three-month-olds' detection of alliteration in syllables. *Infant Behavior & Development* 31, 153–156.

Hayne, Harlene, & Simcock, Gabrielle. (2009). Memory development in toddlers. In Mary L. Courage & Nelson Cowan (Eds.), *The development of memory in infancy and childhood* (2nd ed., pp. 43–68). New York, NY: Psychology Press.

Hayward, Diane W., Gale, Catherine M., & Eikeseth, Svein. (2009). Intensive behavioural intervention for young children with autism: A research-based service model. *Research in Autism Spectrum Disorders,* 3, 571–580.

Heaton, Tim B., & Darkwah, Akosua. (2011). Religious differences in modernization of the family: Family demographics trends in Ghana. *Journal of Family Issues.* Advance online publication. doi:10.1177/0192513x11398951

Heine, Steven J. (2007). Culture and motivation: What motivates people to act in the ways that they do? In Shinobu Kitayama & Dov Cohen (Eds.), *Handbook of cultural psychology* (pp. 714–733). New York, NY: Guilford Press.

Hemminki, Kari, Sundquist, Jan, & Lorenzo Bermejo, Justo. (2008). Familial risks for cancer as the basis for evidence-based clinical referral and counseling. *The Oncologist,* 13, 239–247.

Henning, Anne, & Striano, Tricia. (2011). Infant and maternal sensitivity to interpersonal timing. *Child Development,* 82, 916–931.

Herek, Gregory M. (2010). Sexual orientation differences as deficits: Science and stigma in the history of American psychology. *Perspectives on Psychological Science,* 5, 693–699.

Herman, Khalisa N., Paukner, Annika, & Suomi, Stephen J. (2011). Gene × environment interactions and social play: Contributions from rhesus macaques. In Anthony D. Pellegrini (Ed.), *The Oxford handbook of the development of play* (pp. 58–69). New York, NY: Oxford University Press.

Herman-Giddens, Marcia E., Wang, Lily, & Koch, Gary. (2001). Secondary sexual characteristics in boys: Estimates from the National Health and Nutrition Examination Survey III, 1988–1994. *Archives of Pediatrics & Adolescent Medicine,* 155, 1022–1028.

Herring, Ann, & Swedlund, Alan C. (Eds.). (2010). *Plagues and epidemics: Infected spaces past and present.* New York, NY: Berg.

Herrmann, Esther, Call, Josep, Hernàndez-Lloreda, María Victoria, Hare, Brian, & Tomasello, Michael. (2007, September 7). Humans have evolved specialized skills of social cognition: The cultural intelligence hypothesis. *Science,* 317, 1360–1366.

Herschensohn, Julia Rogers. (2007). *Language development and age.* New York, NY: Cambridge University Press.

Hetherington, E. Mavis. (2006). The influence of conflict, marital problem solving and parenting on children's adjustment in nondivorced, divorced and remarried families In Alison Clarke-Stewart & Judy Dunn (Eds.), *Families count: Effects on child and adolescent development* (pp. 203–237). New York, NY: Cambridge University Press.

Higgins, Matt. (2006, August 7). A series of flips creates some serious buzz. *New York Times,* p. D7.

Higuchi, Susumu, Matsushita, Sachio, Muramatsu, Taro, Murayama, Masanobu, & Hayashida, Motoi. (1996). Alcohol and aldehyde dehydrogenase genotypes and drinking behavior in Japanese. *Alcoholism: Clinical and Experimental Research,* 20, 493–497.

Hill, Denise M., Hanton, Sheldon, Matthews, Nic, & Fleming, Scott. (2010). Choking in sport: A review. *International Review of Sport and Exercise Psychology,* 3, 24–39.

Hill, Nancy E., Bush, Kevin R., & Roosa, Mark W. (2003). Parenting and family socialization strategies and children's mental health: Low-income, Mexican-American and Euro-American mothers and children. *Child Development,* 74, 189–204.

Hill, Nancy E., & Tyson, Diana F. (2009). Parental involvement in middle school: A meta-analytic assessment of the strategies that promote achievement. *Developmental Psychology,* 45, 740–763.

Hill, Patrick L., Duggan, Peter M., & Lapsley, Daniel K. (2011). Subjective invulnerability, risk behavior, and adjustment in early adolescence. *The Journal of Early Adolescence.* Advance online publication. doi:10.1177/0272431611400304

Hill, Shirley A. (2007). Transformative processes: Some sociological questions. *Journal of Marriage and Family,* 69, 293–298.

Hillier, Dawn. (2003). *Childbirth in the global village: Implications for midwifery education and practice.* New York, NY: Routledge.

Hillman, Richard. (2005). Expanded newborn screening and phenylketonuria (PKU). In Merlin Gene Butler & F. John Meaney (Eds.), *Genetics of developmental disabilities* (pp. 651–664). Boca Raton, FL: Taylor & Francis.

Hilton, Irene V., Stephen, Samantha, Barker, Judith C., & Weintraub, Jane A. (2007). Cultural factors and children's oral health care: A qualitative study of carers of young children. *Community Dentistry and Oral Epidemiology,* 35, 429–438.

Hindman, Annemarie H., Skibbe, Lori E., Miller, Alison, & Zimmerman, Marc. (2010). Ecological contexts and early learning: Contributions of child, family, and classroom factors during Head Start, to literacy and mathematics growth through first grade. *Early Childhood Research Quarterly,* 25, 235–250.

Hines, Melissa. (2004). *Brain gender.* Oxford, UK: Oxford University Press.

Hipwell, Alison E., Keenan, Kate, Loeber, Rolf, & Battista, Deena. (2010). Early predictors of sexually intimate behaviors in an urban sample of young girls. *Developmental Psychology,* 46, 366–378.

Hirsch, Eric Donald, Jr. (2008). Plugging the hole in state standards. *American Educator,* 32, 8–12.

Hirsh-Pasek, Kathy, Golinkoff, Roberta Michnick, Berk, Laura E., & Singer, Dorothy G. (2009). *A mandate for playful learning in preschool: Presenting the evidence.* New York, NY: Oxford University Press.

Ho, Caroline, Bluestein, Deborah N., & Jenkins, Jennifer M. (2008). Cultural differences in the relationship between parenting and children's behavior. *Developmental Psychology,* 44, 507–522.

Ho, Emily S. (2010). Measuring hand function in the young child. *Journal of Hand Therapy,* 23, 323–328.

Hofer, Scott M., & Piccinin, Andrea M. (2010). Toward an integrative science of life-span development and aging. *The Journals of Gerontology: Series B: Psychological Sciences and Social Sciences, 65B,* 269–278.

Hoff, David J. (2007, April 18). Not all agree on meaning of NCLB proficiency. *Education Week,* pp. 1, 23.

Holden, Constance. (2009, October 16). Fetal cells again? *Science, 326,* 358–359.

Holland, James D., & Klaczynski, Paul A. (2009). Intuitive risk taking during adolescence. *Prevention Researcher, 16,* 8–11.

Holland, John L. (1997). *Making vocational choices: A theory of vocational personalities and work environments* (3rd ed.). Odessa, FL: Psychological Assessment Resources.

Hollich, George. (2010). Early language. In J. Gavin Bremner & Theodore D. Wachs (Eds.), *The Wiley-Blackwell Handbook of Infant Development* (pp. 426–449). Oxford, UK: Wiley-Blackwell.

Hollich, George J., Hirsh-Pasek, Kathy, Golinkoff, Roberta Michnick, Brand, Rebecca J., Brown, Ellie, Chung, He Len, et al. (2000). Breaking the language barrier: An emergentist coalition model for the origins of word learning. *Monographs of the Society for Research in Child Development, 65*(3, Serial No. 262), v–123.

Holm, Stephanie M., Forbes, Erika E., Ryan, Neal D., Phillips, Mary L., Tarr, Jill A., & Dahl, Ronald E. (2009). Reward-related brain function and sleep in pre/early pubertal and mid/late pubertal adolescents. *The Journal of Adolescent Health, 45,* 326–334.

Holodynski, Manfred, & Friedlmeier, Wolfgang. (2006). *Development of emotions and emotion regulation.* New York, NY: Springer.

Holsti, Liisa, Grunau, Ruth E., & Shany, Eilon. (2011). Assessing pain in preterm infants in the neonatal intensive care unit: Moving to a brain-oriented approach. *Pain Management, 1,* 171–179.

Holtzman, Jennifer. (2009). Simple, effective—and inexpensive—strategies to reduce tooth decay in children. *ICAN: Infant, Child, & Adolescent Nutrition, 1,* 225–231.

Hooper, Stephen R., Roberts, Joanne, Sideris, John, Burchinal, Margaret, & Zeisel, Susan. (2010). Longitudinal predictors of reading and math trajectories through middle school for African American versus Caucasian students across two samples. *Developmental Psychology, 46,* 1018–1029.

Hormann, Elizabeth. (2007). Sleeping with your baby: A parent's guide to co-sleeping. *Birth, 34,* 355–356.

Horowitz, Frances Degen, Subotnik, Rena F., & Matthews, Dona J. (Eds.). (2009). *The development of giftedness and talent across the life span.* Washington, DC: American Psychological Association.

Hougaard, Karin S., & Hansen, Åse M. (2007). Enhancement of developmental toxicity effects of chemicals by gestational stress. A review. *Neurotoxicology and Teratology, 29,* 425–445.

Hout, Michael, & Elliott, Stuart W. (Eds.). (2011). *Incentives and test-based accountability in education.* Washington, DC: National Academies Press.

Howe, Mark L. (2004). The role of conceptual recoding in reducing children's retroactive interference. *Developmental Psychology, 40,* 131–139.

Howell, Diane M., Wysocki, Karen, & Steiner, Michael J. (2010). Toilet training. *Pediatrics in Review, 31,* 262–263.

Howlin, Patricia, Magiati, Iliana, Charman, Tony, & MacLean, William E., Jr. (2009). Systematic review of early intensive behavioral interventions for children with autism. *American Journal on Intellectual and Developmental Disabilities, 114,* 23–41.

Hrabosky, Joshua I., & Thomas, Jennifer J. (2008). Elucidating the relationship between obesity and depression: Recommendations for future research. *Clinical Psychology: Science and Practice, 15,* 28–34.

Hrdy, Sarah B. (2009). *Mothers and others: The evolutionary origins of mutual understanding.* Cambridge: Harvard University Press.

Hsia, Yingfen, & Maclennan, Karyn. (2009). Rise in psychotropic drug prescribing in children and adolescents during 1992–2001: A population-based study in the UK. *European Journal of Epidemiology, 24,* 211–216.

Huang, Chiungjung. (2010). Mean-level change in self-esteem from childhood through adulthood: Meta-analysis of longitudinal studies. *Review of General Psychology, 14,* 251–260.

Huang, Chien-Chung. (2009). Mothers' reports of nonresident fathers' involvement with their children: Revisiting the relationship between child support payment and visitation. *Family Relations, 58,* 54–64.

Huesmann, L. Rowell, Dubow, Eric F., & Boxer, Paul. (2009). Continuity of aggression from childhood to early adulthood as a predictor of life outcomes: Implications for the adolescent-limited and life-course-persistent models. *Aggressive Behavior, 35,* 136–149.

Hugdahl, Kenneth, & Westerhausen, René. (2010). *The two halves of the brain: Information processing in the cerebral hemispheres.* Cambridge, MA: MIT Press.

Hughes, Julie Milligan, & Bigler, Rebecca S. (2011). Predictors of African American and European American adolescents' endorsement of race-conscious social policies. *Developmental Psychology, 47,* 479–492.

Hughes, Sonya M., & Gore, Andrea C. (2007). How the brain controls puberty, and implications for sex and ethnic differences. *Family & Community Health, 30*(Suppl. 1), S112–S114.

Huijbregts, Sanne K., Tavecchio, Louis, Leseman, Paul, & Hoffenaar, Peter. (2009). Child rearing in a group setting: Beliefs of Dutch, Caribbean Dutch, and Mediterranean Dutch caregivers in center-based child care. *Journal of Cross-Cultural Psychology, 40,* 797–815.

Huntsinger, Carol S., Jose, Paul E., Krieg, Dana Balsink, & Luo, Zupei. (2011). Cultural differences in Chinese American and European American children's drawing skills over time. *Early Childhood Research Quarterly, 26,* 134–145.

Hussey, Jon M., Chang, Jen Jen, & Kotch, Jonathan B. (2006). Child maltreatment in the United States: Prevalence, risk factors, and adolescent health consequences. *Pediatrics, 118,* 933–942.

Hust, Stacey J. T., Brown, Jane D., & L'Engle, Kelly Ladin. (2008). Boys will be boys and girls better be prepared: An analysis of the rare sexual health messages in young adolescents' media. *Mass Communication and Society, 11,* 3–23.

Huston, Aletha C., & Aronson, Stacey Rosenkrantz. (2005). Mothers' time with infant and time in employment as predictors of mother-child relationships and children's early development. *Child Development, 76,* 467–482.

Huston, Aletha C., & Ripke, Marika N. (2006). Middle childhood: Contexts of development. In Aletha C. Huston & Marika N. Ripke (Eds.), *Developmental contexts in middle childhood: Bridges to adolescence and adulthood* (pp. 1–22). New York, NY: Cambridge University Press.

Huver, Rose M. E., Otten, Roy, de Vries, Hein, & Engels, Rutger C. M. E. (2010). Personality and parenting style in parents of adolescents. *Journal of Adolescence, 33,* 395–402.

Hyde, Janet Shibley. (2007). New directions in the study of gender similarities and differences. *Current Directions in Psychological Science, 16,* 259–263.

Hyde, Janet S., Lindberg, Sara M., Linn, Marcia C., Ellis, Amy B., & Williams, Caroline C. (2008, July 25). Gender similarities characterize math performance. *Science, 321,* 494–495.

Hyson, Marilou, Copple, Carol, & Jones, Jacqueline. (2006). Early childhood development and education. In William Damon & Richard M. Lerner (Series Eds.) & K. Ann Renninger & Irving E. Sigel (Vol. Eds.), *Handbook of child psychology: Vol. 4. Child psychology in practice* (6th ed., pp. 3–47). Hoboken, NJ: Wiley.

Iacoboni, Marco. (2009). Imitation, empathy, and mirror neurons. *Annual Review of Psychology, 60,* 653–670.

Iacovidou, Nicoletta, Varsami, Marianna, & Syggellou, Angeliki. (2010). Neonatal outcome of preterm delivery. In George Creatsas & George Mastorakos (Eds.), *Annals of the New York Academy of Sciences: Vol. 1205. Women's health and disease* (pp. 130–134). Malden, MA: Blackwell.

Imai, Mutsumi, Kita, Sotaro, Nagumo, Miho, & Okada, Hiroyuki. (2008). Sound symbolism facilitates early verb learning. *Cognition, 109,* 54–65.

Inan, Hatice Zeynep, Trundle, Kathy Cabe, & Kantor, Rebecca. (2010). Understanding natural sciences education in a Reggio Emilia-inspired preschool. *Journal of Research in Science Teaching, 47,* 1186–1208.

Inhelder, Bärbel, & Piaget, Jean. (1958). *The growth of logical thinking from childhood to adolescence: An essay on the construction of formal operational structures.* New York, NY: Basic Books.

Inhelder, Bärbel, & Piaget, Jean. (1964). *The early growth of logic in the child.* New York, NY: Harper & Row.

Insel, Beverly J., & Gould, Madelyn S. (2008). Impact of modeling on adolescent suicidal behavior. *Psychiatric Clinics of North America, 31,* 293–316.

Institute of Medicine, Committee on Food Marketing and the Diets of Children and Youth. (2006). *Food marketing to children and youth: Threat or opportunity?* Washington, DC: National Academies Press.

Irwin, Scott, Galvez, Roberto, Weiler, Ivan Jeanne, Beckel-Mitchener, Andrea, & Greenough, William. (2002). Brain structure and the functions of FMR1 protein. In Randi Jenssen Hagerman & Paul J. Hagerman (Eds.), *Fragile X syndrome: Diagnosis, treatment, and research* (3rd ed., pp. 191–205). Baltimore, MD: Johns Hopkins University Press.

Ispa, Jean M., Fine, Mark A., Halgunseth, Linda C., Harper, Scott, Robinson, JoAnn, Boyce, Lisa, et al. (2004). Maternal intrusiveness, maternal warmth, and mother-toddler relationship outcomes: Variations across low-income ethnic and acculturation groups. *Child Development, 75,* 1613–1631.

Iverson, Jana M., & Fagan, Mary K. (2004). Infant vocal-motor coordination: Precursor to the gesture-speech system? *Child Development, 75,* 1053–1066.

Iyengar, Sheena S., & Lepper, Mark R. (2000). When choice is demotivating: Can one desire too much of a good thing? *Journal of personality and social psychology, 79,* 995–1006.

Izard, Carroll E. (2009). Emotion theory and research: Highlights, unanswered questions, and emerging issues. *Annual Review of Psychology, 60,* 1–25.

Izard, Carroll E., Fine, Sarah, Mostow, Allison, Trentacosta, Christopher, & Campbell, Jan. (2002). Emotion processes in normal and abnormal development and preventive intervention. *Development & Psychopathology, 14,* 761–787.

Jackson, Richard J. J., & Tester, June. (2008). Environment shapes health, including children's mental health. *Journal of the American Academy of Child & Adolescent Psychiatry, 47,* 129–131.

Jacob, Jenet I. (2009). The socio-emotional effects of non-maternal childcare on children in the USA: A critical review of recent studies. *Early Child Development and Care, 179,* 559–570.

Jacobson, Matthew Frye. (1998). *Whiteness of a different color: European immigrants and the alchemy of race.* Cambridge, MA: Harvard University Press.

Jaffe, Eric. (2004). Mickey Mantle's greatest error: Yankee star's false belief may have cost him years. *Observer, 17*(9), 37.

Jaffee, Sara R., Caspi, Avshalom, Moffitt, Terrie E., Polo-Tomás, Monica, & Taylor, Alan. (2007). Individual, family, and neighborhood factors distinguish resilient from non-resilient maltreated children: A cumulative stressors model. *Child Abuse & Neglect, 31,* 231–253.

James, Raven. (2007). Sexually transmitted infections. In Annette Fuglsang Owens & Mitchell S. Tepper (Eds.), *Sexual health: Vol. 4. State-of-the-art treatments and research* (pp. 235–267). Westport, CT: Praeger/Greenwood.

Jansen, Jarno, Beijers, Roseriet, Riksen-Walraven, Marianne, & de Weerth, Carolina. (2010). Cortisol reactivity in young infants. *Psychoneuroendocrinology, 35,* 329–338.

Jenson, Jeffrey M., & Fraser, Mark W. (2006). *Social policy for children & families: A risk and resilience perspective.* Thousand Oaks, CA: Sage.

Johnson, Elizabeth K., & Tyler, Michael D. (2010). Testing the limits of statistical learning for word segmentation. *Developmental Science, 13,* 339–345.

Johnson, Mark H. (2005). Developmental neuroscience, psychophysiology and genetics. In Marc H. Bornstein & Michael E. Lamb (Eds.), *Developmental science: An advanced textbook* (5th ed., pp. 187–222). Mahwah, NJ: Erlbaum.

Johnson, Mark H., Grossmann, Tobias, & Kadosh, Kathrin Cohen. (2009). Mapping functional brain development: Building a social brain through interactive specialization. *Developmental Psychology, 45,* 151–159.

Johnson, Mark H. with Michelle de Haan. (2011). *Developmental cognitive neuroscience: An introduction* (3rd ed.). Malden, MA: Wiley-Blackwell.

Johnson, Monica Kirkpatrick, Crosnoe, Robert, & Elder, Glen H. (2011). Insights on adolescence from a life course perspective. *Journal of Research on Adolescence, 21,* 273–280.

Johnson, Susan C., Dweck, Carol S., Chen, Frances S., Stern, Hilarie L., Ok, Su-Jeong, & Barth, Maria. (2010). At the intersection of social and cognitive development: Internal working models of attachment in infancy. *Cognitive Science, 34,* 807–825.

Johnson, Scott P., & Shuwairi, Sarah M. (2009). Learning and memory facilitate predictive tracking in 4–month-olds. *Journal of Experimental Child Psychology, 102,* 122–130.

Johnson, Teddi Dineley. (2011). Report calls for examination of chemical safety: National coalition notes difficulty determining exposures. *The Nation's Health, 41,* 9.

Johnson, Wendy. (2010). Understanding the genetics of intelligence: Can height help? Can corn oil? *Current Directions in Psychological Science, 19,* 177–182.

Johnston, Lloyd D., O'Malley, Patrick M., Bachman, Jerald G., & Schulenberg, John E. (2008). *Monitoring the Future national results on adolescent drug use: Overview of key findings, 2007* (NIH Publication No. 08–6418). Bethesda, MD: National Institute on Drug Abuse.

Johnston, Lloyd D., O'Malley, Patrick M., Bachman, Jerald G., & John E. Schulenberg. (2010). *Monitoring the Future national results on adolescent drug use: Overview of key findings, 2009* (NIH Publication No. 10–7583). Bethesda, MD: National Institute on Drug Abuse.

Johnston, Lloyd D., O'Malley, Patrick M., Bachman, Jerald G., & Schulenberg, John E. (2009). *Monitoring the Future national survey results on drug use, 1975–2008: Vol. II. College students and adults ages 19–50* (NIH Publication No. 09–7403). Bethesda, MD: National Institute on Drug Abuse.

Jones, Diane, & Crawford, Joy. (2005). Adolescent boys and body image: Weight and muscularity concerns as dual pathways to body dissatisfaction. *Journal of Youth and Adolescence, 34,* 629–636.

Jones, Edward P. (2003). *The known world.* New York, NY: Amistad.

Jones, Edward P. (2003). *Lost in the city: Stories.* New York, NY: Amistad. (Original work published 1992)

Jones, Mary Cover. (1965). Psychological correlates of somatic development. *Child Development, 36,* 899–911.

Jones, Randall M. (2011). Psychosocial development and first substance use in third and fourth grade students: A short-term longitudinal study. *Child Development Research, 2011.* doi:10.1155/2011/916020

Jones, Steve. (2006, December 22). Prosperous people, penurious genes. *Science, 314,* 1879.

Jong, Jyh-Tsorng, Kao, Tsair, Lee, Liang-Yi, Huang, Hung-Hsuan, Lo, Po-Tsung, & Wang, Hui-Chung. (2010). Can temperament be understood at birth? The relationship between neonatal pain cry and their temperament: A preliminary study. *Infant Behavior and Development, 33,* 266–272.

Juan, Shan. (2010, January 14). C-section epidemic hits China. Retrieved from http://www.chinadaily.com.cn/index.html

Juvonen, Jaana, Nishina, Adrienne, & Graham, Sandra. (2006). Ethnic diversity and perceptions of safety in urban middle schools. *Psychological Science, 17,* 393–400.

Kagan, Jerome. (2008). In defense of qualitative changes in development. *Child Development, 79,* 1606–1624.

Kagan, Jerome. (2011). Three lessons learned. *Perspectives on Psychological Science, 6,* 107–113.

Kagan, Jerome, & Herschkowitz, Elinore Chapman. (2005). *Young mind in a growing brain.* Mahwah, NJ: Erlbaum.

Kagan, Jerome, & Norbert Herschkowitz (with Herschkowitz, Elinore Chapman). (2005). *A young mind in a growing brain.* Mahwah, NJ: Erlbaum.

Kagan, Jerome, Snidman, Nancy, Kahn, Vali, & Towsley, Sara. (2007). The preservation of two infant temperaments into adolescence. *Monographs of the Society for Research in Child Development, 72*(Serial No. 287), 1–95.

Kagitcibasi, Cigdem. (2003). Human development across cultures: A contextual-functional analysis and implications for interventions. In T. S. Saraswati (Ed.), *Cross-cultural perspectives in human development: Theory, research, and applications* (pp. 166–191). New Delhi, India: Sage.

Kahana-Kalman, Ronit, & Walker-Andrews, Arlene S. (2001). The role of person familiarity in young infants' perception of emotional expressions. *Child Development, 72,* 352–369.

Kakihara, Fumiko, & Tilton-Weaver, Lauree. (2009). Adolescents' interpretations of parental control: Differentiated by domain and types of control. *Child Development, 80,* 1722–1738.

Kalambouka, Afroditi, Farrell, Peter, Dyson, Alan, & Kaplan, Ian. (2007). The impact of placing pupils with special educational needs in mainstream schools on the achievement of their peers. *Educational Research, 49,* 365–382.

Kalliala, Marjatta. (2006). *Play culture in a changing world.* Maidenhead, England: Open University Press.

Kalra, Suleena Kansal, & Barnhart, Kurt T. (2011). In vitro fertilization and adverse childhood outcomes: What we know, where we are going, and how we will get there. A glimpse into what lies behind and beckons ahead. *Fertility and Sterility, 95,* 1887–1889.

Kanner, Leo. (1943). Autistic disturbances of affective contact. *Nervous Child, 2,* 217–250.

Karabinus, David S. (2009). Flow cytometric sorting of human sperm: MicroSort® clinical trial update. *Theriogenology, 71,* 74–79.

Karama, Sherif, Ad-Dab'bagh, Yasser, Haier, Richard J., Deary, Ian J., Lyttelton, Oliver C., Lepage, Claude, et al. (2009). Positive association between cognitive ability and cortical thickness in a representative US sample of healthy 6 to 18–year-olds. *Intelligence, 37,* 145–155.

Kärnä, Antti, Voeten, Marinus, Little, Todd D., Poskiparta, Elisa, Kaljonen, Anne, & Salmivalli, Christina. (2011). A large-scale evaluation of the KiVa antibullying program: Grades 4–6. *Child Development, 82,* 311–330.

Kärtner, Joscha, Keller, Heidi, & Yovsi, Relindis D. (2010). Mother infant interaction during the first 3 months: The emergence of culture-specific contingency patterns. *Child Development, 81,* 540–554.

Kärtner, Joscha, Keller, Heidi, & Yovsi, Relindis D. (2010). Mother–infant interaction during the first 3 months: The emergence of culture-specific contingency patterns. *Child Development, 81,* 540–554.

Kastenbaum, Robert. (2006). *Death, society, and human experience* (9th ed.). Boston, MA: Allyn and Bacon.

Kavanaugh, Robert D. (2011). Origins and consequences of social pretend play. In Anthony D. Pellegrini (Ed.), *The Oxford handbook of the development of play* (pp. 296–307). New York, NY: Oxford University Press.

Keating, Daniel P. (2004). Cognitive and brain development. In Richard M. Lerner & Laurence D. Steinberg (Eds.), *Handbook of adolescent psychology* (2nd ed., pp. 45–84). Hoboken, NJ: Wiley.

Keating, Daniel P. (Ed.). (2011). *Nature and nurture in early child development.* New York, NY: Cambridge University Press.

Kedar, Yarden, Casasola, Marianella, & Lust, Barbara. (2006). Getting there faster: 18- and 24-month-old infants' use of function words to determine reference. *Child Development, 77,* 325–338.

Keel, Pamela K., & Brown, Tiffany A. (2010). Update on course and outcome in eating disorders. *International Journal of Eating Disorders, 43,* 195–204.

Keil, Frank C. (2011, February 25). Science starts early. *Science, 331,* 1022–1023.

Kelemen, Deborah, Callanan, Maureen A., Casler, Krista, & Perez-Granados, Deanne R. (2005). Why things happen: Teleological explanation in parent-child conversation. *Developmental Psychology, 41,* 251–264.

Keller, Heidi, Borke, Jörn, Chaudhary, Nandita, Lamm, Bettina, & Kleis, Astrid. (2010). Continuity in parenting strategies: A cross-cultural comparison. *Journal of Cross-Cultural Psychology, 41,* 391–409.

Keller, Heidi, Lamm, Bettina, Abels, Monika, Yovsi, Relindis, Borke, Jörn, Jensen, Henning, et al. (2006). Cultural models, socialization goals, and parenting ethnotheories: A multicultural analysis. *Journal of Cross-Cultural Psychology, 37,* 155–172.

Keller, Heidi, Yovsi, Relindis, Borke, Joern, Kärtner, Joscha, Jensen, Henning, & Papaligoura, Zaira. (2004). Developmental consequences of early parenting experiences: Self-recognition and self-regulation in three cultural communities. *Child Development, 75,* 1745–1760.

Kellman, Philip J., & Arterberry, Martha E. (2006). Infant visual perception. In William Damon & Richard M. Lerner (Series Eds.) & Deanna Kuhn & Robert S. Siegler (Vol. Eds.), *Handbook of child psychology: Vol. 2. Cognition, perception, and language* (6th ed., pp. 109–160). Hoboken, NJ: Wiley.

Kempe, Ruth S., & Kempe, C. Henry. (1978). *Child abuse.* Cambridge, MA: Harvard University Press.

Kemple, James J. (with Cynthia J. Willner). (2008). *Career academies: Long-term impacts on labor market outcomes, educational attainment, and transitions to adulthood.* Retrieved from MDRC website: http://www.mdrc.org/publications/482/full.pdf

Kempner, Joanna, Perlis, Clifford S., & Merz, Jon F. (2005, February 11). Forbidden knowledge. *Science, 307,* 854.

Kennedy, Colin R., McCann, Donna C., Campbell, Michael J., Law, Catherine M., Mullee, Mark, Petrou, Stavros, et al. (2006). Language ability after early detection of permanent childhood hearing impairment. *New England Journal of Medicine, 354,* 2131–2141.

Keogh, Barbara K. (2004). The importance of longitudinal research for early intervention practices. In Peggy D. McCardle & Vinita Chhabra (Eds.), *The voice of evidence in reading research* (pp. 81–102). Baltimore, MD: Brookes.

Kéri, Szabolcs. (2009). Genes for psychosis and creativity: A promoter polymorphism of the neuregulin 1 gene is related to creativity in people with high intellectual achievement. *Psychological Science, 20,* 1070–1073.

Kerns, Kathryn A., Brumariu, Laura E., & Seibert, Ashley. (2011). Multi-method assessment of mother-child attachment: Links to parenting and child depressive symptoms in middle childhood. *Attachment & Human Development, 13,* 315–333.

Kerr, Margaret, Stattin, Håkan, & Burk, William J. (2010). A reinterpretation of parental monitoring in longitudinal perspective. *Journal of Research on Adolescence, 20,* 39–64.

Keysers, Christian, & Gazzola, Valeria. (2010). Social neuroscience: Mirror neurons recorded in humans. *Current Biology, 20,* R353–R354.

Khaleque, Abdul, & Rohner, Ronald P. (2002). Perceived parental acceptance-rejection and psychological adjustment: A meta-analysis of cross-cultural and intracultural studies. *Journal of Marriage & the Family, 64,* 54–64.

Khan, Laura Kettel, Sobush, Kathleen, Keener, Dana, Goodman, Kenneth, Lowry, Amy, Kakietek, Jakub, et al. (2009, July 24). Recommended community strategies and measurements to prevent obesity in the United States. *Morbidity and Mortality Weekly Report Recommendations and Reports, 58*(RR07), 1–26.

Khanna, Sunil K. (2010). *Fetal/fatal knowledge: New reproductive technologies and family-building strategies in India.* Belmont, CA: Wadsworth/Cengage Learning.

Khoury-Kassabri, Mona. (2009). The relationship between staff maltreatment of students and bully-victim group membership. *Child Abuse & Neglect: The International Journal, 33,* 914–923.

Kiang, Lisa, & Harter, Susan. (2008). Do pieces of the self-puzzle fit? Integrated/fragmented selves in biculturally-identified Chinese Americans. *Journal of Research in Personality, 42,* 1657–1662.

Kiang, Lisa, Witkow, Melissa, Baldelomar, Oscar, & Fuligni, Andrew. (2010). Change in ethnic identity across the high school years among adolescents with Latin American, Asian, and European backgrounds. *Journal of Youth and Adolescence, 39,* 683–693.

Killen, Melanie. (2007). Children's social and moral reasoning about exclusion. *Current Directions in Psychological Science, 16,* 32–36.

Killen, Melanie, Kelly, M., Richardson, C., Crystal, D., & Ruck, M. (2010). European-American children's and adolescents' evaluations of interracial exclusion. *Group Processes and Intergroup Relations, 13,* 283–300.

Killen, Melanie, Lee-Kim, Jennie, McGlothlin, Heidi, & Stangor, Charles. (2002). How children and adolescents evaluate gender and racial exclusion. *Monographs of the Society for Research in Child Development, 67*(4, Serial No. 271).

Killen, Melanie, Margie, Nancy Geyelin, & Sinno, Stefanie. (2006). Morality in the context of intergroup relationships. In Melanie Killen & Judith G. Smetana (Eds.), *Handbook of moral development* (pp. 155–183). Mahwah, NJ: Erlbaum.

Killen, Melanie, & Smetana, Judith. (2007). The biology of morality: Human development and moral neuroscience. *Human Development, 50,* 241–243.

Killgore, William D. S., Vo, Alexander H., Castro, Carl A., & Hoge, Charles W. (2006). Assessing risk propensity in American soldiers: Preliminary reliability and validity of the Evaluation of Risks (EVAR) scale-English version. *Military Medicine, 171,* 233–239.

Kilmer, Ryan P., & Gil-Rivas, Virginia. (2010). Exploring posttraumatic growth in children impacted by Hurricane Katrina: Correlates of the phenomenon and developmental considerations. *Child Development, 81,* 1211–1227.

Kim, Dong-Sik, & Kim, Hyun-Sun. (2009). Body-image dissatisfaction as a predictor of suicidal ideation among Korean boys and girls in different stages of adolescence: A two-year longitudinal study. *The Journal of Adolescent Health, 45,* 47–54.

Kim, Geunyoung, Walden, Tedra A., & Knieps, Linda J. (2010). Impact and characteristics of positive and fearful emotional messages during infant social referencing. *Infant Behavior and Development, 33,* 189–195.

Kim, Heejung S., Sherman, David K., & Taylor, Shelley E. (2008). Culture and social support. *American Psychologist, 63,* 518–526.

Kim-Cohen, Julia, Moffitt, Terrie E., Caspi, Avshalom, & Taylor, Alan. (2004). Genetic and environmental processes in young children's resilience and vulnerability to socioeconomic deprivation. *Child Development, 75,* 651–668.

Kimbro, Rachel Tolbert, Brooks-Gunn, Jeanne, & McLanahan, Sara. (2011). Young children in urban areas: Links among neighborhood characteristics, weight status, outdoor play, and television watching. *Social Science & Medicine, 72,* 668–676.

King, Pamela Ebstyne, & Furrow, James L. (2004). Religion as a resource for positive youth development: Religion, social capital, and moral outcomes. *Developmental Psychology, 40,* 703–713.

King, Pamela Ebstyne, & Roeser, Robert W. (2009). Religion and spirituality in adolescent development. In Richard M. Lerner & Laurence Steinberg (Eds.), *Handbook of adolescent psychology: Vol. 1. Individual bases of adolescent development* (3rd ed., pp. 435–478). Hoboken, NJ: Wiley.

King, Sara, Waschbusch, Daniel A., Pelham, William E., Frankland, Bradley W., Corkum, Penny V., & Jacques, Sophie. (2009). Subtypes of aggression in children with attention deficit hyperactivity disorder: Medication effects and comparison with typical children. *Journal of Clinical Child and Adolescent Psychology, 38,* 619–629.

Kinney, Hannah C., & Thach, Bradley T. (2009). The sudden infant death syndrome. *New England Journal of Medicine, 361,* 795–805.

Kirby, Douglas, & Laris, B. A. (2009). Effective curriculum-based sex and STD/HIV education programs for adolescents. *Child Development Perspectives, 3,* 21–29.

Kirkorian, Heather L., Pempek, Tiffany A., Murphy, Lauren A., Schmidt, Marie E., & Anderson, Daniel R. (2009). The impact of background television on parent-child interaction. *Child Development, 80,* 1350–1359.

Kiuru, Noona, Burk, William J., Laursen, Brett, Salmela-Aro, Katariina, & Nurmi, Jari-Erik. (2010). Pressure to drink but not to smoke: Disentangling selection and socialization in adolescent peer networks and peer groups. *Journal of Adolescence, 33,* 801–812.

Klaczynski, Paul, Daniel, David B., & Keller, Peggy S. (2009). Appearance idealization, body esteem, causal attributions, and ethnic variations in the development of obesity stereotypes. *Journal of Applied Developmental Psychology, 30,* 537–551.

Klaczynski, Paul A. (2001). Analytic and heuristic processing influences on adolescent reasoning and decision-making. *Child Development, 72,* 844–861.

Klaczynski, Paul A. (2011). Age differences in understanding precedent-setting decisions and authorities' responses to violations of deontic rules. *Journal of Experimental Child Psychology, 109,* 1–24.

Klahr, David, & Nigam, Milena. (2004). The equivalence of learning paths in early science instruction: Effects of direct instruction and discovery learning. *Psychological Science, 15,* 661–667.

Klassen, Terry P., Kiddoo, Darcie, Lang, Mia E., Friesen., Carol, Russell, Kelly, Spooner, Carol, et al. (2006). *The effectiveness of different methods of toilet training for bowel and bladder control* (AHRQ Publication No. 07–E003). Rockville, MD: Agency for Healthcare Research and Quality.

Klaus, Marshall H., & Kennell, John H. (1976). *Maternal-infant bonding: The impact of early separation or loss on family development.* St. Louis, MO: Mosby.

Kleinspehn-Ammerlahn, Anna, Riediger, Michaela, Schmiedek, Florian, von Oertzen, Timo, Li, Shu-Chen, & Lindenberger, Ulman. (2011). Dyadic drumming across the lifespan reveals a zone of proximal development in children. *Developmental Psychology, 47,* 632–644.

Kline, Kathleen Kovner. (2008). *Authoritative communities: The scientific case for nurturing the whole child.* New York, NY: Springer.

Klöppel, Stefan, Vongerichten, Anna, Eimeren, Thilo van, Frackowiak, Richard S. J., & Siebner, Hartwig R. (2007). Can left-handedness be switched? Insights from an early switch of handwriting. *Journal of Neuroscience, 27,* 7847–7853.

Klug, William, Cummings, Michael, Spencer, Charlotte, & Palladino, Michael. (2008). *Concepts of genetics* (9th ed.). San Francisco, CA: Pearson/Benjamin Cummings.

Kochanska, Grazyna, Aksan, Nazan, Prisco, Theresa R., & Adams, Erin E. (2008). Mother-child and father-child mutually responsive orientation in the first 2 years and children's outcomes at preschool age: Mechanisms of influence. *Child Development, 79,* 30–44.

Kochanska, Grazyna, Barry, Robin A., Jimenez, Natasha B., Hollatz, Amanda L., & Woodard, Jarilyn. (2009). Guilt and effortful control: Two mechanisms that prevent disruptive developmental trajectories. *Journal of Personality and Social Psychology, 97,* 322–333.

Kochanska, Grazyna, Gross, Jami N., Lin, Mei-Hua, & Nichols, Kate E. (2002). Guilt in young children: Development, determinants, and relations with a broader system of standards. *Child Development, 73,* 461–482.

Kogan, Michael D., Blumberg, Stephen J., Schieve, Laura A., Boyle, Coleen A., Perrin, James M., Ghandour, Reem M., et al. (2009). Prevalence of parent-reported diagnosis of autism spectrum disorder among children in the US, 2007. *Pediatrics, 124,* 1395–1403.

Kohl, Patricia L., Jonson-Reid, Melissa, & Drake, Brett. (2009). Time to leave substantiation behind. *Child Maltreatment, 14,* 17–26.

Kohlberg, Lawrence. (1963). The development of children's orientations toward a moral order: I. Sequence in the development of moral thought. *Vita Humana, 6,* 11–33.

Kohlberg, Lawrence, Levine, Charles, & Hewer, Alexandra. (1983). *Moral stages: A current formulation and a response to critics.* New York, NY: Karger.

Kolb, Bryan, & Whishaw, Ian Q. (2008). *Fundamentals of human neuropsychology* (6th ed.). New York, NY: Worth.

Kolling, Thorsten, Goertz, Claudia, Frahsek, Stefanie, & Knopf, Monika. (2009). Stability of deferred imitation in 12- to 18-month-old infants: A closer look into developmental dynamics. *European Journal of Developmental Psychology, 6,* 615–640.

Konner, Melvin. (2007). Evolutionary foundations of cultural psychology. In Shinobu Kitayama & Dov Cohen (Eds.), *Handbook of cultural psychology* (pp. 77–105). New York, NY: Guilford Press.

Konner, Melvin. (2010). *The evolution of childhood: Relationships, emotion, mind.* Cambridge, MA: Harvard University Press.

Kopp, Claire B. (2011). Development in the early years: Socialization, motor development, and consciousness. *Annual Review of Psychology, 62,* 165–187.

Koretz, Daniel. (2009, November 6). Moving past No Child Left Behind. *Science, 326,* 803–804.

Kovacs, Maria, Joormann, Jutta, & Gotlib, Ian H. (2008). Emotion (dys)regulation and links to depressive disorders. *Child Development Perspectives, 2,* 149–155.

Kovas, Yulia, Hayiou-Thomas, Marianna E., Oliver, Bonamy, Dale, Philip S., Bishop, Dorothy V. M., & Plomin, Robert. (2005). Genetic influences in different aspects of language development: The etiology of language skills in 4.5-year-old twins. *Child Development, 76,* 632–651.

Krebs, Dennis L. (2008). Morality: An evolutionary account. *Perspectives on Psychological Science, 3,* 149–172.

Krebs, John R. (2009). The gourmet ape: Evolution and human food preferences. *American Journal of Clinical Nutrition, 90,* 707S–711S.

Krentz, Ursula C., & Corina, David P. (2008). Preference for language in early infancy: The human language bias is not speech specific. *Developmental Science, 11,* 1–9.

Kroger, Jane, Martinussen, Monica, & Marcia, James E. (2010). Identity status change during adolescence and young adulthood: A meta-analysis. *Journal of Adolescence, 33,* 683–698.

Kronenberg, Mindy E., Hansell, Tonya Cross, Brennan, Adrianne M., Osofsky, Howard J., Osofsky, Joy D., & Lawrason, Beverly. (2010). Children of Katrina: Lessons learned about postdisaster symptoms and recovery patterns. *Child Development, 81,* 1241–1259.

Kruger, Daniel J., & Polanski, Stephen P. (2011). Sex differences in mortality rates have increased in China following the single-child law. *Letters on Evolutionary Behavioral Science, 2,* 1–4.

Kruk, Margaret E., Prescott, Marta R., & Galea, Sandro. (2008). Equity of skilled birth attendant utilization in developing countries: Financing and policy determinants. *American Journal of Public Health, 98,* 142–147.

Kryzer, Erin M., Kovan, Nikki, Phillips, Deborah A., Domagall, Lindsey A., & Gunnar, Megan R. (2007). Toddlers' and preschoolers' experience in family day care: Age differences and behavioral correlates. *Early Childhood Research Quarterly, 22,* 451–466.

Kuehn, Bridget M. (2011). Scientists find promising therapies for fragile X and Down syndromes. *The Journal of the American Medical Association, 305,* 344–346.

Kuh, George D., Gonyea, Robert M., & Williams, Julie M. (2005). What students expect from college and what they get. In Thomas E. Miller, Barbara E. Bender, John H. Schuh, & Associates (Eds.), *Promoting reasonable expectations: Aligning student and institutional views of the college experience* (pp. 34–64). San Francisco, CA: Jossey-Bass.

Kuhn, Deanna. (2009). The importance of learning about knowing: Creating a foundation for development of intellectual values. *Child Development Perspectives, 3,* 112–117.

Kuhn, Deanna, & Franklin, Sam. (2006). The second decade: What develops (and how). In William Damon & Richard M. Lerner (Series Eds.) & Deanna Kuhn & Robert Siegler (Vol. Eds.), *Handbook of child psychology: Vol. 2. Cognition, perception, and language* (6th ed., pp. 953–993). Hoboken, NJ: Wiley.

Kuhn, Louise, Sinkala, Moses, Thea, Don, Kankasa, Chipepo, & Aldrovandi, Grace. (2009). HIV prevention is not enough: Child survival in the context of prevention of mother to child HIV transmission. *Journal of the International AIDS Society, 12,* 36.

Kulkofsky, Sarah, & Klemfuss, J. Zoe. (2008). What the stories children tell can tell about their memory: Narrative skill and young children's suggestibility. *Developmental Psychology, 44,* 1442–1456.

Kun, Jürgen F. J., May, Jürgen, & Noedl, Harald. (2010). Surveillance of malaria drug resistance: Improvement needed? *Future Medicine, 7,* 3–6.

Kuppens, Sofie, Grietens, Hans, Onghena, Patrick, & Michiels, Daisy. (2009). Associations between parental control and children's overt and relational aggression. *British Journal of Developmental Psychology, 27,* 607–623.

Kutob, Randa M., Senf, Janet H., Crago, Marjorie, & Shisslak, Catherine M. (2010). Concurrent and longitudinal predictors of self-esteem in elementary and middle school girls. *Journal of School Health, 80,* 240–248.

Kwok, Sylvia Y. C. Lai, & Shek, Daniel T. L. (2010). Hopelessness, parent-adolescent communication, and suicidal ideation among Chinese adolescents in Hong Kong. *Suicide and Life-Threatening Behavior, 40,* 224–233.

LaBar, Kevin S. (2007). Beyond fear: Emotional memory mechanisms in the human brain. *Current Directions in Psychological Science, 16,* 173–177.

Labouvie-Vief, Gisela, Grühn, Daniel, & Mouras, Harold. (2009). Dynamic emotion-cognition interactions in adult development: Arousal, stress, and the processing of affect. In Hayden B. Bosworth & Christopher Hertzog (Eds.), *Aging and cognition: Research methodologies and empirical advances* (pp. 181–196). Washington, DC: American Psychological Association.

LaFontana, Kathryn M., & Cillessen, Antonius H. N. (2010). Developmental changes in the priority of perceived status in childhood and adolescence. *Social Development, 19,* 130–147.

Laible, Deborah, Panfile, Tia, & Makariev, Drika. (2008). The quality and frequency of mother-toddler conflict: Links with attachment and temperament. *Child Development, 79,* 426–443.

Lamb, Michael E. (1982). Maternal employment and child development: A review. In Michael E. Lamb (Ed.), *Nontraditional families: Parenting and child development* (pp. 45–69). Hillsdale, NJ: Erlbaum.

Lamb, Michael E. (Ed.). (2010). *The role of the father in child development* (5th ed.). Hoboken, NJ: Wiley.

Lamb, Michael E., & Lewis, Charlie (2005). The role of parent-child relationships in child development. In Marc H. Bornstein & Michael E. Lamb (Eds.), *Developmental science: An advanced textbook* (5th ed., pp. 429–468). Mahwah, NJ: Erlbaum.

Lamb, Stephen, Markussen, Eifred, Teese, Richard, Sandberg, Nina, & Polesel, John (Eds.). (2011). *School dropout and completion: International comparative studies in theory and policy.* New York, NY: Springer.

Lambert, Nathaniel M., Fincham, Frank D., Stillman, Tyler F., Graham, Steven M., & Beach, Steven R. H. (2010). Motivating change in relationships. *Psychological Science, 21,* 126–132.

Lamm, Bettina, Keller, Heidi, Yovsi, Relindis D., & Chaudhary, Nandita. (2008). Grandmaternal and maternal ethnotheories about early child care. *Journal of Family Psychology, 22,* 80–88.

Lane, Scott D., Cherek, Don R., Pietras, Cynthia J., & Steinberg, Joel L. (2005). Performance of heavy marijuana-smoking adolescents on a laboratory measure of motivation. *Addictive Behaviors, 30,* 815–828.

Langenkamp, Amy G. (2010). Academic vulnerability and resilience during the transition to high school. *Sociology of Education, 83,* 1–19.

Långström, Niklas, Rahman, Qazi, Carlström, Eva, & Lichtenstein, Paul. (2010). Genetic and environmental effects on same-sex sexual behavior: A population study of twins in Sweden. *Archives of Sexual Behavior, 39,* 75–80.

Lapsley, Daniel K. (1993). Toward an integrated theory of adolescent ego development: The "new look" at adolescent egocentrism. *American Journal of Orthopsychiatry, 63,* 562–571.

Lara, Marielena, Akinbami, Lara, Flores, Glenn, & Morgenstern, Hal. (2006). Heterogeneity of childhood asthma among Hispanic children: Puerto Rican children bear a disproportionate burden. *Pediatrics, 117,* 43–53.

Lara-Cinisomo, Sandraluz, Fuligni, Allison Sidle, & Karoly, Lynn A. (2011). Preparing preschoolers for kindergarten. In DeAnna M. Laverick & Mary Renck Jalongo (Eds.), *Transitions to early care and education* (Vol. 4, pp. 93–105). New York, NY: Springer.

Laraway, Kelly A., Birch, Leann L., Shaffer, Michele L., & Paul, Ian M. (2010). Parent perception of healthy infant and toddler growth. *Clinical Pediatrics, 49,* 343–349.

Larson, Nicole I., Neumark-Sztainer, Dianne, Hannan, Peter J., & Story, Mary. (2007). Trends in adolescent fruit and vegetable consumption, 1999–2004: Project EAT. *American Journal of Preventive Medicine, 32,* 147–150.

Larson, Reed, & Wilson, Suzanne. (2004). Adolescence across place and time: Globalization and the changing pathways to adulthood. In Richard M. Lerner & Laurence D. Steinberg (Eds.), *Handbook of adolescent psychology* (2nd ed., pp. 299–330). Hoboken, NJ: Wiley.

Larzelere, Robert, Cox, Ronald, & Smith, Gail. (2010). Do nonphysical punishments reduce antisocial behavior more than spanking? A comparison using the strongest previous causal evidence against spanking. *BMC Pediatrics, 10,* 10.

Lassiter, G. Daniel, & Meissner, Christian A. (Eds.). (2010). *Police interrogations and false confessions: Current research, practice, and policy recommendations.* Washington, DC: American Psychological Association.

Laursen, Brett, Bukowski, William M., Nurmi, Jari-Eri, Marion, Donna, Salmela-Aro, Katariina, & Kiuru, Noona. (2010). Opposites detract: Middle school peer group antipathies. *Journal of Experimental Child Psychology, 106,* 240–256.

Laursen, Brett, & Collins, W. Andrew. (2009). Parent-child relationships during adolescence. In Richard M. Lerner & Laurence Steinberg (Eds.), *Handbook of adolescent psychology: Vol. 2. Contextual influences on adolescent development* (3rd ed., pp. 3–42). Hoboken, NJ: Wiley.

Laursen, Brett, & Mooney, Karen S. (2007). Individual differences in adolescent dating and adjustment. In Rutger C. M. E. Engels, Margaret Kerr, & Håkan Stattin (Eds.), *Friends, lovers, and* groups: *Key relationships in adolescence* (pp. 81–92). Hoboken, NJ: Wiley.

Lavelli, Manuela, & Fogel, Alan. (2005). Developmental changes in the relationship between the infant's attention and emotion during early face-to-face communication: The 2-month transition. *Developmental Psychology, 41,* 265–280.

Layden, Tim. (2004, November 15). Get out and play! *Sports Illustrated, 101,* 80–93.

Leach, Penelope. (1997). *Your baby & child: From birth to age five* (3rd ed.). New York, NY: Knopf.

Leach, Penelope. (2009). *Child care today: Getting it right for everyone.* New York, NY: Knopf.

Leadbeater, Bonnie J., & Hoglund, Wendy L. G. (2009). The effects of peer victimization and physical aggression on changes in internalizing from first to third grade. *Child Development, 80,* 843–859.

Leather, Nicola C. (2009). Risk-taking behaviour in adolescence: A literature review. *Journal of Child Health Care, 13,* 295–304.

Lee, Joyce M., Kaciroti, Niko, Appugliese, Danielle, Corwyn, Robert F., Bradley, Robert H., & Lumeng, Julie C. (2010). Body mass index and timing of pubertal initiation in boys. *Archives of Pediatric and Adolescent Medicine, 164,* 139–144.

Leerkes, Esther M., Blankson, A. Nayena, & O'Brien, Marion. (2009). Differential effects of maternal sensitivity to infant distress and nondistress on social-emotional functioning. *Child Development, 80,* 762–775.

Lefkowitz, Eva S., & Gillen, Meghan M. (2006). "Sex is just a normal part of life": Sexuality in emerging adulthood. In Jeffrey Jensen Arnett & Jennifer Lynn Tanner (Eds.), *Emerging adults in America: Coming of age in the 21st century* (pp. 235–255). Washington, DC: American Psychological Association.

Lehmann, Martin, & Hasselhorn, Marcus. (2010). The dynamics of free recall and their relation to rehearsal between 8 and 10 years of age. *Child Development, 81,* 1006–1020.

Lehmann, Wolfgang. (2004). "For some reason, I get a little scared": Structure, agency, and risk in school-work transitions. *Journal of Youth Studies, 7,* 379–396.

Lei, Joy L. (2003). (Un)necessary toughness?: Those "loud black girls" and those "quiet Asian boys". *Anthropology & Education Quarterly, 34,* 158–181.

Leman, Patrick J., & Björnberg, Marina. (2010). Conversation, development, and gender: A study of changes in children's concepts of punishment. *Child Development, 81,* 958–971.

Lengner, Christopher J. (2010). iPS cell technology in regenerative medicine. In Mone Zaidi (Ed.), *Annals of the New York Academy of Sciences: Vol. 1192. Skeletal biology and medicine* (pp. 38–44). Boston, MA: Blackwell.

Lenneberg, Eric H. (1967). *Biological foundations of language.* New York, NY: Wiley.

Lenroot, Rhoshel K., & Giedd, Jay N. (2008). The changing impact of genes and environment on brain development during childhood and adolescence: Initial findings from a neuroimag-

ing study of pediatric twins. *Development and Psychopathology, 20,* 1161–1175.

Lepper, Mark R., Greene, David, & Nisbett, Richard E. (1973). Undermining children's intrinsic interest with extrinsic reward: A test of the "overjustification" hypothesis. *Journal of Personality & Social Psychology, 28,* 129–137.

Lerner, Claire, & Dombro, Amy Laura. (2004). Finding your fit: Some temperament tips for parents. *Zero to Three, 24,* 42–45.

Lerner, Richard M., & Steinberg, Laurence D. (2009). *Handbook of adolescent psychology* (3rd ed.). Hoboken, NJ: Wiley.

Lesane-Brown, Chase L., Brown, Tony N., Tanner-Smith, Emily E., & Bruce, Marino A. (2010). Negotiating boundaries and bonds: Frequency of young children's socialization to their ethnic/racial heritage. *Journal of Cross-Cultural Psychology, 41,* 457–464.

Lester, Patricia, Leskin, Gregory, Woodward, Kirsten, Saltzman, William, Nash, William, Mogil, Catherine, et al. (2011). Wartime deployment and military children: Applying prevention science to enhance family resilience. In Shelley MacDermid & David S. Riggs (Eds.), *Risk and resilience in U.S. military families* (pp. 149–174). New York, NY: Springer.

Leung, Angel Nga-Man, Wong, Stephanie Siu-fong, Wong, Iris Wai-yin, & McBride-Chang, Catherine. (2010). Filial piety and psychosocial adjustment in Hong Kong Chinese early adolescents. *The Journal of Early Adolescence, 30,* 651–667.

Levi Setti, Paolo E., Albani, Elena, Cesana, Amalia, Novara, Paola Vittoria, Zannoni, Elena, Baggiani, Annamaria M., et al. (2011). Italian Constitutional Court modifications of a restrictive assisted reproduction technology law significantly improve pregnancy rate. *Human Reproduction, 26,* 376–381.

Lewallen, Lynne Porter. (2011). The importance of culture in childbearing. *Journal of Obstetric, Gynecologic, & Neonatal Nursing, 40,* 4–8.

Lewin, Kurt. (1943). Psychology and the process of group living. *Journal of Social Psychology, 17,* 113–131.

Lewin, Tamar (2009, October 23). No Einstein in your crib? Get a refund. *New York Times,* p. A1.

Lewin-Benham, Ann. (2008). *Powerful children: Understanding how to teach and learn using the Reggio approach.* New York, NY: Teachers College Press.

Lewis, Charlotte W., Linsenmayer, Kristi A., & Williams, Alexis. (2010). Wanting better: A qualitative study of low-income parents about their children's oral health. *Pediatric Dentistry, 32,* 518–524.

Lewis, Lawrence B., Antone, Carol, & Johnson, Jacqueline S. (1999). Effects of prosodic stress and serial position on syllable omission in first words. *Developmental Psychology, 35,* 45–59.

Lewis, Michael. (2008). The emergence of human emotions. In Michael Lewis, Jeannette M. Haviland-Jones, & Lisa Feldman Barrett (Eds.), *Handbook of emotions* (3rd ed., pp. 304–319). New York, NY: Guilford Press.

Lewis, Michael, & Brooks, Jeanne. (1978). Self-knowledge and emotional development. In Michael

Lewis & L. A. Rosenblum (Eds.), *Genesis of behavior: Vol. 1. The development of affect* (pp. 205–226). New York, NY: Plenum Press.

Lewis, Michael, & Ramsay, Douglas. (2005). Infant emotional and cortisol responses to goal blockage. *Child Development, 76,* 518–530.

Lewkowicz, David J. (2010). Infant perception of audio-visual speech synchrony. *Developmental Psychology, 46,* 66–77.

Li, Yibing, & Lerner, Richard M. (2011). Trajectories of school engagement during adolescence: Implications for grades, depression, delinquency, and substance use. *Developmental Psychology, 47,* 233–247.

Libertus, Melissa E., & Brannon, Elizabeth M. (2009). Behavioral and neural basis of number sense in infancy. *Current Directions in Psychological Science, 18,* 346–351.

Lichter, Daniel T., Qian, Zhenchao, & Mellott, Leanna M. (2006). Marriage or dissolution? Union transitions among poor cohabiting women. *Demography, 43,* 223–240.

Lillard, Angeline, & Else-Quest, Nicole. (2006, September 29). Evaluating Montessori education. *Science, 313,* 1893–1894.

Lillard, Angeline Stoll. (2005). *Montessori: The science behind the genius.* New York, NY: Oxford University Press.

Lim, Boo Yeun. (2004). The magic of the brush and the power of color: Integrating theory into practice of painting in early childhood settings. *Early Childhood Education Journal, 32,* 113–119.

Limber, Susan P. (2011). Development, evaluation, and future directions of the Olweus Bullying Prevention Program. *Journal of School Violence, 10,* 71–87.

Lincove, Jane A., & Painter, Gary (2006). Does the age that children start kindergarten matter? Evidence of long-term educational and social outcomes. *Educational Evaluation and Policy Analysis, 28,* 153–179

Lindfors, Kaj, Elovainio, Marko, Wickman, Sanna, Vuorinen, Risto, Sinkkonen, Jari, Dunkel, Leo, et al. (2007). Brief report: The role of ego development in psychosocial adjustment among boys with delayed puberty. *Journal of Research on Adolescence, 17,* 601–612.

Linn, Susan, & Novosat, Courtney L. (2008). Calories for sale: Food marketing to children in the twenty-first century. In Amy B. Jordan (Ed.), *Annals of the American Academy of Political and Social Science: Vol. 615. Overweight and obesity in America's children: Causes, consequences, solutions* (pp. 133–155). Thousand Oaks, CA: Sage.

Lipton, Jennifer S., & Spelke, Elizabeth S. (2003). Origins of number sense: Large-number discrimination in human infants. *Psychological Science, 14,* 396–401.

Liszkowski, Ulf, Schäfer, Marie, Carpenter, Malinda, & Tomasello, Michael. (2009). Prelinguistic infants, but not chimpanzees, communicate about absent entities. *Psychological Science, 20,* 654–660.

Liszkowski, Ulf, & Tomasello, Michael. (2011). Individual differences in social, cognitive, and morphological aspects of infant pointing. *Cognitive Development, 26,* 16–29.

Liu, David, Sabbagh, Mark A., Gehring, William J., & Wellman, Henry M. (2009). Neural correlates of childrens theory of mind development. *Child Development, 80,* 318–326.

Liu, David, Wellman, Henry M., Tardif, Twila, & Sabbagh, Mark A. (2008). Theory of mind development in Chinese children: A meta-analysis of false-belief understanding across cultures and languages. *Developmental Psychology, 44,* 523–531.

Livas-Dlott, Alejandra, Fuller, Bruce, Stein, Gabriela L., Bridges, Margaret, Mangual Figueroa, Ariana, & Mireles, Laurie. (2010). Commands, competence, and *cariño*: Maternal socialization practices in Mexican American families. *Developmental Psychology, 46,* 566–578.

Lloyd-Fox, Sarah, Blasi, Anna, Volein, Agnes, Everdell, Nick, Elwell, Claire E., & Johnson, Mark H. (2009). Social perception in infancy: A near infrared spectroscopy study. *Child Development, 80,* 986–999.

Lobstein, T., & Dibb, S. (2005). Evidence of a possible link between obesogenic food advertising and child overweight. *Obesity Reviews, 6,* 203–208.

LoBue, Vanessa, & DeLoache, Judy S. (2011). Pretty in pink: The early development of gender-stereotyped colour preferences. *British Journal of Developmental Psychology, 29,* 656–667.

Lockhart, Kristi L., Chang, Bernard, & Story, Tyler. (2002). Young children's beliefs about the stability of traits: Protective optimism? *Child Development, 73,* 1408–1430.

Lockhart, Kristi L., Nakashima, Nobuko, Inagaki, Kayoko, & Keil, Frank C. (2008). From ugly duckling to swan? Japanese and American beliefs about the stability and origins of traits. *Cognitive Development, 23,* 155–179.

Loe, Irene M., & Feldman, Heidi M. (2007). Academic and educational outcomes of children with ADHD. *Journal of Pediatric Psychology, 32,* 643–654.

Loeb, Susanna, Bridges, Margaret, Bassok, Daphna, Fuller, Bruce, & Rumberger, Russell. (2005). *How much is too much? The influence of preschool centers on children's social and cognitive development.* Retrieved from National Bureau of Economic Research website: http://www.nber.org/papers/w11812

Loeber, Rolf, & Burke, Jeffrey D. (2011). Developmental pathways in juvenile externalizing and internalizing problems. *Journal of Research on Adolescence, 21,* 34–46.

Loland, Sigmund. (2002). *Fair play in sport: A moral norm system.* London, England: Routledge.

Loman, Michelle M., & Gunnar, Megan R. (2010). Early experience and the development of stress reactivity and regulation in children. *Neuroscience & Biobehavioral Reviews, 34,* 867–876.

London, Kamala, Bruck, Maggie, Poole, Debra Ann, & Melnyk, Laura. (2011). The development of metasuggestibility in children. *Applied Cognitive Psychology, 25,* 146–155.

Longmore, Monica, Eng, Abbey, Giordano, Peggy, & Manning, Wendy. (2009). Parenting and adolescents' sexual initiation. *Journal of Marriage and Family, 71,* 969–982.

Lord, Catherine, & Bishop, Somer L. (2010). Autism spectrum disorders: Diagnosis, prevalence, and services for children and families. *Social Policy Report, 24*(2), 1–26.

Losin, Elizabeth A. Reynolds, Dapretto, Mirella, & Iacoboni, Marco. (2009). Culture in the mind's mirror: How anthropology and neuroscience can inform a model of the neural substrate for cultural imitative learning. *Progress in Brain Research, 178,* 175–190.

Lovecky, Deirdre V. (2009). Moral sensitivity in young gifted children. In Tracy Cross & Don Ambrose (Eds.), *Morality, ethics, and gifted minds* (pp. 161–176). New York, NY: Springer.

Lowell, Darcy I., Carter, Alice S., Godoy, Leandra, Paulicin, Belinda, & Briggs-Gowan, Margaret J. (2011). A randomized controlled trial of Child FIRST: A comprehensive home-based intervention translating research into early childhood practice. *Child Development, 82,* 193–208.

Lucast, Erica K. (2007). Informed consent and the misattributed paternity problem in genetic counseling. *Bioethics, 21,* 41–50.

Luna, Beatriz, Padmanabhan, Aarthi, & O'Hearn, Kirsten. (2010). What has fMRI told us about the development of cognitive control through adolescence? *Brain and Cognition, 72,* 101–113.

Luthar, Suniya S., Cicchetti, Dante, & Becker, Bronwyn. (2000). The construct of resilience: A critical evaluation and guidelines for future work. *Child Development, 71,* 543–562.

Luthar, Suniya S., D'Avanzo, Karen, & Hites, Sarah. (2003). Maternal drug abuse versus other psychological disturbances: Risks and resilience among children. In Suniya S. Luthar (Ed.), *Resilience and vulnerability: Adaptation in the context of childhood adversities* (pp. 104–129). New York, NY: Cambridge University Press.

Lynn, Richard, & Mikk, Jaan. (2007). National differences in intelligence and educational attainment. *Intelligence, 35,* 115–121.

Lynne, Sarah D., Graber, Julia A., Nichols, Tracy R., Brooks-Gunn, Jeanne, & Botvin, Gilbert J. (2007). Links between pubertal timing, peer influences, and externalizing behaviors among urban students followed through middle school. *Journal of Adolescent Health, 40,* 181. e187–181.e113.

Lyon, Thomas D., Malloy, Lindsay C., Quas, Jodi A., & Talwar, Victoria A. (2008). Coaching, truth induction, and young maltreated children's false allegations and false denials. *Child Development, 79,* 914–929.

Lyons, Kristen E., Ghetti, Simona, & Cornoldi, Cesare. (2010). Age differences in the contribution of recollection and familiarity to false-memory formation: A new paradigm to examine developmental reversals. *Developmental Science, 13,* 355–362.

Lyons-Ruth, Karlen, Bronfman, Elisa, & Parsons, Elizabeth. (1999). IV. Maternal frightened, frightening, or atypical behavior and disorganized infant attachment patterns. *Monographs of the Society for Research in Child Development, 64*(3, Serial No. 258), 67–96.

Ma, Lang, Phelps, Erin, Lerner, Jacqueline V., & Lerner, Richard M. (2009). Academic competence for adolescents who bully and who are bullied: Findings from the 4-H Study of Positive Youth Development. *The Journal of Early Adolescence, 29,* 862–897.

Maas, Carl, Herrenkohl, Todd I., & Sousa, Cynthia. (2008). Review of research on child maltreatment and violence in youth. *Trauma, Violence & Abuse, 9,* 56–67.

Maccoby, Eleanor E. (2000). Parenting and its effects on children: On reading and misreading behavior genetics. *Annual Review of Psychology, 51,* 1–27.

Macgregor, Stuart, Lind, Penelope A., Bucholz, Kathleen K., Hansell, Narelle K., Madden, Pamela A. F., Richter, Melinda M., et al. (2009). Associations of ADH and ALDH2 gene variation with self report alcohol reactions, consumption and dependence: An integrated analysis. *Human Molecular Genetics, 18,* 580–593.

MacMillan, Harriet L., Wathen, C. Nadine, Barlow, Jane, Fergusson, David M., Leventhal, John M., & Taussig, Heather N. (2009). Interventions to prevent child maltreatment and associated impairment. *Lancet, 373,* 250–266.

Macmillan, Ross, & Copher, Ronda. (2005). Families in the life course: Interdependency of roles, role configurations, and pathways. *Journal of Marriage and Family, 67,* 858–879.

Madden, Mary, & Lenhart, Amanda. (2009). *Teens and distracted driving: Texting, talking and other uses of the cell phone behind the wheel.* Washington, DC: Pew Internet & American Life Project.

Magnuson, Katherine, & Berger, Lawrence M. (2009). Family structure states and transitions: Associations with children's well-being during middle childhood. *Journal of Marriage and Family, 71,* 575–591.

Maguire, Kathleen. (2010). *Sourcebook of criminal justice statistics.* Washington, DC: U.S. Department of Justice.

Mahler, Margaret S., Pine, Fred, & Bergman, Anni. (1975). *The psychological birth of the human infant: Symbiosis and individuation.* New York, NY: Basic Books.

Mahmoud, Adel. (2004, July 9). The global vaccination gap. *Science, 305,* 147.

Majercsik, Eszter. (2005). Hierachy of needs of geriatric patients. *Gerontology, 51,* 170–173.

Makimoto, Kiyoko. (1998). Drinking patterns and drinking problems among Asian-Americans and Pacific Islanders. *Alcohol Health and Research World, 22,* 270–275.

Malina, Robert M., Bouchard, Claude, & Bar-Or, Oded. (2004). *Growth, maturation, and* *physical activity* (2nd ed.). Champaign, IL: Human Kinetics.

Malloy, Michael H. (2009). Impact of cesarean section on intermediate and late preterm births: United States, 2000–2003. *Birth: Issues in Perinatal Care, 36,* 26–33.

Mandler, Jean Matter. (2004). *The foundations of mind: Origins of conceptual thought.* Oxford, UK: Oxford University Press.

Mandler, Jean M. (2007). On the origins of the conceptual system. *American Psychologist, 62,* 741–751.

Manfra, Louis, & Winsler, Adam. (2006). Preschool children's awareness of private speech. *International Journal of Behavioral Development, 30,* 537–549.

Mann, Joshua R., McDermott, Suzanne, Bao, Haikun, & Bersabe, Adrian. (2009). Maternal genitourinary infection and risk of cerebral palsy. *Developmental Medicine & Child Neurology, 51,* 282–288.

Mann, Ronald D., & Andrews, Elizabeth B. (Eds.). (2007). *Pharmacovigilance* (2nd ed.). Hoboken, NJ: Wiley.

Manzi, Claudia, Vignoles, Vivian L., Regalia, Camillo, & Scabini, Eugenia. (2006). Cohesion and enmeshment revisited: Differentiation, identity, and well-being in two European cultures. *Journal of Marriage and Family, 68,* 673–689.

Mao, Amy, Burnham, Melissa M., Goodlin-Jones, Beth L., Gaylor, Erika E., & Anders, Thomas F. (2004). A comparison of the sleep-wake patterns of cosleeping and solitary-sleeping infants. *Child Psychiatry and Human Development, 35,* 95–105.

Mar, Raymond A. (2011). The neural bases of social cognition and story comprehension. *Annual Review of Psychology, 62,* 103–134.

Mar, Raymond A., Tackett, Jennifer L., & Moore, Chris. (2010). Exposure to media and theory-of-mind development in preschoolers. *Cognitive Development, 25,* 69–78.

Marazita, John M., & Merriman, William E. (2010). Verifying one's knowledge of a name without retrieving it: A U-shaped relation to vocabulary size in early childhood. *Language Learning and Development, 7,* 40–54.

March, John S., Franklin, Martin E., Leonard, Henrietta L., & Foa, Edna B. (2004). Obsessive-compulsive disorder. In Tracy L. Morris & John S. March (Eds.), *Anxiety disorders in children and adolescents* (2nd ed., pp. 212–240). New York, NY: Guilford Press.

Marcia, James E. (1966). Development and validation of ego-identity status. *Journal of Personality & Social Psychology, 3,* 551–558.

Marcia, James E., Waterman, Alan S., Matteson, David R., Archer, Sally L., & Orlofsky, Jacob L. (1993). *Ego identity: A handbook for psychosocial research.* New York, NY: Springer-Verlag.

Marcovitch, Stuart, Boseovski, Janet J., Knapp, Robin J., & Kane, Michael J. (2010). Goal neglect and working memory capacity in 4- to 6-year-old children. *Child Development, 81,* 1687–1695.

Marcus, Gary F., & Rabagliati, Hugh. (2009). Language acquisition, domain specificity, and descent with modification. In John Colombo, Peggy McCardle, & Lisa Freund (Eds.), *Infant pathways to language: Methods, models, and research disorders* (pp. 267–285). New York, NY: Psychology Press.

Margueron, Raphaël, & Reinberg, Danny. (2010). Chromatin structure and the inheritance of epigenetic information. *Nature Reviews Genetics, 11,* 285–296.

Marks, Amy K., Patton, Flannery, & Coll, Cynthia García. (2011). Being bicultural: A mixed-methods study of adolescents' implicitly and explicitly measured multiethnic identities. *Developmental Psychology, 47,* 270–288.

Marlow-Ferguson, Rebecca (Ed.). (2002). *World education encyclopedia: A survey of educational systems worldwide* (2nd ed.). Detroit, MI: Gale Group.

Marsh, Louise, McGee, Rob, Nada-Raja, Shyamala, & Williams, Sheila. (2010). Text bullying and traditional bullying among New Zealand secondary school students. *Journal of Adolescence, 33,* 237–240.

Marsh, Lauren E., & Hamilton, Antonia F. de C. (2011). Dissociation of mirroring and mentalising systems in autism. *NeuroImage, 56,* 1511–1519.

Marshall, Eliot. (2011, February 4). Waiting for the revolution. *Science, 331,* 526–529.

Marshall, Peter J. (2009). Relating psychology and neuroscience: Taking up the challenges. *Perspectives on Psychological Science, 4,* 113–125.

Martin, Andrew J. (2009). Motivation and engagement across the academic life span: A developmental construct validity study of elementary school, high school, and university/college students. *Educational and Psychological Measurement, 69,* 794–824.

Martin, Carol Lynn, & Ruble, Diane N. (2010). Patterns of gender development. *Annual Review of Psychology, 61,* 353–381.

Martin, Carol Lynn, Ruble, Diane N., & Szkrybalo, Joel. (2002). Cognitive theories of early gender development. *Psychological Bulletin, 128,* 903–933.

Martin, Joyce A., Hamilton, Brady E., Sutton, Paul D., Ventura, Stephanie J., Mathews, T. J., & Osterman, Michelle J. K. (2010). Births: Final data for 2008. *National vital statistics reports, 59*(1).

Masche, J. Gowert. (2010). Explanation of normative declines in parents' knowledge about their adolescent children. *Journal of Adolescence, 33,* 271–284.

Mascolo, Michael F., Fischer, Kurt W., & Li, Jin. (2003). Dynamic development of component systems of emotions: Pride, shame, and guilt in China and the United States. In Richard J. Davidson, Klaus R. Scherer, & H. Hill Goldsmith (Eds.), *Handbook of affective sciences* (pp. 375–408). Oxford, UK: Oxford University Press.

Mashburn, Andrew J., Justice, Laura M., Downer, Jason T., & Pianta, Robert C. (2009). Peer effects on children's language achievement during pre-kindergarten. *Child Development, 80,* 686–702.

Maslow, Abraham H. (1954). *Motivation and personality.* New York, NY: Harper.

Maslow, Abraham H. (1971). *The farther reaches of human nature.* New York, NY: Viking Press.

Maslow, Abraham H. (1999). *Toward a psychology of being* (3rd ed.). New York, NY: J. Wiley & Sons. (Original work published 1962)

Masten, Ann S. (2004). Regulatory processes, risk, and resilience in adolescent development. In Ronald E. Dahl & Linda Patia Spear (Eds.), *Annals of the New York Academy of Sciences: Vol. 1021. Adolescent brain development: Vulnerabilities and opportunities* (pp. 310–319). New York, NY: New York Academy of Sciences.

Masten, Carrie L., Guyer, Amanda E., Hodgdon, Hilary B., McClure, Erin B., Charney, Dennis S., Ernst, Monique, et al. (2008). Recognition of facial emotions among maltreated children with high rates of post-traumatic stress disorder. *Child Abuse & Neglect, 32,* 139–153.

Mathison, David J., & Agrawal, Dewesh. (2010). An update on the epidemiology of pediatric fractures. *Pediatric Emergency Care, 26,* 594–603.

Matsumoto, David. (2004). Reflections on culture and competence. In Robert J. Sternberg & Elena L. Grigorenko (Eds.), *Culture and competence: Contexts of life success* (pp. 273–282). Washington, DC: American Psychological Association.

Mayes, Rick, Bagwell, Catherine, & Erkulwater, Jennifer L. (2009). *Medicating children: ADHD and pediatric mental health.* Cambridge, MA: Harvard University Press.

Mayeux, Lara, & Cillessen, Antonius H. N. (2007). Peer influence and the development of antisocial behavior. In Rutger C. M. E. Engels, Margaret Kerr, & Håkan Stattin (Eds.), *Friends, lovers, and groups: Key relationships in adolescence* (pp. 33–46). Hoboken, NJ: Wiley.

Mazin, Alexander L. (2009). Suicidal function of DNA methylation in age-related genome disintegration. *Ageing Research Reviews, 8,* 314–327.

Mazzocco, Michèle M. M., & Ross, Judith L. (2007). *Neurogenetic developmental disorders: Variation of manifestation in childhood.* Cambridge, MA: MIT Press.

McAdams, Dan P., Bauer, Jack J., Sakaeda, April R., Anyidoho, Nana Akua, Machado, Mary Anne, Magrino-Failla, Katie, et al. (2006). Continuity and change in the life story: A longitudinal study of autobiographical memories in emerging adulthood. *Journal of Personality, 74,* 1371–1400.

McAdams, Dan P., & Olson, Bradley D. (2010). Personality development: Continuity and change over the life course. *Annual Review of Psychology, 61,* 517–542.

McAdams, Dan P., & Pals, Jennifer L. (2006). A new big five: Fundamental principles for an integrative science of personality. *American Psychologist, 61,* 204–217.

McCarthy-Keith, Desireé M., Schisterman, Enrique F., Robinson, Randal D., O'Leary,

Kathleen, Lucidi, Richard S., & Armstrong, Alicia Y. (2010). Will decreasing assisted reproduction technology costs improve utilization and outcomes among minority women? *Fertility and Sterility, 94,* 2587–2589.

McCartney, Kathleen, Burchinal, Margaret, Clarke-Stewart, Alison, Bub, Kristen L., Owen, Margaret T., Belsky, Jay, et al. (2010). Testing a series of causal propositions relating time in child care to children's externalizing behavior. *Developmental Psychology, 46,* 1–17, 17a.

McCarty, Cheryl, Prawitz, Aimee D., Derscheid, Linda E., & Montgomery, Bette. (2010). Perceived safety and teen risk taking in online chat sites. *Cyberpsychology, Behavior, and Social Networking, 14,* 169–174.

McClain, Paula D., Johnson Carew, Jessica D., Walton, Eugene, Jr., & Watts, Candis S. (2009). Group membership, group identity, and group consciousness: Measures of racial identity in American politics? *Annual Review of Political Science, 12,* 471–485.

McClintock, Elizabeth Aura. (2010). When does race matter? Race, sex, and dating at an elite university. *Journal of Marriage and Family, 72,* 45–72.

McConkie-Rosell, Allyn, & O'Daniel, Julianne. (2007). Beyond the diagnosis: The process of genetic counseling. In Michèle M. M. Mazzocco & Judith L. Ross (Eds.), *Neurogenetic developmental disorders: Variation of manifestation in childhood* (pp. 367–389). Cambridge, MA: MIT Press.

McCormick, Cheryl M., Mathews, Iva Z., Thomas, Catherine, & Waters, Patti. (2010). Investigations of HPA function and the enduring consequences of stressors in adolescence in animal models. *Brain and Cognition, 72,* 73–85.

McCowan, Lesley M. E., Dekker, Gustaaf A., Chan, Eliza, Stewart, Alistair, Chappell, Lucy C., Hunter, Misty, et al. (2009). Spontaneous preterm birth and small for gestational age infants in women who stop smoking early in pregnancy: Prospective cohort study. *BMJ, 338,* b1081. doi:10.1136/bmj.b1081

McGrath, Susan K., & Kennell, John H. (2008). A randomized controlled trial of continuous labor support for middle-class couples: Effect on cesarean delivery rates. *Birth, 35,* 92–97.

McGuigan, Leigh. (2008). Systems thinking and culture change in urban school districts. In Wayne K. Hoy & Michael F. DiPaola (Eds.), *Improving schools: Studies in leadership and culture* (pp. 99–116). Charlotte, NC: Information Age.

McIntyre, Donald A. (2002). *Colour blindness: Causes and effects.* Chester, UK: Dalton.

McKinley, Jesse. (2010, June 24). Whooping cough kills 5 in California; State declares an epidemic. *New York Times,* p. A15.

McKown, Clark, & Strambler, Michael J. (2009). Developmental antecedents and social and academic consequences of stereotype-consciousness in middle childhood. *Child Development, 80,* 1643–1659.

McKusick, Victor A. (2007). Mendelian Inheritance in Man and its online version, OMIM. *American Journal of Human Genetics, 80,* 588–604.

McLanahan, Sara. (2009). Fragile families and the reproduction of poverty. *The Annals of the American Academy of Political and Social Science, 621,* 111–131.

McLeod, Bryce D., Wood, Jeffrey J., & Weisz, John R. (2007). Examining the association between parenting and childhood anxiety: A meta-analysis. *Clinical Psychology Review, 27,* 155–172.

McLeod, Jane D., Pescosolido, Bernice A., Takeuchi, David T., & Falkenberg White, Terry (2004). Public attitudes toward the use of psychiatric medications for children. *Journal of Health and Social Behavior, 45,* 53–67.

McLoyd, Vonnie C., Aikens, Nikki L., & Burton, Linda M. (2006). Childhood poverty, policy, and practice. In William Damon & Richard M. Lerner (Series Eds.) & K. Ann Renninger & Irving E. Sigel (Vol. Eds.), *Handbook of child psychology: Vol. 4. Child psychology in practice* (6th ed., pp. 700–775). Hoboken, NJ: Wiley.

McLoyd, Vonnie C., Kaplan, Rachel, Hardaway, Cecily R., & Wood, Dana. (2007). Does endorsement of physical discipline matter? Assessing moderating influences on the maternal and child psychological correlates of physical discipline in African American families. *Journal of Family Psychology, 21,* 165–175.

McManus, I. Chris, Moore, James, Freegard, Matthew, & Rawles, Richard. (2010). Science in the making: Right Hand, Left Hand. III: Estimating historical rates of left-handedness. *Laterality: Asymmetries of Body, Brain and Cognition, 15,* 186–208.

McNally, Richard J., & Geraerts, Elke. (2009). A new solution to the recovered memory debate. *Perspectives on Psychological Science, 4,* 126–134.

McNeil, Nicole M., & Uttal, David H. (2009). Rethinking the use of concrete materials in learning: Perspectives from development and education. *Child Development Perspectives, 3,* 137–139.

McNeil, Nicole M., Uttal, David H., Jarvin, Linda, & Sternberg, Robert J. (2009). Should you show me the money? Concrete objects both hurt and help performance on mathematics problems. *Learning and Instruction, 19,* 171–184.

McShane, Kelly E., & Hastings, Paul D. (2009). The New Friends Vignettes: Measuring parental psychological control that confers risk for anxious adjustment in preschoolers. *International Journal of Behavioral Development, 33,* 481–495.

Meadows, Sara. (2006). *The child as thinker: The development and acquisition of cognition in childhood* (2nd ed.). New York, NY: Routledge.

Meaney, Michael J. (2010). Epigenetics and the biological definition of gene–environment interactions. *Child Development, 81,* 41–79.

Medscape Psychiatry & Mental Health. (2005). *Autism first-hand: An expert interview with Temple Grandin, PhD.* Retrieved from http://cme.medscape.com/viewarticle/498153

Meece, Judith L., & Eccles, Jacquelynne S. (2010). *Handbook of research on schools, schooling, and human development.* New York, NY: Routledge.

Meeus, Wim. (2011). The study of adolescent identity formation 2000–2010: A review of longitudinal research. *Journal of Research on Adolescence, 21,* 75–94.

Mehta, Clare M., & Strough, JoNell. (2009). Sex segregation in friendships and normative contexts across the life span. *Developmental Review, 29,* 201–220.

Meier, Ann, Hull, Kathleen E., & Ortyl, Timothy A. (2009). Young adult relationship values at the intersection of gender and sexuality. *Journal of Marriage and Family, 71,* 510–525.

Melhuish, Edward, & Petrogiannis, Konstantinos. (2006). An international overview of early childhood care and education. In Edward Melhuish & Konstantinos Petrogiannis (Eds.), *Early childhood care and education: International perspectives* (pp. 167–178). London, England: Routledge.

Melhuish, Edward C., Phan, Mai B., Sylva, Kathy, Sammons, Pam, Siraj-Blatchford, Iram, & Taggart, Brenda. (2008). Effects of the home learning environment and preschool center experience upon literacy and numeracy development in early primary school. *Journal of Social Issues, 64,* 95–114.

Meltzoff, Andrew N. (2007). 'Like me': A foundation for social cognition. *Developmental Science, 10,* 126–134.

Meltzoff, Andrew N., & Moore, M. Keith. (1999). A new foundation for cognitive development in infancy: The birth of the representational infant. In Ellin Kofsky Scholnick, Katherine Nelson, Susan A. Gelman, & Patricia H. Miller (Eds.), *Conceptual development: Piaget's legacy* (pp. 53–78). Mahwah, NJ: Erlbaum.

Melzi, Gigliana, & Caspe, Margaret. (2005). Variations in maternal narrative styles during book reading interactions. *Narrative Inquiry, 15,* 101–125.

Mendle, Jane, Harden, K. Paige, Brooks-Gunn, Jeanne, & Graber, Julia A. (2010). Development's tortoise and hare: Pubertal timing, pubertal tempo, and depressive symptoms in boys and girls. *Developmental Psychology, 46,* 1341–1353.

Meririnne, Esa, Kiviruusu, Olli, Karlsson, Linnea, Pelkonen, Mirjami, Ruuttu, Titta, Tuisku, Virpi, et al. (2010). Brief report: Excessive alcohol use negatively affects the course of adolescent depression—One year naturalistic follow-up study. *Journal of Adolescence, 33,* 221–226.

Merriman, William E. (1999). Competition, attention, and young children's lexical processing. In Brian MacWhinney (Ed.), *The emergence of language* (pp. 331–358). Mahwah, NJ: Erlbaum.

Mervis, Jeffrey. (2008, March 21). Expert panel lays out the path to algebra—and why it matters. *Science, 319,* 1605.

Merz, Emily C., & McCall, Robert B. (2010). Behavior problems in children adopted from psychosocially depriving institutions. *Journal of Abnormal Child Psychology, 38,* 459–470.

Meshcheryakov, Boris G. (2005). Psychometric approach to child animism. *Cultural-Historical Psychology, 1,* 70–86.

Mesquita, Batja, & Leu, Janxin. (2007). The cultural psychology of emotion. In Shinobu Kitayama & Dov Cohen (Eds.), *Handbook of cultural psychology* (pp. 734–759). New York, NY: Guilford Press.

Messer, Karen, Trinidad, Dennis R., Al-Delaimy, Wael K., & Pierce, John P. (2008). Smoking cessation rates in the United States: A comparison of young adult and older smokers. *American Journal of Public Health, 98,* 317–322.

Messing, Jacqueline. (2007). Multiple ideologies and competing discourses: Language shift in Tlaxcala, Mexico. *Language in Society, 36,* 555–577.

Messinger, Daniel S., Mahoor, Mohammad H., Chow, Sy-Miin, & Cohn, Jeffrey F. (2009). Automated measurement of facial expression in infant-mother interaction: A pilot study. *Infancy, 14,* 285–305.

Meteyer, Karen, & Perry-Jenkins, Maureen. (2010). Father involvement among working-class, dual-earner couples. *Fathering, 8,* 379–403.

Miklowitz, David Jay, & Cicchetti, Dante (Eds.). (2010). *Understanding bipolar disorder: A developmental psychopathology perspective.* New York, NY: Guilford Press.

Mikulincer, Mario, & Goodman, Gail S. (2006). *Dynamics of romantic love: Attachment, caregiving, and sex.* New York, NY: Guilford Press.

Milardo, Robert M. (2010). *The forgotten kin: Aunts and uncles.* New York, NY: Cambridge University Press.

Miles, Lynden K. (2009). Who is approachable? *Journal of Experimental Social Psychology, 45,* 262–266.

Milkman, Katherine L., Chugh, Dolly, & Bazerman, Max H. (2009). How can decision making be improved? *Perspectives on Psychological Science, 4,* 379–383.

Miller, Greg. (2006, March 31). The thick and thin of brainpower: Developmental timing linked to IQ. *Science, 311,* 1851.

Miller, Greg. (2008, June 13). Growing pains for fMRI. *Science, 320,* 1412–1414.

Miller, Greg. (2010, November 26). New clues about what makes the human brain special. *Science, 330,* 1167.

Miller, Joan G. (2004). The cultural deep structure of psychological theories of social development. In Robert J. Sternberg & Elena L. Grigorenko (Eds.), *Culture and competence: Contexts of life success* (pp. 111–138). Washington, DC: American Psychological Association.

Miller, Kevin F., Smith, Catherine M., Zhu, Jianjun, & Zhang, Houcan. (1995). Preschool origins of cross-national differences in mathematical competence: The role of number-naming systems. *Psychological Science, 6,* 56–60.

Miller, Orlando J., & Therman, Eeva. (2001). *Human chromosomes* (4th ed.). New York, NY: Springer.

Miller, Patrick, & Plant, Martin. (2010). Parental guidance about drinking: Relationship with teenage psychoactive substance use. *Journal of Adolescence, 33,* 55–68.

Miller, Patricia H. (2011). *Theories of developmental psychology* (5th ed.). New York, NY: Worth.

Miller, Patricia Y., & Simon, William. (1980). The development of sexuality in adolescence. In Joseph Adelson (Ed.), *Handbook of adolescent psychology* (pp. 383–407). New York, NY: Wiley.

Miller, Torri W., Nigg, Joel T., & Miller, Robin L. (2009). Attention deficit hyperactivity disorder in African American children: What can be concluded from the past ten years? *Clinical Psychology Review, 29,* 77–86.

Mills, Britain, Reyna, Valerie F., & Estrada, Steven. (2008). Explaining contradictory relations between risk perception and risk taking. *Psychological Science, 19,* 429–433.

Mills, Jon (Ed.). (2004). *Psychoanalysis at the limit: Epistemology, mind, and the question of science.* Albany, NY: State University of New York Press.

Mills, James L., McPartlin, Joseph M., Kirke, Peadar N., Lee, Young J., Conley, Mary R., Weir, Donald G., et al. (1995). Homocysteine metabolism in pregnancies complicated by neural-tube defects. *Lancet, 345,* 149–151.

Mills, Ryan E., Walter, Klaudia, Stewart, Chip, Handsaker, Robert E., Chen, Ken, Alkan, Can, et al. (2011). Mapping copy number variation by population-scale genome sequencing. *Nature, 470,* 59–65.

Mills-Koonce, W. Roger, Garrett-Peters, Patricia, Barnett, Melissa, Granger, Douglas A., Blair, Clancy, & Cox, Martha J. (2011). Father contributions to cortisol responses in infancy and toddlerhood. *Developmental Psychology, 47,* 388–395.

Minagawa-Kawai, Yasuyo, van der Lely, Heather, Ramus, Franck, Sato, Yutaka, Mazuka, Reiko, & Dupoux, Emmanuel. (2011). Optical brain imaging reveals general auditory and language-specific processing in early infant development. *Cerebral Cortex, 21,* 254–261.

Mindell, Jodi A., & Owens, Judith A. (2010). *A clinical guide to pediatric sleep: Diagnosis and management of sleep problems* (2nd ed.). Philadelphia, PA: Lippincott Williams & Wilkins.

Mindell, Jodi A., Sadeh, Avi, Wiegand, Benjamin, How, Ti Hwei, & Goh, Daniel Y. T. (2010). Cross-cultural differences in infant and toddler sleep. *Sleep Medicine, 11,* 274–280.

Minogue, Kristen. (2010, November 5). China's brain mappers zoom in on neural connections. *Science, 330,* 747.

Mintz, Toben H. (2005). Linguistic and conceptual influences on adjective acquisition in 24- and 36-month-olds. *Developmental Psychology, 41,* 17–29.

Mishra, Ramesh C., Singh, Sunita, & Dasen, Pierre R. (2009). Geocentric dead reckoning in Sanskrit- and Hindi-medium school children. *Culture & Psychology, 15,* 386–408.

Misra, Dawn P., Caldwell, Cleopatra, Young, Alford A., & Abelson, Sara. (2010). Do fathers matter? Paternal contributions to birth outcomes and racial disparities. *American Journal of Obstetrics and Gynecology, 202,* 99–100.

Mitchell, Edwin A. (2009). SIDS: Past, present and future. *Acta Pædiatrica, 98,* 1712–1719.

Mitchell, Philip B., Meiser, Bettina, Wilde, Alex, Fullerton, Janice, Donald, Jennifer, Wilhelm, Kay, et al. (2010). Predictive and diagnostic genetic testing in psychiatry. *Psychiatric Clinics of North America, 33,* 225–243.

Miyake, Akira, Kost-Smith, Lauren E., Finkelstein, Noah D., Pollock, Steven J., Cohen, Geoffrey L., & Ito, Tiffany A. (2010). Reducing the gender achievement gap in college science: A classroom study of values affirmation. *Science, 330,* 1234–1237.

Mize, Krystal D., Shackelford, Todd K., & Shackelford, Viviana A. (2009). Hands-on killing of intimate partners as a function of sex and relationship status/state. *Journal of Family Violence, 24,* 463–470.

MMWR. (2002, September 13). Folic acid and prevention of spina bifida and anencephaly: 10 years after the U.S. public health service recommendation. *MMWR Recommendations and Reports, 51*(RR13), 1–3.

MMWR. (2005, August 26). Surveillance for dental caries, dental sealants, tooth retention, edentulism, and enamel fluorosis—United States, 1988–1994 and 1999–2002. *MMWR Surveillance Summaries, 54*(3), 1–44.

MMWR. (2005, January 14). Reducing childhood asthma through community-based service delivery—New York City, 2001–2004. *Morbidity and Mortality Weekly Report, 54,* 11–14.

MMWR. (2005, May 27). Blood lead levels—United States, 1999–2002. *Morbidity and Mortality Weekly Report, 54,* 513–516.

MMWR. (2008, January 18). School-associated student homicides—United States, 1992–2006. *Morbidity and Mortality Weekly Report, 57,* 33–36.

MMWR. (2008, July 11). Disparities in secondhand smoke exposure—United States, 1988–1994 and 1999–2004. *Morbidity and Mortality Weekly Report, 57,* 744–747.

MMWR. (2009, June 12). Assisted reproductive technology surveillance—United States, 2006. *MMWR Surveillance Summaries, 58*(SS5), 1–25.

MMWR. (2009, October 9). Availability of less nutritious snack foods and beverages in secondary schools—Selected states, 2002–2008. *Morbidity and Mortality Weekly Report, 58,* 1102–1104.

MMWR. (2010, June 4). Youth Risk Behavior Surveillance—United States, 2009. *MMWR Surveillance Summaries, 59*(SS5), 1–142.

MMWR. (2010, May 14). Progress toward interruption of wild poliovirus transmission—Worldwide, 2009. *Morbidity and Mortality Weekly Report, 59,* 545–550.

MMWR. (2011, February 25). Abortion surveillance—United States, 2007. *MMWR Surveillance Summaries, 60*(SS1), 1–39.

MMWR. (2011, January 7). Notifiable diseases and mortality tables. *Morbidity and Mortality Weekly Report, 59,* 1704–1717.

Moffitt, Terrie E. (2003). Life-course-persistent and adolescence-limited antisocial behavior: A 10-year research review and a research agenda. In Benjamin B. Lahey, Terrie E. Moffitt, & Avshalom Caspi (Eds.), *Causes of conduct disorder and juvenile delinquency* (pp. 49–75). New York, NY: Guilford Press.

Moffitt, Terrie E., Caspi, Avshalom, & Rutter, Michael. (2006). Measured gene-environment interactions in psychopathology: Concepts, research strategies, and implications for research, intervention, and public understanding of genetics. *Perspectives on Psychological Science, 1,* 5–27.

Moffitt, Terrie E., Caspi, Avshalom, Rutter, Michael, & Silva, Phil A. (2001). *Sex differences in antisocial behaviour: Conduct disorder, delinquency, and violence in the Dunedin Longitudinal Study.* New York, NY: Cambridge University Press.

Mofidi, Mahyar, Zeldin, Leslie P., & Rozier, R. Gary. (2009). Oral health of Early Head Start children: A qualitative study of staff, parents, and pregnant women. *American Journal of Public Health, 99,* 245–251.

Molina, Brooke S. G., Hinshaw, Stephen P., Swanson, James W., Arnold, L. Eugene, Vitiello, Benedetto, Jensen, Peter S., et al. (2009). The MTA at 8 years: Prospective follow-up of children treated for combined-type ADHD in a multisite study. *Journal of the American Academy of Child & Adolescent Psychiatry, 48,* 484.

Molitor, Adriana, & Hsu, Hui-Chin. (2011). Child development across cultures. In Kenneth D. Keith (Ed.), *Cross-cultural psychology: Contemporary themes and perspectives* (pp. 75–109). Malden, MA: Wiley-Blackwell.

Mollenkopf, John, Waters, Mary C., Holdaway, Jennifer, & Kasinitz, Philip. (2005). The ever-winding path: Ethnic and racial diversity in the transition to adulthood. In Richard A. Settersten, Jr., Frank F. Furstenberg, Jr., & Rubén G. Rumbaut (Eds.), *On the frontier of adulthood: Theory, research, and public policy* (pp. 454–497). Chicago, IL: University of Chicago Press.

Møller, Signe J., & Tenenbaum, Harriet R. (2011). Danish majority children's reasoning about exclusion based on gender and ethnicity. *Child Development, 82,* 520–532.

Monahan, Kathryn C., Steinberg, Laurence, & Cauffman, Elizabeth. (2009). Affiliation with antisocial peers, susceptibility to peer influence, and antisocial behavior during the transition to adulthood. *Developmental Psychology, 45,* 1520–1530.

Monastersky, Richard. (2007, January 12). Who's minding the teenage brain? *Chronicle of Higher Education, 53,* A14–A18.

Moncloa, Fe, Wilkinson-Lee, Ada M., & Russell, Stephen T. (2010). Cuídate sin pena: Mexican mother-adolescent sexuality communication. *Journal of Ethnic and Cultural Diversity in Social Work, 19,* 217–234.

Monks, Claire P., & Coyne, Iain. (2011). *Bullying in different contexts.* New York, NY: Cambridge University Press.

Monroe, Kristen Renwick, Hankin, James, & Vechten, Renée Bukovchik Van. (2000). The psychological foundations of identity politics. *Annual Review of Political Science, 3,* 419–447.

Monteiro, Carlos A., Conde, Wolney L., & Popkin, Barry M. (2007). Income-specific trends in obesity in Brazil: 1975–2003. *American Journal of Public Health, 97,* 1808–1812.

Montgomery, Leigh, & Williams, Stacie. (2010). *Countries with the highest college graduation rates.* Retrieved from Christian Science Monitor website: http://www.csmonitor.com/USA/Education/2010/0809/Countries-with-the-highest-college-graduation-rates/Ireland-43.9–percent

Moore, Ginger A., & Calkins, Susan D. (2004). Infants' vagal regulation in the still-face paradigm is related to dyadic coordination of mother-infant interaction. *Developmental Psychology, 40,* 1068–1080.

Moore, Keith L., & Persaud, Trivedi V. N. (2003). *The developing human: Clinically oriented embryology* (7th ed.). Philadelphia, PA: Saunders.

Moore, Keith L., & Persaud, Trivedi V. N. (2007). *The developing human: Clinically oriented embryology* (8th ed.). Philadelphia, PA: Saunders/Elsevier.

Moore, Susan, & Rosenthal, Doreen. (2006). *Sexuality in adolescence: Current trends* (2nd ed.). New York, NY: Routledge.

Morasch, Katherine C., & Bell, Martha Ann. (2009). Patterns of brain-electrical activity during declarative memory performance in 10-month-old infants. *Brain and Cognition, 71,* 215–222.

Morelli, Gilda A., & Rothbaum, Fred. (2007). Situating the child in context: Attachment relationships and self-regulation in different cultures. In Shinobu Kitayama & Dov Cohen (Eds.), *Handbook of cultural psychology* (pp. 500–527). New York, NY: Guilford Press.

Moreno, Carmen, Laje, Gonzalo, Blanco, Carlos, Jiang, Huiping, Schmidt, Andrew B., & Olfson, Mark. (2007). National trends in the outpatient diagnosis and treatment of bipolar disorder in youth. *Archives of General Psychiatry, 64,* 1032–1039.

Moreno, Luis A., Pigeot, Iris, & Ahrens, Wolfgang (Eds.). (2011). *Epidemiology of obesity in children and adolescents prevalence and etiology.* New York, NY: Springer.

Morgan, Ian G. (2003). The biological basis of myopic refractive error. *Clinical and Experimental Optometry, 86,* 276–288.

Morón, Cecilio, & Viteri, Fernando E. (2009). Update on common indicators of nutritional status: food access, food consumption, and biochemical measures of iron and anemia. *Nutrition Reviews, 67*(Suppl. s1), S31–S35.

Morris, Amanda Sheffield, Silk, Jennifer S., Steinberg, Laurence, Myers, Sonya S., & Robinson, Lara Rachel. (2007). The role of the family context in the development of emotion regulation. *Social Development, 16,* 361–388.

Morris, John A., Jordan, Cynthia L., & Breedlove, S. Marc. (2004). Sexual differentiation of the vertebrate nervous system. *Nature Neuroscience, 7,* 1034–1039.

Morris, Pamela, & Kalil, Ariel. (2006). Out-of-school time use during middle childhood in a low-income sample: Do combinations of activities affect achievement and behavior? In Aletha C. Huston & Marika N. Ripke (Eds.), *Developmental contexts in middle childhood: Bridges to adolescence and adulthood* (pp. 237–259). New York, NY: Cambridge University Press.

Morrison, Frederick J., Ponitz, Claire Cameron, & McClelland, Megan M. (2010). Self-regulation and academic achievement in the transition to school. In Susan D. Calkins & Martha Ann Bell (Eds.), *Child development at the intersection of emotion and cognition* (pp. 203–224). Washington, DC: American Psychological Association.

Morrissey, Taryn. (2009). Multiple child-care arrangements and young children's behavioral outcomes. *Child Development, 80,* 59–76.

Moshman, David. (2005). *Adolescent psychological development: Rationality, morality, and identity* (2nd ed.). Mahwah, NJ: Erlbaum.

Mosholder, Andrew D., Gelperin, Kate, Hammad, Tarek A., Phelan, Kathleen, & Johann-Liang, Rosemary. (2009). Hallucinations and other psychotic symptoms associated with the use of attention-deficit/hyperactivity disorder drugs in children. *Pediatrics, 123,* 611–616.

Moulson, Margaret C., Westerlund, Alissa, Fox, Nathan A., Zeanah, Charles H., & Nelson, Charles A. (2009). The effects of early experience on face recognition: An event-related potential study of institutionalized children in Romania. *Child Development, 80,* 1039–1056.

Mrozek-Budzyn, Dorota, Kieltyka, Agnieszka, & Majewska, Renata. (2010). Lack of association between measles-mumps-rubella vaccination and autism in children: A case-control study. *The Pediatric Infectious Disease Journal, 29,* 397–400

Mueller, Christian E., Bridges, Sara K., & Goddard, Michelle S. (2011). Sleep and parent-family connectedness: Links, relationships and implications for adolescent depression. *Journal of Family Studies, 17,* 9–23.

Müller, Ulrich, Dick, Anthony Steven, Gela, Katherine, Overton, Willis F., & Zelazo, Philip David. (2006). The role of negative priming in preschoolers' flexible rule use on the dimensional change card sort task. *Child Development, 77,* 395–412.

Mullis, Ina V. S., Martin, Michael O., & Foy, Pierre. (2008). *TIMSS 2007 international mathematics report: Findings from IEA's Trends in International Mathematics and Science Study at the fourth and eighth grades.* Chestnut Hill, MA: TIMSS & PIRLS International Study Center, Boston College.

Mullis, Ina V. S., Martin, Michael O., Kennedy, Ann M., & Foy, Pierre. (2007).

PIRLS 2006 international report. Chestnut Hill, MA: TIMSS & PIRLS International Study Center.

Munck, Hanne. (2009). Early intervention and fatherhood: Denmark. In Kevin J. Nugent, Bonnie J. Petrauskas, & T. Berry Brazelton (Eds.), *The newborn as a person: Enabling healthy infant development worldwide* (pp. 101–111). Hoboken, NJ: Wiley.

Mundy, Peter, & Jarrold, William. (2010). Infant joint attention, neural networks and social cognition. *Neural Networks, 23,* 985–997.

Muñoz, Carmen, & Singleton, David. (2011). A critical review of age-related research on L2 ultimate attainment. *Language Teaching, 44,* 1–35.

Munroe, Robert L., & Romney, A. Kimbal. (2006). Gender and age differences in same-sex aggregation and social behavior: A four-culture study. *Journal of Cross-Cultural Psychology, 37,* 3–19.

Murphy, Kevin, & Delanty, Norman. (2007). Sleep deprivation: A clinical perspective. *Sleep and Biological Rhythms, 5,* 2–14.

Murphy, Laura M. Bennett, Laurie-Rose, Cynthia, Brinkman, Tara M., & McNamara, Kelly A. (2007). Sustained attention and social competence in typically developing preschool-aged children. *Early Child Development and Care, 177,* 133–149.

Mutti, Donald O., & Zadnik, Karla. (2009). Has near work's star fallen? *Optometry & Vision Science, 86,* 76–78.

Naci, Huseyin, Chisholm, Dan, & Baker, T. D. (2009). Distribution of road traffic deaths by road user group: A global comparison. *Injury Prevention, 15,* 55–59.

Nadeau, Joseph H., & Dudley, Aimée M. (2011, February 25). Systems genetics. *Science, 331,* 1015–1016.

Nagda, Biren A., Gurin, Patricia, & Johnson, Shawnti M. (2005). Living, doing and thinking diversity: How does pre-college diversity experience affect first-year students' engagement with college diversity? In Robert S. Feldman (Ed.), *Improving the first year of college: Research and practice* (pp. 73–108). Mahwah, NJ: Erlbaum.

Naninck, Eva F. G., Lucassen, Paul J., & Bakker, Julie. (2011). Sex differences in adolescent depression: Do sex hormones determine vulnerability? *Journal of Neuroendocrinology, 23,* 383–392.

Narayan, Chandan R., Werker, Janet F., & Beddor, Patrice Speeter. (2010). The interaction between acoustic salience and language experience in developmental speech perception: Evidence from nasal place discrimination. *Developmental Science, 13,* 407–420.

Narvaez, Darcia, & Lapsley, Daniel K. (2009). Moral identity, moral functioning, and the development of moral character. In H. Ross Brian (Series Ed.) & Daniel Bartels, Christopher Bauman, Linda Skitka, & Douglas Medin (Vol. Eds.), *Psychology of learning and motivation* (Vol. 50, pp. 237–274). San Diego, CA: Academic Press.

National Center for Education in Maternal and Child Health. (2011, August). *SUID/SIDS*

Resource Center Consortium: Statistics. Retrieved from Georgetown University website: http://sidscenter.org/statistics.html

National Center for Education Statistics, Institute of Education Sciences. (2009). *The condition of education 2009* (NCES 2009–081). Washington, DC: U.S. Department of Education

National Center for Health Statistics. (2008). *Deaths: Final data for 2005.* Retrieved from U.S. Department Of Health And Human Services website: http://www.cdc.gov/nchs/data/nvsr/nvsr56/nvsr56_10.pdf

National Center for Health Statistics. (2010). *Health, United States, 2009: With special feature on medical technology.* Hyattsville, MD: Author.

National Center for Health Statistics. (2011). *Health, United States, 2010: With special feature on death and dying.* Hyattsville, MD: Author.

National Governors Association Center for Best Practices (NGA Center) and the Council of Chief State School Officers (CCSSO). (2010). *Common Core State Standards Initiative.* Retrieved from National Governors Association website: http://corestandards.org/

National Sleep Foundation. (2006). *Summary findings of the 2006 Sleep in America poll.* Retrieved from http://www.sleepfoundation.org/atf/cf/%7BF6BF2668–A1B4–4FE8–8D1A–A5D39340D9CB%7D/2006_summary_of_findings.pdf

Naudé, H., Marx, J., Pretorius, E., & Hislop-Esterhuyzen, N. (2007). Evidence of early childhood defects due to prenatal over-exposure to vitamin A: A case study. *Early Child Development and Care, 177,* 235–253.

Neave, Nick. (2008). *Hormones and behaviour: A psychological approach.* New York, NY: Cambridge University Press.

Negriff, Sonya, Dorn, Lorah D., Pabst, Stephanie R., & Susman, Elizabeth J. (2011). Morningness/eveningness, pubertal timing, and substance use in adolescent girls. *Psychiatry Research, 185,* 408–413.

Neigh, Gretchen N., Gillespie, Charles F., & Nemeroff, Charles B. (2009). The neurobiological toll of child abuse and neglect. *Trauma, Violence, & Abuse, 10,* 389–410.

Nelson, Charles A., III. (2011). Neural development and lifelong plasticity. In Daniel P. Keating (Ed.), *Nature and nurture in early child development* (pp. 45–69). New York, NY: Cambridge University Press.

Nelson, Charles A., de Haan, Michelle, & Thomas, Kathleen M. (2006). *Neuroscience of cognitive development: The role of experience and the developing brain.* Hoboken, NJ: Wiley.

Nelson, Charles A., III, Zeanah, Charles H., Fox, Nathan A., Marshall, Peter J., Smyke, Anna T., & Guthrie, Donald. (2007, December 21). Cognitive recovery in socially deprived young children: The Bucharest Early Intervention Project. *Science, 318,* 1937–1940.

Nelson, Jennifer A., Chiasson, Mary Ann, & Ford, Viola. (2004). Childhood overweight in a

New York City WIC population. *American Journal of Public Health, 94,* 458–462.

Nelson, Larry J., Hart, Craig H., & Evans, Cortney A. (2008). Solitary-functional play and solitary-pretend play: Another look at the construct of solitary-active behavior using playground observations. *Social Development, 17,* 812–831.

Nelson, R. Michael, & DeBacker, Teresa K. (2008). Achievement motivation in adolescents: The role of peer climate and best friends. *Journal of Experimental Education, 76,* 170–189.

Nesdale, Drew, Maass, Anne, Durkin, Kevin, & Griffiths, Judith. (2005). Group norms, threat, and children's racial prejudice. *Child Development, 76,* 652–663.

Nesselroade, John R., & Molenaar, Peter C. M. (2003). Quantitative models for developmental processes. In Jaan Valsiner & Kevin J. Connolly (Eds.), *Handbook of developmental psychology* (pp. 622–639). Thousand Oaks, CA: Sage.

Neumann, Anna, van Lier, Pol, Frijns, Tom, Meeus, Wim, & Koot, Hans. (2011). Emotional dynamics in the development of early adolescent psychopathology: A one-year longitudinal study. *Journal of Abnormal Child Psychology, 39,* 657–669.

Newman, George E., Keil, Frank C., Kuhlmeier, Valerie A., & Wynn, Karen. (2010). Early understandings of the link between agents and order. *Proceedings of the National Academy of Sciences.* Advance online publication. doi:10.1073/pnas.0914056107

Newnham, Carol A., Milgrom, Jeannette, & Skouteris, Helen. (2009). Effectiveness of a modified mother-infant transaction program on outcomes for preterm infants from 3 to 24 months of age. *Infant Behavior and Development, 32,* 17–26.

Ng, Nawi, Weinehall, Lars, & Öhman, Ann. (2007). 'If I don't smoke, I'm not a real man'—Indonesian teenage boys' views about smoking. *Health Education Research, 22,* 794–804.

Ngui, Emmanuel, Cortright, Alicia, & Blair, Kathleen. (2009). An investigation of paternity status and other factors associated with racial and ethnic disparities in birth outcomes in Milwaukee, Wisconsin. *Maternal and Child Health Journal, 13,* 467–478.

Nguyen, Simone P., & Murphy, Gregory L. (2003). An apple is more than just a fruit: Cross-classification in children's concepts. *Child Development, 74,* 1783–1806.

Nic Gabhainn, Saoirse, Baban, Adriana, Boyce, William, Godeau, Emmanuelle, & The HBSC Sexual Health Focus Group. (2009). How well protected are sexually active 15-year-olds? Cross-national patterns in condom and contraceptive pill use 2002–2006. *International Journal of Public Health, 54,* 209–215.

Niccols, Alison. (2007). Fetal alcohol syndrome and the developing socio-emotional brain. *Brain and Cognition, 65,* 135–142.

NICHD Early Child Care Research Network (Ed.). (2005). *Child care and child development: Results from the NICHD Study of Early Child Care*

and Youth Development. New York, NY: Guilford Press.

NICHD Early Child Care Research Network. (2007). Age of entry to kindergarten and children's academic achievement and socioemotional development. *Early Education and Development, 18,* 337–368.

Nichols, Tracy R., Graber, Julia A., Brooks-Gunn, Jeanne, & Botvin, Gilbert J. (2006). Sex differences in overt aggression and delinquency among urban minority middle school students. *Journal of Applied Developmental Psychology, 27,* 78–91.

Nielsen, Mark. (2006). Copying actions and copying outcomes: Social learning through the second year. *Developmental Psychology, 42,* 555–565.

Nielsen, Mark, Suddendorf, Thomas, & Slaughter, Virginia. (2006). Mirror self-recognition beyond the face. *Child Development, 77,* 176–185.

Nielsen, Mark, & Tomaselli, Keyan. (2010). Overimitation in Kalahari Bushman children and the origins of human cultural cognition. *Psychological Science, 21,* 729–736.

Nieto, Sonia. (2000). *Affirming diversity: The sociopolitical context of multicultural education* (3rd ed.). New York, NY: Longman.

Nightingale, Claire M., Rudnicka, Alicja R., Owen, Chris G., Cook, Derek G., & Whincup, Peter H. (2011). Patterns of body size and adiposity among UK children of South Asian, black African–Caribbean and white European origin: Child Heart And health Study in England (CHASE Study). *International Journal of Epidemiology, 40,* 33–44.

Niji, Rie, Arita, Kenji, Abe, Yoko, Lucas, Milanita E., Nishino, Mizuho, & Mitome, Masato. (2010). Maternal age at birth and other risk factors in early childhood caries. *Pediatric Dentistry, 32,* 493–498.

Nisbett, Richard E. (2009). *Intelligence and how to get it: Why schools and cultures count.* New York, NY: Norton.

Nishida, Tracy K., & Lillard, Angeline S. (2007). The informative value of emotional expressions: 'Social referencing' in mother-child pretense. *Developmental Science, 10,* 205–212.

Nishina, Adrienne, & Juvonen, Jaana. (2005). Daily reports of witnessing and experiencing peer harassment in middle school. *Child Development, 76,* 435–450.

Normile, Dennis. (2007, April 13). Japan picks up the 'innovation' mantra. *Science, 316,* 186.

Norris, Deborah J. (2010). Raising the educational requirements for teachers in infant toddler classrooms: Implications for institutions of higher education. *Journal of Early Childhood Teacher Education, 31,* 146–158.

Norris, Pippa. (2001). *Digital divide: Civic engagement, information poverty, and the internet worldwide.* New York, NY: Cambridge University Press.

Nsamenang, A. Bame. (2004). *Cultures of human development and education: Challenge to growing up African.* New York, NY: Nova Science.

Nucci, Larry P. (2009). *Nice is not enough: Facilitating moral development.* Upper Saddle River, NJ: Merrill/Prentice Hall.

Nugent, J. Kevin, Petrauskas, Bonnie J., & Brazelton, T. Berry. (2009). *The newborn as a person: Enabling healthy infant development worldwide.* Hoboken, NJ: Wiley.

O'Doherty, Kieran. (2006). Risk communication in genetic counselling: A discursive approach to probability. *Theory & Psychology, 16,* 225–256.

O'Donnell, Lydia, Stueve, Ann, Duran, Richard, Myint-U, Athi, Agronick, Gail, Doval, Alexi San, et al. (2008). Parenting practices, parents' underestimation of daughters' risks, and alcohol and sexual behaviors of urban girls. *Journal of Adolescent Health, 42,* 496–502.

O'Leary, Colleen M., Nassar, Natasha, Zubrick, Stephen R., Kurinczuk, Jennifer J., Stanley, Fiona, & Bower, Carol. (2010). Evidence of a complex association between dose, pattern and timing of prenatal alcohol exposure and child behaviour problems. *Addiction, 105,* 74–86.

Oakes, J. Michael. (2009). The effect of media on children. *American Behavioral Scientist, 52,* 1136–1151.

Oakes, Lisa M. (2011). *Infant perception and cognition: Recent advances, emerging theories, and future directions.* New York, NY: Oxford University Press.

OECD. (2010a). *PISA 2009 results: Learning to learn: Vol. 3. Student engagement, strategies and practices.* Retrieved from http://www.oecd-ilibrary.org/education/pisa-2009-results-learning-to-learn_9789264083943–en

OECD. (2010b). *PISA 2009 results: What students know and can do: Vol. 1. Student performance in reading, mathematics and science.* Retrieved from http://www.oecd.org/dataoecd/10/61/48852548.pdf

Offit, Paul A. (2008). *Autism's false prophets: Bad science, risky medicine, and the search for a cure.* New York, NY: Columbia University Press.

Ogbu, John U. (2008). *Minority status, oppositional culture, and schooling.* New York, NY: Routledge.

Ogden, Cynthia, & Carroll, Margaret. (2010, June 4). *Prevalence of obesity among children and adolescents: United States, trends 1963–1965 through 2007–2008.* Retrieved from CDC/National Center for Health Statistics website: http://www.cdc.gov/nchs/data/hestat/obesity_child_07_08/obesity_child_07_08.htm#

Ogden, Cynthia L. (2010). *Childhood obesity in the United States: The magnitude of the problem* [Presentation slides]. Retrieved from Division of Health and Nutrition Examination Surveys, National Center for Health Statistics, Centers for Disease Control and Prevention website: http://www.cdc.gov/about/grand-rounds/archives/2010/download/GR-062010.pdf

Ogden, Cynthia L., Carroll, Margaret D., & Flegal, Katherine M. (2008). High body mass index for age among US children and adolescents, 2003–2006. *Journal of the American Medical Association, 299,* 2401–2405.

Oh, Seungmi, & Lewis, Charlie. (2008). Korean preschoolers' advanced inhibitory control and its relation to other executive skills and mental state understanding. *Child Development, 79,* 80–99.

Oken, Emily, & Bellinger, David C. (2008). Fish consumption, methylmercury and child neurodevelopment. *Current Opinion in Pediatrics, 20,* 178–183.

Oldershaw, Lynn. (2002). *A national survey of parents of young children.* Toronto, Ontario, Canada: Invest in Kids.

Olfson, Mark, Crystal, Stephen, Huang, Cecilia, & Gerhard, Tobias. (2010). Trends in antipsychotic drug use by very young, privately insured children. *Journal of the American Academy of Child and Adolescent Psychiatry, 49,* 13–23.

Olson, Kristina R., & Dweck, Carol S. (2008). A blueprint for social cognitive development. *Perspectives on Psychological Science, 3,* 193–202.

Olson, Kristina R., & Dweck, Carol S. (2009). Social cognitive development: A new look. *Child Development Perspectives, 3,* 60–65.

Olson, Sheryl L., Lopez-Duran, Nestor, Lunkenheimer, Erika S., Chang, Hyein, & Sameroff, Arnold J. (2011). Individual differences in the development of early peer aggression: Integrating contributions of self-regulation, theory of mind, and parenting. *Development and Psychopathology, 23,* 253–266.

Olweus, Dan. (1993). Victimization by peers: Antecedents and long-term outcomes. In Kenneth H. Rubin & Jens B. Asendorpf (Eds.), *Social withdrawal, inhibition, and shyness in childhood* (pp. 315–341). Hillsdale, NJ: Erlbaum.

Olweus, Dan, Limber, Sue, & Mahalic, Sharon F. (1999). *Bullying prevention program.* Boulder, CO: Center for the Study and Prevention of Violence, Institute of Behavioral Science, University of Colorado at Boulder.

Omariba, D. Walter Rasugu, & Boyle, Michael H. (2007). Family structure and child mortality in sub-Saharan Africa: Cross-national effects of polygyny. *Journal of Marriage and Family, 69,* 528–543.

Ontai, Lenna L., & Thompson, Ross A. (2008). Attachment, parent-child discourse and theory-of-mind development. *Social Development, 17,* 47–60.

Oosterman, Mirjam, Schuengel, Carlo, Slot, N. Wim, Bullens, Ruud A. R., & Doreleijers, Theo A. H. (2007). Disruptions in foster care: A review and meta-analysis. *Children and Youth Services Review, 29,* 53–76.

Orlich, Donald C., Harder, Robert J., Callahan, Richard C., Trevisan, Michael S., & Brown, Abbie H. (2009). *Teaching strategies: A guide to effective instruction* (9th ed.). Boston, MA: Cengage Learning.

Osgood, D. Wayne, Ruth, Gretchen, Eccles, Jacquelynne S., Jacobs, Janis E., & Barber, Bonnie L. (2005). Six paths to adulthood: Fast starters, parents without careers, educated partners, educated singles, working singles, and slow starters. In Richard A. Settersten, Jr., Frank F. Furstenberg, Jr., & Rubén G. Rumbaut (Eds.), *On the frontier of* *adulthood: Theory, research, and public policy* (pp. 320–355). Chicago, IL: University of Chicago Press.

Osher, David, Bear, George G., Sprague, Jeffrey R., & Doyle, Walter. (2010). How can we improve school discipline? *Educational Researcher, 39,* 48–58.

Osorio, Snezana Nena. (2011). Reconsidering Kwashiorkor. *Topics in Clinical Nutrition, 26,* 10–13.

Ostfeld, Barbara M., Esposito, Linda, Perl, Harold, & Hegyi, Thomas. (2010). Concurrent risks in sudden infant death syndrome. *Pediatrics, 125,* 447–453.

Over, Harriet, & Gattis, Merideth. (2010). Verbal imitation is based on intention understanding. *Cognitive Development, 25,* 46–55.

Owen-Kostelnik, Jessica, Reppucci, N. Dickon, & Meyer, Jessica R. (2006). Testimony and interrogation of minors: Assumptions about maturity and morality. *American Psychologist, 61,* 286–304.

Owens, Judith A., Belon, Katherine, & Moss, Patricia. (2010). Impact of delaying school start time on adolescent sleep, mood, and behavior. *Archives of Pediatrics & Adolescent Medicine, 164,* 608–614.

Oyekale, Abayomi Samuel, & Oyekale, Tolulope Olayemi. (2009). Do mothers' educational levels matter in child malnutrition and health outcomes in Gambia and Niger? *The Social Sciences, 4,* 118–127.

Padilla-Walker, Laura M., Barry, Carolyn McNamara, Carroll, Jason S., Madsen, Stephanie D., & Nelson, Larry J. (2008). Looking on the bright side: The role of identity status and gender on positive orientations during emerging adulthood. *Journal of Adolescence, 31,* 451–467.

Pagani, Linda S., Japel, Christa, Girard, Alain, Farhat, Abdeljelil, Cote, Sylvana, & Tremblay, Richard E. (2006). Middle childhood life course trajectories: Links between family dysfunction and children's behavioral development. In Aletha C. Huston & Marika N. Ripke (Eds.), *Developmental contexts in middle childhood: Bridges to adolescence and adulthood* (pp. 130–149). New York, NY: Cambridge University Press.

Paik, Anthony. (2011). Adolescent sexuality and the risk of marital dissolution. *Journal of Marriage and Family, 73,* 472–485.

Palmer, Raymond F., Blanchard, Stephen, Jean, Carlos R., & Mandell, David S. (2005). School district resources and identification of children with autistic disorder. *American Journal of Public Health, 95,* 125–130.

Park, D. J. J., & Congdon, Nathan G. (2004). Evidence for an "epidemic" of myopia. *Annals, Academy of Medicine, Singapore, 33,* 21–26.

Park, Hyun, Bothe, Denise, Holsinger, Eva, Kirchner, H. Lester, Olness, Karen, & Mandalakas, Anna. (2011). The impact of nutritional status and longitudinal recovery of motor and cognitive milestones in internationally adopted children. *International Journal of Environmental Research and Public Health, 8,* 105–116.

Park, Hyunjoon, Byun, Soo-yong, & Kim, Kyung-keun. (2011). Parental involvement and students' cognitive outcomes in Korea. *Sociology of Education, 84,* 3–22.

Parke, Ross D., & Buriel, Raymond. (2006). Socialization in the family: Ethnic and ecological perspectives. In William Damon & Richard M. Lerner (Series Eds.) & Nancy Eisenberg (Vol. Ed.), *Handbook of child psychology: Vol. 3. Social, emotional, and personality development* (6th ed., pp. 429–504). Hoboken, NJ: Wiley.

Parke, Ross D., Coltrane, Scott, Duffy, Sharon, Buriel, Raymond, Dennis, Jessica, Powers, Justina, et al. (2004). Economic stress, parenting, and child adjustment in Mexican American and European American families. *Child Development, 75,* 1632–1656.

Parker, Susan W., & Nelson, Charles A. (2005). The impact of early institutional rearing on the ability to discriminate facial expressions of emotion: An event-related potential study. *Child Development, 76,* 54–72.

Parladé, Meaghan V., & Iverson, Jana M. (2011). The interplay between language, gesture, and affect during communicative transition: A dynamic systems approach. *Developmental Psychology, 47,* 820–833.

Parris, Leandra, Varjas, Kris, Meyers, Joel, & Cutts, Hayley. (2011). High school students' perceptions of coping with cyberbullying. *Youth & Society.* Advance online publication. doi:10.1177/0044118x11398881

Pascarella, Ernest T. (2005). Cognitive impacts of the first year of college. In Robert S. Feldman (Ed.), *Improving the first year of college: Research and practice* (pp. 111–140). Mahwah, NJ: Erlbaum.

Pascarella, Ernest T., & Terenzini, Patrick T. (1991). *How college affects students: Findings and insights from twenty years of research.* San Francisco, CA: Jossey-Bass.

Pashler, Harold, McDaniel, Mark, Rohrer, Doug, & Bjork, Robert. (2008). Learning styles: Concepts and evidence. *Psychological Science in the Public Interest, 9,* 105–119.

Passel, Jeffrey S. (2011). Demography of immigrant youth: Past, present, and future. *The Future of Children, 21,* 19–41.

Pathela, Preeti, & Schillinger, Julia A. (2010). Sexual behaviors and sexual violence: Adolescents with opposite-, same-, or both-sex partners. *Pediatrics, 126,* 879–886.

Patrick, Kevin, Norman, Gregory J., Calfas, Karen J., Sallis, James F., Zabinski, Marion F., Rupp, Joan, et al. (2004). Diet, physical activity, and sedentary behaviors as risk factors for overweight in adolescence. *Archives of Pediatrics & Adolescent Medicine, 158,* 385–390.

Patrick, Megan E., & Schulenberg, John E. (2011). How trajectories of reasons for alcohol use relate to trajectories of binge drinking: National panel data spanning late adolescence to early adulthood. *Developmental Psychology, 47,* 311–317.

Patton, George C., Hemphill, Sheryl A., Beyers, Jennifer M., Bond, Lyndal, Toumbourou, John

W., McMorris, Barbara J., et al. (2007). Pubertal stage and deliberate self-harm in adolescents. *Journal of the American Academy of Child & Adolescent Psychiatry, 46,* 508–514.

Pauli-Pott, Ursula, Mertesacker, Bettina, & Beckmann, Dieter. (2004). Predicting the development of infant emotionality from maternal characteristics. *Development & Psychopathology, 16,* 19–42.

Pearson, Barbara Zurer. (2008). *Raising a bilingual child: A step-by-step guide for parents.* New York, NY: Living Language.

Pelham, William E., Jr., & Fabiano, Gregory A. (2008). Evidence-based psychosocial treatments for attention-deficit/hyperactivity disorder. *Journal of Clinical Child and Adolescent Psychology, 37,* 184–214.

Pellegrini, Anthony D. (2009). Research and policy on children's play. *Child Development Perspectives, 3,* 131–136.

Pellegrini, Anthony D., Dupuis, Danielle, & Smith, Peter K. (2007). Play in evolution and development. *Developmental Review, 27,* 261–276.

Pellegrini, Anthony D., & Smith, Peter K. (Eds.). (2005). *The nature of play: Great apes and humans.* New York, NY: Guilford Press.

Pellis, Sergio M., & Pellis, Vivien C. (2011). Rough-and-tumble play: Training and using the social brain. In Anthony D. Pellegrini (Ed.), *The Oxford handbook of the development of play* (pp. 245–259). New York, NY: Oxford University Press.

Peng, Duan, & Robins, Philip K. (2010). Who should care for our kids? The effects of infant child care on early child development. *Journal of Children and Poverty, 16,* 1–45.

Pepler, Debra, Craig, Wendy, Yuile, Amy, & Connolly, Jennifer. (2004). Girls who bully: A developmental and relational perspective. In Martha Putallaz & Karen L. Bierman (Eds.), *Aggression, antisocial behavior, and violence among girls: A developmental perspective* (pp. 90–109). New York, NY: Guilford Press.

Perels, Franziska, Merget-Kullmann, Miriam, Wende, Milena, Schmitz, Bernhard, & Buchbinder, Carla. (2009). Improving self-regulated learning of preschool children: Evaluation of training for kindergarten teachers. *British Journal of Educational Psychology, 79,* 311–327.

Perfetti, Jennifer, Clark, Roseanne, & Fillmore, Capri-Mara. (2004). Postpartum depression: Identification, screening, and treatment. *Wisconsin Medical Journal, 103,* 56–63.

Perner, Josef. (2000). About + belief + counterfactual. In Peter Mitchell & Kevin John Riggs (Eds.), *Children's reasoning and the mind* (pp. 367–401). Hove, East Sussex, UK: Psychology Press.

Perron, Andreann, Brendgen, Mara, Boivin, Michel, Vitaro, Frank, & Tremblay, Richard E. (2011). Playing sports improves academic performances for victimized children. Poster session presented at the SRCD 2011 Biennial Meeting. Montreal, Quebec, Canada.

Perry, William G., Jr. (1981). Cognitive and ethical growth: The making of meaning. In A. Chickering

(Ed.), *The modern American college: Responding to the new realities of diverse students and a changing society* (pp. 76–116). San Francisco, CA: Jossey-Bass.

Perry, William G. (1999). *Forms of intellectual and ethical development in the college years: A scheme.* San Francisco, CA: Jossey-Bass.

Persaud, Trivedi V. N., Chudley, Albert E., & Skalko, Richard G. (1985). *Basic concepts in teratology.* New York, NY: Liss.

Peterson, Jordan B., & Flanders, Joseph L. (2005). Play and the regulation of aggression. In Richard Ernest Tremblay, Willard W. Hartup, & John Archer (Eds.), *Developmental origins of aggression* (pp. 133–157). New York, NY: Guilford Press.

Peterson, Jane W., & Sterling, Yvonne M. (2009). Children's perceptions of asthma: African American children use metaphors to make sense of asthma. *Journal of Pediatric Health Care, 23,* 93–100.

Pew Commission on Children in Foster Care. (2004). *Safety, permanence and well-being for children in foster care.* Retrieved from http://pewfostercare.org/research/docs/FinalReport.pdf

Pew Forum on Religion & Public Life. (2010). *Ten years of changing attitudes on gay marriage.* Retrieved from http://features.pewforum.org/gay-marriage-attitudes/index.php

Pew Research Center. (2009). *Independents take center stage in Obama era.* Washington, DC: Author.

Pew Research Center. (2010). *Teen and young adult internet use.* Retrieved from http://www.pewinternet.org/Infographics/2010/Internet-acess-by-age-group-over-time-Update.aspx

Pew Research Center. (2010). *Millennials: A portrait of "Generation Next." Confident. Connected. Open to change.* Retrieved from http://pewsocialtrends.org/files/2010/10/millennials-confident-connected-open-to-change.pdf

Pew Research Center. (2011). *Living together: The economics of cohabitation.* Retrieved from http://www.pewsocialtrends.org/2011/06/27/living-together-the-economics-of-cohabitation/

Pew Social Trends Staff. (2010, March 18). *The return of the multi-generational family household.* Washington, DC: Pew Research Center, Social & Demographic Trends.

Pew Social Trends Staff. (2010, November 18). *The decline of marriage and rise of new families: VI. New family types.* Washington, DC: Pew Research Center.

Pew Social Trends Staff. (2011). *Is college worth it? College presidents, public assess, value, quality and mission of higher education.* Washington, DC: Pew Research Center.

Pfeifer, Jennifer H., Masten, Carrie L., Moore, William E., Oswald, Tasha M., Mazziotta, John C., Iacoboni, Marco, et al. (2011). Entering adolescence: Resistance to peer influence, risky behavior, and neural changes in emotion reactivity. *Neuron, 69,* 1029–1036.

Philips, Sharon, & Tolmie, Andrew. (2007). Children's performance on and understanding of the Balance Scale problem: The effects of paren-tal support. *Infant and Child Development, 16,* 95–117.

Philipsen, Nina, & Brooks-Gunn, Jeanne. (2008). Overweight and obesity in childhood. In Thomas P. Gullotta & Gary M. Blau (Eds.), *Handbook of childhood behavioral issues: Evidence-based approaches to prevention and treatment* (pp. 125–146). New York, NY: Routledge/Taylor & Francis.

Phillips, Deborah A., Fox, Nathan A., & Gunnar, Megan R. (2011). Same place, different experiences: Bringing individual differences to research in child care. *Child Development Perspectives, 5,* 44–49.

Phillips, Deborah A., Gormley, William T., Jr., & Lowenstein, Amy E. (2009). Inside the pre-kindergarten door: Classroom climate and instructional time allocation in Tulsa's pre-K programs. *Early Childhood Research Quarterly, 24,* 213–362.

Phillips, Mary L. (2010). Coming of age? Neuroimaging biomarkers in youth. *American Journal of Psychiatry, 167,* 4–7.

Phillips, Tommy M., & Pittman, Joe F. (2007). Adolescent psychological well-being by identity style. *Journal of Adolescence, 30,* 1021–1034.

Phillipson, Sivanes, & Phillipson, Shane N. (2007). Academic expectations, belief of ability, and involvement by parents as predictors of child achievement: A cross-cultural comparison. *Educational Psychology, 27,* 329–348.

Phinney, Jean S. (2006). Ethnic identity exploration in emerging adulthood. In Jeffrey Jensen Arnett & Jennifer Lynn Tanner (Eds.), *Emerging adults in America: Coming of age in the 21st century* (pp. 117–134). Washington, DC: American Psychological Association.

Piaget, Jean. (1929). *The child's conception of the world* (Joan Tomlinson & Andrew Tomlinson, Trans.). New York, NY: Harcourt, Brace.

Piaget, Jean. (1952b). *The origins of intelligence in children* (M. Cook, Trans.). Oxford, UK: International Universities Press.

Piaget, Jean. (1954). *The construction of reality in the child* (Margaret Cook, Trans.). New York, NY: Basic Books.

Piaget, Jean. (1962). *Play, dreams and imitation in childhood* (C. Gattegno & F. M. Hodgson, Trans.). New York, NY: Norton. (Original work published 1945)

Piaget, Jean. (1972). *The psychology of intelligence.* Totowa, NJ: Littlefield. (Original work published 1950)

Piaget, Jean. (1997). *The moral judgment of the child* (Marjorie Gabain, Trans.). New York, NY: Simon and Schuster. (Original work published 1932)

Piaget, Jean, & Inhelder, Bärbel. (1969). *The psychology of the child.* New York, NY: Basic Books.

Piaget, Jean, Voelin-Liambey, Daphne, & Berthoud-Papandropoulou, Ioanna. (2001). *Problems of class inclusion and logical implication* (Robert L. Campbell, Trans.). Hove, East Sussex, UK: Psychology Press. (Original work published 1977)

Pianta, Robert C., Barnett, W. Steven, Burchinal, Margaret, & Thornburg, Kathy R. (2009). The effects of preschool education. *Psychological Science in the Public Interest, 10,* 49–88.

Piazza, Manuela, Facoetti, Andrea, Trussardi, Anna Noemi, Berteletti, Ilaria, Conte, Stefano, Lucangeli, Daniela, et al. (2010). Developmental trajectory of number acuity reveals a severe impairment in developmental dyscalculia. *Cognition, 116,* 33–41.

Pietrefesa, Ashley S., & Evans, David W. (2007). Affective and neuropsychological correlates of children's rituals and compulsive-like behaviors: Continuities and discontinuities with obsessive-compulsive disorder. *Brain and Cognition, 65,* 36–46.

Pignotti, Maria Serenella. (2010). The definition of human viability: A historical perspective. *Acta Pædiatrica, 99,* 33–36.

Pikounis, George W. (2010). *How does divorce affect the individual relationships of the children involved?* Unpublished paper written for class, Communication Department, Lycoming College, Williamsport, PA.

Pin, Tamis, Eldridge, Beverley, & Galea, Mary P. (2007). A review of the effects of sleep position, play position, and equipment use on motor development in infants. *Developmental Medicine & Child Neurology, 49,* 858–867.

Pinborg, Anja, Loft, Anne, & Nyboe Andersen, Anders. (2004). Neonatal outcome in a Danish national cohort of 8602 children born after in vitro fertilization or intracytoplasmic sperm injection: The role of twin pregnancy. *Acta Obstetricia et Gynecologica Scandinavica, 83,* 1071–1078.

Pinheiro, Andréa Poyastro (Ed.). (2006). *World report on violence against children.* Geneva, Switzerland: United Nations.

Pinker, Steven. (2007). *The stuff of thought: Language as a window into human nature.* New York, NY: Viking.

Piontelli, Alessandra. (2002). *Twins: From fetus to child.* London, England: Routledge.

PISA. (2009). *Learning mathematics for life: A perspective from PISA.* Paris, France: OECD.

Pitzer, Virginia E., Viboud, Cécile, Simonsen, Lone, Steiner, Claudia, Panozzo, Catherine A., Alonso, Wladimir J., et al. (2009, July 17). Demographic variability, vaccination, and the spatiotemporal dynamics of rotavirus epidemics. *Science, 325,* 290–294.

Pizer, Ginger, Walters, Keith, & Meier, Richard P. (2007). Bringing up baby with baby signs: Language ideologies and socialization in hearing families. *Sign Language Studies, 7,* 387–430.

Plomin, Robert, DeFries, John C., Craig, Ian W., & McGuffin, Peter. (2003). *Behavioral genetics in the postgenomic era.* Washington, DC: American Psychological Association.

Plomin, Robert, Defries, John C., McClearn, Gerald E., & McGuffin, Peter. (2008). *Behavioral genetics* (5th ed.). New York, NY: Worth.

Plotkin, Henry. (2011). Human nature, cultural diversity and evolutionary theory. *Philosophical*

Transactions of the Royal Society B: Biological Sciences, 366, 454–463.

Pluess, Michael, & Belsky, Jay. (2009). Differential susceptibility to rearing experience: The case of childcare. *Journal of Child Psychology and Psychiatry and Allied Disciplines, 50,* 396–404.

Pluess, Michael, & Belsky, Jay. (2010). Differential susceptibility to parenting and quality child care. *Developmental Psychology, 46,* 379–390.

Pogrebin, Abigail. (2009). *One and the same: My life as an identical twin and what I've learned about everyone's struggle to be singular.* New York, NY: Doubleday.

Posner, Michael I., Rothbart, Mary K., Sheese, Brad E., & Tang, Yiyuan. (2007). The anterior cingulate gyrus and the mechanism of self-regulation. *Cognitive, Affective & Behavioral Neuroscience, 7,* 391–395.

Potter, Daniel. (2010). Psychosocial well-being and the relationship between divorce and children's academic achievement. *Journal of Marriage and Family, 72,* 933–946.

Poulin-Dubois, Diane, & Chow, Virginia. (2009). The effect of a looker's past reliability on infants' reasoning about beliefs. *Developmental Psychology, 45,* 1576–1582.

Powell, Douglas R. (2006). Families and early childhood interventions. In William Damon & Richard M. Lerner (Series Eds.) & K. Ann Renninger & Irving E. Sigel (Vol. Eds.), *Handbook of child psychology: Vol. 4. Child psychology in practice* (6th ed., pp. 548–591). Hoboken, NJ: Wiley.

Powell, Kendall. (2006). Neurodevelopment: How does the teenage brain work? *Nature, 442,* 865–867.

Powlishta, Kimberly. (2004). Gender as a social category: Intergroup processes and gender-role development. In Mark Bennett & Fabio Sani (Eds.), *The development of the social self* (pp. 103–133). Hove, East Sussex, England: Psychology Press.

Pratt, Michael W., Norris, Joan E., Lawford, Heather, & Arnold, Mary Louise. (2010). What he said to me stuck: Adolescents' narratives of grandparents and their identity development in emerging adulthood. In Kate C. McLean & Monisha Pasupathi (Eds.), *Narrative development in adolescence: Creating the storied self* (pp. 93–112). New York, NY: Springer Science + Business Media.

Pressley, Michael, & Hilden, Katherine. (2006). Cognitive strategies: Production deficiencies and successful strategy instruction everywhere. In William Damon & Richard M. Lerner (Series Eds.) & Deanna Kuhn & Robert S. Siegler (Vol. Eds.), *Handbook of child psychology: Vol. 2. Cognition, perception, and language* (6th ed., pp. 511–556). Hoboken, NJ: Wiley.

Priess, Heather A., Lindberg, Sara M., & Hyde, Janet Shibley. (2009). Adolescent gender-role identity and mental health: Gender intensification revisited. *Child Development, 80,* 1531–1544.

Print, Murray, Ugarte, Carolina, Naval, Concepción, & Mihr, Anja. (2008). Moral and human rights education: The contribution of the United Nations. *Journal of Moral Education, 37,* 115–132.

Pruden, Shannon M., Hirsh-Pasek, Kathy, Golinkoff, Roberta Michnick, & Hennon, Elizabeth A. (2006). The birth of words: Ten-month-olds learn words through perceptual salience. *Child Development, 77,* 266–280.

Pryor, J. H., Hurtado, S., DeAngelo, L., Palucki Blake, L., & Tran, S. (2010). *The American freshman: National norms fall 2010.* Los Angeles, CA: Higher Education Research Institute, UCLA.

Pullmann, Helle, & Allik, Jüri. (2008). Relations of academic and general self-esteem to school achievement. *Personality and Individual Differences, 45,* 559–564.

Pulvermüller, Friedemann, & Fadiga, Luciano. (2010). Active perception: Sensorimotor circuits as a cortical basis for language. *Nature Reviews Neuroscience, 11,* 351–360.

Puri, Sunita, & Nachtigall, Robert D. (2010). The ethics of sex selection: A comparison of the attitudes and experiences of primary care physicians and physician providers of clinical sex selection services. *Fertility and Sterility, 93,* 2107–2114.

Purves, Dale, Augustine, George J., Fitzpatrick, David, Hall, William C., LaMantia, Anthony-Samuel, McNamara, James O., et al. (Eds.). (2004). *Neuroscience* (3rd ed.). Sunderland, MA: Sinauer Associates.

Qin, Lili, Pomerantz, Eva M., & Wang, Qian. (2009). Are gains in decision-making autonomy during early adolescence beneficial for emotional functioning? The case of the United States and China. *Child Development, 80,* 1705–1721.

Quas, Jodi A., Bauer, Amy, & Boyce, W. Thomas. (2004). Physiological reactivity, social support, and memory in early childhood. *Child Development, 75,* 797–814.

Quinn, Paul C. (2004). Development of subordinate-level categorization in 3- to 7-month-old infants. *Child Development, 75,* 886–899.

Race, Ethnicity, and Genetics Working Group of the National Human Genome Research Institute. (2005). The use of racial, ethnic, and ancestral categories in human genetics research. *American Journal of Human Genetics, 77,* 519–532.

Rajaratnam, Julie Knoll, Marcus, Jake R., Flaxman, Abraham D., Wang, Haidong, Levin-Rector, Alison, Dwyer, Laura, et al. (2010). Neonatal, postneonatal, childhood, and under-5 mortality for 187 countries, 1970–2010: A systematic analysis of progress towards Millennium Development Goal 4. *Lancet, 375,* 1988–2008.

Rajaratnam, Julie Knoll, Marcus, Jake R., Flaxman, Abraham D., Wang, Haidong, Levin-Rector, Alison, Dwyer, Laura, et al. (2010). Neonatal, postneonatal, childhood, and under-5 mortality for 187 countries, 1970–2010: A systematic analysis of progress towards Millennium Development Goal 4. *Lancet, 375,* 1988–2008.

Ramachandran, Vilayanur S. (2011). *The tell-tale brain: A neuroscientist's quest for what makes us human.* New York, NY: Norton.

Ramón, Rosa, Ballester, Ferran, Aguinagalde, Xabier, Amurrio, Ascensión, Vioque, Jesús, Lacasaña, Marina, et al. (2009). Fish consumption during pregnancy, prenatal mercury exposure, and anthropometric measures at birth in a prospective mother-infant cohort study in Spain. *American Journal of Clinical Nutrition, 90,* 1047–1055.

Ramscar, Michael, & Dye, Melody. (2011). Learning language from the input: Why innate constraints can't explain noun compounding. *Cognitive Psychology, 62,* 1–40.

Rankin, Jane L., Lane, David J., Gibbons, Frederick X., & Gerrard, Meg. (2004). Adolescent self-consciousness: Longitudinal age changes and gender differences in two cohorts. *Journal of Research on Adolescence, 14,* 1–21.

Raspberry, Kelly Amanda, & Skinner, Debra. (2011). Negotiating desires and options: How mothers who carry the fragile X gene experience reproductive decisions. *Social Science & Medicine, 72,* 992–998.

Raver, C. Cybele, Jones, Stephanie M., Li-Grining, Christine, Zhai, Fuhua, Bub, Kristen, & Pressler, Emily. (2011). CSRP's impact on low-income preschoolers' preacademic skills: Self-regulation as a mediating mechanism. *Child Development, 82,* 362–378.

Ravizza, Kenneth. (2007). Peak experiences in sport. In Daniel Smith & Michael Bar-Eli (Eds.), *Essential readings in sport and exercise psychology* (pp. 122–125). Champaign, IL: Human Kinetics.

Raymond, Neil, Beer, Charlotte, Glazebrook, Cristine, & Sayal, Kapil. (2009). Pregnant women's attitudes towards alcohol consumption. *BMC Public Health, 9,* 175–183.

Ream, Geoffrey L., & Savin-Williams, Ritch C. (2003). Religious development in adolescence. In Gerald R. Adams & Michael D. Berzonsky (Eds.), *Blackwell handbook of adolescence* (pp. 51–59). Malden, MA: Blackwell.

Reche, Marta, Valbuena, Teresa, Fiandor, Ana, Padial, Antonia, Quirce, Santiago, & Pascual, Cristina. (2011). Induction of tolerance in children with food allergy. *Current Nutrition & Food Science, 7,* 33–39.

Reese, Elaine, Bird, Amy, & Tripp, Gail. (2007). Children's self-esteem and moral self: Links to parent-child conversations regarding emotion. *Social Development, 16,* 460–478.

Reilly, Sheena, Eadie, Patricia, Bavin, Edith L., Wake, Melissa, Prior, Margot, Williams, Joanne, et al. (2006). Growth of infant communication between 8 and 12 months: A population study. *Journal of Paediatrics and Child Health, 42,* 764–770.

Reis, Harry T., & Collins, W. Andrew. (2004). Relationships, human behavior, and psychological science. *Current Directions in Psychological Science, 13,* 233–237.

Reith, Gerda. (2005). On the edge: Drugs and the consumption of risk in late modernity. In Stephen Lyng (Ed.), *Edgework: The sociology of risk taking* (pp. 227–246). New York, NY: Routledge.

Renk, Kimberly, Donnelly, Reesa, McKinney, Cliff, & Agliata, Allison Kanter. (2006). The development of gender identity: Timetables and influences. In Kam-Shing Yip (Ed.), *Psychology of gender identity: An international perspective* (pp. 49–68). Hauppauge, NY: Nova Science.

Renzulli, Joseph S. (2011). The multiple menu model for developing differentiated curriculum. In Joseph S. Renzulli, E. Jean Gubbins, Kristin S. McMillen, Rebecca D. Eckert, & Catherine A. Little (Eds.), *Systems and models for developing programs for the gifted and talented* (2nd ed., pp. 353–381). Mansfield Center, CT: Creative Learning Press.

Rettig, Michael. (2005). Using the multiple intelligences to enhance instruction for young children and young children with disabilities. *Early Childhood Education Journal, 32,* 255–259.

Retting, Richard A., Ferguson, Susan A., & McCartt, Anne T. (2003). A review of evidence-based traffic engineering measures designed to reduce pedestrian-motor vehicle crashes. *American Journal of Public Health, 93,* 1456–1463.

Reutskaja, Elena, & Hogarth, Robin M. (2009). Satisfaction in choice as a function of the number of alternatives: When "goods satiate." *Psychology and Marketing, 26,* 197–203.

Reynolds, Arthur J. (2000). *Success in early intervention: The Chicago child-parent centers.* Lincoln, NE: University of Nebraska Press.

Reynolds, Arthur J., & Ou, Suh-Ruu. (2011). Paths of effects from preschool to adult well-being: A confirmatory analysis of the child-parent center program. *Child Development, 82,* 555–582.

Rhee, Kyung. (2008). Childhood overweight and the relationship between parent behaviors, parenting style, and family functioning. In Amy B. Jordan (Ed.), *Annals of the American Academy of Political and Social Science: Vol. 615. Overweight and obesity in America's children: Causes, consequences, solutions* (pp. 12–37). San Diego, CA: Sage.

Riccio, Cynthia A., & Rodriguez, Olga L. (2007). Integration of psychological assessment approaches in school psychology. *Psychology in the Schools, 44,* 243–255.

Riccio, Cynthia A., Sullivan, Jeremy R., & Cohen, Morris J. (2010). *Neuropsychological assessment and intervention for childhood and adolescent disorders.* Hoboken, NJ: Wiley.

Richardson, Rick, & Hayne, Harlene. (2007). You can't take it with you: The translation of memory across development. *Current Directions in Psychological Science, 16,* 223–227.

Richert, Rebekah A., Robb, Michael B., & Smith, Erin I. (2011). Media as social partners: The social nature of young children's learning from screen media. *Child Development, 82,* 82–95.

Riordan, Jan (Ed.). (2005). *Breastfeeding and human lactation* (3rd ed.). Sudbury, MA: Jones and Bartlett.

Riordan, Jan, & Wambach, Karen (Eds.). (2009). *Breastfeeding and human lactation* (4th ed.). Sudbury, MA: Jones and Bartlett.

Ripke, Marika N., Huston, Aletha C., & Casey, David M. (2006). Low-income children's activity participation as a predictor of psychosocial and academic outcomes in middle childhood and adolescence. In Aletha C. Huston & Marika N. Ripke (Eds.), *Developmental contexts in middle childhood: Bridges to adolescence and adulthood* (pp. 260–282). New York, NY: Cambridge University Press.

Rivas-Drake, Deborah, & Mooney, Margarita. (2009). Neither colorblind nor oppositional: Perceived minority status and trajectories of academic adjustment among Latinos in elite higher education. *Developmental Psychology, 45,* 642–651.

Rivers, Ian, Poteat, V. Paul, Noret, Nathalie, & Ashurst, Nigel. (2009). Observing bullying at school: The mental health implications of witness status. *School Psychology Quarterly, 24,* 211–223.

Rizzolatti, Giacomo, & Fabbri-Destro, Maddalena. (2010). Mirror neurons: From discovery to autism. *Experimental Brain Research, 200,* 223–237.

Robelen, Erik W. (2011, April 5). Study finds more students learning Mandarin Chinese. *Education Week,* p. 5.

Roberts, Donald F., & Foehr, Ulla G. (2004). *Kids and media in America: Patterns of use at the millennium.* New York, NY: Cambridge University Press.

Roberts, Leslie. (2007, October 26). Battling over bed nets. *Science, 318,* 556–559.

Roberts, Soraya. (2010, January 1). *Travis Pastrana breaks world record for longest rally car jump on New Year's Eve.* Retrieved from New York Daily News website: http://www.nydailynews.com

Roche, Alex F., & Sun, Shumei S. (2003). *Human growth: Assessment and interpretation.* Cambridge, UK: Cambridge University Press.

Rodgers, Joseph. (2003). EMOSA sexuality models, memes, and the tipping point: Policy & program implications. In Daniel Romer (Ed.), *Reducing adolescent risk: Toward an integrated approach* (pp. 185–192). Thousand Oaks, CA: Sage.

Rodkin, Philip C., & Roisman, Glenn I. (2010). Antecedents and correlates of the popular-aggressive phenomenon in elementary school. *Child Development, 81,* 837–850.

Roebers, Claudia M., Schmid, Corinne, & Roderer, Thomas. (2009). Metacognitive monitoring and control processes involved in primary school children's test performance. *British Journal of Educational Psychology, 79,* 749–767.

Rogaev, Evgeny I., Grigorenko, Anastasia P., Faskhutdinova, Gulnaz, Kittler, Ellen L. W., & Moliaka, Yuri K. (2009, November 6). Genotype analysis identifies the cause of the "royal disease." *Science, 326,* 817.

Rogers, Carl R. (2004). *On becoming a person: A therapist's view of psychotherapy.* London, England: Constable. (Original work published 1961)

Rogoff, Barbara. (2003). *The cultural nature of human development.* New York, NY: Oxford University Press.

Rogoff, Barbara, Correa-Chávez, Maricela, & Cotuc, Marta Navichoc. (2005). A cultural/historical view of schooling in human development. In David B. Pillemer & Sheldon H. White (Eds.), *Developmental psychology and social change: Research, history and policy* (pp. 225–263). New York, NY: Cambridge University Press.

Rondal, Jean A. (2010). Language in Down syndrome: A life-span perspective. In Marcia A. Barnes (Ed.), *Genes, brain, and development: The neurocognition of genetic disorders* (pp. 122–142). New York, NY: Cambridge University Press.

Rose, Amanda J., & Asher, Steven R. (2004). Children's strategies and goals in response to help-giving and help-seeking tasks within a friendship. *Child Development, 75,* 749–763.

Rose, Steven. (2008, January 31). Drugging unruly children is a method of social control [Correspondence]. *Nature, 451,* 521.

Rose, Susan A., Feldman, Judith F., & Jankowski, Jeffery J. (2009). A cognitive approach to the development of early language. *Child Development, 80,* 134–150.

Rose, Susan A., Feldman, Judith F., Jankowski, Jeffery J., & Van Rossem, Ronan. (2008). A cognitive cascade in infancy: Pathways from prematurity to later mental development. *Intelligence, 36,* 367–378.

Roseberry, Sarah, Hirsh-Pasek, Kathy, Parish-Morris, Julia, & Golinkoff, Roberta M. (2009). Live action: Can young children learn verbs from video? *Child Development, 80,* 1360–1375.

Rosenbaum, James E. (2011). The complexities of college for all. *Sociology of Education, 84,* 113–117.

Rosenberg, Rebecca, Mandell, David, Farmer, Janet, Law, J., Marvin, Alison, & Law, Paul. (2010). Psychotropic medication use among children with autism spectrum disorders enrolled in a national registry, 2007–2008. *Journal of Autism and Developmental Disorders, 40,* 342–351.

Rosenfield, Robert L., Lipton, Rebecca B., & Drum, Melinda L. (2009). Thelarche, pubarche, and menarche attainment in children with normal and elevated body mass index. *Pediatrics, 123,* 84–88.

Rosenthal, Miriam K. (1991). The relation of peer interaction among infants and toddlers in family day care to characteristics of the child care environment. *Journal of Reproductive and Infant Psychology, 9,* 151–167.

Ross, Colin A. (2009). Ethics of gender identity disorder. *Ethical Human Psychology and Psychiatry, 11,* 165–170.

Rossi, Eleonora, Schippers, Marleen, & Keysers, Christian. (2011). Broca's area: Linking perception and production in language and actions. In Shihui Han & Ernst Pöppel (Eds.), *Culture and neural frames of cognition and communication* (pp. 169–184). New York, NY: Springer Berlin Heidelberg.

Rossignol, Daniel, Rossignol, Lanier, Smith, Scott, Schneider, Cindy, Logerquist, Sally, Usman, Anju, et al. (2009). Hyperbaric treatment for children with autism: A multicenter, randomized, double-blind, controlled trial. *BMC Pediatrics, 9,* 21.

Rothbart, Mary K., & Bates, John E. (2006). Temperament. In William Damon & Richard M. Lerner (Series Eds.) & Nancy Eisenberg (Vol. Ed.), *Handbook of child psychology: Vol. 3. Social, emotional, and personality development* (6th ed., pp. 99–166). Hoboken, NJ: Wiley.

Rothbaum, Fred, Pott, Martha, Azuma, Hiroshi, Miyake, Kazuo, & Weisz, John. (2000). The development of close relationships in Japan and the United States: Paths of symbiotic harmony and generative tension. *Child Development, 71,* 1121–1142.

Rothenberg, Paula S. (2010). *Race, class, and gender in the United States: An integrated study* (8th ed.). New York, NY: Worth.

Rothrauff, Tanja C., Cooney, Teresa M., & An, Jeong Shin. (2009). Remembered parenting styles and adjustment in middle and late adulthood. *The Journals of Gerontology Series B: Psychological Sciences and Social Sciences, 64B,* 137–146.

Rouchka, Eric C., & Cha, I. Elizabeth. (2009). Current trends in pseudogene detection and characterization. *Current Bioinformatics, 4,* 112–119.

Rovee-Collier, Carolyn. (1987). Learning and memory in infancy. In Joy Doniger Osofsky (Ed.), *Handbook of infant development* (2nd ed., pp. 98–148). New York, NY: Wiley.

Rovee-Collier, Carolyn. (1990). The "memory system" of prelinguistic infants. In Adele Diamond (Ed.), *The development and neural bases of higher cognitive functions* (Vol. 608, pp. 517–542). New York, NY: New York Academy of Sciences.

Rovee-Collier, Carolyn. (2001). Information pick-up by infants: What is it, and how can we tell? *Journal of Experimental Child Psychology, 78,* 35–49.

Rovee-Collier, Carolyn, & Cuevas, Kimberly. (2009a). The development of infant memory. In Mary L. Courage & Nelson Cowan (Eds.), *The development of memory in infancy and childhood* (2nd ed., pp. 11–41). New York, NY: Psychology Press.

Rovee-Collier, Carolyn, & Cuevas, Kimberly. (2009b). Multiple memory systems are unnecessary to account for infant memory development: An ecological model. *Developmental Psychology, 45,* 160–174.

Rovee-Collier, Carolyn, & Hayne, Harlene. (1987). Reactivation of infant memory: Implications for cognitive development. In Hayne W. Reese (Ed.), *Advances in child development and behavior* (Vol. 20, pp. 185–238). San Diego, CA: Academic Press.

Rovi, Sue, Chen, Ping-Hsin, & Johnson, Mark S. (2004). The economic burden of hospitalizations associated with child abuse and neglect. *American Journal of Public Health, 94,* 586–590.

Rovner, Alisha J., Nansel, Tonja R., Wang, Jing, & Iannotti, Ronald J. (2011). Food sold in school vending machines is associated with overall student dietary intake. *Journal of Adolescent Health, 48*(1), 13–19.

Rubie-Davies, Christine M. (2007). Classroom interactions: Exploring the practices of high- and low-expectation teachers. *British Journal of Educational Psychology, 77,* 289–306.

Rubin, Kenneth H., Coplan, Robert J., & Bowker, Julie C. (2009). Social withdrawal in childhood. *Annual Review of Psychology, 60,* 141–171.

Ruble, Diane N., Martin, Carol Lynn, & Berenbaum, Sheri. (2006). Gender development. In William Damon & Richard M. Lerner (Series Eds.) & Nancy Eisenberg (Vol. Ed.), *Handbook of child psychology: Vol. 3. Social, emotional, and personality development* (6th ed., pp. 858–932). Hoboken, NJ: Wiley.

Ruder, Debra Bradley. (2008, September-October). The teen brain. *Harvard Magazine, 111,* 8–10.

Rueda, M. Rosario, Rothbart, Mary K., Saccomanno, Lisa, & Posner, Michael I. (2007).

Modifying brain networks underlying self regulation. In Daniel Romer & Elaine F. Walker (Eds.), *Adolescent psychopathology and the developing brain: Integrating brain and prevention science* (pp. 401–419). Oxford, UK: Oxford University Press.

Russell, Stephen T., Chu, June Y., Crockett, Lisa J., & Lee, Sun-A. (2010b). Interdependent independence: The meanings of autonomy among Chinese American and Filipino American adolescents. In Stephen Thomas Russell, Lisa J. Crockett & Ruth K. Chao (Eds.), *Asian American parenting and parent-adolescent relationships* (pp. 101–116). New York, NY: Springer.

Russell, Stephen T., Crockett, Lisa J., & Chao, Ruth K. (2010a). Conclusions: The role of Asian American culture in parenting and parent-adolescent relationships. In Stephen Thomas Russell, Lisa J. Crockett, & Ruth K. Chao (Eds.), *Asian American parenting and parent-adolescent relationships* (pp. 117–128). New York, NY: Springer.

Rutter, Michael. (2010). Biological and experiential influences on psychological development. In Daniel P. Keating (Ed.), *Nature and nurture in early child development* (pp. 7–44). New York, NY: Cambridge University Press.

Rutter, Michael, Colvert, Emma, Kreppner, Jana, Beckett, Celia, Castle, Jenny, Groothues, Christine, et al. (2007). Early adolescent outcomes for institutionally-deprived and non-deprived adoptees: I. Disinhibited attachment. *Journal of Child Psychology and Psychiatry, 48,* 17–30.

Rutter, Michael, Sonuga-Barke, Edmund J., Beckett, Celia, Castle, Jennifer, Kreppner, Jana, Kumsta, Robert, et al. (2010). Deprivation-specific psychological patterns: Effects of institutional deprivation. *Monographs of the Society for Research in Child Development, 75,* 1–252.

Rutters, Femke, Nieuwenhuizen, Arie G., Vogels, Neeltje, Bouwman, Freek, Mariman, Edwin, & Westerterp-Plantenga, Margriet S. (2008). Leptin-adiposity relationship changes, plus behavioral and parental factors, are involved in the development of body weight in a Dutch children cohort. *Physiology & Behavior, 93,* 967–974.

Ruys, Jan H., de Jonge, Guus A., Brand, Ronald, Engelberts, Adèle, C., & Semmekrot, Ben A. (2007). Bed-sharing in the first four months of life: A risk factor for sudden infant death. *Acta Pædiatrica, 96,* 1399–1403.

Ryan, Michael J. (2005, June 8). Punching out in Little League. *Boston Herald.*

Ryan, Suzanne, Franzetta, Kerry, Manlove, Jennifer, & Holcombe, Emily. (2007). Adolescents' discussions about contraception or STDs with partners before first sex. *Perspectives on Sexual and Reproductive Health, 39,* 149–157.

Ryan, Suzanne, Franzetta, Kerry, Manlove, Jennifer S., & Schelar, Erin. (2008). Older sexual partners during adolescence: Links to reproductive health outcomes in young adulthood. *Perspectives on Sexual and Reproductive Health, 40,* 17–26.

Rydell, Robert J., & Boucher, Kathryn L. (2010). Capitalizing on multiple social identities to prevent stereotype threat: The moderating role

of self-esteem. *Personality and Social Psychology Bulletin, 36,* 239–250.

Rymer, Russ. (1994). *Genie: A scientific tragedy.* New York, NY: Harper Perennial. (Original work published 1945)

Saarni, Carolyn, Campos, Joseph J., Camras, Linda A., & Witherington, David. (2006). Emotional development: Action, communication, and understanding. In William Damon & Richard M. Lerner (Series Eds.) & Nancy Eisenberg (Vol. Ed.), *Handbook of child psychology: Vol. 3. Social, emotional, and personality development* (6th ed., pp. 226–299). Hoboken, NJ: Wiley.

Sacks, Oliver W. (1995). *An anthropologist on Mars: Seven paradoxical tales.* New York, NY: Knopf.

Sadeh, Avi, Mindell, Jodi A., Luedtke, Kathryn, & Wiegand, Benjamin. (2009). Sleep and sleep ecology in the first 3 years: A web-based study. *Journal of Sleep Research, 18,* 60–73.

Sadeh, Avi, Tikotzky, Liat, & Scher, Anat. (2010). Parenting and infant sleep. *Sleep Medicine Reviews, 14,* 89–96.

Sadler, Philip M., Sonnert, Gerhard, Tai, Robert H., & Klopfenstein, Kristin (Eds.). (2010). *AP: A critical examination of the Advanced Placement program.* Cambridge, MA: Harvard Education Press.

Sadler, Thomas W. (2009). *Langman's medical embryology* (11th ed.). Baltimore, MD: Lippincott Williams & Wilkins.

Saewyc, Elizabeth M. (2011). Research on adolescent sexual orientation: Development, health disparities, stigma, and resilience. *Journal of Research on Adolescence, 21,* 256–272.

Saey, Tina Hesman. (2008, May 24). Epic genetics: Genes' chemical clothes may underlie the biology behind mental illness. *Science News, 173,* 14–19.

Safe Kids USA. (2008). *Report to the nation: Trends in unintentional childhood injury mortality and parental views on child safety.* Washington, DC: Safe Kids Worldwide.

Saffran, Jenny R., Werker, Janet F., & Werner, Lynne A. (2006). The infant's auditory world: Hearing, speech, and the beginnings of language. In William Damon & Richard M. Lerner (Eds.), *Handbook of child psychology: Vol. 2. Cognition, perception, and language* (pp. 58–108). Hoboken, NJ: Wiley.

Salkind, Neil J. (2004). *An introduction to theories of human development.* Thousand Oaks, CA: Sage.

Salmivalli, Christina. (2010). Bullying and the peer group: A review. *Aggression and Violent Behavior, 15,* 112–120.

SAMHSA (Substance Abuse and Mental Health Services Administration). (2009). *Results from the 2008 National Survey on Drug Use and Health: National findings* (Office of Applied Studies, NSDUH Series H-36, HHS Publication No. SMA 09-4434). Rockville, MD: U.S. Department of Health and Human Services.

Sandstrom, Marlene J., & Zakriski, Audrey L. (2004). Understanding the experience of peer rejection. In Janis B. Kupersmidt & Kenneth A. Dodge (Eds.), *Children's peer relations: From development* to intervention (pp. 101–118). Washington, DC: American Psychological Association.

Sangrigoli, Sandy, Pallier, Christophe, Argenti, Anne-Marie, Ventureyra, Valérie A. G., & de Schonen, Scania. (2005). Reversibility of the other-race effect in face recognition during childhood. *Psychological Science, 16,* 440–444.

Santelli, John S., & Melnikas, Andrea J. (2010). Teen fertility in transition: Recent and historic trends in the United States. *Annual Review of Public Health, 31,* 371–383.

Santosh, Paramala J., & Canagaratnam, Myooran. (2008). Paediatric bipolar disorder—An update. *Psychiatry, 7,* 349–352.

Santosham, Mathuram. (2010). Rotavirus vaccine—A powerful tool to combat deaths from diarrhea. *New England Journal of Medicine, 362,* 358–360.

Sapienza, Julianna K., & Masten, Ann S. (2011). Understanding and promoting resilience in children and youth. *Current Opinion in Psychiatry, 24,* 267–273.

Saulny, Susan, & Steinberg, Jacques. (2011, June 13). On college forms, a question of race, or races, can perplex. *New York Times,* p. A1.

Savic, Ivanka (Ed.). (2010). *Progress in Brain Research: Vol. 186. Sex differences in the human brain, their underpinnings and implications.* Amsterdam, The Netherlands: Elsevier.

Saw, Seang-Mei, Cheng, Angela, Fong, Allan, Gazzard, Gus, Tan, Donald T. H., & Morgan, Ian. (2007). School grades and myopia. *Ophthalmic and Physiological Optics, 27,* 126–129.

Saxe, Geoffrey B. (1999). Sources of concepts: A cultural-developmental perspective. In Ellin Kofsky Scholnick, Katherine Nelson, Susan A. Gelman, & Patricia H. Miller (Eds.), *Conceptual development: Piaget's legacy* (pp. 253–267). Mahwah, NJ: Erlbaum.

Saxe, Geoffrey B. (2004). Practices of quantification from a socio-cultural perspective. In Andreas Demetriou & Athanassios Raftopoulos (Eds.), *Cognitive developmental change: Theories, models and measurement* (pp. 241–263). New York, NY: Cambridge University.

Saxton, Matthew. (2010). *Child language: Acquisition and development.* Thousand Oaks, CA: SAGE.

Saylor, Megan M., & Sabbagh, Mark A. (2004). Different kinds of information affect word learning in the preschool years: The case of part-term learning. *Child Development, 75,* 395–408.

Scales, Peter C., Benson, Peter L., & Mannes, Marc. (2006). The contribution to adolescent well-being made by nonfamily adults: An examination of developmental assets as contexts and processes. *Journal of Community Psychology, 34,* 401–413.

Scambler, Douglas J., Hepburn, Susan L., Rutherford, Mel, Wehner, Elizabeth A., & Rogers, Sally J. (2007). Emotional responsivity in children with autism, children with other developmental disabilities, and children with typical development. *Journal of Autism and Developmental Disorders, 37,* 553–563.

Scannapieco, Maria, & Connell-Carrick, Kelli. (2005). *Understanding child maltreatment: An ecological and developmental perspective.* New York, NY: Oxford University Press.

Schachner, Adena, & Hannon, Erin E. (2011). Infant-directed speech drives social preferences in 5-month-old infants. *Developmental Psychology, 47,* 19–25.

Schafer, Graham. (2005). Infants can learn de-contextualized words before their first birthday. *Child Development, 76,* 87–96.

Schanler, Richard. J. (2011). Outcomes of human milk-fed premature infants. *Seminars in Perinatology, 35,* 29–33.

Schardein, James L. (1976). *Drugs as teratogens.* Cleveland, OH: CRC Press.

Scheffler, Richard M., Brown, Timothy T., Fulton, Brent D., Hinshaw, Stephen P., Levine, Peter, & Stone, Susan. (2009). Positive association between attention-deficit/hyperactivity disorder medication use and academic achievement during elementary school. *Pediatrics, 123,* 1273–1279.

Scheibehenne, Benjamin, Greifeneder, Rainer, & Todd, Peter M. (2010). Can there ever be too many options? A meta-analytic review of choice overload. *Journal of Consumer Research, 37,* 409–425.

Schenkman, Lauren. (2011, February 25). Second thoughts about CT imaging. *Science, 331,* 1002–1004.

Schermerhorn, Alice C., D'Onofrio, Brian M., Turkheimer, Eric, Ganiban, Jody M., Spotts, Erica L., Lichtenstein, Paul, et al. (2011). A genetically informed study of associations between family functioning and child psychosocial adjustment. *Developmental Psychology, 47,* 707–725.

Schick, Adina, & Melzi, Gigliana. (2010). The development of children's oral narratives across contexts. *Early Education & Development, 21,* 293–317.

Schlarb, Angelika A., Velten-Schurian, Kerstin, Poets, Christian F., & Hautzinger, Martin. (2010). First effects of a multicomponent treatment for sleep disorders in children. *Nature and Science of Sleep, 2011,* 1–11. doi:http://dx.doi.org/10.2147/NSS.S15254

Schmader, Toni. (2010). Stereotype threat deconstructed. *Current Directions in Psychological Science, 19,* 14–18.

Schmader, Toni, Johns, Michael, & Forbes, Chad. (2008). An integrated process model of stereotype threat effects on performance. *Psychological Review, 115,* 336–356.

Schmeer, Kammi K. (2011). The child health disadvantage of parental cohabitation. *Journal of Marriage and Family, 73,* 181–193.

Schmidt, Marie Evans, Pempek, Tiffany A., Kirkorian, Heather L., Lund, Anne Frankenfield, & Anderson, Daniel R. (2008). The effects of background television on the toy play behavior of very young children. *Child Development, 79,* 1137–1151.

Schneider, Wolfgang, & Lockl, Kathrin. (2008). Procedural metacognition in children: Evidence for developmental trends. In John Dunlosky & Robert A. Bjork (Eds.), *Handbook of metamemory and memory* (pp. 391–409). New York, NY: Psychology Press.

Schofield, Thomas J., Martin, Monica J., Conger, Katherine J., Neppl, Tricia M., Donnellan, M. Brent, & Conger, Rand D. (2011). Intergenerational transmission of adaptive functioning: A test of the interactionist model of SES and human development. *Child Development, 82,* 33–47.

Schön, Daniele, Boyer, Maud, Moreno, Sylvain, Besson, Mireille, Peretz, Isabelle, & Kolinsky, Régine. (2008). Songs as an aid for language acquisition. *Cognition, 106,* 975–983.

Schorge, John O., Schaffer, Joseph I., Halvorson, Lisa M., Hoffman, Barbara L., Bradshaw, Karen D., & Cunningham, F. Gary. (2008). *Williams gynecology.* New York, NY: McGraw-Hill Medical.

Schreck, Christopher J., Burek, Melissa W., Stewart, Eric A., & Miller, J. Mitchell. (2007). Distress and violent victimization among young adolescents: Early puberty and the social interactionist explanation. *Journal of Research in Crime and Delinquency, 44,* 381–405.

Schroedel, Jean Reith, & Fiber, Pamela. (2001). Punitive versus public health oriented responses to drug use by pregnant women. *Yale Journal of Health Policy, Law, and Ethics, 1,* 217–235.

Schulenberg, John, O'Malley, Patrick M., Bachman, Jerald G., & Johnston, Lloyd D. (2005). Early adult transitions and their relation to well-being and substance use. In Richard A. Settersten, Jr., Frank F. Furstenberg, Jr., & Rubén G. Rumbaut (Eds.), *On the frontier of adulthood: Theory, research, and public policy* (pp. 417–453). Chicago, IL: University of Chicago Press.

Schumann, Cynthia Mills, Hamstra, Julia, Goodlin-Jones, Beth L., Lotspeich, Linda J., Kwon, Hower, Buonocore, Michael H., et al. (2004). The amygdala is enlarged in children but not adolescents with autism; the hippocampus is enlarged at all ages. *Journal of Neuroscience, 24,* 6392–6401.

Schwartz, Carl E., Kunwar, Pratap S., Greve, Douglas N., Moran, Lyndsey R., Viner, Jane C., Covino, Jennifer M., et al. (2010). Structural differences in adult orbital and ventromedial prefrontal cortex predicted by infant temperament at 4 months of age. *Archives of General Psychiatry, 67,* 78–84.

Schwartz, David, & Collins, Francis. (2007, May 4). Environmental biology and human disease. *Science, 316,* 695–696.

Schwartz, Pepper. (2006). What elicits romance, passion, and attachment, and how do they affect our lives throughout the life cycle? In Ann C. Crouter & Alan Booth (Eds.), *Romance and sex in adolescence and emerging adulthood: Risks and opportunities* (pp. 49–60). Mahwah, NJ: Erlbaum.

Schwartz, Paul D., Maynard, Amanda M., & Uzelac, Sarah M. (2008). Adolescent egocentrism: A contemporary view. *Adolescence, 43,* 441–448.

Schweinhart, Lawrence J., Montie, Jeanne, Xiang, Zongping, Barnett, W. Steven, Belfield, Clive R., & Nores, Milagros. (2005). *Lifetime effects: The High/Scope Perry Preschool Study through age 40.* Ypsilanti, MI: High/Scope Press.

Schweinhart, Lawrence J., & Weikart, David P. (1997). *Lasting differences: The High/Scope Preschool Curriculum Comparison Study through age 23.* Ypsilanti, MI: High/Scope Educational Research Foundation.

Schwekendiek, Daniel. (2009). Height and weight differences between North and South Korea. *Journal of Biosocial Science, 41,* 51–55.

Schytt, Erica, & Waldenström, Ulla. (2010). Epidural analgesia for labor pain: Whose choice? *Acta Obstetricia et Gynecologica Scandinavica, 89,* 238–242.

Scott, Lisa S., & Monesson, Alexandra. (2010). Experience-dependent neural specialization during infancy. *Neuropsychologia, 48,* 1857–1861.

Scott, Lisa S., Pascalis, Olivier, & Nelson, Charles A. (2007). A domain-general theory of the development of perceptual discrimination. *Current Directions in Psychological Science, 16,* 197–201.

Sebastian, Catherine, Burnett, Stephanie, & Blakemore, Sarah-Jayne. (2008). Development of the self-concept during adolescence. *Trends in Cognitive Sciences, 12,* 441–446.

Sebastián-Gallés, Núria. (2007). Biased to learn language. *Developmental Science, 10,* 713–718.

Seifer, Ronald, LaGasse, Linda L., Lester, Barry, Bauer, Charles R., Shankaran, Seetha, Bada, Henrietta S., et al. (2004). Attachment status in children prenatally exposed to cocaine and other substances. *Child Development, 75,* 850–868.

Seligman, Hilary K., & Schillinger, Dean. (2010). Hunger and socioeconomic disparities in chronic disease. *New England Journal of Medicine, 363,* 6–9.

Selin, Helaine, & Stone, Pamela Kendall (Eds.). (2009). *Childbirth across cultures: Ideas and practices of pregnancy, childbirth and the postpartum.* New York, NY: Springer Verlag.

Senju, Atsushi, Southgate, Victoria, Miura, Yui, Matsui, Tomoko, Hasegawa, Toshikazu, Tojo, Yoshikuni, et al. (2010). Absence of spontaneous action anticipation by false belief attribution in children with autism spectrum disorder. *Development and Psychopathology, 22,* 353–360.

Setlik, Jennifer, Bond, G. Randall, & Ho, Mona. (2009). Adolescent prescription ADHD medication abuse is rising along with prescriptions for these medications. *Pediatrics, 124,* 875–880.

Settle, Jaime E., Dawes, Christopher T., Christakis, Nicholas A., & Fowler, James H. (2010). Friendships moderate an association between a dopamine gene variant and political ideology. *The Journal of Politics, 72,* 1189–1198.

Shah, Prakesh, Balkhair, Taiba, Ohlsson, Arne, Beyene, Joseph, Scott, Fran, & Frick, Corine. (2011). Intention to become pregnant and low birth weight and preterm birth: A systematic review. *Maternal and Child Health Journal, 15,* 205–216.

Shahin, Hashem, Walsh, Tom, Sobe, Tama, Lynch, Eric, King, Mary-Claire, Avraham, Karen, et al. (2002). Genetics of congenital deafness in the Palestinian population: Multiple con- nexin 26 alleles with shared origins in the Middle East. *Human Genetics, 110,* 284–289.

Shanahan, Lilly, McHale, Susan M., Osgood, Wayne, & Crouter, Ann C. (2007). Conflict frequency with mothers and fathers from middle childhood to late adolescence: Within- and between-families comparisons. *Developmental Psychology, 43,* 539–550.

Shanahan, Timothy, & Lonigan, Christopher J. (2010). The National Early Literacy Panel: A summary of the process and the report. *Educational Researcher, 39,* 279–285.

Shanks, Laurie. (2011). *Child sexual abuse: How to move to a balanced and rational approach to the cases everyone abhors.* Retrieved from SSRN website: http://ssrn.com/abstract=1739767

Shannon, Joyce Brennfleck (Ed.). (2007). *Eating disorders sourcebook: Basic consumer health information about anorexia nervosa, bulimia nervosa, binge eating, compulsive exercise, female athlete triad, and other eating disorders* (2nd ed.). Detroit, MI: Omnigraphics.

Shapiro, Edward S., Zigmond, Naomi, Wallace, Teri, & Marston, Doug (Eds.). (2011). *Models for implementing response to intervention: Tools, outcomes, and implications.* New York, NY: Guilford Press.

Shapiro, James A. (2009). Revisiting the central dogma in the 21st century. In Günther Witzany (Ed.), *Annals of the New York Academy of Sciences: Vol. 1178. Natural genetic engineering and natural genome editing* (pp. 6–28). New York, NY: Wiley-Blackwell.

Sharma, Monica. (2008). Twenty-first century pink or blue: How sex selection technology facilitates gendercide and what we can do about it. *Family Court Review, 46,* 198–215.

Shattuck, Paul T. (2006). The contribution of diagnostic substitution to the growing administrative prevalence of autism in US special education. *Pediatrics, 117,* 1028–1037.

Sherblom, Stephen. (2008). The legacy of the "Care challenge": Re-envisioning the outcome of the justice-care debate. *Journal of Moral Education, 37,* 81–98.

Shields, Margot, & Tremblay, Mark S. (2010). Canadian childhood obesity estimates based on WHO, IOTF and CDC cut-points. *International Journal of Pediatric Obesity, 5,* 265–273.

Shirtcliff, Elizabeth A., Dahl, Ronald E., & Pollak, Seth D. (2009). Pubertal development: Correspondence between hormonal and physical development. *Child Development, 80,* 327–337.

Shonkoff, Jack P. (2010). Building a new biodevelopmental framework to guide the future of early childhood policy. *Child Development, 81,* 357–367.

Shonkoff, Jack P., Boyce, W. Thomas, & McEwen, Bruce S. (2009). Neuroscience, molecular biology, and the childhood roots of health disparities: Building a new framework for health promotion and disease prevention. *Journal of the American Medical Association, 301,* 2252–2259.

Shuler, Carly. (2009). *Pockets of potential: Using mobile technologies to promote children's learning.* New York, NY: The Joan Ganz Cooney Center at Sesame Workshop.

Siebenbruner, Jessica, Zimmer-Gembeck, Melanie J., & Egeland, Byron. (2007). Sexual partners and contraceptive use: A 16–year prospective study predicting abstinence and risk behavior. *Journal of Research on Adolescence, 17,* 179–206.

Siegler, Robert S. (2009). Improving the numerical understanding of children from low-income families. *Child Development Perspectives, 3,* 118–124.

Siegler, Robert S., & Chen, Zhe. (2008). Differentiation and integration: guiding principles for analyzing cognitive change. *Developmental Science, 11,* 433–448.

Siegler, Robert S., & Mu, Yan. (2008). Chinese children excel on novel mathematics problems even before elementary school. *Psychological Science, 19,* 759–763.

Siegler, Robert S., Thompson, Clarissa A., & Schneider, Michael. (2011). An integrated theory of whole number and fractions development. *Cognitive Psychology, 62,* 273–296.

Silk, Timothy J., & Wood, Amanda G. (2011). Lessons about neurodevelopment from anatomical magnetic resonance imaging. *Journal of Developmental & Behavioral Pediatrics, 32,* 158–168.

Sillars, Alan, Smith, Traci, & Koerner, Ascan. (2010). Misattributions contributing to empathic (in)accuracy during parent-adolescent conflict discussions. *Journal of Social and Personal Relationships, 27,* 727–747.

Silva, Katie G., Correa-Chávez, Maricela, & Rogoff, Barbara. (2010). Mexican-heritage children's attention and learning from interactions directed to others. *Child Development, 81,* 898–912.

Silverman, Wendy K., & Dick-Niederhauser, Andreas. (2004). Separation anxiety disorder. In Tracy L. Morris & John S. March (Eds.), *Anxiety disorders in children and adolescents* (2nd ed., pp. 164–188). New York, NY: Guilford Press.

Simpkins, Sandra D., Fredricks, Jennifer A., Davis-Kean, Pamela E., & Eccles, Jacquelynne S. (2006). Healthy mind, healthy habits: The influence of activity involvement in middle childhood. In Aletha C. Huston & Marika N. Ripke (Eds.), *Developmental contexts in middle childhood: Bridges to adolescence and adulthood* (pp. 283–302). New York, NY: Cambridge University Press.

Simpson, Jeffry A., Collins, W. Andrew, Tran, SiSi, & Haydon, Katherine C. (2007). Attachment and the experience and expression of emotions in romantic relationships: A developmental perspective. *Journal of Personality and Social Psychology, 92,* 355–367.

Simpson, Jeffry A., & Rholes, W. Steven. (2010). Attachment and relationships: Milestones and future directions. *Journal of Social and Personal Relationships, 27,* 173–180.

Singh, Gopal K, & Siahpush, Mohammad. (2006). Widening socioeconomic inequalities in US life expectancy, 1980–2000. *International Journal of Epidemiology, 35,* 969–979.

Singh, Leher. (2008). Influences of high and low variability on infant word recognition. *Cognition, 106,* 833–870.

Singleton, David, & Muñoz, Carmen. (2011). Around and beyond the critical period hypothesis In Eli Hinkel (Ed.), *Handbook of research in second language teaching and learning* (Vol. 2, pp. 407–425). Mahwah, NJ: Erlbaum.

Sinnott, Jan D. (1998). *The development of logic in adulthood: Postformal thought and its applications.* New York, NY: Plenum Press.

Siu, Angela F. Y. (2007). Using friends to combat internalizing problems among primary school children in Hong Kong. *Journal of Cognitive and Behavioral Psychotherapies, 7,* 11–26.

Skinner, B. F. (1953). *Science and human behavior.* New York, NY: Macmillan.

Skinner, B. F. (1957). *Verbal behavior.* New York, NY: Appleton-Century-Crofts.

Slater, Alan, Quinn, Paul C., Kelly, David J., Lee, Kang, Longmore, Christopher A., McDonald, Paula R., et al. (2010). The shaping of the face space in early infancy: Becoming a native face processor. *Child Development Perspectives, 4,* 205–211.

Slavin, Robert E., Lake, Cynthia, & Groff, Cynthia. (2009). Effective programs in middle and high school mathematics: A best-evidence synthesis. *Review of Educational Research, 79,* 839–911.

Slining, Meghan, Adair, Linda S., Goldman, Barbara Davis, Borja, Judith B., & Bentley, Margaret. (2010). Infant overweight is associated with delayed motor development. *The Journal of Pediatrics, 157,* 20–25.e1. doi:10.1016/j.jpeds.2009.12.054

Sloan, Mark. (2009). *Birth day: A pediatrician explores the science, the history, and the wonder of childbirth.* New York, NY: Ballantine Books.

Slobin, Dan I. (2001). Form-function relations: How do children find out what they are? In Melissa Bowerman & Stephen C. Levinson (Eds.), *Language acquisition and conceptual development* (pp. 406–449). Cambridge, UK: Cambridge University Press.

Smetana, Judith G., Metzger, Aaron, & Campione-Barr, Nicole. (2004). African American late adolescents' relationships with parents: Developmental transitions and longitudinal patterns. *Child Development, 75,* 932–947.

Smith, Chris. (2006). *Including the gifted and talented: Making inclusion work for more gifted and able learners.* New York, NY: Routledge.

Smith, Christian (with Denton, Melinda Lundquist). (2005). *Soul searching: The religious and spiritual lives of American teenagers.* Oxford, UK: Oxford University Press.

Smith, Margaret G., & Fong, Rowena. (2004). *The children of neglect: When no one cares.* New York, NY: Brunner-Routledge.

Smith, Peter K., Mahdavi, Jess, Carvalho, Manuel, Fisher, Sonja, Russell, Shanette, & Tippett, Neil. (2008). Cyberbullying: Its nature and impact in secondary school pupils. *Journal of Child Psychology and Psychiatry, 49,* 376–385.

Smith, Peter K., Pepler, Debra J., & Rigby, Ken. (2004). *Bullying in schools: How successful can interventions be?* New York, NY: Cambridge University Press.

Smith, Tom W. (2005). Generation gaps in attitudes and values from the 1970s to the 1990s. In Richard A. Settersten, Jr., Frank F. Furstenberg, Jr., & Rubén G. Rumbaut (Eds.), *On the frontier of adulthood: Theory, research, and public policy* (pp. 177–221). Chicago, IL: University of Chicago Press.

Smokowski, Paul Richard, Rose, Roderick, & Bacallao, Martica. (2010). Influence of risk factors and cultural assets on Latino adolescents' trajectories of self-esteem and internalizing symptoms. *Child Psychiatry & Human Development, 41,* 133–155.

Smyth, Joshua M. (2007). Beyond self-selection in video game play: An experimental examination of the consequences of massively multiplayer online role-playing game play. *CyberPsychology & Behavior, 10,* 717–727.

Snow, Catherine E., Porche, Michelle V., Tabors, Patton O., & Harris, Stephanie Ross. (2007). *Is literacy enough? Pathways to academic success for adolescents.* Baltimore, MD: Brookes.

Snow, David. (2006). Regression and reorganization of intonation between 6 and 23 months. *Child Development, 77,* 281–296.

Snyder, James, Schrepferman, Lynn, Oeser, Jessica, Patterson, Gerald, Stoolmiller, Mike, Johnson, Kassy, et al. (2005). Deviancy training and association with deviant peers in young children: Occurrence and contribution to early-onset conduct problems. *Development & Psychopathology, 17,* 397–413.

Snyder, Thomas D., & Dillow, Sally A. (2010). *Digest of education statistics, 2009.* Washington, DC: National Center for Education Statistics.

Snyder, Thomas D., & Dillow, Sally A. (2011). *Digest of education statistics, 2010.* Washington, DC: National Center for Education Statistics.

Social Security Administration. (2009, May 8). *Popular baby names.* Retrieved from http://www.ssa.gov/OACT/babynames/

Soenens, Bart, & Vansteenkiste, Maarten. (2010). A theoretical upgrade of the concept of parental psychological control: Proposing new insights on the basis of self-determination theory. *Developmental Review, 30,* 74–99.

Soley, Gaye, & Hannon, Erin E. (2010). Infants prefer the musical meter of their own culture: A cross-cultural comparison. *Developmental Psychology, 46,* 286–292.

Soons, Judith P. M., & Kalmijn, Matthijs. (2009). Is marriage more than cohabitation? Well-being differences in 30 European countries. *Journal of Marriage and Family, 71,* 1141–1157.

Sowell, Elizabeth R., Thompson, Paul M., & Toga, Arthur W. (2007). Mapping adolescent brain maturation using structural magnetic resonance imaging. In Daniel Romer & Elaine F. Walker (Eds.), *Adolescent psychopathology and the developing brain: Integrating brain and prevention science* (pp. 55–84). Oxford, UK: Oxford University Press.

Spandorfer, Philip R., Alessandrini, Evaline A., Joffe, Mark D., Localio, Russell, & Shaw, Kathy N. (2005). Oral versus intravenous rehydration of moderately dehydrated children: A randomized, controlled trial. *Pediatrics, 115,* 295–301.

Spelke, Elizabeth S. (1993). Object perception. In Alvin I. Goldman (Ed.), *Readings in philosophy and cognitive science* (pp. 447–460). Cambridge, MA: MIT Press.

Spencer, John P., Blumberg, Mark S., McMurray, Bob, Robinson, Scott R., Samuelson, Larissa K., & Tomblin, J. Bruce. (2009). Short arms and talking eggs: Why we should no longer abide the nativist–empiricist debate. *Child Development Perspectives, 3,* 79–87.

Spinillo, Arsenio, Montanari, Laura, Gardella, Barbara, Roccio, Marianna, Stronati, Mauro, & Fazzi, Elisa. (2009). Infant sex, obstetric risk factors, and 2-year neurodevelopmental outcome among preterm infants. *Developmental Medicine & Child Neurology, 51,* 518–525.

Spittle, Alicia J., Treyvaud, Karli, Doyle, Lex W., Roberts, Gehan, Lee, Katherine J., Inder, Terrie E., et al. (2009). Early emergence of behavior and social-emotional problems in very preterm infants. *Journal of the American Academy of Child and Adolescent Psychiatry, 48,* 909–918.

SRCD Governing Council. (2007, March). *SRCD ethical standards for research with children.* Retrieved from http://www.srcd.org/index.php?option=com_content&task=view&id=68&Itemid

Sroufe, L. Alan, Egeland, Byron, Carlson, Elizabeth A., & Collins, W. Andrew. (2005). *The development of the person: The Minnesota study of risk and adaptation from birth to adulthood.* New York, NY: Guilford Press.

Staff, Jeremy, Messersmith, Emily E., & Schulenberg, John E. (2009). Adolescents and the world of work. In Richard Lerner & Laurence Steinberg (Eds.), *Handbook of Adolescent Psychology* (pp. 270–313). Hoboken, NJ: Wiley.

Staff, Jeremy, & Schulenberg, John. (2010). Millennials and the world of work: Experiences in paid work during adolescence. *Journal of Business and Psychology, 25,* 247–255.

Staiger, Annegret Daniela. (2006). *Learning difference: Race and schooling in the multiracial metropolis.* Stanford, CA: Stanford University Press.

Stanley, Scott M., Rhoades, Galena Kline, & Markman, Howard J. (2006). Sliding versus deciding: Inertia and the premarital cohabitation effect. *Family Relations, 55,* 499–509.

Statistics Canada. (2011, September 26). *Vital statistics—Death database.* Retrieved from http://www.statcan.gc.ca/cgi-bin/imdb/p2SV.pl?Function=getSurvey&SDDS=3233&lang=en&db=imdb&adm=8&dis=2

Stearns, Elizabeth, & Glennie, Elizabeth J. (2010). Opportunities to participate: Extracurricular activities' distribution across and academic correlates in high schools. *Social Science Research, 39,* 296–309.

Steele, Claude M. (1997). A threat in the air: How stereotypes shape intellectual identity and performance. *American Psychologist, 52,* 613–629.

Steemers, Jeanette. (2010). *Creating preschool television: A story of commerce, creativity and curriculum.* New York, NY: Palgrave Macmillan.

Stein, Arlene. (2006). *Shameless: Sexual dissidence in American culture.* New York, NY: New York University Press.

Steinberg, Laurence. (2001). We know some things: Parent-adolescent relationships in retrospect and prospect. *Journal of Research on Adolescence, 11,* 1–19.

Steinberg, Laurence. (2004). Risk taking in adolescence: What changes, and why? In Ronald E. Dahl & Linda Patia Spear (Eds.), *Adolescent brain development: Vulnerabilities and opportunities* (Vol. 1021, pp. 51–58). New York, NY: New York Academy of Sciences

Steinberg, Laurence. (2007). Risk taking in adolescence: New perspectives from brain and behavioral science. *Current Directions in Psychological Science, 16,* 55–59.

Steinberg, Laurence. (2009). Should the science of adolescent brain development inform public policy? *American Psychologist, 64,* 739–750.

Steinberg, Laurence. (2010). A dual systems model of adolescent risk-taking. *Developmental Psychobiology, 52,* 216–224.

Steinberg, Laurence, Lamborn, Susie D., Darling, Nancy, Mounts, Nina S., & Dornbusch, Sanford M. (1994). Over-time changes in adjustment and competence among adolescents from authoritative, authoritarian, indulgent, and neglectful families. *Child Development, 65,* 754–770.

Steinberg, Laurence, & Monahan, Kathryn C. (2011). Adolescents' exposure to sexy media does not hasten the initiation of sexual intercourse. *Developmental Psychology, 47,* 562–576.

Steiner, Meir, & Young, Elizabeth A. (2008). Hormones and mood. In Jill B. Becker, Karen J. Berkley, Nori Geary, Elizabeth Hampson, James P. Herman, & Elizabeth Young (Eds.), *Sex differences in the brain: From genes to behavior* (pp. 405–426). New York, NY: Oxford University Press.

Sterck, Elisabeth H. M., & Begeer, Sander. (2010). Theory of Mind: Specialized capacity or emergent property? *European Journal of Developmental Psychology, 7,* 1–16.

Sternberg, Robert J. (1996). *Successful intelligence: How practical and creative intelligence determine success in life.* New York, NY: Simon & Schuster.

Sternberg, Robert J., Jarvin, Linda, & Grigorenko, Elena L. (2010). *Explorations in giftedness.* New York, NY: Cambridge University Press.

Stevenson, Olive. (2007). *Neglected children and their families* (2nd ed.). Malden, MA: Blackwell.

Stevenson, Richard J., Oaten, Megan J., Case, Trevor I., Repacholi, Betty M., & Wagland, Paul. (2010). Children's response to adult disgust elicitors: Development and acquisition. *Developmental Psychology, 46,* 165–177.

Stewart, Endya B. (2008). School structural characteristics, student effort, peer associations, and parental involvement: The influence of school- and individual-level factors on academic achievement. *Education and Urban Society, 40,* 179–204.

Stigler, James W., & Hiebert, James. (2009). *The teaching gap: Best ideas from the world's teachers for improving education in the classroom* (Paperback ed.). New York, NY: Free Press. (Original work published 1999)

Stigum, Hein, Samuelsen, Sven-Ove, & Traeen, Bente. (2010). Analysis of first coitus. *Archives of Sexual Behavior, 39,* 907–914.

Stiles, Joan, & Jernigan, Terry. (2010). The basics of brain development. *Neuropsychology Review, 20,* 327–348.

Stillman, Robert J., Richter, Kevin S., Banks, Nicole K., & Graham, James R. (2009). Elective single embryo transfer: A 6-year progressive implementation of 784 single blastocyst transfers and the influence of payment method on patient choice. *Fertility and Sterility, 92,* 1895–1906.

Stokstad, Erik. (2003, December 12). The vitamin D deficit. *Science, 302,* 1886–1888.

Stone, Richard. (2011, April 8). Daring experiment in higher education opens its doors. *Science, 332,* 161.

Stoneking, Mark, & Delfin, Frederick. (2010). The human genetic history of East Asia: Weaving a complex tapestry. *Current Biology, 20,* R188–R193.

Strasburger, Victor C., Wilson, Barbara J., & Jordan, Amy B. (2009). *Children, adolescents, and the media* (2nd ed.). Los Angeles, CA: Sage.

Straus, Murray A., & Paschall, Mallie J. (2009). Corporal punishment by mothers and development of children's cognitive ability: A longitudinal study of two nationally representative age cohorts. *Journal of Aggression, Maltreatment & Trauma, 18,* 459–483.

Streissguth, Ann P., & Connor, Paul D. (2001). Fetal alcohol syndrome and other effects of prenatal alcohol: Developmental cognitive neuroscience implications. In Charles A. Nelson & Monica Luciana (Eds.), *Handbook of developmental cognitive neuroscience* (pp. 505–518). Cambridge, MA: MIT Press.

Strouse, Darcy L. (1999). Adolescent crowd orientations: A social and temporal analysis. In Jeffrey A. McLellan & Mary Jo V. Pugh (Eds.), *The role of peer groups in adolescent social identity: Exploring the importance of stability and change* (pp. 37–54). San Francisco, CA: Jossey-Bass.

Stubben, Jerry D. (2001). Working with and conducting research among American Indian families. *American Behavioral Scientist, 44,* 1466–1481.

Štulhofer, Aleksandar, Graham, Cynthia, Božičević, Ivana, Kufrin, Krešimir, & Ajduković, Dean. (2009). An assessment of HIV/STI vulnerability and related sexual risk-taking in a nationally representative sample of young Croatian adults. *Archives of Sexual Behavior, 38,* 209–225.

Suchy, Frederick J., Brannon, Patsy M., Carpenter, Thomas O., Fernandez, Jose R., Gilsanz, Vicente, Gould, Jeffrey B., et al. (2010). National Institutes of Health Consensus Development Conference: Lactose intolerance and health. *Annals of Internal Medicine, 152,* 792–796.

Sun, Min, & Rugolotto, Simone. (2004). Assisted infant toilet training in a Western family setting. *Journal of Developmental & Behavioral Pediatrics, 25,* 99–101.

Sunstein, Cass R. (2008). Adolescent risk-taking and social meaning: A commentary. *Developmental Review, 28,* 145–152.

Suomi, Steven J. (2002). Parents, peers, and the process of socialization in primates. In John G. Borkowski, Sharon Landesman Ramey, & Marie Bristol-Power (Eds.), *Parenting and the child's world: Influences on academic, intellectual, and social-emotional development* (pp. 265–279). Mahwah, NJ: Erlbaum.

Suomi, Stephen J. (2004). How gene-environment interactions shape biobehavioral development: Lessons from studies with rhesus monkeys. *Research in Human Development, 1,* 205–222.

Super, Charles M., & Harkness, Sara. (2009). The developmental niche of the newborn in rural Kenya. In J. Kevin Nugent, Bonnie Petrauskas, & T. Berry Brazelton (Eds.), *The newborn as a person: Enabling healthy infant development worldwide* (pp. 85–97). Hoboken, NJ: Wiley.

Super, Charles M., Harkness, Sara, Barry, Oumar, & Zeitlin, Marian. (2011). Think locally, act globally: Contributions of African research to child development. *Child Development Perspectives, 5,* 119–125.

Suris, Joan-Carles, Michaud, Pierre-André, Akre, Christina, & Sawyer, Susan M. (2008). Health risk behaviors in adolescents with chronic conditions. *Pediatrics, 122,* e1113–1118. doi:10.1542/peds.2008-1479

Susman, Elizabeth J., Dockray, Samantha, Schiefelbein, Virginia L., Herwehe, Suellen, Heaton, Jodi A., & Dorn, Lorah D. (2007). Morningness/eveningness, morning-to-afternoon cortisol ratio, and antisocial behavior problems during puberty. *Developmental Psychology, 43,* 811–822.

Susman, Elizabeth J., Houts, Renate M., Steinberg, Laurence, Belsky, Jay, Cauffman, Elizabeth, DeHart, Ganie, et al. (2010). Longitudinal development of secondary sexual characteristics in girls and boys between ages 9½ and 15½ years. *Archives of Pediatrics & Adolescent Medicine, 164,* 166–173.

Sutton-Smith, Brian. (2011). The antipathies of play. In Anthony D. Pellegrini (Ed.), *The Oxford handbook of the development of play* (pp. 110–115). New York, NY: Oxford University Press.

Swanson, Christopher B. (2011, June 9). Analysis finds graduation rates moving up: Strong signs of improvement on graduation. *Education Week,* p. 23.

Syed, Moin, & Azmitia, Margarita. (2010). Narrative and ethnic identity exploration: A longitudinal account of emerging adults' ethnicity-related experiences. *Developmental Psychology, 46,* 208–219.

Taber, Daniel R., Stevens, June, Evenson, Kelly R., Ward, Dianne S., Poole, Charles, Maciejewski, Matthew L., et al. (2011). State policies targeting junk food in schools: Racial/ethnic differences in the effect of policy change on soda consumption. *American Journal of Public Health*, AJPH.2011.300221.

Taga, Keiko A., Markey, Charlotte N., & Friedman, Howard S. (2006). A longitudinal investigation of associations between boys' pubertal timing and adult behavioral health and well-being. *Journal of Youth and Adolescence, 35*, 401–411.

Takahashi, Hidehiko, Kato, Motoichiro, Matsuura, Masato, Mobbs, Dean, Suhara, Tetsuya, & Okubo, Yoshiro. (2009, February 13). When your gain is my pain and your pain is my gain: Neural correlates of envy and schadenfreude. *Science, 323*, 937–939.

Talge, Nicole M., Neal, Charles, & Glover, Vivette. (2007). Antenatal maternal stress and long-term effects on child neurodevelopment: How and why? *Journal of Child Psychology and Psychiatry, 48*, 245–261.

Tamay, Zeynep, Akcay, Ahmet, Ones, Ulker, Guler, Nermin, Kilic, Gurkan, & Zencir, Mehmet. (2007). Prevalence and risk factors for allergic rhinitis in primary school children. *International Journal of Pediatric Otorhinolaryngology, 71*, 463–471.

Tamis-LeMonda, Catherine, Kahana-Kalman, Ronit, & Yoshikawa, Hirokazu. (2009). Father involvement in immigrant and ethnically diverse families from the prenatal period to the second year: Prediction and mediating mechanisms. *Sex Roles, 60*, 496–509.

Tamis-LeMonda, Catherine S., Bornstein, Marc H., & Baumwell, Lisa. (2001). Maternal responsiveness and children's achievement of language milestones. *Child Development, 72*, 748–767.

Tamis-LeMonda, Catherine S., Way, Niobe, Hughes, Diane, Yoshikawa, Hirokazu, Kalman, Ronit Kahana, & Niwa, Erika Y. (2008). Parents' goals for children: The dynamic coexistence of individualism and collectivism in cultures and individuals. *Social Development, 17*, 183–209.

Tanaka, Yuko, & Nakazawa, Jun. (2005). Job-related temporary father absence (Tanshinfunin) and child development. In David W. Shwalb, Jun Nakazawa, & Barbara J. Shwalb (Eds.), *Applied developmental psychology: Theory, practice, and research from Japan* (pp. 241–260). Greenwich, CT: Information Age.

Tangney, June Price, Stuewig, Jeff, & Mashek, Debra J. (2007). Moral emotions and moral behavior. *Annual Review of Psychology, 58*, 345–372.

Tanner, Jennifer L., Arnett, Jeffrey J., & Leis, Julie A. (2009). Emerging adulthood: Learning and development during the first stage of adulthood. In M. Cecil Smith (Ed.), *Handbook of research on adult learning and development* (pp. 34–67). New York, NY: Routledge/Taylor & Francis Group.

Tarullo, Amanda R., Garvin, Melissa C., & Gunnar, Megan R. (2011). Atypical EEG power correlates with indiscriminately friendly behavior in internationally adopted children. *Developmental Psychology, 47*, 417–431.

Tarullo, Amanda R., & Gunnar, Megan R. (2006). Child maltreatment and the developing HPA axis. *Hormones and Behavior, 50*, 632–639.

Tauber, Alfred I. (2010). *Freud, the reluctant philosopher*. Princeton, NJ: Princeton University Press.

Tay, Marc Tze-Hsin, Au Eong, Kah Guan, Ng, C. Y., & Lim, M. K. (1992). Myopia and educational attainment in 421,116 young Singaporean males. *Annals, Academy of Medicine, Singapore, 21*, 785–791.

Taylor, Donald H., Jr., Cook-Deegan, Robert M., Hiraki, Susan, Roberts, J. Scott, Blazer, Dan G., & Green, Robert C. (2010). Genetic testing for Alzheimer's and long-term care insurance. *Health Affairs, 29*, 102–108.

Taylor, James A., Geyer, Leah J., & Feldman, Kenneth W. (2010). Use of supplemental vitamin D among infants breastfed for prolonged periods. *Pediatrics, 125*, 105–111.

Taylor, Marjorie, Carlson, Stephanie M., Maring, Bayta L., Gerow, Lynn, & Charley, Carolyn M. (2004). The characteristics and correlates of fantasy in school-age children: Imaginary companions, impersonation, and social understanding. *Developmental Psychology, 40*, 1173–1187.

Taylor, Marjorie, Shawber, Alison B., & Mannering, Anne M. (2009). Children's imaginary companions: What is it like to have an invisible friend? In Keith D. Markman, William M. P. Klein, & Julie A. Suhr (Eds.), *Handbook of imagination and mental simulation* (pp. 211–224). New York, NY Psychology Press.

Taylor, Ronald D., Seaton, Eleanor, & Dominguez, Antonio. (2008). Kinship support, family relations, and psychological adjustment among low-income African American mothers and adolescents. *Journal of Research on Adolescence, 18*, 1–22.

Taylor, Rachael W., Murdoch, Linda, Carter, Philippa, Gerrard, David F., Williams, Sheila M., & Taylor, Barry J. (2009). Longitudinal study of physical activity and inactivity in preschoolers: The FLAME study. *Medicine & Science in Sports & Exercise, 41*, 96–102.

Teachman, Jay. (2008). Complex life course patterns and the risk of divorce in second marriages. *Journal of Marriage and Family, 70*, 294–305.

Tedeschi, Alberto, & Airaghi, Lorena. (2006). Is affluence a risk factor for bronchial asthma and type 1 diabetes? *Pediatric Allergy and Immunology, 17*, 533–537.

ter Bogt, Tom, Schmid, Holger, Gabhainn, Saoirse Nic, Fotiou, Anastasios, & Vollebergh, Wilma. (2006). Economic and cultural correlates of cannabis use among mid-adolescents in 31 countries. *Addiction, 101*, 241–251.

Terman, Lewis M. (1925). *Genetic studies of genius*. Stanford, CA: Stanford University Press.

Tessier, Karen. (2010). Effectiveness of hands-on education for correct child restraint use by parents. *Accident Analysis & Prevention, 42*, 1041–1047.

Tester, June M., Rutherford, George W., Wald, Zachary, & Rutherford, Mary W. (2004). A matched case-control study evaluating the effectiveness of speed humps in reducing child pedestrian injuries. *American Journal of Public Health, 94*, 646–650.

Thaler, Richard H., & Sunstein, Cass R. (2008). *Nudge: Improving decisions about health, wealth, and happiness*. New Haven, CT: Yale University Press.

The American College of Obstetricians and Gynecologists Committee on Obstetric Practice. (2011). Committee opinion no. 476: Planned home birth. *Obstetrics & Gynecology, 117*, 425–428.

The EXPRESS Group. (2009). One-year survival of extremely preterm infants after active perinatal care in Sweden. *Journal of the American Medical Association, 301*, 2225–2233.

Thelen, Esther, & Corbetta, Daniela. (2002). Microdevelopment and dynamic systems: Applications to infant motor development. In Nira Granott & Jim Parziale (Eds.), *Microdevelopment: Transition processes in development and learning* (pp. 59–79). New York, NY: Cambridge University Press.

Thelen, Esther, & Smith, Linda B. (2006). Dynamic systems theories. In William Damon & Richard M. Lerner (Series Eds.) & Richard M. Lerner (Vol. Ed.), *Handbook of child psychology: Vol. 1. Theoretical models of human development* (6th ed., pp. 258–312). Hoboken, NJ: Wiley.

Thomaes, Sander, Reijntjes, Albert, Orobio de Castro1, Bram, Bushman, Brad J., Poorthuis, Astrid, & Telch, Michael J. (2010). I like me if you like me: On the interpersonal modulation and regulation of preadolescents' state self-esteem. *Child Development, 81*, 811–825.

Thomas, Alexander, & Chess, Stella. (1977). *Temperament and development*. Oxford, UK: Brunner/Mazel.

Thomas, Lori M. (2008). The changing role of parents in neonatal care: A historical review. *Neonatal Network, 27*, 91–100.

Thomas, Michael S. C., & Johnson, Mark H. (2008). New advances in understanding sensitive periods in brain development. *Current Directions in Psychological Science, 17*, 1–5.

Thomas, Michael S. C., Van Duuren, Mike, Purser, Harry R. M., Mareschal, Denis, Ansari, Daniel, & Karmiloff-Smith, Annette. (2010). The development of metaphorical language comprehension in typical development and in Williams syndrome. *Journal of Experimental Child Psychology, 106*, 99–114.

Thompson, Clarissa A., & Siegler, Robert S. (2010). Linear numerical-magnitude representations aid children's memory for numbers. *Psychological Science, 21*, 1274–1281.

Thompson, Elisabeth Morgan, & Morgan, Elizabeth M. (2008). "Mostly straight" young women: Variations in sexual behavior and identity development. *Developmental Psychology, 44*, 15–21.

Thompson, Ross A. (2006). The development of the person: Social understanding, relationships, conscience, self. In William Damon & Richard M. Lerner (Series Eds.) & Nancy Eisenberg (Vol. Ed.), *Handbook of child psychology: Vol. 3. Social, emotional, and personality development* (6th ed., pp. 24–98). Hoboken, NJ: Wiley.

Thompson, Ross A., & Nelson, Charles A. (2001). Developmental science and the media: Early brain development. *American Psychologist, 56*, 5–15.

Thompson, Ross A., & Raikes, H. Abigail. (2003). Toward the next quarter-century: Conceptual and methodological challenges for attachment theory. *Development & Psychopathology, 15*, 691–718.

Thornton, Arland, Axinn, William G., & Xie, Yu. (2007). *Marriage and cohabitation.* Chicago, IL: University of Chicago Press.

Thurber, James. (1999). The secret life of James Thurber. In James Thurber (Ed.), *The Thurber carnival* (pp. 35–41). New York, NY: Harper Perennial.

Tikotzky, Liat, Sharabany, Ruth, Hirsch, Idit, & Sadeh, Avi. (2010). "Ghosts in the Nursery:" Infant sleep and sleep-related cognitions of parents raised under communal sleeping arrangements. *Infant Mental Health Journal, 31*, 312–334.

Tilton-Weaver, Lauree, Kerr, Margaret, Pakalniskeine, Vilmante, Tokic, Ana, Salihovic, Selma, & Stattin, Håkan. (2010). Open up or close down: How do parental reactions affect youth information management? *Journal of Adolescence, 33*, 333–346.

Tishkoff, Sarah A., Reed, Floyd A., Friedlaender, Françoise R., Ehret, Christopher, Ranciaro, Alessia, Froment, Alain, et al. (2009, May 22). The genetic structure and history of Africans and African Americans. *Science, 324*, 1035–1044.

Titus, Dale N. (2007). Strategies and resources for enhancing the achievement of mobile students. *NASSP Bulletin, 91*, 81–97.

Tluczek, Audrey, Koscik, Rebecca L., Modaff, Peggy, Pfeil, Darci, Rock, Michael J., Farrell, Philip M., et al. (2006). Newborn screening for cystic fibrosis: Parents' preferences regarding counseling at the time of infants' sweat test. *Journal of Genetic Counseling, 15*, 277–291.

Tokunaga, Robert S. (2010). Following you home from school: A critical review and synthesis of research on cyberbullying victimization. *Computers in Human Behavior, 26*, 277–287.

Tolman, Deborah L., & McClelland, Sara I. (2011). Normative sexuality development in adolescence: A decade in review, 2000–2009. *Journal of Research on Adolescence, 21*, 242–255.

Tomalski, Przemyslaw, & Johnson, Mark H. (2010). The effects of early adversity on the adult and developing brain. *Current Opinion in Psychiatry, 23*, 233–238.

Tomasello, Michael. (2006). Acquiring linguistic constructions. In William Damon & Richard M. Lerner (Series Eds.) & Deanna Kuhn & Robert S. Siegler (Vol. Eds.), *Handbook of child psychology: Vol. 2. Cognition, perception, and language* (6th ed., pp. 255–298). Hoboken, NJ: Wiley.

Tomasello, Michael. (2009). Cultural transmission: A view from chimpanzees and human infants. In Ute Schönpflug (Ed.), *Cultural transmission: Psychological, developmental, social, and methodological aspects* (pp. 33–47). New York, NY: Cambridge University Press.

Tomasello, Michael, & Herrmann, Esther. (2010). Ape and human cognition. *Current Directions in Psychological Science, 19*, 3–8.

Tomicic, Catherine, Berode, Michèle, Oppliger, Anne, Castella, Vincent, Leyvraz, Fabienne, Praz-Christinaz, Sophie-Maria, et al. (2011). Sex differences in urinary levels of several biological indicators of exposure: A human volunteer study. *Toxicology Letters, 202*, 218–225.

Tomopoulos, Suzy, Dreyer, Benard P., Berkule, Samantha, Fierman, Arthur H., Brockmeyer, Carolyn, & Mendelsohn, Alan L. (2010). Infant media exposure and toddler development. *Archives of Pediatrics & Adolescent Medicine, 164*, 1105–1111.

Tonn, Jessica L. (2006). Later high school start times: A reaction to research. *Education Week, 25*, 5, 17.

Toppelberg, Claudio O., & Collins, Brian A. (2010). Language, culture, and adaptation in immigrant children. *Child and Adolescent Psychiatric Clinics of North America, 19*, 697–717.

Toutain, Stéphanie. (2010). What women in France say about alcohol abstinence during pregnancy. *Drug and Alcohol Review, 29*, 184–188.

Tracy, Erin E. (2009, August). Does home birth empower women, or imperil them and their babies? *OBG Management, 21*, 45–52.

Trautmann-Villalba, Patricia, Gschwendt, Miriam, Schmidt, Martin H., & Laucht, Manfred. (2006). Father-infant interaction patterns as precursors of children's later externalizing behavior problems: A longitudinal study over 11 years. *European Archives of Psychiatry and Clinical Neuroscience, 256*, 344–349.

Tremblay, Richard E. (2011). Origins, development, and prevention of aggressive behavior. In Daniel P. Keating (Ed.), *Nature and nurture in early child development* (pp. 169–187). New York, NY: Cambridge University Press.

Trenholm, Christopher, Devaney, Barbara, Fortson, Ken, Quay, Lisa, Wheeler, Justin, & Clark, Melissa. (2007). *Impacts of four Title V, Section 510 abstinence education programs final report.* Retrieved from Mathematica Policy Research website: http://www.mathematica-mpr.com/publications/PDFs/impactabstinence.pdf

Trickett, Penelope K., Negriff, Sonya, Ji, Juye, & Peckins, Melissa. (2011). Child Maltreatment and Adolescent Development. *Journal of Research on Adolescence, 21*(1), 3–20.

Trickett, Penelope K., Noll, Jennie G., & Putnam, Frank W. (2011). The impact of sexual abuse on female development: Lessons from a multigenerational, longitudinal research study. *Development and Psychopathology, 23*, 453–476.

Trommsdorff, Gisela, & Cole, Pamela M. (2011). Emotion, self-regulation, and social behavior in cultural contexts. In Xinyin Chen & Kenneth H. Rubin (Eds.), *Socioemotional development in cultural context* (pp. 131–163). New York, NY: Guilford Press.

Tronick, Ed, & Beeghly, Marjorie. (2011). Infants' meaning-making and the development of mental health problems. *American Psychologist, 66*, 107–119.

Tronick, Edward Z. (1989). Emotions and emotional communication in infants. *American Psychologist, 44*, 112–119.

Tronick, Edward Z., & Weinberg, M. Katherine. (1997). Depressed mothers and infants: Failure to form dyadic states of consciousness. In Lynne Murray & Peter J. Cooper (Eds.), *Postpartum depression and child development* (pp. 54–81). New York, NY: Guilford Press.

Trzesniewski, Kali H., Donnellan, M. Brent, Moffitt, Terrie E., Robins, Richard W., Poulton, Richie, & Caspi, Avshalom. (2006). Low self-esteem during adolescence predicts poor health, criminal behavior, and limited economic prospects during adulthood. *Developmental Psychology, 42*, 381–390.

Tsao, Feng-Ming, Liu, Huei-Mei, & Kuhl, Patricia K. (2004). Speech perception in infancy predicts language development in the second year of life: A longitudinal study. *Child Development, 75*, 1067–1084.

Tu, Wanzhu, Batteiger, Byron E., Wiehe, Sarah, Ofner, Susan, Van Der Pol, Barbara, Katz, Barry P., et al. (2009). Time from first intercourse to first sexually transmitted infection diagnosis among adolescent women. *Archives of Pediatrics & Adolescent Medicine, 163*, 1106–1111.

Tucker-Drob, Elliot M., Rhemtulla, Mijke, Harden, K. Paige, Turkheimer, Eric, & Fask, David. (2011). Emergence of a gene × socioeconomic status interaction on infant mental ability between 10 months and 2 years. *Psychological Science, 22*, 125–133.

Tudge, Jonathan. (2008). *The everyday lives of young children: Culture, class, and child rearing in diverse societies.* New York, NY: Cambridge University Press.

Tudge, Jonathan R. H., Doucet, Fabienne, Odero, Dolphine, Sperb, Tania M., Piccinini, Cesar A., & Lopes, Rita S. (2006). A window into different cultural worlds: Young children's everyday activities in the United States, Brazil, and Kenya. *Child Development, 77*, 1446–1469.

Turiel, Elliot. (2006). The development of morality. In William Damon & Richard M. Lerner (Series Eds.) & Nancy Eisenberg (Vol. Ed.), *Handbook of child psychology: Vol. 3. Social, emotional, and personality development* (6th ed., pp. 789–857). Hoboken, NJ: Wiley.

Turiel, Elliot. (2008). Thought about actions in social domains: Morality, social conventions, and social interactions. *Cognitive Development, 23*, 136–154.

Turkheimer, Eric, Haley, Andreana, Waldron, Mary, D'Onofrio, Brian, & Gottesman, Irving. (2003). Socioeconomic status modifies heritability of IQ in young children. *Psychological Science, 14*, 623–628.

Turley, Ruth N. López, & Desmond, Matthew. (2010). Contributions to college costs by married, divorced, and remarried parents. *Journal of Family Issues.*

Turner, Val D., & Berkowitz, Marvin W. (2005). Scaffolding morality: Positioning a socio-cultural construct. *New Ideas in Psychology, 23,* 174–184.

Twenge, Jean M., Gentile, Brittany, DeWall, C. Nathan, Ma, Debbie, Lacefield, Katharine, & Schurtz, David R. (2010). Birth cohort increases in psychopathology among young Americans, 1938–2007: A cross-temporal meta-analysis of the MMPI. *Clinical Psychology Review, 30,* 145–154.

Twenge, Jean M., Konrath, Sara, Foster, Joshua D., Campbell, W. Keith, & Bushma, Brad J. (2008). Egos inflating over time: A cross-temporal meta-analysis of the narcissistic personality inventory. *Journal of Personality, 76,* 875–902.

Tzeng, Shih-Jay. (2007). Learning disabilities in Taiwan: A case of cultural constraints on the education of students with disabilities. *Learning Disabilities Research & Practice, 22,* 170–175.

U.S. Bureau of the Census. (2009). *Statistical abstract of the United States: 2010* (129th ed.). Washington, DC: U.S. Government Printing Office.

U.S. Bureau of the Census. (2010). *Statistical abstract of the United States: 2011* (130th ed.). Washington, DC: U.S. Government Printing Office.

U.S. Bureau of the Census. (2010). *America's families and living arrangements: 2009.* Retrieved from http://www.census.gov/population/www/socdemo/hh-fam/cps2009.html

U.S. Bureau of the Census. (2011). *Statistical abstract of the United States: 2012* (131st ed.). Washington, DC: U.S. Government Printing Office.

U.S. Department of Agriculture and U.S. Department of Health and Human Services. (2010). *Dietary Guidelines for Americans, 2010.* Washington, DC: U.S. Government Printing Office.

U.S. Department of Health and Human Services. (2010). *Head Start impact study: Final report.* Washington, DC: Author.

U.S. Department of Health and Human Services. (2011). *The Surgeon General's call to action to support breastfeeding.* Washington, DC: U.S. Department of Health and Human Services, Office of the Surgeon General.

U.S. Department of Health and Human Services, Administration for Children and Families. (2010). *Head Start impact study: Final report.* Washington, DC: Author.

Uddin, Monica, Koenen, Karestan C., de los Santos, Regina, Bakshis, Erin, Aiello, Allison E., & Galea, Sandro. (2010). Gender differences in the genetic and environmental determinants of adolescent depression. *Depression and Anxiety, 27,* 658–666.

Uekermann, Jennifer, Kraemer, Markus, Abdel-Hamid, Mona, Schimmelmann, Benno G. , Hebebrand, Johannes, Daum, Irene, et al. (2010). Social cognition in attention-deficit hyperactivity disorder (ADHD). *Neuroscience & Biobehavioral Reviews, 34,* 734–743.

Umana-Taylor, Adriana J., & Guimond, Amy B. (2010). A longitudinal examination of parenting behaviors and perceived discrimination predicting Latino adolescents' ethnic identity. *Developmental Psychology, 46,* 636–650.

UNESCO. (2009). *Global education digest 2009: Comparing education statistics across the world.* Montreal, Quebec, Canada: UNESCO Institute for Statistics.

UNESCO. (2010). *Global education digest: Comparing education statistics across the world.* Montreal, Quebec, Canada: UNESCO Institute for Statistics.

UNICEF. (2007). *Progress for children: A world fit for children statistical review.* New York, NY: Author.

UNICEF. (2009). *The state of the world's children 2009: Maternal and newborn health.* New York, NY: Author.

UNICEF. (2011). *The state of the world's children 2011: Adolescence–An age of opportunity.* New York, NY: Author.

United Nations Department of Economic and Social Affairs. (2011). *Population and Vital Statistics Report: Vol. 62. Series A.* Retrieved from http://unstats.un.org/unsd/demographic/products/vitstats/Sets/Series_A_2011.pdf

United Nations Development Programme. (2011, January). *Human development indices: A statistical update, 2010.* Retrieved from United Nations Statistics Division website: http://data.un.org/Default.aspx

United States Department of Transportation. (2010). *Traffic safety facts: 2009 data* (DOT HS 811 387). Washington, DC: National Center for Statistics and Analysis.

Unnever, James D. (2005). Bullies, aggressive victims, and victims: Are they distinct groups? *Aggressive Behavior, 31,* 153–171.

Utendale, William T., & Hastings, Paul D. (2011). Developmental changes in the relations between inhibitory control and externalizing problems during early childhood. *Infant and Child Development, 20,* 181–193.

Vaala, Sarah E., Linebarger, Deborah L., Fenstermacher, Susan K., Tedone, Ashley, Brey, Elizabeth, Barr, Rachel, et al. (2010). Content analysis of language-promoting teaching strategies used in infant-directed media. *Infant and Child Development, 19,* 628–648.

Valentino, Kristin, Cicchetti, Dante, Rogosch, Fred A., & Toth, Sheree L. (2008). True and false recall and dissociation among maltreated children: The role of self-schema. *Development and Psychopathology, 20,* 213–232.

Valkenburg, Patti M., & Peter, Jochen. (2009). Social consequences of the internet for adolescents. *Current Directions in Psychological Science, 18,* 1–5.

Valsiner, Jaan. (2006). Developmental epistemology and implications for methodology. In William Damon & Richard M. Lerner (Series Eds.) & Richard M. Lerner (Vol. Ed.), *Handbook of child psychology: Vol. 1. Theoretical models of human development* (6th ed., pp. 166–209). Hoboken, NJ: Wiley.

van den Akker, Alithe, Deković, Maja, Prinzie, Peter, & Asscher, Jessica. (2010). Toddlers' temperament profiles: Stability and relations to negative and positive parenting. *Journal of Abnormal Child Psychology, 38,* 485–495.

van den Ban, Els, Souverein, Patrick, Swaab, Hanna, van Engeland, Herman, Heerdink, Rob, & Egberts, Toine. (2010). Trends in incidence and characteristics of children, adolescents, and adults initiating immediate- or extended-release methylphenidate or atomoxetine in the Netherlands during 2001–2006. *Journal of Child and Adolescent Psychopharmacology, 20,* 55–61.

van den Berg, Stéphanie M., & Boomsma, Dorret I. (2007). The familial clustering of age at menarche in extended twin families. *Behavior Genetics, 37,* 661–667.

van Hof, Paulion, van der Kamp, John, & Savelsbergh, Geert J. P. (2008). The relation between infants' perception of catchableness and the control of catching. *Developmental Psychology, 44,* 182–194.

van IJzendoorn, Marinus H., & Bakermans-Kranenburg, Marian J. (2010). Invariance of adult attachment across gender, age, culture, and socioeconomic status? *Journal of Social and Personal Relationships, 27,* 200–208.

van IJzendoorn, Marinus H., Bakermans-Kranenburg, Marian J., Pannebakker, Fieke, & Out, Dorothée. (2010). In defence of situational morality: Genetic, dispositional and situational determinants of children's donating to charity. *Journal of Moral Education, 39,* 1–20.

Van Leijenhorst, Linda, Zanolie, Kiki, Van Meel, Catharina S., Westenberg, P. Michiel, Rombouts, Serge A.R.B., & Crone, Eveline A. (2010). What motivates the adolescent? brain regions mediating reward sensitivity across adolescence. *Cerebral Cortex, 20,* 61–69.

Van Puyvelde, Martine, Vanfleteren, Pol, Loots, Gerrit, Deschuyffeleer, Sara, Vinck, Bart, Jacquet, Wolfgang, et al. (2010). Tonal synchrony in mother-infant interaction based on harmonic and pentatonic series. *Infant Behavior and Development, 33,* 387–400.

van Schijndel, Tessa J. P., Singer, Elly, van der Maas, Han L. J., & Raijmakers, Maartje E. J. (2010). A sciencing programme and young children's exploratory play in the sandpit. *European Journal of Developmental Psychology, 7,* 603–617.

van Soelen, Inge L. C., Brouwer, Rachel M., Peper, Jiska S., van Beijsterveldt, Toos C. E. M., van Leeuwen, Marieke, de Vries, Linda S., et al. (2010). Effects of gestational age and birth weight on brain volumes in healthy 9 year-old children. *The Journal of Pediatrics, 156,* 896–901.

Van Zundert, Rinka M. P., Van Der Vorst, Haske, Vermulst, Ad A., & Engels, Rutger C. M. E. (2006). Pathways to alcohol use among Dutch students in regular education and education for adolescents with behavioral problems: The role of parental alcohol use, general parenting practices, and alcohol-specific parenting practices. *Journal of Family Psychology, 20,* 456–467.

Varnum, Michael E. W., & Kitayama, Shinobu. (2011). What's in a name? Popular names are less common on frontiers. *Psychological Science, 22,* 176–183.

Vartanian, Lesa Rae. (2001). Adolescents' reactions to hypothetical peer group conversations: Evidence for an imaginary audience? *Adolescence, 36,* 347–380.

Veenstra, René, Lindenberg, Siegwart, Munniksma, Anke, & Dijkstra, Jan Kornelis. (2010). The complex relation between bullying, victimization, acceptance, and rejection: Giving special attention to status, affection, and sex differences. *Child Development, 81,* 480–486.

Vered, Karen Orr. (2008). *Children and media outside the home: Playing and learning in after-school care.* Houndmills, Basingstoke, Hampshire, England: Palgrave Macmillan.

Verona, Sergiu. (2003). Romanian policy regarding adoptions. In Victor Littel (Ed.), *Adoption update* (pp. 5–10). New York, NY: Nova Science.

Véronneau, Marie-Hélène, & Dishion, Thomas. (2010). Predicting change in early adolescent problem behavior in the middle school years: A mesosystemic perspective on parenting and peer experiences. *Journal of Abnormal Child Psychology, 38,* 1125–1137.

Véronneau, Marie-Hélène, Vitaro, Frank, Brendgen, Mara, Dishion, Thomas J., & Tremblay, Richard E. (2010). Transactional analysis of the reciprocal links between peer experiences and academic achievement from middle childhood to early adolescence. *Developmental Psychology, 46,* 773–790.

Verté, Sylvie, Geurts, Hilde M., Roeyers, Herbert, Oosterlaan, Jaap, & Sergeant, Joseph A. (2005). Executive functioning in children with autism and Tourette syndrome. *Development & Psychopathology, 17,* 415–445.

Viadero, Debra. (2007, April 5). Long after Katrina, children show symptoms of psychological distress. *Education Week,* p. 7.

Victora, Cesar G., Adair, Linda, Fall, Caroline, Hallal, Pedro C., Martorell, Reynaldo, Richter, Linda, et al. (2008). Maternal and child undernutrition: Consequences for adult health and human capital. *Lancet, 371,* 340–357.

Vieno, Alessio, Nation, Maury, Pastore, Massimiliano, & Santinello, Massimo. (2009). Parenting and antisocial behavior: A model of the relationship between adolescent self-disclosure, parental closeness, parental control, and adolescent antisocial behavior. *Developmental Psychology, 45,* 1509–1519.

Vitale, Susan, Sperduto, Robert D., & Ferris, Frederick L., III. (2009). Increased prevalence of myopia in the United States between 1971–1972 and 1999–2004. *Archives of Ophthalmology, 127,* 1632–1639.

Vitiello, Benedetto, Zuvekas, Samuel H., & Norquist, Grayson S. (2006). National estimates of antidepressant medication use among U.S. children, 1997–2002. *Journal of the American Academy of Child & Adolescent Psychiatry, 45,* 271–279.

Vogel, Gretchen. (2010, November 26). Diseases in a dish take off. *Science, 330,* 1172–1173.

von Mutius, Erika, & Vercelli, Donata. (2010). Farm living: Effects on childhood asthma and allergy. *Nature Reviews Immunology, 10,* 861–868.

Vonderheid, Susan C., Kishi, Rieko, Norr, Kathleen F., & Klima, Carrie. (2011). Group prenatal care and doula care for pregnant women. In Arden Handler, Joan Kennelly, & Nadine Peacock (Eds.), *Reducing racial/ethnic disparities in reproductive and perinatal outcomes: The evidence from population-based interventions* (pp. 369–400). New York, NY: Springer.

Vouloumanos, Athena, & Werker, Janet F. (2007). Listening to language at birth: Evidence for a bias for speech in neonates. *Developmental Science, 10,* 159–164.

Vygotsky, Lev S. (1986). *Thought and language* (Eugenia Hanfmann & Gertrude Vakar, Trans. Revised ed.). Cambridge, MA: MIT Press. (Original work published 1934)

Vygotsky, Lev S. (1987). *Thinking and speech* (Norris Minick, Trans. Vol. 1). New York, NY: Plenum Press. (Original work published 1934)

Vygotsky, Lev S. (1994). Principles of social education for deaf and dumb children in Russia (Theresa Prout, Trans.). In Rene van der Veer & Jaan Valsiner (Eds.), *The Vygotsky reader* (pp. 19–26). Cambridge, MA: Blackwell. (Original work published 1925)

Vygotsky, Lev S. (1994). The development of academic concepts in school aged children (Theresa Prout, Trans.). In Rene van der Veer & Jaan Valsiner (Eds.), *The Vygotsky reader* (pp. 355–370). Cambridge, MA: Blackwell. (Original work published 1934)

Waber, Deborah P. (2010). *Rethinking learning disabilities: Understanding children who struggle in school.* New York, NY: Guilford Press.

Wagner, Carol L., Greer, Frank R., & and the Section on Breastfeeding and Committee on Nutrition of the American Academy of Pediatrics. (2008). Prevention of rickets and vitamin D deficiency in infants, children, and adolescents. *Pediatrics, 122,* 1142–1152.

Wagner, Laura, & Lakusta, Laura. (2009). Using language to navigate the infant mind. *Perspectives on Psychological Science, 4,* 177–184.

Wagner, Paul A. (2011). Socio-sexual education: A practical study in formal thinking and teachable moments. *Sex Education: Sexuality, Society and Learning, 11,* 193–211.

Wahlstrom, Dustin, Collins, Paul, White, Tonya, & Luciana, Monica. (2010). Developmental changes in dopamine neurotransmission in adolescence: Behavioral implications and issues in assessment. *Brain and Cognition, 72,* 146–159.

Wahlstrom, Kyla L. (2002). Accommodating the sleep patterns of adolescents within current educational structures: An uncharted path. In Mary A. Carskadon (Ed.), *Adolescent sleep patterns: Biological, social, and psychological influences* (pp. 172–197). New York, NY: Cambridge University Press.

Wakefield, Melanie, Flay, Brian, Nichter, Mark, & Giovino, Gary. (2003). Effects of anti-smoking advertising on youth smoking: A review. *Journal of Health Communication, 8,* 229–247.

Walker, Peter, Bremner, J. Gavin, Mason, Uschi, Spring, Jo, Mattock, Karen, Slater, Alan, et al. (2010). Preverbal infants' sensitivity to synaesthetic cross-modality correspondences. *Psychological Science, 21,* 21–25.

Waller, Erika M., & Rose, Amanda J. (2010). Adjustment trade-offs of co-rumination in mother-adolescent relationships. *Journal of Adolescence, 33,* 487–497.

Walsh, Bridget A., & Petty, Karen. (2007). Frequency of six early childhood education approaches: A 10-year content analysis of early childhood education journal. *Early Childhood Education Journal, 34,* 301–305.

Wang, A. Ting, Lee, Susan S., Sigman, Marian, & Dapretto, Mirella. (2006). Developmental changes in the neural basis of interpreting communicative intent. *Social Cognitive and Affective Neuroscience, 1,* 107–121.

Wang, Qi, Shao, Yi, & Li, Yexin Jessica. (2010). "My way or mom's way?" The bilingual and bicultural self in Hong Kong Chinese children and adolescents. *Child Development, 81,* 555–567.

Wang, Richard Y., Needham, Larry L., & Barr, Dana B. (2005). Effects of environmental agents on the attainment of puberty: Considerations when assessing exposure to environmental chemicals in the National Children's Study. *Environmental Health Perspectives, 113,* 1100–1107.

Wang, Wendy, & Taylor, Paul. (2011, March 9). *For millennials, parenthood trumps marriage.* Washington, DC: Pew Research Center.

Wang, Yonghong, Wang, Xiaolin, Kong, Yuhan, Zhang, John H., & Zeng, Qing. (2009). The Great Chinese Famine leads to shorter and overweight females in Chongqing Chinese population after 50 years. *Obesity, 18,* 588–592.

Ward, L. Monique, Epstein, Marina, Caruthers, Allison, & Merriwether, Ann. (2011). Men's media use, sexual cognitions, and sexual risk behavior: Testing a mediational model. *Developmental Psychology, 47,* 592–602.

Warneken, Felix, & Tomasello, Michael. (2009). The roots of human altruism. *British Journal of Psychology, 100,* 455–471.

Warner, Judith. (2011, January 11). No more Mrs. nice mom. *New York Times Magazine,* pp. 11–12.

Warren, Charles W., Jones, Nathan R., Eriksen, Michael P., & Asma, Samira. (2006). Patterns of global tobacco use in young people and implications for future chronic disease burden in adults. *Lancet, 367,* 749–753.

Warshofsky, Fred. (1999). *Stealing time: The new science of aging.* New York, NY: TV Books.

Wartella, Ellen, Richert, Rebekah A., Robb, Michael B., & National Science Foundation. (2010). Babies, television and videos: How did we get here?

Washington, Harriet A. (2006). *Medical apartheid: The dark history of medical experimentation on Black Americans from colonial times to the present.* New York, NY: Doubleday.

Watson, John B. (1928). *Psychological care of infant and child.* New York, NY: Norton.

Watson, John B. (1998). *Behaviorism*. New Brunswick, NJ: Transaction. (Original work published 1924)

Wax, Joseph R., Pinette, Michael G., & Cartin, Angelina. (2010). Home versus hospital birth-process and outcome. *Obstetrical & Gynecological Survey, 65,* 132–140.

Waxman, Sandra R., & Lidz, Jeffrey L. (2006). Early word learning. In William Damon & Richard M. Lerner (Series Eds.) & Deanna Kuhn & Robert S. Siegler (Vol. Eds.), *Handbook of child psychology: Vol. 2. Cognition, perception, and language* (6th ed., pp. 299–335). Hoboken, NJ: Wiley.

Weichold, Karina, Silbereisen, Rainer K., & Schmitt-Rodermund, Eva. (2003). Short-term and long-term consequences of early versus late physical maturation in adolescents. In Chris Hayward (Ed.), *Gender differences at puberty* (pp. 241–276). New York, NY: Cambridge University Press.

Weikum, Whitney M., Vouloumanos, Athena, Navarra, Jordi, Soto-Faraco, Salvador, Sebastian-Galles, Nuria, & Werker, Janet F. (2007, May 25). Visual language discrimination in infancy. *Science, 316,* 1159.

Weis, Robert, & Cerankosky, Brittany C. (2010). Effects of video-game ownership on young boys' academic and behavioral functioning. *Psychological Science, 21,* 463–470.

Weisgram, Erica S., Bigler, Rebecca S., & Liben, Lynn S. (2010). Gender, values, and occupational interests among children, adolescents, and adults. *Child Development, 81,* 778–796.

Wellman, Henry M., Cross, David, & Watson, Julanne. (2001). Meta-analysis of theory-of-mind development: The truth about false belief. *Child Development, 72,* 655–684.

Wenner, Melinda. (2009, February). The serious need for play. *Scientific American Mind,* 23–29.

Werner, Emmy E. (1979). *Cross-cultural child development: A view from the planet Earth.* Monterey, CA: Brooks/Cole.

Werner, Emmy E., & Smith, Ruth S. (1992). *Overcoming the odds: High risk children from birth to adulthood.* Ithaca, NY: Cornell University Press.

Werner, Emmy E., & Smith, Ruth S. (2001). *Journeys from childhood to midlife: Risk, resilience, and recovery.* Ithaca, NY: Cornell University Press.

Werner, Nicole E., & Hill, Laura G. (2010). Individual and peer group normative beliefs about relational aggression. *Child Development, 81,* 826–836.

Wheatley, Thalia, Milleville, Shawn C., & Martin, Alex. (2007). Understanding animate agents: Distinct roles for the social network and mirror system. *Psychological Science, 18,* 469–474.

Whelchel, Lisa. (2000). *Creative correction: Extraordinary ideas for everyday discipline.* Wheaton, IL: Tyndale House.

Whitbourne, Susan Krauss, Sneed, Joel R., & Sayer, Aline. (2009). Psychosocial development from college through midlife: A 34-year sequential study. *Developmental Psychology, 45,* 1328–1340.

Whitehead, Kevin A., Ainsworth, Andrew T., Wittig, Michele A., & Gadino, Brandy. (2009). Implications of ethnic identity exploration and ethnic identity affirmation and belonging for intergroup attitudes among adolescents. *Journal of Research on Adolescence, 19,* 123–135.

Whiteside-Mansell, Leanne, Bradley, Robert H., Casey, Patrick H., Fussell, Jill J., & Conners-Burrow, Nicola A. (2009). Triple risk: Do difficult temperament and family conflict increase the likelihood of behavioral maladjustment in children born low birth weight and preterm? *Journal of Pediatric Psychology, 34,* 396–405.

Whitfield, Keith E., & McClearn, Gerald. (2005). Genes, environment, and race: Quantitative genetic approaches. *American Psychologist, 60,* 104–114.

Whitlock, Janis L., Powers, Jane L., & Eckenrode, John. (2006). The virtual cutting edge: The internet and adolescent self-injury. *Developmental Psychology, 42,* 407–417.

Whittle, Sarah, Yap, Marie B. H., Sheeber, Lisa, Dudgeon, Paul, Yücel, Murat, Pantelis, Christos, et al. (2011). Hippocampal volume and sensitivity to maternal aggressive behavior: A prospective study of adolescent depressive symptoms. *Development and Psychopathology, 23,* 115–129.

Wicherts, Jelte M., Dolan, Conor V., & van der Maas, Han L. J. (2010). The dangers of unsystematic selection methods and the representativeness of 46 samples of African test-takers. *Intelligence, 38,* 30–37.

Willatts, Peter. (1999). Development of means-end behavior in young infants: Pulling a support to retrieve a distant object. *Developmental Psychology, 35,* 651–667.

Williams, Caroline, Constantine, A., & Sutcliffe, Alastair. (2011). Systematic review and meta-analysis of cancer risk in children born after assisted reproduction. *Archives of Disease in Childhood, 96*(Suppl. 1), A6.

Williams, Lela Rankin, Fox, Nathan A., Lejuez, C. W., Reynolds, Elizabeth K., Henderson, Heather A., Perez-Edgar, Koraly E., et al. (2010). Early temperament, propensity for risk-taking and adolescent substance-related problems: A prospective multi-method investigation. *Addictive Behaviors, 35,* 1148–1151.

Williams, Preston. (2009, March 5). *Proposal to push back high school start time in Fairfax county overlooks reality.* Retrieved from Washington Post website: http://www.washingtonpost.com/wp-dyn/content/article/2009/03/03/AR2009030304052.html

Williamson, Rebecca A., Meltzoff, Andrew N., & Markman, Ellen M. (2008). Prior experiences and perceived efficacy influence 3–year-olds' imitation. *Developmental Psychology, 44,* 275–285.

Wilmshurst, Linda. (2010). *Child and adolescent psychopathology: A casebook.* Los Angeles, CA: SAGE.

Wilson, Kathryn R., Hansen, David J., & Li, Ming. (2011). The traumatic stress response in child maltreatment and resultant neuropsychological effects. *Aggression and Violent Behavior, 16,* 87–97.

Wilson, Stephan M., & Ngige, Lucy W. (2006). Families in sub-Saharan Africa. In Bron B. Ingoldsby & Suzanna D. Smith (Eds.), *Families in global and multicultural perspective* (2nd ed., pp. 247–273). Thousand Oaks, CA: Sage.

Winner, Ellen. (1996). *Gifted children: Myths and realities.* New York, NY: Basic Books.

Winsler, Adam, Manfra, Louis, & Díaz, Rafael M. (2007). "Should I let them talk?": Private speech and task performance among preschool children with and without behavior problems. *Early Childhood Research Quarterly, 22,* 215–231.

Winter, Suzanne M. (2011). Culture, health, and school readiness. In DeAnna M. Laverick & Mary Renck Jalongo (Eds.), *Transitions to early care and education* (Vol. 4, pp. 117–133). New York, NY: Springer.

Witherington, David C., Campos, Joseph J., & Hertenstein, Matthew J. (2004). Principles of emotion and its development in infancy. In Gavin Bremner & Alan Fogel (Eds.), *Blackwell handbook of infant development* (Paperback ed., pp. 427–464). Malden, MA: Blackwell.

Wittrock, Merlin C. (2010). Learning as a generative process. *Educational Psychologist, 45,* 40–45.

Wolak, Janis, Finkelhor, David, Mitchell, Kimberly J., & Ybarra, Michele L. (2008). Online "predators" and their victims: Myths, realities, and implications for prevention and treatment. *American Psychologist, 63,* 111–128.

World Bank. (2010). *What can we learn from nutrition impact evaluations?* Washington, DC: The International Bank for Reconstruction and Development.

World Health Organization. (2005). *Sexually transmitted infections among adolescents: Issues in adolescent health and development.* Geneva, Switzerland: Author.

World Health Organization. (2010, October 5). *WHO global infobase: NCD indicators.* Retrieved from https://apps.who.int/infobase/Indicators.aspx

Worrell, Frank C. (2008). Nigrescence attitudes in adolescence, emerging adulthood, and adulthood. *Journal of Black Psychology, 34,* 156–178.

Worthman, Carol M., Plotsky, Paul M., Schechter, Daniel S., & Cummings, Constance A. (Eds.). (2010). *Formative experiences: The interaction of caregiving, culture, and developmental psychobiology.* New York, NY: Cambridge University Press.

Wosje, Karen S., Khoury, Philip R., Claytor, Randal P., Copeland, Kristen A., Hornung, Richard W., Daniels, Stephen R., et al. (2010). Dietary patterns associated with fat and bone mass in young children. *American Journal of Clinical Nutrition, 92,* 294–303.

Wright, Mathew W., & Bruford, Elispeth A. (2011). Naming 'junk': Human non-protein coding RNA (ncRNA) gene nomenclature. *Human Genomics, 5,* 90–98.

Wu, Pai-Lu, & Chiou, Wen-Bin. (2008). Postformal thinking and creativity among late adolescents: A post-Piagetian approach. *Adolescence, 43,* 237–251.

Xu, Yaoying. (2008). Children's social play sequence: Parten's classic theory revisited. *Early Child Development and Care, 180,* 489–498.

Xu, Yaoying. (2011). Preparing young children for schools in China. In DeAnna M. Laverick & Mary Renck Jalongo (Eds.), *Transitions to early care and education* (Vol. 4, pp. 149–161). New York, NY: Springer.

Yajnik, Chittaranjan S. (2004). Early life origins of insulin resistance and type 2 diabetes in India and other Asian countries. *Journal of Nutrition, 134*, 205–210.

Yamaguchi, Susumu, Greenwald, Anthony G., Banaji, Mahzarin R., Murakami, Fumio, Chen, Daniel, Shiomura, Kimihiro, et al. (2007). Apparent universality of positive implicit self-esteem. *Psychological Science, 18*, 498–500.

Yan, Bernice, & Arlin, Patricia. (1995). Nonabsolute/relativistic thinking: A common factor underlying models of postformal reasoning? *Journal of Adult Development, 2*, 223–240.

Yang, Dahe, Sidman, Jason, & Bushnell, Emily W. (2010). Beyond the information given: Infants' transfer of actions learned through imitation. *Journal of Experimental Child Psychology, 106*, 62–81.

Yehuda, Rachel (Ed.). (2006). *Annals of the New York Academy of Sciences: Vol. 1071. Psychobiology of posttraumatic stress disorder: A decade of progress.* Boston, MA: Blackwell.

Yen, Ju-Yu, Ko, Chih-Hung, Yen, Cheng-Fang, Chen, Sue-Huei, Chung, Wei-Lun, & Chen, Cheng-Chung. (2008). Psychiatric symptoms in adolescents with internet addiction: Comparison with substance use. *Psychiatry and Clinical Neurosciences, 62*, 9–16.

Yerys, Benjamin E., & Munakata, Yuko. (2006). When labels hurt but novelty helps: Children's perseveration and flexibility in a card-sorting task. *Child Development, 77*, 1589–1607.

Yeung, W. Jean, & Conley, Dalton. (2008). Black-White achievement gap and family wealth. *Child Development, 79*, 303–324.

Yli-Kuha, Anna-Niina, Gissler, Mika, Luoto, Riitta, & Hemminki, Elina. (2009). Success of infertility treatments in Finland in the period 1992–2005. *European Journal of Obstetrics, Gynecology, and Reproductive Biology, 144*, 54–58.

You, Danzhen, Jones, Gareth, & Wardlaw, Tessa. (2010). *Levels & trends in child mortality: Report 2010.* Geneva, Switzerland: UN Interagency Group for Child Mortality Estimation.

Young, Elizabeth A., Korszun, Ania, Figueiredo, Helmer F., Banks-Solomon, Matia, & Herman, James P. (2008). Sex differences in HPA axis regulation. In Jill B. Becker, Karen J. Berkley, Nori Geary, Elizabeth Hampson, James P. Herman, & Elizabeth Young (Eds.), *Sex differences in the brain: From genes to behavior* (pp. 95–105). New York, NY: Oxford University Press.

Young, John K. (2010). Anorexia nervosa and estrogen: Current status of the hypothesis. *Neuroscience & Biobehavioral Reviews, 34*, 1195–1200.

Zachry, Anne H., & Kitzmann, Katherine M. (2011). Caregiver awareness of prone play recommendations. *American Journal of Occupational Therapy, 65*, 101–105.

Zahn-Waxler, Carolyn, Park, Jong-Hyo, Usher, Barbara, Belouad, Francesca, Cole, Pamela, & Gruber, Reut. (2008). Young children's representations of conflict and distress: A longitudinal study of boys and girls with disruptive behavior problems. *Development and Psychopathology, 20*, 99–119.

Zalenski, Robert J., & Raspa, Richard. (2006). Maslow's hierarchy of needs: A framework for achieving human potential in hospice. *Journal of Palliative Medicine, 9*, 1120–1127.

Zalesak, Martin, & Heckers, Stephan. (2009). The role of the hippocampus in transitive inference. *Psychiatry Research: Neuroimaging, 172*, 24–30.

Zani, Bruna, & Cicognani, Elvira. (2006). Sexuality and intimate relationships in adolescence. In Sandy Jackson & Luc Goossens (Eds.), *Handbook of adolescent development* (pp. 200–222). Hove, East Sussex, UK: Psychology Press.

Zehr, Mary Ann. (2011, April 6). Study stings KIPP on attrition rates. *Education Week*, pp. 1, 24–25.

Zehr, Mary Ann. (2011). Schools strengthen counseling on postsecondary options. *Education Week*, pp. 16–17.

Zeller, Meg H., Reiter-Purtill, Jennifer., & Ramey, Christine. (2008). Negative peer perceptions of obese children in the classroom environment. *Obesity, 16*, 755–762.

Zentner, Marcel, & Bates, John E. (2008). Child temperament: An integrative review of concepts, research programs, and measures. *European Journal of Developmental Science, 2*, 7–37.

Zhang, Donghui. (2010). Language maintenance and language shift among Chinese immigrant parents and their second-generation children in the U.S. *Bilingual Research Journal, 33*, 42–60.

Zhang, Shuangyue, & Kline, Susan L. (2009). Can I make my own decision? A cross-cultural study of perceived social network influence in mate selection. *Journal of Cross-Cultural Psychology, 40*, 3–23.

Zhang, Ying. (2009). *State high school exit exams: Trends in test programs, alternate pathways, and pass rates.* Washington, DC: Center on Education Policy.

Zhu, Qi, Song, Yiying, Hu, Siyuan, Li, Xiaobai, Tian, Moqian, Zhen, Zonglei, et al. (2010). Heritability of the specific cognitive ability of face perception. *Current Biology, 20*, 137–142.

Zhu, Weimo, Boiarskaia, Elena A., Welk, Gregory J., & Meredith, Marilu D. (2010). Physical education and school contextual factors relating to students' achievement and cross-grade differences in aerobic fitness and obesity. *Research Quarterly for Exercise and Sport, 81*, S53–64.

Zhu, Ying, Zhang, Li, Fan, Jin, & Han, Shihui. (2007). Neural basis of cultural influence on self-representation. *NeuroImage, 34*, 1310–1316.

Zigler, Edward, & Styfco, Sally J. (Eds.). (2004). *The Head Start debates.* Baltimore, MD: Brookes.

Zimmer-Gembeck, Melanie J., & Collins, W. Andrew. (2003). Autonomy development during adolescence. In Gerald R. Adams & Michael D. Berzonsky (Eds.), *Blackwell handbook of adolescence* (pp. 175–204). Malden, MA: Blackwell.

Zimmer-Gembeck, Melanie J., & Ducat, Wendy. (2010). Positive and negative romantic relationship quality: age, familiarity, attachment and well-being as correlates of couple agreement and projection. *Journal of Adolescence, 33*, 879–890.

Zimmerman, Frederick J., & Bell, Janice F. (2010). Associations of television content type and obesity in children. *American Journal of Public Health, 100*, 334–340.

Zuvekas, Samuel H., Vitiello, Benedetto, & Norquist, Grayson S. (2006). Recent trends in stimulant medication use among U.S. children. *American Journal of Psychiatry, 163*, 579–585.

Subject Index